A History of Modern Political Thought

To Suzi,
for Jessica, Sam and Olivia

A History of
Modern Political Thought

Major Political Thinkers from Hobbes to Marx

IAIN HAMPSHER-MONK

BLACKWELL
Oxford UK & Cambridge USA

Copyright © Iain Hampsher-Monk, 1992

The right of Iain Hampsher-Monk to be identified as author of this work has been asserted in   .
accordance with the Copyright, Designs and Patents Act 1988.

First published 1992
Reprinted 1993, 1994

Blackwell Publishers
108 Cowley Road
Oxford OX4 1JF
UK

238 Main Street
Cambridge, Massachusetts 02142
USA

British Library Cataloguing-in-Publication Data
A CIP catalogue record for this book is available from the British Library.

Library of Congress Cataloging-in-Publication Data
Hampsher-Monk, Iain, 1946–
    A history of modern political thought : major political thinkers
from Hobbes to Marx / Iain Hampsher-Monk.
        p.   cm.
    Includes bibliographical references and index.
    ISBN 1-55786-146-3 (alk. paper). – ISBN 1-55786-147-1 (pbk. :
alk. paper)
    1. Political science – History. I. Title.
JA83.H256   1992
320'.09–dc 20   92-17205
                                                                           CIP

Typeset by the author and Archetype, Stow-on-the-Wold, UK
Printed in Great Britain by T.J. Press (Padstow) Ltd., Padstow, Cornwall

This book is printed on acid-free paper

Contents

Acknowledgements

Living under such a drearily philistine government as we have endured over the period of this book's composition would be far more unbearable than it has been without the warmth and academic friendship which the community of political theorists and historians of political thought has afforded. In particular the January meetings at Oxford of the Political Thought Conference have been an annual source of invigorating, and often bracing, inspiration.

I should like particularly to thank the following friends and colleagues who have patiently and speedily read various individual chapters and offered good advice which has not always been followed: Maurice Goldsmith, Harro Höpfl, Dick Ashcraft, Bill Jordan, Dario Castiglione, John Charvet, John Hope-Mason, the late John Dinwiddy, Eldon Eisenach, Chris Berry, Andrew Lockyer, Joe Melling and Terrell Carver.

I have shared with my colleagues in the Department of Politics at Exeter a congenial if increasingly overworked academic home for most of the last twenty years. In particular I have benefited from the company and conversation of many students, as well as the 'regular team' of theorists, Maurice Goldsmith, Peter Butler, Janet Coleman, and now Dario Castiglione, but also Alison Frazer, Barry Smith, Peter Stirk, Mark Stewart, Emma Murphy and Giuseppi Saccone, all of whom at various times helped to teach the 'Exeter HPT Course' from which this book grew.

Thanks are due to Sue Ridler and Fay Burgoyne who, early in the career of the text managed to insert the typing of two draft chapters into an increasing mound of administrative business. However, the combined effects of cuts on university resources and the division of labour to which the new IT leads has meant that the bulk of the book has been typed by myself. For invaluable assistance with typesetting – a further task transposed onto the academic by the need to meet the volatile UFC research selectivity deadline – thanks are due to Keith Sutherland of Imprint Academic. His wizardry in virtually instantaneously converting word-processed files into embryonic typeset text was as vital as it was impressive. Thanks are also due to the staff at Blackwell Publishers, in particular Romesh Vaitilingam whose initial enthusiasm for the project supported me through some difficult patches, and his successors, Mark Allin and Simon Prosser, and to John Keston-Hole in the production department who supported the editorial and proofing process.

Finally I must endorse all those expressions of thanks and admiration which authors customarily express to their partners at this point. Despite meeting the needs of at first one and eventually three very young children, serving on a ministerial advisory committee and drafting European Food legislation, Suzi still managed to provide time for me and my ever-gestating textbook; moreover we are still talking to each other.

Introduction

This book has been written primarily with the undergraduate or interested lay reader in mind, and makes no great claims for originality. I have tried to reflect something of the current state of scholarship in each of the thinkers treated. Given these aims elaborate introductions are largely out of place, but the curious reader is entitled to some excuse, and the writer to pre-empt speculation about authorial intentions.

The study of political thought is a kind of intellectual no-man's land, a subject of border disputes between (at least) the adjacent territories of politics, philosophy and history. As its practitioners are well aware, the past twenty years or so have seen a vigorous offensive on the part of history, and the journal *History of Political Thought*, which Janet Coleman and I started in Exeter in 1980, has played a part in that movement. Part of the consequence of this has been to focus attention on a wider range of texts, and indeed other sources, than hitherto in our attempt to understand the past environment and movement of political ideas.

Nevertheless the 'history of political thought', or 'political theory since Hobbes' as it is encountered by undergraduates in any of the three disciplines mentioned above, tends to remain the study of the 'great texts' which the 'historical revolution' has done so much to dethrone. There are good and defensible pedagogical reasons for this.

Whether students are approaching the subject from History, Philosophy or Politics, the major political philosophers of the past are felt to have something to say. For philosophers they present a range of problems and approaches to political questions and their possible relationship to epistemology, moral philosophy and the philosophy of the social sciences, and, increasingly recognised recently, a necessary sense of philosophy's own history in this area. For historians, however much the serious study of sources has shifted to the more manageable arena of an episode or particular controversy in which the minor texts, and context, can be brought into focus, there is still a need for an 'outline' understanding of what the major theoretical statements have been, if only as a wider context for closer studies of theory, or indeed, of other branches of history. For students of politics, the study of theory provides a way of forcing confrontation with normative issues which are otherwise often concealed, a necessary counterpoise to the constant threat of relapsing into descriptivism in comparative government; the analysis of texts also provides the most disciplined basis for the appraisal of ideologies. For those who make serious claims to be 'political scientists' there is even greater need to be reminded of the hermeneutic basis of the concepts and vocabulary they deploy.

In each of these cases what the student is required to read (at least, so it is very much to be hoped) is the author's original text. Whilst some 'histories of political thought' such as the venerable and still useful work by Sabine, are indeed histories in the now re-asserted sense, they cover so much ground that they cannot help to guide the modern student through the text before them. The modest aim of this work is to do that. I have tried to bring to the texts what historical sensitivity I have acquired during the recent revolution (I was trained in philosophy and political science, not in history), and to use the authors to provoke students to philosophize themselves without committing any truly crass errors (it was a long time ago). The political content of the works discussed is, I hope, incapable of being concealed even by my treatment.

This does not, then, claim to be a true 'history of political thought' as we have come to understand the term. Our available knowledge is now such that I doubt whether it would be possible, or indeed prudent, to attempt such a work, certainly over this period within a single volume. What it aspires to be is a kind of travellers' guide, for students following courses *called* the History of Political Thought, something to have by them whilst grappling with the text, or to turn to when temporarily recuperating from the struggle.

The introductory and pedagogical intent of the work affects the treatment of the thinkers, which is not uniform. Whilst not entirely suppressing the authorial voice I have tried to reflect the different preoccupations of current research on the various authors. Thus the chapters on Hobbes and on Marx involve some discussion of recent attempts to reformulate their theories in terms that might have seemed somewhat strange to those authors. The chapter on Hegel, once having sketched a background, focuses on overcoming the considerable difficulty of simply getting to terms with the logic of his argument; an approach which both reflects the effort of much recent work, and also seeks to meet the needs of the student. The range of texts chosen for discussion is also driven largely by an estimation of those works the student is most likely to be asked to read. Accordingly it ranges from a single work of Hobbes, Locke and Hegel, to several by Marx and Mill. I have not attempted to provide a full indication of the position of commentators on the various issues raised, or of the ultimate source of every position advanced. Rather, footnotes have been used, firstly and primarily to establish the basis of my interpretive claims in the primary text; secondly to elaborate arguments or make qualifications that might have confused the line of my text; and intermittently to indicate important interpretive standpoints or secondary works on which I was particularly aware of drawing.

Methodological

In attempting a book like this one is very conscious of two audiences, the undergraduate, or interested general reader one is hoping to reach, and one's colleagues, whom I have often imagined peering (indeed grimacing) critically over my shoulder as I wrote, and whom I must first convince if the book is to be recommended to a student audience. To them, and with some trepidation, I would advance a further claim for the work. One consequence of the reassertion of the importance of historical context, aided in a curious, if not always strictly logical way, by influential developments in French interpretive philosophy, is the tendency for a text, and indeed an author to be so securely located in their historical and intellectual milieu as to be submerged and overcome by it. In extreme, but by no means uncommon cases this denies them intellectual agency and the desire, or certainly capacity, to formulate statements with any referent beyond the historically parochial. In so doing it denies them any political import for the present.

In a possibly rather naive and distinctly old fashioned way I believe this view to be both mistaken as history and pernicious as philosophy. Whilst an understanding of the identity of the conceptual 'language' being deployed is necessary to understand historical meaning, an exclusive preoccupation with it can distract attention from the fact that it is being used to make a statement. As a result, writer and text can actually fragment and disappear into context, appearing no more than the sum of its hermeneutical parts. Languages indeed cannot be private, nor, except inasmuch as they parasitize public meaning, the work of an individual. Languages are irreducibly social products, and recent scholarship has transformed our understanding of the history of political theory in recognising the persistence through time of particular patterns of thought, and the way in which certain key terms relate to one another in a way that mimics the 'grammar' of natural languages. Nevertheless the work of a particular theorist is not itself a language, but a unique statement, or rather a set of statements, which constitute an *argument*. Each of the writers discussed here was a highly energetic agent in pulling together, out of what was at the time an often bewildering intellectual environment, an account of human political life which achieved some considerable level of coherence. To be able to demonstrate the sources on which they drew, the logic which (retrospectively) we can see them following, or the sub-texts that can be conjured from them, does nothing in my view, to alter their achievement in constructing the arguments discussed here.

Such a view of intellectual agency is as important for present as for past political theory. If, as our modern critics tell us, there is no more such a thing as truth than there are authors or texts, we must fall back on consequentialist criteria by which to establish what can be said. To believe that human philosophical agency can achieve nothing that goes beyond the fragmentary intellectual materials on which it must, necessarily, work, could serve no purpose except to undermine our endeavours to make our world coherent, or to help reorder it in accordance with such coherence. It is a view therefore, which, whilst rejecting any standard of truth on which it could establish its own credentials, fails the only remaining principle of discrimination which could be advanced in these matters.

I have tried to bring out what I see as the *achievement* of each of these authors in drawing coherence out of contradiction, incoherence or chaos. In contrast to the claims often advanced for the distinctive character of post-modern or post-nietzschean political theory, it may be pointed out that the sceptical epistemological context in which so many of the thinkers in this book operated had surprising parallels to those claimed as so uniquely a feature of postmodernity.

However, in stressing the creative effort involved in producing each text, I in no way wish to deny that their authors operated from within a set of inherited ideas and political vocabulary, a context also, it should be said, of real events, political pressures and crises, which nevertheless had to be understood, at least initially, in terms of the existing languages of political thinking. The historical revolution in political theory has taught us to be far more respectful of the constraining effects of available language in offering interpretations, and in stressing the author's intellectual agency I would not wish to deny the importance of intellectual context and the resonances provided by a tradition in which that agency must be exercised; but these are not antithetical. The presence of a cultural hermeneutic no more impedes the creativity of the thinker than the presence of air impedes the flight of the dove, rather in each case the one is the very condition of the other.

A final word of historical introduction. The reader will want to know why the work starts where it does, and what has gone before. A long term, and long range answer to the second question lies in a companion volume to this one currently being written by my friend and colleague, Janet Coleman. This will cover the political thought of the ancient world, the medieval period and the Renaissance. Shorter term, and shorter range answers will, I hope, be found embedded in various discussions in the first chapter of this work, on Hobbes. Some of the reasons why there is not a separate treatment of such material in this volume are entirely pragmatic ones to do with the already excessive length of the work, and the fact that I have chosen to organise discussion around the key texts which students traditionally study. Until the recent and excellent 'Cambridge Texts' series, lesser works from this period have simply not been available in undergraduate editions, or even in institutional libraries.

Nevertheless, the tradition of starting from Hobbes has something to be said for it. The English Civil Wars were a forcing-house of European significance for political theory, and *Leviathan* was its most vigorous growth. Through Hobbes, despite his self-conscious claims as an innovator, flowed many of the intellectual preoccupations and devices of his predecessors and contemporaries, and those moreover, that set much of the agenda for the succeeding two or more centuries. The new approaches to physical science, moral, religious and epistemological scepticism, the vocabulary of subjective rights, state of nature and social contract as adapted by Protestant theorists from the Catholic neo-Thomists, the tension between demands for order at virtually any cost and the desire for civil and religious liberty – in England as in France an outcome of a long period of religiously-inspired unrest – all of these can be seen in Hobbes's philosophy. Perhaps the most distinctive sense in which Hobbes represents a starting point is his thorough-going attempt, not only to subordinate the church to the state, but to subordinate the epistemological claims of religion and faith to those of 'natural knowledge'. Neither Marsilio of Padua nor Machiavelli, each of whom had articulated a purely secular account of government, had been able to locate it within a fully developed, secular, moral psychology. In this sense, Hobbes's long account of psychology and epistemology grounded in a materialist physiology is an extremely political statement, and was seen as such by his opponents. It attempted for the first time since antiquity to give an account of politics within a detailed and unified secular world view. This is not of course to say that Hobbes was an atheist, or even an agnostic, it is simply that God played no essential *role* in his account of the world. With the exception of Locke, no subsequent mainstream thinker was able to rest his arguments on essentially theological premises, and even in Locke's case his philosophical psychology squared awkwardly with the political assumption of a theologically grounded 'law of nature'. Instead, thinkers increasingly argued on Hobbes's assumptions, namely, that both moral standards, and the possibility of constructing the motives needed to adhere to them, must be discovered in the psychology of human beings and the structure of their society. Social circumstances were, moreover, increasingly seen to shape psychology, making an understanding of historical processes a vital part of any respectable political theory.

This brings us to the one major tradition which is absent from Hobbes's thought, the tradition of civic humanism, or republicanism. For it is through the resources provided by this tradition that thinkers in the early modern period were best able to think through the relationship between the citizen's experience, political, military and economic, and his psychology. Hobbes's contemporaries, James Harrington, John Milton, and Algernon

Sidney are the most important vehicles for this pattern of thought in English. It has been a major omission of the tradition of the 'great texts' that it has not included any representative figures from it. Two major and related developments in modern political thought drew extensively on this pattern of thinking. The first deepened the civic tradition's ability to theorize about the political qualities of the individual by applying to it the intellectually powerful philosophical psychology of Locke. This had been developed in order to understand the psychology of personal belief and so was in fact, if not essentially, a product of Protestantism. The result however, was the development of extremely sophisticated accounts of the social and individual psychology of moral and political belief that we find, for example, in Hume.

A second development relates to the essentially dynamic nature of civic thought. Whereas Christian psychology was, within historical time, static, civic psychology was preoccupied with change, especially decline and corruption. Harnessing a complex philosophical psychology to a social and political theory preoccupied with dynamics proved a stimulus for the development of thought about long-term social processes, and about the inter-dependence of ideas and social institutions. Characteristically modern ideas then become conceivable, ideas about progress, claims about the paradoxical interplay between individual vices and public benefits, about the social production of ideology, and about historicism. Some at least of what Rousseau, 'Publius', Burke, Mill, Hegel and Marx are saying draws vitally on this civic or republican tradition, which consequently receives a good airing in this volume, particularly in the background to the *Federalist*.

With this proviso made, Hobbes is not at all a bad figure with which to open a book on modern political theorists, and so to the man.

I

Thomas Hobbes

Introduction

Life and intellectual concerns

Thomas Hobbes was born on the 5th April 1588, near Malmesbury in Wiltshire. He claimed his birth was premature, his mother's labour having been induced by news of the Spanish Armada. After graduating from Oxford he was for most of his life family retainer and tutor to the Earls of Devonshire. He travelled extensively on the continent, living in France during the Civil War. He died in 1679, and his life thus covered a period of both scientific and political revolution.[1] In both of these fields Hobbes played a part, and in an audacious way he attempted to link them, seeking a solution to the political instability of his time through the application of the burgeoning natural sciences.[2]

His master work is *Leviathan*, published in the midst of the constitutional upheavals of the Civil War and Commonwealth. But he had rewritten his political philosophy three times, changing various details, some clearly in response to political events, before he was satisfied.[3] However Hobbes's interest in politics may be said to predate even the first version of his theory in the *Elements of Law*. His first publication – a translation of Thucydides' *The Peloponnesian Wars* (1629) – being already, he claimed, an attempt to prevent civil war, by warning his countrymen of the illusionary benefits of a republic. As he wrote in his own verse *Life* (originally in Latin):

[1] The conflict and eventual civil war between Charles I and Parliament culminating in Charles' execution in 1649, was followed by a period of constitutional experimentation and uncertainty before the Restoration in 1660. For a good narrative history: Ivan Roots, *The Great Rebellion* (London, 1966). During this period too, scientific and intellectual activity was at a perhaps surprisingly vital pitch, culminating in the foundation of the Royal Society after the Restoration. Hobbes was never a member – possibly because of his supposed atheism. But see most recently Noel Malcolm, 'Hobbes and the Royal Society', in *Perspectives on Thomas Hobbes*, ed. G.A.J. Rodgers and Alan Ryan (Oxford, 1988).

[2] Hobbes wrote his own *Life* in Latin verse, of which there is an English translation (not by him), see *The Life of Mr Thomas Hobbes of Malmsbury* (repr. Exeter, 1979). There is also Aubrey's witty and anecdotal sketch in John Aubrey, *Aubrey's Brief Lives*, ed. O.L. Dick (Harmondsworth, 1972). See also the life in chapter I of S. Mintz, *The Hunting of Leviathan* (Cambridge, 1962) and most recently the biography by A. Rogow, *Hobbes*, (New York, 1986), and Tuck's short biography in his *Hobbes*, (Oxford, 1989) in the Past Master series.

[3] Hobbes's first version of his political theory, *The Elements of Law*, was circulated privately in 1640, and the second, *De Cive* (On the Citizen) published on the eve of the Civil War in 1642. *Leviathan*, was published in 1651 when Hobbes was in exile in France following the victory of the parliamentarians and the execution of King Charles I in 1649.

Plautus, Euripides, Aristophanes,
I understood, nay more; but of all these,
There's none that pleas'd me like *Thucydides.*
He says Democracy's a Foolish Thing,
Than a Republick Wiser is one King.
This author I taught *English,* that even he
A Guide to Rhetoricians might be.[4]

In humanist conceptions of the intellectual disciplines, prevalent in Hobbes's day, history was considered a branch of rhetoric, and the task of history as rhetoric, was to exhort men by example, to lead good lives. In *Leviathan,* Hobbes seeks to undermine both rhetorical history and our knowledge of the past as a source of political science, but its companion monster – *Behemoth,* a history of the Civil War – did illustrate the origins of the war, and claimed to expose the same errors as *Leviathan.*[5] Although Hobbes undermined history as a source of scientific knowledge, its rhetorical role may be said to have been passed to science itself, for Hobbes expresses the hope that his work could be 'profitably taught in the Universities . . . which are the Fountains of Civill, and Morall Doctrine.'[6] His aim throughout was to warn against the consequences of political conflict, the only cure for which, he thought, was an absolute and undivided sovereignty.[7]

The separation of religion from politics

One major significance of Hobbes's adoption of the new science was the possibility he saw in it of establishing the autonomy of politics from clerics, theology and metaphysics in general. For he believed 'the dispute . . . betweene the spirituall and civill power, has,

---

[4] *The Life of Mr Thomas Hobbes,* pp. 4–5. Hobbes drew on Thucydides' analysis, and even on his images in his later works, see R. Schlatter, 'Thomas Hobbes and Thucydides', *Journal of the History of Ideas,* 6 (1945); G. Klosko & D. Rice, 'Thucydides and Hobbes's State of Nature', *History of Political Thought,* VI, 3 (1985); and G. Slomp, 'Hobbes, Thucydides, and the Three Greatest Things', *History of Political Thought,* XI, 4 (1990).

[5] For Hobbes's rejection of history as moral rhetoric, G. Rossini, 'The criticism of rhetorical historiography and the ideal of scientific method: History, nature and science in the political language of Thomas Hobbes', in *The Languages of Political Theory in Early Modern Europe,* ed. A. Pagden (Cambridge, 1987).

[6] *Leviathan,* p. 395. All page references to *Leviathan,* are to the pagination of the original edition of 1651 which is indicated [in square brackets] in the margins of the editions by Pogson-Smith (Oxford, 1909), Macpherson (Harmondsworth, 1968), and Tuck (Cambridge, 1991). The first two of these texts use the Head version of the 1651 edition, as does that of Oakeshott (Oxford, 1946), although the latter omits the original pagination. Tuck's edition uses a text derived from a comparison between the corrected large-font version of the 1651 edition, and the amended manuscript copy presented by Hobbes to Charles II in 1651. Thus his text is probably closest to Hobbes's original intentions. The Cambridge edition also contains a useful concordance with the other editions mentioned here, as well as by far the most helpful critical apparatus for the student, including biographical notes and references and a good index.

[7] Interest in the rhetorical aspect of *Leviathan* is increasing, see, e.g., D. Johnston, *The Rhetoric of Leviathan* (Princeton, 1986); and Conal Condren, 'On the Rhetorical Foundations of *Leviathan*', *History of Political Thought,* XI, 4 (1990).

of late more than any other thing in the world, bene the cause of civille warre'.[8] Hobbes denied the existence of metaphysics but not, wisely for him – for there were still those seeking to make heresy an offense – of God. Aubrey reported that shortly after the Restoration in 1660 'some of the Bishops made a motion to have the good old Gentleman [Hobbes] burn't for a Heretique.'[9] Rather he sought to so separate the realm of religion from that of politics that no religious arguments affecting political legitimacy could be mounted. Whilst most of his contemporaries thought it essential that political obligation should derive from some religious premise, Hobbes's tactic was first either to subordinate or incorporate religion within the limits of 'natural knowledge', and then to try to show that natural knowledge leads to unequivocal obedience to the political ruler. This aim required him to undermine two important strands of English Protestant religious belief, stemming ultimately from the two major figures of the continental Reformation, Luther and Calvin, namely a belief in the integrity and transcendent authority of the Bible, and a belief in the sufficiency and authority of the believer's faith.

Either of these, taught Hobbes, is destructive of political authority and hence of political order, for on either of these grounds believers might be led to disobey their rulers. Hobbes, probably using arguments acquired during his trips to France, questions the textual integrity of the Bible. He tries to show that, as it comes down to us it is a work of human composition, like any other history, subject to human adjudication both as to what was included in it, and as to its provenance and internal consistency.[10] He also points out that any book, however sacred, will also require authoritative interpretation. Even allowing the sacredness of the text of the Bible, there was no guarantee that readers would find the correct meanings in it. Therefore, to prevent religious and hence political conflict, the public interpretation of the Bible must ultimately be the sovereign's. This was not an attack on religion itself, merely an attempt to deny it any authority independent of politics. Secondly Hobbes converts the Reformation 'Christian liberty' of inward conviction, from a potentially radical and subversive principle into an a-political and quietist one. Whilst many in the English Revolution saw the inwardness of faith and the guide of conscience as a licence to resist the imposition of what they believed to be ungodly forms of government, or church leadership, or liturgy, Hobbes argued that the Protestant stress on the importance of inner conviction made all of these 'outward things' a matter of indifference: for if true belief (as Protestantism taught) was a private, inward thing, a matter of the quality of one's faith, what did it matter what outward forms were used to express it? He wanted to persuade men that 'The controversies of religion, are altogether

[8] Letter 23.7/2.8, cited by D. Johnston, 'Hobbes's Mortalism', *History of Political Thought*, X, 4 (1989), p. 656.

[9] John Aubrey, *Aubrey's Brief Lives*, ed. O.L. Dick (Harmondsworth, 1972), p. 316. The threat could not have been carried out without a change in the law since heresy was no longer a capital offence in England, although there were several attempts to revive it. For a brief account of the situation see Richard Tuck, 'Hobbes and Locke on Toleration', in *Thomas Hobbes and Political Theory*, ed. Mary Dietz (Lawrence, Kansas, 1990). Not surprisingly Hobbes had a more than professional interest in the issue and devoted much of his *Dialogue of the Common Laws of England* (1665) to it. His preoccupation was quite justifiable: as late as 1697, almost twenty years after Hobbes's death, the poor student Thomas Aikenhead was burnt to death in Scotland for denying the Trinity.

[10] *Leviathan*, pp. 200ff.

about points unnecessary to salvation.'[11] In this Hobbes was adapting (considerably) an argument of orthodox Anglicans that extended back at least to Hooker.[12] However Hobbes's adaptation of it pushed its implications to the limits. If a ruler asked a Christian to deny Christ, Hobbes said, he was at liberty to do so for 'profession with the tongue is but an outward thing'. With a religion which has retreated as far inward as this, there would seem indeed to be no possible way in which it could disturb political obedience.

Modern scepticism and modern natural rights

A second major feature of Hobbes's argument is his adoption of the new natural rights theory. The ideas of seventeenth century natural law thinkers were a response to a moral scepticism associated with the French thinkers Michel de Montaigne and Pierre Charon. Its growth in France owed much to the dogmatism and conflict which were a consequence of, amongst other things, the moral and religious differences produced by the Reformation. This produced a very sophisticated agnosticism about all moral and political issues and a withdrawal from the political altogether, later epitomised in Voltaire's sardonic remark that 'we must cultivate our gardens'. Modern natural law thinkers accepted these sceptics' attacks on earlier attempts to construct universalist principles, but rejected the relativism implicit in them. Whilst it was indeed true that the diversity of moral codes and social practices around the world revealed no common moral *customs*, these thinkers denied that it therefore followed that there was nothing upon which to establish a universal ethics. 'Part of their response consisted equally simply in demonstrating that there were actually at least two universal moral beliefs (the right of self-preservation and the ban on wanton injury) and that this minimalist ethics could be used as the basis for a universal moral science.'[13]

Gradually assembled from a number of component ideas, some of which had existed for two thousand years, these arguments rejected the Christian-Aristotelian view of human life as inherently social and political, and instead attributed to human beings in their pre-political state – a 'state of nature' – certain (variously defined) individual and thus a-social natural rights. This vocabulary of natural rights exercised in a pre-political natural state had been elaborated by Spanish neo-Thomists such as Suàrez, Molina and De Soto, who, however located their discussions within the context of an all-embracing natural law.[14] The new thinkers however, increasingly decoupled the notion of 'right' from 'law' as an objective system of (what is) right, and instead asserted right as an area of virtually unqualified subjective freedom for individuals. Linked with the device of a

---

[11] *Elements of Law*, ed. Tönnies, 2nd ed., intr. M.M. Goldsmith (London, 1969), Pt. 2, vi, §9.

[12] In *De Cive*, the argument is used to justify the imposition of a national church claiming apostolic succession, under the political sovereign, essentially Anglicanism. In *Leviathan*, p. 385, the same argument is used to defend a toleration for Christians outside the national church, albeit always under the ultimate authority of the sovereign, although there remain elements of the Anglican position in the later work.

[13] Richard Tuck, 'The "Modern Theory" of natural law', in (Pagden) *The Languages of Political Theory*, p. 114–15.

[14] See Quentin Skinner, *The Foundations of Modern Political Thought* (2 vols, Cambridge, 1978), vol. 2, p. 154ff.

'social contract' in which these rights were granted (in whole or in part) to political ruler(s) in order to effect a transition from the 'state of nature' and establish political society, natural rights arguments became a widespread and influential pattern of argument, used chiefly to determine the kinds and degree of obligations citizens and rulers owed each other. Although we are used to thinking of natural rights as claims which can be made against governments by citizens, so placing limits on the former's powers, the emphasis in many early modern theorists is quite the other way – natural right and the contract were used primarily to explain, and to justify, the increasingly extensive authority claimed by the emergent modern state over its citizens.[15]

The context of political and moral uncertainty within which Hobbes wrote was thus both local and relatively short term (the English Civil War or the threat of it), and international and long term (the European discovery of other cultures and intra-European conflict produced by religious differences.)[16] Hobbes's ability to draw on the work of scholars and thinkers reflecting on the latter undoubtedly enriched and strengthened his response to the former. This has given his work not only a British but the widest European significance, testified by the international interest in his ideas ever since.

The seminal figure in this wider context and the natural rights tradition was the famous Dutch jurist Hugo Grotius. He clearly articulated the concept of subjective right as the origin of political authority quite independent of moral or juristic side-constraints: 'A people can select the form of government which it wishes; and the extent of its legal right in the matter is not to be measured by the superior excellence of this or that form of government, in regard to which men hold different views, but by its free choice.'[17] In addition Grotius insisted, to the scandal of his contemporaries, that his principle could be sustained on purely secular grounds. His theory would obtain, he wrote, 'even if we should concede that which cannot be conceded without the utmost wickedness, that there is no God, or that the affairs of men are of no concern to Him.'[18] In England Grotius' ideas were the subject of intense discussion before the Civil War amongst a royalist intellectual group known as the Tew Circle, of which Hobbes was a member, as indeed was Grotius' antagonist in the debate about natural rights on the high seas, John Selden.[19] Emerging from this *milieu* Hobbes yet moved away from crucial elements of the theory.

---

[15] See Richard Tuck, *Natural Rights Theories, their origin and development* (Cambridge, 1979); and Quentin Skinner, *Foundations*, vol. 2, pp. 148–73.

[16] Note, however, the long rearguard action fought, especially by Jesuits such as d'Acosta, to demonstrate that traditional natural law standards were perfectly consistent with the range of cultural diversity discovered by the new explorations. Book Six of his *Natural and Moral History of the Indies* (Salamanca, 1589), was devoted to 'confute the false opinion many doe commonly hold [of the indians] that they are a gross and brutish people . . . have little understanding.' As a good neo-Aristotelian the best way of demonstrating that the indians were not natural slaves was to relate how 'they lived under their owne lawes . . . worthy of great admiration . . . by nature capable to receive any good instructions; and . . . did in some things pass many of our commonweales.' Joseph d'Acosta, *The Natural and Moral History of the Indies*, tr. Edward Grimstone [1604], intr. Clements R. Markham (New York, 1880, repr., 2 vols, 1970), Vol 2, p. 390–1. I am grateful to Harro Höpfl for stressing this point to me.

[17] Hugo Grotius, *De Iuri Belli ac Pacis* (1625), Bk.I, Ch.III, sect.viii, 2; *On the Law of War and Peace*, tr. F. W. Kelsey (Indianapolis, 1925), p. 104.

[18] Grotius, *Law of War and Peace*, Prolegomena, p. 13.

[19] On the Tew Circle see Irene Coltman, *Private Men and Public Causes* (Oxford, 1962); and Tuck, *Natural Rights Theories*, ch.5.

In particular he rejected the historical content given to the notion of contract by Selden. For Selden, human beings within a society had evidently contracted away their natural rights. There were virtually no limits on such a contract: contracts to establish absolutist or tyrannical regimes were as permitted as those to establish limited ones – this freedom followed from the subjective quality of natural right. However, contracts once made had to be kept – this was one of the few restrictive laws of nature; moreover contracts by earlier generations established obligations binding subsequent ones. The nature of the contract was for Selden a matter of historical demonstration, for the legal-historical record of any particular country effectively constituted an account of the terms of the contract. Thus whether the King or Parliament was in the right at the outbreak of the Civil War, was for him, a matter only to be settled, as he did settle it, by looking at the strict legality of the actions of each of the two parties. In the end Selden sided with Parliament because he believed the King's method of raising an army fell outside the legal framework constitutive of the state of England.[20]

Arguments about the nature of the English past were, of course, rife during the civil-war period, and something needs to be said here about Hobbes's attitude to history, since it is relevant both to the rejection of Selden's natural rights theory and to the idea, mentioned earlier, of the historicity of the Bible – both, in negative ways, foundations for Hobbes's science of politics.

Science versus history and religion

In a traditional society, even a divided one such as Civil-War England still largely was, the assumption that what had been, ought to be, pervaded minds on both sides. Parliamentarians sought to demonstrate the longevity of Parliament and the unbroken pedigree of the 'Ancient Constitution' that would, in a traditionalist society guarantee the assembly's continued existence, whilst some royalists were gradually developing the view that England had originally been a feudal state in which all power – and indeed all property – derived from the King, who could therefore – on this view – resume either at will.[21] Hobbes disagreed politically with the parliamentarians, but unlike virtually all royalists, urged the irrelevance of past practice as grounds for political legitimacy. Instead he sought to persuade his readers that it was possible to establish a basis of political legitimacy on the grounds of something less contentious than religious belief or historical interpretation, and that something was natural reason alone. But to do this he had to create a science of politics.

Hobbes's decision to write a work of political philosophy was, as he put it, 'occasioned by the disorders of the present time'; these being struggles between King and Parlia-

---

[20] Richard Tuck, 'The Ancient Law of Freedom: John Selden and the Civil War', in *Reactions to the English Civil War*, ed. John Morrill (London and Basingstoke, 1982). Hobbes disagreed. Whatever law might have stated, the power to raise troops was 'in effect the whole sovereign power', *Behemoth*, intr. M.M. Goldsmith (London, 1969), pp. 80, 99, 118ff, 145. For my use of the word 'state' see below, fn. 193.

[21] The classic discussion is J.G.A. Pocock, *The Ancient Constitution and the Feudal Law* (Cambridge, 1957) now dated, but see the very substantial retrospective essay in the revised edition (1987). See also recently, J.P. Sommerville, *Politics and Ideology in England 1603–1640* (London, 1986), ch. 3, 'The Ancient Constitution'. Hobbes identifies the doctrine that subjects have absolute rights in their property as one of a set of beliefs which was subversive of political sovereignty and led to civil war; *Leviathan*, p. 169.

ment.[22] Hobbes intended his political thought to be not merely speculative but a contribution and a solution – as we have seen, he hoped it would be taught in universities – to a political situation which led, during his lifetime to civil war, regicide and military rule.[23] Hobbes was trained both as a rhetorician and in the emerging natural sciences. His argument was designed both to meet, and even set, standards of scientific rigour, *and* to appeal successfully to a wide range of readers and was accordingly originally written in English.[24] Only if the truths offered by *Leviathan* were accepted by the citizens could civil tumult be avoided; it was therefore important for his arguments not only to be widely understood, but to avoid appearing partisan. Since any positions starting from premises in religion or history were bound to be, or to appear partisan, Hobbes wisely avoided them as foundations.[25] At the same time, religion was a vital issue in the civil conflict, certain interpretations of scripture being, as Hobbes put it 'the Outworks of the Enemy, from whence they impugne the Civill Power'.[26] So, although rejecting religion as a basis of politics, Hobbes spends, and 'necessarily' so he remarks, over half the book explaining the relationship between them.

In championing the new scientific initiatives Hobbes is outspoken in his rejection of inherited traditions of knowledge, blaming both the classical republican idea of the mixed constitution derived from Aristotle, and the Christian adaptation of Aristotle's metaphysics by the 'schoolmen' both prevalent in the universities, for spreading political dissent and conceptual confusion.[27] Hobbes was overly flamboyant in this rejection of traditional learning: in his *Brief Lives* Aubrey recounts how Hobbes 'was wont to say that if he had read as much as other men he should have knowne no more than other men.'[28] This is, however, misleading, since as we shall see his thought is deeply structured by recognisable intellectual debts, some very old. Nevertheless Hobbes's remark catches something

---

[22] *Leviathan*, p. 395.

[23] The desire that his political theory be widely taught as a way of preventing dissidence was a constant theme. See, e.g., *The Elements of Law*, 'it would be an incomparable benefit to commonwealth, if every man held the opinions concerning law and policy here delivered.' 'The Epistle Dedicatory', p. xvi; and *Leviathan*, 'A Review and Conclusion': 'it may be profitably printed, and more profitably taught in the Universities . . . the Fountains of Civill and Morall Doctrine . . . '. p. 395.

[24] There is a Latin translation dating from 1668 with some interesting modifications evidently written for a different audience; see *Leviathan*, ed. Tuck, 'Introduction', p. xxv.

[25] Hobbes's attempt to appeal to fundamentals as a way of outflanking controversy turned out, in the short term to be disastrous. *Leviathan* outraged both sides in the interregnum and his views on religion incensed Restoration Bishops as we have seen (fn. 9 above). In the longer term, however, he may be seen as part of a movement which, by the middle of the next century, forced his opponents to adopt more rational approaches and to argue on Hobbes's own terms.

[26] *Leviathan*, 'The Epistle Dedicatory'. It was the attempt to impose the *Book of Common Prayer* on the Scots which had provoked the initial conflict leading to the Civil War. It had been the need to raise money in order to subdue them that had forced Charles, in 1640, to call the Long Parliament which opposed him.

[27] *Behemoth* develops at some length Hobbes's views about the role of these ideas and of the universities ('which have been to this nation, as the wooden horse was to the Trojans') in spreading them: 'such curious questions in divinity are first started in the Universities, and so are all those politic questions concerning the rights of civil and ecclesiastic government; and there they are furnished with arguments for liberty out of the works of Aristotle, Plato, Cicero, Seneca, and out of the histories of Rome and Greece, for their disputations against the necessary power of their sovereigns.' *Behemoth*, pp. 40, 56.

[28] Aubrey, *Brief Lives*, p. 314. Clarendon also took him to task because he 'consulted too few authors and made use of too few books.' Cited Richard Ollard, *Clarendon and his Friends* (Oxford, 1988) p. 337.

of his abrasive intellect and the perverse pleasure he seems to have taken in shocking and disconcerting his adversaries, a quality of his thought which however, was at odds, not only with what he liked to say was his timorous personality, but also his rhetorical aim of gaining wide consent for his views.

The nature of reality and the method of true science

At the most obvious level, Hobbes based his argument on what seemed to him the most exciting intellectual development of his day: the new mathematical sciences. Aubrey claims that Hobbes came to geometry late in life, when, aged about 40, he saw a book of Euclid's *Geometry* open on a table. Hobbes was convinced that the proposition he read there was 'impossible', but on following through the proof saw that it was indeed true. 'This', relates Aubrey, 'made him in love with Geometry'.[29] But if the conversion was as dramatic as this it had well laid foundations. His first job, as tutor to the Cavendish family, provided him not only with a superb library at Chatsworth, but access to the scientific circle and interests of Charles Cavendish at Welbeck Abbey. The story, moreover, is only the tip of an iceberg, for Hobbes was a natural philosopher, if not of the first rank, of international reputation, familiar with Bacon,[30] an acquaintance of Galileo, disputer with Descartes and correspondent of Mersenne. Hobbes's method, as both the infatuation with geometry, and the predominantly continental origin of his influences suggests, was not the cautious empiricism so characteristic of Bacon and of other English science at the time. It was, rather, a science constructed on the model of mathematics, and based primarily on deduction rather than observation: 'reasoning from the definitions of the terms of a proposition we suppose true, and again from the definitions of the terms of those definitions, and so on, till we come to some things known.'[31]

Hobbes thought this method could be applied throughout all areas of human knowledge to give a unified understanding of the world of natural science, psychology and politics – the three sections of his *Elements of Philosophy*.[32] In this way he seems to have hoped to either incorporate or to outflank forms of knowledge (such as history or religion) which offered alternative and hence divisive theories of political duty. Hobbes's view of the

[29] Aubrey, *Brief Lives*, p. 309.

[30] Aubrey, *Brief Lives*, p. 308. Hobbes was said to have taken dictation from Bacon who enjoyed his conversation and admired the accuracy of his notes. On Hobbes's scientific standing see Malcolm, 'Hobbes and the Royal Society'.

[31] *De Corpore*, in *The English Works of Thomas Hobbes* (Hereafter *E.W.*), ed. Sir Wm. Molesworth (11 vols, London, 1839–45), vol. I, p. 309. On the sceptical empiricism of English science see Henry van Leeuwen, *The Problem of Certainty in English Thought 1630–90* (The Hague, 1963). The implications of the mathematical model have been misunderstood. They clearly did not convey to Hobbes the possibility of quantification, but rather the possibility of establishing proof by chains of logical entailment from hypotheses to 'things known'. See, most recently, D.W. Hanson, 'The Meaning of "Demonstration" in Hobbes's Science', *History of Political Thought*, XI, 4 (1990). Notice also that Hobbes, unlike Plato, excused his rulers their maths (*Leviathan*, p. 194).

[32] The *Elementorum Philosophiae* was planned in the late 1630s in three parts. *De Cive* (On the Citizen) was to have been the third, but was published first in 1642, *De Corpore* (on Body) was published in 1655, and *De Homine* (on Man) in 1658.

kind of knowledge arrived at by scientific method, was however, quite distinct from his view of knowledge arrived at by ordinary experience and he is at great pains to distinguish the two.

Reality as matter in motion

Hobbes's epistemology – his view of human knowledge – was intimately related to his ontology – his theory of the ultimate nature of existence. The basis and origin of all human knowledge was sensation. The basic and irreducible component of existence for Hobbes was moving matter.[33] Hobbes attributed this latter insight to Galileo, who, as far as Hobbes was concerned, had invented modern science.[34] Although the two positions do not entail each other, there is nevertheless a neat fit between them, a fit which is emphasised at the start of *Leviathan* by Hobbes's determinedly mechanistic account of sensation.

Human perception, says Hobbes, is the result of moving matter impinging on our sense organs, transferring motion to the nerves and eventually the brain which reacts by repressing this intrusion from the external world. This repression is experienced as a sensation of some kind or other – a sight, sound, smell, taste or touch. Experience is then the body's response to matter in motion; it is itself a reactive motion in the human body. Hobbes's implied metaphor in his Introduction – 'what is the *Heart*, but a *spring*; and the *Nerves*, but so many *Strings* – and the *Joynts*, but so many *Wheeles,* giving motion to the whole Body,' turns out to be less metaphor and more literal description. Human 'life itselfe', and our very consciousness is, claims Hobbes, like the rest of existence, 'but Motion'.[35]

Hobbes uses a particular – inertial – conception of motion which reveals his debt to the new science. For despite the novelty of Galileo's claims, motion and substance had also been central categories for the Aristotelian philosophers – the 'Schoolmen' whom Hobbes so derided. But the way they characterised them were very different. For Aristotelians motion (like matter) is structured, and purposive, it is directed towards the end-point or resting place appropriate for the nature of the thing which is moving. Thus

---

[33] In Hobbes's own *Life* he wrote:

> One only thing i'th'World seem'd true to me,
> Tho' several ways that Falsified be.
> One only True Thing, the basis of all
> Those Things whereby we any Thing do call.
> . . .
> And he that studies Physicks first must know
> What Motion is, and what Motion can do.
> To Matter, Motion, I myself apply,
> And thus I spend my Time in Italy. (p. 6.)

[34] 'Galileo first opened up to us the gateway of a universal natural science, which is *motion.* The age of natural science can be reckoned back no further than him.' *De Corpore,* in *The Latin Works,* ed. Sir Wm. Molesworth (V vols, London, 1839), Vol. I, Epistola Dedicatoria, p. [iv].

[35] *Leviathan,* p. 29; and 'life is but a motion of Limbs', *Leviathan,* Introduction, p. 1; 'Nor can a man any more live, whose desires are at an end, than he whose Senses and Imaginations are at a stand', *Leviathan,* p. 47.

apples fall to earth, acorns rise into oak trees and human beings come together to form communities. The world of material, living and acted movements were, on this old but persistent view, all purposive or teleological, that is they all involved motion towards the position or state required of them by their natures, at which point they ceased to move and came to rest.

Although retaining a central role for these two categories of matter and motion, Hobbes so drastically transformed their meaning that he totally disrupted the ordered Aristotelian world view. If motion is inertial, movement, not rest, becomes the 'natural' state of any body, which once 'in motion will eternally be in motion, unless somewhat els stay it'.[36] On this view there is no 'end point' at which a particular motion ceases, having, as it were, 'arrived' at a destination, for there are no destinations. Motion of a particular body only ceases through having imparted its motion to something else which it has struck. Motion for Hobbes is not end-directed, but ceaseless. The situation of 'rest' is a singularly unusual one for Hobbes, a 'special case' rather than the norm or end towards which all motion tends; his universe is therefore, almost literally 'restless', a continuum of moving matter.[37]

Matter too changes its character in Hobbes's system. It becomes uniform, and it is also ubiquitous. Body – *'that, which having no dependence upon our thought, is coincident or co-extended with some part of space'*[38] – is all that there is: and there is nothing but material being.[39] Even God, claimed Hobbes, was material, although he allowed that his substance may be 'very subtle'. Biblical stories of spirits coming upon people must be understood as the intervention of actual physical beings, or else as metaphorical, signifying excessive zeal, or enthusiasm. His views brought Hobbes much criticism from contemporary churchmen who were well aware of the long association between materialism and atheism. 'By taking away all incorporeal substance,' wrote Bishop Bramhall, Hobbes 'taketh away God himself'.[40] Against such charges Hobbes replied in characteristically polemical fashion: it was, he pointed out, surely the Bishop, in asserting that God was *not* a material being who was courting atheism: 'to say that God is an incorporeal substance, is to say, in effect there is no God at all'!'[41] The issue of materialism involved

---

[36] *Leviathan*, p. 4.

[37] See Thomas Spragens, 'The Politics of Intertia and Gravitation' *Polity*, v, 3 (1973). and his book *The Politics of Motion* (Lexington, 1973).

[38] *E.W.*, I, p. 102. Space and time for Hobbes were not themselves the object of sensation, they were, it followed, 'phantasms'. Had space been real – and, as Torricelli showed, at times empty – this would have suggested incorporeal existence, the target of Hobbes's greatest ridicule. On Hobbes's protracted dispute with Boyle about the existence of a vacuum see the brilliant study by S. Shapin & S. Schaffer *Leviathan and the Air Pump* (Princeton, 1985).

[39] '. . . *the Universe*, that is, the whole masse of all things that are is Corporeall, that is to say, Body; and hath the dimensions of magnitude . . . every part of the Universe is Body, and that which is not Body, is no part of the Universe: and because the Universe is All, that which is no part of it, is *Nothing*; and consequently *no where*. Nor does it follow from hence, that Spirits are *nothing*; for they have dimensions, and are therefore really *Bodies*; . . . ', *Leviathan*, p. 371.

[40] Bishop John Bramhall, *The Catching of Leviathan* (1658), in *Works* (Dublin, 1676), III, p. 873, cited Mintz, *The Hunting of Leviathan*, p. 67. For a brilliant succinct account of the religious response to *Leviathan*, see Mark Goldie, 'The Reception of Hobbes', in *The Cambridge History of Political Thought in the Seventeenth Century*, ed. J.H.Burns with Mark Goldie (Cambridge, 1990).

[41] Thomas Hobbes, *An Answer to a book published by Dr Bramhall, late Bishop of Derry, . . .* , in *E.W.*, vol. IV, p. 305.

more than the nature of God. Subsumed under it were the questions of his very existence, whether, without a God, matter could think, and whether there could be any secular basis for morality. These issues were to remain contentious for a century and more, and unorthodox opinions on them would evoke charges of 'Hobbism'. Hobbes's method too, stressing as it did, even in religious matters, the role of reason over faith, was characteristic of the more advanced thinkers of the coming century.[42]

Hobbes's position on the nature of matter was logically implicated in his peculiar view of scientific method. For Aristotle and his Christian followers, the forms in which matter manifested itself – the 'objects' of perception with differentiated qualities and characteristics – were themselves real: they constituted an objectively differentiated range of beings. The natural forms revealed by experience were true 'natural kinds'. The definition and classification of the animal world, for example, was not an invention of the human mind but was somehow (inasmuch as it was right) a revelation of their natural forms. The existence of such 'kinds' was thought to be a condition of the world's being understood, since the otherwise somewhat shadowy 'first matter' which underlay the existence of individual beings did not enable one to explain anything about their behaviour or characteristics, but only the fact that they existed.

Hobbes's position was different. Whilst it is the real basis of existence, he denies to matter any suggestion of possessing other than the most abstract of corporeal qualities: extension, position, mass. What strictly differentiates one 'thing' from another for Hobbes, is its position. Matter is otherwise undifferentiated, and although it displays accidents which do enable us to differentiate and categorise it, these are purely subjective responses elicited in us, and Hobbes does not seem to believe them capable of constituting, or at any rate of allowing, knowledge of 'real kinds'.[43] At least, if such real kinds exist, the identity of them is, since the tower of Babel, lost to humans.[44] Consequently, in assigning words to objects of experience, Hobbes does not seem to think that we are marking the intrinsic items of a creation – 'considering how many new names are daily made, and old ones laid aside; . . . how can any man imagine that the names of things were imposed from their natures.' Rather names are 'words taken at pleasure to serve for a mark' which 'have their constitution not from the species of things, but from the will and consent of man.'[45]

For an Aristotelian, motion and the nature of the body moving are defined interdependently. Motion is always purposeful, moving towards an appropriate and predetermined end, because it takes place in a world of distinct beings which are all seeking to realise

---

[42] *Leviathan*, p. 195. Hobbes writes that in turning to matters of religion 'we are not to renounce our Senses, and Experience; nor (that which is the undoubted word of God) our naturall Reason.' Later in assessing the authority of the scriptures he says 'As far as they differ not from the Laws of Nature, there is no doubt, but they are the Law of God, . . . but this is no other Authority, then [sic] that of all other Morall Doctrine consonant to Reason . . . ' p. 205.

[43] Thus : accidents are 'that faculty of any body, by which it moves in us a conception of itself.' *E.W.*, I, p. 103. And in the *Answer to . . . Bishop Bramhall*, he insisted 'I have denied, that there is any reality in accidents.' *E.W.*, IV, p. 306.

[44] In *Leviathan* Hobbes recounts how God taught Adam to name animals at the creation, but how, 'all this language . . . was again lost at the tower of *Babel*', and the diverse natural languages which subsequently grew up created new names 'in such manner, as need (the mother of all inventions) taught them'. *Leviathan*, p. 12.

[45] *Elements of Philosophy*, *E.W.*, p. 16; words are 'arbitrarily imposed', *Elements of Law*, Pt. 1, v, §2; 'words have their signification by agreement, and constitution of men;' *Leviathan*, p. 192.

their potential by moving, growing or developing in such a way as to fulfill their intrinsic natures. Thus scientific problems concerning the description and understanding of motion and change could be related to the supposed purposes or fully developed states (natures) of the bodies or substances moving or changing in the world. Such explanations are particularly plausible in biology, since living things do exhibit apparently end-orientated activity and processes. This form of argument proved particularly attractive, and organic accounts of politics were a common feature of early modern political homilies, encouraging the different members of the state to sink their differences by regarding themselves as parts of a body, performing necessarily complementary functions which reappear.[46]

However, this familiar organic analogy appears in the Introduction to *Leviathan* already grotesquely transmogrified into a *mechanized* body. Hobbes takes the concept of merely mechanical motion and makes it theoretically fundamental: the explanation of all phenomena must ultimately be reducible to the description of the action of matter in motion impinging on other matter. Not only physical phenomena but the activities of the human body and mind are also to be explained in this way. The circulation of the blood, described by his friend William Harvey in 1628, in what must have been, for Hobbes, encouragingly mechanical terms, was a spur to the conceptual invasion by mechanics of the field of biology: 'what is the heart but a spring; and the nerves but so many strings?' Life is indeed but a 'motion of the limbs' and since motion is inertial this motion is unceasing, for 'as to have no Desire is to be Dead, so to have weak passions, is Dullness.'[47]

Moral and political implications of the issue of materialism

Hobbes's mechanical materialism however, explicitly subverted not only the idea of the political community as a natural body, but also the more general idea of 'final' or 'teleological' cause, whether in animate nature, or in humans (apart from their wills).[48] If matter is undifferentiated then motion cannot be teleological, for there can be no distinctive or particular ends available to an undifferentiated creation. Motion itself must

---

[46] For example Edmund Dudley's treatise *The Tree of Commonwealth*, ed. D.M.Brodie (Cambridge, 1948) [written 1509–10], argued: 'The comon wealth of this realme or of the subiectes or Inhabitauntes thereof my be resemblid to a faier and mighte tree growing in a faier feild or pasture, under the couerte or shade wherof all beastes, both fatt and leane, are protectyd and comfortyd from heate and cold as the tyme requireth' p. 31. King James I's classic statement of divine monarchical right, *The Trewe Law of Free Monarchies* (1598), which was nothing if not eclectic in its arguments, observed, very much to his own advantage, that as 'for the similitude of the head and the body, it may very well fall out that the head will be forced to gar cut off some rotten members . . . to keep the rest of the body in integrity. But what state the body can be in if the head, for any infirmity that can fall to it, be cut off, I leave to the reader's judgement.' Excerpted in *Divine Right and Democracy*, ed. & intr. D. Wootton (Harmondsworth, 1986), p. 100. It was a topic on which his unfortunate son did not, in the end, have to speculate.

[47] *Leviathan*, p. 35.

[48] 'As if [*per impossibile*] Stones, and Metalls had a desire, or could discern the place they would bee at, as Man does; or loved Rest, as Man does not;' *Leviathan*, p. 375. 'A *final cause* has no place but in such things as have sense and will; and this also I shall prove hereafter to be an efficient cause.' (*De Corpore*, *L.W.*, vol. I, p. 117.

become at best uniform, at worst random, and the kind of explanations in terms of purpose, to which the Christian Aristotelian's world is susceptible, are impossible. But if the universe is unstructured, it must also seem irrational and so incapable of explanation. How, an Aristotelian might have asked, can we understand (as opposed to merely describe) a concept of motion which is merely change of place, in a world where substance is merely undifferentiated matter and has no 'places' peculiarly appropriate for it to go to, or developments proper to its 'nature'?[49] There are important ethical implications, too, since it is the proper 'nature' of things that validates their actions, or their importance in relation to the 'ends' pursued by others. If no particular actions are in accordance with nature, then no actions – not even, perhaps, murder – are unnatural.

Hobbes accepted this implication and in doing so both rejected the Aristotelian world and invoked one with extraordinary parallels to our own – a world drained of all intrinsic evaluative significance, where what is natural is morally indifferent, or even hostile; where no thing is of intrinsically greater value than another; and where all moral judgements seem to have to be created and imposed from without.

Some of Hobbes's arguments against Aristotelians are purely methodological, others focus on the political properties of their world view. Firstly, Hobbes thought the neo-Aristotelian schoolmen's explanations were bogus, based on what he called 'insignificant speech'. Here is a typical gibe dealing with the central concept of motion:

> If you desire to know why some kind of bodies sink naturally downwards toward the Earth, and others goe naturally from it; the Schools will tell you out of Aristotle, that the bodies that sink downwards, are *Heavy*; and that this Heaviness it is that causes them to descend. But if you ask what they mean by *Heaviness*, they will define it to bee an endeavour to goe to the center of the Earth: so that the cause why things sink downward, is an Endeavour to be below: which is as much as to say that bodies descend or ascend, because they doe.[50]

These kinds of explanations, however, are not only 'empty words', they are, he thinks, something more sinister, part of a whole language of abstractions propagated by the 'Kingdome of Darknesse', explored in the last, and, until recently, mostly unread part of *Leviathan*. Why should Hobbes bother himself with these obscure issues of metaphysics in a work on political obedience? 'It is to this purpose, that men may no longer suffer themselves to be abused by them, that . . . would frighten them from obeying the Laws of their Countrey with empty names.'[51]

Hobbes' target here, and in his last book generally, is Catholicism, which, by depriving people of the right to read the Bible in their own language promoted religious gullibility. But this is deliberately compounded by their

> introducing the Daemonology of the Heathen Poets, that is to say, their fabulous Doctrine concerning Daemons, which are but Idols, or Phantasms of the braine . . . such as . . . dead men's Ghosts, and Fairies . . . [and] mixing with the Scripture diverse

---

[49] Amongst Hobbes's critics, Bishop William Lucy ridiculed the 'universe of motion madly fancied by Mr. Hobbes.' Mintz, *The Hunting of Leviathan*, p. 65.

[50] *Leviathan*, p. 374–5.

[51] Ibid., p. 372–3.

reliques of the Religion, and much of the vain and erroneous Philosophy of the Greeks, especially of Aristotle.[52]

This heady cocktail of biblical obscurantism, Aristotelian metaphysics and pagan demonology led not only to bad science: it was, he thought, politically disruptive, because it opened the door to arguments based on unverifiable spirits, powers and agents, which affect our political obedience. Belief in the powers of priests to ease suffering after death, or in the capacity of God to 'fill' men with obedience or defiance, or in the church's control over ghosts and spirits, all gave men reason for disobeying their sovereign.[53] Nor, as contemporary Anglican churchmen were well aware, did such arguments apply only to the Catholic church. Hobbes's argument was generally anticlerical: as he pointed out at the very end of the book: 'it is not the Romane Clergy onely, that pretends the Kingdom of God to be of this World, and thereby to have a Power therein, distinct from that of the Civil State'.[54] Any clergy claiming any power with implications for human *action* in this world were potential sources of political dissidence: neo-Aristotelian views of science were part and parcel of this danger and true science exposed it.

These objections to scholastic science apart, Hobbes did believe that there was an alternative mode of explanation uniquely fitted to the world of bodies in motion. The application of the method of geometry, 'the onely Science that it hath please God hitherto to bestow on mankind', thought Hobbes, was this key to success.[55] For a major spur to the development of geometry at the time had been ballistics, the science of the paths traced by moving objects – in this case cannon balls. Geometry modelled mechanics, and a world of matter in motion was ultimately a mechanical world. Both the substance and the method of Geometry, made it a discipline peculiarly suited to the exploration of a conceptual universe inhabited only by matter in motion, and where any further definition of the objects of our attention had to be created by men in the way that geometric axioms were.

One of the most important consequences of this view of reality is the sort of explanations which it allows. Since all that exists is matter and all that happens takes place as a result of mechanical causes, all there is to be known must be known, or knowable through our senses.[56] To assert the existence of entities not susceptible to our senses was for Hobbes unaccountable:

> . . . a man can have no thought, representing any thing, not subject to sense. No man therefore can conceive any thing, but he must conceive it in some place; and indued with some determinate magnitude; and which may be divided into parts; nor that any thing is all in this place, and all in another place at the same time; nor that two, or more things can be in one, and the same place at once; for none of these things ever have,

---

[52] *Leviathan*, p. 334.

[53] 'If this superstitious fear of Spirits were taken away, and with it, Prognostiques from Dreams, false Prophecies, and many other things depending thereon, by which, crafty ambitious persons abuse the simple people, men would be much more fitted than they are for civill Obedience.' Ibid., pp. 7–8.

[54] Ibid., p. 387.

[55] Ibid., p. 15.

[56] 'The Original of them all [our thoughts], is that which we call SENSE: For there is no conception in a man's mind, which hath not at first , totally, or by parts, been begotten upon the organs of *Sense*.' Ibid., p. 3.

nor can be incident to Sense; but are absurd speeches, taken upon credit (without any signification at all,) from deceived Philosophers, and deceived, or deceiving Schoolemen.[57]

Epistemological implications

As indicated above, this view rules out any non-material agency as a causative force, and hence as a basis of explanation. But in a subtler way both religion and history, potent and subversive sources of contemporary explanation and argument concerning political allegiance, are ruled out. There are, according to Hobbes, two kinds of knowledge, and neither really enables us to escape from the limitations of the present, which alone 'has a being in Nature'.[58] These two are knowledge of fact and knowledge of causes.

Concerning knowledge based on the accumulation of fact Hobbes is fairly contemptuous. Firstly, the accumulation of factual knowledge is dependent on either our own memory or the testimony and records of others. However vivid present experience, it fades with time. This is explained by Hobbes's materialistic account of experience. The impressions caused in the mind by sensation – being inertial motion – continue, like ripples, in motion after the particles have ceased to hit us. This is called memory or imagination. But their movement – subject to friction and interference by other movements and sensations in the mind – becomes progressively more sluggish. Memory is therefore at best only 'decaying sense'. Secondly, the worth of records depends on the integrity of the recorder and the circumstances under which such records have come down to us. How well have manuscripts been copied? Do they exhibit internal consistency? And so on. Accepting records, or even personal testimony, becomes a matter of assessing the likelihood of their claims in the light of our personal knowledge. Undermining 'knowledge of fact' in this way weakens both political and religious arguments which rely on a particular set of historical facts. The notion that history rests on the shaky foundation of faith in the integrity of the historical records casts doubt on the use of history as a source of political argument and in justifications for political allegiance.

Religious arguments are also undermined, and in two ways. Hobbes shows that it is possible to deny the status claimed for personal revelations without any disrespect to God. Thus, even if a contemporary has a vision in which he receives personal instructions from God, his hearers are not bound to believe him, since, for someone 'To say he [God] hath spoken to him in a Dream is no more than to say he hath dreamt that God spake to him; which is not of force to win belief from any man, that knows dreams are for the most part natural and may proceed from former thoughts.'[59] This, at a stroke, sweeps aside all 'enthusiastic' claims to divine inspiration, so common in that chiliastic age. Secondly, the arguments above about the unreliability of the historical record have the effect of secularizing the epistemological status of conventionally organised religion too, since most of the content of Christian religion – the Bible, and the historical identity of the church for example, or even Christ's ministry – is based on historical records and reported facts. Most people's religion is not based on a personal revelation, but on an acceptance of what the church tells them, and the church is an organisation of men whose

[57] Ibid., p. 11.
[58] Ibid., p. 10.
[59] Ibid., p. 196.

assertions are to be subject to the same intellectual criteria as those of other men. Much of Book 3 of *Leviathan* is devoted to a hermeneutic and historical critique of the Bible, pointing out its inconsistencies, the activity of human beings in constructing it and the long periods that often passed between events and the time when they were written down.[60] Empiricism of Hobbes's kind thus has serious consequences for a religion – such as Christianity – that is both aspirantly transcendent, and claims a basis in historical fact.

The impossibility of a science based on experience

Hobbes's account of everyday knowledge thus uses the limitations inherent in sensory knowledge to undermine historical and religious claims. But such empiricism is not the basis of Hobbes's account of science. Hobbes in fact denies the possibility of constructing science out of empirical knowledge and instead advances a deductive theory of science which is completely at odds with his commonsense, empiricist epistemology. Hobbes's objections to an empirically based science stress the irreducibly particular nature of experience, and the problem of generating from it – as science tries to – statements of a universal kind. The mere accumulation of individual facts about the world does not, Hobbes argues, lead in itself to any kind of science. In this sense it is merely history, and history, simply as a chronicle or record of events has no explanatory power. Hobbes includes in this judgement the accumulation of scientific observation, which is, for him, no different from other kinds of history: empiricism in science is simply *natural* history. Bringing out Hobbes's reasons for believing this requires us to return to Hobbes's account of the human mind in order to understand the status of the different operations of which it is capable.

Decaying sense impressions can be re-evoked in us by re-exposure to other impressions which were originally experienced close in time to them. A whole train of thought associated in this way can be evoked by exposing the thinker to the first of a series he has previously experienced. This 'association of ideas' was to have enormous consequences in the next century, but it plays only two limited if important roles here in Hobbes's thought. Firstly it explains how we can use signs, and thus language – a version of signs peculiar to humans. The explanation is clearer in the *Elements of Law*. Animals, says Hobbes, who hide their food, use the connection between the impression of the food and the impression of some feature of the place where they hid it in order to remember hiding, and recover their food, but they nevertheless easily forget. Humans may themselves make a mark in such a place, and so remember more easily.[61] The ability to use one impression to evoke another is thus common to man and beast. But the ability to

---

[60] Impugning the possibility of religious certainty as a basis for faith – sceptical fideism – had become a tactic of the Counter-reformation, pursued in France by Catholics such as Pierre Charron to undermine the claims of Protestants that believers could discern, in the Bible, and so without the aid of the Catholic Church, God's message to mankind. The key figure of Hobbes's generation – whom Hobbes probably knew – was Isaac La Peyrère who developed a specifically biblical critical hermeneutic, denying Moses's authorship of the Pentateuch. In England a follower, Richard Simon was taken up and used by deists to discredit revelation in favour of natural or rational religion. Hobbes's use of such arguments in England is, however, early. See Richard H. Popkin, *The History of Scepticism, from Erasmus to Spinoza* (Berkely, L.A., & London, 1979), ch.xi.

[61] *Elements of Law*, Pt.1, v, §1.

understand, which is to raise impressions in another's mind by the use of conventional signs, is peculiar to humans. Only human beings therefore develop associations between conventional signs and objects – speech – and are thereby able to co-ordinate their thoughts both with one another and through time – a capacity Hobbes immediately connects with the construction of societies.[62]

The second role of association is to explain one way in which humans (and beasts) gain knowledge of the consequences of events or actions. That is, by thinking of similar events or actions in the past and seeing what the 'associated' consequences were: such as, for example, the association between grey skies and rain. The accumulation of this kind of experience is what enables us to make 'better guesses' at outcomes. But knowledge of this kind is always 'a *Praesumtion* of the *Future*, contracted from the *Experience* of time *Past*'; it is called prudence.[63] In a significant devaluation of this once prized quality, Hobbes points out that prudence, this accumulation of experienced associations, is common to men and beasts. Animals can gain prudence because it is simply the acquisition of associations between signs in the mind. Signs can be natural – grey skies – or conventional – the master's call that brings the dog running to heel. What animals lack is the capacity voluntarily to construct sequences of signs – to reason. Prudence is at best the memory or knowledge of (sometimes many) individual facts, and can never, Hobbes claims, give rise to science. That is, it never entitles us to make universally valid statements concerning the object we are trying to understand.

This is essentially a widely recognised philosophical problem – that of induction. No matter how many times we observe that a certain event follows another one, or that a certain kind of thing exhibits certain properties, we cannot, on such grounds, be justified in asserting that this will always be the case. Here this may follow in part from Hobbes's ontology, according to which there are no 'natural kinds' of things to provide a basis for such regularity. 'Events' and 'things' are, after all, conventionally designated itemizations of a reality which is either inherently undifferentiated, or, as the next generation of scientists was to insist, differentiated in a way inscrutable to humans. However, if we know the mechanism of cause and effect that is operating between an event y and its cause x, then, claims Hobbes, we can assert that y will always follow x. Observation of the facts themselves, however, never reveals causes, only regular sequences; experience is always and only experience of particulars, and so, '*concludeth nothing universal*', whereas the achievement of universal propositions is the very object of science.[64] So, claims Hobbes, the only true science, is not knowledge of facts, but knowledge of causes, and knowledge of causes cannot be got from observation alone but must involve the use of analysis and reason.[65]

---

[62] *Leviathan*, pp. 10–11, and 12–13.

[63] Ibid., pp. 10, 11.

[64] *E.W.*, IV, p. 18

[65] As Harro Höpfl – who has tried to keep me honest – reminds me, Hobbes's usual assertion is that science enables us to achieve knowledge of 'consequences'. (*Leviathan*, pp. 14, 18, etc.) But that Hobbes considers the 'consequences' so arrived at to reveal causes is clear both because lack of science is 'ignorance of causes', and from the following passage, which also clearly illustrates Hobbes's Baconian conception of science as a source of control and power: '*Science* is the knowledge of Consequences, and dependence of one fact upon another; by which, out of that we can presently do, we know how to do something else when we will . . . : Because when we see how any thing comes about, upon what causes, and by what manner; when the like causes come into our power, wee see how to make it produce the like effects.' *Leviathan*, p. 21.

There is then, a fundamental split in Hobbes's epistemology.[66] Our everyday epistemology is resolutely empiricist: we should believe only the evidence of our senses. Science however – the attempt to explain by causes – must reject empiricism, which can never proceed beyond the particular. Accounts of causal regularities – because they aspire to universality – can only be achieved through the one medium that transcends the particular, namely language.

The nature of true science

Although language – the use of names as signs – enables us to make general statements, and so opens up the possibility of science, language is subject to one major drawback. This is its equivocal nature.

> This equivocation of names maketh it difficult to recover those conceptions for which the name was ordained; and not only in the language of other men, wherein we are to consider the drift, and occasion, and contexture of the speech, as well as the words themselves; but also in our own discourse, which being derived from the custom and common use of speech, representeth not unto us our own conceptions.[67]

In common with other thinkers of his time, many of whom in England were later to form the Royal Society, Hobbes saw the creation of an unequivocal scientific language as one of the prerequisites of science.[68] 'In the right Definition of Names, lyes the first use of Speech; which is the Acquisition of Science: And in wrong, or no Definitions, lyes the first abuse.'[69] This defining activity includes, of course, ridding ourselves of the terminology and sometimes the meanings of earlier thinkers. For as he says in a famous passage, 'words are wise mens counters, they do but reckon by them: but they are the mony of fooles, that value them by the authority of an *Aristotle*, a *Cicero*, or a *Thomas*, or any other Doctor whatsoever, if but a man.'[70] Hobbes clearly has particularly in mind the misleading metaphysical terminology of the scholastics.

The sense in which the foundation of science is 'the apt imposition of names' (or as above, their 'right definition') cannot be that of isolating and correctly defining a natural kind – *essential definition* as it is called – for there can be no such activity. Firstly because matter is uniform: there are no natural kinds, or if there are we cannot know them; and secondly because (as a result) names are purely conventional. Hobbes's seemingly extraordinarily modernist project is to construct not only politics, but the very intelligibility of the world itself out of purely conventional materials. However, this 'nominalism'

---

[66] 'There be two sorts of knowledge, whereof the one is nothing else but sense, or knowledge original . . . ; and the other is called science or knowledge of the truth of propositions, and how things are called, and is derived from understanding.' *Elements of Law*, Pt. 1, vi, §1.

[67] *Elements of Law*, Pt. 1, v, §8; also *Leviathan*, p. 17.

[68] The Bishop of Chester, John Wilkins, founder member of the Royal Society, was the most famous advocate, arguing for the creation of a new language the terms of which, being without other associations, would be precise, unambiguous and international: *Essay Towards a Real Character, and a Philosophical Language* (1668).

[69] *Leviathan*, p. 15.

[70] Ibid. p. 15.

of Hobbes's invites comparison not only with the Wittgensteinian claim that our investigations are limited and constrained within the linguistic world which we have created for ourselves, but with that of the famous fourteenth century heterodox nominalist, William of Occam. Although there is no direct evidence of Hobbes's familiarity with Occam, the similarities extend to aspects of their social theory too.

How can definitions be, as Hobbes puts it 'apt', or 'got right'? It may be that Hobbes did not see the full implications of his conventionalism, for if there are no natural kinds and language is as arbitrary as he suggests, it is difficult to see what criteria there could be for a 'right' or a 'wrong' definition.[71] Even so there were other ways in which definitions could be 'got wrong'. That is not only by definitional equivocation – defining a term so loosely it could mean different things, and so confound a chain of argument – but also by ambiguity between the definitions and the use: defining a term to mean something different from what we had in mind (and so deceiving ourselves) or using it metaphorically or guilefully (and so deceiving others).[72]

The major way, though, in which language can go wrong, relates back to Hobbes's materialism. If language is to reflect reality, it must and can only deal in that which is body or matter, or a property of body or matter, or the properties of our own bodies, senses or conceptions of matter, or the terms we use to describe these things.[73] Language which purports to be about anything else, like statements containing contradictory terms, is 'insignificant sounds'. To give rise to science then, language must consist of strict and consistently held definitions, and be about material body and its movements or properties and the conceptions in our mind arising therefrom.

Although science must be *about* matter or body, it is an essentially linguistic or logical activity. It *consists* in a verbal process moving

> from the Elements, which are Names, to Assertions made by Connexion of one of them to another; and so to Syllogismes, which are the Connexions of one Assertion to another, till we come to a knowledge of all the consequences of names appertaining to the subject in hand; and this is it, men call SCIENCE.[74]

Science is essentially a process of calculating the logical consequences of definitions, precisely analogous to the way the geometer establishes the truth of theorems from definitions.[75] Only science will give us knowledge of causes, and so give us knowledge of consequences, which no knowledge of fact can reliably do. The logical links in our deductions, Hobbes believes, can parallel the causal links in the world. Hobbes believes this to be possible where our definitions are related in ways that verbally replicate the generation or composition of the object being defined. However because all that exists is material, they can do this only where the definitions refer to bodies in motion. The

---

[71] The problem of induction exists even if there are real kinds, for there must be uncertainty that we have identified them; however the problem seems quite intractable in their absence. Only at one point, however, does Hobbes seem to make explicit the connection between the difficulties of induction and the necessarily arbitrary nature of language: 'we cannot . . . conclude . . . from any proposition *universal* whatsoever, except it be from the remembrance of the use of names imposed arbitrarily by men:', *E.W.*, IV, p. 18.

[72] *Leviathan*, p. 13.

[73] Ibid, p. 16.

[74] Ibid, p. 21.

[75] Ibid, p. 18.

logic of the geometrical method represents the causality of the world and this is possible because fundamentally all causality is movement, and geometrical deduction is a verbal representation of mechanical consequence. Although he never makes it explicit, the existence of geometry provides a conceptual bridge between a mechanical reality and Hobbes's nominalistic science.

There is an important limitation, though, to Hobbes's nominalistic rationalism. Despite his championing of the sort of knowledge produced by reasoning, he insists that this knowledge is nevertheless only conditional. It is dependent on the kinds of definitions we give to the objects of our discourse. Indeed, for Hobbes, all human knowledge is limited. Science:

> is not Absolute, but Conditionall. No man can know by Discourse, that this, or that, is, has been, or will be: which is to know absolutely: but onely, that if This be, That is; if This has been, That has been; if This shall be, That shall be: which is to know conditionally;[76]

Consequently the sort of knowledge that even scientific reasoning attains is a matter of the relationship of its conclusions to reality, and is contingent not only on the correctness of our chains of reasoning, but on the conformity of the world to our definitions of it. Just as in geometry the proofs of the qualities possessed by right-angled triangles would only apply to a real triangle inasmuch as it possessed the ideal characteristics of the definition of a right-angled triangle – being a closed figure having three straight sides etc. – so in Hobbes's analogous reasoning the proof is conditional on the objects in the world conforming to the definitions in our argument.

There is therefore, a role for empiricism in Hobbes's science, but it lies not in the accumulation of data to ground hypotheses, but in checking the plausibility of the conclusions derived from hypotheses through strict deductive chains of reasoning.

This is the promised method of *Leviathan*; the structure of the first two parts of which at least, is presented by Hobbes as a long series of deductions from axioms, intermittently checked against reality for plausibility. Having presented the world as matter in motion, Hobbes aspires to construct a scientific account of it by deducing an ever more complex series of propositions based on the few axioms from which he starts.[77]

The science of man

The basic axiom that the world consists of matter in motion is true for human beings also. We have already seen how Hobbes claimed to account for sensation and memory through the motion of sensed waves or particles.[78]

---

[76] Ibid, p. 31.

[77] This is currently a slightly unfashionable view to take of Hobbes. It is one, however, which seems to me to bear the closest relationship to his own declared aspirations.

[78] Hobbes equivocated over the form taken by light as moving matter. Starting with a particle theory, he rejected it because of the difficulty of accounting for the persistence of bodies (such as the sun) which continually lose matter. He then proposed a wave theory which ran into difficulties because of the demonstration of the existence of the vacuum by Torricelli. See the account in Goldsmith, *Hobbes's Science of Politics*, pp. 17–20.

Human action as matter in motion

The activities of human beings too are based on the inertial movements of the matter which comprises them. There are two broad categories of motion in humans: vital, or involuntary motion such as breathing, digestion, jumping with fright etc., and animal, or deliberate motion or actions. These latter result at least in part from our imaginations. When animal motion is towards an object it is called appetite; when away, aversion; and where indifferent it is called contempt. The words 'good' and 'evil' says Hobbes are names of what we desire or hate, they do not relate in any way to moral qualities of objects themselves, for it is a consequence of his mechanistic, causal picture of the world that they have none. Hobbes here underscores the way in which he has drained the world of any inherent value or meaning of right and wrong. There is 'nothing simply and absolutely so; nor any common Rule of Good and Evill, to be taken from the nature of the objects themselves.'[79] This denial of an objective basis for morality once again provoked tremendous outrage amongst Hobbes's clerical opponents. Since things cannot be good or bad in themselves, the only possible source for such values seems to lie in human preferences. What can we say about these preferences?

Pleasure, claims Hobbes, derives from those sensations which help us to continue our vital motion, which is ultimately life itself. But because human beings have language and the ability to imagine the future, they can describe to themselves, and attempt to bring about, states of affairs which assist this motion (and so produce pleasure). Primitive humans organised to catch deer, and the modern organisation of a political society to enjoy security, differ only (if crucially) in the extent to which human beings have used their reason to foresee and bring about that situation which will enable them to continue their vital motion. The attempt to maintain one's vital motion is, in subjective terms, the desire to remain alive; the instinct for self preservation is the behavioural counterpart of the inertial motion of all matter: it is the psychological manifestation of the physical properly. The succession of desires, like the threats to their satisfaction, is constant whilst men live; no one end, therefore, is capable of making us content, but 'felicity' is continual success in satisfying our desires. It is not that men's appetites are individually insatiable – we get bored – but they are infinitely varied.

In any circumstance humans (and indeed animals) will have a number of possible choices. *Deliberation* is the process by which those choices are resolved into action. In humans possessing science this takes the form not only of assessing how strong the various desires are but how they could be satisfied (their *causes*), what other consequences satisfying them may have (their *effects*) and how likely they are to be achieved (*hope* and *fear*). Deliberation is necessarily directed at satisfying the deliberator's desires, altruism is at best a peculiarly directed form of egoism – 'of the voluntary acts of every man, the object is some *Good to himselfe*'[80] – not that we are always correct in our

---

[79] *Leviathan*, p. 24.

[80] Ibid, p. 66. Hobbes didn't deny the existence of apparently altruistic actions, but he claimed they still derived from essentially egoistic motives. Aubrey records a minister, seeing Hobbes give money to a beggar, asking how he could have done this consistently with the purely egoistic premises of his psychology. Hobbes replied there was no inconsistency 'because I was in paine to consider the miserable condition of the old

calculations. Once these calculations are over, the strongest remaining desire determines our *Will*. The will is simply *'the last Appetite in Deliberating'*.[81] The circumstances entering into our calculations make no difference as to whether our wills are free or not. Threats of violence, or other unacceptable alternatives do not render our wills the less free. Only where we are physically constrained are we unfree.

It is important to notice the radical devaluation of the role of reason in Hobbes's account of human nature compared with classical views. Hobbes reduces reason to the capacity to calculate the likely outcomes of our appetites: nothing is inherently reasonable, and reason does not, for Hobbes, provide us with any superior or sublime insights or moral truths. It simply enables us to calculate outcomes better.[82]

Will, too, is reduced to the outcome of the clash of appetites. This view has important implications. A man's will – for Christians at least – is highly relevant to questions of morality. We are commonly held responsible for actions that result from our free wills, and responsibility carries with it the burden of moral praise – or blame worthiness. Yet Hobbes's account of deliberation seems most to resemble a play of forces within a passive vessel: there seems no role for a personality which does the deciding. Deciding is simply the emergence of the strongest desire, something that happens to us rather than something we do. We might well argue that our actions can only be subject to, and involve, morality when they are considered voluntary – which, despite his determinism, he insisted our uncoerced actions were.[83] But Hobbes's account of human decision-making seems to reduce it to simply the more complex consequences of bodies in motion. Has he successfully crossed what many like to think of as the boundary between the description of physical particles and the language of human behaviour and morality?

Hobbes anticipates no problems in reducing the phenomena of human consciousness to the sort of language used about the physical world, because ultimately all experience is reducible to physical phenomena. The debate as to whether this is possible has persisted, in different forms, amongst philosophers, physiologists and psychologists ever since. It seems to be no nearer any resolution. Can the signal on a cerebral monitoring device or the electro-chemical reaction in a brain cell or cells actually be *identified* with a thought (as opposed to merely accompanying it)? Or isn't the world of meanings and intentions involved in language and thought about ourselves and our motives irresolvably distinct from the merely mechanical operations of the brain considered as a part of nature? This barrier between the two categories: that of consciousness and that of even living matter has seemed a central feature of modern thought. Hobbes, in developing the view

---

man; and now my almes, giving him some reliefe, doth also ease me.' John Aubrey, *Brief Lives*, p. 317. F.S. McNeilly, *Anatomy of Leviathan* (London, 1968), argues that *Leviathan* contains a retreat from Hobbes's earlier commitment to the ubiquity of egoistic motivation.

[81] *Leviathan*, p. 28.

[82] Contemporary critics, even the Cambridge Platonists, with whom he differed most, complained curiously little about Hobbes's dethronement of reason. Mintz, *Hunting of Leviathan*, p. 83. But the sage Clarendon noted that the assumption of a calculating rationality was one of the least plausible of Hobbes's positions: 'We have too much cause to believe that the major part of mankind do not think at all.' Cited, John Bowle, *Hobbes and his Critics* (London, 1951), p. 163.

[83] Hobbes engaged in a long controversy with Bishop Bramhall on the question of freedom and determinism in which he maintains a compatibility thesis on the grounds that although wills are necessarily determined by chains of causality, actions are free if they result from the will. *The Questions Concerning Liberty, Necessity, and Chance, clearly stated and debated . . .* , in *E.W.*, vol. V.

of the material world as unspiritual, dis-enchanted and inert, helped to establish the distinction, with all the moral difficulties that position entailed. Yet he ultimately denies it by seeking to reduce consciousness to a merely emergent property of moving matter.[84] The churchmen who so denounced Hobbes were at the very least right in identifying this as a crucial and far-reaching issue.

The natural condition of mankind

Having outlined his conceptions of scientific method and of human psychology, Hobbes next considers what properties might be exhibited by human beings assembled together in some kind of aggregate (we cannot assume this will constitute a social whole). True to his method, this involved an attempt to logically deduce such properties from those of individuals, in the hope of isolating the relevant universally effective causes.

The deduction of the state of nature

Since all seek to satisfy their desires, and since there is no one *summum bonum*, or highest good, for men, but rather a constant succession of appetites, what each human most wants is not any particular thing but the generalised capacity to satisfy new desires as they emerge: 'to assure for ever, the way of his future desire'.[85] This is effectively *power*: 'The POWER *of a Man* . . . is his present means, to obtain some future apparent Good.'[86] Power is not confined simply to physical force: it includes any attribute which enables a man to affect the world to what he deems to be his advantage. In social terms it includes attributes such as wealth, servants, friends, reputation and honour. Hobbes conceives of power, at this point, in specifically social terms; that is, he is not concerned so much with the way nature might thwart our desires, rather than with the way other humans do.[87] Power consists in 'eminence' and is therefore the marginal advantage of control enjoyed

---

[84] J.W.N. Watkins seems to conclude, rather unhistorically, that since [in principle?] 'psychological conclusions . . . cannot be deduced from materialist premises', Hobbes must have detached his psychology and politics from his physics. ('Philosophy and Politics in Hobbes', in *Hobbes Studies*, ed. K.C. Brown (Oxford, 1965), p. 238) But conclusions about Hobbes's beliefs can hardly follow from premises about Watkins's, however true the latter. For a more sympathetic discussion of the problems in Hobbes's position see Tommy L. Lott, 'Hobbes's Mechanistic Psychology', in *Thomas Hobbes His View of Man*, ed. J.G. van der Bend (Amsterdam, 1982).

[85] *Leviathan*, p. 47. That all human beings want this, presumes of course that they reason rationally about their long-term interests, rather than being swept along by their current desire. This presumption is a central one in Hobbes's argument, but not made explicit until chapter 15, where he argues, that for a man to try and foresee or 'reckon upon' the 'errours of other men' is 'against the reason of his preservation' (p. 73). In any attempt to reason about human behaviour, therefore, we should presume that people make correct, and not false, reasonings about their interests, as does Hobbes, throughout *Leviathan*.

[86] Ibid., p. 41.

[87] Although he is clearly aware of this dimension. For example, one of the consequences of the inability to co-ordinate effort in the pre-political state is human feebleness in the face of natural forces. Without social co-operation there are, 'no Instruments of moving, and removing such things as require much force'. Ibid., p. 62.

by one human over other human beings: it is a relative, and therefore 'zero-sum', quality.[88]

The interaction of humans with the characteristics described by Hobbes, produces his version of the 'state of nature'. This, he argues will be a situation of conflict, uncertainty and violence in which the survival of each is threatened by the very means each adopts to secure it. Men, Hobbes observes, are all roughly equal in physical size and strength, in intellectual powers, and consequently, in the hope of attaining their ends. In fact there is a sinister, if perfectly explicable, asymmetry of such hope: inasmuch as men, being proud, 'will hardly believe there be many so wise as themselves: For they see their own wit at hand, and other men's at a distance'.[89] Overestimating our own chances of success in any conflict is dangerously destabilizing. A direct consequence of this is that should any two or more men desire the same thing there will be conflict, violence and perhaps even death. Conflict can arise from any attempt by humans to satisfy their desires, for they may go to any lengths to do so. In the state of nature there are no moral limits to men's action: 'The notions of Right and Wrong, Justice and Injustice have there no place' and they may kill another for anything they deem necessary to their life, even, Hobbes insists, 'for trifles, as a word, a smile, a different opinion'.[90] Hobbes's 'low view' of human nature was not merely a conclusion of his science. Aubrey writes that 'Thomas Hobbs said that if it were not for the gallowes, some men are of so cruell a nature as to take a delight in killing men more than I should to kill a bird.'[91]

It is instructive to notice in detail the causes of this violence. It derives from the very qualities which are commonly thought of as being the basis of human political sociability, our supposed equality and rationality. Although Hobbes uses the device of a state of nature, the conflict in it does not arise because men there are intellectually primitive or beast-like; quite the opposite: it arises from their equality, and a presumption of their equal skill and sophistication at reasoning. Not the least of Hobbes's paradoxes is that the worst features of human life derive, not from their lapses into beastliness, but from their very humanity.

---

[88] 'Power is the eminence of the Faculties' *Leviathan*, pp. 41, 61.

[89] Ibid., p. 61.

[90] Ibid., pp. 63, 62. Some commentators question the apparently limitless nature of the rights Hobbes allows to men in a state of nature. See esp. R.Tuck, *Natural Rights Theories*, pp. 125ff.; and his 'Hobbes' in *Plato to Nato*, intr. B.Redhead, (London, 1984); and also Goldsmith, *Hobbes's Science of Politics*, p. 88: 'The right of nature . . . should not be regarded as an absolute and unlimited right. Hobbes does overstate the situation somewhat.' (Although see his later position in 'Hobbes on Liberty', *Hobbes Studies*, II (1989)) It's not clear how Hobbes could overstate a situation of which he is himself the author. As Goldsmith goes on to point out, the right is to anything men *regard* as necessary for their survival, not anything that is *in fact* necessary for it. But since individuals, in a state of nature are the only judges, this is no effective limit on their actions. This argument is most clearly made by Hobbes in the *Elements of Law*, Pt. 1, xiv, §10: 'every man by nature hath right to all things, that is to say, to do whatsoever he listeth to whom he listeth, to possess, use, and enjoy all things he will and can.' Although, as Tuck points out, (*Natural Rights Theories*, p. 125), in the next version of his theory (*De Cive*, [1642]) Hobbes warns against pretending that we need something for our preservation when we don't, in *Leviathan* once again Hobbes goes out of his way to demonstrate how reasonable it would be for men to assert their right over seemingly infinitely trivial matters – for 'trifles, as a word, a smile, a different opinion, and any other sign of undervalue'; *Leviathan*, p. 62.

[91] Aubrey, *Brief Lives*, p. 317. The remark perhaps reveals as much about Aubrey's attitude to wildlife as Hobbes's to his fellows.

The explanation of conflict is, in line with Hobbes's rule of scientific method, a logical deduction from the situation and properties of natural man. Initially conflict may arise from the desire of individuals for the same objects. Where individuals have worked upon and improved nature, for example by tilling the ground and sowing a crop, the likelihood of others wishing to take advantage of these goods is high, for there is no property and no right and wrong apart from what individuals deem to be to their advantage. But conflict is not to be explained, as often suggested, by natural scarcity. It is primarily a result of men's reasoned reflections on their social interaction. Where all outcomes (all 'future goods'), and indeed all existing advantages and possessions are uncertain, the most rational course for a man is to anticipate (which he can do through reason) others' invasions of his goods, and to pre-empt it by attempting to gain power over them. Scarcity might be said to result from men's actions rather than vice-versa. The situation is already unstable, but it is worse: for there may be men who simply enjoy the possession of power and who therefore extend their power 'further than security requires'. Given the existence of some such men, it becomes even more reasonable for others, more moderate, to try to extend their power also, in a purely defensive effort to retain their position relative to everyone else. Finally men are essentially proud creatures who desire to have others esteem them at their own inflated valuation, and this is a further cause of quarreling. This may seem trivial, yet to be esteemed is a kind of power, and to show contempt for a man is therefore an invasion of his security. Aggressive defence of one's honour is accordingly quite rational.[92]

In these circumstances an escalation in the degree and likelihood of conflict between men is always to be reckoned on, and pre-emptive action is, in principle, invariably rational. Although this is not an outcome that any man individually desires, it is a necessary result of each individual reacting rationally to preserve their own interest. Hobbes's genius here is point out how, in the absence of authority, unrestricted competition driven by quite rational individual calculation, brings about an unwished for and disastrous outcome for all concerned. The situation has clear similarities to an arms race, or the pursuit of a limited natural resource such as fish stocks, or to unionized groups of workers competing through inflationary wage bargaining to protect their standards of living. In each case, the reasonable defensive reactions of individuals to the general situation has the effect of making it worse. It is one of the most powerful and generalizable political models ever constructed, and Hobbes's famous description of it, as so often in his work, adds dramatic and rhetorical force to an already compelling logic:

> In such condition, there is no place for Industry; because the fruit thereof is uncertain: and consequently no Culture of the Earth; no Navigation, nor use of the commodities that may be imported by Sea; no commodious Building; no Instruments of moving, and removing such things as require much force; no Knowledge of the face of the Earth; no account of Time; no Arts; no Letters; no Society; and which is worst of all, continuall feare, and danger of violent death; And the life of man, solitary, poore, nasty, brutish, and short.[93]

[92] *Leviathan*, p. 61; and p. 41, 'Reputation of power, is Power; because it draweth with it the adhærence of those that need protection.'

[93] Ibid., p. 62. The formalization of Hobbes's intimations has spawned a vast subject beyond the possibility of this work to explore, and which far surpasses anything which could be ascribed to Hobbes himself. For recent studies see works in the bibliography by Gauthier, Hampson, Kavka and McLean.

Hobbes now breaks off from his argument to consider whether the picture of men created by his method conforms at all to our ordinary experience. For although Hobbes denies that science can be established on the basis of empirical evidence, science is only 'conditionally true' and, he acknowledges, requires an experiential check on the validity of the results achieved. If we consider his picture is too pessimistic he asks us: consider the measures taken for security when a man sleeps (locking his doors), goes on a journey (arming himself and taking servants), or is absent from his valuables (locking them away): 'Does he not there as much accuse mankind by his actions, as I do by my words?' If we consider parts of the world such as America, where there is no government, there men live 'in that brutish manner' and Hobbes reminds his readers that they know from experience the sort of behaviour men resort to in a civil war. Finally in inter-state relationships we find individual states behaving in this fashion towards each other in the absence of any power (which we call sovereignty) to control their aggression and thus minimize their fear.[94] Empirical evidence, Hobbes claims, supports the results of his deductive science.

The sources, character and status of Hobbes's state of nature

The status and origins of Hobbes's state of nature have been a source of both moral horror and intellectual fascination to contemporaries and modern commentators alike. As to the question of its status – Hobbes disconcertingly admits that he is not claiming it was a generalised historical epoch: there 'was never generally' such a state, 'over all the world'.[95] It is rather a condition which emerges whenever political authority fails: Hobbes might – as indeed he does – admit that men have always been involved in some degree of association with each other, even if only through the 'natural lust' which gives rise to authority within the family, without having to abandon the theoretical role of the state of nature.[96] It was, on one view at least, immaterial to his argument whether the state of nature ever fully existed: he did not, after all, wish to get bogged down in (in his view) irrelevant historical questions. For Hobbes, the attempt to construct scientific knowledge was a-temporal, in the sense that it pursued the logical implications of refined definitions: the state of nature was an 'Inference, made from the Passions'.[97] Just as Galileo had never actually seen or measured bodies falling in a vacuum, nor would Newton be able to

---

[94] *Leviathan*, pp. 62, 63.

[95] Ibid., p. 63.

[96] Ibid. Despite this famous, and theoretically central role of atomised individuals in Hobbes's state of nature, there are persistent references by him to the possibility of small, familial and proto-political social groups in the state of nature. It is unclear how important a role such groups are supposed to play in Hobbes's basic argument. For a discussion which considers both what Hobbes says on this issue and the persuasive role it may have played for his readers, despite its apparent incongruence with what has been (and is here taken to be) his 'theory', see Richard Ashcraft, 'Political Theory and Practical Action: A reconsideration of Hobbes's State of Nature', *Hobbes Studies*, I (1988).

[97] *Leviathan*, p. 62. Although this is true of his science, Hobbes's thought shows a keen awareness of the issues raised by time and history, especially within a Christian framework. By far the best discussion of this is J.G.A. Pocock's 'Time, History and Eschatology in the thought of Thomas Hobbes', in his *Politics, Language and Time* (Chicago and London, 1971).

measure frictionless reacting forces, but each could nevertheless usefully postulate laws involving such conditions, so Hobbes could postulate the state of nature, to explain the underlying regularity of human behaviour, even though this postulate appeared strange to men. 'For Science is of that nature, as none can understand it to be, but such as in a good measure have attayned it.'[98]

Although the postulates of science cannot be arrived at through common sense, it is interesting that Hobbes commonly asserts, as in the passage above, that ordinary practical knowledge is consistent with its conclusions.[99] It was important to him that his science be accessible. In demolishing old mysteries he did not want to establish new ones in their place.

The state of nature is simply the condition of men without a sovereign power to compel order. Just as we may never have a perfect vacuum, perhaps we can never have a situation where there are no vestiges of the restraints that sovereignty provides, but *inasmuch* as sovereignty is absent, to that extent men will begin to exhibit behaviour typical of the state of nature.[100]

The second question that arises with respect to Hobbes's picture of the state of nature is the question of his sources. In a sense there is a simple answer and it is the answer that is provided in Hobbes's text itself: the picture of the state of nature is deduced from the characteristics of human psychology. But are there other explanations?

Some have sought to explain Hobbes's account in terms of widespread socio-economic changes taking place in the early modern period. Although the state of nature reveals not 'natural' (in the sense of aboriginal) man, but social man without the normal constraints of society, it seems too limiting (although not altogether false) to say, as some have done, that Hobbes's picture of natural man simply displays the characteristics of a new 'bourgeois' social order.[101] Hobbes's attitude to these changes seems more complex. Certainly he emphasises the egoistic calculating aspect of human beings; but pride – a theoretically central and worrying manifestation of egoism on Hobbes's account – is a characteristic of aristocracies, and much of the detail of Hobbes's account of social terms reveals an endorsement of some of the qualities of an aristocratic class, and is in turn scornful of the opportunism and calculation required of the new commercial and upwardly mobile groups, and of those aristocrats who had joined them.[102] Both the ideal, and destructive

---

[98] *Leviathan*, p. 42.

[99] Further examples occur in the 'Review and Conclusion' where he claims his doctrines are based on knowledge, 'of which no man, that pretends but reason enough to govern his private family, ought to be ignorant' (p. 394); and where he points out that although men like to parade their book learning in politics and religion, when it came to organising their private affairs, they rightly adhered to more practical views – a rather different attitude to 'prudence' than Hobbes normally shows, Ibid. p. 24.

[100] Goldsmith puts it well: 'the residue of anarchy and insecurity exists wherever and whenever the effective control of the society begins to weaken. In areas remote from the power of the sovereign, bandits lurk. In the interstices of the society, psychological as well as physical, in the contempt of law-enforcing power as well as in the darkened back-alley, the state of nature is evident.' *Hobbes's Science of Politics*, p. 173.

[101] Most notably C.B. Macpherson, *The Political Theory of Possessive Individualism* (Oxford, 1962); but see also Leo Strauss, *The Political Philosophy of Hobbes* (Oxford, 1936[Chicago, 1952]).

[102] Macpherson makes much of the passage (*Leviathan*, p. 42) beginning 'The *Value*, or WORTH of a man, is as of all other things, his Price; that is to say, so much as would be given for the use of his Power:' as exemplifying a market view of social power. *Possessive Individualism*, p. 37. But other observations in

qualities in Hobbes's humans are aristocratic; for despite the underlying role of self-interest it is in the form taken by pride or vainglory that it destabilizes political society.[103]

Others stress the influence of religious thought. Whilst it is common to assume, as does Hobbes himself, a prevalent Christian-Aristotelian orthodoxy in matters of social and political philosophy, this is of course the crudest shorthand. There were strands in Europe's intellectual tradition which questioned the Aristotelian and Thomistic view of human beings as naturally suited and fitted to social life. Indeed, within the 'republican tradition' for which political Aristotelianism is so often a convenient shorthand, there was a tradition of stoicism and a reading of Cicero which stressed the necessary role of artifice in constructing societies.[104]

Within Christianity the Augustinian tradition regarded man's sociability as brought seriously into question by the Fall. Politics, on this view was a necessary consequence of our *im*perfections. There was often a particular stress on this in countries influenced by Lutheran Protestantism which had placed renewed emphasis on the Augustinian view of original sin, and man's continuing and irredeemable wickedness. Religious wars and dynastic struggles on the continent had brought home to humans the degree of suffering societies were prepared to inflict on each other, and had given rise – especially in France as we saw – to a political tradition which questioned whether such issues were important enough to warrant killing and bloodshed. Also important was the fact that travel and exploration were beginning to provide a wider perspective to Europeans' views of themselves. Hakluyt's famous *Voyages* was only one of an increasing number of books detailing the strange and apparently barbaric practices of non-Europeans. Without the kind of anthropological perspective which might enable appreciation of these often complex and subtle cultures, Europeans saw in them frightening testimony of the possibility of human existence without most of the things they had regarded as distinctly human. The French essayist Montaigne, a sceptical 'politique' coming under both these influences, and in turn, an influence on Hobbes himself, describes the culture of 'cannibals' in an admittedly more ironic vein than Hobbes, as the negation of all that constitutes, for Europeans, civilisation's very existence. It is in effect a description of the state of nature, and the literary device is clearly an ancestor of Hobbes's. Amongst the cannibals, writes Montaigne, there is 'No kinde of traffike, no knowledge of Letters, no intelligence of numbers, no name of magistrate, nor of politike superioritie, no use of service, of riches or of povertie; no contracts, no successions, no partitions, no

---

the same chapter seem dismissive of bourgeois values and to endorse an aristocratic ethos. 'To be descended from conspicuous Parents, is Honourable . . . from obscure Parentage, is Dishonourable . . . Magnanimity is a signe of Power. On the contrary, Craft, Shifting, neglect of Equity, is Dishonourable . . . Covetousness and ambition, of little gaines or preferments is Dishonourable' (pp. 44, 46). The man honoured in the dedication of the book, Sidney Godolphin, possessed virtues which were not 'acquired by necessity, or affected upon occasion [as Hobbesian psychology, might lead us to expect], but inhærent, and shining in a generous constitution of his nature.' sig. B2.

[103] For an exploration of the view that *Leviathan* was 'a masterfull project designed to salvage, rejuvenate and contain a disorderly peerage and gentry instead of a complex machine to prevent the self-destruction of bourgeois man' see N.Wood, 'Hobbes and the Crisis of the Aristocracy', *History of Political Thought*, I, 3 (1986), p. 437. For another discussion of the social context see K. Thomas, 'The Social Origins of Hobbes's Political Thought', in *Hobbes Studies*, ed. K.C. Brown (Oxford, 1965).

[104] The following section owes much to Richard Ashcraft's discussion 'Hobbes's Natural Man' *Journal of Politics*, 33 (1971).

occupations but idle, no respect of kindred, but common, no apparell but naturall, no manuring of lands, no use of wine, corne or mettle.'[105]

There were then, plenty of suggestions in the inherited culture to suggest that men were not always quite as naturally fitted to civilised, cultured and sociable life as Aristotle, Aquinas and Hooker had suggested, in the right circumstances, they might be. Part of Hobbes's originality lies in the fact that, instead of seeing such unsociability as deviations from a norm, he presents it as inherent and constitutive of man's nature. He inverts the prevailing view, representing the exceptions as typical, and what was considered 'natural' – human sociability – as the fragile product of human artifice, capable of being sustained only through a full understanding of the contrived and voluntary nature of its construction. It was important to dispel illusions about man's nature because natural man was the building block from which this artifice called society was constructed, and a misunderstanding of the nature of one's material is disastrous in the practice of any art.

Whatever the historical and psychological sources for Hobbes's picture of man's natural condition there is little doubt about the degree to which it outraged contemporaries. However, although Hobbes shared an Augustinian view of man's fallen nature, he is much more optimistic than Augustine about the ability of political science to contribute some measure of real security and happiness. He does this through adapting the notion of 'Natural Law'. As we have seen, in Christian and Aristotelian tradition, natural law is presented as something like an immanent moral imperative applicable to, and recognisable by all men in view of their common ability to reason or by virtue of all being creations of the same God.[106] But Hobbes's universe of matter in random motion contains no inherent moral imperative, he is insistent that the only source of values – the meaning of good and bad – are our own desires, and it is the clash of those desires which has produced the state of nature. What then does – indeed what *could* – Hobbes mean by natural law?[107]

Natural law

The derivation of natural law

In the *Elements of Law* Hobbes had asserted that previous thinkers were mistaken in attempting to define natural law in terms of the common customs of men, for there could be no agreement about which customs are to count, and if all are to count, then to derive

[105] *The Essayes of Michael Lord of Montaigne*, tr. John Florio (London and New York, 1928), 'Of the Caniballes', p. 220. Montaigne already insinuates the idea that Europeans' advantages might be illusory.

[106] For example, Cicero, *The Laws*, I, vii, 23: 'there is nothing better than reason, and since it exists in both man and God, the first common possession of man and God is reason. But those who have reason in common must also have right reason in common. And since right reason is Law, we must believe that men have Law also in common with the gods.' Consider also the Leveller contemporary of Hobbes, John Lilburne: 'The Law of God, or Law of Reason is written in the heart of every man teaching him what is to be done.' *The Afflicted Man's out-cry* (1653).

[107] Contemporaries were quick to seize on the apparent incongruity between Hobbes's state of nature and his assertion of natural law; thus Clarendon: 'How should it come to pass that Mr Hobbes, while he is demolishing the whole frame of nature for want of order to support it, and makes it unavoidably necessary

uniform, general prescriptions is impossible because of the diversity of customs deriving from men's various passions.[108] The pursuit of a universal human *good* proved an illusory basis for human society.[109] But, there was another way of deriving general principles: 'Reason is no less of the nature of man than passion, and is the same in all men, because all men agree in . . . that which they desire to attain, namely their own good, which is the work of reason.'[110] In *Leviathan* too, the variety of custom and of men's views of good and evil, is presented as an insuperable difficulty in establishing from them a universally applicable moral philosophy, the science of good and evil. But here he is clearer on the source of the law of nature. Reason for Hobbes has no real content, it is 'nothing but *Reckoning* . . . of the Consequences of generall names agreed upon, for the *marking* and *signifying* of our thoughts'.[111] As a result, and strictly speaking, reason, cannot – as the account in the *Elements* might imply – direct our actions in the place of the passions. Only a passion, a desire or an aversion, can motivate us.

But although – indeed because – human judgements of what is good and bad are so various as to lead to violent conflict, there is one thing that all men fear, and that is death. Since avoiding death is an absolute condition of satisfying their other, more various desires, peace, which renders premature death less likely, must be sought by all rational men: 'all men agree on this, that Peace is Good, and therefore also the way, or means of Peace'.[112] This is what the laws of nature are to Hobbes – ways to peace. Their universality derives from the fact that all men seek peace, at least as a way of avoiding the greatest evil – death.[113] The avoidance of death is not a duty (this has important implications later) merely a necessary means to an almost universal aim. Hobbes (unusually for his time) recognised the possibility of rational suicide, which would make the avoidance of death a part of our animal motion. Yet he seems to have thought that for the most part, 'man shuns death by a certain impulsion of nature'.[114] Given Hobbes's

---

for every man to cut his neighbour's throat . . . that . . . he should in the next chapter, set down such a body of laws prescribed by nature itself as immutable and eternal?' *Brief view of the dangerous and pernicious errors of Mr Hobbes his Leviathan*, cited Bowle, *Hobbes and his Critics*, p. 165.

[108] Hobbes seems here to be referring to the Roman *Ius Gentium* or Law of Nations (laws which the different nations had in common), which was sometimes identified with the Law of Nature.

[109] 'There is no such *Finis Ultimis* (utmost ayme,) nor *Summum Bonum* (Greatest Good,) as is spoken of in the Books of the old Morall Philosophers.' *Leviathan*, p. 47.

[110] *Elements of Law*, I, xv, 1. In the Epistle dedicatory to the *Elements*, he refers to 'the two principal parts of our nature, Reason and Passion', p. xv.

[111] *Leviathan*, p. 18.

[112] Ibid. pp. 79, 80. In *claiming* to base the laws of nature on reason, Hobbes was consistent with the classical natural law inheritance. In actually basing it on the passion of avoiding death he follows the new Grotian tradition. Most insistent on the view that Hobbes subverts the classical inheritance is Leo Strauss, *Natural Right and History* (Chicago and London, 1950), Ch. V, esp. p. 182ff.

[113] There is an echo here of Augustine, who insists that the most evil of men and the most immoral monster one could imagine would still desire peace in which to enjoy his ill gotten gains. *The City of God*, ed. D. Knowles & tr. Henry Bettenson (Harmondsworth, 1972) Bk.XIX, 12.

[114] *Philosophical Rudiments, E.W.* v2, Ch 1. §7 Hobbes thought suicide usually irrational, never immoral. It resulted from the normally mistaken fear that there could be something worse than death. (*E.W.*, VI p. 88) However in *De Homine* he acknowledged that 'the sorrows of life may be so great, that, . . . death may be numbered amongst the goods.' ('nam tantae possunt esse vitae aegrotudines, ut, nisi earum finis propinquus praevideatur, faciant mortem inter bona numerari.') *L.W.* II, p. 98. See the discussion in Goldsmith, *Hobbes's Science of Politics*, p. 123.

conception of nature this would make the avoidance of death part of our vital motion, and a desire beyond reflective choice.

Although the rational pursuit of their survival is paradoxically what led men into the state of nature, men are capable of seeing further than their immediate situation. Because they have the art of speech and reasoning they have the ability to picture to themselves not only their long-term interests but the sort of situation in which these could most likely be fulfilled. The laws of nature are nothing more than the rules for bringing this situation about. A law of nature, then, 'is a Precept, or generall Rule, found out by Reason, by which a man is forbidden to do, that, which is destructive of his life, or taketh away the means of preserving the same; and to omit, that, by which he thinketh it may be best preserved.'[115] These rules are advisory, they are not moral absolutes, nor commands: 'men use[d] to call [them] by the name of Lawes, but improperly: for they are but Conclusions, or Theoremes concerning what conduceth to the conservation and defence of themselves.'[116] The first part of the first law of nature: the right of nature 'consisteth in liberty to do, or to forbeare;' it is not, as Hobbes is at pains to point out, a duty.[117] The desire to ensure our survival may be taken as a manifestation at the level of consciousness of our animal motion; the motive for obeying the laws of nature derives from the perception that such obedience will (under the appropriate circumstances) fulfill that appetite for continued life.

This seems fairly straightforward, but it has been a point of great controversy in interpreting Hobbes. Some have argued that whilst Hobbes stressed the role of egoistic calculation in *motivating* men to obey the natural laws, the sense in which they oblige is not grounded in egoism, but in their being the commands of God.[118] This interpretation of the law of nature has its attractions, for it solves serious difficulties about the adequacy of purely egoistic motives in sustaining political obligation, difficulties which raise issues far wider than the interpretation of Hobbes. On the other hand it seems to contradict what Hobbes has said thus far about the absence, not merely of moral motives, but of moral standards in the pre-political world. Moreover it is entirely inconsistent with a major thrust of *Leviathan*, which is to deny to religion any independent source of authority which might undermine the secular power.[119] If God's will – revealed or natural – were independently knowable apart from the sovereign's determination of it, then men might claim what many had done in the Civil War, and what it was Hobbes's intention to render impossible: they could claim 'for their disobedience to their Soveraign, a new Covenant,

---

[115] *Leviathan*, p. 64.

[116] Ibid., p. 80.

[117] Ibid., p. 64.

[118] A.E. Taylor, ' There are really two distinct questions . . . why I *ought* to behave as a good citizen, and . . . what inducement can be given me to do so if my knowledge of the obligation to do so is not in itself sufficiently effective. Hobbes's ethical doctrine proper, disengaged from an egoistic psychology with which it has no logically necessary connection, is a very strict deontology . . . Hobbes simply meant what he said about the natural law as a command of God.' 'The Ethical Doctrine of Hobbes' pp. 20–21, 34. Reprinted in *Modern Political Theory from Hobbes to Marx, key debates*, ed. J. Lively and A. Reeve (London and New York, 1989), originally published in *Philosophy* (1938). Howard Warrender's formulation is that 'the laws of nature are eternal and unchangeable and, as the commands of God, they oblige all men who reason properly . . . ', Warrender, *The Political Philosophy of Hobbes* (Oxford, 1957), p. 322.

[119] On this see in particular D. Johnston, *The Rhetoric of Leviathan* (Princeton, 1986), chs. 6, 7.

made not with men, but with God . . . an act of an unjust, but also of a vile, and unmanly disposition.'[120]

This interpretive issue will be discussed further towards the end of the chapter. Meanwhile let us take the laws of nature to be instrumental rules, telling us what we must do if we wish to realise certain passions. These passions include not only the avoidance of death, but a desire for what Hobbes, quaintly to modern readers, calls 'commodious living'.[121] As it is close to being a physiological necessity and at least an almost universally valid empirical generalisation that men wish to avoid death, and to increase their chances of felicity – that is to create peace – the laws of nature are theorems which almost everyone will wish to make use of.[122] Nevertheless on the view taken here, they are adopted, if they are adopted, by choice, or even physical necessity, and not out of any absolute moral or religious obligation, for, in the state of nature there are none of these things.

What the laws of nature prescribe

The first law of nature points out that since peace would benefit all men's chances of staying alive it is in everyone's interests to attempt to bring it about; but where peace is not possible there is no limit to what a man may do to defend himself. This second half of the law is in fact the right of nature, by which Hobbes implies no moral claim but simply

> the Liberty each man hath, to use his own power, as he will himselfe, for the preservation of his own Nature; that is to say, of his own Life; and consequently, of doing any thing, which in his own Judgement, and Reason, hee shall conceive to be the aptest means thereunto.

By 'liberty' Hobbes simply means 'the absence of externall Impediments' (and perhaps also the absence of obligations which might create such impediments).[123]

The second law of nature is an expansion of the first part of the first law: it explains what men must do in order to obtain the peace which will allow them to satisfy their desires:

> *That a man be willing, when others are so too, as farre-forth, as for Peace, and defence of himselfe he shall think it necessary, to lay down this right to all things; and be contented with so much liberty against other men, as he would allow other men against himselfe.*[124]

[120] *Leviathan*, p. 89.

[121] Ibid., p. 63.

[122] *Almost* everyone. If the avoidance of death were a physiological necessity, the laws of nature would indeed have been grounded in a physical law. But suicide would then be impossible, and Hobbes seems to have recognised the possibility of rational suicide. See above, fn. 114.

[123] Ibid., p. 94.

[124] Ibid., p. 64.

The proviso ('when others are so too') is important. No man, says Hobbes, could be required unilaterally to give up his natural right of defence, for he would expose himself to destruction, and we cannot be obliged to do that which destroys us.[125] Moreover the proviso applies generally to the laws of nature, which oblige only in conscience, 'in foro interno' or 'to an endeavour' unless we can act on them without detriment to ourselves.[126] Nevertheless, since the exercise of each man's natural right is what produces the condition of war, each would be rational, if others will do so too, to give it up, since no one desires war.

Before dealing with the third and subsequent laws of nature Hobbes discusses the definition and terminology of contracts. A right has already been defined by Hobbes as a 'liberty or freedom,' not in the positive sense of a right guaranteed by law, but simply as the absence of a particular prohibition or impediment. In the state of nature all men have a right to all things. This clearly doesn't mean that they all actually get them, since they may be thwarted by men stronger than they are.[127] In these circumstances exercising a right is simply participating in an uninhibited scramble or struggle for things.

Moreover 'laying down a right' doesn't mean giving it to anyone, although Hobbes confusingly talks of 'transferring' it. Since in the state of nature, all men already have a right to all things, there is no one who could be a possible recipient of such a right. What giving up a right involves is 'to *devest* himselfe of the *Liberty*, of hindring another of the benefit of his own right', i.e, it involves a commitment to the non-exercise of that right, or to refrain from the scramble. There are two ways in which a right can be given up: firstly by simply renouncing the right, which leaves anyone free to benefit, and secondly by transferring, where your aim is that a particular individual should benefit.

Imagine a field full of wild berries with a party of berry pickers, none of whom have been assigned to particular portions of the field, each of whom therefore has an equal 'liberty' right to any of the berries in the field. A person giving up their rights to berries might simply refrain from picking, in which case any other pickers are free from competition by that picker. Alternatively he might resign his right in favour of a particular person, in which case they might agree to hand over their share to him or not to compete with him but only with the others, or some such arrangement which favours the individual who is the object of the transfer.[128] If we declare that we have given up our right to someone, and then fail to abide by that declaration, we have injured that person, says Hobbes, pointing out the derivation of 'in-jure'.[129]

---

[125] Since 'the end of all voluntary acts is the thought of some good to the doer', such obligations could never be fulfilled: ought implies can.

[126] *Leviathan*, p. 79.

[127] The *Elements* is brutally frank about this: 'that right of all men to all things, is in effect no better than if no man had a right to any thing. For there is little use and benefit of the right a man hath, when another as strong, or stronger than himself, hath right to the same.' (*Elements of Law*, Pt. 1, xiv, §10.)

[128] This analogy fails (like most) ultimately to catch the structure of the original, but it's not clear that this isn't a problem in Hobbes rather than in the analogy. A 'giving up' of our right would establish only a duty of passive non-resistance to the sovereign and Hobbes is concerned to establish a duty of positive compliance. However, it's not clear that *any* mere renunciation could effect this; and the idea of authorisation may be designed to supply it. See the exchange between Orwin and Pitkin, and the works cited there. *Political Theory*, 3, 1 (1973).

[129] *Leviathan*, p. 65. Hobbes's account of the derivation fits his theory better than the real etymology. He claims injury is formed from 'in' (= against) plus the verb 'iuro-iurare', to swear, hence injury is 'against a swearing, or oath'. In fact in-iuria is against law, or right (O.E.D.).

Transferences of right are made by a promise or some similar sign. The promise, or transfer of right, may be separated in time from the transference of the object, or the performance of the action which is the object of the agreement. Mutual exchanges of right are contracts in which the exchange may be immediate, as in barter, when two goods are exchanged at the same time. But the good may be contracted for at some later date, as for example in a wage agreement, where an employer gives me a promise that if I labour for him he will give me a wage at the end of a specified time. Such contracts which involve a time-lag between the agreement and the fulfillment of its terms on the part of one or other of the contractors are called covenants, and presume good faith and the keeping of promises.[130]

The third law of nature states that men shall keep their covenants once they've made them.[131] Transferences of right are voluntary acts, and the end or aim of all such acts is the hope of some good to the actor. Even apparent one-way transfers which we call gifts, are, Hobbes claims, made in the hope of some future benefit. Such observations are clear implications of his egoistic psychology. Another is his observation that there is one right that we cannot transfer, despite any apparent protestation to the contrary, and that is the ultimate right to defend our lives or, in a significant extension of which little has been made by commentators, 'the means of so preserving life, as not to be weary of it'.[132] Clearly such an outcome could never be the motive for a contract, nor would it be possible for human beings as described by Hobbes to fulfill such a promise to lay down their lives, the continuance of which is the aim of all desire and activity.

Since covenants are voluntary acts it follows that covenants undertaken through fear, like other acts undertaken through fear or threats, are still free, they are still morally significant, and they still oblige us. There is nevertheless an important limitation on the performance of covenants. Since a covenant involves a promise to perform part of an agreement at some future date, the party who performs his part of the bargain first, puts himself at risk as to the performance by the other party, and, as Hobbes puts it, 'does but betray himselfe to his enemy; contrary to the Right (he can never abandon) of defending his life, and means of living'.[133]

Since this would be irrational, covenants of mutual trust may be void upon any reasonable suspicion of failure to perform, and in a state of nature there are almost always grounds for such suspicion, and consequently no such contracts.[134]

The third law of nature – that men shall keep their agreements or promises – is therefore only binding, or indeed even relevant, in conditions of security, and security only exists where there is a power to coerce possible defaulters into keeping their contracts. For as Hobbes reiterates,

[130] *Leviathan*, p. 66.

[131] Ibid., p. 110.

[132] Ibid., p. 66.

[133] Ibid., p. 68.

[134] The situation turns out to be more complex than this. In the unlikely event of such a contract being agreed to in the state of nature, the reason for withdrawing from it must have arisen subsequent to the agreement. For reasons to be discussed below, although it would be irrational to initiate such a covenant, Hobbes thinks it would be irrational not to complete it, if, unlikely as he thinks it, one found oneself facing a satisfactory first performer. See below p. 57.

he that should be modest, and tractable, and performe all he promises, in such time, and place, where no man els should do so, should but make himselfe a prey to others, and procure his own certain ruine, contrary to the ground of all Lawes of Nature, which tend to Nature's preservation.'[135]

The making and keeping of covenants, says Hobbes, is the origin of, indeed is constitutive of, justice.[136] Since there is no right and wrong prior to human agreement, justice is fundamentally dependent on such agreement. Once right has been transferred by a covenant the breaking of that promise is injustice. But it is only where there is a power to ensure that neither side defaults that covenants of mutual trust are possible, and that justice can emerge. Justice then is the keeping of valid covenants, and the possibility of valid covenants begins with a superior power sufficient to enforce their validity.

If the laws of nature show us what calculations we must make if we are to preserve our lives, should those calculations extend beyond this life 'to the attaining of eternal felicity after death'? Hobbes denies this. The laws of nature are based on 'naturall knowledge' of which we have none about the afterlife. Moreover, considerations of eternal punishment had been made the pretext for breaking obligations here on earth. A major issue with Catholics in the Reformation, and, long before 1651, it appeared, with Protestants too, was the doctrine that religious beliefs might lead them to 'think it a work of merit to kill, depose, or rebell against, the Soveraign Power constituted over them by their own consent'.[137]

The remaining laws of nature promote survival by proscribing conduct which might be a source of enmity amongst men: ingratitude, intolerance, bearing grudges, vengeance, provocation, pride and arrogance; and secondly by specifying procedures such as equity, rules of distribution, mediation and the judging of quarrels. Finally there are some laws which regulate only individual conduct, such as that prohibiting drunkenness.[138]

The laws of nature, then, mark out a world very different from the state of nature, a world of possible human co-operation, of improvement and security, a world where, since industry is rewarded, agriculture, commerce, building and technology can flourish, where there may be knowledge and science, art and culture, but most of all security from fear and physical harm; and life may be sociable, rich, pleasant, cultivated and long. The

---

[135] *Leviathan*, p. 79.

[136] Ibid., p. 71.

[137] Ibid., p. 73–4. In 1638 the General Assembly of the Scottish Kirk (Church) had, in a key episode leading to the Civil War, produced the Scottish National Covenant. Whilst still respectful to the King, the covenanters could not accept the 'papist' practices introduced in the new Scottish prayer book, and to justify this resistance invoked 'their covenant with God'. (The Scottish National Covenant, Feb., 1638, in *Constitutional Documents of the Puritan Revolution, 1625–1660*, ed. S.R. Gardiner (Oxford, 1906), p. 133. Hobbes thought that 'the very entering into the Covenant with the Scottish nation against the King is by itselfe a very great crime.' 'Considerations upon the Reputation, Loyalty, Manners and religion of Thomas Hobbes.' *English Works*, iv, p. 418. On the political theory of the covenanters see I.M. Smart 'The Political Ideas of the Scottish Covenanters, 1638–88', *History of Political Thought*, I, 2 (1980). For the development within Calvinist Protestantism of the justification for political resistance see Quentin Skinner, 'The Origins of the Calvinist Theory of Revolution' in *After the Reformation, essays in honour of J.H. Hexter*, ed. Barbara C. Malament (Manchester, 1980).

[138] Despite this imprecation, Hobbes, according to Aubrey, used to get drunk about once a year 'to have the benefit of vomiting', though no oftener since he believed that even in moderation, regular alcohol 'spoiles the Braine'. *Brief Lives*, p. 315.

laws of nature show what rules must be followed within such a world, but they also warn how foolish would be the attempt to initiate it on one's own. The problem then remains, how is man to enter such a world?

The institution and nature of commonwealths

The social contract

Hobbes describes two ways of entering the world of society and peace, two methods by which commonwealths may be formed, if one considers Hobbes's argument a historical one, or two analyses, if one reads him be simply giving a logical account of the relationship between rule and protection. Commonwealths can be established either by institution – that is by the mutual agreement of free individuals, or by acquisition – by conquest of a previously existing sovereign. Both sovereignty by institution and by conquest, or acquisition, involve convention, or agreement. The social organization 'of men, is by Covenant only, which is Artificiall', whereas the social organisation of species such as bees and ants is natural, or unreflective. Natural society would be impossible for human beings, for unlike the social insects, men distinguish between their public and private interests, they are proud (the characteristic quality both of sinful, fallen man, and of the biblical monster after whom Hobbes named his book). Man's 'Joy consisteth in comparing himselfe with other men'; he has the use of speech, and consequently the ability to deceive. Ultimately humans do not, as do bees and ants, involuntarily subordinate themselves to the good of the whole. Hobbes's important if contentious claim is that for humans social community can only be established through the exercise of political power.[139] Political society amongst men has to be *constructed*; it is, he often reminds us, a work of artifice, requiring skill and science, resting on nothing more than the conventions men themselves create.

Commonwealths by institution

The more difficult of the two cases, although the rarest, is when a commonwealth is created out of the chaos of the state of nature, where men, to avoid its horrors, establish political authority from nothing. Although more unusual, it is logically prior to sovereignty by conquest, for conquest can only occur once a sovereign already exists, and so, there must be some explanation of how, at some point, sovereignty originally comes about.[140] In this case, says Hobbes, it results from the mutual agreement of a group of men, numerous enough to repulse attacks, to give up the exercise of their natural right, and acknowledge an individual or collective body as their ruler. It is, says Hobbes, as if every man were to say to every man:

[139] *Leviathan*, pp. 86–7. But see the discussion of an earlier view in François Tricaud, 'Hobbes's Conception of the State of Nature from 1640 to 1651': in Rogers and Ryan, *Perspectives on Thomas Hobbes*.

[140] Modern political anthropologists agree with Hobbes's account in arguing that the earliest states came about in one of two ways: by the uniting together of groups for defence either against natural or human enemies, or by the incorporation of non-political populations into already existing states. See R. Carniero, 'A Theory of the Origin of the State', *Science* 169 (1970).

I Authorise and give up my Right of Governing myselfe, to this Man, or to this Assembly of men, on this condition, that thou give up thy Right to him, and Authorise all his Actions in like manner.[141]

The sovereign so created, which can be either a council or an individual, has absolute power and almost absolute authority, the full range of which Hobbes will spell out at some length. The subjects agree to 'authorize' its actions, that is, to regard them as in some sense, their own. Thus the frontispiece of *Leviathan* showed the Sovereign composed of his citizens. The sovereign 'bears their person' or represents them publicly – 'person' being nothing more than a representation of an individual.[142]

Commonwealths by acquisition

The second origin or species of sovereignty Hobbes calls a commonwealth by acquisition. Here the motivation for obedience is not so much fear of the state of nature, but fear of the power of a sovereign power already in existence, where, for example, men have been defeated by, or even merely surrendered to an opposing army. A related instance of such sovereignty is generation: Parents exercise sovereignty over children – in fact, interestingly, Hobbes insists, primarily our mothers. We owe our lives to them, not because they bore us, but because they nourished us when we were helpless, or more starkly, did not kill us when they could have.

The contract in the case of the child is not expressed, but Hobbes insists that the child's consent is to be understood from the protection it enjoys. Many patriarchal theorists who argued for parental dominion derived it from the act of generation itself, but for Hobbes it derives from the same reciprocal relationship between obedience and protection which underlies political obedience. For this reason, it is the mother – who first has the power of life and death over the infant – who gains, in the absence of positive agreement, the right to its obedience:

For it ought to obey him by whom it is preserved; because preservation of life being the end, for which one man becomes subject to another, every man is supposed to promise obedience, to him, in whose power it is to save, or destroy him.[143]

---

[141] *Leviathan*, p. 87.

[142] Ibid., in general, Ch.xvi. Hobbes puts the definition to startlingly good effect in suggesting a way of conforming to trinitarian orthodoxy, without resorting to metaphysics – 'God, who has been Represented (that is, Personated) thrice, may properly be said to be three Persons'! Ibid., pp. 268–9.

[143] Ibid., p. 103. In terms of the rights and duties existing within them, each family is 'a little Monarchy', but cannot be considered a Commonwealth 'unless it be of that power by its own number . . . as not to be subdued without hazard of war.'Ibid., p. 105. On Hobbes and the family see above fn. 96.

Although within political societies the law normally prescribes obedience to the father, Hobbes disarmingly explains that this is 'because for the most part Common-wealths have been erected by the Fathers, not by the Mothers of families'.[144]

Despite allowing this 'tacit' submission of the infant, sovereignty by acquisition yields dominion over those defeated in war not by the mere fact of conquest itself, but by agreement. It occurs

> when the Vanquished, to avoyd the present stroke of death, covenanteth either in expresse words, or by other sufficient signes of the Will, that so long as his life, and the liberty of his body is allowed him, the Victor shall have the use thereof at his pleasure.[145]

Power, contract and the theory of 'authorization'

Here, as in the case of generation, Hobbes seeks to hold on to an attenuated notion of contract, because it will enable him to distinguish political authority from mere over-whelming power.[146] He is insistent that it 'is not therefore the Victory, that giveth the right of Dominion over the Vanquished, but his own Covenant. Nor is he obliged because he is Conquered; . . . but because he commeth in, and Submitteth to the Victor'.[147] Hobbes wants to distinguish slaves, who have no duty of obedience 'but may break their bonds, or the prison; and kill, or carry away captive their Master, justly:' from servants, who are obliged.[148] Consent is thus important for Hobbes's theory of obligation, for it is through consent, he claims, that the subject is obliged to obey by more than the mere threat of punishment.

It may be helpful here to illuminate the difference between prudential and political obligation by drawing a further distinction between 'natural' and 'political' obligation. There is a sense in which the consequences caused by foolish actions can be seen as natural punishments of them. In the sense then, that causes bind or oblige us by their effects, the laws of nature oblige through the natural sanctions in their consequences.[149] However, as Hobbes points out, if someone is ignorant of these consequences, as indeed

---

[144] *Leviathan*, p. 103. For a historically speculative reconstruction of the assumptions which enabled Hobbes to combine his radical assertion of sexual equality in the state of nature with an assumption of patriarchs entering civil society, see Carol Pateman, '"God hath ordained to Man a Helper": Hobbes, Patriarchy and Conjugal Right', *British Journal of Political Science*, 19, 4 (1989).

[145] *Leviathan*, p. 103.

[146] The 'authorisation' becomes so attenuated as to be derivable: 'either . . . from the expresse words . . . or from the Intention of him that submitteth (which Intention is to be understood by the End for which he so submitteth) . . . namely, the Peace of the Subjects . . . and their Defence against a common Enemy.' Ibid., p. 111.

[147] Ibid., p. 104.

[148] Ibid., p. 104.

[149] All human actions issue in 'so long a chayn of Consequences', that we cannot see to the end. Nevertheless, 'he that will do any thing for his pleasure, must engage himselfe to suffer all the pains annexed to it; and these pains, are the Naturall Punishments of those actions.' So 'Intemperance, is naturally punished with Diseases, . . . Negligent government of Princes, with Rebellion; and Rebellion with Slaughter. For seeing Punishments are consequent to the breach of Lawes; Natural Punishments must be naturally consequent to the breach of the Laws of Nature.' Ibid., p. 193.

if they are ignorant of any other law then, 'to speak properly, that Law is no Law to him'.[150]

The idea of being obliged by irresistible power, natural or coercive, is the residue of an older theory of obligation, but it still does some work in Hobbes's argument. Any overwhelming power creates *some* kind of obligation (but not necessarily duty). The case of God is analogous. Although man is not so naturally powerful as to be able to rule by might, this is the case with God; and as a result God is capable of obliging all men to obey him, whether they will or not for:

> To those . . . whose power is irresistible, the dominion of all men adhæreth naturally by their excellence of Power; and consequently it is from that Power that the Kingdome over men, and the Right of Afflicting men at his pleasure, belongeth Naturally to God Almighty; not as Creator and Gracious; but as Omnipotent.[151]

However this 'natural kingdom of God' is distinct from his political or 'civil' kingdom, for *political* rule operates only where a sovereign 'governs his subjects, by his Word, and by promise of Rewards to those that obey it, and by threatning them with Punishment that obey it not'.[152] God can do this as much as (indeed better than) a human sovereign. Thus the distinction between political and natural power, and between political and natural *obligation*, rests on the fact that political power works via *words*, and, 'ariseth from pact'.[153] The only members of God's kingdom in *this* sense are those who, by believing in him, *acknowledge* his power of punishing and rewarding and covenant to obey; the rest are still in his power, but as enemies: their position is that of slaves or captives who do not acknowledge their masters, or those who remain in the state of nature when others incorporate politically: they may be destroyed by the right of nature. Thus prudential obligation is, for Hobbes, something of an equivocal category, since prudential foresight necessarily involves recognition (in the subjective sense) of the power that brings about the consequences of actions; it does not, however involve covenant (in the sense of an objective acknowledgement). The natural consequences of our irrational acts, like the absolute power of God, punish us in a way, and in that sense oblige us, if only to accepting the consequences of our actions. But such obligation is not political and cannot – as exemplified in the case of mere slaves – impose duties on us.[154] Thus consent, no matter how minimized, is a crucially important dimension of Hobbes's argument in enabling him to distinguish between mere 'slaves' or 'captives' – subject to their lord's power, but unobligated – and subjects or citizens – also subject to the sovereign's power – but who truly owe him an unfeigned obligation. These positive properties of covenants also enable him to distinguish different degrees of obligation incurred by citizens in different roles which they have entered *by contract*. Thus the military obligations of soldiers, who have agreed to enlist, are considerably more demanding than those laid on

---

[150] *Leviathan*, p. 140. The distinction seems to be a scholastic one. See on the difference between the way the law of nature operates on unreflective nature, and the way it operates on man – via reflection and foresight – in St. Thomas Aquinas, *Summa Theologica*, I, II, Qu.91, art.ii reply obj.3, in *The Political Ideas of St Thomas Aquinas*, ed. D. Bigongiari (London and New York, 1953), p. 14.

[151] *Leviathan*, p. 187.

[152] Ibid., p. 186. See Ch.31 passim, for 'the Kingdom of God by Nature'.

[153] Ibid., p. 187.

[154] Ibid., p. 193.

ordinary citizens, who may normally plead fear or 'naturall timourousnesse' to avoid military service.[155]

Hobbes makes the further claim, new in *Leviathan*, that in the covenant, the subjects 'authorize' the sovereign, who becomes their 'representative'.[156] The idea of authorization derives from medieval developments in the Roman Law theory of corporations, giving rise to the useful notion of an artificial or 'legal' personality which could bear rights and own property on behalf of a collectivity.[157] Hobbes's idea is that the public *persona* of the citizen is concentrated in the sovereign so exhaustively and irrevocably that there is no political agency left for the individual to exercise and so no source of political conflict. It is not clear how much this adds to the notion of contract. But one important implication may be in absolving the citizen from worries about their religious culpability. Authorization seems to work asymmetrically. The subject authorizes all the actions of the sovereign, and so cannot gainsay them. Yet the sovereign incurs external responsibility – to God – for both his own actions and those which he commands of his subjects. Subjects therefore, claims Hobbes, do not need to fear sinning, as long as they obey the sovereign.[158] It is also interesting to note here, against those who insist only on the modernity of Hobbes's theory, that this is a secularized restatement of Divine Right theory, which also, to the scandal of Protestant theologians, relieved men of their conscience in return for their obedience.[159] Moreover in the 'acquisition' version of sovereignty, what Hobbes describes is virtually a personal (albeit one-sided) Feudal Contract of fealty.

By stressing, through his analysis of sovereignty, the importance of recognizing what the terms of the subject-sovereign relationship necessary to preserve peace should be, rather than what those of any supposed historical contract actually were, Hobbes had hoped to lead men to adopt those political attitudes and behaviour that avoided the breakdown of political order. Taken *this* way Hobbes's argument does not actually require there to have been a contract at all: its purpose lay simply in demonstrating to subject (and to sovereigns) what would constitute rational behaviour on each of their parts, as he puts it, merely 'to set before men's eyes the mutuall Relation between Protection and Obedience'.[160] *Leviathan* could therefore constitute a political lesson for all men at all times, and in all situations. The contract is, after all, introduced by the words: 'it is as if every man were to say to every man . . . '.

[155] For a citizen 'to avoyd battell, is not Injustice, but Cowardice. But he that enrowleth himselfe a Soldier, or taketh imprest mony, taketh away the excuse of a timorous nature.' *Leviathan*, p. 112. See the helpful discussion in Deborah Baumgold, *Hobbes's Political Theory* (Cambridge, 1988), ch.5.

[156] David P. Gauthier, *The Logic of Leviathan*, (Oxford, 1969), was the first to emphasise this aspect of Hobbes's thought, although the full problem of its relationship to other aspects of his theory did not become apparent until Tuck's treatment of Hobbes's relationship to his predecessors (*Natural Rights Theories*).

[157] See Brien Tierney, *Religion, Law and the Growth of Constitutional Thought* (Cambridge, 1982), p. 19ff.

[158] On this see Clifford Orwin, 'On the Sovereign Authorization', *Political Theory*, 3, 1 (1975).

[159] Thus in Shakespeare's *Henry V*, the night before Agincourt, the King goes disguised amongst his men urging 'I could not die any where so contented as in the king's company, his cause being just and his quarrel honourable.' To which the common soldiers reply: (Williams) 'That's more than we know', and (Bates) 'Ay, or more than we should seek after; for we know enough if we are the king's subjects. If his cause be wrong, our obedience to the king wipes the crime of it out of us.' William Shakespeare, *Henry V*, VI, i, ll.132–140.

[160] *Leviathan*, pp. 395–6.

This 'virtual contract' view of his argument, however, cannot incorporate the theory of authorization, with its important role. Authorization would seem to require an actual contract. The same kind of obligation cannot be deduced from the fact that it would be rational for me to have promised, as could be deduced from my actually having promised. I advance this not only as a generalised truth, but as something that seems true also for Hobbes, for despite this emphasis on the subject's 'authorization' of the sovereign in *Leviathan*, Hobbes retains elements of his earlier theory; and the equivocation in his account over the need for an actual contract, as for example in the case of the infant, has implications for any parts of the theory which rely on an actual contract. It relates, for example to the issue of how contracts bind subsequent generations.

It was a common assumption amongst earlier natural law theorists, that the act of consent establishing society continued to bind later generations.[161] This seems illogical to modern readers because we presume that the contract is being used to explain how as individuals we incur the personal obligation; and we fail to see how later generations can be obliged without themselves contracting, for which such theories make no provision. But even for Hobbes's immediate predecessors this was not a problem because they commonly separated their accounts of obligation from their account of the origin of political authority. For Selden you were obliged simply if there was a power to punish you, the contract only explained the *origins* of such a power. His theory of obligation didn't presume that subsequent generations needed to have played any part in its establishment. It was difficult, on this view, to distinguish between the slave's obedience because he must, and the subject's obedience because he ought: people were obliged by, and to the extent of, the actual powers established over them.[162] Hobbes adopted the notion of authorization to explain *both* the existence of political authority, *and* an individual's obligation to obey it. This latter was quite distinct from Selden's account of obligation which seems to derive from the mere susceptibility to punishment. Confusingly, however, Hobbes sometimes retains hints of this argument too. Hobbes's modified account then, runs something like this: The sovereign power exists because all have abjured their natural rights in its favour. The subject then has a political obligation to obey the sovereign because a) he has covenanted to do so; b) he has agreed to authorize its actions, they are therefore his own; and c) because he is susceptible to punishment by the sovereign. Only a and b are truly political obligations which enable Hobbes, in principle at least, to distinguish himself from mere de-facto theorists, such as Anthony Ascham, who relied on c. Hobbes insists that the sovereign's right of punishment was quite distinct from the subject's duty to obey, the latter derives from the right conveyed in the contract, which the former cannot, because one cannot contract to harm oneself. Rather the sovereign's right of punishment derives from his right of nature.[163] However, this left a problem about the status of government in relation to the obligation of future generations. They are still obliged in the Seldenian sense (because there exists a power

---

[161] See for example the discussion of the Spanish neo-Thomist school in Skinner, *Foundations*, vol 2, p. 155ff.

[162] See the discussion in Tuck, *Natural Rights Theories*, pp. 92–4.

[163] *Leviathan*, p. 161. Because no one could voluntarily be thought to give 'any right to another to lay violent hands upon his person . . . It is manifest therefore that the Right, by which the Common-wealth (that is, he, or they that represent it) hath to Punish, is not grounded on any concession, or gift of the Subjects . . . But [in the right] every man had . . . to every thing.'

to enforce obedience), yet they are excluded from actively consenting for, as Hobbes points out, once it is established, sovereignty must involve the right of succession. If it is left to each generation to consent anew 'then is the Common-wealth dissolved' every time; and men 'should return into the condition of Warre in every age'.[164] This threat of return to a state of nature constitutes a further level of natural obligation, but it is not, any more than the fear of punishment, the *political* obligation of the original covenantors. The requirements of stable sovereignty are in some tension with the theory of political obligation – a situation not uncommon in liberal political thought.

Features of the contract

The rights and consequences of sovereignty, whether established by a contract of institution or of submission are identical, and it is important to remark on a number of their characteristics.

Hobbes's care in formulating this contract (he reworked it several times) was motivated by a recognition of the important political consequences that follow from different versions of it. Firstly, Hobbes is very careful to characterize the contract as one that does not impose on the sovereign obligations to the subjects. In sovereignty by institution the sovereign is not a party to the contract.[165] It is a contract amongst the potential subjects to yield up their rights in favour of a sovereign. Indeed since the original contract takes place in the state of nature (in which all men have a right to all things) there are no rights which the subject could give to the sovereign, since he, in common with them, until the moment of contract, has a right to all: the right of nature.[166] In commonwealths by acquisition on the other hand, the contract between the sovereign and the subject is an agreement to spare the vanquished's life, but this is provisional on the subject's obedience. If the subject disobeys, or, more precisely if the sovereign deems him to have disobeyed, he may be punished. The subject has the right to protect his life, but it is not a right that the sovereign is obliged in any sense to respect. In neither case does the sovereign incur any obligation to the subject.

As either the sovereign is not a party to the contract, or there is no condition (although there may be expectations) attached to the creation of sovereignty, there can be no claim that the sovereign has broken any agreement.[167]

If individuals have no rights against the sovereign, neither does the community as a whole, since they only become a community by virtue of the existence of the sovereign whom they have authorized to act in their names. The right of defending one's life against the sovereign is one that may only be exercised by individuals, and only in extremis,

---

[164] *Leviathan*, p. 99.

[165] 'There can happen no breach of Covenant on the part of the Soveraign' since 'he which is made Soveraign maketh no Covenant with his Subjects before-hand.' Ibid., p. 89.

[166] On which his right of punishment rests. Ibid., p. 162, and see above, fn. 163.

[167] Ibid., p. 89. Because 'the right of bearing the Person of them all, is given to him they make Sovereign, by Covenant onely of one to another, and not of him to any of them; there can happen no breach of Covenant on the part of the Soveraigne; and consequently none of his Subjects, by any pretence of forfeiture, can be freed from his Subjection.'

since all his other acts have been authorized by the subject.[168] Since the community has no being without the sovereign, it cannot act against him.[169] Without the sovereign the community is merely an aggregate of warring individuals.[170] The isolated relationship of the individual to the sovereign is clearer in the case of sovereignty by acquisition, but Hobbes's concern to make this apply also in the case of instituted sovereignty is revealed by the way he developed his argument from the *Elements of Law* through to *Leviathan*. In the early version of his theory, Hobbes describes a two-stage contract, in which the individuals first incorporated themselves into a sovereign community or democracy which then authorized a sovereign.[171] This gives to the community a pre-political identity which would open the possibility – later exploited by Locke – of it acting against the sovereign. In *Leviathan* Hobbes closes off this possibility, by collapsing the two contracts into one. He stresses that if the sovereign fails, this

> leaves the Multitude . . . without any Representative in whom they should be united, and be capable of doing any one action at all . . . which is a returne to Confusion, and to the condition of a War of every man against every man.[172]

The notion of any kind of social contract (much less the kind Hobbes outlines) might strike us today as odd, but the middle of the seventeenth century was a period when the notion of the social contract had a very real existence outside the libraries and studies of academics. In social life the increasing importance of contractual, rather than customary relations, had been the subject of comment for well over a century. Protestant theology revived and stressed Old Testament notions of the role of God's covenant with his chosen people (a relationship which Hobbes firmly denied could apply to post-Judaic communities). The Scottish Presbyterians had formed a national covenant to protect their religion in 1638.[173] Constitutionalist thinkers on the continent and in Great Britain, commonly construed the kings' coronation oaths as enforceable contracts.[174] Both Houses of Parliament, and the famous parliamentary pamphleteer, Henry Parker, had asserted that both Magna Carta and the subsequent coronation oath comprised a contract in which the King bound himself to uphold the laws chosen by the people (as expressed by Parliament).[175] During the Civil War the Levellers, a grass roots constitutionalist

---

[168] *Leviathan*, p. 112, 'To resist the sword of the Common-wealth, in defence of another man . . . no man hath liberty . . . '.

[169] Ibid., p. 89.

[170] Here Hobbes may have been countering attempts by both parliamentary apologists such as Henry Parker, and, in a more thoroughgoing way, the Levellers, to assert the rights of a presupposed 'community' of 'the people' against the King, and in the Levellers' case, eventually against the Long Parliament.

[171] *Elements of Law*, Pt. 2, i, §3; Pt. 2, ii, §1. As Harro Höpfl has pointed out, this may owe something to the contract formulations of Suárez. See Skinner, *Foundations*, II, pp. 164–66.

[172] *Leviathan*, p. 100; in the formulation at p. 121 there is still a vestige of the *Elements* version.

[173] The text is reprinted in S.R.Gardiner's *Constitutional Documents*, p. 124.

[174] This was asserted in the *Vindiciae Contra Tyrannos*, a widely translated and reprinted French work of the sixteenth century. See *A Defence of Liberty Against Tyrants*, ed. and intr. Harold J. Laski (London, 1924).

[175] *A Remonstrance, Or the Declaration of the Lords and Commons* (1642), p. 6; Henry Parker, 'Observations on some of his Majesties Late Answers and Expresses' (1642), reprinted in *Revolutionary Prose of the English Civil War*, ed. H. Erskine-Hill & G. Storey (Cambridge, 1983), pp. 39–40.

movement, had also invoked the coronation oath.[176] Claiming that all legitimate authority had collapsed, they proposed establishing a new constitution by appealing to the people to sign 'Agreements of the People' which were in fact social contracts, intended to establish a new and constitutionally limited political regime.[177] A contract of a less explicit or far reaching kind was offered by the Commonwealth in 1650 when office-holders were required to sign the 'Engagement' to the effect that they recognised the new regime and denied the validity of the claims of Charles Stuart.

Hobbes's view of the Engagement controversy was complex. It has been suggested that *Leviathan* was a contribution to the debate, and the addition of the 'authorization' strand to his argument, and in particular the material of the 'Review and Conclusion' is consistent with this view.[178] However, there is a sense in which historical events overtook Hobbes's theory, and the argument which utterly denied a right of resistance to the sovereign King in 1642, or even as late as 1648, looked, in the context of late 1649, like an argument for accepting the, now sovereign, victorious rebels' Engagement.[179] Looking back, Hobbes claimed that *Leviathan* was 'written in the behalf of those many and faithful servants and subjects of his majesty, who had taken his part in the war, or otherwise done their utmost endeavour' to sustain him. Having discharged their duty, they were at liberty to submit to the new rulers: 'imposing of the Engagement' was nevertheless, 'a very great crime'.[180] The concern to derive legitimacy or at least obligation (the Levellers sought the former, the Rump only the latter) from covenant was clearly a burning issue, and one which implicitly recognised that rightful authority could not derive from mere coercive force.[181]   However, despite the widespread social penetration of the idea of contract, Hobbes's argument was not a rhetorical success. The groups to whom the language of contract was most congenial were those most opposed to his political views, and those – the royalists – closest to his political conclusions found the individualist premise and contractarian argument he used to support them too threatening to accept his support.[182] Hobbes's stress on the absence of any natural community – particularly any kind of natural order – offended conservatives of many kinds, and his denial that sovereignty could survive any constitutional limitation offended more radical parliamentarians and traditional defenders of 'mixed government' and

---

[176] Some Levellers claimed that Magna Carta was 'an absolute contract betwixt the Kings of *England* and the People thereof, which, at their Coronations ever since, they take an Oath inviolable to observe'; *A Remonstrance of many thousand Citizens,* in *Leveller Manifestoes of the Puritan Revolution,* ed., D.M. Wolfe (New York, 1944), p. 122.

[177] See I.W. Hampsher-Monk, 'Putney, property and Professor Macpherson, the political theory of the Levellers', *Political Studies,* xxiv, 4 (1976).

[178] See Quentin Skinner, 'The Ideological Context of Hobbes's Political Thought', *Historical Journal,* 9 (1966); and 'Conquest and Consent: Thomas Hobbes and the Engagement Controversy', in *The Interregnum : The Quest for a Settlement, 1646–1660,* ed. E.G. Aylmer (London, 1972); and Baumgold, *Hobbes's Political Theory,* p. 124ff.

[179] See the excellent discussion by Glen Burgess, 'Contexts for the writing and publication of Hobbes's *Leviathan*', *History of Political Thought,* XI, 4 (1990).

[180] *Considerations on the Loyalty, EW,* IV, p. 418.

[181] On the Levellers see Hampsher-Monk, 'Political Theory of the Levellers'; on the Engagement, John Wallace, 'The Engagement Controversy, 1649–52, an annotated list of pamphlets', *Bulletin of the New York Public Library,* 68 (1964).

[182] At the Restoration Charles II did grant Hobbes a pension, and tried to protect him, but he was almost alone in his support.

mixed monarchy alike. Under these circumstances it is not difficult to see why he lacked immediate political influence. Nevertheless the assumption of natural community, like the existence of a shared historical tradition of legitimacy, was seriously undermined by the Civil War, and in recognising the problems posed by social breakdown and discontinuity, Hobbes's thought achieved a higher and necessarily philosophical level of generality which has over the centuries received greater and greater recognition.

The rights of sovereigns

The rights of the sovereign are as extensive as the right of nature, and effectively unlimited. However, although no subject can call the sovereign to account, sovereigns are still subject to natural laws in the sense, outlined above, that their actions naturally lead to certain consequences. So as well as outlining the rights constitutive of sovereignty, Hobbes also, although this is far less remarked on, provides advice on what will be most conducive to the sovereign's own survival, the maintenance of his sovereignty, the internal peace and external security of his state.

Although there are many things it would be prudent for the sovereign to do, there are some powers without which he cannot be considered sovereign. In outlining such constitutive sovereign powers, Hobbes points to issues which had all been major points of controversy between parliament and king in the prelude to the Civil War. It is the sovereign's responsibility, for which he is not answerable to his subjects, to judge what is necessary for peace and for warfare, what doctrines are to be taught, what are the rules or laws of property, to arbitrate on all quarrels within the state, to make war and levy the troops and funds necessary to do so, to choose his own ministers and to award honours.[183] During Charles's reign the Short Parliament had refused supplies for war on Scotland, the church had failed to suppress Puritan preachers and Parliament had disputed property rights in the context of taxation in a long battle going back to Charles's first Parliament of 1625; Parliament had abolished the King's Star Chamber, and lawyers such as Coke had successfully asserted the independence of the law and the courts, thus denying the king's ultimate right to 'arbitrate on quarrels'. The right of levying troops and funds for them figured prominently in the contentious Militia Bill of 1642, and in the last peacetime pamphlet exchange between the King and Parliament before the outbreak of the Civil War, the 'Nineteen Propositions sent by the Two Houses of Parliament to the King at York' (1642) and 'His Majesties Answer ... to the Nineteen Propositions of Parliament'. Parliament had again bitterly disputed Charles's ministerial choices. It had attempted, unsuccessfully, to impeach Buckingham in 1626, and Strafford in 1641, although the latter was subsequently executed under a bill of attainder. Hobbes warns that advisory assemblies, summoned by the sovereign to assist him – a status which he clearly accorded to the House of Commons – must not be confused with a situation where sovereignty is vested in assemblies, and such consultative assemblies should not be referred to as the people's representative, which the sovereign alone can be.[184]

Hobbes's responses to these pressing political issues illustrate the differences between him and even those intellectually quite close to his position such as John Selden. Selden was like Hobbes a contract theorist. Like Hobbes he agreed that the right of nature gave

---

[183] *Leviathan*, pp. 88–92.   [184] Ibid., p. 95.

men wide discretion over their actions, including what political institutions they might agree to set up. But unlike Hobbes, he did not move in the direction of stipulating what, logically, such a contract must prescribe if it is to work. Instead, Selden took the contract literally and historically. He held that citizens' obligations derived from the specific forms of contract discoverable from their society's legal history.[185] Thus even for Selden, a sophisticated modern natural rights thinker, legitimacy was still – even in the Civil War, and of course at other times – based on historical conceptions of legality. In continuing to base legitimacy on a kind of legal precedent, Selden was more within the mainstream of English political thinking down at least as far as Burke, on whom he exercised a significant influence.

The trouble with the idea of legal precedent, like the idea of a mixed, balanced or distributed sovereignty, each (and often both) of which were widely supported in the 1640s, was that in the event of a dispute about the extent of a particular power someone was required to be judge of it. If the judge was an external authority the state was not independent. If there was no internal authority it was up to individuals to decide. In this latter situation, as Philip Hunton was wearily forced to admit in his *Treatise of Monarchy* (1643), it meant that 'the people are unbound, and in a state as if they had no government'.[186] This was a dire strait for Hunton, but it becomes in time a positive argument in favour of an ultimate popular resolution for such issues.[187] For Hobbes it simply shows the incoherence of any theory of government that does not recognise the necessity of sovereignty as a 'SYSTEME[S] . . . Regular . . . *Absolute,* and *Independent*, subject to none but their own Representative'.[188] This strand of Hobbes's argument – in contrast to the theory of authorization – appeals to a priori and deductive considerations independent of what has been enacted, considerations which would apply to any truly political society which must exhibit both hierarchy and closure.[189] Hobbes is particularly aware of the threat posed by religion to a unified sovereignty. For this reason the erastian subordination of both religious doctrine and church organisation to the sovereign is vital.[190]

The analytical core of Hobbes's conception of sovereignty is the idea that the guarantee of an absolutely authoritative and decisive outcome for all political decisions is more

---

[185] Tuck, *Natural Rights Theories*, p. 97 ff. Selden, himself a man with strong royalist sympathies, in trying to decide who was in the right over the outbreak of the Civil War, felt the crucial issue was who had the legal right to summon the militia, and whether they could be used outside their home counties. This was to be decided on the basis of statute and precedent (the embodiment of the social contract), and could not be pleaded by the King on grounds of prerogative. (See R.Tuck 'The Ancient Law of Freedom', in Morrill, ed., *Reactions*.)

[186] Cited M.M. Goldsmith, 'Hobbes's "Mortall God"', *History of Political Thought*, I, 1 (1980), p. 47. There is no modern edition of Hunton's work, but it is excerpted in Wooton, *Divine Right and Democracy*. On Hunton see more generally J.H. Franklin, *John Locke and the Theory of Sovereignty: Mixed Monarchy and the Right of Resistance in the Political Thought of the English Revolution* (Cambridge, 1978), and C.Condran, *George Lawson's 'Politica' and the English Revolution* (Cambridge, 1989).

[187] See C.C. Weston, 'Co-ordination: a radicalising principle in Stuart Politics', in *The Origins of Anglo-American Radicalism*, ed. M.Jacob and J.Jacob (London, 1984).

[188] *Leviathan*, p. 115.

[189] Goldsmith, 'Hobbes's "Mortall God"'.

[190] The sovereign has the right of judging what doctrines are fit to be taught, which parts of scripture are to be taken as the word of God, of covenanting with God on the subject's behalf, of interpreting God's will, and of appointing clergy. *Leviathan*, pp. 91, 295, 69, 149–50, 295–6.

important than the quality of the decisions themselves: 'the reason of him that hath the sovereign authority, . . . whether it be right or erroneous in itself, ought to stand for right to us that have submitted ourselves thereunto . . . '[191]

Hobbes's conception of sovereignty is not only demonstrably shaped by contemporary issues, but it marks the emergence of the modern idea of the concept as the defining quality of political bodies. The idea of sovereignty as definitive had already been articulated in this form by the French theorist Jean Bodin, whom Hobbes approvingly cites.[192] In Hobbes's prewar discussion group – the Tew Circle – John Selden had already started to talk about the 'state' in an abstract way to refer to an assemblage of political powers.[193] Hobbes himself moves easily from talking about the sovereign as a person or a body, which would be the normal referent in a European world of increasingly absolutist monarchies, to sovereignty as the particular collections of powers exercised by such a person, and so to sovereignty as those powers constitutive of the authority needed to maintain a state in being.[194]

Hobbes recognised that his absolutist conclusion was unpalatable. Many Englishmen, who had just fought a civil war to establish limits on the king's powers, might think the 'Condition of [such] subjects is very miserable'. Yet, he insisted no power strong enough to protect men could be less than absolute. Men's passions made them unwilling to recognise this, and their lack of political science unable 'to see a farre off the miseries that hang over them, and cannot without such payments be avoyded'.[195] Sovereignty could not be limited, or worse, divided, without the destruction of the commonwealth. Moreover, given his abstract conception of sovereignty Hobbes insists that this is true of all forms of government: his argument about absolutism is an argument about the nature of sovereignty itself, and not an argument in favour of locating sovereignty in any particular form of government.[196] Hobbes did believe there were good *prudential* grounds for preferring monarchy – there is closer identity between individual and public good,

---

[191] 'Liberty and necessity . . . ', E.W., V, p. 176; and *Elements*, Pt. 2, x, §8, 'seeing right reason is not existent, the reason of some man, or men, must supply the place thereof; and that man, or men, is he or they, that have the sovereign power'. As Goldsmith points out, Hobbes's argument is fallacious – it might be called a fallacy of decomposition – in that it assumes that the properties of a system (closure) must be possessed by an identifiable element of the system. Goldsmith, 'Hobbes's "Mortal God"', p. 40.

[192] In the *Elements of Law*, Pt. 2, viii, §7. For a comparison of the two see Preston King, *The Ideology of Order* (London, 1974).

[193] Selden was perhaps the first English writer to use the word in this sense. As early as 1616, in answer to the question of how old was the Common Law, he replied '*When there was first a state in that land which the common law now governs*', Selden *Opera*, III, col. 1892, cited, but unremarked on by Tuck, *Natural Rights Theories*, p. 84.

[194] *Leviathan*, ch. 21 *passim*, but especially the following: 'The sovereignty is the Soule of the Commonwealth; which once departed from the Body, the members doe no more receive their motion from it. . . . And though Sovereignty, in the intention of them that make it, be immortall; yet is it in its own nature not only subject to violent death, by forreign war; but also through the ignorance and passions of men it hath in it, from the very institution, many seeds of a natural mortality, by Intestine Discord.' p. 114.

[195] Ibid., p. 94.

[196] Ibid., p. 94: 'Power in all formes, if they be perfect enough to protect them, is the same'; again, 'the Soveraign Power, whether placed in One Man, as in Monarchy, or in one assembly of men, as in Popular, and Aristocraticall Common-wealths, is as great, as possibly men can be imagined to make it', pp. 106–7; and conversely, 'Whether a Common-wealth be Monarchicall, or Popular, the Freedome is still the same', p. 110.

wider consultation, more effective secrecy, less division, less scope for corruption – but he did not claim that his theory of sovereignty entailed an absolute monarchy.[197] It was the unique exercise of unbounded authority that characterised sovereignty, not the person or persons in whom it was located. The crucial characteristic of governments for Hobbes was whether or not they were possessed of all the necessary powers constitutive of sovereignty.[198] Hobbes rejects, like so much else in Aristotle, that thinker's distinction between 'good' and 'bad' forms: tyranny is merely monarchy 'misliked'.[199]

To be sure of peace then, the sovereign's powers had to extend potentially into all areas of outward life. But although no constraints could be placed on him (or her or it), there are some things Hobbes thought the sovereign should (although under no obligation) do. These give a more benign picture of Hobbes's politics than is usually presented.

Firstly although Hobbes acknowledged a sovereign is not subject to the law and may do anything by his mere power, he nevertheless in a curious way propounds a weak and limited version of the rule of law. The exercise of his office 'should be done, not by care applyed to Individuals . . . but by a generall Providence . . . in the making of good Lawes, to which individuall persons may apply their own cases.'[200] Punishment moreover, cannot (logically) be arbitrary, it is *'an Evill inflicted by publique Authority, on him that hath done, or omitted that which is Judged by the same Authority to be a Transgression of the Law'*.[201] Still, although Hobbes's point is definitional, it has teeth: Punishment without transgression of the law is an unequivocal violation of the law of nature, punishment must be preceded by due public process, legislation cannot be used to punish retrospectively, and so on.[202] Thirdly sovereigns have a general obligation under the law of nature to promote equity. They should 'cause Justice to be taught', and 'equally administred to all degrees of People; . . . as well the rich, and mighty, as poor and obscure persons'. They should see to the 'Equall imposition of Taxes', which should, to hit the prodigal, be levied on consumption not possessions. Sovereigns also have an obligation under the law of nature (for which they are answerable to God 'and to none but him') to do more than barely preserve their subjects, but to ensure them 'all other Contentments of life' which the subjects' 'lawfull industry . . . shall acquire'.[203] Moreover there should be laws to encourage the arts of commerce, agriculture and manufacture, and those unable to work through no fault of their own were not to be left to private charity, but supported by public money. If despite these measures there are still unemployed people, they are to be transported to colonies, 'where neverthelesse, they are not to exterminate those they find there; but constrain them to inhabit closer together, and not range a great deal of ground'. In general, although the sovereign right of lawmaking is unlimited, and no law

---

[197] *Leviathan*, pp. 95–7. The multivalency of Hobbes's conception of sovereignty, particularly at the time of *Leviathan*'s publication in 1651, meant it could be read, despite its clear criticism of the parliamentary rebels, as a justification for obedience to the existing sovereign, Parliament, or the Council of State.

[198] The 'Soveraign is absolute . . . ; or else there is no Soveraignty at all;' Ibid., p. 105.

[199] Ibid., p. 95.

[200] Ibid., p. 175.

[201] Ibid., p. 161.

[202] Ibid., pp. 165, 162, 163.

[203] Ibid., p. 175.

can technically be unjust, laws made for the benefit of the sovereign, which do not benefit the people are not good laws. Above all, a good legal code is a short one.[204]

These remarks should modify the view, sometimes taken, of Hobbes as an enthusiastic defender of capricious absolutism or exploitative tyranny. But although good policy, and even required of the sovereign by the law of nature, none of these things can be claimed by subjects as a right.[205] It is crucial to Hobbes's argument to deny citizens either any rights against the sovereign beyond the bare natural right to seek the preservation of one's life, and perhaps even more insistently, to deny them the right to exercise judgement about political matters in defiance of the sovereign's command.

The rights and liberty of subjects

Where then does this leave the subject? The subject can expect to enjoy only such liberty as is consistent with political society, says Hobbes; which – since the sovereign must be absolute – means only such liberty as the sovereign chooses to allow him. Those who seek liberty in any other sense, thinks Hobbes, do not consider seriously what they are asking for.

Although it is now conventional to distinguish the question of political liberty from the issue of philosophical determinism, in Hobbes's view a proper understanding of this latter question was crucial to the political issue. Misuse of the term 'liberty' had, he thought, been partly responsible for the outbreak of the Civil War. For Hobbes '*A FREE-MAN is he, that in those things which by his strength and wit he is able to do, is not hindred to doe what he has a will to.*'[206] Actions are voluntary and free if they proceed from the agent's will, and unfree if physically constrained. However, properly speaking, for Hobbes, liberty is applicable only to agents considered as bodies and their actions considered as movements, and not to properties of agents (such as their wills), or their internal motions (such as motives or reasoning).[207] To be free is not to suffer *external* impediment to a body's movement. Analogously, political bodies too, are free if their external movement is not impeded, irrespective of what is going on inside them.[208] So with individuals, internal freedom is an illusion, for whereas, as long as not constrained, a man is '*free to do if he will, and to abstain if he will . . . he is not free to will*'.[209] Our wills are part of a universal causality. Our liberty, is in a sense, only a manner of speaking

[204] *Leviathan*, pp. 165 (equity), 179 (teach justice), 180 (to all classes), 181 (taxation and public charity), 182 (brevity).

[205] The sense in which the sovereign is here 'obliged' is presumably that in which actions (or inactions) oblige us with their natural consequences, here, the 'Negligent government of Princes, with Rebellion'. (Ibid., p. 194) Although it is a paradox of his position that if all subjects heeded Hobbes's argument there would be no such consequences.

[206] Ibid., p. 108.

[207] Or indeed to unmoving material objects, such as roads: 'When 'tis said . . . The way is Free, no Liberty of the way is signified, but of those that walk in it without stop.' Ibid., p. 108.

[208] Ibid., p. 149.

[209] *Liberty, Necessity, and Chance, EW*, vol.V, p. 189. See also briefly, *Leviathan*, p. 108: 'from the use of the word *Freedom*, no Liberty can be inferred of the will, desire, or inclination, but the Liberty of the man; which consisteth in this, that he finds no stop, in doing what he has the will, desire, or inclination to doe.'

about one particular cause of movement – that which proceeds from the agent's will. Both scripture, which asserts both God's omnicompetence and foreknowledge, and Hobbes's science, which supposes the ubiquity of mechanically caused motion, presupposed that all events have causes sufficient to bring them about. It is, thinks Hobbes, our ignorance of the way they operate that leads us to ascribe liberty to human will: which is (like all things) the result of a chain of causality.[210] We cannot distinguish between free and unfree acts on the basis of some external factor impinging on the will that gives rise to them, for *all* action results from motives impinging on the will and is therefore caused: 'because every act of a man's will and every desire . . . proceedeth from some cause . . . and that from another cause, in a continuall chaine . . . they proceed from *necessity*'.[211] Liberty in this sense is therefore, consistent with being (mentally) caused, and something that all subjects not physically constrained manifestly possess. The political upshot of all this is that since liberty is acting according to our will, and since all wills are causally motivated, the discrimination between free and unfree acts cannot be made on the basis of the kind of causes that motivate us: 'Feare and liberty are consistent; as when a man throweth his goods into the Sea for *feare* the ship should sink, he doth it nevertheless very willingly and may refuse to doe it if he will'.[212] So also 'all actions which men doe in Commonwealths, for *feare* of the law, are actions, which the doers had *liberty* to omit.'[213]

Nevertheless, within Commonwealths it may be said that men create 'artificial chains' which bind them to the commands of the sovereign. These are needed for, however rational, the laws of nature 'are contrary to our naturall Passions, that carry us to Partiality, Pride, Revenge and the like'.[214] If by political liberty is meant freedom from these artificial chains, or laws, this is clearly an absurd demand; it is, in effect, to demand the re-introduction of the state of nature. Recognising the need for the sovereign power and his laws to protect us from this is no more an infringement of our liberty than is the storm to the mariner who must decide whether to abandon his cargo.[215] Each is simply the circumstance in which we must decide how to exercise our liberty.[216]

Within the state the greatest liberty of the subject depends on the silence of the law, for what is not forbidden by the law may legally be done: indeed a subject may sue a

---

[210] For Hobbes 'liberty of the will' is, like natural religion, a result of 'ignorance of causes': 'consider as much as we will, and understand as clearly as we will, . . . [we] are never the nearer to the knowledge of their necessity; and that, I said, was the cause why we impute those events to liberty, and not to causes.' *Liberty, Necessity, and Chance* , EW., vol.V, p. 294.

[211] *Leviathan*, p. 108.

[212] Ibid., p. 108.

[213] Ibid., p. 108.

[214] Ibid., p. 85. The passions are natural 'multiplying [sc. magnifying] glasses', which exaggerate our private interests, and inhibit the motivational influence of our true, long-term, interests, p. 94.

[215] Indeed, he suggests it is much less so. Flirting with the notion of positive liberty, to which his own is so often thought the antithesis, Hobbes suggests that the use of 'Lawes is not to bind the People from all Voluntary actions: but to direct and keep them in such a motion, as not to hurt themselves by their own impetuous desires, rashnesse, or indiscretion; as Hedges are set, not to stop Travellers, but to keep them in the way.' *Leviathan*, p. 182. The image is also used by Locke, *Second Treatise*, §57 'that ill deserves the Name of Confinement which hedges us in only from Bogs and Precipices.'

[216] For two excellent recent discussions see Quentin Skinner, 'Thomas Hobbes on the Proper Signification of Liberty', *Transaction of the Royal Historical Society*, 5th Ser., 40 (1990); and M.M. Goldsmith, 'Hobbes on Liberty', *Hobbes Studies*, II (1989).

sovereign at law within a purely legal framework. Nevertheless it is always open to the sovereign to demand something simply in virtue of his mere power.[217] The rights retained by the subject are the minimal rights of self-preservation – the right to defend his person, not to testify against himself, not to assist in his own punishment.[218] These do not prevent the sovereign from justly punishing people who do not acquiesce in his commands. In other words there is no symmetry between the all-embracing rights of the sovereign and the limited residual natural right of the subject. Ultimately the right of capital punishment exercised by the sovereign over the individual is no more than the last vestige of the right of nature, and the relationship between the sovereign and a condemned man is essentially that of the state of war.

The debate about the nature of obligation

Ever since Hobbes wrote, the most contentious issues, both in understanding Hobbes's argument, and in assessing its cogency have been those connected with his account of the nature and origin of political obligation.

In *Leviathan* political obligation comes about as a result of a grant of right to another: and once made, a man, says Hobbes, *'ought*, and it is his DUTY, not to make voyd that voluntary act of his own: . . . such hindrance is INJUSTICE, and INJURY, as being *Sine Jure*, the Right being before renounced, or transferred'.[219] This obligation is, however, only indefeasible where there is a sovereign power to enforce agreements, for most men's sense of honour is weak and insufficient to keep them to their word: 'Covenants, without the Sword, are but Words, and of no strength to secure a man at all'.[220] In a state of nature, Hobbes suggests, there may be immediate exchanges, but there would be no covenants, for there could be no trust that bargains would be fulfilled. Yet the social contract is a form of covenant – 'a promise of future performance' – which takes place in the state of nature. The establishment of the sovereign is a very special form of covenant in that it is the covenant which itself creates the conditions under which covenants – including that very one – become enforceable and therefore binding. The power to enforce

[217] The 'King's word, is sufficient to take any thing from any Subject, when there is need; and the King is Judge of that need', *Leviathan*, p. 106. It's possible that this claim contains an echo of a famous legal judgement, known as Bate's Case. The case occurred in 1606 but the argument about its implications rumbled on until the Civil War. Bate was an importer of currants from the Middle East who refused to pay a tax imposed by James I on the grounds that it had not been passed by Parliament. The judge in that case asserted, what Stuart monarchs clearly believed in general, that the ultimate judgement of public matters (and of what was and wasn't public) was not for the courts but to be made 'according to the wisdom of the King, for the public good'. Parliament's worry about this judgement were well expressed by Sir John Strangeways: 'if the king be judge of the necessity we have nothing and are but tenants-at-will.' It was just this position that Hobbes wished to assert. Conrad Russell, *The Crisis of Parliaments* (Oxford, 1971), pp. 274–5, and Johann Somerville 'Ideology, Property and the Constitution' in *Conflict in Early Stuart England*, ed. R. Cust and A. Hughes (London, 1989).

[218] *Leviathan*, p. 114, The 'right men have by Nature to protect themselves, when none else can protect them, can by no Covenant be relinquished.'

[219] Ibid., p. 65. As noted above, fn.149, there is a wider sense in which we can be said to be obliged, by an overwhelming power, such as God's, or by the natural effects of our actions, such as when excessive drinking leads to sickness.

[220] Ibid., p. 85.

obedience is an essential prerequisite for the existence both of active political obligations and of laws. The logical compliment of this view is the notion that when the power to enforce obedience (which is effectively the same as that required to protect) has gone, the state of nature supervenes and the individual is free to take measures for his own safety and to acknowledge allegiance to a new sovereign. This happens, for example, when the subject is captured and offered his liberty on condition that he acknowledge the captor's sovereignty, or if the existing sovereign banished him, and so puts him beyond his protection. Similarly if the sovereign himself dies without providing for a successor, or if he submits himself to another (but not if he is merely held captive leaving a deputy to exercise power in his place), the subject is free to seek a new sovereign.[221] Hobbes criticised the parliamentarians for undermining Charles's power whilst he was still King. But once the King was captured and executed, his loyal subjects were free to swear allegiance to the Commonwealth: 'They that had done their utmost endeavour to perform their obligations to the King, had done all that they could be obliged unto; and were consequently at liberty to seek the safety of their lives and livelihood wheresoever, and without treachery.'[222]

There are two things to notice about this account which bear on the effectiveness of the 'hypothetical' contract as an argument for political obligation. The first is again the strong emphasis placed on self-preservation as a fundamental *motive* and on contract or agreement as a basis for achieving the political condition. As stressed above, it is not the mere *capture* of either subject or sovereign that breaks the bonds of allegiance, but the act of acknowledging submission to another.[223] This militates against the plausibility of a hypothetical account, although is a useful guide for those in the midst of civil war. But the second point is the political implications of this account. Political allegiance is a voluntary undertaking (an aspect of Hobbes's theory that unsettled royalists) but it need not bind us until death. The desire to avoid death, being both an axiom of Hobbes's science and a natural fact about human beings, must be built into any realistic theory of obligation – we cannot be required to do that of which most of us, at any rate, are motivationally incapable. Hobbes, in allowing individuals the right to shift loyalty to save their skins seems to acknowledge the insufficiency of honour and the prevalence of a more ignoble, self-interested and distinctively modern mentality.

This raises crucial issues as to whether his account (indeed whether any account grounded on egoistic and secular premises) could succeed in generating an obligation effective enough to sustain political society. Hobbes's preoccupation with this problem has made him appear an astonishingly prescient theorist of the modern, secular, age. Moreover, the method he used has proved a great attraction for modern commentators and theorists, whose 'rational choice' premises, derived from economics, they see as startlingly similar to Hobbes's own.[224]

---

[221] *Leviathan*, p. 114, 'The Obligation of Subjects to the Soveraign, is understood to last as long, and no longer, than the power lasteth, by which he is able to protect them.'

[222] 'Considerations upon the reputation', *E.W.*, IV, pp. 420–1.

[223] *Leviathan*, pp. 114, 391.

[224] For example most recently and exhaustively Jean Hampton's *Hobbes and the Social Contract Tradition* (Cambridge,1987) and Gregory S. Kavka, *Hobbesian Moral and Political Theory* (Princeton, 1986).

This is not just a modern issue in rational choice theory which has followed Hobbes's intimations by collapsing all issues of political morality into questions about the possible logics of egoistic motivation. Seventeenth and eighteenth century thinkers clearly recognised and consciously sought to reject this approach. However they did so not simply because they believed there were other sources of moral standards, but also because they regarded a complete theory of morality as one which demonstrated not only the content of a moral code, but also provided sufficient psychological motivation to adhere to it. Thinkers identified, though not by name, the modern problem of the morally opportunist 'free rider' as a crucial objection to any secularly based morality. The practical advantages of Christianity, it was claimed, were not only that it told you what you ought to do, but through the alternatives of salvation and damnation, it provided adequate motives to *do it*.[225] Many of Hobbes's contemporary critics certainly thought that the insufficiency of egoism was the vital weakness in his case. John Eachard saw the problem about whether Hobbes's egoistic men could actually subordinate themselves to political rule when he remarked that 'To fasten *de Homine* and *de Cive* [i.e. 'man' and 'citizen'] cleverly together requires a little more knocking and hammering'.[226] Alexander Rosse in *Leviathan drawn out with a Hook* (1653) encapsulated numerous objections to the project of a secular moral theory when he argued that it was only 'the curb of conscience that restrains men from rebellion: there is no outward law or force so powerful . . . there is no judge so severe, no torturer so cruel, as an accusing conscience.'[227] But Hobbes, painfully aware – through the Civil War – of the terrible effects of tying political allegiance to the dangerously subjective base of religious or moral belief, deliberately sought, in *Leviathan,* to construct a politics without the aid of religious conscience.[228] In this Hobbes certainly anticipated a central development of modern politics – its secularization and even its autonomy.

The question of the plausibility of Hobbes's account of obligation raises for social theorists the more general question of whether a state could survive, if populated by the purely secularly motivated hedonists that the most obvious interpretation of Hobbes suggests men to be. A negative answer to this issue has led many to seek to save Hobbes by questioning whether this most obvious interpretation of Hobbes is in fact correct, or whether there is not some other source of obligation in Hobbes's theory.

---

[225] In the next generation the moralist John Balguy for example (1686–1748), is as clear about the need to reject self-interest as the source of moral principle as he is about the need to recruit it as a motive for moral action: 'nothing can tend more to the disparagement of virtue than to found it thus on self-interest . . . yet 'tho interest can never enter into the nature and constitution of Virtue, yet why may it not be allowed to stand beside her?' Would a benevolent atheist become less so for being converted to a belief in the rewards of an afterlife? To expect moral behaviour without some self-interested motive is to expect 'the greatest Part of mankind should become philosophers.' John Balguy, *A Letter to a Deist*, (1726), pp. 9, 17.

[226] John Eachard, *Mr Hobbs's State of Nature Considered* (London, 1672), p. 14, cited Mintz, *Hunting of Leviathan*, p. 18.

[227] Cited in Bowle, *Hobbes and his Critics*, p. 67. For further discussion of contemporary criticisms of Hobbes, see Goldie, 'The Reception of Hobbes'.

[228] But notice Hobbes's equivocation over this. Hobbes was anxious to stress that the 'Christian liberty' the Reformation had granted men, should minimize religious grounds for political disobedience since it allowed them to do what their secular rulers required of them without disobeying God in their hearts. Yet Hobbes also feared the consequences of a political obedience which was merely perfunctory and lacked commitment.

Problems of the political obligation of prudential egoists

One extreme way of presenting the problem of the tension between political obligation
and calculated egoism is by postulating the situation of the 'first performer'. The problem
is presented as that facing the first individual having to fulfill the covenant which
inaugurates society. The first performer must be in *some* doubt as to whether the contract
is going to hold, and whether that security, which society alone affords, that our covenant
won't be taken advantage of, in fact exists. The covenant is, in a sense, or rather in two
senses, a confidence trick. The exercise of sovereignty depends on all *believing* that the
ruler will be able to exercise power, in order that he can in fact do so; if all were to
disbelieve, and so withhold obedience until he demonstrated his power, he would have
none, for political power is, in the last analysis, nothing but the obedience of subjects,
all men being equal and equally able – and in a state of nature entitled – to kill one another.

In one sense this problem of trust only arises because of the discrepancy – discounted
by Hobbes's assimilation of mechanical reality to geometry – between the real world
and the world of logic. Within the terms of a logical argument, the instant the covenant
is agreed, the sovereign exists (logically), since the two facts are but different aspects of
the same act and the sovereign can immediately use its power to ensure that the
consequences of our promising are not to our disadvantage, and prevent the whole
agreement from unravelling. Viewed in this way the Covenant is hardly a 'contract of
future performance'. But if we consider the first covenant not as a logical construct but
in the real world, the interposition of the dimension of time makes a crucial difference,
since although right can be transferred in an instant (by promising), power is not
verifiably conveyed at the same instant, but only when the sovereign subsequently issues
a command and subjects do in fact obey. The successful transfer of power thus depends
on those whom the sovereign appoints to do its bidding, actually obeying as they said
they would, when the fulfilling condition for their own obedience is in fact the power of
the sovereign i.e. their own obedience. There is clearly an element of Catch 22 in the
situation.[229] Unless some prior obligation exists to fulfill, and not merely to endeavour
to fulfill, covenants – or at least this one – *despite* some risk to ourselves, political society
could never begin.[230] Yet Hobbes emphasises that we cannot be obliged to risk our safety.
Is the founding contract perhaps the one supererogatory act humans are called on to
perform?

---

[229] As Hobbes and Warrender seem both to acknowledge, see *Leviathan*, p. 138, on which Warrender
comments: 'The obligation of the citizen to obey the civil law is based on his having made a political
covenant: his obligation to keep his covenant is based on his obligation to obey natural law; his obligation
to obey natural law is then based upon his obligation to obey civil law, or the commands of the sovereign;
this is then based on the political covenant, and so on.' Warrender, *Political Philosophy of Hobbes*, p. 167.

[230] Hobbes's conception of endeavour may help here. Endeavour is 'the small beginnings of Motion
within the body of man', *Leviathan*, p. 23. 'To be obliged to an endeavour' then is literally 'to be obliged
to have small beginnings of motion in one's body', a locution which exposes the difficulty Hobbes has in
sustaining his attempt to reduce consciousness and will to mechanics. More charitably, it may be read as
to be obliged to take small trusting initiatives without fully committing, and so endangering, oneself; thus
a showing of goodwill may be to endeavour peace.

To this it can of course be objected that we are now to consider the contract, not literally, but as a hypothetical device, directed primarily not to men in a state of nature, but to men already in society – to discourage them from doing what is destructive of it.

However, renouncing historical claims for the covenant will not dispose of worries about narrowly egoistic motivations; and it shows also that the conundrum about the 'first covenantor' is more than an interesting logical puzzle: for the argument that suggests that first covenantors might have grounds for withholding obedience, also suggests that a non-covenanting subject (such as all after the first generation might be) might disobey whenever they had reasonable grounds for believing the sovereign temporarily incapable of providing protection or enforcing law, or where the advantages to be gained from lawbreaking outweighed the costs. In a world of time and place there will always be moments and areas where the protection provided by the sovereign will seem unreliable or remote, sapping the confidence on which rests men's willingness to keep their covenants, whether from greed or fear. Will not man, without some entrenched disposition towards civility – what Hobbes calls 'an unfeigned and constant endeavour' – be constantly tempted to revert to behaviour typical of the state of nature?[231]

Against this it might in turn be argued that the conversion of human beings from the unsociable wretches of Hobbes's state of nature to the civilized, law abiding inhabitants of the Commonwealth is unlikely, or even inconceivable, and so, to put the same argument in reverse, the immediate relapse into state-of-nature behaviour would be equally unlikely. Perhaps each of these changes is implausible if we take these descriptions of men as patterns of behaviour to which men have become *habituated*. But there is no role for habit in Hobbes's theory, since men, he claims, are invariably calculators of their interest, not simply in terms of long term strategy, but also in the face of every action they take.[232] Consequently the only difference between the behaviour of men outside and inside society can be the structure of the choices facing them. Inside society there is reasonable security, outside there is none. To the self-interested rational individual these suggest different patterns of behaviour, yet the pattern can be reversed the moment the situation changes, or appears to – for Hobbes's account of motivation invariably stresses that it is the subjective *appearance* of good that determines actions. It may be true in logic that the covenant creates the sovereign and civil society and consequently the power to enforce that covenant, i.e. to render it obliging 'in foro externo'. But will it always appear that such power is present to individuals in actual

---

[231] *Leviathan*, p. 79. Michael Oakeshott, as perceptive (if elusive) on Hobbes as he is on all else, suggested as much when he pointed out the existential qualities of this particular covenant never permit completion in that 'on account of the character of what is transferred . . . what each undertakes is to maintain a certain state of will . . . the daily keeping of a promise, which can never attain the fixed and conclusive character of a contract performed once and for all time.' Introduction, *Leviathan*, (Oxford, n.d.) p. xxxviii. The version reprinted in his *On Civil Association* (London, 1975), interestingly omits this passage and refers merely to the subject's covenant 'to be continuously active in supplying the power required to exercise [right]', p. 40.

[232] *Leviathan*, p. 66: 'of the voluntary acts of every man, the object is some *Good to himselfe*'; again p. 132, 'the proper object of every man's Will is some Good to himselfe.' Hobbes of course recognised the existence of habit, which is 'motion made more easy and ready by custom; that is to say by perpetual endeavour, or iterated endeavours . . . ' *E.W.*, I, p. 349, but he allots it no place in his account of political motivation.

societies? Nor is it only fear of danger from others that might lead men to revert to state-of-nature behaviour: hope of advantage might also lead to the re-emergence of selfish behaviour:

> Of all the passions that which inclineth men least to break the laws is fear. Nay excepting some generous natures it is the only thing, when there is appearance of or profit or pleasure by breaking the laws, that makes men keep them.[233]

The problem is that it is not enough for Hobbes to show theoretically that it is in the interests of self-motivated men to covenant to *establish* a society; what he has to show is that they will also see it as in their interests to obey the laws and defend that society *once it is in being*; and this is a much less abstruse matter. Even potential thieves and robbers see it as in their interests to *be* in society, and consequently would presumably promise to obey. But they might well deny that it is in their interests always to *obey* the rules of that society – where they could get away with it. Is this incoherent? Certainly not logically so. 'What', one might say, 'would happen if all were to behave like you?' Yet such an appeal is clearly of a moral nature and has no obvious effect on a self-interested calculator such as Hobbes depicts. Self-interested agents might want to consider the chance that this particular crime would itself lead to the collapse of civil society, yet clearly such a chance is remote; and in any case if civil society were in such imminent danger of collapse, the motivation to profit from it before its demise would be even stronger.

Hobbes seems keenly aware of this and yet if we look closely at some passages it seems that he expects a good deal more from his subjects than would be possible if we considered their behaviour to be purely self-interested. In his Review and Conclusion we have seen that Hobbes adds another law of nature: *'That every man is bound by Nature, as much as in him lieth, to protect in Warre, the Authority, by which he is himself protected in time of Peace.'*[234] It is doubtful whether this could be the result of any self-interested calculation for the existence of that security which renders the laws of nature fully operable is, in this case, precisely what is in question, since the power of the sovereign – and consequently his ability to protect us – depends on his chances of winning the war. Should not the rational egoist be calculating those chances rather than saying to himself that he has a duty to turn out and fight for the sovereign who has hitherto provided peace and security? If not only subjects, but the agents of the sovereign too – officials and soldiers – are always calculating their interests and assessing the ability of the sovereign to protect or punish in each situation they find themselves in, his real power will become very fragile indeed. Indeed there are examples of such quasi-states in every age.

It often seems not only that Hobbes realizes that self-interested calculation endangers political obligation, but that he thinks that his argument has indeed provided something more. For at various points he himself recognises the need for a consummate commitment to the laws of nature – that 'unfeigned and constant endeavour' as he calls it.[235] Hobbes's

---

[233] *Leviathan*, p. 155.

[234] Ibid., p. 390.

[235] Ibid., p. 79. The point is underscored at p. 179: where Hobbes insists that subjects are to be taught (although he does not himself insist on its truth), 'that not onely the unjust facts, but the designes and intentions to do them (though by accident hindred,) are Injustice; which consisteth in the pravity of the will, as well as in the irregularity of the act.' The margin heading, which I believe to be Hobbes's own, at this point reads: 'And to do all this sincerely from the heart.'

attempt to meet this problem, at one level at any rate, is to attempt to show how self-interest, under the guidance of reason, is capable of considerable refinement. Although the calculations of immediate self-interest is the position from which any model of human behaviour must start, this is not the only kind of behaviour possible.[236] Reasoned reflection itself, he suggests, may transform self-interest itself into something that looks more like morality.

In a famous passage Hobbes discusses the case of 'the (atheistic) Foole' who reasons that since by nature each of us is allowed to act for our own preservation (and advantage), we must be entitled to break promises and renege on agreements whenever we can do so without discovery, or if the pay off is sufficiently great to make the risk worthwhile. This seems a clear deduction from our natural liberty, and the presumption of egoism: but Hobbes judges such reasoning to be false. Although we would indeed be foolhardy to be first performers in a state of nature, we would be foolish *not* to be second performers if first-performers had done their part.[237] Such reasoning would *a fortiori* apply to agreements within a commonwealth with an effective sovereign. The reason why it would be foolish, suggests Hobbes, is that it is reasonable to calculate on the assumption that all other men will successfully pursue their own preservation. Whilst it is true that men will sometimes err in this (and that defaulters might gain as a result) such a possibility can never make it a rational tactic to pursue, for the consequences of failure are too serious. Assuming others were to pursue their own interests successfully they would identify and exclude such deceivers from society.

> He therefore that breaketh his Covenant, and consequently declareth that he thinks he may with reason do so, cannot be received into any Society, that unite themselves for Peace and Defence, but by the errour of them that receive him; . . . which errours a man cannot reasonably reckon upon as the means of his security: and therefore if he be left, or cast out of Society, he perisheth; and if he live in Society, it is by the errours of other men, which he could not forsee, nor reckon upon; and consequently against the reason of his preservation.[238]

Not only is it in our interests to be *seen* to be trustworthy, suggests Hobbes, but because it is irrational to assume we can fool people, our interests require us to actually *be* trustworthy. Truly rational calculators would *act* in a trustworthy way, and do so in their own interests, and indeed they would sincerely intend to so act.[239]

---

[236] The most prominent example of such a personality in *Leviathan* is the brother of the dedicatee, Sidney Godolphin, described as a man whose virtues appeared 'not as acquired by necessity, or affected upon occasion, but inhaerent, and shining in a generous constitution of his nature.' *Leviathan*, Sig, B2. This description, so strikingly at odds with the model of man developed in the book itself, has led some scholars to discuss the possibility of a second theory of human nature in Hobbes.

[237] And immoral too, *Leviathan*, p. 74: 'For if any fault of a man; be sufficient to discharge our Covenant made; the same reason ought to have hindred the making of it.' Such reasoning might also be argued to constrain (morally, but not of course legally or politically) the sovereign, who is not bound as a result of the contract, but *is* thereby freed from fear of non-performance and so enabled to obey the laws of nature, *in foro externo*. The fourth law of nature seems to apply especially to sovereigns: '*That a man which receiveth Benefit from another of meer Grace, Endeavour that he which giveth it, have no reasonable cause to repent him of his good will.*' Ibid., p. 75.

[238] Ibid., p. 73.

[239] Ibid., p. 179. For a formal treatment of The Foole's argument see D. Gauthier *Morals by Agreement* (Oxford, 1986) ch. vi.

This argument goes to the heart of Hobbes's moral psychology. However, in salvaging, if it does, the viability of self-interest as a constructive natural motive for morality within commonwealths, Hobbes is in danger of undermining the crucial role it had played in establishing the state of nature. For if it were true that the importance of a reputation for justice would make it always in one's interests to perform the second half of a covenant of mutual trust, even in a state of nature; then this knowledge must become part of the calculations made by potential first performers in that situation, and the fear of 'non-performance' which militates against the initiation of such ventures without a sovereign to ensure obedience, would be largely assuaged. It would become possible to perform all sorts of covenants of trust in the state of nature, relying only on the security of each person's need for a good reputation. Pursuing this logic to its extreme: a situation driven by men acknowledging the vital need for trustworthiness could lead to the development of a pleasant and cultivated environment operating quite anarchically.[240] This is clearly not Hobbes's intention. He argues that the partiality of men's passions make reliance on such logic irrational in a state of nature, yet such a logic can be supportive within society. His problem is to obtain sufficient credit on the swings of sociability to make political society viable, without running into such deficit on the state-of-nature roundabouts as to make it unnecessary.

Deontology versus conditional morality: the problem stated

The discussion so far has tended to focus on the practical issue of whether Hobbes has managed to generate a sufficient *motive* for moral behaviour. But the more we apprehend the need to transcend egoism as either a motivational, or a moral foundation, the more we are pushed towards the deeper problem, which is whether, having created a world devoid of moral standards, Hobbes can logically have recourse to anything other than egoism at all. This problem is often presented, somewhat anachronistically, as deriving from a distinction first clearly insisted on by the philosopher David Hume. Hume, and many subsequent philosophers, argued that there is an absolute distinction between statements of fact and evaluative statements. You cannot, they claim, without violating the rules of logic, move an argument from statements of fact to statements of value. That is, no number of statements that x, or y, or z is the case, will enable you to deduce that you ought to do a, or b, or c.[241]

The question is often posed in the following way: either Hobbes seems to argue from certain facts about human nature to conclusions that we *ought* to do certain things (a move which modern philosophy has regarded with grave suspicion), or he must have had in mind, some pre-existent source of morality which has escaped the apparent nihilism of the state of nature. This may be to oppose as alternatives, what as we have seen, were

[240] A modern formal exploration of such 'anarchic solutions' to rational choice problems is Michael Taylor's *The Possibility of Cooperation* (Cambridge, 1987).

[241] The gulf between factual and evaluative statements was first clearly asserted by David Hume (*A Treatise of Human Nature*, ed. Selby-Bigge (Oxford, 1956), Bk III, Pt 1, i, p. 469). For a modern discussion of this see *Fact and Value* (Proceedings of the Royal Philosophical Society, 1974). A presentation particularly relevant to Hobbes's claim that it is the making of *covenants* that initiates justice and political morality is 'How to derive "ought" from "is"', John R. Searle, *Philosophical Review*, 73 (1964), and in *Theories of Ethics*, ed. Philippa Foot (Oxford, 1967) and the ensuing discussion.

capable of being conceived as two distinct issues for Hobbes and his contemporaries, one being the motive of obligation, the other being the grounds or basis of morality.

If we take seriously Hobbes's account of science, premised on statements about body and motion, and proceeding deductively it seems that Hobbes must argue from (psychological) facts to reach moral obligations. Need this involve Hume's illicit move, if indeed it is illicit? Or, grasping the other horn of the dilemma, does Hobbes's account of the state of nature, despite its apparently amoral character, already contain the moral imperatives needed to generate a theory of obligation? This raises, amongst other things, the issue, touched on earlier, of the status of the laws of nature.

Conditional morality

However, not all propositions of the form 'you ought to do x' are 'moral', i.e. statements of the kind that are excluded by the fact/value distinction alluded to above. There are statements of the kind: 'If you want y, then you ought to do x', where x is a condition of getting y. These are hypothetical imperatives, whereas the notion of a moral imperative implicit in the 'fact-value' controversy is an absolute or categorical imperative. Now hypothetical imperatives are not normally considered to be moral imperatives, moreover Hobbes regards it as axiomatic that the motive of all voluntary actions is the hope of some advantage, so if the hypothetical attached to doing x is that I will then get something that I want, the proposition certainly ceases to look like anything involving morality at all.

However let us consider. There are some hypothetical imperatives which involve conditions so wide and all embracing that they are almost invariably validated. One could regard Aristotle's attempt to deduce the proper forms of political and individual life from the 'natures' of men as involving a hypothetical imperative of the kind: 'If one wants to fit the world as it has been formed, realise one's own nature and place within it, then one ought to live in the following way'. Hobbes too is recommending to us behaviour which fits his much more chaotic world, and our own rather more egocentric natures. If says Hobbes, we want to a) stay alive, and b) be received into society (which is a condition of realising a), then we 'ought' to obey the laws of nature.[242] Furthermore, pursuing our survival is for Hobbes, not something he believes we normally have a choice about, but rather something which we are usually bound to pursue, because of the inertial nature of the motion of particles that constitute our physical make-up. Given this, and remembering Hobbes's determinism, one might regard the very knowledge of the laws of nature as a strong causal factor obliging us to obedience to them, for they are a means to that which we necessarily (and not simply by choice) seek, and consequently one might regard us as necessarily bound to at least endeavour to fulfill them. Such a view opens Hobbes to criticism for confusing reasons and causes of actions, a distinction which seems important to him in distinguishing political and natural obligation, but given his particular deterministic position it seems likely that he is vulnerable to some sort of criticism here in any case, and we have at least explained the puzzling sense in which the laws of nature could be said to 'oblige' us even in the state of nature where there seems to be no one able to 'bind' us to obligations. Clearly causes bind their effects; and as we've seen

---

[242] It is in this sense, and this sense alone that we 'ought' to seek peace. See Oakeshott, 'The Moral Life . . . ' in *Civil Association*, p. 90.

Hobbes is quite capable of conceiving of apprehended consequences acting as causes and affecting action.[243]

But we might ask is this not still all hypothetical rather than moral? Formally speaking, in terms of logic, of course the answer is yes. But we must be careful not to deny Hobbes's moralism purely by definition. On one view all moral assertions are ultimately reducible to absolute moral principles for which further reasons cannot be given (since to give further reasons would render them not ultimate). However, another property of Hobbes's science is that it is conditional, and if Hobbes, as he seems to, regards his moral statements as being derived from his factual assertions about human physiology and psychology in an unbroken chain, uniformly informed by the same method, then what is true about factual statements will also be true of moral assertions, and the name we give to conditional assertions in the field of morality is a hypothetical imperative. Hobbes also seems to want at all costs to avoid a regress to any supposedly absolute moral presuppositions, since there would then be nothing in principle to choose between his own, and those of anybody else: men basing their assertions of how subjects should behave on their views of God, the nature of English history or simply their own prejudices. One cannot in principle argue men out of positions based on their particular prejudices and Hobbes recognises this. But reason *is* the same in all men, therefore to base our moral or political obligations on reason is to establish the possibility of agreement, at least where our reason is good. But to 'base' arguments on reason is to make them hypothetical for a second reason: for to base them on reason is to allow them to be questioned. If moral or political duties are to be open to question, then they must be hypothetical in the sense of being conditional on the reasons given.

It seems that any attempt to base morality on reason, in the sense of reasoned argument for the principles constituting that morality, must make morality hypothetical in status. But that is not to say that it is nothing more than the selfish desires given as the ultimate grounds for holding it, nor to disqualify it as morality at all, except by definition.

The case against a Hobbesian deontology

However, as we have seen there is another possible interpretation of Hobbes's argument. That is to say that Hobbes commits no move from ought to is, because his account of natural law establishes that law, even in the state of nature, as a strict and pre-existing deontology. All the argument about 'obligation' in *Leviathan* should then be construed, not as a search for moral standards, but as a search for an adequate moral *motive*. We touched on this briefly in discussing the status of the laws of nature. What has become known as the Taylor – Warrender Thesis argues that we take seriously Hobbes's admission that the laws of nature may be considered as the laws of God.[244] The *motive*

---

[243] In his controversy with Bishop Bramhall, which took the form of a long correspondence, Hobbes refers to one of his arguments as physically causing the Bishop's response: 'I doubt not but he had therefore the will to write this reply, *because* I had Answered his treatise concerning true liberty. My answer therefore was, at least in part, the *cause* of his writing; yet that is the cause of the nimble local motion of his fingers. Is not the cause of the local motion physical? His will therefore was physically, and extrinsically, and antecedantly, and not morally caused by my writing.' *Questions concerning Liberty* . . . E.W., V, p. 188.

[244] The characterisation 'Taylor-Warrender' is extremely crude. As Warrender points out both in his study, and in an answer to Quentin Skinner's criticism of it, his position is quite distinct from that of Taylor

for obeying natural law might be prudential, but the *status* of the law is established by God's having commanded them. This separation of the motive of obligation from the moral standard is much in line with the position of Hobbes's opponents – whose theory of motivation, at least, in stressing the importance of the fear of hell, was disarmingly close to Hobbes's own. Consummate, and not opportunistic, obedience to any contract, on this view, would be a moral requirement from the start. There is no problem in deriving a duty to a specific covenant where there is a general duty to obey all laws of nature under God.

Now whilst it is true that Hobbes acknowledges that the laws of nature *might* be considered as commands of God, he stresses that it is only if they are so considered that they are laws in the true 'positive' sense, unless and until they are enforced by a civil sovereign.[245] Moreover, he doesn't *insist* that we read them this way; and he makes it clear that he wants nothing in his argument to depend on God providing any independent content or deontological status for his laws of nature.[246] Taylor's version of this argument for example, hinges at least at one point, on a crucial misconstrual of Hobbes's very carefully worded text. Taylor claims 'Hobbes regularly says of his natural law that it is a 'theorem' *which forbids* certain actions'.[247] This is precisely wrong. In the passage he himself quotes from *Leviathan* immediately after this assertion Hobbes writes that the laws are 'theorems *by which* a man is forbidden . . . ' (my emphasis), and not theorems 'that forbid'. Hobbes's point seems to be to stress the difference between, for example, laws which command us to play cricket and laws by which cricket is played.

Moreover *Leviathan*'s account differs significantly from earlier versions of Hobbes's theory where he does talk about obligation deriving simply from power. Such 'Irresistible Power' in God – effectively the right of nature, but one which cannot be controverted – still, in *Leviathan*, gives him who has it 'right', but not those under it any duty – they obey because they must, not because they ought.[248] In *Leviathan*'s political theory Hobbes stresses that sovereignty and political duty 'ariseth from pact'.[249] And since

---

who sees in Hobbes an anticipation of Kant. (Warrender, *The Political Philosophy of Hobbes*, p. 336; 'Political Theory and Historiography', *Historical Journal* (1979), p. 932.) Warrender's position is nevertheless similar in asserting 'that Hobbes bases the duties of the citizen ultimately upon a fundamental natural law that imposes obligations antecedently to, and independently of, the commands of the civil sovereign', Warrender, *Philosophy of Hobbes*, p. 336; and for our limited purposes here, that is enough to bracket them together. For a discussion of Hobbes's commitment to natural law which draws useful comparisons with other near-contemporary natural law theorists see S.A. State, *Hobbes and the Debate over Natural Law and Religion* (New York and London, 1991) esp. pp. 185–6, 237.

[245] *Leviathan*, pp. 80, 138.

[246] Ibid., p. 80, 'These dictates of Reason, men use to call by the name of Lawes; but improperly: for they are but Conclusions, or Theoremes concerning what conduceth to the conservation and defence of themselves; . . . yet if we consider the same Theoremes, as delivered in the word of God, that by right commandeth all things; then are they properly called Lawes.' Hobbes reminds the reader of this point again at p. 138, and in the Review and Conclusion Hobbes insists not on the supposed theological sanctions of his argument but that : 'I ground the Civil Right of Soveraigns, and both the Duty and Liberty of Subjects, upon the known naturall Inclinations of Mankind, and upon the Articles of the Law of Nature . . . ' p. 394

[247] Taylor, 'The Ethical Doctrine', in Reeve and Lively, pp. 23–4.

[248] *Leviathan*, p. 187. And see also the discussion of God's 'Natural Kingdom', above, p. 39 and in *Leviathan*, p. 216.

[249] Ibid., p. 187.

Hobbes does not believe it possible for men to covenant directly with God this makes the derivation of a duty to obey the laws of nature directly from God practically impossible.

The only way in which Hobbes does allow contract with God highlights what is surely his real concern, and is a strong argument against the theological interpretation of obligation. For Hobbes 'there is no covenant with God, but by mediation of some body that representeth Gods Person' and the only person who can do this is God's lieutenant, the secular ruler, 'who hath the sovereignty under God'.[250] Moreover Hobbes is insistent that for those within society, law, whether the civil law, or law of nature (which he says, is contained within the civil law) or even the revealed law of God 'obliges not, but to them that acknowledge it to be the act of the soveraigne'.[251]

So whilst God's will may in principle provide an independent source of obligation, in practice Hobbes allows no access to it except through its manifestation in the political sovereign, and so it turns out not to be an alternative at all.

Hobbes invariably goes to extraordinary lengths to armour his theory against such religious tactics. If Hobbes's intention had been to distinguish in this way between the egoistic motivation and the absolute duty to obey, it would not have been at all a strange distinction for his contemporaries. As he knew 'fear of damnation' is alone capable of outweighing the 'fear of temporal death'[252] and the hope of paradise and fear of hell-fire were used with disarming frankness by those in authority (and by Hobbes in earlier versions of his theory) to supply self-interested motives for obeying God's law. But in *Leviathan* Hobbes evidently decided that whatever motivational incentives might be gained from recruiting the fear of divine punishment to the cause of political obedience, were outweighed by the uncertainty of being able to do so. He not only insists that as far as politics is concerned, our religious duties are fulfilled by political obedience, he even argues that hell itself is not eternal torment, but simply annihilation, and the reason he gives for adopting this notoriously heterodox position is that 'it is impossible a Commonwealth should stand, where any other than the Soveraign, hath a power of giving greater rewards than Life; and of inflicting greater punishment than Death'.[253]

Hobbes is insistent that authority and obligation in modern Christian commonwealths is not derived directly from God as it was by the Old Testament Jews but indirectly, through our senses and capacity for rational knowledge: 'the talents he has put into our hands to negotiate'.[254] We must always judge for ourselves whether what a man claiming revelation tells us is true or not, or even what a passage of scripture means: 'As far as they differ not from the Laws of Nature, there is no doubt, but they are the Law of God, and carry their Authority with them, legible to all men that have the use of naturall reason . . . '[255] So, if even scripture appears to contradict reason and the laws of nature as known by reason, we must reject it. Most specifically of all, for it relates directly to this issue of the *status*, rather than the *content* of Law: Hobbes insists that the knowledge that any law is God's command (as opposed to knowledge of its content) is available only to those individuals to whom he has personally revealed this to be their status (clearly a very small group!), the rest of us 'is not obliged to obey them by any other Authority, then that of the Commonwealth'. For to say that we are obliged to obey, as God's natural

---

[250] *Leviathan*, pp. 89, 69.
[251] Ibid., p. 282.
[252] *De Cive*, VI, xi.

[253] *Leviathan*, p. 245 (Hell eternal death), p. 238.
[254] Ibid., p. 195.
[255] Ibid., p. 205.

law, whatever any man claims to have received, 'on pretence of private Inspiration, or Revelation,' is a recipe for conflict and strife.[256] If men do not take their understanding of religion from their Christian sovereigns

> they must either take their owne Dreames, for the Prophecy they mean to bee governed by, and the tumour of their own hearts for the spirit of God; or they must suffer themselves to bee lead by some strange Prince or some of their [rebellious] fellow subjects, that can bewitch them . . . and by this means . . . reduce all Order, Government, and Society, to the first Chaos of Violence, and Civill warre.[257]

It is the sovereign – God's vice regent on earth – who tells us the status of laws. This again seems a crucial objection to the deontological account, for it amounts to a denial by Hobbes, that we could have the kind of natural knowledge that would endow the laws of nature with the status that would have to be claimed for them by it.

More positively Hobbes himself tells us in his Review and Conclusion on what logical grounds *he* thinks his case for political obedience rests:

> I ground the Civil Right of Sovereigns, and both the Duty and Liberty of Subjects, upon the known and natural Inclinations of Mankind, and upon the Articles of the Law of Nature; of which no man, that pretends but reason enough to govern his private family, ought to be ignorant.[258]

Hobbes himself, then, claimed his case for obedience rested on his psychology and the ability of men to reason, and not on theology. Whilst the declared intentions of an author are not an infallible guide to the logical structure of his work, we ought to try very hard indeed to see whether they are successful before insisting on some other account of what he has said.

The argument from context, internal and external

However, perhaps the most telling arguments against the cleverly worked out theory are two much wider considerations which militate against the view that God is, in any effective sense, the source of Hobbes's morality. Firstly, if we consider the deontological interpretation against the context of Hobbes's careful exclusion of theological consider-ations so as to preclude sources of moral and political disagreement, it would be almost inconceivable that he should revert to allowing God to play such a crucial independent role as being the source of moral duty.

Hobbes, throughout *Leviathan*, is extremely careful to deny to God any properties which impinge on political allegiance: 'The nature of God is incomprehensible; that is to say, we understand nothing of *what he is*, but only *that he is*'.[259] Even more precisely, the question of interpreting what moral doctrine follows from the fact of God's existence 'is in all Common-wealths inseparably annexed . . . to the Soveraign Power Civill'.[260]

---

[256] *Leviathan*, p. 205.
[257] Ibid., p. 232.
[258] Ibid., p. 394.

[259] Ibid., p. 208.
[260] Ibid., p. 295.

At the end of Part 2, when he starts his attack on the possibility of religious interference with political sovereignty, he insists that he has

> derived the Rights of Soveraigne Power, and the duty of Subjects hitherto, from the Principles of Nature onely; such as Experience has found true, or Consent (concerning the use of words) has made so; that is to say, from the nature of Men, known to us by experience, and from Definitions (of such words as are Essential to all Politicall reasoning) universally agreed on.[261]

There must be, Hobbes claims, in matters of biblical interpretation, no less than in other religious matters, as in legal and political judgement, a final arbiter; moreover, lest their opinions conflict, it must be the same arbiter in each case:

> There is therefore no other Government in this life, neither of State, nor Religion, but Temporall; nor teaching of any doctrine, lawfull to any Subject, which the Governour both of the State, and of the Religion Forbiddeth to be taught: And that Governor must be one; or else there must needs follow Faction, and Civil war in the Common-wealth, between the *Church* and *State*.[262]

The second more general point to be made against this interpretation of Hobbes is that he was so often criticised for not holding these very views: no contemporary, critic or ally, read Hobbes in this (then) much more congenial way; and although he replied to other criticisms he never, despite all the opprobrium it brought, subsequently denied that he sought to ground both the duty and the motive of law-abiding behaviour on self-interest, rather than on an independently knowable duty to obey God.[263]

Hobbes sought to drive a massive wedge between earthly rule and God's kingdom, so as to preclude any arguments about the latter's relevance to, or imminent arrival on, earth, an event which would result in the destruction of all existing secular powers. Such views had been propagated with various degrees of certainty and fervour during the Civil War, and were to come close to gaining power through the influence of fifth-monarchists on Cromwell in 1653.[264] Hobbes indeed brings God's kingdom 'down to earth' but in a diametrically opposed way. Denying the eschatological claims of the millenarians, Hobbes, instead of sacralising the secular, secularizes the sacred. 'The Kingdome of God is a Civill Kingdome; which consisted, first in the obligation of the people of Israel to those Laws, which Moses should bring unto them from Mount Sinai', and after Christ's return, as his personal rule as a Hobbesian sovereign – 'by force of our Covenant'.[265] In between these times, concludes Hobbes, there is no conflict between religion and the

---

[261] *Leviathan*, p. 195.

[262] Ibid., p. 248.

[263] See Skinner, 'The Ideological Context', p. 316: To read Hobbes's natural law as premised on an obligation to obey God's law would 'make the entire intellectual milieu impossible to understand. Hobbes must be represented as presenting a traditional type of natural law theory of politics in a manner so convoluted that it was everywhere taken for the work of a complete utilitarian . . . .And despite Hobbes's predilection for the quiet life, his terror at being arraigned for heterodoxy, he never once attempted either to disown the alarmingly radical writers who cited his authority, or to disarm his innumerable critics by pointing out their misconception of his intentions.'

[264] On the Millenial tradition generally see N.Cohn, *The Pursuit of the Millenium* (1957); on the fifth-monarchists in particular, B.S. Capp, *The Fifth Monarchy Men: a study in seventeenth-century English millenarianism* (London, 1972).

[265] *Leviathan*, p. 219.

secular, because within the necessary limitations of natural knowledge, there is no access to God's will except through the sovereign who interprets it to us. All Christians are required to believe for salvation is 'that JESUS IS THE CHRIST . . . the King which God had before promised by the Prophets of the Old Testament, to send into the world, to reign (over the Jews, and over such other of other nations as should beleeve in him.) under himself eternally'.[266]

Hobbes firmly subordinates religion to political sovereignty at every point where it could possibly provide grounds for political disobedience. No religious revelation, he believed, was genuine if it contradicted what reason showed was necessary for civil peace. One of the tests of a true prophet was his 'not teaching any other Religion than that which is already established', or so as to 'stir up revolt against the King.'[267] Since reason demonstrated the necessity for an absolute sovereign with command over both public worship and 'what doctrines may be taught', we must disbelieve those who claim to challenge that sovereign by God's direct instruction. It is the sovereign who guarantees the status of the scriptures, and 'the ordinary cause of our beleeving that the Scriptures are the Word of God' is the fact that they are taught to us under the sovereign's direction.[268]

It is always true that God may speak directly to an individual, rather than through man's reason, but this could at most only justify that individual in acting on that revelation, for such is our natural knowledge that there is no politically legitimate or epistemologically convincing way in which that conviction can be communicated to others. We, who only hear the individual, have no way of assessing his inspiration except by comparing it with what our reason tells us is true.

The same may be said of the authority of the Bible: Hobbes recognised, what was obvious in seventeenth-century England, that the range of interpretations to which the Bible was susceptible was a rich source of heterodoxy, enabling many different views to claim scriptural authority for their subversive opinions. The question, as Hobbes points out, 'is not of obedience to God, but of *when* and *what* God hath said; which to Subjects that have no supernatural revelation, cannot be known, but by that naturall reason, which guided them, for the obtaining of Peace and Justice, to obey the authority of their severall Common-wealths; that is to say of their lawful sovereigns.'[269] Since reason tells us that there must be a single arbiter in all matters of potential difference, it is the responsibility of the sovereign: 'to be Judge of what Opinions and Doctrines are averse, and what conducing to Peace'.[270] It follows that 'it is not the Writer but the authority of the Church that maketh a Book Canonicall' and the political sovereign, as head of the Church of England, is the ultimate interpreter of these.[271] Thus revelation, Bible and church are all subordinated to the sovereign political power.

Hobbes pushes to the very limit the claims of political authority over the church. Using the Puritan stress on the importance of the inner belief of the individual to draw

---

[266] *Leviathan*, p. 324, and p. 272.

[267] Ibid., p. 197.

[268] Ibid., p. 324.

[269] Ibid., p. 199, and see p. 32.

[270] Ibid., p. 91.

[271] Ibid., pp. 204–5. Although it is true that in *Leviathan* Hobbes expresses some sympathy for a more congregationalist view of church organisation, the last word in such matters, as in that of doctrine, lies with the sovereign.

conclusions diametrically opposed to those of many radicals, Hobbes claims men may obey even a monarch who commands them to deny Christ, for, he claims: 'Profession with the tongue is but an externall thing, and no more than any other gesture whereby we signifie our obedience . . . that action is not his, but his sovereign's.'[272] As for bearing witness to Christ, such a course is legitimate, but not required. The alternative between this kind of religious profession and politics is absolute: subjects cannot both have their civil cake and consume it in religious fervour. The principles of secular peace and safety are simply incompatible with the enactment of all subjectively held religious convictions. Of course, men *may* choose martyrdom: 'But if they do, they ought to expect their reward in Heaven, and not complain . . . '[273]

For men of Hobbes's generation their religious freedom was perhaps the single most important political issue, yet the pursuit of it had produced the most devastating consequences. The strength of Hobbes's concern with religious differences is shown in his willingness to grant even to Muslims in Christian countries, the same liberty of conscience he claimed for Protestants. Anyone who refused them this, and said that the Muslim commanded to Christian worship by his sovereign is, if sincere, bound to refuse, 'authorizeth all private men, to disobey their Princes, in maintenance of their Religion', and if he says he should obey, then 'he alloweth to himself, that which hee denyeth to another, contrary to the words of our Saviour, *Whatsoever you would that men should doe unto you, that doe yee unto them*; and contrary to the Law of Nature'.[274]

Hobbes's theory claimed to safeguard civil peace whilst granting freedom of conscience on condition that it was exercised only in that private space allowed by the sovereign and by the constitution of human consciousness. To do this he had to interpret Christianity in such a way that its demands, by way of outward action, were minimal, whilst asserting that what remained private or inward, could not reasonably be the cause of conflict, nor, lying as it did beyond the reach of coercive power, an object of political command. But to guarantee such external peace, the sovereign had to assert at least a potential claim to *all* that lay outside – including public expressions of belief. This was a drastic solution. Was it the only way that autonomous individuals could survive together? A very different answer was given some forty years later, using surprisingly similar intellectual materials, by John Locke.

As often stressed here, Hobbes's political theory found almost no significant champions at the time. In that sense he is not part of the mainstream of political ideas. Yet his boldness and stridency were clearly fascinating and challenging to many. Reading responses to him one sometimes feels that his views were rejected because they were distasteful rather than incoherent or obviously false. For much of the succeeding century moralists complained (sometimes by name) about the increasingly Hobbesian nature of people's behaviour, their egoism and their lack of religion. This suggests that Hobbes had touched a raw nerve. Since the nineteenth century Hobbes has enjoyed increasing reputation as a political philosopher, to the point where Professor Oakeshott, could reasonably assert that '*Leviathan* is the greatest, perhaps the sole, masterpiece of political philosophy written in the English language'.[275] It is now less fashionable than it was to

---

[272] *Leviathan*, p. 271.
[273] Ibid., p. 331.

[274] Ibid., p. 271.
[275] *Leviathan*, ed. Oakeshott, p. vii.

rank political philosophy, but it's worth pausing to consider what might lay behind such a claim.

Hobbes's waxing reputation suggests that in the long term he made more sense than in the short. Or rather, that in the long term we can accept and admire the insights that made him so unacceptable to his contemporaries. If Hobbes's mechanics now seem crude, they are at least recognisable ancestors of the modern world-view. Moreover the moral problems which he raised about the sources and status of ethical values are still with us. Although the absolutist method of reconciling the egoistic motivations he discovered to the world was repugnant, the problem of the containment of egoism remained. Thinkers such as Mandeville, and Adam Smith, Shaftesbury, Hutcheson and Hume, sought in different ways to solve this problem, either by attempting to show that individual egoism bore a paradoxically supportive relationship to other social ends, and was reconciled through institutions such as the market, or that egoism was counteracted by an innate 'moral sense' or could be moderated and refined by the processes of social development. But such solutions, particularly the latter, were always provisional, they depended on a political society creating and sustaining morals, manners and opinions amongst its citizens which were, even if stable, in a dynamic and evolving tension. Royalists were right to fear Hobbes's 'democratic' premises, despite his absolutist conclusion. The validation of the individual's will and appetite, has proved, in the long run, to be a crucial aspect of the modern state, challenged only, and in historical terms, briefly, by the collectivist alternatives of fascism and communism. The modern commercial state can stress the importance of individual choice, and allow it full reign only because it has succeeded - for the while, and for those who have mattered - in channelling it within manageable limits. But those limits are constantly threatened, and the source of the threats, some more apparent recently than for some time, are those which Hobbes identified, unrestrained egoism and the 'enthusiastic' assertion of religious certainty. When they arise, civil peace is threatened, and the state if it is to survive, is forced to cast aside its benign liberal mask and assert its ultimately absolutist authority. There is a neat fit between Hobbes's two most paradoxical assertions – the unbounded and disparate desires of individuals and his political authoritarianism. For only an ultimately absolute and arbitrary sovereign could guarantee to control such unpredictable individualism.

II

John Locke

Introduction

The historical background to the composition of the two treatises

In important ways the English Civil War and the experiments of the Commonwealth failed to resolve the issues which led to them. The restoration of the monarchy in 1660 took place largely through the exhaustion of other possibilities. The dynastic principle was deeply rooted and had already re-asserted itself with the short-lived succession of Cromwell's son Richard to the office of Protector. So although it seems that Londoners welcomed General Monck and the soon-to-be-Charles II with some genuine relief, once the monarchy was re-established Parliament continued to be worried about the same issues as under his father, Charles I.

They were worried about religion: the court's long exile in France had not allayed the fears of many that the royal family's sympathies lay with the Catholic rather than the Protestant religion. They were also worried about their property: that is they wanted to be sure they could control the King's power to raise taxes. Nor were the issues of religion and property as distinct as they might appear today. The royal claim to rule by prerogative and to tax without the consent of Parliament was effectively seen as a kind of arbitrary government; and arbitrary government in turn was associated in people's minds with Catholicism. The reason for this was partly that those neighbouring nations which were Catholic – notoriously France and Spain – were also absolutist monarchies, but partly also because Catholicism was seen as a kind of religious absolutism – giving, as Protestants saw it, the Pope the right to determine men's religious consciences. The Earl of Shaftesbury warned 'slavery and popery, like two sisters go hand in hand'.[1] A major Whig pamphleteer succinctly linked the fears of absolutism in government, insecurity of property, and Catholicism in religion:

> Your neighbours in France, Spain, and other Popish governments have no other security either for their estates or beings, save for the grace or favour of their prince; which renders them vassals to the crown . . . There you may see the poor tenant ground to beggary, . . . merchants, tradesmen and artifacers paying excessive . . . excise . . . for every egg or bit of bread they put in their mouths. Their very labours are not their own . . . These and a thousand more inconveniences are incident to absolute monarchy, and absolute monarchy incident to popery.

[1] Shaftesbury's speech in the House of Lords, 25 March, 1679.

Another Whig, Sir Henry Capel claimed:

> There are but two sorts of monarchy in the whole world: one absolute without limitation, as that of France whose subjects are at the disposal of the King for life and limb, and to invade other nations' property for the luxury of the court: and little men of low fortunes are ministers of state and whoever does that I shall suspect him of absolute monarchy.[2]

The other of course was England, which was Protestant not papist, free not subject and constitutional not absolutist.

Effectively the Whig circles around Shaftesbury were still fighting the Civil War issue of establishing parliamentary limitations on royal power (the 'Good Old Cause'); the King's power of prerogative, or indeed any of the King's powers were only to be used in the public's interest, and the only proper judge of that interest was Parliament. The problem came to a head in what is known as the Exclusion Crisis of 1680. Anti-Catholic feelings were running very high, boosted by the fears aroused by the 'Popish Plot'. The plot, a supposed attempt by Jesuits to assassinate the King, was invented in 1678 by Israel Tongue and Titus Oates, fuelled by anti-Catholic sentiment, and gratefully, but probably innocently, taken up by Shaftesbury and other Whig politicians.[3] The Earl of Shaftesbury who had first employed Locke as his physician in 1667, had by 1679, become his patron, political associate and friend. As Lord President of the Council, Shaftesbury was prime mover of an attempt to pass a Bill through Parliament to exclude the next in line of succession, James, Duke of York, Charles's younger brother, from the throne. Charles II was childless, or rather, had no legitimate heirs.[4] James was a Catholic. The purpose of the 'Exclusion Bill' was to prevent a Catholic succeeding to the throne. This involved Parliament changing, or putting aside a rule – the rule of hereditary succession – which was fundamental to the whole concept of monarchy. If Parliament could legislate to determine who should or should not succeed, then had not sovereignty, in effect passed to them? Certainly James himself, perhaps predictably, thought so. He declared: 'The exclusion bill destroys the very being of monarchy, which, I thank God, yet has had no dependency on parliaments nor on nothing but God alone, nor ever can, and be a monarchy.'[5]

James's Catholicism and some parliamentarians' attempts to exclude him, thus led to a discussion of the fundamentals of political authority and obligation. But it was a discussion based not, as were those of Hobbes and the Levellers during the Civil War, on the problem of the breakdown of sovereignty, but on its presence and its limits. The question being asked was: Was it ever right to resist a sovereign, and if so when?

---

[2] Sir Henry Capel, *A Character of Popery and Arbitrary Government*, p. 2, cited Richard Ashcraft, *Revolutionary Politics & Locke's Two Treatises of Government* (Princeton, 1986), p. 205.

[3] J.P. Kenyon, *The Popish Plot* (London, 1972), esp. ch. 5.

[4] His illegitimate son, the Duke of Monmouth, was to lead a rebellion agains his half-brother in 1685. The rebellion was organised and financed from the emigré community in Holland, activities in which, it now seems, Locke himself took a significant part. See Ashcraft, *Revolutionary Politics*, p. 452ff.

[5] James II, cited M. Ashley, *The Glorious Revolution of 1688* (London, 1966), p. 26; on the constitutional issues see C.A. Edie, 'Succession and Monarchy: the Controversy of 1678–1681', *American Historical Review*, LXX (1964–5).

The attempt to exclude James failed when Charles dissolved Parliament. A group of Whigs led by Shaftesbury and Locke himself began to move towards treason. Shaftesbury fled to Holland in November 1682, and died there the following January. In June 1683, what became known as the Rye House Plot was discovered and two leading Whigs, Lord Russell and Algernon Sidney were arrested and executed. Others fled England for Holland, amongst them Locke himself, anxiously arranging with his friends for the safety of his papers on 'The French Disease'.[6] Locke never returned home until the flight of Charles's brother and successor, James II, and the Glorious Revolution of 1688.

From his accession in 1685 James pursued a series of policies which succeeded in alienating virtually all leading elements of English political life. These included promulgating or dispensing with laws in defiance of Parliament, the establishment of special courts, the preferment of Catholics to high places in the army and universities, and a dubious foreign policy in which James was suspected, rightly as we now know, of secretly accepting French money in return for engineering the restoration of Catholicism. Ironically, as part of the rehabilitation of Catholics, James pursued a policy of imposed toleration which outraged not only the Anglican establishment, but even some dissenters who, although they had suffered under the Anglican restoration saw toleration as a Trojan horse for Catholicism.[7] There was thus a complex of issues at stake, and it is not always clear which people saw as the most salient. Non-conformists in particular had to choose between rejecting toleration or accepting it at the cost of repudiating the rule of Parliament (since the King imposed the toleration and never succeeded in legislating for it). More generally the Whig opponents of Charles, to whom James made overtures in an attempt to undermine the high Anglican Tories, had to choose between principled isolation or a share of office and a chance to revenge themselves on the Tories who had driven them out under Charles. It is almost as convincing to see 1688 as an anti-Catholic putsch, as it is to see it as a high-minded defence of constitutionalism. At any rate, the birth of a son to James and the prospect of an unending line of Catholic monarchs was the final straw. It was widely put about that the child was that of a serving woman, smuggled into the royal bed chamber some said, in a warming pan.

When James attempted to impose toleration by decree, the famous 'seven bishops' refused instructions to read his 'Declaration of Indulgence' from the pulpit. High Court judges and a jury in turn refused instructions to convict them of seditious libel. Leading English aristocrats had for some time been sounding out William of Orange – married to James's Protestant daughter Mary who was next in line of succession if James had died without issue. William and Mary now indicated their willingness to accept the throne. When William landed in Torbay in November 1688, it was in a situation fraught with irony. A Dutch Presbyterian ruler who supported toleration was intervening to prevent an English King from imposing it, at the request of an Anglican regime, in which,

---

[6] Locke, by the standards of his day an impressive doctor, ambiguously and wittily labelled his critical notes on absolutism 'De Morbo Gallico' (On the French Disease) which was contemporary slang for syphilis. On his concern with the whereabouts of his treasonable manuscript see M. Cranston, *John Locke, A Biography* (Oxford, 1985), pp. 227–30ff.

[7] Good narrative histories include Ashley, *The Glorious Revolution of 1688*. The constitutional issues are brought more to the fore in J.R. Western, *Monarchy and Revolution: The English State in the 1680s* (London, 1972).

as a private individual he could not, because of his religion, officially have held even local government office!

James fled on hearing the news of the landing and William and Mary became joint monarchs, occupying the 'vacant' throne. The supposed 'vacancy' of the throne was intended to evade constitutional embarrassment. James's flight could be presented as a kind of unofficial 'abdication', thus avoiding the issue of whether Parliament had indeed appointed William and Mary. This was, however, clearly a convenient fiction.[8]

It was at the time of the Exclusion Crisis that we now know Locke began a work on politics that was to become the *Two Treatises of Government*.[9] Before it emerged in this form Locke had fled the country, threatened with arrest for treason, and throughout the events of the 1680s he remained on the continent, embroiled in the community of political exiles, probably laundering money sent out from England to help the cause. His concern was justifiable: the case against Sidney had rested almost entirely on his authorship of an unpublished work of political theory, his *Discourses Concerning Government*. Locke was known to have advised Shaftesbury, and may already have had a hand in some of his works.[10] The cautious Locke never in his life acknowledged authorship of the *Two Treatises*, even after the successful revolution which enabled their revision and publication.[11]

The work was thus not originally written to justify the successful revolution of 1688, but almost wholly to incite a future one in the early 1680s.[12] It is possible, however, to discern in Locke's argument, references to both circumstances, for he revised the work immediately before publication. But before trying to trace such detail it is important to remember the wider conditions of the debate and the terminology in which it was cast.

Although some of Locke's associates in the revolutionary movement had republican sympathies, the movement was not in essence republican. Locke's concern was to construct an argument which justified, in exceptional circumstances, the expulsion of a ruler (or rulers – his argument, as he several times repeats, is directed as much at tyrannical parliaments as at tyrannical kings) who had ceased to act constitutionally. It

---

[8] On the theoretical problems of the Whigs in justifying what they decided they would rather not call a revolution see J.P. Kenyon, 'The Revolution of 1688, Resistance and Contract', in *Historical Perspectives, Studies in Honour of J.H.Plumb*, ed. N. McKendrick (London, 1974).

[9] Laslett concludes that Locke had written quite possibly a substantial portion of a version of the *Second Treatise*, by 1680, at which point he abandoned it to write the *First Treatise*, in direct repudiation of Filmer's *Patriarcha* which had been republished by the Court party that year. *Locke's Two Treatises of Government*, ed. Peter Laslett (Cambridge, 1967), p. 59. (This edition used for all citations to Locke's work, cited hereafter either as *First Treatise* or *Second Treatise*, by paragraph and page number in that edition where Locke's words are quoted, otherwise by paragraph alone). Ashcraft points out that Locke did not acquire a copy of Filmer's *Patriarcha* until January 1680, and acquired many other works cited in the *Second Treatise* over the next two years. Moreover, although the *First Treatise* fits the Exclusion Crisis in dealing with the need to undermine the support for James's succession given by the republished patriarchal theories of Filmer, the revolutionary import of the *Second Treatise* fits much better the political context of the early 1680s — in particular the refusal of Charles to call a parliament — and Shaftesbury's Whigs response to that by threatening resistance. Richard Ashcraft, *Locke's Two Treatises of Government* (London, 1987), pp. 286–297: Appendix 'The Composition and Structure of the *Two Treatises of Government*'.

[10] Laslett, *Two Treatises*, pp. 29, 31, and Ashcraft, *Revolution Principles*, pp. 85, 120.

[11] Locke finally acknowledged authorship in an amendment to his will.

[12] See Laslett's introduction to his edition of the *Two Treatises*, and his 'The English Revolution and Locke's *Two Treatises of Government*' *Cambridge Historical Journal*, xii (1956).

was not an argument against monarchy as such, nor did he seem to want to base his arguments on principles which might lead to such a position. Fear of the democratic forces unleashed during the Civil War undoubtedly deterred many opponents of Charles from making such appeals, and would certainly have deterred many to whom some kind of appeal had to be made.[13] However it is now clear that Shaftesbury and Locke were much closer to such views than has long been thought – John Wildman for example, the ex-Leveller leader was amongst their conspirators, as were old Cromwellian officers and known republicans such as Slingsby Bethel.[14] Like most political activists, their views were more extreme than theirs whose support they had to attract. But whatever the personal opinions of their more active collaborators, it seems clear that Shaftesbury and Locke realised that maximum support could be attracted by a minimalist programme. The main focus of Locke's political argument therefore, was simply to demonstrate a right of resistance and the circumstances in which it could be exercised. His text nevertheless contains innumerable and multivalent references to specific issues in the controversy aroused by Charles and James. This rendered it an extraordinary mine of arguments for both radical and conservative interpretations of those events and no doubt contributed to its eventual success.

The intellectual context: the inheritance of parliamentary thought

The intellectual context, however, from which Locke began to argue, was not an easy one in which to establish even this limited right. There was, within continental (and Scots) Protestantism a strong tradition which viewed the king as an executive officer of the parliament, assembly or estates in which the constituent authority of the people lay. Even where a regime did not regard the king as subordinate, Protestant resistance theory allowed 'lesser magistrates' a right of resistance and deposition in the event of the monarch's delinquency.[15]

If the monarch was seen merely as a chief executive officer, using powers delegated by the parliament, as in the continental Monarchomach tradition there was no problem about parliamentary intervention. But such a view involved asserting either the supremacy of Parliament over the monarch (and possibly of the Commons over the Lords too, as many of those peers had realised who slipped away from London to join the King in Nottingham in 1642); or it involved asserting that Parliament in some way represented

---

[13] Mark Goldie has pointed out that many of Locke's West-Country friends were distinctly cool about radical political action at the time of Monmouth's Rebellion and more so as the eighties wore on. He has other evidence which contradicts some of the detail of Ashcraft's case, but in my view leaves it substantially uncontroverted. [Unpublished paper]. I am grateful to the author for the opportunity to read this research.

[14] Ashcraft, *Revolution Principles*, pp. 247–8.

[15] On this tradition see J.H. Franklin (tr. & ed), *Constitutionalism and Resistance in the Sixteenth Century: Three Treatises by Hotman, Beza and Mornay* (New York, 1969); and on the rights of lesser magistrates, most famously the *Vindiciae Contra Tyrannos*, which was seasonally published in translation in London as 'A Defence of Liberty against Tyrants' in 1689 (its eighth printing that century — the dates are almost a barometer of political crisis: 1622, 1631, 1648, 1660, 1688). On the relationship of these traditions to Locke's own ideas on resistance see Quentin Skinner, 'The Origins of the Calvinist Theory of Revolution', in *After the Reformation, Essays in Honour of J.H. Hexter*, ed. Barbara C. Malament (Manchester, 1980).

'the people' directly, and, because of this, had precedence over the other elements in the constitution. This in turn involved a flirtation with dangerously populist conceptions of authority, an idea which in the early 1640s, and even more by the Restoration, most were anxious to reject.

Most Englishmen on both sides in 1642 and in the 1680s, were anxious to operate – or at least to appear to be operating – within the constraints of legality. They were attached to the notion that the English constitution was 'balanced' or 'mixed' in such a way that the mixture stood or fell as a totality. King, Lords and Commons were 'co-ordinate' – intertwined so subtly that no one part could claim overall precedence, nor could any one part act in the absence of any other. Yet at the same time, and by the same token, each part was 'independent' in status in the sense that it was not answerable to either of the others. Moderate seventeenth-century opposition theorists thus had a problem: they acknowledged the independent but 'co-ordinate' status of the monarch within the constitution, yet they wished to call him to account.[16]

Any resistance theorists of the 1680s had a similar problem, exacerbated by the memory of the civil wars and the threat of social revolution that had within living memory, resulted from 'popular' theories of sovereignty.

Royalists moved in another direction. Some, including the King's official defenders in the pamphlet battle that preceded the outbreak of the Civil War, had adopted a constitutionalist position which acknowledged the co-ordinate nature of the English constitution, and the constitutional boundaries to the King's power.[17] But with the confidence of the restored monarchy many had reasserted the royal absolutist position outlined earlier in the century in James I's *Trewe Law of Free Monarchy*. Amongst these, the most prominent of the works used to support this assertion of royal supremacy in the 1680s was one by a long-dead Kentish Knight, Sir Robert Filmer.

Filmer's patriarchal defence of monarchy

Born in 1588, the same year as Hobbes, Filmer's major work *Patriarcha*, had circulated in manuscript during the Civil War amongst royalist intellectuals. Parts of it, with critical discussions of other writers, were published by Filmer in the late 1640s. But although *Patriarcha* itself was never fully published in the author's lifetime, it was published in 1680 by a Court party anxious for an intellectual justification to relieve itself of the pressure from the exclusionists and Whigs. Collections of Filmer's tracts were published three times in 1679-80 and again in 1684, *Patriarcha* twice in 1680 and in 1685.[18] There was no doubt who it was that had to be answered. Sidney, executed for his anti-patriarchal *Discourses*, denounced Filmer from the scaffold with his dying breath.[19]

[16] The best account of the relationship of this political theory to Locke is Julian Franklin, *John Locke and the Theory of Sovereignty* (Cambridge, 1978).

[17] The most celebrated expression of this was Falkland and Culpepper's 'His Majesty's Answer to the Nineteen Propositions' (1642).

[18] There is a short bibliography in Sir Robert Filmer, *Patriarcha and other Political Writings*, ed. Peter Laslett (Oxford, 1949) pp. 47–8.

[19] 'Memoirs of Algernon Sidney' and his 'Apology' in Algernon Sidney, *Discourses Concerning Government* (1751, repr., Farnborough, 1968), pp. xxv and xxxviii. In his *Apology for Himself*, which

In the Oxfordshire countryside Locke and Tyrrell, although friends, seem independently to have formed the project of writing an attack on Filmer's arguments. Locke bought a copy of *Patriarcha* (and *The Freeholder's Grand Inquest*) in January 1680.[20] Tyrrell's essay *Patriarcha non Monarcha* appeared in 1681. Thus three of the major works of the opposition were directed at Filmer's influential defence of absolute monarchy.

Recent scholarship has questioned the representativeness of Filmer's royalism.[21] Whether his patriarchalism was the only royalist position can be questioned. What is beyond doubt is that Sidney, Tyrrell and Locke all perceived it to be, if not typical, at least the most dangerous of the royalist apologetics. Locke, in the *Two Treatises* is replying to Filmer's *Patriarcha*, and to the specific conditions of the Exclusion Crisis and the resulting proscription of Parliament.[22] So closely is Locke's argument determined by these concerns that it is often impossible to understand why he introduces certain topics, why he treats them in the way he does, or yet again why he leaves out certain other things, without some awareness of his concern to refute Filmer's patriarchalism. Consequently we shall need to look at Filmer's case in some detail.

---

according to one contemporary Sidney 'had read', but was at any rate printed and distributed at his death, Sidney claimed the case against him rested on 'somme scraps of a large treatise, in answeare to Filmer's book, which, being full of abominable maximes, might be opposed by any man'. On this period of Sidney's life see Jonathan Scott, *Algernon Sidney and the Restoration Crisis*, (Cambridge, 1991). Scott explores links in the theory of rebellion held by Locke and Sidney in a forthcoming paper: The Law of War: Grotius, Sidney, Locke and the Political Theory of Rebellion which I thank the author for allowing me to read.

[20] M.Cranston, *John Locke*, p. 190 (purchase of *Patriarcha*), p. 202 (ignores Tyrrell's request for information about plans). Filmer's authorship of the *Freeholder's Grand Inquest*, is disputed, see below, fn.34.

[21] James Daley, *Sir Robert Filmer and English Political Thought* (Toronto, 1979) argues for Filmer's peculiarity amongst royalist writers, albeit by a very narrow definition of Filmerianism. Gordon Schochet's assessment seems only a slight exaggeration: 'The Filmerian position very nearly became the official state ideology', Gordon Schochet, *Patriarchalism in Political Thought* (New York, 1975), p. 193. However, there were other Royalist ideologues too, see Mark Goldie, 'John Locke and Anglican Royalism', *Political Studies*, XXXI, 1 (1983), pp. 66–70.

[22] As Laslett points out, *Second Treatise*, p. 301, fn. Locke's reference here, and in his *Tablet* (Notebook), is not to *Patriarcha* itself, but to Filmer's *Observations upon Aristotle's Politiques*, republished in various versions of Filmer's *Tracts*. However, for the present purposes I have used *Patriarcha* as the epitome of Filmer's and the patriarchalist argument, which I believe does no serious violence to Locke's intentions in rebutting the patriarchalist case. Such details however *are* important for the dating of the various stages of composition of the two treatises. According to Laslett Locke began with the *Second Treatise* in 1679, but broke off to write the *First Treatise* early in 1680, on the appearance of *Patriarcha*. He then returned to and revised the incomplete *Second Treatise*, in 1681, and finally, immediately prior to publication, after the Glorious Revolution in 1689. Laslett, *Locke's Two Treatises*, pp. 60–66. Ashcraft argues persuasively for the reverse order of composition and a later date (1680–1 and 1681–2), *Revolutionary Politics*. Laslett has defended his original position in *Locke's Two Treatises of Government*, (Student Edition, Cambridge, 1988), p. 123. See above, fn.9.

The patriarchalist case

Filmer's argument is to modern ears a bizarre one. It is that paternal authority is absolute, and that all political authority is an analogue of paternal authority.[23] Indeed, paternal authority was for Filmer, the original type and exemplar of all authority presented to us as a model in the Bible story of the creation of Adam. Having created Adam, God, we are told, gave him authority over his family (Eve) and over the earth and its products. All rightful authority, Filmer argues, must be derived from this grant.[24] Some patriarchal theorists argued that descent could be literally established by constructing a family tree from Adam down to Charles II![25] But Filmer is not as crude as this. Locke does not always do justice to the subtlety of Filmer's argument. Although concerned to deal precisely with Filmer's criticism of contractualism, in his asides Locke sometimes attacks a more general 'straw patriarch' position, implicating Filmer by association. Filmer does however argue that originally kings, as heads of clans, were biological heads of families, and that their authority descends naturally, through the act of procreation, from one monarch to another, as does parental authority. One strength of this position is his ability to insist on the existence of 'natural communities', which contractualists cannot, since they must start from isolated individuals and somehow derive a social group from them. Filmer doesn't claim that kings were still literal patriarchs, nor that there was an unbroken line of legitimate succession which has actually filled up historical time. Men have been both wicked and ignorant of God's intentions for them. The line of descent has consequently been broken, indeed sometimes usurpers are the unwitting instrument of God's justice.[26] It is also true that men have attempted to establish other forms of government; but, Filmer thinks, they are neither in accordance with God's wishes, nor do they work. He thus adds a utilitarian argument to his theological one; and for good measure argues that nature also demonstrates the suitability of paternal authority in all other spheres. By an excruciatingly perverse reading of Aristotle on the family and kingship he even manages to invoke his authority for this view – despite, as a heathen, his not having had the advantage of scripture.[27]

---

[23] Locke succinctly quotes from Filmer (*Observations on Mr Hobb's Leviathan*) the core of his position: 'If God created only Adam, *and out of a piece of him made the Woman, and if by Generation from them two, as parts of them, all Mankind be propogated: If also God gave to* Adam *not only the Dominion over the Woman and the Children that should Issue from them, but also over the whole Earth to subdue it, and over all the Creatures on it, so that as long as* Adam *lived, no Man could claim or enjoy any thing but by Donation, Assignation, or permission from him.* '(Locke, *First Treatise*, §14, p. 168). My outline of Filmer's argument here is necessarily a summary. For the texts see Laslett, *Patriarcha . . . and other Political Works.* Extended discussions of Filmer and patriarchalism can be found in the works by Schochet and Daly mentioned above. Shorter treatments can be found in R.W.K. Hinton, 'Husbands, Fathers and Conquerers', *Political Studies*, XV (1967) [and XVI (1968)], and W.H. Greenleaf, *Order, Empiricism and Politics* (Oxford, 1964), ch. v.

[24] *Patriarcha and other Works*, p. 57.

[25] William Slayter, *Genethliacon* (1630)

[26] *Patriarcha and other Works*, p. 62.

[27] Ibid., pp. 79, 85.

What hinges on Filmer's claim that political authority is, rightly understood, patriarchal? A great deal: since God's original grant to Adam was unconditional, it followed that monarchical rule could not be limited. As a result, all positions of power or authority, or representative institutions such as parliaments, and all titles to estates and possessions are held at the pleasure of, and revocable by, the monarch.[28] Since all legitimate political power is derived from the monarch, all powers and titles are dependent on his continuing recognition of the legitimacy of such claims. There is, it follows, no sense in which the monarch could be accused of depriving someone of their personal or political rights, since all such rights were given by the king in the first place. Nor is there any sense in which subjects could complain about the king taxing them without their consent: he is simply recalling what is only held by them through his good grace in the first place.[29]

At the most abstract level Filmer's argument involves the permeation of time and place with political authority to such an extent that there is no way in which the notion of an individual right, held independently of the monarch, could be relevant. Since God gave Adam dominion over the world there is no possibility of anyone other than his modern representative establishing private property. And since throughout time men are born into families and states (or should be) there is no point at which one could identify a 'free' individual who could deny the claims of paternal or patriarchal authority.[30] This is strong stuff: although Filmer is no apologist for tyranny, and insists on the monarch's duties to obey God's law, there is nothing subjects can do to ensure it; the most he will countenance is passive resistance. His point is that the institution of monarchy has such good theological and natural credentials that it is inappropriate and impious to demand institutional constraints on it.

One might wonder how such an argument could be convincing. But whatever its intellectual limitations there is no doubt that it had a strong psychological appeal. For Stuart England, although it was capable of producing substantial radical movements, remained overwhelmingly a patriarchal society: and when a political theory portrays what conforms to our everyday experience, we are apt to be far less critical in our responses to it. We are talking of a society before the existence of a separate police force, tax inspectorate, civil service or any of the now widespread state functionaries whom citizens might meet; of a society in which the commonest experience that most people had of authority was that of their father's. Moreover outside the family the nearest source of authority was the church, and ministers were still addressed as 'father'. When priests preached political obedience from their pulpit by using the commandment that we honour our fathers and mothers, it was explained that by 'father' was meant all in authority over

[28] Ibid., p. 95 (monarchical power unlimited), p. 114 (parliaments 'from the grace of Princes'), p. 71 (natural and private dominion of Adam).

[29] Once again Locke tendentiously summarises the conclusions to be drawn from the patriarchalist position: 'This *Fatherly Authority* then, or *Right of Fatherhood*, in our A[thors]'s sense is a Divine unalterable Right of Sovereignty, whereby a Father, or a prince hath an Absolute, Arbitrary, Unlimited, and Unlimitable Power, over the Lives, Liberties, and Estates of his Children and Subjects; so that he may take or Alienate their Estates, sell, castrate, or use their Persons as he pleases, they being all his Slaves, and he Lord or Proprietor of every Thing, and his unbounded Will their Law.' Locke, *First Treatise*, §9, pp. 165–6.

[30] As Locke ironically paraphrases again: 'we are all born Slaves, and we must continue so; there is no remedy for it: Life and Thraldom we enter'd into together, and can never be quit of the one, till we part with the other.' *First Treatise*, §4, pp. 160–1.

us (and by mother was meant nothing of any political import).[31] The national economy
and administration were still capable of being identified with the royal 'household' and
its monarchical father; and the rule of a father within the household was a severe and
authoritative one extending well into the adulthood of his offspring. At a time when 'the
deliberate breaking of the young child's will, first by the harshest physical beating and
later by overwhelming psychological pressures . . . were thought to be the key to
successful child-rearing'[32] it is no wonder that the political theory of patriarchalism had
a receptive audience.[33]

However there were, in the world of Stuart England, other congruities between
patriarchalism and more overtly political ideas. The absolutist claims of patriarchalism
fitted well with the embryonic notions of a feudal past then emerging from the studies
of antiquarians and the pens of royalist historians. Indeed Filmer, no mean legal
antiquarian himself, used an incipiently feudal legal history in arguing, in the closing
chapters of *Patriarcha*, that parliament as it was then known had been the king's
creation.[34] Idealized feudalism presented a picture of a pyramidal society in which
authority descends hierarchically from the king, depends on the king, and in which no
autonomous sources of authority exist. On this view, representative institutions such as
parliaments, where they exist, have been created by the king to advise him and help him
rule, and this implies no independent locus of power or authority, either in that body or
in the people who elect them. Although the intellectual grounds on which feudalism was
established – legal history – were different from that used to assert patriarchy, the
structure of the society they depicted and their absolutist conclusions were very similar.

[31] The assumption is so pervasive that Filmer himself takes the commandment 'Honour thy Father' to
be a law enjoining obedience to kings, and explains that the terminology used rests on the assumption that
all power originated in fathers! *Patriarcha and other Works*, p. 62. Locke continually takes him to task for
this: 'I hope 'tis no injury to call an half an Quotation an half Reason, for God says, *Honour thy Father
and Mother*; but our Author contents himself with half, leaves out *thy Mother* quite, as little serviceable to
his purpose. But more of that in another place.' *First Treatise*, §6, p. 163. The other places are §§11, 29,
61. It is interesting to note that Locke persistently denies that any of the patriarchal Genesis texts (including
even God's curse, which he reads as a 'foretelling' and not as a command) can be construed as subjugating
Eve to Adam, or women to men; although I do not mean to imply by this that Locke proposed an active
political role for women. Locke, *First Treatise*, §§29, 47, 55, 62.

[32] Lawrence Stone, 'Children and the Family' in *The Past and the Present Revisited*, Lawrence Stone
(London, 1987), p. 315.

[33] There is a discussion of patriarchalism as an anthropological phenomenon in Schochet, *Patriarchalism . . .* ch. iv.

[34] *Patriarcha and other Works*, chs. xxviii — xxxii, pp. 109–126. The classic discussion of the emergence
of the concept of feudalism is still J.G.A. Pocock, *The Ancient Constitution and the Feudal Law*,
(Cambridge, 2nd ed. 1987). For Filmer, who was ignorant of the full implications of the phenomenon, see
pp. 152–4. As Pocock deftly puts it 'the point at issue was less whether the Commons had originated in
this year or that, than whether they could be shown to have originated in any identifiable year at all. If they
could not then they were immemorial and their privileges were secure; but if they could, then they owed
their being to some pre-existing authority — always assumed to be the king — which must to the end of
time retain the sovereignty over them. What the king's remotest ancestor had given, his remotest descendent
could take away', p. 153. Pocock documents Filmer's attack on the antiquity of parliaments from *The
Freeholder's Grand Inquest*, the authorship of which is disputed (see Corinne C. Weston, 'The Case for
Sir Robert Holbourne Reasserted', *History of Political Thought* VIII, 3 (1987). But *Patriarcha* itself tries
to prove 'that the anscientist and most usual summons [of parliament] was of earls and barons and that Kings
did vary their summons at their pleasure.' (Patriarcha and other Works, p. 117)

Filmer is also on common ground with much seventeenth-century thinking in deriving political authority from God. Those few thinkers who denied this assumption outright (as Hobbes was notoriously held to have done) signally failed to convince an audience unprepared for such premises. The question was, though, did basing political authority on God mean, for a Christian, basing it on the story of Adam in Genesis? Filmer's was not the only way the Bible, or indeed, even the story of Adam, could be used; but if Locke's argument was to be persuasive it had at least to grapple with Filmer's religious assumptions.[35]

The patriarchal challenge to contractualism

Even though I have stressed the associative rather than the logical strengths of Filmer's argument, he nevertheless set some interesting intellectual puzzles for his contractualist opponents. This raises interesting questions as to the basis of our contemporary liberal politics, a remote but recognisable intellectual descendent of seventeenth-century contractualism. For of course, living in an individualistic society we are as unlikely to be aware of the weaknesses of our intellectual presuppositions as Filmer's patriarchal contemporaries were of the weaknesses of theirs.

The division of labour between the two *Treatises*, reflects the positive and critical aspects of Filmer's own work. The *First Treatise* attacks Filmer's positive assertions about patriarchy and its supposed biblical authority. It continually draws back from developing the positions implicit in its criticism, promising to take them up later. The *Second Treatise*, whilst developing Locke's own position, also deals with Filmer's criticisms of contractualism. For Filmer, although writing forty years before Locke, was well aware of the kind of arguments Locke was to use. The opening lines of *Patriarcha* relate how 'within the last hundred years' the following opinions have become widespread, that:

> Mankind is naturally endowed and born with freedom from all subjection, and at liberty to choose what form of government it please, and that the power which any one man hath over others was at the first by human right bestowed according to the discretion of the multitude.[36]

This view, needless to say, Filmer regards as pernicious, and he stresses that the originators of it were Catholics.[37] The theory not only conflicted with the true origins of government as described in scripture, the Christian fathers, the law of nature, and 'the

---

[35] This is not meant in the least to suggest that Locke's invocation of Christian premises was opportunist. Far from it, we know that he was a devout, if questionably orthodox member of the Church of England. But it is unlikely, that without the spur of Filmer he would have spent so much time demolishing the supposed political implications of the creation story.

[36] Filmer, *Patriarcha and other Works*, p. 53.

[37] Catholic Counter-Reformation theorists, and especially the Jesuits, had developed a theory justifying popular deposition and even tyrannicide of ungodly (e.g. Protestant) princes. It was quite true that 'modern' social contract theorists derived their ideas from these sources. (See Figgis, *From Gerson to Grotius* (Cambridge, 1907), pp.151–2; and J.W. Allen, *A History of Political Thought in the Sixteenth Century* (London, repr. 1977), pp. 356–66. Moreover it was an important element of English Royalist polemic to

constant practice of all ancient monarchies', but contractualism had implications which its supporters refused to acknowledge, and which rendered the position incoherent. It is Filmer's attack on the failings of contractualism which provides Locke with the specific intellectual problems he had to face in the *Second Treatise*. [38]

If contractual arguments were true, says Filmer, two consequences follow which must be unacceptable even to their advocates.

Firstly, no continuing, valid political authority would be possible. For, argued Filmer, if all political authority rests on consent, any individual who cannot be shown to have consented is not bound by the laws – minorities, dissenters, non-voters (and women and those under age) need not obey the law, and no one need obey a new ruler at all, until they have been consented to. [39] If the original contractors who establish society are free, then so must each generation be, and until they give such consent they are not bound to obey the laws. But this would make each generation of society unstable and pose the problem of individuals continually growing up within society who were not yet obliged to obey its laws. For if we say that they are obliged to obey because their fathers or forefathers consented to the laws, then we have reverted to patriarchalism.

Secondly, on the issue of property rights, Filmer points out that contractualists, such as Grotius and Selden, escape the absolutist implications of Adam's dominion over the world only by construing God's grant as a general one given to all mankind in common, and not a private grant to an individual.[40] But, thought Filmer, this is even more problematic for the defender of private property, for it raises the spectre of communism in economics just as contractualism had raised the spectre of anarchy in politics. How, he asked, could a communal grant give rise to private property? Why should God have originally ordained community of possessions if it were not to last, and how could the abandonment of this primitive communism be morally binding unless every single individual had consented to it – of which consent we have no record? How, in any case, could such a decision be binding on posterity, who would surely be born – according to the contractualist – with their original common right to all?[41]

Filmer thought that those who derived government from the consent of free individuals would find it impossible to establish either workable or morally defensible political authority, or rightful private possession of goods. So as well as refuting the patriarchal thesis, to which Locke devoted the *First Treatise*, Locke had to meet Filmer's claims about the absurdity of contractual arguments. In particular, the problem of giving contractual accounts of the origins of political power and private property. The agenda

---

expose this relationship, thus paradoxically turning widespread anti-Catholic sentiment against the radicals. See Goldie, 'Locke and Anglican Royalism', pp. 71–5.

[38] The fact that these criticisms were available in works before the publication of *Patriarcha* in 1680/1 is consistent with Laslett's account of the date and order of composition.

[39] Filmer, *Patriarcha and other Works*, pp. 81–2, and see Laslett's 'Introduction', pp. 15–17.

[40] Grotius reads the grant to Adam as a grant to all men in Adam, rather than to him exclusively. Seldon accepts the original grant to Adam was exclusive, but thinks common ownership came about after the flood, with the separate grant to Noah. *Patriarcha and other Works*, pp. 63–4. Locke endorses Selden's interpretation of the Noadic grant against Filmer, *First Treatise*, §32. On Grotius and Selden see R.Tuck, *Natural Rights Theories* (Cambridge, 1979), chs. 3 and 4.

[41] Filmer, *Patriarcha and other Works*, pp. 64–6. The problem is a continuing one for theorists of natural law, using contractualist arguments. It is only finally overcome in Hegel's thoroughgoing historicisation of the content of natural law and social development.

for his *Second Treatise* was determined, as Locke acknowledged at the start, by the need to demonstrate 'another rise of Government, another Original of Political Power, and another way of designing and knowing the Persons that have it, than what Sir *Robert F.* hath taught us', and secondly 'how men might come to have a *property* in several parts of that which God gave to Mankind in common, and that without any express Compact of all the Commoners.'[42]

Locke's response to Filmer: the basic assumptions of political right

Locke rejected Filmer's interpretation of the biblical account of the origin of political power, but he did not by any means abandon religious foundations. Far from it. Locke bases his politics firmly and explicitly on the moral relationship between man and God. The following famous passage, which is in danger of being read by the modern reader as a pious aside, contains in fact the basic premise of his argument.

> For Men being all the Workmanship of one Omnipotent, and infinitely wise Maker; All the Servants of one Sovereign Master, sent into the World by his order and about his business, they are his Property, whose Workmanship they are, made to last during his, not one anothers Pleasure. And being furnished with like Faculties, sharing all in one Community of Nature, there cannot be supposed any such *Subordination* among us, that may Authorize us to destroy one another, as if we were made for one anothers uses, as the inferior ranks of Creatures are for ours. Every one as he is *bound to preserve himself*, and not to quit his Station wilfully; so by the like reason when his own Preservation comes not in competition, ought he, as much as he can, *to preserve the rest of Mankind*, and may not unless it be to do Justice on an Offender, take away, or impair the life, or what tends to the Preservation of the Life, the Liberty, Health, Limb or Goods of another.[43]

This shared duty to God to preserve ourselves as part of his creation is, for Locke, the basic moral law of nature. It operates in, and even characterises the state of nature. Locke's tactic is to insist that political power can only be understood if we 'derive it from its Original, [and] consider what State all Men are naturally in, and that is a state of perfect freedom to order their actions and dispose of their possessions and persons as they think fit within the bounds of the law of nature.'[44]

The state of nature as a moral code

This state of nature is a state of equality amongst men. It is a created equality based on their common membership of a single species. Some royalists based their argument for the supremacy of the king on a theory of natural hierarchies, in which the king corresponded to the 'natural superiors' of the animal world – such as the superiority of the eagle amongst birds. But such correspondence arguments, Locke hints, could not

---

[42] *Second Treatise*, §1, p. 286, §25, p. 304.

[43] Ibid., §6, p. 289.

[44] Ibid., §4, p. 287.

operate within a single species in which all are 'promiscuously born to all the same advantages of Nature' except where God has granted some special authority and by some 'manifest Declaration of his Will set one above another . . . '.[45] Locke, in common with other Christian writers of the seventeenth century acknowledged that in the *Old Testament* God is described as laying down particular forms of government, and sometimes appointing individual rulers. Argument about whether Protestant states were obliged to adopt these forms, or to be ruled by a religious elect, formed a considerable part of Reformation political theology. Yet, like Hobbes, Locke thinks that such 'prophetic kingdoms' existed no longer, and where we were given no such direct command from God we were to make use of our natural reason in deciding how to establish government.

The 'Law of Nature' which imposes limitations on our natural freedom does not set bounds on what is actually physically possible for humans – it is a moral law which we are capable of disobeying if we so choose. However to do so would be to thwart God's purpose in the world and to contradict our own (God-given) natures. Locke argues that since God made the world, everything within it (including ourselves) has a purpose. Thus the more lowly created beings – animals and plants – are available to man to use for his survival, but not to waste. Even our own lives are not ours to dispose of, they are a trust from God, we have no right to destroy ourselves (to 'quit our station wilfully') nor to destroy, injure, enslave or rob other beings who are equal to us before God.

In Locke's argument here we can see the radical Protestant belief in the responsibility of all believers before God being used to ground a principle of political equality. The individualist implications of Reformation theology are being cashed out in political terms. So often such arguments had been used by more conservative groups in political debate, without seeming awareness of their radical implications when taken literally.[46] But with Locke and Shaftesbury, it now appears, they were being consciously deployed as a political tactic to involve groups sympathetic to a Protestantism more radical than that currently supported by the Church of England. These kinds of arguments had been used by the Levellers in the English Civil War, and appealed to social groups well below the gentry and politically enfranchised classes. Although politically radical, Locke's argument is far from being secular. It is because we are all beholden to God that we are equal. Political authority, like all moral claims for Locke, must rest ultimately on our religious obligations, which are for him, the source of all morality. The law of nature then, is a set of duties owed to God by men, which requires them to seek their preservation.

Locke's position can be highlighted by noticing the difference between it and that of Hobbes. Because Hobbes's fundamental postulate was an unlimited *right* of nature claimed by each individual on his own behalf, the state of nature is one of strife, whereas Locke's fundamental postulate is a natural *duty* of preservation which we owe to God as a result of his having created us. This duty does not lead to strife (if it is followed) because it requires not only our own preservation but that of all men, since even though we are all special to ourselves, we are all equal before God.

---

[45] Ibid., §4, p. 287.

[46] A classic example was the radical exploitation of Henry Parker's often sweepingly populist justifications of *parliamentary* authority. See recently A .Sharp, 'John Lilburne and the Long Parliament's *Book of Declarations*: A Radical's Exploitation of the Words of Authorities', *History of Political Thought*, IX, 1 (1988).

If the rule of behaviour which constitutes the law of nature (preserve God's creation) is to be effective, it requires enforcement. When men are in a state of nature the task of enforcement will obviously remain with individuals. Since the state of nature is, by definition, one in which we have not modified our original, equal and individual obligations to God, no other authority can exist.[47] As a result, anyone is individually entitled to exact punishment from those who have broken the law of nature, even though they may not themselves have been the ones who were wronged. Locke points out that, contrary to what Filmer claimed, far from the state of nature making government impossible, the acknowledged practices of political society do not make sense without the assumption of a state of nature. For effectively what governments do when they punish a foreigner who disobeys the law, is to exercise a natural right of punishment over them; for there are no grounds, patriarchal or contractual, on which such an individual could be considered to be subject to that government. Nevertheless in disobeying rightful government (which must embody the law of nature) the stranger has transgressed that law and so deserved punishment, which government, like any other moral agent, is entitled to impose if it can.[48] Punishing offenders against ourselves derives from our duty and right of self-preservation, and includes a further right to exact reparations. The right of non-victims to punish (but not exact reparations) derives from the general right and duty to uphold the law preserving mankind (God's creatures). This right goes so far as to countenance the killing of men who commit murder or show contempt for the law of nature. Men who

> having renounced Reason, the common Rule and Measure, God hath given to Mankind, hath by the unjust Violence and Slaughter he hath committed upon one, declared War against all Mankind, and therefore may be destroyed as a *Lyon* or a *Tyger*, one of those wild Savage Beasts with whom Men can have no Society nor Security.[49]

Locke acknowledges two questions that might be raised against his account of the state of nature as a basic moral code. First of all he agrees that men's selfishness will render the application of the law of nature very uncertain, resulting in confusion, partiality and occasional violence. Indeed, he argues, this partiality may be one of the reasons for establishing government. However, by way of softening up the apparent strength of Filmer's case, or indeed of any argument for 'strong government' which this might seem to imply, Locke points out that absolute monarchs of the kind the Royalists endorse are also simply men with interests of their own, who are likely to judge partially in their own case. The consequences of such partiality would be far worse in a man with the powers of an absolute monarch, and consequently men might well be better off – in terms of being able to discharge their duties to God – in a state of nature than under such a 'government', which would be in effect simply a kind of state of nature with two sorts of inhabitants, ordinary men, powerless to protect themselves and the all-powerful sovereign.[50]

Secondly, Locke considers a recurrent objection to arguments based on the 'state of nature', and that is the question of whether it ever existed. Locke gives the standard example of states in an international situation, cites Hooker on the existence of a moral,

---

[47] *Second Treatise*, §7, p. 289
[48] Ibid., §9, p. 290.
[49] Ibid., §11, p. 292.
[50] Ibid., §13, pp. 293–4.

pre-political law of nature, but reiterates 'That all Men are naturally in that State, and remain so, till by their own Consents they make themselves Members of some Politick Society'.[51]

If the meaning of Locke's state of nature is relatively clear, the question of its import and status is more complex. How are we to take it, and what part is it to play in Locke's argument?

First of all, whilst tempting, it is most misleading to think of Locke's state of nature in the same terms as Hobbes's: to suggest for example that the essential difference between the two thinkers lies simply in the degree of unpleasantness to be found in their respective states of nature, and to argue that Hobbes disallows rebellion whilst Locke can defend both it and limited government simply because the more pleasant state of nature makes the consequences of a return to it less disastrous. To think in this way is to miss most of the importance of Locke, for it is to miss the essentially moral status of Locke's conception of natural man and of the state of nature.

By status is meant the level, mode or import of an argument. For example, arguments about human behaviour can operate at a variety of levels. We could argue factually (that people actually do behave in this fashion), historically (that they have done), morally (that they ought to), causally (that they must). Hobbes's state of nature purports to be a description of people's actual behaviour in that situation, even though the situation is an imaginary one – an inference made on the assumptions of the effects of the unconstrained passions. For Locke, on the contrary, the state of nature is not descriptive of a pattern of actual behaviour at all; it refers to the rules which men are morally obliged to obey when they have not contracted or promised to modify their behaviour in any way. Thus the status of Locke's state of nature is essentially moral, whilst the status of Hobbes's is essentially behavioural. However arguments or concepts possessing one status may have implications for others. The absolute primacy of selfish motions is central to Hobbes's descriptive account, and yet both the suggestion that the development of reason enables us to overcome it, and the claim that economically and culturally primitive men approximate more closely to the model state of nature, suggests – if no more – a historical dimension to his argument.

Emphasising the moral status of Locke's state of nature, has important implications within his theory, and highlights its differences from another, then fairly pervasive, model of political apologetic which appealed to history in vindication of its case. Any account of legitimacy which relied on the actual political behaviour of men, like one which drew exclusively on historical experience (which after all included tyranny and flagrant abuses of power) was vulnerable to this criticism. Indeed Filmer himself was vulnerable here.[52] Seventeenth-century political argument, at least on its constitutional side was immensely historical. Since Filmer's use of Genesis might be seen as an attempt to trump ancient constitutionalists who claimed the antiquity of Parliament in its favour against the King, it is tempting to read Locke's state of nature as a kind of secular earliest history seeking in turn to outdo other histories. Yet the whole attempt to recruit history for polemical purposes, although still popular, was becoming distinctly vulnerable. As political radicals in the 1640s had pointed out: if history was a record of man's sinfulness since the Fall

---

[51] Ibid., §15, p. 296.

[52] As Locke sarcastically points out, 'if the Example of what hath been done be the Rule of what ought to be', then even cannibalism could be justified. *First Treatise*, §57, pp. 199–200.

(or secularly speaking, a record of conquest and subjection), it was pointless to look to it, or to the human nature revealed in it, for the standards of good government.[53]

So for Locke, the state of nature is moral and a-historical, it is the condition men are in before contracting to change it. This, far from implying that they have no obligations at all, means they are still morally bound by God's original law of nature to act for their own and others' preservation. It is therefore primarily that state in which the axioms of human morality are uncomplicated by any man-made commitments.[54] The axioms of human political morality derive directly from each person's relationship to God, and not from their prior subjection to any actual or archetypical father. Since each of us is answerable to God for our actions, we are all in principle, and at some point in our lives – for example when we come of age – free to agree to modify our duties by entering into a relationship with any existing legitimate authority, or indeed to create a new one. By identifying the moral core of the state of nature with the Protestant's individual answerability to God, Locke shows, that at least for Protestants, there must be a point when human beings are in this simple and politically unobligated state.[55] He thus breaks the grip which patriarchalism seemed to exert over the whole of history. In doing so he clears the way to establishing an alternative, contractual, yet fundamentally Christian account of the nature and authority of government.

Although we have insisted that the state of nature is not *defined* by Locke in historical terms, it nevertheless follows that such a situation obtains at any point in history when there were no political obligations. Clearly, early history, before the development of complex social institutions, is such a situation, since institutions, at least to be legitimate, would have required agreements modifying our original moral obligations. Specific empirical social characteristics could be derived from the fact that men had entered into no binding social obligations with each other. Thus Locke can treat the state of nature as a kind of historical fiction with descriptive content. For example, it would follow from the fact that men have not contracted with each other, that there will be no social institutions designed to impose or enforce rules of behaviour which avoid conflict between men. It also follows that any economic institutions or relationships will be of a primitive kind, involving direct exchange, since only long-term contracts, agreement to conventions such as the use of money, and widespread regularization of titles and their enforcement could permit the development of a more complex economy. So, although not primarily historical in conception, the state of nature provides a point from which a speculative history of man's political and economic development might be started, as well as providing a set of rules to which such a history ought to adhere if it is to produce morally acceptable results.

---

[53] On the state of nature and historical arguments see John Dunn, *The Political Thought of John Locke* (Cambridge, 1969), p.100ff. On radicals' claims about the irrelevance of history, see for example the Leveller Richard Overton's, observation that, as a result of the Norman Invasion, 'Our very laws were made by conquerors': *A Remonstrance* (1646), in D.M. Wolfe ed., *Leveller Manifestoes of the Puritan Revolution* (London, 1967).

[54] Here, and at many other points I have been greatly influenced by Dunn, *Political Thought of John Locke*, p. 96ff., esp. p. 111.

[55] The qualification is of considerable importance. For Catholics, salvation was tied to membership of the church, and they recognised no such individual duty. They were thus (so held Protestants) unreliable citizens of free states. The importance of anti-Catholicism both as a general political prejudice of the time, and in the more sophisticated form held by Locke can hardly be underestimated.

Far from identifying legitimate authority with the competent exercise of power as Hobbes does, and as Filmer effectively does,[56] Locke's argument is designed to show, not only that criteria of legitimacy exist outside political society, but also that within it, what passes for political power is often illegitimate coercion.

The attempt to subject anyone to absolute power is to be understood as an attempt on that person's life; for their freedom is what enables them to protect their life. Freedom is 'the Foundation of all the rest. . . . I have no reason to suppose, that he, who would *take away my Liberty*, would not when he had me in his Power, take away everything else.'[57] Thus those who aim at our freedom are no different from those who aim at our lives – they are like the wild beasts that we may kill with impunity for they threaten our ability to discharge our responsibility to God for our own survival. Nevertheless, the existence of this threat is not confined to the state of nature. Although some men there behave in this way and so produce a state of war, war is neither identified with, nor confined to the state of nature.[58] Within political society itself there are people who aim at absolute power, and where this happens, individuals are as free, and as obliged, to resist it as they were in the state of nature. Even within political society

> where an appeal to the Law and constituted Judges lies open, but the remedy is deny'd us by a manifest perverting of Justice and a barefaced wresting of the Laws . . . *there* it *is* hard to imagine any thing but *a State of War*. For wherever violence is used, and injury done, though by hands appointed to administer Justice, it is still violence and injury however colour'd with the Name, Pretences, or Forms of Law . . . [59]

For Locke, injustice, and even a state of war, can take place within what appears to be civil society, for the standards of justice are independent of positive institutions, the moral authority of the laws of nature 'cease not in Society, but only in many Cases are drawn closer, have by Humane Laws known Penalties annexed to them, to inforce their observation'.[60] The passage clearly further undermines Filmer's absolutism. Locke is hinting, and will make explicit, that far from being the only proper form of government, absolute monarchy is not even a candidate.

Avoiding the inconveniences of the state of nature, or even the state of war which might intermittently occur in it, involves establishing civil, i.e. political, society, which men can only do by establishing an arbiter with authority to interpret and enforce the law of nature. Since men are naturally free from each other's (although not God's) dominion, such an authority can only be set up with their consent. If done properly this is hardly an

---

[56] As stated above, Filmer did not make the improbable claim that the Stuarts' title existed by direct eldest male heir descent, but this meant, that on a charitable reading, he was defending royal absolutism as a *type*, irrespective of who exercised it, or, less charitably, that he was defending de facto power. *Patriarcha and other Works*, p.61. As Locke says, 'And being not able to make out any Princes Title to Government, as Heir to *Adam*, which therefore is of no use, and had been better let alone, he is fain to resolve all into present Possession, and makes Civil Obedience as due to an *Usurper* as to a lawful King.' *First Treatise* , §121, p. 247.

[57] *Second Treatise*, §17, p. 297; §18, p. 298.

[58] Laslett suggests this is perhaps one of Locke's rare references to Hobbes. See Laslett, *Second Treatise*, §19, p. 298, fn.

[59] Ibid., §20, p. 299.

[60] Ibid., §135, p. 376.

infringement on our freedom, which is in any case only a freedom to act within the limits of the law of nature which the civil authority will be enforcing. But freedom has a more positive side to it as well. If we are not free we cannot act to preserve our lives, and this we have a duty to God to do. There may be a certain background duty to establish political authority as the best way of discharging our duty of self-preservation, just as we have not only a right to resist arbitrary power, but a duty to do so.

It is a logical impossibility for us to attempt to establish, by consent, an absolute authority over ourselves. Locke is not always consistent over his use of terms, especially in the odd but crucial little chapter IV. Political authority is not mere power but power plus right. Because right can only originate with a grant of already existing right, and because humans have no right to grant away their duty to preserve themselves, they could not (logically or morally) grant rightful power to an absolute authority.[61] So anyone who contracted obedience to an absolute sovereign would (possibly unwittingly) be contracting to give the sovereign something he did not have, the contract would thus be void and the resulting government could not be legitimate. Locke is not arguing that there are no such things as absolute governments. What he is claiming is that they can never be legitimate. What Filmer suggests is not only wrong but wicked. It involves giving up to another a right which we cannot part with, because it is God's, and ours only on trust.

Although we cannot enslave ourselves by agreement, we can rightfully incur it 'by some act that deserves death'. Locke does seek to justify slavery. Criminals convicted of capital offences could, Locke thinks, justifiably be kept alive as slaves rather than executed. Slavery is thus a possible legitimate state, but not one that we can enter into by contract.

It might be asked how, if it is wicked to put ourselves under an absolute ruler because he might kill us, it could ever be permissible to put ourselves into any kind of political society at all, since all political societies claim, as Locke points out 'a *Right* of making Laws with Penalties of Death . . . '. The Christian anarchist might ask: Doesn't *any* political society threaten our ability to discharge our God-given duty of self-preservation? The answer to this would be 'yes' if political society claimed rights over us which other individuals did not already have in the state of nature; if, in some way the agreement to establish government was an agreement to *create* new and wider powers with authority to limit our capacities for legitimate self defence. But it is precisely Locke's point that that cannot be what the establishment of government is about. It's because we each have a right to punish – with death if necessary – offenders against the law of nature, that we can entrust a government with carrying out that task.[62] As long as government does no more than that, we have not at all increased our vulnerability by entering political society. Only those who offend the law of nature are vulnerable, and they are anyhow, rightly to be punished. It is precisely because the absolutist claims *more* rights over individuals than individuals themselves possess under the law of nature that their regimes cannot be legitimate. Political society properly speaking represents a concentration and greater

---

[61] Ibid., §23, p. 302.

[62] As Locke points out, it is not necessary for an individual to have formally consented to a political authority for them to be susceptible to punishment by it. How else could governments exercise jurisdiction over criminal strangers for crimes carried out within their territories? Ibid., §9, p. 291. This important argument reappears at §74, p. 335. See below p. 97.

effectiveness of, but not an increase in the range or degree of, natural-law rights of coercion over others.

The establishment of individual property rights

Before Locke could embody in institutions the theory of political authority outlined above he needed to deal with two problematic institutions which according to his polemical adversary, Filmer, disqualified any contractualist account of government: property and paternal authority.

Filmer had argued that property, like political authority, deriving from God's grant to Adam described in Genesis, had either been a grant to Adam as private property, or a communal grant to all mankind. Indefeasible private property rights were, argued Filmer, impossible either way, since in the former case 'dominion' had descended from Adam to the various monarchs of the world, and subjects thus held private property only at the pleasure of the king. Alternatively, if God had sanctioned communism then how could one justify private property at all? The Bible seemed to require either absolutism or communism. Contractualists had to show that this apparent dilemma could be overcome, and it is this that Locke attempts to do in the very important chapter V.

Locke argued that through God's grants to Adam and Noah, he gave men the world in common,[63] and he derives the subsequent right to private property, like the right to limit political power, from our duty of self-preservation. In answer to the question: how could men make private use of this common gift? he replies that there is, even in a world of common goods, one part of it which is already private property – ourselves. Locke claims 'every Man has a *Property* in his own *Person*'.[64]

This is a difficult notion. Our 'persons' are certainly not a property in the sense of being something we could sell to someone else (slavery not being possible by contract); and the right to trade away or alienate something is certainly a major part of the modern meaning of the notion of property. Yet 'property' in the seventeenth century was often used more widely to denote any rights of a fundamental kind, and fundamental rights were often claimed to be inalienable.[65] For Locke, human beings are primarily centres of rights and duties (rather than, as with Hobbes, centres of appetites). The right and duty or 'property' of humanity requires, first and foremost, our survival. What we take and eat from nature in order to survive becomes our 'property' in a number of senses.

Digesting something, Locke almost jokes, certainly makes it ours – perhaps even 'us'. But this is simply a fact of biology: persons are not only bodies but possessors of rights,

---

[63] Locke had demolished Filmer's claim that either Adam's or Noah's grant could be construed exclusively in *First Treatise*, §§ 30, 32.

[64] *Second Treatise*, §26, p. 304.

[65] See the contemporary dictionary definitions in I.W. Hampsher-Monk, 'The Political Theory of the Levellers', *Political Studies*, XXIV, 4 (1976). For a discussion see G. Aylmer, 'The Meaning and Definition of "property" in seventeenth century England', *Past and Present*, 86 (1980), and Karl Olivekrona, 'The Term "Property" in Locke's Two Treatises of Government', *Archiv für Rechts — und Sozialphilosophie*, LXI/1 (1975). The best discussion of the philosophical basis of Locke's conception of property is James Tully, *A Discourse on Property, John Locke and his adversaries*, (Cambridge, 1980), esp. ch. 5. The 'meaning of "property" is, for Locke, independent of reference. Locke means by property . . . any sort of right, the nature of which is that it cannot be taken without a man's consent.' p.116.

and it is in the establishment of the right that Locke is primarily interested. Gathering something natural and unowned for our sustenance involves us imposing our rightful, survival-orientated purposes on it.[66] So, by extension, any such 'mixing our labour' with the products of nature makes them ours and establishes a *prima facie* right to private property. If some such procedure were not available then it would indeed – as Filmer pointed out – have required the universal agreement of all mankind before we could eat so much as a mouthful and 'Man had starved, notwithstanding the Plenty God had given him'.[67] Locke turns the absurdity of Filmer's dilemma into an argument that this could not possibly have been what God meant. The very 'Condition of Humane Life, which requires Labour and Materials to work on, necessarily introduces *private Possessions*.'[68]

However, the fact that private property derives from God's common grant and our duties to preserve both self *and* others, entails that our right to appropriate through our labour must be limited by a recognition of the similar rights of others. This leads to two further conditions on our acquisitive activity, there must be 'enough, and as good left in common for others' in nature,[69] and secondly, since God gave men the world to enjoy, not to spoil and waste, we must take only what we can use without spoiling.[70] On these three conditions: labour, leaving sufficient for others, and non-spoilage, men can acquire private property from what is common, without 'the express consent of all the Commoners' and (and because) no one is worse off for it.[71]

It's important to note that although labour is what individuates and so establishes a private right, Locke doesn't assume the right will in all circumstances accrue to the labourer. Although Locke does not, in the *Second Treatise*, formally introduce the topic of employed labour, he clearly assumes both it, and the fact that employees' labour creates property rights for the employer: 'Thus the Grass my Horse has bit; the Turfs my Servant has cut; and the Ore I have digg'd . . . become my *Property*'.[72] The political implications of this account of the origin of property would seem to be ambivalent. The central importance of labour, its almost religious significance in discharging our duty of self preservation, and of being industrious – and its role, both in establishing property rights in the first place, and in subsequently creating value, have suggested to one recent author that Locke was appealing to a predominantly artisan audience, and this may be read as having important political implications for the social complexion both of the resistance movement he was prepared to support, and the resulting regime.[73] However as Marxist critics have pointed out following C.B. Macpherson, the easy assumption that employers rightfully acquire the property rights (and presumably also the increased value) deriving from their employees' labour, can also lead to Locke being read as defender of a primarily employer class, and, if specifically wage employment is assumed,

---

[66] See Tully's linking of personality, purposefulness and action to property through the concept of 'maker's rights', and his contrast of such a justification for property with one grounded on utility (which he shows Locke to have rejected). Ibid., pp. 104–11, 116–18.

[67] Filmer, *Patriarcha and other Works*, pp. 64–6 (see above, p. 80); *Second Treatise*, §28, p. 306.

[68] Ibid., §35, p. 310.

[69] Ibid., §27, p. 306.

[70] Ibid., §31, p. 308.

[71] Ibid., §28, p. 307.

[72] Ibid., §28. For a classic discussion of this passage see C.B. Macpherson, *The Political Theory of Possessive Individualism* (Oxford, 1962), p. 215.

[73] See Ashcraft, *Revolution Politics*, pp. 257–77.

an emergent bourgeoisie.[74] The indeterminacy of Locke's text on this issue is typical, accounting for the possibility of its subsequent exploitation by both conservatives and radicals, but its openness may just actually have been a deliberate ploy to appeal to as wide an audience as possible.

The development of the complex economy

Locke's discussion of economic life up to this point has envisaged a very simple economy indeed, one which in modern anthropology would be called a 'hunter-gatherer', or (in some of Locke's examples) possibly a 'herding' economy, where humans simply appropriated the fruits or captured or culled the animals that nature provides. He has shown, against the claims of Filmer that it was impossible, that at least such a primitive level of private property was defensible according to the law of nature. But this was obviously far from the kinds or amounts of property that existed in the relatively complex economy of the seventeenth century. Yet the justification of such properties – against the claims of the King – was precisely Locke's aim. To justify that, he tried to show how this sophisticated system of property rights could have developed, by a justifiable process, from the primitive sort of private property sanctioned by the laws of nature. That is, he attempted a kind of speculative economic history which would demonstrate the legitimate development of the modern economy with its inequality and 'large estates' from the egalitarian aboriginal property rights of the state of nature.

Although Locke thought that there were still some parts of the world where this primitive original economy was possible, notably America, he also clearly recognised the existence of local pressures on population. Drawing on biblical history he describes how originally men simply followed herds and flocks around the wild landscape without laying any claim to the land itself until:

> . . . there was not room enough in the same place, for their Herds to feed together, they, by consent, . . . separated and inlarged their pasture, where it best liked them.[75]

The right of enclosure and appropriation of land, brought about in this instance by localized pressure of stock, could, it seems, operate even under a pastoral economy. But to till and cultivate land is much more productive than simply to live off the grazing animals it supports, and since the productive and 'industrious' use of his gifts is one of God's purposes for humans, it is always open to men to enclose land for cultivation, subject always to the proviso that they labour on it, do not take more than they can use and leave enough and as good for others.[76]

---

[74] Two more recent accounts which provide good arguments for reading Locke in this way are Ross Poole, 'Locke and the Bourgeois State', *Political Studies*, XXVIII, 2 (1980) and, more distinctively, Neal Wood, *John Locke and Agrarian Capitalism* (Berkeley and Los Angeles, 1984).

[75] *Second Treatise*, §38, p. 314; and see §45, p. 317, 'in some parts of the world . . .' In both of these passages Locke seems to conflate the private appropriation of land with the territorial consolidation of states.

[76] Ibid., §§32–3; and §34, p. 309, 'he gave it to the use of the Industrious and Rational'.

Mixing one's labour with land has, of course, several much more far-reaching implications than simply appropriating its products. Each man, claims Locke, has a right to that in which he has mixed his labour, it is his property, and so excludes others from the use of it. If I gather wild apples off a tree I have a right only to those apples, I do not prevent others from gathering the rest, or next year's crop. But if I improve the ground by my labour, and prune and cultivate the trees, I have, by mixing my labour with the source of the fruit, acquired a capital resource in the land and the trees which will yield me apples (and exclude others from those apples) for years to come.

Secondly, although the produce of nature (fruits and animals) replace themselves annually and so ensure there is 'enough and as good for others', land is an absolutely finite resource. In some parts of the world such as England, it was in very limited supply indeed. Once individual appropriation of it is allowed, there will at some point, not be 'enough and as good left for others'. Clearly there were men in England in Locke's time without land. Did this offend the proviso of the law of nature for legitimate appropriation of property?[77]

Thirdly, Locke seems to presume that by improving land with respect to one resource – its fertility for crops – we acquire the whole physical terrain, together with all the other rights that could relate to that land: fallow grazing, wood gathering and hunting wild game for example. This would not seem to be strictly entailed by the law of nature. My right is only to that part, or aspect of nature that my labour has modified; although it was certainly becoming more and more true that cultivation disqualified any other right, as commoners' rights were abolished under the spread of enclosure, the presumption that cultivation absorbs and extinguishes other users' rights to land is clearly a bias stemming from an agrarian economy. Such an argument had important consequences in America, where Indians could be presented (usually incorrectly) as nomadic hunters who had not mixed their labour with the land, and whose title to it could therefore be ignored by European settlers.[78]

Locke's general answer to doubts about the legitimacy of private property in land is that enclosing and cultivating land is much more productive than hunter-gathering, or pastoralism.[79] Although enclosure will eventually exhaust the available stock of common land, Locke also implies that there will be employment for those without land working

---

[77] Although he recognised local shortages of land had ended the right of private enclosure from nature in most of the world, Locke (correctly) still thought it possible in America and Spain, see Ibid., §36, p. 311, Laslett's fn. to ll.26–34.

[78] See: Wilcomb E. Washburn, 'The Moral and Legal Justification for Dispossessing the Indians', in *Seventeenth Century America: Essays in Colonial History*, ed. James Morton Smith (Chapel Hill, 1959), pp. 15–32, pp. 22–3, 27. I am not, of course, suggesting that in the absence of such arguments Europeans would not have found some other pretext for taking aboriginal people's land, as they are still doing today. Interestingly, nomadism is still being used in English law to disqualify otherwise plausible claims to possession. In October 1990 the Court of Appeal ruled that Miss Rita Myra Davies' claim of an intention to possess land in a disused quarry where she lived in her caravan could not be sustained on the grounds that her claim to be a gypsy, entailed a travelling way of life which was inconsistent with the necessary '*animus possidendi*' (resolution or intention of possessing)!

[79] *Second Treatise*, §37, p. 312, 'he who appropriates land to himself by his labour, does not lessen but increase the common stock of mankind . . . the provisions . . . produced by one acre of inclosed and cultivated land, are (to speak much within compasse) ten times more, than those, which are yielded by an acre of Land, of equal richnesse, lyeing wast in common.'

for those who have, thus increasing the amount of 'labour' brought to bear on these enclosures. This has important beneficial consequences, since, Locke claims, it is labour that '*puts the difference of value* on every thing'; the ability to employ extra labour on privately owned plots will increase its productivity still further. In consequence, the day labourer in England is, he thinks, better off than the richest king in America where there is no cultivation.[80]

Following the enclosure and cultivation of land comes, what is for Locke, the second revolution in human political economy, the invention of money. Implicit in Locke's suggestion that many landless labourers could be employed to increase productivity is the notion that the size of landholdings would increase – only if one possessed more land than one could work on one's own would one employ someone else. The acquisition of holdings larger than one can work oneself *also* presupposed the accumulation of wealth to pay the labour (and possibly to purchase land). But the accumulation of wealth would be severely limited as long as it took the form of perishable consumables, because natural law prohibited the acquisition of property which spoiled in one's keeping or which laid idle in one's possession. Under such circumstances, the acquisition of land more than one could cultivate oneself would therefore be immoral, as well as pointless, unless it could be worked by others, and they in turn would be unlikely to seek paid employment, as long as there was land 'enough and as good left' for them.

The invention of money held out the possibility of enabling people to 'enlarge' their possessions without transgressing the natural law spoilage limitation, for money does not spoil in storage as grain or fruit does. But money would also, in enabling an increase in wealth, and through that, the amounts of land held, increase the rate at which land was enclosed, and the likelihood of its exhaustion. The accumulation of wealth in money for capital and wage funds, the increase in the size of landholdings, and creation of landless labourers seeking work, are all mutually re-enforcing. The money economy also stimulates production through the possibility of trading one's surplus, without which all production must hover around subsistence.[81]

The introduction of money thus has enormous impact on the operation of human economies. Nevertheless, Locke suggests, although money made these developments possible, it was not invented with this, or indeed any specific purpose. Money has its origins in 'fancy', the chance delight that an individual finds in a sparkling stone or an ore of pleasing colour.[82] But it is barter that establishes their role as specie: once such tokens become generally accepted they make possible both exchange, and accumulation: mutually re-enforcing aspects of the sophisticated economy which Locke is concerned to explain.

---

[80] Ibid., §40, p. 314; §41, p. 315.

[81] I have reorganised and helped Locke's somewhat compressed and scattered argument on its way a little here. The suggestion that money accelerated the accumulation and size of land holdings is made at the end of §36 and at §48, its role as a store of value, §48 and §49, larger landholdings pointless without money and commerce, §48. Locke nowhere makes explicit the crucial role played by the landless labourer in his account; but see Adam Smith: *The Wealth of Nations* (2 vols, Oxford, 1976), vol. I, Bk. 1, viii, 6, p. 83, 'As soon as land becomes private property, the landlord demands a share of almost all the produce which the labourer can raise, or collect from it.'

[82] *Second Treatise*, §46, p. 318.

Thus the enclosure of land and the introduction of money together account for the trend towards larger possessions, the landless labourer and the trading economy: and the sort of economy and possessions the Whig parliamentarians wanted to defend against the King. Locke argues that these are in accordance with the law of nature since the law of nature commands preservation, and although the original limitations on property were designed to secure individual men's preservation, the accumulation of money and the enclosure of land lead to more productive forms of property capable of supporting larger populations, and thus better able to fulfill our duty of self-preservation.[83] Moreover Locke is careful to insist that these economic developments, 'This partage of things, in an inequality of private possessions', came about before the establishment of government ('out of the bounds of Societie'), and thus independently of any political authority. So that even quite complex private property rights are pre-political.[84] The importance of this claim being of course, that rights, the establishment of which pre-dated the emergence of political authority, could not be denied or invaded by the sovereign on the grounds that, as Hobbes claimed, they depended on it for their very existence.

An important issue raised here by many commentators is Locke's assumptions about distribution. The rules for possessing property in the primitive state of nature ensured that each individual had access to nature sufficient to preserve himself (or himself and his family).[85] The new and much more unequal economic regime is justified by Locke as being more productive (in general), the intensity of labour creating far more wealth than before: 'This shews, how much numbers of men are to be preferd to largenesse of dominions'.[86] But Locke is less than explicit about the process by which this greater productivity is distributed to individuals. This has led writers to interpret Locke as providing a justification for the capital accumulation of an emerging bourgeois class. There are many aspects of Locke's argument which have become part of the repertoire of bourgeois political thought: the presumption that it is *individuals* who work land and extract value from it in the primitive state, [87] the presumption of a market in labour which shows through, or seems required by his argument at various points, and perhaps most important of all, the labour theory of value which became the basis of classical bourgeois economics. None of this is surprising. Locke was carefully read by many of these later thinkers, including Adam Smith, the great theoretician of bourgeois political economy, and Marx who claimed to have unmasked it. But we must not credit Locke with prescience. His purpose at the time of writing was to defend the claims of private property against royal appropriation: in order to do that he had to show that the kinds of property that existed were in accordance with the standards of what was just and natural. Some of these were implicitly critical of bourgeois behaviour. Locke's typically puritan insistence on 'industriousness' would seem to tell against the absentee landlord and rentier, although Locke himself fell into this class. In general those standards required

---

[83] Ibid., §37, p. 312, enclosure and consequent intensive cultivation 'does not lessen but increase the common stock of mankind'.

[84] Ibid., §50, p. 320.

[85] The justification is carried on largely in terms of individuals but the assumption that it is a family group that has to be supported is mentioned from time to time: *First Treatise*, §142, *Second Treatise*, §§38, 48.

[86] *Second Treatise*, §42, p. 315.

[87] Although see Ibid., §83, p. 340, where marriage is described as involving a 'community of goods'.

that humans be able to preserve themselves, and that they not be made worse off as a result of entering into social institutions. Locke believed the sophisticated economy met these requirements. Many people from the seventeenth century right through to the present day have believed this, despite far more evidence than was available to Locke who need have been neither naive or dishonest to have believed it true in his day.

Moreover there is a strong case to be made for saying that property rights in the modern economy are *only* justified for Locke as long as the proviso that even the poor are better off holds good.[88] In the *First Treatise* he strenuously denied that any claim to property right could be upheld against the need or pressing want of the indigent, or that such poverty could be made use of to force undesired employment contracts, or indeed any kind of authority on people.[89] It is a point reiterated in the *Second Treatise* that even in the extreme situation where reparations are justly being sought against the aggressor that 'he that hath, and to spare, must remit something of his full Satisfaction, and give way to the pressing and preferable Title of those, who are in danger to perish without it.'[90] In favour of the 'bourgeois apologist' view of Locke it is common to cite the harsh treatment he prescribed for unlicensed beggars in his document on the reform of the Poor Law — three year's naval impressment or hard labour for adult males, flogging and the work-house for children, ears cut off for forging a begging licence. However the severity of these punishments may be more a reflection on the age than any particular determination on Locke's part to 'mobilize and discipline the unemployed into a docile labour force'.[91]

---

[88] J.W. Kendall has argued that if we take seriously our duty to God to preserve others there are strong collectivist strands in Locke. On this view it might well be implied by the law of nature, that if the development of the economy deprived some of that opportunity to preserve themselves which obtained in the state of nature, then there was a collective duty (to be exercised through government) to provide such people with at least work, if not property. J.W. Kendall, *John Locke and the Doctrine of Majority Rule* (Urbana, 1941). Something like this was argued by radicals such as Paine and Thelwall, using Lockean notions of labour derived property right in the the 1790s, see Tom Paine, *Agrarian Justice* (1795), and John Thelwall, *The Rights of Nature* (1795). For a discussion, my 'John Thelwall and the eighteenth-century radical response to political economy', *Historical Journal*, 34, 1 (1991). James Tully goes further and argues not only that such an argument is implicit in Locke, but that it was Locke's intention to stipulate such criteria as a condition of legitimate government: 'Government is obliged to distribute to each member the civil rights to life, to the liberty of preserving himself and others, and to the requisite goods or "means of it"'. This would have required governments to ensure not only the citizen's right to property, but to ensure they had property — a far more stringent stipulation that would make Locke very radical indeed. Tully, *A Discourse on Property*, p. 166.

[89] The passage is an important one, often overlooked by critics of Locke's supposedly proto-bourgeois apologetic in the *Second Treatise*. Its implications for Macpherson's interpretation are discussed at some length by Tully, *A Discourse on Property*, pp. 131–43. 'God . . . has given no one of his Children such a Property, in his peculiar Portion of the things of this World, but that he has given his needy Brother a Right to the Surplusage of his Goods; so that it cannot justly be denied him, when his pressing Wants call for it. And therefore no Man could ever have a just Power over the Life of another, by Right of property in land or Possessions; since 'twould always be a Sin in any Man of Estate, to let his Brother perish for want of affording him Releif out of his Plenty' . . . nor can a man 'justly make use of another's necessity to force him to become his Vassal, by with-holding that Relief, God requires him to afford to the wants of his Brother . . .' *First Treatise*, §42, p. 188. This idea of property limited by need has clear ancestors in medieval notions of property as stewardship.

[90] *Second Treatise*, §183, p. 409.

[91] As suggested by Wood, *John Locke and Agrarian Capitalism*, p. 106, and Macpherson, *Possessive Individualism*, pp. 222–6.

For there is another side to the coin: the same document proposes to make the parish authorities criminally responsible for any individual dying of hunger within their boundaries, and Locke insists that individuals, working or not, are entitled to meat, drink, clothes, shelter and heat.[92] No such necessities may be witheld to threaten people into obedience. In this sense, the property right to subsistence can be read as the absolutely fundamental right which is retained within political society (even without labour!), and which that society has authority to supply through the action of its democratically elected representatives 'regulating' or 'determining' more complex (and provisional) property rights, in other words government may have an overriding duty of redistributive taxation where failure to act would result in starvation.[93] The right to land or other complex properties is a right which derives, as a means, from the fundamental right and duty of human self-preservation. It would be strange if a derivative, secondary right were to override the fundamental right to which it was a means. This is what conventional property rights would do, if they were to justify denying to the poor a right to a decent self-subsistence. Nothing Locke says suggests he would support such a position, and what he does say suggests that the right to subsistence seemed perfectly consistent *to him* with an emphasis on the benign role of large and well-managed productive estates.

Distinguishing paternal from political power

Besides showing that the state of nature could have a meaning and that private property was possible, Locke also has to refute Filmer by distinguishing political from paternal power. The central thrust of Locke's argument was to show that men did ultimately have the right to resist a government which was tyrannical. This required him to show that citizens did not – as patriarchalists argued – incur irresistible obligations of obedience simply as a result of their birth. He does this both by demonstrating the limits of a natural father's authority, and by severing its association with political authority.

Locke does not offend his Christian readers by disagreeing with the biblical injunction to obey our fathers and mothers. What he does firstly is to point out that this injunction establishes something that more properly might be called parental than paternal authority, and being shared, cannot be a model for the rule of an individual as patriarchal monarchists insist.[94] Secondly, even in the case of our parents, he points out, the obedience owed is only temporary, and a consequence of our ignorance and lack of reason, it lasts only until we become morally responsible.[95] Thirdly, the rights our parents exercise over us are not 'natural' in the sense of being inseparable from the act of generation. These rights can be exercised by fosters on behalf of our parents,[96] and indeed

---

[92] H.R. Fox-Bourne, *The Life of John Locke* (2 vols, 1876), vol. 2, pp. 382, 390.

[93] *Second Treatise*, §§45, 50. This is argued by both Tully and Ashcraft. In support of this view note the right to a subsistence property is strikingly referred to by Locke as 'The Fundamental Law of Nature' §183. But see J. Waldron, 'Locke, Tully and the Regulation of Property', *Political Studies*, XXXII, 1 (1984).

[94] Ibid., §53, p. 322. The stress on the equality of the woman's role, as recipient both of God's grant, and the obedience and honour of children is remarked on above, fn.31.

[95] Ibid., §55, p. 322.

[96] Ibid., §59, p. 325.

they may be taken away from our parents if they neglect their duties.[97] Once again, as ever in Locke's argument, rights derive from and are limited by duties. Parent's rights are a consequence of their duty to care for their children, the attempt to exercise those rights beyond the limits of those duties is void.[98] Clearly the implications of this for a theory of monarchy based on an analogy with paternity are serious indeed. The real reason that we are subject to our parents' authority is because of their moral maturity, yet such maturity comes to us all in time: 'If this *made* the Father *free*, it shall *make* the Son *free* too'.[99] The argument identifying political as paternal power involved another more basic logical flaw: by assimilating political authority to paternal, and yet claiming that political authority was absolute, Filmer had left the true original model of paternal authority, the father, with none to exercise, 'For then, all Paternal Power being in the Prince, the Subject could naturally have none of it'.[100]

Then, as if worried that he had undermined paternal authority too much, Locke emphasises the honour which we must owe our parents all our lives. A further influence on our obedience to parents is 'the Power Men generally have to *bestow their estates*', that is to grant or withhold inheritance. This, Locke remarks, in one of his more wry asides, is 'no small Tye on the Obedience of Children'.[101] Nevertheless inheritance is, in the *First Treatise*, discussed as something which children have a virtual right to, following from the duty parents have not only to provide for their children's survival but 'to the conveniences and comforts of Life, as far as the conditions of their parents can afford it'.[102] It is a practice with important implications, for although a father cannot oblige his offspring to obey the laws of a government he has established or consented to (for this would be patriarchalism at the second generation), accepting such laws, where they are consistent with the law of nature, can legitimately be 'a necessary Condition annex'd to the Land', and so a condition of inheritance.[103]

At this point Locke appears to do something quite breathtaking. Having spent the whole of the *First Treatise* and almost a whole chapter of the *Second* in demolishing the shared identity of political and patriarchal power, and in trying to keep the two apart in order to deny that political authority derives its qualities from paternal, he now appears to confound the distinction he had spent so much time and sarcasm establishing, by remarking:

> tis obvious to conceive how easie it was in the first Ages of the World, and in places still, . . . for the *Father of the Family* to become the Prince of it.

and again

> Thus the natural *Fathers of Families*, by an insensible change, became the *politick Monarchs* of them too.[104]

---

[97] Ibid., §65, p. 328.

[98] Ibid., §58, p. 324.

[99] Ibid., §59, p. 325.

[100] Ibid., §71, p. 332. The point is also made at length in *First Treatise*, 'if the Magistrate hath all this Paternal Right as he must have if *Fatherhood* be the Fountain of all Authority, then the Subjects, though Fathers, can have no Power over their Children, . . . for it cannot be all in anothers hands, and a part remain with the Parents.' §65, p. 206.

[101] *Second Treatise*, §72, p. 333.

[102] *First Treatise*, §89, p. 225.

[103] *Second Treatise*, §73, p. 333.   [104] Ibid., §75, p. 335; §76, p. 336.

The explanation, however, is that these are historical observations, they are not meant to have any moral implications. Locke had no need to deny the existence of patriarchal monarchies as a historical fact, because he had, unusually for many English political thinkers of his time, rejected the past as the source of political legitimacy. But patriarchalism was invoked by Locke as a historical explanation for the origin of early political societies: their legitimacy, where they were legitimate, was to be explained on quite different grounds, namely their operating within the bounds of the law of nature, and the continuing consent of the maturing offspring. It is also worth remarking here, despite what Locke later says about the need for express consent in forming societies, that he describes this particular form of transition from family group to (evidently legitimate) political society, as taking place by an 'insensible change' and with the 'tacit, and scarce avoidable consent' of the children.[105]

It is important to notice what Locke seems to imply by consent at this point. It is not a piece of behaviour such as voting or acclamation (hardly something one could do without noticing it). Rather Locke regards people as having consented when they (being adults) could legitimately have withheld their consent, by denying the father's right to punish. Locke's curious 'criminal stranger' argument appears again as it did in §9. A stranger who entered the family and killed one of the children could rightly be executed by the father, points out Locke, under the law of nature, without claiming any patriarchal authority over him or the children. And by the same token the father could punish his adult child without claiming patriarchal authority over them. All he needs is the acquiescence of the group that he is the one who enforces the law of nature about the place.[106] The question of how to identify when acquiescence has taken place does not seem to worry Locke, so he does not bother to identify it with any behaviour on the part of the consenters: the children of the primitive patriarch do not even seem to be aware that they have consented. Locke seems to assume that because of the moral equality and freedom which human beings enjoy (or endure) they are to be described as consenting whenever they acknowledge the exercise of legitimate power over them. Although that authority is not *created* by their wills, as they are free and equal, it is only through their consent, actual or presumed that such power can be exercised on their behalf.

The character of legitimate commonwealths: the role of consent

Locke has successively demolished Filmer's objection to the state of nature, private property and the notion that political power must be identical with paternal. He has cleared the ground for his own account of political society. Political society is then defined by Locke as where 'any number of Men are so united into one Society, as to quit every one his Executive Power of the Law of Nature, and to resign it to the publick, there, and there only is a *Political, or Civil Society.*'[107]

---

[105] Ibid., §76, p. 336; §75, p. 335.
[106] Ibid., §74, p. 335.

[107] Ibid., §89, p. 343.

Locke stresses the importance of 'a Judge on Earth, with Authority to determine all the Controversies, and redress the Injuries [of members]',[108] so that although the name given to this body is the Legislative, it is its judicial or arbitrary character that is most important, indeed definitive of the very existence of political society. Yet it is precisely this subjection to the rule of law that the absolute sovereign denies. Where men have no public arbiter to appeal to they are still in a state of nature. Locke draws attention to the fact that where a society is ruled by an absolute sovereign who is not himself under the law of that society it is in a state of nature with regard to him, since they have no common judge to appeal to in case of dispute. Even worse, since the sovereign is much more powerful than an ordinary human being would be, the dangers to the individual are considerably greater than they would otherwise be. To be concerned about the inconveniences of the state of nature as we normally think of it, and yet to ignore the danger posed by an arbitrary sovereign is

> to think that Men are so foolish that they take care to avoid what Mischiefs may be done them by *Pole-Cats*, or *Foxes*, but are content, nay think it Safety, to be devoured by *Lions*.[109]

Consent in the establishment of commonwealths

How do men come to be under a mutual judge? Since men are morally free and independent beings subject only to God's natural law it can only be by their consent.[110] Locke now argues that express consent *is* necessary to form a political community. Notice also that the establishment of political authority takes place in two stages. Firstly all men agree to form a political community, and to accept whatever form of government the majority subsequently decide to adopt. Secondly the community so formed establishes a government. This involves entrusting the rights of judging and executing the law to a man or body of men. Government is thus a trust, not a simple contract: the body which does the entrusting is society, which *is* the result of a contract. This account is consistent with many different forms of government, including constitutional monarchy. Locke has been misconstrued as stipulating majoritarian democracy as the only legitimate form of government. But his argument that the majoritarian principle must obtain, applies to the *process* by which a form of government is chosen, and men's natural freedoms regulated, *not* to the *constitutional form* the government must take.[111]

Locke anticipates objections that there never were such contracts and that men have never been free to enter them. Government precedes all records so we should not expect to find contracts recorded in history, although even so the Bible records some. Using a principle of interpretive charity Locke argues that although early records show the establishment of monarchies, they could never have been absolutist, because it could never have occurred to people that monarchs would claim the kind of absolute powers they now do, and if it had, people would never have acquiesced in such a form of government. Only in this sense may states have had a patriarchal origin. Such early

---

[108] Ibid., §89, p. 343.
[109] Ibid., §93, p. 346.

[110] Ibid., §95, pp. 348–9.
[111] Ibid., §§95, 96, 99.

'patriarchal' states were a result of political naivete, yet as long as the ruler obeyed the law of nature, authority in them was legitimate.[112]

Consent in established commonwealths

The notion of consent is clearly of importance to Locke in demolishing Filmer's assertion that we incur political obligations simply as a result of our birth. But we have seen his equivocation over how strong he wants that consent to be, when he suggested that as families grew into political communities consent to the patriarch could be assumed. In his more formal account of the origins of political society Locke argues not only that an initial consent is necessary to establish government, but also that a continuing consent is necessary if governmental power is to be legitimate. This can be of two sorts: express consent which, once given, binds a man to that government until it ceases to exist, and tacit consent which involves simply enjoying the benefits of the society; indeed 'barely travelling freely on the Highway; and in Effect, . . . the very being of anyone within the Territories of that Government'.[113]

Tacit consenters can leave, they seem identical with the visiting or resident foreigner who is obliged to obey because he shares the benefits of civilized living: 'submitting to the Laws of any Country, living quietly, and enjoying Priviledges and Protection under them, *makes not a Man a Member of that Society*' nor he adds, significantly, does it even make him a subject.[114] However the situation becomes confused when we look for examples of what counts as express and tacit consent. Locke tells us that express consent is necessary to establish a government, and yet, in the discussion of the patriarchal origins of magistracy, twice talks of their emerging 'tacitly'. He distinguishes the tacit from the express consenter, suggesting that aliens and citizens are the groups referred to in each case, and yet he gives inheritance as an example of both express and tacit consent.[115] Moreover terms for the possession of land, as Locke intermittently emphasizes, have crucial implications for the territorial integrity of the state. There must be some way in

[112] Ibid., §§111, 112.

[113] Ibid., §119, p. 366.

[114] Ibid., §122, p. 367. Significant, because some commentators, e.g. Macpherson, have wanted to suggest Locke is making a distinction between two kinds of membership — full members, who own property, expressly consent (construed by him as having the vote), and are bound to the civil association on the on hand, and mere 'subjects' who own no property, tacitly consent (are disenfranchised), and who may, if they can, leave, on the other. Macpherson, *Possessive Individualism*, p. 250. This won't do because even the kind of Locke Macpherson wants to paint would certainly need to make the propertyless 'subjects' of the regime, and Locke says consent is necessary for any men to be '*Subjects or Members of* [a] *Commonwealth*'. Ibid. On the issue of voting his case seems initially more plausible, but see the discussion below, pp. 104, 106.

[115] Ibid. The example of inheritance as express consent describes how the son, by inheriting his father's possessions 'puts himself presently under the Government he finds there established, as much as any other Subject of that Commonwealth. And thus *the Consent of Free-men, born under Government, which only makes them Members of it*, being given separately in their turns, as each comes to be of Age . . . '§117, p. 364. Compare only a few sections later where Locke describes non-members of the society who have acquired property in it, 'by Inheritance, Purchase, Permission or otherwise,' as having only tacitly consented, and so being under the kind of obligation which '*begins and ends with the Enjoyment*'. §120, p. 366; §121, p. 367.

which landowners can have their rights safeguarded without at the same time rendering the state liable to dismemberment. Achieving this is crucial to the difference between the theory of the modern liberal, and the feudal state. Locke's solution is to bind proprietors to the state through their consent to the ownership of protected, but ultimately inseparable territories.[116]

A major problem in taking seriously Locke's requirement of continuing consent in an express sense is that there would then seem to have been large sections of the English population who were not under any obligation to obey their lawful government. Even most men did not have the vote and it is difficult for us to see what else might be construed as express consent. However exercised Locke was about the subversive activities of Charles II, and later James II and his advisors, he surely did not have it in mind to suggest that the very form of English government which he was about to recommend to his readers was inherently illegitimate with regard to a large section of its subjects.

John Dunn has suggested that there are a number of occasions on which seventeenth-century Englishmen could be said to have consented to their government. Oaths of allegiance could be, and were, demanded by kings from their subjects (since 1609 by statute), attendance at church involved prayers for and spiritual endorsement of the regime, liability for militia service also involved such oaths. He concludes 'there are enough occasions in a man's life in which he uses verbal formulae which imply a recognition of his membership of the national society to which he belongs for any adult to be held to have made some express declaration of membership.'[117] Even so it seems extraordinarily remiss of Locke not to have specified them.

One solution is the suggestion of Macpherson that the example of inheritance is to be taken as constitutive of express consent. Thus only those who inherit property would be express consenters. This has some relevance to contemporary conditions, for enfranchisement extended only to those with property. It conveniently also fits Macpherson's casting of Locke as an apologist of bourgeois interests.

Nevertheless Locke's text will not bear this: he is at great pains to insist that although an act of personal allegiance commits both oneself and one's possessions to the commonwealth 'as long as it hath a being', the mere ownership of possessions which are already a part of a commonwealth, although it does, whilst one enjoys the possessions, make one subject to that government: *'makes not a Man a Member of that Society'*. Resident foreigners, bound as they are to obey the law, are nevertheless not properly *subjects or Members of that Commonwealth'* without 'positive Engagement, and express Promise and Compact'.[118]

Part of an answer to Locke's carelessness over identifying what counts as express consent can, I think, be got by reminding ourselves of what it was in Filmer that Locke wanted to deny. Locke wanted to deny Filmer's claim that men incur binding political obligations simply as a result of their birth. As stated this assertion contains at least two claims. Firstly, that because political obligations are fixed by birth they are absolute and cannot be revoked; and secondly that the location of those obligations is determined by

[116] This fascinating aspect of Locke has been rarely discussed; there is, however, an excellent, but rarely cited article by John Gale, 'John Locke on territoriality: an unnoticed aspect of the Second Treatise', *Political Theory*, 1 (1973).

[117] Dunn, *The Political Thought of John Locke,*, pp. 137–41.

[118] *Second Treatise*, §§120, p. 366; §122, p. 367.

birth, i.e., being born in England or of English parents determines that it is the English king (and not the French) to whom we owe obligation. For much of his text it is on the first of Filmer's claims that Locke wishes to focus. Getting good Christians to accept that they might have moral grounds for resistance *at all* involved overcoming the influence of the considerable campaign of non-resistance that the Anglican Church had mounted since 1660. Instead he wants to stress that because we are morally responsible for our own obligations they are ultimately limited and consensual, and so we can withdraw that consent when the limits are transgressed. For this limited case no issue of express consent is raised, for consent functions here only to justify (when necessary) the withdrawal of allegiance, not as a positive sign or creator of it. If consent is used to replace the second part of Filmer's assertion as well, then we do indeed need an express consent to determine where our political allegiance lies. But however far Locke strays – wittingly or not – in this direction, he does not need to be so explicit for it was not an issue for Locke or his adversaries, and the reason why he did not bother to clear up the confusion may well have been because he made the perfectly commonplace (although patriarchal) assumption, that the Englishness of English children could be assumed from their birth even though the absolute nature of their obligations to an English monarch could not. We might presume, in the case of English children that they wished to join their native commonwealth. Although they were at liberty not to, this would require an act of withdrawal.[119]

What at least emerges clearly is that Locke is concerned to argue and separate two points: firstly to establish criteria of legitimate government, and secondly to persuade people that they could do something about it if they found themselves under an illegitimate government. The role of consent in relation to the first of these is both complex, and, at times, unclear; it is vital at the founding but less so in established commonwealths. But it is not merely because a government is consented to that it is legitimate, indeed it may only be consented to if and when it is legitimate, the ground of its legitimacy is its conformity to the law of nature. However, it is because legitimate governments are consented to that illegitimate governments can be dissented *from*. Consent then is concerned most forcefully with the second of the two above issues, that of what might be done about illegitimate governments. An express, continuing consent is not ultimately required by Locke to validate all governments, and that is why he shows very little concern to establish what sorts of actions might count as such an endorsement. Rather the main thrust of Locke's arguing that government is based on consent is to establish that consent can be withdrawn if need be, not that it has to be shown to have been given in the first place. The consensual nature of government in the end seems to be an assertion about its moral status, rather than a claim about what precise sort of actions must have accompanied its creation or continuance.[120]

This lack of precision about the role of consent may seem to diminish Locke's importance, for we regard Locke as a founder figure of liberal thought and expect him to have something to say on the subject. Certainly from the mid-century or so after his

---

[119] Locke overstates the degree of discretion allowed under existing positive law in ibid., §118, see Laslett's footnotes, p. 365.

[120] John Dunn, 'Consent in the political theory of John Locke', *Historical Journal*, 10, 2 (1967); Iain Hampsher-Monk, 'Tacit Concept of Consent in Locke's *Two Treatises of Government*: A note on citizens, travellers and Patriarchalism', *Journal of the History of Ideas*, XL, 1 (1979).

death many people interpreted what he had to say about consent in modern ways. But it is clear that Locke does not regard the consent of the people as in itself conferring legitimacy on a government. Locke denies that a monarch who claimed absolute authority over his subjects could be legitimate. Yet he could hardly deny that, in his wide sense of the word, people might consent to him, not least because he spent some twenty years of his life in opposition to two of them who did enjoy that passive consent from most of the population. Even if a people explicitly promised to accept an absolutist's rule, this would not, in Locke's view, make it legitimate. For the responsibility we owe to God for ourselves, as Locke continually stresses, is not actually something we can morally transfer to another, and so such an apparent consent will be void of any legitimizing content. For Locke the criteria of legitimacy are laid down, not very clearly it is true, in the law of nature. But for Locke at least the law of nature is an objective moral order which is not affected by the subjective desires of men, and to which therefore subjective consent is irrelevant.

There is thus an important difference between the kind of regime which can be justified by Locke's account of consent, and the sort of regime that could be justified by a doctrine of popular sovereignty where consent itself formed not only the justification for resistance, but the criterion of legitimacy itself. Under the latter doctrine it is clear that all sorts of unpleasant laws might be agreed to by the majority, affecting racial, religious or class minorities, and we would have to say that these were just because we would have defined what is just in terms of what the majority consent to. But Locke himself was involved in opposition to Charles and James at least in part on grounds of their pursuit of a religious policy which he regarded as morally wrong independently not only of their views but also of those of the majority. Even the express consent of a majority to a measure cannot make it legitimate if it is contrary to the law of nature. Let us return to Locke's argument where these issues will recur.

The reasons for initiating commonwealths

In chapter IX Locke summarizes the reasons that lead men to seek government, rather than simply the logic of the consent by which it may be legitimately established. The law of nature, although, in principle, it provides a moral rule for men to operate by, is in the natural state a very uncertain restraint on men's behaviour. There is no guarantee that men, biassed and partial as they are, will obey its commands as they ought, nor that effective judgement will be made where wrong has been done, or that punishment will be impartially and effectively applied.[121] In his religious writings Locke explained these shortcomings in terms of Christian beliefs about men's fallen natures. However in the *Second Treatise* Locke stresses that 'The great and *chief end* therefore, of Mens uniting into Commonwealths, and putting themselves under Government, *is the preservation of their Property*',[122] and hints at more secular explanations of quarrelsomeness amongst men based on the increase in property holding and the invention of money.[123] This is of

---

[121] *Second Treatise*, §§124, 125, 126.

[122] Ibid., §124, pp. 368–9; see also §134, p. 376

[123] These are hints scattered through the text. The invention of money, is not an unmixed blessing, it 'alters the intrinsick value of things' and leads to a 'desire of having more than Men needed'. §37, p. 312.

some interest since it exemplifies the general trend in the eighteenth century towards the development of socio-economic explanations of moral and political belief.[124] The development of a more sophisticated economy, although initially pre-dating government, is seen by him to require social, and eventually political organisation. The latter involves individuals entrusting to some mutually agreed authority, two of their natural rights: that of interpreting the law of nature with respect to human preservation, and the right to punish offenders of the law. This allows us to overcome the three inherent difficulties of the state of nature: the absence of a clear law, the partiality of our judgements concerning it and the uncertainty of punishment.

The structure of legitimate polities: limitations of powers

At this stage in his argument Locke is unconcerned about the *form* of government adopted. It could be an oligarchy, a democracy or indeed a monarchy.[125] What is crucial to its legitimacy is the degree of power which it claims over individuals. Legitimate power is power plus right. The powers surrendered by the citizens are limited by the constraints on their own original rights. Because the individual's rights are limited (by his duties of self-preservation etc. owed to God) so must be the powers of the government if it is to remain legitimate. A related, but not identical, limiting factor is the intentions of the contractors. It must, thinks Locke, be illegal for a government to use its powers in a way contrary to the intentions of those who gave it the powers. Moreover since we don't know what the founders of government intended, Locke uses the principle of what it is reasonable to think they intended.[126] Locke outlines the general characteristics legitimate government must possess with reference in each case to these two general criteria – the law of nature and the intentions of the people.

Firstly this means that government cannot be arbitrary. Because the rights of action that individuals themselves possess under the law of nature are not arbitrary, arbitrary authority cannot be given to another: 'no Body can transfer to another more power than he has in himself; . . . so that the Legislative can have no more than this.' Neither, on any reasonably charitable interpretation of what the founders of a state intended, could individuals entering political society have wanted to put themselves in this defenceless position, so on this criterion too, such governments are illegitimate.[127]

It follows as a corollary of this first condition that government must proceed by general laws and not by individual (and therefore always potentially arbitrary) decree. These laws must be public, and the individual(s) who decide them must themselves be subject

---

Accumulation and a money economy make land scarce and so requires for it political regulation. §45, p. 317. At §111, p. 360, he refers to the *'Golden Age* (before vain Ambition, and *amor sceleratus habendi,* evil Concupiscence, had corrupted Mens minds . . .), ' as one where there was 'no contest betwixt Rulers and People'.

[124] See, especially on Locke, although as his title suggests, he stresses the discontinuities rather than the continuities, John Dunn, 'From applied theology to social analysis: the break between John Locke and the Scottish Enlightenment', in *Wealth and Virtue: The Shaping of Political Economy in the Scottish Enlightenment*, ed. Istvan Hont and Michael Ignatieff (Cambridge, 1983).

[125] *Second Treatise*, §132, p. 372.

[126] Ibid., §131, p. 371.

[127] Ibid., §135, p. 375.

to these same rules that govern everyone else. If they were not, this would not only offend against the natural moral equality of men, it would also immeasurably increase the possibilities for partiality within political society. In such a society men would actually be worse off than in a state of nature, and, once again, this could not have been their intention in establishing government.[128] That the people making the laws should effectively be subject to them requires a separation of the legislative and judicial functions of government. This criterion then has one important institutional implication: all legitimate governments must at least have separate bodies, one to make, another to apply the laws.[129]

Thirdly Locke argues that since property is a natural (i.e. a pre-political) right, established in accordance with the law of nature, and because the preservation of it is the main reason for entering civil society, it follows that it cannot be a legitimate act of government to appropriate, through taxation, the possessions of its subjects without their consent. This seems to require the *individual* express consent of each property owner, since it differs from the transfer of the rights of judging and punishing in a most important way. In that case, what is transferred are the enforcements of a pre-existing natural right, in the case of the right of taxation what is transferred is the right to abrogate a right. Since the general abrogation of a right of nature would be tyranny, this can only be avoided where each alienation of that right, i.e. each act of taxation, is specifically consented to. So, whilst Locke can be relatively unconcerned about the mechanism of consent to government's powers of applying the law of nature, consent to taxation must have some institutional expression. Despite this, Locke slips, without justification, from insisting on the individual's consent to taxation – which seems perfectly consistent with everything he has so far said – to assuming the consent of only a majority, or even a majority of representatives – which is not.[130] Nor were all Englishmen represented in the Parliament which made decisions about taxation. If Locke assumed, as was commonplace where the major source of revenue was still the land tax, that it was only landowners who bore the burden of taxation then since all those with any substantial land were represented in Parliament, the existing representation might seem to meet Locke's point. However, as Locke well knew, indirect and local taxation extended to virtually all economically active individuals; his argument, particularly its concern that 'every one who enjoys his share of Protection, should pay out of his Estate his proportion of for the maintenance of it',[131] taken together with the claim that all contributions must be levied with the specific consent of the individual, or his representative, could be taken as easily for an argument in favour of the enfranchisement (and liability for taxation) of all those protected, as it could for one that assumed the limiting of protection to the propertied taxpayers.[132]

The twin roles of consent and the law of nature in identifying legitimate government then seem to be something like the following. Political society can only be established by explicit consent of all the founders. The majority must then agree on the form of

---

[128] Ibid., §137, p. 377 'It cannot be supposed that they should intend, had they a power so to do, . . . to . . . put force into the Magistrates hand to execute his unlimited Will arbitrarily upon them.'

[129] Ibid., §§131, 136, 137.

[130] The slippage at §140, p. 380 takes place within a single phrase. However fair or necessary taxation is 'still it must be with his own Consent, *i.e.* the Consent of the Majority, giving it either by themselves, or their Representatives chosen by them.'

[131] Ibid., §140, p. 380.

[132] M. Hughes, 'Lock on Taxation and Suffrage', *History of Political Thought*, XI, 3 (1990).

government to be established, but this form must have certain characteristics, and consent to a government without them would not endow it with legitimacy. These are that it must operate through known laws to which all are subject, ruler and ruled alike. There must be an independent judiciary. There must be a body representative of the whole of those liable to taxation, which must consent to specific acts of taxation. The body entrusted with making the laws (which might, but need not strictly be the same as the body that authorizes taxation) must pass nothing contrary to the law of nature (even though people might consent to such enactments).

Finally government cannot delegate its powers. This follows from the fiduciary nature of government whose powers are a trusteeship from the people and to whom they revert if given up: a trust cannot be discharged by proxy.[133]

These are the conditions that a government must fulfill if it is to be legitimate. It is worth noticing that they are conditions which Protestants believed a Catholic monarch was incapable of fulfilling. Because the Pope had excused Catholics from the need to keep faith with Protestants, there simply could not be the required relationship of trust between Catholic ruler and Protestant subjects.[134] But if the relationship of rule were not based on trust, it must be one of conquest and subjection.[135]

Nevertheless although ruling out certain forms of government, particularly those associated with Catholicism, these are wide and general requirements. They do not, except in requiring legal regularity, a separate judge, and a mechanism for consenting to taxation, specify particular institutions. If these criteria are satisfied, the form that government takes cannot in itself, compromise its legitimacy. But it may well be that some arrangements foster legitimacy better than others. Theorising about politics is a composite activity. Locke distinguishes between that part of it which belongs to moral philosophy – deciding what is required of a legitimate government – and that part of it which belongs to what Locke might have called prudence or what we would call political science or institutional theory – how best to embody these principles in, or sustain them by, institutions.

The 'well ordered commonwealth'

Locke goes on to consider the sort of institutions which prevail under 'well ordered Commonwealths', these being those polities which are most likely to sustain legitimacy successfully. Clearly the kind of commonwealth Locke has in mind is late seventeenth-century England, and in the course of his discussion Locke touches on a number of issues which had surrounded both the Exclusion Crisis and the eventual abdication of James II.

The legislative power is that which makes the laws that govern the community. Although it is supreme over the other powers of government, and although it is entrusted

---

[133] *Second Treatise*, §142, p. 381.

[134] Locke stresses this point in the *Letter Concerning Toleration*, (1689) [Indianapolis, 1955], p. 50.

[135] 'Seeing a papist successor can be obliged by no contract or oath, therefore he cannot succeed by contract. And if he succeed not by contract, then he will succeed by conquest for there are but two ways of succession, either by contract or conquest.' William Lawrence, *The Right of Primogeniture* (1681), p. 148, cited Ashcraft, *Revolutionary Politics*, p. 200.

by the people with defining and encoding the law of nature, its powers can still be forfeit to them if they judge it delinquent.[136] It is a striking measure of Locke's radicalism and his rejection of purely formal criteria of legitimacy that he sanctions popular resistance even to representative bodies.[137] The legislature does not need to be in constant existence, nor should it be, for it might be tempted to interest itself in the application of its own laws, or to promote its own interests. Consequently, 'in well order'd commonwealths' it consists of a body of persons 'who duly Assembled, have by themselves, or jointly with others, a Power to make Laws, which when they have done, being separated again, they are themselves subject to the Laws, they have made.'[138]

The executive power designates for Locke both the administrative and judicial functions of government, necessarily continuously in existence. The third power he calls the federative power, that of engaging in relationships, friendly or otherwise, with other political communities. The organisational form of, and relationships between, these different functions of government vary, and it is here that the possibility lies of constructing institutions which are more or less likely to sustain legitimacy.

The legislative power is morally superior, for it lays down the rules which the whole society must adhere to. Locke presumes this will be a representative body of some kind although he tells us nothing explicitly about how they are to be chosen or by whom. On the one hand Locke, and the whole revolutionary movement recognised the importance of protecting property rights as a means of ensuring confidence and productivity, to this end 'the Landholder ... ought to have the greatest care taken of him, and enjoy as many Privileges, and as much Wealth, as the favour of the Law can (with regard to the Public weal) confer on him'.[139] The fear of egalitarian levelling which pervaded the Civil War period was not only a recent but an enduring political preoccupation. On the other hand there is an undoubted strand of egalitarianism in Locke's thinking and in view of recent evidence concerning the social complexion of Locke's revolutionary connections it would be rash even to presume, as many have done, that he considered the existing franchise in England – possession of freehold land to the value of 40/– per annum in the counties, and a variety of wider and narrower franchises in the boroughs – to be adequate.[140] Although even this may not seem much to modern readers, the late-seven-

---

[136] *Second Treatise*, §149, p. 385, 'thus the *Community* perpetually *retains a Supreame Power* of saving themselves from the attempts and designs of any Body, even of their Legislators, whenever they shall be so foolish, or so wicked, as to lay and carry on designs against the Liberties and Properties of the Subject.'

[137] Ibid., §201: ''Tis a Mistake to think this Fault [tyranny] is proper only to Monarchies; other Forms of Government are liable to it, as well as that.' Locke defended certain rights, notoriously, but not exclusively, those of religious conscience, against interference by *any* political power, however constituted, including, as in the passage cited above, a representative legislature. This insistence that the legislature itself may constitute a source of tyranny, might seem odd in the light of the conflict between parliament and Charles II and James II, but memories of the self-perpetuating Long Parliament (1640–1660) during the Civil War and Interregnum were still strong. In an unpublished tract written jointly with Tyrrell in 1681, whilst also composing the *Second Treatise*, Locke expressly committed himself 'to a natural rights defense of liberty of conscience against the claims of all forms of political authority, including representative government.' Ashcraft, *Revolutionary Politics*, pp. 496–7.

[138] Ibid., §143, p. 382.

[139] John Locke *Some Considerations of the Lowering of Interest, and raising of the Value of Money* (1692), repr. in *Several Papers Relating to Money, Interest and Trade* (N.Y., 1968), p. 100.

[140] Ashcraft, *Revolutionary Politics*, ch.6, 'Class Conflict and Electoral Politics', passim.; esp. p. 228; the Whigs 'wanted to forge an alliance between merchants, tradesmen, artisans, shopkeepers, *and* yeoman

teenth-century franchise was wider than any enjoyed in England until the passing of the Great Reform Act in 1832.[141] The distribution of representation, however arrived at, stresses Locke, must be reviewed from time to time as the balance of population changes.

These were real issues. Uninhabited boroughs with one or two electors such as Gatton and Old Sarum were to become notorious in the eighteenth century for the opportunities they provided for the sale and hire of parliamentary seats. Locke's patron, the Earl of Shaftesbury, had introduced a Bill to reform the electoral districts in 1679, about the time we know Locke was starting work on the *Second Treatise*. There is another more sinister contemporary episode related to this question. Both Charles II and James II had attempted to control their parliaments by 'remodelling' the charters which determined the extent of the franchise, narrowing them so as to ensure the return of members sympathetic to their policies.[142] Locke cites such a practice,[143] as an example of an explicit attempt to undermine government. Again although the legislature is supreme it does not need to be in session all the time, whereas the executive clearly does need to have a continuous existence. The calling of the legislature must then be left to the executive; but this does not mean that it can choose not to call it. It has a duty to do so; a duty which is entrusted to it, and for the neglect of which it can be called to account. Once again their failure regularly to call parliaments was part of the radicals' objection to the Stewart monarchs.[144]

The third, or Federative power, that of dealing with other political communities, is usually combined with the executive. Locke sees the relationship between these branches of government as a hierarchy of trusts. The executive branch of the government, dealing with the day-to-day affairs of government, cannot have its hands tied absolutely by the legislature. It must therefore be entrusted with a degree of discretionary 'prerogative power', to act without always seeking particular legal permissions. Yet this power cannot, Locke argues be understood as it had often been claimed – as a right by the monarch-executive to pursue his own interests or to deny individuals their natural rights of property, and due process of law. Prerogative power, like any other species of political power, must be presumed limited by natural law, and the intentions of the entrusters, and it is only when so directed that it is legitimate. From this it follows that the executive clearly acts on trust when the legislative is not assembled, and even in some areas such as foreign policy, when it is. Ultimately even the legislative body itself is in possession of a trust from the community. In this respect the community itself may be said to be the supreme power in the nation. But this power is never realised until the particular political form which the government has taken has been destroyed. Thus Locke is not advocating the direct intervention of all individuals in the normal course of political life. What he claims instead is that since it is (or, strictly, ought to be) the desire of the community to ensure the observance of the laws of nature and to further their own good that brings about the political society, it must ultimately be community that judges when that end is

---

farmers and the gentry.' The difficulty lay in appealing to the former without frightening the latter. This may account for Locke's reticence to be clear about the scope of representation.

[141] J.H.Plumb, 'The Growth of the Electorate in England from 1600–1715', *Past and Present*, XLV (1969).

[142] J.H.Plumb, *The Growth of Political Stability in England 1675–1725* (London, 1967) pp. 52–62.

[143] *Second Treatise*, §216.

[144] Ibid., §215

not being pursued.[145] This does not mean that a referendum has to be taken before the legislative or executive can act, but it does mean that the people are entitled to resist when it considers the legitimate purposes of political power are being abused. There is nothing treasonable in this assertion, insists Locke. For our political obligation is to legal forms and roles, and not to individuals. Even where monarchs (as in England) exact oaths of personal loyalty, these are not binding if rulers go beyond the law: '*Allegiance* being nothing but an *obedience according to Law*, which when he violates, he has no right to Obedience'.[146] This is a crucial claim, denying as it does the central feature of feudalism: the personal bond of fealty between ruler and subject, whilst asserting in its place the modern principle of legal regularity, albeit still underpinned by theological premises.

Two features of patriarchalism entailed its complete disqualification of any active form of resistance to a hereditary monarch. It held that all rightful political rule was absolute, and that such rule was conveyed through descent, or exceptionally through God's special providence. On neither of these grounds could one envisage the possibility of legitimate resistance to a monarch. Locke asserted a criterion of legitimacy based on conformity to a law of nature, and he had argued that the status of such government must be thought of as consensual, allowing the withdrawal of obedience in specific circumstances. Because successful conformity with the law of nature entailed some formal properties in the government (minimally, the existence of independent judges and the requirement of rule by law), allegiance must always be to the constitutional *forms* of a properly constituted government, and not to the persons who were officeholders. They could be resisted in the event of their misbehaviour or if they sought to abrogate the proper, or possibly even the agreed forms of government and the reason why they could be resisted was because government was premised on consent. Locke is not here saying that some institutionalized act of consent by each individual had to be elicited to accompany the ongoing activity of governments (although some such consent is necessary for certain kinds of acts - raising taxes, changing the basic institutions of government for example): rather he is emphasizing that the community could withdraw its consent when a government, by breaking its trust, becomes tyrannical.[147] How, precisely, do we know when a government may properly be resisted?

Exercising the right of resistance

Locke begins an answer to this question (ch. XV) by discussing a number of illegitimate forms of government. Yet again he distinguishes political from paternal power, emphasizing the limited nature of paternal power and the consensual nature of the political community. He re-emphasizes that any claim to unlimited, i.e. despotic power (such as was made by Charles and James) is unnatural, the consequence only of an aggressive renunciation of the laws of nature and a denial of 'Reason, . . . the Rule betwixt Man and

---

[145] Ibid., §149

[146] Ibid., §151, p. 368

[147] Locke uses consent 'not to discriminate between governments which may be resisted and governments which should not be resisted. It is merely to explain why any government is in principle subject to just resistance, if it behaves wickedly'. Dunn, *Political Thought of John Locke*, p. 143.

Man, and the common bond whereby humane kind is united'. Anyone claiming absolute dominion over another, far from claiming a political power, is claiming something which denies that right and responsibility on which political power rests, that is the responsibility each man has to preserve and order his own life. They are 'liable to be destroied by the injur'd person and the rest of mankind.'[148]

Locke then considers the case of conquest. Once again this has a basis in the party polemics of the time. Many political arguments in the seventeenth century were preoccupied with justifying institutions and practices by demonstrating their antiquity. Parliamentarians and royalists before, during and after the Civil War had each claimed the antiquity of their institution and the innovatory and dependent nature of their opponents'. Two conflicting interpretations of history were emerging. One of these, espoused by the parliamentarians and then the Whigs, saw English history as a (more or less) unbroken line of libertarian institutions and principles. Despotic deviations were explained by reference to numerous attempts to subvert this tradition, by imposing the 'yoke' of slavery on the people. Examples of such attempts were those of William the Conqueror, the early Tudors, the Stuarts. The other view was beginning to recognise the existence of such a thing as feudalism. In a curious way Harrington had perceived its existence as 'Gothic Prudence', but criticised it for its instability rather than its absolutism. Hobbes of course had derided the whole style of historical argument in politics but one of the two methods of establishing sovereignty – the less problematical and more likely – was effectively conquest. And he had acknowledged the historicity of such a method in *Behemoth* and his *Dialogue of the Common Laws*, where he talked of William the Conqueror establishing his right by conquest. More recently polemicists such as Brady using the more scholarly works of Spelman and Dugdale had elaborated the whole theory of feudal government as a set of rights descending from the king in whom they had originated. Clearly the nature of the English past was becoming an increasingly delicate political matter. When William and Mary replaced James II, Brady was relieved of his position as Keeper of the Records of the Tower and replaced by Petit and Atwood, advocates of the politically more acceptable if historically erroneous Whig interpretation of history.[149]

Locke insists that conquest in itself never founds any right of government. A conqueror may subject his beaten enemy but they always retain a right to revolt whenever they can do so without causing worse trouble to themselves than by submitting. An aggressor claiming rights over a conquered people is exactly like an extortioner in private life. But even supposing the war leading to the conquest to be a 'just war', the right of conquest extends only to those who actively fought against the victor. As Locke makes clear, this is directly relevant to the argument over English history. William the Conqueror, even if one assumes his war to have been just, gained no absolute rights over his fellow Norman soldiers who came and settled in England, and only over the enemy soldiers did he have any right of conquest at all. Their properties are not forfeit, except to the extent necessary to repair the damage done, and the lives and properties of non-combatants, women,

---

[148] *Second Treatise*, §172, p. 401.

[149] The classic account is Pocock's, *The Ancient Constitution and the Feudal Law*. For an interesting discussion of the ways in which rational criteria intertwined with those proposing an 'ancient' or precedent-based, constitution, and thus paved the way for thinkers like Locke, see Johann P. Somerville, 'The Norman Conquest in Early Stuart Political Thought', *Political Studies*, XXIV, 2 (1986).

children and descendants, are not legally vulnerable at all.[150] Once again Locke uses his peculiarly limited notion of consent to excuse the rest of a community whose army had fought an unjust war. The rest of the community cannot be held responsible for this because they merely acquiesced (tacitly consented?) to their government fighting an unjust war.[151] Yet soldiers, by actively participating, do incur moral responsibility, and culpability.

The reparations exacted by the victors must never amount to the value of the land itself. Locke here recognises the difference between money, riches and treasure which are only of a 'Phantastical imaginary value': and 'Natures Goods, in land itself which is a perpetual inheritance'. Whatever damage has been done by an unjust aggressor (Locke presumably discounts here the loss of life which is beyond valuation), it cannot be more that 'the destruction of a Year's Product or two', whereas land itself is productive for ever. This stress on the difference between a right to the product of a piece of land and the right to the repeated produce (the 'perpetual inheritance') that follows from the possession of the land itself (especially 'where all is possessed, and none remains waste to be taken up') had, however, played no part in Locke's discussion of the development of property rights, which might have taken a very different turn if Locke had taken account of this distinction.[152] For the differential in future returns established between those who did and those who did not possess land would then have been recognised as a moral issue.

A second form of illegitimate political authority is usurpation. A usurper is one who gains legitimate office by illegitimate means. The means by which people gain office (inheritance, election, appointment etc.) is just as much a part of the rules of a common-wealth, as the offices themselves. Usurpers, therefore need not be obeyed. But a usurper, in breaking the rules of accession, need not break the rules circumscribing the office. A usurper therefore, can become a legitimate ruler if the people are at liberty to and do consent to him in that legitimate office.[153] By 'at liberty to' Locke had already explained that he means 'either they are put in a full state of Liberty to chuse their Government and Governors, or at least till they have such standing Laws, to which they have by themselves or by their Representatives, given their free consent'.[154]

This circumstance would fit the constitutionally irregular expulsion of James and the recruitment of William and Mary to occupy his office. The date of this chapter, and that on conquest (ch.XVI), to which it is related, is unclear. Laslett thinks it likely to be 1681 or 2, but allows that this is only an opinion.[155] His reason, that an argument about conquest would have been irrelevant in 1689, seems strange. Although conservative supporters of the Glorious Revolution stressed the kinship claims of William and Mary, for radicals of Locke's circle, who wished to stress the right of the community to replace tyrants, the

[150] *Second Treatise*, §177, pp. 404–5; §180, p. 406. Reparations cannot reach the extent of jeopardizing the livelihoods of the dependants or successors (an anti-patriarchal point) of combatants.

[151] Ibid., §179. Yet in the preceding sentence we find Locke using consent, in the stronger form, to designate those who might be considered as having 'actually assisted, concurr'd or consented to that unjust force'. §179, p. 406.

[152] Ibid., §184, p. 409.

[153] Ibid., §197, p. 415.

[154] Ibid., §192, p. 412.

[155] Ibid., Laslett's notes pp. 415, 402.

legitimation of an irregularly recruited ruler would seem to be a highly topical issue. Locke himself seemed to want to legitimize William and Mary within the framework of the existing constitution without endorsing their claim from either heredity or conquest theory.[156] The legitimation of usurpation does precisely this.

Tyranny however, is the exercise not of another person's (legitimate) power, but the exercise of power beyond moral right. Such power cannot be legitimized no matter how many indications of consent are made by those subject to it.[157] The use of political power for private or sectional gain, rule by the mere will of an individual, and abrogation of the rule of law, are examples of tyrannical practices.[158]

The practice of revolution

Up to now Locke has been talking about what counts as illegitimate government. But what follows from this? Does all illegality imply resistance? Must we revolt whenever governments err? Will not such a wide right 'unhinge and overturn all Polities, and instead of Government and Order leave nothing but Anarchy and Confusion'?[159]

Locke denies this. He denies both the moral argument that illegitimate action on the part of the government invariably sanctions resistance by the people, and he also denies the sociological observation that such action will in fact always lead to such resistance. The question 'when is a government acting illegitimately?' does not have the same answer as the question 'when may a people properly resist their government?' Moreover the form and extent of resistance is to be proportionate to the severity of the departure from legitimacy. There are clear limitations on our rights of resistance.

In some countries (including England), the king's person is sacred. This means that although we might be entitled to resist his officers we may not attack him physically in person, unless by actually declaring war on his people, he dissolves the government and with it the statutory limitations on his personal treatment (Locke thus appears to endorse the execution of Charles II). This Locke thinks, is a prudent device, for it justifies us in resisting the monarch's officers when they are attempting to do something improper, without actually overturning the government.[160]

Secondly, it is always improper to resort to force where there is a legal process available for redress. The highwayman demanding 1/– at sword point may be lawfully killed, whereas someone who obtains 100 by fraud must be taken to law, for in this case our lives are not endangered, and there is the possibility of resort to a legal arbiter. We are not here, as we are with the highwayman, in a state of nature in relation to him.

---

[156] Locke endorsed the existing constitutional framework at a time when he might have regarded himself free to speculate on alternatives, i.e. in the first weeks of the Convention parliament of 1689 when it was unclear what constitutional settlement would be made. He wrote to Edward Clarke: 'the setle ment of the nation upon the sure grounds of peace and security . . . can noe way soe well be don as by restoreing our ancient government, the best possibly that ever was if taken and put together all of a peice in its originall constitution.' *Correspondence of John Locke*, ed. De Beer, (8 vols, Oxford, 1978) vol 3, p. 545.

[157] Locke thus firmly denies the (now apparently commonly held) belief that a popular mandate can in itself justify any government action.

[158] *Second Treatise*, §§199 (private advantage), 200 (will), 202 (rule of law).

[159] Ibid., §203, p. 419.

[160] Ibid., §§205, 206.

But even where power is being used illegitimately, and where there is no redress to be had at law, there are further considerations to be satisfied before resistance is justified. The subjects' right to resist says Locke, will 'not easily ingage them in a Contest, wherein they are sure to perish.'[161] This would likely be the case where an individual sought, alone, to rebel against injustice. Moreover, there is a strong implication that it would be wrong for them to do so, both on personal grounds – by pointlessly endangering their God-given lives – and also by overturning the public peace in pursuit of a private grievance.[162] But where the wrong done represented an attack on the general principle of citizens' rights the presumption is that more people will become involved. Locke's discussion involves an interplay between the strict moral grounds of resistance and the sociology of belief that makes it possible. Ultimately, he seems to suggest, the two coincide. It is only when there is a serious attempt to invade the nation's liberties that a large number of people will be sufficiently aggrieved to be roused to action, and it is only under such circumstances that rebellion is either likely to succeed or fully justified. Certainly he regards people as being so generally disposed to accept government that their being discontented is a sufficient presumption against the government.

> It being as impossible for a Governor, if he really means the good of his People and the preservation of them and their Laws together, not to make them see and feel it as it is for the Father of a Family, not to let his Children see he loves, and takes care of them.[163]

Once again it is important to emphasize that it is not the mere discontent of the people that itself constitutes their moral right to resist government. Rather, because of his belief in what Laslett has called the 'natural political virtue' which Locke presumes in men, widespread discontent is presumptive evidence for the government's serious illegality.

Collective resistance is not justified, then, simply when a government does things the people do not want, nor even when it is guilty of casually and isolated illegal actions, nor even when individuals become dissatisfied with the undoubtedly arbitrary persecution of a government impinging on them. However, when 'a *long Train of Actings shew the Councils* all tending that way [towards arbitrary rule]' then the people will be driven to resistance, and revolution will be both legitimate and possible.[164] Resistance is then justified when the three interrelated criteria of legitimate government have all been transgressed; when the government's acts are not in accordance with law and there is no legal redress, when the government's actions are not in accordance with the general good, and when the government's no longer enjoys the consent of the people, and the sufficient proof of each of these is demonstrated by the fact of their rebellion.

The dissolution of the government is thus distinguished from the resistance either of an individual to the government, or of the whole of the people to an individual act of government.[165] However, even the overthrow of the government does not involve the

---

[161] Ibid., §208. p. 422

[162] Ibid., §230, p. 435. Turbulent men, over-keen to stir up political dissent, will do so only 'to their own just ruine and perdition'.

[163] Ibid., §209, p. 423; and see §230.

[164] Ibid., §210, p. 423.

[165] See my 'Resistance and economy in Dr Anglim's Locke', *Political Studies*, XXVI, 1 (1978).

dissolution of society, for both the trust that established government and the revocation of that trust which is what resistance is, are acts involving the previously existing society. By deriving government from a previously existing society, rather than following Hobbes in making society and government coeval, Locke explains how resistance, and the overthrow of a government can occur without reversion to the state of nature. Such a task is invariably undertaken by a *people*, for the powers of enforcing the law of nature 'can never revert to the Individuals again, as long as the Society lasts, but will always remain in the Community'.[166]

How can the government be dissolved? Either from within by subversion or from outside by conquest. Here Locke prepares the reader for a dialectical twist in the identity of the threat to government. Up to now the argument has presumed the threat to come from rebellious (albeit rightfully so) subjects. Locke now leads the reader to consider dissolution to result from the delinquent acts of government itself. Drawing attention again to the practices of the Stuart monarchs in influencing elections he says such action destroys the legislature, the 'soul' of the state, and the people are then at liberty to replace it or reassert the original form.[167] The example of a legislature involving the co-ordination of powers, of 'A single hereditary Person . . . An Assembly of Hereditary Nobility . . . An Assembly of Representatives Chosen *pro tempore*, by the People'[168] is transparently meant to refer to England itself. Locke is not designating this form of government as the definitive form of political legitimacy, merely as the form that exists in England. But having, in some sense been endorsed by the people, its subversion by a ruler would be a destructive and rebellious act. In this situation the legislature is changed if the 'single person' asserts laws on his own initiative, [169] if the freedom of the legislative assembly to meet and discuss is hindered, [170] if the electoral process is arbitrarily changed, [171] or if the ruler delivers his people to foreign powers,[172] all of which were charges laid – and justly so – at Charles and James. Finally, the abandonment of government by the executive – almost certainly a late insertion referring to James's flight in 1688 – dissolves not only the government, but (confusingly in view of what Locke says elsewhere about its capacity to survive the demise of government) even society itself.[173]

Peoples' rights to resist tyranny extend to a right to resist in anticipation of it. For 'Men can never be secure from Tyranny, if there be no means to escape it, till they are perfectly under it: and therefore it is, that they have not only a Right to get out of it, but to prevent it.'[174] Pressing home his radical twist to the source of rebellion, Locke insists that the

---

[166] *Second Treatise*, §243, pp. 445–6.

[167] Ibid., §212.

[168] Ibid., §213, p. 426.

[169] Ibid., §214, p. 426.

[170] Ibid., §215.

[171] Ibid., §216.

[172] Ibid., §217.

[173] Ibid., §219. The Bill of Rights, brought in by parliament in 1689, listed precisely these, amongst other misdemeanours of James II. He had assumed 'a power of dispensing with and suspending laws, and the execution of laws without the consent of parliament.' The bill felt it necessary to assert the 'freedom of speech, and debates or proceedings in parliament'. It charged him with 'violating the freedom of election of members to serve in parliament' and in the end described him as 'having abdicated the government' (E.N. Williams, *The Eighteenth-Century Constitution* (Cambridge, 1970), pp. 26–28.

[174] *Second Treatise*, §220, p. 429.

resistance of the people to government in these circumstances cannot be, strictly speaking, rebellion. For to rebel is, literally, to re-introduce a state of war. The point of Locke's earlier discussion about the distinction between the state of nature and the state of war now acquires full significance. For in overriding the agreed institutional limitations on the exercise of power, governments and magistrates – indeed elected legislatures too, no matter how representative – will have made that very bid for absolute power which Locke earlier identified with the state of war, a state in which contractual agreements – between people and rulers – are void, and the society recovers the full right to exercise its natural rights of self-preservation. Rulers who have perverted the ends of their rule in such a way as to pose a threat no longer exercise authority, they may retain power but they have no right on their side; it is, properly speaking, they who are rebels.[175] Resistance to such rulers is not resistance to authority, for authority exists only where force and right coincide.

This stress on delinquent governors as the true rebels meshed well with the meaning of 'revolution', later applied to the events of 1688-9, although used only twice by Locke in his *Treatise*. Since the French Revolution the term has conjured up for us the idea of the innovative transformation of the political and social order of a society. In the seventeenth century this was not so. A revolution was literally that, a turning back in the process of history, cyclically conceived following the ideas made famous by Plato, Polybius or Machiavelli. It was a return to a principle or rule from which there had been a corruption or deviation.

Although Locke thus provides an ultimate justification for resistance to government, resistance is conceived of as leading to the re-establishment of a political order which had been upset or lost, rather than, as in most modern revolutions, to the creation of an innovative social order. The political principles to which the people make appeal are not, or rather for Locke, should not be, a matter of their mere subjective will; they are the objectively discoverable principles of the law of nature. This said, Locke of course recognizes that principles require interpretation, and he is insistent that in the event '*The People shall be Judge*'.[176]

Despite Locke's stress on the difference in principle that exists between what is objectively right and what the people decide, between natural law and popular sovereignty, the possibility of the people mistaking is not one which appears to worry Locke unduly, at least in the context of his political thought. But the notion that the people's beliefs were in some sense the ultimate arbiters if not of political right, then of political power, that is, as so many thinkers of the next century were to put it, that 'government

---

[175] The explicit claim of executive or legislative rebellion is made at ibid., §227, p. 434, 'In both the forementioned Cases . . . those who are guilty are *guilty of Rebellion*'. That legislatures as well as executives can be tyrannical is also asserted there, and at §222, p. 430.

[176] Ibid., §240, p. 445; again at §242, p. 445, 'the proper *Umpire*, in such a Case, should be the Body of the People'. This is a practical maxim; the real arbiter, Locke seems to feel, is God, who decides the outcome of such conflicts (§241). The implicit congruency between the decision of the people and the will of God was taken up in the title of one of the most popular pamphlets of the century, *Vox Populi, Vox Dei* (The voice of the people, the voice of God). The text of the pamphlet comprised substantial unattributed quotations from the *Second Treatise* and it is one of the most plausible vehicles for the popularisation of Locke's views. On this see Richard Ashcraft and M.M .Goldsmith, 'Locke, revolution principles and the formation of whig ideology', *Historical Journal* 26, 4 (1983).

is founded on opinion', did raise two vital questions: what was the relationship between opinion and the objective moral law? and secondly how were the people's opinions shaped and formed?[177] This 'sociology of belief' as we would today call it, was not only to be one of the major preoccupations of the next century, it was to acquire a permanent place in the political topography of modernity.

---

[177] Amongst the major thinkers who explicitly subscribed to the view that government was founded on opinion, were Montesquieu, Hume, Madison, Burke, J.S. Mill and, via his theory of ideology, Marx.

III

David Hume

Introduction

Hume's political thought is elusive. The *Enquiries* and the *Treatises* are full-scale works of philosophy, and only towards the end do they contain material which is obviously political. Even this by no means seems to amount to a theory of politics. The *Essays* do indeed contain a lot of political material; but the essay form has the effect of fragmenting their impact. Furthermore, they deal with issues which relate quite closely to eighteenth-century concerns and controversies, which makes them seem irrelevant today. Finally, the intellectual relationship between the sceptically thrusting philosophical system, and the discursive and occasional material in the *Essays* is difficult to articulate. Yet Hume is a thinker of immense importance. His account of the operations of the human mind exercised a strong influence on philosophy in general and on moral philosophers in particular until well into the next century, indeed arguably down to today. Major English philosophical works of the twentieth century such as A.J. Ayer's *Language, Truth and Logic* are heavily influenced by Hume and it is common to read books on Hume from which one might assume he was alive and well today. This can be misleading, since like any other thinker, many of his formulations sprang from the philosophical preoccupations of his own time, and are best understood as responses to those questions. Moreover to treat Hume's theory of understanding and moral philosophy in isolation from his wider social theory is to isolate them from the very context in which he was most concerned to locate them. For Hume was preoccupied with the way in which our experience, including our social, political and economic experience, formed and shaped our beliefs about the world. Identifying the forces shaping our moral and political beliefs was a major concern for eighteenth-century thinkers, preoccupied as they were with maintaining political stability, and painfully aware of how easily it could be undermined if religious fanaticism, political bigotry or sheer greed gained the upper hand. Like most thinkers of the Enlightenment, Hume saw the new elegance and civility of polite society as a token of the refinement and progress of humanity. But he did not take this for granted, he was aware that progress could be reversed, that support for the existing order depended on a proper understanding and nurture of the opinions and beliefs that sustained it.

Hume's methodological assumptions and the limits of understanding

The theological origins of the philosophy of belief and morals

At the start of the eighteenth century questions of epistemology and questions about the basis of morality were still inextricably entwined in theology. Questions about the limits of human knowledge, had, as Locke himself acknowledged in his famous essay on the subject, grown out of attempts to establish the limits of religious certainty.[1] This in turn had important political implications, for what could be established by way of dogma and ceremonial could legitimately be imposed. Toleration was only important in things where certainty was unachievable, or in 'matters indifferent'.

From the 1690s an acrimonious debate was waged about the limits of religious certainty, in which Locke's philosophy played a significant role.[2] This was largely, although not completely, an argument about the propriety of using rational and empirical criteria in assessing matters of religious belief. The Anglican church was, against Catholicism – a considerable threat under Charles II and James II – committed to an empirical epistemology. On their view, the evidence for Christ's life, and especially his resurrection, the proof obtained by 'doubting' Thomas, rested on empirical evidence.[3] The Catholic church, in its insistence on the doctrine of transubstantiation confused the status of the evidence of our senses, and so threw into doubt the basis on which Christianity rested. Some Anglican critics went further and charged Catholics with going against 'reason' as well as against 'evidence'. Here however, Anglicans were on more difficult ground. For as well as Catholics they had to beware of Dissenters, many of whom distinguished themselves from Anglicans by denying the Trinity – support for which united Catholics and Anglicans. Anglicans did not argue that there was empirical evidence for the Trinity, but they did argue – using the old scholastic line that there were some things that were not against reason, but above it – that there were no reasons for refusing to accept the Trinity on faith. Their deist opponents argued that we could not be asked to believe propositions which contravened either our normal experience or our reason, and that consequently the Trinity was an indefensible, indeed, an

[1] John Locke, *An Essay Concerning Human Understanding* (Oxford, 1975), 'The Epistle to the Reader', p. 7. Cranston explains the nature of the 'Subject very remote from this', as 'the principles of morality and revealed religion'. M. Cranston, *John Locke, a biography* (Oxford, 1985), pp. 140–1.

[2] For the beginnings of the debate, John W. Yolton, *John Locke and the Way of Ideas* (Oxford, 1956); chapters two and three of Robert Sullivan *John Toland and the Deist Controversy* (Harvard, 1982), contains a good recent treatment of the religious and epistemological issues, and an overview is provided by Leslie Stephen, *English Thought in the Eighteenth Century* (2 Vols, London, 1881), vol. 1, chs 2–4. But there is no modern overall treatment which relates these concerns to politics, as they clearly were related for many contemporaries, although see the extremely suggestive essay by J. G. A. Pocock, 'The Problem of the Enlightenment', in *Culture and Politics from Puritanism to Enlightenment*, ed. Perez Zagorin (Berkeley, 1980), who suggests reasons why the British focus of the Enlightenment debate shifted away from the religious faith–secular epistemology axis which it largely assumed on the continent.

[3] Bishop Edward Stillingfleet, *The Doctrine of the Church of Rome Truly represented by a Protestant of the Church of England* (1686), pp. 50–4: 'some of the most important articles of the Christian faith do suppose the evidence of our senses to be true.'

incomprehensible article of faith.[4] The more extreme traditionalists tended to reply that it was precisely because these 'mysteries' were irreducible to reasonable propositions that they were articles of faith, whilst hard-line deists argued that it was psychologically impossible to assent to an article of faith to which a clear meaning could not even be given. The religious argument thus opened up a path into the psychology of under-standing, belief and faith on which more determinedly secular thinkers later drew.

As well as discussing the secular limitations of knowledge, the second major area thrown up by these debates was the question of whether there could be a secular grounding for morals. Indeed the two questions could hardly be separated as long as morality was seen to be absolutely dependent on religion, and a matter of knowledge or ignorance of God's command. For the traditionalist, God played two essential and related roles in moral theory. Firstly by issuing moral commands (the Ten Commandments, the Sermon on the Mount, etc.), he declared what the content of morality was, to an otherwise confused humanity who might be unable to deduce it from their circumstances, an operation which some, at any rate, thought should be possible. Secondly, by revealing to humanity an eschatology of judgement and damnation, religion provided motives sufficient to make man to adhere to that moral order. Attempts to establish a secular basis for morality had therefore to operate at two distinct levels to meet objections that 'natural morality' failed to parallel these divine roles. They had first to show that clear and unequivocal moral insights were attainable without revelation, and secondly they had to show that the motives needed to sustain moral behaviour could be established without the fear of hell fire.

Such attempts pursued broadly speaking three tactics. There were those, following Shaftesbury, and Hutcheson, who accounted for morality as a kind of intuited or innate 'moral sense', almost a natural faculty, which, whilst it might require cultivation (a great deal for Shaftesbury, less so for Hutcheson), was in principle available to all. Then there were those who following Hobbes attempted to establish morality on the untrustworthy grounds of psychological egoism. Indeed at the motivational level, traditional moralists fell into this group, and were amongst the most outspoken here, quite unashamedly making morality a matter of weighing paradisical gains against earthly pleasure. Thirdly there were those who attempted to demonstrate that morals were a matter of pure reasoning, immorality a kind of contradiction.[5]

It was from within this context that Hume began his investigations. We know that he burnt a massive essay book in which he had discussed various theological arguments. He also submitted some of his moral philosophy to Hutcheson for criticism.

The experimental method

Although he repudiated (unsuccessfully) the term deist, there is also no doubt that Hume was determined, like them, to try and establish a wholly secular and naturalistic theory

---

[4] The notorious deist John Toland wrote that God's revealed religion couldn't contradict experience since 'if what he said did not agree with their common notions' they wouldn't understand him; why should God not want to be understood? John Toland, *Christianity not Mysterious* (1696), p. 133.

[5] For an anthology see *British Moralists*, ed. L. A. Selby-Bigge (2 vols, Oxford, 1897, repr. New York, 1967).

of human understanding, morality and politics. In doing so he acknowledged the influence of the two figures who dominated the intellectual life of the century, Newton in the natural sciences and Locke in epistemology and the human sciences.[6] Hume attributed the success of these thinkers to two methodological devices which he determined to follow himself. These were the principles of economy of explanation, and that of empiricism.

Newton's methodology included the recommendation that we should, other evidence being equal, always prefer that explanation which is simplest and most economical in that it used the least number of explanatory categories in order to account for the event in question. Thus, to take a then-current example: Hume argued that in explaining how human beings make judgements – of fact, and about morality, and in art – we should, if at all possible, relate all these to a single mental process, or the fewest possible elements of mental activity, rather than attributing to human beings different faculties or 'senses' to account for each of the various kinds of judgement they made: factual, moral and aesthetic.[7]

This is a self-conscious application of Newtonian method. Newton's famous claim that he would not 'feign hypotheses' in order to provide explanations of what he could not empirically verify, led him to resist invitations to attribute a non-material 'force' to gravity, which was known only through its effects. Instead, for the most part, he claimed ignorance of how gravity worked and only that he had created a mathematical account of observable effects. This sceptical caution informs Hume's method throughout, and, although he does frame hypothetical accounts of the origins of the virtues and political institutions, he tries to anchor them rigorously in appeals to the experienced properties of consciousness. Expressing the ambitious hope that he can advance the moral sciences as much as the natural had been, Hume clearly alludes to Newton in suggesting he has found, in the association of ideas 'a kind of ATTRACTION, which in the mental world will be found to have as extraordinary effects as in the natural, and to shew itself in as many and various forms.'[8]

Hume repeats Hobbes's sarcastic criticism of the 'schoolmen' for supposedly multiplying fictitious explanatory entities which were as numerous as the different events to be explained.

> I found that the moral Philosophy transmitted to us by Antiquity, labour'd under the same Inconvenience that has been found in their natural philosophy, of being entirely

---

[6] Hume also mentions Shaftesbury, Mandeville, Hutcheson (with whom he corresponded) and Butler; see David Hume, *A Treatise of Human Nature*, ed. L .A. Selby-Bigge (Oxford, 1888 [London, 1739]), xxi. (All references are to this edition, hereafter referred to as *Treatise*) Although Hume adopted the methods of Locke and Newton in his attempts to found a secular understanding of man and morals, this should not be taken to imply that either of those thinkers thought their methods had secular implications. Each was a devout, if dubiously orthodox Anglican.

[7] *Treatise*, p. 282, as in the natural sciences: ' 'tho' the effects be many, the principles, from which they arise, are commonly but few and simple, and . . . 'tis the sign of an unskilful naturalist to have recourse to a different quality in order to explain every different operation'; so in moral philosophy 'to invent without scruple a new principle to every new phænomenon, instead of adapting it to the old; to overload our hypotheses with a variety of this kind; are certain proofs, that none of these principles is the just one, and that we desire, by a number of falsehoods, to cover our ignorance of the truth.'

[8] Ibid., p. 13.

Hypothetical, and depending more upon invention than Experience. Every one consulted his Fancy in erecting Schemes of Virtue and Happiness, without regarding human Nature, upon which every moral Conclusion must depend. This [human nature] therefore I resolved to make my principle Study, and the source from which I wou'ld derive every Truth in Criticism, as well as Morality.[9]

Explanations of how moral judgements could be made, should, he thought, be constructed from the simplest and most intuitively obvious properties of consciousness as we experience it. At a philosophical level then, Hume was intent on establishing the basis for human understanding, and judgements of all kinds on an 'experimental' basis; a slightly misleading term since by it he means not active intervention in, or control of phenomena, but allowing as evidence or explanation only that which was capable of being experienced by the senses, or through introspection. In this sense history is (or should be) experimental being 'so many collections of experiments, by which the politician or moral philosopher fixes the principles of his science', a science made possible by the assumption of a certain basic uniformity in our underlying human natures.[10] Thus in the Introduction to the *Treatise* he says:

And tho' we must endeavour to render all our principles as universal as possible, by tracing up our experiments to the utmost, and by explaining all effects from the simplest and fewest causes, 'tis still certain we cannot go beyond experience.[11]

In the first of his three *Treatises*, that on understanding, this method is applied to the question of human beings' understanding of the world. The analysis of Hume's project has occupied scholars for two and a half centuries now, with the level of interest quickening in this century, since Anglo-American philosophy returned to similar concerns. There will only be space to pick out those issues which proved most relevant for his moral and political thought.

Human psychology

Perceptions of the mind, insists Hume, are of two kinds, *impressions* and *ideas*. Impressions are the most vital and involuntary, and result from our senses. Ideas are less immediate and distinct, and result from our reflection and thinking about those impressions, or parts of them; for the mind is capable of analysing and reworking ideas which originate from impressions. This accounts, for example, for our ability to conceive the idea of a mermaid or a unicorn, without ever having seen either: they are composed of parts of beings of which we have had impressions. Hume's first principle then, is that 'all our simple ideas proceed either mediately or immediately from their corresponding

---

[9] *The Letters of David Hume*, ed. J. Y. T. Greig (2 vols, Oxford, 1932), vol. I, p. 16.

[10] David Hume, *Enquiries Concerning Human Understanding and Concerning the Principles of Morals*, ed. L.A.Selby-Bigge (2nd Ed., Oxford, 1902 [London, 1777]) p. 83. (All references are to this edition, hereafter refered to as *Enquiries*) Hume believed there were real and regular causes operating in nature, but denied we could ever know them. The best we could achieve was a kind of 'harmony between the course of nature and the succession of our ideas'. Ibid., p. 54.

[11] *Treatise*, p. xxi.

impressions'. The extent of Hume's scepticism is made apparent when he immediately draws our attention to the fact that this does not prove or disprove the issue of innate ideas. Impressions, it is true, do not derive from anything else we are aware of, any 'precedent perception', and they do appear to be 'conveyed by our senses', but this does not permit the conclusion to be drawn that they, as it were, come from outside. Impressions are distinguished from ideas *in our consciousness*, merely by their force and liveliness, and not by their external origin, they 'arise in the soul originally from unknown causes'.[12] The extraordinary fact is, as Bishop Berkeley had already shown, that the most scrupulous empiricism – reliance on the evidence of experience – does not support a secure belief in an external world independent of consciousness. Instead it stops short at the content of our experiencing minds, a content which remains resolutely idealist. It is this conclusion which, in a curious way, links Hume, the paradigmatic British empiricist, as we shall see, with Hegel, the paradigmatic idealist.[13]

Hume next notes a fact of human psychology noted by both Hobbes and Locke and much remarked on by philosophers and writers of the century: that the mind appears to connect or to associate together quite different impressions, in such a way that the occurrence of one idea leads, almost involuntarily, to the other. The idea of association had already claimed the attention of essayists and was soon to form the basis of an entire sprawling novel – Lawrence Stern's *Tristram Shandy*. Yet Hume claims he is the first to analyse and classify the principles by which association operates. Particular impressions, he points out, can become associated in the mind through resemblance to one another, they can be located close in space to one another, and they can follow sequentially – as cause and effect.

Resemblance is of the greatest importance in discussing the issue to which Hume next turns, that of general or abstract ideas. The problem of abstract ideas or of the general words which designate them is, for an empiricist, or 'experimental' philosopher, that such abstract ideas do not correspond to any particular impression or idea (at least, if by idea we mean something like a mental picture). When we think of a house, or a triangle, it must always be a *particular* house or triangle. So it seems, either we must (contrary to the fact of our everyday use of them) deny the existence of abstract ideas, or we must relax our criterion of empiricism to allow the mental existence of something that could not be known through experience. The assertion (by Locke) that general ideas are nothing but particular ones attached to a single word is, claims Hume 'one of the greatest and most valuable discoveries of late years'.[14] Hume offers an explanation of how abstract ideas arise, which relies on observations about the natural characteristics of the mind. There is, he observes elsewhere 'a kind of laziness of the mind', by which we do not take note of the individual characteristics of each particular thing that we see. Rather we lump together experiences that have a certain rough and ready resemblance to one another. It is as though the mental effort of remembering each particular thing's characteristics were

---

[12] Ibid., p. 7; *Enquiries*, pp. 19, 22.

[13] Bishop George Berkeley's *Treatise Concerning the Principles of Human Knowledge*, had been published in 1710. It's subtitle indicates the connections between epistemological and religious and moral issues outlined above: 'wherein the chief causes of error and difficulty in the sciences, with the grounds of scepticism, atheism, and irreligion are enquired into.' The unusual, and for some, paradoxical likeness, between Hegel and Hume is explored in detail by Chris Berry, *Hume, Hegel and Human Nature* (The Hague 1982).

[14] *Treatise*, p. 17.

too much for us. Instead, our mind seems to sort ideas out into conceptual boxes or categories containing those with roughly similar characteristics.[15] Thus whilst we have names for individual people, whom we learn to identify as individuals; when dealing with trees or plants we will normally be satisfied with tree or plant – unless we are botanists. But even if we are botanists we only label *kinds*, of plants, and not individuals. Hume emphasises the role of habit, custom and socialisation into what our society considers useful distinctions: 'A particular idea becomes general by being annexed to a general term; that is, to a term, which from a customary conjunction has a relation to many other particular ideas and readily recalls them in the imaginations.'[16] Habit, which is to play such a large part in his political thought, is already given a pivotal role even in his account of understanding, a role which is made even more explicit in the *Enquiry*'s claim that 'Custom is the great guide of human life'. Custom, for Hume, sustains our epistemology, our practical knowledge and our society.[17]

That the connection between ideas we learn to think of as the 'same', is one made in the mind, and not in the world, emphasises a pervasive and radically disturbing feature of Hume's analysis: subtly, but insistently, Hume's account of understanding draws into, and ascribes to the mind, relations and properties which commonsense might attribute to the world. It thus lays the foundation for both a sociology of belief (a theory that belief is determined by the circumstances of the believer), and the move towards idealism (the doctrine that the only kinds of things of which we can have direct knowledge are ideas). This becomes particularly important in his account of causation.

Causation is important for Hume, as it is for every investigator of the social world, because it is upon the presumption of uniformity of causation that we base our claim that there are general truths about the nature of humankind and the world to be discovered. But it is also important because his account of how we form ideas (which we use when reasoning) from impressions (which we experience via our senses) presumes that there is some regular causal link, not only between the ideas and the impressions but between them and the objects believed to cause them. Thus the link between reality, our impressions, and our reasoning, and therefore between our thinking and the real world, is, we presume, causal. Causation is what guarantees, or seems to guarantee this link. But Hume's analysis renders this guarantee very frail indeed.

Cause and effect is one of the three 'relations' or 'associations' between ideas or impressions, pointed out earlier by Hume. What, according to him, is the nature of the cause and effect relationship? Hume takes this question to mean what are the component experiential units of the idea of causation. He picks out three characteristics: contiguity – for two things to appear as cause and effect they must appear at some point to touch, either directly or *via* some series of intermediaries; secondly priority – cause must precede effect in time. But these two experiences are not in themselves enough to complete the idea of a cause; temporal succession and physical contact occur without causation. What we take to be absolutely necessary for causality is the idea of necessary

---

[15] Ibid., pp. 17–25.

[16] Ibid., p. 22; socialisation, p. 20; and see p. 60.

[17] *Enquiry Concerning the Human Understanding,* Oxford, 1902), p. 44; and 'Without the influence of custom, we should be entirely ignorant of every matter of fact beyond what is immediately present to the memory and senses. We should never know how to adjust means to ends, or to employ our natural powers in the production of any effect. There would be an end at once of all action, as well as of the chief part of speculation.' Ibid., p. 45.

connection.[18] Whilst we feel it to be true, there is, Hume argues, no reason to believe in the ubiquity of causation. More destructively, there is no sensory evidence of the 'necessary connection' that seems so essential a part of the idea of causality. What looks like an ability to discern causes, is simply an ability to state a general principle under which the individual example falls, but this is no more than a generalisation of past experiences. Take for example the bursting of a balloon near a fire. We could say that heat caused the balloon to burst because we know Boyle's law asserts that heated gases expand, and that balloons have limited elasticity. But in our *experience*, the bursting of a balloon is a unique event, and Boyle's law is simply a general statement of similar unique events: neither the particular experience, or the 'law' induced from a number of them, reveal the 'necessary connection' which we like to think so essential for a true cause to exist. However hard we look, Hume argues, we never perceive a *cause*, what we see is one event following another. There is no warrant in experience, or through rational analysis for believing in the real existence of necessary connection. This aspect of causation, far from being a natural fact about the world is simply an idea that the *mind* contributes to contiguous sequential events in its experience. Causation is simply one of the ways in which the 'laziness of the mind' brings together, or allows ideas to associate:

> When the mind, therefore, passes from the idea or impression of one object to the idea or belief of another it is not determined by reason, but by certain principles, which associate together the ideas of these objects, and unite them in the imagination. Thus tho' causation be a philosophical relation as implying contiguity, succession, and constant conjunction yet 'tis only so far as it is a natural relation, and produces an union among our ideas, that we are able to reason upon it or draw any inferences from it.[19]

Hume's position, as he recognises, is a very destructive one. It destroys the basis of our most fundamental beliefs about the regularity of phenomena in the external world and the integrity of our relationship to it. This profound scepticism is called pyrrhonism, after the founder of the ancient school of scepticism, and the only escape Hume sees from it is not an intellectual one, but to simply let our natural dispositions reassert their presumption of reality and regularity on which we act, but cannot prove:

> Most fortunately it happens, that since reason is incapable of dispelling these clouds, nature herself suffices . . . by relaxing this bent of mind, or by some avocation . . . I dine, I play a game of backgammon, I converse, and am merry with my friends; and when after three or four hours amusement I would return to these speculations, they appear so cold, so strained, and ridiculous, that I cannot find it in my heart to enter into them any further.[20]

The implication here would seem to be that philosophy leaves everything as it is. Since it can do nothing but establish universal doubt, we had perhaps better let it alone, and revert to what common sense suggests is the case. This would have no political implications at all since there would be no *philosophical* criteria for being more sceptical

---

[18] *Treatise*, pp. 75–7.

[19] Ibid., pp. 92, 94.

[20] Ibid., p. 269.

of one political position than another – all would be equally vulnerable. But although the *Treatise* perhaps gives that impression, it is not quite where the matter rests.[21] There is a sense in which Hume regards himself as having established a position which he believes *does* bear differentially on the wilder and more enthusiastic political positions which had been adopted within the last century and were still held by some of his contemporaries. For if scepticism concerning the reliability of some of our most everyday experiences is in order, how much more sceptical ought we to be of the extravagant claims to certainty of religious, moral or political bigots? Hume's politics can be considered then 'philosophical' in the colloquial sense of recommending our being, as one study has deftly put it, 'rationally or sensibly calm under trying circumstances'.[22]

In the second version of his philosophy, written some ten years later, the *Enquiry Concerning Human Understanding*, Hume is clearer about distinguishing different degrees of scepticism. Here he rejects extreme scepticism as incompatible with our natures since 'though I may doubt that a piece of bread will effect its usual course and nourish me, I invariably eat it, and doubting the existence of other beings I nevertheless talk and discuss with them.' But he claims 'there is indeed, a more *mitigated* scepticism, or *academical* philosophy, which may be both durable and useful' and he goes on to point out the role of 'mitigated scepticism' in curbing dogmatism, obstinacy and pride in opinions. By way of criteria for distinguishing between reasonably and unreasonably grounded assertions Hume introduces a famous distinction between different kinds of mental activity each of which is limited but competent in its sphere, and which between them comprise all the human mind is truly competent to perform. They are abstract reasoning, which concerns itself with the logical properties of words or numbers, and empirical demonstration which ascertains the truth or otherwise of matters of fact. Whilst the first sort of argument can supply us with guaranteed and necessarily true statements, they are truths which are dependent on the meanings we ourselves have assigned to the terms in which they are stated. Thus for example, the truth that two plus two equals four is a truth consequent solely on the conventional meanings we have given to the words 'two' and 'plus' and 'equals' and 'four'. By contrast, any assertion of a matter of fact – for example the claim that there is grass outside my study window – is dependent on empirical evidence about the case which it asserts. We don't need to collect *examples* of pairs of twos adding up to four to verify the claim about the mathematical relationship, whereas we would need to look outside my study to verify the claim about the grass. Now, whereas the first kind of reasoning is, if correct, incontrovertible, the second case could, given a snowfall, or a dry summer, quite easily be otherwise. These two principles thought Hume, would, if strictly applied, destroy much of what passed for the accumulation of knowledge in human history:

> When we run over our libraries, persuaded of these principles what havoc must we make? If we take in our hand any volume of divinity or school metaphysics, for instance; let us ask, 'Does it contain any abstract reasoning concerning quantity or

[21] See R. H. Popkin, 'David Hume: his Pyrrhonism' *Philosophical Quarterly* I (1951) and in *Hume*, ed. V. C. Chappell (New York, 1966); see also David Miller, *Philosophy and Ideology in Hume's Political Thought* (Oxford, 1982), p. 37.

[22] Duncan Forbes, *Hume's Philosophical Politics* (Cambridge, 1975), p. 219. Forbes's book is the most important attempt to locate Hume's political thought in its immediate political context.

number?' No. 'Does it contain any experimental reasoning concerning matter of fact and existence? No. Commit it then to the flames: for it can contain nothing but sophistry and illusion.[23]

Hume's limited scepticism rules out the more outlandish religious and metaphysical enthusiasms. But his focus on the operations of the human mind has implications for what should most concern the sceptical social scientist, and that is the assessment of social and political belief in the terms of the natural properties of the mind, that is to say a focus on how beliefs *come to be held*, and how they *work*, rather than whether they are *true*.

Moral and political philosophy is, in an important way less troubled by Hume's empirical scepticism than natural philosophy. For whilst Hume's account of understanding undermines our faith in the coherence and knowability of the external material world by claiming many of its supposed characteristics to be properties of the mind, it nevertheless for that reason holds out higher hopes for the investigation of the world of consciousness, of which morals and politics form such an important part. In an important way, Hume's empiricism, or reliance on the senses, paves the way for idealism, although the full implications of this are not drawn until the work of Hegel some sixty years later. The way in which the mind forms moral and political ideas, and applies them in judgements is the subject of Hume's third *Treatise*, of morals.

The natural history of morality

The theory of the natural virtues

Hume's account of morality is heavily structured by the observations he had already made about the working of the human understanding, and the limiting of reasonable and true propositions to the two cases of dealing with the relations between ideas and those describing matters of fact.

The first is his claim that reason can only deal in matters of fact or the relations between ideas. Consequently, if reason can treat of morality, morality must turn out to be one or the other, or some combination of these.

Secondly he makes strong claims, reminiscent of Hobbes, about the relationship between reason and desire. In a famous and dramatic phrase he declared 'reason is and ought to be the slave of the passions', and insisted that as a result 'tis not contrary to reason for me to prefer the destruction of the whole world to the scratching of my little finger'. His point here is the same as Hobbes's: reason can never be a motive to action. Moreover, particular desires cannot be considered reasonable or unreasonable in themselves, but only inasmuch as they are based on true or false beliefs, or are consistent with or contradict other projects or desires which we have.[24]

Hume's target here is, at least in part, those rationalist moralists who attempted to reduce immorality to some kind of contradiction, or in Hume's terms 'relation between ideas'. Such a view was famously put forward by William Wollaston in *The Religion of*

---

[23] *Enquiry*, p. 165.   [24] *Treatise*, pp. 414–16.

Nature Delineated (1722). Wollaston argued all wrongdoing is a kind of lying. Theft is pretending that something which is not your property actually is. Fornication is to act as if you were married when you are not. Moral censure then involves the identification of contradictions between what is true and what is falsely presented as true.[25] Hume points out that such arguments do not in any case reveal the grounds of morality, since the ability to identify individual acts as contradictions presupposes previously known moral principles, which cannot be based on the identification of contradictions without creating a vicious circle.[26]

This objection is important in signalling a major feature of Hume's discussion of morality, and a distinction which, if ignored, can cause great difficulty in understanding Hume's account. That distinction is between explaining how an individual moral judgment can be made (which can invoke the notion of a moral rule), and explaining how a moral rule or convention arises in the first place (which cannot). This will be discussed further below.

The third point he makes is about the relationship between moral judgements and the other sort of reasoning we can sensibly engage in: empirical demonstration. Once again Hume denies that moral qualities are simple empirical properties. Morality is not a fact about the world; good and bad are not qualities that inhere in things, or act in the way that size and shape, or even the less objective qualities of colour or taste do.[27] Nor are they in any way analogous to those qualities, in such a way that they could be intuited by a special faculty of the mind. Once again there is a polemical thrust to this claim. Francis Hutcheson, to whom Hume had submitted his *Treatise* before publication, was the most famous of previous philosophers who had experimented with the notion of a 'moral sense' capable of identifying inherently good or bad actions. Although Hutcheson was trying to steer a path between the shockingly secular moral theory of the third Earl of Shaftesbury who tried to ground morality in taste, and those severe churchmen who wanted to maintain the identification of morality with the will or command of a terrifying God, he was himself criticised for reducing morality to an animal instinct or feeling, by religious moralists, as well as by rationalists who thought morality must derive from something more dignified than the feelings we share with animals. The clergyman John Balguy for example typically acknowledged the role of feeling or sentiment in *motivating* our moral actions, but insisted that this could never itself *constitute* their morality.[28] Hume's position was even more outrageous, in that he sought to sever not only the mechanism by which moral feeling is experienced, but the very standards of morality itself, from any connection with God or the transcendent. Instead he sets out to show how morality emerges from a series of interactions between the natural world and the known (through introspection) properties of our minds. In effect instead of trying to discover what Moral Good essentially is, he tries to discover how we come to believe it

---

[25] Wollaston's work is excerpted in *British Moralists*, vol. 2, p. 361ff. Hume's relationship to his contemporary moralists is well discussed in D. Fate Norton, *David Hume: Common Sense Moralist, Sceptical Metaphysician* (Princeton, 1982).

[26] *Treatise*, p. 462 (note).

[27] Ibid., pp. 468–9.

[28] John Balguy, *The Foundation of Moral Goodness*, part II, pp. 42, 65ff. in part in *British Moralists*, vol. 2, pp. 196–97.

to be constituted in the way we do. In effect he sets out to write an anatomy and natural history of our moral beliefs.

Given Hume's rejection of metaphysics, and his denial that morality could either be deduced from reason or be a fact about the world, there would seem to be little left that it could be. There are however some matters of fact which are not about the external world at all but about our own psychologies, and Hume believes that moral, and political judgement are primarily phenomena of the human mind and are to be understood as such. Although extreme in form, Hume's position here is consistent with other major political thinkers of the century such as Montesquieu, Rousseau and Burke, all of whom insist that the basis of politics lies in the 'opinion' or beliefs of the citizens. Political philosophy as a result becomes greatly preoccupied with the properties and characteristics, as we should say today the sociology, of belief. Explicit recognition of this, and the radical decoupling of belief from its rational content would not occur until the aftermath of the French Revolution, in the invention of the term 'ideology' by Destutt De Tracy. But here, as so often, the phenomenon precedes the term.

Moral praise or blame, then, claims Hume, arises from a feeling or sentiment experienced within us at the contemplation of certain acts. Since, he insists there is no moral content in acts themselves, and since he denies the existence of intuitive moral standards, these feelings or sentiments must be explained by reference to something other than themselves.[29] The question is: How do we come by the feelings we do, and what differentiates them from other feelings – what, if anything, makes them peculiarly moral? Is there anything to differentiate our preference for benevolence and aversion to murderers from our preferences for certain types of ice-cream and aversion to say, spinach?

The moral role of the passions

To make these kind of distinctions we need to understand Hume's theory of the passions. By passions Hume does not mean the kind of uncontrollable urges supposedly extinguished by long woollen underwear. Passions for Hume, as for most writers of his time, include all of those desires and aversions which might motivate us to action. There are calm as well as violent passions.

Hume distinguishes between primary and secondary passions. These parallel a cognitive division between original and secondary impressions. Primary passions seem to 'arise originally in the soul, or in the body, whichever you please to call it, without any preceding thought or perception.'[30] Such passions are what we would call the natural or instinctual drives of hunger, sexuality and physical ease. Hume is less interested in these than in the secondary or reflective passions which result from a combination of primary passions and reflective ideas. Such passions may be calm or violent, a division which Hume seems to think conforms roughly to the feelings evoked by art or nature, and those evoked by human actions which once again he divides into direct (desire,

---

[29] 'No action can be virtuous, or morally good, unless there be in human nature, some motive to produce it distinct from the sense of its morality.' *Treatise*, p. 479.

[30] Ibid., p. 276.

aversion, grief, joy, hope, fear, despair and security) and indirect (pride, humility, ambition, vanity, love, hatred, envy, pity, malice, generosity). These latter passions are the most obviously social. The first pair: pride and humility (which turn out to be intimately related to morality)[31] derive, Hume suggests, from the consideration of some object of either value or derision associated with the self.[32] Hume's interest in the general principles which give rise to these feelings, and his relative unconcern for what they actually attach themselves to, is illustrated by his treatment of the latter. If we want to know what particular goods or qualities are the cause of pride or humility we need only consult ordinary usage: 'as custom and practice have . . . settled the just value of everything . . . and guide us by means of generally establish'd maxims, in the proportions we ought to observe in preferring one object to another.'[33]

Since morality moves us to action as well as to make judgements, something neither reason nor mere knowledge of facts is capable of, morality must be a form of passion.[34] But morality is different from other forms of passion in that it applies only to certain objects, and only under particular circumstances. Analysis of the circumstances in which morality comes into play, Hume thinks, will tell us much about it's nature and origins.

Firstly we do not apply moral judgements to inanimate objects. Although we may admire or fear natural phenomena such as earthquakes and volcanoes, we do not judge them morally good or bad. Even in the animal world, patricide or incest is not considered blameworthy in animals, as it is in humans. Moralists, such as those from Cicero onwards, who argue that these actions are culpable in men because they have knowledge of morality, whereas animals don't, still have the problem of explaining how we know, and what it is that immorality consists in.[35]

Secondly, moral judgements do not tell us more about the facts of the situation than we already knew. Just as a closer examination of a cause and effect relationship yields no further evidence of the necessary connection, so no close examination of, for example a ritual human sacrifice, will reveal empirical qualities which distinguish it from a failed operation – the same preparation of the subject, the same careful ritual surrounding the incision in the body, use of valuable substances, the same hierarchy of assistants etc.[36]

Thirdly, moral judgements, although connected with what is beneficial and harmful, cannot be applied simply to what benefits or harms the judge as an individual. To put it more formally, they are not, in any simple sense, identified with selfish passions. It cannot be simply because I benefit from it, that I judge an action morally good.[37] Moreover moral judgements are properly applied to the *motives* and character of the person

---

[31] Ibid., p. 473.

[32] Ibid., pp. 277–9.

[33] Ibid., p. 294.

[34] Ibid., p. 457.

[35] Ibid., pp. 467–8.

[36] 'Morality consists not in any *matter of fact*, which can be discovered by the understanding . . . The vice entirely escapes you as long as you consider the object. . . . [but] turn your reflection into your own breast, and find a sentiment of disapprobation . . . Here is a matter of fact; but 'tis the object of feeling, not of reason.' Ibid., pp. 468–9.

[37] 'Tis only when a character is considered in general, without reference to our peculiar interest, that it causes such a feeling or sentiment, as denominates it morally good or evil.' Ibid., p. 472.

performing the action (and this again explains why they are not applied to animals as beings supposed not to reflect on their actions).[38]

Miller points out that Hume here only assumes, but does not explain why moral blame should only attach to motive or settled dispositions rather than to actions and outcomes, and that the reason why this distinction should operate is problematic. Whilst it's true Hume offers no explanation of this it is also true that, in general both in law and in morality we do acknowledge the distinction he makes. A motorist who kills someone quite by accident, is not as culpable as a bank robber discharging a shotgun at his pursuer. Therefore, inasmuch as Hume is summarizing the evident characteristics of moral judgement, which, at this point in the *Treatise*, he is, there is every warrant for bringing it in. Explaining the basis of the distinction is a different enterprise which we must deal with next. But we could at least note here that the utility of our moral practices (of which Hume wants to make much) is surely best served by praising or blaming only those acts which are deliberate; and that the supply of good actions is most likely to be furthered by fostering dispositions to perform them rather than rewarding randomly accomplished examples of them. In this sense Hume's insistence on the motive rather than the act or its outcome is quite consistent both with our actual practice and with the utilitarian explanation of how such practice emerges and comes to be valued.

Vice and virtue then 'are not qualities in objects but perceptions in the mind' and they express approval or disapproval of actions in view of their general character rather than simply as they affect the individual speaker, on a particular occasion. These are not prescriptions, they are rather observations about the properties that moral terminology seems to have, they are, true to Hume's method, based on our own experience of what moral judgement (in general) seems to involve.

Given that morality is a complex response of this kind, which is not innate, how does it arise?

The moral role of sympathy

Hume attributes to human beings the capacity of sympathy. This is not an ad-hoc attribution brought in merely to plug a gap in the theory. Nor is it (yet) a moral virtue. It is, he thinks an observable fact about human beings; explicable through the powerful mental property of associating ideas. Passions can pass most easily between ideas or impressions linked in the mind on one or other of the grounds of association – resemblance, contiguity and cause and effect. We therefore find ourselves vicariously suffering, as it were through imagination, the passions we observe in other beings who resemble us or are close to us. This explains why we (mostly) feel more sympathy for humans than for animals, and amongst animals, more sympathy for those that resemble us, such as

---

[38] 'If any action be either virtuous or vicious, 'tis only as a sign of some quality or character. It must depend upon the durable principles of the MIND which extend over the whole of conduct, and enter into the personal character. Actions themselves, not proceeding from any constant principle, have no influence on love or hatred, pride or humility and consequently are never considered in morality.' Ibid., p. 575.

mammals, than for those such as reptiles, that do not.[39] Contiguity too is relevant. Hume notes that sympathy is more easily evoked by what is closer to us: the beggar before our eyes – destitute but perhaps not starving – than for the starving victims of a famine thousands of miles away in China. Nevertheless when we consider things in a moral light, we recognise that the accident of such proximity is not strictly speaking a relevant consideration.[40] Moral judgement then seems to be related to sympathy, but to have been modified in some way. How does this modification come about?

Since humans are similar, and tend to suffer in similar ways, in viewing someone in pain or suffering, the mind passes irresistibly , through the operation of association, from the spectacle of another's pain to the contemplation of ourselves in the same situation; and the hatred or dislike of the pain we would be suffering is transferred to theirs. Where what causes pain is a human being operating from apparently deliberate motives, the hatred will naturally be attached to the motives which give rise to the suffering. Since some dispositions are constantly productive of the motives giving rise to actions causing suffering, the censure that attaches to the acts is carried back to the disposition. Where there is a sufficient consensus amongst humans as to what dispositions and actions lead to agreeable, and what to disagreeable consequences for others, these judgements will tend to form a consistent pattern. This pattern, once recognised as such, can form the basis of a general and shared convention about which dispositions and actions lead to beneficial and which to harmful consequences. These will accordingly be subjected to praise and blame, thereby encouraging individuals to cultivate or avoid dispositions as appropriate. Subsequently the process of socialisation inducts individuals into those rules or principles which, as a result of association and the consensus of experience, have been adopted by the community.

There are thus three levels of explanation for moral action. The explanation of why an individual acts morally on a particular occasion is that such action is attached in the individual's mind to sentiments of approbation. At this level Hume is a 'moral sense' theorist. But unlike most such theorists he does not let matters rest here by arguing for, or worse, simply assuming, the givenness of such sentiments. We need to know *why* individuals feel this way. The answer to this question, and the next level of analysis, is that we internalise (if we have been socialised properly) from our fellows, those standards or principles which we see evoking praise or blame from those around us. But even this explanation does not yet get to the root of the matter, for it still begs the question as to why those standards or principles emerged in the first place. And the answer to that is that they arise from the connections established through association in the human mind between certain dispositions and actions, and their widely recognised painful or

[39] *Treatise*, pp. 317–9, 340–3, 369. There is of course, a more rational explanation for this in terms of our knowledge that mammals have more developed nervous systems and can therefore suffer more pain. However Hume clearly has a point: it is easier to drum up public support for the protection of animals which are soft and cuddly and have appealing faces. Endangered species of wart-hog have a harder time! Questioned about the grounds and extent of his vegetarianism, a friend of mine exhibited a clear application of Hume's principle: 'I don't eat 'owt wi' a FACE!'

[40] Except inasmuch as Hume characteristically observes that we can only affect what is close to us. Our moral duty he notes (passing from analysis to prescription) is to do good to those with whom we come into contact. Once again we may note the effectiveness of television, in bringing home to people's *senses*, the horrors of war and famine, and in leading to public outrage and action against both.

pleasurable outcomes. Hume, unlike his moralistic contemporaries, can reject a supposedly objective and given morality without being thrown back on Hobbesian egoism, because he can explain the *development* of more or less permanent moral sentiments from simple, non-moral properties of the mind. Moreover it is ironically because those properties include the irrational principle of association, that moral dispositions can be stable, and not, as Hobbes's seem to be, constantly subject to erosion by the persistence of rational egoistic calculation as a motive. This latter problem was a constant ground for criticism of Hobbes, and persistently led either to reassertions that morality must be grounded in God's command if it was to be effectual, or to rather lame assertions of the 'natural' existence of moral sentiments. The significance of Hume is that he provides the first convincing naturalistic account of morality, and shows that morality, like so much else in human nature has a discoverable natural history. Since the properties of the human mind which give rise to morality are themselves natural, there is a sense in which these virtues are natural, being a continuous outgrowth of the property of sympathy, itself derived from the natural association of ideas. However some virtues are more natural than others, and the 'natural history' of justice involves a different story from that of benevolence, the archetypical natural virtue.

Hume's account of the artificial virtues

In the case of the 'natural virtues' it is our natural sympathy which provides the original motive for the kind of actions that are then regularized, reinforced and sanctioned by social approbation. But, Hume points out, the range over which the sympathetic response is capable of operating is strictly limited. Because it is so closely tied to the associative mechanisms and experiences which give rise to it, sympathy does not easily extend to those with whom we do not have personal or relational ties. Sympathy is therefore inadequate as a foundational motive for those moral rules and practices which operate beyond the realm of personal association. Different rules are necessary in a large, impersonal, i.e. a commercial, society. Since justice (the general term by which Hume denotes these rules), often requires us to do things which are not conducive to our own immediate benefit, it cannot, either, in any simple sense derive from that other natural disposition, self-interest. Since the virtues necessary to regulate impersonal relations between individuals do not arise directly from natural motives, they must derive indirectly, and that is why Hume calls them artificial. They 'arise artificially, tho' necessarily from education, and human conventions.'[41] Nevertheless although not the direct motive for justice, self-interest must be the indirect principle at work, Hume thinks, if only because the passion justice is called on to restrain is the powerful and socially threatening one of self-interest, and only a similarly strong passion could counter it.[42]

Although produced indirectly, the artificial virtues must nevertheless be a response to some natural qualities of the human mind and the natural facts of human existence. In this qualified sense they are still 'natural', and indeed could even be considered 'laws of nature'. These qualities and facts are 'the selfishness and confin'd generosity of men,

---

[41] *Treatise*, p. 483.   [42] Ibid., pp. 491–2.

along with the scanty provision nature has made for his wants.'[43] If nature freely provided all our wants or if other humans were generous to the point of being unconcerned to secure their goods for themselves we should never have invented private property. Private property – the central category of Hume's conception of justice – grows up in the gap between human need and nature's provision, both facts of our existence.

A remarkable and very unsatisfying aspect of Hume's account is the very narrow scope he ascribes to the operation of 'justice'. He has virtually nothing to say about legal procedure, and is dismissive about the threat posed by the possibility of personal violence. The major, and virtually only rational threat to society which Hume sees comes from the vulnerability of our property to the acquisitiveness of others. Once this has been overcome 'there remains little or nothing to be done towards settling a perfect harmony and concord. All other passions besides this of interest are either easily restrain'd or are not of such pernicious consequence when indulged.' In establishing this he tells us he thinks there are only three kinds of goods which humans enjoy, the internal satisfaction of the mind, the enjoyment of our bodily freedom and integrity, and the possession of external goods. Nothing, he seems to suggest, can rob us of the first, and whilst 'the second can be ravish'd from us' he implies that this is unlikely since it 'can be of no advantage to him who deprives us of them' – a remark which reveals an astonishing degree of short-sightedness about the general level of violence, including sexual violence, in the eighteenth century.[44] Hume invites us to accept that it is only our external goods, that are both exposed and vulnerable to the violence of others. He concludes: 'As the improvement, therefore, of these goods is the chief advantage of society, so the instability of their possession, along with their scarcity, is the chief impediment.'[45] Whatever these limitations might lead us to think of Hume's general knowledge of human nature – on the street as it were – it clearly shows us one of his central concerns, namely to provide a theoretical basis for property rights and what was then known as 'commercial society', that is a society based on the impersonal exchange of goods and services amongst individuals not otherwise bound to each other through the natural ties of sympathy. The issue of a moral philosophy appropriate for a modernizing, commercial society had been a crucial one for Scots thinkers for over a generation.

The desirability or otherwise of Scotland accepting the modern economy of England had been a subject of heated debate since the Union of the Crowns in 1707. Initiated by Andrew Fletcher of Saltoun the debate continued to stimulate a tradition of reflection on the nature of property and the processes of economic change to which Scotland was so markedly subject, and culminated most famously in the work of Adam Smith. Modernizers and traditionalists clashed on the social effects of instituting modern notions of property rights and the exchange economy that went with it. Modernizers, picking up the challenge of Mandeville that 'Private vices, [yielded] Publick Benefits' strove to show how egoism, properly channeled, led to a coherent social world. As Smith famously put it, characterizing the motivational basis of commercial society 'It is not from the benevolence of the butcher, the brewer, or the baker, that we expect our dinner, but from

---

[43] Ibid., p. 495.

[44] Homicide rates fell dramatically in the eighteenth century, but violence against the person increased in the first part of it and was so much complained of Hume could not have been unaware of it. Lawrence Stone, 'Homicide and Violence', in *The Past and the Present Revisited*, (London, 1987).

[45] Ibid., p. 488.

their regard to their own self-interest'.[46] Smith however was no isolated figure, and Hume's concerns here, and later, more explicitly in his *Essays*, are firmly informed by this context in which the fundamental nature and characteristics of property rights in an exchange economy were explored and debated. The origin as well as the moral force of such rules, argues Hume, lies in the fact that they do, ultimately, serve our interests.[47]

The difficulty, however, with grounding justice in self-interest is, as Hume points out, that there are many particular occasions when justice is not in our individual, or even the general, interest, even though overall, and most of the time, it is. What is needed is some psychological account of how it is that we can become so attached to a rule as being in our interests, that we stick to it even when it isn't.[48] Since justice is artificial – a convention – and derives from self-interest, we seem to be well on the way to some kind of social contract. But Hume, briefly in the *Treatise*, and at greater length in the essay 'Of the Original Contract', goes out of his way to deny the plausibility of such an explanation. Hume is in fact famous for having demolished the whole notion of the social contract by arguing that it is logically dependent in the first place upon having established the convention of promising, since we cannot promise to obey until we have promises. But in that case he argues, whatever explains the origin of promising, could be used also to establish other social or political institutions directly, without the intervention of a formal contract, which is thus rendered redundant. What are the mechanisms by which Hume thinks these rules and institutions could have come into existence?

The conventional origins of social practices

Anxious as ever to show that moral and political practices derive from sentiment and experience, rather than rational constructs, Hume wishes to show that although we can demonstrate the rationality of the rules of justice after the event, such rationality could not have brought them into existence in the first place.[49] Hume points to a different sense of 'convention' than that implied by an explicit social contract. He argues that just as the meanings of words in a language, and the acceptability of those metals which first stand for money (an example also used by Locke) become established, not through formal agreement, but through a gradual and inexplicit acceptance, so also, the institutions of justice and property could have been derived from a gradual experience of their utility.[50]

There is a chicken-and-egg problem here. Hume wants to explain that we recognise the benefit of justice through experience, rather than by inventing it through rationalising our ideas. But, surely, it could be objected, before justice exists we cannot have experience of it? Experience of its benefits cannot quite, then, explain its remotest origin, it must have a beginning in something else. If we follow Hobbes, the existence of justice seems to be an all or nothing matter: there is either a sovereign (and therefore justice), or not. If not, we cannot have experience of justice; recognition of its benefits must, therefore, for Hobbes, be created through a rational process of theorising, and it must be

---

[46] Adam Smith, *The Wealth of Nations* (2 vols, Oxford, 1976) vol. 1, p. 27.

[47] *Treatise*, p. 492.

[48] Ibid., p. 497.

[49] 'The sense of justice, therefore, is not founded on our ideas, but on our impressions.' Ibid., p. 496.

[50] Ibid., p. 490.

established, initially, and all at once, through contract, since any attempt to 'experiment' with just behaviour would lead to our exploitation by others not so minded. Hume rejects this, both on philosophical grounds – because he is even less convinced than Hobbes that rational argument leads to determinate conclusions – and on the grounds of a more sophisticated historical sense – because the idea of justice 'wou'd never have been dream'd of among rude and savage men'.[51] Hume's move is to destroy the outright contrast between the state of nature and society, which is implicit in Hobbes's formulation of the social contract. Instead, like the Stoics whom he so admired, he suggests experiences which, in the most elementary society we can imagine would still have given us enough awareness of the benefits of sociability that we would be able to reflect on the experience and seek to extend them further.[52]

Hume invites us to consider ways in which appreciation of the benefits of regularity and reciprocality could emerge without their having been deliberately formulated. As a hint of the kind of gradual accommodation which could establish rules without an explicit contract, Hume uses the analogy of two men rowing a boat. Without some agreement between the two rowers, it might be thought, the boat could never keep a straight course. Yet the strength and cadence of their oar strokes, he suggests, will gradually accommodate to one another, enabling the boat to pursue a straight course rather than a circular or irregular one. Thus without explicit contract, the convention that each pulls as fast and as often as the other will emerge.[53] Once emerged, and its benefits are experienced, it can be explicitly formulated as a rule; but Hume's argument is that the rules are subsequent to the experience of the practice. Reflecting on the beneficial consequences of such conventions enables us to express them as rules or principles. And once they are so expressed we can 'obey' them; but the principles are historically subsequent to, and derived from the practice, they were not, and could not have been, instrumental in the establishment of it. The family or small social group bound by sympathy cannot create justice, but it does enable us to experience the advantage of rule-governed behaviour, and this experience can then be applied to the wider social field where justice operates. Justice, Hume concludes, arises from our impressions and sentiments (of self-interest), and not from our ideas or reason. [54]

The story of the rowing boat reveals some deeper assumptions of Hume's argument. For the analogy will only produce the desired outcome as long as the two rowers share a common destination. Hume's assumption is that all will have an interest in *some* rule of possession, which is greater than any inconvenience or undesired inequality which results from its *particular* distributional properties. Another example illustrates this line of thought. Two drivers 'cannot even pass each other on the road without rules' as to which side of the road to drive on.[55] In this case it is clearly as immaterial what the rule is, as it is vital that there be one. Most political matters, Hume suggests, are like this. Amiable and phlegmatic as he personally was, Hume is here at his most complacent. For

---

[51] Ibid., p. 488.

[52] Ibid., pp. 485, 489. On Hume's interest in Stoicism, particularly Cicero, see E.C.Mossner, *The Life of David Hume* (Oxford, 1954) pp. 52, 54–5; and letter to Francis Hutcheson, *Letters*, I, p. 34, 14; and further, in Peter Jones, *Hume's Sentiments, Their Ciceronian and French Context* (Edinburgh, 1982).

[53] *Treatise*, p. 490.

[54] Ibid., p. 496.

[55] *Enquiries*, p. 210.

whether this is true or not, seems very much an empirical question. That is to say, whether citizens regard any particular rule as better than none does seem to depend on the properties of the rule, and how much particularly disadvantaged groups stand to lose by it. Only by insisting that having no rule is *always* worse than any possible one can the position hold. Against this objection Hume has to revert to Hobbesian scare tactics, and we find the previously underplayed state of nature assuming frightening proportions. With the stability of possessions

> every individual person must find himself a gainer . . . since, without justice, society must immediately dissolve, and every one must fall into that rude and savage solitary condition, which is infinitely worse that the worst situation that can possibly be supposed in society.[56]

Even if Hume's claim about the utility of *any* rule of property is true at the outset, and helps to explain its origin, he readily admits that our perception of this interest becomes remote as society advances, and men do not so 'readily perceive that disorder and confusion follow upon every breach of these rules, as in a more narrow and contracted society'.[57] Consequently although this above account explains the origin of justice, as a social rule, it does not explain how the sense of justice and injustice operates in the individual. The psychological, or what Hume, confusingly for us, calls the moral obligation, that is the motive that activates the individual, is a result of the socialisation process and the ambient attitudes of praise or blame attaching to acts of justice or injustice, which the individual internalizes.[58]

The origins of what Hume calls the 'moral' obligation, and what we might call the subjective feeling of right or wrong – is distinct from the explanation of the emergence of the rule of justice itself. Here says Hume there is a role, both for sympathy and for the feelings of those close to us. It is sympathy for the general principles which sustain society (once we've got it) which enables us to extend our condemnation to actions which, although unjust, do not directly affect us (or might even advantage us). It is the general practice of praising or blaming according to these criteria which, together with our concern to be thought well of by those around us, instills in us a desire to adhere to those rules. Vanity, in the sense of being concerned what others think of us, is hardly a fault, it is 'rather to be esteemed a social passion, and a bond of union among men.'[59] Such a process of internalizing these values is re-enforced not only in an informal sense by our parents and educators and those all around us in society, but also by the deliberate artifice of politicians.[60] Nevertheless, such re-enforcement and conditioning is only possible, Hume suggests, because there is a basis in nature for the rules in the first place:

[56] *Treatise*, p. 497.

[57] Ibid., p. 499.

[58] '*Thus self-interest is the original motive to the* establishment *of justice: but a* sympathy *with public interest is the source of the* moral approbation *which attends that virtue*', ibid., pp. 499–500; and 'What farther contributes to encrease their solidity, is the interest of our reputation, after the opinion, *that a merit or demerit attends justice or injustice*, is once firmly establish'd among mankind', ibid., p. 501.

[59] Ibid., p. 491.

[60] A point emphasised by Hume's predecessor Bernard Mandeville in both *The Female Tatler* and *The Fable of the Bees*. See the discussion in M.M. Goldsmith, *Private Vices, Public Benefits: Bernard Mandeville's Social and Political Thought* (Cambridge, 1985), ch. 3, 'The Skilful Politicians'.

'The utmost politicians can perform, is to extend the natural sentiments beyond their original bounds; but still nature must furnish the materials, and give us some notion of moral distinctions.'[61]

The content of the rules of justice

What then is the content of the rules established in this way? Clearly it is very minimal, since it emerges from the common yet unexamined self-interests of natural individuals. The basic rules of justice, claims Hume are three: the stability of possessions, the transfer of them by consent, and the keeping of promises. These rules have a basis both in their utility – which of course could only be recognised retrospectively, and in natural passions and cognitive operations.

The first rule, stability of possession, Hume suggests would emerge both from the natural desire of human beings to keep what goods they already possessed, and from the natural associations formed in the mind by continually seeing an object and a person together. Extensions of the associative principle further explain the origin of the major titles to property resulting from occupancy, long possession (prescription), and accession – when something we already possess gives rise to something else. All of these are in fact Roman Law principles, better known in Scotland whose legal system was, unlike that of England, derived from the Roman Law tradition so prevalent on the continent. But whatever influence Roman Law may have played in providing the categories of his thought, Hume himself is more interested in showing that they have a grounding in the associative principle.[62]

Property is a relationship with its origin in the mental associations formed by repeatedly seeing a particular object in connection with a particular person: this association would eventually come to raise expectations which, re-enforced by our desire to keep what we own, could on reflection be formalized into the rule that people should be secure in the possession of those things they already had, which is the first principle of justice. This is the explanation of rights arising from prescription. Long possession produces no real change in the object, it is 'the offspring of sentiments'. Whilst the original principle seems straightforward enough, the further specification of it in the particular titles by which property is acquired is more contentious.

(i) Occupation, or first possession. Hume acknowledges the flimsiness of this relation. It lies simply in the (psychological) fact that the first possession somehow 'engages the attention most'. In general occupancy or possession involves control or power over something, the relation between the owner and object is one of cause to effect, this kind of association is then the one that operates here. Hume is particularly dismissive of Locke's theory of 'mixing our labour', showing that it reduces to a number of different arguments. We do not, except figuratively 'mix our labour', rather we alter something by our labour. This establishes a relation in the mind between the thing and the person, sufficient, on the principle of cause and effect, to generate the idea of property. Mere

---

[61] *Treatise*, p. 500.

[62] Hume studied Scots and Civil (Roman) Law as a youth, and was proficient enough to practise (successfully) on behalf of friends at various times, and to gain a legal post with the military in 1746. See Mossner, *Life of Hume* (Oxford, 1954), pp. 54–6.

occupancy, which he explains above, on different principles, does not involve labour; and titles generated by the labour of others belonging to me (as in Locke's famous 'Grass my Horse has bit; the Turfs my Servant has cut:' passage)[63] are really examples of accession. This dismissive attitude to Locke reveals the gulf that has opened up between the naturalism of Hume, and Locke's basic assumption of human personality as *essentially* the locus of deontological rights and duties.

(ii) By accession the products or appurtenances of any of our property become ours. Hume instances the fruits of trees, the young of animals we possess and the work of slaves we own; all become ours because the offspring are associated with their origins in the imagination, and the relationship of being possessed passes from the one to the other, especially if the second is smaller. Such 'smooth transition of the imagination' also explains the accession of smaller islands and territories to larger ones: the incorporation of the Orkney (ceded to Scotland from Norway in 1469) and Hebridean islands to Great Britain (and possibly also – although Hume does not mention it – of Scotland to England!). These 'offsprings' of our property are ours because 'the objects are connected together in the imagination . . . and are commonly supposed to be endowed with the same qualities.'[64]

(iii) Finally, succession or inheritance derives again from the nearness of the relationship. On the death of the proprietor, the mind, already linking the property to the offspring via the dead parent 'is apt to connect them still further by the relation of property'.[65] This relationship is re-enforced by what Hume claims as a fact, that 'men's possessions shou'd pass to those, who are dearest to them, in order to render them more industrious and frugal.'[66]

Thus in some cases Hume stresses the utility of particular claims to property, as well as the utility of stability of property in general. But perhaps the most extraordinary feature of his account is his stress on the way in which these particular claims to property 'are principally fix'd by the imagination, or the more frivolous properties of our thought and conception.'[67] As we descend to the more particular rules about property, the role of imagination or chance association increases. Thus an individual discovering and claiming a small deserted island can be thought the possessor of it, but not if the island is as big as a continent, simply because, in the first instance the extent of the property can be imagined to ourselves, and is related, proportionally to the possessor. The idea of an individual claiming in this way a whole continent is somehow incongruous. But these are only properties, as Hume points out, of our fancy. Hume does not pretend that all and every rule of property to be found can be shown to be *the* one that best fits the operation of the mind, let alone to be justified by utility. What he argues is that they all can be shown to have *some* basis in associationist psychology – and in this way their origin can be explained independently of rational invention. Moreover, since any rule is better than none, and there are rarely non-experiential grounds for demonstrating the superiority of one over another, any rule embodied in practice and habit is to be preferred to another not so embodied. Hume's scepticism here characteristically results not in practical

---

[63] John Locke, *Two Treatises of Government*, Second Treatise, §28.

[64] Hume, *Treatise*, p. 509.

[65] Ibid., p. 513.

[66] Ibid., p. 511.

[67] Ibid., p. 504.

anarchy or diffidence, but rather in an acceptance of existing practice, not because it is best, but because it's existence as a practice is a better proof of its workability than any reasons that might be given for an imaginary one.

Considered as a justification, as opposed to an explanation, Hume's was a tenuous and even 'fantastic' basis on which to put property rights.[68] Yet given Hume's scepticism about metaphysical reasoning, and his denial that pure reason or historical fact could produce moral conclusions, it was the firmest basis there was. Moreover, to all but philosophical rationalists and partisans it was the most likely to foreclose argument, since it derived from reflections on the nature of the human mind, from the workings of which, whatever our views about reason, history or religion, there was no escaping. Moreover there was something about this 'fantastic' basis for property rights which equalized the status of different kinds of property, and this had important political implications in Hume's time.

The notion that certain kinds of wealth – especially since the advent of credit – were based on fantasy, or men's imaginations, had a well established literary pedigree before Hume daringly enshrined it in philosophy. Daniel Defoe had personified credit as Fortuna – the fickle pagan goddess – who made the most demanding political conditions, 'if you will entertain this Virgin, you must act upon nice principles of Honour, and Justice; you must preserve Sacred all the Foundations, and build regular structures upon them; you must answer all Demands, with respect to the solemnity and Value of the Engagement; with respect to Justice, and Honour; and without any respect to Parties – If this should not be observed, Credit will not come; No, tho' the Queen should call; tho' the Parliament should call, or tho' the whole Nation should call.'[69] But the most extraordinary version of this popular image was that of Addison in *The Spectator*. Addison describes 'a kind of methodical dream' he had after visiting the Banking Hall of the Bank of England. In the dream he returned to the hall and saw a beautiful virgin on a golden throne, behind and beside which were piled bags of gold and money. The walls were hung not with pictures but, at the side with the acts of parliament relating to the establishment of the National Bank and Debt, and at either end with Magna Carta and the Act of Settlement (settling the throne on Anne and then the House of Hanover and precluding the Catholic line of James Stuart). Her name was Public Credit, and she had King Midas' property of turning all she touched to gold. The lady was subject to swoons and faints, and anxious about her acts of parliament. Suddenly into the hall came three pairs of figures: Tyranny and Anarchy, Bigotry and Atheism, and the 'Genius of a Commonwealth (republicanism) with a figure who turns out to be the Stuart pretender. The lady swoons and her bags of gold and money collapse like deflated balloons, whilst others turn into little bundles of paper. However, on the arrival of a second set of more 'aimiable phantoms': 'Liberty with monarchy at her right hand . . . Moderation leading in Religion', and a figure that turns out to be George Ist with the genius of Great Britain, the first set vanish, the lady

---

[68] Despite Hume's denial that descriptions (of origins or of anything else) could never produce obligations, it is quite clear that Hume regarded his account as, at least in part, a vindication, as well as an explanation of property rights. Ibid., p. 469.

[69] Daniel Defoe, *A Review* vol.vii, no.116, p. 463, cited J.G.A. Pocock, *The Machiavellian Moment*, p. 455.

comes round, the bags of gold are reflated and the paper turns again into guineas.[70] Addison's image stressed the support that political freedom and a Protestant state religion were believed to provide to the national debt and a credit-based economy, but it also emphasized the volatility of such a new economic order.

Landed property was somehow more real than this claimed the 'country' opposition against the modernizing policies of Walpole's Whigs, who, with their array of modern economic devices such as a national bank and debt, a market in stocks and bonds, and the pursuit of an empire based on trade, represented an opposed 'monied' interest. Hume's argument about the nature of property was anti-partisan in that it made landed property, as much as property in money or shares alike a consequence of the associative operations of the mind. Yet this very equalization of the status of different kinds of property favoured – albeit for scientific rather than vulgar or partisan reasons – the modern Whig view over that of the more nostalgic country Tories.

Government

Although property and justice are, and can be seen to be, in our interest, human beings are apt to be more impressed by what strikes them immediately and is present to their senses, than what is a long way off. We are, therefore, more highly motivated by our immediate advantage, than by the long term, no matter how disproportionate the actual advantage is, and often, even though we recognise the disproportion. The only way of overcoming the 'narrowness of soul, which makes them prefer the present to the remote' is to institute government and appoint magistrates who can 'render the observance of the laws of justice our nearest interest, and their violation the most remote'. Governments are conventional devices. They exist not to change our natures, but to alter our calculations; not to make us altruistic citizens, but to ensure our immediate self-interest coincides with our long term. [71] Once again, since Hume denies the idea of an original social contract, he is careful to show how experience of the benefits of magistracy and political rule could have grown up piecemeal, without our having to 'invent' political authority from nothing. Even societies without government (such as he believed the American Indians to be) acknowledge a chief in time of war, and this could have enabled men to experience briefly the benefits of government, gradually extending it to a more regular operation.[72] Once the benefit of government is established, as in the case of other artificial institutions, praise or blame will attach to actions which promote or undermine it, and the virtues and vices of loyalty and sedition grow up: '*Education* and *the artifice*

[70] Joseph Addison, *The Spectator*, no. 3 (March 1711).

[71] Hume's brief account in *Treatise*, pp. 538–9 is a remarkable and succinct anticipation of the kind of modern arguments about the logic of collective action spawned by Mancur Olsen's work of that name. Where small groups are concerned with indivisible goods (two men planning to share in the draining of a common meadow), no compulsion is necessary to achieve their long term good. For each knows that if either fails to act the whole scheme fails. Where thousands of men are involved, such factors do not operate, the default of any one is not crucial and 'each seeks a pretext to free himself of the trouble and expence, and wou'd lay the whole burden on others.' Magistrates (governments), who because of their privileged position have every interest in the prosperity and continuance of society, have therefore an interest in enforcing contributions to the public good. See also *Treatise*, p. 552.

[72] Ibid., p. 540.

of politicians, concur to bestow a further morality on loyalty, and to brand all rebellion with a greater degree of guilt as infamy.'[73]

Although the idea of government as a social contract is a fiction ('no-one whose judgement has not been led astray by too strict adherence to a system of philosophy, has ever yet dreamt of ascribing it to that origin')[74] the principles which are derived from it are nevertheless roughly those on which government stands or falls. Obedience does last only as long as government provides protection and security. However, the reason is not because government is based on a contract; but because protection and security are in our interests, and continued obedience to a government that fails to deliver them is not. True enough, most people are incapable of following the subtle argument which justifies and explains the existence of government; but this does not mean that the points at which they will cease to obey it are not the same as those at which the argument suggests they would be right to. 'There is evidently no other principle than common interest; and if interest first produces obedience to government, the obligation to obedience must cease, whenever the interest ceases, in any degree, and in a considerable number of instances.'[75]

So much for the nature of obligation. But having explained the origin of political obligation in general, there remains another question: to whom is it due? And the stunningly simple answer is to whoever, or whatever, has long held it. 'The only rule of government' as he puts it in the *Essays,* 'is long use and practice'.

> An established government has an infinite advantage, by that very circumstance, of its being established. Custom and habit, where (happily) they exist, tell us who is the rightful government. Disputes over the origins of titles long held is pointless. Neither history, nor reason is capable of providing authoritative answers to disputes about legitimacy.[76]

If, unhappily, there is no long established government, then the present one is the next best choice. We should, suggests Hume, not be too scrupulous about the means by which a government gained power: 'Few governments will bear being examin'd so rigorously.'[77]

The issue of legitimacy

Discussion of political allegiance at this time was no academic issue. Fear of a Stuart restoration was a continuing feature of lowland Hanoverian Britain and not without reason. Six years after the publication of the *Treatise*, in 1745, Charles Stuart, the Young Pretender to the throne, grandson of the deposed James II, landed in Scotland, was declared King and marched as far south as Derby, causing panic in London. Although this was a last and desperate shot, achieving through luck and surprise more than could reasonably have been hoped, it did not look that way to contemporaries, and indeed, even

[73] Ibid., p. 546.

[74] Ibid., p. 547.

[75] Ibid., p. 553.

[76] *Essays, Moral, Political and Literary* (Oxford, 1963) (hereafter *Essays* followed by individual essay title), p. 480, 'Of the Coalition of Parties'; p. 499, 'Idea of a Perfect Commonwealth'.

[77] *Treatise*, p. 558.

after the defeat of Charles, Hume did not regard the Jacobite threat as over.[78] Certainly the ideological embarrassment of the Hanoverian dynasty – seeking to reassert the trappings of hereditary monarchy when they owed their position to parliamentary usurpation – were considerable.

Through this political briar patch Hume treads warily. Writing in the *Treatise*, before the '45 rebellion, he phlegmatically notes that although tyranny and oppression will, and rightly so, lead men to rebel, there are no *'particular* rules, by which we may know when resistance is lawful'. Moreover he more than hints that the removal of James was at least a marginal case (although he paradoxically provides an 'associationist' account of why it was natural, having excluded him, to exclude his heir also).[79] But whatever happened at that time, he says, the question of its origins is now irrelevant: because the House of Hanover is so well established it should be accepted. 'Time and custom give authority to all forms of government, and all successions of princes; and that power which at first was founded only on injustice and violence, becomes in time legal and obligatory.'[80] This, as Hume could not but be aware, was a pretty lukewarm case for allegiance. And although he makes substantially the same case in his essay 'On the Protestant Succession' written in 1748, he evidently felt sufficiently nervous about it in the aftermath of the '45 rebellion to delay publication until 1752.[81]

The danger of even mitigated scepticism was the same in politics as in religion. In undercutting fervour and the volatile 'enthusiasm' of sectarian and party attachment, which could give (and had given) rise to destructive conflict, there was a danger that belief and allegiance were rendered altogether too fragile. For most of his life Hume clearly thought the dangers of enthusiasm posed by far the greater threat, and his writings attempt as much to insinuate diffidence in politics as they do agnosticism in religion. Towards the end of his life however he glimpsed with dread, in the radicalism of Wilkes's London, the rise of a secular superstition. But there is no evidence that he saw, as Burke was to see in the descendants of that radicalism in the 1790s, the influence of sceptical rationalism itself; *that* fear of reason belongs to another chapter.[82]

The indifference Hume expressed to the competing dynastic claims of his day extended to the wider debate about constitutional forms and the question of corruption. About politics, if not quite as about religion, Hume, shared Pope's consequentialism:

> For forms of government let fools contest,
> What'er's administered best is best.
> For modes of faith, let graceless zealots fight
> His can't be wrong whose life is in the right.[83]

---

[78] 'The claims of the banished family, I fear, are not yet antiquated; and who can tell that their future attempts will produce no greater disorder.' *Essays*, p. 494, 'Of the Protestant Succession'.

[79] *Treatise*, p. 563; dubious case. Ibid., pp. 564–5, 566, and *Essays*, p. 497 ,'Protestant Succession'.

[80] *Treatise*, p. 566.

[81] See Forbes, *Hume's Philosopical Politics*, p. 97.

[82] On Hume's political views at the end of his life, and their relationship to his theory of history see J.G.A. Pocock, 'Hume and the American Revolution: the dying thoughts of a North Briton' in his *Virtue, Commerce and History* (Cambridge, 1985).

[83] Alexander Pope, *Essay on Man*, III, 303–6.

However, because Hume's theory of politics rested so heavily on the properties of the human mind, and because the interaction of the mind's intrinsic qualities with social and economic circumstance produced a variety of outcomes, Hume could not be indifferent about regimes and their characteristics. Indeed, in the *Essays* Hume exhibits a rich understanding of what today would be called the sociology of political belief. Moreover because beliefs were, in relation to the circumstances that gave rise to them, either more or less stable, there were important points to be made about the emergence and successful management of public opinion in the modern commercial state.

Political economy

Hume's political economy is contained for the most part in his *Essays* published in several instalments in 1741, 1742 and 1752, as well as in passages in his famous and vastly popular *History of England*. It is connected to his political philosophy through their mutual concern with the workings of the human mind and the formation of our opinions on moral and political matters. In his philosophical works, Hume had followed through the implications of a strict empiricism applied to the philosophical psychology of his immediate predecessors – Locke, Mandeville, Shaftesbury and Hutcheson. In the *Essays* Hume follows up the implications of a tradition of historical sociology, and implicitly integrates it with the findings of his philosophy. Thus the political economy moves from the general and historical, the political philosophy from the individual and particular, each to the social institutions they explain and support.

The sociological tradition mentioned above is the one that is associated most, in the modern world, with Machiavelli. In his attempts to identify the circumstances under which *virtù* would flourish, Machiavelli had re-initiated a discussion of the impact of laws and the economy on citizens' personalities which had laid the foundations for a secular sociology of moral belief. This pattern of thought had been introduced into English politics during the Civil War, notably in the work of James Harrington (a writer much admired by Hume[84]) and it had, in the course of the constitutional disputes of 1640–1720 been grafted onto perceptions about the development of English political economy which were inextricably entwined in partisan issues. In common with his aims in his philosophical work, Hume's treatment of political economy was designed to dissolve merely ideological partisanship and substitute a cool assessment of the impact of political and economic changes on the beliefs and hence the behaviour, of citizens. Ultimately Hume believed that a certain kind of political economy best fosters the calm and deliberative philosophical attitude to politics that minimizes conflict. Although the vocabulary and approach derive from the Machiavellian tradition, the conclusions reached by Hume are diametrically opposed to those of Machiavelli, or his eighteenth-century heirs. In this sense Hume's argument, if accepted, signals an end of 'Classical Republicanism'.[85]

---

[84] Hume's essay 'The Idea of a Perfect Commonwealth' owes and acknowledges a debt to Harrington.

[85] James Moore, 'Hume's Political Science and the Classical Republican Tradition', *The Canadian Journal of Political Science* 4 (1977), explores this aspect of Hume's enterprise.

Whig and Tory: the ideological positions

The background to these partisan positions must now be briefly sketched. Under Bolingbroke, the opposition Tories, and country Whigs, stressed the classical connection between land ownership, and political independence. Incongruously for the owners of great estates, they recruited the idealized view of the early Roman republic, where political heroes left their ploughs to come to the defence of their state, returning modestly again, to work, when the danger was over. However outdated it might seem in the economy of eighteenth-century England, the ideal of the citizen-peasant-freeholder died very hard (it was alive and well at the time of the American Revolution), and it was just such an economy, warned Andrew Fletcher, that the Scots were seen to be giving up in entering economic as well as political union with England. The stress on the English past as on of a peasant-freeholder-citizenship, which involved identifying the English long-bowman as Machiavelli's citizen militiaman, linked two lines of thinking, one historical and the other constitutional.

The historical line ran something like the following. Political society is dependent for its success on the *virtù* of the citizens. But that *virtù* is a response to their political rules and their economy. As Machiavelli had shown, where a people become soft and luxurious, moral decline and the rise of private interests is irresistible. Harsh laws and material austerity, as well as material independence and social discipline are preconditions for survival. Therefore, where a society grows rich, where the means of acquisition dissociates the citizen from hard work and discipline, or its politics from the economic independence of a peasant farmer, corruption sets in. The acquisition of empire and tribute, the growth of financial institutions, the enclosure of land and spread of paid labour all facilitated this degeneration. Thus many of the processes we now associate with the successful transition to modernity, the growth of manufactured goods, trade and increased consumer activity, on this view, constituted corruption, and recent history was identified with degeneration. Some defeated Tories used such views as a stick with which to beat Walpole's Whigs. Moreover many 'country Whigs' supported them because such views integrated well with the constitutional line of thinking, deployed successfully in the opposition to James, which related *virtù* to the operation of the constitution, and so explained in detail, how corruption would actually affect the British constitution.

The constitutional argument pointed out that the success of England in avoiding both anarchy and tyranny was a result of her balanced or mixed constitution, whereby King, Lords and Commons kept a mutual check on each other's operation and so prevented any one (or the order of persons it represented) exercising tyranny over the rest. However, the capacity of the Commons to restrain the Crown was dependent on its control over the revenue, and the independence of the Commons was itself dependent on the independence of the electors. Arbitrary government could result from the bribery of, or influence of the court over MPs and constituents. The possibility of governments borrowing money, as well as the existence of indirect imperial revenues (through taxes on trade), undermined the financial control exercised by the Commons through the right to withhold taxation; and the independence of the electors was undermined by the growing influence-through-patronage that the Crown – via the government of the day –

exercised, as the military needs resulting from imperial growth swelled the government bureaucracy and expenditure.[86]

In an ironic switch of ideologies, the displaced Tories had adopted as ideal the Whig view of history as containing an ancient, balanced constitution, guaranteed by the virtue of an economically frugal citizenry – now undermined by Walpole's modern Whigs. The Whigs in turn had adopted the old Tory history, although depicting the feudal past now as a bogey, to be contrasted with the civilized present.[87]

In this confrontation Hume is generally on the Whig side – despite his reputation as a Tory (which derives mainly from his history). But it is, as one commentator has remarked, a 'scientific Whig' position which avoids the chauvinistic extremes of 'vulgar Whiggism'.[88] Hume does not for example join the contemptuous excoriation of the French for their supposed submission to absolutism, pointing out that the arts – for him an essential index of civilization – had progressed at least as far with them as with the British. Moreover in the field of civil liberty, modern civilized monarchies had achieved what formerly only republics had done, 'the rule of laws not men'. No citizen in a modern monarchy thought Hume could justifiably feel less secure for their personal safety, or personal property than formerly in a republic. If commerce suffered under modern monarchies, it was not because property rights were insecure, for they were not; but because commerce was less honourable. It was not the absolutism of French government that inhibited commerce, but the social prestige of aristocracy and the resulting ethic that downgraded the life of the merchant.[89]

The inadequacies of the agrarian city-state model

To start with the historical story: Hume accepts the story of the virtuous classical republic handed down and embellished by Machiavelli, at more or less face value; but in a number of ways he undermines its claim to be a model society.

Firstly he argues that the austerity and single-minded preoccupation with military matters required by the classical republic was against human nature: it was 'violent, and contrary to the more natural course of things'. Although such a civic morality could be seen to be the appropriate outcome of certain conditions – small independent egalitarian states, continually under threat from neighbours, and with primitive economies – these unusual conditions constituted 'an extraordinary concurrence of circumstances'; and if the existence of the states to which they gave rise were not so well documented they 'would appear a mere philosophical whim or fiction, and impossible ever to be reduced to practice'.[90]

---

[86] The emergence of this line of thinking owed much to the analysis of the republican poet Andrew Marvell's *Growth of Popery and Arbitrary Government*, (1677). See the discussion of this and other works in J. G. A. Pocock, 'Machiavelli, Harrington and English Political Ideologies in the Eighteenth Century', in Pocock, *Politics, Language and Time*, (Chicago and London, 1971).

[87] On this see Isaac Kramnick , *Bolingbroke and his Circle, The Politics of Nostalgia in the Age of Walpole*, (London, 1968).

[88] The terms are broached by Duncan Forbes in his *Hume's Philosophical Politics*. See also James Moore, 'Humes's Political Science . . .' which argues that Hume's target was somewhat narrower.

[89] *Essays*, pp. 93–4, 'Of Civil Liberty'.

[90] Ibid., p. 264, 'Of Commerce'.

Secondly he sets out to debunk judgements about the greatness of such states. Discussion about the relative sizes of the populations of ancient and modern states was a topic of considerable interest at the time: population was commonly felt to be an index of the political success of states. The issue relates inextricably, Hume points out, to other important domestic and political issues. The absence of slavery for example must make modern nations far superior in the account of liberty than ancient ones. But it also makes them more populous. Contrary to the supposition that slave owners had an interest in breeding from their possessions, Hume points out, they no more bred their slaves in the city than butchers breed their cattle there. The expense of maintaining a slave child in the town until it could be of service was prohibitive. It was cheaper to import them. Like a number of eighteenth-century cities, although probably to a lesser extent, ancient Rome was incapable of sustaining its own population, the growth or even maintenance of which was dependent on replenishment from outside. Ancient and early modern cities, claimed Hume, were human sumps which drew into themselves and destroyed the population of their environs. [91]

In warfare and politics too, ancient practice militated against great numbers. Since the consequences of losing – slavery or massacre – were so much worse, ancient warfare was far more furious and destructive than modern, and engaged a larger proportion of the population. Moreover it was practised more continuously, and more effectively.[92] Politically, the eventual extension of the franchise to absurdly poor levels of the population engendered such deep factions in 'free governments' that when any one group achieved the upper hand they slaughtered, or banished the other. Moreover such endemic political instability also rendered property precarious.

For this and other reasons, the economies of ancient republics were undeveloped. Their citizens had simple tastes, so there was little demand for variety. Although some cities were based on commerce, none were founded on manufacturing. They developed no mechanical skill, no new trade routes, no system of public communications and no institutions of credit.

On these grounds alone it seems unlikely that ancient states could have been large, and the figures he cites confirmed this impression. Athens at her height was 'not larger than Yorkshire'[93] and her population 21, 000 citizens and 40, 000 slaves. Indeed the whole population of the classical Greek states was hardly more than that of modern Scotland, at one and a quarter million.[94] Although Rome as a city became possibly as large as contemporary London, and did establish a great Empire, as a republic it was, in common with others of the ancient world no more than a 'petty Commonwealth'.

This excursion into historical demography has already raised the central issue of the relationship of political regime to different patterns of economic activity and mental propensities which lies at the heart of Hume's analysis.

[91] Ibid., 'Of the Populousness of Ancient Nations' *passim*.

[92] More continuously, effectively, furiously, ibid., pp. 403–4 ('Of the Populousness . . .'). Hume's remark that the move away from citizen armies towards the 'low set of people' who comprise the modern soldiery has had the beneficial effect of making fighting less effective, is typical of the delight he takes in showing that in politics, 'first appearances deceive'. Ibid., p. 399; larger armies, p. 263, 'Of Commerce'.

[93] Ibid., p. 400, 'Of the Populousness' ; p. 263, 'Of Commerce'.

[94] Ibid., p. 423ff. Modern accounts suggest Hume seriously underestimates these numbers.

The origins and advantages of the commercial state

As well as casting doubt on the claims made for the ancient republican city state, Hume attacks the previously Whig, and now Tory argument of classically influenced thinkers which claimed for the agrarian peasants of late medieval and early modern Europe the independent qualities of the ancient republican citizen. Truer to Harrington than to his neo-Harringtonian followers, Hume regards the late-medieval agrarian economy as feudal, not free. It is he argues, characterised by two classes, proprietor and tenant. The one 'petty tyrants' the other 'necessarily dependent, and fitted for slavery and subjection.' Such poverty and simplicity, far from being, as nostalgic neo-classical republicans suggest, the seed bed of independent *virtù*, produces servility and 'meanness of spirit'.[95] The most prominent mental quality of such a society would have been 'a habit of indolence'.[96] Hume's account of the relationship of politico-economic change to the progress of the human mind is in fact the reverse of the Machiavellian cycle, according to which the spirit and vigour of the austere agrarian republic is replaced by the laziness and *ozio* of cultivated life made possible through wealth and luxury. Not so, argues Hume. Although he retains concerns about the dangers of 'unlimited conquest'[97] Hume sees the onset of luxurious consumption – derived instead from commerce and manufacture – as generally beneficial. Indeed it is intimately related to a whole range of phenomena associated with the modern state, which, based on increased agricultural production, lead to economic diversification, the increase in the power and resilience of the state, the emergence and spread of political liberty, and the mental development of mankind.

Hume's theory of economic growth is demand led. The most effective means of increasing agricultural production is by the production of manufactured goods. Without these the farmers 'have no temptation . . . to increase their skill and industry; since they cannot exchange that superfluity for any commodities which may serve either to their pleasure or vanity.'[98] The increased agricultural production serves not only to feed the manufacturers. Both it, and the labourers employed off the land, act as a kind of public reservoir of labour which the state can draw on in time of war 'since persons engaged in that [inessential] labour may easily be converted to the public service.'[99] Moreover the existence of an exchange economy facilitates not only military service, but that other pressing requirement of the early modern state – taxation. In the absence of luxury commodities, violence and compulsion are necessary to get the peasant to produce more goods than he needs, and to extract them. Moreover such violence is often ineffectual. But as Hume notes, an exchange economy makes both the eliciting and extraction of a taxable surplus relatively painless. 'Furnish him [the peasant or farmer] with manufactures and commodities, and he will do it [grow extra crops] of himself; afterwards you will find it easy to seize some part of his superfluous labour.' The state is thus not weakened but strengthened, economically and militarily by the promotion of exchange, manufactures and luxury. Hume, like his friend Adam Smith, tries to show that all this may come about through giving reign to the basic human instinct for self-interest, rather

---

[95] Ibid., p. 284, 'Of Refinement in the Arts'.
[96] Ibid., p. 266, 'Of Commerce'.
[97] Ibid., p. 282, 'Of Refinement in the Arts'.
[98] Ibid., p. 266, 'Of Commerce'.
[99] Ibid., p. 268, the point is repeated, p. 279.

than applying the classical ideal of suppressing it in favour of the public good. The one civic activity which is a casualty of the new scheme of things is the duty of military service, which classical republican values stressed so much. Hume notes the 'remarkable custom' of impressment for military service in a state such as Britain, with an otherwise good record for civil liberties, but evidently failed to see the link between the need to resort to compulsion here and the abandonment of the civic ideal in favour of self-interest.[100]

Both commerce and the flourishing of the arts and sciences were seen by some ancient authors to depend originally on free government, and to decline along with the growth of wealth and empire. It had been an article of Whig faith since the 1688 revolution that Britain's successful economy was owing to her Protestant, liberty-safeguarding mixed monarchy. But Hume points out that modern experience contradicts this supposed maxim of politics. Modern Rome, Florence and France all produced prodigies in the sciences and the arts under absolute rule; and the commercial development of France under her absolute monarchy rivalled that of Britain.[101] Moreover ancient writers and their modern epigones, although they recognised the role of free government in stimulating the arts and sciences, invariably saw the further development of refined taste and sophistication as ultimately destructive of the self-denying morality and martial qualities necessary for its survival. The widely read and respected Roman historian Sallust (no shrinking violet in his own private life) most popularized this view, which, Hume claims, is nevertheless false: 'these writers mistook the cause of the disorders in the Roman state , and ascribed to luxury and the arts, what really proceeded from an ill-modelled government, and unlimited extent of conquests.'[102]

In fact, Hume claims, there is a positive causal link flowing the other way: between the cultivation of the arts and political liberty. It is indeed such a strong connection that modern absolute monarchies, where taste and the arts are cultivated, are almost indistinguishable, in respect of civil liberty and security, from the republics in which such cultures originated.[103] To explain why this is so we must proceed to the fourth consequence of economic progress, the mental development of mankind.

Commercial and mental development

We have already seen how Hume denies to the agrarian life, the values of vigorous, independent, civic pride. Such a life is instead, he suggests, slothful and ignorant, servile and parochial. The progress of the human character takes place under the spur provided by the growth, both of the economy and of its partners, the arts and sciences. The epithets Hume applies to this progress reveal the important emphasis he places on mental culture. Where economic and artistic stimulation provide 'perpetual occupation . . . The mind acquires new vigour'; 'enlarges its powers and faculties'; it is 'put into a fermentation'; 'profound ignorance is banished'; 'the tempers of men, as well as their behaviour, refine apace'; they are 'softened as well as their knowledge improved'. 'Thus *industry*,

---

[100] Ibid., p. 378, 'Of Some Remarkable Customs'. [103] Ibid., 'Of the Rise and Progress of the Arts and
[101] Ibid., p. 89ff, 'Of Civil Liberty'.   Sciences', *passim*.
[102] Ibid., p. 282, 'Of Refinement in the Arts'.

knowledge and *humanity*, are linked together, by an indissoluble chain, and are found, from experience, as well as reason, to be peculiar to the more polished, and, what are commonly denominated, the more luxurious ages.' [104]

It is, argues Hume, precisely the *refinement* that results from the cultivation of taste and the arts which makes *excess* (one of the things that worried the defenders of austerity) less likely. Sexual 'gallantry' is a more likely 'vice' in such a society than drunkenness, and, he notes, a less harmful one.

The progress of the mind of a nation has a direct effect on its politics. Refinement and polish make a people less prone to the destabilizing effects on government of superstition; and an understanding of the nature of government 'begets mildness and moderation . . . humanity . . . [makes] authority less severe, and sedition less frequent'. [105]

The management and discrimination of beliefs

Thus, whilst the notion that all government rests on opinion is a truism, the kind of opinion on which it rests, is a product of general factors of cultural and economic development, and some factors are more productive of stability than others. Either way opinion is a major factor in political stability, and needs to be managed successfully. Whilst much of this way of thinking derives from the republican tradition, there is another source too. This lies in religious debates between deists and Anglicans about the source of superstition and irrationality. As we have seen, whilst Anglicans claimed that some beliefs and practices (the argument was usually about articles of belief, but often explicitly extended to political institutions) were 'above reason' and had to be accepted on trust, rationalists tried to deny this. They developed proto-sociologies of religion, explaining the origin of the sacrament in pagan ceremonies, and, as Hobbes had done, the origins of priestly authority in the manipulation of the fears of the ignorant. [106] Hume was well aware of this literature. [107] Indeed, although he rejected the title, he can be seen as a deist in the tradition going back through Anthony Collins and John Toland to Lord Herbert of Cherbury.

The difficult point is that Hume is neither a cultural relativist, nor like the deists, a believer in the effectiveness of critical rationalism. He does not believe that society will automatically generate the appropriate moral and political beliefs, and that the matter can be left there. Nor, given his position on the limited role of reason, can he believe that one set of opinions are intrinsically rational and another false. However he clearly believes there is a distinction to be made between superstitious, and therefore useless or even harmful, beliefs, and reasonable or appropriate ones. Although custom and habit form, and quite properly so, the basis of political culture and institutions, criticism, especially in the form of a free press, has an important role to play. It both enables reflection on whether the operation of habit is beneficial, and guards against the

---

[104] Ibid., pp. 278–282, 'Of Refinement in the Arts'.

[105] Ibid., pp. 280–1 'Of Refinement in the Arts'.

[106] See especially Mark Goldie, 'The Civil Religion of James Harrington', in *The Languages of Political Theory in Early-Modern Europe*, ed. Anthony Pagden (Cambridge, 1987).

[107] Hume recounts his struggles with religious belief in a famous letter, where he records burning a book written in his teens in which he had recorded his reasoning. *Letters*, I, p. 154.

emergence of sinister practices by governments bent on the destruction of political liberty.[108] This criterion is consequentialist, based on judgement about the way in which moral beliefs operate, on their effects, rather than on their truth as corresponding to something. Indeed, on Hume's view this is the only way moral belief can be appraised. Since as we have seen, what moral language describes is not some metaphysical super-reality but feelings, there can be little disputing the factual element in a moral judgement made by someone, since they are best judge of the feelings they are experiencing. On the other hand they have no such privileged knowledge of the consequences of the beliefs they hold.

On this view the study of moral belief acknowledged both cultural relativism, *and* a belief in critical standards capable of assessing the utility or disutility of holding particular beliefs under particular circumstances. For Hume all moral belief *has* a natural history explanation, but it is not always, as tends to be the case in the *Treatise*, an explanation which is also a justification by revealing the continuing benefits of holding such a belief. The 'monkish virtues' of austerity and self-denial may have had utility in the context of the small economically primitive, warlike state, but they are not relevant, indeed they are counterproductive in the modern economy. Some moral beliefs seem never to have been useful, but to result from absurd associations in the mind, and between citizens, in the form of factions. So far was Hume from believing in a rational basis to politics that he thought the formation of political parties on the basis of abstract principles to be not only a destructive but 'the most extraordinary and unaccountable *phenomenon*'.[109] Another source of absurdity was the tendency of the mind to generalise rules of behaviour desirable only within particular circumstances. Denial of self-gratification might be justifiable in order to benefit another person but self-denial *for its own sake* 'can never enter into a head, that is not disordered by the frenzies of enthusiasm.'[110]

Thus although the third *Treatise* seems to betray an optimistic belief in the automatic generation by the mind of the appropriate patterns of morality and political belief, in the *Essays* Hume combats the survival of beliefs which although possibly once appropriate in other circumstances, are no longer so.

Modern sources of ideological and social instability

As well as recognising the survival of spurious belief patterns, Hume increasingly acknowledged that modern society could itself generate destabilizing beliefs. Much of this came too late to be incorporated in his major works, but is expressed clearly enough in his letters. Two particular sources of irrational belief, destructive to stable politics, refer back to the classical tradition and emphasise his continuing debt to it. They are his concern about British imperial expansion and his fears about the public debt.

Whilst civic thought in British political culture had made strenuous efforts to accommodate itself to the necessity of trade and commerce, it had had great difficulty with the

---

[108] These rational appraisals are of benefit 'to all forms of government except the ecclesiastical' to which 'it would be fatal'. Ibid., p. 11ff., 'Of the Liberty of the Press'.

[109] Ibid., p. 58, 'Of Parties in General'.

[110] Ibid., p. 275, 'Of Refinement in the Arts'.

illusionary worlds of credit and finance. Here too, Hume drew the line. In a popular government there is no clear guarantee that the passions will be regulated by reason; and public debt and empire both provoke the passions in a way destructive of political stability.

At one obvious level, the ability to borrow money encouraged financial irresponsibility in politicians by dissociating them from the consequences of their actions. It would, he wrote, 'be scarcely more imprudent to give a prodigal son a credit in every banker's shop in London, than to empower a statesman to draw bills, in this manner on posterity'.[111] The temptation for politicians to mortgage the future rather than face unpleasant choices in the present would be more irresistible, the more responsive to popular opinion politicians became, and this practice would have complex implications in its effect on social structure and belief.

An economy with a creditor class distorts the size and economy of the capital where those living on unearned income tend to congregate. As wealth concentrated in the hands of stockholders, the country would be increasingly 'owned' by men with no identity of interest with the state, men 'who have no connection with the state, who can enjoy their revenue in any part of the globe in which they chose to reside'. [112] Moreover capital in this form, as opposed to that in landed property, creates no enduring social ranks 'which form a kind of independent magistracy in a state' and which might form a hedge against tyranny. Indeed, even the residue of such a landed aristocracy would become 'despised for their poverty and hated [by their tenants] for their oppressions' as they struggled to service the national debt owed to the financiers.[113] These speculated outcomes were only instances of the general truth that in the last resort, an economy based on credit was an economy based on the irrational, fluctuating and unstable beliefs of market participants, 'it was the economic equivalent of religious superstition'.[114] There was in the end nothing to underpin it. As the national debt grew the temptation to declare a bankruptcy must grow, and with it suspicions as to the nation's creditworthiness. But in a free state the debt holders are likely to *be* the governing class and it will therefore never be in their interests to default on the public debt. In that event says Hume, instead of the thousands (of stockholders, who he calculated numbered 17, 000) being sacrificed to millions, the millions (whose taxes have to pay the interest) may be sacrificed to the thousands. Factional struggle is therefore endemic in the burden of debt.[115]

This debt was increased by foreign military campaigns, in particular the attempt to hold an overseas empire in America. Hume was therefore opposed to the extension of empire and the war, not on abstract grounds of American liberty or self-determination, but because it increased public debt. Unfortunately the war had also raised the abstract issue of political liberty, support for which, Hume pointed out, had grown hugely, and in his view, dangerously in the fifty years since the Glorious Revolution. [116] The rise of

---

[111] Ibid., p. 357, 'Of Public Credit'.

[112] Ibid., p. 363, 'Of Public Credit'.

[113] Ibid., p. 363, 'Of Public Credit'.

[114] Pocock, 'Hume and the American Revolution' in *Virtue, Commerce and History*, p. 139.

[115] Hume, *Essays*, p. 370, 'Of Public Credit'.

[116] Ibid., p. 51ff., 'Whether the British Government inclines more to Absolute Monarchy, or to a Republic'.

a 'faction for liberty' encouraged by 'that wicked Madman, Pitt' was another, and related source of irrationality in the structure of modern public opinion.[117]

Hume's enterprise of showing that neither faith nor rationality provide a secure guide to stable politics, and that only experience itself can tell us what will and what will not work, did not in the end quite come off. It failed because, as he himself recognised, the dynamic of political and economic change was capable of, if not likely to continue, generating unstable and incoherent opinions which overcame those of reflective experience. Head of the agenda of any social thinker was therefore the problem of the relationship (and gap) between philosophy, as the reflective attempt to create a theory of a coherent world, and ideology, as the process by which ideas are socially produced. Unless the ideas with which people are furnished by the conditions of their social life are the same as those which the sceptical philosopher correctly identifies as supportive of a civilized social order, barbarism will reassert itself. Before we turn to those who attempted to solve this problem however, we must consider the view that even the temporary humane equilibrium between liberty and authority which Hume thought had been achieved – and was more likely to be sustained by – the modern commercial monarchy, was in fact an illusion; that the happy reconciliation of luxury and liberty was a failure, and that the whole project of modern political economy was fatally flawed. The thinker who most persistently asserted these themes was the Frenchman whom Hume had once invited, with such disastrous results, to visit Britain.[118] He was Jean-Jacques Rousseau.

---

[117] On Hume's views on Pitt, empire and liberty see *Letters*, II, pp.301–5.

[118] For the story of the encounter see Chapter 35 of Mossner, *Life of Hume*.

IV

Jean-Jacques Rousseau

Introduction

An ancient with a modern soul

Rousseau's political thought is a strange and disturbing combination. He seems, some-how, to run together nostalgia for the freedoms of a simple pastoral age, still then to be glimpsed in alpine villages, an idealization of the classical military republics of Sparta and early Rome and a terrible awareness of the complex forms of meaninglessness and oppression – both liberal and totalitarian which have, in the mass societies of the twentieth century, insinuated themselves into our lives. He is an ancient with a modern soul. He would have us believe that the very cultural forms through which we live our lives crush and distort our natures: 'Civilized man is born and dies a slave. The infant is wrapped up in swaddling clothes, the corpse is nailed down in his coffin. All his life man is imprisoned by our institutions.'[1]

A thinker of the Enlightenment, he subverts and denies the values and properties so often ascribed to it, opposing pessimism to its optimism, sentiment and will to its rationalism, and in particular rejecting its view of progress. In this he was of course, not alone, Voltaire had already impishly satirized the facile optimism of some in *Candide*. There is a strong strand of historical pessimism in the Enlightenment; as Peter Gay writes 'A program for progress, it is worth insisting, is not a theory of progress . . . the philosophes . . . were haunted by antique metaphors which they thought they had discarded; they pictured civilizations as individuals, with a distinct life-cycle ending in decay and death'.[2] If Rousseau differed from his contemporaries more than in the depth of his pessimism, it was perhaps that their pessimism arose from the fear that their ideals would not be realised, and his from the fear that they would. So, though often differing from their judgement, Rousseau nevertheless shares with the Enlightenment thinkers a preoccupation with certain issues, and an inheritance of certain ways of thinking.

The suspicion of reason

Rousseau's subversion of the common view of the Enlightenment is exemplified in Rousseau's rejection of what was, at least for many early Enlightenment thinkers, an

---

[1] Jean-Jacques Rousseau, *Emile*, tr. Foxley (London, 1911) p. 10.
[2] Peter Gay, *The Enlightenment: An Interpretation* (2 vols, London, 1966–9), vol.2, p. 100.

article of faith, and that is a belief in the progressive effects of the power and clarity of reason.

Although the Enlightenment's faith in reason is almost an intellectual cliché, it can be overemphasized. Locke's vastly influential *Essay on Human Understanding* could be (and was) read two ways, either as a sceptical critique of the limits of 'knowledge' considered precisely – without thereby undermining the existence of that which could not be so known (as, largely, in Britain) or, much more optimistically, using a definition of knowledge to establishing prescriptively what could be said to exist and what could not (as he tended to be read in France).[3] In the British Enlightenment, and especially amongst Scottish and Irish thinkers the focus was on the role of feelings and the sentiments.[4] Scepticism has an important and still under-acknowledged role in the development of political thinking. We should remember Hume's dictum about reason quite properly being the slave of the passions. But even though Hume and others played down the role of reason in everyday life, he remained confident enough about reason's limited reflective role in discovering the operations of the mind. In France moreover, the legacy of Descartes' rationalism led (against his intentions) to a more sustained, and potentially disruptive, optimism about the social and political benefits to be expected from the application of critical rationality.[5]

But Rousseau differed from all these, his rejection of rationalism was based, not on the view that it overestimates the role of reason in our lives, but on the observation that its role has increased, and with disastrous results. Reason, he thought, had overcome ignorance only to make us sceptics, it had tempered our chauvinism to the point where it had destroyed our patriotism. It had been used to suppress and distort our natural responses of sympathy and pity, and to construct, as objects of rational belief, 'vain sophisms' which crumble under attack because they do not engage the feelings. The very roots of the rational sciences lie in our least admirable qualities – astronomy came from astrology, resulting from our superstition, mathematics from accounting, needed by our avarice, law from our inequality and injustice. Everywhere the consequences of reason's work for morality was disastrous. The application of technology in warfare had undermined courage and personal bravery. And the progress of medicine had destroyed our capacity to face death.

> I do not know what the doctors cure us of, but I know this: they infect us with very deadly diseases, cowardice, timidity, credulity, the fear of death. What matter if they make the dead walk, we have no need of corpses; they fail to give us men, and that is what we need.[6]

---

[3] See for example Rousseau's contemporary, Turgot, *On Universal History*, in *Turgot, on Progress, Sociology and Economics*, ed. & intr. R. Meek (Cambridge, 1973), p. 95.

[4] For Rousseau's famous predecessor Montesquieu, the 'principle' of a government is 'the human passions which set it in motion'. So, 'Virtue in a republic is a most simple thing; it is love of the republic; it is a sensation, and not a consequence of acquired knowledge'. Baron Montesquieu, *The Spirit of the Laws*, tr. Thos. Nugent (New York and London, 1949), Bk. III, §1; Bk. V, §2. Francis Hutcheson, an Irish Scot, the Scots Adam Smith and David Hume, and the Irishman, Edmund Burke, all stress the operation of sentiment over reason in human nature.

[5] N.O. Keohane, *Philosophy and the State in France, the Renaissance to the Enlightenment* (Princeton, 1980), pp. 210–12.

[6] *Emile*, p. 21.

The perils of socialisation

Rousseau subverted a second major theme of the Enlightenment. He viewed with despair the growing belief in the adaptability of the human mind. Numerous philosophers in France during this period adopted or adapted the philosophical psychology popularized by Locke.[7] Locke's attempt to show how the mind might come to build up a coherent picture of the world from sense-perception and without the aid of any 'innate ideas' excited both fear and optimism. Fear – widely expressed in Britain – that his position might (as indeed it did) support atheistic tendencies, in denying the role of God in at least establishing and enforcing moral belief. Optimism about social reform – more particularly in France – in that the mind, if only it could be furnished with appropriately selected experiences, could be formed to education, cultivation and a benevolent disposition. 'Education', wrote Helvetius, one of the most optimistic of its proponents, 'could do everything'.

Nor was philosophical psychology the only discipline which emphasised the way in which personality and belief were a product of circumstance. The historical sociology implicit in the early forms of political economy stressed the influence of socio-economic and geo-political circumstance on the formation of customs, manners and temperament.[8] Although a recognizable historical political economy was only emerging in France at the time Rousseau wrote, legal thought had already provided there the basis for an essentially similar development. Comparative legal study, and the increasingly reflective and sophisticated 'travellers' tales' of foreign societies led to attempts to characterise the 'Spirit' of different peoples as suffused through their culture and institutions, and internalized by the individual.[9]

The variety of cultures demonstrated the adaptability of the human mind and the way it was shaped by experience, and this held out to many reformers the infinite possibilities inherent in education. But the very plasticity of mind also implied for Rousseau, that it could be infinitely degraded. Hume seemed almost happy to dissolve problems about the standards of morality into the natural history of how moralities emerge, and our growing understanding of the process of socialisation. For Rousseau this merely raised the question at another level – what values should we be socialised into? He sees with

---

[7] Turgot's *Philosophical Review of the Successive Advances of the Human Mind* (1750), asserts that 'The most exalted mental attainments are only and can only be a development or combination of the original ideas based on sensation'; 'the senses constitute the unique source of our ideas'. *Turgot . . .*, ed. Meek, pp. 42, 46. D'Alembert's 'Preliminary Discourse' to the famous *Encyclopaedia*, is truly Lockean in denying innate ideas and stressing their origins in experience and reflection. In a Lockean subversion of Descartes he almost (but not quite) asserts 'I experience therefore I am': 'The fact of our existence is the first thing taught us by our sensations, and indeed is inseparable from them.' *Preliminary Discourse to the Encyclopaedia of Diderot*, Jean D'Alembert, tr. & intr. R.N. Schwab with W.E. Rex (Indianapolis and New York, 1963).

[8] Once again Turgot's earlier works and the later Montesquieu explore and develop these themes.

[9] The most famous example being Montesquieu's *Esprit des Lois* (see especially books 14–19). Montesquieu's work was however the culmination of a long tradition of such reflections discussed in Ira O.Wade, *The Intellectual Origins of the French Enlightenment* (Princeton, 1971).

frightening clarity that we could be made *victims* of our sensations and experiences, if we were not taught how to master them; and that the content of the educational or socialising process cannot be assumed to be morally benign. Rousseau, typically, harnesses the new psychology to an old story, and uses it to elaborate the classical and Machiavellian theme of the enervation of virtue and decline into a servility where men lose even their desire to be free. His new version however, makes a return on Fortune's wheel even less likely than before, and instead leads him to explore not the possibility of returning to the past (however attractive), but of constructing an alternative future.

Freedom and the self

Rousseau's central preoccupation is freedom – his greatest fear, dependency. But he carries these preoccupations to levels of experience which had previously only been the concern of religion. Indeed his episodic concern to sustain the idea of an inviolable and authentic 'self' untouched by the pressures of socialisation and education seems to have an obviously religious, and indeed Protestant, source in a will which was ever inwardly retreating, and was ultimately unknowable even to its possessor. For thinkers in the British tradition, freedom had purely physical dimensions. For Hobbes and Hume freedom was an attribute of the person only as a body, the freedom of the will was they thought (though for different reasons) a non-question. Anyone having bodily freedom: 'not a prisoner and in chains', was free. Even the severity of the options facing us – coercion, life or death – was not a relevant issue; much less the question of the psychological constraints that may have been imposed on us through custom or our upbringing. But Rousseau shows deep awareness of these issues; awareness of the informal and structural constraints on our range of realistic choices. He sets out in the first *Discourses* to show the modern individual psyche as under constant and degrading assault from its social environment, and in the second to reveal the process by which that came about. In works such as *Emile*, *La Nouvelle Héloïse*, and the *Reveries of a Solitary Walker* he explores the always elusive, and often illusionary possibility of an individual refuge from its pressures.

But to sustain both the claim that freedom is the essential property of humans and that modern forms of socialisation render us unfree – that 'man is born free but everywhere in chains' – Rousseau has to be able to demonstrate a social alternative. He has to be able to demonstrate the possibility of a socialisation – and a society – that would not constrain us, because it would neither require of us, nor lead us to demand, things which conflicted with each other, or our natures. The difficulty of doing so perhaps explains why, both in his personal and in his literary life Rousseau so often found himself exploring individualist and reclusive solutions. It is this possibility of a whole social environment which supported rather than harassed the individual personality which Rousseau explores in *The Social Contract*, the possibility of a form of association which will defend and protect with the whole common force the person and goods of each associate and in which each, whilst uniting himself with all, may still obey himself alone and be as free as before. [10]

The Social Contract thus provides an answer to the question raised in the *Discourses* of whether humans can enjoy both civilization and freedom, society and moral integrity. The two works need to be read together if sense is to be made of either.[11]

The Discourse on the Arts and Sciences

The arts, sciences and morals

The first of Rousseau's *Discourses* was written in response to an essay competition set by the Academy of Dijon on the question 'Whether the Restoration of the Arts and Sciences has had the effect of purifying or corrupting morals.' It won the prize – a solid gold medal – in July 1750, but more important it was also published and promoted in Paris, thanks to efforts by Rousseau's friends the Abbé Raynal and the Encyclopaedist and philosopher Denis Diderot.[12] Born in 1712, Rousseau was already thirty-eight; previously a musicologist and composer existing on the margins of the fashionable salon society, known but not famous, he was soon, as a result of this and his next *Discourse* to become a figure of enormous controversy. The essay, if it does not quite, as Diderot later claimed, provide the knot from which Rousseau teased his whole social and political philosophy, [13] did nevertheless provoke a debate which enabled Rousseau to clarify his eventual position.

The issue was not a new one. It was a recognizable civic variant of the 'ancients *vs* moderns' topic, a popular Renaissance genre, which had survived down to the eighteenth century. The questionable relationship between virtue, the arts and the luxury that made them possible was an aspect of revived civic humanism which in France, as in Britain, formed a major context through which contemporaries sought to judge the progress of that commercial century. Hume's parallel essay 'Of Refinement in the Arts' had given a resounding YES! to the Dijon question about the beneficial effect of the Arts and sciences. Rousseau's answer was an equally resounding NO!

[10] Jean-Jacques Rousseau, *The Social Contract*, p. 12. References to *The Social Contract* and the *Discourses*, are to the Everyman's Classics edition, tr. G. D. H. Cole, revised J. H. Brumfitt and John C. Hall (London, 1973). Note that pagination in this edition differs from that of earlier ones. Where I have varied the translation I have given a reference to the French text, in C. E. Vaughan, *The Political Writings of Rousseau* (2 vols, Cambridge, 1915), or, if a work is not there, to the relevant volume of the Pléade Edition *Oeuvres* (Paris, 1959–69).

[11] There is also a biographical aspect to their unity. Although *The Social Contract*, was not published until 1762, work on the larger project of which it was a part had begun as early as 1744, and he was heavily involved in it in 1750–51, at the time when his first discourse was published (Vaughan, *Political Writings*, vol. 2, p. 2.)

[12] Maurice Cranston, *Jean-Jacques, the early life and work of Jean-Jacques Rousseau, 1712–1754* (London, 1983), p. 240.

[13] Cited Cranston, *Early Life*, p. 242; see also Robert Wokler 'The *Discours sur les arts* and its offspring' in *Reappraisals of Rousseau, studies in honour of R. A. Leigh*, ed. S. Harvey et al. (Manchester, 1980).

There is a discrimination to be made here. Whilst Machiavellian republicanism stressed the impact of *luxury* on morals, Rousseau's topic is the effect of *learning and culture* on morals. Whilst the wide tradition focussed generally on the baneful moral effects of economic growth, modernization and the emergence of a bourgeois culture, the focus on the arts is to be found in a narrower epistemological channel of influence running from the Cynics and Stoics, and into Christian and Protestant scepticism.[14] Moreover the insistent defence of modernity had increased the salience of this tradition. Hume's *Essays* in particular countered the traditional view that luxury must corrupt since morals are based on austerity, with the claim that manners and refinement – if not a part of morals then a reasonable substitute for them – are increased by luxury and commercial progress. The impact of the arts – through cultivating manners – and the sciences – through stimulating and promoting economic progress – were thus central to the conflict between ancient agrarian virtue and modern commerce and manners, although understanding of their impact changed the centre of the conflict from the military/ political/ economic arena to that of the personal, cultural and economic.[15]

Ancient and Machiavellian themes

The broad argument of Rousseau's *Discourse on the Arts and Sciences* is then, not original, although the precise articulation of it is. It is, broadly, the theme popularized by Machiavelli, and still being worked over in Rousseau's lifetime by Montesquieu in his *Considerations on the Greatness of the Romans and their Decline*, that of the relationship between luxury and growth, on the one hand, and moral decline and loss of liberty on the other: 'rectitude of morals is essential to the duration of empires, and luxury is diametrically opposed to such rectitude . . . The politicians of the ancient world were always talking of morals and virtue; ours speak of nothing but commerce and money.'[16] The relationship of the arts and sciences to luxury and corruption was complimentary and mutually reinforcing. On the one hand the arts and sciences originate in our vices, on the other they mask and make bearable our depravity. They both bring about our corruption, and 'fling garlands of flowers over the chains' that result. They are wisely cultivated by despots to divert their subject people from awareness of their loss of liberty. The Barbarian invaders of the dark ages were not stupid in ignoring mental cultivation –

[14] Scepticism was a particularly important tradition in French culture. Amongst the most famous exponents are Charron and Montaigne. On Montaigne see most recently D.L. Schaefer, *The Political Philosophy of Montaigne* (Ithaca, 1991). However such ideas are already present in the late Italian Rennaissance, indeed it is in the writings of the famous humanist Pico della Mirandola that the strikingly Rousseauian assertion 'we are born free, we make our own bonds' is to be found. See John Hope Mason, 'Reading Rousseau's First Discourse', *Studies on Voltaire and the Eighteenth Century*, 249 (1987), p. 253, n.11.

[15] On this see the excellent analysis offered in J. G.A. Pocock's 'Virtue, rights and manners, a model for historians of political thought' in Pocock, *Virtue, Commerce and History, Essays on Political Thought and History, Chiefly in the Eighteenth Century* (Cambridge, 1985).

[16] *Arts and Sciences*, p. 17. The popularity of the theme is stressed by Keohane, *Philosophy and the State*, p. 381.

they *knew* its effects, and so left the Greeks their libraries, convinced that they would, as a result, be easier to rule.[17]

The mood of the whole piece is severely stoic. The expansion of commodities, no less than the increase in our wants, undermines our natural independence. The less we desire, the more free we are: 'What yoke, indeed, can be imposed on men who stand in need of nothing?'[18] Sparta 'a republic of demigods, rather than of men . . . eternal proof of the vanity of science' which has 'left us nothing but the memory of their heroic actions' is Rousseau's ideal, not Athens, or Imperial Rome.[19]

Like the later Stoics too, notably Cicero (although he was hardly an ascetic), Rousseau insists on the destructive effect of a philosophy not tied to practical political needs. He has in mind here the sceptical effect of such philosophy on the strength of customary belief.[20] Every civilization that has nourished philosophy has subsequently been destroyed: Egypt by the Persians, Greece by the Macedonians, Rome by the Goths, China by the Tartars.[21] Philosophy's 'fatal paradoxes sap the foundations of our faith and nullify virtue', it cultivates wit but undermines sincerity and conviction without which society cannot cohere.[22] Simplicity, innocence, poverty and virtue are throughout opposed to refinement, wit, wealth and decadence.

New themes: authenticity and the irreversibility of history

There are though, two newer themes which Rousseau was to develop more fully in his subsequent works.

The first is the notion that the arts, manners and politeness are not merely effete and destructive of martial virtues, they also, in some way deny our natures, and force us to conceal our real selves. In the modern society 'we build our happiness in the opinions of others, when we [should] find it in our own hearts.'[23] Art highlights this truth, for art *is* deceit. Reflecting perhaps the emergence of commercial rather than patronage-based art, Rousseau observes that to gain the applause he seeks the artist must 'lower his genius to the level of the age'.[24] The arts and sciences originate 'in two wretched sources that are enlarged and sustained by scholarship: idleness and the desire for distinction'.[25]

---

[17] *Arts and Sciences*, pp. 15 (origins), 5 (flowers on the chains), 5fn (cultivated by despots), 20 (libraries divert Greeks from military pursuits).

[18] Ibid., p. 5.

[19] Ibid., pp. 10–11.

[20] See the 'Preface' to Rousseau's play *Narcisse*: 'Customs are the moral life of a people, and as soon as they cease to respect them, there is no rule but the passions, no restraint but the law . . . when philosophy once teaches a people to scorn customs, they soon uncover the secret of evading laws.' 'Preface to *Narcisse*' tr. *Political Theory*, 6, no. 4 (1978), p. 551.

[21] *Arts and Sciences*, pp. 8–10.

[22] See especially the 'Preface to *Narcisse*': philosophy 'loosens all the bonds of esteem and goodwill which tie men to society.' By learning to be critical, philosophers lose the capacity to respect men for 'it is diffcult to hold in respect that which, on merit is despised . . . . Family and fatherland are, for him, words void of meaning. He is neither parent nor citizen, nor man: he is philosopher'; pp. 548–9.

[23] *Arts and Sciences*, p. 29.

[24] Ibid., p. 19. It extends beyond art to social attitudes at large: 'everyone wants to be a nice fellow, while nobody is content to be a good man.' 'Preface to *Narcisse*', p. 547.

[25] Ibid., p. 547.

Although the reason for this is not made clear until the second *Discourse*, deceit is clearly for Rousseau, the central characteristic of modern manners, and particularly of modern art.[26] His work is littered with images of falsehood and concealment: mirrors, clothes, veils, masks and roles, hide us from each other, and all too often from ourselves. In his *Confessions* he declared he was 'resolved on an enterprise which has no precedent . . . to display to my kind a portrait in every way true to nature, and the man I shall portray will be myself.'[27] It has been suggested that the peculiar vehemence of the denunciation to be found in this *Discourse* results from Rousseau's recognition of the effect of the pursuit of artistic fame on his own psyche: '[it] was the voice of Rousseau condemning himself'.[28] This side of Rousseau anticipates in striking form the modern existentialist polarities of authenticity and bad faith, and it is clearly no accident that existentialism should have so flowered in France, where every school child reads some Rousseau.[29]

The second new theme is the implied irreversibility of the process of corruption, identified as it seems to be, with the very forces of civilization itself. Once again this is an idea which is not fully clarified until the second discourse and *The Social Contract*, and the reasons are, even there, ambiguous. There are two reasons implicit in the account in the *Arts and Sciences* . The first is geo-political. Like his near contemporary Gibbon, Rousseau accounts for the renewal of virtue and the destruction of corrupt imperial societies through their conquest by barbarians on the edges of civilization. It was already apparent to most eighteenth-century thinkers that there was no reservoir of barbarism to effect the task in the modern world.[30] Part of Rousseau's recurrent despair derives from his perception of the corruption *and stability* of the modern state – a new combination. The peroration of the *Discourse* is concerned, not with the hopeless task of renewing simple virtue, but of preventing its further corruption by 'restraining men of letters' and keeping from the ordinary reading public the more destructive conclusions of modern culture. One might cynically say, that the part of the *Discourse* that won him the prize is the part praising the Academies as guardians, indeed, almost isolation wards, of 'the dangerous trust of human knowledge'.[31]

The second reason for the supposed irreversibility of corruption lies in the way Rousseau personalizes the process of social development. Once again there is an ancient

---

[26] 'There prevails . . . a servile and deceptive conformity.' *Arts and Sciences*, p. 6.

[27] *The Confessions of Jean-Jacques Rousseau*, tr. & intr. J.M. Cohen (Harmondsworth, 1957[1953]), p. 17

[28] Hope Mason, 'Reading Rousseau's First Discourse', p. 257. In the Preface to *Narcisse*, Rousseau records 'having explored the effect of literary success on my soul', p. 552.

[29] The most striking explorations of Rousseau's ideas from this perspective are those of Jean Starobinski, *Le Transparence et l'Obstacle* (tr. Arthur Goldhammer as *Transparency and Obstruction* (Chicago and London, 1988)), and, Marshall Berman *The Politics of Authenticity* (London, 1971).

[30] But notice Rousseau conjures up an impending barbarian invasion of Europe by the Tartars for his *Social Contract*, p. 219.

[31] *Arts and Sciences*, pp. 24–5. In the 'Preface to *Narcisse*', the reason is more sinister, and harks back to the strategy of the Goths towards the Greeks. 'Leave be the academies, the colleges, the universities, the libraries and the theatres; indeed support them along with all the other entertainments that divert the wicked.' The arts and the sciences 'destroy virtue . . . in virtue's place they introduce decorum and propriety'; a poor substitute but better than nothing; 'Preface to *Narcisse*', p. 551 (cf. Pocock 'Virtue, Rights and Manners').

and classical, as well as a modern aspect to this. Like the Roman historians on whom he draws, Rousseau sees history in moral terms. He describes social change using the moral vocabulary appropriate for describing the corruption of an individual. But there is a modern, and indeed a religious aspect to this. For the movement from virtue to corruption describes not only the substitution of selfish interest for public spirit, as it had for the Romans, but also a movement from innocence to knowledge. If the Romans moralized their history, Rousseau personalizes it. Rousseau's equation of virtue with innocence was much questioned by critics of the first *Discourse*.[32] Rousseau cites Socrates as his source for the praise of ignorance, but the story of the Christian fall also haunts these passages, whilst the modernist aspect of his account is the notion of personal development as a process of self-knowing, and consequently irreversible – one cannot regain lost innocence.[33]

The reason for his despair is clear. Rousseau's view of history is a combination of pagan and Christian, it is quasi-cyclical yet linear. There may be a linear universal history, yet each people may pass through but one round of growth and decline. The cycle is not connected at the base.

The reaction to the . . . Arts and Sciences

Rousseau's work provoked a storm of controversy.[34] Ironically – in view of his preoccupation with sincerity – he was praised for his eloquence and cleverness, but his paradoxes were taken by many as clear evidence of the fact that he could not be in earnest![35] Among those who replied to Rousseau's work was the King of Poland, and Rousseau was also delighted (at this stage) to be distinguished by criticism in the preliminary 'Discourse' to the *Encyclopaedia*, which began publication in the same

---

[32] Wokler, 'The *Discourse* . . . and its offspring', p. 258, ff.

[33] In the Preface to his play *Narcisse* he wrote shortly after — as he was to later in *The Social Contract*, 'The morals of a people are like the honour of a man: a treasure, to be preserved, but one which when lost, can never be recovered. . . . since a vicious people can never return to virtue there can be no question of restoring the goodness of those who are no longer good.' 'Preface to *Narcisse*' p. 551. Rousseau was careful to warn critics against drawing the conclusion from his work that any return to a state of simple virtue was possible. In a note to the *Discourse on Inequality*, p. 229, (Vaughan, *Writings I*, p. 207), he added a passage ridiculing the possibility of a return to nature: 'must society be destroyed, mine and yours be abolished, and we return to the forests to live amongst bears?' To the King of Poland he wrote ' Beware of concluding that we ought today to burn the libraries and destroy the universities and academies.' Cited Cranston *Early Life*, p. 243.

[34] Most of the replies discussed here are reprinted in *Jean-Jacques Rousseau, The First and Second Discourses together with the replies to the critics and the Essay on the Origin of Languages* ed. and trs. Victor Gourevitch (New York, etc., 1986). I have drawn heavily on Robert Wokler's excellent discussion, 'The *Discourse* . . . and its offspring'.

[35] S.S.B. Taylor, 'Rousseau's Reputation in Contemporary France', *Studies in Voltaire and the Eighteenth-Century*, XXVII (1963), pp. 1548–9.

[36] Denis Diderot and Jean d'Alembert, *L'Encyclopédie, ou Dictionnaire Raisonné*, (repr. 5 vols, Elmsford, New York, N. D.), *Discours Préliminaire*, vol. 1, p. xxxiii. Praising Rousseau's work as eloquent and philosophical they argued that the evils he attributed to the arts and sciences arose from other sources.

year.[36] Those who took him seriously however, raised objections which provoked Rousseau to further elaborate his position, and he published no less than seven replies.[37]

Rousseau, his critics claimed, had confused ignorance with virtue. Without the cultivation of the arts men were not innocent, but barbaric and cruel; the uncorrupted state was an illusion. Rousseau's history, they complained, was vague and shaky: ancient stoics *were* supporters of the world of learning, Sparta notwithstanding, and in any case when, exactly, did Rousseau see corruption setting in? What was the relationship between the barbarism that preceded classical learning, and the barbarism of the ensuing dark ages and medieval period, on the escape from which, Enlightenment thinkers were still busy congratulating themselves? Corruption, inasmuch as it existed, was surely a consequence of riches rather than of learning. Others argued that nations declined from political, rather than moral causes.[38] These and other criticisms spurred Rousseau to clarify and systematize his thought.

Rousseau's various replies were first synthesized in the brilliant preface to his play *Narcisse,* revived for publication at the time. There, and in his 'Reply to the King of Poland' he starts to focus on the problem of chronology and causality. Rather than simply *associating* together wealth, the spread of learning and moral corruption, he begins the process of sorting out the causal relationships between them, presenting the move from virtuous simplicity to immoral complexity as a temporally structured process, a true genealogy of corruption.[39] In the 'Reply to the King of Poland' he asserts the centrality of what was to prove a new and continuing focus of his political thinking from then on, inequality:

> I never said that luxury was born from learning, but that they were born together, the one could not have gained strength without the other. . . . The first source of evil is inequality, from inequality comes wealth; for these words wealthy and poor are relative, and wherever men are equal there are neither rich nor poor. From wealth is born luxury and idleness; from luxury comes the refined arts and from idleness the sciences.[40]

In answer to critics' assertions of the violence and rapacity of uncultured man, Rousseau begins to develop an understanding of the necessary role played by institutions in any serious depredations which humans might impose on each other.

> Before these hideous words *yours* and *mine* were invented; before there existed that cruel and brutal sort of men which we call masters, and that other sort, knavish and deceitful, called slave; before there were men so loathsome as to dare possess more whilst others died of hunger; before mutual dependence forced all to become deceitful,

---

[37] The following list of objections is abridged from the discussion of the replies in Wokler, 'The *Discourse* . . . and its offspring', pp. 258–261.

[38] A point made by Hume in his essay 'Of the Rise and Progress of the Arts and Sciences', but against Rousseau by his friend Charles Borde of Lyons.

[39] 'For to admit that these things go hand in hand is not to admit that one has led to the other. I have still to demonstrate a causal connection.' 'Preface to *Narcisse*', p. 547

[40] 'Observations, by Jean-Jacques Rousseau of Geneva on the Answer to his Discourse [by King Stanislas of Poland]', in *The First and Second Discourses*, ed. Gourevitch, p. 45, and in *Oevres Complétes*, III, pp. 49–50.

jealous and treacherous; I wish someone would explain to me in what it was that these vices and crimes with which [primitive man] is charged could have consisted.[41]

The *Origins of Inequality*

Apart from an unpublished *Essay on Wealth,*[42] which explores what was to become for Rousseau an important theme – the effect of wealth and poverty on personality – the major fruit of Rousseau's reflections on his critics was his *Discourse on the Origins of Inequality*, completed in 1754, again in response to a competition from the Academy of Dijon (who clearly recognised good publicity when they saw it). The second *Discourse* elaborates in an extraordinary fashion a speculative history of human psychology and social institutions. As well as dealing with the issue of inequality it attempts to answer the question implicit in his earlier criticism of contemporary culture – if modern society is false and artificial, what would it be to be true and natural?

The problem of 'nature'

The question of what was 'natural' was of course, an exceptionally difficult one to answer, not least, as Hume had pointed out, because it was a word with so many meanings. If 'natural' is opposed to 'artificial' there are two senses in which its meaning could be explored. Our natural qualities might be thought of as essences which underlay our acquired characteristics in such a way that we might, by a process of philosophical analysis, succeed in stripping away what our selves owed to civilization to discover our true 'natures'. Yet this enterprise was fraught with difficulty. As Rousseau himself pointed out in the first pages of the *Discourse*, philosophers continually made the mistake of reading back into 'nature ideas which were acquired in society'.[43] The alternative, to conceive of 'the natural' historically, also posed difficulties. Thinkers of Rousseau's time, had to struggle both conceptually and politically to establish a developmental conception of humanity against the religious orthodoxy of the creation story in Genesis. To suggest that speculation about secular origins could answer questions about our nature was to virtually reject the Bible as a fable.[44] Even accepting that human nature could be identified with human origins which pre-dated civilization, or even speech, the 'nature' discovered there was, as his critics had pointed out, likely to be nothing but savagery, and irrelevant to the standards and criteria of civilized men. In the end Rousseau hovers between the two. This is hardly surprising given the leap of imagination needed at the time to think about human development in truly evolutionary terms. He

---

[41] 'Last Reply, by J-J. Rousseau of Geneva', in *The First and Second Discourses*, ed. Gourevitch, p. 73, in *Oevres Complétes*, III, p. 80.

[42] The *Discours sur les richesses*, eventually published in 1853. The essay is discussed in C.E. Ellison, 'The Moral Economy of the Modern City: Reading Rousseau's *Discourse on Wealth*', *History of Political Thought*, xii, 4 (1992).

[43] *Discourse on the Origins of Inequality*, p. 50.

[44] 'Religion commands us to believe that God Himself having taken men out of a state of nature immediately after the creation, they are unequal only because it is His will they should be so: but it does not forbid us to form conjectures based solely on the nature of man, and the beings around him, concerning what might have become of the human race, if it had been left to itself.' Ibid., p. 51.

evaded criticisms about the accuracy of his ancient history by denying that what he was asserting could be tied down to specific historical episodes or sequences. In his response to the Abbé Raynal he denied having committed himself on these issues, he claims 'I cast my thesis in the form of a general proposition . . . I found the progress in these two things [decadence and literary culture] always to be directly proportional'.[45] Gradually, and emblematically (for social thought was in the process of shedding its preoccupation with the classical world) Rousseau substitutes anthropology for ancient history, the Abbé Prévost's *Histoire générale des voyages* for Plutarch's *Lives* as a primary source.[46] Confusingly, he warns that his investigations 'must lay facts aside'. His arguments 'should not be considered as historical truths but only as mere conditional and hypothetical reasonings, rather calculated to explain the nature of things than to ascertain their actual origin'. Yet the form of his argument is sequential: it is a speculative moral prehistory, and he tells us 'the times of which I am going to speak are remote', that it is 'the life of the species which I am going to write'.[47] The confusion is more apparent than real, for there is a sense in which for truly developmental beings our essences are our pasts, and we can never know what we are except by knowing how we have come to be so.[48]

Rousseau tells us his concern in the *Discourse* was precisely to 'mark, in the progress of things, the moment at which right took the place of violence and nature became subject to law, and to explain by what bizarre chain of events the strong submitted to serve the weak, and the people to purchase an imaginary repose at the expense of real happiness.' This is an interesting and carefully worded account. The real disasters do not appear until the end of the sequence. The initial transition from violence to right does not seem an objectionable one. The progress from nature to corruption is not an uninterrupted decline. Rousseau recognises both the moral appeal of natural simplicity as well as the primitivism inherent in the idea of the 'natural'. He sets out to explain how humans advanced to the point where they *could* have become moral, as well stressing that from that point they *in fact* became vicious. There has been, in human history, a moment of moralization, but it has passed. There is, he suggests to the reader, 'an age at which you would have wished your species had stopped'.[49]

The natural condition (i) physical

Rousseau assures us that man 'as he comes from the hand of nature' would have been, in terms of bodily skills and endurance, vastly superior to his modern descendants, whose reliance on the tools and contrivances of civilization has undermined their natural, unaided capacities. Mentally too, he would have had few, and easily gratified desires, and would have been accepting of natural processes such as ageing and death. His senses

---

[45] 'Letter to Monsieur L'Abbé Raynal' in *The First and Second Discourses*, ed. Gourevitch, p. 28.

[46] The antithesis is suggested by Wokler, 'The *Discourse* . . . and its offspring', p. 263.

[47] *Inequality*, pp. 50–1; Brumfitt and Hall suggest that 'the facts' to be laid aside are those concerning human origins related in the Old Testament, direct repudiation of these might well have caused Rousseau trouble, hence the confused attempt to sidestep the issue. See note, p. 345, and above, n.44.

[48] Jean Starobinski, 'The Discourse on Inequality', in Starobinski, *Transparency and Obstruction*, pp. 291ff.

[49] Ibid., pp. 50, 51; (Vaughan, *Writings*, vol.1, p. 140).

of taste and touch being unrefined, would have conveyed to him no dissatisfaction with the coarseness of his existence; whilst his superior senses of smell, sight and hearing would have enabled him to discern things at as great a distance as we can with optical aids such as telescopes. We could never have guessed at these characteristics from any empirical investigations into cultivated men; for like domesticated animals, socialised man is weak and timid. But evidence of these qualities is given by travellers' tales of aboriginal peoples alive at his time.[50]

The natural condition (ii) moral

The moral or psychological qualities of such men would have exhibited equally extraordinary differences. It is not in their knowledge or understanding that natural men differ from animals, so much as in their possession of free will. Animals operate intuitively, by instinct, men by choice.[51] That capacity for choice often proves their undoing, but it also allows for improvement, the quality of 'perfectibility' by which human beings successively change their way of living, incorporating innovations, which, starting as conveniences, become necessities. The inventor of a blanket responded not to a necessity (he or she *had* done without it), but to an inconvenience. Once we are used to blankets however, the lack of them is unacceptable and they become necessities.[52] The accumulation of such acquired necessities is what goes under the name of progress.

However, whilst free will offers the *possibility* of adaptation and improvement, it does not explain how individuals could become motivated to seek the initiation of such improvements. Reason develops only because the passions stimulate it. But the passions themselves can only motivate us beyond blind instinct, once we can depict to ourselves new possibilities, which in turn we cannot do without the further development of reason. Rousseau, in attempting to rely on sensationalist empiricism – 'seeing and feeling must be his first condition' – is in fact pushing at the limits of the doctrine. It seems we have to be able to imagine improvements before we can be motivated to attempt them, yet we cannot gain empirical knowledge of what is possible in advance of experience, 'so great appears the distance between pure sensation and the most simple knowledge'.[53] How then could progress begin? Chance and necessity must have played initially the major part.

However invention was explained, Rousseau points out, ideas and acts perish with their performers unless they could be communicated to another, nor would communication necessarily help unless men were sociable. Language and society were necessary for innovation to be sustained. Rousseau raises extraordinarily penetrating questions in this short diversion on the then popular topic of the origin of language. Is language inventable prior to abstract thought, or abstract thought prior to language? How did men move from naming of individual things to universal terms for general kinds? He cannot answer these questions; but he is clear that some explanation is needed: neither language

---

[50] Ibid., pp. 52–58.

[51] A distinction in the operation of natural law emphasised by Aquinas (see Ch. 1 Hobbes, n.150). Note that the question of whether inequality is authorised by natural law is the second part of the title.

[52] *Inequality*, p. 58.

[53] The gist of the problems raised at ibid., pp. 61–2.

nor sociability can be assumed to be a natural quality of humans, and neither is possible without the other – 'speech is the first social institution'.[54]

Although he cannot unravel the chicken-and-egg problem of language and sociability, Rousseau is decided on another issue, the question of whether humans are motivated by sympathy as well as by their own interests. A major problem posed by Hobbes, and recognised, especially by his critics, is that once we abandon God and try to give a secular account of morality, we seem thrown back on the pervasiveness of self-interest. And self-interest is, as Hobbes's and modern theorists' difficulties reveal, an unpromising ground on which to construct a morality. As Rousseau points out, even Hobbes's followers, such as Mandeville, acknowledged pity as a further natural impulse. This is not, in conventional terms, a virtue – a self-conscious principle which we use to limit our desire – but a natural sentiment of compassion which on occasion, and prior to any kind of reflection, 'tempers the love he has for his own well-being, through an innate repugnance at seeing his own like suffer'.[55] Anticipating his theme of the effect of civilization on our moral natures, Rousseau notes how reasoned reflection undermines the spontaneity of compassion. It is the cautious philosopher who stands aside from the street-brawl, whilst the mob and the common market-women intervene to prevent injury.[56]

The absence of natural conflict

Hobbes's picture of the state of nature, is then, decisively rejected by Rousseau, but for complex and subtle reasons. It is not simply the existence of compassion which limits conflict between natural men, it is the poverty of their imaginations that limits the causes of it. Rousseau stresses how most serious causes of conflict and unhappiness are *introduced* by the civilizing of our tastes and the developing sense of a social self. Think these away and 'To what kind of misery is a free being subject whose heart is at peace and whose body in health?'[57] Two particular cases exemplify how natural life denies causes of conflict common in cultured society.

The coarseness of taste and indifference to particulars severely limit the motives for conflict in the natural condition. One tree is as good as another to shelter under, another fruit as good as the one I have just had taken from me. Where difference is unperceived there is less motive to fight over losses.[58] This is even more true in the case of sexual passion, characteristically viewed by Rousseau from a male perspective. Before the emergence (and cultivation) of individuality, of ideas of beauty and moral worth, or the capacity to make comparisons based on these, sexual passion could not be directed at a particular individual. Such an element of love in sexuality must, thinks Rousseau, be a

---

[54] Ibid., p. 64ff.; and *Essay on the Origin of Languages*, in *First and Second Discourses*, ed. Gourevitch, p. 240. Rousseau worked on the *Essay on the Origin of Languages* during the 1750s and 60s, but never published it (Cranston, *Early Life*, p. 289). Its theme parallels that of the *Discourse on Inequality*, language at first honest, open, expressive, becomes deceitful, exact, dry and abstract.

[55] *Inequality*, p. 73 (Vaughan, *Writings*, vol. 1, p. 160).

[56] Ibid., p. 75.

[57] Ibid., p. 180 (Vaughan, p. 158).

[58] Ibid., p. 79.

creation of civilization. In the natural state 'man is attuned only to the disposition received from nature, not to the taste he could not yet have acquired; and one woman is as good as the next'.[59] Quarrels resulting from possession or envy would therefore be minimal, even in the extreme case of sexual jealousy.

A second, and more far reaching example of the limitations which simplicity places on conflict lies in the quality of natural egoism itself. In an important note, Rousseau warns that we must not confuse natural egoism or self-love (l'amour de soi-même) with the social passion of pride, or vanity (l'amour-propre).

> Self-love is a natural feeling which leads each animal to care for its own preservation, and which in mankind, guided by reason and modified by pity, produces humaneness and virtue. Pride, or vanity is an artificial and relative feeling, born of society, which leads each individual to make more of himself than of anyone else, which inspires men to all the harm they do one another, and is the real source of social distinction.[60]

Without this sense of pride, as Hobbes himself had pointed out, conflict would be limited to the immediate object, or rather to the satisfaction of the desire to which the object in question related.[61] If I desire fruit, and have had my apple taken from me, the only question is whether I can more easily satisfy that desire through fighting to regain the apple or by picking another. Where our palate is not discriminating, and we have no sense of face to lose, we will normally choose the other apple. Social man, however, always thinking of the figure he cuts with others, has a new repertoire of motives for conflict. In nature, by contrast, neither pride nor the uniqueness of the object exacerbates any tendency to conflict.

There is one last and vital observation about conflict which relates to the professed theme of the *Discourse*. Not only would conflict be minimised by the natural condition, so also would be the results of conflict – subordination and inequality. In fact they would not only be minimised but temporary to the point of being fleeting. In a state of nature it is sometimes said, the strong would oppress the weak. But how, asks Rousseau, under the conditions described, could anyone, in any continuous sense, oppress anyone else? Someone could chase me from my tree, steal the fruits I have gathered or the game I have killed, but how could anyone get themselves obeyed, or be rendered dependent?[62] It is only once we depend on others that we must obey them, and it is only once they

---

[59] Ibid., p. 78 (Vaughan, p. 164). The word 'moral' used, both in French by Rousseau, and in English by translators, to distinguish the non-physical element of sexual attraction is misleading (for example at the start of the quoted paragraph: 'Let us begin by distinguishing the moral from the physical in feelings of love.' Ibid., p. 77) It has to do not with moral in the sense of ethical duty, but, as so often in eighteenth-century writing, to the psychological or dispositional, as opposed to the purely instinctive.

[60] Ibid., p. 73 (Vaughan p. 217).

[61] Hobbes of course, stresses that pride, although not innate, is a rational individual response to any threat from another — since 'reputation of power is power'. Rousseau argues that such reasoning could not occur to ignorant unsophisticated natural beings, but only to clever, civilized men, whose rationally reinforced aggression Hobbes has projected back onto the state of nature. Ibid., pp. 71–2; and, implicitly, *The Social Contract*, p. 183.

[62] *Inequality*, p. 81; and Appendix, p. 120.

have something we need that we can be brought to depend on them.[63] The increase and multiplication of human needs – 'opening up inlets to pain and death'[64] – is thus the central hinge on which humanity is swung from the isolation and independency of nature into the dependency of the social condition.

The emergence of dependency (i) material causes

Rousseau opens his account of the 'fall' into social life, and the second part of the *Discourse*, with a striking claim about the central role of private property: 'The first who having enclosed some land, thought to assert "this is mine", and found people simple enough to believe him, was the true founder of civil society.'[65] However before even this can come about he must explain how to overcome the isolation of natural men. The key to this loss of isolation is man's perfectibility, a blessing and a curse, the source of both his knowledge and his stupidity, his virtues and his vices, his sociability and his wickedness.[66]

For these developments to follow, given only the qualities and potential of natural man, certain external and material causes must be applied. Rousseau's moral history rests on a firm economic base. These causes are initially the natural difficulties placed in the way of survival, difficulties arising from scarcity, competition, pressures of population, extremes of climate and natural disaster. Rising to these challenges involved human beings in innovative responses including the devising of weapons, the invention of clothing and the domestication of fire. But interesting too are the psychological changes which Rousseau speculates must have accompanied these developments. Human reflection on the qualities and relationships that affect successful hunting must have given rise to comparative mental conceptions of size, speed, strength, boldness etc., and man's own successful innovation in hunting must have led him to reflect on his own superiority to animals, leading in turn to making such comparisons between himself and other men. Our domination of nature thus prepared the way conceptually for our domination of each other.[67]

The emergence of dependency (ii) social and psychological

As we have seen, in our original state the persistence of domination was impossible because of the isolated nature of existence. How then did men come together? Partly again, Rousseau argues, as a natural outgrowth of man's inventiveness in overcoming difficulties. Observing the regularities in the behaviour of other men would follow naturally from observing the regularities of nature – part of a purely natural prudence.

---

[63] Ibid., p. 190, 'bonds of servitude are formed merely by the mutual dependence of men . . . it is impossible to make any man a slave unless he be first reduced to a situation in which he cannot do without the help of others . . . '.

[64] Ibid., appendix, p. 120.

[65] Ibid., p. 84, (Vaughan, p. 169).

[66] Ibid., pp. 60, 82.

[67] Ibid., pp. 85–7.

Recognising in them behavioural similarities to himself would lead him to attribute to them the motives that operated in his own case, and thus to realise the possibility of combined action for such mutually beneficial enterprises as could not be accomplished alone – the catching of large game for example. This would encourage the development of simple communication. But the other main stimulation to sociability was the establishment of the family. This Rousseau seems to link in some way to the construction of houses. There is no real explanation here of why the hitherto solitary sexes should now start to cohabit. The effects of it, were, however, far reaching. It produced the first developments of sentiment and feeling; it led to a differentiation of roles by sex, women becoming more sedentary, men foraging abroad. As family networks increased, society, and the feelings it engendered, became more extensive; it accelerated the development of language; and the increased leisure time allowed for the further invention of conveniences.[68]

The development of the social group speeds the growth of self-awareness. Since we wish to be accepted by the group, we seek to acquire qualities, or the appearance of them, which are acceptable to others. We start to see ourselves through others' eyes, and this leads us to deny (or conceal) our real wishes and present ourselves in a favourable light:[69] 'Man's being and man's appearance, now became two completely different matters'.[70] It is, once again, interesting to note that the process being described here is essentially that described by Hume as part of his natural history of morality. For Rousseau too it leads to morality – morality *is* seeing ourselves through others' eyes.[71] However it is a situation that for him is fraught with danger and is morally highly ambiguous.[72] The crucial difference arising from the social and primitive states is that 'the wild man lives within himself; social man, always outside himself, only knows how to live in the

[68] Modern studies intriguingly suggest Rousseau was right here. Both the remarked-on sexual role-differentiation and extensive leisure time are prominent features of hunter-gatherer societies. See Marshall Sahlins, *Prehistoric Economics* (London, 1970).

[69] The achievement of a secular 'distance', a standpoint outside ourselves or our society from which we might better view ourselves was a preoccupation of Enlightenment thought. Montesquieu's *Persian Letters*, supposedly describing French society in the letters home of an oriental outsider, was a sophisticated, and typical literary device. At the more demotic level there is Robert Burns's epigramatic plea: 'Ah wid some power the giftie gie us tae see oorselves as ithers see us'. The device was exploited even by popular entertainers in France; see Keohane, *Philosophy and the State*, p. 422. It is characteristic of Rousseau that, unlike most of his contemporaries he sees this distancing process in negative terms. See further, n.72.

[70] Ibid., p. 95, (Vaughan, p. 178).

[71] Rousseau stresses this, ibid., p. 90, 'hence arose the first obligations of civility'. Adam Smith's notion of justice as the judgement that would be given by an 'impartial spectator' is another, more abstract and prescriptive embodiment of the idea. See Adam Smith, *The Theory of Moral Sentiments*, ed. D. D. Raphael and A .L. MacFie (Oxford, 1976) p. 83 & passim.

[72] *Inequality*, p. 112. Where we judge ourselves through the eyes of others our morality will be dependent on theirs. True political morality is for Rousseau a singular and unusual instance of the more general desire to be approved of and acclaimed by other people, hence the equivocation over the moral status of viewing ourselves through others' eyes: 'it is to this desire of being talked about, and this unremitting rage of distinguishing ourselves, that we owe the best and the worst things we possess, both our virtues and our vices, our science and our errors, our conquerors and our philosophers; that is to say a great many bad things and a very few good ones.' To internalise the judgements of dissolute fellow-citizens is to collude in our own corruption, but to judge ourselves, as Rousseau would have us do in *The Social Contract*, through the eyes of an idealised universal citizen is to elevate our morality above the standards of any actual person.

opinions of others; which is to say that he draws his very sense of his own existence only from their judgement.'[73] Hume was complaisant about vanity, it provided a motive for the internalization of social norms. For Rousseau it is in the growing dependency on others that human pride, deception and inequality, as well as the possibility of morality, emerges. The core of this process is the loss of independence:

> As long as men only applied themselves to tasks which could be accomplished alone, and skills which didn't require the collaboration of many hands, they lived as free, healthy, well and happily as could be, consistent with their natures . . . But from the moment that one man had need of help from another, as soon as it was understood there was advantage in one man having provisions for two, equality disappeared, property was introduced, work became necessary; and the vast forests were changed into smiling fields which had to be watered with men's sweat and in which one soon saw slavery and misery sprout up and grow along with the harvest.[74]

Specialization, dependency and inequality

Economic innovations that increase men's interdependence reinforce these factors. The introduction of metallurgy and arable farming are identified by Rousseau as the two crucial steps in human moral, as well as economic history. Smiths are not self-subsistent, they must exchange their products with the farmers who produce food. Farmers in turn must be made to need iron in order to be willing to exchange food for it. It is in the growth of need that independence is destroyed.[75] Cultivation leads to the private possession of land, even though its origin, in labour, could only have justified ownership of the harvest, not the land itself. Once private property exists, any natural inequalities between men (for there are many) are reinforced and perpetuated. Once all the land is possessed, theft or slavery are the only courses open to men to survive.[76] Whether by force or stealth all need to get others to do their will. The complimentary vices of a divided society, indifference and sycophancy, had their roots here. He could not have wished to become rich, Rousseau wrote later, for to have done so he would have to have done what one needs to do to become rich: 'to be insolent and degraded, sensitive and feeling only on my own behalf, harsh and pitiless to all besides, a scornful spectator of the sufferings of the lower classes'.[77]

Although the property owners seem to have the better of this, they are in reality as dependent on the poor as the poor are on them. Man 'became in some sense a slave [his own kind] to even in becoming their master'.[78] Moreover the rich, used to luxury and

---

[73] *Inequality*, p. 116, (Vaughan, p. 195).

[74] Ibid., p. 92, (Vaughan, pp. 175–6).

[75] Ibid., pp. 92, 94.

[76] Ibid., p. 96.

[77] *Emile*, p. 310.

[78] *Inequality*, p. 95, (Vaughan, p. 179).

slaves to their own discriminating tastes, are more vulnerable – they 'have feelings in every part of their possessions'.[79]

It is this insecurity of the privileged and wealthy which Rousseau thinks must have led to the second great revolution in society. The position of the property owners was morally indefensible. The universal consent of humanity would have been needed before such private property could be justified.[80] The rich therefore contrived a confidence trick of epic proportions designed to convert usurpation into what appeared to be right. They suggested that everyone associate together to use their common force to 'secure the weak from oppression, restrain the ambitious, and assure to every man the possession of what belongs to him'. Crude and ingenuous as the poor were, they agreed and 'all ran headlong to their chains believing they were ensuring their liberty'.[81] The political association of one social group forced others to associate defensively in their turn, and the world became one of states.[82]

The final step, and the third great historical revolution, was to transfer public authority from the people as a whole to a private individual, and the loss of liberty was complete.[83]

At the end of this still astonishing work Rousseau reiterates his two main themes, the psychological transformation man undergoes in the course of his development, and the role of social and political life in opening up the possibility of serious inequality. He hopes the reader will understand first

> ... how the soul and the human passions altering insensibly, change so to speak their nature; why the objects of our needs and pleasures eventually change; why, as original man disappears by degrees, society presents to the thoughtful spectator only a collection of artificial men and counterfeit passions which are the product of these new relations, and have no real basis in nature[84]

[79] Ibid., p. 101. The idea recurrs in *Emile*, p. 46, where civilized man is criticised for 'grasping at everything . . . We spread ourselves so to speak, over the whole world , and all this vast expanse becomes sensitive.'

[80] The problem of whether and what kind of consent was needed to establish private property from a common stock was a crucial and much debated one amongst the early contract theorists of the seventeenth century, some of whom, such as Grotius (later and weakly) and Pufendorf (more insistently) actually speculated on the existence of such a contract, which it was the intention of Locke, through his theory of individual appropriation to circumvent. Locke was known to Rousseau both directly and through the eighteenth-century French natural lawyer and commentator Jean Barbeyrac. Rousseau's claim here, was made by Filmer as an ironic way of showing the impossibility of private property, as Rousseau, who discusses Filmer, must have known. See above pp. 88ff. Barbeyrac's role in interpreting the Grotian-Pufendorf-Locke tradition is stressed by James Tully, *A Discourse on Property* (Cambridge, 1980) pp. 5–7 and ff.

[81] *Inequality*, p. 98, (Vaughan, p. 181).

[82] Ibid., p. 99. Once again Rousseau's account of the catalytic effect of one state on the formation of others finds substantial agreement in modern commentators. See work by Carniero, cited p. 36.

[83] Once again Rousseau here touched on a crucial and ongoing debate amongst social contract theorists. Was there both a contract of institution and a contract of subjection, or, as Hobbes finally argued, one contract which embodied both moves? Rousseau thinks there must have been two, for it would have been absurd for men seeking to escape the tyranny of the powerful in the state of nature, 'to begin by casting into the hands of a ruler the very things, which they needed his help to conserve for themselves. ' *Inequality*, p. 102, (Vaughan, p. 184).

[84] Ibid., p. 115, (Vaughan, pp. 194–5).

and secondly how

> It follows from this demonstration that inequality, being almost absent in the state of nature, grows and draws strength from the development of our faculties and the progression of the human intellect, and becomes at last established and legitimated through the institution of property and the laws.[85]

The possibilities for freedom

Striking as this work is, Rousseau's view is one of almost unrelieved gloom. The idea that discovering what human beings were 'naturally like' could settle arguments about the legitimacy or otherwise of civilized institutions proved to be an illusion. Natural man although 'good' is not even capable of morality, and the processes by which he might become so seem inseparable from those that corrupt and degrade him. Civilized life is degenerate and yet 'natural' life unfulfilled. Moreover, even if nature were fulfilling, 'progress' is irreversible. We cannot pretend to an innocence we have lost, nor can we 'go back to living in the forests with the bears'.[86] Is there an alternative?

In fact there may be several. One way of viewing Rousseau's various works is as explorations of possible ways out of the seeming cul-de-sac of civilized life.[87] The tension Rousseau depicts between nature and civilization, and between the individual and society – the two axes of his social thought – is absolute as long as the individual is identified with nature, and society with civilization. But if individuality can be sustained outside the natural state, or if a society can be described which avoids what passes for civilization, possibilities begin to emerge for other, more fulfilling forms of existence.

In *Emile*, an attempt is made to educate an individual to moral independence. One who would be capable of resisting the pressures to internalise the values and aspirations of a corrupt society around him. This is exceptionally difficult. Our education comes from three sources, from our nature, from things and from men. One source of our unhappiness in the modern world is the conflict between the lessons learned from these three. Emile's education is to consist in removing him from the influence of society – taking him out of the traffic of the social 'highway', and placing a protective wall around him – until he is strong enough to resist society's values. Emile can never be a natural man, or fully socially integrated, but he can be independent.

On the other hand, in *Emile*, Rousseau also acknowledges the possibility of a drastic collective solution to the problem. 'Good social institutions are those best fitted to make a man unnatural, to exchange his independence for dependence, to merge the unit in the group, so that he no longer regards himself as one but as a part of the whole, and so is

---

[85] Ibid., p. 116, (Vaughan, p. 196).

[86] Ibid., Appendix, p. 125.

[87] See, initially, the suggestions made in Judith Shklar, 'Rousseau's Two Models, Sparta and the Age of Gold,' *Political Science Quarterly*, LXXXI, no.1 (1966), especially pp. 40–43. The exploration of the suggestions that Rousseau's major works consist of different attempts to solve the tensions between an unfulfilled, and unfulfilling nature, and a corrupting civilization is a popular interpretive theme, see, Keohane, *Philosophy and the State*, p.432ff.; and in brilliant, if historically precocious fashion, Berman, *The Politics of Authenticity*.

only conscious of the common life.'[88] In the *Government of Poland*, Rousseau describes the true republican in these terms:

> [love for his country] makes up his whole existence; he sees nothing but his country, he lives only for her; the minute he is alone, he is nothing, the moment he loses his country, he is no more; if he is not dead, he is worse than dead. [89]

This seeming endorsement of the radically denatured and socialised individual seems at odds with Rousseau's ideal, not only for Emile, but for a traditional society arrested at some point short of the onset of corruption, a 'golden age', as suggested briefly in the *Discourse on Inequality*. Although Rousseau's enthusiasm for natural independence, Emile's autonomy, the golden age, and the unnatural dependence of 'Good social institutions' represent clearly different ideals, do they represent confusion or vacillation in Rousseau's mind, or can they be related to a consistent theoretical position? I believe they can, through some general reflections on what Rousseau persistently regarded as his major political theme – freedom.

Dimensions of freedom

At the start of this chapter I emphasised the way in which Rousseau, as well as recognising that freedom involved physical constraint, opened up the inner dimension of political thought, and of freedom in particular. Allowing questions about whether our wills are free (as opposed to merely our actions) suggests that there are at least two ways in which our freedom can be denied. Firstly, in the more conventional sense, we might will something which we cannot attain. In this case our will is restrained *via* the incapacitating effects of the world in which we act – we are chained up, someone will prevent or threaten us, we do not have the resources and so on. But secondly, in a more unusual sense, our wills themselves might not be free; either in the sense of being riven by conflicting and irreconcilable desires, or through being totally enervated by some debilitating belief or doctrine, or again by being directed at something that is in principle unattainable. In all of these cases, whether the world or the will limits us, unfreedom arises from some discrepancy between what we will and the possibilities of realising that will in the world around us.

If this is so, it follows that there are in principle two ways of tackling the problems of unfreedom. The first involves reorganising the world so that the will is never presented with those objects which it is incapable of realising. The second involves so disciplining the will that it resolves never to will what it cannot possibly achieve. Freedom is either the rejection of the unattainable or the realisation of necessity: in either case will and possibility are once again brought into harmony. Although Rousseau does not develop his arguments in a philosophically rigorous form, there are clear indications that he structures his thought on freedom in this way.

---

[88] *Emile*, p. 7.

[89] Rousseau, *The Government of Poland*, ed. Willmoore Kendall (Indianapolis, 1972), p. 19, (Vaughan, II, p. 437).

The strong Stoic dimension of Rousseau's thought generally contains the notion of disciplined self-denial as the path to equanimity.[90] We have seen in the *Discourse on the Origins of Inequality*, how the increase in human desire and need disrupts both the internal integrity of the will – by making us live through others – and its capacity to realise its aims through increasing material reliance on others. Freedom, Rousseau asserts briefly in *The Social Contract*, is the concurrence of will and power.[91] But there is an explicit formulation of the doctrine, in his discussion of the principles to be applied in the education of Emile. Firstly 'dependence on things', it is claimed, does not infringe our freedom, and produces no vices, as does dependence on men.[92] It is at the most only an illusion of freedom that can be offended by desires for what is practically impossible. Emile is to be educated through maximum exposure to natural necessity, and the minimal use of human commands. For most of his education, indeed, his tutor must contrive to constrain Emile without appearing to command him (as must the Legislator of *The Social Contract* with respect to his society). The general spirit of the rules governing children's upbringing is to give them

> more real liberty and less power, to let them do more for themselves and demand less
> of others; so that by teaching them from the first to confine their wishes within the
> limits of their powers they will scarcely feel the want of whatever is not within their
> power.[93]

The congruency of will and power is here the crucial consideration. This is outlined by Rousseau in quite general terms, which go far beyond the schooling of Emile: 'Our wretchedness consists in the disproportion between our desires and our powers', or, more positively, 'True happiness consists in decreasing the difference between our desires and our powers, in establishing a perfect equilibrium between the power and the will, then only ... man will find himself in his true position.'[94] The practical implications are swiftly drawn: 'The world of reality has its bounds, the world of imagination is boundless; as we cannot enlarge the one, let us restrict the other'.[95]

But if this tactic produces happiness does it also produce freedom? Tranquillity, as he elsewhere sinisterly remarks, is found also in dungeons.[96] That Rousseau does believe this is suggested in his seemingly prescient and since then doubly poignant advice to the Poles to retain their freedom by building the national republic in their souls, so that even though physically conquered they could never be extinguished.[97] Again, at the end of

---

[90] See K.F. Roche, *Rousseau Stoic and Romantic*, (London, 1974), p. 8 note 2.

[91] *The Social Contract*, p. 229.

[92] *Emile*, p. 49, & see, p. 6 'we are taught by three masters, nature, men and things'. The idea that subjection to the natural world — it being an expression of rationality — was no infringement of freedom, has stoic roots. See generally on this theme Roche, *Stoic and Romantic*, esp. pp. 6–10. It is also interesting to note the assertion in a work entitled *Discours sur l'inéglité*, by Rousseau's much admired Marquis d'Argenson that 'nature dictates to us only laws that are easy to execute'. Cited Keohane, *Philosophy and the State*, p. 390.

[93] *Emile*, p. 35.

[94] Ibid., p. 44.

[95] Ibid., p. 45.

[96] *The Social Contract*, p. 186.

[97] *Poland*, p. 11, (Vaughan, II, p. 431).

Emile's education he reflects that his tutor has 'made me free by teaching me to yield to necessity'. Restraining his desires for anything external – even his bodily liberty – he realises he can feel the lack of nothing, he is not unfree.[98]

Could one, using these principles, create a society which presented only realisable aims, to a human psyche structured to desire only them? Could there be a society where not only the material aspirations of the citizens were so structured as to be capable of mutual satisfaction without engendering dependency, but where the desire for selfish aggrandizement so criticised in the *Discourse on Inequality* was uprooted at the psychic and not merely constrained at the legal level?[99] Moreover, if this could be done, could such a society be characterised as free? Or as Rousseau puts it, is it possible

> To find a form of association which defends and protects with the whole collective force the person and goods of each associate, and through which each one, in uniting with all, would obey no-one but himself, and remain as free as before.[100]

It is this question that *The Social Contract* seeks to answer.

The Social Contract

Introduction

The Social Contract was, Rousseau tells us, part of a larger projected work on political institutions. In 1759 this was evidently well under way, though requiring several more years work, when he decided to abandon it, and extract from it what was to become *The Social Contract*, published in 1762.[101]

As the name of the work implies, the form of Rousseau's argument derives from the traditions of the social contract, a theory little used in France since the sixteenth century. He refers frequently to the inadequacies of other social contract thinkers. But although it is less obvious he also draws on important traditions and debates in French thought.[102] Perhaps his most extraordinary feat was to try and merge two important, and opposed,

---

[98] *Emile*, p. 436.

[99] 'One does not stamp out luxury with sumptuary laws. You must reach deep into men's hearts, and uproot it by implanting there healthier and nobler tastes . . . the law's disapproval is never efficaceous except as it reinforces the disapproval of the citizen's own judgement.' *Poland*, p. 18.

[100] *The Social Contract*, p. 191, (Vaughan, II, p. 32).

[101] *The Confessions of Jean-Jacques Rousseau*, tr. & intr. J. M. Cohen (Harmondsworth, 1957[1953]), bk.x, p. 478. The idea of writing a book on political institutions seems to have been provoked in Rousseau by his experience of the labyrinthine government of republican Venice, when he was secretary to the French ambassador there, as far back as 1743–44. Cranston, *Early Life*, p. 175 & ch.10 passim. Another fragment from this abandoned work is probably the *State of War* (*Vaughan*, I, p. 283). See the recent reconstruction and discussion of the fragment by Grace G. Roosevelt, 'A Reconstruction of Rousseau's Fragments on the State of War' *History of Political Thought*, VIII, 2(1987).

[102] Keohane's *Philosophy and the State in France* is quite indispensible in providing this context, in particular the two figures referred to by Rousseau, the Abbé Saint-Pierre, and René-Louis de Voyer de Paulmy, Marquis d'Argensen. See esp. ch. xiii.

French traditions of political thinking by installing a very French absolutist sovereign in a popular constitutionalist republic, a tactic pursued, in a much more literal way by his mentor, cited several times in the work, the Comte d'Argenson.[103]

Rousseau equivocated over the use of the term Social Contract in the title.[104] But his decision to do so heightens his originality in using it to decisively reject the other central feature of contract theory, namely the transfer of political authority from a people to a sovereign.[105] That, as he famously puts it, 'man is born free, and is everywhere in chains' (a conclusion derived from his *Discourse on Inequality*) is a denial of the claims to the legitimacy of any contemporary polity, and an implicit criticism of all existing political theories.[106] The first part of his assertion denied any natural or given hierarchy, such that claimed by Filmer and the patriarchalists, as well as the assertions of *de facto* theorists – whether secular or religious – who argued that the holder of effective power is all we need concern ourselves with.[107] Natural equality is, of course, the assumption on which social contract theory is premised. Without equality a social contract would be difficult, and quite possibly unnecessary. But as we have seen, the major school of contract theory, taking its rise from Grotius, and numbering Hobbes amongst its most famous exponents, had used the contract to establish the possibility of virtual enslavement, solving the paradox of natal liberty and social subordination by claiming that men had, as their freedom entitled them to, given away their freedoms. It is precisely this that Rousseau denies is possible – morally possible.

That there are, or may have been, people who have contracted in this way, Rousseau does not deny, but that any right derives from it cannot be. This is not because such an act might offend against natural law – Rousseau is not, in any normal sense, a natural

---

[103] Keohane, *Philosophy and the State*, p. 390.

[104] In fact the Geneva MSS reveal that Rousseau changed his mind twice over the main title, at one time preferring *Of Civil Society*, before reverting to *The Social Contract*. Moreover the subtitle was changed even more often. See Vaughan, *Writings*, vol. 1, p. 22.

[105] As discussed in the chapter on Hobbes the modern 'contract tradition' synthesized ideas concerning two contracts — the social contract by which isolated humans (usually men) joined together to form a society, and contract of government or political contract, in which power was transferred to a sovereign. Rousseau's title implicitly rejects the latter.

[106] In the *Letters written from the Mountain* Rousseau characterised the starting point of *The Social Contract* in terms of his agreement and his differences from his contemporaries: 'What is it that makes the State one? It is the union of its members. And how is the union brought into being? From the obligations they lie under. Everyone agrees up to this point. But what is the basis of this obligation? Here is where authors disagree. For some it is force, for others paternal authority, for others the will of God. Each establishes his principle, and attacks those of the others. I do no more myself; and, following the most sane group of those who have discussed these things, I have suggested as the foundation of the political body the agreement of its members.' Letter VI, Vaughan, II, p. 200. Rousseau gives another account of what he was up to in *The Social Contract* towards the end of *Emile*, pp. 423ff.

[107] Rousseau, in common with many others takes Hobbes to be a *de facto* theorist. As we have seen this is not *quite* right, although the differences may not amount to much in practice. But he is also critical of thinkers such as Bossuet, a late-seventeenth-century divine right theorist, who base absolute obligations to *de facto* rulers on the assumption that God's providence must have placed them there: 'all power comes from God I admit; but all sickness does so too: is this to say we are not to call a doctor?' *The Social Contract*, p. 185 (Vaughan, p. 27). On Bossuet see Keohane, *Philosophy and the State*, pp. 252ff. There is a new edition, of his central work *Politics Drawn from the very words of Holy Scripture*, tr. and ed. Patrick Riley (Cambridge, 1990).

law thinker (a point in which he departs from previous radical contract theorists)[108] – but because to make such a contract would clearly have been an act of madness, and 'madness creates no right'. More certainly it creates no right over posterity. The paradox is that even if absolute and arbitrary government could be legitimate, it would have required endorsement from each generation.[109]

But Rousseau's more strategic objection to these interpretations of contract theory is that they assume what is most to be explained. The establishment of political authority – the *pactum subjectionis* 'is itself a civil act; that is, it presupposes a public deliberation. So before examining the act by which a people chooses a king, it would make good sense to examine the act by which a people is made a people; for it is this act logically prior to the other, is the real foundation of society'[110] – the *pactum sociale*.

Becoming a people

The problem of how individuals become a collective unity is seen and approached by Rousseau in a way analogous to Hobbes, though his answer is very different. Without a principle of unity, Rousseau agrees, a group is only an 'aggregation', not an association. Yet to even establish the political authority that would provide the principle of unity they would have already to act as a collectivity. Hobbes solves the problem, by making the act of association identical with that of subordination – the contract establishes at one and the same time both the community and the sovereign who unifies it. Rousseau follows the same tactic, yet for him, the community and the sovereign turn out to be the same thing, in different roles. Despite the fact that contract theories characteristically describe the grant of sovereignty to an individual or assembly, such a grant, in Rousseau's view, far from establishing an association, immediately dissolves it, and disbands the 'people'. Legitimacy is only possible if sovereignty is *retained* by the people.[111] The sovereign must therefore be identical with the citizens themselves. Radical as this undoubtedly is however, Rousseau is less radical than he can seem: the citizens need not be all the inhabitants, nor need all citizens be equal in their influence.

Rousseau's account of the establishment of political community involves far more than agreement: it changes the members' personalities. As he showed in the *Origins of Inequality*, and as he reiterates here 'This passage from the natural to the civil state produces a very remarkable change in man, substituting justice for instinct in his conduct,

---

[108] 'There neither is nor can be any kind of fundamental law binding on the body of the people — not even the contract itself'; *The Social Contract*, pp. 193–4 (and see *Inequality*, 'Preface', p. 45–6). In the first version of the *Contrat Social*, Rousseau rejects more clearly the idea of a natural jurisprudence preceding positive law. 'It is only from the social order established amongst us that we draw the ideas we imagine to be about it. We conceive of society in general after the pattern of particular societies . . . and we begin to become truly men only after having been citizens.' Vaughan, *Writings*, I, pp. 452–3. This objection would not hold against a view of natural law as a kind of abridgement of the collective social experience of mankind such as the Roman Law of Nations was, and such inductive generalisations were often thought to be the basis of natural law. But as we saw in Hobbes, modern, i.e., post-Grotian natural law theorists rejected this source in favour of a more abstract approach.

[109] *The Social Contract*, p. 186

[110] Ibid., p. 190; (Vaughan, p. 31).

[111] Ibid., p. 200

and giving to his actions the moral quality they had hitherto lacked.'[112] Although, as he has shown, the transition is fraught with the danger of tyranny and corruption, it holds out the possibility of true human ennoblement, above anything possible in his natural condition. *The Social Contract* picks up the story at the point he suggests we would have wished it to stop in the *Discourse on Inequality*, and invites us to consider a different outcome.[113] The terms of the contract which allows this are exacting: 'Each one of us places in common his person and all his powers under the supreme direction of the general will; and we receive back as a corporate body, each member, as an indivisible part of the whole.'[114] Perhaps we should better translate 'personne' here as 'personality' to empha-sise how much is at stake in entering the social condition.

How are our 'personnes' to be affected? The issue of liberty is crucial: We exchange natural liberty for civil or moral right or liberty. There seem to be two elements to this transition. Natural liberty, as in Hobbes's account, is a freedom to take and hold what we can. Civil right, on the other hand, guarantees proprietorship – secure enjoyment of what is ours. This is relatively unproblematic; although the stress on the importance of property here is interesting in view of Rousseau's jaundiced view of its consequences in the *Discourse*. What is more difficult is the second part of the transition. Natural man's liberty is the freedom to follow physical impulse, whilst the civil individual's freedom consists in acting in accord with the general will. In this sense, Rousseau insists, the move into society is more than a contract, it is a positive transcendence of our previous selves, which alone gains us self-mastery, for 'the impulse of appetite, alone, is slavery, whilst obedience to the law prescribed to oneself is freedom'.[115]

A people, then, is not merely a group of individuals who have made a contract, even a social contract; it is a group who have made a contract of a special kind that has both changed their natures and individual personalities, and created out of their isolated natural selves, a collective agency – the sovereign – capable of both embodying and legislating over their individual wills. Finally, unlike many other contract theorists, Rousseau several times insists that the contract cannot be a once-and-for-all act. To sustain legitimate political authority it must be continually reaffirmed by the citizens in a sovereign assembly.[116]

---

[112] Ibid., p. 195, (Vaughan, p. 36). See also the role of the founding legislator, whose task is that of 'changing human nature, of transforming each individual . . . altering man's constitution . . . [to] take away from man his own resources, and give him instead new ones alien to him, and incapable of being made use of without the help of other men.' *The Social Contract*, p. 214.

[113] Ibid., p. 190, 'I suppose men to have reached the point at which the obstacles in the way of their preservation in the state of nature show their power of resistance to be greater than the resources at the disposal of each individual for his maintenance in that state.'

[114] Ibid., p. 192, (Vaughan, p. 33).

[115] Ibid., p. 196, (Vaughan, p. 37).

[116] Ibid., pp. 185–6, 200–1, 262. Although at p. 201 he then also allows the possibility of 'tacit consent' as long as the sovereign is 'free to oppose'. Noone's claim, *Rousseau's Social Contract* (London, 1981) p. 25, n. 10, p. 191, that his interpretation of the social contract as the 'ongoing constitutive moral principle of society' and not a 'gimmick that is invoked to get civil society going and then quietly pushed into the background' is unique amongst commentators, seems extraordinary. Cf. for example the celebrated article by Shklar, 'Rousseau's Two Models: Sparta and the Age of Gold', p. 40: 'The Social Contract, the creation of a rightful bond of association is not only an act and an agreement. It is a continuing process . . . The Social Contract, is a constant transformation.'

Being forced to be free

The notion that obedience to our own law is freedom is pressed further by Rousseau in his famous claim that 'whoever refuses to obey the general will shall be compelled to do so by the whole of society, which means nothing more or less than that he will be forced to be free.'[117]

It is not the claim that the sovereign can coerce individuals that causes, or should cause, readers problems. All states, even the most liberal and democratic, do this; indeed Max Weber notoriously made the monopoly of such force a defining characteristic of the legitimate state. Rather it is the claim that in so submitting we are being forced to be *free* which liberals find especially disturbing.[118] But even this, although it might be objected to on other grounds, need not be conceptually problematic. 'Free' is an adjective that can be a description of an act, or a condition of either individuals or states. Particular acts may be free or not in view of the conditions under which they are performed. Coercion is clearly a condition which disqualifies acts from being free. Hence the apparent paradox of being 'forced to be free' but the paradox is only apparent. Rousseau does not talk about being forced to commit 'free acts' but of being forced in respect of acts which jeopardize (the state or condition of) freedom, and this is surely unproblematic.

Individual acts which are free in the normal way can certainly lead to conditions or states of being which are not. Indeed, they can lead to conditions in which the commission of free acts is no longer possible. One clear example is the onset of addiction. Whilst the initial acts of taking drugs may be freely performed, such acts can lead to a situation where subsequent actions acquire a compulsive character. *Free acts* here clearly lead to a *condition* which is *unfree*. If we accept that addiction is a state of unfreedom, wouldn't the coercion or restraint of such acts (preventing the slide into compulsive behaviour), or compulsory rehabilitation, both be correctly described as 'forcing someone to be free'? One would have to be a very hard-line libertarian indeed to shrug off such considerations and to press for freedom of traffic in drugs. But can this apply to politics?

The analogy is compelling in structure but difficult to apply. Both political acts and political conditions can be 'free'. Certain free political acts may undoubtedly lead to states of unfreedom. This is classically illustrated in the paradox of democracy. Does a democracy have the right to abrogate itself and grant sovereignty to a tyrant? Either answer seems to limit the sovereign *freedom of action* of democracy. But to place coercive limits on the *free actions* of the democratic sovereign to resign its sovereignty in this way might well be described as coercing or restraining it in order to sustain democratic *freedom as a state of being*[119] (suspending for a moment the problem of whether a sovereign of any kind could be subject to coercive limitation). Although Rousseau claims that 'there neither is nor can be any kind of fundamental law binding on the body of the people', it seems he must here mean fundamental *positive* law, for he

---

[117] Ibid., p. 195, (Vaughan, II, p. 36).

[118] See most famously, Sir Isaiah Berlin, 'Two Concepts of Liberty' in *Four Essays on Liberty* (Oxford, 1969).

[119] As Locke says in discussing natural law restraints: 'that ill deserves the Name of Confinement which hedges us in only from Bogs and Precipices.' *Second Treatise*, §57.

asserts early on in *The Social Contract* that there are some things a people cannot do; for example, to irrevocably transfer sovereignty to an absolute ruler would 'presuppose a people of madmen; and madness creates no right'.[120]

The difficulty with applying the drugs analogy is that we have fairly clear evidence of the compulsive behaviour that results from those kinds of 'free acts'. In the case of politics such clear evidence is less forthcoming. Nevertheless, if we allow for the moment Rousseau's claim that the condition of life in a community subject to the general will is a state of freedom, then attempts to disobey that sustaining will must be considered acts destructive of freedom. The constraint of such acts as a 'forcing to be free' follows by definition. The real problem then, reverts to Rousseau's characterisation of the sovereign general will as the embodiment of freedom. If this is once granted, the sense in which disciplining offenders against it is 'forcing them to be free' is less problematic.

The general will

The general will is what the sovereign assembly of all citizens ought to decide, if its deliberations were as they should be. Rousseau's discussion of the general will is rendered confusing for two reasons. Firstly we are not, as was Rousseau's contemporary audience, heirs to a rich tradition of both theology and social thinking in which the idea of the general will played a prominent role. For them the idea would immediately have elicited a range of positive associations and resonances on which Rousseau's rhetoric was able to draw. The second reason is that Rousseau does not clearly distinguish between abstract claims made about the *principle* of the general will, and the question of the *characteristics of* the political *institutions* and society he thought necessary to embody and realise it.[121] The potential difference between these two means that although 'the general will is always right and always tends to the public benefit; it does not follow that the deliberations of the people are always equally correct.'[122]

The background to the idea of the general will

The terms 'general will' and 'particular will' were much used in the theological literature of the seventeenth century with which Rousseau was familiar. In theological discussions of how, if God had willed the salvation of all, some could be damned, the terms general and particular will referred respectively to God's original intention to save all (frustrated by Adam's sin) and his subsequent intention to nevertheless save some. The issue became embroiled in the wider question of God's justice versus his omnipotence, which interestingly paralleled discussion at the time in England regarding the extent to which justice or reason could be said to constrain God's actions. In particular, important discussions by Malebranche, a disciple of Descartes, linked the terms with the essentially political issues of how to understand God's providence: whether he ruled the world through

---

[120] *The Social Contract*, p. 186.

[121] The distinction is made more clearly in the 'First Draft' of *The Social Contract*, (Vaughan, I, intr. p. 436, and text, p. 483).

[122] *The Social Contract*, p. 203, (Vaughan, II p. 42).

regular and consistent 'volontés générales' – which would show up as natural laws, or by acts of individual – and essentially arbitrary – willing in particular cases. Since the former is inherently more 'law-like', 'universal' and just, God, it seemed, must have chosen to rule in this way, and not by capricious particularity. The desire for miracles – essentially an interruption of 'general willing' – is essentially a selfish desire that God suspend the course of nature especially for us, that God will particularly, and from his sheer omnipotence. In willing generally, God is, he argues, willing not from his mere power, but in accordance with wisdom, justice and goodness. Thus the opposition between particular and general wills took on associations of the opposition between 'power' and 'justice', and between 'selfish' and 'social' which we find in Rousseau. Moreover there are further religio-political parallels in Malebranche's description of the passage from an original, [equal] state of human nature, corrupted by 'the ambition of some and the need of others' to one in which force rules, and men needed 'visible protectors'.

The increasingly secular career of these ideas paralleled that of many concepts as they moved from a theological to a political environment from the mid 17th to the mid 18th century. Two writers in particular confirmed this. The opposition between general and particular pervades the most famous French political treatise of the first half of the century, Montesquieu's *Spirit of the Laws*; and it plays a major role in one of the important articles in the *Encyclopaedia*, written by its editor Denis Diderot.[123] The association between the idea of generality and what was good, just and socially beneficial was therefore, a prominent part of the intellectual landscape, and nothing could have been more natural than for Rousseau to adopt it to express, not, as is sometimes claimed, an abstract metaphysical, and potentially repressive will, opposed to that of concrete individuals, but the will of the individual, when it was morally directed through a law-like concern for the collectivity of which he was a member.[124]

The abstract principles of the general will

The assumption behind the general will is that there is an objective common good, distinct from the particular interests or wishes of the individuals composing society (why else would it have been established?). Moreover it assumes that in any given situation there is always some policy or policies which will serve that common good.[125] Most major thinkers of the period acknowledge that the problem of identifying what is morally good, is quite distinct from that of motivating humans to pursue it. For Rousseau, with his extreme distrust of reason, the problem is more acute than for most. For the general will

---

[123] The principles of natural right are 'perpetual and invariable: one may not depart from them through any convention, nor even any law, nor may one shirk the obligations it imposes', and 'a full understanding of natural right requires an understanding of what obligation is in general.' 'Droit de la Nature, ou Droit Naturel', *Encyclopédie*, ed., Diderot and D'Alembert, vol.5, pp. 131, 133.

[124] The above draws on the excellent account in Patrick Riley's 'The General Will Before Rousseau', *Political Theory*, vol 6, no.4 (1978), and his book, *The General Will Before Rousseau* (Princeton, 1986). The ease with which concepts could be transferred between the fields of theology and politics in the early eighteenth century is commented on by Keohane, *Philosophy and the State*, p.432.

[125] *The Social Contract*, p. 200.

must be shown both to make sense to philosophers as an idea, and to be capable of being incorporated in the moral psychology of a people in such a way as to motivate them to pursue it. The problems are first to identify what the general will could be, and then to devise political institutions – and, it turns out, a political culture – capable of achieving it.

At its simplest level the general will is what identifies and sustains the existence of any collective body. A collectivity exists in some minimal sense as long as people identify with it at some level and they consider themselves members.[126] The sense of abstraction and metaphysical puzzles produced by the concept of the general will, to which Rousseau refers here, should not distract us from its essentially subjective and even nationalistic aspects.[127] If the general will vanishes completely, the society ceases to exist.[128] However, not only the state, but collectivities within it have wills. That is why Rousseau is so wary about allowing to political parties, or other informal associations, any political role. Allegiance to *their* collective will might become stronger than allegiance to that of the state.[129] For although the qualities that define the general will are objective, it is only through the actual willing of the citizens that it can be realized, and allowing particular, or less general wills greater strength in the minds of the citizens than the general will is a recipe for political collapse. But we are already straying into the arena of practicalities.

Although the general will has to be willed by the citizens to come into existence, it is not simply the outcome of whatever they will.[130] The general will is that decision which, if enacted by the people, would sustain the society, and what sustains a society is laid down, at least in part, in natural law. In the *Letters Written from the Mountain* Rousseau, writing in defence of his argument in *The Social Contract* claimed he asserted there that 'it is no more permissible to break the laws of nature by the Social Contract, than it is permitted to break positive laws by particular contracts; and it is only through these very [natural] laws that the liberty exists which gives force to the contract.'[131] As the principle of political right the general will thus has objective aims and characteristics, which the majority of the people, if uninformed, might fail to embody in their decisions. However, the fact that majorities could be wrong does not mean that they may be overridden. For Rousseau, citizen majority opinion is the only means of *realizing* political right, even though it does not *define* what is right. For reasons that should be clear to readers of the

---

[126] Ibid., p. 274

[127] Of necessity these aspects come through more strongly in works such as the *Government of Poland* and the *Project for Corsica*. (See for example the chapter on education in the *Government of Poland*: 'at ten to be familiar with everything Poland has produced; at twelve to know all of its provinces, all its roads, all its towns; at fifteen, to have mastered all his country's entire history, and at sixteen, all its laws; let his mind and heart be full of every noble deed, every illustrious man, that ever was in Poland . . . the content, the sequence, even the method of their studies should be specified by Polish Law. They should have only Poles for teachers . . . ' *Poland*, p. 20. Rousseau entreats us to be patriotic about even the most unworthy of states, see *Emile*, p. 437.

[128] *The Social Contract*, pp. 274–5.

[129] Ibid., p. 203, or if there are parties they should be small and many. The wills of partial associations are general only in relation to their members. Only the will of the society is truly general, although not of course, in relation to other states.

[130] 'What makes the will general is less the number of votes than the common interest uniting them . . . ' Ibid., p. 25.

[131] Letter VI, (Vaughan, p. 200).

Discourse on Inequality, and as Rousseau reiterates, the object of political right must be liberty and equality.[132] The preservation of equality is essential to the preservation of liberty, for it was the onset of inequality that spurred the growth of dependency and thence corruption, and enslavement. It is primarily this process that the general will must avert. Part of the objective content of the general will, therefore, is its 'constant tendency to equality'. By this Rousseau means not only procedural equality – equality before the law, but a strong measure of substantive equality. As an individual Rousseau had a horror of personal dependence extending well across the boundaries of paranoia. This seems to have been re-enforced by his exposure to French culture, a society he often sees as based on personal subservience through patronage rather than on contract.[133] We should not underestimate the importance of this for Rousseau's social theory. The general will 'secures [each citizen] against all personal dependence'.[134] Economic inequality amongst citizens should not be so great as to enable one to exert decisive political influence over another.[135] Resistance, then, to the onset of social obsequiousness and inegalitarian policies, is one curious sense in which the general will is, in Cole's felicitous phrase 'the application of freedom to human institutions'.[136]

There is a second, and initially more procedural sense in which the general will is orientated to equality. Pronouncements of the general will must be in the form of 'general conventions': they must – harking back to the theological debates about the form of God's rule – take the form of absolutely general laws; although here, laws which all create as well as all obey.[137] To be general, the will must 'both come from all and apply to all'.[138] As soon as a sovereign assembly concerns itself with the treatment of individuals, it ceases, for that very reason, to be sovereign.[139] Although strictly formal, this equality of application, Rousseau thinks, at the very least renders groundless fears of loss of personal rights, and at best means we can truly be said to obey only ourselves.

It is a commonly based charge that the theory of the general will lays a ground for totalitarianism through failing to set limits to its sphere of action through the enunciation of incorrigible individual rights. But Rousseau both sees and is concerned to meet this danger. He thinks that sufficient safeguards can be derived from adherence to the correct procedures of sovereignty, without recourse to the pre – or extra – social standards which his own, and the century's deepening sense of historical development seemed to disallow. If all who are to be subject to a rule must be involved in drawing it up, and if the rule

---

[132] *The Social Contract*, p. 225.

[133] Rousseau seems by no means consistent on this. In the *Arts and Sciences* he seems to presuppose a market in art.

[134] *The Social Contract*, p. 195.

[135] Ibid., p. 225 (Vaughan, p. 61), 'Let not any citizen be wealthy enough to have it in his power to buy another, and none so poor as to be forced to sell himself', again, in the note, 'permit neither rich men nor beggars'. Rousseau is not, I think, talking about the possibility of literal slavery — hardly a domestic issue in Western Europe in the eighteenth century, but of using economic power to undermine the citizens' political independence or *virtù*.

[136] *The Social Contract*, p. xxxviii.

[137] Ibid., p. 211.

[138] Ibid., p. 205.

[139] Ibid., pp. 20–6, the one exception is the right of granting pardons which is vested in the sovereign, because only the sovereign (i.e. the people as a collectivity) can be above the law, p. 207.

must be couched in general terms, one can see how, in a rough and ready kind of way, tyranny can be guarded against.[140] Since no rule specifying differential treatment for a specified individual could count as an act of sovereignty, it would be difficult, although admittedly not impossible, to use law as an instrument of arbitrary government.[141] The legalized disadvantaging of specific groups would be further rendered less likely by the social conditions Rousseau specifies for the citizen body – approximate equality and mutual independence of private interests. It is true that this is not quite the same as guaranteeing individual rights, since it says nothing about the allowable limits of what the sovereign might decide to impose (only that they must be imposed by *everyone*) – it even allows for legal privilege and orders or ranks of citizens [142] – so long as the collectivity agrees to this. This is not quite the equality of all before the law, but the equality of all to decide how unequal before the law we should be. Rousseau doesn't believe in pre-social rights, because, firstly, he accepts Hobbes's argument that the pursuit of what is claimed under them is incompatible with society, but also – and a more specifically Rousseauian argument – because the very idea of right is only comprehensible within society. However, he does believe that if uncorrupted, the reason, self-interest and equality of the citizens will operate in such a uniform, regular and law-like way as to enable them to agree about how extensive the influence of their own sovereignty needs to be over their own private lives in order to sustain the society.[143] This degree of legal and political equality may appear minimal, or even inadequate, to those in 'the developed west' today, although smugness and complacency about these matters is always unwarranted and often dangerous. However in *ancien régime* France with its mass of localized jurisdictions, class-based legal privilege, and royal prerogative, it was, and was to prove, a thoroughly subversive ideal.

---

[140] This tactic of attempting to deduce standards of justice from purely procedural considerations allies Rousseau with the method's most famous modern exponent, John Rawls, *A Theory of Justice* (Oxford, 1971). See G. Kateb's lucid defence of Rousseau, 'Aspects of Rousseau's Political Thought', *Political Science Quarterly*, 76, 4 (1961) which sees a Rawlsian conception of justice as central to Rousseau's political thought.

[141] *The Social Contract*, p. 194.

[142] Ibid., p. 211. On this see David Ronsenfeld, 'Rousseau's unanimous Contract and the Doctrine of Popular Sovereignty', *History of Political Thought*, VIII (1987).

[143] *The Social Contract*, pp. 191–2; 206; 'each necessarily submits to the conditions he imposes on others . . . they all bind themselves to observe the same conditions'. The notion that the 'volunté genéral' of God, appeared to human beings as natural law, in both the scientific and moral sense, is perhaps the last trace of the notion that the general will rests on a kind of natural law. But Rousseau's political application of the idea, however much it might owe in *form* to theology, was devoid of theological content. Rousseau explicitly argued that political principles derived from the will of God must be dispensed with partly because 'though it were clear that what God wills, man ought to will, it is not clear that God wishes us to choose one government rather than another, nor [a reference to 1688 in England] that one should obey James rather than William.' *Letters from the Mountain*, letter IV, (Vaughan, II, p. 200), and partly because 'the abuse of them causes as many crimes as they can spare us'. Let us, he continues, 'render to the philosopher, the examination of a question which the theologian has never dealt with but to the prejudice of humankind.' 'First Draft', Vaughan, vol 1, p. 451.

'Obeying ourselves and being as free as before'

The notion that in obeying the general will we are 'obeying ourselves' is more difficult. One simplistic criticism is that the claim merely involves the fallacy of composition: 'Obeying myself', is not the same as being part of a collectivity in which we 'obey ourselves' through some majoritarian procedure – in the latter case I can be out-voted. But Rousseau's argument is much more complex than this.

Rousseau envisages the social individual possessing both a social, or general will, and a private one.[144] One of his major targets was that group of thinkers, prominent in France as well as Britain, who defended the development of a commercial society by arguing that selfish and social goods are ultimately harmonized through, in Adam Smith's famous phrase, 'the hidden hand' of the market.[145] Rousseau sees this as fundamentally mistaken and morally pernicious, although he acknowledges that self-interest has a role to play in leading the individual to recognise a 'common interest' which is not simply an aggregate of selfish wishes.[146] His considered view at the time, of the general relationship between virtue and egoism is that 'We have in all cases a true interest in cultivating virtue, even though there may be cases where it will be insufficient in itself, without the expectation of a life to come.'[147] But if the general will is not merely an aggregate of selfish desires, neither is it or rather should it be, an external authority opposed to the individual. The general will is something of which each individual citizen needs to have a sense within him. As a contributor to and participant in the general will of the society, the individual prescribes rules which, in turn as a private subject, he must obey. In this sense then, he as subject obeys himself as sovereign. Rousseau considers it vital for the health of any community that its members keep a sense of the notion that something could be generally beneficial which did not accord with their personal interest. This sense is the individual's social or general will. But suppose the general will of the community disagreed, not with what the individual recognised as his private will, but with what he regarded as the general will? Then, says Rousseau, he was mistaken about the general will. What we must ask ourselves when we vote, is not whether we approve of the measure under consideration, but whether we think it is in conformity with the general will. If it turns out that my decision was defeated – I was in fact wrong in my assessment. As Rousseau acknowledges, this presupposes that the majority decision does in fact embody the general will, of which there is, and indeed can be, no guarantee. But *if* it did, then the

---

[144] *The Social Contract*, p. 196.

[145] Theoretical arguments in favour of the free market were at least as far advanced in France as in Britain. The major figure was Pierre de Boisguilbert, see Keohane, *Philosophy and the State . . .* , p. 350 ff. On Rousseau's idealization of a pre-monetary economy, see Starobinski, *Transparency*, pp. 104ff.

[146] On the distinction between the widespread belief in a natural harmony of selfish interests and the need to realise the common interest, albeit through the enlightened management of individual interests, see Nannerl O. Keohane ' "The Masterpeice of Policy in Our Century" Rousseau on the Morality of the Enlightenment.' *Political Theory*, vol 6, no.4 (1978). The distinction between the general will, and the will of all is central to Rousseau's theory. Unfortunately the most prominent discussion of it in *The Social Contract*, having made the distinction, immediately obscures it by suggesting that the general will could be elicited from an arithmetical treatment of particular wills. *The Social Contract*, p. 203.

[147] 'A Letter about Morality' (1761), *Religious Writings*, ed. Grimsley (Oxford, 1970), p. 99.

fact that I mistook the general will, means that I should correct myself by adopting the new will as my own, and once again I am obeying my (truly social) self.[148] Finally we might consider the situation where the general will goes against my particular wishes as a private individual – where these are stronger than my commitment to the general will. In this case it seems more difficult to suggest that subordination to the general will can be construed as 'obedience to myself'. Here we need to recall the psychological transformation undergone by the individual on entering society, and Rousseau's claim that only this socialisation makes possible both freedom and moralization, in fact, the realization of the individual's true human potential. He sees this as a political task: 'The better the state is constituted the more public business intrudes it into private concerns in the mind of the citizens.'[149] In placing the egoistic will above the values of morality and freedom which can only be achieved collectively, the individual would be rejecting his true and higher self. Obedience to the state – 'une personne morale'[150] – is thus, as long as the state is legitimate, obedience to my higher, public as opposed to my lower, selfish will; and if that obedience is not forthcoming voluntarily, Rousseau argues that it can legitimately be imposed by the collectivity.

There is a last problem. As Rousseau recognizes, freedom as obedience to ourselves makes less and less sense the larger the state. If I as private citizen obey myself as sovereign in a state of 10, 000 citizens, I contribute 1/10, 000 to the sovereign authority, yet experience to the full its constraints. The larger the state, the more disproportionate the relationship between my obedience as subject and my role as sovereign in prescribing a law to myself – the less in fact my freedom.[151] The clear implication of this, reiterated several times by Rousseau, is that freedom and legitimacy is more easily achieved in small states.[152]

Once again, this whole line of argument is dependent for any validity it may have (as Rousseau openly acknowledges), on the sovereign assembly of citizens successfully realising the general will; for it is not the fact that the majority (or even all) of the citizens have willed something that makes it the general will, but whether what they have willed proves capable of sustaining equality, freedom and the continued existence of the community. Whether it does so or not depends on the major issue referred to earlier: that of whether the citizens are motivated to pursue the good, as opposed to simply being able

---

[148] *The Social Contract*, p. 278.

[149] Ibid., p. 266, (Vaughan, p. 95) and see the extraordinary degree of social identity prescribed for Poland in notes 89 and 127 above.

[150] Cole's original translation had 'moral person' (1913 ed., p. 24), doubtless a source of worries about the sinister nature of Rousseau's claims. The term was drawn from Roman Law, and referred to the legal personality allowed to corporate bodies. The new translation renders this much better: 'corporate body', the English technical equivalent would be 'legal person'. *The Social Contract*, p. 204.

[151] Ibid., p. 231. This renders highly suspect Rousseau's claim that under a legitimate state we would be 'as free as before'. On his own account here our new freedom would be a fraction of the old, the numerator of which was one and the denominator of which was the number of citizens in the state!

[152] *The Social Contract*, p. 268. This is the strongest assertion of the point. However size is not for Rousseau, as some commentators suggest, an absolute disqualification for legitimacy, but a difficulty, which with enough persistence can be overcome. Rousseau instances the late Roman Republic with over four million citizens, four-hundred thousand of them active in the assemblies in Rome (p. 262). He comments 'the bounds of possibilities in moral matters, are less narrow than we imagine: it is our weaknesses, our vices, and our prejudices that confine them'. (p. 261).

to recognize it; and this in turn relates to two topics which have been lurking in the above discussion, firstly the institutional setting of the general will, and secondly the question of the socialisation, or civic education, of the citizens.

The institutional setting for the general will

Rousseau throws out some general comments on the kind of institutional devices that assist in the realization of the general will, as well as discussing more systematically the major relevant distinction: that between sovereignty and government.

Firstly, as already mentioned, Rousseau argues we should guard against the emergence of parties or partial interest groups in the state since these create mini general wills capable of overriding that of the society as a whole.[153] There is every reason to fear this, for our wills are naturally strongest in respect of ourselves and progressively weaker as they relate to social bodies more general and remote from ourselves. We are, therefore, according to the same kind of mathematics as referred to in the previous section, almost bound to be more attached to corporate bodies intermediate between us and the state – parties, regional or local government, economic corporations – such as trade or business associations.[154] The same reasoning implied too that the state must be small. The larger the state, the more attenuated its general will within the individual citizens.[155] It is only by abolishing intermediary associations, weakening them, equalizing them, or as a last resort having as many as possible, thinks Rousseau, that the 'general will' of the state can emerge, but the larger the state the more important it would seem to be to destroy these intermediate focuses of loyalty.[156]

Secondly, Rousseau argues, individuals must, as much as possible, 'think their own thoughts'[157] and not be swayed by others. If the people, fully informed, voted without communication, the general will would always emerge. This reinforces the suggestion, inherent in the previous point, that Rousseau is actually nervous about political activity which goes on outside the confines of political institutions strictly considered. Once again this has provoked liberal charges of totalitarianism, since a marked feature of twentieth century totalitarian regimes has been the abolition, or incorporation into the state, of the private and unofficial associations of society. But for Rousseau it is precisely this area of 'civil society', as it was coming to be called, in which flourished the *amour propre*, private interests and inequality that destroy liberty.

Finally, for the general will to emerge, individuals must be present and vote in person. As long as the state is uncorrupted citizens should vote publicly, for the need to justify one's decision to an honest public is a motive for political virtue. Moreover it signals that voting is a public, not a private right. Secret voting is only needed to discourage bribery.[158] Private interests may be represented, but citizens' wills cannot. Repre-

---

[153] Ibid., p. 204.

[154] Ibid., p. 235.

[155] Ibid., pp. 231–2.

[156] Ibid., p. 204. The solution to the problem posed by such partial interests forms the linchpin of the transition to the modern state. See the discussion of James Madison (following David Hume), in his famous 10th *Federalist Paper*, in chapter V.

[157] *The Social Contract*, p. 204. [158] Ibid., p. 290.

sentation involves at least the intermittent yielding up of sovereignty.[159] Representation in politics is like the hiring of mercenaries in war, each represents a diminution of public spirit through the use of money to evade the performance of public duty. The substitution of money for service – a major feature of the modern state with its elaborate system of taxation and the corollary, professional armies and bureaucracies – is targeted by Rousseau as a crucial index of political degeneracy.[160] This Machiavellian theme becomes more and more important in books three and four, and although it here lacks much of the psychological subtleties of *'amour propre'*, it ties in with the criticisms of the parallel growth of wealth and selfishness made in the *Discourse on Inequality*. It is in these books also that we get a sustained discussion of two major issues relating to the successful realisation of general will, the separation of government from sovereignty and the importance of education and civic religion.

Government

First (and incomplete) readings of *The Social Contract* often seem to produce the impression that Rousseau is simply advocating direct democracy. In fact his argument is more complex, and in some ways less radical than that. It is more complex in that although he argues for a democratic *sovereign*, he is most insistent about distinguishing sovereign and government; and he insists that democratic *government* is impossible (at least for humans). It is less radical in that both what one might call the intensity of activity, and the range of membership of the sovereign body turns out to be much less than he sometimes suggests. Indeed, it could be argued that it is less than is needed to generate the sense of public spirit he so desired.

To take the last point about sovereignty first. Despite his emphasis on the continual re-affirmation of popular legitimacy, Rousseau allows that the consent of the people might be tacit. The commands of the government can pass for the general will, 'so long as the Sovereign, being free to oppose them, offers no opposition. In such a case, universal silence is taken to imply the consent of the people.'[161] Secondly, much of what the sovereign body does is a matter of politicising the minds of the participating citizens

---

[159] The English, he remarks are only free during their elections, and the use they make of that freedom (eighteenth-century elections were notoriously rowdy and corrupt) shows how little they deserve it. Ibid., p. 266.

[160] By paying taxes rather than serving in person 'they end by having soldiers to enslave their country and representatives to sell it. . . . In a country that is truly free, the citizens do everything with their own arms and nothing by means of money . . . I hold enforced labour to be less opposed to liberty than taxes.' Ibid., p. 265. The last striking assertion only makes sense in a Machiavellian, neo-classical republican context. It would have been all the more contentious in France where the *corvée*, a levy of forced labour, was one of the most hated of all *ancien régime* impositions.

[161] Ibid., p. 201.

through ceremonial rather than involving them in significant political action.[162] Thirdly although Rousseau insists that only the consent of the whole people can legitimize the exercise of political power, it is clear that this power is not equally spread amongst the citizens. Apart from the obvious point that he can be assumed to exclude women, he makes reference at several points to different classes of citizenship, and the weight that votes of the different classes might carry.[163]

The major point however is the importance of separating sovereign and government. The everyday running of the state is to be in the hands of the few. A democratic government, as opposed to a democratic sovereign, would leave the actual application of the laws to all the citizens – a situation workable only for angels.

The execution of the laws established by the sovereign requires an intermediary, and this, ideally, should be an aristocracy. By an aristocracy Rousseau includes what we would call a representative democracy, for selection by voting is an aristocratic device – it involves choosing the best, democracy would involve selection by lot, or chance.[164]

The line of demarcation between the role of government and sovereign is set by the criterion of generality. Only commands framed generally – laws – can be acts of the sovereign. The appointment of particular people to office, the application of the law to particular cases, and the declaration of peace and war, are all particular acts, and cannot therefore be acts of the sovereign.[165] They should be left to government.

The most significant of these is the first: denying to the general will the power over individuals, was, as we have seen a safeguard against popular tyranny. But it creates a problem in relation to government. For whilst the establishment of the form of government is a general and abstract provision, and hence a law (not a contract),[166] and a proper subject for the sovereign; the appointment of the personnel in a government – of whatever kind – deals with individuals, and is consequently a particular act, from performing which the sovereign is disbarred. Whilst the people as sovereign may decide on their form of government, they ought not, in their sovereign capacity, to assign positions in it. Instead, Rousseau suggests, they exhibit the 'astonishing property' of being able 'without sensible change' to transform themselves temporarily into a democratic government to perform

---

[162] Such hints are intermittent. The two questions to be asked whenever the sovereign assembles are, though important, limited: whether to preserve the form of the government, and whether to keep the existing office-holders (although this latter, being an act affecting particular individuals, would presumably be an act strictly for the people-as-government, rather than the people-as-sovereign). Ibid., p. 273. This is extraordinarily general. In the admittedly earlier *Discourse on the Origins of Political Economy*, the sovereign is not even required to meet; whilst in discussing the church, Rousseau sees the celebration of the Eucharist as an expression of its general will. *The Social Contract*, fn., p. 302.

[163] Ibid., p. 211, and the whole of the much neglected, and evidently approving discussion of Roman voting methods designed to minimise the influence of poorer classes of citizens, by having block votes of equal weight. Bk IV, ch iv. The example of his native city-state, Geneva, for whom Rousseau was asked at one point to give constitutional advice, is instructive here. Four classes of inhabitant with very different political rights were acknowledged: *Citoyens, Bourgeois, Natifs and Habitants*. See Rosenfeld, 'Rousseau's Unanimous Contract'. In general, on Rousseau's politics as inspired by classical republicanism, Judith Shklar, *Men and Citizens* (Cambridge, 1969), is excellent.

[164] *The Social Contract*, p. 241. This view of voting was a commonplace of classical politics, which survived until around this time; it is found, as Rousseau points out, in Montesquieu, see ibid., pp. 279–80, although Rousseau rejects his reasoning. See also Ch V, pp. 229–32.

[165] Ibid., pp. 211, 209, 202.

[166] Ibid., p. 269.

the task.[167] Whilst this solves (logically) the problem of appointing governments, the facility with which the sovereign changes into a government (on the separation between which so much depends) must raise serious worries about the adequacy of the 'generality' principle as a practical (as opposed to merely theoretical) barrier to majority tyranny. The only further safeguard (and it is perhaps no accident that Rousseau immediately goes on to discuss it), is the stress which he places both on adherence to formal procedures in calling and conducting the sovereign assembly, which is in turn somewhat invalidated by his insistence on its right to meet, if necessary, in defiance of the government.[168]

For government itself poses a threat. It will inevitably possess a corporate identity and a general will of its own. Indeed, to an extent it is desirable that it should.[169] But this general will, will be particular with respect to the truly general will of the society, and hence need to be guarded against. Rousseau produces a complex account of the proportionality of the various wills involved, and the devices required to establish the appropriate relationships between them.

As we've seen, the relationship between sovereign and citizen becomes more tenuous the larger the state. In its place the 'morals and manners' of the citizens' particular wills become more powerful.[170] This required a more powerful government to restrain them, and suggested another reason why large states had less liberty. If liberty is to be sustained in this increase in government power, the sovereign too must be able to exercise greater power to restrain government.[171] Within a government official (magistrate) there are three wills – his own private will, his common will as a member of the government and his will as a member of the whole community. Ideally, the last should be strongest and the first weakest, but their 'natural' strengths are the inverse of that. If the government is a monarchy, the one man's individual will, and the governmental will are one. His will would therefore be much stronger, although almost certainly not more right, than a government of many, or even all, citizens. For in the latter case the individuals' wills are only remotely connected with a widely shared, and therefore indistinct and attenuated governmental will. Although weaker, such a government, where all magistrates' wills are also citizen's wills, will accord more with the popular will. However, to be effective, the number of magistrates (members of government), should be inversely proportional to the number of citizens (members of the sovereign body), or to put it another way the larger a state, the more concentrated governmental power needs to be. Unfortunately, the requirements of legitimacy run in the opposite direction, the more numerous the magistrates, the more likely their magisterial wills are to conform to their wills as citizens.[172] The art of framing constitutions is, amongst other things the art of mixing these advantages and disadvantages. Although the conventional language uses the terms monarchy, aristocracy and democracy to categorise governments, there is, in reality, a

---

[167] Ibid., pp. 270–1, and see p. 279 'the election of rulers is a function of government, and not of Sovereignty.'

[168] Ibid., p. 263, cf. pp. 272–3, and the even more damaging claim there, that there is 'no fundamental law that cannot be revoked'.

[169] Ibid., pp. 232–3.

[170] It was something of a commonplace in republican literature that the austerity characteristic of republican *virtù*, was only sustainable in small states, a major point of discussion in the debates over the American Constitution. See below Chapter V.

[171] Ibid., pp. 231–2.

[172] Ibid., pp. 235–7.

continuum of possibilities from one magistrate to all citizens. Picking up a theme adumbrated by Montesquieu, Rousseau announces that he does not regard monarchy and republic as distinct. A republic is simply any 'state governed by laws', and its government (i.e. administration) may be monarchical, aristocratic or democratic.[173] The existence of a democratic sovereign is quite compatible with government by a monarch, as, in an intermittent and imperfect way, the English had shown.[174] By distinguishing the sovereign from the government, and in his treatment of relations between the two, Rousseau combined the French traditions of absolute sovereignty and constitutionalism, and achieved, in a totally unexpected way, d'Argensen's ideal of combining the two in one polity.

Civic education and religion

The successful operation of Rousseau's society, has, it has frequently been observed, depended ultimately on the opinions and morality of the citizens. To a large degree, the laws and institutions of the society of the social contract are, like those of the ancient city-states he so admired, themselves designed to sustain that morality, but they cannot create them, nor, once lost, can they recover them. This is clearest in the case of the office of the Censor, an office under the Roman constitution, charged with the preservation of public morals, not through law, but through example and ridicule, giving effect to public opinion. This is to the modern reader a disturbing and illiberal recommendation, but Rousseau is primarily concerned with political, not personal liberty. Maintaining a sense of political belonging and autonomy is more important than personal freedom. This is the task of the censor, he as it were, reflects to the citizens, and reminds them of, their best ideals and qualities. His office is a holding operation against the forces of corruption, it is useful for the preservation of morality, but because he cannot work by compulsion, only through appealing to their sense of political virtue, useless to restore it.[175]

This circularity of the relationship, laws – opinion – morality – law, together with Rousseau's insistence on the autonomy of the popular sovereign, raises questions about the origins of the good state. The people ought to establish their own laws, but since the moral opinions that would give rise to good laws are themselves not natural, but a product of law, how can we break into the virtuous circle?

Rousseau's answer is the legislator, a political educator who performs in relation to society, what the tutor performs for Emile. The legislator is not a part of the constitution but wholly outside it, his authority is not legal but charismatic, and having exercised it, he must, like Emile's tutor, leave, if his pupil is to be truly independent.

What he does underscores the transformation that social man undergoes, and the *de*naturing quality of the civic education. He must

---

[173] Ibid., p. 212, and n. 1. However, Rousseau is inconsistent in this, contrasting republics in the conventional sense with monarchy in Bk.iii, chs. 6, and 8.

[174] Montesquieu's famous discussion of the English consitution in Bk xi of *The Spirit of the Laws*, had included the description of England as 'a republic disguised under the form of a monarchy', p. 68.

[175] *The Social Contract*, p. 297.

take away from man his own resources, and give him instead new ones alien to him, and incapable of being made use of without the help of other men. The more completely these natural resources are annihilated, the greater and more lasting are those which he acquires, and the more stable and perfect the new institutions;[176]

Having no powers, the legislator cannot impose his plans upon the society; moreover the people being politically unsophisticated cannot by any normal means be persuaded to see the attractions of civic life, to do so

the effect would have to become the cause; . . . and men would have to be before the laws, what they should become by means of them. The Legislator, then, able to employ neither force nor reason, necessarily has resort to authority of another order, which can drive them on without violence and persuade without convincing.[177]

That 'authority of another order' is religion. Neither philosophical reason, nor self-interest is of any use in founding states. Rousseau is not here endorsing the claims of conventional religion. Like Machiavelli, he is – at least in this context – concerned only with the political use that can be made of it.[178] The legislator is a religious ventriloquist who puts decisions 'into the mouths of the immortals', he 'can make the gods speak'.[179] Founding is a miracle, but not a supernatural one. The miracle lies in the inspired soul of the legislator who like the 'great man' of Cicero's state of nature, can, by his eloquence, gain credence for his falsehoods and so serve the people by founding their state.

This political use of religious belief forms the last of Rousseau's topics in *The Social Contract*.

Civil religion

Rousseau's discussion of religion draws on a century and more of scepticism. In particular he makes use of the application to Christianity of techniques of historical scholarship, and the comparative sociology of religion pioneered originally by the English deists. It was this kind of background that made possible Gibbon's great account of the interplay of politico-military history and the sociology of religious and philosophical belief in his *Decline and Fall of the Roman Empire*.[180] Voltaire and the Encyclopaedists too were impressed with the attempt to treat Christian belief and religion as a social phenomenon to be explained, rather than a truth to be understood.[181]

---

[176] Ibid., p. 214.

[177] Ibid., p. 216, (Vaughan, p. 53).

[178] This is not to say that Rousseau lacked, as Machiavelli seems to have, at least a desire for a personal faith, and a religious sense. However his attempt to sort these issues out, the 'Confession of Faith of the Savoyard Vicar', provoked more opposition than he anticipated. See Ronald Grimsley, *Religious Writings*, (Oxford, 1970), pp. 105ff. In general see Grimsley, *Rousseau and the Religious Quest*, (Oxford, 1968).

[179] *The Social Contract*, p. 216.

[180] See J. G. A. Pocock, 'Gibbon's *Decline and Fall* and the world view of the Late Enlightenment' in *Virtue, Commerce and History*.

[181] This is the context for his famous remark that 'If God had not existed it would have been necessary to invent him' which opens the door to secular explanation, whilst prudently hedging on the issue of his

Rousseau outlines the political history of pagan religion and the peculiar features of the rise of Christianity. He then analyses the political properties of religion in general, and assesses Christianity in the light of them.

The original governments were theocracies, and each state had its own theogony – 'there were as many gods as peoples'. This reinforced national divisions but did not lead to specifically religious intolerance, nor to attempts to convert others: 'the provinces of the gods were, so to speak, fixed by the boundaries of nations'.[182] Followers of one cult might be contemptuous of other gods, but they did allow that they existed, and where a people were conquered they adopted the gods of their new masters. Indeed the Romans generously also adopted the gods of their conquered enemies and so sponsored a tolerant and eclectic polytheism. It was Judaism, and, later, Christianity that began the separation of religious and political authority by refusing, whatever their political plight, to acknowledge other gods. This refusal was (rightly, Rousseau thinks) perceived by their conquerors, who believed in the inseparability of politics and religion, as an expression of political rebellion, and so brought about their persecution.[183]

Pagans' suspicions about Christ's claims that his kingdom was not of this world proved justified, for as soon as Christians gained power they set about establishing 'the most violent of earthly despotisms'. However, having used religion to undermine the classical state, Christian political culture never proved capable of reuniting earthly and religious authority, and the central problem of Europe remained, for Rousseau, the competing jurisdictions of church and state.[184] Rousseau notes that in churches, communion forms a kind of social contract amongst clergy, making them a corporate body (and emphasising the symbolic aspect of sovereignty.) Even in England and Russia, where the attempt has been made to overcome the division between church and state by making the monarchs the head of the church, they are 'not its legislators, but only its princes'.[185] In other words, sovereignty remains with the priesthood.[186] Hobbes was the only person to have dealt with this problem, by insisting that the sovereign should really legislate for the church in all matters as well as for the state, and that is the very reason why the church has been so opposed to him.

Reflecting on this history, Rousseau suggests we can identify three species of religion, each with very different social and political properties. The first, a subject of enormous interest in the eighteenth century, Rousseau calls the 'religion of man'. This he identifies with both primitive Christianity and what contemporaries would have called 'natural religion', i.e. that universal religious and moral code to be found in the New Testament, but which (with the exception of the resurrection) they believed could have been arrived at through rational reflection, without the aid of revelation. The second, of which original paganism is exemplary, consists of a set of gods and cults peculiar to a single nation or

---

existence. On the background see Wade, 'Religion to Holbach and Helvetius', in *French Enlightenment*, vol. 1.

[182] *The Social Contract*, p. 299.

[183] Ibid., p. 300. There are strong similarities with Hobbes's analysis, which Rousseau praises, p. 302.

[184] Ibid., pp. 300–1. Islam, although originally linking church and state under the caliphate, developed the same fatal division.

[185] Ibid., pp. 301–2.

[186] See the intriguing footnote on the Eucharist, ibid., p. 302.

people. The third is the mixed kind of jurisdiction prevalent in developed Christian states with its competing authorities and hierarchies of church and state.

Being socially divisive the third is, at best, politically useless, at worst destructive. The second, in uniting religious belief and nationalism has all the political advantages, it adds the sanction of religion to its legal code, and can give the prize of martyrdom to its dead military heroes. This combination can make it so confident and aggressive that it seeks to convert by conquest and becomes such a danger to other states, that they in turn endanger it. Its disadvantage is that it is untrue, and relies on credulity and superstition.[187]

The first form of religion, on the other hand has truth, but since its effect is to divert its adherents altogether from earthly and political concerns, it is the most harmful politically. Primitive Christianity teaches unconcern about the health of the state, resignation in the face of usurpation or tyranny, irresolution in the face of what it sees as God's providence and indifference to military success.[188] Its aversion to things political deprives members of such a state of 'one of the great bonds that unite society', in short, says Rousseau, 'I know of nothing more contrary to the social spirit'.[189] What then is to be done?

The sovereign only has a right to concern itself with what affects the community. This is nowhere near as liberal as it sounds, for many of the beliefs of citizens, Rousseau recognises, affect the community. The task of a political theology is to distinguish within religion between what does and what does not require political regulation. Firstly all citizens should have *a* religion. This was a widely held view.[190] Without belief in a deity and an afterlife, few thought humans could be trusted to adhere to even the most elementary forms of morality; with atheists, there could be no society. But the content of religious dogma – its confessional creed, beliefs concerning the nature of god, or the afterlife is no concern of the state, the state should therefore tolerate all religions whose dogmata do not undermine the duties of citizenship. This proviso would, however, most probably exclude members of the Catholic church, whose claims of papal supremacy were widely held in Protestant countries to undermine political obligation. However, Rousseau goes considerably further, and would exclude any church or sect making claims of even doctrinal exclusivity.[191] In other words only religions or sects that accept, as part of their doctrine, the possibility of the truths of other religions or sects, can be tolerated. Civil and religious toleration cannot be distinguished, for 'it is impossible to live at peace with those who we regard as damned; to love them would be to hate the God who punishes them.'[192]

But as well as requiring such toleration as a characteristic of the citizen's otherwise private religious beliefs, the state can and should require adherence to a 'civil religion'. This need not intrude on the private religious belief of the individual, it's dogma is either

---

[187] Ibid., p. 303.

[188] Ibid., pp. 304–6.

[189] Ibid., p. 304.

[190] Despite his championship of toleration Locke, in his *Fundamental Constitutions of Carolina*, required all citizens to acknowledge there was a God who should be publicly worshipped. (*Works*, 4 vols, 1777, volume 4, p. 534.)

[191] 'Whoever dares to say: "Outside the Church is no salvation" ought to be driven from the State, unless the State is the Church and the prince the pontiff.' *The Social Contract*, p. 308.

[192] Ibid.

secular or so generally phrased as to be incapable of providing religious offence: belief in an all powerful, rational well disposed god and in an afterlife, in reward and punishment for the just and the unjust, the sanctity of the social contract and the laws. These tenets are not so much a matter of theology as 'social sentiments without which a man cannot be a good citizen or a faithful subject.'[193]

For Rousseau, the state should be concerned with religion from the point of view of the consequences that follow from different forms of belief, not from the truth of its content. But as we can see, because Rousseau has a heightened sense of the role of belief in structuring behaviour, this often involves less toleration than the principle would seem to imply.

---

[193] Ibid.

Chapter V

'Publius': *The Federalist*

Introduction

The immediate context

In the winter of 1787–8 various New York newspapers carried a series of articles headed *The Federalist*, and signed 'Publius'. They sought to persuade New Yorkers to vote in favour of the new constitution drawn up over the previous summer in Philadelphia. The articles pursued this aim by reviewing the constitution's institutional provisions in the light of the preconceptions and concerns of an American people anxious to maintain the liberty dearly won in the revolutionary war against the British barely a decade previously. In the course of this they constructed what has come to be seen as a work of political theory.

The project of writing political theory in a series of newspaper articles does not perhaps strike us today as a plausible one, but it was not uncommon in the eighteenth century.[1] Moreover it was particularly suited to a society in the process of establishing itself as a popular, republican and widely spread political culture.[2]

Those circumstances were briefly as follows. The thirteen British American colonies had declared their independence in 1776 and there followed the five-year-long War of Independence. Seven months before the British surrender at Yorktown on 19th October 1781, the representatives of the new American States had met at a Continental Congress in March 1781, and ratified a document defining their collective identity and relations, the 'Articles of Confederation'. A loosely federal government was conducted under the provisions of this document until 1787, when the Congress – a meeting of the constituent

---

[1] There were the beginnings during the English Civil War; see, for example Jurgen Deithe '*The Moderate*: Politics and allegiances of a revolutionary newspaper', *History of Political Thought*, IV, 2 (1983). From the eighteenth century on there are many examples, *Cato's Letters*, by Trenchard and Gordon, and *Letters of Junius*, being the best known. During the revolutionary period in America John Dickinson's twelve *Letters from a Farmer in Pennsylvania* published in the *Pennsylvania Chronicle* (1767–9), and widely reprinted, established the genre.

[2] Whether the constitution argued for by *The Federalist* was in fact as republican or as democratic as claimed, is a vast subject of scholarly (and polemical) debate. In seeking to defend a continental-scale republic *The Federalist* arguably redefined all the key terms in the debate: 'democracy', 'republic' and 'federal'. See the outstanding collection of essays *Conceptual Change and the Constitution* ed. Terence Ball and J.G.A.Pocock (Lawrence Ka., 1988), and in particular 'The American Founding in Early Modern Perspective', by Pocock, also in *Social Science Quarterly*, 68 (1987); ' "A Republic — If you can keep it"', by Terence Ball, and ' "Commons" and "Commonwealth" at the American Founding: Democratic Republicanism as the New American Hybrid' by Russel Hanson. See the extended discussion below.

states, called another assembly, subsequently known as the Constitutional Convention, to meet in May in Philadelphia, Pennsylvania 'for the sole and express purpose of revising the Articles of Confederation'.[3] In fact they so far exceeded their formal brief that they drew up a new constitution.[4] This constitution, the basis of the present American Constitution, was forged over a period of six months of intensive and – by the participants' own agreement – secret debate, by 55 delegates from twelve states, and signed, not without misgivings, on 17th September 1787.[5] However, the delegates had no authority to establish the constitution, although interestingly they took on themselves authority to decide how this should be done.[6] The Constitutional Convention had decided that the new constitution must be ratified by special conventions, called for the purpose, in at least nine of the individual states, and it was by no means clear that this would happen.[7] New York ratified by only 30 votes to 27, Rhode Island, which had been the last to agree to the convention (and then did not attend), by 34–32, as late as 1790. Both it and North Carolina made ratification dependent on the passing of a Bill of Rights.[8]

The heated ratification debate was dispersed and fragmented, focussed still in the different states. The debate was particularly hard fought in New York, which was not only one of the larger and more important states, without the agreement of which ratification would have been practically impossible, but it had a strongly anti-centrist government. It contained two prominent individuals with diametrically opposed views about the desirability of strong central government – George Clinton the State Governor, an extreme proponent of local state power, and Alexander Hamilton, youthful military hero of the War of Independence, a brilliant lawyer and ardent nationalist, without whom New York might not even have been represented at Philadelphia.[9] It was Hamilton, along with the Virginian James Madison and John Jay, also from New York, who wrote *The*

---

[3] Cited Clinton Rossiter, *1787 The Grand Convention* (London and N.Y., 1966), p. 55.

[4] A common criticism of the new constitution, both at the convention and in the ensuing ratification debate, was that the convention had no authority to draw up a new constitution. See R.S. Kay, 'The Illegality of the Constitution', *Constitutional Commentary*, IV (1987)

[5] In fact three delegates refused to sign, George Mason, and Edmund Randolph from Virginia, and Elbridge Gerry from Massachusetts, whilst a further fourteen had already left for home. Rossiter, *Grand Convention*, pp. 237, 234. Some delegates, unsympathetic to the idea of a stronger national government had not even attended, a fact which was given as a reason for the aristocratic leanings of the resulting constitution. (. . . *Letters from the Federal Farmer*, in *The Complete Anti-Federalist* 7 vols. ed. Herbert J.Storing (Chicago, 1981), vol. 2, no.8, 7, and in the abridged version, *The Anti-Federalist* ed. Murray Dry (Chicago, 1985), p. 37.

[6] The Congress' decision to call the convention (Feb. 1787) had specified that the revisions be reported 'to Congress and the several legislatures'. Cited Rossiter, *The Grand Convention*, p. 55. The extra-legal 'Annapolis Convention' (September, 1786) which had precipitated Congress' action had called for the revisions to the constitution to be reported to and agreed by 'the United States in congress assembled . . . and afterwards confirmed by the legislature of every state'. *The Federalist*, ed. Max Beloff (Oxford, 1987), appendix, p. 461.

[7] The proposal to seek popular ratification provoked considerable debate, Max Farrand, ed., *Records of the Federal Convention of 1787* (IV vols, New Haven, 1966) — hereafter Farrand — vol. I, pp. 122–3, II, 88–96, etc. In opting for this mode of ratification the convention was already undermining the sovereignty of the states, and the Articles of Confederation by seeking to establish a direct link between the individual and the Federal government. Despite the resistance to centralisation this point was explicitly made by Madison at the Convention and accepted unanimously. Farrand, I, p. 122.

[8] Rossiter, *Grand Convention*, pp. 293, 303, 304.

[9] Ibid., p. 95.

Federalist as part of the New York ratification campaign. Thus whilst *The Federalist* tried to articulate the new conception of government arrived at in the convention, it also sought to rebut the criticisms made of it in numerous other contemporary publications, most famously the *Essays of Brutus*, and the *Observations* of a writer signing himself 'A Federal Farmer', also published in New York that winter. *The Federalist* was thus a vindication of the new constitution against its detractors. As we shall see, its very title signalled how large a part of the task of vindication was to lie in proving that the constitution's supporters were indeed justified in calling it Federal.[10]

The problem of *The Federalist* as a text

The Federalist poses problems that are almost unique in political theory. Firstly, virtually all other major works in the history of political thought are the product of an individual author. In reading them we are entitled to assume that the coherence of a single mind is at work, and in interpreting the theory, if we fail, initially, to find coherence, we seek further for it. In the case of *The Federalist* our author is fictional, 'Publius' being the pen-name of three individuals, James Madison, Alexander Hamilton and John Jay, each of whom wrote some of the essays. Their views were not identical. Hamilton favoured a much stronger executive and a much stronger national government than Madison, indeed shortly after the ratification they were to become bitter political opponents.

The second problem concerns the episodic form of the work, which was determined both by its multi-authorship and the circumstances in which it was published. Most political theories of our period take the form of a continuous argument moving, as do Hobbes and Locke, from epistemological considerations through to a theory of political society. *The Federalist* does not proceed in this systematic way.[11]

The writers of *The Federalist* were constrained in two important ways by its context. *The Federalist* is a defence of *another* document, one that already existed – the Federal Constitution, its range of arguments circumscribed by the provisions of that document. Moreover the constitution itself was not the result of a unified theory, but the outcome of a series of compromises at the convention between interested parties 'compelled to sacrifice theoretical propriety, to the force of extraneous considerations'.[12]

Secondly, the authors' approach to issues was determined by how salient they were in the public debate. As a result they often defended positions they themselves had opposed

---

[10] 'Federal' up to this point in the debate was largely contrasted with 'national'. 'Federal' and its cognates, had referred, as in Locke's *Second Discourse*, to an attribute of a state's authority — that of engaging in treaties (*Foedera*) with others; and federations were collections of states which had used (and might be thought still to retain) this power in uniting themselves. (Pocock, 'American Founding' pp. 58, 59, 69.) In arguing for a stronger national government, constituted by, and deriving powers *directly from the people*, rather than from treaties between states, under the name of 'Federalist', Madison, Jay and Hamilton, were seeking to attract for themselves the positive connotations of a word that belonged strictly to their opponents.

[11] It seems unlikely that such different personalities as Madison and Hamilton agreed on the whole range of positions relevant to a characterization of human nature. Attempts to extract coherent philosophical assumptions present and informing the authors' writing, include Morton White, *Philosophy, The Federalist and the Constitution* (Oxford, 1987).

[12] *Federalist*, 37, p. 180.

in the convention and used arguments they themselves rejected because they hoped (or knew) they would be persuasive.

In general these very complexities make the study of *The Federalist* a good case in which to exemplify the now well established view, that the meaning of an author's work must be discovered by relating it to the context and circumstances, intellectual and political, in which he – or in this case they – wrote. Here, above all, then, close attention must be paid to these contexts, for whatever its wider merits, the purpose of *The Federalist* is explicitly and intimately concerned and conditioned by them. *The Federalist* was designed to persuade ordinary voters. It shows political theory at work in the world; It is a permanent reproof to those who assert the irrelevance of political theory to political reality. Its immediate role in winning over its public, is debated[13] but its subsequent influence has been great. Practical politicians and lawyers too, believed – and continue to believe – that it helped them to understand the reasoning of the framers of the American constitution, the first, and longest lived, modern, written constitution.[14] Whether it does so or not is another matter. *The Federalist* was written to persuade a contemporary electorate, not to clarify for posterity the intentions of the founders. Indeed, at the time, the proceedings of the convention were still a closely guarded secret. The quasi- constitutional role *The Federalist* plays in modern American life and law, makes it difficult, particularly for Americans, to distance themselves from the present, and recover its historicity in reading it.[15] This is particularly ironic given the degree of historical sophistication with which its framers operated.

The lessons of 'experience' (i) practical

One of the most quoted phrases from the Constitutional Congress, often echoed in *The Federalist* itself, has been John Dickinson's famous claim that 'Experience must be our only guide. Reason may mislead us'. This has been used to stress the 'practical' approach of the framers and to deny the impact of theories or of intellectual traditions on the debate. However, the next few lines of his speech show that he, like most of his highly educated colleagues, construed 'experience' widely, to include history, both ancient and modern, and perhaps more surprisingly, as embodied in the principles of the English constitution

[13] Opposition to adoption in New York had been very strong indeed, one of the newspapers in which *The Federalist* appeared dropped the articles after opposition to them from subscribers, and elections to the convention originally contained a majority of anti-federalists. James MacGregor Burns, *The Vineyard of Liberty* (New York and Toronto, 1983[1982]) p. 44, 56; historians however seem to think *The Federalist* did not have a great impact on the ratification vote. See Charles R. Kesler, ed., *Saving the Revolution:* The Federalist Papers *and the American Founding* (New York, 1987) and other works cited by Peter S. Onuf, 'Reflections on the Founding: Constitutional Historiography in Bicentennial Perspective', *William and Mary Quarterly*, XLVI, 2 (3rd Ser., 1989), fn. 77.

[14] Jefferson, for example thought *The Federalist* 'the best commentary on the principles of government that was ever written' and included it, along with Locke and Sidney in the undergraduate Law curriculum of the University of Virginia which he drafted in 1824. Noble E. Cunningham, Jr., *In Pursuit of Reason, the life of Thomas Jefferson*, (Baton Rouge and London, 1987) pp. 343–4

[15] The question of how historical or immediate an interpretation may be given to the constitution is one that frequently arises in American legal controversy, for a discussion see W.E. Nelson, 'History and Neutrality in Constitutional Adjudication' *Virginia Law Review*, LXXII (1986).

and in institutions such as trial by jury.[16] The issues involved in judging the constitution, and the way they were conceptualized in this debate, were set by at least three layers of experience, which often suggested different conclusions and so producing a complex pattern of ideals, beliefs and 'lessons', about political reality which shaped participants' possible responses to the new constitution. The writers of *The Federalist* exploited the diversity of this shared experience to the full, showing that the 'lessons of history' or the constitutional practices of the various American states were by no means as unequivocal as their opponents claimed.

The most recent and immediate of these layers consisted of the personal experiences of Americans since achieving independence. There were positive and constructive lessons to be learnt in the burst of state-constitution making between 1776 and 1784, lessons which were cited and recounted in the Committee of Detail and elsewhere at the Constitutional Convention, in the ratification debates and in *The Federalist* itself.[17] There were more men with experience of making constitutions in the State House in Philadelphia in the summer of 1787 than in the whole of the rest of the world: for only in America had constitutions in this sense been made.[18] But there were also negative experiences of political life under the Articles of Confederation, frustration with which had precipitated the Constitutional Convention, and thus indirectly the new constitution itself.

These negative experiences, it was widely agreed, derived primarily from the weakness of the central government. The Articles of Confederation, born of the war against the arbitrary colonial executives mostly imposed on Americans by the British, was a very loose association of states. For example it provided for no continuing national executive: 'Americans . . . were in no mood to give a faraway, central regime in the United States what they were busy denying to a faraway central regime in Britain.'[19] The only national body was the Congress, of representatives of states' governments. The Congress could solicit revenue from the individual states but had no *power* to impose taxes, or to regulate commerce; it issued but could not impose currency. Its powers, such as they were, and when it managed to use them, extended only over the states, and not over individuals within states. What residual authority it might have arrogated to itself was eroded by the advent of the states' own constitutions.[20] As Edmund Randolph was to put it near the start of the Constitutional Convention, the authors of the Articles 'had done all that patriots could do, in the then infancy of the science of constitutions and confederacies',

---

[16] Dickinson's speech is in Farrand, II, p. 278. The same claims about privileging experience over reason are to be found in *The Federalist*, together with the same broad and historical interpretation of 'experience', see *Federalist*, 5, p. 17 ('We may profit by their [the British] experience, without paying the price which it cost them.'), 6 ('Let experience . . . be appealed to' [Sparta, Athens, Rome, Carthage, Venice, etc.]) 52, p. 270, etc.

[17] Rossiter, *The Grand Convention*, pp. 46, 64, 207. On state constitution-making see D. Lutz, *Popular Consent and Popular Control* (Baton Rouge, 1980); on the impact of the experience of popular control of legislatures, see L.F. Goldstein, 'Popular Sovereignty, the Origins of Judicial Review, and the revival of Unwritten Law', *Journal of Politics*, 48 (1986).

[18] Eleven states had, between them made seventeen constitutions between Independence and the Constitutional Convention, Rossiter, *The Grand Convention*, p. 64.

[19] Ibid., p. 47, Article II of the *Articles of Confederation* was quite clear on the issue: 'Each state retains its sovereignty, freedom, and independence, and every power, jurisdiction, and right, which is not by this Confederation expressly delegated to the United States in Congress Assembled.'

[20] Robert Middlekauf, *The Glorious Cause* (Oxford, 1982), p. 603.

but it was not enough.[21] In two particular areas, which had wide repercussions, it was seen to fail badly.[22] It was insolvent, and it was incapable of exercising external sovereignty.

Even during the War of Independence insolvency had led to the risk of a military coup because Congress had been unable to pay its soldiers; America finished that war, like many winners, in debt. By 1786 the Federal income was only one third of what was needed even to pay the interest on its debt.[23] America was therefore in a poor condition to attract credit from abroad.

Individuals too were in debt, and often those who had fought hardest and lost most in the struggle for independence. Wealthy Tory loyalists, whose property was protected under the peace treaty, seemed too often to have done better than poor farmers who had lost capital and family fighting for liberty.[24] Populist movements in many of the hinterland areas, but especially in Massachusetts and Rhode Island, sought, and in some cases succeeded in achieving, the abolition of debt. This could be crudely done as in Shays's rebellion in Massachusetts, where mobs surrounded and coerced the law courts. In New Hampshire, rioters successfully besieged the legislature demanding paper money, which was issued in seven of the states. Rhode Island, in the grip of agrarian radicals, used paper money as an instrument of policy to depreciate the value of the currency (and hence debts), in which creditors were then forced to accept payment. The division between creditor and debtor varied from state to state, influencing states' policies on financial matters (as on those of trade) which the continental government was powerless to control. The tension between debtor and creditor thus also became an issue between states, which cried out for decisive arbitration.[25]

External sovereignty was weakened by the lack of internal authority. Although it had powers of representing the nation abroad, the Congress had no continuing administration through which to sustain its decisions. Nor, as Madison amongst others complained, was it capable of ensuring that the individual states honoured international agreements signed in their name by the Congress.[26] Finally there was the issue of how to deal with the vast western lands. This posed delicate problems of foreign relations between the United States and Spain, France and its recent enemy Britain, all of whom had a presence there, as well as raising difficult inter-state issues. The accession of further territory to the Union, either as national domain, or incorporated as new states would affect the balance of political power within the whole. Yet the Union could not ignore its vast hinterland. The Congressional Government (through John Jay) nearly allowed the signing away of the rights to navigate to the mouth of the Mississippi. Such an act would have put all

---

[21] Farrand, I, p. 18.

[22] I stress that the Articles were *seen* to fail badly. Historians divide still, as did the federalists and anti-federalists, on how bad things actually were. For an old but clear review see Richard B. Morris 'The Confederation Period and the American Historian', *William and Mary Quarterly*, 13 (1956).

[23] Curtis P. Nettels, *The Emergence of a National Economy, 1790–1860* (Englewood Cliffs, N.J., 1961), cited Rossiter, *The Grand Convention*, p. 49.

[24] One of whom wrote a threatening letter to Governor Bowdoin in Boston, pointing out that if things didn't change blood would be spilt. 'We', he reminded the Governor, 'fought of our liberty as well as you did.' Cited Burns, *The Vineyard of Liberty*, p. 14.

[25] Madison, 'Vices of the Political System of the United States', in James Meyers, *The Mind of the Founder*, revised ed. (Hanover and London, 1981), p. 58.

[26] Ibid., p. 58.

settlers west of the Appalachians at the mercy of the Spanish.[27] It was the fear of 'rendering ourselves ridiculous and contemptible in the eyes of all Europe' that prompted Washington, in the autumn of 1786, to fire off a salvo of letters to notables about the need for action.[28] The need for a coherent and *domestically enforcible* foreign policy was apparent to all the more far-seeing thinkers of the time. Without it the states could be set against one another and picked off singly by the European powers.[29]

The common source of this financial and diplomatic paralysis, was, by general, if often reluctant consent, the degree of autonomy enjoyed by individual states – particularly their legislatures. As Noah Webster, America's Dr. Johnson, put it: 'So long as any individual state has power to defeat the measures of the other twelve, our pretended union is but a name and our confederation but a cobweb.'[30] The inability of the Federal Government to coerce *individuals*, except through the assistance of the states, and its inability to control the states, on all but a few issues, without their unanimous consent, left it without the effective attributes of sovereignty. For if states were not willing to follow or enforce federal law it was effectively inoperable. Madison, reflecting on the 'vices' of the political system of the United States in preparation for the Congress, referred to the Articles of Confederation contemptuously as a 'treaty' rather than a constitution, for it lacked the essential attribute of sovereignty: it possessed no sanctions by which punish those who disobeyed the government established under it.[31] The inability to coerce individuals was, thought Hamilton, 'The great and radical vice, in the construction of the existing confederation.'[32]

The lessons of '*experience*' (ii) inherited

Yet if life as Americans was beginning to show the difficulties inherent in decentralized government, a second, and by now more remote, layer of experience, taught another lesson. Life under the British, and indeed, life *as* British, which is what Americans were until the Declaration of Independence[33] had created a strong mistrust of the executive branch of government. In the colonial era, locally elected legislatures had often struggled,

---

[27] Middlekauf, *Glorious Cause*, pp. 586–90.

[28] *Writings of George Washington*, ed. J.C.Fitzpatrick (Washington, 1931–44), vol. XXIX, p. 27, and pp. 34, 52 and XXVIII, p. 51, cited Morris, 'The Confederation Period . . . ', p. 140.

[29] These issues were raised in early numbers of *The Federalist* as vital reasons for a more effective central government. Since virtually all agreed on the diagnosis it was the strongest line on which to lead. *Federalist*, ensuring execution of treaties no. 3; vulnerability to European colonial powers in America, no. 4; differing interests of states, leads to different foreign policies, no. 5, Union territory in the Western Lands a source of quarrel, public debt, states conflicting over recognition of other states' citizens' private debt, no. 7.

[30] Cited in Rossiter, *The Grand Convention*, p. 50, and see Madison, 'Vices of . . . the United States', in Meyers, *Mind of the Founder*, pp. 57–65.

[31] Ibid., p. 60.

[32] *Federalist*, 15, p. 69.

[33] Indeed eight of the framers had been born in Great Britain, including James Wilson, one of the most learned men there, and Hamilton, one of the co-authors of *The Federalist*, was born a British subject in the West Indies. Others had arrived in America as children, whilst yet others had degrees from British universities. Rossiter, *The Grand Convention*, pp. 140, 146.

fruitlessly, against the imposition of laws and latterly taxes drawn up and enacted by the British legislature, but imposed locally by the chief executive, the governor, usually an appointee of the British Crown. Executives, and indeed judiciaries – all-too-pliable creations of the executive under British rule – were everywhere downgraded in the post-war state constitutions.

Nevertheless, suspicion was not directed only at the executive branch. Some insisted that it was in fact the British *Parliament* – the source of tax legislation – that had been oppressing them.[34] This led to a concern with the answerability of legislatures, especially when remote and corruptible, as well as worries about unconstrained executive officers. This was a crucial issue in which the political experience of Americans and British diverged. Because the British had used the supremacy – or at least the independence – of Parliament twice in the seventeenth century to overthrow royal absolutism, they tended to identify parliamentary supremacy with political liberty itself. Because the Americans suffered under the actions of an unrepresentative imperial parliament, and had fought against its authority to achieve their liberty, for them no such identity was possible. Liberty was identified with rights held *against* government, and legislatures were only exempted inasmuch as they were intimate reflectors of their constituents' wills. More-over, as disillusion set in concerning the degree of responsibility displayed by popular legislatures in the 1780s they too, as we shall see, came under suspicion.

Nor must the influence of more purely legal thinking be forgotten. American law, was, in origin and practice, English law. Thirty-five of the fifty-five framers were lawyers by training. The American Revolution began, and indeed continued for a long time, as an attempt by Englishmen – on both sides of the Atlantic – to secure their native legal and constitutional rights, fundamental amongst which was no taxation without represen-tation![35] In the twenty years from 1780 to 1800 the English constitutional lawyer, William Blackstone was the most cited individual author in American political literature.[36] This institutional and legal inheritance modified the more immediate experience of tyranny at the hands of the British. For many of the most learned and articulate Americans, it was the *perversion* of the English constitution, complained of by opposition thinkers in England as well as in America, which had caused the oppression; their revolution was 'not against the English constitution, but on behalf of it'.[37] Forced to choose between

---

[34] 'It was never a dispute between royal prerogative and parliamentary privilege, whether in Britain or in the colonies. It was a dispute over the powers and authority of the British Parliament.' John Derry, *English Politics and the American Revolution* (London, 1976) p. 21. As late as July 1776 the Congress addressed the Olive Branch petition over the head of the British Parliament to the King and to the British people, as they had often done in the decades before.

[35] See, for example Derry, *English Politics . . .* , ch. 1. Over a third of political pamphlets dealing with the American crisis published before 1776 were written in England by critics of the English government. T.R. Adams, *American Independence, the growth of an idea* (Providence, 1965). A good selection of such English pamphlets is *English Defenders of American Freedoms 1774–1778* ed. P. Smith (Washington, 1772).

[36] Donald S. Lutz 'The Relative Influence of European Writers in Late-Eighteenth Century American Political Thought', *American Political Science Review* 78 (1984), Table 2, 'Most cited Thinker by Decade'.

[37] Gordon S. Wood, *The Creation of the American Republic 1776–1787* (Chapel Hill, N.C., 1969), pp. 10, 44.

adherence to Britain itself, or adherence to the ideals it proclaimed, they chose the latter.[38] 'Right to the end [of the War of Independence] and even after' writes Gordon Wood, an 'uncorrupted English constitution remained for most Americans the model of what a constitution should be.' Nor was this heritage abandoned on achieving independence: continually during the Constitutional Convention, and in *The Federalist* itself, the excellence of the English constitution (when not corrupted) was proclaimed and precedents and warnings from it urged in argument.[39] The British constitution *was* an embodiment of political experience. As John Dickinson had urged at the convention, Americans would be foolish to 'oppose to this long experience the short experience of eleven years which we had ourselves on this subject.'[40]

The lessons of 'experience' (iii) drawn from the history and theory of republics

The American founders inherited well established British and European patterns of thought both to justify resistance and critically to analyse constitutions. This 'Whig' oppositionist political theory reached back to the ideas used by Locke and Sidney in the 1670s, and to Harrington in the 1660s and his heirs, William Trenchard, Walter Moyle and Henry Neville. All of these provided ideas which were used as a starting point by Americans both in attempting to understand and analyse the operation of the tyranny they felt themselves to be under, and in seeking ways to prevent its re-emergence.[41]

These ideas in turn constituted the third and broadest level of 'experience'. The fervour of an at least rhetorical identification with the republican legacy of classical history is shown by the pen-names used in the pamphlet war of ratification which evoked republican heroes from Roman and Greek history, as did Madison, Jay and Hamilton by signing themselves 'Publius'.[42]

By the end of the War of Independence most Americans had come to agree that their government must be republican, at least in the now everyday sense that it should be popular, that there should be no hereditary monarch, nor any hereditary aristocracy. This

[38] Thus Patrick Henry at the Virginia Ratification Debate appealed to Virginians whether the King had had any more loyal subjects than in Virginia: 'We entertained from our earliest infancy, the most sincere regard and reverence for the mother country . . . predilection for her customs, her habits, manners and laws.' Yet forced to choose between liberty and loyalty Virginians were right to *'Sell all and purchase liberty.'* Dry, *Anti-Federalist*, p. 317.

[39] M. Duffy, 'The Making of the Constitution' in J. Smith ed., *The American Constitution, the first 200 years 1787–1987* (Exeter, Exeter studies in History, 1987); *Federalist*, 4, 5, 26, 34, 41, 47, 53, etc.

[40] Farrand II, p. 278.

[41] On the influence on America see Bernard Bailyn, *The Ideological Origins of the American Revolution* (Cambridge, Mass., 1967) Ch. II; Wood *The Creation*, Ch. I; for details of the individuals mentioned see C.Robbins, *Two English Republican Tracts* (Cambridge, 1969), 'introduction', and more extensively, her *The Eighteenth-Century Commonwealthsmen* (Cambridge, Mass., 1959).

[42] Publius was the Roman hero who had established the Republic by ejecting Tarquin the Proud and overthrowing the monarchy. Many of the place names in upper New York State, which were settled by revolutionary war veterans, also reveal this concern to identify with classical republican places or heroes, thus Rome, Syracuse, Ithaca, Macedon, Cato, Tully (Cicero), Cicero, Seneca, Camillus, Fabius. I am grateful to Isaac Kramnick for pointing out this neat and unusual example of the geography of political theory to me. As he shows, other political traditions are also invoked, there is a Locke, N.Y. and a Geneva, N.Y. too. See his 'The "Great National Discussion": the Discourse of Politics in 1787', *William and Mary Quarterly*, XLIV (1987) p. 32.

was uncontentiously written into the constitution, and received the merest passing mention in *The Federalist.*[43] This aspiration marked a significant shift, for it was only after 1776 that the word 'republican' and its cognates acquired unambiguously positive connotations. As Rufus King, speaking for an earlier generation, reminded the younger men at the convention, whilst those 'who have been born since the Revolution, look with horror on the name of a king, and upon all propositions for a strong government. It was not so with us. We were born subjects of a king and were accustomed to subscribe ourselves, His Majesty's most faithful subjects.'[44]

When modern historians refer to the influence of 'republicanism' in the founding period they mean something both looser and yet more historically specific than simply anti-monarchism. After the restoration of the monarchy in 1660, the public and rhetorical use of the term 'republican' was always pejorative in the English context, yet political categories and an analysis derived from republican thinking were nevertheless widely deployed by Englishmen and about England despite the fact that it was a monarchy. A fairly thickly textured set of beliefs about politics had been built up during the late seventeenth and eighteenth centuries, which it requires some effort for us now to recover. Describing this situation is further complicated by the fact that reference to the influence of a founding 'republicanism' commonly reveals a scholar's engagement in a modern controversy about whether founding Americans were (to put the matter over-crudely) modern liberals or classical republicans. This is something of an academic minefield where a scholar may lose not only his way, but his friends, so one must tread warily. But whether they accepted or rejected it the republican legacy formed a vital background to Americans' political thought and we need to know what it told them.

Classical republicanism, as it developed in Greece and Rome focussed on the problem of creating in citizens those personal qualities necessary to sustain the republic; possession of them rendered a man virtuous, and the loss of them signified corruption.[45] Originally these qualities were primarily military. A state which could not defend itself, could not survive. But a state had to sustain itself politically too. Citizens had to be independent – of bribes, of poverty, of foreign influence – to sustain the autonomy of the state. The two roles interlocked and reinforced each other. Military valour paid dividends in political courage too. A man who risked his life for his state's freedom in battle, it was thought, would not be shy of standing up for it in peacetime; and comrades who trusted each other to maintain a phalanx need not fear political treachery. However, the susceptibility of individuals and states to corruption was a continual republican theme.

---

[43] *Constitution of the United States* (1787), art. I, sect.9. There was some fear that the elite Officers of the Revolutionary Army, who formed themselves into a club, the 'Cincinnati' might become a hereditary class. Rossiter, *The Grand Convention,* pp. 44–5. *Federalist,* 84, p. 438.

[44] Farrand, III, p. 446. On the habilitation of 'republicanism' see: W. Paul Adams, 'Republicanism in Political Rhetoric before 1776', *Political Science Quarterly* LXXXV, no.3 (1970).

[45] The most famous Renaissance discussion of these qualities was to be found in Machiavelli. I shall follow the now common practice of using his Italian term *virtù* to refer to them rather than risk confusion with the rather different assemblage of qualities which the English term 'virtue' connotes. However, it is worth noticing that Americans did not mark such a distinction. A certain blurring took place both between pagan *virtù* and puritan virtue, hinging on their common concern with frugality (see Edmund Morgan, 'The Puritan Ethic and the American Revolution', *William and Mary Quarterly,* XXIV, 1, (1967)) and between some of the more technical requirements of the classical model and a more generalised concern with political life. See Lance Banning, 'Second Thoughts on Virtue and Revolutionary Thinking' in Ball and Pocock, ed., *Conceptual Change.*

Since the re-creation of political qualities was required in each generation (*virtù* was an acquired, not a natural or inherited property) the success of a state was dependent on it finding and maintaining those institutions and laws which conditioned the citizen's *virtù*. Unfortunately, the success of one generation overcame those circumstances and usually led to corruption and decline in the next. This was true of all kinds of regimes: Heroic kings bred cossetted tyrannical heirs, noble, dutiful aristocrats bred selfish and idle oligarchs, thoughtful, public spirited democrats bred fickle and factious mobs.[46]

One line of thought, not without its representatives in America, stressed the importance of maintaining the simplicity and austerity of character and the military experience which did so much to reinforce it. During the War of Independence, at the Continental Congress in Philadelphia in 1776, John Adams, a great student of the political thought of antiquity, privately expressed the hope that the British might take the town. Such a reverse 'would cure Americans of their vicious and luxurious and effeminate Appetites, Passions and Habits, a more dangerous Army to American Liberty than Mr. Howes' [the British General]'.[47] The strong associations of civic *virtù* with material simplicity and independence continued for many to mean that it could only be sustained in a society dominated by agrarian freeholders. This provided an ideological underpinning for the lively interest in whether the new constitution would give prominence to the 'landed' or the 'commercial' interests. To many, the growth of trade and manufacture, and the complex forms of dependence fostered by urban life posed a continuing threat to republicanism, and such a view informs a continuing antithesis in American life between the 'virtuous' west, and the 'corrupt' east.

In republican thinking the construction of a 'mixed constitution' in which both the principles and the social groups represented by monarchy, aristocracy and democracy each played a separate political role, and checked and balanced the other was believed to prevent degeneration. The mixed or balanced constitution was thus the answer to republican instability; and Britons, as they had realised in the seventeenth century, were especially fortunate in already having, in the King, Lords and Commons, a mixed constitution. What the British had done was to identify the medieval estates with the classical republican elements of the balance. America however, was to be a society without 'estates', that is without legal differentiations in the status of the citizens (slaves of course, awkwardly, and women without much reflection, excepted). If America was to seek republican stability without monarch or aristocrats, she would have to find other means of 'balancing' her constitution.

However this was not the only problem. Continuing success of even the mixed constitution – of which classical Rome's was the best-known example – could lead to corruption and decline. Successful states grow, in growing they acquire empires. Imperial rule accustoms them to domestic despotism, just as the wealth of empire, whether acquired through plunder or trade, accustoms them to soft living. The size of the Roman Empire eventually made it impossible for ordinary citizens to be soldiers, for the distances covered, the length of campaigns and the need for continual garrisoning meant that only a professional army could do the job. Republican zealots – and even Whig English country gentlemen – dated the decline of Rome from the establishment of a

---

[46] Aristotle, *Politics*, 1304b; Polybius, *History*, 6. v; Cicero, *On the Commonwealth*, I, xlii; Machiavelli, *Discourses*, I, ii.

[47] John to Abigail Adams 22 Sept. 1776, cited Morgan, 'Puritan Ethic . . . ' p. 19.

professional standing army. Once the roles of citizen and soldier were separated out, the *virtù*-ous circle of their mutually supportive interaction ceased – citizens were denied the disciplining influence of military life, and soldiers the political responsibility of citizenship. The possibility arose of military takeover and civic incapacity to resist it. Thus the suspicion of any political authority with its own professional military – the dreaded standing army of opposition theorists – was built into republican thinking, and it heavily influenced both resistance to stronger central government, and the creation of a national military force in America.[48]

Reflection on the history of Rome was one of the most pervasive sources of political ideas for early modern theorists.[49] But Rome, although the most glorious, was not the only model of a republic. Other republics were as long lived, if less glorious. Venice for example, situated on an island, enjoyed geographical isolation. She needed no army – militia or standing – to defend her territory: the sea, and her navy, could do it for her, whilst each also provided a livelihood through trade. Since a navy posed no threat to domestic politics, her citizens did not need to be so inured to military and civic austerity. Unlike land-based, necessarily expansive republics, which needed many citizen-soldiers – and so had to be democratic in nature – Venice could be stable, allowing full reign to the self-interested motives prompted by commercial growth. She could dispense with '*virtù*', sustaining her constitution by complex artifices rather than public spirit. It was a different ideal from Rome's; it presupposed a different, though still stable and supportive, set of relationships between the citizens' natures and their political institutions.[50]

The geographical and constitutional parallels between Venice and Great Britain were not lost on Englishmen of the seventeenth or eighteenth century wishing to deploy a republican analysis. For Harrington, who first did so, Venice's trading economy was not

---

[48] There had been a huge pamphlet debate on the dangers of maintaining a full-time army following the Peace of Ryswick at the end of the seventeenth century in England. (See Lois G. Schwoerer, 'The Literature of the Standing Army Controversy' *Huntington Library Quarterly* V, xxviii, 3 (1965).) The title of the most widely circulated pamphlet of the exchange — indeed possibly of the century — clearly asserted the central tenet of republicanism; it was Trenchard and Moyle's *An Argument Shewing that a Standing Army is inconsistent with a Free Government, and absolutely destructive to the Constitution of the English Monarchy.* (1697, reprinted, The Rota, Exeter, 1971). The claim about its circulation is made by Caroline Robbins, *Two English Republican Tracts* (Cambridge, 1969), p. 29. For the influence of its ideas in America see Bailyn, *Ideological Origins*, p. 62ff. Standing armies are evoked as a symbol of centralised despotism throughout the opposition pamphlets of the ratification debate. See, for example the 'Letters of Brutus', the 'Impartial Examiner', 'Report . . . of the Pennsylvania Minority', 'Agrippa', etc., in Dry, *Anti-Federalist*, pp. 152, 159, 284, 220, 238, and Jefferson, *Jefferson, His Political Writings*, ed. Edward Dumbauld (Indianapolis, 1955), p. 138. The ideological constraints which these ideas placed on military organisation in the young republic are discussed by Lawrence Delbert Cress, 'Republican Liberty and National Security: American Military Policy as an Ideological Problem, 1783 to 1789', *William and Mary Quarterly*, XXXVIII, 1 (1981).

[49] Three thinkers who heavily influenced the founders were dominated by it, and two of them devoted major works to it, Machiavelli (*Discourses*), Harrington, and Montesquieu (*Considerations on the causes of the Greatness of the Romans and their Decline* (1734).

[50] Machiavelli drew attention to the distinctive politico-military-economic dynamics of Venice at the start of the *Discourses* (Bk. I, chs. 5, 6.) On Venice see Eco Haitsma Mulier, *The Myth of Venice*, tr. G.T.Moran (Assen, Netherlands, 1980), and J.G.A. Pocock *The Machiavellian Moment* (Princeton, 1975), ch. ix.

the significant factor – his preferred economy was still agrarian – but by the beginning of the eighteenth century an increasingly and self-consciously commercial Britain was producing thinkers such as Charles Davenant who tried to apply Venetian lessons to Britain's island situation.[51] Even in mainland, absolutist France Montesquieu was prepared to see a new kind of *trading virtù* as the spirit of great cities such as Marseilles.[52] The Venetians had such a dubious moral reputation that they were hardly ever directly invoked as an ideal. Yet it could be argued that if England alone of European states escaped (domestic) despotism, this owed much to her maritime, Venetian situation. The idea occurred to both Hamilton and Madison that despite her vast size, a united America might, relative to the European world, be in such a fortunate, isolationist situation. A disunited America, by contrast, would quickly find herself recreating the divisions and dissensions so endemic in Europe, and with them the resulting militarization and the threats it posed to political freedom.[53]

British opposition Whig thought, to which Americans had long been exposed, embodied other strands too, amongst them the radical notion, common to Locke and Paine, of inalienable individual natural rights, and the constitutional separation of powers, central, if in rather different ways, to the thought of both Locke and Montesquieu. The fortunes of Locke's influence in America have waxed and waned. According to an old and relatively uncritical view he was the major influence on American thinking; whereas recent interpretations have stressed the influence of the republican-derived analysis outlined above.[54] Natural rights and the separation of powers have been presented as liberal concerns, placing subjective and economic freedoms of the individual above the demands of the political community; and so a rigorously conceived republicanism seems to be inconsistent with any theory of natural rights.[55] However, this may not always have

[51] See the discussion of Davenant's pivotal role in Pocock, *Machiavellian Moment*, p. 437ff.

[52] Montesquieu, *Spirit of the Laws*, XX, 5. Montesquieu's commercial appropriation of Machiavelli's hallowed assertion that virtù is the product of *necessità* is striking, recalling the latter's conjecture in *Discourses* I, 1 that it might be better for the virtue of the inhabitants to found a city in barren land. Montesquieu writes 'the sterility of the adjacent country determined the citizens to an economical commerce. It was necessary that they should be laborious to supply what nature refused.... We everywhere see violence and oppression give birth to a commerce founded on economy, while men are constrained to refuge in marshes, in isles, in the shallows of the sea, and even on the rocks themselves.'

[53] *Federalist*, 8 (Hamilton), 41 (Madison); and see Madison's argument at the convention about how a united America might escape the rule that 'means of defence agst foreign danger, have always been the instruments of tyranny at home' by drawing on Britain's island experience which allowed naval defence 'a kind of defence wch cd not be used for the purpose of oppression.' Farrand, I, p. 465.

[54] The older view is typified by Louis Hartz's claim that 'Locke dominates American political thought as no other thinker anywhere dominates the political thought of the nation.' *The Liberal Tradition in America* (N.Y., 1955) p. 140; a claim all the more striking for having been made at the height of the Cold War! For a more cautious assessment see John Dunn, 'The Politics of Locke in England and America' in J. Yolton, ed., *John Locke Problems and Perspectives* (Cambridge, 1969). Don Lutz's work on citations makes Locke the most cited author in the literature of the fifteen years *preceeding* the Declaration of Independence, yet in the ratification debate he is way behind Montesquieu and Blackstone. Donald S. Lutz, 'The relative influence of European Writers on Late-Eighteenth-Century American Political Thought' *American Political Science Review* 78 (1984). The works by Bernard Bailyn and Gordon S. Wood established the outlines of the new paradigm, the broader context for which was set by John Pocock in 'Civic Humanism and its role in Anglo American Thought' in *Politics, Language and Time* (Chicago, 1971).

[55] See 'Virtue, Rights, and Manners: A Model for Historians of Political Thought', *Political Theory*, 9, no. 3 (1981); and in Pocock, ed., *Virtue, Commerce and History* (Cambridge, 1985).

appeared to be the case to historical actors.[56] Certainly *The Federalist* shows both a concern with the protection of individual rights and a stress on the need for virtue or some compensatory mechanism in its absence. Moreover it does so under an overarching concern to demonstrate its own republican credentials.

Whilst the 'republican syndrome' of ideas form an indispensable starting point for any understanding of *The Federalist*, and the debate of which it is a part, the role of such a starting point is not in showing whether *The Federalist* was or was not 'essentially' a liberal or republican work, so much as showing how its authors creatively used the available political languages and ideas at their disposal in trying to forge a theory for dealing with a wholly new situation, the creation of a free state on a continental scale. In doing so they made a permanent contribution not only to American statehood but to our present-day resources for conceptualizing the liberal-democratic state.

The Federalist case for closer unity

The Federalist begins with a group of essays (1–8) which set out the general case for a stronger union. They do so by rehearsing the argument about how the difficulties Americans currently faced lay in the deficiencies of the Articles of Confederation. But first, in introducing this theme, Hamilton raises two other issues so fundamental to modern politics that we perhaps take them for granted.

The first is to point out that the issues faced by Americans will decide 'whether societies of men are really capable or not, of establishing good government from reflection and choice, or whether they are forever destined to depend, for their political constitutions, on accident and force.' The very idea that societies could deliberately construct their own political institutions is a recurrent feature of modernity, and one that has been constantly referred back to the American, no less than the French Revolutions. If such a task, unprecedented at that time, was to be possible anywhere, it was possible in America where human beings had (or so many of them believed), rid themselves of the inherited corruption and inequality which disqualified European nations from attempting such a fresh start.[57]

Hamilton's second point also has great relevance to modern conceptions of politics. It is his claim that political possibilities are to be determined not by questions of absolute right and by means of coercion, but, as Hume had stressed, by opinion and interest: Madison agreed that 'the regulation of . . . interests forms the principal task of modern legislation'.[58] This recognition of private interests is also highly relevant to the delicate issue of interpretation mentioned in the introductory section. Paraphrasing John Pocock's

---

[56] As Lance Banning suggests in his 'Jeffersonian Ideology Revisited: Liberal and Classical Ideas in the New American Republic', *William and Mary Quarterly*, XLIII (1986), p. 12.

[57] It was, ironically, an immigrant English Radical, Tom Paine, who had most successfully articulated this aspect of Americans' culture to them by invoking a shared and natural *'Common Sense'* which could substitute for the misrule characteristic of corrupt European political institutions. See Mark Philp, *Paine* (Oxford, 1989) esp. pp. 32–3. On English reformers' recognition that America held out possibilities for popular government which were unrealizable in Britain see my 'Civic Humanism and Parliamentary Reform: The Case of the Society of the Friends of the People', *Journal of British Studies* 18 (Spring 1979).

[58] *Federalist* 10, p. 43.

influential analysis one may say that recognising and protecting private interests and rights is a liberal project; establishing institutions which will bring about civic behaviour is a republican one.[59] However eighteenth-century thinkers, aware, particularly in America, of the increasingly politically mobilized nature of the community, were coming to recognise that not even an objectively right order could survive unless it also nourished subjective approval of its claims. This dual strategy could be pursued in one of two broad directions: by conditioning individuals' acceptance of a given order, or by shaping an order conducive to individuals given opinions and interests. Recent discussion of republicanism has perhaps overstressed those strands in the tradition which emphasised the shaping of civic *virtù* in a moralized individual personality, a strand which runs from Machiavelli to Milton and Sidney in seventeenth-century England, and, picking up puritan elements in its conception of *virtù* along the way, on to America.[60] But as we have seen, another part of the tradition is represented by Venice and particularly by the Venetian thinker Contarini, and in Anglo-American thought by his follower Harrington. For them, cleverly constructed constitutional devices could simply preclude the possibility of politically destructive behaviour, so that *virtù* did not need to be internalized in the individual; rather, it resided in the whole ensemble of institutions.[61] This view is considerably closer to the modern liberal's moral agnosticism about motives, than the former, and Harrington – particularly through Hume – was an influential figure in late-eighteenth century American debates.[62]

Both Hamilton and Madison follow Hume and Harrington in assuming that politics cannot be conducted successfully on the basis of unrealistic assumptions about human motivation: 'The supposition of universal venality in human nature is little less an error in political reasoning than that of universal rectitude . . . ' We should be 'disposed to see human nature as it is, without either flattering its virtues, or exaggerating its vices . . . '[63] To this end their arguments typically seek out the 'causes, as well physical as moral, which may, in a greater or less degree, permanently nourish different propensities and inclinations'.[64] Having discovered these causes, Madison sought to pursue a 'policy of supplying by opposite and rival interests, the defect of better motives, in such a manner . . . that the private interests of every individual, may be a sentinel over the public rights.' That is to say, he thought that the juxtaposition of, and tension between sectional

---

[59] See Pocock 'Virtue, Rights and Manners', in *Virtue, Commerce and History.*

[60] As mentioned above there is an ambivalence of virtuous austerity as between puritan and republican paradigms which enabled each to feed on the other's language. E.S. Morgan 'The puritan Ethic . . .'

[61] Pocock, *Machiavellian Moment*, p. 325.

[62] Cf. Lutz's citation count in 'The Relative Influence . . . '. The influence of Hume on Madison was first identified by Douglas Adair. ' "That Politics may be reduced to a Science": David Hume, James Madison and the tenth *Federalist*', *Huntington Library Quarterly* 20 (1957), and almost simultaneously by Ralph Ketcham 'Notes on James Madison's Sources', *Midwest Jol. of Pol. Science.* Vol I, part 1 (1957). See most recently, Edmund S. Morgan 'Safety in Numbers, Madison, Hume, and the Tenth *Federalist*', *Huntington Library Quarterly*, 49 (1986). On Adams' and Hamilton's debt to Harrington see Stourzh, *Alexander Hamilton and the Idea of Republican Government* (Stanford, 1970) p. 56ff. On Hume's engagement with Harrington, Fred. G. Whelan, *Order and Artifice in Hume's Political Philosophy,* p. 342ff, and Forbes, *Hume's Philosophical Politics*, p. 183. One supporter of the new constitution, Benjamin Rush, went so far as to write under the pen-name Harrington.

[63] *Federalist*, 76, pp. 389–90.

[64] *Federalist*, 60, p. 307.

interests could be used to create a politically stable whole instead of relying on an individually internalized *virtù*. Moreover Publius often chose to express this aim in the language of rights. This is the republican world of Contarini, Harrington and Hume, more than that of Machiavelli, Sidney or Rousseau – for all the latter's claim to be taking 'men as they are'. Within the very institutions of government itself the same principle applied: political liberty could be assured only in a balanced constitution – or its liberal near-relation – one embodying the separation of powers. The principle gave 'to those who administer each department, the necessary constitutional means, and personal motives, to resist the encroachments of the others . . . ambition must be made to counteract ambition'.[65] Hamilton too makes no apology for appealing to his readers' interests, rather than to their morals. If one apparent opposition – between political liberty and private interests – could be overcome, so, he thought could another, that between liberty and a strong central government. His task was one of showing that a federal government such as that proposed, was in conformity '*to the true principles of republican government* . . . and . . . *will afford . . . the preservation of that species of government, . . . liberty . . . and property*'.[66]

Recognising the possibility of human control over political futures, and seeing that the ability to exercise this control required an understanding of mass political behaviour are two perceptions which lead very directly into modern political science. In this sense both Hamilton with his 'rational calculation of probabilities'[67] and Madison with his embryonic sociology of interests, articulate modes of political thinking which reveal the intimate connections between the historical emergence of democratic political institutions and the transition between classical theory and modern political science itself.[68]

The issue of size

Crucial to the task of showing that liberty was consistent with the new proposed constitution was that of showing that a free republican government could be *large*. For the anti-federalists used the widely accepted argument that republican liberty was possible only in small states; a consolidated continental government would, it was thought, like all large governments lead to tyranny.[69] Brutus, Publius' pamphleteering antagonist, urged the lessons of both classical experience and modern theory. Rome, the greatest republic in history had lost her republican liberty as she had gained her empire.

---

[65] *Federalist*, 51, pp. 264–5.

[66] *Federalist*, 1, p. 4.

[67] *Federalist*, 60, p. 307.

[68] Judith Shklar, 'Alexander Hamilton and the languages of Political Science', in Pagden, ed., *Languages of political theory in early-modern Europe* (Cambridge, 1987), pp. 344–5

[69] *Federalist* 9, p. 37, 'The opponents of the PLAN proposed have, with great assiduity cited and circulated the observations of Montesquieu on the necessity of a contracted territory for a rebublican government.' For a discussion of such views see Cecilia M.Kenyon *The Antifederalists*, Boston, 1985 [1966]) 'Introduction' section II, p. xxxixff.; and various selections; Cathy D. Matson and Peter S. Onuf, *A Union of Interests: political and economic thought in revolutionary America.* (Lawrence, Kansas, 1990), pp. 129–30: and the following original works all reprinted in Dry, *Anti-Federalist*: 'Agrippa' (James Winthrop) 'no extensive empire can be governed upon republican principles'; George Mason, 'popular

Montesquieu argued, like Rousseau after him, that the further government had to extend, the more concentrated must its power be. Great states produce great material inequalities, tempting rich citizens to usurp the political equality on which liberty depended. The public good is more difficult to identify in large than in smaller communities. A free republic is one in which the people give their consent to the laws, but again, this is not meaningfully possible, even with representation, in an extended republic. The population and their customs are too diverse, the laws too difficult to enforce, the people too remote from their rulers, to enable any government but that of force to succeed.[70]

Although the issue of size itself may have become something of a polemical cliché, it was inextricably linked to a number of others which decidedly were not. The argument about state's rights versus national government was one such. Republican theory seemed to demonstrate that, as Montesquieu, by far the most frequently cited author in the debates, put it: 'A large empire supposes a despotic authority in the person who governs . . . ' whereas it was 'a natural property of small states to be governed as a republic'.[71] The more powers were vested in the centre the more the national government not the state, became the political unit, making America, if governable at all, necessarily an empire, in the pejorative sense used of later Rome, and opposed to a republic.[72] On this view, only by keeping power devolved and under popular control, could republicanism survive. The more powers were retained by the states, the more the political unit could be construed as each individual state, and the small size which republican liberty required was preserved. Hence to urge the impossibility of republican liberty in a large political unit was by patent logical implication to reject closer union and defend states' sovereignty, at least internally. Rebutting such an argument, based as it was on that always-formidable combination of the best intellectual authorities and deep-seated prejudice, required major conceptual and polemical effort. Yet there was one immediate point to be scored. For against the views of academic defenders of the small classical

---

governments can only exist in small territories'; 'Brutus' (probably Melacton Smith) 'A free republic cannot succeed over a country of immense extent'.

[70] Brutus, *Essays*, Anti-Federalist, p. 113ff. The most succinct summary of the objections to liberty posed by size; but see also the appeals to 'the greatest writers on the subject' in *Letters of a Federal Farmer*: 'a free elective government cannot be extended over large territories'. Ibid., p. 39; *Letters of Centinel*: 'a very extensive country cannot be governed on democratical principles, on any other plan than a confederation of a number of small republics, possessing all the powers of internal government'. Ibid., p. 18; *Address . . . of the Minority . . . of the Convention of Pennsylvania*: 'a very extensive territory cannot be governed on the principles of freedom, otherwise than by a confederation of republics, possessing all the powers of internal government.' Ibid., p. 209; 'Agrippa' *Letters*: 'no extensive empire can be governed upon republican principles, [it] . . . will degenerate to a despotism . . . '. Ibid., p. 235; Patrick Henry: 'One government cannot reign over so extensive a country as this is, without absolute despotism.' Ibid., p. 317; etc.

[71] Montesquieu *The Spirit of the Laws*, VIII, 19–20; or again as Rousseau put it, 'the larger the State, the more concentrated should the government be, so that the number of the rulers diminishes in proportion to the increase of the people.' *Social Contract*, p. 53 (London, 1968). On Montesquieu, P.M. Spurlin, *Montesquieu in America* (Baton Rouge, 1941) is still very useful.

[72] Confusingly, as Pocock has pointed out, it was possible to find the term 'republic' used as the generic term for any political entity — even of the Holy Roman Empire; Pocock, 'American Founding . . . ' in Ball and Pocock, ed., *Conceptual Change*, pp. 67–8. This need not delay us here. All Americans knew that by a republic they meant a government which was tolerably popular and devoted to the defence of liberty, whatever was meant by either of these two protean terms.

republic, Hamilton iconoclastically pointed out that even the *individual* American states were already far larger than any ancient republic on whose experience such wisdom was based.[73] Moreover, the very existence of the previous continental congresses told against the claim that a unified national government was impractical. Continental government, *of some kind*, was sanctioned both by the geography of America, and the shared culture and history of its people.[74] Given its possibility, the argument for federal unity was pressed firstly, in terms of security from foreign enemies, and secondly in terms of ensuring domestic liberty, harmony and prosperity, although there were numerous ways in which these issues interconnected.

The 'external' argument for closer union

The primary and most general argument in favour of a unified sovereign power illustrates this interconnection. A national government would render impossible independent international action by individual states. This would make it impossible for foreign powers to 'divide and rule' by seeking out individual states whose interest on any one particular issue might deviate from the whole. This argument applied in the field of both diplomacy and trade; presenting a unified commercial front to Europe was as important as political unity. As one supporter of the new constitution neatly put it, without the new constitution 'we may be independent of each other but we will be slaves to Europe'.[75]

The argument is justified, like many others in *The Federalist*, by a psychology of interests. As long as the individual states see themselves as one of a group of individuals, they will conceive of their interest individually, and be tempted (and able) to pursue that interest, if strong enough, to the detriment of the whole. By arguing that the most serious threats to the interest of *each and every* state are external to them all and can only be dealt with collectively by a strong federal government, *The Federalist* seeks to make its readers reconceptualize their ultimate sense of their 'interest' at the federal level, and so to see that states' particular interests could never override the larger issue of collective security. On this view, even where strong passions (such as the injured pride of a border state at territorial violation by a foreign neighbour) might lead states to dangerous overreaction, the national government, in checking those passions, would in fact be acting in their long term interests.[76]

By beginning his case with this foreign dimension Publius had cleverly chosen a topic on which there was some agreement between him and his opponents. The need for some consolidation of the union's external powers was widely acknowledged. Existing theory too, had provided a way forward: for the oracle to whom all sides deferred –

---

[73] *Federalist*, 9, p. 37.

[74] Ibid., 2, pp. 6, 8. 'The people' being implicitly, the white, European section of the population.

[75] Thomas Dawes in the Massachusetts ratification debate, cited, Matson and Onuf, *A Union of Interests*, p. 138.

[76] *Federalist*, 3, pp. 11–12. The psychological assumption is that short term passions have 'a more active and imperious control over human conduct' (Ibid., 6, p. 22), and need to be controlled by 'reason'. The trick is to construct a government that controls such destructive short term passions, which is itself responsive to 'the people' when acting from rational motives. (Ibid., 49, p. 260) See Daniel Walker Howe 'Faculty Psychology in *The Federalist Papers*', in Ball and Farr, *Conceptual Change*.

Montesquieu – had allowed an exception to the impossibility of large, free republics which offered hope for the American case. Montesquieu's reasoning about popular republics was that if they became large they lost that love of equality and frugality which was the spirit or virtue of such governments.[77] On the other hand, if they remained small, they became prey to other, larger, states. Republican states seeking to preserve liberty could, however, provide for their external safety without endangering that liberty by the device of confederation, a form of government 'that has all the internal advantages of a republican, together with the external force of a monarchical, government'.[78] By starting his defence of the new constitution with the topic of foreign relations, Publius selects that very dimension of government which Montesquieu himself recognized as inadequate in the isolated republic.

To the safety from foreign (i.e. European) intervention promised by the new constitution would be added the advantage of national concord. The establishment of several different confederations in America – one of the alternatives to the new constitution at which *The Federalist* constantly hints – would effectively be the establishment of several nations.[79] Once again experience showed that, riven by warfare when separated into the kingdoms of England, Wales and Scotland, Britain's true interest lay in being one nation – Americans 'may profit by their experience, without paying the price which it cost them'.[80] Of such disunited states Hamilton observes 'A man must be far gone in Utopian speculation who can seriously doubt that the subdivisions into which they might be thrown, would have frequent and violent contests with each other.'[81] Readers were pressed to consider a simple dichotomy between a constitution which 'shall be the wonder of the universe' and the otherwise inevitable slide of its constituent states into 'the wild and extended field of nature, unrestrained by any former compact'. Such Hobbesian responses came easily to mind. Pelatiah Webster urged the paramount need for an – any – authoritative arbiter, even 'a wrongful decision [would be] preferable to the continuance of such destructive controversies.'[82]

There were certainly a wide range of issues which could cause inter-state conflict: the various states' claims to the Union Territories, the different geographical situations – coastal, inland, northern, central, southern, the different economic interests – commercial, agricultural or manufacturing, slave holding or free, debtor or creditor.[83] *The Federalist* argued that the consequences of inter-state disputes would be as disastrous for political liberty as for economic prosperity. Whilst upholders of states'-rights republicanism voiced traditional fears about the danger posed to liberty by centralisation and a standing army in a new national government, they failed, says Hamilton, to realise that the inevitable result of inter-state conflict would be the creation of permanent

[77] Montesquieu *Spirit of the Laws*, V:3; VIII:2.

[78] So, 'If a republic be small, it is destroyed by a foreign force; if it be large, it is ruined by internal imperfection.' Ibid., IX:1.

[79] *Federalist*, 5, p. 19.

[80] Ibid., 6, p. 17.

[81] Ibid., 6, p. 20.

[82] See the suggestive discussion on this theme in Matson and Onuf, *A Union of Interests*, pp. 134–7. The quotations are respectively from Hugh Henry Brackenridge at the Pennsylvania ratification convention, 1787 and Pelatiah Webster *The Weakness of Brutus Exposed: Or Some Remarks in Vindication of the Constitution* (Philadelphia, 1787), cited, Matson and Onuf, pp. 135, 137.

[83] *Federalist*, 7, *passim*, 60, etc.

standing armies in each of the states, or future confederations of states, now forming the union. The result of this would be the militarization of public life, the suppression of liberty and the strengthening of the executive at the expense of legislatures, the very things most feared by those who opposed the new constitution as centrist and a threat to liberty.[84] The resolution of this issue is begun by Hamilton in rather typical power-political fashion in *Federalist* IX, where he cites Montesquieu's point that a federal government can always intervene to 'regulate' the subversion of republican liberty in one of their members.[85]

The Federalist here also recruited the political implications of the new economic history pioneered by Hume and Smith in Scotland to stress the differences between ancient militaristic, and modern commercial republics.[86] The continual warfare of ancient republics posed no internal threat to political liberty, indeed it sustained it, by ensuring that all citizens were soldiers. But the modern republic, based on more productive agriculture, commerce and a cash economy, divorced the role of citizen from that of the soldier, and made an army, where needed, necessarily professional. Where such a state is habitually under military threat, the consequences of professional militarization in terms of the erosion of civil liberties, will necessarily follow.[87] Thus in the modern state, the logic of the relationship between size, republican liberty and military necessity is reversed. In ancient, small and economically austere states, republicanism and military necessity were mutually reinforcing factors in the preservation of liberty. In modern large, commercial states, they were not. Indeed as Hume observed, the practice of impressing for military service was a peculiar blemish on the liberty of the modern limited state.[88] However, even in unprecedentedly large states, Hamilton argued, popular republicanism was possible if military necessity was limited, as it could be by minimizing the possibility for both inter-state conflict and foreign intervention; and this was something which both large size, distance from other powers and purposeful unity could achieve.

Nevertheless, stressing the dangers from the conflicting interests of independent states, raised the question about whether it would be wise to try and contain them in an all-embracing national state. The 'traditional wisdom' held that faction and party division were a serious problem, rather than a healthy sign of political liberty.[89] In stressing the danger to a loose federation from internal divisions was there not a danger that those very divisions, might undermine the possibility of maintaining liberty or even stability

---

[84] Ibid., 8, pp. 32–3; Madison returns to the theme in 41, pp. 205–6.

[85] Ibid., 9, pp. 39–40, the point recurs in ibid., 43, p. 224 his citation in both cases is from Montesquieu, *The Spirit of the Laws*, I, bk. ix, ch. 1. Interestingly both Montesquieu and Hamilton refer here to the 'popular' internal subversion of the individual state's constitution, as well as to the danger of its usurping power over the other members of the confederation. Needless to say this former danger was not one which preoccupied the anti-federalists.

[86] See especially Hume's Essays 'Of Commerce', and 'Of Refinement in the Arts.' David Hume, *Essays, Moral, Political and Literary* (Oxford, 1963).

[87] *Federalist*, 8, pp. 33–4.

[88] 'Of Some Remarkable Customs', Hume, *Essays*, pp. 378–9.

[89] This needs to be qualified. Those in opposition tended to draw on an analysis, stemming from Machiavelli's account of Rome, that internal conflict was essential to liberty. See J. Gunn, *Factions No More, Attitudes to Party in Government and Opposition in Eighteenth-Century England* (London, 1972) for an analysis and a selection of original texts.

in a closer union? 'Brutus' certainly thought so. One of his objections to a 'consolidated' national government was that in a country the size of the United States the diversity of interests and customs would be so great that if they were represented effectively in a national legislature they would 'not only be too numerous to act with any care or decision, but would be composed of such heterogeneous and discordant principles, as would constantly be contending with each other.'[90]

Madison championed the view that 'an extinction of parties necessarily implies either an universal alarm for public safety, or an absolute extinction of liberty.'[91] This well-worn cliché of English oppositionist thought was to be transformed by Madison in the tenth and possibly most famous issue of *The Federalist*. There, in an argument of great scope and subtlety he effectively transforms the fear of faction into a celebration of pluralism, and helped to redefine republicanism in the process.

The enlarged and commercial republic

The tenth Federalist

No. X is one of the nerve centres of *The Federalist*, resynthesizing the worrying issues about size, faction and democracy into a mutually supportive whole. It provides support and nourishment for a wide range of other arguments at various points in the rest of the series. It is also revealing about the kind of otherwise unexpressed psychological assumptions which underpin its authors' arguments.[92]

Like Hume, Madison recognises that not only inequality of property (to which he gives the greatest weight) and the self-interest of various economic groups, but also more 'frivolous and fanciful distinctions' have been made the basis of party and faction. Like Hume too, he supposes that this derives from a basic human propensity to 'fall into mutual animosities', about 'even . . . the most speculative and indifferent opinions'.[93]

The psychological origins of these differences lie in the disparate uses that human beings make of their reason in working out how to satisfy their various desires. Reasoning differently about how to achieve different ends soon produces different perceptions of interest.[94] Some of these will be 'fallible' or 'frivolous' but some will not; and there is no guarantee that harmony can be created, even amongst individuals correctly perceiving their interests.[95] Moreover, as these differences derive from the different use men make of their liberty, it would be inconsistent with liberty to suppress them, no matter how misguided, unless more important considerations supervene. Differences of interest are

---

[90] Brutus, *Essays*, Dry, *Anti-Federalist*, pp. 114–5.

[91] *Federalist*, 50, p. 263.

[92] For an excellent overview of the arguments and interpretations of the Essay, see A. Gibson, 'Impartial representation and Extended Republic: towards a Comprehensive and Balanced Reading of the Tenth *Federalist Paper*', *History of Political Thought*, XXII, 2 (1991).

[93] Madison, *Federalist* 10, p. 43, Hume 'Of Parties in General' p. 59. Hume distinguishes between parties based on interest, those based on principle and those based on affection. *Essays* (p. 58), Madison duly notes, as well as interest based on property, 'a zeal for different opinions concerning religion [and] government' and 'an attachment to different persons . . . or leaders', p. 42.

[94] Ibid., 10, p. 42.

[95] Ibid., 10, p. 44.

then, a natural consequence of human psychology and liberty. Yet they are only a matter of political concern if factious. A faction is defined as

> a number of citizens, whether amounting to a majority or minority of the whole, who are united and actuated by some common impulse of passion, or of interest, adverse to the rights of other citizens, or to the permanent and aggregate interests of the community.[96]

The other considerations that justify interference with liberty are principally two: 'the rights of other citizens' and 'the permanent and aggregate interests of the community'.[97]

Now, as anyone who has reached this point in the history of political theory will be aware, concepts such as 'the rights of other citizens', and even more 'the permanent and aggregate interests of the community' are not without their problems. Madison had no doubt that there were such rights; he had given a list of them in advice on a constitution for Kentucky.[98] The question was, could they be legally expressed, and even if they could, who would interpret them? In the absence of the definitive hereditary, cultural or theological authority which the Americans had self-consciously repudiated, the task of assessing what rights and interests are proper had devolved on popular legislatures whose majorities were clearly liable to be 'factious'. Legislation is often effectively an act of judgement between two interest groups, and in popular government such groups are at large in the people doing the deciding. Legislating to prevent leisure parks in nature reserves is simply endorsing the wildlife lobby's claim to represent the permanent interests of the community and denying the similar claims of the leisure industry. Less obviously, but even worse, the very concepts of interest and right can be confused: Madison pointed out that legislative decisions about the rules of property, debt and taxation are in effect 'but so many judicial determinations . . . concerning the rights of large bodies of citizens and what are the different classes of legislators, but advocates and parties to the causes which they determine?'[99] Allocative decisions such as these, are, or should be, matters of determining right and justice. Yet when they are decided politically, not only are they treated like interests, but the contending parties are also judge and jury in their own case, and the strongest faction wins.

Madison had confronted these issues in the 1780s when majoritarian popular legislatures began to interfere with religious liberty, and even with the judicial process. Identifying the protection of rights with popular government had seemed unproblematic when the threat to rights came from an unrepresentative imperial power; with independence it was clear that the threat could come from popular government itself. Democratic or republican government now seemed incapable of guaranteeing that protection of individual rights and avoidance of faction which would allow the permanent interests of the society to emerge.

---

[96] Ibid., 10, p. 42.

[97] Ibid., 45, p. 234. Madison asserts that the ultimate value of government is 'the public good, the real welfare of the great body of the people.'

[98] To Caleb Wallace, 23 August, 1785, he listed constitutional limitations which might be placed on the legislative power as 'medling with religion, abolishing juries . . . Habeas Corpus, forcing a citizen to give evidence against himself . . . controuling the press . . . enacting retrospective laws . . . abridging the right of suffrage . . . taking private property . . . licensing the importation of slaves . . . infringing the Confederation.' Meyers, Mind of the Founder, p. 28.

[99] Federalist 10, p. 43.

These were central objections to large and popular government. In small classical republics faction might be averted by engendering a shared collective identity which, as Rousseau hoped, would create a psychology in which the public interest would be clearly identifiable, and from which individuals would differentiate their rights less sharply. But the larger the electorate, the less clear is the public good and the less powerful moral motives are, for their 'efficacy is diminished in proportion to the number which is to share the praise or the blame'. Nor can religion, except when zealous – and it is then hardly an aid to political stability – guarantee disinterested motives.[100] This erosion of political cohesion and disinterestedness in large communities was one of the reasons held to limit successful republicanism to small states. For as we have seen, at least on one view, republics relied on an ethic of unselfish public service. Even large republics required *some* sense of virtue and public responsibility.[101] Nevertheless, we also noted an alternative story – of republics which contrived to immunize themselves – as far as possible – from human failings by institutional balance and complexity.[102]

Seeking institutional means to cope with human 'interest' was, as we have seen, the acknowledged core of Madison's conception of constitution-making. But merely formulating the problem in these, rather than in classical republican terms did not dispose of the issue. Our natural partiality required that no man should judge his own case, but neither should any group of men, and the central problem with unrestrained popular government is that the majority do. Moreover, in expressing these worries there was a particular majority that many had in mind. The 'majority' had carried, since Aristotle's time, the in-built notion of a faction, and, since the majority were invariably the poorer members of the community, a faction composed of the poor. Indeed this possibility was an expressed concern of Madison's, rising to something of an obsession in the 1780s. The whole constitutional debate was sparked by and preoccupied with the populist threat to property.[103] By pointing out the implications of interest-expressive legislation under popular government, Madison brilliantly refocused the whole issue, from the problem of the divisive factions when popular government became too large to generate solidarity, to the threat to liberty – and property – posed by a single dominant faction, from democracy as anarchy, to democracy as majority tyranny.[104] In doing so he made size and faction redeeming virtues, rather than a threat to the popular republic.[105]

[100] Madison, 'Vices of the Political System of the United States' in *The Mind of the Founder*, p. 63. See also Hamilton, *Federalist* 15, 'regard to reputation, has a less active influence, when the infamy of a bad action is to be divided among a number than when it is to fall singly upon one' p. 72.

[101] *Federalist*, 54, p. 287.

[102] The American career of these two concepts of republicanism is picked up in Hanson's 'Democratic Republicanism. . .' in *Conceptual Change*, ed. Ball and Pocock.

[103] Jack N. Rakove's 'The Madisonian Theory of Rights' *William and Mary Law Review*, 31 (1990), p. 253. At the Constitutional Congress Madison had painted a very frank picture of the possible threat posed to property rights as the American Republic grew and with the gap between rich and poor, under equal suffrage 'power will slide into the hands of the [indigent]', Farrand, I, p. 423.

[104] 'To secure the public good, and private rights, against the dangers of such a [majority] faction, and at the same time preserve the spirit and form of popular government is then the great object to which our inquiries are directed.' *Federalist* 10, p. 44.

[105] At the convention Madison had rehearsed many of the arguments of *Federalist* 10, pointing out that the threat to property posed by universal suffrage — if it proved necessary — could only be overcome by larger electoral districts. Farrand, III, p. 454.

Madison is notorious for rejecting one possible safeguard to individual rights, the idea of a bill of entrenched rights. His scepticism about this however, was firmly based on a belief in its ineffectuality, and not on any denial of the danger of majority domination. He had conducted a struggle in Virginia under the Confederation to maintain freedom of religion *against* both a popular campaign to re-impose it, and an elected legislature minded to do so. A bill of rights *might* remedy such incursions, but Madison doubted that these 'parchment barriers' would hold; in Virginia such entrenched rights had been 'violated in every instance where [they had] been opposed to a popular current.' What Madison sought to do was to counter interest with interest, power with power, and a bill of rights did not establish a countervailing power, however much it might in time establish a countervailing sentiment.[106] On Madison's view, and it is a view with still a great deal to be said for it 'Wherever the real power in a Commonwealth lies, there is the danger of oppression.' If, as in the American republic the real power lay in the majority, the implication could not be shirked:

> the invasion of private rights is chiefly to be apprehended, not from acts of Government contrary to the sense of its constituents, but from acts in which the Government is the mere instrument of the major number of the Constituents.[107]

Madison's experience in Virginia left him in no doubt that legislatures, even popular legislatures, indeed especially popular legislatures, could threaten individuals' interests and rights as effectively as had colonial executives. However, this experience also provided a clue as to how the threat could be minimised (for it could never be completely disposed of). In *The Federalist* 51 Madison drew a clear lesson about how he thought he could secure civil liberty in the new state from the circumstances that had, in the end, preserved religious liberty in Virginia:

> It consists in the one case in the multiplicity of interests, and in the other in the multiplicity of sects. The degree of security in both cases will depend on the number of interests and sects; and this may be presumed to depend on the extent of country and the number of people comprehended under the same government.[108]

---

[106] Madison did later acknowledge that if such a bill 'acquired by degrees the character of a fundamental maxim of free Government, and . . . became incorporated in national sentiment' it might 'counteract the impulses of interest and passion'. Madison to Jefferson, Oct. 17th, 1788, in Meyers, *Mind of the Founder*, pp. 157, 158.

[107] Ibid., p. 157.

[108] *Federalist*, 51, p. 267. The evolution of Madison's views on this and the role of his experiences in Virginia is well analysed in Rakove, 'The Madisonian Theory of Rights', on which this section has drawn.

The nub, and rhetorical genius of Madison's argument in *Federalist* 10 should now be clear. By reconceptualizing the issue of self-interested factions as a problem of oppressive majorities, the issue of size becomes a benign factor rather than the source of the problem. 'In the extended republic of the United States . . . a coalition of a majority of the whole society could seldom take place upon any other principles than those of justice and the general good.' This was so, not because people were virtuous enough to set aside their own interest, but because they could never construct a majority stable enough to impose its interests on others.[109] It was this 'enlargement of the sphere' which offered a cure for the threat posed to political life by the pursuit of interests which liberty makes possible. Just why should this be? Madison's argument is extremely close, occupying barely three pages. There are in fact three principles involved, that of representation, the greater numbers of citizens and the greater extent of territory.

The principle of representation was one which 'America can claim the merit of making the . . . basis of unmixed and extensive republics.'[110] The nature of representation was a crucial point of difference between the federalists and anti-federalists which it was in Publius's interests to underplay by meeting only indirectly. 'Brutus', the anti-federalist champion, held a view of representation not unlike that of the modern opinion pollster's 'stratified sample':

> the farmer, merchant, mecanick and other various orders of people, ought to be represented according to their respective weight and numbers; and the representatives ought to be intimately acquainted with the wants, understand the interests of the several orders . . . , and feel a proper sense and becoming zeal to promote their prosperity.[111]

On this view a representative assembly had to replicate, in miniature, the 'people' it was supposed to represent. A representation which blurred the divisions between, or diffused the passions of, the constituents was defective. Moreover, for Brutus, the fact that a directly elected national assembly entailed larger constituencies, had two deleterious consequences.[112] Firstly the proportionality implied by the direct form of representation would be distorted, for only an assembly numerous in proportion to its electorate could truly represent its various groupings. Secondly, what is a specific and serious

---

[109] *Federalist*, 51, p. 268. As Madison and others were painfully aware there was at least one permanent minority who were not beneficiaries of this principle, black slaves. Nevertheless, he, James Wilson and others all argued that the acceptance of slave-holding states into the Federation at least held out the hope of federal control over, and eventual abolition of, the institution. Letter to Robert Walsh, 27 Nov. 1819, in Meyers, *The Mind of the Founder*, p. 321.

[110] *Federalist*, 14, p. 62.

[111] Dry, *Anti-Federalist*, p. 125. This juxtaposition between the two views of representation and its importance for the conceptual issues at stake draws on Ball's excellent discussion in ' "A Republic . . . "' in Ball and Pocock, *Conceptual Change*.

[112] The new constitution fixed the size of Congressional constituencies at a maximum of 30, 000, and pending a census, the first House was to have in any case 65 members. The constituencies were very large indeed by eighteenth-century standards. The largest eighteenth-century constituency in Britain was the County of Yorkshire, where two members were returned each election by 20, 000 voters. But this was nearly twice the size of the next largest, Westminster, at 12, 000, and Kent, Lancashire and Somerset at 10, 000. Most English counties had electorates of 3–4, 000, and in the 203 borough constituencies electorates varied from that of Westminster to as low as two (Gatton), with most being well below a thousand. John Brooke, *The House of Commons 1754–1790* (Oxford, 1964), pp. 1, 30, and Ch.1 *passim*.

example of the latter, larger constituencies would absolutely exclude 'the great body of the yeomen . . . the farmers . . . [and] mechanicks of every branch' from election, because 'the station will be too elevated for them to aspire to' so that 'there will be no part of the people represented, but the rich'.[113] For anti-federalists, representation was at best a risky expedient which might enable popular republicanism to be extended to a federal America. For Madison it was a necessary means of inhibiting the volatile, parochially interested and badly informed wills of the state electorates from being reflected at national government level. For Hamilton, never one to mince his words about the qualities to be expected of the ordinary citizen, the brilliance of the American experiment was, not merely the use of representation, which had, after all, been known in the ancient world, but that 'to the most advantageous superiority in favour of the United States' it applied the principle 'to the total exclusion of the people' in direct popular politics, which had never been done before. The full advantage could, however, only be reaped if representation were applied over large constituencies.[114]

The issue of representation was a crucial prism through which to analyse both Publius' claim and Brutus' denial that the new constitution was a popular federal republic. Though they were focussed through disputes about the meanings of certain key terms, the differences between the two positions were real and substantial. For Brutus the predominance of power in the federal government meant that the government was national and not federal. It was therefore at the national level that the question of its representativeness was to be assessed. Since a national assembly in a country the size of the US could not represent in the literal and immediate sense, the government could not claim either to be a popular, nor, in his view, could it long remain a free republic.

Madison's view of representation, together with the size and extent of constituencies 'promised a cure' for the typical ills of popular republics without deviation from their spirit. Larger political units 'refine and enlarge' the electorate's demands by filtering them through the more educated and public spirited characters who are likely to be elected. This is not guaranteed; representatives may be intemperate, parochial or plain corrupt; but other things being equal, a larger state with larger constituencies will have a better chance of avoiding such men than smaller. For, as constituency size increases, as it must to keep the size of the assembly within reasonable bounds, the pool of available talent also increases.[115] Moreover larger constituencies – and wider franchises – make bribery and corruption, legendary in British eighteenth-century elections, more difficult, or at least more expensive. Larger constituencies also make a representative's preoccupation with *excessively local* interest less likely.[116] Of course, if the constituency is too large the representative loses his connection with the community. But the federal principle, by allowing two tiers of government, overcomes this too, 'the great and aggregate interests being referred to the national, the local and particular to the state legislatures.'[117] Most fundamentally of all, Madison's conception of representation does

---

[113] *Essays of Brutus*, Dry, *Anti-Federalist*, pp. 125–6.

[114] *Federalist*, 63, p. 325.

[115] Ibid., 10, p. 45.

[116] See also Ibid., 57, it 'cannot be said . . . that five or six thousand citizens are less capable of choosing a fit representative, or more likely to be corrupted by an unfit one, than five or six hundred' and where Madison cites the experience of various states with large constituencies for their upper house.

[117] Ibid., 10, p. 46.

not, unlike that of his opponents, involve attempting to create a microcosm of the constituency. It is actually an advantage, he claims, that legislatures should not mirror precisely their constituents' divisions. This is one of the means of filtering out faction, and the larger the constituency the greater this effect. Conversely, by diminishing constituency size and increasing the number of representatives, the representative assembly itself becomes liable to the 'confusion and intemperance of a multitude' or to being captured and manipulated by sinister forces: 'the countenance of the government may become more democratic; but the soul that animates it will be more oligarchic'.[118]

Greater numbers of electors in themselves make for more varied groupings of interests within the assembly, and the possibility of a permanent majority is then less likely. Wider extent of territory weakens possibility of sinister combinations successfully communicating their plans in secret. Conspiracies are simply more difficult when more people are involved over a wider area. Finally the distinct federal tier of government could act as a safeguard, guaranteeing the restoration of republicanism in any state unfortunate enough to have its constitution subverted.

Thus, representation, particularly in combination with 'greater extent of territory' made possible in turn by the division of responsibilities between local, state, and federal business, makes more likely the creation and maintenance of an enlightened, distinguished and independent national legislature. Such a legislature might not only prove enlightened and independent enough to realise a truly common interest at national level, but also, by being the ultimate safeguard against factious majorities within a state from oppressing minorities there, it could defend rights as well.[119] In terms of the psychology deployed in *The Federalist*: it could exercise the people's own reason in controlling their passions.

A republic large, federal and widely representative thus has advantages which spring from what, on a more traditional reading of republicanism, are its defects. Each characteristic renders any majority 'by their number and local situation, unable to concert and carry into effect their schemes of oppression' because they will be checked by another 'representative' body, thus providing 'a republican remedy for the diseases most incident to republican government.'[120]

Madison's solution is theoretically extremely elegant. However in order to be also rhetorically powerful Publius had not only to overcome doubts about the viability of large republics, he had largely to reconceptualize what was meant by, and to integrate, the two terms 'republic' and 'federal'.[121] If he could do so he could deny them to his opponents. By capturing the positive associations of the term 'federal' for his own position, his opponents were forced to become anti-federalists. In substituting an opposition between 'federal' and 'anti-federal', for one between 'national' or 'consolidated'

---

[118] Ibid., 55, pp. 284; 58, 301.

[119] See further Robert J. Morgan, 'Madison's theory of representation in the Tenth Federalist' *Journal of Politics*, 37 (1974). Discussion of the constitutional mechanism by which such a safeguard would operate must wait until the section on the division of powers, p. 237ff.

[120] *Federalist*, 10, pp. 47, 44, 47–8.

[121] As Madison hints, by suggesting that, at least in the American context, one could not be a republican without also being, in this sense a federalist. Ibid., 10, p. 48. On the reconceptualization of 'republic' and 'federal' see Ball ' "A Republic — if you can keep it" ' and Pocock 'States, Republics, and Empires': both in Ball and Pocock (ed) *Conceptual Change*.

on the one hand, and 'federal' or 'confederal' on the other, he immeasurably improved the position of the supporters of the new constitution

Madison returns to the issue of size in no.14, where again terminology becomes important. Size is an objection to large democracies, because, Madison stresses, in a democracy the people must meet in person. In this he implied what was untrue, that his opponents, by championing 'popular' government sought direct democracy. A republic, by contrast, he now defines as government by representatives.[122] Only by confusing democracy and republicanism, which he claims monarchist Europeans have done to frighten their populations from the pursuit of republican liberty, could the vices of democracy be attributed to republics. The only size limits to a republic are those which enable representatives to attend some central place for discussion, and it cannot be said that the United States is too large for this because such continental assemblies have existed since the revolution! The furthest states are no further from Philadelphia than northern Scotland is from London. Far-flung states may find it less convenient to attend, but to balance this they have a stronger interest. Having borders with potential enemy territories, the French to the south and west, the British to the north, they have more to gain from adherence to the union. If only the central authority were given enough power to protect the periphery, the theory of interest and the theory of extended representation argued not for but against disintegration. The vitality and diversity of interests predicted the viability of the 'extended republic.'[123]

The political economy of the commercial republic

The arguments that applied to the political benefits of a strong federal republic, applied also in the field of economics. Here again traditional republican arguments provided a framework, for thought and argument.

For virtuous republicans, undoubtedly the surest way to expand without corruption was to extend the margins of cultivation. Working the land produced independent, self-reliant, characters who were virtuous whether in a republican or puritan sense. There is no quarrelling that such an ideal played a role in the thinking of many at the time – and since. It was clearly an important ideal for Jefferson. The Louisiana Purchase was still some years away, but the existing opportunities for westward settlement already promised growth without the need to expand manufactures, city life and its attendant moral dubiety.

Nevertheless there were other ways to grow. In a world increasingly dominated by international trade, even thinkers as important to Americans and as influenced by the language of the virtuous republic as Tom Paine and Montesquieu saw the egalitarian and civilizing influence of trade.[124] The War of Independence had been generated ultimately

---

[122] Madison slips in this not uncontentious stipulative definition in *Federalist*, 10, p. 45.

[123] Ibid., no. 14.

[124] In *Common Sense* Paine rhetorically invoked the argument from austerity to assert the superiority of the Americans over the English, whose 'Commerce has diminishe[d] the spirit of patriotism and military defence.' Paine, *Common Sense*, in *Foner* (ed.), *Complete Writings* (2 vols, New York, 1969) vol I, p. 36. But the influence of trade is later asserted as a virtue. He claims 'I have been an advocate for commerce, because I am a friend to its effects. It is . . . the greatest approach toward universal civilisation, that has yet

by the issue of taxes intimately connected with control of trading activity.[125] The central issue for Americans now, claimed Hamilton, was to ensure that American vessels carried their own produce and so not only benefited from the 'carrying trade', but reaped the full benefits of the profits to be gained in European markets.[126] Once again a *United* States would be able to negotiate – and impose – much more favourable trading terms than a divided confederation. A united America could force a divided Europe to bid competitively for her trade.

Not only traders but the national exchequer would benefit from unity. Divided states would have different excise policies and tariffs. Foreign traders would land produce where it was cheapest. It would be impossible to control contraband movements between the states – indeed the liberal temper of the Americans (and the association of excise men with the hated British), would make attempts at such control highly unpopular. States with higher tariffs would be forced to reduce them in competition with those with lower rates. A United States with a single tariff, would force traders back into the ports or would-be evaders to turn smuggler, and land on perilous coasts.[127] A United States would therefore be able to sustain a higher revenue, for any given rate of excise.[128]

A successful carrying trade would not only secure better terms and revenue for the new national government, it would create a merchant navy providing the basis for maritime power with which to protect both the trade and, if necessary the territory of the new nation, thus completing a virtuous circle. Yet more benefits may accrue, since the creation of a national navy – something of a preoccupation with Hamilton – not only safeguards the nation's economic and territorial integrity, it generates work and trade in supplying naval requisites – wood for ships, iron for fittings, pitch and tar, rope and cloth – which stimulates the economy of even the non-trading states. This was no small issue. The naval dockyard was by far the largest economic or organizational enterprise in the eighteenth-century state, exceeding by whole orders of magnitude that of any manufacturer. The generation of such operations and the subsequent pursuit of government contracts was widely held to produce corruption – through patronage – in the English Parliament. Hamilton, however, who has some insight into the dynamics of what

---

been made by any means not immediately flowing from moral principles.' *Rights of Man* (I) in Foner, I, p. 400. For a discussion of Paine which gives due prominence to the nuances of his views on commerce see Gregory Claeys, *Thomas Paine, Social and Political Thought* (London, 1989), esp pp. 46–9, and 96ff.On Montesquieu and trade see, e.g. *The Spirit of the Laws* XX, 7, and V, 6, and my 'British and European Background to the Ideas of the Constitution' in J.Smith (ed), *The American Constitution, the first 200 years* (Exeter, 1987).

[125] To be precise, the major issue was whether they were or not. The British had always taxed to regulate the Atlantic traffic. What became an issue from the middle of the eighteenth century was whether they were entitled to levy taxes for the purpose of raising revenue, and which taxes could be said to be of this kind.

[126] *Federalist*, 11, p. 48. America's European competitors will try to deprive her of 'an ACTIVE COMMERCE in our own bottoms [i.e., ships]'; and p. 51, 'compelled to content ourselves with the first price of our commodities, and to see the profits of our trade snatched from us, to enrich our enemies and our persecutors.'

[127] 'There will be . . . but one side to guard, the ATLANTIC COAST.' Ibid., 12, p. 57.

[128] Ibid., 12, pp. 56–7. Ironically this very fact was urged against a federal impost by anti-federalists who argued that to maintain the importers' option of smuggling between the states would act as a natural limit on the temptation of states to increase their excise – and a good thing too. Matson and Onuf, *Union of Interests*, p. 153.

John Brewer has called the eighteenth-century fiscal-military state, and was perhaps least worried of all the founders about a strong government's threats to political virtue, holds it out as a potential benefit to the emergent American nation.[129]

Eighteenth-century arguments about economic development, invariably involved political considerations.[130] The argument between the federalists and their opponents is not a simple one between the apologists of a modern liberal economic order and the defenders of austerity in the name of republican virtue – even if they had been capable of formulating it in this way. The terms involved in the argument – and the values pursued by the two sides – were too multivalent to enable such clear distinctions to hold. Although it's true that classical learning taught that virtuous popular republics were brought down by economic growth and luxury, various thinkers had already developed the language of republicanism to envisage other possibilities. The easily-evoked praise for frugality and thrift could be recruited both in support of nostalgic agrarian republican simplicity, and – often with the significant addition of 'industry' – in support of developing commerce and manufacture. There were defenders of free trade on each side of the federalist – anti-federalist divide.[131] Such arguments were invariably subordinated to the test of national political interest: whilst *The Federalist* argues for free and equal trade *within* the union, it seeks the imposition of tariffs and controls – and where possible a carrying monopoly – *without*.

We can see this unified conception of a political economy in the discussion about the best way of raising revenue. This was to be through a levy on manufactured imports. Since America was, at this time, an exporter of basic and raw materials, which the Old World needed, it made little sense to tax them. On the other hand taxing manufactured imports provided revenue for the state, inhibited luxury, and provided a sheltered environment for the growth of American manufactures, a set of motives mixed enough to appeal to agrarian republicans, state-builders and the manufacturing and commercial lobby. The extension of taxation was always a sensitive issue, however, since the ability of governments to raise funds was directly related to their ability to act independently of the legislatures that normally granted them. Granting the federal government powers to tax imports gave it a source of revenue independent of the states legislatures and which would grow automatically with the economy. Whilst it was one which would, Brutus conceded, at least impinge equally on the states, the granting of unrestricted powers of taxation was politically dangerous.[132] Yet in arguing that government could not be constitutionally restricted to rely for its revenue on import duties, Madison clearly recognized the necessarily shifting political economy on which the American state must rest. Foreseeing, in all but these words, the closure of the frontier, he anticipates a time when American manufacturing will overtake agriculture, at which point it may need

[129] John Brewer *The Sinews of Power* (London, 1989), pp. 35–6, and passim.

[130] See for example the classic statement by Donald Winch, *Adam Smith's Politics* (Cambridge, 1978).

[131] Kramnick, 'The "Great National Discussion"', esp. pp. 16ff; Matson and Onuf, *Union of Interests*, p. 156ff. The 'oracle' Montesquieu had pointed out that although in general democracies require frugality, in 'a democracy founded on commerce, private people may acquire vast riches without a corruption of morals. This is because the spirit of commerce is naturally attended with that of frugality, economy, moderation, labour, prudence, tranquillity, order, rule.'*Spirit of the Laws*, V, 3, 5.

[132] 'Essays' of Brutus, Dry, *Anti Federalist*, pp. 149–50.

some raw, or other imported materials. Taxation on imports would then be a foolish way to raise revenue, and other sources of it will be needed.[133]

Economic development was not to be feared, a commercial and manufacturing economy would extend the range of interests in the community, and this could be further integrated into Madison's account of how diversity could enable free republics to be large without suffering the onset of corruption and decline at the hands of a dominant faction.

Defining the terms

Publius' arguments in *Federalist* X and elsewhere about the way size and diversity of interests impinge on the operation of representation and republican liberty in large states were concerned to dispel fears about the new constitution by demonstrating its systemic properties – the mutually supportive relationship between its various characteristics – at what we might today call the level of political sociology. But Publius also sought to show that the formal institutions and offices of the constitution itself possessed similarly beneficial interactive qualities. More specifically, he argued that the various branches and powers of government both within the federal government, and between the federal government and the states, were articulated in such a way as to prevent any one branch – or tier – of government gaining control of the others, and so becoming tyrannical.

This topic was essentially that of the separation of powers which preoccupies much of the second half of *The Federalist*. But the discussion also raised conceptual issues about the identity of 'republicanism' and of 'federalism' which were intimately bound up with the question of the need for such checks and balances and, if they were needed, where they were best located. However these were also rhetorical issues, for such was the prestige of 'republicanism', and, given the suspicion of a strong centralised government, so great the attachment to the federal ideal, that it was vital for Publius to persuade his readers that the new constitution embodied both characteristics. To realise these two aims some subtle conceptual moves had to be accomplished. These definitional issues are raised head-on in *Federalist* 39, but it draws on ground prepared elsewhere in the work. We shall discuss them now before moving on to the more explicit consideration of the separation of powers.

'Republics', 'democracy' and 'aristocracy'

Both English republican theory and Lockean natural rights thinking provided theoretical justification for the widespread popular belief that absolute, i.e. unlimited and unrestrained, power was tyrannical in itself. Both the idea of the balanced, or mixed constitution, which emerged from republican thinking, and the doctrine of the separation of powers asserted by Locke on natural rights grounds, were theories devised to meet the threat of unlimited political power in the hands of one person or body. Within the

---

[133] *Federalist* 51, pp. 209–10.

British context the balancing of the influence of social orders (King, Lords and Commons), the balancing of constitutional principles (unity, wisdom, liberty) and the separation of functional powers (particularly executive and legislative) could be said to be achieved all at once. The two houses of Parliament and the King simultaneously represented the different socio-legal estates, embodied different virtues and disposed of different powers. However it was inherent in this balance that Britain remained only partly a popular regime – the Commons was the only 'popular' part of the constitution. Since, within the British political tradition, these different 'estates' of citizens also provided the limiting, or checking elements of the mixed constitution, a republic in America, which had rejected two of those elements, could easily be thought of as an unmixed constitution, a government wholly popular.[134] This left the issue of majoritarian tyranny very much exposed, but individuals differed as to how much of a worry this was. As Jefferson put it, with rather more popular fervour than Publius would have: though the 'sacred principle' of a republic was that 'the will of the majority is in all cases to prevail, that will, to be rightful, must be reasonable; . . . the minority [must] possess their equal rights, which laws must protect and to violate which would be oppression.'[135] Just how the will of the majority and what was 'reasonable' and consistent with the rights of minorities, could be made to coincide without so curbing majorities as to offend the 'sacred principle' was the crucial issue.

For Jefferson popular majority rule was actually the defining characteristic of a republic. This could, however, be legitimately exercised through representatives, and he later identified this as a new democratic variant:

> The first principle of republicanism is that the *lex majoris partis* is the fundamental law of every society of individuals of equal rights; to consider the will of society enounced by the majority of a single vote as sacred as if unanimous is the first of all lessons in importance, yet the last which is thoroughly learnt.[136]

Although a public supporter of the new constitution, he was privately critical of those aspects of it which departed from republican principles, i.e. which impeded the operation of majority will. He believed in a bill of rights, but he also believed that even individual rights were best preserved by popular majoritarianism.[137] Such an innovatory republic 'democratical but representative', or, as Jefferson went on to call it (so inaugurating a famous phrase) 'this new principle of representative democracy', required of its constitution only a government that truly and directly reflected the will of the people. This was close to the anti-federalists' 'sample' theory of representation. If the government could

---

[134] Merrill Jenson, 'Democracy and the American Revolution' *Huntingdon Library Quarterly*, XX (August, 1957); Wood, *Creation*, pp. 553–652; Hanson, 'Democratic Republicanism as the New American Hybrid' in Ball and Pocock, ed., *Conceptual Change* , esp. p. 171.

[135] Jefferson *Political Writings*, p. 42 (Inaugural Presidential Address, 1801).

[136] To Alexander Humboldt, June, 1813, Jefferson *Political Writings*, pp. 83–4.

[137] 'Governments are more or less republican as they have more or less of the element of popular control in their composition; and believing, as I do that the mass of the citizens is the safest depository of their own rights . . . I am a friend to that composition of government which has in it the most of this ingredient.' As a result he thought the House of Representatives, the purest republican institution of the new constitution 'the executive less so . . . [and] the Judiciary seriously anti-republican'. Letter to John Taylor, May, 1816. Ibid., p. 52. Jefferson was, of course not present at the Constitutional Convention and played no part in it, being at the time American ambassador in France.

only be made close and answerable to the people then there could be no tyranny. The development of the idea of constitutional checks and balances had come about, after all, only to check and balance the *government* from tyrannizing over the people. If, through the new device of representation, the people could exercise a close and direct control over their government, the intervention of further checks and balances were at best unnecessary, at worst sinister. If the *people themselves* were the check then any further check was a limitation on their power and reopened the possibility of governmental tyranny. If this went counter to conventional wisdom on the matter (and it did) then that was because the new form of government invalidated so much of what had gone before: 'The introduction of this new principle of representative democracy has rendered useless almost everything written before on the subject of government' wrote Jefferson some years later.[138]

If this analysis had prevailed in 1787 it would have been difficult to reject the anti-federalist claim that sovereignty should be located at state level, or to allay their fears that shifting power to the national tier simply re-introduced the threat of governmental tyranny, by making government remote and uncontrollable by the people. However, this drift towards identifying 'republic' with 'democracy' as the most direct possible form of popular control by no means went unnoticed or unchecked. John Adams famously declared that the 'true meaning' of a republic was not democracy but 'a government, in which all men, rich and poor, magistrates and subjects, officers and people, masters and servants, the first citizens and the last are equally subject to the law.' On this view the abolition of King and Lords – effected by the separation from Britain – established a republic, not because of its implications for popular political control but because it abolished formal legal privilege. However, although Adams stressed that republics might not be democracies, he acknowledged that all democracies were republics: 'A democracy is really a republic as an oak is a tree or a temple a building'.[139]

The Federalist, however, in seeking to reverse the growing tendency to identify republicanism with a mandated representative democracy, disagreed with Adams. Madison denied that democracy was a species of republic, rather they were two distinct genera. A pure democracy was 'a society consisting of a small number of citizens, who assemble and administer the government in person'; by contrast, a republic is 'a government in which a scheme of representation takes place', or more fully: 'a government which derives all its powers directly or indirectly from the great body of the people, and is administered by persons holding their offices during pleasure, for a limited period, or during good behaviour.'[140] These mutually exclusive and contentious definitions were obviously designed to deny the anti-federalist claim that republics were only so to the extent they were democratic, and to keep apart the two forms which Jefferson was to identify as the American hybrid.

[138] Letter from Jefferson to Isaac H.Tiffany, August 1816, Ibid., p. 87. Hamilton was prepared to use this argument too when seeking to dismiss the authorities cited by anti-federalists against the possibility of a large republic: 'The science of politics . . . has received great improvement. The efficacy of various principles is now well understood, which were either not known at all, or imperfectly known to the ancients.' *Federalist*, 9, p. 37.

[139] John Adams, *Defence of the Constitutions of Government of the United States of America, Works*, 10 vols. (Boston, 1850–56), vol. V, p. 453, and vol. X, p. 378; both cited Stourzh, *Alexander Hamilton*, pp. 56, 55.

[140] *Federalist*, 10, p. 45; 39, pp. 190–1.

Commentators have recently emphasised the way in which Madison's definitional dexterity sought to marginalise the anti-federalists by seeking to secure for the new constitution the now positive connotations of the term 'republican'.[141] But his denial that democracy is one form of republic also cleverly masks the extent to which both the new constitution, and Publius' defence of it, must therefore be the other, an aristocracy.[142] It was a charge to which they were clearly vulnerable.

The Federalist openly acknowledged that representation at the national government level, though in principle 'equally open to all' will in fact 'consist almost entirely of proprietors of land, of merchants, and of members of the learned professions'. This is proper in terms of their ability, nor is it dangerous since, it claimed, their interests are not threatening to those of the rest of society.[143] Yet such an argument was essentially aristocratic, albeit aimed at a natural aristocracy of wealth or ability rather than heredity.

Anti-federalists commonly charged defenders of the new republic with seeking to introduce an aristocracy. 'Centinel' predicted of the new government that 'so far from being a regular balanced government, it would in practice be a *permanent* ARISTOC-RACY'. 'A Federal Farmer' thought the difficulties and uncertainties of the post-war period had been used 'to furnish aristocratic men with weapons . . . and . . . means, with which they are rapidly achieving their favourite object'. The new constitution had been pushed through by 'the consolidating aristocracy'. Brutus warned that 'the natural aristocracy of the country will be elected. . . . in reality there will be no part of the people represented, but the rich, even in that branch of the legislature which is called democratic'.[144] Such charges were well grounded in classical republican thinking, where election itself is an aristocratic or oligarchic device, a way of choosing the best men, the 'aristoi' – or, more realistically, the wealthiest. Democracy, by contrast, was thought of as direct democracy, and any long-term offices were normally selected by lot.[145] Anti-federalists were well aware of this.[146] They were however, as we saw, prepared to allow representation only inasmuch as it was so exact a sample of the people 'that a person who is a stranger to the country might be able to form a just idea of their character, by knowing that of their representatives' a view of representation dismissed by Hamilton as 'altogether visionary'.[147] In place of a representative body which reflects the feelings and interests of the people through the 'actual representation of all classes of people, by

---

[141] See especially Ball ' "A republic – if you can keep it"' and Hanson 'Democratic Republicanism . . . ' in Ball and Pocock, ed., *Conceptual Change and the Constitution.*

[142] Montesquieu, *Spirit of the Laws*, Bk II:1, 2.

[143] *Federalist* 36, p. 169, and 35, pp. 167–8. Publius later refers to the effective representation of property, despite the relatively open conditions of election, as operating through the 'imperceptible channel' of deference. Ibid., 54, p. 281.

[144] Centinel Letter I, Dry, *Anti-Federalist*, p. 19; Letters of a Federal Farmer, Ibid., p. 36, 37; Essays of Brutus, III, Ibid., pp. 125–6; and Melancton Smith, Speech at the New York Ratification Convention, Ibid., pp. 340–1.

[145] Aristotle, *The Politics*, 1294b 5 (Aristotle here actually contrasts democracy with oligarchy, but see Barker's note on the use of terms at 1273 b.) Montesquieu traces the origins of modern representative institutions from the invading Gothic peoples' needs to find a substitute for their warriors' assemblies after they dispersed and settled in Western Europe. He also, therefore, but for different reasons, assigns to representative institutions an aristocratic origin and character. Montesquieu, *Spirit of the Laws*, Bk XI, 8.

[146] A [Maryland] Farmer, insisted on the essentially aristocratic nature of representative government, *Essays* II, V, Dry, *Anti-Federalist*, pp. 258, 263.

[147] *Essays* of Brutus, Ibid., p. 124; *Federalist*, 36, p. 166.

the persons of each class', he and Madison substituted representation by those who have 'a knowledge of the interests and feelings of the people', for this is 'all that can reasonably be meant' by representation.[148]

Madison shamelessly suggests that the anti-federalists' pursuit of literal 'representation' is, effectively a support for classical 'direct democracy', and draws the traditional contrast between the instability of democracy and the calm and wisdom of the rule of the 'better sort' promised by the improved quality of politician resulting from representation in larger and more diverse units. Yet having revived the classical categorisation to the detriment of his opponents, it was difficult to deny the corollary that his own position was aristocratic Thus the final brilliant flourish to his 'linguistic turn' was not simply that by defining 'democracy' as an *alternative* to 'republic' he denies the latter epithet to his opponents; it is that in defining the two to be alternatives he also *substitutes* the category 'republic' for one subdivision of the old category 'aristocracy'. The term aristocracy was now entirely reserved for what was originally only one variant of it, namely hereditary aristocracy: the other, elective aristocracy, was to be called a republic, or, as Jefferson's phrase took hold, a representative democracy.[149]

'Federal' and 'national' government

The second major conceptual and rhetorical issue concerns the 'federal' identity (or otherwise) of the new constitution. This was not only – for the reasons suggested above – a rhetorical question. It intimately concerned the very real issue of the separation of powers, since Publius defends a separation of powers on two distinct axes – both within the national government – that is between legislative, executive and judicial – and between the national and the state governments. In one major respect both Madison and Hamilton had already made this point: the national government could provide a backstop to guarantee the rights of minorities threatened by majorities within, or even of majorities threatened by, the legislatures of the states.[150] Yet this was to argue in the opposite direction from the anti-federalists. For them, as for Publius, republics were to guarantee liberty, and liberty required limited government. The anti-federalists' view was that the 'enlarged' national government, far from providing a fail-safe device which guaranteed rights and liberty by intervening where necessary at the state level, actually posed,

---

[148] Ibid., 35, pp. 166, 169. Once again, in terms of the psychology employed this was prudent. Government by those who *know* the feelings of the people is quite different from direct, or mandated government by those who *have* the feelings. In the former case reason and prudence can intervene to judge the propriety or validity of the desires experienced, in the latter case passions will be expressed directly as government action.

[149] Completely purging 'democracy' of its lawless and opprobrious overtones took some time; according to Chute it was not until the franchise debates of the 1830s. Marchette Chute *The First Liberty* (London, 1970), pp. 299–305.

[150] The oppression of huge black minorities in the southern states was hardly what was in mind here, even though the tension between the claims of the federal government to oversee rights and those of the states to abrogate them was recognised as a potential issue, as the provision (Art I, sect.9) that Congress reserved the right to restrict the importation of 'persons' after 1808 makes clear. However, the constitution (IV, 2) also denied slaves the right of sanctuary in other states, even where, as in the case of Massachusetts, slavery had already been abolished.

through its remoteness from the people, a special threat to that liberty. For them the looser – i.e. more confederal – was the national government the more this danger could be alleviated, and the more popular liberty – republicanism – could be guaranteed. For Publius to demonstrate that the new government was indeed federal was therefore not only to score more rhetorical points in the battle for popular acceptance, it was a crucial plank in its claim to guarantee republicanism.

Federalist 39 discusses this claim under a number of headings, relating to the foundation, derivation and operation of powers. But it draws on a discussion of the definition of 'federal' by Hamilton in *Federalist* 9. At issue was whether a central government which exercised jurisdiction over individuals within the states, as opposed to one which merely treated of relations between sovereign and equal states could claim to be federal. There was some basis for this in usage. Federal derives from *foedum*, a treaty: Locke had defined the 'federative' power to be that which a state exercised externally in relation to other states, through treaty, war, etc.[151] A federal government could be thought of as one which derived from a treaty amongst states, as well as one that dealt with the foreign policy of the resulting entity. The implication of this, insisted on by most anti-federalists, was that 'one of the essential distinctions between one entire or consolidated government, and a federal republic . . . [was that its laws] operate immediately on the persons and property of individuals, and not on the states'.[152] That this was the normal usage of the time can hardly be denied. In the secrecy of the convention Madison himself had explicitly contrasted a constitution where 'acts of the Gen'l Govt. would take effect without the intervention of the State legislatures' as a national government in direct contrast to a federal.[153] But to admit that the new government was not federal would be to admit that it was a national one, and endanger its claim to support republicanism.

To assert that no government claiming to be federal could exercise any internal jurisdiction within the states, Hamilton claimed, was to make a distinction, 'in the main, arbitrary . . . supported neither by principle nor precedent'. For the precise nature of state-federal relations were 'mere matters of discretion'. His trump card was again Montesquieu, so often cited by the anti-federalists for his claim that republican government can only survive in small states. Montesquieu's assistance to *The Federalist* case did not end in pointing out that the federal association of republics overcame the normal limitations of size imposed by the republican form (thereby enjoying 'internal happiness . . . and with regard to its external situation, by means of association, it possesses all the advantages of large monarchies'.[154]) For, in discussing examples of republican federal associations Montesquieu had particularly highlighted the ancient Lycian

---

[151] John Locke, *Two Treatises of Government*, II, 146.

[152] 'Letters of a Federal Farmer', XVII. See also *Essays of Brutus*, I, where he claims because 'there is no need of any intervention of the state governments, between the Congress and the people, to execute any one power . . . The government . . . is a complete one and not a confederation.' Dry, *Anti-Federalist*, pp. 87–8, 110.

[153] Farrand, I, p. 37; and see p. 141 where Madison, in rejecting an attempt to have federal representatives elected by state legislatures stressed that their decision in favour of 'a national government . . . was intended to operate to the exclusion of a federal government', so indicating again that at that time a federal government meant for him one which derived from and operated on the states and only indirectly on their inhabitants.

[154] Montesquieu, *The Spirit of the Laws*, Bk. IX:1.

confederacy. This confederacy both gave differential voting rights to larger member states, and allowed the federal government powers of judicial appointment within the individual states, thus breaching each of the principles claimed by the anti-federalists as constitutive of the difference between a federal (or confederal) state, and a consolidated, or national one. 'The distinctions insisted upon', Hamilton triumphantly concludes, 'were not within the contemplation of this enlightened writer: and we shall be led to conclude, that they are the novel refinements of an erroneous theory.'[155]

In addressing the federal identity of the constitution, Hamilton's method is to brusquely dismiss the anti-federalist's terminology. Madison, although he too points to the fluidity and imprecision of political terminology, proceeds to make an assessment which broadly accepts the anti-federalists' distinction, that is to say by considering whether the constitution is a union of people or a union of states.[156] He does so firstly, by considering the terms of the constitution's foundations: since the new constitution is to be ratified on a state-by-state basis it can be considered federal. Its adoption required the agreement of (a majority of) sovereign states, not a majority of American people. The significance of this procedure though, could be read in two ways. The adoption through the device of popular conventions, rather than by the existing state governments, had, after all, been imposed on the states by the Constitutional Convention. To Brutus, it seemed that even voting state-by-state, a convention presupposes 'the people of the several states as one body corporate, and is intended as an original compact'. This directly contradicted the federal or confederal idea of: 'a number of independent states entering into a compact.'[157]

Once the constitution was established, the way the powers of the individual branches of government *derived* from the people differed. The membership of the House of Representatives, drawn from roughly equal constituencies, was national, that of the Senate – two per state, irrespective of size, chosen by each state legislature, was unequivocally federal. Madison here defended a compromise, against which he had fought at the convention. The original Virginia plan, like today's constitution, derived both branches of the legislature from the people, although the Senate was to be elected indirectly from the House. Madison had opposed the involvement of state legislatures on grounds of their proven irresponsibility.[158] The measure adopted led to the mixing of state and national governments which Madison had originally sought to keep distinct. Thus originally Madison proposed a national government which *in itself* had no federal elements, although, in that it existed alongside the state governments, the *system* of which it formed a part was arguably federal.[159]

The President was to be chosen by an electoral college in which each state contributed members equal to the total number of combined representatives for that state and the two senators. If that failed to produce a candidate with an absolute majority, the House of representatives was to hold a run-off election. This was clearly a mixed derivation of power.

---

[155] *Federalist* 9, pp. 39–40.

[156] *Federalist* 37, pp. 178–9 on the difficulty of terminology. *Federalist* 38 begins the assessment.

[157] Brutus 13. Dec. 1787, in Dry, *Anti-Federalist*, p. 133.

[158] Farrand, I, pp. 46, 154.

[159] See the excellent analytical discussion of the various possibilities in Michael P. Zuckert, 'Federalism and the Founding', *Review of Politics*, 48, 2 (spring, 1986).

In terms of the *operation* of its powers, Madison concedes that the national government's powers do indeed extend to the individuals within states, but only, he insists, with
respect to enumerated areas. It is true, that in areas of conflict the national government
was the arbiter, but some final decision is necessary. Although Madison, unlike Hamilton
seems to have rejected an abstract conception of sovereignty, he here recognises the
necessity for a principle of closure in a political system and seeks to combine it with the
idea of limited and popular government. Without some such device disagreements
between the national and state governments, or between different state governments
could ultimately lead to conflict.[160] Madison seeks to resolve these differences *within* the
constitution, and they must, he argued, be determined at the national level.[161] Madison's
attempt to smooth the differences between himself and the anti-federalists would not
allow him to deny what, for him and them, was a fundamental point of difference. For
the question of the existence and location of the ultimate power of arbitration between
state and national governments was the crucial issue which had brought the Articles of
Confederation into disrepute and precipitated the Constitutional Convention; they had

> endeavoured to accomplish impossibilities; to reconcile a partial sovereignty in the
> union, with complete sovereignty in the states; to subvert a mathematical axiom, by
> taking away a part, and letting the whole remain.[162]

So concerned had Madison been not to repeat the errors of the Articles by imprecision
as to where the power of last resort lay, or delusive hopes that it might be shared, that he
had insisted (vainly) both in the convention, and in correspondence that a national
government veto *'in all cases whatsoever'* on state laws was 'absolutely necessary' and
'essential to the efficacy and security of the general government'.[163] Although he failed
in this, Madison insisted that the federal government's powers to make and enforce all
laws as they relate to foreign states, national, and internal inter-state issues (including
fiscal and monetary measures) must be unconstrained, or the ability of the United States
to act effectively would be undermined. It was simply not possible to enumerate such
powers because of the unpredictable nature of what might be needed. This is, in essence,
Locke's 'prerogative power' institutionally unlimited, but only to be used for the public
good.[164]

[160] Indeed the New Jersey plan, which allowed coercion only of states, envisaged such conflict as part
of the constitution. Farrand, I, pp. 243, 245.

[161] For Locke, recourse to popular resistance had been a regrettable necessity. Jefferson seems to have
regarded it as a virtue. Of Shays's rebellion, which had done so much to precipitate the convention, he
wrote: 'God forbid, we should be twenty years without such a rebellion . . . The tree of liberty must be
refreshed from time to time with the blood of patriots and tyrants.' Jefferson to Wm. Smith, Nov. 1787;
Jefferson *Political Writings*, p. 69. Publius cannot quite get by either, without the 'appeal to heaven': in
Federalist 60 he refers to the *threat* of a popular revolution as a factor curbing any attempt by the national
government to subvert its own elections, p. 307.

[162] Ibid., 42, p. 216. Brutus agreed in insisting that sovereign powers represented a zero sum which could
not meaningfully be shared. He simply disagreed about their proper location. Dry, *Anti-Federalist*, p. 142.

[163] Meyers, *Mind of the Founder*, p. 67 (Letter to Washington); Farrand, II, pp. 27–8.

[164] *Federalist*, 44, passim.

Finally if one considered the avenues for *amendment*, the constitution was mixed. Madison concludes, in conciliatory fashion, that it is 'in strictness neither a national nor a federal constitution; but a composition of both.'[165] Madison's final argument subverts the whole federal issue by charging that those who make crucial this 'secondary enquiry' about the effect of the union on the powers of the states 'have lost sight of the people altogether'. State-national power relations are relevant only to the primary issue: 'the public good, the real welfare of the great body of the people is the supreme object to be pursued; and that no form of government whatever has any other value, than as it may be fitted for the attainment of this object.'[166]

There is, however, a deeper issue lurking behind Publius' attempts to satisfy those who needed persuading the new constitution could carry a 'federal' tag. This has to do with a certain tension between the claim that the states retained some internal sovereignty and the earlier line of argument which saved republicanism from faction and instability by 'enlarging the sphere'. If it is only larger political units that are capable of not only of giving popular republicanism that combination of 'stability and energy . . . essential to security against external and internal dangers', but also of providing what seemed equally important to Madison, namely the defence of individual and minority rights, can this enlarged sphere operate consistently with the claim that the state-national government represents some real federal interface which cannot legitimately be transgressed? How was the 'enlarged sphere' to intervene in the smaller one, as it must do to achieve these objects. Could one gain on the federal swings without losing on the roundabouts of the 'large sphere'? This issue can only be fully resolved by looking more closely at the division of powers between the state and federal tiers of government; but before we can address that we must discuss what Publius meant by the division or separation of powers.

The division of powers

The continued relevance and meaning of the division of powers

Arguments then, about what the ancients or Montesquieu, regarded as federal, however important rhetorically, did not dispose of important aspects of these problems. For quite apart from what one *called* the thing there were substantial issues involved in how to arrange the allocation of powers between the state and federal governments. Madison's rejection of small-scale, direct, or almost direct, democracy and his praise of the advantages of 'larger representation' in a more remote 'consolidated' government, kept alive, indeed heightened the issue of the appropriate way to limit or control the powers of government. Madison's 'enlarged sphere' pointed precisely in the direction of the remote, unresponsive and potentially tyrannical government which the anti-federalists saw in the new constitution. He clearly had to assuage fears that the powers of the federal government were too concentrated, both internally with respect to each other, and externally with respect to the states, to meet the requirements of early modern authorities such as Montesquieu and Locke that the powers of government in a free state be divided

---

[165] Ibid., 39, p. 195; amendments could be proposed either by two thirds of Congress or two thirds of the state legislatures. Federal Constitution, Art. V.

[166] *Federalist*, 46, p. 239; 45, pp. 234–5.

and limited.[167] Anti-federalists were concerned about the separation and balancing of powers because they feared oppression from an over-powerful central government. Because they thought the danger of tyranny to come from government, they thought safety could be found in a dominant legislative branch closely tied to the people. Madison did not deny the danger from irresponsible government but Madison's concern about the danger of tyranny was unrequited by the legislature's responsiveness – indeed it was increased. This was because, for him, there was not one but two potential sources of tyranny, government and majority. In a republic one must 'not only guard against the oppression of its rulers; but . . . guard one part of the society against the injustices of the other part.'[168] Since it was the peculiar property of popular republics to be dominated by the legislative and representative branch, increasing the responsiveness of the legislature to popular will simply increased the ability of a majority to use it to tyrannize minorities. As he argued in *Federalist* X, following both Locke and Montesquieu in this point, uncontrolled legislatures as much as uncontrolled power anywhere else, could prove tyrannical.[169]

The problem lay 'in combining the requisite stability and energy in government, with the inviolable attention due to liberty, and to the republican form.'[170] The traditional protection of liberty was mixed, or balanced government, which in England had relied on the existence of different legal estates to provide the different agencies of government. As we have seen, Americans linked republicanism with the abolition of privileged classes, or, more extremely, to the dominance of the 'people'.[171] They had, Madison claimed, discovered *unmixed* republicanism.[172] There was however – and this was one reason why the name was so much fought over – a tendency to assume that republics *per se* embodied liberty. The revered Montesquieu had not thought the issue so clear cut. 'Democratic and Aristocratic states', [the two species of republic], he argued, 'are not in their nature free. Political liberty is to be found only in moderate governments; and

---

[167] Ibid., 41, p. 203.

[168] Ibid., 51, p. 266.

[169] 'In a representative republic, where the executive magistracy is carefully limited . . . and where the legislative power is exercised by an assembly . . . inspired . . . with an intrepid confidence in its own strength . . . it is against the enterprising ambition of this department, that the people ought to indulge all their jealousy and exhaust all their precautions.' Ibid., 43, p. 253. The worry is a continual one, e.g., nos. 51, p. 265; 63; 73, p. 375, etc. One of Locke's observations is that even representative legislatures may be resisted if they act tyrannically, *Second Treatise*, 221–2; for Montesquieu one of the greatest threats to Rome's republic was the 'extravagance of liberty' enjoyed by the popular assembly's ability to legislate freely on certain issues without the intervention of the patricians. Montesquieu, *Spirit of the Laws*, XI:16. America, committed to the equality of its citizens, could not balance this danger by dividing powers between groups of citizens of different status.

[170] *Federalist*, 37, p. 177.

[171] Amongst the most strident formulations of the latter view was that of the otherwise unknown Ben Hinchborn: 'I define civil liberty to be, not a "government by laws" . . . but a power in the people at large, at any time, for any cause, or for no cause, but for their own sovereign pleasure, to alter or annihilate both the mode and the essence of any former government, and adopt a new one in its stead.' 'Oration Delivered at Boston' (1777) cited, Stourzh, *Alexander Hamilton*, p. 56. Such a view virtually abolished the need for a constitution by denying any distinction between it and the laws.

[172] *Federalist*, 14, p. 62.

even in these it is not always found.'[173] The question then arose from a number of quarters, of how a remote national government less immediately responsive to the people, and one in which legally differentiated estates could not form the basis of the separation of powers could be limited and free.

Because the distribution of power between the federal and state levels would determine the extent of the concentration of power in the central government, the federal–state power ratio was directly relevant to the question of the degree to which the federal powers themselves needed to be internally divided. However, the permeability of the federal-state divide also affected the extent to which the 'larger sphere' could guarantee liberty by ensuring diversity of interests for: 'in exact proportion, as the territory of the union may be formed into more circumscribed confederacies or states, oppressive combinations of a majority will be facilitated.'[174] Madison however, once again seeks to convert two problems into one solution, by arguing that the division of powers *between* the federal and state levels can be used to reinforce the guarantees provided by the division of powers *within* both the federal and the state governments:

> In a single republic, all the power surrendered by the people is submitted to the administration of a single government; and the usurpations are guarded against, by a division of the government into distinct and separate departments. In the compound republic of America, the power . . . is first divided between two distinct governments, and then the portion allotted to each subdivided among distinct and separate departments. Hence a double security arises to the rights of the people. The different governments will control each other; at the same time that each will be controlled by itself.[175]

It remains to show how this 'double security' is worked out in practice.

The true meaning of the separation of powers

The new constitution established clear identities and responsibilities for the President (executive), Senate and House of Representatives (legislative), and Supreme Court (judiciary), and ensured certain necessary immunities and disqualifications. Members of Congress, for example had immunity from arrest for most crimes during session, and were conversely excluded from government office whilst elected (I, 6); judges' salaries were guaranteed and they held their offices during good behaviour (III, 1). Yet the powers normally associated with 'Legislature, Executive and Judiciary' were not wholly given respectively to Congress, President and Supreme Court, nor, partly in consequence, were they independent of each other.[176] The Senate had to validate by a two-thirds majority

---

[173] See, e.g., Montesquieu, *Spirit of the Laws*, XI:4; by liberty Montesquieu seems to have meant, not Machiavelli's active and civic participation in a free republic, but something much more private and modern: 'political liberty of the subject is a tranquillity of mind arising from the opinion each person has of his safety.' XI:6.

[174] *Federalist*, 51, p. 267.

[175] Ibid., 51, p. 266.

[176] Although note that Publius prefaces the whole discussion with a philosophical reflection on the difficulties of classification and definition. Ibid., 37, p. 179.

treaties negotiated by the President (II, 2) and Congress jointly had the power to declare war, and supervise the raising and supply of the armed forces (I, 8) – all of which were normally considered an executive role. The President had a veto on legislation unless it were returned to Congress and achieved a two-thirds majority. (I, 7). Congress chose the timing of the electoral college which elected the President, and, in the final stages would play a role in his election (II, 1). The President appointed Supreme Court judges, but again only with the support of the Senate (II, 2). The Senate acted as a judicial court for impeachments (I, 3).[177]

In *Federalist* 47 therefore, Publius is led to consider the objection that the constitution fails to observe the principle of the separation of powers, which, he acknowledges, if true, is a very serious fault. The immediate source of this principle is, again, Montesquieu, and Montesquieu's model in this case is England.[178] Yet in the English constitution powers were not separate but intermingled: the Commons could not make laws without the Lords; the two together could not pass laws without the King's assent; the Parliament could not meet without the King's writ; the King could not raise a militia or taxes without the Parliament's consent; the King's ministers sat in the Commons, and had to command the confidence of the House; the Lords were the supreme court of appeal, as well as comprising the judiciary for peers; the King appointed the judges, Parliament could remove them. In this form the separation of powers involved a doctrine of 'co-ordination' according to which tyranny in any one department of government was evaded through requiring the 'co-ordination' of another before authority could be exerted. Moreover despite numerous American assertions of the doctrine of the separation of powers, such 'interference' was to be found in virtually all of the existing states' constitutions.

How was this 'interference' to be reconciled with the doctrine of 'separation'? The separation of powers, claims Publius, did not mean that ' . . . departments ought to have no *partial agency* in, or no *control* over, the acts of each other.' Rather, it meant only 'that where the *whole* power of one department is exercised by the same hands which possessed the *whole* power of another department, the fundamental principles of a free constitution are subverted'[179] Moreover, in making this distinction between exercising some interference in, and wholly taking over powers, Publius is in no way making excuses for Montesquieu, the British or the states' constitutions. The apportionment to a second department of the powers of one, does not represent the beginnings of tyranny. The whole point about the doctrine is, paradoxically, that unless the different 'departments are so far *connected* and blended, as to give each a constitutional control over the others the degree of separation which the maxim requires, as essential to a free government, can never in practice be duly maintained.'[180]

The doctrine of the separation of powers then, although it was commonly taken to mean the allocation of the whole of each analytically distinct power to a discrete governmental department was, properly understood, rather the *division* of each analyti-

[177] References to articles and sections of *The Federal Constitution as agreed upon by the Convention* (September 17, 1787).

[178] Despite having escaped British tyranny, the strengths of the English constitution were widely acknowledged and cited during the constitutional convention, see the evidence assembled in Michael Duffy, 'The Making of the Constitution' in Smith, ed, *The American Constitution*, p. 25.

[179] *Federalist*, 47, p. 247.

[180] Ibid., 47, p. 252 [my emphasis].

cally distinct power and the distribution of its parts amongst two or more departments.[181] The confusion arises in part because the terms 'legislative', 'executive' and so on are used to refer both to the abstract power, and to the particular department of government in which they are mostly exercised. Madison undoubtedly contributes a real development to the theory, assisting its move from the notion of a segregation of powers wholly identified with particular departments, to the notion of powers separated in such a way that they were not uniquely distributed to a particular department.

The psychology of balancing powers

This task of separating the powers of government is not merely a matter of demarcating in legal terminology what Madison sniffily referred to as 'parchment barriers'.[182] Real security 'consists in giving to those who administer each department, the necessary constitutional means, and personal motives, to resist the encroachments of the others. Ambition must be made to counteract ambition. The interests of the man must be connected with the constitutional rights of the people.'[183] What Madison calls 'This policy of supplying by opposite and rival interests, the defect of better motives' is directly relevant to our earlier discussion of the extent to which *The Federalist* abandons republican concern with political virtue. It is easy to over-interpret Madison's remarks at this point. When we come to the motives which he does consider operate on men they are not uniformly selfish or ignoble. Just as there is 'a degree of depravity in mankind which requires a certain degree of circumspection and distrust: So there are other qualities in human nature which justify a certain portion of esteem and confidence.'[184]

The task of a constitution is to make the most of the human material available to it. It must structure government so that representatives are selected who have the 'wisdom to discern, and most virtue to pursue, the common good'. Its second task is 'to take the most effective precautions for keeping them virtuous.'[185] This is to be done less by harsh laws than by prudent ones, laws which reinforce good but weak motives with strong and self-interested ones. One view of republican political virtue, prevalent amongst both Publius' contemporaries and some modern commentators, is that it was pitched resolutely and austerely against private interest. Yet many thinkers, including those British opposition thinkers most influential in American circles denied this antithesis. The authors of *Cato's Letters* insisted that to

---

[181] Montesquieu cites the common meaning at the start of his famous chapter on England, when, after enumerating the three powers, legislative, executive and judicial, he comments: 'There would be an end of everything were the same man or the same body . . . to exercise those three powers . . . ' But after describing the operation of the King's veto on legislation and on the timing of elections, as well as the legislature's right to scrutinize the executive and the judicial role of the legislature in extreme cases, he concludes: 'Here, then, is the fundamental constitution of the government we are treating of. The legislative body being composed of two parts, they check one another by the mutual privilege of rejecting. They are both restrained by the executive power as the executive is by the legislative', Montesquieu, *The Spirit of the Laws*, XI:6, p. 161.

[182] *Federalist*, 48, p. 252, again, p. 254.

[183] Ibid., 51, p. 265.

[184] Ibid., 55, p. 287.

[185] Ibid., 57, p. 292.

call a man disinterested, we should intend no more . . . than that the Turn of his Mind is toward the Publick, and that he has placed his own personal Glory and Pleasure in serving it. To serve his Country is his private Pleasure, Mankind is his Mistress, and he does good to them by gratifying himself.[186]

Such a view is endorsed by Madison and perhaps even more strongly by Hamilton, who in a tellingly Machiavellian image observed, 'Men will pursue their interests. It is as easy to change Human Nature, as to oppose the strong current of the selfish passions. A wise legislator will gently divert the channel and direct it, if possible to the public good.'[187] It was observed of Hamilton himself, by Gouverneur Morris that Hamilton could be trusted with power 'for he was more covetous of glory than of wealth or power'.[188] The possibility of recruiting egoistic motives in the public service is a continuous tactic revealed in these texts. The founders did not, like some modern liberals, enthusiastically endorse egoism as a fundamental postulate of moral discourse, nor did they seek, like Spartan zealots to banish its every expression. It was a fact of human psychology, but not the only one. The moral and political demands of republican life had to take egoistic motives into account, but the republic could not be a passive articulator of egoism and survive. It was not that men had no virtue, but neither were they angels. Humans were fallible, and those placed in positions of public trust were morally exposed: good institutions should offer as much psychological and motivational support as was possible. 'Duty, gratitude, interest, ambition itself, are the cords by which [the representatives] will be bound to fidelity and sympathy with the great mass of the people. . . . these may all be insufficient . . . But are they not all that government will admit, and that human prudence can devise?'[189]

Publius is here perhaps too modest in enumerating the range of means at his disposal. For there is another dimension to the constitution which he brings out here, and that is time. The moral psychology which underpins *The Federalist* is to a degree plastic and circumstantial. That is to say our moral responses (although not our moral standards), are seen to derive ultimately from impressions and are subject to similar processes. One of these is the effect of time. In an almost Hobbesian sense our moral dispositions are potentially 'decaying' impressions. Anti-federalists argued that the distance, both physical and social of the National Congress from the constituent would lead to a separation of sentiment and feeling between the electors and their representatives. Publius responds with a check, or balance that operates in a further dimension, that of time. Biennial elections will place representatives in such a situation that

Before the sentiments impressed in their minds by the mode of their elevation, can be effaced by the exercise of power, they will be compelled to anticipate the moment when their power is to cease, when the exercise of it is to be renewed, and when they must descend to the level from which they were raised . . . '[190]

[186] Thomas Gordon and John Trenchard: *Cato's Letters*, no.40, cited Stourzh, *Alexander Hamilton*, p. 106.

[187] Hamilton, *Papers*, ed. Syrett and Cooke, vol. V, p. 85, cited Stourzh, *Alexander Hamilton*.

[188] Cited ibid., p. 202.

[189] *Federalist*, 57, p. 294.

[190] Ibid., 57, pp. 293–4.

Thus, although 'neither moral or religious motives can be relied on as an adequate control',[191] interests, a sense of honour and a sense of gratitude can all be combined with the aid of time to ensure, inasmuch as is humanly possible the preservation of free government in the interest of the people as a whole.

The same argument operates in a reverse direction to provide stability in the Senate. There, a longer term, and staggered pattern of elections insulates the members from volatile popular pressures, as is wholly appropriate for a body whose purpose, being concerned mainly with longer term issues of strategy and finance, 'is to consist in its proceeding with more coolness and with more wisdom than the popular branch'.[192]

The separation of national and state powers

In persuading his opponents that there is a satisfactory separation of power between the federal and state levels Publius has to be careful not to undo the work he has done in persuading them that the constitution has a good claim to be federal. He does not therefore claim that individual powers are separated in the above sense of being *shared* between the two tiers of government – indeed, for the most part they are not.[193] He also has to keep in mind his claim that popular republicanism can be stable and preserve rights and liberty, only where we have 'enlarged the sphere' within which it works, two claims which we noted above, were in some conflict.

Any power may be viewed as divided either in terms of its sources or its exercise. The observations made above about how the separation of powers was to be understood, i.e. as a separating out of individual powers amongst different agencies, refers to the *exercise* of power. Madison did not, for the most part, apply the same arguments to the derivation, or source of power. The separation of powers ideally required each agency to have 'a will of its own'. Although they all derive ultimately from the people they should do so 'through channels having no communication with each other' and without depending on one another for finance.[194] In practice, some deviation from this ideal had to be accepted, and although originally Madison denied that the federal government should derive in any way from the states, and had fought at the convention to exclude the states as governments from electing organs of the national government, he had had to accept a compromise. In presenting the new constitution he now sought to minimize distinctions he had sought to sustain. Considered as to its source, Madison claimed that there is a division of the *derivation* of power in the federal government. Half of the federal legislature is derived from the union considered as an undifferentiated population, and half – the Senate – derived from the union considered as a union of states. The selection of the executive

---

[191] Ibid., 10, p. 44.

[192] Madison, speech at the Federal Convention, Farrand, I, p. 151.

[193] The innovation which emerged at the convention was a national government the institutions of which did not owe their election to the state governments, but to the people, and which exercised its sanctions on individuals and not on states. It was thus truly a national government. (Madison, Farrand, III, p. 473) But it was to co-exist with the state governments in a Federal Scheme. Boundaries of competence between the two — such as Madison's 'negative on state laws', had therefore to be set. See Zuckert, 'Federalism and the Founding'.

[194] *Federalist*, 50, pp. 264–5.

involves the potential for both principles, whilst the judiciary is appointed from within the federal government itself, although subject to confirmation by the Senate – the representative of the states. In sum Madison concludes: 'The state governments may be regarded as constituent and essential parts of the federal government; whilst the latter is nowise essential to the operation or organisation of the former.'[195]

The claim that a dual derivation of power – from people and the other tier of government – provides a safeguard applies only to the federal government, for the state governments derive all *their* powers from the people and not from the federal government. If they did the constitution would hardly be federal be at all.[196]

If we consider the *operation* of the two tiers of government on each other, whilst there is a demarcation of areas of responsibility, the case that particular powers are in any way shared between the two tiers is weak. The state governments do not in the normal course of events participate in the operation of federal government. In the one case where such a sharing might be thought most likely – the judicial execution of federal issues – Publius is most insistent on the insertion of federal courts into the states' legal systems.[197]

However although given no *constitutional* role in or authority over the federal government, Publius frequently refers to the anticipation of extra-constitutional resistance from the state legislatures as a curb on the possible encroachment of the federal. Looking on this darker side Publius evokes familiar arguments about the balancing effect of different tiers of government and about the effects of size and – through staggered elections – time in limiting the capacities of the legislature to endanger the liberty of the people – or the states. A successful federal usurpation supposes

> That the people and the states should, for a sufficient period of time, elect an uninterrupted succession of men ready to betray them both . . . silently and patiently behold the gathering storm, and continue to supply the materials, until it should be prepared to burst on their own heads.

Such a scenario, which the opposition depicts, is 'more like the incoherent dreams of a delirious jealousy . . . than . . . the sober apprehensions of genuine patriotism.'[198] Moreover, Publius again puts the ball back in the anti-federalists' court by continuing his tactic of stressing that the dangers they fear at the federal level are no less – indeed more – to be feared at the state level, and indeed, that they cannot be brought about without the connivance of the state government. If the federal legislature were to make an attempt on the liberties of the people, it would have to involve the Senate, and the Senate is elected by the state legislatures, so such a move cannot take place without the connivance of a body in which the anti-federalists repose their greatest confidence.[199] Thus although the state governments have no *constitutional* role in (though they have some in the appointment of) national government, they can still, through the threat of unconstitutional resistance, act as watchdogs:

[195] Ibid., 39.

[196] Hamilton, whose instincts were for a wholly central government, had suggested at one point that the state governors should be appointed by the federal government. Farrand, I, p. 293.

[197] *Federalist*, 80, p. 408. Full discussion of this is reserved to the section on the judiciary.

[198] Ibid., 46, p. 243.

[199] Ibid., 60, p. 308.

The executive and Legislative bodies of each state will be so many sentinels over the persons employed in every department of the national administration . . . Their disposition to apprize the community of whatever may prejudice its interests from another quarter may be relied upon, if only from the rivalship of power.[200]

If the states' governments can prevent tyranny in the federal government, Publius also claims that the federal government can guarantee liberty to the states. This guarantee of liberty seems to be meant in two senses, which Madison would dearly have loved to extend to a third. Firstly in Montesquieu's sense, the external power created by the confederation ensures the states' freedom from foreign intervention or conquest. Secondly – a point also mentioned by Montesquieu – the republican form of government is guaranteed to the states, by the federal government (whether they wish it or no!).[201] However Madison had clearly wished to extend this constitutional guarantee to a third point, that the federal government should act as a guarantor of minority rights within the states by holding a veto over all state legislation.[202] The introduction of this 'heretofore kingly prerogative' had in fact been the cornerstone of the project he announced to Washington that he intended to take with him to the Philadelphia Congress.[203] Such an empowered national government could not only arbitrate between states, and overcome the evasions that he expected them to practise on 'every positive power that can be given on paper'; a further 'happy effect of this prerogative would be its controul on the internal . . . aggressions of interested majorities on the rights of minorities and of individuals.' Such a measure was 'absolutely necessary, and the least possible encroachment on the state jurisdictions.'[204] This hardly fits the notion of separation as sharing powers out, and is in clear contrast with the idea of the separation of powers as expressed within the federal government.

Madison stressed the importance of this 'negative on state legislation' many times, perhaps most vigorously in the convention. Such a veto was 'the great pervading principle that must controul the centrifugal tendency of the States; which, without it, will continually fly out of their proper orbits and destroy the order and harmony of the political system.' The impossibility of a bill of rights meeting all possible exigencies, and the fact that enumerating rights might lead to a presumption that unlisted rights might not be protected, led him to assert that such a veto must be unconstrained. The imperatives of Hobbesian sovereignty reasserted themselves: all laws must be interpreted, the power of interpretation is, in the final resort, the power of sovereignty. Madison wished 'that the line of jurisprudence could be drawn . . . but on reflection he finds it is impossible'. Any such attempted 'discrimination wd. only be a fresh source of contention between the two

---

[200] Ibid., 84, p. 442: and see 46, p. 242; and 85, p. 451, 'We may safely rely on the disposition of the state legislatures to erect barriers against the encroachments of the national authority'. The one exception to the exclusion of state governments from the operation of national government is that two thirds of the states' legislatures can initiate a constitutional amendment, and three quarters must ratify them. *Constitution*, Article V. This is however, clearly an extraordinary event.

[201] *Constitution*, Article IV, Sect. 4; Montesquieu, *Spirit of the Laws*, IX, 1. Montesquieu specifies *'popular* insurrection' as the internal danger to republics.

[202] Farrand, I, p. 165.

[203] See Ketcham, 'Madisonian Theory of Rights', p. 253; and Hobson, 'The Negative . . . ', pp. 225–6.

[204] Letter to Washington, April 16th, 1787, in Meyers, *Mind of the Founder*, p. 67.

authorities'.[205] However, to his bitter disappointment, Madison's efforts to provide a federal veto were rejected. With it went what was effectively the keystone of Madison's theory of the enlarged republic. For the virtuous, or at least necessarily disinterested, majorities of a national government could only operate to protect minorities within the states if the internal government of the states were open to its (the national government's) effective intervention. Without the veto, federal government only had jurisdiction over issues relating to foreign, inter-state, or enumerated areas such as that concerning trade.[206] This is surely one reason why Madison subsequently came round to enshrining rights in a bill. It was not that he thought a bill of rights could in itself counter the wills of determined repressive majorities, but, as he wrote to Jefferson immediately after the convention, it could prevent the very emergence of such wills if entrenched rights could, by being 'declared in that solemn manner, acquire, by degrees the character of fundamental maxims of free Government, and . . . become incorporated with the national sentiment'.[207]

In *The Federalist* Madison made the best of a bad job, assuaging fears of over centralization, by pointing to the restricted sphere of federal action, a restriction which he had so opposed, and praising the 'partly federal partly national' government which he had denounced in a letter to Jefferson as a 'feudal system of republics'.[208] His own views are closer to the surface in his warnings that the greatest danger lay not in the excess of power but in the inefficacy of the federal government, whose 'powers are few and defined' whilst those 'which are to remain in the state governments are numerous and indefinite'.[209] Yet again in terms of popularity state governments must clearly have the 'predilection and support of the people' whilst the federal, being remote and detached from citizens' immediate interests will be 'at no time the idol of popular favour'.[210]

The record of the state assemblies shows their difficulties to derive from representatives pursuing their local interests to the exclusion of the state, and the states would pursue the same role in the national government, inhibiting the emergence of enlightened, broader, and longer term views in the 'larger sphere' of national government: 'the states will be to the [federal Congress] what the counties and towns are to [state]'. Whilst Madison manages to express confidence that the new government will indeed take a larger than local view, the worry must be all on that side and the presumption from past experience must certainly be that they would be 'disinclined to invade the rights of the individual states'.[211]

---

[205] *Federalist*, 84, p. 439; for arguments against a bill of rights. The quotations are from Madison at the Federal Convention, Farrand, I, pp. 169, 165.

[206] For a discussion of the importance of the veto in Madison's vision of the extended republic, see Charles F. Hobson, 'The Negative on State Laws: James Madison, the Constitution, and the Crisis of Republican Government', *William and Mary Quarterly*, XXXVI, 2 (1979).

[207] Rejection of veto, vote June 8th, Farrand, pp. 171, 173. Madison's hope that popular majorities might be inhibited by a bill of rights status as 'a solemn charter' was expressed in a famous letter to Jefferson, Oct. 17, 1787. See Meyer, *Mind of the Founder*, p. 158. On the development of the need for a bill of rights, see Rakove, 'Madisonian theory of rights'.

[208] *Federalist*, 46, p. 240; to Jefferson 24 Oct., 1787, cited Hobson, 'The Problem of the States', pp. 233–4.

[209] *Federalist*, 46, pp. 237–8.

[210] Ibid., 45, pp. 236; 46, pp. 240–1.

[211] Ibid., 46, pp. 241–2.

The separation of powers within the national government

Publius sets out very baldly the contradictory principles demanded of a republican form of government:

> The genius of republican liberty seems to demand on one side, not only that all power should be derived from the people; but that those entrusted with it should be kept in dependence on the people, by a short duration of their appointments; and that even during this short period, the trust should be placed not in a few, but in a number of hands. Stability on the contrary, requires, that the hands, in which power is lodged, should continue for a length of time the same. A frequent change of men will result from a frequent return of elections; and a frequent change of measures, from a frequent change of men: whilst energy of government requires not only a certain duration of power, but the execution of it by a single hand.[212]

The success of a constitution in making republican liberty consistent with its ability to function in a world of states will depend on its success in balancing the conflicting demands that power should be at once popular, stable and energetic.

The degree of attention paid to each of these requirements in any constitution will depend on an estimate of the peculiar dangers or deficiencies obtaining in any particular case. In a hereditary monarchy – the pre-revolutionary form of government in America – the greatest dangers to liberty came from the permanent centralization of executive power in a single hand – a source of energy but a danger to liberty. By contrast, in a representative republic such as America now was, it should be 'against the enterprising ambition of [the legislative] department that the people ought to indulge all their jealousy and exhaust all their precautions.'[213] Monarchy was controlled, or balanced, by 'mixing' it with aristocratic or popular elements. How could a republic be balanced?

The abolition of nobility in America had, as we saw, forced her to experiment with the innovative form of an 'unmixed republic', unmixed in the sense of having no 'orders' or divisions amongst its citizens on which to base different constitutional powers.[214] This raised the issue of how power in such a government could be countered or 'balanced', indeed, of whether it needed to be. In Publius' view it did. Not only did the different functions of government need to be divided and balanced against each other in the sense described above; but the legislature itself, because it was, in republican governments, invariably the most powerful branch, needed to be internally divided. In England this had been achieved by giving one branch of the legislature to the commons and one to the nobility. But America had abolished such distinctions. The solution to the issue of

---

[212] Ibid., 37, p. 178.

[213] Ibid., 48, p. 253, the point is repeated, 71, p. 367.

[214] Ibid., 14, p. 62. The device was not only embodied in the British constitution, through the House of Lords, it was a commonplace of republican thinking, one influential version being articulated by Harrington, who accorded to his landholding senators the function of 'debate' and to his freeholding yeomen that of 'result' or decision. Separation of powers was ensured here by respect between two socially differentiated groups for the different political functions accorded them. Pocock, 'Introduction', *The Complete Works of James Harrington*, p. 66.

how to divide the legislature without a principle of separate estates was ; 'to render them by different modes of election and different principles of action, as little connected with each other as . . . will admit'.[215] Thus although both the bodies of the federal legislature fulfill the now established 'republican' principle of being popular representatives, yet by being elected in different ways, they can still be given a sufficiently different character as to create different motives and interests in their incumbents, and so by rivalry check any departure from the proper role of the other.

In discussion of the House of Representatives the issue of representation recurs. In the convention Madison had objected to attempts to have Congress elected by the states legislatures, partly because in making the national government a creature of the states it would have deprived it (and left the states securely in possession of) the necessary popular base: 'he was an advocate for the policy of refining popular appointments by successive filtrations, but thought it might be pushed too far'.[216] However the other reason had to do with his concern to deny the irresponsible state legislatures such a large role in the national government, a government which he hoped would be able to curb their excesses through the exercise of veto. A truly representative House, one which was 'an exact miniature of the society: each element – farmers, artisans, Germans, Baptists, and so on . . . to speak for its particular interest in government' would be huge.[217] But to Madison more meant worse, and less morally resolute members, more meant greater influence of demagogues.[218] The representative would begin to take on the same characteristics of direct democracy which it was designed to avoid.[219] A further criticism derived from Publius' moral psychology which accorded much importance to the motive of public reputation. Love of fame 'the ruling passion of the noblest minds' was a vital motive to republics.[220] The pursuit of fame, by recruiting egoism in the service of the public good, provided motivational support for republicanism without making unrealistic demands on human nature. But the institutional framework had to be right. Very large bodies promote moral irresponsibility because this motive 'has a less active influence when the infamy of a bad action is to be divided among a number of men.'[221] Under the anonymity of numbers, factious cabals and conspiracies can thrive, 'passion never fails to wrest the sceptre from reason. Had every Athenian Citizen been a Socrates; every Athenian assembly would still have been a mob.'[222]

In a sense this line of argument played into the hands of the anti-federalists for whom the impossible size of a proper national representative was a strong argument in favour of keeping the federal government a relation purely between states. But Publius drew different implications. For one, he had, as we saw earlier a different sense of represent-ation. This allowed him to be more than happy with larger constituencies and a less than literally representative body which 'filtered' the more volatile demands of the people. Secondly, he points out, different representational roles required different degrees of

---

[215] *Federalist*, 51, pp. 265–6.
[216] Farrand, I, p. 50; deprived of popular legitimacy, *Federalist* 39, p. 191.
[217] Gordon S. Wood, 'Foreword' to Kenyon, *The Antifederalists*, pp. vii-viii.
[218] *Federalist*, 58, p. 301.
[219] Ibid., 58, p. 301
[220] Ibid., 72, p. 370; and see Stourzh, *Alexander Hamilton . . .* , pp. 95–106.
[221] Ibid., 15, p. 72.
[222] Ibid., 55, p. 284.

'representation' in even the anti-federalists' case. Since the federal government was to be concerned only with national issues, there was no need to represent the detailed political complexion of the states at national level, such knowledge was important for state legislatures, and the more local representation they afforded would provide it there.[223]

The third objection to the House of Representatives was that it will be a class biased, even class dominated body comprising 'citizens which will have least sympathy with the mass of the people'.[224] This objection is more difficult for Publius to meet. It had been an important part of his case for a national government, covering the larger sphere, that it will select more enlightened, better educated representatives. He cannot then deny anti-federalist charges that mechanics and poor farmers will be unlikely to be represented. He can only point out that if not chosen, at least such men will – as much as in the states themselves – be the choosers. The franchise qualifications for federal elections will be those obtaining in the states and the most important sense in which representatives will be an elite will be that they 'will have been distinguished by the preference of their fellow citizens.' Natural gratitude to their electors, no less than a self-interest in keeping in with them will, combined with a short term of office, make for an identity of interest and sympathies even where it might not naturally exist.[225] When Publius discusses in detail the possible different kinds of special interest that might be served, he doesn't refute the property less – property-owner divide so often stressed by the opposition (indeed he praises the 'imperceptible channel' of deference by which property will gain the recognition it is not legally given).[226] Instead he focuses on the potential opposition of interests amongst different sorts of property-owners – primarily that between land-owners and merchants. Here he is on safer ground: for the likelihood of any one such group gaining the ascendancy must be even greater in the state legislatures, the autonomy of which such critics are defending. For the economies – and therefore the political sociology – of individual states are less diverse than that of the union as a whole. Competing elites, as they have come to be called, are more likely in a larger than in a smaller political unit. In any case given the necessary predominance of landowners amongst members of any national elite, that interest would be ensured without threat to commerce since such men 'accustomed to investigate the sources of public prosperity . . . must be too well convinced of the utility of commerce to inflict upon it so deep a wound . . . '[227]

The separation of federal powers (i) between legislature and judiciary

The above arguments against tyranny in the legislature are probabilistic ones, based on the likely concatenations of groupings of interests based on economic activity. However, Publius' strongest arguments rely on the division of powers, which, combined with the republican principle of equality of legal status, gives rise to an immensely important – if still embryonic – version of the principle of the rule of law. This was expressed in John

---

[223] Ibid., 56.
[224] Ibid., 57, p. 292.
[225] Ibid., 57, pp. 293–4.

[226] Ibid., 54, p. 281.
[227] Ibid., 60, p. 310.

Adams' famous ideal of 'a government of laws and not of men', and it was most assiduously cultivated by Hamilton's Publius.

The formal safeguard against oppressive legislative measures is legal equality. Legislators 'can make no law which will not have its full operation on themselves and their friends, as well as on the great mass of society.' It was a common complaint that under the Articles of Confederation, state legislatures intervened to suspend the operation of the law when it suited them or interested parties. As early as 1784 Hamilton had been active in seeking to prevent the New York legislature from doing this. The particular case also involved in part, the doctrine of internal sovereignty which *The Federalist* was still trying to establish. Hamilton argued that because the United States had incurred Peace Treaty obligations to protect loyalists, the individual states could not abrogate them by victimizing loyalist citizens. More generally, he appealed to the 'fundamental principles' of republican government, which, at that time, he identified with a universal right to due process of law under laws which were themselves expressed in completely general terms.[228] There was, needless to say, a tension between that notion of republicanism, and the notion of republican government as one embodying the will of the majority, a tension which pervades the whole work, as it does the constitution and indeed American political culture itself.

A crucial plank in the establishment of the rule of law was the separation of legislature and judiciary. Collusion between them could break that uniformity in the application of law which, through guaranteeing the legislators' own susceptibility to it, ensured fairness and care in its formulation.[229] This plank however, was not yet the whole ship. If one asked what there was to stop the legislature 'making legal discriminations in favour of themselves, and a particular class of society' the answer as yet was only 'the genius of the whole system; the nature of just and constitutional laws; and above all, the vigilant and many spirit which actuates the people of America'.[230] Such an argument not only invoked again the residual 'virtue' on which even a modern republican government ultimately depends, but pointed towards a doctrine of constitutionalism which is not fully articulated until *Federalist* 78, and perhaps beyond that to the bill of rights and to a doctrine, and a system of judicial review which did not, at this stage exist, but which could provide judicial compensation for Madison's lost federal veto on legislation.

The separation of powers (ii) within the national legislature: the Senate

This brings us back to division of legislative power within the legislative department itself, between the House of Representatives and the Senate. *The Federalist* justified the split legislature in two different ways. Firstly Madison justified the split as a way of diminishing what he saw as the otherwise dangerously preponderant power in this branch

---

[228] The case is put in the essays published by Hamilton under the pseudonym of 'Phocion'. Their significance for this issue is discussed in Stourzh, *Alexander Hamilton . . .* p. 57ff.

[229] 'Necessity of being bound . . . by the laws to which he gives his assent, are the true, and they are the strong cords of sympathy between the representative and the constituent.' *Federalist*, 35, p. 168.

[230] Ibid., 57, p. 294.

of the government.[231] Secondly Hamilton argues that representing the people via different mechanisms will go far to ensure that diversity of views and interests which inhibits majority tyranny, even if the original causes of that diversity are eroded by time.[232] The Senate is too, a representative of the whole people although it represents them via the state legislatures who elect it. It is therefore federal in character. In a federal scheme of government laws need the agreement of both the people and the states. The equal representation of the states in the Senate is an acknowledgement of their equal sovereign character within the union, and a form of safeguard for the smaller states against the larger ones, a protection of minority rights in the population of states, just as Madison sought a protection of minority rights in the population of citizens. At the same time the indirect representation of the senators means they are representatives of representatives; they are selected as the best, by those whom the people of the state have already chosen as their best, – they are, suggests Madison, swallowing his usual impatience with state legislatures, a republican aristocracy of merit. The age and residence qualifications for senators are more demanding, their term of office longer, and their elections staggered. All of these qualities make it a more conservative body and less immediately responsive to the 'passions' associated with popular opinion.[233] This is in keeping with the specific responsibilities of the Senate, particularly its foreign policy role which requires a longer term and less localized view of interests. Responsibility 'must be limited to objects within the power of the responsible party; and . . . must relate to operations . . . of which a ready and proper judgement can be formed by the constituents.' If the term of office were short, constituents could not form a judgement about senators' success in dealing with long term policies. Moreover senators would have no personal incentive to choose to pursue policies directed at long term success – which may entail, for their constituents short term hardship – rather than ultimately destructive short term successes. Whilst the spirit of republicanism may demand short terms to maintain popular supervision over govern-ment, representatives of short duration cannot be expected to act responsibly with respect to the long term.[234] Thus the relative independence of representatives from their constituents is not, as we so often think today, inconsistent with their responsibility; nor is greater responsiveness any guarantee of it. Yet another dimension of political bodies affects responsibility when it is opposed in this way to responsiveness, and that is size. Smaller bodies are more responsible, because it is more difficult for each individual to shirk their role in the action.[235] Indeed when Publius comes to consider the executive the argument is extended to its ultimate conclusion.

Stability is particularly important too, in international relations, where the state most takes on the character of a person, the persistence of qualities through time being a characteristic of personality. However not only in foreign but in domestic affairs is a sense of national identity, and identification with the nation important. Whilst the general

[231] Ibid., 51, p. 265.

[232] Ibid., 60, p. 308. The two justifications are in some tension with each other for they appeal to different concerns about the central government, the first that it will be too powerful, the second that it will too weakly represent the people's will.

[233] Ibid., 62, passim.

[234] Ibid., 63, p. 322.

[235] Ibid., and see n.100.

thrust of *The Federalist*'s argument is to stress the importance of difference and diversity within the new nation, this is one of the few places where an appeal to an as-yet-tenuous national identity makes an appearance.[236] Much of the justification for the Senate stresses its necessary distance from the people and its aristocratic character. However, although stability is not a characteristic associated with the popular will, it is a characteristic from which the people at large benefit. Numerous laws, a complex and changing legislation – all of which could result from a legislature over-responsive to popular feelings and passions – does not benefit the people, it gives 'unreasonable advantage . . . to the sagacious, the enterprising, and the monied few, over the industrious and uninformed mass of the people'. Any legislative measure 'affecting the value of the different species of property, presents a new harvest to those who watch the change, and can trace its consequences'.[237] Thus a paradoxical consequence of popularly responsive government is that it provides opportunity for the speculator, the evil genius who haunts modern republicanism, to prey on the people's honest toil.

The executive

Publius' concerns about the need to check and refine a representative legislature had to be stressed to a public which, in his view naively, regarded that branch as the least likely source of oppression. His task in relation to the executive was different and much greater. For he had to overcome prejudices about powerful and centralised executives which had deep roots in the historical experience of Americans. Anti-federalists had reserved their most extreme invective for the executive branch of the new constitution. Particularly singled out was the President's role as commander in chief of the army. 'Philadelphiensis' assured his readers that 'the *president general* will be a *king* to all intents and purposes' (by the next issue he had become 'the most *despotic monarch* . . . in modern times'). Whilst acknowledging that the constitution-makers had conceded enough to democracy to grant an initial election for the President, they were sceptical that this could last: 'let the wheels of this government be once cleverly set in motion, and I'll answer for it, that the people shall not be much troubled with future elections, especially in choosing their *king*. The *standing army* will do that business for them'.[238]

Publius regarded such a response as a complete (and calculated) over-reaction, and seeks to show this by a running comparison between the powers of the executive and those of the governor of New York. But his difficulty in meeting such criticisms was not merely that he regarded them as unfounded in this particular case. Supporters of the new constitution were convinced that in republics the executive was actually an inherently weak arm of government, which, if anything needed strengthening, for a weak executive was a fault in any government.[239] In the convention Madison had stressed the executive's weakness in the republican forms of government. This arose from the impossibility of having, within a republic, an individual so pre-eminent, independent and with such a personal interest in the regime as a king. As a result the chief executive would be envied by others hoping to take his place and vulnerable to subversion by foreigners. He would

---

[236] Ibid., 62, 63, pp. 320–1.

[237] Ibid., 62, p. 320; and c.f. Burke, Ch VI, p. 294.

[238] Letters of 'Philadelphiensis', Kenyon, *Antifederalists*, p. 72.

[239] *Federalist*, 70, p. 358.

need support against the first and checks to prevent the second, moreover he would have to be a man of pre-eminent moral qualities.[240] An executive veto was here proposed by Madison, not only to protect minorities but to enable the executive to protect itself.[241] The importance of a vigorous executive is something Publius works gradually round to, not fully broaching it until the third of the issues devoted to the subject.

When he does so he produces one of the clearest and succinct analyses of the whole work, clearly outlining the conditions which will maximise energy and the further qualities required of a republican executive. An energetic executive needs to be united, needs a reasonably long period of office, needs material means and adequate powers to discharge its tasks. To satisfy republican standards it must be popularly elected and responsible for its actions.[242] Earlier Publius had pointed out the unconstitutionality of the view – inherent in the states' legislatures' intervention in the legal process – that executive power was somehow less legitimate than legislative.[243] The idea of popular constitutionalism is to give the constitution itself a popular sanction. All powers exercised under that constitution then have the same degree of legitimacy. Legislatures cannot usurp the role of executives, or judiciaries on the grounds that they alone derive their authority from popular mandate. There is a qualitative difference between the popular mandate that establishes the constitution and the one that elects the legislature, which makes it impossible, even in a popular republic, to appeal through the legislature to the people above the head, as it were, of the constitution.[244] This relationship between popular will and constitutionalism is such an important, and misunderstood issue in democracies that Hamilton's robust statement of it bears extended quotation:

> [There is] a right of the people to alter or abolish the established constitution whenever they find it inconsistent with their happiness; yet it is not to be inferred from this principle that the representatives of the people, whenever a momentary inclination happens to lay hold of a majority of their constituents incompatible with the provisions of the existing constitution, would, on that account, be justifiable in a violation of those provisions; . . . Until the people have, by some solemn and authoritative act, annulled or changed the established form, it is binding upon themselves collectively as well as individually; and no presumption, or even knowledge of their sentiments can warrant their representative is a departure from it prior to such an act.[245]

Having established the equal legitimacy of the executive branch under the constitution it is still a requirement for a republican executive that it be derived from the people. This rules out hereditary monarchy, which nevertheless has some revealing things to be said in its favour. The hereditary monarch's guarantee of security and independence, both for himself and his descendants deprives him of any temptation which might befall a private individual to 'sacrifice his duty to his complaisance for those whose favour was

---

[240] Farrand, I, p. 138.

[241] Farrand, I, p. 108; *Federalist*, 66, p. 338.

[242] *Federalist*, 70, pp. 358–9.

[243] Ibid., 64, p. 331; cf. Sherman's view at the convention, Farrand, I, p. 65.

[244] 'A constitution is . . . a fundamental law. . . .the Constitution ought to be preferred to statute, the intention of the people to the intention of their agents.' *Federalist*, 78, p. 398. Legislatures sometimes 'seem to fancy they are the people themselves', *Federalist*, 71, p. 367.

[245] Ibid., 78, p. 400.

necessary'.[246] Such personal pre-eminence was incompatible with republicanism, but the institutional framework must try to supply it. On the other hand monarchy, without checks, degenerated into tyranny. How could the checks not cancel out the independence? How could the demands of popular derivation not 'constantly counteract those qualities in the executive which are the most necessary ingredients in its composition – vigour and expedition'?[247] The executive needs to be derived from the people, not from the other organs of government, for it needs to be independent of them, if the separation of powers is to be maintained. This required that the executive be elected neither from the state governments, nor from the federal government, but through a channel having no connection with them.[248] A further consideration is the requirement of pre-eminent ability and virtue in the chief executive, exposed as he would be to temptation and flattery.[249] The answer in each case was the electoral college. Since it only came together for the purpose of the election it was completely separate from the existing organs of state or federal government, and since its existence was transitory it was not prone to corruption or manipulation. Moreover since the people would choose the best of their number to then choose the President, a judicious and informed choice might be expected. By diffusing the act of election through a process involving time and space, the violence and disorder so feared in eighteenth century elections, and which might be redoubled in the choice of such an important post, would be avoided. Finally by making the executive owe his office to the people assembled as an electoral college, he would be independent of the people in any other form once elected.[250]

If the demands of a popular derivation were satisfied, how could the prerequisites of strength and vigour – unity, duration, adequate resources and powers – be reconciled with responsibility?

Unity was required for energy.[251] An internally divided executive would waste energy on internal conflict. This could arise because someone was not consulted over a particular policy – or because they were, but were unheeded. Motives of pride, certainty or bigotry could all play a part. Such dissension was inescapably a part of republican government, quite possibly benign in its operation within the legislative branch where it ensured, from whatever motives, that all legislation was subject to proper scrutiny, but it was quite unsuited to the executive.[252]

However despite the worries about an elected 'king' Publius argues that unity is not at odds with the requirement that the executive be responsible. Where authority is vested in a single individual, the motive of public praise or blame for his actions is strongest, it is not diluted through having to be shared with others. 'Love of fame, the ruling passion of noble minds', must be allowed to operate to the fullest extent possible.[253] By contrast, where the executive is a plurality, responsibility is diminished through loss of clarity

[246] Ibid., 68, p. 349.

[247] Ibid., 70, p. 361.

[248] Ibid., 51, p. 264.

[249] Ibid., 68, p. 350.

[250] Ibid., 68, pp. 348–9. It is true that the House of Representatives, voting by states, would conduct a run-off election in the event of there being no clear winner in the popular vote. Constitution II, 1.

[251] On 'energy' see David Epstein, *Political Theory of the Federalist* (Chicago, 1984) chapter 2, passim.

[252] *Federalist*, 70, pp. 360–1.

[253] Ibid., 70, p. 362.

about agency.[254] If shared, or uncertain, moral censure does not work as a curb.[255] At the extreme this takes the form of the President's liability to impeachment. So the principle of a unitary executive conforms to the demands of both vigour and responsibility. Once elected, a major guarantee of responsibility in the executive is his desire to avoid the opprobrium of his fellow citizens. The moral and political arithmetic coincides.

The next dimension of energetic power is duration in office. The importance of duration lies in the ability of the incumbent to resist as he must the influence of transitory shifts in public opinion. Republicanism is to be understood as popular government, and the executive is, as we've seen, to owe his office to popular if indirect election. But neither of these propositions 'requires an unqualified complaisance to every sudden breeze of passion.' Like Rousseau, Publius perceives that while 'the people commonly *intend* the PUBLIC GOOD' it would be foolish to 'pretend that they always *reason right* about the *means* of promoting it.'[256] In such cases, where 'the interests of the people are at variance with their inclinations' the duty of the public representative must be 'to withstand temporary delusion, in order to give them time and opportunity for more cool and sedate reflection.'[257] The moral analysis here reflects that which pervades the work. Short term passions, or even prudential self-interest are more powerful motivators, yet less reliable guides than reason and justice. It was 'the reason of the public alone that ought to control and regulate the government'; the art of the founder was so to construct institutions that it did.[258]

Given that the executive must resist the swings of public mood, what institutional arrangements will assist *him* psychologically in doing this? The answer is a reasonably long term of office and the prospect of re-election. We can only have an interest in that which we know with some certainty will remain in our possession for at least some time, this is 'no less applicable to a political privilege, or honour, or trust, than to any article of ordinary property.' To be committed to the office and to face the unpopularity which the proper discharge of its duties might require (and which a mischievous legislature might exploit) the term must be long enough that 'the prospect of annihilation would be sufficiently remote, not to have an improper effect upon the conduct of a man endued with a tolerable portion of fortitude; and in which he might reasonably promise himself that there would be time enough . . .to make the community sensible of the propriety of the measures he might incline to pursue.'[259] Whilst a reasonable term rightly frees the executive from 'servile pliancy to the prevailing current' the possibility of re-election is both an inducement to good behaviour and offers further benefits in terms of stability. Publius recognises that these two arguments cut across one another to a degree, but the approaching end of a term of office will not reduce to servility someone who had through

---

[254] Publius cites the characteristic excuses: 'I was overruled by my council. The council were so divided on the issue that it was impossible to obtain any better resolution on the point.' Ibid., 70, p. 362.

[255] Ibid., 70, p. 363.

[256] Ibid., 71, p. 366. Cf. Rousseau, *The Social Contract* (London, 1973), 'Our will is always for our own good, but we do not always see what it is.' p. 203.

[257] *Federalist*, 71, p. 367.

[258] Ibid., 49, p. 260. On the moral psychology of *The Federalist*, see Daniel Walker Howe, 'Faculty Psychology in *The Federalist Papers*' in Ball and Pocock, *Conceptual Change*.

[259] *Federalist*, 71, p. 368.

the 'proofs he had given of his wisdom and integrity' gained the 'respect and attachment of his fellow citizens'. There is a kind of moral calculus at work here too. The more a statesman had proved himself to his public when, as in mid-term, he was beyond their censure, the less likely they would be to exercise it, but put faith in his judgement if he found unpopular measures were necessary close to re-election.[260] Thus the dimension of 'duration in office' exhibits a balance, along the dimension of time itself between the short which would render him responsive, but incapable of fulfilling his task, and the long term which would make him independent but risk his being irresponsible.

The provision of the requisite support and powers of the President concerns his ability to sustain himself personally and his post constitutionally. They consist of a requirement not to alter his initial salary (upwards or downwards), and a qualified veto over the acts of the legislature, so as to return them to Congress for reconsideration.[261] This latter power is presented here as a power of self-defence against the ever-invasive legislature. In such circumstances, Publius suggests, the danger is not the irresponsible use of his power so much as that he wouldn't use it at all. The popular nature, and natural pre-eminence of the legislature might inhibit the executive from exercising a full veto; the advantage of making it only a power of referral is that the executive will actually dare to use it. Even its very existence will inhibit the legislature from seeking to overstep its proper sphere by a series of legislative usurpations.[262]

The assessment of the executive concludes by stressing that the direction of war, the initiation (but not the ratification which requires the Senate) of treaties, and the nomination (subject to senatorial approval) of diplomatic personnel are all appropriate tasks for an individual. In rebutting the fears and accusations of anti-federalists Publius here again stresses the general issue of trust, and the role of honour. The very 'institution of delegated power implies that there is a portion of virtue and honour among mankind, which may be a reasonable foundation of confidence.' The way in which a sense of honour functions is to inhibit the executive from acting in ways that would be seen as shameful – 'proposing candidates who had no other merit than that of coming from the same state . . . or of being personally allied to him'.[263] Whether this is seen as shameful or not depends on the morality of the people at large, and in this sense republics do rely on the acknowledgement of a *standard* of public political virtue to which people are prepared to accord honour, even if they do not themselves live up to it. Honour, however, is a kind of cement, which fills in the gaps and binds together the institutional structure, it is not the fabric. The requirement of senatorial confirmation for posts, and the exclusion of any member of Congress from civil office is an additional and vital component in the separation of powers, preventing the executive from doing what they had so notoriously done in Britain: undermining the independence of the legislature by the promise of lucrative appointments.

---

[260] Ibid., 71, p. 368.
[261] Ibid., 73, pp. 374–5, 'The power over a man's support, is a power over his will.'
[262] Ibid., 73, pp. 375–8.
[263] Ibid., 74, pp. 389–70.

The judiciary

The final department in the constitution is 'beyond comparison, the weakest of the three'. Its weakness derives from its lack of access to 'either the sword or the purse'. It has 'total incapacity to support its usurpations by force'. Fear of encroachment on the other organs of government from it is therefore 'in reality a phantom', and as a result 'all possible care is requisite to enable it to defend itself against their attacks'.[264] Partly for this reason the argument that the division of powers must be understood as each having a 'partial agency' in the other does not apply to the judiciary. Being itself so weak it needs no curbing through dependence on the acquiescence of another – particularly the legislature.[265] On the contrary, it must be rendered as independent of other branches of the national government as possible, through its mode of appointment which is not popular, and through its tenure of office which is, during 'good behaviour' unlimited.[266] The ultimate supremacy of the federal judiciary over the states has already been discussed and this makes it clear that just as the judiciary is to be guarded from the invasive acts of the other branches of the federal government, so too it is to be assured and unimpeded in the exercise of its jurisdiction over the states.

This independence of the judiciary raises, once again, the question of the popular will. 'Brutus' pointed out that the power of the judiciary to determine the constitutionality of legislation will ultimately comprise a kind of legislative authority. For legislatures will not continue to pass laws 'which they know the courts will not execute' and as a result 'the judgement of the judicial on the constitution, will become the rule to guide the legislature.' He acknowledged that elective judges did not make sense, but thought nevertheless that the 'supreme controlling power [of the judiciary] should be in the choice of the people, or else you establish an authority independent and not amenable at all, which is repugnant to the principles of free government.'[267]

The counter to this argument involves stressing – as with the executive – the equal legitimacy of the various powers under the constitution. The power of judicial review is essential to a limited constitution, such as that of the United States, where, even before the bill of rights, and the famous judgement of Marbury versus Madison, there were limits placed on what laws the legislature might enact. Allowing judges to overrule legislatures in cases of legal conflict, or possible constitutional impropriety does not 'suppose a superiority of the judicial to the legislative power. It only supposes that the power of the people is superior to both'.[268]

---

[264] Ibid., 78, pp. 396–7; 81, p. 414; 78, p. 397.

[265] Ibid., 81, p. 412–3.

[266] Ibid., 80, pp. 396–7.

[267] *Essays of Brutus,* XII, and XVI, Dry, *Anti-Federalist,* pp. 169, 188. Publius draws attention to what he sees as the beneficial effect of the anticipated judgement of the judiciary in curbing the legislature. *Federalist,* 78, p. 401.

[268] Ibid., 78, pp. 397–8.

Establishing the primacy of the constitution within a popular republic is one of the major achievements of the American founding.[269] The idea of the constitution as a written 'fundamental law' with a different and more entrenched status than other laws is the culmination and integration of a whole series of theoretical reflections on developments in early modern European and American history.[270] Many of these developments involved the identification of 'fundamentals' with the idea of what was most ancient and lay at the 'founding' of the state, and the idea of the political 'constitution' with that which was 'constitutive of' the polity. The American constitution was self-consciously new, it was constituted by 'the people'. Since the basic principle as well as the historical origin of the popular republic was the political expression of the popular will, many found it difficult to concede that will should be impeded in any way. Since the legislature was a more obvious expression of popular will than the judiciary, it seemed to many wrong that the judiciary should be able to disqualify its acts.

But if the will of the people could be seen as contrary to established or constituted power,[271] a 'constitution' could also be seen as a bulwark against the 'encroachment' of even popularly constituted power. The townspeople of Concord, Massachusetts, had asserted at the outset of the War of Independence 'We conceive that a constitution in its proper idea intends a system of principles established to secure the subject in the Possession and enjoyment of their rights and privileges, against any encroachments of the governing part.'[272] One notorious and oft-cited example of such encroachment was the passing in Britain, of the Septennial Act of 1716 by which Parliament had increased the gap between elections from three to seven years and its own life by four years. Where such 'fundamental articles of the government' which are 'corner stones' of liberty can be changed by ordinary acts of the legislature because there was 'no constitution paramount to the government' then liberty is unsafe.[273] The English, as Paine was to point out, *had* no constitution, for Parliament could at any moment legally take away their rights.[274]

The idea that it was the constitution – and not the government – which was the fundamental expression of the people's will resolved the tension between the popular sovereignty and constitutionalist strands of thought in the representative republic. Publius cleverly uses the representative, and therefore derivative nature of the legislature to disadvantage it in relation to the constitution, turning the populists' principle against them: 'the constitution ought to be preferred to the statute' where they clashed because this was simply preferring 'the intention of the people to the intention of their agents'.[275]

---

[269] See the excellent overview of the meanings applied to 'constitution' and the significance of the American debate by Gerald Stourzh in '*Constitution*: Changing Meanings of the Term from the Early Seventeenth to the Late Eighteenth Century', in Ball and Pocock, *Conceptual Change*.

[270] As well as the previously cited chapter, and references there see J.W.Gough, *Fundamental Law in English Constitutional History* (Oxford, 1955); and Harro Höpfl, 'Fundamental Law and the Constitution in Sixteenth-Century France', in R. Schnur ed., *Die Rolle der Juristen bei der Entstehung des Modernen Staates* (Berlin, 1986).

[271] As the telling title of the English radical, John Thelwall's response to Burke put it, constitutionalism pitted: 'The Rights of Nature Against the Usurpation of Establishments'.

[272] Cited Stourzh, '*Constitution*. . . ', in Ball and Pocock, *Conceptual Change*, p. 46.

[273] *Federalist*, 53, p. 274.

[274] *Rights of Man*, II, Foner, *Complete Writings*, vol. I, p. 382.

[275] *Federalist*, 78, p. 398.

Although the constitution was based on the people's will in the sense of having been established through popular vote, the expression of the people's will was thereafter to be confined to the forms and channels laid down in the constitution, for that – together with the judiciary's role in safeguarding it – would have been the intention of the people in establishing the constitution.

Such arguments may justify the role of an independent judiciary in a popular federal republic. There is, however, still room for argument about its relationship to, and effect on the states' governments. The constitution established federal courts and a supreme court, with jurisdiction over all issues concerning federation as a whole, the constitution, all inter-state conflict, and conflicts between individuals and other states, and between individuals of different states. It also has a general duty to promote equity and the aims provided in the preamble of the constitution – 'to provide a more perfect Union, establish Justice, insure domestic Tranquillity, provide for the common Defence, promote the general Welfare, and secure the Blessings of Liberty to ourselves and our posterity'.

Far from agreeing with Publius' claims about the weakness and unthreatening nature of the judiciary, anti-federalists saw the formulation of jurisdiction as one which meant 'that all questions [even] between citizens of the same state are to be decided by the local laws and not by general ones'; thus increasing the 'tendency of the proposed system . . . to consolidate the whole empire into one mass, and, like the tyrants bed, to reduce all to one standard.'[276] In New York, Brutus spelled out with absolute clarity the implications that constitutional control by the courts would have in terms of limiting popular power exercised through the state legislatures. The constitution 'vests the courts with authority to give the constitution a legal construction' a process which necessarily 'gives a certain degree of latitude of explanation'. Furthermore the requirement to interpret the law according to equity, or a conception of fairness which departs from the strict letter of the law, allows them to 'determine according to what appears to them, the reason and spirit of the constitution' and no one can set aside such a judgement for the court is 'authorized by the constitution to decide in the last resort.' Brutus has no doubt that the 'legal construction' which the federal judiciary will give 'will give such an explanation to the constitution, as will favour an extension of its [the general government's] jurisdiction.' As a result

> The judicial power will operate to effect, in the most certain, but yet silent and imperceptible manner, what is evidently the tendency of the constitution: – I mean an entire subversion of the legislative, executive, and judicial powers of the individual states.[277]

Agrippa exaggerates, but Brutus, from the perspective of state-sovereignty, perhaps not much. The constitution does enumerate the areas of competence of the federal judiciary but it does not do so with such precision as to inspire confidence in defenders of states' rights, covering as they do all cases concerning 'the execution of the provisions expressly contained in the articles of union'. Hamilton confirms the wide interpretation that 'whatever practices may have a tendency to disturb the harmony of the states, are

---

[276] Agrippa, *Letters of Agrippa*, V (Dec. 1787); Storing, *Anti-Federalist*, p. 236–7.
[277] Brutus, *Essays of Brutus*, XI (Jan., 1788); Ibid., pp. 164–5.

proper objects of federal superintendence and control.'[278] However the sticking point is the issue of legal sovereignty. The anti-federalists were reluctant to concede what the federalists regarded as absolutely necessary: a constitutional mechanism for the ultimate determination of all points of conflict. Since it was not possible to anticipate all sources of conflict, some catch-all jurisdiction had to be given at some point in the constitution.

The federal court system is to have appeal jurisdiction 'in all the enumerated cases of federal cognizance, in which it is not to have an original one'. Now since the constitution 'gives no definition of [the jurisdiction] of the subordinate [state] courts', and if only because even (state) judiciaries can 'be judge in [their] own cause'[279] it follows that disagreements over what counts as state jurisdiction must be open to appeal to the federal courts. If we think of legal sovereignty in terms of a legal system having determinate closure, there is little doubt that the federal government exercised internal sovereignty.[280] Whilst the federal judiciary cannot, therefore, intervene directly in the internal judicial processes of states, there is no ultimate legal autonomy in the states.[281] In the language of legal sovereignty 'the national and state systems are to be regarded as ONE WHOLE.'[282]

Conclusion

The conceptual innovations associated with the American founding, to which *The Federalist* contributed so much, helped to redefine the language of modern politics.[283] They clearly articulated for the first time the notion of a written constitution as a fundamental law; helping to initiate a widespread process to which Gerald Stourzh has called attention as the 'positivisation of natural rights'.[284] Although the constitution did not initially contain, nor did *The Federalist* support, a bill of rights, all the essential

---

[278] The preamble to the constitution lists 'to form a more perfect Union, establish Justice, insure domestic Tranquillity, provide for the common Defence, Promote the general Welfare, and secure the Blessings of Liberty' which is sufficiently broad to cover most things. If 'within the Articles' were construed strictly, to include only those provisions mentioned under an article, there is still a long list under Article I, section 8. *Federalist*, 80, p. 408.

[279] Ibid., 80, p. 408.

[280] However, whilst Hamilton drew this conclusion, Madison denied the premise. Hamilton thought dissension could only be avoided 'by such a compleat sovereignty in the general Governmt. as will turn all the strong principles and passions . . . on its side.' Farrand, I, 286. Madison thought there was 'a gradation. . . from the smallest corporation, with the most limited powers, to the largest empire with the most perfect sovereignty.' Farrand, I, p. 464.

[281] Indeed when Madison came to make the case for a bill of rights he argued that a bill of rights was necessary precisely *because* the federal government was effectively legislatively as well as juridically sovereign: 'It is true the [legislative] powers of the General Government are circumscribed . . . but even if the Government keeps within those limits, it has certain discretionary powers, [and] power to make all laws which shall be necessary and proper for carrying into execution powers vested in the Government of the United States [and] it is for them to judge of the necessity and propriety . . . ' Speech Introducing the Bill of Rights, 8 June, 1789 in Meyers, *Mind of the Founder*, p. 170.

[282] *Federalist*, 82, pp. 422, 423, 422.

[283] See especially Pocock, 'The American Founding', in Ball and Pocock, *Conceptual Change . . .*

[284] Gerald Stourzh, *Fundamental Laws and Individual Rights in the Eighteenth-Century Constitution*, Bicentennial Essays, 5 (Claremont, Ca., 1984).

ingredients are present. The constitution is a limited one, in which certain acts are prohibited (even to state governments), the maintenance of the constitution is entrusted to an independent judiciary, and is therefore placed beyond majoritarian pressures which could endanger minorities. Secondly, in converting representation into a 'republican', and eventually also a 'democratic' institution America provided a language, and a legitimizing framework within which large modern states who needed to mobilize their populations could do so.

The universality of the claims made in 1787 took some time to be realised in law, and even longer in practice. Blacks were not legally enfranchised until 1870 but effective enfranchisement had to wait until federal officials were imposed on some states to guarantee voting rights in 1965. Women had no federally guaranteed vote until 1920, The first black woman did not sit in Congress until 1968. Yet once these rights had been established other worries remained. The low, and decreasing turnout in elections seems to raise many issues about civic identity and commitment which worried the anti-federalists. America, like other modern republics, needs to continuously create a public with the political will to sustain it in being. In *The Federalist*, there are, as J.G.A.Pocock has put it 'clear and unmistakable signs . . .of a tendency to separate the maintenance of a republican balance from the operations of any moral principle within the personality of the individual as citizen.'[285] As we suggested Publius shows an awareness that as well as balanced institutions some 'political virtue' is needed, in both politicians and citizens, if the republic is to survive. What is missing is any clear account of how those institutions engender that *virtù*. Emulation, the desire for fame, glory and the praise of one's fellows engenders *virtù* only as long as *virtù* is the currency of public life. When other values predominate and are accorded pre-eminence, these are the values that will be engendered in those seeking power through public approval: as Burke had put it 'Whatever be the road to power, that is the road which will be trod'.[286]

Democratic, or at least popular politics was to be now the focus of theorists' attention. In moving away from traditional republican concern with replenishing the qualities that made citizenship possible, and redefining citizenship in terms of certain basic, and eventually universal rights which were largely optional or private, new and representative democracy seemed to set a new agenda which could be much more agnostic about civic personality. Yet as we shall see, a concern with the moral and intellectual properties of citizens remained a matter of intense concern to political theorists who saw, as the federalists saw, that stable popular government required something more than a mere *ascription* of political rights. Indeed that concern is, or should be, with us still.

The Federalist's immediate legacy was rather different from that status which it subsequently attained. The constitution was of course, ratified. However, even the federalists soon found themselves in disagreement with the interpretation of it, Madison expressing opposition to Hamilton's centrist and aristocratic aspirations.[287] As a defence

---

[285] 'American Founding . . . ' in Ball and Pocock, p. 72

[286] Edmund Burke, 'Thoughts on the Causes of the Present Discontents', *Works of the Right Honourable Edmund Burke* (6 vols, London, 1886), vol. I p. 335.

[287] Madison however, acknowledged, what was true, that the political system of his Virginia was an aristocracy. Barely a quarter of the people — if one included slaves and disenfranchised whites — had the vote. Drew McCoy, *The Last of the Fathers, James Madison and the Republican Legacy* (Cambridge, 1991), p. 234.

of popular government *The Federalist* was a very conservative document indeed. We must remember that the 'popular' legislatures whose power it spent so much effort countering and balancing, were hardly popular at all by modern standards. The constitution did not specify any revision of suffrage rights from those which obtained in the individual states, and even the most radical of them limited the vote to free males who paid taxes, whilst the majority imposed a property qualification. By the middle of the nineteenth century, reformers in England identified with Jacksonian Democrats against the Federalists, and English Tories, who had denounced the founders, looked back to the Federalists as 'that party . . . which has been most averse from the irreligious and levelling principles of the Jacobins, and which contains the most respectable portion of the American people . . . they were desirous that such improvements might be made in their system of government, as should strengthen the executive power, remunerate more liberally the officers of government, render the judges less dependent. . .'[288] This is not an unfair assessment, and amongst the events which had intervened to emphasise the importance of discriminating amongst different forms of 'popular government' was the French Revolution. It was also to play a crucial role in provoking a major critique of democratic forms, Burke's *Reflections on the Revolution in France.*

---

[288] William Jacob in *The Quarterly Review*, 21 (1829), cited in David Paul Crook, *American Democracy in English Politics*, p. 139 (Oxford, 1965).

VI

Edmund Burke

Introduction

Burke is still an extremely potent political figure. In his opposition to the French Revolution he not only became for his time the acknowledged champion of the conservatives then ranged against it, but he put forward a view of human nature and society on which conservatives have drawn and to which they have appealed ever since. Not only did the right recruit Burke for their purposes in the Cold War of the fifties, but the collapse of communism in Eastern Europe has been followed there by renewed interest in Burke's writings.[1]

In this, ideological sense then Burke is very much alive. Yet ironically, and because of their very practical involvement in the politics of his own time, it is difficult for his writings to speak directly to us. Burke wrote no systematic treatise on politics, but as a practising politician, mostly in opposition, wrote mainly about the political controversies of his day – the reform of eighteenth-century government and finance, the revolt of the American Colonies, British relations with their colonies in Ireland and India, and finally the French Revolution.[2] The enthusiastic conservative looking for a succinct theoretical statement or credo is apt to be disappointed. It requires some effort from today's reader to understand the nature of these issues, and once we have made that effort, the more general relevance of Burke's observations can be lost. Burke forces us to face one of the most difficult issues in the study of political theory: the tension between the particular historical meaning of an author, and the more general truth to which their writing might aspire. In the case of a thinker such as Hobbes, his aspiration to achieve such universality is constant and unmistakable, it is built into the abstract structure of his argument, it even requires some considerable presence of mind to recognise the aspects of contemporary context when they occur. With Burke the converse is the case, the focus and the narrative are always carried by the particular political issue he is addressing, the more general theory is hinted at in passages of reflection, brilliant epigrams, or general observations aside from the apparent subject.

However, although this may be disappointing there is a sense in which it is integral to Burke's whole conception of conservatism and indeed politics that one should avoid such

---

[1] There are a number of interesting surveys of Burke's reputation and the ideological importance he has held for those of different persuasions, for example chapter 6 in F.P. Locke, *Burke's Reflections on the Revolution in France* (London, 1985), and in Isaac Kramnick, *The Rage of Edmund Burke* (New York, 1977), chapter 1, p. 39ff. as well as his 'The Left and Edmund Burke' *Political Theory*, 11, 2(1983).

[2] The best survey of Burke's career as a politician who was also a theorist remains C.B. Cone's *Burke and the Nature of Politics* (2 vols, Lexington, 1957–64).

abstraction and systematization. For Burke, political wisdom was inseparable from practice. It was more likely to be found in the skilled practitioner's response to particular issues, not in the construction and application of general truths.[3] I nevertheless believe it is possible to show that he did indeed speak and act from within some.

Biographical

Burke was born in Dublin in January 1729 the son of a Protestant attorney and a Catholic mother.[4] This background was, in the context of the oppressive anti-Catholic regime imposed on Ireland at the time, of considerable importance. He studied at the Anglican Trinity College, reading mostly classical works, and won a scholarship. After graduation he founded and briefly edited a literary weekly called *The Reformer* – aimed at reforming the taste and morals of Dublin society – before, in 1750, moving to London to study law at the Middle Temple.[5] Burke never completed his law studies and we know little about his life in what has been called his 'lost years', but that he travelled and kept literary company.

In 1756 and 1757 Burke published two literary works, his ironic *Vindication of Natural Society* and his *Philosophical Enquiry into the Origins of our Ideas of the Sublime and Beautiful*, and a year later was hired to edit the *Annual Register* a review of news and events. Burke had long hoped to make a literary career, and as part of it he hired himself as secretary and speech writer to politicians. After a false start with William Hamilton in Ireland, Burke began an enduring political relationship with the Marquis of Rocking-ham, leader of the so called Rockingham Whigs, and entered Parliament as Member for Wendover in 1765.

In 1769 and 1770 Burke published his first major political pamphlets *Observations on . . . The Present State of the Nation* and *Thoughts on the Causes of the Present Discontents*, the latter virtually a manifesto for the Rockinghamites. In 1774 he became MP for Bristol and began a series of speeches aimed at healing the rift between Britain

---

[3] A good introductory study which pursues this by trying to show not that Burke's thought was 'prompted by political theory' but 'relates to his career and to the political and social situation which evoked it' is Frank O'Gorman's, *Edmund Burke, his political philosophy* (London, 1973). The difficulty is not merely that for the theorist the more Burke's thought seems *merely* a response to events the less impressive it appears as theory, but rather more generally, as John Brewer argued, that an actor, or for that matter a theorist does not come to any 'political and social situation' cold; they come to it with preconceptions. Such preconceptions may be consciously and conscientiously held and articulated, or they may not be, either way they may be said to constitute a mental set from which arguments are drawn and by which they are structured and this relationship can be presented as a theory. The problem with Burke lies in striking a balance between the underlying presuppositions and the historical circumstances which were filtered through those presuppositions to result in his actions and writings, to 'gain on the historical swings and not lose on the philosophical roundabouts'. John Brewer, 'Rockingham, Burke and Whig Political Argument' *Historical Journal*, XVIII, 1 (1975), p. 201.

[4] Whilst not written from a theorist's perspective there is a new biography which makes use of the recently completed edition of Burke's letters, S. Ayling *Edmund Burke, his life and opinions* (London, 1988).

[5] The early life is still best covered in A. I. P. Samuels, *Early Life, Correspondence and Writings of Edmund Burke* (1923), which reprints early material by Burke still not available in the new edition of his works.

and her rebellious American Colonies. In 1780 he withdrew from Bristol in anticipation of defeat and was installed as MP at Malton. He campaigned with his friend Fox on the reform of government finances, and was able to implement changes in 1782 when he was briefly Paymaster General in the second Rockingham Administration.

From 1783, when he supported Fox's East India Bill, to 1787–95 when he conducted the impeachment of the Governor of Bengal, Warren Hastings, Burke was enmeshed in Indian affairs and their British repercussions. In the last eight years of his life, from 1790 when he published his most famous work *Reflections on the Revolution in France* until his death in 1797 he campaigned and wrote with increasing vehemence against the French Revolution and the influence of its ideas.

Even this brief outline reveals the many facets of Burke's life, and in particular shows something that puzzled contemporaries. The Rockinghamites were essentially an opposition party, the bulk of Burke's writings were essentially reformist. Critical of government patronage and influence over members of the House of Commons, of Lord North's government's intransigent policy towards the rebellious Americans, critical of loose housekeeping in the Royal exchequer and of the exploitation of Indian society and economy, Burke was essentially an agent for change, rationalization even, and reform. It is then, not only ironic that his greatest work, and the one for which he is best remembered should be the classic statement of conservatism, the *Reflections*, it is something that requires explanation. More, perhaps, than any other thinker Burke's reputation hinges on this question of consistency. Since he never tried to distill his political thought in a single work, the tensions between different statements made at different times are thrown into greater relief for him than for other thinkers. Since he was involved in such a diversity of practical political issues he had more occasion than the reflective philosopher, to contradict himself. If Burke's actions and statements are 'ad hoc' – 'pragmatic' responses to circumstance it is difficult to save his status as a theorist, however successful we judge his purely political career. Burke himself, for all his criticism of 'abstract theorising', was no irrationalist, and recognised consistency as an important virtue. By focusing on *Reflections* yet using it to provoke discussions of Burke's earlier and later positions, we can hope to demonstrate the underlying coherence of a mind that came to be seminal for European conservative political thought.

Edmund Burke's *Reflections on the Revolution in France*

The structure and nature of 'Reflections'

Whilst *Reflections* reads well – at times even pyrotechnically – it is one of the most difficult of works to analyse. This is partly because it appears to have, neither as regards form or content any very obviously coherent structure or shape; this is a characteristic for which Burke apologizes several times, and which the 'letter' format is perhaps designed to excuse.[6] The difficulty runs deeper than that, however, for to the absence of

---

[6] He was attacked for this by his opponents. Paine, introducing a 'miscellaneous' chapter in his famous *Rights of Man*, written against Burke, felt no compunction since, he said, 'Mr. Burke's Book is *all* Miscellany'. Turning Burke's invocation of the fear of the mob against him, Paine continues 'His intention was to make an attack on the French Revolution; but instead of proceeding with an orderly arrangement,

a formal structure seems intimately linked to Burke's longstanding determination to avoid systematic abstract theorising about politics altogether; and this seems to entail a rejection of the deductive, or at least cumulative and logically linked, pattern of argument we have come, at least since Hobbes, to associate with 'political theory'. The attack on abstract theorising forms a major theme of the book. Whatever 'political theory' Burke himself subscribed to (if any), is therefore, not coherently elaborated in the work. *Reflections* is, like most of his writings, an occasional work, in the sense of being at least overtly concerned with particular issues of the day; and it is a polemic. The polemic is directed firstly against those Englishmen who welcomed the French Revolution on the supposed grounds that it embodied the principles of the English Glorious Revolution of 1688, and who then re-apply those mistaken principles in the cause of reform at home. Secondly it is directed against the French Revolution itself, against the ideas which Burke believed inspired it, the men who perpetrated it and the policies which it pursued. The Revolution, Burke came increasingly to believe, constituted a threat to the whole edifice of Christian, European civilization.

Nevertheless, despite Burke's distaste for theorizing about foundations, the Revolution posed such a challenge to them that he was required to make his assumptions about the basis of a civilized order more explicit than he might otherwise have cared to. It is also possible to discern a kind of organisation of topics within *Reflections*, although the dazzling prose often obscures this, and Burke rarely resists the temptation to deviate or refer back to other issues.[7]

Introduction and epilogue apart, the body of the work comprises a first third which is devoted to an analysis and refutation of Price's sermon, the three principles it espouses, and the tactics supposedly underlying it, branching out along the way to consider such issues as the social composition of the National Assembly, and to contrast the 'French' doctrine of natural rights with the 'English' one of custom and tradition. In the central section Burke focuses primarily on the role of religion and the church in the state, in both England and France. In the last third he discusses in much more orderly turn the various principal institutions of the new French state. However the ostensible topic is interwoven by a series of latent issues which occasionally surface briefly in their own right, but are more often visible as episodic, but rhetorically powerful and evocative images and allusions. In this way Burke keeps two levels of discourse going at once and renders his text richer for the resonances each is able to sound in the other. Ironically the major and patent themes of *Reflections* are more historically parochial than the subtexts for which it has become best known.

Burke's major purpose is to evoke, in a way that would have been familiar to most eighteenth-century readers, the way in which an established church, a particular kind of social order and a particular arrangement of property rights contributed to the stability

---

he has stormed it with a mob of ideas tumbling over and destroying one another.' Tom Paine, *Rights of Man* (Harmondsworth, 1969), p. 116.

[7] Particularly good accounts of the structure of *Reflections* are to be found in David McCracken, 'Rhetorical Strategy in Burke's *Reflections*' in *The Yearbook of English Studies*, vol. 1 (1971), and in F.P. Locke *Burke's Reflections . . .* ch.4.

of public opinion necessary for settled and civilized life.[8] A recurrent setting for this theme is the contrast between Britain and revolutionary France – clearly designed to stymie the claims of English reformers who wanted to use France as a model for domestic political reform. What is, for most of the time the subtext, is a fragmented set of more abstract reflections on the nature of political identity and continuity, the roles of reason, superstition and prejudice in politics. Let us consider in sequence the topics outlined in the overt structure of the work and look thematically at some of the persistent undercurrents along the way.

Reflections Part One:
Price's sermon, natural rights and inherited rights

Reflections opens not with an account of anything in France but with a long section, almost a third of the work, devoted to attacking Richard Price's sermon 'On the Love of Our Country' preached at a dinner of the Revolution Society, an association of religious dissenters celebrating the events of 1688, and the expulsion of a Catholic king. The pretext for this is that the Frenchman Depont, to whom is addressed the 'letter' that *Reflections* claims to be, had asked for information on them. In fact he had not, the claim is a rhetorical device enabling Burke to broach his major theme – the connection between the Revolution in France and radicalism in Britain.[9] In this sermon Price put forward an interpretation of the 'principles' of 1688 which was not only, in Burke's view historically inaccurate, but were principles which, if widely believed would have been incapable of supporting any government at all.[10] These principles relate to the legal basis of political rule, which Price, and the French, wished to base on some principle of popular choice, and Burke wishes to base on custom, and specifically, heredity.

Price's sermon, in general concerned patriotism, which he sought to distinguish from chauvinism, and to identify with certain universal values, some of which even involved a duty to be critical of possible aspects of one's own government. In this sense it typified the different approaches of the two men which had already become clear when they each

---

[8] We are only now recovering the full complexity of this analysis. By far the best piece on this context so far is J.G.A. Pocock's Introduction to his edition of *Reflections* (Indianapolis, 1987), and his earlier articles on Burke cited below.

[9] F.P. Locke, *Burke's Reflections* p. 118, is the first to draw attention to this ploy.

[10] In fact those involved in the 'Glorious Revolution' of 1688 held a variety of views as to the status of the events surrounding the ejection of James II and the installation of William and Mary. It is true to say that leading politicians at least were anxious to avoid giving the impression that the action involved any assertion of popular sovereignty. This down-playing of a popular basis for the regime was reinforced at the famous trial in 1710 of Dr. Sacheverell, a Tory, who had asserted the divine hereditary right of kings and so impugned the Revolution, Act of Settlement and, indeed Queen Anne's title to the Crown. Tory support was so strong that the Whig prosecution almost backfired on them and a very moderate interpretation of 1688 and the 'right of resistance' had to be put. See Geoffrey Holmes *The Trial of Doctor Sacheverell* (London, 1973). It is the view of 1688 presented at the trial that Burke uses as the basis for his view of the 'Old Whig' position, in his *Appeal from the New to the Old Whigs*, published the year after *Reflections*.

attacked Lord North's repressive policy to the America colonies.[11] Price now argued, amongst other things, that the revolution of 1688 had established the English right

> to Choose our Governors
> to Cashier them for misconduct
> to Frame a Government for ourselves

In fact, argues Burke, although, if ever there was an opportunity to establish such principles, 1688 was it, these were not the rights then appealed to and 'It's not being done at this time is a proof that the nation was of the opinion that it ought not to be done at any time'.[12] Although there was a constitutional irregularity at the succession of William and Mary, Burke is determined to minimize it ('a small and temporary deviation'). The fact that the English found it necessary to suspend a part of their constitutional practice provides no grounds for asserting that they were at liberty to renegotiate the whole thing at their pleasures. In Burke's view in England in 1688 the institutions were preserved, though the personnel changed. In France they have changed the institutions and kept the person, they could have done as the English did, but they didn't.

The argument from precedent versus abstract principle: the appeal to the past

In the course of this defence of continuity Burke invokes a very famous pattern of argument and gives it an additional twist. The argument is the Common Law argument – used politically since the early seventeenth century – that since precedent has always prevailed in English legal practice, our law, including our constitutional law, must be immemorial, or at least derived from ever more ancient models. Burke is prepared to concede, what with the increasing historical sophistication of the eighteenth-century had become unarguable, that this belief may be an exaggeration, but it leads him to a subtle adaptation of the argument, for he goes on

---

[11] Price had argued in the abstract fashion which Burke so deprecated: 'I have' wrote Price, reviewing his own argument, 'from one leading principle, deduced a number of consequences that seem to me incapable of being disputed.' The one leading principle was that 'civil government is an expedient contrived by human prudence for the gaining of security against oppression and that, consequently, the power of civil government is a delegation or trust from the people for the accomplishment of this end.' The alternative principle was that 'Civil governors' . . . power is a commission from Heaven, unbounded in extent, and never to be resisted.' Price is puzzled by Burke's claim that government is an institution of divine authority, and tries to explain away his position. (Richard Price *Observations on Civil Liberty*, and 'General Introduction and Supplement to the Two Tracts on Civil Liberty . . . etc.' in *Richard Price and the Ethical Foundations of the American Revolution: Selections from his pamphlets*, ed. & intr. Bernard Peach (Durham, N.C., 1979), pp. 81, 48. Burke rejected the attempt to 'split and anatomies the doctrine of free government, as if it were an abstract question concerning metaphysical liberty and necessity.' He thought that 'one sure symptom of an ill conducted state is the propensity of the people to resort to them [abstract theories of government]'. 'Letter to the Sheriffs of Bristol', in *The Works of the Right Honourable Edmund Burke* (6 vols, London, 1886) the 'Bohn' edition, vol. II, pp. 29, 31. Apart from *Reflections*, which will be cited in the Penguin edition, and unless otherwise stated, references to Burke's works are to this edition.

[12] Edmund Burke, *Reflections on the Revolution in France* (Harmondsworth, 1968) p. 101.

if these lawyers mistake in some particulars, it proves my position still the more strongly; because it demonstrates the powerful prepossession towards antiquity, with which the minds of all our lawyers and legislators and all of the people whom they wish to influence, have been always filled; and the stationary policy of this kingdom in considering their most sacred rights and franchises as an *inheritance*.

What Burke says is that it is not the fact that the English constitution, as it now stands, actually *is* as old as is claimed, that is the point; it may not even be true. The important point is the propensity of the English to claim their rights by appealing – rightly or wrongly – to past practice. We justify our rights 'not on abstract principles "as the rights of men", but as the rights of Englishmen, and as a patrimony derived from their forefathers.'[13] Justification through appeals to antiquity – whether historically tenable or not – are part of English political culture. The English are culturally and temperamentally suited to appeals to the past, to regarding their constitution as an inheritance – entailed for posterity – so it may not be sold off or dismantled. Each generation thinks of itself only as a temporary possessor and a 'life renter' in the constitution, not as 'entire masters', they have no right of 'destroying at their pleasure the whole original fabric of society' or even to take the risk of leaving behind 'to those who come after them a ruin instead of a habitation'.[14]

However, not only is this the way we are, Burke says, but to be this way is both natural and beneficial. Without it 'the whole chain and continuity of the commonwealth would be broken.' The continuity which alone makes progress possible, would be severed, and generations of men would be born and die 'like flies of a summer' without learning from, or perhaps even knowing of their predecessors.[15]

The appeal to the past is beneficial because it 'furnishes a sure principle of conservation, and a sure principle of transmission; without at all excluding a principle of improvement'; it is natural because 'we receive, we hold, we transmit our government and our privileges, in the same manner in which we enjoy and transmit our property and our lives', that is to say through familial inheritance. In a famous rhetorical passage Burke goes on to eulogize this policy by which, he says, 'our political system is placed in a just correspondence and symmetry with the order of the world'. For nature itself uses the familial principle to ensure a stable blend of continuity and variation. Burke draws the constitution, domestic affection and religion all together into a metaphor for the very thread that takes us through time:

In this choice of inheritance we have given to our frame of polity the image of a relation in blood; binding up the constitution of our country with our dearest domestic ties: adopting our fundamental laws into the bosom of our family affections; keeping inseparable, and cherishing with the warmth of all our combined and mutually reflected charities, our state, our hearths, our sepulchres, and our altars.[16]

---

[13] Ibid., p. 118.

[14] Ibid., p. 192. Entailment was a legal form of inheritance which carried with it the condition that the inherited estate not be partitioned or sold, but bequeathed entire to the next generation.

[15] Ibid., p. 193.

[16] Ibid., p. 120.

A set of images which are contrasted with those of the family are related to sexual vulnerability. The actions of the French are frequently portrayed as sexually threatening – the attack on Marie Antoinette is an unconsummated, or one might say sublimated, rape:

> a band of cruel ruffians and assassins, reeking with blood, rushed into the chamber of the queen, and pierced with an hundred strokes of bayonets and poinards the bed, from whence this persecuted woman had but just time to fly almost naked . . . .[17]

The Revolutionaries 'rudely tear off the decent drapery of life'. The loss of ancient manners is felt as 'a stain like a wound' to the 'chastity of honour'.[18] There are numerous others. The cumulative effect of these images is to reinforce Burke's claims about a traditional government, based on inheritance in all its forms, being like a family – 'binding up our nation with its dearest domestic ties' – a family in which the calm and decent domestic sentiments prevail. Energetic sexuality is linked with violence, rapine and murder.

The other form in which murder so often appears in Burke's work – patricide – also stresses its opposition to the natural family. The stressed harmony between the political, and the natural (and Christian) virtues of English domesticity produces the idea of the constitution as a father to be revered and looked after in old age, violently contrasted with the unnatural alchemical patricide of the demonic and occult revolutionary French:

> those children of their country who are prompted rashly to hack their parent into pieces, and put him in a kettle of magicians, in hopes that by their poisonous weeds, and wild incantations, they may regenerate the paternal constitution, and renovate their father's life.[19]

The argument from precedent versus abstract principle: abstract and natural rights argument

By contrast to the English appeal to the past, the French appeal to the much more general principle of natural rights. Whereas arguing from precedent always tends to sustain continuity, arguing from general principles invariably tends, claims Burke, to be subversive. For general principles which sound innocuous, in a settled political context, can be violently disruptive outside it. The principle that kings are only legitimate when they owe their office to the choice of the people, exercising their natural right, seemed innocuous in a Britain where there was no challenge to the legitimacy of the King, but in legal and constitutional fact this was not the basis of the English monarchy, and if the doctrine were allowed to gain ground, the government would be overturned as soon as there was any popular discontent. The spreading of this doctrine Burke thought, was a

---

[17] Ibid., p. 164.

[18] Ibid., pp. 171, 170.

[19] Ibid., p. 194.

deliberate radical tactic which he had identified amongst reformers as early as 1782.[20] Those who propagate it:

> are in hopes that their abstract principle . . . would be overlooked whilst the king of Great Britain was not affected by it. In the meantime the ears of their congregations would be gradually habituated to it, as if it were a first principle admitted without dispute. . . . By this policy, whilst our government is soothed with a reservation in its favour, to which it has no claim, the security, which it has in common with all governments, so far as opinion is security, is taken away.[21]

Before he read the sermon, wrote Burke, 'I really thought I had lived in a free country, . . . [but] . . . The Revolution Society has discovered that the English nation is not free.'[22] It is clear that the French example is 'held out to shame us': starting out by claiming to admire our constitution for its principles which the French now aspire to, Price and the radicals now invite us to believe that the French have realised them much better than we did ourselves, and we should imitate them. In by far the most famous of the replies to Burke, Tom Paine was to confirm all these fears by denying our obligations to any existing institutions and asserting natural rights as the basis of all government, everywhere, and at all times. His message was simple and devastating: 'Every age and generation must be as free to act for itself, *in all cases*, as the ages and generations which preceded it.'[23]

Natural rights

Price's sermon does not make prominent use of the language of natural rights, which was to be so important in the controversy following the publication of Burke's *Reflections*. It is Paine who is the most vociferous champion of them. Paine, like Burke was a polemicist, indeed a very successful one. He had already been credited with a major role in persuading the Americans to declare independence through his pamphlet *Common Sense*. It and the *Rights of Man* were amongst the most printed, and certainly the most widely read pamphlets of the century.[24]

Brilliant polemicist as he was Paine is not an elaborate theorist and only gradually refined his theory of natural rights. In the *Rights of Man*, his view of them was extremely inclusive. Men have an equal natural right 'of acting as an individual for his own comfort and happiness,' wherever it is 'not injurious to the natural rights of others'. This is an extremely subjective and indeterminate definition of right. To exercise such a right we would need to know *what* it was that other individuals were going to claim under this

---

[20] In the 'Speech on a motion for a Committee to Enquire into the State of Representation' 7th May, 1782, Burke had urged not to give credence to arguments for parliamentary or franchise reform based on ideas of natural right, for 'When you come to examine [it] . . . you find the thing demanded [the degree of reform asked for] infinitely short of the principle of the demand.' *Works*, vol. IV, p. 146.

[21] *Reflections*, p. 97.

[22] Ibid., pp. 143, 145.

[23] Tom Paine, *Rights of Man* (Harmondsworth, 1984 [1791]), p. 41.

[24] On Paine see most recently Mark Philp *Paine* (Oxford, 1989) and Gregory Claeys *Thomas Paine, Social and Political Thought* (London, 1989).

rubric, and Paine does not, at this point, go into the matter. What he does do is to clarify the relationship between government and natural right. Civil rights are simply those natural rights of the individual 'to the enjoyment of which his individual power is not, in all cases, sufficiently competent.' Every positive right, at least every justifiable positive right 'has for its foundation, some natural right pre-existing in the individual'. One important such right is the 'right to judge in our own cause' (a right we shall see Burke specifically identified – here following Hobbes – as a specific cause of anarchy). This right is one which we can only imperfectly exercise in nature, that is, we cannot execute our judgement by imposing punishment on those who invade our rights. It is this right 'deposited into the common stock of society' which constitutes the proper origins of civil power.[25] The final central point about radical natural rights doctrines as they were to be articulated by Paine is that the 'deposition' of certain rights with the civil power doesn't disqualify individuals from reclaiming them, each generation has the same rights as the first, each individual the same as each other.[26] Although chronologically speaking Paine of course wrote after *Reflections*, his views are characteristic of those Burke sets out to attack, and had already been tersely expressed in the French *Declaration of the Rights of Man and Citizen*, which Burke had before him when he wrote.[27]

In dealing with the challenge of natural rights Burke employs two main tactics. One is to adopt a Hobbesian conception of natural rights which views their exercise as totally opposed to and inconsistent with civilization and society. The other is to emphasise that whilst there may be certain rights that all humans should be guaranteed, these, far from being in any sense natural, can only be a result of convention, the artificial creation of society.

It is often asserted as a truism that Burke opposed the whole concept of natural rights, but this is false; he certainly opposed the radical conception of natural rights; but he does so within his own, fairly well worked out theory of natural right, with strong similarities to Hobbes's.[28] Man's natural right is indeed 'to judge for himself and assert his own cause'; but for Burke, this is the source of the whole problem. Despite the Lockean affinities that might be expected from Burke's long association with the Whigs, he denies that the assertion of natural right against a government can be viewed as the act of a coherent society recovering a trust, rather, it leads to a Hobbesian state of nature. This is a view that Burke elaborates a year later in the *Appeal*:

> When men . . . break up the original compact or agreement which gives its corporate
> form and capacity to a state, they are no longer a people; they have no longer a corporate

---

[25] Paine, *Rights of Man*, p. 68.

[26] Ibid., pp. 66–7.

[27] The *Declaration of the Rights of Man and Citizens* (27 August 1789) had endorsed Paine's central points: that 'Men are born and remain free and equal' (1), that the 'aim of every political association is the preservation of the natural and inalienable rights of man' (2), 'sovereignty resides essentially in the nation' (3), and that the 'enjoyment of natural rights . . . has for its limits only those that assure other members of society the enjoyment of those same rights'. (4) John Hall Stewart, *A Documentary History of the French Revolution* (New York, 1951), p. 113.

[28] In fact it seems likely that John Selden, Hobbes's older contemporary, who is one of the few people Burke cites directly, was the stronger influence.

existence . . . They are a number of vague, loose individuals, and nothing more . . . .in that state of things each man has a right, if he pleases, to remain an individual.[29]

The assertion of natural rights pitches us back into a state of uncertainty and unpredictability which is every bit as 'rude' and barbarous as Hobbes's state of nature and which even carries an echo of the magnificent rhetorical figure with which *Leviathan* characterises it:

> No certain laws . . . would keep the actions of men in a certain course or direct them to a certain end. Nothing stable in the modes of holding property, or exercising function, could form a solid ground on which any parent could speculate in the education of his offspring . . . No principles would be early worked into habits . . . . no man could know what would be the test of honour in a nation . . . No part of life would retain its acquisitions. Barbarism with regard to science and literature, unskilfulness with regard to arts and manufactures would infallibly succeed to the want of a steady education and settled principle; and thus the commonwealth itself would, in a few generations, crumble away, be disconnected into the dust and powder of individuality, and at length dispersed to all the winds of heaven.[30]

The sources of this disastrous deconstruction lie in the same unrestrained assertion of individual right which Hobbes, Locke and Paine all agree to be fundamental. Where they differ, and where Burke sides with Hobbes and against Locke and Paine is in what follows from such a right. For Locke and Paine the residual claim to exercise such a right is the basis of limited and accountable government. Whereas for Burke, as for Hobbes, men: 'by having a right to everything . . . want everything'.[31] For both thinkers man's transition to society is accomplished by an irrevocable 'divesting himself of the first fundamental right of uncovenanted man, that is, to judge for himself, and to assert his own cause', and in addition he 'in great measure abandons the right of self-defence, the first law of nature'.[32] Also Hobbesian is Burke's view of the need for a power, independent of the citizens, which can control their potentially disruptive wills. What men need is 'a power out of themselves' which is a 'sufficient restraint on their passions', which are so threatening as to need 'subjection' and 'thwarting': there must be something that can 'bridle and subdue' men's natural wills before society is possible.[33]

The essentially Hobbesian structure of Burke's theory of natural right lies in the fact that, instead of viewing natural rights as Locke and Paine do, that is as both recoverable, and constituting in some sense a persisting standard, within society – Burke regards the attempted exercise of natural right as inconsistent with, and destructive of society.[34] As

---

[29] Burke, *An Appeal from the New to the Old Whigs, Works*, vol. III, p. 82.

[30] *Reflections*, pp. 193–4.

[31] Ibid., p. 151.

[32] Ibid., p. 150.

[33] Ibid., p. 151.

[34] 'How can any man claim, under the conventions of civil society, rights which do not so much as suppose its existence? Rights which are absolutely repugnant to it? . . . Men cannot enjoy the rights of an uncivil and civil state together . . . natural rights exist in total independence of it [government].' Ibid., p. 150.

a consequence the entry into society signals the end of the exercise of natural rights and the construction of conventional ones.[35]

The parallels with Hobbes are instructive, but the differences too are particularly worth noting. Where Burke departs from Hobbes – and is closer to Selden – is in his insistence that it is the particular historically acquired conventions of each individual society that determine its liberties and constraints, that determine what one might call the clauses of the social contract. Purely rational argument cannot resolve these issues: 'they cannot be settled upon any abstract rule; and nothing is so foolish as to discuss them upon that principle'.[36] There is no obvious abstract answer to even such a basic matter as how the collectivity should express its will. Even the idea of accepting majority rule, far from being 'a law of our original nature . . . is one of the most violent fictions of positive law'.[37] Burke endows all his concepts with a much stronger historical content. Consequently although, as for Hobbes, the decline into the state of nature is precipitated by the reassertion of natural right, there is for Burke a major additional reason why this causes chaos, and that is because it breaks the historical continuity of the commonwealth. Moreover, re-entry into society involves not merely the renegotiation of what is for Hobbes an admittedly tricky social contract, it presupposes the need to traverse the long and hazardous *historical* process which, in Burke's view, must mark the passage from barbarism to civilization. If we revert to the natural state 'all is to begin again'. A people, such as the French, foolish enough to make such a move 'little know how many a weary step is to be taken before they can form themselves into a mass, which has a true, politic, personality'.[38] It is a little-remarked paradox of Hobbes's argument, that because he depicts the transition to society as an instantaneous possibility constantly available to rational men, the state of nature, whilst horrendous enough in itself, must in principle be relatively easy to escape from, once one has learnt the trick. This might be thought to lessen the terrors it holds, and its role in inhibiting the reassertion of natural rights. However, for Burke men are not rational actors, but creatures of habit. Acquiring the habits of sociability is a long, and hit-and-miss, historical process, the work of many minds over many generations. This refinement of accumulated experience, cannot be simply renegotiated: once gone, it is lost and, he suggests irrecoverable. Only the passage of time can restore it or rather, has to create it anew. So to the barbarism of the state of nature is added the impossibility of any immediate escape from it.

What then does Burke mean by the *'real* rights of men' which he claims to champion in contrast to the abstract and destructive 'natural' rights? These are the conventional rights established within society to meet men's undoubted needs. Political society was not, in his view, established to guarantee men's natural rights; it was established to meet men's needs which were far from being met when natural right prevailed. These needs are, for Burke, primarily social, economic, cultural and religious: a right to justice, to 'the fruits of their industry, .. to instruction in life, and to consolation in death'.[39] Political

---

[35] 'The moment you abate anything from the full rights of men, each to govern himself, and suffer any artificial positive limitation upon those rights, from that moment the whole organisation of government becomes a consideration of convenience.' Ibid., p. 151.

[36] Ibid., p. 151.

[37] *Appeal* . . . , Works, vol. III, p. 83.

[38] Ibid., p. 82.

[39] *Reflections*, p. 149.

rights, such as the vote, a 'share of power, authority, and direction . . . in the management of the state' are not natural rights, they are 'a thing to be settled by convention'.[40]

Religion and politics

In this opening section Burke introduces another theme that will dominate the centre of the work: the relationship between religion and politics. The preaching of political sermons reminds Burke not of the bloodless coup of 1688 which Price is supposedly celebrating, but the bloody Civil War of the 1640s when religious fanatics fuelled civil and military conflict from the pulpit.[41] There are two aspects to this. One is the fear of religious 'enthusiasm'. This was common enough at the start of the century as people looked back on the previous hundred years of religiously inspired conflict, but became dormant as an increasingly secular-minded century wore on. Burke, with his Irish background, was more aware than most contemporaries of the threat posed by religious dogmatism. Moreover he had received a rude reminder – if he needed it – when as a supposedly covert Catholic he narrowly escaped with his life during the anti-Catholic Gordon Riots of 1780. Jacobinism, he would later remark, resembled nothing so much as the Reformation: 'The last revolution of doctrine and theoretic dogma' which wrought havoc and imposed destructive divisions within and between all the states of Europe.[42] What Burke perceived and warned against was a new form of fanaticism which was only quasi-religious, and which we would today call ideological. The French Revolution provided the first example of the fact 'that a theory concerning government may become as much a cause of fanaticism as a *dogma* in religion'. Discontent with bad government can be appeased, where possible, by remedying the cause, but ideological opposition cannot be met through ordinary politics, once it has taken hold: 'mere names, will become sufficient causes to stimulate people to war and tumult'.[43]

This argument, whether correct or not, operates at the level of the sociology of belief: it considers the objective social and political consequences of people coming to hold certain ideas in certain ways. Even unbelievers such as Hume recognised the importance of this sociology of religious belief, and acknowledged the important effect religion might have on political stability. Burke, as a sincere believer, also had a second, more partisan and committed concern with religion. He believed the Revolution to be fundamentally atheistic, and regarded himself as conducting a defence of European Christianity against it, an assumption which underlies the discussion of the central section of the work.[44]

---

[40] Ibid., p. 150.

[41] Ibid., p. 158.

[42] 'Thoughts on French Affairs', Works, vol. III, p. 350.

[43] *Appeal . . .* Works, vol III, pp. 98–99.

[44] Another issue which must be deferred is Burke's discussion of the social composition of the National Assembly, this is part of Burke's applied political sociology, and will be discussed with the third and last section of *Reflections*.

A difference of method: the sociological versus the logical

Quite apart from Burke's religious commitment, there are some quite general propositions concerning the relationship between politics, social structure and belief, which Burke advances early in the work and which are constantly used as another foil to the abstract natural rights argument.

As the contrast developed with Hobbes above suggests, if Hobbes can be claimed as in some sense an ancestor of 'rational choice' or economic theories of human beings as social actors, Burke in contrast is an ancestor of a more sociological pattern of argument, and a more sociological picture of human beings. Whereas Hobbes's method, like that of the abstract theoreticians of natural right whom Burke so deprecated, was to deduce consequences from the content of ideas, and to depict men acting as constant calculators of their interest, Burke, as we noted, sees men as creatures of habit, and stresses the rational unpredictability of responses to new ideas which break those habits.

There are a cluster of terms, 'habit', 'custom', 'prejudice', which Burke continually employs to denote patterns of behaviour which are not derived from the reasoning of individuals, but are acquired as the result of a thorough and irresistible process of socialisation. However, habit, and even prejudice, are not, claims Burke, irrational. Although they are not chosen nor critically appraised by the individual, habits are the result of a kind of collective rationality accumulated over time by generations of individuals who deployed and adapted them to circumstance.[45]

Acting from such motives has two important advantages over reasoning things out for oneself, Burke believes. Firstly, by a kind of Darwinian process of selection, the very survival of certain habits, customs and prejudices is a presumption of their benefit or utility, and the fit or congruency of one social practice with another into the more or less coherent social whole we call a society. Thus the mutual adjustment of customs through time obviates much of the need for a violence-wielding sovereign to create order. The reason for and coherence of social practices is not always immediately apparent to casual analysis and may even be quite resistant to rational demonstration. However by sustaining them we enable individuals to 'avail themselves of the general bank and capital of nations and of ages' and avoid putting 'men to live and trade each on his own private stock of reason'.[46]

Secondly, even if reasons were available, Burke would rather they were not made the justification for the practice or custom. This is to do with his theory of motivation. Drawing on the increasingly common eighteenth-century notion that reason is not itself

---

[45] This idea is drawn from the English Common Law tradition alluded to above. Burke refers to law as 'the collected reason of ages', a phrase which is straight out of Coke or Hale, *Reflections*, p. 193. The work which securely located Burke within this tradition was J.G.A. Pocock's 'Burke and the Ancient Constitution: A Problem in the History of Ideas', *The Historical Journal*, III, 2 (1960); reprinted in Pocock, *Politics, Language and Time* (New York, 1971).

[46] *Reflections*, p. 183. Hume's assertion that 'reason is and ought to be the slave of the passions' was only an exceptionally stark assertion of the view that reason is merely a calculating or analytical faculty, it is the passions or the sentiments that provide motivation.

a good motivator, [47] Burke points to the advantage of having 'latent wisdom' already enmeshed in sentiments and passions – as they are in the case of prejudices.[48] The advantage is that 'it does not leave a man hesitating in the moment of decision, sceptical, puzzled, and unresolved. Prejudice renders a man's virtue his habit; and not a series of unconnected acts. Through just prejudice, his duty becomes a part of his nature.'[49] Thus even irrational prejudice is preferable to fallible reason, since it motivates us surely and regularly.

Another important part of Burke's argument against the rationalist model is to assert that what we should pay attention to in politics, is not the formal properties – or even the truth – of abstract arguments about political right, so much as what the consequences would be of those arguments being widely believed:

> The practical consequences of any political tenet go a great way in deciding on its value. Political problems do not primarily concern truth or falsehood. They relate to good or evil. What in the result is likely to produce evil, is politically false: that which is productive of good, politically true.[50]

The point is that it is not the *conformity* of any theory to reality that counts, but the *effect* that it has on reality. It is this property of ideas that Burke is so often concerned about. 'I have said that in all political questions the consequences of any assumed rights are of great moment in deciding upon their validity.'[51] Nor is it only a way of assessing theories, institutions too should be viewed pragmatically: 'old establishments are tried by their effects. If the people are happy, united, wealthy, and powerful, we presume the rest. We conclude that to be good from whence good is derived.'[52]

However irrational its basis in reason, a stable social order has huge benefits over instability. Judged by this standard, the new natural rights theories are disastrous and anarchic. Against natural rights arguments thought Burke 'there can be no prescription; against these no agreement is binding: these admit of no temperament, and no compromise: any thing withheld from their full demand is so much of fraud and injustice.'[53] Under them every man has a right 'in his own particular to break the engagements which bind him to the country in which he lives . . . to make as many converts to his opinions as he can procure'.[54]

Burke's objection is that the mentality encouraged by natural rights thinking is not conducive to sociability. If we undermine the existing loyalties and attachments of people, by encouraging them to think, and judge, in terms of abstract conceptions of their individual entitlements, which continually disposes them to adopt a critical, rather than an indulgent habit of mind towards our institutions, then the habitual sentiments and beliefs – irrational as many of them no doubt are – on which a society depends, will be

---

[47] 'Prejudice, with its reason, has a motive to give action to that reason, and an affection which will give it permanence.' *Reflections*, p. 183.

[48] Ibid., p. 183.

[49] *The Appeal . . .* , *Works*, vol. III, p. 81.

[50] Ibid., p. 92.

[51] *Reflections*, p. 285.

[52] Ibid., p. 148.

[53] *The Appeal . . .* , *Works*, vol. III, p. 93.

[54] Ibid., p. 81.

dissolved. But once these 'public affections' as Burke calls them, are undermined, once the 'decent drapery of life' is torn aside, and the 'pleasing illusions, which made power gentle' are exposed, we are back in the violence of the state of nature in which all moral duties are suspended.[55] The only forces capable of creating order or co-ordination in society, are naked power or self-interest. It is to this that the French philosophy leads: 'at the end of every visto, you see nothing but the gallows.'[56]

The role of ancient manners in modern society

If we look, not at the abstract defensibility of existing political belief and morals, argues Burke, but at the way they *work*, we find old ideas and manners playing an interesting role. In the wake of his effusive and emotional panegyric to Marie Antoinette, Burke launches into a more general praise of chivalry in a wider sense. The feudal system of manners, of which chivalry is a part, is not merely praised for being *old*, nor is it desirable merely for being familiar, although that too is important for 'when antient rules of life are taken away, . . . we have no compass to govern us'.[57] Chivalrous social and religious codes are 'the shade' under which commercial society grew. Chivalrous sentiments, manners and morality form as it were, an ethical medium in which modern commercial society, like modern learning, have developed. Burke's argument here refers undoubtedly to a discussion amongst the Scottish historical sociologists about the causal relationships between economic and cultural or ethical life. Smith, Hume and others had stressed the degree to which economic changes brought about moral changes beneficial to the emerging economic regime – exchange, specialization, and enterprise led to culture, manners and enlightenment which in a virtuous circle provided political stability and in turn assisted the development of the economy. But suppose the causality operated in the opposite direction? According to Robertson and Millar, it was feudalism and chivalry, not commerce that had began the process of civilizing manners after the barbarism of the dark ages.[58] Commerce, rather than being an autonomous *creator* of manners and refinement, was late on the scene, and heavily reliant on other contributory factors as a condition of its own development. The civilized and orderly exchange of

---

[55] *Reflections*, p. 172.

[56] Ibid., pp. 171–2.

[57] Ibid., p. 172.

[58] William Robertson, *A View of the Progress of Society in Europe*, ed. Felix Gilbert (Chicago, 1972[1769]). Although feudalism was originally barbarous and warlike, from about the 11th century a series of developments took place *within it* which Robertson identifies as productive of more polished and refined manners. 'Sentiments more liberal and generous had begun to animate the nobles. These were inspired by the spirit of Chivalry, which though considered, commonly, as a wild institution, the effect of caprice, and the source of extravagance . . . had a very serious influence in refining the manners of the European nations.' p. 57. William Millar describes how the completion of feudalism involves the regularization of property rights and the unification of law, lead to a lessening of physical conflict within society. This pacification of society is what enables the 'improvement of the arts and manufactures'. William Millar, *Observations concerning the Origin of the Distinction of Ranks in Society* (Bristol, 1990 [1771]), pp. 201, 208–9, 222.

refined products requires a pacific, respectful, cultured and moderate society. However, all thinkers (Adam Smith included) recognised there were tendencies within any commercial society which pushed in the direction of barbarism, philistinism and unstable immoderation. If these gained the upper hand, Burke implies, commercial society would not be capable, from within its own resources, of re-establishing the ethical and cultural norms which make commercial exchange possible.[59]

Burke's argument about the relationship between manners and economics is extremely compressed, but it is important and worth trying to tease out. One of the points he may have had in mind is what might be called the necessity of 'honour'. A commercial society operating purely on principles of selfish gain, would not even be able to conduct commerce – so much does commercial activity involve trust and the observance of norms. Yet trustworthiness and the keeping to the spirit of agreements are, as Hobbes, perhaps despite himself, had shown, unable to sustain themselves in a wholly egoistic environment. Burke foresees the collapse, not only of what he calls the spirit of religion and of a gentleman, but of the commercial economy as well, and as a result.

A second and more specific worry, is the possibility of an undisciplined popular government indulging itself through allowing public borrowing to get out of control, leading to the possibility of national bankruptcy, and further expropriation of property, domestic or foreign, to satisfy creditors. Either course would be extremely destabilizing, not only for France, but for Europe. Both issues (of which we shall have more to say) bring out Burke's extreme ambivalence to the free market.[60]

One important way in which Burke characterises the revolution is as 'the revolt of the enterprising talents of country against its property', that is to say in sociological terms, the revolt of the entrepreneurial classes against the landed. In the eighteenth century it was not at all odd, despite endorsing the operation of what we today call market forces, to discriminate between different economic sectors, and to do so on the basis of whether their activity was essentially productive. The physiocrats certainly gave support to free market principles whilst claiming agriculture was the only essentially productive sphere. Smith too, although he denied this latter claim, distinguished productive from unproductive labour. Thus support for free market conditions in agriculture, was not inconsistent with worries about the effects of the 'entrepreneurial spirit' elsewhere. On such a view, the role of the market within society must be kept subordinate, both as a cultural influence, and in terms of the social groups who champion it.

This analysis is Burke at his most analytical, striving to demonstrate, what he believes it is often impossible to show, and if possible, not always desirable to be shown, namely the sociologically supportive role of ideas within a given social structure. It is not always desirable to demonstrate these things, for, as was argued above, rational demonstration was not a good basis for conviction. 'What' he had asked with horror, in the *Vindication*

---

[59] For the seminal account of this analysis see, J.G.A. Pocock, 'Burke's Analysis of the French Revolution', *Historical Journal*, XXV, 2 (1982), reprinted in Pocock, *Virtue, Commerce and History* (Cambridge, 1985), p. 197ff.

[60] Much has been made of Burke's *Thoughts and Details on Scarcity*, a private memorandum written to Pitt during the dearth year of 1795, seeking, on free-market principles, to persuade him not to intervene in the operation of the market in agricultural produce. But it cannot be deduced from this (or indeed from the much quoted claim that Adam Smith found Burke the only person who thought as he did on economic matters) that Burke did not have deep reservations about the extent, pervasiveness and *moral* influence of the unrestricted market mentality. (Doubts which, despite constant attempts to recruit him by the more rabid of modern libertarians, were shared by Smith himself.)

of Natural Society, 'would become of the world, if the practice of all moral duties, and the foundation of society, rested upon having their reasons made clear and demonstrative to every individual?'[61] Much safer, and in a sense more natural, is the recourse to sentiment, particularly religious sentiment, in support of our social institutions. Burke criticizes the French philosophers not only for their ultimately shallow analysis of society, but for their disrespect for religion as one of it's major supports, and the attack on the religion of French philosophy forms the transition to the second major section of *Reflections*, in which he defends the role of religion and religious establishments in the state.

Part Two:
Church, state and political economy

Burke was a Christian thinker. This undoubted, but little remarked on fact, is central to any understanding of his thought, as his contemporaries and immediate followers in England and perhaps even more so on the continent clearly saw.[62] His commitment to Christianity was, however instrumental as well as consummate. Burke saw no conflict between the possession of a sincere personal faith and emphasising the social usefulness of religion. It was 'one of the great bonds of human society'.[63] On a visit to France he had been shocked by the open atheism of the Paris salons, and on his return home had taken the opportunity of a Parliamentary debate on the extension of toleration to condemn atheism vigorously: toleration must be extended to dissenters in charity, but not out of indifference: the perpetration of atheism was 'The most horrid and cruel blow that can be offered to society', and its propagators 'the infidels', were 'outlaws of the constitution; not of this country, but of the human race'.[64]

---

[61] *A Vindication of Natural Society* (1756), in *Works*, vol. I, p. 4.

[62] The anti-Christian character of the revolution became explicit in the Decree of 24th November 1793 inaugurating the Revolutionary Calendar numbering the years, not from the birth of Jesus Christ, but from the establishment of the Republic in 1792. Secondly in the dechristianization campaign which began spontaneously in 1793 in the conversion of churches into 'Temples of Reason' and culminated in the Decree of 7 May 1794 establishing the cult of the Supreme Being, in the place of Christianity. John Hall Stewart, *A Documentary Survey of the French Revolution* (London and New York, 1951) pp. 511, 526. The translation into English of the Abbé Barruel's *Memoirs Illustrating the History of Jacobinism* (3 vols, London, 1797) dramatically endorsed Burke's view of the revolution as an anti-Christian conspiracy. This aspect of the reception of the revolution which owes much to Burke is discussed at various points in Seamus Deane, *The French Revolution and Enlightenment in England, 1789–1832* (Harvard, 1988), and Robert Hole, *Pulpits, Politics, and Public Order in England 1760–1832* (Cambridge, 1989).

[63] *Speech on the Petition of the Unitarians* (1792), *Works*, VI, p. 115.

[64] *Speech on a Bill for the Relief of Protestant Dissenters* (1773), *Works*, VI, p. 112. True religion, Burke wrote is 'obedience to the will of the sovereign of the world; in a confidence in his declarations; an imitation of his perfections. The rest is our own.' *Reflections*, p. 269. Burke followed the central line of Anglicanism since Hooker of arguing that since Protestantism stressed the importance of *inner* belief no offence could be taken if the state regulated the 'indifferent' matter of the outward form of worship. He also defended religious toleration for those outside the Anglican Church (but not toleration for the atheism which he saw inherent in some forms of Christianity such as unitarianism) on the grounds that suppression politicizes sects 'to raise a faction in the state'. *Speech on a Bill for the Relief of Protestant Dissenters, Works*, VI,

Religion was not then, to Burke, merely a matter of subjective individual conviction. Whilst theological speculation about the nature of God or the content of religious dogma was not a matter on which human beings could hope to progress very far (and consequently not something worth contending for politically) nevertheless, ensuring the persistence of some kind of institutional form in and through which religious belief could be sustained, renewed and channelled was an essential part of statecraft as he understood it.[65] This is a recognisable issue for all early modern thinkers, identifiable as a topic in its own right, that of the role of 'civil religion'.[66] Burke's treatment of it represents a crucial step in the transformation of this topic into the modern, and purely secular subject, of the formation of political and social ideology – an irony which, as a devout believer, he would not at all have appreciated. The Christian religion, he thought has been the 'one great source of civilisation amongst us, and . . . we are apprehensive . . . that some uncouth, pernicious, and degrading superstition, might take place of it.'[67]

As Burke's rage at the Revolution grew, he saw, in atheistical Jacobinism a threat to the whole cultural tradition of Western Europe which shared religion (Christianity) its law (Roman) and its manners (chivalry) to the extent that it could be and had, by some writers been considered 'a commonwealth . . . virtually one great state having the same basis of general law, with some diversity of provincial customs and local establishment . . . from this resemblance in the modes of intercourse, and in the whole form and fashion of life, no citizen of Europe could be altogether an exile in any part of it.'[68] His account of Jacobinism as a secular religion which departed 'from every one of the ideas and usages, religious, legal, moral, or social, of this civilized world' of European Christendom was taken up by conservative social theorists of the next generation – De Maistre and Bonald in France, Coleridge and Wordsworth in England, and Gentz and Müller in Germany – seeking to account for the French Revolution – and they formed important sources for the construction both of traditions of national identity and of sociological theorising.

What, in more general terms, did Burke think, was the civil role of religion? The primary role of religion was to provide human beings with a motive for good behaviour.

---

pp. 108, 107, 113. However, Burke's attitude to dissent differed between trinitarians and non-trinitarians, and also changed over time. Objections based on the likely political orientation of particular sects were, to him, more or less salient depending on how popular or active they were, and on how stable or unstable the political situation. The degree of political control over religious issues 'depends on the state in which you find men' and 'The whole question is on the reality of the danger'. The emergence of a Jacobin threat saw his attitude harden considerably. *Speech on the Petition of the Unitarians* (1792), *Works*, VI, p.115.

[65] 'Religion is so far, in my opinion, from being out of the province of the duty of a Christian magistrate, that it is, and ought to be, not only his care, but the principle thing in his care'; p. 115. For a discussion which identifies Burke's position with a high Anglican political theology see J.C.D. Clark, *English Society, 1688–1832* (Cambridge, 1986), esp. ch. 4 parts 3 and 5.

[66] Cf. chapter IV Rousseau; Mark Goldie, 'The Civil Religion of James Harrington' in Pagden (ed.) *The Languages of Political Theory*'; and for the grounds of the controversy that still dominated the intellectual life during Burke's undergraduate days: 'A Religion fit for Gentlemen' in R.E. Sullivan: *John Toland and the Deist Controversy* (Harvard, 1982); and 'Civil Theology', ch. 6 in J.A.I. Champion, *The Pillars of Priestcraft Shaken* (Cambridge, 1992).

[67] *Reflections*, p. 188.

[68] *Letters on a Regicide Peace II*, *Works*, V, pp. 214–5. The homogeneity of European culture is stressed as a general theme by Robertson, *Progress of Society*, e.g., p. 97.

Like most men of his century, Burke believed that only the hope of everlasting life or the fear of hell fire could prevent the baser aspects of human beings from asserting themselves. Cultivated men may understand the kind of arguments he offers in *Reflections* (discussed below), but 'the less enquiring receive them from an authority which those whom Providence dooms to live on trust need not be ashamed to rely on'.[69] More specifically, the political role of religion was to impress particularly those in political office, some sense of awe and even dread at their terrible responsibilities. For Burke, as for most conservatives, human beings are fallen creatures, we ought to take care that those who exercise responsibility over others are 'infused' with the 'sublime principles' which only religion can generate.[70] This is even more necessary in democratic states. For where political power is diffused, the holder of each portion can imagine they will escape the consequences of its irresponsible use. It is highly dangerous for men to imagine they could evade their responsibility in this way, and the greater the numbers involved in an action the more likely this is, since 'the people at large can never become the subject of punishment by any human hand'. However democratic a society becomes, it is vital that it should not believe in a doctrine of complete popular sovereignty: 'It is . . . of infinite importance that they should not be suffered to imagine that their will, any more than that of kings, is the standard of right and wrong.'[71] As one way of reminding us of this Burke talks continually of the need for the state and its offices to be thought of as 'consecrated' so as to ensure our reverence for them, and to imply some criterion of right over and above popular will.[72]

Reverence for the state both requires and supplies a religious sense of its continuity through time, and this 'consecration of continuity' leads to the notion of the state's history being providentially guided. Burke here brings off a considerable rhetorical coup by subverting the popular and potentially radical notion of a social contract and recruiting it into his own arsenal of conservative images. The radical idea of a social contract, from the Levellers, through Locke onwards, provided precisely the idea that Burke wished to deny, namely that the people could call their political leaders to account, or renegotiate their political institutions to suit their convenience. To counter this view, Burke stresses the difference between the state and 'a partnership agreement in a trade of pepper and coffee . . . or some other such low concern, to be taken up for a little temporary interest.' The state deals with higher things: it was ordained by God as a vehicle through which human virtue could be realised and transmitted.[73] As a result 'It is a partnership in all art; a partnership in every virtue, and in all perfection.' Not only does the social contract deal in things far more elevated than our normal contractual activities, but both its scope and the identity of the contracting parties is vastly enlarged: 'it becomes a partnership, not only between those who are living, but between those who are living, those who are dead and those yet to be born.' 'Each contract of each particular state is but a clause in the great primeval contract of eternal society . . . '[74] Extricating oneself from such a contract,

---

[69] *Reflections*, pp. 195–6.

[70] Ibid., p. 189.

[71] Ibid., p. 191.

[72] E.g., ibid., pp. 190, 192, 194.

[73] 'He who gave our nature to be perfected by our virtue, willed also the necessary means of its perfection — He willed therefore the state — . . . ' Ibid., pp. 196. (Cf. Hegel 'The state is the path of God in the world').

[74] Ibid., pp. 194–5.

becomes an impossible task, and this is precisely Burke's point. Contracting into – or out of – a historically existent state is not, indeed cannot be a matter of choice, of will. Since Burke believes that stable political life and institutions can only emerge through many generations, if states are to exist at all it is a matter of necessity that individuals born into them should not regard either the state itself, or their membership of it, as a matter of mere subjective assent.[75] States simply could not survive if their inhabitants regarded their own membership as optional. This is as much a law of nature as the laws of physics, and consequently a matter which it lies beyond human will to change. There is, in this sense a law of nature under which no one has 'a right to free themselves from that primary engagement into which every man born into a community as much contracts by his being born into it, as he contracts an obligation to certain parents by his having been derived from their bodies. The place of every man determines his duties.'[76]

However, if this reverential attitude to the state and its history is to be perpetuated, there must be some institutional and organisational means of sustaining it, and this in turn must be financed. It is this that leads to Burke's defence of the 'church establishment'. The established church seems for Burke to have responsibilities that extend beyond religion and even the sanctification of the political order; they include the perpetuation of the national culture in the widest sense, and clearly informed Coleridge's later idea of a 'Clerisy' to preserve culture against the philistinism he perceived in the nineteenth century.[77] A church establishment, no less than any large endowed property, Burke argues, constitutes a kind of cultural repository:

> the accumulation of vast libraries, which are the history of the force and weakness of the human mind; .. great collections of antient records, medals and coins, which attest and explain laws and customs; .. paintings and statues ... grand monuments of the dead which continue the regards and connexions of life beyond the grave; ... collections of the specimins of nature ... that by disposition facilitate, and, by exciting curiosity, open the avenues to, science.[78]

However, in order to perform these functions and guarantee its survival the church must be financially independent of the state, and this can only be guaranteed through its possessing property large enough to yield an income sufficient for its needs. If this produces over-wealthy bishops, says Burke, so be it. It is no worse than having over-wealthy lords. Once we grant the need for a church property in order to guarantee its independence, we cannot allow political arguments about whether the property is too much, without undermining the independence the property is designed to protect.[79]

---

[75] Contrast, for example the speech of Mirabeau summing up the debate on the nationalization of church lands in October 1789: 'there is no Legislative act that a Nation may not revoke; that it can change, when it so pleases, its laws, its constitution, its organisation, and its mechanism: the same might which has created can destroy, and everything which is simply the effect of a general will must cease the moment that this will has changed.' Quoted in Florin Aftalion, *The French Revolution: An Economic Interpretation* (Cambridge and Paris, 1990), p. 63.

[76] *Reflections*, p. 195; *The Appeal* ... , *Works*, vol. III, p. 80.

[77] There is an interesting comparative discussion in John Morrow, *Coleridge's Political Thought* (London, 1991), pp. 69–72.

[78] *Reflections*, p. 272.

[79] Ibid., p. 203.

This discussion of church property is designed to prepare the reader for another sustained contrast between Britain and Revolutionary France. In November 1789 the French Assembly had voted to tackle the fiscal crisis of the state by adopting Talleyrand's suggestion of appropriating the wealth of the church, whilst taking over responsibility for meeting its expenses out of the national income.[80] France had thus done what Burke claimed the British House of Commons would never do, 'seek their resource from the confiscation of the estates of the church and poor.'[81]

The arguments advanced in France to justify this involved making a distinction between personal property and property vested in corporations. Since the latter were merely 'fictive persons' their rights were, it was claimed, not as real or secure as those of real persons.[82] The distinction was one that had been developed in Roman Law to allow corporate bodies to possess property, although the actual term *persona ficta* is medieval. Thus the confiscation of church property to save that of the creditors could plausibly be presented as an attempt to defend property rights rather than undermine them. Burke was clearly aware of this speech and rehearses the argument.[83] There was however, no grounds for the claim that such property should be less secure than that of persons, although there may be a shady basis for it in the fact that the establishment of a corporate identity required a concession from the state.[84]

Burke then develops the question of the nature and status of corporations into a major theme. Human lives are short, but the state, if civilisation is to be transmitted, must somehow endure, the longevity of corporations becomes a vital means to this end. Corporations are more susceptible to political direction than unincorporated individuals. The habits, property and way of life of their members render them more regular and tractable.[85] Corporate bodies are in a sense the material stuff of the commonwealth, the fibre from which it is formed, like the material used by any craftsman they cannot be made, we find them as they are. Their origins are neither here nor there, they may lie in superstition, they may be the 'products of [past] enthusiasm'; but they are, or should be 'the instruments of wisdom'. If we lose them we cannot build afresh because we have, in a sense, destroyed the properties of the material we would work with. Like the forces of nature: steam, magnetism, electricity, we must learn how to use them, not seek to destroy them. The French politicians 'do not understand their trade; and therefore they sell their tools.'[86]

---

[80] In the last year of its life the *ancien régime* was expending over 46% of its income on debt-related payments. Aftalion, *Economic Interpretation*, Appendix 1.

[81] *Reflections*, p. 204. As Burke was aware of course, two hundred and fifty years earlier, Henry VIII had performed a similar move, solving his financial problems by selling off monastic lands appropriated by him through Acts of Parliament (1537, 1540). However Burke regarded even this as more excusable than the French since he had at least had the decency to do it under the *pretext* of punishment, and by a legal Act of Parliament. Ibid., p. 218.

[82] These points were made by the jurist Thouret. Aftalion, *Economic Interpretation*, p. 63.

[83] *Reflections*, p. 206.

[84] W.W. Buckland, *A Textbook of Roman Law*, 3rd edn., revised Peter Stein (Cambridge, 1963), pp. 174, 179.

[85] *Reflections*, p. 273.

[86] Ibid., p. 268.

The political economy of the Revolution

Sandwiched in the middle of the discussion about religious corporations is an extraordinary, and self-contained passage analysing what might be called the political and moral economy of the Revolution. Because this involved the sale of church lands this is an appropriate place to put it, but it relates also to the wider analysis of the economic and social processes of the Revolution dealt with in the final section, and with the discussion of the sociological composition of the National Assembly, which we deferred from the first.

The sale of church lands had been advocated as a way of overcoming the huge debts inherited from the French *ancien régime*. This financial crisis had been identified by Burke as early as 1769, when he wrote 'no man . . . who has considered their affairs with any degree of attention or information, but must hourly look for some extraordinary convulsion in that whole system; the effect of which on France, and even on Europe it is difficult to conjecture.'[87] The financial situation had actually worsened in the first years of the Revolution through, amongst other things, the non-payment of taxes.[88] The state's debt holders were themselves Frenchmen, whose rights had been assured in one of the earliest declarations of the National Assembly. The problem, given the deficit in the national budget, was how to honour this pledge without infringing the property rights of other individuals. Many potential solutions seemed unavailable: increasing taxation was thought to be politically impossible. The disastrous scheme for an unbacked paper currency conducted by the Scots financier John Law in the first decades of the century had frightened the French from any further such experiment – although paper notes circulated in Paris, provincial merchants refused to accept them, threatening the economic isolation of the capital.[89] However, the church lands, and later, other 'national goods' (*biens nationaux*), could be regarded as in some sense not owned by any particular person, their appropriation would not therefore infringe any individual's property right.[90]

[87] *Observations on . . . 'The Present State of the Nation'*, *Works*, vol. I, p. 230.

[88] In its report to the Assembly in August 1790, the Committee for Finance estimated that the state would have to spend 281m *livres* to service its debts, and was committed to 360m on current expenditure, a total expenditure of 641m *livres*. This was 11m more than in the last year of the *ancien régime*. Modern reconstructions show that in the first half of 1790 the gap between income and expenditure grew from 18m–28m in January, to 18m–70m in September. (Aftalion, *Economic Interpretation*, p. 76–7. Henri Lefebvre, *The French Revolution, from its origins to 1793* (London and New York, 1962), p. 97 estimates the *ancien régime*'s recurrent deficit at 126m, or 20% of the annual budget.

[89] During the debate the Abbé Maury waved Law's discredited banknotes in the air during his speech, saying he had seen great piles of the worthless things 'soaked in the tears and blood of our fathers' they should be considered as a dangerous reef which the ship of state must avoid at all costs. Aftalion, *Economic Interpretation*, p. 85. Burke later compares Law's scheme favourably with the current one, claiming that Law at least built an incentive for economic expansion into his sale of bonds in overseas trading rights, whereas the current scheme merely encouraged asset stripping; moreover Law's investors could choose to hold the bonds rather than being forced to accept them as was the case with the *assignats*. *Reflections*, pp. 368–9, asset stripping: pp. 308–9.

[90] Burke picks up this argument, ibid., p. 206, cf. Aftalion, *Economic Interpretation*, pp. 62–3.

As Burke pointed out, if a debtor defaults, either the borrower or the lender must lose, but to make a third party pay is a strange way of imposing justice.[91]

However it was not merely the injustice but the political and economic consequences of the solution on which Burke focussed. The debts were not to be discharged simply by exchanging land to the actual value of the debts. Instead the scheme was formed of issuing promissory notes – *assignats* – which would be redeemed against an eventual sale value of the lands which were to be brought onto the market gradually in order to avoid lowering the price. In order to make the *assignats* more attractive they would also bear interest; on the other hand they would be compulsorily exchanged for the debt. The *assignats* also came to be regarded as a medium of exchange, a way of increasing liquidity in the economy at large, although initially – and again this hit at the poor – they were only issued in relatively large amounts of 50 *livres*.[92]

In Burke's view this was no less than an act of robbery perpetrated by the state on the church, fiendishly constructed in such a way as to implicate the meanest citizen in the crime – 'to bind the nation in one guilty interest to uphold this act'.[93] Since eventually the smallest transaction would involve the *assignat* as money: 'They have compelled all men, in all transactions of commerce . . . to accept as perfect payment and good and lawful tender, the symbols of their speculations on a projected sale of their plunder.'[94] Indeed, as Burke, who followed the debates in detail, must have known, the widest possible implication of citizens in the *assignat* scheme had been pressed by some as crucial to its success.[95] The notion being that confidence in the *assignat* would be greater the more people had a personal interest in its viability.[96] The scheme attracted popular support because it was seen as a way of recovering the national finances without increasing the incidence of taxation; but some warned, correctly as it turned out, that the temptation to print *assignats* would lead to inflation and increasing difficulties for the poor, whilst allowing speculators to make huge windfall gains.

To make matters worse, stress on the injustices of the finances of the ancient regime had undermined the Assembly's ability to collect the existing taxes while a new system was being worked out. The revenue, and therefore the creditworthyness of the regime during the transition was thus fatally undermined, with disastrous consequences for confidence in the new *assignats*. This was what Burke quite correctly foresaw.[97] Indeed

---

[91] *Reflections*, p. 214.

[92] Burke's account of the scheme is at ibid., pp. 223–6.

[93] Ibid., p. 225. As Burke had foreseen, in May 1791 the *assignats* were issued in 5 *livre* denominations acknowledging that they were indeed to be used as money, and not simply as redemption pledges for the capital of the national debt.

[94] Ibid., p. 261.

[95] Burke's knowledge of contemporary French events is often impugned. However, any fair reading of *Reflections* reveals his assiduous concern to master the sources then available, including both the statistical reports and the verbatim proceedings of the debates in the Assembly. E.g. Ibid, , p. 284; see further Locke, *Burke's Reflections . . .* , pp. 102–3.

[96] Aftalion, *Economic Interpretation*, p. 72.

[97] *Reflections*, pp. 310–11: 'What he receives in the morning will not have the same value at night' and as a result, 'industry will wither away . . . Who will labour without knowing the amount of his pay . . . Who will accumulate, when he does not know the value of what he saves?..' But worst of all since 'all are forced to play, [but] few can understand the game . . . The many must be the dupes of the few who conduct the machine of these speculations.'

it was already happening. During the summer of 1790 whilst Burke was completing the *Reflections*, the value of the *assignat* already fallen by 20% against coin. He correctly predicted the mechanism by which attempts to enforce the acceptance of the inflationary *assignats* on primary producers would lead to the dislocation of the economy, and in particular affect the supply of food to the large towns, especially Paris, leading to further instability there. He does so in a plain and easily comprehensible manner:

> When the peasant first brings his corn to market, the magistrate obliges him to take the corn at par; when he goes to the shop with this money, he finds it seven percent worse for crossing the way. This market he will not readily resort to again. The townspeople will be inflamed! They will force the country people to bring their corn. Resistance will begin, and the murders of Paris and St. Denis may be renewed through all France.[98]

However Burke was concerned not merely with the immediate economic consequences of the policy, bad as he thought they would be. He placed the issue in a longer term context, attributing a broad stratagem, in fact a conspiracy, to particular social groups which provided the social base for the Revolution, and explained both its course and the ideological means it had adopted.

The financial borrowings of the *ancien régime* had produced a 'great monied interest'. Money is an 'enterprising', not, like land, a 'sluggish, inert and timid' principle; by which Burke meant, as did many of his time, that commercial and financial classes were more opportunistic and innovative than landowners. Both forces were necessary, states must innovate as well as survive, indeed 'A state without the means of some change is without the means of its conservation'.[99] However, in France 'Those of the Commons who approached to or exceeded many of the nobility in point of wealth, were not fully admitted to the rank and estimation which wealth, reason and good policy ought to bestow..' (another contrast with Great Britain where 'money' and 'land' could intermingle socially). As a result, those who held the debt were not only anxious about its being honoured, they were also resentful of their social exclusion, and they 'struck at the nobility through the crown and the church'.[100] At the same time there had grown up another group, now disaffected, not only to the constitution itself but to the whole enterprise of a Christian state: the philosophers and 'men of letters'. Rashly cultivated to glorify his court by the 'impolitic' Louis XIV, these intellectuals had been out of favour since, but had, through the establishment of the Academies and the 'vast undertaking' of the *Encyclopedie* managed to form themselves into a corporation, or less kindly a 'cabal' with, Burke thought, as its object 'the destruction of the Christian religion'.[101] This they pursued through the long slow process of undermining opinion, monopolizing literary outlets and ridiculing the faithful, whilst at the same time they 'pretended to a great zeal for the poor and the lower orders'.[102] It was an alliance between these two groups that fomented the revolution. The literary men performed for the monied classes the invaluable service of diverting the envy of the poor away from them, and towards

---

[98] Ibid., p. 311; cf. Aftalion, *Economic Interpretation*, p. 101.

[99] *Reflections*, pp. 140, 106.

[100] Ibid., p. 210.

[101] Ibid., p. 211.

[102] Ibid., p. 213.

the court, nobles and the church.[103] To Burke it seems inconceivable that there could otherwise have been such an unnatural alliance between 'obnoxious wealth and restless poverty . . . All the envy against wealth and power was artificially directed against other descriptions of riches.'[104]

The church already contributed handsomely to the state, through taxation, and had made over-generous offers to ease the fiscal crisis.[105] But the destruction of the church as a corporation was essential to this conspiracy, not merely to provide finances for the new regime, but because in order to accomplish the violent and immoral acts of the revolution religious sentiments had to be undermined.[106] Burke identifies a kind of vicious spiral, foreseen as a nightmare possibility by Hume, in which the national debt has created a class whose interest is opposed to the stability of property and the morality which supports it. In pursuit of that interest they are driven to undermine the property which denies them theirs. To do so they must attack the moral sentiments that would normally inhibit such actions. But religion, being the strongest support for such sentiments, must itself be a target. The social strength of religion relies in turn on the corporate, propertied, independence of the church. What better, then, than to select the church's property for attack, and appear to distribute some of it as widely as possible, securing at one and the same time, the original object of the conspiracy, and removing those sentiments which might have proved an obstacle to its success? The scheme was a true nightmare, for it involved a horrid but frighteningly coherent rearrangement of all the conceptual pieces of the eighteenth-century commercial state. Instead of property ownership, bolstered by religion, providing a stable social order and liberal politics, which in turn made property secure, property now pitched the whole cycle into a maddeningly unstable set of relationships where each undermined instead of mutually supported the whole.

What often reads as pure imagery here, has a basis in reality. And the equivocation between metaphor and description adds powerfully to the rhetorical effect of Burke's argument without it becoming in the least fanciful. For example in his later discussion of the finances of the new regime Burke, wishing to emphasize the flimsy basis of its political economy, talks about land being 'volatilized', and the 'transmutation of paper into land, and land into paper'. This image is prepared and reinforced by the continual use of terms such as 'alchemy', 'arcane', 'hermetic', 'philosopher's stone', 'magician' to describe the skills, learning, equipment and persons engaged in the process.[107] The capacity to transmute land, the most stable form of property – indeed church land – into promissory notes, the most unstable, contravening and confounding as it did the most basic categorical assumptions of eighteenth-century political economy, might indeed

---

[103] 'All this violent cry against the nobility I take to be a mere work of art.' Ibid., p. 245.

[104] Ibid., pp. 213–14.

[105] Ibid., pp. 222–3.

[106] The revolutionaries intended 'the utter abolition . . . of the Christian religion, whenever the minds of men are prepared for this last stroke against it, by the accomplishment of the plan for bringing its ministers into universal contempt.' Ibid., p. 256.

[107] Ibid., pp. 308, 369, 359 (Hermetic and philosopher's stone). Alchemy was a forerunner of chemistry, famous for its supposed preoccupation with how to turn base metals into gold — a process which 'the philosopher's stone', if it could be found, was believed to be able to accomplish. 'Hermetic' refers to a secret, anti-Christian, or at least unorthodox tradition of philosophizing, supposedly tracing its origins to the shadowy Egyptian sage Hermes Trismegistus.

appear, to conventional minds, to require the assistance of the occult forces Burke ascribes to the revolutionary government. And the occult forms a (for Burke) rhetorically convenient polarity with the Christian.

This magical 'volatilization' is however, emphatically not merely an image, it is an actual process. Landed property, together with religion, form the most stabilizing influence on society because of the effect they each have on the moral qualities of those who possess and believe. But the possession of bonds backed by land has no such effect. The holders of *assignats* 'will purchase to job out again, as the market of paper, or of money, or of land shall present an advantage'. They have no commitment to land as a productive physical resource, merely as a potential for speculative gain; as a result the normal properties of land and the behaviour and attitude of those who own and work it will be subverted. The decision whether to hold land or *assignats* will be determined by subjective opinions (a volatile factor) about the changing value placed by the market (itself simply an aggregate of opinions) on these two forms of wealth. Church and property, are converted into mere speculative economic value, and this becomes the underlying principle of the political and moral economy of the state. To re-emphasise this Burke points to the plan to supply the shortage of coin by melting down the church bells.[108]

Another strength of Burke's synthesis of imagery and reality is his exploitation of the possibility of different referents sharing the same vocabulary. He consistently insinuates a connection between the languages of economics and epistemology. Credit for example is given alike to what is either economically trustworthy or believably true. The key critical concept here is speculation. Speculation is at once a destablizing and irresponsible economic activity, and (for Burke) an irresponsible and destablizing philosophical one. Both involve the indulgence of individual fancy, and the pursuit of mere opinion, to the contempt, and hence danger, of what is real. The French pursue both, the English, by temperament, 'have chosen our nature rather than our speculations' (in either sense) as a basis for their politics. The habit of moral philosophizing through discussing extreme and speculative cases serves merely 'to turn our duties into doubts', thus destabilizing our moral relations.[109] Likewise the pursuit of wealth through speculation undermines the real economy on which it is parasitic, destabilizing property relations.[110] But economic speculation also undermines the moral qualities of honesty and hard work on which that economy also relies. Economy and epistemology are ultimately causally linked for those disciples of Locke who saw that humans' cognitive repertoire must grow out of their experience. The French government too links them, they are 'desperate adventurers in philosophy and finance'.[111] The speculative philosophy and unstable

---

[108] Ibid., p. 369.

[109] *Appeal . . . , Works*, vol. III, p. 81.

[110] 'Too many of the financiers by profession are apt to see nothing in revenue but banks, and circulations, and annuities on lives, and tontines, and perpetual rents . . . In a settled order of the state these things are not to be slighted, nor . . . of trivial estimation. They are good, but then only good, when they assume the effects of that settled order and are built upon it. But when men think these beggarly contrivances may supply a resource, for the evils which result from breaking up the foundations of public order, or . . . suffering the principles of property to be subverted . . . they will, in the ruin of their country, leave a melancholy and lasting monument of the effect of preposterous politics, and presumptious short-sighted, narrow-minded wisdom.' *Reflections*, pp. 372 – 3.

[111] Ibid., p. 360; again, it is a scheme of 'philosophical credit', p. 366.

credit-based economy are mutually supportive expressions of a single principle. The French are

> the first who have founded a commonwealth upon gaming, and infused this spirit into it as its vital breath. The great object in these politics is to metamorphose France into one great play table; to turn its inhabitants into a nation of gamesters; to make speculation as extensive as life; to mix it with all its concerns; and to divert the hopes and fears of the people from their usual channels, into the impulses, passions, and superstitions of those who live on chances. They loudly proclaim their opinion, that this, their present system of a republic, cannot possibly exist without this kind of gaming fund; and the very thread of its life is spun out of the stable of these speculations.[112]

Although there is a kind of logic to what the French are doing, it is an insane logic which cannot lead to any new equilibrium; rather, the insidious role of credit will, he thinks, continue to destabilize the whole. For the payment of the church lands is to be by instalment, thus the new owners need not actually possess the funds to acquire the property which they are being sold. They could acquire their subsequent instalments from the rents of the properties they buy, from stripping it of its assets, or from extorting the peasants who work it.[113] Moreover if, as Burke predicted, the *assignats* decrease in value, yet are imposed as a currency, the state can hardly refuse to accept them as such. The state will find itself being paid for its violently seized capital, with the increasingly worthless currency which it tried to palm off in exchange for its own debts. The purchasers will have increased their holdings at the expense of everyone else: the state will be as in debt as before, the church will have lost its property in return for an income paid in worthless *assignats*, and the poor, through inflation will be worse off than ever. No one can imagine that property would be safe under such discontent, and a new cycle of expropriations will begin.

Burke offers a limited defence of the *ancien régime*'s economy, its aristocracy and its priesthood. There were errors, vanities, excesses, but nothing that merited what Burke exaggeratedly (at this stage) sees as its destruction.[114] To account for this Burke presciently picks up on the strain of austere moralizing – what he later calls the 'malignity of disposition' which was eventually to fuel the Terror and the Revolution's consumption of its own heroes as ever more 'pure' leaders disposed of their discredited predecessors. The revolutionaries are critical by temperament and 'those who are habitually employed in finding and displaying faults, are unqualified for the work of reformation'.[115] Abstract theorising plays a malign role here. Our moral beliefs and customs are never as rational as we pretend them to be, and following our moral rules or customs to extreme conclusions can produce paradoxical results. This Burke concedes, is a suitable

---

[112] Ibid., p. 310. It is impossible to resist observing that it is ironically a Conservative Government that has, over the last decade been following the French Revolutionaries in such an experiment, with similar consequences for rich and poor respectively, as well, one suspects, as the lasting social and economic damage referred to in fn. 110 above.

[113] Ibid., p. 226.

[114] Ibid., pp. 231–246; exaggeration it clearly was at the time of his writing, when a constitutional monarchy was a plausible, and the intended outcome.

[115] Ibid., pp. 246–7, 283.

amusement to exercise our intellects in private.[116] With the revolutionaries, however, 'these paradoxes become serious grounds of action'. The irresponsibility of thinkers like Rousseau in seeking literary fame by undermining customary moral belief is now become apparent.[117]

To counter this potential vindictiveness and the destabilization of the disorientated individual intellect, Burke returns to his theme of the benign social role of corporations. Corporate bodies including nations themselves are 'immortal for the good of the members, but not for their punishment'. The benefits of corporations accrue to the individual because as individuals we inherit the practices, wisdom, art or whatever it provides. But we cannot for that reason be held responsible for violence or wrong committed by previous members in the past. The English and the French might otherwise be justified in waging war on each other simply for what their ancestors did to each other. History should not be a source of quarrels, it is 'a volume of instruction', it should not be 'a magazine, furnishing offensive and defensive weapons . . . the means of keeping alive . . . dissensions and animosities'. Burke is very much aware that the historical record, filled as it is with the horrors and injustices that result from men's vices can easily be used as a pretext for more.[118]

The institutions of the revolutionary state

Burke's final section, which is more methodical than much of the earlier part of the work, discusses the political institutions established or envisaged at that time, by the Assembly.[119] Since the new constitution was not settled at the time of his writing at least some of his criticisms were, as he acknowledged, speculative.[120] He deals successively with the legislature, the role of the king (the executive) and the judiciary, the role and nature of the army, and, again, the finances. His detailed criticism of the Assembly's constitutional provisions commands much less attention today than his more general critique of the 'abstract method' of theorising which led to them. The former reveals however more of the mind which impressed his contemporaries, not only the great orator, but the painstaking worker and analyst, one who was quite capable of thinking in the kind of 'computing' manner which he so criticised, if only to indicate its failures.

The discussion is prefaced by yet another expatiation on the importance of gradualism in politics. Constitutions such as Britain's which have grown up over time are 'the results of various necessities and expediencies . . . ' they provide 'means taught by experience'. By contrast the French behave like builders levelling and clearing a site.[121] In doing so

[116] 'Let it [theorising about moral right] be their amusement in the schools.' Ibid., p. 149.

[117] Ibid., p. 283.

[118] Ibid., pp. 247–8.

[119] He announces the final section at ibid., pp. 274–5, after apologizing for the length of the 'letter'. He does not, however, begin it until page 285, being unable to resist another excursion.

[120] Burke seems to have been adding to the book over the summer of 1790. A friend read a draft in April, yet all references in it to events or material published after April occur in the last third of the work. Locke, *Burke's Reflections*, pp. 58–9. The constitution was not completed until 3 September 1791; but the decree establishing the electoral assemblies, on which Burke bases his discussion, was published in December 1789. Stewart, *Documentary History*, p. 127ff.

[121] *Reflections*, p. 285.

they make things more difficult for themselves, destroying the authority of 'any antient usage or settled law' on which they might have based their actions, creating 'sudden alterations' in the condition and habits of people. Politics, as distinct from coercion, involves the continuous engendering of consensus, 'mind must conspire with mind', and 'those who will lead, must also, in a considerable degree follow. They must conform their propositions to the taste, talent, and disposition of those they wish to conduct.'[122] The revolutionaries operate under the illusion that they can cut loose from habits, traditions and institutions which however imperfect, are actually in existence. It is an illusion, either because it is impossible, or because if it is effected, it will have the most disastrous consequences making politics, as opposed to the mere exercise of force, impossible.

Representation: the legislature

The basis on which the members of the single-chamber legislative assembly are to be elected has regard to three principles, those of territory, population and wealth. This, Burke points out, immediately undermines the principle of universal natural right proclaimed by the Assembly, which would require that attention be given only to population.[123] The country was to be divided into eighty-three Departments, each further subdivided into districts, cantons and communes: electors at the commune level sent representatives to the canton, and the canton elected to the Department, which chose the deputies to the National Assembly. So much for the principle of territory.

Burke's main objection here is one that has been heard often since: that by making election indirect you sever the personal link between the member and his constituents.[124] For elective representation to be meaningful, he claims, 'you must first possess the means of knowing the fitness of your man; and then you must retain some hold upon him by personal obligation of dependence'; but under the French system of successive electoral colleges 'they can never know anything of the qualities of him that is to serve them.' Even worse, because sitting members are ineligible to stand again, they are given no incentive to act responsibly in order to gain re-election. No sooner do they gain experience than they are disqualified.[125]

In a famous speech, given to his constituents on election at Bristol in 1774, Burke had outlined his view of the proper relationship between MP and constituency. The member should consult, consider and respect his constituents, but he should not receive instructions from them. He owes them not his obedience but his judgement, and he betrays them if he sacrifices it to their opinions.[126] This view of representation is tied to a view of the

---

[122] Ibid., pp. 276, 281, 128.

[123] Ibid., p. 289; as Burke would have been aware from reading the Assembly's *Journals*. This criticism had already been made by Marat and Robespierre, but was, for the time being, overridden. R. Ben Jones, *The French Revolution* (London, 1967), p. 65.

[124] *Reflections*, pp. 288n., and 298.

[125] Ibid., p. 305. The comparison between the French arrangements and Madison's much more subtle reasoning is instructive. Cf. Chapter V, pp 240, 249.

[126] '. . . but *authoritative* instructions; *mandates* issued, which the member is bound blindly and implicitly to obey, to vote, and to argue for, though contrary to the clearest conviction of his judgement

nature of parliament itself which is 'not a *congress* of ambassadors from different and hostile interests . . . but . . . a *deliberative* assembly of *one* nation, with *one* interest . . . You chose a member indeed; but when you have chosen him, he is not a member of Bristol, but he is a member of *parliament*.[127] The contrast here, with the French is not immediately apparent.[128] For it might be thought that an electoral college, although it precludes electors from making a personal choice of their representative, for this very reason, by severing the direct link between elector and deputy, would best guarantee the independence of the representative that Burke aims at. However, he thinks this is not so. For the very artificiality of the separation will encourage the ultimate candidates to attempt to influence primary voters to instruct their electoral colleges on how to vote. Thus whilst the method of election precludes the public recognition of responsibility, it is incapable of preventing the secret operation of control.[129]

The principle of population is already influenced by the principle of wealth for there is a property qualification for electors at each level, varying from the primary electors, who must contribute taxation equivalent to three days' labourer's wages, to the deputies who must contribute a silver mark.[130] However, wealth is also allowed to weight representation in the aggregate, in the following way. Districts are given extra weight in electing to the Department level according to the tax revenue they yield. This extra representation is not given to those *individuals* whose wealth yields the revenue, but to the *district* as a whole.[131] But this, Burke points out, is neither consistent with their principle of equality, nor is it a security for the wealthy (who need it). It exacerbates, rather than harmonizes the tensions between rich and poor:

Let us suppose one man in a district to contribute as much [tax] as an hundred of his neighbours. Against these he has but one vote. If there were but one representative for the mass, his poor neighbours would outvote him by an hundred to one for that single representative. Bad enough. But amends are to be made him. How? The district, in virtue of his wealth, is to choose, say, ten members instead of one: that is to say, by paying a very large contribution he has the happiness of being outvoted, an hundred to

---

and conscience, — these are things utterly unknown to the law of this land, and which arise from a fundamental mistake of the whole order and tenour of our constitution.' 'Speech at the conclusion of the Poll', Bristol, Nov. 1774, *Works*, vol. I p. 447.

[127] Ibid. The irony of this famous statement is that Burke was rejected by his constituents at the next election, having failed to pursue their wishes on the American War, trade with Ireland, and the treatment of debtors, and Catholic emancipation. 'Speech at the Guildhall Previous to the Election', 1780, *Works* II, p. 131.

[128] The constitution of 1791 in fact stated that 'The representatives elected in the departments shall not be representatives of a particular department, but of the entire nation, and no mandate shall be given them'. Title III, sect. 3, §7, Stewart *Documentary Survey*, p. 238.

[129] *Reflections*, pp. 304, 306; 'your constitution has too much of jealousy to have much sense in it.'

[130] Even the low qualification for primary electors admitted only four and a half million 'active citizens' to the franchise out of a total population of 26 million. Jones, *French Revolution*, p. 65.

[131] Decree of 22 December, 1789. The number of representatives was to be nine times the number of Departments. Each Department had three representatives as of right, the next third of the total number of seats was to be distributed amongst Departments on the basis of the proportion of the national population they possessed, and the final third on the basis of the proportion of the direct taxation contributed by each Department. Stewart, *Documentary History*, pp. 131–2. Each individual's vote, rich or poor, however, carried the same weight within his Department.

one, by the poor for ten representatives, instead of being outvoted exactly in the same proportion for a single member.[132]

Burke's point is that by *aggregating* the principle of wealth, allowing it representation comes to have the opposite effect from that intended. In democratic governments 'the rich do require and additional security', but by providing for it in this way 'the rich do not feel it . . . for the aristocratic mass is generated from purely democratic principles . . . and has no sort of connexion with the persons on account of whose property this superiority of mass is established.'[133]

Thus, irrespective of Burke's own views, the Assembly's planned constitution failed to achieve its own ends: by imposing a property qualification 'it excludes from a vote, the man of all others whose natural equality stands most in need of protection and defence': and by aggregating the influence of property, it failed to defend what it intended to defend, the interest of the propertied.[134] Although the constitution is mathematically clever, in practice it is incompetent.

Burke also finds fault with the assessment of contribution on the basis of capital wealth, favouring instead, indirect taxation levied on consumption, both as a way of raising revenue, and as a way of 'discovering wealth'.[135] There are good economic reasons for this: for example, direct tax in the form of import duties raise large sums, and on this criterion major ports would be huge 'contributors to the national income', and receive correspondingly larger representation. But in reality, the duties are paid by all the widely scattered consumers of goods passing through the port. A great deal of 'local wealth will itself arise from causes not local' and 'in equity ought not to produce a local preference.'[136]

The three principles of population, territory and tax contribution, are, Burke concludes, neither well formulated individually nor melded together to form a coherent whole. Rather, they are 'like wild beasts shut up in a cage, to claw and bite each other to their mutual destruction.'[137] This seems less than fair. Burke's normal criticism of the revolutionaries is that they simplistically follow through the logic of single principles. In contrast, he says, we English 'compensate, we reconcile, we balance . . . to unite into a consistent whole the various anomalies and contending principles that are found in the minds and affairs of men.'[138] Balancing principles would seem to be precisely what the French are attempting to do here. As one, admittedly broadly sympathetic historian of the Revolution, remarks of this episode: 'To bend principles or to contradict them

---

[132] *Reflections*, p. 292.

[133] Ibid., p. 291.

[134] Ibid., pp. 288, 290.

[135] This once again is implicitly a comparison in favour of Britain, a state which had avoided the financial difficulties of almost all her European competitors by three means: efficient management of the national debt, refusal to alienate control of taxation and the substitution of direct by indirect taxation. During the Nine-years War land tax provided over 50% of the English state's revenues, the excise less than 20%. By the outbreak of the Revolution the proportions were roughly reversed: 18:45. In terms of net tax revenue the figures are even more startling: 2000m:500m in 1695 becomes 2500m:6500m by 1790. See John Brewer, *The Sinews of Power: War, Money and the English State, 1688–1783* (London, 1989), pp. 98, 96–7

[136] *Reflections*, pp. 293–4.

[137] Ibid., p. 296.

[138] Ibid., p. 281.

altogether, sometime in an effort to fight the aristocracy and sometimes in an attempt to restrain or court the people, was to build a structure based on reality, not on abstraction.'[139] Burke does not see it this way. The principles themselves, no matter how cleverly combined, are abstract: there is no reference to 'the concerns, the actions, the passions, the interests of men' no attempt 'to place them in such situations in the state as their peculiar habits might qualify them to fill, and to allot to them such appropriate privileges as might secure to them what their specific occasions required.'[140] Instead all citizens are treated alike: as 'one homogeneous mass', they are pulled apart from that place in the social fabric which gives them their acquired, or second natures, and reduced to 'loose counters'.[141]

This atomization of the individual citizens is not merely unfortunate, it becomes a major issue in defence of the kind of liberty Burke championed, and, as many have since reiterated, makes possible the kind of political system we might want to call totalitarian, and which Burke, although he did not use that term, was one of the first to identify. Burke believed the individual was integrated into society through a series of primary associations, local attachments, family connections: 'to love the little platoon we belong to in society is the first and necessary step that leads us to patriotism.'[142] These connections were not necessarily rational – perhaps indeed they were necessarily not rational –

> We begin our public affections in our families . . . We pass on to our neighbourhoods, and our habitual provincial connections. These are inns and resting places. Such divisions of our country as have been formed by habit, and not by a sudden jerk of authority, were so many little images of the great country in which the heart found something which it could fill.

By erasing the old and imposing a new local administration on France the revolutionaries have severed another of the cords of sentiment that bound a people together, and to its past. 'In that general territory itself, as in the name of old provinces, the citizens are interested from old prejudices and unreasoned habits, and not on account of the geometric properties of its figure.'[143]

However these local attachments not only integrated the individual; these primary groupings, these local and the secondary associations, form a locus of power, a political defence against the emergence of centralised absolutism. Montesquieu, a thinker much admired by Burke, had pointed out this role of 'intermediate powers' in distinguishing modern French monarchy from the Eastern absolutisms which had become a byword for tyranny.[144] Like Montesquieu, Burke placed particular emphasis on the independence of the regional judiciaries of the *ancien régime* who, whatever else may be said against them, 'possessed one fundamental excellence; they were independent. . . They composed permanent bodies politic, constituted to resist arbitrary innovation. . . ..' Indeed, any judiciary ought to be so far independent of the sovereign as to be 'as it were, something

---

[139] Lefebvre, *French Revolution*, p. 152.

[140] *Reflections*, pp. 297, 300.

[141] Ibid., p. 300, 'second nature', p. 299.

[142] Ibid., p. 135.

[143] Ibid., p. 315.

[144] Montesquieu, *The Spirit of the Laws*, Bk. II, 4, and Bk. IX, 7.

exterior to the state.'[145] By dismantling these powers, and by reducing all citizens to the same status in relation to the national government, the French had prepared the way for absolutism: 'all the indirect restraints which mitigate despotism are removed . . . if monarchy should ever again obtain ascendancy' Burke presciently observed, 'it will be the most complete arbitrary power that has ever appeared on the earth'. The makers of the new French constitution behave, not like citizens seeking to safeguard their liberty, but conquerors establishing a military administration.[146]

In the meantime, the people who will gain political power from such a dissolution will not be those who seem, on the face of it, to be accorded more representation. Burke's political sociology pierces below the legal provisions of the constitution in extending the franchise. It was true that some of the poorer and middling people will have a vote, but the real power 'will settle in the towns among the burgers and the monied directors who lead them'. Those who work the land, are incapable of sustained political organisation for their very way of life 'means they are always dissolving into individuality'. [147] For townspeople, however, the formation of groups is natural: 'their occupations, their diversions, their business, their idleness, continually bring them into contact.' Even Adam Smith thought that sinister combinations amongst employers were the norm.[148] Burke sees a regular oligarchy being forged from the social groups originally responsible for the revolution and who had benefited from its new system of property: 'directors of assignats, and trustees for the sale of church lands, attornies, agents, money-jobbers, speculators and adventurers composing an ignoble oligarchy . . . '[149]

Burke turns briefly to the National Constituent Assembly, and its possible successor as legislature. His main complaint is the lack of a second chamber. Its functions would be three: foreign policy, to provide an example of statesmanship to the more popular house and to give 'bias and steadiness, and preserve something like consistency in the proceedings of state'.[150] He also refers to the likely institutional culture of the new body, which, if his worries about the electoral system outlined above were well founded, would be less independent even, than the present body.

In the opening section of the book Burke had discussed the sociological and ideological composition of the National Assembly. He had emphasised first their lack of practical experience: 'the best were only men of theory'. But the majority of them were lawyers, not judges, nor leading advocates or jurists, but 'obscure provincial advocates . . . conductors of the petty war of village vexation'. Burke's belief in the dominating role of habit in human character-formation is such that he believes it will be impossible for

---

[145] *Reflections*, pp. 325, 326.

[146] Ibid., pp. 301, 297–8 and 225, where Burke complains 'the old independent judicature of the parliaments . . . was wholly abolished' 'to bring the whole under implicit obedience to the dictators in Paris.'

[147] Ibid., p. 312. One is reminded both of Aristotle's point that in an agrarian democracy participation rates are low, for citizens are busy with their farms, and of Marx's contemptuous simile: the peasantry is like a sack of potatoes, they cannot cohere except with the assistance of some external force. Aristotle, *Politics*, 1318b, Karl Marx, *18th Brumaire of Napolean Bonaparte*, in *Surveys from Exile*, ed. D.Fernbach (Harmondsworth, 1973), p. 239.

[148] Adam Smith, *Wealth of Nations*, I, viii, 13.

[149] *Reflections*, p. 313.

[150] Ibid., p. 316. The first and third of these functions, interestingly, featured in the American Constitution, adopted three years before. See *The Federalist* on the role of the Senate, Ch. V.

such country-lawyers to rise above the qualities that were elicited in their professional life.[151] How could one expect anything but that 'men who are habitually meddling, daring, subtel, active, of litigious dispositions and unquiet minds, would easily fall back into their old condition . . . ?' Not only habitual disposition, but self-interest will prevent the settling of France's constitution with any degree of stability. For lawyers positively thrive on instability:

> was it to be expected that they would attend to the stability of property, whose existence had always depended on whatever rendered property questionable, ambiguous, and insecure? Their objects would be enlarged with their elevation, but their disposition and habits and mode of accomplishing their designs must remain the same.[152]

The second largest occupational category in the Assembly – doctors of medicine – were no better: 'the sides of sick beds are the not academies for forming statesmen and legislators.'[153] Those of the clergy – originally a separate first estate in its own right – who had joined the third estate when it broke away from the original three separate bodies, were also not men of eminence in their field, but predominantly 'mere country curates', men who 'immersed in hopeless poverty, could regard all property, whether secular or ecclesiastical, with no other eye than that of envy.'[154] Whilst Burke thought it proper for some professionals to sit in a legislature, he thought it improper for it to be comprised of them, particularly to the absolute exclusion of the 'landed interest'. A professional training was, in his view, a kind of narrowing of the mind, men

> too much confined to professional and faculty habits, and, as it were inveterate in the recurrent employment of that narrow circle, they are rather disabled than qualified for whatever depends on the knowledge of mankind, on experience in mixed affairs, on a comprehensive connected view of the various complicated external and internal interests which go to the formation of that multifarious thing called a state.[155]

The combined effect of overwhelming numbers of small minded men in high places was to invert the natural process of political socialisation by which new elites emulate the principle and selfless public service of the old. Burke was an elitist, but he believed

---

[151] Burke elsewhere refers to jurisprudence as 'the pride of the human intellect . . . the collected reason of ages, combining the principles of original justice with the infinite variety of human concerns.' Ibid., p. 193. In the case of law, Burke's preference for the theoretical end of the subject — jurisprudence, as against practical experience of it, is the opposite of his usual position. Jurisprudence — at least under the English Common Law system — was not an abstraction *from* experience but the embedding of experience. For an excellent historically sensitive analysis of this see G.J. Postema, *Bentham and the Common Law Tradition*, (Oxford, 1986), ch. 1, 'Elements of Classical Common Law Theory'.

[152] Ibid., pp. 128–31.

[153] Ibid., p. 132.

[154] Ibid., p. 134. The marginalization of the higher clergy had begun even in the election to the first estate, for hardly any bishop, not even the primate of all France, the Archbishop of Lyons was elected. Of the lay clergy the vast majority — 205 — were *curés* who voted, more or less *en bloc*, to joint the third estate. Jones, *The French Revolution*, pp. 47, 51.

[155] *Reflections*, p. 133.

an aristocracy must comprise merit as well as heredity.[156] There was this much to be said for both the English and the French civil wars that men rose to the top 'not so much like men usurping power, asserting their natural place in society'. Burke praises even the regicide Cromwell ('a great bad man') in this respect.[157] The fact that Burke could do this illustrates the distinctive character he already saw in the new Revolution in France. In the political convulsions of the past 'conscious dignity, noble pride, a generous sense of glory and emulation, was not extinguished. . . . the prizes of honour and virtue, all the rewards, all the distinctions, remained.' Ambition was endemic, it was holding out the right objects to men's ambition that was 'the fountain of life itself'. The new legislature, by preaching the rights of man and the equality of all occupations, cannot aspire to these values. The principle of emulation will still operate, men being what they are, but in the opposite way: seeking to outdo their predecessors in levelling and destruction, men will be tempted 'to enterprises the boldest and most absurd'.[158]

One further observation should be made here, although it really belongs to Burke's political sociology of the revolution discussed in the previous section: that is the role of traitorous aristocrats in deserting the King and going over to the popular side.

The executive: the constitutional monarch under the new constitution

Burke refers to the constitutional monarch as 'a degraded king'. He endorses the view – on which he claimed all the French were agreed from the very start of the revolution – that absolutism was gone forever. [159] But the French have taken away so much of both the dignity and powers of the King that he has not the authority to exercise those few responsibilities that are left him.[160] As the head of the executive he has no control over the judiciary, no right of pardon and no veto over public order issues; yet as head of the executive he must bear responsibility for all punitive acts. He is 'deprived of all that is venerable' and 'every thing in justice that is vile and odious is thrown upon him.' This is not just a plea for more power for the King. Burke's point is that any office, but especially the most elevated, is in danger of losing legitimacy and authority, if, because of the range of tasks it performs, it incurs the odium of the public, or the contempt of its own officers. A judicial head perceived as 'one degree above the executioner' is not one whose staff will 'love and venerate' in a way necessary for institutions to work well.[161] A king, he later remarks 'is not to be deposed by halves', he must have the authority

---

[156] 'There is no qualification for government, but virtue and wisdom, actual or presumptive. Wherever they are actually to be found, they have, in whatever state, condition, profession or trade, the passport of Heaven to human place and honour.' Ibid., p. 139.

[157] Ibid., p. 137.

[158] Ibid., p. 316; and 'Woe to that country, too, that . . . considers a low education, a mean and contracted view of things, a sordid and mercenary occupation, as a preferable title to command. Everything ought to be open, but not indifferently to every man.' p. 139.

[159] Ibid., p. 241, 'Upon a free constitution there was but one opinion in France. The Absolute Monarchy was at an end.' It is not clear that Louis himself was committed to this view.

[160] Ibid., p. 317, and see p. 142, 'the person whom they persevere in calling king has not the power left to him by the hundredth part sufficient to hold together this collection of republics.'

[161] Ibid., pp. 317–9.

needed to perform the tasks allotted to him, otherwise he should not be given those tasks.[162]

Burke's criticisms here refer constantly to the need to harmonize institutions with human nature. The French subordinate the monarch and his ministers absolutely to the Assembly. How can such a merely nominal head of the executive command respect from those with whom he must deal? 'Will foreign states seriously treat with him who has no prerogative of peace or war . . . ?' A King situated in this way, cannot rest content, but will inevitably attempt to reassert his position. Burke anticipates the objection: 'This you will say is not his duty. That may be; but it is his Nature; and whilst you pique Nature against you, you do unwisely to trust to duty.'[163]

The ministers too, are placed in an intolerable position in which their duties must be exercised in contradiction to all the natural propensities created by their situation. Chosen by the Assembly, in which they are precluded from sitting, they must work for the King (who has not chosen them) as chief executive, whilst being nominally responsible to the Assembly. The honorific aspects of the ministry are discharged by committees of the Assembly, thus, as in the case of the King, dissociating what Walter Bagehot was later to call the efficient and the dignified parts of the office in such a way as to undermine that authority which the latter might impart to the former. 'They are to execute without power; they are to be responsible, without discretion; they are to deliberate, without choice, . . . under two sovereigns, over neither of whom they have any influence, they must act in such a manner as (in effect, whatever they may intend) sometimes to betray the one, sometimes the other, and always to betray themselves.'[164]

The judiciary

With regard to the judiciary itself, Burke's central point of contention is the point made so forcefully by Locke of the need for judicial independence. Since this independence is not guaranteed, there can be no assurance that the legislative authority will itself be under the law. The old legal *parlements* under the ancient regime were at least independent – Burke acknowledges that the fact that offices could be bought and sold was a 'doubtful circumstance' yet it added to their independence from the government! Making judges elective is a recipe for partiality, since successful candidates can hardly fail to favour supporters over those who voted against them. Even worse, the judiciary is to operate according to rules laid down by the National Assembly, which amounts, in Burke's view, to the ability of the legislature to direct the judges. Finally, the judiciary is not only denied judicial review of legislation, but administrative bodies are exempt from its jurisdiction: 'That is, those persons are exempted from the power of the laws, who ought to be the most entirely submitted to them'.[165]

---

[162] Ibid., p. 341.

[163] Ibid., p. 322. The acknowledgement that we need to supply men with some motive to act virtuously — here, self-interest or fame — was one of Burke's enduring themes, backed by a line from Juvenal. 'The separation of fame and virtue is a harsh divorce'. 'Letter to the Sheriffs of Bristol', *Works*, II p. 41. Burke had grave doubts 'Whether it will be right, in a state so popular in its constitution as ours, to leave ambition without popular motives . . . ' *Present Discontents*, *Works* I, p. 335.

[164] *Reflections*, p. 325.

[165] Ibid., pp. 325, 328–9. The last point was of course, virtually definitive of tyranny for Locke. See above Ch. II, p. 111.

The army

The breakdown of discipline in the army is used by Burke to reveal in a magnified and prescient way, the actual and likely consequences of the breakdown of social and political order. This is ultimately traced by Burke to the ideology of the rights of man. The problem of discipline in a revolutionary army had first been faced by Fairfax and Cromwell in England in the 1640s, and it has arisen many times since. Quite apart from the fact that it was notoriously more difficult for a popular assembly than an individual ruler to control an army, it is also more difficult to impose discipline when, it is in the very nature of a revolutionary situation to 'have destroyed the principle of obedience'.[166] The Assembly has only come to have control of the army in the first place 'by debauching the soldiers from their officers' so undermining the chain of honour and obedience linking the sovereign to the private. How can they now hope to inculcate obedience? The French revolutionary ideology vastly exacerbates these problems. Not only does it deliberately undermine religion, and with it the effective motive of fear of eternal punishment, by preaching the rights of man they indoctrinate soldiers with views which make them quite indisposed to accept any discipline:

> The soldier is told, he is a citizen, and has the rights of man and citizen. The right of a man, he is told, is to be his own governor, and to be ruled only by those to whom he delegates that self-government. It is very natural he should think, that he ought most of all to have his choice where he is to yield the greatest degree of obedience . . . they see elective justices of the peace, elective judges, elective curates, elective bishops, elective municipalities, . . . Why should they alone be excluded?[167]

If the power of military appointment passes, as these principles suggest, from the hands of the state into the hands of the soldiers then a military coup is inevitable.[168] Burke warns his French readers that 'you have infused into that army by which you must rule, as well as into the body of the whole nation, principles which after a time must disable you in the use you resolve to make of it.'[169]

If the example and the doctrines of the revolution threatened to undermine both military discipline and the possibility of excluding the military from politics, then the measure taken to remedy this threat, in Burke's view, only added to an already explosive mixture. This involved trying to ensure the soldiers' loyalty through involving them with civilians in the civic festivals which the Revolution promoted. However, since part of the problem is already that of imposing central rule on the provinces and municipalities (Burke had talked about the revolutionaries having dismembered France into a number of quasi-autonomous republics) this fraternization of 'mutinous soldiers with seditious citizens' cannot augur well, for it will either equip the secessionist municipalities with

---

[166] Ibid., p. 342.

[167] Ibid., p. 343.

[168] Burke effectively predicts the phenomenon of Bonapartism, ibid., p. 342.

[169] Ibid., pp. 344–5.

their own military force, or subject them to military rule, but it will render neither the military or the local government more obedient to the national.[170]

Burke then returns again to the topic of the French national finances which we have already discussed. He closes the work abruptly, with a brief but studied conclusion. The close contrasts again the French and British constitutions, the one a venerable but solid building, to be restored, where necessary, in the original style, the other a flimsy hot-air balloon, which may be admired from a distance, but would be terrifying to ride in. He doubts if his warnings will have any effect in France which is doomed 'to be purified by fire and blood'. Finally, perhaps anticipating the charges that would be made of his abandoning the cause of liberty, Burke refers to his own career. He clearly hoped that his attack on the revolution would gain credence by pointing out that it came from one 'almost the whole of whose public exertion has been a struggle for the liberty of others' and who 'in his last acts does not wish to belye the tenour of his life.' He finishes by implicitly invoking the image of the ship of state as a metaphor for his own career. Burke valued his reputation for consistency very highly.[171] Yet to steer a consistent course we must, under different conditions, trim the vessel differently, so Burke asserted that he was one who

> would preserve consistency by varying his means to secure the unity of his end; and, when the equipoise of the vessel in which he sails, may be endangered by overloading it on one side, is desirous of carrying the small weight of his reasons to that which may preserve its equipose.[172]

So ends an extraordinary work. Despite my attempt to reveal a coherent plan to it, it is a work which continually threatens to run out of control, its own form perhaps subconsciously revealing the anarchic character of its subject matter. What saves the work is the power and vigour of the writing, which carries the reader through the disorganised and circuitous path of its argument, the evocation of emotion alternating with his dissection of political incompetence. In a revealing response to one reader of an early draft who complained about the inaccuracy and 'foppishness' of the emotional passage describing the mob's breaking in on Marie Antoinette, Burke revealed his concern to prioritize the communication of emotion over the establishment of literal accuracy. 'I felt too for Hecuba when I read the fine Tragedy of Euripides upon her Story: and I never enquired into the Anecdotes of the Court or City of Troy before I gave way to the Sentiments which the author wished to inspire.'[173]

However much this, if convincing, pays tribute to Burke's rhetorical skill, it is less than satisfying to the student of political theory. He or she will seek either a clearer historical understanding of the larger patterns of political thinking on which Burke drew,

---

[170] Ibid., pp. 339–40.

[171] *The Appeal* . . . , *Works*, vol. III, p. 24, 'strip him of this and you leave him naked indeed'.

[172] *Reflections*, pp. 376–7. Coleridge, at this time a radical journalist, supporting revolutionary principles was perhaps the most spectacular of those who came to agree. In dealing with the American and French revolutions he reflected, some years later, Burke's '*principles* [remain] exactly the same . . . the practical inferences almost opposite . . . ; yet in both equally legitimate and in both equally confirmed by results . . . He was a *scientific* Statesman; and therefore a *seer*.' S. T. Coleridge, *Biographia Literaria* (2 vols, Oxford, 1939), pp. 124–5.

[173] Burke to Sir Philip Francis, 20th Feb. 1790, *Correspondence*, vol. 6, p. 90.

or (or perhaps also) they will want to expose more clearly the analytical structure, rather than the rhetorical qualities of the work. In a systematic work of philosophy the author is concerned to clarify their principal concepts and the nature of the connections between them, in a work of rhetoric they will commonly be concealed or at least unexpressed.[174] In this sense at least *Reflections* is a work of rhetoric, not all of the assumptions made in the arguments of *Reflections* are established, or even mentioned there. But we can go some way further towards establishing them. There is enough in Burke's other work and in the beliefs and attitudes of those of his contemporaries with whom he agreed, to sketch out in broad terms the deeper philosophical assumptions against which *Reflections* may be set.

Edmund Burke: context and overview

It is common to see Burke as a harbinger of Romanticism, *Reflections* a kind of dark requiem for Enlightenment optimism, indeed one famous study described him in revolt against the eighteenth century.[175] However, Burke was born and educated in conservative Dublin in the first half of the century and his upbringing and education took place in a world not only very different from that of the French Revolution, but one in which the major works that supposedly influenced that event – Rousseau's *The Social Contract* (1762), Montesquieu's *Spirit of the Laws* (1748) Diderot and D'Alembert's *Encyclopaedia* (1751-65) – were as yet unwritten.

The agenda in social and political philosophy during the early part of the century focussed on a number of interrelated issues in moral psychology.

There was firstly the question of whether morality was possible without religion. We have several times referred to the widespread belief that only an afterlife can supply adequate motives for moral action. But the role of religion, and indeed the way it was conceived was undergoing change, and subject to different emphases by different people. There was considerable desire to downplay religious fervour, 'enthusiasm' was the current term, following the turbulence it had caused in the previous century. Yet there was also anxiety as to whether sociability and orderly behaviour would be possible without it.

---

[174] The characteristic logical form is the syllogism in which two statements, one of which must be general are shown to stand as premises in a certain logical relationship to each other and to a conclusion. Thus a syllogistic form of the natural rights argument would be

All men have natural rights
Natural rights entail political rights
All men have political rights.

The characteristic rhetorical form is the enthymeme in which one or more of the premises is unexpressed, or unargued for, but which appeals to some belief (whether true or not), which the audience either already possesses or has been insinuated in other parts of the speech. Thus when the French cast aside the 'coat of prejudice' and appeal to 'naked reason'. The suppressed premises, alluded to throughout the work, are that nakedness is undesirable, and that prejudice and custom function as clothes. For a detailed discussion see Locke, *Burke's Reflections*, ch.4, who does not, however deal with enthymeme, and my 'Rhetoric and Opinion in the Politics of Edmund Burke', *History of Political Thought*, IX, 3 (1988).

[175] Alfred Cobban, *Edmund Burke and the Revolt Against the Eighteenth Century* (London, 1960).

This is directly related to the question of whether a satisfactory account of moral behaviour could be given by the kind of philosophical psychology available at the time. There are two issues here. One is the question of natural religion: whether the *standard* of morality is in some way deduceable without religious revelation, the other is the issue of whether psychological conditioning or association could bring about adherence to such a standard.

This in turn relates to a third area which concerned the effect of an increasingly commercial economy on the patterns of conditioning and associations received by humans. To put it brutally: if commercial society rewards and so promotes egoism, and egoism is destructive of society (much less our hopes of salvation) what is to be done?

One answer, apparent in the reaction to both Hobbes and Mandeville on the part of churchmen, and to be found even at the end of the century was of course to insist on the wickedness of egoism and the absolute necessity of obeying God's commands, if for no other reason than that they were commanded by God. Another, elaborated by Mandeville, Hutcheson, Hume and Smith was to deny the premise that egoism was destructive of society, either by showing (Mandeville) that private vices created public virtues – that gluttony for example created jobs, or (Hutcheson) that moderated egoism need not be vicious, and produced beneficial social outcomes, or again (Hume and Smith) that, not only was this true, but that the very development of commerce itself, softened and civilized the desires and demands of the ego. The detail of such an answer was worked out primarily in terms of the kind of moral psychology made available by Locke in his *Essay Concerning Human Understanding*, and adapted so brilliantly by Hume. Nevertheless to many this remained a radical and daring line of thought, dispensing as it did with the need for a God to set standards and restrain men's passions.[176]

However, there was, strictly speaking, no need to make a choice. After all, Locke himself had remained a believer. An associationist psychology could be made perfectly compatible with Christian religion: without abandoning a belief in absolute moral standards the processes by which humans were to be led to adopt them could indeed involve the secular mental operations of the mind. It was thus possible for devoutly religious and avowedly secular thinkers to share a synthesis of some of the above positions, building up a picture of human nature and belief determined by the laws of mental association as then understood, even showing how the natural development of society brought about changes in moral belief, appropriate to the changes in society. Whilst the agnostic would regard this as a 'natural' process and the morality as purely conventional, the believer would regard the process as providential and the morality having a religious authority and sanction.

One further way in which the attempt to analyse the human mind had threatened to undermine religion was in Locke's claim that knowledge was '*the perception of the*

---

[176] Robert Hole, *Pulpits, Politics and Public Order*, is an excellent overview, for the Lockean versus natural sense view of morality see, p. 63 and the ensuing discussion. Josiah Tucker, Dean of Gloucester, thought it 'hard to imagine a more pernicious Set of opinions' than Locke's formulation of natural rights, and the theological objectors to the revolution commonly ran together natural rights arguments and the attempt to deploy material and secular explanations as all part of the same atheistical package, or, more sinisterly, conspiracy. Tucker, *A Treatise Concerning Civil Government* (London, 1781), p. 112. On the ecclesiastical attack on secularism see Robert Hole 'English Sermons and Tracts as media of debate on the French Revolution 1789–99' in *The French Revolution and British Popular Politics*, ed. Mark Philp (Cambridge, 1991).

connexion and agreement, or disagreement and repugnancy of any of our Ideas.'[177] To perform this operation ideas had to be '*clear and determinate*'.[178] Since many of the truths asserted by Christianity – including the nature of God himself – were anything but clear and determinate, religious truths, Locke insisted, could not themselves be a matter of knowledge, only – although this was in itself something of a virtue – a matter of faith. This was a reformulation of a time-honoured way of reconciling what common reason and sense told us with what the tenets of revealed religion demanded. For it had long been claimed that the way to reconcile the competing claims of faith and reason was to distinguish between statements which contradicted experience or reason, and what was 'above' it. What was above it was faith, and whilst we could form no clear idea of what the Trinity was, we could have faith in it. However Locke's insistence that we could nevertheless criticise articles of faith and supposed revelation '*if it be contradictory to our clear intuitive Knowledge*' of other things, since this 'must overturn all the Principles and Foundations of Knowledge he has given us' provoked a storm of controversy, and suspicions about whether his views on the Trinity could possibly be orthodox. The sceptical implications of Locke's psychology were insistently pressed by John Toland's scandalous *Christianity not Mysterious* (1696), and helped to fuel the 'Deist controversy' which was still rumbling on in Burke's student days.[179] One way in which churchmen sought to deal with the controversy, especially in Ireland, was to stress the lack of clarity and utter inscrutability of religious notions which rendered them in some way more engaging and the resulting need for faith more of a virtue.[180]

Burke is thoroughly steeped in these issues and this literature. No matter how subtle a grasp he had on the secular forces shaping public opinion he clearly regarded religious belief as an essential prerequisite for political life. He was well versed in religious controversy and his early essay on aesthetics reveals a clear understanding and adaptation of Lockean psychology.[181] Burke regarded an understanding of aesthetic susceptibilities as crucial for 'an exact theory of the passions' so necessary to those, such as artists and politicians, 'whose business it is to affect the passions'.[182] In discussing the origins of our responses to the sublime and the beautiful, Burke draws on Lockean psychology in a curiously inverted way. The qualities that excite the beautiful are the small, the smooth, the polished, the light, the delicate, all of which are, in terms of Lockean philosophical psychology, capable of being properly known, since they can excite 'clear and determinate' ideas. A far more powerful response than the beautiful is the sublime, produced by the vast, the great the rugged, the negligent, the obscure and gloomy, the massive.[183] There are good reasons why 'Too make anything very terrible, obscurity seems in general

[177] John Locke, *Essay Concerning Human Understanding*, IV, i, §2.

[178] Ibid., II, xi, §3.

[179] Ibid., IV, ch. xviii, §5. On the controversy over Locke's views see John Yolton, *John Locke and the Way of Ideas* (Oxford, 1956).

[180] An excellent context for this aspect of Burke is provided by David Berman, 'The Irish Counter-Enlightenment' in, *The Irish Mind, exploring intellectual traditions*, ed. Richard Kearney (Dublin, 1985).

[181] Burke alluded to his knowledge of theological controversies of his youth in a speech in the House of Commons (*Parliamentary History*, 21 710). On Burke's debt to Locke's analysis, and Locke's followers see *A Philosophical Enquiry . . . concerning . . . the Sublime and the Beautiful*, ed. J.T. Boulton (London and New York, 1958), p. lxxix, etc.

[182] *Sublime and Beautiful*, ed. Boulton, preface to 1st. edn., pp. 1, 124.

[183] Ibid., p. 124.

to be necessary'.[184] The mechanism through which both immense size and obscurity 'rob us of our reasoning, and hurry us on by an irresistible force' is explained by Burke in impeccably Lockean fashion: such ideas cannot be 'known' in the Lockean sense since 'the mind is so entirely filled with its object, that it cannot entertain any other, nor by consequence reason on that object which employs it'.[185] Reasoning is impossible where the imprecision of ideas does not permit the mind to perform the necessary comparative operations on them. Once the mind can encompass an idea it can be clear and so known, compared (reasoned about) and it loses its sublimity.[186]

What does this have to do with politics? Well, the effect of the sublime is astonishment, admiration, reverence and respect.[187] Burke draws the reader's attention to the political implications of this analysis. Despotic governments conceal their rulers 'as much as may be from the public eye.' Heathen religions were similarly concerned that their temples should be dark so as to inspire awe.[188] Power under our control is never affecting, but the power of wild animals is sublime because it is 'unmanageable'. 'The power which arises from institutions in kings and commanders has the same connection with terror. Indeed, in considering God's power 'we are in a manner annihilated before him'.[189] Sociable qualities are beauteous, and excite affection; political qualities, fortitude, justice, and wisdom, 'are of the sublimer kind, produce terror rather than love'.[190]

Thus it is on the effects of the sublime, the awesome and the powerful that political society, for Burke, depends. Reasoning and analysis renders ideas 'clear', 'small' and unaffecting, it is 'an enemy to all enthusiasms'.[191] Burke's fear of the rationalising philosophy of the French philosophes, and indeed of any attempt to reduce the sublime complexity of social institutions to the simplistic rationalisations of the individual mind, was one that was based on their resulting incapacity to motivate us strongly. As Hume had observed, reason was the slave of the passions. A people and a state that rested its institutions on reason would soon be slaves. Human psychology is such that only the sublime can 'overwhelm' our reason, as it needs to be overwhelmed if we are not to be cut adrift from God's providential path by the destructive effects of our own analysis.

Burke thus tells us two intertwined stories about the revolution, an epistemological one and a social one. The epistemological story is a tale about how the newly politicized classes are inadequately socialised into the political culture, how they are therefore prey to the desire for novelty – a mental property of untutored minds – and whoever can suggest it to them, how they are further undermined by attacks on their religion. This is already a dangerously volatile political situation, but it is re-enforced by the political economy story. This depicts not only the unleashing of egoism from the normal social controls provided by the church and the aristocracy but the institutionalization of gambling in property-rights (through the sale of church lands and the *assignats*) so

---

[184] Ibid., p. 58.

[185] Ibid., p. 57.

[186] 'When we know the full extent of any danger . . . a great deal of the apprehension vanishes.' Ibid., p. 58.

[187] Ibid.

[188] Ibid., p. 59.

[189] Ibid., pp. 67–8.

[190] Ibid., p. 110.

[191] Ibid., pp. 60–3.

subjecting to hazard and chance the interests and opinions that property would otherwise, normally fix and stabilize.

The French Revolution thus threatened each and all of the sources from which eighteenth-century thinkers had sought to construct an assurance that the emergence of a commercial society and a political public was consistent with political stability and liberalism. It attacked the stability of property, it attacked the conservative implications of associationism (habit) and it attacked Christianity itself. In the face of this onslaught Burke resorted to a rhetorical attempt to convince his readers of the greater eligibility of the status quo. It is, and must be a rhetorical attempt because on Burke's own version of Lockean psychology, a rational argument would be incapable of securing firm or deep conviction. Instead Burke has to evoke the existing 'prejudices' of his readers without tempting them to analyse their origins. Although he in some ways anticipates the far more rationalist Hegel, Burke's fear of the inadequacies of individual reason has only an obscure counterpart in his belief in collective wisdom. It is part of Burke's purpose to remain elusive, he wants and needs to persuade his readers, not enlighten them, for his psychology suggested the two enterprises were hardly compatible. This may explain one source of the enduring scepticism or even hostility that conservatives have had for those who claimed to reveal to them truths about society that contravened their deeply held convictions.[192]

---

[192] The most interesting exception to this are the truths discovered by classical economics, the laws of which Burke himself referred to confidently as 'the laws of nature, and consequently the laws of God'. 'Thoughts and Details on Scarcity', *Works*, vol. V, p. 100. The most provocative treatment of this aspect of Burke's thought is C. B. Macpherson's, *Burke* (Oxford, 1980).

VII

Jeremy Bentham

Introduction

Bentham's fame rests, as he would have wished, on having popularized the 'greatest happiness of the greatest number' as the overriding criterion of good law and good morals. More than most other philosophers he was successful in inspiring practical men to put his ideals into practice. He even donated his own mummified remains as a rather gruesome founding reliquary to the movement he hoped to inspire. Edwin Chadwick, Lord Brougham, James Mill and a generation of Victorian reformers in the fields of poor relief, factory reform, local government and the provision of public utilities were variously informed and inspired by Bentham's doctrine.[1] Moreover the passage of the Great Reform Act of 1832 owed a considerable amount to the propaganda offensive mounted by Bentham and James Mill in the cause of radicalism since the second decade of the century.[2]

Yet Bentham is an unlikely figure to have inspired such promotional success. A recluse and an almost compulsive writer and reviser, he was continually being sidetracked into some other area of study which had to be clarified before he could finish the work in hand. One contemporary observed that he could not play a game of badminton without wanting to redesign the shuttlecock.[3] As a result he failed to complete many works, and saw very few of them through the press himself. Indeed the book that laid the basis of his reputation, the *Traités de législation civile et pénale*, was in fact a compilation published in a French translation by a disciple, Etienne Dumont. Vast boxes of manuscripts lay unpublished at his death, written and rewritten in the crabbed and indecipherable hand of which his editors and Bentham scholars so perpetually complain.[4] These

---

[1] The ways in which Benthamism impinged on these reforms varied and is a matter for some debate. See S.E. Finer, 'The Transmission of Benthamite Ideas, 1820–1850', in *Studies in the Growth of Nineteenth-Century Government*, ed. G. Southerland (London, 1972); L.J. Hume, 'Jeremy Bentham and the Nineteenth-Century Revolution in Government', *Historical Journal*, 10 (1967) and W. Thomas, *The Philosophical Radicals* (Oxford, 1979). For a recent discussion and further reading see: R. Pearson and G. Williams, *Political Thought and Public Policy in the Nineteenth-Century* (London, 1984), ch. 1, 'Utilitarianism'.

[2] The classic study is J. Hamburger, *James Mill and the Art of Revolution* (Yale, 1963).

[3] Leigh Hunt, cited Ross Harrison, *Bentham* (London, 1983), p. 131.

[4] There is a bibliography of Bentham's work by C.W. Everett, in Elie Halevy, *The Growth of Philosophical Radicalism* (London, 1972 [1928]) and another, more recent one in Harrison, *Bentham*. See also *The Bentham Newsletter*, nos. 1, 2, 4, 6 & 7, further updates may be expected in the new journal *Utilitas* which supersedes it.

difficulties were only overcome through his sheer persistence and the immense loyalty he inspired in his disciples.

One result of Bentham's own constant reworking of his ideas, and of the role of others in their preparation for publication has been great difficulty in establishing the precise identity of Bentham's political thought. For one thing there are serious problems about the textual integrity of individual works. A recent study commented that comparison of the printed text with the manuscripts revealed that Bowring, Bentham's nineteenth-century editor 'at times seems to have shuffled the manuscript as if it were a pack of cards'. Even worse, he was, it seems, 'incapable of leaving a single sentence in the form in which Bentham wrote it.'[5] This problem is slowly being resolved by the publication of Bentham's *Collected Works* from the original manuscripts under the aegis of the Bentham Project at University College, London. However, there is another, and not unrelated problem, and that is in deciding which of Bentham's works should be regarded as representative for the purposes of the student of the history of political thought. When the works that were in fact available to the public were effectively rewritten by others, and those by Bentham were not available, we have not only problems of authenticity, but an interesting conundrum about the operation of historical influence. Bentham's 'real' thought has lain in manuscript in cardboard boxes in University College. What has been popularized and discussed as Bentham's thought has often been the work of others.[6] The situation is an extreme, but recognisable variant of a general problem in the history of ideas. The history of political thought, is not simply a matter of recovering the thought of a thinker as they thought it. It also involves rediscovering the subsequent career of that thought once their ideas were, so to speak, in the public domain, open as they were, to misunderstanding, misinterpretation and distortion.[7]

Whilst these problems have led to unjust criticisms of the crudity of Bentham's thought, now seen to be deeper and more coherent than was once believed; they do not blur the central messages he wished to impress on posterity. They were, firstly, that clarity in the understanding of any legal and political system can only be achieved by rejecting metaphysics and a commitment to positive descriptions, reducible to accounts of individuals' experience and behaviour; and secondly that there is only one criterion for evaluating or even analysing legal systems: the maximization of the happiness of the greatest number under that law. These two principles were held by Bentham from the start, and his very self-conscious career as a legal philosopher and reformer was devoted to justifying, clarifying and working through their implications. The third and final principle was a conclusion which he arrived at during the course of that career: it is that the only government with the will to implement this utilitarian criterion was a democratic one. Accordingly, to cut through the Gordian knot of the twisted strands of Bentham's literary legacy and Benthamism we shall organize the discussion around these three principles and the works which are readily available, textually unproblematic and

---

[5] Harrison, *Bentham*, p. x. Harrison's work begins with a useful and sensible assessment of the textual problems besetting the study of Bentham's works.

[6] The issue is well discussed in the first part of J.R. Dinwiddy, 'Bentham and the Early Nineteenth Century', *The Bentham Newsletter* (June, 1984).

[7] See John Dunn, 'The Identity of the History of Ideas' and an exemplification of this problem in J. Yolton ed. *John Locke, Problems and Perspectives* (Cambridge, 1969), 'The Politics of Locke in England and America.'

exemplify these principles, two of them published by Bentham himself, and one written by his close colleague and associate, James Mill.

Bentham was born in London in 1748.[8] A withdrawn but precocious child, who had graduated from Oxford by 1763, he was called to the bar in 1769. His pushy father had ambitions for him to be Lord Chancellor. But Bentham was temperamentally unsuited to the 'society life' such a career would have required. Thoughtful and retiring as he was though, he was ambitious. Reading the French philosophe Helvetius in 1769 he self-consciously responded to that author's reflections on genius with the question 'What do you have a genius for?' and answered 'legislation' and determined to devote the rest of his life to it.[9] The date of this story is at least as remarkable as the story itself in that Bentham is often thought of as an English nineteenth century thinker. In fact his roots lie deep in the eighteenth-century European Enlightenment, and his fame and influence in his lifetime was if anything greater abroad than at home.[10] He wrote letters to Voltaire, D'Alembert and Chastellux.[11] He sought the patronage of Enlightenment statespersons such as James Madison, Catherine the Great and William Pitt. Moreover he thought of himself as a member of the progressive and enlightening group responsible for the 'busy age, in which knowledge is rapidly advancing towards perfection' in which he lived.[12] And he was proud to acknowledge his major intellectual debts to Locke, Hume and the French philosophe Helvetius, to rejoice that Gibbon's first volume of *The Decline and Fall of the Roman Empire*, revealed him to be 'quite one of us', and to celebrate the Italian Beccaria as 'the father of *Censorial Jurisprudence*'.[13] Although he spent his life as a scholar and writer, he was, in the mid 1790s and early 1800s, unsuccessfully involved in political lobbying on behalf of his panopticon scheme, an experience which may have enriched his understanding of the way vested interests operate to inhibit legal and other reform.[14]

In terms of his political theory his life falls into two not quite distinct periods. Up to the outbreak of the French Revolution, Bentham was relatively uninterested in political reform. He saw his task as that of clarifying the greatest happiness principle and constructing a legal code which embodied it. As to the question of how the implemen-

---

[8] There is no standard biography. Vol. I of the *Correspondence*, ed. T.L.S. Sprigge (London, 1968), contains an extended biographical essay.

[9] Cited in Harrison, p. 114, from, *The Works of Jeremy Bentham*, ed. J. Bowring (11 vols, London, 1843), vol. X, p. 27; hereafter cited as Bowring.

[10] As already noted, the first widely influential work was assembled and published abroad, in French in 1802 by Dumont. Bentham had already been made an honorary French Citizen during the Revolution in 1792 for his work on penal reform. He was consulted officially by both the Spanish and Portuguese revolutionary governments of 1820 in drawing up their criminal codes, and was an influence (ultimately ineffectual) on the founding figures of South American politics Rivadavia in Argentina, and Bolivar in Columbia. Hazlitt wrote he was known 'best of all in the plains of Chili and the mines of Mexico'. See Dinwiddy, 'Biographical Outline' in his *Bentham* (Oxford, 1989), and 'Bentham and the Early Nineteenth Century', *The Bentham Newsletter* (1984).

[11] Even if he appears not always to have sent them. See J.H. Burns 'From Radical Enlightenment to Philosophic Radicalism', *The Bentham Newsletter* (June, 1984), pp. 5, 11.

[12] *A Fragment on Government*, intr. Ross Harrison (Cambridge, 1988) p. 3. All citations are to this edition.

[13] 'Preface' to *Fragment on Government*, p. 14; the letter about Gibbon's work is cited in Burns, 'From Radical Enlightenment . . . '.

[14] As argued by L.J. Hume *Bentham and Bureaucracy* (Cambridge, 1981), esp. p. 176 ff.

tation of such a code would come about, he had given less thought, or at least thought no determinate answer could be given.[15] He sought to catch the ear of a 'legislator', a governor or ruler capable of imposing beneficial laws on a people, although his numerous introductions and rewritten letters of dedication of the period bear witness to his uncertainty as to how this was to come about.[16] 'I address myself', he wrote at this time 'to Princes'. However, at first briefly, in 1789–92 before, like many other English radicals, being frightened by the progress of the French Revolution, and then more permanently from about 1809, he became converted to political reform, and a champion of democracy. His later works therefore focus on Constitutional Law rather than on Criminal, but they are informed by the same utilitarian premise. The shift signals a recognition that the capacity for evil of those 'whose means of evil-doing are derived from the share they respectively possess, in the aggregate powers of the government' is much greater than that of the ordinary criminal.[17]

Critical method: the *Fragment on Government*

The establishment of critical jurisprudence

The title of Bentham's first work is symptomatic of his whole output, made up as it is of 'fragments', 'drafts', 'outlines' and 'introductions'. The *Fragment on Government* is a part of a larger critique of one of the most influential English language works on jurisprudence and government of the eighteenth century, Blackstone's *Commentaries on the Laws of England*.[18] Although he selects only a small section of Blackstone's introduction for his massive attack, it is there, Bentham claims, that the author reveals mistaken principles which pervade the whole. Although the work is critical[19] Bentham's purpose is clearly also to use Blackstone's views as a foil against which to elaborate his own principles. In the *Fragment*, the full depth of these principles is often only hinted at. They were worked out more fully by Bentham in later works to which we will refer in order to bring out the implications of his position more fully.

---

[15] Dumont's introduction to the *Traités* specifically rejected the view that Bentham's legislative principles entailed commitment to any particular political form; happiness could be maximized by proper legislation, irrespective of political emancipation. *Traités* (3 vol., Paris, 1802) I, p. xvi, cited, Dinwiddy, 'Bentham and the Early Nineteenth-Century'.

[16] Harrison, *Bentham*, p. 198.

[17] Cited, ibid., p. 120. (Bowring, ii, p. 270).

[18] The larger work was the *Comment on the Commentaries*, published this century. (*A Comment on the Commentaries and a Fragment on Government*, ed. J.H. Burns and H.L.A. Hart, in *The Collected Works of Jeremy Bentham* (vols 1–8, London, 1968–81, vols 8 — , Oxford, 1981 — [continuing]); hereafter referred to as *Collected Works*. Volumes are not numbered. They are cited here by individual title and editor. Blackstone was not only a respected authority in England, his work was the second most cited title (after Montesquieu's *The Spirit of the Laws*) in the debates on Independence and the Constitution in Revolutionary America. See Donald S.Lutz, 'The Relative Influence of European Writers in Late-Eighteenth Century American Political Thought' *American Political Science Review*, 78 (1984).

[19] 'The chief employment of this Essay, . . . has necessarily been *to overthrow.*' *Fragment on Government*, p. 31.

The two related conceptual issues which Bentham is concerned to press in the work are the importance of maintaining a distinction between descriptive and critical juris- prudence and, as one condition of that, the importance of absolute clarity of analysis. His attack on Blackstone's use of natural law and natural right (itself an odd target since Blackstone's reference to it was fairly adventitious in the context of a largely descriptive work of English Common Law) was an attack both on the propensity to mix description and justification, and on the lack of clarity which in Bentham's view was entailed by the language of natural jursiprudence.

There is to modern readers a certain oddity in Bentham's insistence on the distinction between descriptive and critical – or what he calls 'censorial' – jurisprudence, in modern terms, the distinction between factual and evaluative statements. To recover Bentham's target, we must remember the nature and pervasiveness of the English Common Law, and the prescriptive mentality which it was Blackstone's purpose to illustrate and extol. The essence of Common Law was precedent. What must be understood is the way precedent functioned *both* as a means of identifying what the law was, *and* as a means of justifying the law. In Common Law preceding judgments were seen as expressions of other preceding judgments which were claimed ultimately to derive from custom.[20] The identification of relevant precedent, rather than the application of appropriate statute was therefore seen as the paradigmatic judicial act. Correct identification of precedent determined what the law was. But it also, in a legal system, and indeed in a culture, based on what Burke delighted in calling the Englishman's 'constant prepossession with antiquity' constituted a justification. For the *assumption* simply was that oldest was best. To demonstrate the (factual) antiquity of a law, was, in a precedent based culture, itself to justify its perpetuation.[21] Blackstone's 'professed object was to explain to us what the Laws of England *were*'.[22] Whilst this is, for Bentham a far inferior task than the work of critical jurisprudence, it is, in its own limited way, perfectly respectable. What incensed Bentham was that Blackstone furtively passed beyond description and 'by oblique glances and sophistical glosses, he studies to guard from reproach, or recommend to favour, what he knows not how, and dares not attempt to justify . . . not content with this humbler function, he attempts to give *reasons* in behalf of it. . . . For the very idea of a reason betokens approbation . . . '[23] To explain the origins of a thing, is, in a way, and certainly in the context of Common Law, to justify it, and it is precisely this kind of conflation of the positive and evaluative that Bentham is out to detect and destroy. So much is a commonplace; but it is far less clear to the modern reader why this should have been such a radical move. Only appreciation of the precedential nature of the Common Law that was Bentham's target highlights the nature of the conflict.

---

[20] See J.G.A. Pocock 'The Common Law Mind' in *The Ancient Constitution and the Feudal Law*, (2nd edn. Cambridge, 1987). There is an excellent historical and analytical discussion in G. Postema *Bentham and the Common Law Tradition* (Oxford, 1986), Ch. I, passim.

[21] Sometimes there was, as in Burke, a hint at a utilitarian justification in that the very survival of practices and laws was held to be a presumption of their utility. However this would be so only if their perpetuation was accompanied by a critical rather than precedent-dominated mentality. For custom to be justified as a utilitarian filter it has, ironically, not to have been followed over-reverently or – as Burke claimed it should be – for its own sake.

[22] *Fragment on Government*, p. 8.

[23] Ibid., p. 9.

In the preface Bentham points out the paradoxes of this idealization of precedent and rejection of innovation. Not only was 'Whatever *now* is established, *once* ... innovation' but because of our misguided reverence for the past, the institutions and laws we have perpetuated are those that originated when the human intellect was at its most primitive: in 'a desolate and abject state'. In his later mocking *Book of Fallacies*, Bentham identifies this as one of the major categories of political deception, calling it the 'Wisdom of our Ancestors, or Chinese Argument'.[24] Characteristically, and in a self-consciously Lockean move, Bentham thinks it important to expose the role of indistinct ideas in explaining the plausibility of the argument. This hinges on an equivocation in the meaning of 'old'. Whilst an old *individual* may have more experience than a young, an older period of *history* must have less. The 'wisdom of our ancestors' then, 'as their talents could only be developed in proportion to the state of knowledge at the period in which they lived' must, in terms of the life of the species, be 'the wisdom of the cradle' and it is therefore 'absurd to rely on their authority, at a period and under a state of things altogether different'.[25]

This is a crucial radical argument. It identifies Bentham as a direct opponent of Burke, and as a characteristic figure of the Enlightenment, committed not only to the emblematic substitution of reason for custom, but also to a broadly Enlightenment historiography in which clarity and reason progressively banish superstition and ignorance.[26] As in the progress of the Enlightenment itself, Bentham at first simply assumed without explanation, the existence of superstition, and that the very act of intellectual clarification would evaporate it: his task, he wrote, 'was to help [the reader] emancipate his judgment from the shackles of authority'.[27] Eventually, however, as we shall see, Bentham, like other later Enlightenment thinkers, found that the resistance to its message required other, deeper explanations for the persistence of irrationalism, explanations which invoked malign and sinister interests in places of power. The desire to explain and overcome such irrationality pushed Bentham, as it did others, both towards psychology, and in the direction of democratic politics.

Within the Common Law environment, then, Bentham's emphasis on the descriptive – evaluative distinction was clearly radical. But the obscuring of this distinction was only one source of the confusion which Bentham sought to dispel. There were two other major sources, one revealed in Blackstone's organization of his material, and the other in his account of the nature of government and obligation.

---

[24] This was prepared from Bentham's manuscripts by a lawyer in his circle, Peregrine Bingham. The most accessible edition is published as a *Handbook of Political Fallacies*, ed. Crane Brinton (New York, 1962), see 'The Wisdom of Our Ancestors', ch. 2.

[25] Ibid., pp. 44–5.

[26] *Fragment on Government*, pp. 12–13. Reasoned criticism poses no threat to the laws. But the suppression of it produces 'a passive and enervate race, ready to swallow anything, and to acquiesce in anything: with intellects incapable of distinguishing right from wrong, and with affections alike indifferent to either: insensible, short-sighted, obstinate: lethargic, yet liable to be driven into convulsions by false terrors: deaf to the voice of reason and public utility: obsequious only to the whisper of interest and to the beck of power.' Such, according to Bentham, are the common lawyers.

[27] Ibid., p. 126. He later wrote in his own copy of the work that it was 'the very first publication by which men at large were invited to break loose from the trammels of authority and ancestor-wisdom in the field of law.' Cited Harrison, 'Introduction' to *A Fragment on Government*, p. vi.

The principles of classification

The first was the problem of classification. Classification, and the coining of neologisms were to become something of an obsession with Bentham. Yet he rightly claimed that the progress of science presupposed the capacity correctly to classify its material. A major hindrance to the development of a scientific jurisprudence was the disordered state of the law, an 'immense and unsorted heap'. Trying to get a training in the law was, he said, in a memorable if pungent image, like wallowing about in a night-soil cart.[28] To overcome this, wrote Bentham

> I know of but one remedy; and that is by *Definition* , perpetual and regular definition
> . . . which explains terms less familiar by terms more familiar, terms more abstract by
> terms less abstract, terms with a larger assemblage of simple ideas belonging to them,
> by terms with an assemblage less extensive.[29]

Like other Enlightenment social theorists, Bentham was impressed with the progress of the natural sciences; like Hume, whom he so much admired, he sought to emulate the great Newton. But he also praised the Swedish naturalist and botanist Carl Linnaeus, whose classification system helped organize the increasing amount of empirical knowledge being collected in the field of natural history. However Linnaeus' system of classification, inherited from Aristotle, involved division 'per genus et differentiam'. That is by specifying the larger category, and then identifying the particular characteristics of the sub-category. At the lowest level this involved specifying what differentiated a species from other members of its genus; at the higher level what differentiated say, an order from a class. Thus chimpanzees are a species differentiated from other great apes, whilst at a higher level of generality the class of mammals is subdivided into primates (apes, monkeys and prosimians) and, amongst others, cetaceans (whales and dolphins) and ungulates (hoofed animals). This form of classification, however, will not work for abstract ideas, for they are not hierarchically related, have no common genus, and therefore cannot be used to create an exhaustive and mutually exclusive classification.[30] It cannot therefore be applied to the subject matter of law or government, comprising as it does, a mass of abstractions.

In the *Introduction to the Principles of Morals and Legislation*, Bentham is more explicit about the kind of categorization which he thinks will work: and that is the method of bifurcation (interestingly exemplified in the first nine chapters of Machiavelli's *Prince*). Bifurcation involves the successive division into two (and only two) of any large whole to be categorized. (Classification *per genus et differentiam* allows as many sub-categories in each class as seem to be relevant). Bentham gives a reason for thinking the method of bifurcation more generally successful than that of *species* and *genus*, a reason which is also illustrative of his materialist, even mechanical, conception of the

---

[28] Cited Harrison, ibid., p. vi.

[29] From a 'Draft Preface', Appendix B, ibid., p. 123.

[30] Bentham, *Introduction to the Principles of Morals and Legislation*, ed. J.H. Burns and H.L.A. Hart (London, 1970), p. 53, note 1 (to page 52); and *Fragment on Government*, p. 108, note 7.

mind. It is that there are 'but two objects that the mind can compare together at exactly the same time.'[31] There is therefore a general psychological reason why one particular logical system works better than another, as well as an argument that bifurcation is better suited to abstract topics.

But a system of classification requires not merely a formal structure, it requires principles of distinction to be applied to that structure. Blackstone had organized his subject matter in a technical arrangement, that is, according to the technical language and distinctions developed within English Common and Civil law.[32] But to assume the adequacy of this would beg the whole question of the relationship of the English system to a scientific jurisprudence. More especially, Bentham stresses, it would allow the persistence of categories and terms which may have no precise meaning at all, a worry which will have to wait until we get to Bentham's theory of meaning and fictions.

Instead of the 'technical' arrangement of English law, deriving in fact from its haphazard and accidental growth, Bentham proposes what he calls a 'natural arrangement'. By this he means an arrangement which uses 'criteria which men in general are, by the common constitution of man's *nature*, disposed to attend to'. Like Hume, Bentham is using what he takes to be a natural property of the mind as the empirical basis for his science. The natural property of an action, which Bentham claims we are most likely to attend to, is the tendency it has to promote or diminish happiness.[33] This is, of course, one guise of the principle of utility, which has already been announced in the preface.[34] A full consideration of this principle will have to wait until Bentham's discussion of it in the *Introduction to the Principles of Morals and Legislation*; it here has the status of an empirical observation as to the quality in actions that most strikes the attention, and therefore, in a Humean sense, is the most natural principle of analysis.[35]

Bentham's explanation of the application of this principle, needs careful attention, for it seems to render him guilty of what he had imputed to Blackstone, namely the confusion of description and evaluation. Using the principle of utility, he claims, legal institutions would be characterized in terms of the kinds of offences they prohibit, and offences in turn according to the kind and extent of pains they cause.[36] Such a classification would immediately expose laws which penalized behaviour that caused no pain; and which therefore, ought not to be criminal. The classification derived from utility would, he claims 'at once be a compendium of *expository* and of *censorial* Jurisprudence . . . a

---

[31] *Principles of Morals and Legislation*, p. 187, note a.

[32] English law comprised, for the most part Common Law which was largely customary and peculiar to England. However some parts of her legal system derived from Roman Law, areas originally dealt with by Church (Cannon) Law for example such as divorce or probate, or those concerning relationships with foreigners which had to conform to the law of nations, such as certain areas of trade and laws applying at sea. Roman Law was generally referred to as 'civil law', i.e. the law of the civilians, or the commentators on Roman Law.

[33] *Fragment on Government*, pp. 25–6.

[34] On page one Bentham had announced as an 'incompletely noticed' 'matter of fact', the axiom that '*it is the greatest happiness of the greatest number that is the measure of right and wrong*'. Ibid., p. 3.

[35] Again, ibid., p. 28, 'the only consequences (of Laws) that men are at all interested in, what are they but *pain* and *pleasure*?'

[36] Bentham attempts to carry this out in Chapter XVI of the *Principles of Morals and Legislation*, 'Division of Offences', see below.

map . . . of Jurisprudence as it *is*, and a slight but comprehensive sketch of what it ought to be.'[37]

The criticism of legal fictions and Bentham's theory of 'fictions'

One aspect of the system Bentham is beginning to oppose to Blackstone's is his preference for categories or principles which are empirically verifiable in some way. In his argument about classification systems he chooses methods – bifurcation – and criteria – the principle of utility – which rely on what he takes to be empirical properties of human psychology. This stress on empirical verification becomes a mainstay of his method and is developed further in his attack on the final major source of confusion he sees in Blackstone, that is Blackstone's uncritical use of fictions.

At an obvious level Bentham's analysis exposes the illogicality of Blackstone's argument and the equivocation amongst his terms, how he uses 'society' sometimes to mean what existed before government, and sometimes to mean government itself, how he seems both to believe, and disbelieve in a literal state of nature, how Blackstone quite wrongly regards the familial origin of society to be inconsistent with a contractual one (despite endorsing both). Exasperated, he concludes: 'what distresses me is not the meeting with any positions, such as, thinking them false, I can find a difficulty in proving them so: but the not meeting with any positions, true or false (unless it be a self-evident one,) that I can find a meaning for.'[38]

But there lies behind this rather knockabout demolition of poor Blackstone, the elements of a more general and theoretically sophisticated critique of legal and political language which centres on the exposure of legal fictions.

One prominent and fairly obvious fiction which Bentham set out to expose was the idea of the social contract. Finding that its defenders acknowledged it was not a historical fact, but a fiction designed to 'reconcile the accidental necessity of resistance with the general duty of submission'. Bentham points out the absurdity of the move: 'Indulge yourself in the license of supposing that to be true which is not, and as well may you suppose that proposition itself to be true, which you wish to prove, as that other whereby you hope to prove it.'[39] Bentham rehearses Hume's argument that to rest political obedience on contract begs the question of the basis of contracts. If promise- keeping is justified on the grounds of utility (as it must be), why then, not ground obligation itself directly on utility, rather than on a promise, especially when there hadn't ever been one![40] Moreover, even if there had, potential resistors of delinquent rulers would still have to judge whether they had ruled in accordance with their happiness, i.e. with utility, since what else could the promise have been about?[41] Talk about a social contract simply puts off having to deal with the issue of utility.

In one sense the social contract is a simple falsehood. It is however a kind that recurs in social life. Bentham blamed much of the confusion in English law on fictions, whose 'pestilential breath . . . poisons the sense of every instrument it comes near.'[42] However fictions have a general structure which must be understood, for they are widespread

---

[37] *Fragment on Government*, p. 27.
[38] Ibid., pp. 36–50, 50.
[39] Ibid., p. 52, note.

[40] Ibid., p. 55.
[41] Ibid., p. 54.
[42] Ibid., p. 21, note r.

linguistic phenomena and are even, Bentham later came to argue, in some sense, necessary.[43] Although the assertion of a social contract was literally untrue (for there was no agreement between people and rulers), the fact that it could be reduced to an argument about utility, showed in a way that there was something for it to be about (it was about making rulers rule for the people's happiness). Moreover there is an explanation as to how the fiction of a social contract came about which has its roots in men's experience. Men *experienced* promises being kept and hence neglected to enquire into their basis.[44] This experience thus formed the basis for a reasonable fiction designed to keep kings in order. Fictions, even indefensible ones, thus have a basis in reality.[45] The real question is then, what distinguishes the defensible ones? To answer this we must go a little deeper into Bentham's epistemological foundations which he only fully develops later and of which there are but hints in the *Fragment*.

Bentham was self-consciously an intellectual heir of Locke, and more particularly of Locke's more materialist French disciples such as Helvetius. Every idea which can be made clear and distinct must, he thought, derive from experience either of the senses, or the emotions.[46] Bentham was fairly unequivocal that the sources of such sensory ideas were corporeal, that is material objects.[47] However he realized that science no less than speech would be impossible if speech were restricted to material objects. For one thing, classificatory terms, even informal ones such as general nouns, would be impossible; but furthermore so would the abstract and relational terms that we take so much for granted – motion, rest, etc.[48] Bentham here occupies a position on a line of development from Hobbes to Kant. Hobbes, with whom Bentham has much in common (and whom

[43] The invention of fictitious entities 'is a contrivance, but for which language, or, at any rate, language in any form superior to that of the language, of the brute creation, could not have existence'. *Fragment on Ontology*, Bowring, vol. viii, cited *Bentham's Political Thought*, ed. Bikhu Parekh (London, 1973), p.46. See also, fictitious entities are 'objects, which in every language must, for the purposes of discourse, be spoken of as existing'. (*Fragment on Ontology*, cited Harrison, *Bentham*, p. 83.).

[44] *Fragment on Government*, p. 53: ' The observance of promises they had been accustomed to see pretty constantly enforced. They had been accustomed to see Kings, as well as others, behave themselves as if bound by them. This proposition then, 'that men are bound by *compacts*' . . . were propositions which no man had any call to prove.'

[45] Parekh, *Bentham's Political Thought*, p. 46, 'Every fictitious entity bears some relation to some real entity', (from *Fragment on Ontology*).

[46] Ibid., p. 45 'A perceptible entity is every entity the existence of which is made known to human and other beings by the testimony of one or more senses' (from *Fragment on Ontology*); and *Fragment on Government*, p. 108, n.6.

[47] *Of Laws in General* ' . . . the only objects which have any real existence are those which are corporeal . . . that which is styled a corporeal object is one single and entire corporeal thing.' *Of Laws in General*, ed. H.L.A. Hart (*Collected Works*), p. 284. The issue is clouded, but not I believe, irretrievably so, by Bentham's claim that our perception of our ideas 'is still more direct and immediate than that which we have of corporeal substances.' (*Fragment on Ontology*, Bowring, vol. viii, p. 196 — I am grateful to John Dinwiddy for supplying this reference.) Not irretrievably so, at least from the point of view of Bentham's utilitarianism, because, of all our 'psychological entities', our ideas of pain and pleasure are both the most immediate and indubitable — 'a matter of universal and constant experience' — and the source of all others — 'without these no . . . others ever had . . . existence'. *Deontology, and A Table of the Springs of Action*, ed. Amnon Goldworth (Oxford, 1983, *Collected Works*), p. 98, and in part in Parekh, *Bentham's Political Thought*, p. 62.

[48] Parekh, *Bentham's Political Thought*, pp. 47, 46 (*Fragment on Ontology*).

Bentham acknowledges as an influential predecessor)[49] also recognized that relational words could not be expressed in terms of material objects, and was reduced to calling them 'phantasms'. For Kant, however, such ideas as space and time have virtually overtaken the objects of perception in the ontological stakes. They have a reality which, whilst inferential, is not merely grounded in our experience but is the very condition of it. Bentham's position is an intermediate one. For him time is a 'physical fictitious entity'.[50] The use of fictions 'is a contrivance, but for which language . . . could not have existence.' Our minds for example are such that we can give no account of its content 'otherwise than by speaking of it as if it were a portion of space, with portions of matter, some of them at rest, others moving within it.'[51] As with Hobbes, the paradigm of a mechanical, material world is overwhelming, although Bentham recognizes that this paradigm creates for the mind, a mode of thinking and talking which whilst it imitates, does not stand in a one-to-one relationship with that reality. A fictitious entity is then, 'an entity to which, though by the grammatical form of the discourse employed in speaking of it, existence be ascribed, yet in truth and reality existence is not meant to be ascribed.'[52] Fictions are indispensable, if potentially dangerous aspects of human language.

We can now return to Bentham's earlier critique of law: most legal and political terms are in fact fictions, for they do not directly denote perceptible entities. English law made extensive use of fictions since the widespread adaptation of procedures and actions to areas different from their original one led to numerous 'conventional' uses of them which bore no relation to their reality. Thus the notion of 'legal personality' enabled corporations to be treated as persons, accorded rights, own property etc. In politics various offices were filled in order to reward supporters, and not for them to perform the (redundant) tasks to which they originally related.[53] However, not all fictions were pernicious or nonsensical, and one test is whether they can be redescribed in terms of perceptible entities.

'Political Society' is an obviously abstract term, as is 'duty', but both of these, Bentham insists, can be expressed in the form of propositions which denote experiencable situations. Thus a 'Political Society' can be said to exist 'where a number of persons (whom we may style *subjects*) are supposed to be in the *habit* of paying *obedience* to a person, or an assemblage of persons, of a known and certain description (whom we may call *governor* or *governors*).'[54] The terms in this definition are all, Bentham would insist, perceptible entities: 'persons', 'habits' (an assemblage of acts), 'obedience' (act done in

---

[49] 'The philosopher of Malmesbury' had, according to Bentham only just failed to make the breakthrough to a positivist theory of law. The passage he cites, is interestingly, one of those that most modern commentators believe shows Hobbes to have succeeded! See *A Comment on the Commentaries*, p. 13, fn.d.

[50] Parekh, *Bentham's Political Thought*, p. 49 (*Fragment on Ontology*).

[51] Ibid., p. 47.

[52] Ibid., p. 45.

[53] Again in the *Handbook of Political Fallacies* Bentham parodies (but not by much) the 'Particular Demand for Fallacies under the English Constitution' where we find 'deaf auditors of the Exchequer . . . blind surveyors of melting irons, non-registering registrars of the Admiralty Court..' etc. *Political Fallacies*, p. 246.

[54] *Fragment on Government*, p. 40.

pursuance of an express will on the part of the person governing), are all susceptible of experience, and thus not fictions.[55]

In the case of 'duty', a duty is that 'which you (or some other person or persons) have a *right* to have me made to do' and to be subject to a right in turn means 'I am liable, according to law, upon a requisition made on your behalf, to be punished for not doing [it]' and to be punished is 'to be subject to a pain'.[56] It is for these reasons that it is nonsense to talk, as Blackstone does, about the 'duties' of the supreme political power in a state. Thus duty, power, right, government and other such fictions, are 'a kind of allegory: a riddle', 'a sort of paper currency', which, must be unpacked in terms, either of perceptible entities, or else in terms of other fictions (rights) which can in turn be converted to perceptible entities, that is of persons, actions, consequences, feelings etc.[57] The crucial point is that the paper currency of fictions must *stand for* something, it must be convertible, or it is unreal and worthless, as Bentham clearly thought most of the legal and political discourse of his day was.

However we must not attribute to Bentham too crude a representationalist theory of meaning. This act of conversion – paraphrasis – as he called it, was an operation that applied not so much to words as to propositions.[58] Whilst Bentham wants to insist that language depicts a state of physical affairs in the world, he is not committed to the view that individual words, stand for irreducible components of it. Rather the unit of understanding is the proposition, or sentence. Paraphrasis, or redescription of *situations* in terms of perceptible states of affairs, rather than redefinition of *things* was what Bentham aimed at. So, although, like his revered predecessor, Locke, Bentham sometimes talks as though the unit of meaning that had to be cashed out was the individual word, standing for a Lockean simple idea, his position was actually more subtle than that.

But even this is still crude. For there is a sense in which 'description' is too static to catch Bentham's conviction that the dynamic of a situation is part of what we need to know about it. So to have a duty is to be in a situation where certain action or inaction from you will itself subject you to an action constituting a sanction on the part of another actor. Understanding such sentences involves understanding potential practical consequences in the world. There is a sense in which not merely this kind of pragmatism but the very principle of utility itself enters into Bentham's epistemology. Bentham is not interested in the more metaphysical issues surrounding epistemology, he is interested in it from a practical and utilitarian point of view. The problem of the reality of external existence is brusquely dealt with from a consequentialist position: 'no bad consequences can possibly arise from supposing it to be true and the worst consequences can not but arise from supposing it to be false.'[59] Moreover at the particular level, it was not so much with 'meaning' that he was concerned as what he called the 'import' or practical

---

[55] See below, on 'Custom', p. 335.

[56] *Fragment on Government*, p. 108.

[57] *Of Laws in General*, p. 251.

[58] *Fragment on Government*, p. 108: 'A word may be said to be expounded by *paraphrasis*, when not that *word* alone, is translated into other *words*, but some whole *sentence* of which it forms a part is translated into another *sentence*; the words of which are expressive of such ideas as are *simple*, or more immediately resolvable into simple ones . . . ' See also *A Table of the Springs of Action*, paraphrasis: 'the name of the fictitious entity in question is made parcel of a *phrase*, which contains in it the correspondent and *expository* real entity . . . 'In the case of a *right*: 'a man is said to have a right when, ' etc. *Springs of Action*, p. 7.

[59] UC 69.52, cited Harrison, *Bentham*, p. 54.

implications of a proposition. Clarifying the import of 'fictions' was primarily explaining the consequences of them. Thus, to explain what is meant by having an obligation one has to assert that certain consequences follow from one's not doing whatever it is one has an obligation to do. What law does is to articulate fictions which nevertheless affect the world in such a way that different actions (criminal or non-criminal) will lead to different consequences (punishment or non-punishment). Explaining law involves explaining the outcomes because it is these that constitute the 'perceptible entities' into which the fictions must be resolved if they are to be meaningful. At a more general level his famous attack on judge-made law, is based on a consequentialist argument. Common Law judges make laws for us the way we train our dogs: 'wait till he does it, then beat him for it . . . this is the way that judges make law for you and me. They won't tell a man before hand what it is he *should not do*'.[60] Lack of clarity, like retrospective legislation (which is what judge-made law effectively is) is rejected because the uncertainty it creates prevents people from acting to maximize their happiness.

Bentham's initial critique of law is thus positivistic in two senses. It is adamant that description must be distinguished from evaluation (although he thought the principle of utility could be applied both to the organization of legal descriptions *and* made to form the basis of evaluation.) Secondly he is insistent that any account of law or institutions must be reducible to statements about the behaviour or relations between perceptible entities.

The positivism of Bentham's approach, his insistence on the distinction between description and evaluation might seem an uncongenial starting point for a radical reformer. But the reason it is not is to do with Bentham's psychology. This is more or less hedonistic. Although the greatest happiness principle is the standard of laws, it would be naive to presume it could be the motive for our actions. Consequently, great clarity was needed about the motivational impact of the penal system in order to ensure it was made in each person's interests to refrain from acting to diminish the general happiness. It's not that Bentham thought that the *content* of the claims made by natural rights theorists weren't desirable – he agreed, or came to agree with many of them, it's that claiming they were *rights* confused the whole analysis.

The basic premise: *The Introduction to the Principles of Morals and Legislation*

The principle of utility

At the time of the publication of the *Fragment* Bentham was at work on a detailed study of the application of the principle of utility to legislation and punishment. *The Introduction to the Principles of Morals and Legislation* is a part of that study; it was printed in 1780, but not published until 1789, by which time it had led to a more extensive work *Of Laws in General,* which remained unpublished.[61] In the *Introduction* Bentham sets out briefly, the basic premise of his social theory, the 'principle of utility', or 'greatest

---

[60] Cited, ibid., p. 35.

[61] Unpublished, that is, by Bentham, but first published this century by C.W. Everett under the title *The Limits of Jurisprudence Defined*, which, although not Bentham's title, half catches the relationship between

happiness principle' and, in considerably more detail, how it could be applied to the laws and to the conduct of a society. Bentham's basic thesis is that an understanding of utility can inform us *what* behaviour ought to be prohibited (that which causes pains), and also *how* best to prohibit it (by the threat of just enough pain to dissuade potential criminals from committing it).

The principle is presented by Bentham in a famous passage at the start of the *Introduction* :

> Nature has placed man under the governance of two sovereign masters, *pain* and *pleasure*. It is for them alone to point to what we ought to do, as well as to determine what we shall do. On the one hand the standard of right and wrong, on the other the chain of cause and effects, are fastened to their throne. . . . The *principle of utility* recognizes this subjection. . . . By the principle of utility is meant that principle which approves or disapproves of every action whatsoever, according to the tendency which it appears to have to augment or diminish the happiness of the party whose interest is in question: or, what is the same thing in other words, to promote or oppose that happiness.[62]

The first thing that would have struck an eighteenth-century reader is what is missing from this principle; and that is the total absence of any theological basis for morality.[63] Although the principle cannot be 'proved' he asks us to consider two alternatives, that of asceticism, or pleasure-denial, which is the opposite of utility, and that of 'sympathy and antipathy' which he mischievously calls 'caprice'. He suggests that, in a broad way, calculating utility is in fact how we do mostly act, and that objections to the utility principle hinge on examples of its misapplication.[64]

In defending it, Bentham emphasizes two aspects of his principle which relate closely to his critique of legal fictions in the *Fragment*. Firstly, he thinks it one of the great advantages of his system that 'Pleasures and pains are, doubtless, real entities'.[65] Inasmuch as his political theory is based on the analysis or computation of pleasures and pains, it is, he would claim, unlike those of his predecessors, rooted, not in fictions, but in those perceptible entities which render language of proper and real import. Secondly, his principle is what we should today call methodologically individualist. Given that sensations of pleasures and pains are the ultimate content of evaluative judgments, it follows that collective principles – like 'the interests of the community' – must be nothing more than assessments of the sum of the interests of the individuals in it. And the interest of an individual is what 'tends to add to the sum total of his pleasures'.[66] Whatever

---

the two works. Bentham seems to have held back the publication of the *Principles of Morals and Legislation* because, having been preoccupied with the penal or criminal aspects of law he now wanted to clarify the relationship between it and civil law. The chapter in the *Introduction* from which the larger work, now known as *Of Laws in General*, eventually grew was entitled 'The Limits of the Penal Branch of Legislation'. See 'Introduction' *Of Laws in General*, p. xxiv, in *Complete Works*.

[62] *Principles of Morals and Legislation*, pp. 11–12.

[63] Earlier versions of this principle had been put forward by Hobbes and Mandeville, each of whom had been denounced as atheists by churchmen. Dumont's edition of Bentham was itself attacked by theologians and put on the papal index in 1819. Dinwiddy, 'Bentham and the Early Nineteenth-Century', p. 20.

[64] *Principles of Morals and Legislation*, pp. 13–14.

[65] *Springs of Action*, p. 6.

[66] *Principles of Morals and Legislation* p. 12.

advantages this approach brings (and commentators claim for Bentham anticipations of or advances towards methods not fully realized until the present century)[67] Bentham's principles raise a whole series of questions, the answers to which are not immediately apparent.

The first amongst these is the dual character of the principle. The principle of utility is presented as both a psychological principle (that is the principle of motivation) *and* as a moral criterion, or standard of judgment and action.[68] This is confusing: for on one obvious interpretation the first ought to render the second redundant; if considerations of pleasure and pain do *strictly* determine all we do, then there would seem no room for moral choices at all, and so no role for moral principles, unless, that is, there is an equivocation as to *whose* pleasure and pain motivates us. It is clear that this is what Bentham has in mind, and he acknowledges early on that in applying the principle, the 'utility' to be considered can be either that of the community in general, or the individual.[69] But now we have a second pair of variables. As well as being both a psychological and a moral principle, utility could, it appears, be individualist or generalized. Bentham seems to be claiming some or all of the following: that we are *caused psychologically* to pursue either (1) our own or (2) the community's pleasure, or that we *ought* to pursue either (3) our own or (4) the community's pleasure. The clarification of his position occupies some time (and several works) but even in the *Introduction* it is fairly clear that what he wants to argue is that (1) we are in fact motivated by a mixture of egoistic and (to a much lesser extent) an altruistic concern for others' pleasure; but that (2) the foundational moral and legislative principle is that we ought to maximize the utility of as many people as possible; or rather, as Bentham puts it, that all we can *mean* when we say that a certain action is 'right' or that we 'ought' to do it is that it promotes the principle of utility, i.e. maximizes happiness.[70]

This leads to at least a part of the second problem. This is the issue of precisely what content should be given to the notion of utility. There are two questions here. One is whether altruistic acts count as part of egoism, and are thus included or excluded from utility. The second is what kind of sensations or experiences count as a basis of utility. Is utility a psychological quality of whatever we actually choose to do, no matter how altruistic, or painful it might appear to be? Or is it a property of only some actions, i.e. those that produce pleasure? The principle that we act to maximize our own utility can

[67] See for example the assessment of Bentham's jurisprudence by H.L.A. Hart, *Essays on Bentham, Jurisprudence and Political Theory*, (Oxford, 1982), his economics by W. Stark, in *Bentham's Economic Writings*, his politics, Ian Budge, 'Bentham in the light of modern political science' *Political Studies* in politics and Amnon Goldworth in psychology, are amongst those who have advanced such claims on Bentham's behalf.

[68] 'It is for them alone to point to what we ought to do, as well as to determine what we shall do.'

[69] *Principles of Morals and Legislation*, p. 12.

[70] Ibid., p. 21 Bentham's characterisation of the principle of personal asceticism ('not a political principle') as the opposite of the principle of utility reveals his conception of utility there to be a principle regarding personal pleasure. Although in the *Principles of Morals and Legislation* Bentham characterises the principle of 'sympathy' as one opposed to the principle of utility, he increasingly acknowledged 'sympathy' as a source of pleasure and pain for individuals, allotting it a separate heading in his *Table of the Springs of Action* (p. 84). However, it was, in his view always a subordinate one, whereas self-regarding motives are 'at once the most powerful, most constant, and most extensive' (*Principles of Morals and Legislation*, p. 155). For utility as the meaning of right and duty, ibid., p. 13.

be taken either as an empirical observation, or as a universal axiom of human behaviour. The trouble is that the former seems clearly false, for people do, often act in apparently altruistic fashion. If, on the other hand, we make personal utility-maximizing axiomatic, effectively redefining even altruistic acts so that they are egoistic ones, this contradicts Bentham's methodological claim that utility provides an *objective* standard, distinct from mere individual approbation or eligibility.[71]

Bentham does, disconcertingly, frequently use the term 'axiom' when referring to the principle, and so implies a definitional conception of it.[72] At times in the *Introduction* he seems to wish to characterize all behaviour in such a way that contravention of the utility principle would be logically impossible. Possibly prompted by Adam Smith's famous example of the baker (who is prompted to bake our bread for us by self-interest, not generosity) he asks us to consider a baker who distributes free bread to the poor in time of famine. The motive here, Bentham suggests is 'love of reputation', but whether this is egoistic or not is, he thinks, hardly relevant, the tendency of the act is *good* (i.e. it promotes utility).[73] The shift in focus required by utilitarianism away from the mental intention behind the act and towards its consequences, has the effect of directing attention away from precisely those criteria that we would need to decide whether an action was inherently (i.e. motivationally) altruistic, which becomes largely irrelevant, there are simply 'certain pleasures and pains which suppose the existence of some pleasure or pain of some other person'.[74] On this account Bentham seems to have believed that being motivated by considerations of one's own utility is a necessary psychological truth.

However, against this view, it can be pointed out that from the first Bentham consistently argues that egoistic motives are *stronger* than others (and therefore presumably not the only ones), and this suggests that he sees psychological egoism as an empirical and so falsifiable generalization. Narrow egoism does not, therefore comprise the whole of utility. This is made explicit in his increasing recognition that 'sympathy' is a specific motivational sanction, quite distinct from egoistic ones. Whilst no human actions are literally 'disinterested' – i.e. unrelated to any human interests at all (this is 'a state of things which, consistent with voluntary action, is not possible') – there are, nonetheless some actions consistent with 'the absence of all interest of the self-regarding class'.[75]

---

[71] Ibid., p. 15.

[72] For example in the *Deontology*, 'the very fact of his pursuing it is, subject to the limitations above mentioned, [experience had of it by the person] conclusive proof of its goodness — of its relative goodness, relations being had to the person himself, and his particular well-being.' p. 150.

[73] *Principles of Morals and Legislation*, p. 129. Even though the baker acted out of concern for his reputation and may have no feeling for the sufferings of those he relieved, Bentham thinks only 'some very idle prejudice' could judge his disposition other than 'good' in view of the consequences.

[74] Ibid., p. 49. The claim that motive, when evidence of a disposition, is irrelevant cannot, in the final analysis be strictly true for a utilitarian, as Bentham himself acknowledged. For altruistically motivated actions, at least if evidence of an altruistic disposition, are more likely to be followed by further such acts, and therefore, even on strictly utilitarian grounds, are better than other-benefiting actions which are not so motivated. Ibid., p. 95. However, a) everything cannot be said at once, and b) Bentham is concerned to construct legal and political institutions which work on the most generalisable assumption, and that is that men are largely motivated by a 'self regarding interest' in the stricter sense.

[75] Parekh, p. 64 (*Springs of Action*, pp. 99–100). As suggested above, in the *Principles of Morals and Legislation* Bentham tends to reduce apparently 'altruistic' actions to special cases of personal pleasure, and although he makes an analytical distinction between pleasures dependent on the pleasures of another (extra-regarding) and those not (self-regarding), the pleasures of the former are still egoistic and personally

Although Bentham thinks it important to allow the *possibility* of altruistic action, it is marginal to his system, which not only acknowledges, but requires, the predominance of a robust, if restrained sense of self-interest. Indeed, he thought it was one of the most disastrous characteristics of Christianity that it was so concerned with the suppression of self-regarding motives which he regarded as essential to human survival.[76] The upshot of the last two paragraphs seems to be that on the issue of whether utility is a universal motive of action Bentham wants to both have his cake and eat it. Is this right?

One way round this is to note that there are two quite distinct elements to Bentham's presentation of the principle of utility, the notion of calculation, and the idea of utility itself. Calculation, he seems to want to say is a universal characteristic of (rational) action. 'All men calculate' insists Bentham several times.[77] Some do it well, some badly: the purpose of clarifying the kinds and dimensions of pleasure and pain is to increase the accuracy of our calculation, particularly for the legislator. However the notion of utility also refers to *what* it is that people are calculating *about*, here some account only their own, whilst some include others' interests. Some include imaginary, some real pleasures and pains. The notion of utility excludes some (illusory) objects of desire or action, by showing their lack of any basis in reality, but by acknowledging both egoistic and other-directed concerns, it allows that both the actor's, and others' pleasures can be fed into the computation. By seeking to maintain one sense of 'interest' which is a definitional antecedent of all [rational] action, whilst defining more narrowly a contingent sense of (selfish) interest, Bentham seeks to sustain all three relevant implications of the principle of utility, a general account of action, the powerful explanatory role of self-interest, and the possibility of moral (i.e., altruistic) action.

It is in fact most important for Bentham's whole system that the principle of utility is given an empirical status and not an axiomatic one. If we were to define utility as 'revealed preference' that is, as *whatever* individuals in fact choose, no preferences could be excluded; but then utility would be indistinguishable from the purely capricious principle of 'sympathy and antipathy', which Bentham demolishes as one of the untenable alternatives to utility.[78] What distinguishes the utility principle, as we showed Bentham claiming above, is precisely that it points to 'some external consideration, as a means of warranting and guiding the internal sentiments of approbation' and the external consideration is the production of happiness. It is this that enables our judgments to escape mere subjective preference. As Bentham had put it in the *Fragment*, where

---

felt. In the *Springs of Action*, he asserts however that a virtuous disposition is one motivated by the self-denying pursuit of good to others (p. 99) and introduces a new category of pleasures and pains, those of sympathy. (Introductory table, p. 84) Bentham retains an 'other-regarding' category of personal pleasure — 'amity' — defined in Hobbesian terms as 'PLEASURES derivable from the *Good-will,* thence from the *Free-Services,* of this or that individual'. (p. 82); whereas the meaning of sympathy is, by contrast, defined wholly in terms of altruistic sentiments (p. 84).

[76] On Bentham's attitude to religion see Steintrager, *The Bentham Newsletter,* no. 4 (1980) p. 7.

[77] *Principles of Morals and Legislation,* pp. 40, 173–4.

[78] 'That principle which approves or disapproves of certain actions, not on account of their tending to augment the happiness, nor yet on account of their tending to diminish the happiness of the party whose interest is in question, but merely because a man finds himself disposed to approve or disapprove of them.' Ibid., p. 25. Note that there is still a gap between 'approving of' and 'choosing' but these are both in the realm of expressed subjectivity, and not what Bentham would have us believe is an objective fact: pleasure and pain.

disputes were 'conducted under the auspices of this principle . . . [the parties] would at
any rate see clearly and explicitly, the point on which the disagreement turned' and the
issue would become 'manifestly a question concerning so many future contingent matters
of fact.'[79]

Utility then, is what pleases (i.e. produces pleasure), but not whatever we please (i.e.
choose). Since Bentham believes utility to be both an explanatory and a critical principle
he needs some account of why it does not in fact inform our institutions and our choices.
This is partly due to ignorance, and partly to 'sinister interests'.[80] Initially, in the
Fragment, this referred to the legal profession, who had an interest in maintaining
obscure law so they could gain a living; but sinister interests widened, as Bentham's
perceptions of the power structure of the unreformed constitution became clearer. The
church and the nobility were powerful sources of what would today be called ideological
control. They stopped people perceiving where their true interests lay, and thus perpetuated ignorance and gave rise to 'false consciousness'.[81]

But it is not only ignorance and false consciousness that enable utility to be applied as
a critical standard of what people actually choose. There are other stipulations about what
is to count as utility which have important implications for the kind of society capable
of being justified by the principle of utility. It is sometimes claimed that Bentham's
principle would support the imposition of the majority's moral views on a minority if
the summation of pleasures would thereby be maximized. This is a classic problem for
utilitarianism, since, denying individual natural rights, it has no principle for limiting the
degree of intrusion which a utilitarian majority could imposed on minorities if utility
were thereby maximized. Suppose you were to claim that you experienced detestation
and so pain at the thought of a certain action taking place, even though you were not
present and the individuals involved were consenting: numerous examples spring to
mind, boxing, pornography, prostitution, homosexuality. Would the claim that one felt
pain count as a utilitarian objection to it? Should such pains be added up in calculating
whether to allow such actions? Absolutely not, claims Bentham. If no disutility follows
from the action or practice, apart from that which comprises the detestation or belief that
it is wrong, there is no grounds for prohibition. In such a case 'It is for you to get the
better of your antipathy, not for him to truckle to it.'[82] So once again the objectivity of
the content of utility, in Bentham's view, saves it from being the mere aggregation of
preferences, and so justifying majority tyranny. It is only objective (not imaginary) pains
that it is the task of legislation to minimize.[83] Bentham's specification of the kinds and

---

[79] *Fragment on Government*, pp. 104–5.

[80] A sinister interest is one, the 'tendency of which is to serve a *less* at the expense of a *more* extensive
interest.'*Springs of Action*, p. 18.

[81] The phrase is actually used by Bentham, *Principles of Morals and Legislation*, p. 75. See the account
of Bentham's growing recognition of the ideological control and its social sources in relation to his theory
of fictions, in 'The Political Function of Bentham's Theory of Fictions' L.J. Hume, *The Bentham Newsletter*,
3 (1979).

[82] *Principles of Morals and Legislation*, p. 29, note d to p. 26. This long note is a potted survey of
eighteenth-century moralists.

[83] Not that some 'imagined' pains aren't real, in the sense of being well grounded. Although perhaps not
(yet) a physical pain, the fear produced by an insecurity grounded in a reasonable likelihood of some
eventually painful outcome is real enough in the way that was not the case say, for the 'pain' experienced

dimensions of pleasures and pains that there are, is therefore, not merely classificatory, it is, in its application, also critical.

The application of the principle

Bentham's famous classification of pleasures and pains was designed to assist lawmakers in assessing the appropriate punishment needed to inhibit particular forms of crime, or indeed deciding whether they were fit subjects for punishment at all. It did so by suggesting the dimensions through which a 'quantum' of pleasure or pain could be assessed, and thereby aggregated and compared. Although he goes to considerable lengths in trying to achieve this, Bentham was quite candid about the difficulties of strict quantification.[84] In particular, he recognized a problem which undermined the supposed 'objectivity' of pains and pleasures as a basis of calculation, and which has bedeviled recent welfare economics. That is the difficulty of comparing the 'utility' of different, or indeed even the apparently 'same' pleasure in different people: "'Tis vain to talk of adding quantities which will continue distinct as before, one man's happiness will never be another man's happiness: a gain to one man is no gain to another: you might as well pretend to add 20 apples to 20 pears.'[85] Bentham did not completely identify the 'quantum' of utility either with the objective source of the pleasure or pain (for people's susceptibilities vary), or with the subjective claims of the individual suffering it (for some pains are wholly imaginary), but with a unit which was produced by the first and could only be approached through the second means.

However there were two ways round this. One was to make a virtue out of the vice of the relative indeterminacy of human pleasures and to seek to accommodate it through maximizing liberty. Because the person with the strongest motive to promote, and the best knowledge of, an individual's happiness is that individual, by and large, they will maximize their pleasure themselves if left free to.[86] The greatest happiness could therefore be achieved simply by laws which maximize people's freedom to pursue happiness in their own way, subject, of course, to their not causing pain to others.[87] The principle of utility therefore, in Bentham's eyes, offered strong support for the ideal of liberty, as, if not a good in itself, a most important means to the good.

The second way round the problem of the commensurability of pleasures was his belief that there existed a medium which functioned as a crude, if adequate measure of happiness, and that is money. If one would give the same money for two pleasures, the pleasures are equal. If we equivocate over whether to buy a bottle of wine or give the

---

by someone who detests homosexuality, and cannot bear the idea of homosexual activities going on, even though s/he is never, nor ever likely to witness or be involved in them.

[84] *Principles of Morals and Legislation*, p. 40. 'It is not to be expected that this process should be strictly pursued . . . It may, however, be always kept in view.'

[85] Unpublished manuscript, U.C. xiv 3, cited Dinwiddy, *Bentham*, p. 50.

[86] *Principles of Morals and Legislation*, p. 244; and 159: 'No man can be so good a judge as the man himself, what it is gives him pleasure or displeasure.'

[87] Parekh, *Bentham's Political Thought*, p. 118: 'There is no operation whatever which the legislator could be certain would . . . give pleasure . . . To produce pleasure therefore the Legislator has but one course to take, which is to lay in a man's way some instrument of pleasure, and leave the application of it to himself.' (UCL Box xxvii, 29–30).

money to famine relief we are revealing an equivalent pleasure in indulging our palate and saving human life respectively.[88] It is here that Bentham comes closest to the 'revealed preference' definition of utility. However, he always acknowledges it is only an approximation, and moreover recognizes that some pleasures – those of reputation for example – cannot adequately be compensated for by a sum of money. The role of money is most seriously limited by an extraordinary anticipation of Bentham's which plays an important part in his views on social policy. Bentham clearly articulates a notion of decreasing marginal utility; that is to say, he held that every additional unit of money given to a person increases their happiness by less than the previous unit. This is true interpersonally as well. The value of £10 to a pauper is much greater than the value of £10 to someone comfortably off; more obviously the loss of £10 if it is all I have, is greater to me than the loss of £10 if I am a millionaire.[89] Consequently there is no linear exchange-rate as it were, between money and utility. A given sum of money produces more utility the poorer its owner. This has far reaching consequences for social policy. For, other considerations aside, it suggests that utility will be maximized when wealth is equalized.

Although the first answer to the problem of the indeterminacy of human happiness can be solved by maximizing liberty, the application of the law would, by the same criterion, be undermined. For if we were as uncertain about what causes pain, as about what causes happiness, how could the legislator know what will work as a sanction to prevent unhappiness to others? For Bentham's system to work there needs to be some kind of asymmetry between pleasure and pain. However, once again the very flexibility of Bentham's principle proves a virtue rather than a vice. Indeed one of the more frequent criticisms made of his system turns out to be an advantage.

It is often remarked that Bentham's apparent assumption that pleasures and pains stand on opposite ends of a single spectrum is not a tenable one. His claim that pleasures and pains are ultimately physical sensations seems truer for pains than pleasures.[90] At the most trivial level, pains have a physical location, – you say 'I have a pain in my foot', but never a 'pleasure in my foot'. Pleasure is a *consequence* of (amongst other things)

---

[88] 'The thermometer is the instrument for measuring the heat of the weather, the barometer for measuring the pressure of the air. Those who are not satisfied with the accuracy of these instruments must find out others that shall be more accurate, or bid adieu to Natural Philosophy. Money is the instrument for measuring the quantity of pain or pleasure. Those who are not satisfied with the accuracy of this instrument must find out some other that shall be more accurate, or bid adieu to Politics and Morals.' UCL Box xxvii; 'On the Measurement of Subjective States', ed. Amnon Goldworth, *The Bentham Newsletter* no.2 p. 13 (1979).

[89] 'Measurement of Subjective States', pp. 7–8. More generally 'the quantity of happiness produced by a particle of wealth (each particle being of the same magnitude) will be less and less at every particle; the second will produce less than the first, the third than the second, and so on . . . ' The passage reappears in the *Pannomial Fragments*, Bowring, iii, p. 229, cited Dinwiddy, *Bentham*, p. 52. The germ of the idea is already present in the *Principles of Morals and Legislation*, : 'it is manifest, that there are occasions on which a given sum will be worth infinitely more to a man than the same sum would be another time . . . [e.g.] in cases of extremity.' p. 59. However, Bentham is not consistent in this, or at least notes a contradictory force at work where this principle is applied to a policy of redistribution, and that is that '*ceteris paribus*, it is more painful to lose a given sum than it is pleasurable to gain it, the pain produced by the *taking* is upon average always more than equivalent to the pleasure produced by the *giving*.' *Of Laws in General*, p. 135.

[90] 'Homogeneous real entities', *Principles of Morals and Legislation*, p. 53, '*Pleasures and Pains the basis of all the other entities: these the only real ones:* . . . a matter of universal and constant experience'. *Springs of Action*, p. 98.

physical sensation; pain, at least some kinds of pain, simply *is* the sensation. Some pain can even be pleasurable. Although Bentham claims that both pleasures and pains, of all kinds, derive from physical sensation, the claim seems stronger in the case of some pains than any pleasures. Yet it is precisely this asymmetry that can justify, indeed require, liberty to maximize our (indeterminate) pleasure, whilst giving the legislator the common sanction he needs to inhibit the pain we all (normally) avoid. In the case of pain the physical basis of it in its elemental form, claims Bentham, makes generalizing easier than in the case of pleasure, giving it a kind of ontological priority over pleasure.[91] There may be a few people who like physical pain, or are relatively indifferent to it, but not enough that the legislator need worry that threatening to impose it won't act as a deterrent.[92] Most of us enjoy our liberty, ease and freedom from pain sufficiently to regard confinement, hard labour and privation as detestable. However this may be, there is in both cases a range of possible pleasures and pains going from the very ordinary and general to the esoteric and therefore unpredictable. Although there are some people, ascetics and masochists, say, who reject what most of us like, they are few and far between. So the fact that people's tastes ultimately differ needn't unduly handicap the legislator. The *ultimate* indeterminacy of both pleasures and pain is quite consistent with both the need for freedom for individuals to realize the variety of the former, and the virtually universal susceptibility of humans to particular varieties of the latter. All the legislator needs in order to persuade people not to limit the freedom or happiness of others are some very basic effective and widespread dislikes. He does not need to know the more exquisite forms of pain to which particular individuals might be susceptible.[93]

Bentham's psychology

Bentham's psychology is complex and we shall not be able to go farther into it than to indicate its implications for his legal and political thinking. He starts with what he calls the sanctions. These are simply the different sources of pleasure and pain when the prospect of them acts on us as motives to action. They are physical, by which he means the natural consequences of actions, so that fear of drowning – a natural consequence of imprudent bathing – might inhibit us from swimming in stormy water; political, by which he means consequences resulting from the power of rulers to punish by law; moral, by which he means not what we tend to think of, but something closer to public opinion (as he puts it in his marginal note 'popular'), and finally religious, either in this or the next life.[94] All of these, he believes, are ultimately based on the physical sanction, in that it is through the operation of the physical effects of the natural world that the others can affect

---

[91] After discussing the difficulties of characterizing money as a universal source of pleasure, Bentham continues rather sinisterly: 'of producing pain there is another means which is strictly universal: for every man has a body.' 'On the Measurement of Subjective States', ed. Goldman, p. 11. There are other hints of an asymmetry between the two, thus 'any man can at any time be much surer of administering pain than pleasure.' *Of Laws in General*, p. 135.

[92] The apparent indifference to pain and death of the religiously or ideologically motivated terrorist is what renders the state so powerless to control them. Nor only the terrorist, consider Socrates, Jesus, Ghandi.

[93] It is of course conceivable that knowledge of particular weaknesses might help in particularly tough cases, e.g., Winston's paranoia about rats in *1984*.

[94] *Principles of Morals and Legislation*, p. 35.

us.[95] The use of all of these sanctions is recommended to the legislator. To ignore one or more of them would be to allow the possibility that the ignored sanction might overweigh, in the mind of the individual, those employed by the legislator.

Bentham held that each pain or pleasure, whether actually suffered or enjoyed, or held in prospect as a potential motive, can be evaluated in terms of both its intensity and its duration. This is not only a tool of legislators but something we commonly do in our own lives. Rather as we might, on visiting the dentist, compare the long drawn out discomfort of the anaesthetic with the short intense pain of the drill hitting the nerve. Prospective pleasures and pains can also be considered from the point of view of the certainty with which they will come about, and the nearness or remoteness of that happening (weighing up the certain but limited pain of visiting the dentist soon, or the greater, but remote and uncertain pain of toothache at some indefinite point in the future). Moreover the consequences of pleasures and pains, in terms of further pleasures and pains can be considered too. For example I may get more immediate pleasure from not sharing some delicacy with others, for the extra pleasures of taste may not be outweighed by the pleasures of sociability that come from sharing. However, if I include the further pleasures that will likely come about from sharing in their goodies too, that might swing the balance in favour of generosity. A final consideration is the extent to which any pain is necessarily involved with a pleasure. Not guilt perhaps, as religious moralists are prone to suggest – for Bentham the 'moral' sanction is one of social pressure – but more intrinsically related pains. Those, say that (necessarily) follow the pleasures of over-indulgence.[96] These dimensions of intensity, duration, certainty, propinquity, fecundity, purity, will, if 'kept in view', assist in the calculation of utility, both at the individual and at the collective level.

Not only are there different dimensions of pleasure and pain, there are different kinds. Pleasures and pains are described by Bentham as 'interesting perceptions', and can be either simple – incapable of further analysis – or complex, that is compound. This seems a deliberate allusion to one of Bentham's intellectual heroes, John Locke, who had analysed ideas into simple and complex.[97] Locke's ideas were derived from the mental representations of sensible objects conveyed to our mind by our senses, these Locke called perceptions . Bentham is concerned with 'interesting perceptions', i.e. those that excite an interest in that they give rise to desire, or indeed aversion. Pleasures and pains thus provide a bridge between the cognitive and appetitive faculties of the mind.[98] Bentham lists some fourteen sources of simple pleasure, and twelve of pain.[99] Pains are not simply antitheses of pleasures, there are no simple pains paralleling the physical

---

[95] *Principles of Morals and Legislation*, p. 37.

[96] Bentham explains the origin of the peculiar moral system of asceticism as an immoderate extension of the observation that over-indulgence has harmful consequences. This, he points out, is merely a misapplication of the principle of utility. *Principles of Morals and Legislation*, p. 21.

[97] John Locke, *An Essay Concerning Human Understanding*, Bk II, ii, xii.

[98] See Parekh, *Bentham's Political Thought*, pp. 58–61, from UCL Box ci, pp. 406–14.

[99] They are those of sense, wealth, skill, amity, reputation, power, piety, benevolence, malevolence, memory, imagination, expectation, association and relief. *Principles of Morals and Legislation*, p. 42. In the later *Springs of Action*, Bentham created a different list differentiating amongst the pleasures of sense and intellect which would seem to contradict (or abandon) his earlier identification of pleasure with sensation : Palate, sex, sensuality, wealth, power, curiosity, amity, reputation, religion, sympathy, antipathy. He allowed only poverty, ill-will, ill repute and thwarted vindictiveness, as opposing pains, but added two

pleasures of sex or those of novelty, only the general pain of privation which Bentham does not further subdivide.

Sensibility

Although pleasure and pain are externally and objectively caused, there is no one-to-one relationship between the external cause and the pain suffered. The objectivity Bentham claims for pain does not lie in any identity with the external source which gave rise to it.[100] Although real, the degree of experienced pain produced by common causes is influenced by ineliminable subjective factors present in different degrees in different individuals, such as health, strength, hardiness and so on.[101]

The point about this orgy of classification is that pleasure and pain are, for Bentham, as we have seen, the only possible candidates for motives, or 'springs of action' as he puts it.[102] The task of the legislator is to understand in particular, the operation of pain. For he needs to know, not only what causes pain to people, so that laws may be enacted to prevent it, but what painful motives will operate successfully in order to inhibit the criminal from causing such pain.[103] Together, the kinds, values and susceptibility to pain can be used to give an idea of the *quanta* of punishment necessary both in framing general legislation and in particular cases. Strict, formal equality of punishment is ruled out here. 'Making the punishment fit the crime' involves, not applying the same punishment, but the same amount of pain. Since our susceptibilities vary, this evidently may involve different punishments although Bentham (for once!) refuses to elaborate on this at this point.

For example, a wealthy person should be fined more than a poor one for the same offence. Perhaps more contentiously, someone unused to physical hardship should receive a shorter term of hard labour than someone who is. In each case, their differential susceptibility to punishment requires different sentences to achieve the same *quanta* of pain. Value can be used in interesting ways too. Crimes with a low rate of detection, where punishment is therefore uncertain, should have correspondingly more intense or longer sentences to compensate. The religious sanction of damnation is perhaps the most

---

particular pains with no accompanying pleasures: those of labour and fatigue, and those of death and bodily pain. *Springs of Action*, pp. 79–86 .

[100] *Principles of Morals and Legislation*, p. 51.

[101] Once again there are extensive lists, see *Principles of Morals and Legislation*, p. 52ff. Many of these 'circumstances influencing sensibility' seem simply to parallel categories identified in the kinds of pleasures and pains, others are quite extrinsic: age, climate and so forth.

[102] Motives which influence only the intellect, such as motives to believe for example, are acknowledged but irrelevant for Bentham. By a motive he means 'any thing whatsoever which by influencing the will of a sensitive being, is supposed to determine him to act, or voluntarily forbear to act, upon any occasion.' *Principles of Morals and Legislation*, pp. 96–7. 'Of the sort of motive which has thus been in operation, no clear idea can be entertained otherwise than by reference to the sort of *pleasure* or *pain* which has such a motive for its *basis*: viz. the pleasure or pain, the idea, and eventual expectation of which is considered as having been operating in the character of a motive.' *Springs of Action*, p. 98.

[103] 'On the one hand the mischievous acts, which it is his business to prevent; on the other hand, the punishments, by terror of which it is his endeavour to prevent them.' *Principles of Morals and Legislation*, p. 70.

striking example of this. This nakedly utilitarian appeal was insisted on with disarming candour as a necessary cornerstone of morality by churchmen throughout the century, reaching its fullest development in the theological utilitarianism of William Paley, an elder contemporary of Bentham's. In the absence of an effective police force they were perhaps right to do so. The religious sanction is gravely deficient in the fields of certainty and propinquity, for we are not sure that God or damnation exists, and the latter, if it does, seems a long way off. For this reason, the intensity and duration of the punishment in hell have to be presented as extreme.

The utilitarian case for democratic government: James Mill's *Essay on Government* and Bentham's *Plan of Parliamentary Reform*

> The stricter the dependence of the governors on the governed, the better will the government be.[104]

The case that Bentham and his followers made for democratic reform was essentially instrumental to the greatest happiness principle. As utilitarians neither Bentham nor Mill regarded political participation, much less the vote as a human or natural right; neither did they regard it, even in utilitarian terms, as a good thing in itself.[105] Although Bentham and most of his followers came to see it as indispensable, it remained essentially a means to an end. Moreover, it was a means that involved certain costs, costs that could be compared with other means to the end.

James Mill's *Essay on Government* – the most convenient precis of classical utilitarian principles applied to the theory of government particularly exemplifies this view.[106] Government is essentially a means to ensuring the greatest happiness of the greatest number.[107] There are two sources of happiness, our fellow humans, and material goods. By and large government is concerned with the second of these. Most material goods require the expenditure of labour, so happiness is maximized by encouraging labour on goods which produce it, and the best way to ensure this is by giving people the greatest incentive to work, and that is provided by ensuring each person gets the maximum amount of the product of their labour. So the greatest happiness comes down to 'insuring to every man the greatest possible quantity of the product of his labour.'[108] Such happiness

---

[104] *c*.1790, cited Dinwiddy, 'The Transition . . . ', p. 685.

[105] See Alan Ryan, 'Two Views of Democracy and Politics, James and John Stuart Mill', in *Machiavelli and the Nature of Political Thought*, ed. M. Fleisher (New York, 1972).

[106] Mill's *Essay* has long been held to be a convenient distillation of late Benthamite politics. Fred Rosen has shown how different in fact were the views of the two men on a number of important issues. However, as he acknowledges, 'The Benthamites . . . did not distinguish between the views of Bentham and Mill . . . ' (F. Rosen, *Jeremy Bentham and Representative Democracy* (Oxford, 1983), p. 168), consequently Mill's *Essay*, which is still the most accessible source for students, can still fairly be used to characterize the historical face of Benthamite reformist politics. Important differences between the two thinkers will be noted below.

[107] James Mill, *An Essay on Government* (Cambridge, 1937), pp. 1–2.

[108] Ibid., p. 5. Once again Bentham took a larger view. In his own essay on *Utilitarianism* he attacked Locke for the view that property was 'the only thing entitled to be the object of care to government'. Locke 'missed sight of so many other valuable subject matters of possession, namely power, reputation, condition

is jeopardized by the observation – a deduction from the narrow conception of psychological egoism – that one person 'will desire to render the person and property of another subservient to his pleasures, notwithstanding the pain or loss of pleasure which it may occasion to that other individual'. The need to deal with this problem is 'the foundation of government'.[109]

The next issue is how government is to assure this. In part the answer to this is through power – by the imposition of appropriate painful sanctions sufficient to dissuade opportunists from taking, by fraud or violence, the sources of happiness away from those who had created them, and thereby destroying the incentive to produce them.[110] Bentham's voluminous legal writings showed how this power was to be used. However, the psychological premise on which utility, both as a moral and as a descriptive theory was based – that each individual will pursue their pleasure as a basic good – applies also to government. By giving governors more power (which they need to ensure society's security) they are also provided with greater ability to appropriate resources for their own pleasure at the expense of their subjects. [110] The central problem of government was, then, how to minimize the costs which the misuse of power would impose, without rendering government impotent to secure the goods for which it was originally instituted.[111] This could only be done by ensuring what Bentham called 'Democratical ascendency'. By making the individuals occupying government answerable to, and therefore their interests indistinguishable from, the governed.[112] What were the alternatives?

James Mill reviewed the classical forms of government. Although under democracy, as classically understood, the interests of governed and the government would be identical, democracy is inefficient and would diminish happiness. Not only is democratic government notoriously emotional and unstable, but if all were involved in government, no one would be involved in production, and the total resources of happiness available would fall.[113] Aristocracy and monarchy conversely provide the *possibility* for efficient government, what they notoriously fail to guarantee is governments with an *interest* in ensuring it. However even efficiency is only a possibility for, says Mill, drawing on eighteenth century psychology, intelligence is a consequence of labour, and the aristocracy, as Bentham had impishly classified them, were part of the unemployed classes.[114] Whilst a democracy would not act wrongly from design, aristocracy and

---

in life in so far as beneficent ... exemption from *pain* in all the several shapes in which either body or mind is the seat of it, ... ' Parekh, *Bentham's Political Thought*, p. 313, UCL Box xiv, 392–3.

[109] James Mill, ... *on Government*, p. 17. Cf Bentham, *First Principles..to a Constitutional Code*, p. 270 'Of the principle of self preference the effect is — that, as in every other situation so in that of ruler, generally speaking, a man pursues his own happiness in preference to that of all other individuals put together ... and thence ... to the sacrifice of their happiness.' *First Principles Preparatory to Constitutional Code*, ed. Philip Schofield (Oxford, 1989; *Collected Works*), p. 270.

[110] James Mill, ... *on Government*, p. 6.

[111] Ibid., pp. 21–5.

[112] See Bentham 'A Political Catechism' in Parekh, *Bentham's Political Thought*, pp. 295–6; UCL Box clx, pp. 117–47.

[113] James Mill, ... *on Government*, p. 9.

[114] The notion that intelligence was a product of work, rather than, as in classical thought, leisure is promoted, amongst others, by Hume. See above p. 148. For the aristocracy as the unemployed see Bentham, *Constitutional Code*, ed. F. Rosen and J.H. Burns (Oxford, 1983 *Collected Works*) IX, 25.A47, p.433.

monarchy, if they perceive and follow their selfish interests, will.[115] Once again they will diminish happiness, since by depriving others of the means of it they will lessen the incentives to produce it. In all cases of government by less than the whole community the very 'principles of human nature which imply that Government is necessary, imply that those persons will make use of them to defeat the very end for which Government exists.'[116]

The classical solution to such 'corruption' was of course the notion of the mixed or balanced constitution. Here again utilitarians discerned either muddled thinking or deliberate misrepresentation. If a balanced constitution is truly balanced, power is blocked, Bentham observed. When forces are in balance, the machine is at a stand still.[117] However both Bentham and Mill suggest even this is implausible. True balance is extremely unlikely, and even if it were the case would not last.[118] Alternatively, if there is no true balance, two of the branches will combine to exclude the third. Since the democratic branch represents the interests of the whole, no sectional interest could benefit by combining with it. As a result aristocracy and monarchy will invariably combine against the general interest.[119]

If the people cannot rule themselves, and any smaller group has 'the strongest motives' to abuse their power, the possibility of good government hinges on the fashionable 'doctrine of checks'.[120] Psychology tells us that

> there is no individual or combination of individuals except the community itself, who would not have an interest in bad Government . . . and the community itself is incapable of exercising those powers . . . the conclusion is obvious: The Community itself must check those individuals . . . [121]

It is then, only through representative democratic government that the cost of government from both sources – inefficiency and exploitation – can be minimized. Representative government involves, unlike direct democracy, the election of a body with interests not significantly different from those of the whole community, to, as it were 'police' the government.[122] This leaves most people free to labour to create the means to happiness,

---

[115] James Mill, . . . *on Government*, pp. 11–12.

[116] Ibid., p. 13.

[117] *Political Fallacies*, p. 164.

[118] Mill's argument recalls Hobbes's account of vainglory as a cause of conflict. Even if each power *were* equal, the 'known law of human nature', 'the disposition to overrate one's own advantages, and underrate those of other men', would still lead to conflict and the destabilization of the equilibrium. James Mill, . . . *on Government*, p. 29.

[119] Ibid., p. 32.

[120] Ibid., p. 33. The doctrine of checks refers to what was already a rather heterogeneous literature preoccupied, as so many eighteenth-century writers were, with limiting political power. It included the classical idea of a mixed constitution embodying monarchy, aristocracy and democracy, Locke's notion of the separation of the judiciary from the legislature, Harrington's notion of electoral colleges and Montesquieu's notion of 'intermediate powers'. This amalgam had already received a practical and theoretical endorsement in the American Constitution of 1787 and in *The Federalist*.

[121] James Mill, . . . *on Government*, p. 34.

[122] Mill claims this is not only the sole theoretical solution, but that on which 'the very theory of the British Constitution is erected.' Ibid., pp. 36–7. It was presumably on the basis of such disingenuous claims that Mill assured his anxious editor: 'You need be under no alarm about my article on *Government*: I shall say nothing capable of alarming even a Whig . . .' cited ibid., p. ix.

whilst still minimizing government's opportunities for abuse. The rest of the *Essay* is a discussion of how to identify and weigh up the costs of different ways of constituting the representative body.

The discussion of the extent of political activity, in terms of both the number of people involved and the frequency of their involvement nicely indicates the purely instrumental value attributed to political participation. Mill's concern is to balance the costs of participation (or 'inconveniences' as he calls them, in terms of the numbers of people involved, i.e. the breadth of the franchise) and the intensity of their involvement (i.e. the frequency of elections), against the benefits to be gained by limiting government abuses. The less frequent or extensive the contact between the representative body and the people, the easier it will be for it, like government, to pursue its own good at the expense of the people. The power of the representative body cannot be limited without thereby limiting its ability to do good. But although its power cannot be limited, the length of time for which it is held, can. The more quickly representatives return to the community 'the more difficult it will be to compensate the sacrifice of the interests of the longer period [as a member of the community at large] by the profits of misgovernment during the shorter.'[123]

But just how frequent should elections be? And how much of the population needs to be involved? Mill assumes that being involved in politics constitutes a cost, and that each election is a cost – it involves time away from productive, utility satisfying activity. Neither was an unrealistic assumption in nineteenth-century terms (nor is it obviously false today). Participation could therefore be minimized, consistent with the limitation of the costs of unconstrained government. The inconveniences of political participation were to be traded off against the risks of increased government corruption. One dimension of political activity was its frequency. Representatives need time to learn their task, on the other hand, the longer they are in power before having to be re-elected, the less concerned they will be to consult their constituents' interests. Parliaments should be as 'short as is consistent with the trouble of election and the performance of services'.[124] The other dimension of participation too, thought Mill, should be minimized. The franchise should be as limited as is consistent with the election of a representative body whose interests are those of the community itself. What was 'pretty clear' to Mill was 'that all those individuals whose interests are indisputably included in those of other individuals may be struck off without inconvenience.' What is more staggering to the modern reader is that this disqualified group included all women, and the 'young' males below the age of forty. Mill's conclusion is that since 'scarcely any laws could be made for the benefit of all the men of forty which would not be laws for the benefit of all the rest of the community' the franchise could safely be restricted to that group. [125]

Whilst Mill and Bentham agreed that these were the kind of arguments by which issues of political reform should be decided, the conclusions they drew from them were not always the same.[126] Bentham and Mill thought parliaments should be elected annually –

---

[123] Ibid., p. 38.

[124] Ibid., pp. 38–40.

[125] Ibid., p. 47.

[126] See the interesting discussion in Rosen, *Jeremy Bentham* , ch.ix.

long a traditional demand of radicals.[127] But Mill eagerly endorses re-election, since 'there is good reason for re-electing the man who has done his duty', he has shown his trustworthiness and has his valuable experience to put to the service of the community. Bentham, far more suspicious of the development of cosy relationships, would have disqualified incumbents from re-election, at least until a pool of experienced candidates existed to provide electors with a real choice.[128] Again unlike Mill, Bentham thought constituents should not only be able to unseat delinquent deputies (and for that matter any other officeholder), but that those so unseated should be liable to prosecution.[129] Bentham's insistence on the term 'deputy' indicated a rejection of the paternalistic overtones of the English legal idea of representation, which are assumed in Mill's claim that the working class electorate could be counted on to defer to the middle classes. In these ways Bentham sought to make the elected more accountable to the elected. However, despite this, and again, unlike Mill he retained something of the Burkean idea of the representative, acting, or at least speaking according to his own view of the best interests of all. Their biggest single difference was over the franchise. Mill argued that the franchise could be restricted to men over the age of forty. Since fathers would not act against the interests of their sons or daughters, nor husbands against those of their wives, there was, he claimed, no representational benefit to be gained from the cost of involving these extra groups.

Bentham disagreed. In a set of manuscript comments on James Mill's article, he argued that Mill provided no positive grounds for excluding women and young men, and, moreover, that there were good utilitarian grounds to *include* them.[130] Excluding the young discouraged them from developing the moral and intellectual qualities required by political participation. It would exclude the most vigorous members of the population, and rested on a presumption about the incapacity of the young which, in the case of James Mill's own son, John Stuart Mill, then only eighteen, was manifestly untrue. Including women would, he felt sure, lead to an enlightened revision of the oppressive matrimonial legislation. There were, Bentham insisted, serious distortions of interest to be expected from adult males at the exclusion even of their sons, daughters, and wives.

> ... a selfish and tyrannical husband ... [would] make out of it a pretence for aggravating the already universally existing tyranny of the male sex over the female.
>   A selfish and severe father ... [would] make out of it a pretence for converting into puppets, the wires of which are in his hands, the minds as well as the bodies of his children of both sexes![131]

In his *Constitutional Code* Bentham expresses the general view that groups could not be excluded from the vote unless their happiness was to be excluded from the sum of happiness that government was supposed to maximize. The only other grounds for

---

[127] Major John Cartwright, like Bentham, a reformer with a career going back to the 1770s, was perhaps the most famous campaigner for annual parliaments since then. Mill did not press for annual parliaments in the *Essay*, but supported it in his articles in the *Westminster Review*.

[128] See the discussion of Bentham's views on 'dislocation' in the *Constitutional Code*, Ch. VI, by Rosen, *Bentham and Democracy*, pp. 171–4, cf. James Mill, ... *on Government*, pp. 41–2.

[129] Bentham, p. 286, and see Parekh, p. 211. cf. James Mill, ... *on Government*, pp. 40–1.

[130] The notes are reprinted as Appendix B in Parekh, *Bentham's Political Thought*, p. 311.

[131] Ibid., p. 312.

exclusion were immaturity or incompetence. As regards the former Bentham thought the existing age of majority, then 21, was 'long enough' to wait. As regards the latter, the ability to read and write. Traditional arguments about the intellectual shortcomings of women were unfounded, indeed the examples of the prosperous reigns of Queen Elizabeth and Queen Ann tilted expectations if anything the other way. If women could successfully occupy the executive (the 'operative power' as Bentham termed it) there was no case for excluding them from the electorate (constitutive power). Moreover, it followed from the greater susceptibility of women to pain – both from natural causes and from the violence of men – that the greatest happiness principle required not only their equal, but if anything their disproportionate representation.[132] Despite this Bentham recognized that women's emancipation was at the time too extreme a demand for the reformers to pursue without jeopardizing the rest of the programme: 'The contests and confusion produced by the proposal of this improvement would engross the public mind and throw improvement in all other shapes to a distance.'[133]

In their moves towards a wider franchise, utilitarian thinkers were very conscious of objections involving arguments about the uneducated characteristics of the 'lower sort' of people.[134] Mill's counter-argument once again encapsulates the utilitarian, interest-based view of politics. Even if the people are ignorant, they will at least have an *interest* in acting aright. Unchecked partial government, no matter how competent, will, and can only ever have its own interests at heart. Although education will help a popular electorate to correctly perceive their interests, other groups 'have the strongest possible interest to deceive themselves and to endeavour to deceive others.'[135] A large part of Bentham's political propaganda – most famously the *Book of Fallacies*, was devoted to exposing those arguments designed to conceal from the wider public, the operation of sinister interests.

Bentham's utilitarian public policy

Democratic government was a means to an end; Bentham did not believe that the popular will replaced the principle of utility as the criterion of social or political rectitude. For Benthamites all government, being concerned as it was with the imposition of painful sanctions, was by definition, in itself an evil.[136] Nor, by and large, did Bentham regard even popular government as a proper positive agent in the provision of happiness: 'The care of providing for his enjoyments ought to be left almost entirely to each individual; the principal function of government being to protect him from sufferings'.[137] However,

---

[132] *First Principles . . . to a Constitutional Code*, pp. 97–8. Bentham had stressed the differences in susceptibility to pain as far back as the *Principles of Morals and Legislation*, p. 64; but see: Terence Ball, 'Utilitarianism, Feminism and the Franchise', *History of Political Thought*, I, 1 (1980).

[133] *First Principles . . . to a Constitutional Code*, p. 100.

[134] Here again, Bentham and Mill differed. Bentham would have imposed a literacy test on voters (Parekh, p. 208). Mill makes no such condition.

[135] James Mill, . . . *on Government*, pp. 65, 67.

[136] *First Principles . . . to a Constitutional Code*, p. 4.

[137] Cited Dinwiddy, p. 107, Bowring, i, p. 301, cf. earlier, less political statements of the principle in *Principles of Morals and Legislation*, pp. 159, 244. But note that this conviction *pre*dates Bentham's conversion to political radicalism.

this libertarian principle was quite instrumental to the maximization of utility and distinctly subordinate to other intermediate principles by which he thought it could be realized.

Bentham reformulated the principle of utility several times during his life, with an eye both to precision and its publicity value.[138] As a slogan designed to undermine uncritical acceptance of custom, the detailed policy implications were perhaps less important than its general thrust.[139] However, the more utilitarians developed their theory as a theory of government, the more important it became to articulate, in general terms, what the greatest happiness consisted in, and in addition to decide what balance needed to be struck between individual and aggregate happiness. These questions led Bentham to develop his earlier ideas in exciting directions.

The maximization of happiness *could* justify the imposition of majority opinion on that of a minority. If the majority claimed to experience 'pain' as a result of some purely private practice of minorities – sexual practices or religious worship say – they might argue that utility would be maximized by criminalizing the practice to relieve their feelings. As we've seen, Bentham's insistence on the objective quality of pain would tend to disqualify such arguments, although it is unclear quite how, institutionally, given his championship of democracy whilst rejecting fundamental rights, they could be resisted in practice.[140] This majoritarian threat operated in other areas too. Amongst the traditional fear of any democratization of government was that of 'levelling' – the appropriation of the goods of the wealthy by the poor. Bentham was of course aware of such charges – during the 1790s support for the French Revolution by British radicals had given rise to widespread fears, some of them deliberately promoted by government, of 'levelling'.[141] He had at the time, reversed his own tentative moves towards democracy.

Bentham's later formulations of the principle indicate serious concern to address the problem of how to assess the competing claims for happiness of the few and the many.[142]

---

[138] For a history see R.Shackleton, 'The Greatest Happiness of the Greatest number: the History of Bentham's Phrase.'*Studies on Voltaire and the Eighteenth Century*, XC (1972).

[139] As Bentham suggests in the *Principles of Morals and Legislation*, p. 40, where he writes that his analysis is not meant to be precisely applied but 'held in view'.

[140] Such examples were actually advanced even by sympathetic contemporary critics of Bentham's proposals. Sir James Mackintosh, for example pointed out that the consequence of Bentham's scheme in Ireland would be the establishment of a Catholic tyranny over the Protestant minority, and the same would be true in any society 'divided, by conspicuous marks, into a permanent majority and minority'. *The Edinburgh Review*, xxxi, 184–5, cited J.R. Dinwiddy, review of Frederick Rosen, *Bentham and . . . Democracy* , *The Bentham Newsletter* (June, 1984).

[141] One of the principal loyalist groups was Reeves's Association for the Preservation of Property against Republicans and Levellers.

[142] For example, at the start of *First Principles . . . to a Constitutional Code*, 'The greatest happiness of the greatest number is the only right and proper end of government: of all, in so far as the happiness of all can be encreased without lessening the happiness of any: of the greatest number in so far as the happiness of some can not be encreased unless by defalcation made from the happiness of others', *First Principles . . . to a Constitutional Code*, p. 3. Fred Rosen has noted a later formulation in which Bentham offers a lexical ordering which prioritizes a principle of equal utility over a principle of maximizing total utility. There Bentham claims that it is the task of government to maximise the happiness 'of all of them, without exception, in so far as possible: the greatest happiness of the greatest number of them, on every occasion on which the nature of the case renders the provision of an equal quantity of happiness for every one of

The principle Bentham seems to be working towards is that there are two principles to be applied in succession, the first to be realized as far as possible before the second. They are that increases in happiness should be equally distributed to all if possible, and then, when equal distribution was no longer possible, to the greatest number. This later fine tuning of the general principle perhaps incorporates some of Bentham's earlier claims about the intermediate policy objectives which governments pursuing the greatest happiness need to pursue.

The policy aims of constitutions informed by the greatest happiness principle will be, claims Bentham, subsistence, abundance, security and equality.[143] By subsistence Bentham means everything 'the non-possession of which would be productive of physical suffering'.[144] By abundance, both the proliferation of the means of happiness, and security that subsistence will be sustained. Security itself relates to the propensity (analysed in the *Introduction*) for human's present happiness to be undermined by their uncertainty that it will continue. Thus abundance contributes indirectly to it, whilst continuity and the rule of law – knowing what the rules are and that they will continue to operate in the same way – do so directly. Finally, in urging equality Bentham expresses the view, inherent in the later formulations of the greatest happiness principle, that the distribution and not merely the total sum of goods is relevant to the question of utility.

It is the second two of these four policy objectives which most modify any crude view of Bentham's utilitarianism. The principle of security is in part the utilitarian counterpart of the doctrine of checks and balances: it requires of any constitution the utmost limitation (consistent with the proper discharging of their duty) on the capacity of those placed in authority to harm those under them to their individual advantage. However, looked at more generally, the principle is a (for Bentham) surprisingly powerful conservative one which militates against change, even through utilitarian policies, if there is any doubt about the benefit of the outcome: 'Reason silent or hesitating, custom should on every occasion decide the scale. By departure from custom, disappointment is produced: and by disappointment, disquietude, uneasiness, pain.'[145]

The case of equality appears the most extreme departure from utility. Inasmuch as utility can be regarded (as Bentham suggests) as roughly equivalent to wealth or money, the principle of utility seems to be concerned only with the total amount available, and to be indifferent about its distribution amongst people. Thus, to take an apparently extreme example which in fact obtains in most countries, if ninety per cent of the wealth were possessed by ten per cent of the people, this would be indistinguishable (in utilitarian terms) from an equal distribution of that same amount of wealth. In fact the two positions are not indistinguishable, for two reasons.

Firstly Bentham argued that the amount of happiness engendered by the instruments of happiness – primarily wealth – *was* altered by changes in the overall distribution;

---

them impossible.' *Parliamentary Candidate's Declaration*, p. 7, cited, Rosen, *Bentham and ... Democracy*, p. 212.

[143] *First Principles ... to a Constitutional Code*, in Parekh, *Bentham's Political Thought*, p. 196.

[144] As he negatively prefers to put it. *First Principles ... to a Constitutional Code*, in ibid. p. 196, note.

[145] *First Principles ... to a Constitutional Code*, p. 97.

specifically, that inequality diminished the sum of happiness.[146] The explanation of the basis for this assertion lies in Bentham's notion of decreasing marginal utility, explained in an earlier section. Because each additional sum of money possessed creates less happiness for the possessor than the one before, redistributing wealth to the rich produces less happiness than redistributing it to the poor would. Secondly, it was axiomatic that the more power individuals had, the easier it would be for them to diminish others' pleasure to benefit themselves, and Bentham recognized that 'between power and wealth such is the connexion, that each is an instrument for the acquisition of the other'.[147] The first is the more fundamental and theoretical reason, the second a practical one, albeit an acknowledgement which much libertarian theory would be the better for recognizing.

Does the acknowledgement of marginal utility then commit utilitarians to a policy of imposed equality – the much feared levelling? The answer is no. The demands of equality have to be set against the claims of security and abundance. The knowledge that property was to be periodically redistributed would itself, through the resulting uncertainty of possession, cause widespread fear and unhappiness: disutility. Furthermore such uncertainty would have serious implications for the creation of wealth, by discouraging investment and wealth-creating activity. It was only, thought Bentham, through the freedom of the market that abundance could be achieved, and abundance itself indirectly promoted security. Thus, once subsistence was satisfied, equality, security and abundance had to be played off against one another. Whilst an a priori case for absolute equality could be made on utilitarian grounds, in practice, it had to be modified by utilitarian claims based on security of possession and abundance, or, as we should say today, growth.

Despite this general support for free market policies, Bentham was a decidedly unusual economic liberal, especially for his time. Bentham appears to start out from the classical view that the market equilibrates supply and demand. Certainly this is his view with regard to investment: government could only redistribute the allocation of investment, not increase the amount of it. The clear policy implication was therefore that government-induced increases in growth were an illusion. But he later observed that increases in the money supply, although incapable of affecting growth at full employment, could do so if there was unemployment 'in so far as it gets extra hands, or sets them to work at extra hours'.[148] To this Keynesian insight was added another: that private investment might fall, not due to diversion into expenditure, but due to hoarding, causing a kind of 'savings trap'.[149] The implication that government should stimulate growth in the economy by the judicious increase of the money supply was one that Bentham explicitly drew from these observations, it was a view that was not drawn again until J.M. Keynes's brilliant work in the 1920s. In this Bentham was quite out of line with his contemporaries. The most famous economist of the day, David Ricardo, shown Bentham's manuscript

---

[146] 'The more remote from equality are the shares possessed by the individuals in question, in the mass of the instruments of felicity, the less is the sum of the felicity, produced by the sum of those shares.' *First Principles . . . to a Constitutional Code*, in Parekh, *Bentham's Political Thought*, p. 200.

[147] *First Principles . . . to a Constitutional Code*, in Parekh, ibid., p. 200.

[148] *Manual of Political Economy* (1793–5), in Stark, *Economic Writings*, vol.1, pp. 270–1, discussed in T.W. Hutchison, 'Bentham as an Economist', *The Economic Journal* (1956).

[149] In *The True Alarm* (1801), in *Jeremy Bentham's Economic Writings*, ed. W. Stark (3 vols, London, 1952–4), vol.III, p. 120.

of this work, commented that he could not understand why any increase in the money supply should affect production.

The issue of the relationship of the money supply to economic growth is a technical, and still widely debated one. It is however part of the general classical view of the free market economy as a virtually self-regulating system. It was a view Bentham came deeply to distrust. In the field of economic intervention he wrote 'I never had, nor ever shall have, any horror . . . of the hand of government.' There was no more reason, in his view, for humans to be passive in the face of the operation of natural economic laws, than there was for them to be passive in the face of any other natural laws, after all 'when water, in the search after a level is making its way too fast into a ship, pumps are employed by men to prevail on it to get the better of that propensity, and betake itself to a higher level.' There was absolutely no reason, in Bentham's view, why the politician should not similarly attempt to regulate supposedly 'natural' levels in economics.[150]

Several particular issues exemplify this willingness to intervene where utilitarian criteria allowed. Apart from regulation of the money supply, Bentham defended a maximum price for bread, forced savings, governmental regulation of education, health care and transport communications, he recommended a national statistical service, government supervision of banking and the nationalization of insurance. Moreover, although Bentham, like most other economic thinkers of the time, did not believe that labourers' wages could be raised significantly above subsistence (the level that avoids painful privation), he did believe labourers could be made to feel and be *secure* at those levels. To this end Bentham endorsed a final great heresy of laissez-faire, he recommended the state storage of grain and its release to prevent the exceeding of a maximum price. 'horror in which [this policy] has been held, ' he wrote, 'has nothing but prejudice, and a too indiscriminate attachment to general principles for its foundation.'[151]

More generally Bentham's inclusion of both subsistence and security as policy ideals runs directly counter to liberal economic doctrine, and were recognized to do so at the time. Only by inhibiting the rise and fall of wages and prices could subsistence or security (let alone equality) be pursued. The operation of these forces was explicitly seen at this time as involving the periodic privation, destitution and death by starvation of the labouring classes.[152] In asserting their claims to a secure subsistence Bentham consciously rejected that doctrine.[153]

Once we get past the well known clichés of Bentham's thought we find a subtle and inventive mind at work. However, as we suggested at the start, little of this subtlety survived, and his immediate historical influence comprised rather crude slogans, which,

---

[150] *The Defence of a Maximum* (1801), in *Economic Writings*, vol. III, pp. 257–8.

[151] See Hutchison, 'Bentham as an Economist', pp. 302–3. Once again James Mill differed significantly from Bentham on these economic issues.

[152] The most notorious exponent of the view was Thomas Robert Malthus. The nub of his argument is contained in his *Essay on the Principle of Population*, ed. Anthony Flew (Harmondsworth, 1970), first published 1798. Malthus argued that since invariably population grew faster than the food supply, even the redistribution of money to the poor would only raise the price of food or the size of the population. The poor laws were thus either ineffectual or encouraged irresponsibility. ' . . . considering the state of the lower classes altogether, both in the towns and in the country, the distresses which they suffer from the want of proper and sufficient food, from hard labour and unwholesome habitations, must operate as a constant check to incipient population' (chapter V, passim, and p. 103).

[153] Hutchison, 'Bentham as an Economist', p. 304.

whilst politically powerful, attracted criticism as inadequate and superficial accounts of human beings and their relationship with their society.[154] Ironically such criticisms were made even by an individual brought up at the centre of the utilitarian movement and educated to carry its principles forward to the next generation, James Mill's son, John Stuart Mill.

---

[154] The history of utilitarianism as a propaganda movement is well told in Hamburger's *James Mill and the Art of Revolution*. The wittiest and most famous contemporary attack on utilitarianism is in Macaulay's review of James Mill's *Essay on Government* which will be discussed in the next chapter.

VIII

John Stuart Mill

Introduction: Mill and utilitarianism

John Stuart Mill's interests were wide-ranging, but the keystone of his career as a political theorist was, at an obvious level, the *Essay on Representative Government* (1861): it contained, he wrote in the preface, 'the principles to which I have been working up during the greater part of my life'.[1] Accepting this self-assessment of his we shall try to trace his development from faithful pupil of Bentham and his father, James Mill, to the, in some ways, quite different position he had achieved by the end of his life.[2] One other of his works will receive detailed consideration, and that is his essay *On Liberty*, important both in its own right as a statement of the value of freedom in a civilized society, and in characterizing a particularly significant deviation from his inherited views.

Education

John Stuart Mill was, as is notorious, raised and educated to be the champion of the utilitarian philosophy worked out by his father and Jeremy Bentham. This involved a gruelling educational regime under which he started Greek at the age of three, and Latin at eight. By age seven he was reading – in the original Greek – those dialogues of Plato which nowadays first or second year undergraduates tackle. By the time he was twelve Mill had absorbed a considerable proportion of classical literature, as well as mastering mathematics as far as differential calculus. As for natural science, reading it was at this time, he wrote, 'one of my greatest amusements'. From twelve onward Mill studied logic, a subject he regarded as the most valuable part of his education.[3]

Of a second aspect of his education Mill was aware only in retrospect. That was not only the absence of any emotional education, but his father's denigration and contempt for 'passionate emotions of all sorts'. This Mill later saw as something of a national

---

[1] J.S. Mill, *Representative Government*, p. 173, in *Utilitarianism, On Liberty,* and *Considerations on Representative Government*, ed. H. B. Acton (London, 1910, repr. 1972). All references to these works cite this edition.

[2] It is a perspective Mill himself wanted his readers to be aware of, expressing in his *Autobiography* his 'desire to make acknowledgement of the debts which my intellectual and moral development owes to other persons.' J.S. Mill, *Autobiography,* ed. Jack Stillinger (Oxford, 1969), p. 3. A similar, more detailed examination of this kind, focused more precisely on Mill's political programme is conducted by J. H. Burns, in 'J.S. Mill and Democracy, 1829–61', *Political Studies*, V (1957), and reprinted in *Mill, A Collection of Critical Essays*, ed. J. B. Schneewind (London, 1968) to which citations here refer.

[3] *Autobiography*, pp. 5–13.

character trait of the English when he compared it with the 'habitual exercise of the feelings' to be found on the Continent.[4]

This punishing programme was part of a self-conscious project: to educate the young Mill as the leader and champion of the next generation of utilitarian reformers. In 1812 James Mill wrote to Bentham:

> If I were to die before this poor boy is a man, one of the things that would pinch me most sorely, would be, the being obliged to leave his mind unmade to the degree of excellence, of which I hoped to make it . . . the only prospect which would lessen the pain, would be the leaving him in your hands . . . then we may perhaps leave him a successor worthy of both of us.[5]

The project, initially at least, achieved its end, and Mill writes that he and his peers modelled themselves, as a school of thinking, on the French Enlightenment *philosophes*. Although youthful zealots in pursuit of utility, this enthusiasm was, Mill later felt 'speculative', not rooted 'in genuine benevolence, or sympathy with mankind, although these qualities held their due place in my ethical standard'. Of himself at the time he wrote: 'I conceive that the description so often given of a Benthamite, as a mere reasoning machine, although extremely inapplicable to most of those who have been designated by that title, was during two or three years of my life not altogether untrue of me.'[6]

Mental crisis

This rigorous upbringing, not surprisingly, took its toll on Mill's personality in adult life. He suffered what he described as a 'mental crisis' in 1826, aged 20, which led him – cautiously during his father's life, for Mill senior exercised a form of censorship over his son's writings – to distance himself from inherited views. The tension seems only to have been finally resolved on the death of his father in 1836.[7] Then Mill, duly distressed, nevertheless felt able to write: 'Deprived of my father's aid, I was also exempted from the restraints and reticences by which that aid had been purchased. I did not feel that there was any other radical writer or politician to whom I was bound to defer'.[8] Mill's crisis involved not only, as we shall see, a strictly intellectual re-alignment. Mill's concern in the *Autobiography* is not, as it is often taken, to provide an awful warning about how not to educate a child, but rather to demonstrate his ideal of self-culture by giving a personal account of an exercise in self-redefinition. From the time he first read Bentham (aged fourteen), he wrote 'I had what might truly be called an object in life; to

---

[4] Ibid., p. 38.

[5] *Works of Jeremy Bentham*, ed. John Bowring, (XI vols, Edinburgh, 1843), vol. X p.473.

[6] *Autobiography*, p. 66.

[7] Thomas warns that we should be cautious about the interpretation of Mill's 'crisis' and of reading into the Victorian phrase 'mental crisis' modern notions of mental breakdown and psychological trauma 'without which' as he nicely puts it 'no biographer nowadays feels it possible to retain a reader's attention'. (William Thomas, *The Philosophical Radicals: nine studies in Theory and Practice, 1817–1841* (Oxford, 1979), p. 151ff.).

[8] *Autobiography*, p. 123.

be a reformer of the world. My conception of my own happiness was entirely identified with this object.' But from the autumn of 1826 he 'awakened from this as from a dream', and suffered an acute sense of the inadequacy of this end both as a social and as a personal ideal. 'I seemed', he wrote, 'to have nothing left to live for.'[9]

Disillusionment with Benthamism undoubtedly, and in the long term, forms one strand in the crisis, but this is not what is stressed in the *Autobiography*. There Mill focuses more generally on the inadequacies of the psychological theory behind his education, rather than on Benthamism itself, to which, as we have seen, he had been introduced only quite late. The theory informing his education had been that most influential eighteenth-century doctrine of association. On this view a good character is formed by creating purely associative connections in the mind between virtuous action and personal pleasure. Mill now saw two things: firstly that such ties had been formed for him by only the crudest means: praise and blame, reward and punishment, and that they were therefore 'artificial and casual' unless reinforced in some way. Secondly that 'the habit of analysis has a tendency to wear away the feelings . . . to weaken and undermine whatever is the result of prejudice . . . and [that] no associations whatever could ultimately resist this dissolving force [except for] the real connexions between Things, not dependent on our will and feelings.' Mill, was, in a sense, personally living out the dire consequences predicted by Burke for those who forsake prejudice to live on reason alone. The nihilistic conclusion Mill drew was that his education had failed to establish strong enough associations to sustain his enterprise, and that there was 'no power in nature sufficient to begin the formation of my character anew, and create in a mind now irretrievably analytic, fresh associations of pleasure with any of the objects of human desire.'[10] Mill's characterization of his situation depicts the hopelessness of one who, believing in the causal determination of human action and personality, nevertheless believes that process to have failed them. Mill's subsequent belief in and pursuit of self-culture, was the only route of escape from his situation, although he had to wrestle to reconcile this belief with his doctrine of the pervasiveness of causation.[11] The interest scholars have in Mill's personality as opposed to his arguments thus has considerable warrant in his own ideas, for he stressed that a concern with the development of personality was an essential part of the political culture of a civilized society.[12] Indeed one of his reasons for writing his biography was to chart for others the course of his own personal development, and so demonstrate for others each person's capacity to take command of their own personality and to remedy its deficiencies.[13]

The cultivation of one's personality was, however, threatened in various ways in modern society and he sought to defend it against that threat. These threats were both

---

[9] Ibid., pp. 80–1.

[10] Ibid., pp. 83–4.

[11] John Stuart Mill, *A System of Logic* (London, 1967: the text of the eighth edition), Bk VII, ch.2, p. 547ff.

[12] A view expressed as early as the essay on 'Civilization'. For this view of Mill's enterprise see E .J. Eisenach, 'Mill's *Autobiography* as Political Theory' *History of Political Thought*, VIII, 1 (1987). Mill's Essays and Reviews are cited both from the new *Collected Works of John Stuart Mill*, ed., J. M. Robson (Toronto, 1963 – 1991), hereafter *CW*; and, where possible, from the older *Dissertations and Discussions, political, philosophical, and historical, chiefly from the Edinburgh and Westminster Reviews*, J. S. Mill, (3 vols. London, 1867), cited as *D&D*, or failing that from another easily available edition.

[13] *Autobiography*, p. 3.

political and ideological, and indeed at one important level, even the associationist utilitarianism in which he was schooled posed such a threat, for it assumed and required most individuals to respond predictably to environmental appeals to their self-interest. Mill's development can therefore quite properly be seen as an interplay between his own mental crisis, springing from the inadequacy of his educational upbringing, and external influences in terms of the new social and political circumstances and range of intellectual traditions to which he was exposed – indeed which he deliberately sought out as a corrective. It is the consequences of *these* that then feed into and modify his utilitarianism, rather than utilitarianism itself being the immediate object of change.

Mill's adjustments to utilitarianism

The effects of this crisis on Mill's social and moral beliefs were, as described by him, quite distinct. He saw firstly that whilst happiness was still the *criterion* of moral action it could not, psychologically speaking, be the *aim*. Happiness was the consequence of pursuing some other ideal. The pursuit of happiness as a self-conscious project was, at least for the majority of mankind, self-defeating. According to Bentham, the presumption of egoistic pleasure seeking had been both the psychological axiom from which his descriptive theory of morals and government derived *and* the consideration which validated utilitarianism as an immediate moral principle. Mill now questioned each of these positions. He doubted that egoism was either a universal or an adequate explanatory principle of society, and he certainly doubted whether even an idealistic desire to maximize other's pleasure was in itself an adequate, or psychologically satisfying expression of the utilitarian principle – and it was crucial to the utilitarian project that morality and psychology should mesh in this way. This led him to develop or modify utilitarianism, both psychologically – by showing a much greater concern with generating altruistic motives than had Bentham – and morally – by considering the claims of other ideals than the immediate maximization of pleasure.[14] For, secondly, Mill saw that the happy life was not one where capacities and action were seen as mere instruments to pursue given desires and ends, laudable though they may be. The happiest lives, he thought, were those in which our sensibilities have themselves been refined. 'The cultivation of the feelings became one of the cardinal points in my ethical and philosophical creed.'[15] In pursuit of this Mill turned to poetry and music.[16] He read

---

[14] For example in the essay on *Bentham* written in 1838: 'we think utility, or happiness, much too complex and indefinite an end to be sought except through the medium of various secondary ends . . . those who adopt utility as a standard can seldom apply it truly except through secondary principles; those who reject it, generally do no more than erect those secondary principles into first principles.' *CW*, vol X, pp. 110–11; and in *Mill on Bentham and Coleridge*, ed F. R. Leavis (London, 1967), pp. 90–1.

[15] *Autobiography*, pp. 85–6.

[16] He wrote, in 1833: 'Poetry, when it really is such is truth; and fiction also, if it is good for anything, is truth.' The truth that it describes, is not the literal truth of whatever is the subject of the poem but something, in a way far more important, the truth of poetry lies 'not in the object itself, nor in the scientific truth itself, but in the state of mind in which the one and the other may be contemplated.' 'Thoughts on Poetry and its varieties', *CW*, vol. I, p. 347; *D&D*, I, p. 69. As Mill pointed out, for Bentham 'all poetry is misrepresentation.' *Bentham* p. 95.

Wordsworth and Coleridge, Goethe and German philosophy.[17] He tried to persuade other utilitarians of the importance of the emotions.[18]

Mill sought quite self-consciously to integrate his new ideas with his old into a coherent pattern of thought, adjusting where possible, rejecting only where necessary. Amongst the inadequacies of his inherited theory in the field of politics was, he recognized, an insufficient attention not only to the sheer diversity of political experience and practice, but to the diversity of ends to which government should be directed. A related and deeper problem, he recognized, was that of the correct method to be applied in the study of politics, an argument which continues today as to the extent to which politics is properly a deductive *a prioristic* science, or an essentially empirical and descriptive one. The issue was brought to a head by Macaulay's review of his father's *Essay on Government* in the *Edinburgh Review*, and it led Mill to focus more generally on the utilitarians' failure to acknowledge the dimension of history.[19]

Intellectual influences contradicting utilitarianism

Macaulay's attack

In 1829, the historian Thomas Babington Macaulay published a devastating review of James Mill's *Essay on Government* in the *Edinburgh Review*. It caused consternation in the ranks of the philosophical radicals for its target was much wider than Mill senior's *Essay*. It threatened the whole utilitarian enterprise: it undermined its psychology, its methodology and its policy.[20]

---

[17] There is not space here to do justice to all of the important influences on Mill, but of those not discussed Coleridge is possibly the most important. From Coleridge Mill gained a critical perspective on the threat a commercial society posed to cultural and aesthetic continuity, and the importance of sustaining, in some body of people — for Coleridge an institutionalised 'Clerisy' — the advances thus far made by civilization. One of the high-points of Coleridge's influence was the essay on 'The right and wrong of State interference with Corporation and Church Property' (1833) in which Mill defended the appropriation of church property to sustain a kind of secularized clergy as a 'lettered class..appointed to study and diffuse all those impressions, which constituted mental culture . . . fitted the mind of man for his condition, destiny, and duty as a human being.' *CW*, vol. IV p. 220; *D&D*, I, p. 38. The most recent study of Coleridge's political thought is John Morrow, *Coleridge's Political Thought, property, morality and the limits of traditional discourse* (London, 1990).

[18] Ironically — or perhaps cunningly? — using appropriately empiricist arguments: 'the imaginative emotion which an idea when vividly conceived excites in us, is not an illusion but a fact, as real as any of the other qualities of objects;' *Autobiography*, p. 91. Mill's attempts were not notably successful, as his account of the relationship with Roebuck in the *Autobiography* shows. John Bowring, literary executor of Bentham's works, remarked sardonically that Mill 'was most emphatically a philosopher, but then he read Wordsworth and that muddled him, and he has been in a strange confusion ever since, endeavouring to unite poetry and philosophy.' Cited, ibid., p. xvi.

[19] Ibid., p. 94.

[20] See James Hamburger, *James Mill and the Art of Revolution* (New Haven, 1963), p. 80. Despite the ferocity of the attack, Mill senior forgave Macaulay, and Macaulay later acknowledged that 'serious as are the faults of the Essay on Government, a critic, whilst noticing those faults, should have abstained from using contemptuous language respecting the historian of British India.' T. B. Macaulay, *Complete Works* (XII vols, London, 1897), vol VII, p. xii. (Macaulay was also, for a time, in the Indian Civil Service).

Mill's *Essay* had the virtue of clarity and simplicity. From very simple premises, the assumption of psychological egoism, and the desirability of maximizing utility, Mill deduced, in a way comparable to the elegant models of classical economics, the form that government should take. Macaulay's target was these very virtues, or at least the deductivism that made them possible. If this method, or the basic assumptions were wrong, everything else fell too, for, as Macaulay remarked 'The style which the Utilitarians admire suits only those subjects on which it is possible to reason *a priori*.' Macaulay denied that politics was such a subject, and the reason for his denial was the sheer variety of human historical experience deliberately ignored by Mill: 'We have here an elaborate treatise on government, from which, but for two or three passing allusions, it would not appear that the author was actually aware that any governments existed amongst men.'[21]

James Mill was able to avoid reference to actual governments because his theory of government proceeds deductively, by drawing out the form of government required to maximize utility where abstractly characterized individuals are assumed to act egoistically. But like geometric theorems, it would only apply to the world inasmuch as the world is characterized by the identical characteristics (and no others) that inform the theory. Mill senior's argument was that this method was forced on social theorists because the diversity of human institutions is so great, and the apparent consequences of even the same institutions so various, that to build up inductive generalizations from the observed or recorded historical experience of mankind would be an impossible task; the facts are simply too diffuse for science to be able to make organizational sense of them. It was for this argument that Macaulay reserved the height of his considerable and effective ridicule.[22]

Experience can only appear 'too' diverse with respect to our expectations of it. If our theoretical models are incapable of coping with experience surely we should change our theory, rather than ignore our experience? To say that the deductive method must be followed because experience is too diverse to form a basis for science is not only 'to believe at once in a theory and a fact which contradicts it . . . an exercise of faith which is sufficiently hard: but to believe in a theory *because* a fact contradicts it . . . [which] neither philosopher nor pope ever before required.'[23]

Macaulay attacked not only the method but the assumptions on which Mill's *Essay* was based. Are the rulers in simple forms of government bound to pursue the exploitation of their subjects to the degree predicted by the theory? 'No man of common sense can live among his fellow creatures for a day without seeing innumerable facts which contradict it. . . . Is it not possible that a king or an aristocracy may soon be saturated with the objects of their desires, and may then protect the community in the enjoyment of the rest?'[24] Even more damaging, Macaulay exposed the inadequacy of Mill's limited conception of self- interest in the *Essay*. Only a small part of what the wealthy spend

---

[21] 'Mill's Essay on Government' in Macaulay, *Complete Works*, vol. VII, p. 330.

[22] Macaulay, early in his career, specialized in literary hatchet-jobs; Boswell was another casualty.

[23] Macaulay, 'Mill's Essay on Government', p. 331. Again: 'Mr. Mill reminds us of those philosophers of the sixteenth century who, having satisfied themselves a priori that the rapidity with which bodies descended to the centre of the earth varied exactly as their weights, refused to believe the contrary evidence of their own eyes and ears.' p. 346.

[24] Macaulay, 'Mill's Essay on Government', pp. 337, 335.

goes on personal physical pleasure, much goes on hospitality, and 'to cement the ties of good neighbourhood.' Amongst the strongest objects of wider human desire 'there is none which men in general seem to desire more than the good opinion of others.' Whatever the egoistic origins of this sentiment, once formed 'men feel extremely solicitous about the opinions of those by whom it is most improbable, nay absolutely impossible that they should be in the slightest degree injured or benefited.'[25] Mill's conclusions about the best form of government are also cruelly tested. If Mill's basic assumption about human egoism were true how *could* mere representation guarantee an identity of interests? 'As soon as they are separated from the people . . . commences that interest which must, according to Mr. Mill produce measures opposite to the interests of the community . . . .if men were what he represents them to be, the letter of the very constitution which he recommends would afford no safeguard against bad government.'[26] Even worse is Mill's arbitrary dropping of his 'worst case assumption' when it comes to the franchise. By cavalierly 'deducing' that the interests of women are to be included in their menfolk he 'placidly dogmatizes away the interest of one half of the human race.' Throughout the world women are 'strictly in a state of personal slavery . . . Is the interest of a Turk the same with that of the girls who compose his harem . . . of a Chinese . . . with that of the woman whom he harnesses to his plough . . . of an Italian . . . with that of the daughter whom he devotes to God?' Needless to say, nearer home, the conservative Macaulay expressed fewer fears on behalf of women, but if it can be said to be true of England that a wife's interest is the same as that of her husband's he thought it is only so 'because human nature is not what Mr. Mill conceives it to be' and if the kindness of husbands and fathers to their womenfolk can be assumed to deny them the franchise, why may not the kindness of monarchs and aristocracies be assumed to deny the necessity for representative government? A supporter of reform, although of an increasingly moderate kind, Macaulay was here playing Devil's advocate by pursuing Mill's assumptions into areas where Mill had been reluctant to go.

The most serious example of this is in the discussion of the franchise. Here Macaulay spells out with arithmetical precision the possibility that haunted Europeans from the seventeenth century to the twentieth, from the English Revolution to the Russian and beyond: the use by the poor of political power to expropriate the wealth of the rich. Mill 'proposes to give the poor majority power over the rich minority. Is it possible to doubt to what, on his own principles, such an arrangement must lead?' Macaulay does the sums and concludes that if property were equally divided, expropriation 'would not repay the other members of the community the trouble of dividing it.' On the other hand:

> If there were a thousand men with ten pounds a piece, it would not be worthwhile for nine hundred and ninety of them to rob ten, and it would be a bold attempt for six hundred of them to rob four hundred. But if ten of them had a hundred thousand pounds apiece, the case would be very different. There would be much to be got, and nothing to be feared.

The argument that it might not be in the long term interests for the poor to expropriate, is no security, for on the utilitarians' own principles (see Bentham's dimension of

---

[25] Ibid., pp. 337–8.
[26] Ibid., p. 352.

'propinquity') the fear of a far off evil will be unlikely to outweigh an immediate benefit.[27]

Thus Mill's method, his premise, and his resulting programme were successively demolished. But the challenge with which Macaulay faced the utilitarian was not simply the demolition of their political programme, nor even the challenge of the historian to the a-prioristic social theorist. It was a challenge to recognize, as neither James Mill, nor historians such as Clarendon did, that the ideas, mental climate, moral presuppositions and such like of an age, form the stuff of history and social reality alike. Neither historians who restrict themselves to 'events', nor social theorists who sacrifice all to logical rigour can grasp the major features of social reality:

> A history in which every particular incident may be true, may on the whole be false. The circumstances which have most influence on the happiness of mankind, the changes of manners and morals, the transition of communities from poverty to wealth, from knowledge to ignorance, from ferocity to humanity – these are for the most part, noiseless revolutions. Their progress is rarely indicated by what historians are pleased to call events.[28]

Macaulay had no way of characterizing what a correct method might be, except, very generally,

> induction; – by observing the present state of the world, – by assiduously studying the history of past ages, – by sifting the evidence of facts, – by carefully combining and contrasting those which are authentic, – by generalizing with judgement and diffidence, – by perpetually bringing the theory which we have constructed to the test of new facts.

'This', he thought 'is that noble Science of Politics, which is equally removed from the barren theories of the Utilitarian sophists, and from the petty craft . . . of intrigue, jobbing and official etiquette.'[29]

Other influences

Macaulay's attack on Mill's father's *Essay* was not the only critical influence he absorbed at this time. He was impressed by the French Saint-Simonian thinkers with their view of a rationally ordered utopian society, and by Auguste Comte's work, both as in attempting to schematize historical change as a movement from 'theological' through metaphysical to a 'positivist' stage, and in his insistence that the advent of 'social science' meant that the formation of opinions on important social questions should be left to qualified 'social theorists'. An important early essay 'The Spirit of the Age' (1831) reveals how far Mill had moved from the utilitarian commitment to egalitarian freedom, even as a condition

---

[27] Ibid., pp. 357–8.

[28] Macaulay, 'History', in *Complete Works*, vol. VII, p. 213.

[29] Macaulay, 'Mill's Essay on Government', pp. 369–70.

of maximizing utility.[30] Mill quickly abandoned the more extreme elitism implicit in some of these ideas, and in those of Carlyle and Coleridge, by whom he was also influenced at the time. However, they left a lasting impression on his thought, and continued in particular to modify his commitment to democratic government right to the end of his life.

Another important pair of newspaper articles contributing to a debate about the right of electors to control their representatives, signalled his growing differences with the radicals. Mill argues that electors should choose the wisest and best to represent them: 'but if I vote for a person because I think him the wisest man I know, am I afterwards to set myself up as his instructor?' No more, he urges, than I should presume to tell my doctor what to prescribe for me. Mill even cites the famous passage from *Ecclesiastes* used by Burke to justify the political monopoly of the aristocracy.[31] Mill recognized that an ultimately popular sovereignty was both irresistible and a necessary constitutional safeguard for the interests of the many. Despite this, he insistently denied that the popular will was therefore the standard of policy:

> We know that the will of the people, even of the numerical majority, must be supreme
> . . . but in spite of that the test of what is right in politics is not the *will*, of the people,
> but the *good* of the people, and our object is, not to compel but to persuade the people
> to impose, for the sake of their own good, some restraint on the immediate and unlimited
> exercise of their own will . . . [32]

The longer term context of Mill's thought

Mill's innovations to, or deviations from utilitarianism and its political programme have preoccupied many thinkers whose concerns have been to assess his relationship to his immediate utilitarian past, or to use him as a jumping-off point for analysing modern problems. However, there is a longer term context in which to consider Mill which has proved much more problematic.

In stressing the innovatory and emancipatory nature of his education and the utilitarianism into which he was inducted, Mill's own account of his upbringing asserts by omission, any significant relationship with other strands within his culture's past. In claiming that a concern with historical process was important, and a matter of balancing elements of stability and innovation in both opinion and political institutions, Mill thought he was enriching a narrow British tradition with a broader continental one, drawing particularly on the influence of German philosophers, and French historians and sociologists who, in their attempts to understand the French Revolution, had been forced to grapple with the problem of explaining massive shifts in cultural ideals and their institutional expression. The British tradition, though, was by no means as impoverished

---

[30] The classic expression of Mill's brief apostasy from defending freedom of expression is his 1831 essay 'The Spirit of the Age', *CW*, vol. XXII; for a discussion on this episode see J. M. Robson, *The Improvement of Mankind* (Toronto and London, 1968), pp. 99ff.

[31] The *Examiner*, 1 July 1832, cited Burns, 'Mill and Democracy', in Schneewind, p. 284; *CW*, vol. XXIII, p. 487

[32] *Examiner*, 15 July 1832, cited Burns, 'Mill and Democracy', p. 285; Ibid., p. 497.

in this respect as Mill's originally narrow philosophical outlook had led him to believe. French and German social thinkers themselves owed a heavy debt to the insights of the Scottish school of historical sociology, and to Burke's idiosyncratic treatment of the subject. Indeed Mill's father had been educated in Scotland under Dugald Stewart, leader of the last generation of such thinkers, and it is almost impossible to suppose that there was not some influence on him.[33]

Despite the innovation stressed in Mill's own account of the formation of his thought there appear nevertheless certain continuities between non-utilitarian British thought of the eighteenth century and his own. These are visible initially more in terms of preoccupations and themes rather than in terms of strict method.

A reading of Mill's essay 'Civilization' published in the *London and Westminster Review*, in April 1836 when he was thirty, reveals an anticipation of the topics and concerns of Mill's maturity which is nevertheless still located within an analysis that owes a considerable debt to Hume and the school of Scottish historical sociology.[34] In the essay, Mill considers the progress of civilization 'only in the restricted sense: not that in which it is synonymous with improvement, but that in which it is the direct converse or contrary of rudeness or barbarism.'[35] Mill's view of what he calls 'savage life' owes not a little to the pervasive individualism of the contract tradition (and here he is at odds with the school of historical sociology). Contrary to modern anthropological views of the solidarity of the aboriginal community, views which were to come increasingly to the fore during the century, Mill appeared to believe at this time that 'in savage communities each person shifts for himself'.[36] Backwardness was also marked by an extreme concentration of property and intellectual powers – 'the two elements of importance and influence amongst mankind'. The consequence of the concentration of property recalls Hume's re-evaluation of the supposedly 'virtuous' peasant-freeholder. In such a society all non-property-owners are servile: 'either military retainers and dependents of the possessors of property, or serfs, stripped and tortured at pleasure by

[33] On Mill's isolation from a broad 'Whig tradition' see J. Burrow, *Whigs and Liberals, continuity and change in English political thought* (Oxford, 1988), p. 15; For James Mill's education: Donald Winch, 'The System of the North: Dugald Stewart and his Pupils', in *That Noble Science of Politics*, Stefan Collini, Donald Winch and John Burrow (Cambridge, 1983). It is sometimes remarked that in James Mill's works other than the *Essay on Government* he reveals a very much richer awareness of politics as a developmental and educational process. For example W. H. Burston, *James Mill on Philosophy and Education* (London, 1973), and Michael Woodcock: 'Educational principles and Political Thought: the case of James Mill', *History of Political Thought*, I, 3 (1980)). Nevertheless, J. S. Mill's account of the impact of his father's education confirms the view implicit in the *Essay*, rather than the wider one.

[34] Mill had read Adam Smith as early as 1819, when he was still only 13, evidently as part of a course of instruction in 'Political Economy' which included Ricardo's *Principles of Political Economy and Taxation*, published only two years earlier (at James Mill's instigation and encouragement). However Mill had already read the histories of Hume, William Robertson, John Millar and Adam Ferguson, and later also read Hume's *Essays*. He was therefore well versed in this group of thinkers considered as theorists of society in general, rather than, as some of them were becoming, progenitors of the distinct study of economics. *Autobiography*, pp. 18, 6–7, 44.

[35] 'Civilization', *CW*, vol. XVII, p. 120; *D&D*, vol. I, p. 161.

[36] Ibid., *CW*, p. 120; *D&D*, p. 162; and: 'what makes all savages poor and feeble: incapacity of co-operation. It is only civilized beings who can combine. . . . the savage cannot bear to sacrifice, for any purpose, the satisfaction of his individual will.' *CW*, p. 122; *D&D*, p. 165.

one master, and pillaged by a hundred.'[37] Like Hume, and the apologists of the modern economy, the young Mill sees the extra-familial development of co-operation, discipline and refinement as a consequence of the division of labour and the spread of the mechanical arts and manufactures, the transfer of the benefits of co-operative and rule-governed behaviour from small to larger scale social contexts. Like Hume too he claims the effect of 'such knowledge as civilization naturally brings' to be 'to undermine many of those prejudices and superstitions which made mankind hate each other for things not really odious.'[38] In short Mill accepts the Scottish account of the growth of civil society as the economically-led diffusion of a new set of urbane manners, values and practices, linked also to the rise of a middle class, a popular press, and their concomitants: a public opinion.

So far so good. Mill, however, wishes to draw to his readers' attention not so much this, by now commonplace, historical sketch, but 'to some of the consequences which [it] . . . has already produced, and of the further ones it is hastening to produce'.[39] This preoccupation with the effect of socio-economic change on the formation of opinion, and its implications for politics, reveals a continuing debt to the historical sociologists' preoccupation with the social determinants of belief and character, issues which were far from the centre of classical utilitarians' concern.

The growth of a middle class is inseparable from the diffusion of property and intelligence, which is a broadly positive development. But one inescapable consequence of this is the impossibility of any one individual exercising influence in comparison to the mass.[40] This contributes to a growing lack of incentive for individuals to exert themselves. The social motives which elicit individuals' energies are the desire for personal and familial survival, the 'desire for wealth or of personal aggrandizement, the passion of philanthropy, and love of active virtue.'[41] Echoing Machiavelli's account of the effects of *necessità* on *virtù*, Mill notes that in barbarous states the very struggle for existence calls forth all an individual's cunning and energy. However the security provided by civilized society largely eliminates these as a motive: indeed it eliminates the isolated individual as a social phenomenon. If we consider the impact of the progress of civilization on the formation of character in each of the three classes of society, Mill argues, we find a weakening of the effect of all of these causes. The increasingly onerous nature of high office together with the need now to compete politically for it, leads to a loss of vigour and energy in the aristocracy, who, already rich and possessing social status, do not, in any case need politics to attain either of them.[42] Amongst the middle classes, the wider access to and distribution of property makes the pursuit of wealth the most likely way of satisfying material and status desires, and as a result these take up whatever energy exists in civilized society. So, writes Mill 'the energies of the middle

[37] Ibid., *CW*, p. 121; *D&D*, pp. 163, 164.

[38] Ibid. *CW*, p. 123, *D&D*, p. 167 (co-operation); *CW*, p. 124, *D&D*, p. 168 (discipline); *CW*, p. 131, *D&D*, p. 180 (delicacy and refinement); *CW*, p. 132, *D&D*, p. 181 (loss of prejudice); see also, 'a great increase in humanity, a decline of bigotry . . . amongst our conspicuous classes.' *CW*, p. 125, *D&D*, p. 171.

[39] Ibid., *CW*, p. 121; *D&D*, p. 163.

[40] Ibid., *CW*, p. 126; *D&D*, pp. 171–2.

[41] Ibid., *CW*, p. 129; *D&D*, p. 177.

[42] Ibid., *CW*, pp. 126, 129; *D&D*, pp. 171, 178.

classes are almost confined to money-getting, and those of the higher classes are nearly extinct.'[43] Meanwhile amongst the lower classes it is not so much a question of lack of energy as lack of learning, and the very survival of civilization depends to a degree on a race between the progress of democracy and that of literacy.[44] To these observations on the class-specific causes of decline Mill adds some general ones.

Civilization's promotion of sensitivity and delicacy of manners, so celebrated by Hume and his followers, has a negative side to it. Our susceptibility to pain, Mill suggests, is culturally determined.[45] The pains and hardships endured by the ancients 'did not appear to them as great an evil, as it appears, and as it really is, to us.'[46] Our increased sensitivity to pains of all kinds is the underside of the coin of which cultured sensitivity is the face.[47] It is therefore a natural consequence of civilization, through the operation of refinement, to bring about an unwillingness to suffer, physically or socially, for worthy objects, in short, a decline in heroism, 'a moral effeminacy, an ineptitude for every kind of struggle . . . ' In consequence men in general 'cannot brook ridicule, they cannot brave evil tongues: they have not the hardihood to say an unpleasant thing to anyone whom they are in a habit of seeing.'[48] As a result public opinion comes to dominate over individuality.

Mill's perception of historical change at this time was much influenced by French sociological thinking, in particular by the idea, which he also found in Coleridge, that civilization progresses through the creative tension provided by the forces of permanence and progression, or order and progress or through stationary and progressive phases.[49] Indeed these may form an illuminating context within which to see Mill's later discussion of the relationship between applying utility to the justification of a rule or set of rules, practices or institutions (appropriate to phases of progression) and applying it to an act within a given context (appropriate within an assumed static environment). One distinctively nineteenth-century way of articulating worries about the dynamics of social change was through these categories, variously seen as intellectual principles – conservatism or reform – or as embodied in social groupings – such as landed and commercial classes. The concern to balance successfully these two forces continued to inform Mill's thinking long after his flirtation with Comte and the Saint-Simonians had faded.

[43] Ibid., *CW*, p. 130, *D&D*, p. 178.

[44] Ibid., *CW*, p. 127, *D&D*, p. 174.

[45] The relatively uniform susceptibility of mankind to pleasure and pain had been for Bentham, the foundation on which the possibility of a universal science of legislation might be erected. See above, pp. 323–5.

[46] Civilization *CW*, vol. XVII, p. 131, *D&D*, vol. I, p. 179.

[47] Ibid., *CW*, p. 131, *D&D*, p. 180: 'it is in avoiding the presence not only of actual pain, but of whatever suggests offensive or disagreeable ideas that a great part of refinement consists.'

[48] Ibid., *CW*, p. 131, *D&D*, p. 181.

[49] 'The two antagonistic powers or opposite interests of the state, under which all other state interests are comprised, are those of PERMANENCE and of PROGRESSION.' S. T. Coleridge, *On the Constitution of Church and State* (London, 1972), p. 16; later in the work Coleridge identifies these forces respectively with the landed, and with the commercial, industrial and professional classes, Ibid, p. 92. For a discussion see Morrow, *Coleridge's Political Thought*, pp. 133–42.

Tocqueville and *Democracy in America*, and Mill and democracy in Britain

Mill's worries about the ambivalence of civilization form a major continuity in his thought and received dramatic confirmation from Tocqueville's influential study *Democracy in America* which Mill reviewed for the *Edinburgh Review*, in 1835 and 1840. The work also exemplified for him the proper way in which historical evidence could be incorporated into the study of society and so helped to crystallize the methodological developments forced on him by his dissatisfaction with his father's deductive approach, thoughts which were to bear fruit in Mill's *Logic*. The contribution of Tocqueville to Mill's thought was, one influential scholar comments, 'unique', its effect was 'to finish the revolution in his political thinking initiated by Macaulay's strictures on the *Essay on Government . . .* '[50]

Alexis de Tocqueville, a French aristocrat, politician and social philosopher, had visited America originally as part of an attempt to understand what he saw as the new and worldwide democratic social revolution – furthest developed, he thought, on the other side of the Atlantic. Mill agreed with Tocqueville that the forces leading to democracy were to be seen everywhere in the modern world. The government in England, as in Europe,

> is progressively changing from the government of a few to the government, not indeed of *the* many but of many; from an aristocracy with popular infusion, to the *régime* of the middle class. To most purposes, in the constitution of modern society, the government of a numerous middle class *is* democracy[51]

Mill was particularly impressed with Tocqueville's insight into the nature of a democratic political culture. Following Tocqueville (who had drawn uncomfortable parallels between centralization in post-revolutionary France and the *ancien régime*) Mill points out that in France, whilst the equalization of status and economic condition begun under the monarchy and pursued with vigour in the revolution, had advanced far, the dispersion of political power had hardly taken place at all: 'everything was done *for* the people, and nothing *by* the people'. By contrast, in America, the most significant aspect of the democracy is the lack of centralization and the involvement of citizens in local government. By this means vast numbers of Americans are kept informed about public affairs and educated for political office. This counterbalances an important aspect of modern society which, Mill stresses several times is a predominantly commercial one. By participating at however low a level in public affairs, people are lifted above their own selfish and narrow concerns.[52]

---

[50] Robson, *Improvement of Mankind*, p. 107.

[51] 'De Tocqueville on Democracy in America', *CW*, vol. XVII, p. 167; *D&D*, vol.II, p. 21. A dominant middle class can constitute a democracy, Mill thought, because large sections of the working classes were becoming 'in point of condition and habits' middle class. Indeed he wrote: 'America is *all* middle class' (although he normally pointed out the exception of the slaves).

[52] Ibid., *CW*, pp. 168–9, *D&D*, pp. 24–5.

This was on the credit side; however, it was the disadvantages of the American political culture which struck a warning note to Tocqueville, and, through him, to Mill. A democratic political culture, wrote Mill, values equality so much that it refuses to elect those whose excellence would fit them best for office; instead it chooses mediocrities. Since political terms are short and the incumbents change frequently, there is no career in politics, and hence no accumulation of political experience, no distinct culture in which the arts of statesmanship can flourish: 'There are no traditions, no science or art of public affairs'. As a result politics is conducted 'without consistent system, long-sighted views, or persevering pursuit of distant objects' (Mill can sound extraordinarily like Burke at such times); a situation which is becoming true also of England and France.[53]

A second major danger was the 'despotism of the majority'. Mill grants that in one important sense this is probably only a theoretical danger for America. Property there is so equal, and the belief that rewards are proportionate to effort so widespread, that the fear of the poor overthrowing the property of the rich (the example that immediately springs to Mill's mind), is unlikely. In England, where the labouring classes are 'less happily circumstanced' the possibility of at least legal interference in the operation of the market is less far fetched.[54] However, the real danger in an egalitarian democracy is not to minorities defined in terms of interests, so much as minorities of opinion, belief or race. And the tyranny is to be expected not so much from the passing of laws disadvantageous to the minority, so much as the unwillingness of judges and juries to give minorities the protection to which they are by law entitled.

This leads to a major theme of Tocqueville's, of Mill's review and of Mill's life work: the threat to independence of thought posed by democratic culture, or as Mill put it, following one of Tocqueville's chapter headings: the influence of democracy on intellect.[55] The paradox of America in this respect is that the fundamental 'habit of mind' of the society seems guaranteed to resist the drift into conformity: that basic American disposition is 'the rejection of authority, and the assertion of the right of private judgement'. America was the country where, if anywhere, tradition, inherited authority and the past generally counted for nothing, and yet, strangely, 'in no country does there exist less independence of thought'. According to Tocqueville, the notorious conformity was paradoxically to be accounted for by this very absence of authority. For whereas 'older societies have found [it] in the traditions of antiquity, or in the dogmas of priest or philosophers, the Americans find [it] in the opinions of each other.' Inheritors of no one authoritative aristocratic, religious or intellectual value-system, yet, like all societies, needing one, the Americans endowed their own collective opinion with the aura and authority Europeans gave to their royalty, nobility, popes, academies and national myths. Mill quotes Tocqueville: 'faith in public opinion, becomes in such countries a species of religion and the majority is its prophet.'[56]

[53] Ibid., *CW*, pp. 173–4, *D&D*, p. 32–3.

[54] Ibid., *CW*, p. 176, *D&D*, pp. 36–7. This was a continuing worry for Mill, see the posthumous *Chapters on Socialism*, *CW*, vol. V, p. 703, and in , *On Liberty and Other Writings*, ed. Stefan Collini (Cambridge, 1989), p. 225.

[55] Alexis de Tocqueville, *Democracy in America*, tr. Henry Reeve (2 vols, New York, 1961), vol. II, Bk i: 'Influence of Democracy on the action of the intellect in the United States'.

[56] 'Tocqueville on Democracy in America', *CW*, vol.XVII, pp. 178–9; *D&D*, vol.II, pp. 40–2.

When Tocqueville looked at how this authoritative opinion is formed he found little comfort. Demand for education as a means of getting on is certainly there, but attention spans are short, and precision and detail wearying. There is therefore no money or even glory to be got from the truly first-rate work; and in the absence of incentive to produce it, none is produced. The market in literature panders to public taste, rather than leading it. Instead of leavening the uniformity of public opinion, democratic literature merely reflects and reinforces it.

In a democracy the sheer size and uniformity of the citizen body makes it as loose as grains of sand; it doesn't cohere. There are none of the 'intermediate bodies' stressed by Montesquieu, no Burkean community here linking the nation with the individual through 'the little platoons', nor any linking of the generations through time. Moreover, in a phenomenon that has since been much remarked on, the chances of one individual affecting political outcomes amongst so many, are remote enough to discourage political action – people turn inward to their own private affairs, to become businessmen, or lead merely domestic lives.[57] Linked to this is the propensity for democratic cultures to produce individuals motivated by interests, rather than (as in aristocratic societies) pride.[58] Political identity and patriotism must be stimulated artificially through proliferating local political institutions.

Both Mill and Tocqueville believed that the progress of democracy was irresistible, but for the reasons given above thought that if democracy was to be viable and continue to be a vehicle for progress, three challenges must be met. A form of democracy must be found which 'exercises and cultivates the intelligence and mental activity of the majority' and 'breaks the headlong impulses of popular opinion, by delay, rigour of forms, and adverse discussion'. Finally there must be resistance to the 'tendency of democracy towards bearing down individuality and circumscribing the exercise of the human faculties within narrow limits. To sustain the higher pursuits of philosophy and art; to vindicate and protect the unfettered exercise of reason, and the moral freedom of the individual.'[59]

Despite this fundamental agreement Mill emphasised some aspects of the new political order more than Tocqueville. He claimed that Tocqueville had mistaken as peculiar to democracy, processes which were endemic to the development of civilization itself – even to an aristocratic culture such as England's. What Tocqueville saw as a result of the 'equality of conditions' which prevailed to such an extreme in America, Mill also saw in far less egalitarian Britain.[60] If inegalitarian Britain shared these tendencies with America, whilst egalitarian but uncommercial Canada was free of them, they must, thought Mill, be the consequence, not of mere equality, but of the growth of commercial society.

Conscious of its economic benefits, Mill was profoundly suspicious of the intellectual and moral consequences of commerce: 'the spirit of a commercial people', he wrote, 'will be . . . essentially mean and slavish, wherever public spirit is not cultivated by an extensive participation of the people in the business of government in detail'.[61] Although hitherto the spirit of commerce and industry had been 'one of the greatest instruments of civilization . . . improvement and culture' it required other, co-ordinate developments

---

[57] Ibid., *CW*, pp. 132–3; *D&D*, pp. 47–8.
[58] Ibid., *CW*, p. 184; *D&D*, p. 51.
[59] Ibid., *CW*, p. 189; *D&D*, pp. 58–9.

[60] Ibid., *CW*, p. 193; *D&D*, p. 64.
[61] Ibid., *CW*, p. 169; *D&D*, pp. 25–6.

to balance it, and these were now threatened: 'the most serious danger to the future prospects of mankind is in the unbalanced influence of the commercial spirit'.[62] In stressing the threat posed by commerce Mill was reasserting in a recognizable form the threat perceived by the generations of Smith and Hume to the fabric of political belief. The achievement of their socio-historical analysis had been to suggest that each successive economic 'mode of living' will tend to promote moral ideals and values appropriate to the survival of that form of society. Mill was now warning that an advanced commercial culture will not necessarily do that, and that the competitiveness, inwardness and instability of personal relations might erode those residual values on which society depended, as well as stultifying the sources from which change, and so the possibility of progress, emerged.[63]

Rejection of democracy was not a possible response to this analysis, but it further reinforced Mill's Coleridgean insight that 'there should exist somewhere a great social support for opinions different from those of the mass' and that the sources of these must be 'an agricultural class, a leisured class, and a learned class'.[64]

The rise of chartism and working-class politics, as a sectional interest, further alienated Mill from the political arena. Its accompanying political theory – 'the master fallacy of all, the theory *of class-representation*' – contrasted with and supplanted the 'philosophic radicalism' through which he had hoped to achieve the euthanasia of party politics and articulate an increasingly elusive general interest.[65]

Throughout this period of his life Mill had been a selective and critical supporter of radicalism. He had opposed universal suffrage under the present conditions. 'The natural laws of the progress of wealth and the diffusion of reading' are the two elements of viable democracy.[66] Until these conditions were fulfilled, 'The motto of a Radical politician should be, Government *by means of* the middle, for the working classes.'[67] By the early 1840s, under the impact of these pessimistic considerations, Mill and many of his generation of reformers had withdrawn from radical politics and even from political debate.[68] They turned, as had (and would) so many previous political actors when denied an active role, to academic work and to theory.[69] Mill returned to his massive *Logic* which

---

[62] Ibid., *CW*, p. 198; *D&D*, p. 73.

[63] Ibid. (Competition and instability), *CW*, pp. 193–4; *D&D*, pp. 65–6; (closing off of innovation by the 'dogmatism of common sense'), *CW*, pp. 196–7; *D&D*, pp. 70–71; (reliance of Commerce on other values, which it nevertheless erodes), *CW*, pp. 197–8,;*D&D*, pp. 72–3. In this last Mill is close to Burke's insistence that earlier values provide the shade in which commerce and learning both grew, and his warning that 'They may decay without their natural protecting principles.' See above pp. 276–7, and Pocock, 'The Political Economy of Burke's analysis of the French Revolution' in *Virtue, Commerce and History*, p. 199.

[64] 'Tocqueville on Democracy in America', *CW*, vol. XVIII, p. 198; *D&D*, vol. II, p. 73.

[65] 'The Master Fallacy' — *London Review*, ii, p. 92n., cited Burns. 'Mill and Democracy', p. 293. On the collapse of philosophical radicalism see James Hamburger, *Intellectuals in Politics: John Stuart Mill and the Philosophical Radicals* (New Haven, 1965), esp. ch. 9, & pp. 264 ff.

[66] Cited Burns, 'Mill and Democracy', p. 296.

[67] Ibid., p. 301.

[68] In a letter of 1842 he wrote 'As for Politics I have almost given up thinking on the subject. Passing events suggest no new thoughts but what they have been suggesting for some time now.' To Barclay Fox, cited, ibid., p. 281.

[69] Hamburger discusses the works we owe to this period of political disillusionment, which include Molesworth's edition of Hobbes, and Grote's *History of Greece*, *Intellectuals in Politics*, p. 267.

was to include a discussion of one of the major issues that had shaken his original naive utilitarianism, Macaulay's methodological criticism of his father.

The methodological discussion in the *Logic* – Mill's principles and his method

Right at the start of *Representative Government* Mill was to draw a distinction to which Bentham and James Mill had paid little if any attention. It was the distinction between considering the best form of government simply as a means to an end and so deducing the best form of government from supposedly universal human characteristics; and on the other hand recognizing that governments are so much the products of particular societies and particular times that to talk about them being a means to an end, as though we could fashion them like a machine or a tool to our needs, is nonsense. Important implications for the reformer follow from this. If the former were true the social engineer would have a free hand; the more the latter is stressed the less room for manoeuvre there seems to be. Sensibly, if unexcitingly, Mill suggests the truth lies somewhere between the two.[70] Thus he believes that utilitarianism can still be shown to be an appropriate standard for appraising government, whilst accepting the criticisms, typified by Macaulay, that utilitarians had paid insufficient attention to the historical character of individual governments.

However this attempt to combine utility, in principle an abstract and a-historical criterion, with a sensitivity to the historical particularity of given societies is, as Mill recognizes, fraught with difficulty. In Bk. VI of his *Logic* he tackles the issue of the relationship between them as competing methods of understanding and explanation in what he calls 'the moral sciences'. Two particular areas may be chosen to illustrate the problems, the application of utility as a moral and political standard, and, as a consequence of this, the capacity of a utilitarian understanding of human society to generate a philosophy of history.

The moral problems of a historically sophisticated utilitarianism

As a moral theory utilitarianism is consequentialist. It rests on the assumption that we can work out the consequences of our actions, for it is on their consequences that their moral desirability or otherwise rests. The attractions of a reasonably simple (e.g. pleasure seeking-pain avoiding) model of human nature, were apparent and stressed by the first generation of utilitarians.[71] For simple actions faced by individuals, or indeed for political or legal actions considered in the short term, calculating utility remains a plausible option

---

[70] *Representative Government*, pp. 175–6.

[71] See above on Bentham and James Mill. It is not, as critics of the utilitarians, including J.S. Mill himself sometimes suggested, that the early utilitarians believed that in some literal and simplistic sense all human beings acted to maximize physical pain and limit physical suffering. Rather that this was the most accurate approximation that could be made by one (such as a legislator) who sought to deal with human behaviour in the aggregate. If, Bentham observed, utilitarian psychology 'held in no more than a bare majority . . . it would suffice for every practical purpose, in the character of a ground for all political arrangements.'

– this is what made it so attractive to Bentham as a legal reformer and so powerful a weapon in nineteenth century social reform. But if Macaulay's type of historical criticism is correct, this model is too simple, for people's motives are in fact more complex than this, and the account needs to be supplemented by an understanding of the culture and customs which embody a particular people's values.[72] Moreover this kind of understanding becomes crucial for the utilitarian if, as Mill insisted, we must regard the wider dimension of culture, and not merely the increase in pleasures and diminution of pains, as being crucial to the progress of a society. Moreover if, as Mill also insists, we are concerned not with the impact of particular pieces of legislation but with the longer term aspects of social development, then again, the difficulties of working out the consequences of policies expose the simplicity of the model of human nature. However, if we try to sophisticate our model of human nature, two things begin to happen, each of which are potentially destructive of utility as a workable moral principle.

Firstly, in taking account of the historically contingent characteristics of human beings, we very soon complicate our picture of the human being to the point where it becomes very difficult to make the necessary calculations about what would lead to the greatest happiness. The same things would not make a 20th century New York teenager happy which would make happy a 16th century French peasant, or a Tibetan monk. This impossible diversity was precisely what, James Mill had claimed, led him to adopt the deductive method!

Secondly, if we try to get over this by integrating our notion of utility into an explicit process of historical change by, as Mill suggests, considering utility 'in the widest possible sense, taking man as a progressive being', then we are forced into a search for a philosophy of history. The reason for this is that we need some kind of knowledge of what the background conditions are going to be (even if they are changing) in order to be able to calculate the utility of outcomes of particular policies or actions at any given time, because the context affects the outcomes; and a knowledge of the general nature of historical changes is what philosophy of history is.[73]

This is perhaps best explained by an example relating to political obligation. When, if ever, are we justified in supporting the revolutionary overthrow of an established regime? This is a good example because it highlights the instability of the background circumstances against which the decision must be made. For a utilitarian there can be no overriding obligation to support government over and above considerations of the general happiness (as both Hume and Bentham insist). If the present regime seems to be seriously undermining it, the citizen's response to a revolutionary appeal must be a purely consequentialist calculation.

Bentham, Introduction to *Constitutional Code*, Bowring IX, 6, cited Ross Harrison, *Bentham* (London, 1983), p. 145.

[72] The criticism is closely allied to the philosophical one, which Bentham acknowledged, namely that if 'pleasures and pains' means more than mere physical sensations (and perhaps even then), then *what* it is people took pleasure in, or found painful, is increasingly subjective. We have only to consider the way in which wealthy middle class people spend much spare time and money pursuing activities — such as sailing and cultivating plants — which their predecessors, who had to do them for a living, would mostly have avoided like the plague if they'd had a choice.

[73] History considered as what has been, the philosophy of history is sometimes also used to refer to the philosophy of historiography, i.e. of what is written. 'History' is ambiguous as between these two, except, as we shall see for idealists such as Hegel for whom they are virtually indistinguishable.

One argument runs that the utilitarian should never support revolution. Civil wars are so terrible, civilization so fragile and outcomes so uncertain that the risk could never be justified by the uncertain result. It's not clear why this should be so. Burke has good grounds for believing civilized government to be fragile, for he has a quite distinct belief in the limitations of human understanding and the integrity of actions based on it. What is unclear, is why anyone subscribing to a utilitarian psychology would believe government to be fragile; since for them it is simply a device for maximizing human happiness, which we all seek. A government or revolution which set out to do what utilitarians said government ought to do, should have no fears, since for a utilitarian, maximizing happiness is not only the objective criterion of political legitimacy, it is, subjectively, also what people will see as right. Moreover if the outcomes of revolution are uncertain, so might be the consequences of continuing to endure tyranny, or of accepting the slide into it. If we really don't understand historical processes, then we don't know the future; but then we don't know it with or without the revolution, and consequential arguments weigh no more heavily on one side than on the other.

To be able to decide in such situations we need either some standards of action which are independent of the (incalculable) consequences – but utilitarians, being moral consequentialists, must deny the existence of these – or we need to know, at least in general, how historical change is occurring, how society is changing, because this historical backdrop will enable us to structure our calculations in such a way as to attempt to maximize happiness. If for example, I as a kind of utilitarian Marxist, claim to know that the hour of the proletariat has come, I could add utilitarian reasons to my Marxist ones for supporting the overthrow of the bourgeoisie. Since their downfall is historically inevitable, the greatest happiness of the greatest number will be served by hastening the inevitable, and not causing pain and suffering by futile resistance. A real life example, close to Mill, was that of Tocqueville. Himself an aristocrat, and suspicious of the new bourgeois order, he nevertheless accepted its inevitability, and as a practicing politician, acted, somewhat nostalgically it is true, within the context provided by that new order.[74]

To act politically concerning culture in general, over a long time span, or even over a short one where change is fast, a utilitarian requires a philosophy of history, both in the sense of a method of historical understanding and in the sense of a grasp of the general shape of historical change.

Mill's treatment of the problem of historical methodology

The moral or practical problem set by utilitarianism – that of calculating outcomes – thus leads to a methodological one, of how a utilitarian can construct a philosophy of history. Its failure to provide this would lead to the collapse of utilitarianism as a theory, since it would be unable to tell us, what, on its own admission, we needed to know (i.e. consequences) in order to do what it says we ought. Whether Mill saw the issue as starkly as this he certainly attempted to provide an understanding of history which, whilst it retained belief in a utilitarian account of human nature, attempted to explain how we could understand history in a broader sense, without a need to resolve everything to the

[74] See, e.g., G.A. Kelly, 'Parnassan Liberalism', *History of Political Thought*, vol. VIII (1987).

level of individual psychologies. His most sustained attempt to construct the tools for a rigorous philosophy of history is in Bk. VI of his *System of Logic*.

One major problem in the way of a utilitarian philosophy of history is that utilitarianism is ontologically individualist. That is to say that for utilitarians the real and basic reality is individuals and their feelings. A philosophy of history, simply because of the scale of the phenomena it has to deal with – big events and processes over long time-spans – is virtually forced to operate at the other end of the scale, to deal in generalities – climates of opinion, the organizing ideas or structural principles of a society, and changes at these levels. In the *Logic*, Mill recognizes the importance, mentioned above, of the distinction between the causality operating between 'two specific and local events' within a particular society, and, on the other hand, the causes of the 'general circumstances of society'. Assuming that the intellectual, moral, economic and political life of a society are linked together in some way, the problem Mill sets himself in the *Logic*, is to establish a logical connection between phenomena at the level of generality required by a philosophy of history, and those at the level of the real entities of individual psychology, or even physiology.

Mill's view of the world is ultimately physicalist and necessitarian.[75] Moreover this is also true of human beings; that is to say, he believes, although he acknowledges that it is not yet possible to demonstrate it, that human acts, like all other natural events, are subject to invariable laws, and that these laws are ultimately connected to the physical sciences through the science of physiology; thus the causal explanation of our actions can ultimately be traced back to the physical laws governing the material which comprises us.[76] Furthermore, Mill regards social phenomena as ultimately reducible to individual phenomena.[77]

However, although we cannot (perhaps only not yet) strictly identify physiological causes with the psychological states which are their effect, we can observe regularities in our mental states – such as those observed by associationist psychologists of the eighteenth century, whose work, Mill observed (including that of his father), had been so much neglected by the previous generation.[78] So although we cannot penetrate to the real physical causes underlying our mental operations and actions, Mill does think we can, by observing the sequence of relationships between our mental states – our thoughts, wishes, emotions and feelings – construct inductive generalizations about their behaviour

---

[75] 'The causes with which I concern myself are not *efficient* but *physical* causes. They are causes in that sense alone in which one physical fact is said to be the cause of another.' *Logic*, Bk.III, v, 2. Mill's conception of causality was rigorously reductionist, see Alan Ryan, *The Philosophy of John Stuart Mill*, 2nd edn. (London, 1987) p. 67.

[76] *Logic*, Bk.VI, ch.iii.

[77] 'All phenomena of society are phenomena of human nature, generated by the action of outward circumstances upon masses of human beings; and if, therefore, the phenomena of human thought, feeling, and action, are subject to fixed laws, the phenomena of society cannot but conform to fixed laws, the consequence of the preceding', although Mill goes on to acknowledge that 'there is . . . no hope that these laws . . . would enable us to predict the history of society' for the variety of causes operating on society are simply too great. Ibid., Bk.VI, ch. vi, 2. Again: 'The laws of the phenomena of society are, and can be, nothing but the laws of the actions and passions of human beings united together in the social state.' Ibid., ch.vii, 1.

[78] Ibid., Bk.VI, ch. iii, 3, on the neglect of eighteenth-century psychology, and its substitution by dogmatic assumptions see 4.

which might be used to make successful predictions. These are not real material causes, although he supposes they must ultimately be linked to them.[79]

From such psychological 'uniformities of succession' even common sense is capable of extracting observations which hold good under a limited range of circumstances. These Mill calls 'empirical laws'. Empirical laws are regularities which are observable but exist as a result of a causality which is as yet unavailable to us; they are 'presumed to be resolvable into simpler laws, but not yet resolved into them'.[80] On this view Mill feels confident that there could be a science of character formation, just as he recognizes that 'little has as yet been done to, and that little not at all systematically, towards forming it'.[81]

If we look at how this might relate to a social science, Mill observes that at the level of society the interaction of causes is again so 'innumerable and perpetually changing ... as to defy our limited powers of calculation'. It is true that apparent regularities are observable in social phenomena, but these must be even further removed from the true physical causality operating at the level of individual physiology, and so ineligible, as they stand, to form the basis of a science. Nevertheless Mill believes that without hoping to reach the exactitude of the physical sciences, we could nevertheless reach an understanding of the tendencies and likelihoods operating on an individual state or culture in given circumstances.[82]

Before outlining what such a social science might look like, Mill diverges briefly to discuss 'two radical misconceptions of the proper mode of philosophizing on society and government.' Called, for reasons relating to their treatment earlier in his book the 'chemical' and 'geometrical' methods, they are in fact a formalized representation of the methods implicitly urged by Macaulay in his criticism of Mill's father, and the method used by Mill senior and Bentham. Mill here makes his most explicit methodological break with classical utilitarianism. Interestingly, Bentham had identified this *problem* with that of the chemist but Bentham's own conception of chemical *method* was different, it was still that of resolving the objects of knowledge into corporeal atomic entities. In Mill's terms, Bentham and James Mill use an essentially geometric method, Macaulay recommends a chemical one.[83]

For Mill the 'chemical method' is that which tries to explain the behaviour of any complex entities *without* trying to reduce them observationally to their composite causal

---

[79] Ibid., Bk.VI, ch. v, 1.

[80] Ibid., Bk.III, ch. xvi, 1. Real scientific truths 'are not these empirical laws, but the causal laws which explain them', VI, v, 1.

[81] Ibid., Bk.VI, ch. v, 6. The method to be pursued by ethology cannot be that of attempting to identify experimentally, or observationally, the 'real' causes of character formation, since these will be too complex to identify. Instead it should try to obtain, by deduction, explanations which link the general laws of the mind (psychology) to the observed 'empirical laws' of character formation by showing how the former would lead to the latter under given circumstances. (4) 'Ethology, the deductive science, is a system of corollaries from psychology, the experimental science.' (5) An example might be to attempt to show how the empirically observed propensity of peasant cultures to avoid risk-taking could be explained by an account of the interaction of basic human psychology with the material and social circumstances of peasant life. On Ethology see Nicolas Capaldi, 'Mill's Forgotten Science of Ethology', *Social Theory and Practice* (1977).

[82] *Logic*, Bk.VI, ch. vi, 2.

[83] There is a brief discussion on this in L. J. Hume, *Bentham and Bureaucracy* (Cambridge, 1981), p. 59.

elements. Instead, by a combination of experiment and deduction, observing the different behaviour of the entities under different combinations of circumstances, general laws about its behaviour are constructed. Thus, by observing the behaviour of different compounds containing say potassium, we can *deduce* the basic properties of K without needing to derive or analyse it in its pure form. This works in chemistry because the causes there are singular and invariable, but as Mill demonstrates in Bk III, such a method cannot work where causes are complex, as they invariably are in historical and social phenomena. Mill's major, and highly topical example is to show how impossible it would be, by this method, to prove whether or not restrictive legislation inhibited economic growth. Fundamentally such legislation is not an 'inherent and ultimate difference' but 'the effect of pre-existing causes' too numerous to imagine. Because of this indeterminacy and possible plurality of causes, the usual logical methods of difference cannot apply: if two libertarian governments have high growth we cannot assume it results from the same causes, if a restrictive government has low growth and another, otherwise apparently similar, but liberal, government high, we still cannot prove anything, for we cannot be sure they are similar in all other relevant respects, that is, we cannot assume that the difference results from the absence or presence of a single real cause, or even if there were only one, that it is represented within the phenomena designated by the term 'restrictive legislation'.

This is, amongst other things, an attack on Macaulay's historical method. For Macaulay had explicitly argued that historical examples, at this level of generality, could be compared using the 'method of difference' to produce reliable conclusions: 'The only mode in which we can conceive it possible to deduce a theory of government from the principles of human nature is this. We must find out what are the motives which, in a particular form of government, impel rulers to bad measures, and which impel them to good measures. We must then compare the two classes of motives [in different governments]; and according as we find the one or the other to prevail, we must pronounce the form of government in question good or bad.'[84]

But if Mill here is rejecting Macaulay and the claims of a simplistically applied history, he also rejects the abstract or geometric method of his father. The reasons for this relate again to Mill's discussions of the methods of the various sciences earlier in the book. In geometry, which Mill describes as a 'science of co-existent facts', there is no possibility of two conflicting antecedents impinging on one another – for the simple reason that there are, in a temporal sense, no antecedents: there is no movement in geometry, and so, strictly, no causation. Contrast this with mechanics, in which forces can operate in a simultaneous and complex fashion. To assume that political events result from a single cause, say fear, as Hobbes did, or material interest, as did the Benthamites, and to attempt to construct a theory of government on this basis (as did Mill senior in his *Essay*) is to operate geometrically, and falsely. For the actions of political actors result from 'the feelings, habits and modes of thought which characterize the particular class in that community of which they are members, as well as [those] . . . which characterize the particular class . . . to which they belong . . . also by the maxims and traditions which have descended to them from their predecessors . . .'[85] Although in practice constitutional

[84] Macaulay, 'Mill's Essay on Government', p. 368.
[85] *Logic*, Bk.VI, ch. viii, 3.

safeguards against the selfishness of rulers are required, Macaulay had been right to say that it was unscientific, and unphilosophical of the Benthamites to deduce everything from the assumption of selfish interest.

The more complex phenomena characteristic of social events and processes are amenable neither to the inductive (historical or chemical) method, nor to the simple deductive method. However, the inductive generalizations which the empirical laws of society provide us with, and the laws of psychology (or, as it progresses, ethology) rest on different evidence: empirical social laws rest on observations of social regularities and uniformities, psychology on knowledge of individuals' behaviour. For this reason the two methods can be combined in a non-trivial fashion to confirm or deny one another and so construct theories which, although still at several removes from physical causality, are more valid than either method could be taken singly: 'instead of deducing our conclusions by reasoning, and verifying them by observation, we in some cases begin by obtaining them provisionally from specific experience, and afterwards connect them with the principles of human nature by *à priori* reasonings, which reasonings are thus a real Verification.'[86]

This is the method which Mill had found actually applied so impressively in Tocqueville:

> a combination of deduction with induction: his evidences are, laws of human nature, on the one hand; the examples of America and France and the other modern nations so far as applicable, on the other. His conclusions never rest on either species of evidence alone; whatever he classes as an effect of Democracy, he has ascertained to exist in those countries in which the state of society is democratic, and has also succeeded in connecting with Democracy by deductions *à priori*, tending to show that such would naturally be its influences upon beings constituted as mankind are, and placed in a world such as we know ours to be.[87]

Thus Mill has demonstrated at least the possibility of a science of society, or sociology ('that convenient barbarism' as Mill terms it), which, although it could never be precise, offered sufficient guidance about the operation and processes of change in society to understand the causes, tendencies and changes obtaining at any particular time, 'and by what means those effects might be prevented, modified, or accelerated or a different class of effects superinduced'.[88] With this knowledge, utilitarianism as a principle of political action could be sustained, for we would now be better able to calculate the impact of political actions on the historical process.

Utilitarianism revised

The *Logic* was published in 1843. Towards the end of the 1840s Mill returned to political writing and to radicalism. Mill's enthusiasm for the French Revolution of 1848 led him to defend a working-class franchise and what he now saw as the intellectually re-

---

[86] Ibid., Bk.VI, ch. ix, 1.
[87] Mill, 'Tocqueville on Democracy in America', *CW*, vol. XVIII, p. 157; *D&D*, vol II, p. 5.
[88] *Logic*, Bk.VI, ch. vi, 2.

invigorating class conflict between the propertied and unpropertied; but it did not move him from his belief that 'the office of a representative body is not to make the laws but to see that they are made by the right persons'.[89] However the enthusiasm for politics and radicalism did not last long. By 1850 Mill thought that 'the low intellectual and moral state of all classes' made political, and other forms of progress impossible. At the end of that decade, however, he published, in as many years, the three political works by which he is best known, *On Liberty, Utilitarianism,* and *Representative Government.* The genesis of each of these works stretches well back into the fifties, and it seems reasonable to regard them as interconnected and complementary pieces.

In reformulating his political position, Mill was convinced of two serious (if rather contradictory) dangers in the development of modern democratic political culture. One was the threat posed to a general utilitarian good by the emergence of a working-class based politics, and the accession to power through a working-class electorate comprised of men as yet insufficiently educated to wield power for the general, or even for their own class's good. The balancing act between the educational and instrumental aspects of political institutions would be explored in *Representative Government.* The other danger, already widespread in America, was the danger, not of instability but of a creeping, suffocating stability, as he put it: 'not of too great liberty, but of too ready submission; not of anarchy but of servility; not of too rapid change but of Chinese stationariness.'[90] It was to this second target that Mill's most famous work, *On Liberty,* was directed. The first of these three works however, *Utilitarianism,* published in instalments in 1861, attempted to recapitulate the modified principle of utility on which the other two still claim to be based.[91]

Qualities of pleasure

In this work, Mill, as well as attempting, perhaps rather unwisely, a limited 'proof' of the principle of utility, made two important modifications to the classical utilitarian doctrine. He firstly asserted, contrary to Bentham's dictum that 'pushpin is as good as poetry', that in applying the principle of utility that 'actions are right in proportion as they tend to promote happiness' consideration was to be given to the quality as well as the quantity of pleasure resulting from an action.[92] The higher quality pleasures are revealed, Mill thought, in the preferences of those who had been exposed to both, thus saving at least the appearance of the principle of objectivity. Amongst the higher

[89] *Daily News,* 19 July, 1848, *Westminster Review* li. 20, both cited Burns, 'Mill and Democracy', pp. 314–315.

[90] 'Tocqueville on Democracy in America', *CW,* vol. XVIII, p. 188, *D&D,* vol. II, p. 56.

[91] The major themes of *Utilitarianism,* the distinction between utility as an immediate and as only an ultimate principle, and the idea of qualities of pleasure, are anticipated in *Bentham,* pp. 92, 95–6, in *CW,* vol. X; pp. 107, 112–14; and the *Logic,* VI, xii, 4.

[92] Mill *Utilitarianism* (ed. cit.), pp. 6, 7–8. 'It is quite consistent with the principle of utility to recognise the fact, that some *kinds* of pleasure are more desirable and more valuable than others.' Bentham's unfortunate and now infamous dictum was never published by him, refers not to the ultimate utilitarian worth of pushpin and poetry, but to the notice governments should take of it (i.e. not subsidizing one if the public value both equally) and owes its notoriety only to Mill's citation of it. See the discussion in Harrison, *Bentham,* p. 5.

pleasures Mill counts an altruistic concern with others, and the cultivation of one's own mind and feelings, thus revealing its ancestry in Mill's 'critical' dissatisfaction with Bentham and his father's thought. In seeking their authority for this innovation Mill misrepresents the continuity between his views and those of his father and Bentham by claiming that 'the happiness which forms the utilitarian standard of what is right in conduct, is not the agent's own, but that of all concerned.'[93] Whilst it is strictly true that the maximization of happiness had always been the ultimate principle and the end sought by the first generation of utilitarian reformers, Mill's point of difference with them was that they had never thought it could be the *motive* of individuals' conduct. Indeed it was this denial that many critics objected to, since it abandoned the possibility of altruism required by Christian ethics. Mill had himself originally pursued this 'party line' on the necessity of egoism. Indeed he had criticised the Owenite Socialists for relying on altruism to establish their social programme. Self-love is a stronger and surer principle, he thought:

> Let things be so arranged that the interests of every individual shall exactly accord with the interests of the whole – thus much it is in the power of laws and institutions to effect; & this done, let every individual be so educated as to know his own interest. Thus by the simultaneous action of a vast number of agents, everyone drawing in the direction of his own happiness, the happiness of the whole will be attained.[94]

Now, however, he saw the insufficiency of egoism, and whilst stressing his agreement with older utilitarians over the ultimate end to be pursued, could hardly disguise his reassessment of the potential importance of altruism as a motive, which he expressed as a qualitative difference in pleasures sought.[95]

One final important implication of the idea of higher quality pleasures, however difficult to defend, was that it at least makes it possible for a utilitarian to acknowledge the developmental nature of human (and therefore social) experience, otherwise capable of being characterized only in quantitative terms; and this, as we shall see, is crucial to Mill's attempt to reconcile utilitarianism to a more historically sensitive social science.

The proper application of the utility principle

Mill's second major modification of the classical principle of utility lay in his discussion of how it should be applied; and in particular whether it should be applied directly to particular situations. This arises in two contexts. The first is his concern that utilitarian morality should be seen to be practically applicable. None of us can constantly concern ourselves with the good of the whole world; at any one time we are confronted with particular individuals in particular circumstances, and utility requires only that we take account of those persons' happiness whilst bearing in mind the need not to violate the 'rights, that is the legitimate and authorized expectations of anyone else', and not to perform an act 'of a class which, if practised generally, would be generally injurious'.

---

[93] *Utilitarianism*, p. 16.

[94] 'Further reply to the Debate on Population' cited in Robson, *The Improvement* . . . , p. 14.

[95] This is quite different from the purely Benthamite grounds on which the pleasures of altruism could be recommended in view of their *fecundity*, or propensity to generate more pleasure in others.

The requirement to maximize utility, therefore, is not a universal one but a requirement bounded by the local circumstances in which we find ourselves. Secondly it is a principle which needs to refer to the type or class of actions with which we are faced. If the type of action is pernicious, Mill suggests, we should not perform it even 'though the consequences in the particular case might be beneficial'.[96]

This raises a large issue which is best tackled by looking at the other context in which the application of utility is discussed: Mill's attempt to show that utilitarianism need involve no radical break with traditional morality. Instead he argued that the everyday rules of morality can be seen as utilitarian rules of thumb: the generalised results of our accumulated experience as to the tendencies of actions, judged by the principle of utility. As such, moral rules are not, as is often claimed, absolute, but can and should be improved as we learn more about human nature, the consequences of following the rules in different circumstances, and become more self-conscious about the regulating role of the principle of utility. But this does not mean *exchanging* the moral rules for the principle of utility: 'to consider the rules of morality improvable, is one thing; to pass over the intermediate generalizations entirely, and endeavour to test each individual action directly by the first principle, is another. It is a strange notion that the acknowledgement of a first principle is inconsistent with the admission of secondary ones.'[97] Utility, Mill argues, is, therefore, a principle for evaluating moral rules, not one for evaluating individual acts; it is not the immediate, but the ultimate standard of morality.[98] Here Mill need not, as commentators anxious to see him presaging a modern debate so often claim, have been innovating; he could well merely be drawing on Hume, who stressed not only the utility of moral rules as an explanation (and justification) of them, but, in the case of justice, the utility of having a hard and fast rule, over the utility of having flexibility in adapting its particular content.[99]

This interpretation of Mill is by no means uncontested, for it opens up problems, not only about what Mill meant, but also about the logical defensibility of the distinction he may be trying to make; and commentators have not always been scrupulous in distinguishing between what Mill may have been intending to say, and what they regard as being logically tenable. Briefly, the major question hinges on whether it is possible, and Mill intended, to characterize rule utilitarianism in such a way that it does not collapse into act utilitarianism. To what extent can, or should, the utility of the 'rule' be isolated

---

[96] *Utilitarianism*, p. 18.

[97] Ibid., p. 22.

[98] The distinction between the two ways in which utility might be applied is marked in modern literature by the terms 'act utilitarianism' and 'rule utilitarianism'. The terms were introduced by R.B. Brandt. For an introduction to the extensive literature see: J.J. Smart and B. Williams, *Utilitarianism For and Against* (Cambridge, 1973), part I, section 2, and a useful bibliography. The interpretation offered here, of Mill as an 'act utilitarian' is not uncontested. See, most clearly, J.O. Urmson, 'The Moral philosophy of J. S. Mill' and 'Interpretations of Mill's *Utilitarianism*', both in P. Foot, ed., *Theories of Ethics* (Oxford, 1967). For further discussion of how to construe Mill here see Maurice Mandelbaum 'Two Moot issues in Mill's *Utilitarianism*' in Schneewind, ed., and H.J. McClosky, *John Stuart Mill: A Critical Study* (London, 1971), pp. 73–90.

[99] On this aspect of Hume see in particular D. Castiglione, 'Hume's Conventionalist Analysis of Justice' *Annali Della Fondazione Luigi Eninaudi* (XXI, 1987), esp. p. 157: 'Hume wished to uphold the *inflexibility* of the laws of justice against those who suggested that justice should *constantly* yield to the welfare of mankind.'

from the utility of the acts falling under it? For example, if I make a promise to meet a friend, but my grandmother falls ill and needs visiting, act utilitarianism would prescribe the breaking of the promise and the visiting of my ailing grandmother, but rule utility would prescribe keeping the promise, because it is the 'rule of keeping promises' rather than utility that applies directly. The problem about preventing appeals to utility from breaking through to the level of action is clearer if the difference between the utility outcomes is geared up. Suppose on my way to meet the promised friend I pass a truly terrible road accident where injured and dying people need help. It is a lonely road and I would have to go out of my way and miss my appointment in order to telephone for help and give assistance until it arrives. Surely in such a situation the benefits that follow from the action so outweigh the keeping of the rule of promising that the boundary between act and rule utility cannot be sustained, or made compatible with the ultimate principle of utility? Put more abstractly, if the utility of keeping to the normal rules is simply *one* of the considerations to be taken into account in deciding on an action, how can rule utility be sustained against act utilitarianism? On the other hand, if rule-obedience absolutely prohibits us from considering the utilitarian consequences of a particular act, we get, as in the above case, some distinctly counter-intuitive, as well as counter-utilitarian results.

One way round this possibility is to see 'helping people in distress' as a rule itself, and the example therefore, as a conflict not between the utility of applying a rule and performing an act, but between two rules. Mill certainly suggested that this was a case in which utility should be appealed to.[100] But this raises two further problems. There is, firstly, a logical difference to be noted between the two rules.[101] 'Helping people in distress' is a rule which generalizes from particular actions. But 'Keeping promises' is a rule which can only be kept if there is a rule by which promises are constituted. The 'helping people' could take place without the rule, 'promising' could not. The utility that we derive from the second kind of rule is logically dependent on the existence of the rule in a way that is not the case in the first, and this gives it a greater claim on our obligation. The implication is that if rules of the second kind were widely believed to be corrigible by utilitarian considerations, promising would collapse as an institution, and we would loose the considerable utility to be gained from its availability. It is this kind of consideration that leads Hume to stress the advantages of mere regularity itself, even where practices are not constituted by rules.

However it's unclear that Mill appreciated this distinction, or intended to use it in this way. In *Utilitarianism* Mill gives examples which seem to imply that he believes that what he says applies indifferently to both kinds of 'moral rule'. He says that because sailors use the information in a nautical almanac, it does not follow that the art of navigation doesn't derive from astronomy. The rules and information in the almanac are simply a shorthand version of what astronomy discovers and proves – in the same way, he invites us to believe that everyday morality is a shorthand form of what utilitarianism, considered as the science on which morality is founded, would be able to tell us if we had recourse to it.[102] Now this is a clear example where the everyday rule (the almanac)

---

[100] *Utilitarianism*, p. 24.

[101] Famously outlined in a paper by John Rawls, 'Two Concepts of Rules', *Philosophical Review*, LXVII (1958), and much anthologized.

[102] *Utilitarianism*, p. 23.

depends immediately on the higher rules or principles of astronomical science. The rules in the almanac would be directly and immediately vulnerable to refinements in our astronomical knowledge. If moral rules are seen to have this relationship to the principle of utility, then 'rule' utility is no more than a convenient shorthand or practical device which relieves us from having to work out our moral problems from first principles. 'Rule utility' may be a psychologically distinctive version of how to apply utility, but it asserts no logical distinction between the application of the principle to rules or acts.

On the other hand, in discussing the connection between utility and justice Mill seems to acknowledge the distinctively rule-based nature of the very idea of justice, which would make adherence to justice, like keeping promises, the second kind of rule: 'the idea of justice supposes two things: a rule of conduct, and a sentiment which sanctions the rule'.[103] If the very identity of justice hinges, as it were, on its 'ruleyness', then abrogating the regularity of it, even for good utilitarian reasons, would in itself do more damage, and would at the least require weightier reasons, than would the abandonment of rules which are mere generalised descriptions of 'good acts'. Accordingly, in assessing the status of justice Mill argues that it refers to 'certain moral requirements, which, regarded collectively, stand higher in the scale of social utility, and are therefore of more paramount obligation, than any others' although he later adds 'though not more so than others may be in particular cases'.[104]

It seems then, that Mill does make a distinction between utility as it applies to acts and as it applies to moral rules, and so defends a limited kind of rule utilitarianism. But he does not seem to formulate the distinction in quite the way that modern utilitarians do. He does not believe that the distinction between rules and acts has to be an uncrossable boundary for it to be an important one. The principle of utility permeates to the level of particular acts only in hard cases. The more significant the rule, the harder the circumstances have to be before this is justified. If this sounds messy, Mill acknowledges that it is, but utilitarianism is not the only moral theory that requires acts of judgement; and, as he remarks, any morality can be shown to be defective 'if we suppose universal idiocy to be conjoined with it'.[105]

Mill's revised conception of utility thus acknowledged the historical and progressive dimension of questions about what it is that men find pleasure in, and the necessarily qualitative issues involved in the attempt to maximise pleasure in a context of social progress. One important implication of this was that individuals could no longer be considered the absolute judge – as they had been for Bentham – of what it was that maximized their utility. For on Mill's view I cannot know what pleasures I will be able to gain from tastes and sensitivities which I have not yet developed. The second major revision, and it may be seen in part as a device for implementing the first, was the notion that the principle of utility should be applied primarily to principles, rules or practices, and not always to individual actions. This second principle implements the first by demonstrating to individuals how the immediate pursuit of what appeared to be utility could reasonably be deferred in pursuit of a greater good.

Although *Utilitarianism* has been seen largely as a starting point for a range of discussions in moral theory, its two central issues were vital to Mill's *political* thinking.

---

[103] Ibid., p. 49.   [105] Ibid., p. 22.
[104] Ibid., pp. 59, 60.

For the inability to view matters in a long and developmental term, together with the failure to recognize the importance of sticking to rules in hard cases, were typical of the mass of the people:

> Want of appreciation of distant objects and remote consequences; where an object is desired, want of both an adequate sense of practical difficulties, and of the sagacity necessary for eluding them; disregard of traditions, and of maxims sanctioned by experience; an undervaluing of the importance of fixed rules, when immediate purposes require a departure from them – these are among the acknowledged dangers of popular government.[106]

The principles outlined in *Utilitarianism*, therefore impinged directly on the very political issues preying on Mill's mind. Indeed one can regard the principle of liberty, defended in the next essay, as the most important example of an intermediate rule or principle designed to sustain the 'distant object' of progress which might conflict with the claims of utility in the more immediate sense.

Mill on liberty

In *On Liberty* all Mill's worries about the effects of democratization were brought to a head. His introduction sketches his interpretation of the changing role of liberty as a political ideal. In previous ages the people had used the ideal of liberty to establish limitations on power, claiming inviolable rights against the sovereign and establishing representative bodies to enforce them, and to otherwise represent their interests. With the progress of democracy, however, the rulers have become less and less distinguishable from the people themselves, and the need for limitations on their power had been brought into question. The rule of the people itself, however, has been recognized as the rule only of the majority amongst them, and so the possibility of a 'tyranny of the majority' becomes a real danger. There is thus still a role for a principle of liberty in placing limits on the proper range of government's powers, even those of democratic governments.

However, Mill goes on, although the danger of such tyranny was originally seen as a danger imposed only through political power, it is also one that can be imposed through the informal sanctions of society; indeed these sanctions may be 'more formidable than many kinds of political oppression . . . it leaves fewer means of escape, penetrating much more deeply into the details of life and enslaving the soul itself'. What the new democratic age needs, therefore, is not protection against the actions of government (only), but protection for the individual against the sanctions of society. Unfortunately, the very same ideals and principles which had underpinned the growth of a more democratic society had rendered that protection more difficult. Moral subjectivism has led many to believe their own *feelings* to be an infallible guide on such matters, when in fact such apparently personal views often merely reflect the beliefs of a dominant class or social group. This reveals how deeply the force of social opinion penetrates our most subjective feelings, aided perhaps by subjective religious conviction. Moreover, organized religion gives a distinctive force to and example of intolerance claiming the supposed authority

---

[106] 'Tocqueville on Democracy in America', *CW*, vol. XVIII, p. 202; *D&D*, Vol. II, pp. 80–1.

of God to determine the limits of the toleration, and the extent to which we should sanction or withhold government interference in personal liberty.

Although sketched in the context of a history of rights and of moral psychology, Mill's worries here are a recognizable descendant of the concerns of eighteenth-century thinkers with the question of whether a liberal society can produce the forms of 'public opinion' necessary for it to sustain itself. This meant assessing patterns of belief in society from the point of view of the social consequences of their being held, rather than strictly from the point of view of their truth. Irrationalities had to be judged on their merits. Amongst defenders of commercial society from Hume and Smith onwards, there is an indulgent, and in the case of Burke, violently protective, agnosticism towards the content of popular beliefs, provided they could be shown to beneficially affect people's behaviour according to independently judged standards of human benefit. Thus Mandeville scandalously, and Smith more calmly, had shown that in a case quite central to the emergence of modern society, the paradoxically opposed consequences of private vices and virtues – profligacy and egoism leading to public economic growth and wealth whilst frugality and charity undermined industry and trade. Hume showed how concepts of property and justice arose in ways quite distinct from what most would have regarded as the basis of them, Burke praised and defended 'prejudice' and Gibbon was indulgent to superstition as long as it was not 'enthusiastic'.[107]

The new 'democratic' tendencies in nineteenth-century society posed again the question of whether the public opinion and belief which it generated were stable and compatible with the continued existence and further progress of civilized society; and if not what could be done to correct them. Seen in this way, Mill's concerns in the *Essay* relate to a persistent problem stretching back to the origins of speculation concerning the viability of a commercial society, although the way that he deals with it has set an agenda for a modern debate which, in many ways has quite lost touch with that original question.

The aim of Mill's essay, was, he claimed,

> to assert one very simple principle, as entitled to govern absolutely the dealings of society with the individual in the way of compulsion and control . . . That principle is, that the sole end for which mankind are warranted, individually or collectively, in interfering with the liberty of action of any of their number is self-protection. That the only purpose for which power can be rightfully exercised over any member of a civilized community, against his will, is to prevent harm to others. His own good, either physical or moral is not a sufficient warrant. . . . The only part of the conduct of any one, for which he is amenable to society, is that which concerns others. In the part which concerns himself, his independence is, of right, absolute. Over his own body and mind, the individual is sovereign[108]

---

[107] The development of a concern with what later comes to be known as public opinion has been explored by J. G. A.Pocock in the relevant section of his *Machiavellian Moment* (Princeton, 1975) and in various essays in *Virtue, Commerce and History* (Cambridge, 1985). The connections between this analysis and nineteenth-century figures, including Mill, has been well drawn by John Burrow in Chapter 3 of his *Whigs and Liberals* (Oxford, 1988).

[108] *On Liberty* (ed.cit.), pp. 65–71, 72.

This claim, Mill asserts, covers liberty of belief and opinion, liberty of action and liberty of combination, and it is clearly directed to place explicit limits on the conformist imperatives present in democratic public opinion.

This is both a most extraordinary and a confusing claim. It is extraordinary in the degree of liberty apparently implied by the principle. Depending, admittedly, on how 'harm' is construed, Mill would appear to be sanctioning the rejection of any laws of censorship, including those affecting pornography, and many forms of libel and potential sedition. The principle might not only disqualify the use of public money (such as 'health warning' campaigns) or legal sanctions (including punitive excise taxes) to dissuade people from consumption of tobacco or alcohol, but would defend the private use, and possibly also the organized sale, of any drug whatsoever, however harmful, and the pursuit and indeed private exhibition of sexual activity of whatever kind, whether involving prostitution, animals or unconventional combinations of numbers and genders, as long as 'only with their free, voluntary, and undeceived consent and participation'.[109] Irrespective of what we might think of the desirability of such policies their advocates would have been unprecedented in the context of Victorian England, and needless to say Mill did not intend – nor did even his critics charge him with advocating – such wide freedoms as others have since derived from the principle. Nevertheless his position provoked widespread attack.

Mill's is not only a potentially shocking but also a confusing claim, as many of his early reviewers pointed out.[110] There is firstly the problem of what is meant by 'harm' to others, for harm can be experienced in all sorts of ways and clearly cannot be confined to physical hurt. Secondly there is the huge problem of whether any actions can really concern only ourselves: how we are to sustain the distinction, crucial to the operation of Mill's principle, between what he goes on to call self- and other-regarding actions? Thirdly there is the problem of how to distinguish liberty of thought and opinion from liberty of action, since Mill includes in the former, the freedom to publish and express, as well as to hold opinions.[111] The critic in the *Dublin Review* pointed out (interestingly anticipating a central theme in the work of the twentieth-century philosopher J.L. Austin) that the putting forward of an argument *is* an action, and since Mill allows legal prohibition of actions that harm others, he should, by this reasoning, also sanction the prohibition of the expression of ideas that harm others – contrary to his assertions about freedom of expression.[112] Finally there are a group of problems which arise, not so much from the principle of liberty itself, as from other things that Mill says about it, in particular the supposedly supportive relationship between it and the principle of utility.

To take this last point first. In advancing his 'one very simple principle', Mill was clearly aware that he might be seen as abandoning the principle of utility of which he was still the most famous living proponent. Anticipating charges of apostacy Mill reiterates: 'I forego any advantage which could be derived to my argument from the idea of abstract right, as a thing independent of utility. I regard utility as the ultimate appeal on all ethical questions;' but he adds, in words the significance of which cannot be fully

[109] Ibid., p. 75.
[110] See John C. Rees, *John Stuart Mill's On Liberty*. (Oxford, 1985), Ch.iii: '*On Liberty* and its Early Critics'.
[111] *On Liberty*, p. 75.
[112] Rees, *Mill's On Liberty . . .* , p. 93.

understood without reference to the reformulation of utility in the essay *On Utilitarianism*, two years later, 'it must be utility in the largest sense, grounded on the permanent interests of a man as a progressive being.'[113] Despite this assertion it is difficult to see, and his critics found it difficult to see, that Mill's assertion of an absolutely protected 'sphere of action' as he put it, was anything other than an assertion of an abstract right, a conception ridiculed by Bentham and the utilitarian school generally.[114] A related, if more far reaching version of this objection was to question the claim that *any* completely general 'principle' such as Mill's could possibly specify when government intervention was or was not justified. Surely – for a utilitarian – it must all depend on circumstance and the severity of the consequences in particular cases? Although it was not then put this way, one way of formulating such an objection, more philosophically worrying to one who, like Mill, claimed to remain a utilitarian, would be to question how one could always be sure, *a priori*, that the consequences of protecting individual liberty would always and in each case realise more utility than abrogating them. For if one could not be sure of this, Mill would seem indeed to be asserting liberty as a right independent of its consequences and therefore independently of, and potentially even in opposition to, the principle of utility.

Mill divides discussion of his principle into three followed by a discussion of their application. The three areas concern liberty of thought and discussion, in which Mill includes liberty of speech and publication, a defence of the principle of individuality, and the limits of authority over individuals' action.

Liberty of thought and discussion

Neither government nor a public acting informally, argues Mill, may legitimately exercise coercion to stifle the expression of opinion, and the reason he gives is a utilitarian, or at least a consequentialist one. If the opinion is right, the human race is deprived of it; if wrong, they are deprived of the opportunity to reinforce – through surviving a challenge – their understanding of what is right. The quashing of opinion is therefore, a much more far-reaching evil than the mere loss of something valuable to the individual, for it deprived society at large of something of benefit. Freedom of thought and expression is a condition both of overthrowing error and of fully understanding the grounds on which truths are held. This in general is Mill's argument for freedom of expression. The elaboration of his argument consists of responses to a series of objections, many of which nevertheless were and are still advanced against his position.

Mill claims that 'All silencing of discussion is an assumption of infallibility'. The accusation is, many have thought from the beginning, a strong charge to make.[115] Surely,

---

[113] *On Liberty*, p. 74.

[114] The same idea occurs in Mill's *Principles of Political Economy* V, xi, 2: 'there is a circle around every individual human being, which no government, be it that of one, of a few, or of the many, ought to be permitted to overstep . . . sacred from authoritative intrusion . . . it ought to include all that part which concerns only the life, whether inward or outward of the individual, and does not affect the interests of others.'

[115] See, e.g., *A Review of Mr. J.S. Mill's Essay 'On Liberty'* by A Liberal (London, 1867), discussed in Rees *Mill's On Liberty*, p. 95, and *passim*.

even if we have given up a belief in absolute truths, and accept the pervasive scepticism of the modern world, this cannot be allowed to paralyse our *actions*? We must, surely, both as a society, and as individuals, act on our best judgement of the situation, aware as we may be that that judgement may be wrong. Mill accepts this as a description of the how we must proceed with regard to controlling *actions*, but denies that it applies to thought and opinion. Indeed, he argues, it is only inasmuch as opinions have been exposed to refutation and contradiction that they become reliable guides to action: 'complete liberty of contradicting and disproving our opinion is the very condition which justifies us in assuming its truth for purposes of action; and on no other terms can a being with human faculties have any rational assurance of being right.'[116]

Next Mill considers the argument, that opinions are not to be assessed by their truth but by the consequences of their being believed: for example, belief in a Christian God and therefore in hell, had been, and was still held by many to be, an absolutely necessary motive to maintain moral behaviour. Once again this is a kind of utilitarian, or at least consequentialist, argument, justifying beliefs, not by their truth, but by the benefits that follow from their being believed. If sound, such an argument puts the utilitarian Mill in the awkward position of seeming to defend as an individual right, something which prevents the operation of a utilitarian principle. But Mill's response is that this argument simply shifts the assumption from one about the infallibility of the truth of an argument to one about the infallible utility its being believed.

Cleverly, for many of his opponents would be (as Mill was not) Christian believers, Mill cites Jesus, along with Socrates, as figures who had suffered at the hands of those who believed they were infallible, and invites his readers to accept that those orthodox Jews involved in the persecution of Jesus were 'in all probability quite as sincere . . . as the generality of respectable and pious men now are in the religious and moral sentiments they profess'.[117] The conventional views of any particular age invariably have an aura of infallibility to those who live under them. This is precisely the danger that may ossify progress in thought. The utilitarian argument merely adds spurious strength to a false doctrine. Christians who believe that the utility of Christianity can bolster up whatever doubts there may be about its truth, should consider the case of the Roman Emperor Marcus Aurelius. Enlightened and civilized as he was – 'a better Christian in all but the dogmatic sense of the word than almost any of the ostensibly Christian sovereigns who have since reigned' – Marcus nevertheless believed, as Christian moralists now did, that society was 'held together and prevented from being worse, by belief and reverence for the received divinities'. Moreover Aurelius saw that Christianity 'openly aimed at dissolving these ties . . . [and so] it seemed to be his duty to put it down.'[118] To judge opinion in terms of its uses, no less than to judge it in terms of its truth, required freedom of expression.

Yet another objection, anticipated by Mill and attributed by him to Dr. Johnson, is the view that persecution of unorthodox views is in a sense right, since 'persecution is an

---

[116] *On Liberty*, p. 81; and 82: 'The steady habit of correcting and completing [our] opinion by collating it with those of others, so far from causing doubt and hesitation in carrying it into practice, is the only stable foundation for a just reliance on it.'

[117] Ibid., p. 87.

[118] Ibid.

ordeal through which truth ought to pass.'[119] Mill gives this argument less than its due. Whilst, as he observes, making martyrs of benefactors is a strange way to behave, if we really believe innovation to be a good, this has no impact on the question of whether or not it is *true* that placing some difficulty in the way of new ideas is a way of testing the conviction of the innovators and the power of the ideas themselves.[120] Mill himself acknowledged what was widely assumed in progressive intellectual circles, that the forces of both innovation and stability had to be harmonized for social progress to take place. Was not a degree of repression one way of regulating the extent of innovation? The issue has curious similarities to recent arguments about the methodology of the natural sciences, and the optimum degree of difficulty which should be placed in the way of new theories as a way of testing them.[121] Once again, it would seem to be, on a utilitarian view, a matter for calculation just how much innovation should be discouraged in personal behaviour, given that no discouragement at all would possibly result in frivolous or irresponsible innovations or, to put the argument at its weakest, large numbers of innovations which might cause confusion or make reasoned anticipation of people's behaviour difficult.[122]

The force of this argument might, in turn, depend on the 'spirit of the times'. In turbulent, heroic or individualistic ages, the courageous championing of new ideas might be more likely (one thinks of Galileo's stubborn 'yet it moves' in the face of the Inquisition). Yet, as Mill had noted in *The Spirit of the Age*, 'the virtues which insecurity calls forth, ceased with insecurity itself'.[123] It is part of Mill's argument that the moral sociology of the present age had undermined such courage, rendering it necessary to pursue some active policy to protect individual expression.[124]

The above arguments rest on at least the possibility that conventional views might be false. A second set of arguments was designed to defend freedom of opinion, even on the assumption (which of course could never be guaranteed) that the prevailing orthodox views were infallibly true. These arguments hinge on the need for even true opinions to be grounded in a vivid understanding of their reasons. Such understanding, Mill urged,

---

[119] Ibid., p. 88.

[120] Both Mill's contemporary critic James Fitzjames Stephen, *Liberty, Equality and Fraternity* (London, 1873) and Lord Justice Devlin, *The Enforcement of Morals* (London, 1965), argue along these lines.

[121] Thomas Kuhn, for example has stressed the utility of having a shared and authoritative paradigm within which progress can take place, and both described and endorsed the sociological and epistemological processes which deter innovative paradigms. Paul Feyerabend, on the other hand would let a thousand flowers bloom and argues for a conceptual pluralism. Neither believe that science can be authoritatively assessed in terms of its *truth*, each argues on the grounds of which methodological procedures are most conducive to meaningful innovation. Feyerabend has drawn attention to this parallel in his essay 'Against Method', *Minnesota Studies in the Philosophy of Science*, vol. 4, Minneapolis (1970). For Kuhn see *The Structure of Scientific Revolutions* (Chicago, 1962).

[122] Mill does in fact use this argument about the utility of following conventions because of the social benefits of predictable behaviour in section four: 'it is necessary that general rules should, for the most part, be observed, in order that people know what they have to expect': *On Liberty*, p. 133. It is an argument which, as we have seen, hovers uncertainly around the discussion of moral rules in *Utilitarianism*.

[123] 'The Spirit of the Age', pt.2 (1831) in *Collected Works*, ed. Robson, vol. XXII, p. 280.

[124] Whilst the popular picture of mid-Victorian Britain is indeed of a stiflingly conformist society, Mill's characterization of it is far from being the whole picture. As Alan Ryan dryly observes 'the belief that, in a decade which culminated in the furor over Darwin's *Origin of Species* there were hardly two persons who could put an unorthodox sentence together was grotesque.' Alan Ryan, *J.S. Mill* (London, 1974), p. 127.

can only be gained from having to defend that opinion or belief against an opposing one. Without opposition the most precious truth becomes a dry cliché which engages no vigorous support. Even false beliefs therefore, perform a service to truth by reminding us of its grounds and re-invigorating the strength with which it is held: 'The fatal tendency of mankind to leave off thinking about a thing when it is no longer doubtful, is the cause of half their errors.'[125]

Finally Mill argues that in many areas, and especially in the field of social or political belief, truth, rather than resting in one or the other of two clashing views, emerges from their conflict; it lies somewhere in between. When Rousseau shocked the complacency of the Enlightenment, the benefit of his doctrines was 'not that the current opinions were on the whole farther from the truth than Rousseau's were; on the contrary, they were nearer to it.' It lay rather in Rousseau reminding society of the 'superior worth of simplicity of life' and of the 'trammels and hypocrisies of artificial society.' And the worth of those reminders has remained ever since.[126]

There are almost undertones of what one might call a kind of conceptual Darwinism in these views of Mill's. Ideas and opinions at least, should be left free to allow the fittest to survive. Of course what that might mean in these circumstances is unclear, but Mill evidently assumes it will in some sense be the 'truest', or most civilized. Discussing the 'threat' (as some saw it) of Mormonism, Mill denied civilization was entitled to resort to oppression. 'If civilization has got the better of barbarism when barbarism had the world to itself, it is too much to profess to be afraid lest barbarism, after having been fairly got under, should revive and conquer civilization . . . if this be so, the sooner such a civilization receives notice to quit the better.'[127]

The worth of individuality

Mill moves next as if to consider what the limits might be of individuals' freedom of action; but in the event he postpones this discussion to chapter IV.[128] Instead we have a discussion of the general desirability of what he calls individuality as an end in life. This is a logical step. There is little point in seeking, as Mill wishes, to engage an audience in a discussion about how to minimize the restrictive role of the state or society on individuals' actions if there is no general presumption that that restriction is a bad thing in the first place. The problem – Mill actually calls it an 'evil' – he must deal with is 'that individual spontaneity is hardly recognized by the common modes of thinking as having any intrinsic worth . . . but is rather looked on with jealousy.'[129]

Mill's argument that individuality and spontaneity has intrinsic worth poses an immediate problem for those (including Mill himself) wishing to see him as a consistent utilitarian; for if liberty's worth is 'intrinsic' it cannot be justified on other, let alone on

---

[125] *On Liberty*, p. 103.

[126] Ibid., p. 106.

[127] Ibid., p. 149.

[128] The opening of Chapter III somewhat confusingly announces the aim of 'examining whether the same reasons do not require that men should be free to act upon their opinions', Ibid., p. 114. In fact detailed discussion of this takes place in the next chapter.

[129] Ibid., p. 115.

consequentialist, utilitarian grounds. On the other hand if it *is* so justified, then the value Mill sets on liberty is in danger of being seen as merely instrumental, and Mill's championship of liberty a means to some other end.[130]

Mill's argument hinges on an opposition between custom, passivity and indolence on the one hand, and innovation, originality and energy on the other. Like Blake, Mill denies any inherent connection between goodness and passivity. Energy is protean.[131] But the power and energy of personality is elicited only through use.[132] The hostility of polite society to eccentricity acts like 'a hostile and dreaded censorship' stifling not only new ideas but the very energy that lies behind them. It is not merely that people 'choose what is customary in preference to what suits their own inclination.' Rather 'It does not occur to them to have any inclination, except for what is customary.' In the modern world 'public opinion' (whites in America, most of the middle class in England) is not merely *held* by the mass, the content of it is actually *provided* by them as well, and the influence of persons of distinction in setting opinion virtually excluded. Under such circumstances 'when the opinions of masses of merely average men are everywhere become or becoming the dominant power, the counterpoise and corrective to that tendency would be the more and more pronounced individuality of those who stand on the higher eminences of thought.' Indeed in such servile cultures 'the mere example of non-conformity, the mere refusal to bend the knee to custom is itself a service.'[133]

Mill sees this repressive and stagnant culture as the consequence of a deliberate policy originating in the Reformation by Calvin, according to whom human nature was so corrupt that 'crushing out any of the human faculties, capabilities, and susceptibilities, is no evil.' The Victorian suppression of individuality to custom and authority is a secularized remnant of this mentality.[134]

Mill's positive arguments for his ideal are less easy to pin down. One is an almost Aristotelian view about human ends. Those circumstances (i.e. liberty) which allow the greatest development human potential are claimed to be intrinsically better than those which inhibit or limit that growth. But much of his argument is suggestive and rhetorical in form and at base aesthetic rather than utilitarian. It shares this aesthetic appeal with an important work which Mill read at the time, and from which he quotes at the start of *On Liberty*, namely von Humboldt's *Limits of State Action*.[135] This kind of argument is in line with what one might expect for a value which is 'intrinsic' and cannot be strictly justified as instrumental to another. In the last chapter of his *Logic*, Mill had drawn a general distinction between art and science. Science is an 'enquiry into the course of nature'. Part of moral philosophy is properly a science – that which deals with the natural consequences of actions (including those which relate to humans' natures). But part of it, that which deals in the ultimate ends, or precepts, lies in the realm of art, for what art tells us is 'that the attainment of a given end is desirable,' what science tells us is in what

---

[130] As urged most strongly by M. Cowling, *Mill and Liberalism* (Cambridge, 1963).

[131] 'Energy may be turned to bad uses; but more good may always be made of an energetic nature.' *On Liberty*, p. 118.

[132] Ibid., p. 117.

[133] Ibid., pp. 119, 124.

[134] Ibid., p. 120.

[135] For a discussion of the aesthetic basis of von Humboldt's liberalism see: Ursula Vogel 'Liberty is Beautiful: von Humboldt's Gift to Liberalism', *History of Political Thought*, III, 1 (1982).

circumstances it will flourish.[136] In resorting to an aesthetic appeal in justifying individuality, and the elevated conception of utility of which he evidently believed it to be a part, Mill is therefore quite consistent with his more explicit views about the division of intellectual labour between art, with respect to promulgating ends, and science as identifying appropriate means to them.[137] The cultivation of individuality, it is claimed, produces humans who are 'noble and beautiful objects of contemplation', it renders human life 'rich, diversified and animating', makes the individual 'more valuable to himself'.[138]

Yet again, and dependent in some sense on the above, there are utilitarian arguments which echo those concerning freedom of speech. Individualists benefit others as well as fulfilling themselves by pointing the way to alternatives from which even the most unoriginal of us might at some point benefit. In the way we lead our lives, as well as in the opinions we promote, innovation, and the conditions which sustain it must be kept alive or progressive civilization may simply die out.

The connection Mill asserts between the 'spirit of liberty' and innovative improvement, allows that liberty may find itself, on occasion, defending the status quo, but he is generally confident that 'the only unfailing and permanent source of improvement is liberty'. Like Hegel he sees those countries (the greater part of the world), where reflective, creative thought was never allowed to develop, as having 'properly speaking, no history, because the despotism of Custom is complete'. And he cites China, a country of undoubted talent and wisdom, but no individuality, as an unfortunate warning of the kind of static conformity to which the yoke of public opinion might doom us.[139] It is not, on Mill's view, any superior moral qualities that have accounted for Europe's remarkable progress, but wholly 'the remarkable diversity of character and culture', a diversity which is rapidly being eroded through national homogenization, the creation of a reading public, improvements in education, communications and commerce, but most of all the dominance of public opinion.[140]

Thus lacing his praise of individualism with jeremiads to the baneful progress of uniformity, Mill rounds off his defence of individuality. It is to be valued both as expressive of the highest in human life itself, and for its role in promoting the further development of civilization, the latter perhaps giving some strength to Mill's claim to retain as his standard 'utility in the largest sense, grounded on the permanent interests of man as a progressive being'.[141] For if the utility to be calculated in considering whether to limit actions (or speech) is not simply the direct consequences of that particular (and

[136] *Logic*, Bk VI, ch xii, 1–2.

[137] For example in his essay *Utilitarianism*, he is insistent that no absolute proof can be given of the principle, since 'questions of ultimate ends are not amenable to direct proof' (pp. 4, 32). The subsequent observation, that utility is 'psychologically true' (p. 36) is therefore, not, as it is often presented, a flawed scientific proof of a necessarily artistic ultimate good, but rather a demonstration, as is required by the *Logic*, of the possible congruency of an end provided by art, with world as depicted by science. It is not because happiness is generally desired that utility *must* be the final ethical aim, but rather the fact (if it is one) that happiness is desired makes it *possible* for utility to be the final principle.

[138] *On Liberty*, pp. 120–1.

[139] Ibid., p. 128.

[140] This did not prevent Mill urging the incorporation of those regional cultures he regarded as primitive, into their metropolitan nationalities. See below, p. 390.

[141] *On Liberty*, p. 74.

quite possibly, to present beliefs, painfully offensive) act, but the much wider utility to be enjoyed through the progress achieved as a result of a policy of liberty promoting individual experimentation and diversity, then the scales are loaded very heavily indeed in favour of liberty.

That this is in fact what Mill means has, as we have seen, some confirmation in his essay *On Utilitarianism*. Here Mill argues that the principle of utility, whilst it is the ultimate moral principle, should not be the one invoked in assessing how to act in a particular case: 'to endeavour to test each individual action by the first principle' is a mistake. 'Whatever we adopt as the fundamental principle of morality, we require subordinate principles to apply it by;' it is impossible to operate in any other way.[142] Liberty, Mill seems to suggest, is such a principle. Although the application of the liberty principle might, in particular cases, seem to diminish rather than increase happiness – he gives the example of defending the eating of pork in a Muslim culture[143] – in the long run having such a principle will create more happiness through allowing progress, a vigorous intellectual defence of the society and the flowering of individuality.[144]

Whether these considerations will always tilt the scales, will of course depend upon just how much disutility the individualist's action itself creates. And it is to consider those limits on the liberty of individual action that Mill next turns.

The limits of liberty of action

Although Mill, in common with other utilitarians, rejects the notion of a social contract and natural rights, he does concede that the idea of a right neatly captures what he wants to defend in this section of the *Essay*. What none of us may do is to injure 'interests, which, either by express legal provision or by tacit understanding ought to be considered as rights.' As well as limiting our actions to this extent, society may also require us to contribute to the cost of defending 'society or its members from injury and molestation'. Mill distinguishes (although not always or clearly) between what 'society' in the sense of the state may impose on us, and what 'society' in the looser sense of public opinion, may do. Actions which are hurtful or inconsiderate to people, even though not 'violating their constituted rights' may be 'justly punished by opinion, though not by law.'[145] So

---

[142] *Utilitarianism*, pp. 22–3.

[143] *On Liberty*, p. 142.

[144] Mill made a somewhat similar point about the relationship of the cultivation of personality to utility in the penultimate paragraph of the *Logic*, 'I do not mean to assert that the promotion of all happiness should be itself the end of all actions or even of all rules of actions . . . the cultivation of an ideal of nobleness of will and conduct should be to individual human beings an end, to which the specific pursuit . . . of happiness . . . should give way. But I hold that the very question what constitutes this elevation of character, is itself to be decided by a reference to happiness as the standard. . . . because the existence of this ideal, or a near approach to it, . . . would go further than all things else towards making human life happy, both in the comparatively humble sense of pleasure and freedom from pain, and in the higher meaning of rendering life, not what it now is almost universally, puerile and insignificant, but such as human beings with highly developed faculties can care to have.' Bk VI, Ch.xii, 7.

[145] *On Liberty*, p. 132. Mill later elaborates on what might be 'punished by opinion': falsehood or duplicity in dealing, unfair or ungenerous use of advantage, 'even selfish abstinence from defending them against injury.' Ibid., p. 135.

Mill, despite his misgivings, does allow public opinion a censorial role in inhibiting behaviour which is not strictly nor properly illegal, and perhaps only selfish. He recognizes that those actions which 'affect other people' are not, all of them, covered by legislation. He also recognizes that people who act imprudently, or in an undignified way, even though only in respect of themselves, will, and quite rightly forfeit others' respect; but whilst we may pity or avoid such people, he insists that this must be distinguished from censuring them. His main point is, that though we may argue and persuade (and indeed we should do it more than we do)[146] there is no case for either legal or informal censure 'when a person's conduct affects the interests of no persons besides himself, or needs not affect them unless they like'.[147]

The grounds Mill gives for this are similar to, but more elaborate than the grounds given by Bentham in his defence of liberty: that the individual has himself not only privileged information about his own feelings and desires, but the strongest interest in what Mill calls 'their own well being', and as a result 'All errors which he is likely to commit against advice and warning are far outweighed by the evil of allowing others to constrain him to what they deem his good.'[148]

Mill's distinction between what we may censure or prohibit (informally as a society, or politically through government) and what we should permit, rests on a crucial distinction between 'self regarding' and 'other regarding' actions. The viability of this restriction rests, amongst other things, on how interconnected we believe individuals to be. On one view there may be almost no, or at least no significant self regarding actions. If we abuse and so ruin our bodily or mental health doesn't this affect our dependents and our capacities to do good to others, or even make us dependent on them? Doesn't all action, even self-regarding, affect others by example? It is an argument often used today that famous figures have a special responsibility, even with regard to their private lives, because, willingly or not they act as a public example. As Mill acknowledges, and numerous critics have asserted, the distinction between self- and other-regarding actions is 'one that many persons will refuse to admit'.[149] How does Mill think it can be sustained?

Perhaps the best defence is along the lines suggested by the late Mill scholar John Rees. His argument was that, although Mill's terminology is not always as precise as we might wish, Mill was concerned, and not merely casually, to distinguish between merely affecting, and affecting *the interests* of, another person.[150] Whilst almost any action may be argued to affect another person in some way, not all actions affect their interests. The distinction is one which appeals, as did Bentham's original notion of utility, to the difference between the objective and the purely subjective properties of personal interaction. Just as Bentham tried to construe pleasure and pain as 'real entities', rather than

[146] Ibid., p. 134. He remarks that it would be better 'if this good office were much more freely rendered than the common notions of politeness at present permit.'

[147] Ibid., p. 132.

[148] Ibid., p. 133.

[149] Ibid., p. 136.

[150] For example twice in *On Liberty*, p. 132, and at p. 149, where Mill, reiterating what he claims are 'the two maxims which together form the entire doctrine of this Essay' writes: 'first, that the individual is not accountable to society for his actions, in so far as these concern the interests of no person but himself . . . Secondly, that for such actions as are prejudicial to the interests of others the individual is accountable . . . '.

mere subjective assessments, and so to disallow as 'pain' someone's claim that what others did in private affected them, so Mill here, very much in the utilitarian tradition, wants to use the more objective notion of 'interest' as the criterion, rather than the more subjective one of 'affect'. Not all cases of 'affecting' are cases of 'affecting interests'. What is the difference?

Conceptually, interests are longer term, capable of being judged by outsiders, and concern a relationship between means and ends. They contrast with mere wishes or desires which are more ephemeral, purely subjective and immediate. My desire to eat an ice-cream is hardly an 'interest', nor is it something that another person could be better informed about than myself, nor is there (except practically) a problem about how to satisfy it. My interests as a professional academic on the other hand, are long term, something about which suitably informed colleagues could give me advice, and do concern a distinction between means and ends, about say, whether those interests will best be served by writing a textbook or concentrating on more original research! Interests are more or less permanent features of individuals' moral and social landscapes. Thus one major point about them is that they can be objectively characterized by others without losing touch with the agent's own perceptions of their life and actions. This is precisely the line we find Mill pursuing.

The sort of cases that affect interests and so justify interference are described by Mill as those where an action 'violates a distinct and assignable obligation' to others, or where 'there is a definite risk of damage, either to an individual or to the public'.[151] The notion of injuring interests as violating distinct obligations is further explained at one point as 'certain interests, which, either by express legal provision or by tacit understanding, ought to be considered as rights'.[152] Now if by 'rights' is here meant positive rights, i.e. legally enforceable,[153] then Mill's argument would simply describe and endorse the legal status quo, it would have no critical edge at all, for, by definition, society takes it on itself to punish violators of legal rights. Since one of the purposes of the *Essay* is to defend a principle which could be used to criticise illiberal, or inadequate laws, it would be odd if this was all that Mill meant here. Instead Mill seems to mean that there are some claims which can be called or considered as rights, quite apart from positive law.

Once again a discussion in *Utilitarianism* helps to clarify Mill's meaning. Right is there identified with justice, since to have a right is to have a claim on another which they have an obligation to fulfill, and justice (as opposed to morality more generally) is concerned with the exercise of sanctions against those who contravene rights.[154] If we look at what justice entails we find Mill describing a list of rights: 'liberty, property or anything held under a [*sc.* just] law, *moral rights*, desert, fulfilment of contracts, express or implied, including the knowing raising of expectations'. This latter seems to be fundamental and to underpin the rest, including as it does, positive law, but extending beyond it.[155] For Mill, to have a right then, would seem to be to have a clear and specifiable expectation of behaviour on the part of someone else (an expectation derived from positive law, custom, desert or agreement) the non-fulfilment of which could materially

[151] Ibid., pp. 137, 138.

[152] Ibid., p. 132.

[153] As suggested by Rees, *Mill's On Liberty*, p. 147.

[154] *Utilitarianism*, p. 46.

[155] Ibid., pp. 40–1.

affect one's identifiable interests (and not just one's feelings). It is these rights that mark the limit between self-regarding and other regarding actions. The broad principle is that as long as their actions respect such rights, individuals should be free to do what they wish.

It must be said that although clarifying his position to some extent, this account leads to further problems for Mill, committed as he is to the very Humean task of giving not only a moral justification for 'what ought to be considered as rights' but also a psychological account of their basis.[156] The question of what 'expectations' might be raised must rest largely on the current state of public opinion. Thus my behaviour could quite legitimately raise expectations because of current convention which I had no wish to raise, but which I could not help raising by doing what I wanted to do. One obvious and pertinent Victorian example would be in sexual matters. If the capacity of the individual or individuals involved to act freely is to be circumscribed by others' rights; and those rights derive from expectations (necessarily) determined by conventional attitudes, Mill's principle will not generate the arena of personal freedom he clearly expects it to. This is a direct consequence of his grounding the identity of liberty in a kind of sociology of belief, which will only generate the 'right' kind of expectations once a more liberal culture is itself established.

Against this, Mill can of course point to the more objective elements of his analysis, the notion of material interests, injury and the idea that the particular subjective feeling that underpins our sense of justice is not the desire to defend particular interests, but the most vital one of all – security.[157]

In applying this principle to the limitation of actions, Mill stresses the need to show that specific individuals, or their interests will be harmed, and not to rely simply on vague assertions of contingent, general or 'constructive injury', through, say setting a bad example. There must be 'a definite damage or definite risk of damage.' The idea of a 'risk of damage' justifying intervention, might seem to allow the thin end of a wedge which could again undermine Mill's principle. But the risk, he urges, has to be strong. It would not be right to punish a soldier or policeman for being drunk, or even a drunkard, in their private lives, but only for being drunk on duty. Since then an assignable right (that of the public to protection) is being denied, there is a definite risk of injury. He goes further in urging that if there is a case to be made for punishing individuals for self-regarding actions, he would rather argue it on openly paternalist grounds than by dubiously extending the notion of the rights members of society can expect from them.

Secondly, in discussing the application of his principle Mill argues that even showing that an act does damage another's interest does not automatically justify interference, for the presumption in favour of liberty may still hold.[158]

The major area where others' interests may be legitimately affected is in competition and trade. The winner in a competitive exam, like the 'winner' in the market place, clearly

---

[156] The following, from *Utilitarianism*, is, despite the intrusion of the notion of vengeance, almost pure Hume: 'The sentiment of justice . . . is . . . the natural feeling of retaliation or vengeance, rendered by the intellect and sympathy applicable to those hurts, which wound us through, or in common with, society at large. This sentiment, in itself has nothing moral in it; what is moral is the exclusive subordination of it to the social sympathies, so as to wait on and obey their call.' p. 48.

[157] Ibid., pp. 50–1.

[158] Ibid., p. 150.

affects those who lose. This, however, cannot justify government intervention on straightforward utilitarian grounds. For it is to the benefit of all that the most meritorious conduct public business and that the cheapest supplier produces our commodities. It is utility that directly justifies free trade. The principle of liberty is not, Mill claims, involved in these arguments, except as a background assumption that it is better to leave people free to do as they wish; and against that, the utilitarian justification of public intervention to impose quality or health controls or safety regulations in the workplace, is 'in principle undeniable'.[159] On the other hand, intervention which affects, not the producer (about which Mill has no qualms), but the consumer, intervention which is designed *per se* to make it difficult to buy something, *is* intervention which affects liberty. Mill's liberty principle does not, therefore, in any simple or direct way translate into an argument for the free-market.

Mill argues a further constraint on the operation of his principle. 'The right inherent in society, to ward off crimes against itself by antecedent precautions, suggests the obvious limitation to the maxim that purely self-regarding misconduct cannot be meddled with in the way of prevention or punishment.'[160] Mill is suspicious of this 'preventive function' of government, it is most 'liable to be abused', but this doesn't rule it out: drugs and poisons are dangerous substances, and although people may have legitimate reasons for wanting to possess them, that liberty must be balanced against the likelihood of harm resulting from their availability. Not only are people whose otherwise self-regarding actions injure others – such as the man with family responsibilities who gambles away his money – liable to punishment, Mill also argues that self-regarding actions themselves which for particular reasons render *likely* a harm to others – such as the man who habitually gets violent when drunk – justify punishment.

Although Mill thinks these examples illustrative of his principles, it's not always clear what implications he wants the reader to draw. For example, to apply Mill's principle to the question of driving whilst under the influence of alcohol. Does the 'likelihood of harm' argument support the present position, under which it is an offence merely to *be* drunk and driving, or should it, as Mill's example of the violent drunkard might suggests, only be the case that increased penalties apply if one is drunk and driving *and* cause injury or harm to another as a result? Drunken driving, at least at the level of 80mg, undoubtedly increases the likelihood of accidents, but does it do so by enough to justify punishing an act which *in itself* has not harmed another?

Mill further allows penalties against actions which 'if done publicly, are a violation against good manners', such as indecent exposure.

But perhaps the most interesting area is that in which the individual tries to propagandize, persuade or reward other individuals to participate or pursue 'self-regarding' actions of a dubious nature. Examples abound: the promotion of, and commerce in, alcohol, gambling, prostitution, pornography, drug-taking. Indulging any of these in private, and by consenting adults, is permissible under Mill's rule; can the commercial exploitation of them also be justified? This is perhaps the hardest test for Mill's and indeed any liberal's nerve, and in some ways Mill's answers indicate a decent and principled retreat from the more exposed implications of his position. The principle of freedom of expression must, at the very least, allow individuals to *advise* others to do

---

[159] Ibid., p. 151.   [160] Ibid., p. 153.

what is itself permitted under the principle. But suppose they are being paid to do it? Surely the mere fact of making a living from something not in itself criminal, cannot turn it into something criminal? On the other hand, it is surely a distinct issue whether individuals should be allowed to make money 'to promote what society and the State consider to be an evil.'[161] Surely society has discharged its duty in respect of the principle of liberty when it has removed penalties from the private practice of evil-seeming but self-regarding actions? It has allowed people to make up their own minds. Why is society obliged to go further and allow people to profit from their practice, providing not only the freedom, but a positive motive to spread what is believed to be evil? Although Mill is undecided on these issues, which, he thinks, represent the 'exact boundary line' between the principle of personal liberty and the protection of rights and interests, he admits 'there is considerable force in these arguments'.[162] But inasmuch as the reason why they have force can only be the desire of society to protect its adult members from a harm that affects only themselves, Mill is in danger of contravening his original principle.

Mill's residual paternalism comes to the fore even more in discussing the question of state discouragement of alcohol sales. Mill objects to the policy of limiting the issue of licenses to sell alcohol in working-class areas as a way of curbing sales, since it treats the working classes as children who cannot decide for themselves. And again in the case of excise taxation Mill points out, correctly, that all increases in cost constitute a form of prohibition that falls differentially on the poor, and there is no reason (except for the paternalist one) selectively to condemn the way they wish to spend their money. But in considering the need of the state to raise revenue from sales, the imposition of such costs is inescapable; and, Mill claims, the state has what is an undisguisedly paternalistic duty 'to consider what commodities the consumers can best spare' and in doing so 'to select in preference those of which it deems the use, beyond a very moderate quantity, to be positively injurious.'[163]

There are other limitations on individuals' freedoms which introduce principles with far reaching consequences. Although part of individual freedom is freedom of contract, there are limits which all civilized countries place on what one may part with. Thus slavery, even when voluntarily entered into, is not an enforceable contract, for it 'defeats . . . the very purpose which is the justification of allowing him to dispose of himself'. The 'far wider application' which Mill recognizes this principle suggests might well include certain kinds of drug dependency which effectively take away individuals' freedom of action, thus recruiting Mill for the restrictive rather than the libertarian party in one of the major issues of personal liberty to arise since his day. However the most obvious application for Mill of the principle inherent in slavery was that of marriage, a contract which had the peculiarity of binding for life, not only the person, but what cannot effectively be contracted for: their affections. Marriage clearly creates rights, not only legal rights, but more generally those which encourage expectations on the part of another person, and the frustration of which would materially affect their interests, in effect Mill's paradigm case of rights. Yet whilst marriage creates such rights and obligations they do not, he thought 'extend to the fulfilment of the contract at all costs to the happiness of

---

[161] Ibid., p. 154.   [163] Ibid., pp. 157, 156.
[162] Ibid., pp. 154–5.

the reluctant party.'[164] The case of women was taken up again immediately after *On Liberty*, in *The subjection of women*, written in 1861, but not published until 1869. Meanwhile in 1867 Mill, as MP for Westminster, had sought to introduce a bill for the enfranchisement of women.

It was not only the 'voluntary' tutelage of married women that the principle of *On Liberty* undermined, for the principle, *a fortiori* also had implications for the involuntary subjugation of children. Valuing the personal freedom of all individuals not only placed restraints on how individuals might treat those in their charge, it also imposed obligations on them. Children, unlike women, cannot be made free in the negative sense of merely being given the rights of adults, they had to be made free in the sense of being positively equipped with the skills and knowledge to enable them to use those rights. It was, thought Mill, therefore 'almost a self-evident maxim' that the education of youth was an obligation which the state must not only enforce, but if necessary discharge, not through providing the education, which Mill was vehemently against, but through enforcing parents to provide it, and providing the resources to pay for it, where they could or would not do so.[165]

Mill's worries about state education derived from his concern for individuality and variety. He feared a state education system would be 'a mere contrivance for moulding people to be exactly like one another.' Even the public examinations designed to check educational progress should 'be confined to facts and positive science exclusively' as a way of excluding the state from 'improper influence over opinion.' Religion, especially, he thought should be taught, if at all, as a body of beliefs, not as a dogma. 'There is no reasonable objection to examining an atheist in the evidences of Christianity, provided he is not required to profess a belief in them.'[166]

Towards the end of this section Mill quietly lets fall a quite astonishing application of his principle. Not only is the state justified in intervening to ensure children are educated where they might not otherwise be, it is also justified in intervening to decide whether they should be born or not. Laws proscribing marriage unless the parties can show they can support children do 'not exceed the legitimate powers of the State: and . . . are not objectionable as violations of liberty.'[167] Mill's argument in support of such an intrusive claim is not elaborate. It rests on what he evidently perceives as a direct application of his other-regarding principle, in that procreation under such circumstances harms others – primarily the self that has to endure such a life. He did not seem to think that the consequence of denying very existence to the self being protected from harm (surely not a plausible case of protecting *interests*!) might make any difference to the application of the principle.[168] He merely draws attention to the oddity of a public opinion which regarded what individuals do in private as a matter for rightful comment and intervention, whilst seeing the other-regarding activity of procreation as properly beyond legitimate control.

---

[164] Ibid., p. 159.

[165] Ibid., pp. 160–1.

[166] Ibid., pp. 161, 162.

[167] Ibid., p. 163.

[168] For a modern discussion of the complexities see Derek Parfit. *Reasons and Persons* (Oxford, 1984), pp. 357ff.

Economic applications of the principle

Mill finally considers the applications of his principle. Most of these have already been discussed. They appreciably limit the libertarian range of his principle. Although the period from the sixties to the present has perhaps seen the greatest growth of personal liberty issues of the kind that Mill had in mind – with sexual and drug experimentation, the repudiation of traditional roles for women (and men), and explorations in a variety of communal living arrangements – the other main area in which his principle impinges is that of the economy. Here the principle of liberty has often been taken as underpinning the laissez-faire economy, and there is no doubt that for great areas Mill regarded it as doing precisely this, and for good utilitarian reasons: 'all the facilities which a government enjoys of access to information; all the means which it possesses of remunerating, and therefore of commanding, the best available talent in the market – are not an equivalent for the one great disadvantage of an inferior interest in the result.'[169] However, the final book of his *Principles of Political Economy*, offers an interesting demonstration of the limitations of that principle.

The operation of the principle that the consumer is the best judge is limited when the utilitarian reason given above (that the consumer has the greatest interest in pursing his own happiness) fails to guarantee the achievement of it. It fails to hold in particular when Mill's qualitative conception of happiness or pleasure is brought into play. Whatever is 'chiefly useful as tending to raise the character of human beings' is, in the nature of things, unlikely to be demanded by them spontaneously. Such education should therefore be provided, and even required by government, particularly since the 'natural wage rate' does not allow labourers to make their own provision for it.[170] Mill also excludes, again, as he does in *On Liberty*, those contracts which are binding in the long term, again explicitly mentioning marriage.

It is the third reason that is perhaps most illuminating in stressing not only how individualist was Mill's thought, but how, on his view, un-individualist the social order known as capitalism is. As Mill points out, the 'firm' or joint-stock company which is the major actor in the free-market economy, is not an individual but a delegated agency. Moreover in view of the largely ineffectual control exercised by shareholders, the managers are no more entitled to claim to act in the interests of the individuals they represent than in the case of 'administration by a public officer', and their work 'will often be as well, and sometimes better done, ... by the state'.[171] Although for reasons to do with overloading government, and the danger of concentrating ability, Mill in the end

---

[169] *Political Economy*, V, xi, 5. Mill also uses arguments, repeated in *On Liberty*, about the importance of political participation as an educative experience, and the danger of concentrating energy and talent in the government, to the exclusion of society at large, 6. Cf. *On Liberty*, pp. 164, 167. Although these implications are not spelt out in full they are at base, utilitarian, not libertarian principles, as the exceptions clearly show.

[170] *Political Economy*, V, xi, 8. Mill makes the same disclaimer as in *On Liberty* about government not itself actually monopolizing educational provision, though here he allows it may provide it in competition with others.

[171] *Political Economy*, V, xi, 11.

rejects this line, he still sees much for government to do, especially where natural monopolies such as railways, water and other utilities are concerned. Left in private hands such companies are 'even more irresponsible, and unapproachable by individual complaints, than the government.' Consequently 'the community needs some other security for the fit performance of the service than the interest of the managers'. This may take the form of regulation, profit taking or maintenance of an ultimate public property right in such enterprises.[172]

In this discussion of the role of the market Mill refuses to make the seductive and common elision from the defence of the freedom of the individual as market actor to the defence of the firm or business corporation, on the assumption that the arguments that support the one support the other. This Mill clearly denies. Rather than assume that firms and individuals can be conflated, or that firms can be presumed to act in individuals' (shareholders') interests, Mill stresses the way in which their interests diverge. Business organizations are not more, but *less* responsible than governments in vigilant and democratic societies, and there can be no assumption about the organizational superiority of the former.

Mill openly deprecated the relationship between entrepreneur and employee under capitalism and thought 'that the various schemes for managing the productive resources of the country by public instead of private agency have a case for a trial, and some may eventually establish their claims to preference . . . '. He thought the idea of a centralized economy 'obviously chimerical'.[173] However, although he regarded competition as 'always an ultimate good' he looked forward to a socialized economy of competing workers' co-operative enterprises, which, he firmly believed, would, by a process of competition, replace the conventional capitalist firm.[174]

Discussion of the economic application of Mill's ideas has taken us some way from the core of the issue in *On Liberty*. Mill's overall aim is to vindicate a limited area of personal liberty of action, and a virtually unhindered freedom of expression. His justification for this rests partly on individualist and partly on social grounds. The exercise of liberty is a precondition for the full growth of personality and the realization of an aesthetic ideal of individuality. But the protection of space and expression for the individual is a condition for the continued vigour and progress of society. Only societies which allow their deepest held beliefs to be questioned can be truly strong, and only those which allow some experimentation can possibly progress. Only a society in which alternatives are considered, can therefore realise the utility 'in the largest sense' that is, considering humankind as capable of making and sustaining progress, and not as static bundles of appetites. The themes of stability and progress thread their way through these aspects of *On Liberty* and they remain important in the last of the three major essays of the 1860s, *Representative Government*.

---

[172] Ibid., V, xi, 11.

[173] 'Chapters on Socialism', in *On Liberty etc.*, ed. Collini, p. 273.

[174] *Political Economy*, Bk IV, 7, p. 142 and *passim*.

Representative government

The *Essay on Representative Government* Mill claimed, illustrated the principles to which he had 'been working up during the greater part of my life'. It was, we may conclude, amongst other things an attempt to demonstrate how Mill's two major developments of utilitarian thinking – the revision of the principle of utility to incorporate quality, moral growth and liberty, and the acknowledgement of the historicity of social questions – applied to political issues. The novelty of the work, he claimed, lay not in the institutional reforms suggested or in the principles asserted in it, but in showing how the one derived from the other, in: 'exhibiting them in their connection'.[175] Despite this disclaimer, the *Essay* contains changes in Mill's views which are new to all but close followers of his development. In particular he abandons certain basic radical tenets which he had held – somewhat incongruously it must be said – through even his more conservative phases. He abandons the demand for a secret ballot, and for shorter parliaments, he proposes plural voting for the more qualified voters and proportional representation to safeguard minorities.[176]

Although Mill's stated intention in the work is to 'exhibit' theoretical principle and institutional device 'in their connection', the structure of the work does not facilitate this. Chapters I – VI deal with general principles, whilst chapters VII – XV deal with the structure and institutions of government, and the last three with issues of national identity, federation and colonialism. The principles and the institutions are thus presented largely independently, and often related to each other only by implication. In the following discussion I shall try to integrate discussion of the principles with illustrations of their institutional embodiment. Even if this does not improve on Mill's presentation it will at the least provide an alternative perspective.

One more prefatory remark should be made about the principles informing Mill's *Essay* which will surface from time to time. This is the observation he had made towards the end of the essay on *Bentham* (1838). There are, he wrote there, 'three great questions in government. First, to what authority is it for the good of the people that they be subject? Secondly, how are they to be induced to obey that authority?' and finally 'by what means are the abuses of this authority to be checked?' Bentham, and his father's generation had 'seriously applied' themselves to only the third of these. Whilst the 'power of the majority' (Bentham's eventual answer to the third question) 'is salutary so far as it is used defensively' there is no guarantee that it will be so used. As we have seen Mill had become increasingly preoccupied with what he there and elsewhere referred to as the 'despotism of Public Opinion'.[177] Mill's own theory of government, as we should expect, fills out what he regarded as this important but 'one-sided' preoccupation with ensuring

---

[175] *Representative Government*, Preface, p. 173.

[176] Burns, 'Mill and Democracy' dates Mill's conversion to the 1852 articles 'Thoughts on the Reform Bill', which were not however published until 1859. Correspondence of the mid 1850s indicates Mill's preoccupation with institutional means of ensuring the influence of the educated over mere numbers. Support for plural voting and other proposals is expressed fully in the 'Thoughts on Parliamentary Reform' of 1859: 'The perfection of an electoral system would be, that every person should have one vote, but that every well educated person in the community should have more than one, on a scale corresponding as far as practicable to their amount of education.' *CW*, vol.XIX, p. 325; *D&D*, vol. III, p. 22.

[177] 'Bentham', *CW*, vol.X, pp. 106, 108, 107; *D&D*, vol.I, pp. 376–7, 381, 378.

the 'identity of interest between the trustees and the community for whom they hold their power in trust'[178] by addressing, not only the danger of the 'despotism of public opinion' but also the other two 'great questions'.

The historicity of government and the role of revised utility

Mill opens his discussion by considering the room for manoeuvre available to those concerned to perfect their political institutions. In insisting on the historicity of government, Mill was recognizing that different points of historical development made possible different forms of government. There is a mid-point, or rather range of points, between the mistaken belief in the kind of historical determinism which argues that forms of government are the absolute given and unalterable results of historical processes, and that illusion which presents government as wholly a matter of open choice.[179] Specifically, what makes a given form of government workable is public opinion, the beliefs of the people who exercise government and of those over whom it exercises rule. The relevant beliefs concern their willingness to tolerate the kind of government in question, to act in order to defend and preserve it and to do whatever is required to operate it.[180] Echoing Burke's point about the American colonists, in a way that emphasises the continuity of concern with 'opinion', Mill points out that 'a people cannot be well governed in opposition to their primary notions of right, even though these may be in some points erroneous'.[181] This is not at all an argument in favour of allowing public opinion to determine government action. Rather it is an attempt to re-admit to the agenda the question of how, despite an often misguided public opinion, governments can realise the true interests of the community, without being seen to deny the now irresistible tide of democracy.

In stressing the importance of opinion and belief in this way Mill is, as we have emphasized, reaching back beyond the classical utilitarians to the Scottish historical sociologists. In rejecting the supposedly objective moral principles of the natural lawyers, the Scots had recognized the variety and potential unpredictability of public opinion, the operation of which could, for many of them, only be established empirically. Bentham and Mill senior had subsumed any problems to do with opinion under utility, believing that if utility was defined in a way sufficiently close to subjectively perceived happiness, government which pursued utility would automatically secure the support of public opinion. But the more the conception that the utility which government pursues is different from the subjective wants of the population the more the question of how support for legitimacy is to be constructed reasserts itself as an independent issue. This is clearly how Mill wished to define utility and how, if we are to consider long-term interests, it must be defined.[182] The possibility of pursuing true utility and the workability

---

[178] Ibid., *CW*, p. 109, *D&D*, p. 382.

[179] *Representative Government*, pp. 175–6.

[180] Ibid., p. 177.

[181] Ibid., p. 322.

[182] Mill thought it absurd to expect any holder of power 'to direct their conduct by their real ultimate interests, in opposition to their immediate and apparent interests.' See below.

of different forms of government, therefore, rest on the state of public opinion, and public opinion is a developing entity, subject to progress (and vulnerable to decline). Opinion, therefore, is something that has to be shaped by the reformer as much as institutions: in asserting this Mill brings into sharp relief the second of the questions omitted by Bentham, namely, how are a people to be induced to obey an authority which is for their good?

The redefinition of the principle of utility as 'the permanent interests of man as a progressive being' was of course, tied up with the historicization of the theories of government. The 'progressive improvement of mankind' now included in the idea of utility, could be used not only to provide criteria for the action of government, but also as a way of understanding and organizing our knowledge of the past. In pursuing the new principle of utility governments were now required do more than simply maximise the existing desires of the population. Government was not simply a means to a given end, for if utility was the standard of good government, and utility is itself progressive, then the end of government was not fixed, but must be a continually evolving possibility of perfectibility.[183] Government was 'at once a great influence acting on the human mind, and a set of organized arrangements for public business.'[184] Consequently in considering possible forms of government, institutions should be selected which are not only 'adapted to take advantage of the amount of good qualities [in the population] which may at anytime exist, and make them instrumental to the right purposes'; but also those which positively develop and 'promote the virtue and intelligence of the people'.[185] In allowing as a good, aims and ideals beyond that which all, or even most, individuals in society might at present recognize, Mill raises the relevance of the first of the 'three great questions': 'to what authority is it for the good of the people that they should be subject'; and the answer must be an authority which, at least in some degree, lies beyond themselves, since:

> it is quite conclusive against any theory of government that it assumes the numerical majority to do habitually what is never done, nor expected to be done . . . by any other depositories of power – namely, to direct their conduct by their real ultimate interest, in opposition to their immediate and apparent interest.[186]

The two above principles – influencing the mind and arranging the public business – together constitute the good of society. Rejecting the two principles Mill had found in various guises in Coleridge, in the Saint-Simonians and in Comte, namely order and progress, Mill nevertheless adopts two values which – even to him – insistently recall

---

[183] Ibid., p. 185.

[184] Ibid., p. 195, and cf. 196: 'an agency of national education, and its arrangements for conducting the collective affairs of the community in the state of education in which they already are.'

[185] Ibid., p. 193, Mill reformulates the two principles two pages later when he defines 'merit of any set of political institutions' as 'the degree in which they promote the general mental advancement of the community, including under that phrase advancement in intellect, in virtue, and in practical activity and efficacy; and partly of the degree of perfection with which they organize the moral, intellectual, and active worth already existing, so as to operate with the greatest effect on public affairs.' (p. 195).

[186] Ibid., p. 251.

them. Pursuing both principles involves some tension, though not, Mill claims, contradiction, for 'progress includes Order, but Order does not include Progress.'[187] So 'the institutions which ensure the best management of public affairs practicable in the existing state of cultivation tend, by this alone to further improvement of the state.'[188] As we shall see, reconciling the two principles is not always as simple as this, and one major theme of the work is to settle the relative importance of each in the different political institutions of the modern state. But before turning generally to consider these it is worth stressing one particular context in which that tension crops up, that is in Mill's acknowledgement, ignored, or underrated by the earlier utilitarians, that societies exist on some sort of developmental continuum characterized by the degree and pervasiveness of intellectual, cultural and political sophistication.[189]

The historical context of politics: barbarism and civilization

Since government can only be sustained by the appropriate public opinion (we should probably say political culture), the sort of government that can exist, and the degree to which these principles can be embodied in government institutions, is dependent on the development of opinion in, or the moral climate of that culture.[190] Thus, to take the most extreme example, an uncivilized or, as Mill refers to them 'rude people', may well be unable, unwilling and incompetent to perform what the operation of a representative democracy requires. They may be unable to suppress personal passions or pride to the demands of the collectivity to enable a public consensus to be engineered; they may be unwilling to assist the police in the preservation of order, or the state in the defence of its territory; or they may be too indolent or selfish to participate in the political institutions which safeguard civilized life. In this case, 'civilized government, to be really advantageous to them, will require to be in a considerable degree despotic: to be one over which they do not themselves exercise control, and which imposes a great amount of forcible restraint upon their actions.'[191] Where there are so few 'good qualities' in society to make use of, and those that are, concentrated in a small elite, monarchy and true aristocratic government will be the best calculated to make use of them.[192] But in these conditions the second task of government, to promote good qualities, will also be much more difficult.

---

[187] Mill rejects the order-progress polarity because, 'if we would increase our sum of good, nothing is more indispensable than to take due care of what we already have'. Ibid., p. 190. However the principles he adopts, although clearer and less abstract, exemplify a similar static-dynamic polarity, and pose similar questions about their compatibility or relative priority.

[188] Ibid., p. 190; and p. 196: 'Nor is there any mode in which political institutions can contribute more effectually to the improvement of the people than by doing their more direct work well.'

[189] Mill does not clearly distinguish between these.

[190] Mill is insistent (against both Benthamite and Marxian positions) that it is not material interests, but changes in moral belief that effected such changes as the abolition of slavery, and the emancipation of serfs in Russia. Ibid., p. 184.

[191] Ibid., pp. 178–9, 178. It is important to stress, and Mill himself acknowledges, that such hindrances to representative government are found in supposedly civilized societies as well as 'rude' ones.

[192] Ibid., pp. 243–5.

The reason for this is that Mill sees participatory government itself as an agent in bringing about that culture; the promotion of 'the virtue and intelligence of the people' is, in a political sense, to be brought about through political participation. Where moral and cultural conditions are such that the successful operation of the government's instrumental tasks requires witholding political participation from the people, politics cannot perform its second, educational role for the excluded group. Ironically the first stages of progress require the denial of that political liberty and participation which mark and hasten its subsequent development.

In the savage state, the first quality needed to progress is obedience – hence political rule must initially be despotic. The second quality needed is industriousness, and given humans' natural aversion to disciplined labour, slavery 'by giving commencement to industrial life . . . may accelerate the transition to a better freedom.'[193] But the psychology of this despotic state is based on an appeal to instinctual qualities: immediate hopes and fears. Although slaves have learnt to obey, the way they have done so means that they must be ordered around and motivated by threats. They cannot or will not internalise rules and precepts – even those relating to their self-interest – in the way citizens must do. Although this must be 'superinduced from without', it cannot simply be imposed, for despotic rule cannot in its very nature stimulate the moral and intellectual qualities needed for civilized self-government.[194] Progress to a political state must involve successful appeals to disciplined self-interest and eventually, at a higher stage, to the general interest.[195] So, however unlikely its occurrence, even if a benevolent despotism were the best form of government for, as it were, 'getting things done', it cannot perform the vastly more important role of educating people. Indeed, in a civilized society, a benevolent is worse than a bad despot, 'for it is far more relaxing and enervating to the thoughts, feelings, and energies of the people.' If the Roman citizens of the early empire 'had not first been prostrated by two generations of that mild slavery [the benevolent despotism of Augustus], they would probably have had spirit enough left to rebel against the more odious one [of Tiberius].'[196]

We begin to see here the implications of a criterion of progressive utility tied to a historical conception of cultural progress. What is justifiable on utilitarian grounds depends on its efficacy in shifting a society along the path of progress. Despotism which was defensible in overcoming barbarism, is indefensible in suppressing (or enervating) peoples who have passed through that stage. If this seems harmless enough, it is perhaps more worrying when applied, however sensitively, to the colonial rule of the 'more civilized' over the less. Whilst despotism is a necessary, if transitory, stage on the path to civilization, there is no guarantee, left to historical chance, that its impact will be benign: but a civilized colonial power

---

[193] Ibid., pp. 197–8. The parallels with Hegel's *Phenomenology*, §§194–6, and *Philosophy of Right*, §93 are inviting but bizarre given the vast differences in the philosophical idiom of the two thinkers.

[194] *Representative Government*, pp. 202ff on the imperfection of even the most determinedly benevolent dictator. The issue of the transition from the despotic single ruler to self-government evokes, but not by name, the concerns of Machiavelli and Rousseau on the same topic. Cf., Ibid., p. 200 'a people of savages should be taught obedience, but not in such a manner as to convert them into a people of slaves.'

[195] Ibid., p. 199.

[196] Ibid., p. 207.

ought to be able to do for its subjects all that could be done by a succession of absolute
monarchs, guaranteed by irresistible force against the precariousness of tenure attendant on barbarous despotisms, and qualified by their genius to anticipate all that
experience has taught to the more advanced nation.[197]

Mill does not quite actively advocate the colonization of 'barbarous' or 'semi barbarous' peoples (amongst whom he includes India!); but he does note that almost all
'backward populations' are, or tend to be in such a colonial relationship, and he claims
that despotic rule over them, if with a view to hastening their political development, is
'as legitimate as any other'.[198] It would perhaps be unfair to criticise Mill for failing to
display a cultural relativism which could hardly be expected of him (and the contemporary moral implications of which are at least as problematic as those of his own progressive
liberalism). However it is important to notice that it is his apparent assumption of a
unilinear conception of social progress that justifies the colonizer's intervention to
short-circuit historical processes, and that this seems at odds with his appeals for
individual variety in *On Liberty*. Although individual *personal* experimentation seems
necessary to ensure the possibility of an unpredictable social progress, the same arguments do not seem to support a diversity of conceptions of progress amongst *societies*.
All societies, it seems, are bound to follow the same route.

This assumption of developmental uniformity – perhaps a legacy of his early admiration for Comte – is even more stark in Mill's discussion of the status of national minority
cultures within the great metropolitan nations of Europe. In general, Mill thinks, states
and nations should coincide. But where small minorities exist within otherwise geographically obvious boundaries, he considers the moral arguments for their cultural and
political assimilation overwhelming: 'Nobody' he thought

> can suppose that it is not more beneficial to a Breton or a Basque . . . to be brought into
> the current of the ideas and feelings of a highly civilized and cultivated people – to be
> a member of the French nationality . . . – than to skulk on his own rocks, the half savage
> relic of past times, revolving in his own little mental orbit . . . The same remark applies
> to the Welshman or the Scottish Highlander as members of the British Nation.[199]

Well, nobody except perhaps a Breton, a Basque, a Welshman or a Highlander. So far
from being desirable and worthy of sustaining, cultural diversity at the national minority
level seems to be, for Mill, simply the residue of earlier and more barbarous times. Liberty
is needed at the cutting edge of progress, but not in its wake. Since the way forward has
already been demonstrated by the advanced nations, subsequently 'whatever really tends
to the admixture of nationalities, and the blending of their attributes and peculiarities in
a common union is a benefit to the human race.'[200]

Thus despite Mill's various disclaimers about progress not necessarily entailing
improvement,[201] it is difficult to see how these views could be justified except on the

---

[197] Ibid., p. 382.

[198] Ibid., p. 382.

[199] Ibid., pp. 363–4.

[200] Ibid., p. 364.

[201] E.g., *Logic*, Bk.VI, ch x, 3; but see *Representative Government*, p. 200 . . . 'all things which have for
their object improvement, or Progress.'

assumption that the progress of the 'advanced nations' did indeed represent an improvement, in the revised utilitarian sense of realising 'the permanent interests of man as a progressive being'.

Discussing the policy implications of Mill's historical contextualization of government has taken us to the issues of nationality and colonialism dealt with right at the end of his work. But these are, however revealing of the principles at work, very much peripheral to his main concern, which was to construct an ideal form of government, suited to the present time and conditions 'that is, [one] which, if the necessary conditions existed for giving effect to its beneficial tendencies, would, more than all the others, favour and promote not some one improvement, but all forms and degrees of it'.[202]

Revised utilitarianism and the principles of civilized government

The two original principles of good government which Mill states near the beginning of his work – the use of existing good qualities and the promotion of virtue – can be crudely summed up in two words: efficiency and education. But there is a third principle hovering in the background, the third of the three 'great principles of government', enunciated by Bentham and Mill senior and the one which had all but dominated their thought – the protective principle of the need to limit the exercise of power. 'Men, as well as women, do not need political rights in order that they may govern, but in order that they may not be misgoverned.'[203]

James Mill and Bentham in his later works had concentrated on the issue of protection because of their psychological assumption that all men acted in their own selfish interests and government must be assumed to do so as well. But whilst Mill recognizes this as a danger against which we must guard, it is not an axiom of his thinking. The prevalence of narrow egoism is a phase in human progress. The task of a progressive government was to assist human development towards a more enlightened self-interest, and eventually to a concern with the general good.[204]

However, even though narrow selfishness is not axiomatic, the implications drawn from it still need attention paid to them. We do not need to assume that the voters are out to exploit the disenfranchised in order to assert that 'in the absence of its natural defenders, the interests of the excluded is always in danger of being overlooked.' Mill argues that although there was no conspiracy against the disenfranchised working class in his time – indeed there was, he claimed, much sympathy for them – this did not prevent the view prevailing in Parliament that the right to strike for example, was 'simply absurd'. Those (like Mill himself) who had studied the issue 'know well how far this is from the case', and if working men were represented in Parliament the issue would be subject to

---

[202] *Representative Government*, p. 201.

[203] Ibid., p. 291. On the original two principles see above, fn.185.

[204] Ibid., pp. 208–9. This links in with Mill's Humean argument in *Utilitarianism,* about the cultivation of a progressively wider spread of sympathy based on an original natural sentiment, ch. iii, pp. 28–30.

fair debate.[205] There are therefore good grounds, without adopting universal egoism as a strict axiom, for asserting that 'each is the only safe guardian of his rights and interests'.[206]

The institutional device that guarantees this is universal suffrage – including, although Mill argues only briefly for it in *Representative Government*, the enfranchisement of women.[207] It is important to recognize here that Mill's argument for the extension of the franchise rests on considerations of utility and not on any conception of natural or innate rights. Utility demands that all who are capable should be enabled to defend their interests through political action. 'It is a personal injustice to withhold from any one, *unless for the prevention of greater evils*, the ordinary privilege of having his voice reckoned.'[208] Although it is difficult to see how a natural-rights based franchise could allow exceptions (although proponents of it almost universally and arbitrarily excluded women), Mill's basis for the franchise, whilst including women, does justify some exclusion. Two utilitarian criteria in particular, Mill thought, disqualified individuals from voting: lack of education shown by illiteracy or innumeracy, and economic dependency, by virtue of receiving poor relief. Ideally Mill would go further than this, to require a more extensive educational test, as well as evidence of payment of direct taxes, but under the existing circumstances these were unrealistic demands. Mill's grounds for excluding these classes of people are not obviously utilitarian, but can, I think, be shown to be so by a brief if premature reference to the other main concern of government – that of increasing the good qualities in the population.

Such groups had been excluded in the past either for fear of the expropriation of property or for fear that their votes might be bought and sold by the rich. The latter remained, throughout the nineteenth century, an argument against extending the franchise which was articulated fiercely by Mill's friend and one-time supporter John Austin. It was an argument that Mill thought was overplayed, but could by no means be ignored.[209] More and more of the working class were effectively being drawn into the middle class, as they already were in America. So whilst the fear of revolution, and class legislation by the utterly ignorant and destitute is a residual utilitarian argument, it was, as time passed, and for England at least, a less compelling one.

Mill's grounds for exclusion seem to relate more to the need to provide an incentive for people to develop those characteristics which constituted the progress of society. If education were freely available (a condition which, Mill recognized, had to be satisfied before his test could be fairly applied) it would be wrong to give the vote to those who

---

[205] *Representative Government*, pp. 208, 209; see also 279: Rulers 'however honestly disposed, . . . are in general too fully occupied in things which they *must* attend to, to have much room in their thoughts for anything which they can with impunity disregard.'

[206] Ibid., p. 208.

[207] In *On Liberty*, Mill had pointed out with some vehemence the divergence between the interests of women and those who supposedly exercised protective political rights for them. In *The Subjection of Women*, written the winter prior to the publication of *Representative Government*, but not published until 1869 for tactical reasons, Mill presented in full his arguments in favour of complete equality for women.

[208] *Representative Government*, p. 279, my italics.

[209] Austin was professor of Jurisprudence at the University of London, and, by 1859, author of the conservative 'A Plea for the Constitution' which Mill attacked as unnecessarily alarmist in an article: 'Recent Writers on Reform' in *Fraser's Magazine*, for April of that year. *CW*, vol. XIX, p. 341ff; *D&D*, vol. III, p. 47ff.

had not taken advantage of it.[210] If people could gain the franchise through taking up the available opportunity to educate themselves (which they ought to do anyhow), then those who failed to qualify themselves would only be those whose votes 'would not in general be any indication of any real political opinion'.[211]

The second excluded group – those in receipt of benefit through indigence[212] – are excluded on one immediate utilitarian ground: that 'those who pay no taxes, disposing by their votes of other people's money, have every motive to be lavish and none to economize.' This is a kind of welfare version of the fear of expropriation; but once again, it is not the only ground.

Neither of these reasons for exclusion are permanent reasons, or in Mill's view, reasons independent of the wills or character of the excluded (as would be exclusion on grounds of race or sex): 'They exact such conditions only as all are able, or ought to be able, to fulfill if they choose' requiring the potential voter only to 'do for its sake what he is already bound to do . . . '[213] There is, in the case of individuals, as much as in the case of whole societies, a sense in which certain political institutions are only appropriate at a certain degree of development. Individuals who voluntarily inhibit their development – by failure to grasp basic educational opportunities or to assert their economic autonomy – fail to qualify themselves for the franchise. So, even though there is a prima-facie case for enfranchising all so that they can protect their interests, this is not a case which is incapable of being overridden. The grounds for doing so are not only the protection of the well being of those whose property and indeed culture might otherwise be sacrificed to the irrationalities of the manifestly careless and ignorant.[214] It is also, if here only by implication, to encourage and ensure the promotion of those qualities which will stimulate, and indeed in some sense constitute, progress for all:

> It is by political discussion that the manual labourer, whose employment is a routine, and whose way of life brings him in contact with no variety of impressions, circumstances, or ideas, is taught that remote causes, and events which take place far off, have a most sensible effect even on his personal interests; and it is from political discussions, and collective political action, that one whose daily occupations concentrate his interests in a small circle round himself, learns to feel for and with his fellow-citizens, and becomes consciously a member of a great community.[215]

[210] *Representative Government*, p. 280: 'no one but those in whom an *a priori* theory has silenced common sense will maintain that power over others, over the whole community, should be imparted to people who have not acquired the commonest and most essential requisites for taking care of themselves; for pursuing intelligently their own interests and those of the persons most nearly allied to them.'

[211] Ibid., p. 281.

[212] This phrasing seems necessary to avoid appearing to limit Mill's exclusion to the particular kind of relief — parish poor relief — obtaining in his day. However, whether a universal contributory *insurance* scheme of unemployment benefit such as Britain has until recently maintained would come under Mill's strictures is one of those historical imponderables. A *contributory* insurance scheme, even though compulsory, seems to fall outside Mill's criticism that it permits the recipient 'helping himself to the money of others'.

[213] *Representative Government*, p. 282.

[214] 'Every person has a claim to a voice, and when his exercise of it is not inconsistent with the safety of the whole, cannot justly be excluded from it.' Ibid., p. 283.

[215] Ibid., pp. 278–9.

Individuals who have shown themselves incapable of enough interest to qualify themselves for enfranchisement are unlikely to be equipped or willing to allow political participation to develop these aspects of their personalities. Although political participation is an education and a stimulus to independent thought, to be 'consistent with the safety of the whole' it can only be extended to those who have already shown some sign of valuing such goods, if only at the most basic level.

Discussion of the protective role of political participation has already led us to stray into another area: the educative role of politics, showing how institutions often fulfilled more than one of Mill's principles. Education must be dealt with in due course, but before passing on there is another aspect of protection which must be addressed.

The earlier generation of utilitarians had assumed that the threat of the misuse of power was one that arose only from non- democratic governments, monarchies and oligarchical cliques. A democratic government was presumed to be one whose interests were more or less identical with those of the people. But, Mill points out, what democracy effectively means is the rule of the majority, and there are no grounds for believing that a majority will not abuse its power with respect to minorities – if one is white and the other black, one Catholic and the other Protestant, one English, one Irish, one rich the other poor, even, one skilled labourers and the other unskilled.[216] Democracy therefore, no less than any other form of government requires protections from the sinister interest of the holders of power; and in a democracy that power is the dominant class. It is important to note here that by 'class' Mill means something much wider and more flexible than what Marx or modern sociologists mean by it. Any coalition of sectional interests can form a class, any persons 'whose direct and apparent interest points towards the same description of bad measures.' Despite this flexibility in the term, Mill believed as a matter of fact that unless racial, religious or national cleavages obtain, modern society is effectively divided into two classes comprising, very roughly, labourers and employers. One safeguard against class-interested abuse of power lies, Mill thinks, in so organizing the representative system as to balance these two as closely as possible so that the selfish majority in each group would cancel out. Allowing a

> minority of each in whom that [class interested] consideration would be subordinated to reason, justice and the good of the whole, and this minority of either, joining with the whole of the other, would turn the scale against any demands of their own majority which were not such as ought to prevail.[217]

Although, as we've seen, Mill thought possession of the vote was vital for minimally educated individuals to protect their interests, this protective principle was in conflict with the danger of tyrannical dominance by the majority over individuals constituting the minority. The classic solution to this, adopted in the United States for example, was to entrench certain rights in the constitution or in a fundamental law requiring special majorities to change it. But England had no tradition of this, and even entrenched clauses can be overridden if the majority is large and determined enough to do so, as, once again, the experience of the United States was even then showing. In any case Mill was interested not merely in the minority's capacity to defend itself but in securing its active contribution. In majoritarian systems where there is a persistent and homogeneous

---

[216] Ibid., pp. 249–50.   [217] Ibid., p. 255.

majority, minorities are effectively disenfranchised, and this affects their capacity to use their political rights protectively, as well as their ability to contribute to policy. Mill so objected to this aspect of majoritarian democracy that he went so far as to make it the basis of a distinction between what he called true and false democracy.[218] True, representative democracy is, or should be, the government of the representative of the whole people, not the government of a majority to the exclusion of the rest. Whilst in any actual debate in the representative the majority may prevail, it is vital that the minority view be present and heard.[219] Mill's argument is that a single member constituency representative system automatically excludes all minorities; even a three member constituency system will exclude all minorities smaller than a third of the electorate.

True democracy, and a truly representative assembly could only be achieved where 'any set of electors amounting to the average number of a constituency, wherever in the country they happen to reside, have the power of combining with one another to return a representative.' This extremely idealistic standard was realizable only under a nationalist system of proportional representation such as recently advanced by Thomas Hare.[220]

There are more subtle arguments about representation too. These relate also to Mill's seemingly rather naive presumption that individuals or 'views' should be represented rather than 'parties'. Under a first, or first two past the post system, majorities are bound to be clumsy coalitions. Even those who support them may only support some, or even one, of the elements in their electoral platform. A national list with proportional representation, however, allows any identifiable minority – proportionately as small as the number of seats at stake – to achieve election. For example, if a representative assembly were of 600 people, and those who thought free trade the most important issue comprised a third of the electorate, they would secure 200 votes, suppose those who thought prioritizing education provision were a quarter, they would get 150. If there were only one six-hundredth + 1 of the population who believed saving the world's eco-system were the most important, they would still – just, get a member. And the important point, Mill thinks, is that in each case the relationship between the member and their electorate, far from being weaker (because it is not, as in the case for single-member constituencies, geographical), is in fact conceptually stronger because the member does not represent a heterogeneous group supporting a varied 'platform', but a group whose very existence is defined in terms of their perception of the salience of a particular issue.[221] Further details of how this balance is to operate takes us too far in the direction of the positive policy of 'making use of the good qualities that exist' and will be dealt with in due course.

---

[218] Ibid., the title, and subject matter of chapter vii.

[219] Ibid., pp. 256–8.

[220] Ibid., p. 261. Mill had written to Hare on 3rd of March 1859 after reading his book: 'You appear to me to have exactly and for the first time, solved the difficulty of popular representation; and by doing so, to have raised up the cloud of gloom and uncertainty which hung over the futurity of representative government and therefore of civilization.' *CW*, vol. XV, p. 598. Mill's first public advocacy of Hare's scheme was in his essay of 1859 'Recent Writers on Reform', cited in fn. 209. The scheme Mill proposed involved roughly what is now known as STV: voters ranking candidates from a national list, if they preferred them to those proposed locally, and votes for candidates failing to reach the quota (the quota is (the no. of votes cast ÷ number of seats) + 1) as well as the superfluous votes of successful candidates being redistributed until all the places had been filled. *Representative Government*, p. 262.

[221] Ibid., pp. 263–4.

There is a second major danger to be guarded against in democracy – that of 'the low grade of intelligence in the representative body.'[222] This cannot be guarded against in the obvious way – by seriously limiting the franchise – without withdrawing from that group the protection given by the vote. Instead, Mill argues that, without undermining the responsibility of government to the whole community and therefore the right of all to protect their own interests, ways must be found 'to obtain, in the greatest measure possible, for the function of government the benefits of superior intellect, trained by long meditation and practical discipline to that special task.'[223] Once again this moves over into the project of making use of the best qualities in the existing society. But there are three issues in which the principles hang nicely in the balance, and which illustrate the subtlety with which Mill is prepared to treat them. They were all highly political issues in the radicals' reformist agitation, that of payment for MPs, the right of constituents to instruct their MPs and the role of a second chamber.

Mill opposed the radical demand for a standardized payment for MPs, to allow poorer men to serve, on the grounds that it would 'become an occupation in itself,' attracting the wrong kind of representative – 'adventurers of a low class'. It would in effect be an offer of '658 prizes for the most successful flatterer'. This, far from increasing the protection democracy offers, would be 'making it the private interest of a number of active persons to urge the form of government in the direction of its natural perversion.'[224] Throughout his discussion of representation Mill regards it as vital that 'electors should choose as their representatives wiser men than themselves.'[225] However, he recognizes the difficulty the lower classes may have in finding amongst the wiser men [and by implication members of the professional, educated middle-classes] those through whom 'their particular moral position and mental point of view can be represented at all'.[226] Consequently, if an eminently qualified but unpropertied individual can be found they should be supported by public subscription of his constituents. This would be a suitable test both of his qualities and their commitment to him.[227]

Similar tension between the need to safeguard the protective principle and ensure quality of representation can be found in Mill's discussion of 'pledges' – the right of constituents to instruct their MP.[228] If poor voters are 'obliged by the expenses of election [which Mill wanted strictly limited and declared] and the general circumstances of society, to select their representative from persons of a station widely different in life from theirs' their desire to extract a commitment to certain policies is both understandable and defensible: if they cannot find candidates of their own class or distinguished members of another whom they can trust, they are, Mill reluctantly concludes, 'justified in taking other measures'.[229]

The question of an upper house highlights the role of political opinion in rendering institutions more or less powerful. Whilst it seems an obvious implication of the

[222] Ibid., p. 256.

[223] Ibid., p. 317.

[224] Ibid., p. 312, Mill, quoting himself from his article, 'Recent Writers on Reform'.

[225] Ibid., p. 319.

[226] Ibid., p. 318.

[227] Ibid., p. 312.

[228] 'If it is important that the electors should choose a representative more highly instructed than themselves, it is no less necessary that this wise man should be responsible to them'; Ibid., p. 317.

[229] Ibid., pp. 318–19, 321.

protective principle that 'there should be in every polity, a centre of resistance to the predominant power in the Constitution – and in a democratic constitution, therefore, a nucleus of resistance to the democracy', it is by no means obvious to Mill that a second chamber in the form of a House of Lords, is that centre. The resisting power must have enough moral authority to challenge the popular majority without seeming to do so from a class interest of its own. 'These conditions', Mill dryly observes, 'are not found in a body constituted in the manner of our House of Lords.' The more truly democratic a society becomes in spirit, the less effective a hereditary aristocratic house will be bound to become: 'so soon as conventional rank and individual riches no longer overawe the democracy, a House of Lords becomes insignificant.'[230] On the other hand, a second chamber, composed, like the Roman Senate, of those who had previously held high (and therefore, elective) office would satisfy the democratic principle, since all would have originally been chosen by the people, and could not be considered to possess a class interest of their own, and would also satisfy the need for quality in the representative by giving additional weight to those of proven ability and experience. It would be impossible, Mill believed 'to cry [it] down . . . as a mere obstructive body, whatever amount of mischief it might obstruct.'[231]

Making use of the best existing qualities (i) electoral systems

Although it is a point in democracy's favour that it 'destroys reverence for mere social position', its egalitarianism worried Mill as likely to be too undiscriminating, downgrading real merit and ability as well as undeserved, inherited status. To allay this tendency Mill argued that even within a democracy (in fact *especially* within a democracy) the political institutions 'should stamp the opinion of persons of a more educated class as entitled to greater weight than those of the less educated.'[232] This had to be done, however, without undermining the protections which derived from access to political power discussed above.

Dominance by a selfish and shortsighted majority seemed almost inevitable in a democratic and commercial society. Its danger was not only that the majority could legislatively overrule the ability of the minority to protect itself; but further, rather as Mill argued in *On Liberty*, even non-tyrannical mediocre majorities might stifle the influence of the most morally enlightened elements in society, and so the progress of society to greater happiness and a more elevated view of its interest would be undermined in favour of the satisfaction of existing desires and interests. Mill's problem was how to increase the influence of those members of society capable of assisting progress towards more enlightened desires, without withdrawing from the great majority the necessary protection which their electoral participation guaranteed them. He had found the beginnings of a solution in the system of proportional representation, discussed above; it was completed by his support for plural voting.

Proportional representation would ensure the presence in parliament of any minority view which enough voters deemed significant. This guarantees a hearing for minority

[230] Ibid., pp. 326–8. [232] Ibid., p. 320.
[231] Ibid., p. 328.

views. However, the minority Mill is mostly concerned to have represented is the '*élite* of the country', those 'able men of independent thought, who . . . have by their writings, or their exertions in some field of public usefulness, made themselves known and approved by a few persons in almost every district of the kingdom.' Proportional representation would enable those discriminating 'few persons in every district' to focus their votes in favour of this elite, rather than inevitably waste them in a local constituency where their numbers were too small to count.[233] The effect of such representation was not to protect the educated but to provide a channel through which the best personal qualities available in the population could play a part in political life greater than their mere numbers might otherwise make possible.

However, proportional voting was not enough, in Mill's view, to ensure the influence of these forces of progress. Contentiously, to most modern readers, he also advocates plural voting for those suitably qualified, such as members of professions and university graduates. He even suggests instituting special public exams by which individuals could qualify themselves for extra votes. Although Mill is at pains to insist that extra votes should not be available merely on a basis of wealth, he is sufficiently concerned about the consequences of impending manhood suffrage to argue that where property is the basis of plural voting, it were better kept than abolished, until a more suitable criterion can be established. Plural voting on the basis of education is not for Mill a mere, or unfortunate expedient: he sees it, in some kind of absolute sense as right and proper. Despite his own argument about the beneficial effects of political participation – which he acknowledges here – it is outweighed by the importance, not only of giving more weight to educated opinion, but of *signalling* that principle to people: 'It is not useful, but hurtful, that the constitution of the country should declare ignorance to be entitled to as much political power as knowledge', which is what it would do if it gave the same weight to an ignoramus' vote as to a scholar's. Mill stresses that the English pay too little attention to the way laws and rules have not merely a controlling but a declaratory function in expressing the values and '*spirit* of the institutions of a country'.[234] The educative benefit that political participation brings must be set against the dangerously unlimited power which its ultimate extension gives to the least educated classes. It is the struggle to achieve power, not the secure enjoyment of it which Mill identifies as the most educative phase of political development, when people are 'strong enough to make reason prevail, but not strong enough to prevail against reason.' To this point, and no further, should popular power proceed.[235]

However, it was never Mill's intention that the elite thus elected should actually outnumber those voted in on the normal franchise, or they too could form a 'class' capable of dominating the rest of the community.[236] Mill tries to characterize the way represent-ative democracy works without thinking in terms of 'block voting' in a parliamentary majority – indeed it is one of the criticisms of his thought that he ignores what was by then already the reality of party allegiance. This criticism is misplaced, he does not so much ignore as deprecate the effects of party. The role for the representatives of the 'instructed minority', the men of distinction, learning and public spirit, was *not to outvote but to educate*, inspire and provoke emulation in their colleagues. Mill places great

[233] Ibid., p. 265.
[234] Ibid., pp. 283ff., 288–9.

[235] Ibid., pp. 289–9.
[236] Ibid., p. 286.

emphasis on the capacity of just a few elevated minds to raise the tone of a representative chamber; the majority 'could always outvote them,' but this is not the point, which is that 'they would speak and vote in their presence, and subject to their criticism'. Any majority would at least have to listen to counter-arguments and, if intellectually honest, consider their strength. As a result 'the influence of these leading spirits is sure to make itself sensibly felt in the general deliberations.'[237] This stress on the important influence of debate itself, quite apart from the decision reached, links up both with the stimulating role accorded to criticism in *On Liberty*, and Mill's earlier rejection of criticisms that representative assemblies are 'mere talking shops'.[238] Moreover, as this influence would spread beyond the chamber itself, any representatives of excellence would function as a benchmark against which other candidates could be measured and found wanting, making it impossible any longer for parties to 'foist upon the electors the first person who presents himself with the catchwords of the party in his mouth and three thousand pounds in his pocket'.[239] The competition to appeal to the lowest motives of the electorate – which is what democracy was in danger of becoming – would be turned instead into a competition to secure the most enlightened and educated representative, thus enabling society to make the most use of the good qualities of such men as already existed.

Making the best use of existing qualities (ii) bureaucracies

The second major way in which a society could make the best use of its existing qualities was by clearly separating out the roles of representation on the one hand, and government and legislation on the other.

The drafting of legislation, the administration of government and the appointment of personnel are clearly tasks that require specific skills and expertise. At best amateurish incompetence and at worst corruption follow the attempt by legislative bodies to engage directly in making appointments. Attempts by assemblies to interfere in the detailed running of public departments with their own stores of acquired wisdom and appropriate departmental culture, is described by Mill as 'inexperience sitting in judgement on experience, ignorance on knowledge', because 'No-one who does not thoroughly know the modes of action which common experience has sanctioned is capable of judging of the circumstances which require a departure from those ordinary modes of action.'[240] The detailed interference of the body of the House of Commons in the passage of legislation commonly has disastrous consequences on its coherence, the suitability of the law for the task for which it was originally designed and the coherence of its fit with existing laws. In legislation, the role of design and intelligence is quite separate from the role of will in enacting laws. The representatives' role is the second. The drawing up of legislation should be the task of a constitutional commission, appointed, not elected.[241]

---

[237] Ibid., pp. 266–7.
[238] Ibid., p. 240.
[239] Ibid., p. 265.
[240] Ibid., p. 232.
[241] Ibid., p. 237.

The instrumental (as opposed to the educational) role of a representative assembly, is then, quite limited. It is

> to watch and control the government: to throw the light of publicity on its acts: to compel a full exposition and justification of all of them which any one considers questionable; to censure them if found condemnable, and, if the men who compose the government abuse their trust, or fulfill it in a manner which conflicts with the deliberate sense of the nation, to expel them from office, and either expressly or virtually appoint their successors.[242]

The reasons for these limitations to participation are quite explicitly rooted in the need to satisfy the two other somewhat contradictory principles we have looked at, the need to advance democratic power as a constitutional safeguard and the need to give expertise a free hand. Mill writes

> There are no means of combining these benefits except by separating the functions which guarantee the one from those which essentially require the other; by disjoining the office of control and criticism from the actual conduct of affairs, and devolving the former on the representatives of the Many, while securing for the latter, under strict responsibility to the nation, the acquired knowledge and practical intelligence of a specially trained and experienced Few.[243]

The educative role of politics: 'promoting the virtue and intelligence of the individual'

Mill's case for the morally educative role of politics depends not only on being able to identify relevant moral criteria; it also requires him to be able to show that political activity in some way stimulates the operation of good moral motives. Knowing what the good is, is a philosophical problem; getting people to act in accordance with it is a psychological and sociological one. Although Mill believed in the (suitably modified) principle of utility as the ultimate moral criterion, he did not believe that human beings were naturally motivated to adhere to it. This depended on their education, experiences and upbringing. We have seen how, in his *Autobiography*, Mill explained the way in which purely artificial associative links between duty and motive, such as his father had used in educating him, are liable to break down once, as an adult, they are subject to rational analysis. Even the principle of utility is not natural, in the sense of being spontaneous, and so any enduring commitments to it must be grounded in 'a natural basis of sentiment'. Mill believed that such a natural basis did in fact exist in 'the desire to be at unity with our fellow creatures'. The progress of civilization involves an increasing degree of association and interdependence amongst human beings and ultimately that association can only proceed on the basis of a recognition of equality. Increasingly 'people grow up unable to conceive . . . a state of total disregard of other people's interests'. The social co-operation on which progress depends makes it not only the individual's interests to consider the views and interests of others, 'it also leads him to identify his *feelings* more and more with their good, or . . . practical consideration for it', and such pressures become more insistent as civilization progresses. Like Hume, Mill stresses the role of social approval and disapproval in fostering the development of these

---

[242] Ibid., p. 239.   [243] Ibid., p. 241.

sentiments, a role in which, again like Hume, Mill believes the politician can play at least a supportive role. Building on these sentiments we can even suppose them to be taught as a civic religion:

> and the whole force of education, of institutions, and of opinion, directed, as it once was in the case of religion, to make every person grow up from infancy surrounded on all sides both by the profession and the practice of it.[244]

The educative criterion of politics required institutions to operate in such a way that they contributed to the moral development of individuals by encouraging them to reflect on and internalize the general good rather than a personal or sectional interest.

Character formation and politics

As we have already seen, Mill wanted to stress that a major role of government and politics was educative.[245] Unlike his father and Bentham, Mill does have a particular view of the kind of character which 'utility in the widest sense' requires. Despite his commitment to personal liberty Mill cannot, therefore, ultimately be indifferent as to the way men and women spend their lives. Because he has a dynamic, progressive view of utility, those personal characteristics which contribute to its development must be given a higher value than those which lead people only to seek and enjoy currently available levels and qualities of happiness. Indeed, as we've seen, much of the utilitarian case to be made for liberty rests on the contribution that diversity and experimentation can make to progress. Speaking generally Mill favours 'active' or 'energetic' characters over 'passive' ones. Although society generally – and Christian religion in the form then prevalent in England – praises the contented acquiescent individual, their contribution to the progress of civilization and the human intellect is at best zero: 'nothing is more certain than that improvement in human affairs is wholly the work of uncontented characters . . . '[246] and are likely negative: 'Inactivity, unaspiringness, absence of desire, are more a fatal hindrance to improvement than any misdirection of energy . . . ' Moreover the prevalence of passive qualities in the people at large is, Mill believes, what makes possible the perversion of politics through its 'formidable misdirection by an energetic few'.[247]

Mill asserts that democratic forms of government *can* promote the active type of personality: equality of condition stimulates competition, political participation

---

[244] *Utilitarianism*, pp. 29–30.

[245] Indeed he writes 'hardly any language is strong enough to express the strength of my conviction — [of] the importance of that portion of the operation of free institutions which may be called the public education of the citizens.' *Representative Government*, p. 347.

[246] *Representative Government*, p. 211. Mill had noted the 'habitual dissatisfaction' of people with their social status in America, and seen it becoming more and more the case with England. 'Tocqueville on Democracy in America', *CW*, vol. XVIII, p. 193, *D&D*, vol II, p. 65. Despite the emasculating effects Mill attributed to Victorian Christianity he recognised that in the past religion had inspired men to both critical reflection and greatness ('Spirit of the Age', nos. IV and V, *CW*, vol. 22, pp. 289ff.) and could perhaps again ('Utility of Religion', *CW*, vol.X, pp. 403ff.).

[247] *Representative Government*, pp. 214–15.

disciplines and invigorates. In general the individual's sense of agency and efficacious-
ness is increased, the more is required of him.[248] This adds an important dimension to
the utilitarian defence of democratic government. Under James Mill, and Bentham,
political participation was primarily instrumental in safeguarding the pursuit of other
logically distinct goods. For Mill, a significant part of the intellectual and moral goods
required for progress are only available through political participation. So even if the
instrumental aspects of politics could have been successfully served by other devices
(and his discussion of the benevolent despot was designed to show they could not), the
moral and intellectual growth of the individual would still not be furthered.[249] Mill's case
here links up with one of his defences of liberty. If the ideals of political freedom are
preserved merely as an abstract truth, and are not acted through, they will lack the vigour
and strength necessary to preserve them; it will be 'but a *dilettante* knowledge, like that
which people have of the mechanical arts who have never handled a tool'.[250]

Although democratic politics stimulates energy and the moral qualities associated with
progress, we have also seen that Mill was aware too, of those forces in a commercial and
democratic society which either undermined energy or diverted it away from politics and
into purely economic or domestic concerns.[251] A successful democratic society would
require some encouragement to develop and focus these qualities into the collective,
political, arena.

The ballot

One consequence of seeing politics as intrinsically educative rather than instrumental is
that Mill is not only out to promote political participation but also to organize it in such
a way as to maximise its morally educative impact. The lowliest civic office – jury service
or parish councillor – brings the citizen out of his normally necessarily routine and
self-interested mentality leading him

> to weigh interests not his own; to be guided, in case of conflicting claims, by another
> rule than his private partialities; to apply, at every turn, principles which have for their
> reason of existence, the common good, [and to work with others] . . . whose study it
> will be to supply reasons to his understanding, and stimulation to his feeling for the
> general interest.[252]

It would be wishful thinking, Mill acknowledged, to attribute these beneficial consequences to the mere act of voting, the commonest, and for most, the only political activity
they will undertake. In reflecting on the low level of political culture in post-revolutionary
France, Mill had pointed to the Revolution's failure to establish any integrating

---

[248] Ibid., p. 216.

[249] Ibid., p. 217. See Alan Ryan's discussion highlighting these differences: 'James and John Stuart Mill'
in *Machiavelli and the Nature of Political Thought*, ed. M. Fleischer (London, 1971).

[250] *Representative Government*, p. 204. Mill was painfully aware that he himself was one of these people.

[251] Democracy promotes energetic types, Ibid., p. 215. The essay on 'Civilization' had outlined the
countervailing enervating, or de-politicising processes operating. See above pp. 349–50.

[252] *Representative Government*, p. 217.

institutions in the place of those swept away, except, and then only for some citizens, the vote. Of the political effect of merely voting he realistically remarks:

> A political act, to be done only once in a few years, and for which nothing in the daily habits of the citizen has prepared him, leaves his intellect and moral dispositions very much as it found them.[253]

Mill is therefore concerned to make the democratic process not simply a more efficient vehicle for views, but a more effective educative experience. This sometimes leads to rather unexpected results. One very striking example of this is his discussion of the ballot.

Until the Ballot Act of 1872, votes in Britain were cast openly, being written down publicly by the clerk of the poll for all to see in an election book. This obviously led to abuses, including the exercise of undue influence by powerful landlords and employers, and even the barely disguised sale of votes. One increasingly insistent radical demand, voiced by Obadiah Hume, James Burgh and Major Cartwright as far back as the 1770s was for voting to be conducted by secret ballot.[254]

Mill concedes straightaway that there is force in the radicals' argument: 'cases are conceivable in which secret voting is preferable to public'.[255] But the issue is not one of principle, it is to be determined on consequentialist and utilitarian grounds: in his view the 'power of coercing voters has declined and is declining' throughout Europe and certainly no longer obtains in Britain. The danger of 'bad voting' is now, he thinks, less from undue external influences on the voter, than from 'the sinister interests and discreditable feelings which belong to himself, either individually, or as a member of a class.'[256] Mill has two inter-linked arguments against the secret ballot. One is an abstract argument concerning the nature of the vote. The related argument is concerned to point out that the rules of institutions as well as governing practices, act semiotically, as signals encoding and communicating the values or 'spirit of the institution' to those living under it.

The abstract argument, while denying that political power can be strictly a right, has extraordinary similarities to Locke's argument about the collective moral and testamentary nature of political power, although Mill, unlike Locke, explicitly identified this trust with possession of the vote. The difference seems largely to do with the change in the meaning of 'right' between the two thinkers. Mill denies the vote can be a right because for him a right is a reasonable expectation of a freedom to pursue a personal interest. Locke asserts political rights (which of course he doesn't unequivocally identify with the vote) precisely because in his view rights are needed to discharge (and can only derive from) our prior duties, established by our relationship to God. For Mill of course, rights are merely shorthand expressions of utilitarian considerations. But once it becomes clear

---

[253] 'Tocqueville on Democracy in America', *CW*, vol. XVIII, pp. 167–8; *D&D*, vol. II, p. 23.

[254] The Chartists, a working class movement named after the document inscribing their aims, and drawn up by the London Working Men's Association in 1838, sought six major reforms: universal adult male suffrage, annual parliaments, voting by ballot, equal electoral districts, abolition of property qualifications for candidates, and payment for MPs.

[255] *Representative Government*, p. 298.

[256] Ibid., p. 301.

that Mill too is arguing that there is more of duty than of right in the vote, the similarities are clearer.

Mill's argument is that we cannot have an unfettered right to exercise power over other human beings: any such power must be (as Locke argued) a trust, in which there were strict limits placed on how such right might be deployed. Mill rightly hints at the irresponsible and absolutist implications lurking in the democrat's assertion of an unlimited subjective right.[257] Like Locke also, but on utilitarian grounds, Mill points out that political right derives not solely from the individual's right of self-protection, but from the more general duty to protect others as well. The way a voter casts his vote is not

> a matter in which he has an option; it has no more to do with his personal wishes than the verdict of a juryman. It is strictly a matter of duty; he is bound to give it according to his best and most conscientious opinion of the public good.[258]

Like Rousseau, comparison with whom commentators have found irresistible on this point, Mill even acknowledges individuals may have both a private and a general or public will; there are 'two sets of preferences – those on private and those on public grounds'.[259] But given, on the one hand, that 'the voter is under an absolute moral obligation to consider the interests of the public, not his private advantage'; and on the other, that 'a man's own particular share of the public interest is not, . . . sufficient to make him do his duty to the public without external inducements' how is the former to be ensured?[260] What institutions could guarantee it? Mill refuses to pursue the potentially totalitarian implications lurking in the idea of a 'higher will': 'The laws cannot prescribe to the electors the principle by which they shall direct their choice.'[261] In fact, as Rousseau also ultimately acknowledged, no institutional provision could guarantee such a thing. In any case – even if possible – to positively require of individuals that they vote according even to very general criteria would be a dangerous move. The most that institutions can do, and what they must be made to do, is to signal and encourage certain ways of thinking, and they must seek to capitalize on whatever public spirit there is.

Now if, as Mill believed, 'the best side of their character is that which people are anxious to show, even to those who are no better than themselves', it follows that 'the bare fact of having to give an account of their conduct is a powerful inducement to adhere to conduct of which at least some decent account can be given.'[262] Public voting is therefore a strong incentive, even to bad characters, to use their vote properly because

---

[257] 'Those who say that the suffrage is not a trust but a right will scarcely accept the conclusions to which their doctrine leads.' And later, to use the vote: 'for his own interest, pleasure or caprice; [awakens] the same feelings and purposes, on a humbler scale, which actuate a despot and oppressor'. Ibid., p. 299.

[258] Ibid., p. 299.

[259] Ibid., p. 306. The comparison with Rousseau does not, however, stand up to any extended analysis, see Dennis F. Thompson, *John Stuart Mill and Representative Government* (Princeton, 1976), pp. 43–50.

[260] *Representative Government*, pp. 300, 306.

[261] Ibid., p. 317.

[262] Ibid., pp. 306, 305.

they may have to explain their reasons for their choice to others.[263] The prospect of having publicly to justify one's electoral choices, Mill argues, will force a resort to public as opposed to private values in the actual choosing, thus shaming those into openly seeking the public good who would not have pursued it in private.

The importance of local politics

Despite the importance of national politics, and even with open voting, the extent of the ordinary citizen's political involvement will be limited. Local, not national, politics must therefore be 'the chief instrument' of that educative role that politics must play in a progressive society. The enlargement of mental and moral horizons, the discipline of being forced to consider long-term consequences and the development of thinking and speaking skills can all be encouraged within the local political environment. Moreover because less is at stake, and because the national government is always available as a backup, freer rein can be given to the educative role of government. Greater numbers and lowlier classes of people can, without compromising national interests, be allowed to participate.[264] The educative role can prevail over the instrumental.

However, in order to effect this educative role, devolution must not be too great. This is true both geographically and functionally. Local representative bodies which represent constituencies too small (such as villages) or are concerned with issues too narrow (such as paving or drainage) to recruit people of talent, cannot perform an educative role.[265] Education, Mill is now saying, is effected not merely by letting or encouraging people to be politically active, but by enabling people without political education to participate alongside those who have. His conception of how we gain a political education is here based less on learning by experience and more on learning from example. Mill doesn't mince words about the expected calibre of local politicians. 'That these should be of a very miscellaneous character is, indeed, part of the usefulness of the institution; it is that circumstance chiefly which renders it a school of political capacity and general intelligence. But a school supposes teachers as well as scholars.'[266] Allowing politics to be so localized that no intellectual high-flyer, or elevated character would be involved, would endanger, not ensure, its educative role.

When it comes to discussing what should be devolved, as opposed to to whom, Mill is, however, in danger of taking away with one hand what he had given with the other: 'all business purely local . . . should devolve upon the local authorities . . . But among the duties classed as local . . . there are many which might with equal propriety be termed

---

[263] The argument is especially strong when there are 'others' who do not have the vote — for example 'are not a man's wife and daughters entitled to know whether he votes for or against a candidate who will support' measures to admit women to universities, increase penalties for domestic violence, or allow married women a right to property in their own name?' Ibid., pp. 303–4.

[264] Ibid., pp. 347–8. There is an efficiency argument as well: 'it is but a small part of the public business of a country which can be well done, or safely attempted, by the central authorities'; p. 346. Representation at the local level should be conducted in the same way as at national — proportional representation and plural voting. Mill's only change is to express greater ease at increasing the representation of wealth since the business of local government consists so much of administering local expenditure. p. 349.

[265] Ibid., p. 352.

[266] Ibid., p. 351; see also p. 359, concerning the tutelary role of central government in relation to local.

national.'[267] Prime and obvious candidates are the administration of justice, and, interestingly, the police, which has – in Britain uniquely in Europe – until recently remained
in local hands. Within this local–national tension there is a principle to be opposed to the
educative principle of devolution, and it turns out to be the instrumental principle of
efficiency. There are more and less efficient ways of securing some of these 'primary
ends' of government; and 'whatever are the best arrangements for securing these primary
objects should be made universally obligatory, and . . . placed under central superintendence.' Thus even issues which have a good case for being locally devolved – such as
education – should, like factories and prisons, be subject to a national inspectorate; and
a supervising national ministry should correspond to every function administered at local
level.[268]

   In trying to balance the principle of expertise against that of educative participation,
it must be admitted that the closer Mill gets to discussing practical arrangements, the
more the demands of expertise seem to prevail. The principles to be applied in any area
of government, the instruction of people in those principles, the supervision of them, the
provision of advice (when needed and not just when asked for!), ensuring the regularity
of proceedings and, in extreme cases, the suspension and dissolution of the local councils,
are all powers Mill accords to the central government. The ascendancy of central over
local authority, in view of its greater intelligence, knowledge and experience he thought
'ought to be prodigious'.[269]

Conclusion

Representative Government does indeed try to apply to politics Mill's enriched conception of historical change and his enlarged definition of utility. His recognition that
representative government is possible only at a certain point in historical development,
and that it must secure for itself the sort of responsible public opinion which will support
it, both derive from the first of these insights. Readmitting historical considerations
excluded by the classical utilitarians also meant acknowledging the role of circumstance
in forming opinion, and the necessarily contingent link between the kind of public
opinion produced by any political society and that needed to sustain it. In Mill's case the
issue was complicated by two further considerations. Firstly Mill acknowledged that the
irresistible tide of democratic politics rightly formed the necessary background against
which any reformer must work. Secondly though, because of Mill's progressive and
advancing conception of utility, a truly utilitarian government must be able not simply
to mirror public opinion, but to give extra weight to its most progressive elements, and
to encourage the rest to follow in their direction. The tensions and interplay between
these two themes – democracy and progress – form the major axis of the work. Students
sometimes claim that the work is unclear, that Mill qualifies and equivocates, articulating
principles to which he does not then seem to keep. This is largely a function of his
attempts to balance and offset the different principles at work, and to recognize the effect
that time and circumstance must have on the operation of principle. For those who like

[267] Ibid., p. 354.   [269] Ibid., pp. 357–8.
[268] Ibid., pp. 355, 357.

their political theory – as so much modern theory is – logically tight, the younger Mill's *Essay* can seem a retreat from the standards set by his father's. Yet Mill is self-conscious about the criticisms that had been made of the earlier work. If his own is less clear, it is more subtle; if it is less logically rigorous, it is more realistic; if it is less unified, it balances principles and weighs probabilities; it might even be said in defence of its apparent eclecticism that it embodies the prescriptions of diversity made in *On Liberty*.

Despite though, its general recognition of history as an inescapable context for the study of politics, it must seriously be doubted whether the work truly embodied that other, methodological, programme laid down in Mill's own *Logic*. In Mill's account of the relationship between opinion and government it is traditional utilitarian deductions from egoism that most often inform Mill's judgement. Although a generalized notion of progress enables him to presume the gradual substitution of the general good for self-interest as a motive, there is no explicit attempt to establish either the general 'laws of social development' or the specific psychological forms corresponding to them. As critics complained, Mill's use of historical *examples* seemed very much *ad hoc*, used simply to prove or disprove a point, which, given the complex causality involved in social phenomena, must, as he argued in the *Logic*, be inconclusive.[270] In retrospect it is something of an irony that the liberal Mill should have been criticised for failing to secure his defence of liberal politics within a sufficiently historicist context, however much he held out that hope himself.

Mill's politics are 'idealistic' in two important technical senses of the term. The principles informing both his analysis and his prescriptions are 'ideal-regarding'; they derive from a particular view of human perfectibility, never quite realised, but always possible of closer approximation. Such individuals will be rational and responsible, reflectively concerned with their own moral and cultural growth and yet capable of spontaneity and innovation. They will be less and less motivated by selfish principles, and more and more by a desire to further the collective good. This would be true even in the field of economic life, where, Mill hoped, co-operative enterprises would take over from the conventional capitalist firm.[271] The very categories and criteria of Mill's analysis derive from this perfectibilist view, so that his 'political science' in no sense even attempts to be 'value free'. The second sense in which Mill's politics are idealistic is that he not only believed that ideals provided a way of organizing our understanding of political phenomena, he also believed that those ideals could, with some luck and perseverance, actually function as motives to bring about the political changes implied by them. Education therefore, in the widest possible sense, plays a crucial role in Mill's thought and in his politics, since it is through education that ideals are transmitted. Through education individuals could learn to transcend the immediate and particular 'class' interests which, in the present state of civilization, tended to dominate their views. It was through emancipation from, not in the acknowledgement of, class and material

---

[270] Stefan Collini, 'The Tendencies of things: John Stuart Mill and the philosophic method', in Collini, Winch and Burrows, *That Noble Science*, pp. 154–9.

[271] The most extreme statement of the case is in Mill's review 'Thornton on labour and its claims', *CW*, vol.V, p. 631ff. But see also 'Chapters on Socialism', in Collini, ed., *Liberty* etc., p. 267 and *Political Economy*, Bk. IV, ch. vii, 6. For the movement from egoistic to collectivist motivation and the economic properties associated with each, see 'Chapters on Socialism', in Collini, ed., *Liberty and other writings*, pp. 262ff.

interests that the political progress and ultimate moral salvation of the human race could be achieved. Ironically both of Mill's aims – his unconsummated aspiration to locate political analysis in a progressive historicist schema, and his hope of a politics transcending material interests and class perspectives – were not far removed from those of his near contemporary, Karl Marx.[272] But for Marx, although the emancipation and moral salvation of humanity were indeed only possible through an understanding of history, they involved the tactic of not rejecting class politics, but of actively pursuing the interests of a particular class: the proletariat.

---

[272] For an interesting comparison see Graeme Duncan, *Marx and Mill: Two Views of Social Conflict and Social Harmony*, (Cambridge, 1973).

IX

G.W.F. Hegel

Introduction: The German Enlightenment and early influences

Life and career

Georg Wilhelm Friedrich Hegel was born in 1770 the son of an important civil servant in Stuttgart, then part of Württemburg, one of the many small states, principalities and cities that made up what was to become Germany.[1] He was educated at the Stuttgart *Gymnasium*, and from 1788 until 1793 at the University of Tübingen, where he studied theology.

On graduating he took up a post as tutor to a family in Berne, and later became a university tutor, first at Frankfurt, and, from 1800 at Jena. During this period of his life Hegel wrote a number of works on religion as well as reading the new Scottish political economists and writing some political tracts.[2] At Jena, for reasons that will become apparent he turned his attention to philosophy. The last work which he wrote there provides a transition to what is normally referred to as his 'mature system' by which he is known today, it was the *Phenomenology of Mind*.

Although Hegel had been an enthusiastic supporter of the ideals of the French Revolution, and indeed of Napoleon's intervention in Germany's backward politics, his university post at Jena was one of the casualties. After an interlude in journalism and as a schoolmaster, he returned to university life, a professor, first at Heidelberg for a year, and then, from 1818 until his death in 1831, in Berlin. It was during this period that Hegel produced his great attempt – perhaps the last in the history of philosophy – to systematize all branches of human thought, his *Encyclopaedia of the Philosophical Sciences in Outline* comprising the *Logic*, (not to be confused with an earlier version, often known as the *Greater Logic*, produced in 1816), the *Philosophy of Nature* and the *Philosophy of Mind*. In 1820 it was followed by the *Philosophy of Right* which was an elaboration of that part of the *Philosophy of Mind* which dealt with the objective institutions of law, social and political life.

---

[1] John Edward Toews, *Hegelianism* (Cambridge, 1980), p. 13 upgrades his status from the usual description of 'petty functionary'. As a member of the professional bureaucracy he was an agent of modernization of the German states.

[2] On Hegel's early theological writings and their relationship to his later political philosophy see G. Lukacs, *The Young Hegel*, tr. Livingstone (London, 1975); and Raymond Plant, *Hegel* (London, 1973). There is a translation of most of the texts by T. M. Knox, entitled *Early Theological Writings* (Chicago, 1948). They are discussed below.

In his final years Hegel devoted his attention to art, religion, philosophy and history but the results of his work were never published in his lifetime. After his death students and followers published his lectures on the *Philosophy of History*, the *History of Philosophy*, *The Philosophy of Religion* and *Aesthetics*.

The importance of religion

The fact that Hegel began his work in theology is of great significance in understanding both his own development and the intellectual background against which it must be understood. The German Enlightenment had not undermined religious thought in the way that the rationalism of the French or the scepticism of the British had. True there were systematic doubters, such as Reimarus whose work in turn influenced the famous critic Gotthold Lessing. But neither became outright unbelievers; rather, in Lessing's case it led to a desire to resynthesize religious experience at a higher and more abstract level.

Lessing, the influential aesthetic theorist of the mid-eighteenth century, despite his doubts about doctrine, like most German thinkers regarded the religious impulse itself as a fundamentally genuine one, and prior to theology and dogma. So, whilst increasingly critical of the forms religion took, Lessing regarded the core of religion as in some sense true. In this he agreed with much Protestant non-conformist thought. What is different, and what synthesizes religion and historical process in a distinctively German way, was his belief that human beings were gradually moving closer and closer to the central truths of religion – which he may not ultimately have seen as transcendent – through a sequence of successively refined historically linked articulations.[3] This is particularly interesting because it highlights two ideas which were to remain persistent strands in the development of German thought down to Marx's writings. They are the conviction that there is some truth at the core of religion, even though it may not be the same truth that orthodox religion claims for it; and the second idea is that truth is to be arrived at through a process of historical development. In Germany religious thought remained a major vehicle for and stimulus to philosophical development.

The Enlightenment and historical thinking

Both the above ideas ran counter to significant early Enlightenment patterns of thought. For the 'modern pagans' of France, religion was superstition. Explaining its origin might require some ingenuity, but would be unlikely to reveal any great truths. As for history it was, for a while, eclipsed as an uncongenial, because imprecise and undemonstrable subject, by the rise of mathematical and rationalist models of thought and explanation.[4] Critical history, most widely in the form of Pierre Bayle's *Dictionary*, had an important but ultimately destructive power, retaining, in France and England, the sceptical impulse

---

[3] Paul Hazard, *European Thought in the Eighteenth Century* (Harmondsworth, 1965[1946]), p. 440ff.; Peter Gay, *The Enlightenment, An Interpretation* (2 vols, London, 1970), vol. I, p. 330.

[4] For a good collection of such deprecations from the early Enlightenment see Isaiah Berlin, 'The Sciences and the Humanities' in *Against the Current* (Harmondsworth, 1982), p. 85ff.

of the early Enlightenment.[5] History exposed human follies or, as in the case of the attack on biblical history, or Hume's attack on Whig history, deconstructed an essentially mythical or ideological past. Historical explanation was not unique, merely the identification of the past operations of universal causal laws. History, as either method, or subject matter, was rendered secondary to philosophical reason. In this way despite the Enlightenment's disdain for many earlier ages the ancient rhetorical role of history as moral edification was paradoxically reinforced, not undermined by the emergence of critical philosophical rationality. As Bolingbroke put it 'History is philosophy teaching us by examples how to conduct ourselves . . . we must apply ourselves to it in a philosophical spirit . . . the application of [particular examples] is dangerous.'[6]

The Scottish historical school, it was true, had developed a progressive secular history based on the interaction between essentially material stages and a universal philosophical psychology. Yet the idea that human intellectual history was a positive process comprising its own essentially unique patterns of development seems peculiarly German. Such a position was not arrived at easily, nor were the religious origins of it easily put aside. It was at first particularly hard for Germans to see in history, as Hegel claimed to, the realization of reason itself, for as we shall see, German intellectuals were not at ease with the hand that history had dealt them.

The question relates to a much wider problem thrown up by the thought of the Enlightenment. In its attempt to expose and eradicate the irrationalities, prejudices and superstitions of the *ancien régime*, the thinkers of the Enlightenment relied on very general universal theories of human nature. They assumed that there were at base, constant and uniform aspects of human beings which constitute their 'natures' in the way that the constant and uniform qualities of the natural world constitute the natures of natural objects. This methodological assumption raises two further questions, one philosophical, one historical. The philosophical question is that if human beings do have such a nature, if they are, as Hobbes says fundamentally continuous with the rest of the natural, material world, in the sense of being subject to the same laws that govern the matter of which they are composed, in what way can humans be said to be free? If we want to save human freedom we must either espouse some compatibility thesis which enables us to hold simultaneously, but at different levels, belief in causality, and libertarianism, or else we must differentiate human beings from the rest of nature, arguing that they, uniquely, possess free will.

The historical problem is how, if human nature is uniform and constant, we are to account for the apparent diversity of human societies? This diversity emerges both spatially, in the distinct traditions and cultures of the world, and temporally, in the sequence of changes which any individual state or culture undergoes during the course of its development.[7]

---

[5] Pierre Bayle, described by Diderot as 'the greatest athlete of scepticism, produced his *Historical and Critical Dictionary* in 1696, it exercised a pervasive influence on the growth of unbelief, see the assessment in Gay, *Enlightenment*, Vol. I, pp. 290–5.

[6] Viscount St. John, Henry Bolingbroke, *Letters on the Study and use of History*, Letter III, in *Lord Bolingbroke, Historical Writings*, ed. Isaac Kramnick (Chicago and London, 1972), pp. 25–6.

[7] Montesquieu's famous attempt to tackle this problem placed great emphasis on the physiological effects of climate and their influence on the development of different cultures: 'It is the variety of wants in different climates that first occasions a difference in the manner of living, and this gave rise to a variety

If we regard the development of human societies as in each case, a unique process, but one which is nevertheless determined in a way which renders that process irreversible, and the stages in it irrecoverable, then the past can never be an ideal for us, it can only be an object of nostalgia. But what account of the development of human society could produce this conclusion? It was one of the presuppositions of natural science, and indeed it still is, that the same events produce the same causes. If the development of human society was to be *explained* and if the model of explanation to be adopted was that of the sciences, then surely we must, if we produce the same causes, produce the same effects? It was part of German thinkers' achievement to produce a model of explanation which challenged, at least for a while, the increasing dominance of this particular scientific view of the world.

The thinker who perhaps did most to initiate this line of thought was Johann von Herder, who pursued a line of thought which did much to transcend the less historical trends of the Enlightenment. Herder's early work *On the Origin of Language* (1769) contributed to a debate on a problem which may seem narrow and academic, but which was then seen to, and does, have wider implications. All thinkers recognized the important part played by language in distinguishing man from the animals. Even as mechanistic and materialist a thinker as Hobbes proclaims this. But how could a purely sensationalist psychology account for language? More particularly, if sensation itself is to account for the development then it becomes difficult to see why animals, if they have the same sensory apparatus as human beings, should not be capable of speech. Was it simply that they lacked vocal chords? There was a wide debate on the subject in the eighteenth century. The French materialist philosopher La Mettrie and the Scots Lord Monboddo argued that it should be possible to teach the orang-utan to speak.[8]

Herder, on the contrary shows how difficult it is to give a purely behaviouristic account of the invention of signs. How can one invent a sign before one has the concept of a sign, and how can one possess the concept of a sign without using signs? The two are so integrally related claims Herder that 'man . . . by his first act of spontaneous reflection invented language.[9] Culture and language (for they presuppose each other) are for Herder essentially *expressive*, not reflective. This militates against any reductive explanation of them in terms of other phenomena.[10] Historically it means that the development of man and his language proceeds in a reciprocal fashion so that it is impossible to attribute causal priority to either component of the process. Herder struggled – not always successfully it must be said – to provide a developmental and creative account of human language and society which does not rely on a rationalist or naturalist causality.[11] Language becomes for Herder the source and symbol of all that he wishes to emphasize

---

of laws.' Montesquieu, *Spirit of the Laws*, XIV, §10. Hobbes's explanation that the elaboration of the more speculative sources of cultural diversity — such as religion — was due to 'ignorance of causes' was followed by many and more elaborate such accounts.

[8] R.J. Richards, 'The influence of the sensationalistic tradition in early theories of the evolution of behaviour', *Journal of the History of Ideas*, XL, 1 (1979).

[9] *Essay on the Origin of Language* in *Herder on Social and Political Culture*, ed. F.M. Barnard (Cambridge, 1969), pp. 134–5.

[10] 'Variations in language. . . are not wholly, or even mainly, attributable to such *external* circumstances as climate or geographical distances but mainly to *internal* factors. . .' , ibid., p. 167.

[11] Herder and Kant violently disagreed on the power and purview of explanations based on interpretive, analogistic reasoning about particulars, as opposed to rule-invoking and hence universalist, accounts. See

about man in contrast to what he saw as the analytical sterility of the old Enlightenment; freedom, creativity, spontaneity, individuality, culture and a new emphasis on art as expressive, not imitative. Herder sees human culture transmitted through language, as continually changing and progressing, it is no longer a static repository or even a growing storehouse, but a flow of individually adapted ideas drawn from and to become part of a common tradition.[12] History has to be seen as a creation of man, rather than as a complex of impersonal forces to which he is subject. However, just as language provides the distinguishing characteristics of man, so individual languages mark off individual national cultures and traditions, and thus provide the basis for a sense of national identity and one of the social and historical grounds of nationalism.[13] There is a certain tension in Herder's thought between the idea of a common human culture and national differentiation.

The idealization of Greece and the historicization of aesthetics

In addition to the persistent religious strand in the German Enlightenment and its emerging innovative conception of historical development there was another strong influence on Hegel and his generation and that was the idealization of classical antiquity, and Greece in particular. Johann Winckelmann, with his *History of the Art of Antiquity* (1764), like Lessing with his *Laocoön* fired a generation of Germans with enthusiasm for classical Greek culture as a model for their own. Yet once again the historical impulse asserted itself, making problematic the immediate application of an ideal drawn from another age. Winckelmann is famous for his insistence that art is embedded in the culture and society that gives rise to it, and is, moreover subject to a similar cycle of birth, maturity and decay, stylistically recognizable as naive naturalism, confident idealization and decadent over-elaboration. Thus Winckelmann's aesthetics provided another channel through which German thinkers were drawn towards historical process as the binding core of other disciples. His stylistic categories functioned both as aesthetic judgements and to identify historical development – of art itself, and of the culture of which they were both a product and symptomatic. Despite this insight into the developmental and social context which art occupied, Winckelmann was not historically relativist enough to perceive that his *own* criteria of beauty might owe as much to social and historical circumstance as those Greek objects in which he saw them exemplified. 'Especially in Germany, Winckelmann's antico-mania did much harm: whilst it inspired some splendid poetry, it also inspired a great deal of woolly-minded utopianism, a longing for a perfection that had never been and could never be.'[14]

H. B. Nisbet, *Herder and the Philosophy of Science* (Cambridge, 1970); and the texts of Kant's reviews in *Kant, Political Writings*, ed. Hans Reiss (2nd edn., Cambridge, 1991).

[12] '*The mind creates a progressive unity out of the multiplicity of its states* . . . we can speak of a *cultural growth* throughout the whole human race . . .' This cultural growth is a consequence of cultural continuity, it consists in the fact that 'No thought created by the human mind was ever lost.' Herder, *Origin of Language*, pp. 170–1.

[13] Ibid., p. 165.

[14] Peter Gay: *The Enlightenment*, vol. 2, Winckelmann, pp. 296–7; on Lessing's, *Laocoön*, pp. 266–70

The unattainable political and social ideal to which Winckelmann's work contributed was that of a society which was immediate and face to face, politically democratic, socially undifferentiated and integrated, where art and religion wove the mind of the citizen both to his state and to nature. In the modern world, on the other hand social differentiation and the division of labour meant that no one man could encompass in his consciousness the whole range of ideas and attitudes which constituted his society. The very social and intellectual specialization that seemed to make the modern world more advanced than that of the Greeks, at the same time separated men from each other and fragmented their consciousness of the totality of life. This is the complaint of Hegel's friend and colleague Freidrich Schiller, Professor of History at Jena University, and great enthusiast of Winckelmann's Greece. In his influential *On the Aesthetic Education of Man* (1793) he writes how the advance of the intellect and specialization had impoverished the social life of man:

> Whence comes this disadvantageous relation of the individuals in spite of all the advantages of the race? Why was the individual Greek qualified to be representative of his time, and why may the individual modern not dare to be so? Because it was all-uniting Nature that bestowed upon the former, and all-dividing intellect that bestowed upon the latter, their respective forms.[15]

But if Greece was an ideal, the question arose of how it related to contemporary experience, of whether, and if so how, such a society could be created. For many that link could only be made aesthetically; Schiller urged Goethe to 'give birth to a Greece of your own from within, by substituting in your imagination through the power of thought the element of which reality has deprived it.'[16] Hegel shared Schiller's belief that the greatness of Greek art lay in the fact that artist and audience 'shared a common life and consciousness' whereas 'The modern poet gleaned his materials from an esoteric intellectual culture and expressed his vision in a . . . language . . . not accessible to the majority of his contemporaries'. Yet that very fact made the creation of an integrating modern aesthetic exceedingly problematic. Moreover Hegel was to become less starry-eyed about the 'mythical integrity' of Greece than the previous generation. Hegel did not believe that the classical Greek enlightenment had ultimately created a fully unified society, there was an uncultured mass in Athens too.[17]

Man and nature: causality and freedom

As suggested above, Herder's ideas provide for the possibility of a new view of man and history based on a recognition of his unique capacity for creative expression. But they also provided for a new view of the relationship between man and nature, and between

---

[15] Friedrich Schiller, *On the Aesthetic Education of Man*, tr. Reginald Snell (London, 1954 [1801]). At a more parochial level the breakup of the Wurttemburg cultural elite during Hegel's own youth and his response to it is recorded in his diaries, Toews, *Hegelianism*, p. 23 ff.

[16] Cited without reference, in Geoffrey Hawthorn, *Enlightenment and Despair* (2nd edn., Cambridge, 1987), p. 42.

[17] Toews, *Hegelianism*, pp. 28, 27.

reason and causality. Notice how, in the quotation from Schiller above, he attributes the unity of the Greeks to nature, and the division of modern society to intellect. Although Schiller here deprecates its effects, it was in the growing self-consciousness of human beings that this alternative explanation of human historical development was to be grounded. For instead of viewing man as either wholly a part of nature as the physical sciences conceived of it, and therefore unfree, or seeing him as split between a causally determined physical frame with which a mind and an intellect was constantly at war, man could now be seen as a creative and expressive unity, ultimately under the control of his own creative personality. Such a view precluded the return to a past ideal, yet it rendered it redundant, by pointing to the necessarily progressive character of human history taken as a whole. Just as we can never, as individuals, regain a state of lost innocence, so we can never recreate past historical cultures, because we now stand outside them and view them as wholes from a position which includes more and wider awareness than was possible from within that state. Instead of philosophy involving the analysis and dissection of a given and static human nature, man became not simply an *object* of investigation, but an active and potentially changing *subject*, who himself created the very subject-matter of his enquiries.

Such an ideal appealed not only at a personal and social level, especially to Germans, preoccupied throughout the eighteenth century with the creation of their own national culture, but in time too, at a political one. Amongst the many feelings and aspirations evoked by the French Revolution in Hegel, and in many of his generation throughout Europe, was the desire for a political state embodying, as he put it in a letter to Schelling 'Reason and Liberty'.[18]

The notion that liberty was to be found in and through the state is of course an idea espoused by Rousseau. But it is also an idea that was practically congenial given German experience. The small states and principalities there not only enjoyed 'liberty' in the sense of holding a range of authorities against the more distant and casual power of the empire; but inasmuch also as the chartered rights and liberties of corporate groups were embedded in the emergent territorial states themselves. This 'internal connection . . . between the governing rights of the princes and the representative rights of the people was the first link in the development which was to associate freedom with the very authority of the state in Germany.'[19] Thus instead, as in England, of liberties being claimed by individuals *against* the sovereignty of the state, liberty came to be increasingly associated with the actual powers of the state itself.

Any initial enthusiasm for the ideals of the French Revolution in some intellectual quarters in Germany was soon dissipated, first, as in England, by the path taken by the Revolution itself; but secondly and more significantly by the fragmented and aesthetic nature of German political culture through which the concept of the revolution had to pass.[20] Political culture, in the sense of a politically aware and sophisticated public,

---

[18] Quoted J. Hyppolite, *Studies on Marx and Hegel* (New York, 1969), p. 37.

[19] Leonard Kreiger, *The German Idea of Freedom* (Boston, 1957), p. 6.

[20] 'The legacy of the French Revolution in Germany was quickly dissipated . . . was refracted into . . . separate stimuli which simply pushed theorists and authorities to expand the established order of thought and action until it neutralized the challenge through piecemeal absorbtion.' Krieger, *German Idea of Freedom*, p. 84; 'The Revolution was . . . a sort of theatrical show, to be enjoyed intellectually.' Rheinhold Aris, *History of Political Thought in Germany, 1789–1815* (London, 1965 [1936]), p. 50.

existed patchily, if at all in Germany. The lack even of a German political identity was something widely complained of, most famously by Goethe who did so much to establish a literary one.[21] The devolution of Imperial power amongst the localized rulers and states paradoxically made any determined censorship more effective than it could ever be in centralized France, and stifled what debate might have emerged.[22] In the absence of an effective social or political context in which to operate, the reforming impulse, as Marx was to observe later, turned in on itself to construct idealized philosophical patterns, resulting in Germany being far in advance of either France or England in the realm of political speculation.

The lack of a broad social base for even a moderate radicalism in Germany and the increasingly alarming course taken by the French Revolution itself posed these theoretical questions in pressing political terms. At least, one writer has seen in Hegel's political journalism of the time the tension resulting from the distance between his ideals and what was politically possible.

Hegel's early pamphlet 'That the municipal authorities of Württemburg should be elected by its citizens' concerns the attempts by the Duke of Württemburg to establish absolute rule in the duchy, and the attempts by the estates, or local parliament, to establish constitutional limitations to his rule. The principles from which Hegel starts are very bold: 'the whole representative system of Württemburg is faulty and in need of thorough-going reform.' Yet given the political inexperience of the population Hegel can suggest nothing better than 'to entrust the franchise to a body of enlightened and upright men independent of the court.' Yet even this mild reform seems impossible: 'I do not see how an electoral system could be devised that would result in such an assembly, however carefully the active and passive franchise were determined.'[23]

The problems facing those of Hegel's generation, derived ultimately from their own and their predecessors' self-consciousness about Germany's backward cultural and political position. In seeking to meet such problems, thinkers had pursued – in the abstract – ideals drawn from the very different societies of contemporary France or antiquity. Yet the gap between these ideals and German reality, together with a distinctive understanding of the unique character of historical subjects – language, culture, nations, led to an impasse. Reform in one area – politics – was impossible without a more generally developed culture. Yet cultural development was embedded in a historical schema which, although, as yet imperfectly understood, seemed to militate against progressive leaps out of one's own time. Greater understanding of the nature of historical process might lead either to a reassessment of this gloomy picture, or to some understanding of the means of altering it – or indeed to both. Characteristically Hegel turned to religion in an attempt to gain these insights. For religion was 'the way in which men generally achieve the consciousness of their being.'[24]

---

[21] See W. H. Bruford, *Germany in the Eighteenth Century: the Social Background of the Literary Revival* (Cambridge, 1971), pp. 295ff.

[22] Aris, . . . *Thought in Germany*, p. 237.

[23] G .Lukács, *The Young Hegel*, p. 134.

[24] Hegel's Berlin Inaugural Lecture, cited Plant, *Hegel*, p. 198.

The early religious writings as experimental social theory

In his early writings Hegel discusses religion as that most universal and pervasive spirit which permeates other aspects of a society. He is preoccupied with the loss of the unity enjoyed by Greek society and sees Christianity as a religion responsible for creating the psychologically and emotionally private individual of the Roman and modern ages. In this he follows the lead of Machiavelli and such Enlightenment predecessors as Rousseau and Gibbon, all of whom had pointed to the central role of religion in providing a pervasive moral basis for the successful operation of political institutions. Religion then is the most important factor in deciding the nature of a community.

> The state could only bring its citizens to submit to these institutions through their trust in them, and this trust it must first arouse. Religion is the best means of doing this, and all depends on the use the state makes of it whether religion is able to attain this end. The end is plain in the religion of all nations; all have this in common, that their efforts always bear on producing a certain attitude of mind and this cannot be the object of any civil legislation.[25]

Initially Hegel sees religious morality as a determining *cause* of the other social factors he is interested in, and he still sees history as a process of decline from the Greek ideal. But already by 1796 in *The Positivity of the Christian Religion*, Hegel has gone further. He sees now an interrelationship between religion and other social forces: 'the main problem . . . [is] of showing religion's appropriateness to nature through all nature's modifications from one century to another.'[26] Nature here means human nature, and not nature as opposed to humanity. What he now sees is that the 'positivization' of Christianity, that is, its transformation into a formal, authoritarian religion, is a symptom and not a cause. 'If man's common life does not afford the feelings which nature demands then forcible institutions become necessary . . . . So too the actions demanded by the most natural religion come to be done only to order and out of blind obedience.'[27] The appeal of Christianity arose from the lack of any political community in Rome, it did not itself *cause* it. 'The capacity for this (positive faith) necessarily presupposes the loss of the freedom, the autonomy of one's reason which henceforth stands helpless before a superior power.'[28]

At around this time Hegel was reading or re-read the works of the Scottish Enlightenment thinkers responsible for the development of political economy. The most famous of these is Adam Smith, but Hegel composed a commentary on the work of a successor, Sir James Steuart.[29] From these works Hegel gained the view that what they called 'civil society', the modern, liberal market society, although it may appear, as Schiller had pointed out, more fragmented, could be, and was by them defended as actually allowing the individual greater freedom than that provided by the closed world of the Polis. The

---

[25] 'Positivity of Christian Religion' in *Early Theological Writings,* p. 98.

[26] *The Positivity of the Christian Religion*, in ibid., p. 173.

[27] Ibid., p. 169.

[28] Cited Lukács, *Young Hegel*, p. 23, not included in *Early Theological Writings*.

[29] Ibid., Ch.v, passim. An edited version of Steuart's major work has recently been republished, *An Enquiry into the Principles of Political Economy*, ed. Andrew Skinner (2 Vols, Chicago, 1966).

Scots theorists seemed to have demonstrated how a modern commercial society could escape the limitations which republican theory placed on growth and the flowering of culture and individuality. If there was such an escape it was possible to conceive of the history of mankind as something other than a repetitive cycle of growth and decline. The idea of seeing history as a sequence of economic stages, commonly found in eighteenth century writers, could be allied to artistic and cultural development in such a way as to present a detailed and general theory of the progress of the intellect.

Although the precise chronology of Hegel's intellectual activity at this time is obscure, Hegel applies these insights to his studies of religion. In the *Positivity of Christian Religion*, Hegel, exploring the Judaic origins of Christianity, emphasised the futility of Abraham's attempts to reject a settled, agrarian life and return to a wandering, pastoral one.[30] Not only is this a futile attempt to turn the path of [economic] history into reverse, to 'struggle against the fate which would have proffered him a stationary communal life with others'. It also restricts him: Abraham's rejection of his 'fate' is responsible for his alienation: 'he was a stranger on earth, a stranger to the soil and men alike... The whole world, Abraham regarded simply as his opposite'. [31]

This alienated posture is related by Hegel to Abraham's alienated vision of God as a stern and distant authority. This objectification of God as an *external* source of rules and values was, for Christians, characteristic of Judaism, but, Hegel argues it is also found in Christianity, and is what Hegel refers to as positivity, it is contrasted with the natural religious impulse, the need 'to recognize a Being who transcends our consciousness of human agency, to make the intuition of that Being's perfection the animating spirit of human life...'[32]

From this period Hegel begins to elaborate a new version of historical development. History is no longer seen as a departure from the Greek ideal. Instead, pursuing the insight into the freedom allowed by modern society, he comes to see history as an ultimately benign development, an advance on earlier stages. Consequently the 'positivity' of Christianity is a necessary stage in human development, turning human consciousness inward to enable it to achieve, ultimately, a fuller and more individualistic personality than could ever have been achieved within Greek society. Secondly, as we have already noted, Hegel has rejected the notion that religion is the determining *cause* of social organization and development, instead he sees it as a part, even a manifestation of something infinitely more complex which he will come to call 'spirit'. Finally, as a result of the historicization of cultural ideals Hegel had become increasingly sceptical of the possibilities for creating political change in Germany. 'As long as the people does not know its rights, as long as there is no public spirit, as long as the power of the officials remains unrestrained, popular elections would only result in the complete overthrow of the constitution.'[33]

---

[30] See the discussion in Raymond Plant, 'Hegel and Political Economy,' *New Left Review*, 103–4 (1977), p. 83.

[31] *Early Theological Writings*, pp. 186–7.

[32] Ibid., p. 176.

[33] *Württemburg Estates*, cited Lukács, *Young Hegel*, p. 134.

Although political reform, for the moment was impossible, if history was, despite apparent backsliding, ultimately a rational progression, then the limitations of the present position might prove to be acceptable in that wider context. What was necessary was for human beings to *understand* their world. As Hegel wrote later in the *Philosophy of Right*, 'I am at home in the world when I know it, still more so when I have understood it.'[34]

Hegel's project of enabling man to understand his world brought him face to face with the problems of philosophy. The philosophical views of the time must be at least in part responsible for man's dissatisfaction with his condition. For philosophy is one of the ways in which creative, self-conscious man depicts his condition to himself. Yet philosophy also *constitutes* that condition, for man is, as a self-conscious being largely what he conceives himself to be. A depressing philosophical outlook cannot, therefore, simply be rejected. We must understand how it is we come to view ourselves the way we do, and yet we must reject any understanding based on a natural science explanation, for natural science explanations, as we have seen, give an inadequate account of man as a thinking subject. Where then are we to start? Just as in the case of religion Hegel had sought to understand *from within* the contradictions and difficulties posed by a Christian view of the world, so now in the case of philosophy Hegel attempted from within, to offer a constructive critique of the dominant philosophy of his time: Kantianism. But before we can see how Hegel built philosophically on his predecessors we need to see how he thought they had contributed to the prevailing conception of the 'subject', the thinking conscious mind.

The history of the subject from Descartes to Hegel

Many modern commentators follow Hegel himself in placing the fundamental revolution in our conception of the self, the thinking subject, in the writings of the French philosopher René Descartes (1596–1650).[35] In an attempt to overcome the prevailing confusion resulting from both cultural relativism and the revival of ancient scepticism, Descartes sought to establish a method which recognized, yet overcame the most fundamental scepticism about all forms of human knowledge.[36] Even if an evil genius were capable of deceiving him in all knowledge that derived from his senses, there was one thing of which he felt he could be certain, and in which his own identity indubitably lay, and that was of his sceptical, thinking activity, hence his famous formulation 'I think therefore I am'.[37] For Descartes, our awareness of our own reasoning activity is the surest possible refutation we can have of scepticism concerning our own existence. As Hegel notes, this comes close to implying a recognition of the fact that thought must underlie

---

[34] Hegel, *Philosophy of Right*, tr. Knox (Oxford, 1952), §226.

[35] For a succinct overview see Richard Schacht, 'The Background of Hegel's Metaphysics' in *Hegel and After, Studies in Continental Philosophy between Kant and Sartre*. (Pittsburgh, 1975).

[36] There is a tendency to emphasize the philosophical sources of scepticism, yet in his *Discourse on Method* Descartes stresses the role of socialisation in forming the diversity of human belief: 'how very different the self-same man, identical in mind and spirit, may become, according as he is brought up from childhood amongst the French or the Germans, or has passed his whole life amongst Chinese or cannibals.' *The Philosophical Works of Descartes*, tr. E. Haldane and G.R.T. Ross (2 vols, New York, 1955[Cambridge, 1931]), vol. 1, pp. 90–1.

[37] The famous argument occurs in the *Second Meditation*, *Philosophical Works*, vol. 1, pp. 151ff.

all existence.[38] Its immediate effects, however, were to contribute to the revival of the epistemological scepticism it was designed to challenge, to create a divide between the individual mind and the world, between our consciousness itself and the world of which we are conscious. Consequently, one focus of post-cartesian philosophy centred around the problems of epistemology: how could the relationship between the aware subject, and the world that subject believed to lie beyond be satisfactorily explained? If we could only initially have certainty of our own mental processes, how could we argue from this to establish certainty about an external world? Descartes' philosophy, far from over-coming doubt, seemed to imprison the subject, the really self-conscious part of our personalities, within a physical body with which it had only the most tenuous links in terms of information about an 'outside world'. We seemed relegated to the status of a 'ghost in a machine'.

Further attempts to solve these problems triggered developments in our view of the world of nature. The view of the natural world advanced by thinkers such as Hobbes, as we have seen, undermined the teleological view of reality put forward by Aristotle and endorsed by later medieval Christianity. For these new 'natural philosophers' as they called themselves, reality was often conceived of as a mass of uniform matter or particles moving according to purely mechanical laws. It was difficult in such a world to find a place for meaning, purpose or moral import, no matter how ardently figures such as Galileo and Hobbes protested their orthodoxy.

This concentration on the more mechanical properties of matter provided a number of theories which attempted to explain how humans gained knowledge of the world. The problem of the body-mind dualism in Descartes' philosophy was overcome through an increasingly mechanical conception of the subject. Despite his concern to distance himself from questions relating to the physiology of perception, Locke's famous – at first infamous – image of the mind as an 'empty Cabinet' to be filled, or as a 'white sheet of paper' to be written on, contributed to a view ascribed to him by both critics, and (especially French) followers which entwined philosophical and psychological issues.[39] If the process by which human beings understood the world itself generated the criteria of claims to truth and knowledge, it was vital that that process itself be scrutinized with the same rigour. As we have seen, Hume, in his most sceptical phase pushed the empiricist critique to such lengths as to undermine its own philosophical foundations, without providing a really satisfactory alternative.

The most pressing of Hume's problems relate to the difficulty of providing an account of the workings of the human mind which was itself empiricist, in the sense of not going beyond experience. The claim that all our knowledge of the world comes to us through experience must be able to account for the processes of experience themselves. The difficulties of doing so in terms of experience without question-begging should be apparent. Yet since the only non-experiential truths allowed by Hume were the tauto-logous truths of logic or mathematics, there was, for him, no answer to the problem.[40] But is Hume's position the only possible one? Might there not be objects of knowledge

---

[38] Hegel, *Logic*, tr. Wallace (Oxford, 1975), p. 100.

[39] John Locke, *An Essay Concerning Human Understanding*, ed. P. Niddich (Oxford, 1975), Bk. I, ch. 1, §2 (unconcern with physiology); II, 1, §2 (white paper), I, 1, §15 (Cabinet).

[40] Ironically, the fact that there seemed no answer was proof enough for German anti-rationalists such as Hamann and Jacobi, that Hume had demonstrated the indispensibility of religious faith — in the sense

which are not dependent on the evidence of our senses, and which were more than simply logical identities between elements of the formal systems of logic or mathematics?

This is the question to which Immanuel Kant (1724–1804) addressed himself.[41] Now whilst it may be the case that there are such truths the problem we are immediately faced with is how to prove them. Clearly to show such propositions to be merely *logically* necessary will not do, that would make them relate to our language rather than to the world; nor can they be capable of proof by demonstration, for that would make them dependent on our senses. Kant attempts to develop a new form of argument to demonstrate the existence of such truths. It is not induction (which argues from experiences of individual examples to generalizations about the world), nor is it deduction which argues from the general propositions implicit in the meaning of our words down to what must be true in individual cases. Kant's argument is strictly neither of these, it is a transcendental argument. A transcendental argument appeals to what must be the case if other propositions, the truths of which are independently known, are to be made sense of.

For example, space, empty space, is clearly not something we could experience; there would by definition, have to be *something* in it (or surrounding it) in order for us to be experiencing anything. Space is nevertheless an absolutely necessary presupposition of our experience of *things*; there must, a priori, be space, if the other things, are to be experienced.[42] Concepts like space, time, causality, number all necessarily accompany any purely empirical account of reality. They are the necessary forms which perception must take. That is, we cannot perceive, or at least make intelligible statements about perceptual experiences without involving these forms. They are not in the world for we cannot have perceptual knowledge of them, yet they are for all that absolutely necessary to the possibility of experience and are therefore more than simply thoughts. These *categories* as Kant calls them are required by the very perceptual and reflective process of the mind's relationship with reality.

As well as the categories, Kant postulated the existence of transcendental ideas such as the subject (thinking self) the world and God, which he held were ideas which were necessary to organize the rest of our experience. An empiricist approach seemed unable to give a satisfactory account of the self, which does not seem directly reducible to the sum of its experiences, yet this in turn, according to empiricist criteria, is all that can provide us with evidence about the world. Intuitively, there must be a self to do the experiencing. The self is a transcendental idea which is presupposed by statements about the world.[43] Transcendental ideas were established by transcendental arguments, and did not refer to objects in the world which were perceived in the ordinary way.

By suggesting that the subject, the perceiving and acting individual, was not a part of the perceived world Kant was able to make a further contribution to the dilemma which had both political and philosophical overtones, concerning whether man was a natural

---

of empirically ungrounded belief, something which, needless to say, was far from Hume's intentions. Isaiah Berlin, 'Hume and the Sources of German Anti-rationalism' in Berlin, *Against the Current*.

[41] Two brief and accessible introductions to Kant are S. Körner, *Kant* (Harmondsworth, 1955) and Roger Scruton, *Kant* (Oxford, 1982).

[42] Immanuel Kant *Critique of Pure Reason*, tr. Kemp-Smith (2nd, corrected edn., London, 1933), p. 67ff.

[43] Ibid., p. 365.

being subject to causality, and so unfree. For Kant, causality is a category that applies to things-in-the-world. It does not apply to transcendental ideas, such as God, or indeed the subject. Kant's important achievement then had been to rescue the concept of a human being from the determinism implicit in a ubiquitous causality by showing how the concept of the subject, being a transcendent idea, belonged to a different conceptual world from that of the phenomena which were subject to causality.[44]

However, the price he had paid for freedom seemed to be a kind of alienation, for in the process he had irrevocably cut the subject off from the 'real' world. This was a curious consequence of his notion of the categories: the direct perception of things in the world was impossible, for Kant had shown that in order to apprehend them properly we must apply the categories. This led Kant to a distinction between what he called things-in-themselves and things-as-perceived (noumena and phenomena). Since things-in-themselves cannot be known without becoming phenomena (having the categories applied to them) we are forever separated from the world as it is by the very faculty which enables us to have some knowledge of it, the mind and its categories.[45] Man could thus never be at one with nature, his mental operations always intervened. If we cannot experience the material world directly but only *via* the categorical phenomena of our own consciousness, what grounds do we have for continuing to assert its existence?

It might be suggested that the *occurrence* as well as the forms and categories of our experiences are contributed by the mind itself, thus doing away with the need to postulate the existence of things-in-themselves which we can never know – a possibility Kant himself denied. Such a move seems to result in pure subjectivism. We certainly do not create our sense experience of our own volition, as we might seem to in a day-dream or in the imagination. Surely the common sense instinct that there is, after all, something 'out there' causing our experiences, must be right? Indeed, but what is 'out there' must arguably now itself be mind since, on the most rigorous empiricist criteria, all we have been able to establish is the existence of experiences and ideas and categories contained in minds. Such a move brings out the subjective implications of Kant's idealism and involves finally cutting adrift the notion of any residual material world of objects causing our sensations, and substituting instead the activity of some transcendent mind or subject.

Fichte, makes just such moves. Whilst Fichte thought of himself as following Kant the differences became clear when Kant publicly dissociated himself from Fichte's position in 1799. Whilst Kant provides a bifurcated view of reality in which nature is determined but the will is free, and never really reconciled the two positions, Fichte had transformed the whole of reality into consciousness. This saved freedom but at the apparent expense of intelligibility, for how was a subject to be understood, or indeed to understand itself, when there was nothing else in the world? Intelligibility, indeed consciousness itself must be predicated on an opposition between subject and object. Under pressure of these kinds of considerations Schelling, originally a collaborator with Fichte in the break away from Kant, gradually adopted a belief in the objectivity of 'nature'. However, this was not a return to empiricism. It was an attempt to combine the idea that intelligibility involves a relationship between a distinct subject and its object with the notion that human beings are essentially free and expressive beings, and that consequently the content of their consciousness cannot be known in advance of their

---

[44] Ibid., p. 409.   [45] Ibid., pp. 267–70.

revelation of it. For Schelling nature 'is itself an intelligence, as it were, turned to rigidity, with all its sensations and perception.' 'Intelligence turned into the rigidity of being; its qualities are sensations extinguished into being; bodies are its perceptions, so to speak, killed.'[46]

Hegel's first published philosophical work was entitled *The Difference between the Philosophies of Fichte and Schelling*. Hegel came down on the side of Schelling. For a time they taught together at Jena and even collaborated on an anti-Fichtean journal. Hegel's subsequent career is a development, and to some extent a transformation of this position, culminating initially in the *Phenomenology of Mind*, which marks the threshold of his mature philosophy.

Put most crudely Hegel was faced with three philosophical positions concerning the nature of ultimate reality (the Absolute). The mechanical materialist position, such as that of Hobbes, which assimilates everything to matter. It can, as we have seen, give no satisfactory account of mind, except to reduce it to matter. Kant on the other hand develops a theory of the mind, but failed, in his critics' view, to relate it successfully to the material world. Thirdly Fichte assimilated everything to mind and has thus serious problems with 'nature'. The problem is to provide a philosophical account of the absolute, not just to posit its existence. The impasse is that any actual formulation of it makes it particular, brings it into the here-and-now, which, being an event in the world must be a part of the world and cannot encompass the absolute nature of it:

> The absolute must be constructed for consciousness – that is the task of philosophy. But since both the production and the products of reflection are just limitations, a contradiction arises. The absolute must be reflected, postulated; but in this manner it is not postulated but annulled; for the very act of positing it, limits it.[47]

This view had implications for any revolutionary social or political philosophy. Since any such philosophy must be a particular formulation it cannot be the whole truth and cannot thus be imposed, *toute court*, upon a society. Hegel is consequently a reformer, rather than a revolutionary in these matters. Fichte's position leads either to revolutionary adventurism, or else to the view that any, and not just this particular, society constitutes an imposition on human freedom. This is either anti-political in an anarchist sense, or a-political in the sense of leading individuals to seek freedom in the realm of fantasy, mysticism or drug induced states, all of which were features of the second generation of European romanticism.

Schelling, and to a greater extent Hegel, sees that what is involved in avoiding either of the three positions outlined above is the recognition of philosophy as *process*. Reality is not static, and cannot be philosophically understood by any position which assumes it to be so. For Hegel philosophy is essentially historical, since truth is continually emerging as thought reflects on successive formulations of it over time. The aspiration to overcome contradiction in thought and in society, is what drives both philosophy and history forward, contradiction *is* the structure of reality. The state of tension is what stimulates both the effort to understand and to act, which combine to produce that development of our understanding which we call history. This is the sense in which thought for Hegel is creative, not simply reflective. Men do not simply reflect on their natures, in doing so

---

[46] Quoted by Hegel, *Logic*, note to Chapter 2, §24, p. 304.
[47] Lukács, *Young Hegel*, p. 280.

both as individuals and as societies, they are, as we argued above, constantly changing and recreating them.

Although some applications of this insight (for example his philosophy of nature) are troublesome and bizarre, the notion that human beings develop in consciousness through the process of reflection, is not itself an implausible one. What is more difficult to grasp is Hegel's notion that the elements of this development are not discrete quasi-mechanical components, but dialectically related moments in a constant state of tension. To see things as isolated facts is, for Hegel, to operate at a low level of cognition, he calls it *Verstand*, usually translated as Understanding. This is the level of empiricism. True philosophical insight can only be gained by viewing the essential contradictions in reality, the dynamic tensions which generate development. This is an attribute of the philosophic mind, a higher faculty altogether, *Vernunft*, Reason. However, this not only gives a truer account of the world, it is also the mode by which our world develops, for philosophy depicts our world to us, and so becomes part of it, reshapes it, and is itself then superseded by our reflecting upon it.

The task of philosophy then is to demonstrate the interconnectedness of the world, which it does in successive formulations as philosophical thinking develops. In most moods Hegel thought his own philosophy represented the culmination of this process, so that whereas earlier philosophies provoked contradictions, his own would, like Wittgenstein's 'leave everything as it is'.

Philosophy achieved this demonstration by using arguments with a striking similarity to Kant's transcendental arguments: showing how concepts could not be understood without invoking their contradictories. A good, and central example of this is the concept of freedom, since freedom is the essential property of mind which differentiates it from nature, and since he regarded it as the task for human social institutions to provide an objective arena in which social freedom could exist.

One aspect, or moment of the concept of freedom is the idea that in claiming to be free I claim a potentiality to be or do anything I will, without external influence of any kind. Yet for that freedom to become a reality I must actually choose *something*, and for it to be a real choice, rather than pure contingency, I must choose according to some criteria or standard of desire, which is in a sense, a limitation on my pure freedom. This abstract thought of freedom then seems to imply its opposite, some form of determination; if I do not make a choice my freedom remains purely abstract, as pure potentiality. The purely abstract moment in the concept of freedom must be determined in order to be made actual.[48] Philosophers of Hegel's generation were, as we have seen, torn between the idea that human freedom was determined by external and natural factors which seemed to destroy the autonomy required by freedom, and on the other hand, the idea that the individual could be wholly self-determining. Hegel's view is that the individual's consciousness is a part of a larger whole, spirit or consciousness general (Geist) which is, like himself, thought. Thus although the individual is not self-determining he is determined by something which is not an alien 'other', but which shares the laws and rules of development which apply to him as an individual, to his culture and to the human race as a whole.

---

[48] *Philosophy of Right*, §5, 6.

Through this view, Hegel came to accommodate the process by which Christianity supplanted the world of the Greeks. History becomes for him a process by which the world and the concepts which constitute it for men become successively more rational. Although, viewed in isolation, certain episodes might appear to be retrograde steps; viewed as part of the whole they are not so, and it is the task of philosophy to reconcile man to this process, to demonstrate its rationality, and thus enable him to feel at home in the world.

In the *Phenomenology of Mind* (1807), a work marking the breakthrough to Hegel's mature philosophical system, he treats the development of consciousness from a purely subjective point of view, exploring the actual forms that consciousness might, and has, taken in its development, as it struggled to deal with the contradictory nature of experience. In his final system there are two complementary approaches to truth, through philosophy, which tells us what there must be in the world, and through history, which demonstrates the emergence of that necessity over time. The *Phenomenology* is strictly neither philosophy nor history alone, but an introduction to Hegel's understanding of those disciplines which starts from, 'our ordinary consciousness of things, and takes us from there to the true perspective of Geist. The work is called a 'phenomenology' because it deals with the way things appear for consciousness, or with forms of consciousness.'[49]

The work starts with the naive mind's emergent awareness of a reality external to it, but the most famous and interesting passage for political theorists occurs where Hegel discusses how mind could come to be aware of itself. Self-consciousness, like other forms of knowledge, is neither innate nor externally induced, it has to come about through the overcoming of contradictions internal to consciousness itself. In that sense it, like other concepts, has to be constructed, out of more primitive conceptual materials. Mere subjective awareness of the world, or even of ourselves, is insufficient to achieve self-consciousness, for subjective awareness cannot give us the complimentary, objective, dimension; it cannot tell us what we are like *in the world*. Moreover this is something for which consciousness strives; for consciousness strives to establish its own reality and, for a being which is consciousness to achieve reality, must mean to achieve an objective recognition of its own consciousness. Only another being can do this, by mirroring, and presenting to that consciousness a sense of its own external being. Objective truth lies in their mutual, and consequently developed recognition of the other as a personality. However, the transition to recognition is not a simple one. The individual initially sees the existence of the other personality *as a negation*, as a threat to his own being.

The reason for this is due to the repertoire of possible modes of understanding available to a mind which has so far existed only in a world of things. To such a mind, to understand a thing is to control and subject it to its own will. It is in this way, by treating the other as a thing, that the individual initially attempts to come to terms with it. In doing so it validates its own self-image as an agent in command of a world of things. Since it is unaware of what consciousness would be like seen objectively, from the outside (for it knows itself as yet only from the inside) it initially treats another consciousness as a thing. We see this exemplified in the political form of despotism, in the way very young children treat others as simply bits of physical stuff, or how some men treat women, and philosophically, perhaps, in Hobbes's account of men in the state of nature, which is an

---

[49] Charles Taylor, *Hegel* (Cambridge, 1975), p. 128.

allegory of this form of consciousness in philosophical dress. Historically the aggressive ego is exemplified in the self-sufficient hero of Hegel's beloved Greece – Hector or Achilles.

But this attitude to the 'other' has two aspects. On the one hand the need to subdue and control the 'other' leads to conflict (since the other also experiences this need), and ultimately to death. Conversely, because conscious recognition by another is a precondition of full self-consciousness, this destruction of the other is also a self-destruction, a denial of the opportunity to create a 'world' of mutual recognition and consensus. There is already a germ of humanity in the desire to risk death for one's self identity, even though the notion of what it is one's identity consists in is mistaken.[50] Such an idea will resurface in a more developed form in the citizen's willingness to die for the sake of his political identity – the state. What is required is recognition, but the only form of recognition known is subordination and control of objects, and in the attempt to reduce the other to an object one of them is destroyed:

> The relation of the two self-conscious individuals is such that they prove themselves and each other through a life and death struggle. They must engage in this struggle, for they must raise their certainty of being *for themselves* to truth, both in the case of other and in their own case. And it is only through staking one's life that freedom is won; only thus is it proved that for self-consciousness, its essential being is not [just] being, not the *immediate* form in which it appears.[51]

Hegel sees encapsulated in the life-or-death struggle the emergence of social life and political union, vestiges of which remain for example in the practice of duelling to settle questions of honour which essentially arise from failures to adequately recognize the 'other'.[52]

However, death, as an outcome, clearly does not solve the problem of recognition and the desire for self-realization which initiated the conflict. Should one individual cling to mere life at the expense of validating its own self-image as dominator and controller it may cede the victory before death is reached. At this point a master-slave relationship is established between the two. This relationship is foundational for the emergence of recognition, self-consciousness and social life. Hegel is not saying – as Rousseau at times comes close to – that all social relationships are enslaving. But neither is he making the rather simple point that the master-slave relationship is an early or primitive form of social structure. Since the development of social relationships is not, for Hegel, simply serial, one leading on from another, but self-inclusive, each later stage incorporating in a higher form the earlier ones, the master-slave relationship is a protean source of the various relationships, political, economic, social and sexual that human beings enjoy. The struggle for recognition is not something that takes place once and for all, it is a continuing feature of social life. This insight has been the source of an immense amount of literature, not only in the Marxist but also in psychological traditions of thought.

---

[50] Judith Shklar, *Freedom and Independence, A study of the Political Ideas of Hegel's 'Phenomenology of Mind'* (Cambridge, 1976), p. 59.

[51] Hegel, *Phenomenology of Spirit*, tr. A. V. Miller (Oxford, 1977), §189.

[52] See the alternative discussion of the version of the master-slave dialectic in Hegel, *Philosophy of Mind*, tr. Wallace (Oxford, 1971), §432.

On the face of things it seems as though the master has won. He has won recognition of himself from another consciousness and thus validated his being not only in a world of things but also in a world of consciousness. But let us look more closely. What consciousness needed to achieve full self-awareness was recognition *by another consciousness*. The master has won recognition only by succeeding in reducing that other consciousness to slavery, to (in his own, the master's eyes,) the status of a thing. There is no other 'self' in the world *for the master* (although there is in fact). His consciousness has progressed no further than its existence in a world of unconscious objects; yet even this is now an illusion, since his independence is now mediated by the slave who creates for him, and without the tension provided by resistant things the mind is passive.[53] For the slave, on the other hand, who would seem to have lost, the world does indeed contain another, for the slave is not, as the master has claimed, a thing, but a conscious being, conscious of this other independent mind in the world. Although the slave is *forced* to recognize this other mind, he nevertheless does so, and has hence progressed from the position where the individual is alone in a world of things with only a subjective awareness of what it is to be a self, to a position where he has an objective awareness of self (the master). In assembling these two perspectives, derived from experiencing consciousness both subjectively, in himself and objectively, in another, he can gain self-consciousness, an objective awareness of his own subjectivity.[54]

Hegel emphasises two interesting positive aspects of the slave's experience: the stimulating mental effect of his subordinating the fear of death, the 'quaking of the single isolated will', the feeling of the worthlessness of egoism, which he says is a necessary moment in the education of men, clearing consciousness of its preconceptions to give it a sense of consciousness as such, rather than any particular form of it. There is an echo here of Hegel's earlier preoccupation with positivity, for 'the fear of the Lord, although an alienating experience for the bondsman, is the beginning of wisdom.'[55] Secondly, he stresses the importance of the slave's labour. It is through his labour, though forced, that the slave achieves an insight into his own agency, and so conceives the possibility of applying his objective perception of the Lord, as independent consciousness, to himself. Labour unifies the self-perception.[56] In a passage strikingly prescient of Marx, Hegel explains how the relationship of the master to reality, being one of mere consumption, provided by the activity of the slave, is thus unreal and incomplete (unmediated), whereas the slave, who labours, increases his awareness of himself and his relationship to an initially intractable Nature, in the course of transforming it for his master.

The dialectic of the master and slave illustrates how well Hegel's method works when dealing with the development of human consciousness, showing how objective and subjective perceptions differ, interact and create new perceptions and how all of the forms taken by thought and consciousness have to be constructed from less developed, less differentiated ones.

The method used in the *Phenomenology of Mind*, and more especially in the passage just discussed, is used extensively in the *Philosophy of Right*, Hegel's major political work. Objective spirit thus deals with that aspect of Geist (World Spirit), which appears in the form of human consciousness, and which is extended in interpersonal space, as

---

[53] Hegel, *Phenomenology,* §§190–1.
[54] Ibid., §194.

[55] Ibid., §195.
[56] Ibid., §195.

human social and political institutions. Hegel is thus pointing to the fact that morality, customs, law, political institutions, art, religion and philosophy are forms of human consciousness applied in particular ways or to particular areas of life.

Consider the institution which we call a university for example. It cannot be understood as a collection of buildings. It is a complicated set of conscious states on the part of those participating in the institution. Students and professors, secretaries, vice-chancellors and deans all possess, and elicit in others, a sense of the role they play within the institution and it is these awarenesses that make the institution what it is. In this important sense the university, like other social institutions is an idea, or set of ideas in people's minds.

Abstract right, with a consideration of which Hegel begins the *Philosophy of Right*, is right abstracted from any historical circumstances which might clothe it. Hegel's method is to attempt to deduce the necessary concepts and institutions required by consciousness through a process of *thought* from the most elementary to the most complex. This is essentially a philosophical argument. Nevertheless the way in which Hegel's general position sees history as the exemplification of philosophical positions means that we might expect to find historical instances of the points that Hegel is making.

Political theory, and indeed what is now called political science, is caught method-ologically between history and philosophy. Are the objects of political speculation – forms of government, ideals, social units – each unique examples of their kind which can be explained and understood only by a historical account of their individual development? Or are they reducible to timeless general categories, either necessary categories such as Plato's forms or the contingent categories of modern social science? Hegel attempts to solve this tension between history and philosophy by pointing out that even philosophy has a history, and that history itself must be understood philosophically. There are no unchanging *empirical* truths; but the concepts, ideas and institutions that have constituted truth for various societies can be shown to have developed in a rational and necessary fashion. Hegel believes that over the long term ideas such as the state realize their *full*, i.e. more coherently articulated, meaning in reality; thus there is an implication that early forms of the state may embody logically less differentiated forms of mind. Consequently we should not be surprised to find earlier thinkers describing the state in incongruous ways: for example as a family (Filmer), or as a contract (Hobbes), or as a system of needs (Bentham). Of course all of these forms are contained *within* the state, and they are part of the passage of spirit *to* the form we recognize as the state, but they are not, as we now recognize, *themselves* the state. They are the kind of errors which we should expect human consciousness to make in the course of its development, and indeed when we look in history, this is precisely what we find. The *Philosophy of Right* does not start from the most primitive, but from the most abstract form of objective mind, the argument is one that derives the concepts necessary for a social system of right, in philosophical order, not the stages it must go through, in historical sequence.

Abstract right

The introduction to the *Philosophy of Right*, like many of Hegel's introductions, is best left until later. The work can be more easily started at §34 where Hegel introduces the subject matter of this first part of the *Philosophy of Right*. This is the free will as abstract right; that is, the idea of right abstracted from any particular social or historical context or content which a particular right would ordinarily possess. For this same reason it is 'immediate', that is it is not mediated by any internal properties (tastes, aims, purposes etc.), or external circumstances. To apply the first category of Hegel's *Logic* to it, it has mere being. Such a condition turns out to be only the capacity for existence: in order to be real or actual, the will needs to take on particular properties which could structure its choices in meaningful ways. The will that was *completely* free, in the sense of undetermined, if indeed, such a will could exist, would be random, its acts a product of mere chance. What Hegel wants to show is that our willing when properly structured, can be free *and* determined, in the sense that it can be shown to be logically implicit in the notion of 'free will' itself. In modern terminology he wants to show that the moral categories and forms of social organization and customs through which we live our lives, are not 'natural' but a product of will, but neither – even though a product of will – are they ultimately relative. The institutions, practices and conventions which constitute, and through which we understand the modern liberal state, are necessarily the way they are, because they represent the only way in which human wills can coherently, and without contradiction interact in a social arena.[57] The *Philosophy of Right* is not a historical argument, although history exemplifies the movement from primitive to more complex social concepts and institutions; nor is it a psychological argument, although our individual personalities – necessarily structured by the society in which we live – will again display aspects of the development. It is instead, an attempt to show how the social and moral forms of the state derive *logically* from more primitive forms and from even the most elementary acts of willing.

The absolutely free will

Hegel begins the section on 'abstract right' with a discussion of the absolutely free will. Why start with will? Because his subject matter is 'objective consciousness', that is those ideas and aspects of consciousness that exist in the social world outside our own minds in the form of mutually recognized institutions, formal and informal. If he is to explain why and how we can form ideas of such things he must first explain how our consciousness can extend beyond the field of our mere subjective awareness. There is an aspect of consciousness that we do project outwards. It is what we call will.[58] Willing is the projection of mind beyond itself, most commonly, and initially, onto our bodies, and thence onto the surrounding world. So we (if we reflect on it) will our limbs to move us

---

[57] It is important to notice that the *Philosophy of Right* is about will, not about consciousness more generally (note to §42 e.g. 'free mind . . . must be distinguished from mere consciousness'). In a more general sense we can externalise our consciousnesses through argument and discussion without any implications for social organisation. The putting of our wills into the world however, because it involves the notion of purpose, raises the possibility of *actual and external* contradictions, the resolution of which requires enduring, objective, independent conventions capable of themselves being sustained, and sustaining the objective existence of individuals' wills in that world. On 'real', 'actual' and 'external' see *Logic*, §142.

[58] The will, he says, is 'practical mind', *Philosophy of Right*, Introduction, §4, note. In the *Philosophy of Mind*, Hegel, after introducing the idea of objective mind claims that 'the purposive action of this will is to realize its concept, Liberty, in these externally objective aspects [of reality]' §484.

to the window to close off a draft, or to pour a drink to slake our thirst. More abstractly, in persuasive speech we try to impose our will on others, without physical intermediary, except the movement of our lips. So the will is a central concept in the derivation of the concept of 'objective mind' (the subject matter of the *Philosophy of Right*) since it is will that describes the mind's first projection beyond its merely subjective, or internal dimension.

However, what is initially implied in this *abstract* conception of free will, is the negation, that is the denial, of any of the particular determinants (circumstances, inclinations, tastes) that would make it recognizable as any particular individual's will, since these would, at the same time, curtail its 'abstract freedom'. For once we attribute elements of a personality to the will, it will undoubtedly 'will' some things and not others. However the attribution to the will of any such determinants could, at this stage, only be arbitrary, and Hegel, anxious to construct a rigorously logical argument wants to press forward without introducing them. The 'social contract' method of political theorising was vulnerable to the charge that it could, by reading certain qualities back into 'natural man' virtually predetermine what kind of political society would emerge from the investigation.[59] Hegel evades such criticisms by refusing to attribute any particular desires or tastes to the free will that he places at the start of his investigation.[60]

What is also implied in the notion of the absolutely free will is the notion of a will which has, as it were, not yet decided to will *anything*. For willing a particular thing, i.e. deciding, determines our will, and thus ends its freedom. The absence of these two aspects from the absolutely free will is related, in that it is only on the basis of a particular personality with particular tastes that any actual will could in fact decide;[61] and in pursuing the progress of will into the world Hegel is concerned to recognize, and attempt to overcome, both of these paradoxical 'limitations' inherent in the absolutely free will.

Thus, although Hegel is claiming that freedom is the essential quality of will, and that the capacity to possess rights in order to exercise that freedom is constitutive of what we would recognize as a person, [62] the lack of any content to such claims (and for right to be abstract there cannot be any such content) makes this expression of the being of will incomplete; it is not yet objective. In having no such content it is divided from the world, and so 'unreal' or, more literally 'unrealized'. To become real the will must give itself a content, determine itself, i.e. decide, and put itself into something outside itself – a project.[63] The process of objectification, the development of, or the creation of content

---

[59] The criticism is made of earlier social contract theorists by Rousseau; and Kant's tactic of situating the subject outside the phenomenal realm clearly evades it. See Patrick Riley, 'On Kant as the most adequate of the social contract theorists', *Political Theory*, 1, 4 (1973). Most recently, John Rawls's attempt to construct an 'abstract' personality, stripped of 'particular' properties or personality traits that would enable it to recognise what version of justice would benefit itself, and so placed beyond a 'veil of ignorance', was designed as an attempt to find a way of 'impartially' choosing the standards of justice, and so also attempt to evade such criticisms.

[60] *Philosophy of Right*, §37

[61] This is not quite true. The will, as Hegel recognises, can be determined by 'nature', in the form of our instinctive or biological drives, or it could be determined by chance. Neither of these, however, is an adequate characterisation, or successful realization of what we want to mean by our 'free will'.

[62] Ibid., §36.

[63] Ibid., §34. Addition to §33: 'If the free will is not to remain abstract, it must in the first place give itself an embodiment, and the material primarily available to sensation for such embodiment is things, i.e. objects outside us.'

for, the personality, and the use of that content in making decisions is the process of the will's coming to terms with, and integrating itself into the logic of the world. Whereas the empirical mind, or what Hegel calls the 'understanding' might see the giving of a particular set of tastes and desires to the will as *impinging* on its freedom, Hegel wants to show that on the contrary, this determination is, paradoxically, necessary to make the free will real. Any conception of freedom which seems to hanker after absolute freedom remains tied to pure indeterminacy or to a determination based on caprice. Disposing of the ideal of a purely undetermined will however, doesn't solve the problem of showing how one way of determining will is to be preferred to another, nor how *any* way of determining it could be compatible with freedom. It is this that the *Philosophy of Right* sets out to do, by showing that a rational will develops the practices and institutions there described in its attempt to project itself into reality.

Although a psychological story would, at this point, have to proceed by providing the will with a personality to enable it to make a decision, Hegel does not, for his account is not here a psychological one. It is rather, an attempt to show the *logical derivation* of the ideas that constitute and support objective mind. He is, therefore content to characterize the *logical necessity* for the will to be determined in order to be realized, without yet having to deal with the tastes or preferences that would be necessary for an actual will to make such a decision; that is, he asks us to proceed on the basis that we can know that the will, to realize itself and overcome indecision, must in fact determine on some project, without yet knowing what kind of project that might be, or how it would choose that one.[64]

The determination of the will and its outward projection into the world, not only terminates the suspension of willing which is indecisiveness, but in doing so, it ends the will's abstract freedom. This is both psychologically, and logically (in Hegel's peculiar sense of logic) true. Psychologically, once our will is determined, 'our mind is made up': we are no longer free (at least with respect to the particular decision we were engaged in). But philosophically, within the context of Hegel's argument, the recognition of the need for an act of determination or negation to realize (or make real) the free will also indicates the end (or negation) of the concept of the abstractly free will, and the transition to another concept. This new concept must characterize and incorporate the argument, or movement of thought achieved so far, if it is to sustain the idea of the 'will in the world', which is our subject matter. That is to say, we are looking for a concept to describe 'the determined will projected into the world'. That concept, Hegel suggests, is the concept of right. 'Right' is simply the name we use to characterize attempts to project our will onto external reality.[65]

Property

If the external projection of our will, through the assertion of right, is to be sustained, it must lodge in a particular thing. That is to say, our act of projection must have an objective destination beyond ourselves. At its most basic that destination is a 'thing'; a thing being

---

[64] Ibid., §§37, 39.
[65] 'An existent of any sort embodying the free will, this is what right is.' Ibid., §29. And again: 'Right is in the first place, the immediate embodiment which freedom gives itself in an immediate way' Ibid., §40.

an entity which does not have rights, except such as are put into it by persons, who do.[66] Once again Hegel invites us to accept that language naturally respects this philosophically necessary conception by possessing a key term 'property' to designate it.[67]

In a more abstract but analogous way to Locke, Hegel is defining the condition of man's social existence as real freedom, and freedom in terms of property. For Hegel, our objective social existence presupposes proprietorship. Just as in understanding, mind creates the conceptual world by projecting thoughts onto it, so in the world of action we create a social world by imposing our wills onto things which have themselves no purposes, and possessing them. And, we might add, just as at the limited level of understanding, the thoughts by which we interpret the world seem to have an objective existence of their own, so, at that same limited level, property can appear to have an objective, pre-social, existence. But the need for property is not based on our physical, or biological natures (on our need, or even duty, to keep alive as Locke suggests). It is, claims Hegel, the necessary form that will must take in order, as it were, to emerge from our heads and exist in interpersonal space. As such, the concept of property would be required by *any* kind of self-conscious, willing, being that sought social existence, irrespective of their bodily needs. Property is an entailment of our consciousness, not of our material being.

The essential aspect of property is therefore not what appears to be essential in particular cases of it: the satisfaction of particular wants or needs. It is, rather, the more general capacity that property has to be an object for will.[68] This explains why property must, if it is to achieve this, be private. Moreover, since will appears as the will of an individual the abolition of private property would deny freedom as the right of the will to realize itself.[69]

What counts as a 'thing'? There is a sense in which one's physical body is a thing, an object in the world, and consequently something which, as those with experience of young babies know, has to be taken possession of, in the sense of our learning how to subject it to our wills. The process is one which we can, if we will, pursue almost indefinitely. Virtuoso musicians, through their dexterity, and athletes through their endurance pursue the imposition of their wills on their bodies to a far greater degree than most of us. This is true not only of bodily but of mental or creative skills. The cultivation of these is the making real of our otherwise only abstract freedom. Recognizing our own freedom, that is, our own potential for self-development, is in a sense a precondition for pursuing it, which *is* the way we take possession of ourselves. Conversely the failure to

---

[66] Ibid., §§42, 44.

[67] Ibid., §40. Seeing Hegel in this way highlights the similarities between his philosophy and that of the later Wittgenstein, also committed to bringing out the rationality or coherence in ordinary language and everyday life. Wittgenstein however abjured, and probably despaired of any attempt to show that this revealed an underlying metaphysic. See *Philosophical Investigations* (Oxford, 1958) §§120–30, 599.

[68] Ibid., §45.

[69] Ibid., §46. Although Hegel's point here is specifically directed against communal property — i.e. communism; it does not preclude the possibility of collectively held property, since the collectivity holding it can be, in Roman Law terms a 'legal person', i.e. an artificial collectivity such as a legal partnership, a marriage or an association. Such entities may be deemed to have a single will. Corporate bodies within the state (note to §46), and even the state, or nation itself (note to §64) can hold property.

develop our capacities is the failure to recognize, use and therefore to realize, our freedom.[70] These skills which result from our wills can be property, in the further sense of being, if not exactly bought and sold, at least made the subject of a contract. What is sold is not of course *exactly* the skill itself which is inherently the possession of the individual, but the outward manifestation of it as performance.[71]

Just as the will takes command of the body, it can, moving in the opposite direction, deny it's relationship to body. Sages and mystics can withdraw out of themselves to the extent that bodily privation seems no longer to bother them. But this withdrawal is precisely a withdrawal *out* of the social, interpersonal realm, and back into an abstract world. These contemplative practices, although an option for individuals, would, if generalised, render impossible the existence of objective mind, i.e. the world of objective or interpersonal social existence.[72] For the objective will to exist, the will must be made objective in a thing. Moreover this possession must become property, a socially recognized right, for it to become securely objective.[73] It is this transition from subjective willing to objectively recognized right with which the first part of the *Philosophy of Right* deals.

But if we must take possession of our bodies as property, can we lose possession of them by becoming the property of another? This is in effect a question about slavery.[74] Hegel's short answer is no. The will is inherently free, and can only objectively be so when recognized as such. Since all actual wills are in fact embodied, and, moreover can only be recognized as will if they are; recognizing the freedom of the will involves recognizing the freedom of the body. Indeed, it is, Hegel suggests *only* because of the freedom of will that the freedom of the body can be defended.[75]

It is, of course true that eminent philosophers, amongst them Aristotle and Locke, have defended slavery. Yet there is a sense in which the very way they have done so reinforces both Hegel's analysis here, and, incidentally, his claim that history represents the clarification and articulation of the necessary categories of consciousness, the true relationships of which are only finally apparent at the end of that process. For both Aristotle and Locke agree with Hegel that truly human beings should not be enslaved. In each case, they argued, slavery was appropriate only for those in apparently human form who nevertheless lacked the distinguishing characteristic of humans – the directive virtue of the citizen for Aristotle, the capacity to acknowledge the moral law for Locke. They can therefore be read as endorsing Hegel's claim that only those things that are sub-human can be property, they differ from him only in deciding how to make that distinction.[76] It is, thinks Hegel, only with the emergence of modern idealism that the role of self-consciousness in making this distinction could at last become clear.

---

[70] Ibid., §57.

[71] Ibid., note to §43.

[72] Ibid., note to §48.

[73] Ibid., note to §48.

[74] The question now applies in ways that Hegel could not have envisaged. *Parts* of our bodies (blood, sperm, kidneys, etc.) as well as bodily functions such as gestation can, due to technical developments in medical science, now be the object of a contract. Are such contracts more like the illegitimate one of slavery, or like the legitimate contract of bodily skills?

[75] Ibid., §48.

[76] Ibid., note to §57.

Property – possession

Although property is the objective form that will takes, property itself must be made objective in some sense. It is not enough that I subjectively consider my will to be projected into something, that projection has to be designated in some outward way that goes beyond my subjective willing. How is property to be designated? The question is deliberately ambiguous, since the categories Hegel uses are both those categories which describe successively more 'objective' conceptualizations of the idea of property, as well as denoting actions by which we designate particular objects as our own. For Hegel, needless to say, the fact that our practices turn out to mirror the philosophical argument both confirms the latter, and philosophy's relationship to history.

There are three dialectically related 'moments', to the concept of property: taking possession, which is the initial putting of a will into a thing, use and alienation, which completes, or ends both the concept of property as well as particular instances of property ownership.

We take possession by grasping, forming or marking a thing which has as yet no will in it, which is not yet anyone else's property. Grasping is the most obvious and physically irrefutable of possessive acts. It is at the same time the most primitive and transitory, since it is dependent on my presence there and then and ceases when my hold on the thing is relaxed. Extensions of the notion of grasping are involved in those possession claims deriving from Roman Law ideas of 'natural accession' where something I already own produces something new, for example where livestock produce young, or rivers wash up extra soil on a bank. But since all such connections are based on physical proximity they are ultimately 'external' to will and so fail to make property-as-will objective.[77]

Forming something (such as a pottery vessel out of a lump of clay) on the other hand, imposes our will on it in a much more obvious and continuing way – a way which embodies the maker's will in the very physical shape of the thing. Forming a thing clearly echoes Locke's idea of 'mixing my labour' with it, although again, for Hegel, it is not the labour so much as the will or idea behind it that is the crucial point.[78]

Marking something is a yet more sophisticated version of forming, for the physical impression that designates the presence of will does not now have to suffuse the whole object, but can be a localized sign – initials or a symbol on one part of something – which 'stand for', or represent, a will in the thing. This sense of possession is an allegory of the whole concept of property itself which 'stands for' or represents 'will in the world'. It is thus a more perfect representation of the notion of property itself.[79]

---

[77] Ibid., §55.

[78] Ibid., §56. It is the Platonic idea of the work of art as the physical representation of an idea in the mind of the artist that Hegel has in mind here.

[79] Ibid., §§57–8.

Property – use

But all these forms of possession are only imperfect representations of will. Even in the idea of marking something there is no intimate connection between marking and the will. The most direct expression of the relationship between my will and the thing is the *use* to which I put it. It is in use that will, as purpose, is externalized in the thing and made objective and recognizable as *my* will in the world. In use too, the thing's own lack of will is made explicit.[80] Use therefore illustrates and makes real (or realizes) the two complementary qualities of purpose and purposelessness which characterize the two elements in property – possessor and possessed. There are, once again, anticipations of this view in Locke's account of appropriation, when he stresses that useless appropriation conveys no property right. Because the use of a thing must derive from a will, and because actual will is invariably the will of an individual, ownership claims Hegel, must be exclusive. [81]

Although the particular use to which things are put is a result of the purpose of the particular subject whose will is in them and therefore owns them, property also has a universal aspect which is expressed by its value. Indeed Hegel seems to give some kind of ontological priority to value: because the value of a thing expresses its universality, it is through value that things become objects of general consciousness and significance, rather than mere subjective expressions of one particular individual's personal need, meaningful only to their owners.[82] The thing-as-property is only a symbol of its value, for value represents universal purpose, and significance is in the particular only when united with the universal. Since value represents the universal element of use in property, but is only expressed in exchange, the realization (unity of the particular and the universal) of property implies its exchange, and the concept of property is already leading us in the direction of the concept of contract. However there are more compelling reasons for invoking the concept of contract.

---

[80] Ibid., §59.

[81] Ibid., §§61–2. This is one of Hegel's least convincing arguments, as his tortuous attempt to deal with the much more flexible implications of the Roman Law tradition shows (note to §62). It would seem, rather, that the important role of use in property might render the question of exclusivity a matter of contingency, to be decided by the nature of each particular case (as he almost seems to hint, start of note to §62). Since the nature of use (and therefore the strength of the case for exclusive ownership) is a matter of practicality and subjective will (§63) there would seem to be no grounds for concluding, at the stage of abstract right, that property must be exclusive. Although modern property right is predominantly a right to exclude, there are many examples, especially in the management of the countryside, and wilderness areas, of attempts to assign compatible but different uses to the same 'thing'. Thus wilderness areas can be used for both water-catchment and backpacking, waterways can be used by both birdwatchers and fishers (but not also by power-boat enthusiasts).

[82] Ibid., §63.

Property – alienation

That property *can* be alienated follows from the fact that it results from an act of will, which can be reversed: we can take our wills out of things as well as putting them in.[83] There are some things we cannot, in a way, relinquish. A painting by Picasso will always, in some sense, be 'his' no matter who owns it.[84] The personalities we increasingly construct for ourselves, what Hegel calls 'ethical life' – our moral and religious belief – cannot irrevocably be lost. Although we can lose them through inattention, or by succumbing to superstition, or the moral authority of a pope or a party: we can always, by an act of will, recover them.[85] One implication of this view is that the personality is always prior to the property in which it realizes itself. There can be no entrenched and overriding rights in properties. Although the right to property is a precondition of freedom, particular property rights may be vulnerable to the more general claims of freedom, subsistence and personality.[86]

However, although personality itself cannot be given up, property in the more conventional sense of an intrinsically external thing can be alienated. But alienation as such is simply the negation of all the concepts created thus far. If alienation means simply the withdrawal of my will out of the thing and into myself, it means returning to page one of the *Philosophy of Right* and to the beginning of the argument. If Hegel's project of deducing all the categories of social and political life from the concept of the free will is to succeed, he needs to discover a concept which, whilst 'ending' or 'rounding off' our understanding of the idea of property, still sustains the will in the world, rather than returning it to mere potentiality in our heads. The concept that does this is contract.

Contract

In contract we see how 'property' can be terminated whilst the will is kept in the world (although not in the same thing). However, contract doesn't simply 'rescue' property from a return to the indeterminacy of our un-made-up wills. Contract is a positive step towards the creation of an objective (i.e. mutually recognized) structure of will, and therefore of freedom, in the world.

From this point of view, what is central to contract is not the objects of the exchange, but the mutual recognition of the two parties as property owners.[87] For in recognizing the property right of another, or getting another will to recognize my property right, property gains a degree of objectivity it could never achieve through the efforts of a single

---

[83] Ibid., §65.

[84] Ibid., note to §68.

[85] Ibid., note to §66. There is surely an echo here of Locke's denial that we can voluntarily acknowledge the authority of an arbitrary will over us.

[86] This later enables claims to be made by the impoverished against the property of others, and state intervention in the operation of property rights where personality is threatened. Ibid., §127note. And see below fn. 129.

[87] Ibid., note to §71.

will.[88] The owner's will strives to establish property but can only do so, as it were, from his or her side, projecting the will from the inside outwards. The recognition of my proprietorship by another defines it, as it were, from the outside as well.[89] Just as in property what appeared as central – the need or desire which motivated the appropriation – turned out to be subordinate to the will's more general need for externalization, so again here, although the hope of a particular object motivates the participants, the existence of the institution of contract can be explained by the imperative that the will (in property) attain objective recognition.[90]

Wrong

Although the objective establishment of the will in property requires contract, any such exchange would involve two as yet unmediated and abstract wills (that is, wills without the shared conventions and customs which normally make exchange possible, and without the kind of personality which would render their desires stable and coherent). The emergence of contract is therefore highly arbitrary, dependent as it would be on the contingent coincidence of such unmediated wills in striking a bargain.[91]

Where the particular wills happen to be in conformity with the universal principle of right (i.e. mutual recognition) inherent in contract, then the concept of right presupposed at this point in the argument is sufficient to effect a successful contract. But it is only implicitly adequate because the conformity is dependent on whether the individual and unmediated wills involved conform to a universalized system of right. Where they do not, individual assertions of right will conflict and negate one another. This negation of right is, simply enough, *wrong*.[92] Wrong is not only (and obviously) the negation of right, it also leads, as we shall see, to the re-establishment of right in a more explicit way which escapes the merely contingent coincidence of particular wills.

Wrong (i) civil wrong

Wrong does not imply 'ill'-will, simply its contradiction. Wrong, is logically, simply the negation of right. It can result merely from the clashing content of two innocent claims of right. For example, in civil, or non-malicious wrong, two parties may quite genuinely assert a right over the same object. We can see how this can happen. Although we have derived the necessity of property, we have no conventions regarding its establishment or transfer.[93] Two individuals might honestly consider they had a right to the same piece of

---

[88] Ibid., §71.

[89] Ibid., §72.

[90] Ibid., note to §71, and §73.

[91] Ibid., §§75, 81.

[92] Ibid., §§82, 111–13.

[93] With the exception of the intuitive principle of first-occupancy (Ibid., §50). But there is still no convention about what counts as occupancy. For example can one acquire a whole continent by planting a flag on the coast? Or as in the case of the Falklands/Malvinas acquire a whole group of islands by leaving, on one of them, a lead plaque asserting one's ownership? International disputes abound in examples of this

land – one basing their claim on first sighting, the other on usage.[94] There is no question of criminal will here. Both acknowledge the existence of right, the question is: who has it?[95] The discrepancy here is between the ideal of the notion of contract – to bring two wills into conformity and so recognize one another – and its fact – two wills claiming, in all honesty, conflicting rights.[96]

Wrong (ii) fraud

As Hegel explores the concept of wrong, we move to a situation in which one of the particular wills comes more and more explicitly to deny the principle of right – so making wrong more objective. In the case of fraud, the particular will represents as right, part of a formally adequate contract, which is nevertheless substantively inadequate in not containing the implicit conditions of universality i.e. rightful possession.[97] The man who sells London or Brooklyn Bridge to a tourist is clearly going through the motions of a formal contract, but something essential is missing, which if missing in all contracts would make a nonsense of the whole logic of the argument of contract, and ultimately of the notion of property, which is necessary to the realization of freedom and the development of social institutions. As our confidence trickster cannot do without the *concept* of property (he wants it to apply to what is *his*), there is, in the case of fraud, still a semblance or representation of right, behind which wrong is perpetrated. But in the further case of coercion the very idea of right is denied, thus making explicit the concept of wrong.

Wrong (iii) coercion

Coercion is only possible inasmuch as we have put our wills into external objects (or other persons in the form of love), since it is only by refusing to withdraw our wills from this external locus that we can be coerced.[98] But the putting of our wills into external objects is necessary, as has been shown, for the objective expression of the will's freedom, and hence its determinate existence as right. Since coercion seeks to destroy the externalized will by forcing a retreat from those external things into which it has been

---

kind precisely because, despite some International Law, the actors are, by and large, 'unmediated' by any shared acceptance of conventions of acquisition.

[94] Ibid., §84.

[95] Ibid., §85.

[96] Ibid., §86.

[97] Ibid., §88.

[98] Ibid., §90–1. Hegel's rather spectacular claim that as a result 'only the will which allows itself to be coerced can in any way be coerced' makes sense only on his insistence that the body is an external thing which we could relinquish, rather than yield our will. In this sense it is true that the *will* cannot be coerced. The victim of the inquisition tortured on the rack, or the modern prisoner of conscience tortured for information about his or her colleagues might both be subject to physical coercion, to the point of being killed, but their wills are not coerced as a result of this if they maintain their silence. However note the more conventional view at §48 where because 'I' can only exist in the body, 'it is only abstract sophistical reasoning which can . . . hold that . . . the soul, is not touched or attacked if the body is maltreated.'

put, it is the antithesis of objective freedom and right, and is therefore inherently wrong.[99] Even within the state, the destructive power of coercion is recognized when it is employed in negating a criminal will, judged to have been itself perpetrating coercion and thus wrong.[100] Even the abstract right we have been talking about contains within itself the right to coerce because it must contain the right to protect itself against force or will which threatens to deny the very principle of right. A criminal will must therefore be negated by the application of coercion. This, claims Hegel, is not something which the criminal merely undergoes, but it is their right![101] The criminal has by implication willed his own punishment by simply willing – by extending his will into the world. For as we have seen, the application of punishment is a logical implication of this process, necessary to protect from wrong all the categories generated by 'willing' – will, right, property, contract – traversed thus far.

The act of punishment, as the negation of the criminal will, is simply an outward or objective expression of the negative nature of the criminal will itself and thus no more than the 'realization' of coercion. However, looked at from a broader perspective it is not a merely contingent and unfortunate necessity, for it is also the objective reassertion of right. Punishment, in a peculiar sense, by making explicit the negation of wrong, reasserts not only the particular right that has been negated, but the very principle of right as well. Through punishment, right is placed on a more objective footing than when it was merely asserted.[102]

Punishment

Punishment is then the reassertion of what Hegel calls 'the implicit will', by which he means the aspiration towards a universally recognizable principle of right. Whilst we might agree that objectively, punishment is needed to safeguard expressions of right which, being wrong, subvert this end, there is no guarantee that, subjectively, the annulment of the crime will be seen in this way by the criminal will. Indeed punishment, in the context of right which is immediate and abstract, is primarily, and is liable to be seen as, revenge, i.e. as the subjective act of a particular will. It is therefore merely another wrong, not universal or objectively right. Not even ensuring the equality of punishment to crime can do this. Such an act of mere revenge will itself require avenging, producing what Hegel calls a 'bad infinity'.[103]

Once again the philosophical category finds a representation in historical reality. For there have been, and are, societies without formal law-enforcement agencies, whose only

---

[99] Ibid., §92.

[100] Ibid., §93.

[101] Ibid., §100. Hegel is therefore a retributivist as regards punishment. However, whilst the question of whether punishment — in the sense of just denial of the criminal's right — can be rightly imposed *at all* depends on the will on which it is imposed being a criminal will (and is therefore settled on retributivist principles) — the *form* that punishment takes is a matter for empirical, even consequentialist, and utilitarian consideration (note to §99, and see later, note to §214). I owe clarification of this point to Andrew Lockyer.

[102] Ibid., §§97, 99. At a sociological level this has some disturbing implications: does a society in some sense 'need' its criminals in order to objectively assert its moral identity?

[103] Ibid., §102.

concept of rectification of wrong is revenge: they are vendetta communities.[104] Moreover, in societies where the respect for the impartiality of law-enforcement agencies such as police and courts has, for whatever reason, been lacking, there law-enforcement is liable to be viewed as an act of aggression, justifying revenge.[105]

The resolution of such a vendetta can only come from outside the immediate situation. Hobbes's perception of the need for a sovereign arbiter, who is above the community seems clearly right. And Hegel will indeed ultimately have recourse to a sovereign for those very reasons. But for the moment Hegel seeks an answer not in a particular political *institution* (such as a monarch), but in a new and different kind of *will*.

The vendetta emerges because each will can see in the other only a particular will, and consequently sees the act of punishment as an assertion of constricting private, not liberating universal right. The assertion of right has led to its negation, wrong. Yet this is not a dead end. Mind invariably seeks to transcend, if it cannot develop, a contradiction. The solution is therefore necessitated, not precluded by the contradiction. The will required to solve the dilemma must be a will which is not particular but universal, which wills not its own right, but right in general, and can therefore rise above the subjectivity which makes punishment appear as revenge. We have, therefore not yet arrived at the need for a sovereign, only at the need for a form of willing which transcends the particular and wills that right in general be done. This kind of will is the moral will, and with it Hegel makes the transition from abstract right to morality, the second part of the *Philosophy of Right*.[106] Because this demand for a universal will has developed out of the contradictions inherent in the subjective will, Hegel wants to say that it is will self-determined, developed in accordance with the logic of its self, or to put it less technically: any attempt to make coherent sense of the notion of the individual free will, is bound to lead to the concept of the moral will.[107]

Morality

The universal principle inherent in will

Morality depicts a will that wills not merely its private right, but which self-consciously wills the (universal) principle of right itself. The moral consciousness involves an awareness of the principles according to which it acts. The will for Hegel, as free mind, is essentially universal but so far this has merely shown itself in universal, i.e. generalized, egoism, leading, as we have seen to revenge and vendetta. True freedom involves a recognition of this universal principle embodied in the will, i.e. of the existence and

---

[104] Hegel did not need modern anthropological studies to tell him this. Greek tragedies, in particular those built around the *Oresteia* legends depicted the punishment of Orestes doomed by the Oracle at Delphi to revenge his father's murder by killing his mother, and so in his turn pursued by the Furies, a fate from which, according to the playwright Aeschylus, he was only released by the emergence of impartial, civic justice in the guise of the Athenian goddess Athene.

[105] For example, where an underclass of poor is allowed to emerge, for 'once society is established, poverty immediately takes the form of a wrong done to one class by another.' Ibid., addition to §244.

[106] Ibid., §103.

[107] Ibid., §104.

rights of other wills.[108] It is this growth-through-self-recognition that differentiates the mind from nature.[109] Without it we would merely be part of nature. We might fancy ourselves free, but we would in reality be the play of purely natural impulses, such as those of pleasure and pain to which Bentham and the utilitarians, who have what for Hegel is a very crudely naturalistic conception of the will, depict man as being subject.

The only conception of the will that overcomes this naturalism and the problem of the vendetta is one that recognizes that the rules according to which we operate must be such that all minds could obey as universal. Freedom is not just, as Rousseau would have it, obedience to a law which we prescribe to ourselves, it is obedience to a law we prescribe to ourselves because we see its necessity in our own moral natures. This is essentially what we do when we moralise about our aims and actions: we attempt to make objective what was purely subjective, in the sense of demonstrating that what we do or aim at is what all other wills should reasonably have aimed at in similar circumstances. Although this is the conception of the will that is demanded, morality does not emerge in this form straightaway. For although the moral will is one that recognizes universal principles, its attempt to grasp what is universal is constantly thwarted by the experience of its own subjectivity. The clearest example of this is in the idea of conscience. Although conscience purports to tell us what is right (in general rather than just for us) it is notoriously subjective. It is capable of subjectively presenting as 'universally right' a point of view that is quite peculiar, and particular to the individual or a small group. In conscience subjective feeling almost overwhelms the universal element in morality.

Hegel distinguishes three aspects of the moral will, purpose, intention and good.[110] A moral act involves a purpose to impinge on a state of affairs which is infinitely complex. Not all of the consequences of that action are thus to count as included in its purpose but only those which result from the actor's knowledge of the situation. This is more than a criterion of moral culpability: purpose is what enables an action to be identified as *mine*.[111] Intention is the underlying unity or aim behind purposive action that makes it more than simply a set of physical movements. Intention is (for example) what makes it impossible for someone to excuse themselves from a charge of arson, by saying that they only actually applied the match to one small piece of wood. Together, purpose and intention make us morally responsible for our actions. Conversely, those regarded as incapable, or imperfectly capable of forming purposes and executing intentions are regarded as not responsible for their actions.[112] The content of a moral intention can at this point only be expounded in terms of the welfare at which a particular will aims.[113] Such welfare is a subjectively assessed element,[114] but only within limits, for particular individuals' welfare may damage others, as when one individual asserts his property rights to the extent that another starves, for example. Since the notion of welfare is now

---

[108] Ibid., §106.

[109] See above, p. 415.

[110] Ibid., §114.

[111] Ibid., §117.

[112] Ibid., note to §120.

[113] Ibid., §123. This can only be expressed abstractly because the will is still abstract; we don't know what in particular would motivate a will until it has a content of tastes, desires, customs, aims etc.

[114] Meaning not merely that welfare is itself a matter of subjective judgement, for it is not wholly so; but that welfare may stand opposed to the universal aim of realizing the principles of right. Ibid., §125.

being advanced within the context of a universal (i.e. moral), and not an individualistic view of right, it cannot support a conception of welfare which offends this principle.[115] A truly universal view of welfare must involve a consideration of the general implications of what is being advanced rather than simply the welfare of the particular agent concerned.[116] Moreover it must discriminate between different levels of human need. The 'right of distress' involves recognizing that claims to a particular right – to property, a debt or whatever – cannot hold against individuals' more basic rights to life, and even to subsistence at their customary level. Hegel reasserts, indeed strengthens the medieval view that we have no property rights against the absolutely, or even relatively, destitute.[117] Neither right or welfare can be what I want simply because I want it – even though I want it for another. Mere altruism is not morality.[118]

The category that ensures the unity of the universal concept of will with the particular will as right or even welfare is the good. The idea of the good contains within it both the recognition of right and the idea of universal welfare.[119] Right cannot be advanced against the welfare of others, nor welfare sought in ways which contravene right. Good must comprise right *and* welfare subject to these two constraints; moreover, in accordance with the element of subjectivity in morality it can only be truly good if it is realized through the expression of a particular will.[120] But because the criteria available for the moral will are still abstract (duty, the pursuit of the right and of welfare should be done for duty's sake but what is my duty?)[121] the content of the morally aspirant will can be provided only subjectively, by the will itself. The attempt to provide an objective characterization of the moral will therefore collapses into subjectivity in the form of conscience – the inner conviction that my action is good. But because conscience lacks objective confirmation that it is what it appears to its owner to be (i.e. the good and right thing to do), conscience can depart wildly from what the principle of right requires. Indeed to have this kind of conscience says Hegel 'is simply to be on the verge of slipping into evil' in the sense of elevating a subjective moral perception into a universal one.[122] Such a subjective view of morality – prevalent in the current relativist climate – is moreover wide open to the most shameless hypocrisy, and to the eventual evaporation of any conception of objective wrong altogether, as though: 'My good intention in my action and my conviction of its goodness make it good'.[123]

So far the concept of morality has been guided by the notion that we must act with intention to do good according to principles which could be binding on all other agents as well. Hegel is here adopting Kant's fundamental moral principle of universalizability: '*Act only on that maxim through which you can at the same time will that it should become*

---

[115] Ibid., §126.

[116] Ibid., §125.

[117] The direct source for Hegel of this view is, as for so much else in his thought, Roman Law. In this case the *beneficium competentiae*, or right to retain the necessities of life, which could be claimed by a defaulting debtor against his creditor (except where advanced as a surety). W.W. Buckland, *A Textbook of Roman Law* (3rd edn. revised by Peter Stien, Cambridge, 1975) pp. 693–4, 657.

[118] *Philosophy of Right*, §127.

[119] Ibid., §§129–30.

[120] Ibid., §130.

[121] Ibid., §§133–4.

[122] Ibid., §139.

[123] Ibid., note to §140.

a universal law.[124] The trouble with this, Hegel argues, is that it is a purely formal principle.[125] It tells us what kind of rules count as moral rules (universalizable prescriptions to do good), but it doesn't tell us in what the good consists, and therefore which of the rules conforming to this criterion we should adopt. It doesn't help us choose between competing moral codes. For example, it doesn't enable us to choose between a system of private property or one of communism. For to act according to the principle that I should be allowed to help myself to other people's property is clearly immoral if I expect to be able to exclude them and keep things myself. But to adopt the notion that we should all share informally in the use of things as a universal rule, so that others can use things I have as well, is not in conflict with Kant's principle, although it might well be almost indistinguishable from the first principle if adopted unilaterally by an individual in a society which retained private property. Kant's rule enables us to distinguish moral, from immoral principles, but it doesn't enable us to choose between different moral orders which we might inhabit: monogamous/polygamous, private property-based/communistic.[126]

It is, as a matter of psychological fact, individuals' consciences that give them the certainty that is necessary to adhere to one set of rules rather than another.[127] But the problem, as we have seen, is that conscience cannot guarantee the moral integrity of its own content. Hegel has been trying to show how, on objective grounds, morality could be shown to be necessary and now having shown the inadequacy of Kant's attempt to derive morality from rationality alone, he seems to be in danger of being thrown back on the individual's purely subjective feelings. Indeed in historical periods when the world or a society is corrupt and there is no social consensus as to the 'good' then philosophers tend to look within themselves or beyond the world for some content to morality instead of accepting its determination by their society.[128]

As Plato's *Republic* exemplifies, amongst the Greeks the ideal of a good man and the possibility of realizing a good life, was impossible outside the good city: virtue seemed to derive from civic circumstance. The failed aspiration to moral self-sufficiency of the stoics is a good example of what happens when society provides no context for a moral life. What excited Hegel about Kant was the latter's claim to have successfully revived the stoic derivation of morality from reason itself; and therefore to hold out the possibility of moral principles not tied to the values of a particular society. What disappointed him was that it remained only an abstract notion of morality devoid of specific content. The idea of the will as free seemed to demand that its content be freed from the inculcation of merely traditional principles, or external circumstances and authority. In art the attempt to establish the autonomy of the individual creative mind, and the attempt to achieve a subjective accord with nature are both aspects of the romantic movement. But the attempt to embody this highly abstract and thus volatile notion of freedom in social

---

[124] Immanuel Kant, *Groundwork of the Metaphysics of Morals,* tr. H.J. Paton, (New York & London, 1964[1948]) p. 88.

[125] *Philosophy of Right*, note to §135.

[126] Ibid., §135 and note. To be fair, Kant too presents his supreme principle as a formal criterion of subordinate moral principles. Yet he does talk about 'deriving' duties from it and claims that 'all duties . . . are fully set out in their dependence on our single principle.' *Metaphysic of Morals*, p. 91.

[127] Ibid., §136.

[128] Ibid., note to §138. See above, pp. 414, 417.

institutions led, according to Hegel, to the disastrous excesses of the French Revolution.[129] On the other hand to accept the content of our wills as determined by historically given tastes, culture and aims, if these are seen as something external to us, or at least something contingent, seems to destroy our freedom. For who we are, and therefore what we will, is determined by the accidents of when and where we were born. It is only if this historically given content of our wills and personalities can itself be seen as a rational subject in which we participate that this opposition is resolved.[130] This of course is Hegel's view of the relationship between the individual and *Geist* or world consciousness. The third part of the *Philosophy of Right* only succeeds as an answer to the questions raised in the first two, if we can accept his philosophy of history, for only then can the customs and institutions of the modern liberal state appear as a necessary expression of our conscious natures, rather than a historical contingency, albeit a reasonable one.

For Hegel the determinate content of our morality, the traditional culture and ethics of a society, is given us by the historical circumstances in which we are born. But these circumstances are not arbitrary.[131] They are a result of the rational unfolding of Spirit through history in the medium of human consciousness. Consequently the social determinants of our personality are not the chance result of something that is essentially external to us; on the contrary they are the rational result of something of which we are ourselves a part: World Spirit or *Geist*.[132]

The culture of an actual community can provide us with customs and duties which provide abstract morality with a rational content. Such duties, although they can, from the position of abstract right appear as an imposition, are in fact a liberation from mere subjection to natural or capricious impulses, and from the aimlessness of a will devoid of any particular desire or aspiration.[133]

An aspect of this view of Hegel's which worries modern liberal thinkers is that it seems to make society prior to, and determinant of the individual and so provide a licence for all sorts of repressive and authoritarian relationships. Hegel does indeed claim such a relationship between the state and individual but the extent to which he believed this justified totalitarian or even authoritarian relationships has been grossly exaggerated. Quite apart from whether or not such claims for the state follow strictly from this view, it can hardly be denied that Hegel is right in pointing out that the notion of an individual having any recognizable identity, wants, aims etc. outside of a particular society, whether in that 'state of nature' so beloved of contract theorists, or as the 'autonomous consumer'

---

[129] *Phenomenology of Spirit*, §§582–590.

[130] *Philosophy of Right*, §147.

[131] Ibid., §141, note: 'Ethical life is a subjective disposition, but one that is imbued with what is inherently right.'

[132] Hegel, *Philosophy of History*, tr. J. Sibree (New York, 1956) p. 10 'the history of the World['s] . . . development has been a rational process; . . . has constituted the rational necessary course of the World-Spirit — that Spirit whose nature is always the same, but which unfolds this its one nature in the phenomena of the World's existence.' Or as he puts it more tersely at the end of the *Philosophy of Right*, 'History is Mind clothing itself with the form of events . . . '§346.

[133] Ibid., §149.

of free-market economics is clearly quite unrealistic as social theory, however desirable or useful it may be as a legal fiction or as economic (or ideological) shorthand.[134]

Hegel has now answered the question he set himself in his youth, concerning the relationship between the immediate community of the Greek polis, and modern society. Although close, the relationship between individual and society in Greece was unself-conscious and unthinking, and so not fully rational. It could be destroyed by rationalism in the way Socrates destroyed Euthyphro's certainty of his beliefs. The differentiation of mind in the Roman world and Christianity was a necessary part of the process of recovering unity at a higher level, through rational understanding rather than the immediate sympathy of the small Greek polis.[135] The modern state, as we shall see, can not only survive rational scrutiny, but reserves for the individual a substantial arena of subjective, private freedom, thus not only realizing the objective freedom that so worries liberals, but comprising within that, and as a part of itself, subjective freedom.

Ethical culture

There are three focal points, or 'moments' as Hegel calls them, in his discussion of ethical culture or the customary ethical institutions of modern society. Each represents a different, and progressively more complex stage of the collective mentality, the family, in which unity is unreflective and therefore immediate, civil society in which unity is mediated by reflective and divisive individualism, and the state itself, in which unity is reasserted at both the subjective and objective levels.

The family

Within the family individuals are bonded together immediately through love and affection. Family relationships, unlike those in civil society, are emotional and altruistic, not calculating or instrumental; or if they are, there is something wrong with the family! Because, through love, individuals' wills are merged with others, rights as such – the expression of a single will in such a way as to exclude other wills – do not appear within the family. Marriage for example is not really a contract so much as an 'agreement to transcend a contract'; parents do not strictly have personal 'rights' over their children, rather they have obligations to educate them out of childishness and into the world of ethical culture. This requires a certain measure of authority which is indeed irresistible, but it is also limited, and forfeitable if abused.[136] Viewed naturalistically marriage is rooted in the natural physical requirements of the species to reproduce itself, and as a subjective impression in the minds of the individuals concerned it is self-conscious love.

[134] In the *Phenomenology*, Hegel denies that a natural 'individual' is possible. Nature being a realm where what individuates individuals from their species *cannot* be spirit or consciousness. Individuality therefore can only be possible within cultures, and more so within some cultures than within others. §489.

[135] *Philosophy of Right*, note to §185 and see above p. 417.

[136] On the marriage contract, ibid., note to §75, note to §163; on parental duties and the inadequacy of rights: ibid., §43, 175; but children, like savages, may be coerced in the interests of their education, §93, note.

But Hegel denies that it is either biology or the contingent attraction of two individuals for each other that is the essential element in marriage (any more than subjective need, or desire was the essential element in property or contract, rather than the need for the objective recognition of will). He even suggests that arranged matches might be, and certainly in less reflective, individualistic societies are, as reasonable as voluntaristic marriages. What is required is the coincidence of the wills of the partners and the institution itself. For Hegel, it does not seem to matter which comes first so long as there is, eventually, congruence.[137]

What initially makes a marriage is the partners' shared awareness of a unifying aim, which necessarily, and properly (in Hegel's view) overcomes the transience of physical passion.[138] It cannot ultimately be a contract, although civil society here as elsewhere may try to insinuate itself into this sphere by attempting to reduce it to one. Kant's notion that marriage is a contract for the exclusive use of the partners' sexual properties is denounced by Hegel as a consequence of this view.[139] A marriage is an agreement to transcend a contract.[140] It is an attempt (and necessarily the first) to create a real and enduring community of wills, but the romantic emphasis on feeling, does not mean that feeling itself is enough to establish marriage's objective existence; for feeling, even if shared, remains purely subjective. What gives it true ethical existence (or should, if it does not become a cold or empty formality) is the ceremonial through which the unity of the pair is given an objective existence in the minds and lives of other members of the family and friends. Rather as property can only be made objective through the recognition that contract provides, so marriage can only be made objective through the recognition that ceremonial provides. The fact that this precedes intercourse (what Hegel coyly calls 'the sensuous moment') is for him, an institutional representation of the philosophical truth that the physical element of marriage is secondary and subordinate to the ideal of unity.[141]

A marriage is not a homogeneous unity. The minds of the partners are characteristically different. Hegel believes that the mind has sexuality. Woman's consciousness is superior in the emotional aspects of life, more subjectively certain, practical. The family, and family loyalties are therefore closer to a woman than the more objective and remote law of society.[142] This is exemplified in the tragedy of *Antigone*, forced to choose between obeying her family duty to bury her rebel brother, and her political duty to obey the king's command that he be left unburied.[143] Men, on the other hand, are supposedly more

---

[137] Ibid., note to §162.

[138] Ibid., §163.

[139] Ibid., note to §75.

[140] Ibid., note to §163.

[141] Ibid., §164 and note.

[142] This also, in Hegel's view, justifies sexual double standards; for, since the female mind is made for the home, sexual 'surrender' outside marriage leads to loss of honour. However, because men have an 'ethical' life outside the home, 'the case is otherwise with them'. Ibid., addition to §164. This is pretty transparent stuff, and Hegel at his worst. He provides no account of why 'ethical life' outside the family should involve sexual relations; and because he is reluctant to rest ethical institutions on biological facts, he cannot even resort to the then conventional 'justification' that the assymetry is based on the risk of pregnancy to the woman.

[143] Ibid., §166.

self-conscious and reflective, end-directed and speculative. A certain Hegelian professor of politics, used to respect these differences by asking his men students what they *thought* about questions in tutorials, whilst asking women what they *felt*! There was a time, quite recently, when such views would have been difficult to defend, evidence of Hegel's failure to transcend the limits of his time. However, the question of whether there is a gender-specific determinant to mentality has now, interestingly become an issue entertained not only by extreme male chauvinists, but also by certain radical feminists.[144]

The marriage effectively creates a new collective personality out of the mutual surrender of the two partners to another (and is therefore essentially monogamous).[145] Like other personalities, the marriage expresses itself in the first instance in property: the family home and capital. Like other personalities if the family lacks property it will not be able to express itself fully.[146]

But the most perfect manifestation of this new unity is in the production of children, who embody the unity and love of the parents.[147] It is through the family, and the education it provides into the way of life of a society, that culture perpetuates itself from generation to generation. This is recognized by the Roman gods of the hearth and home who are identified with the ancestors. Although children are free, and cannot, as the Romans claimed, be treated as property, they do not have a right to resist instruction.[148] For they are originally free only in the limited sense of being subject to natural influences. It is the job of parents to see that these are replaced by an acceptance of ethical and cultural principles which represent not the illusory freedom of following their own natural impulses, but freedom as the social system of objective right.[149]

The family ceases to exist, in two senses. Particular families release their offspring into adulthood, and, sometimes, their parents themselves separate through divorce, either process yielding a collection of isolated individuals – the material of civil society.[150] Secondly, in a wider historical perspective, the family in the looser sense of the clan group, may either disintegrate, or, paradoxically grow into a nation state and thereby lose its family character, but in either case yield place to civil society.[151] Both personally and historically then, civil society – the exchange economy – replaces the clan – the extended-family-as-productive-unit, as the individual's social environment.

---

[144] Liberal feminists tend to deny inherent gender difference, other than biological. A classic liberal rights based statement is Betty Friedan *The Feminine Mystique* (1963). At least some radical feminists, on the contrary, like Hegel, tend to emphasize the biological basis of gender differences, although they differ as to whether this should be endorsed or eradicated. M.Daly *Gyn/Ecology: the Metaethics of Radical Feminism* (Boston, 1978), Shulamith Firestone *The Dialectic of Sex: The Case for a Feminist Revolution* (London and New York, 1971).

[145] Ibid., §167.

[146] Ibid., §169.

[147] Ibid., §173.

[148] Nor to resist being punished. As Hegel has already explained, this is not quite the punishment that rights a wrong, but the right of civilized will to coerce the 'natural' or 'untutored will' which is 'implicitly a force against the implicit idea of freedom which must be protected against such an uncivilised will and be made to prevail in it', note to §93. The untutored will is not yet capable of vice, only savagery, but savagery too denies (the general principle of) right and is therefore wrong. Cf. Rousseau on natural man — amoral, but not immoral. See also Hegel, *Philosophy of Mind*, §480, 'the Rights of the Father'.

[149] *Philosophy of Right*, §§173 — 5.

[150] Ibid., §176. Note Hegel's support for legal divorce, §177, §181.

[151] Ibid., §181, note; and see references to this process at §238, 141.

Ethical culture: civil society

Civil society deals with relationships between individuals outside of the family, relationships which are not immediate in the sense of depending directly on emotional bonds of
feeling or kinship, real or imagined. Instead such relationships are based on the subjective
mutual needs and desires of individuals, mediated by exchange. Civil society depicts
concrete (not abstract) wills – that is individuals with a given repertoire of desires and
preferences, a sense of right and wrong and shared moral perceptions. This doesn't make
them complete altruists. They still pursue their private wants, but the means they are
prepared to use are now modified by contract, the moral principle of universality and the
conventions and customs obtaining in the particular society. Individuals' wills are
therefore so related that their wants are found to mesh rather than clash. The egoistic
pursuit of desire is one of the polarities of civil society; the automatic resolution of them
through the operation of market exchanges is the other. [152]

The first tendency represents individualism, particularity, and in a quite threatening
sense, a centrifugal movement away from the social collectivity. When this individualism
had emerged in the past – as in the Greek city state – it had proved an insuperable threat
to society, and the pursuit of subjective desires was, for example in Plato's *Republic*, for
that reason rejected or suppressed.[153] It is one of the strengths of the modern state, and a
proof of its superiority over its classical predecessors Hegel thinks, that it can accommodate this element of 'subjective freedom' without falling apart. The achievements of
modern societies are accomplished through the freely expressed desires and contracts of
individuals, and not, as were the monuments of ancient Middle Eastern civilizations
through the state direction of human labour. Civil society is, on this face of it, simply a
system for satisfying private wants. Indeed it is all the state itself could amount to when
viewed from the level of understanding, for of what else could the state be composed for
those who only recognize the actual subjective wants of individuals?[154] Thus the
utilitarians – who are both methodological individualists and empiricists – misconceive
the state, they see it as civil society, just as the patriarchalists saw it as essentially a
family.

The second tendency in civil society – towards unity – is, at least at first, hidden. It
operates, as it were, behind the backs of the actors, and without their knowledge. Unity
is a result, although not an intention of their actions, but it nevertheless renders coherent
and rational what appears anarchic and subjective. From Mandeville's scandalous claim
that 'private vices' could add up to 'public virtues', through Adam Smith's famous
'hidden hand' of the market, the eighteenth century had become fascinated with the way
individual's actions produced collectively unintended (and benign) consequences. Hegel
too is fascinated by the 'show of rationality' which economic science manages to reveal

---

[152] Ibid., §182.
[153] Ibid., note to §185.
[154] Ibid., §183.

in the mass of subjective aims which comprise market phenomena.[155] However Hegel argues that for the state to achieve rationality it must not only be socially coherent, it must be seen to be so by its citizens. Otherwise, as in the case of classical Greece, gaps can emerge between the objective and the subjective perception which effectively destroys that unity. So Hegel is also concerned to show how this second principle, of unity, can emerge as a subjective aim or ideal in people, rather than remaining an emergent property of their aggregate egoism. Only if unity can be subjectively *and* objectively realized, alongside individuality, can the state and civil society be coherently interrelated.[156]

Within civil society three sets of institutions embody, and seek the resolution of, these polarities. They are the system of needs, the legal system and the police and corporations.[157]

Civil society: the system of needs

This system of needs is essentially the modern commercial economy, an idea particularly explored by thinkers of the Scottish Enlightenment of whom Adam Smith is the most famous. From them Hegel had gained not only insights into the nature of a society dominated by exchanges carried out in a free market, but also the notion of history as a series of phases characterized primarily by different forms of economic activity, on which moral, social and political relationships were clearly dependent. In Hegel's early works the basis of economic determinism in his analysis is still prominent.[158] In his mature works, however, Hegel plays down this element, emphasising instead the primacy of a certain frame of mind, as evidenced in social culture as characterizing the stages of development, and hence the pattern of economic activity.

---

[155] Ibid., note to §189. Mandeville's *Fable of the Bees* had scandalised a generation and more by setting out to show systematically how individuals' vices nevertheless benefited society as a whole, primarily by showing how avarice sets the wheels of commerce in motion:

'Thus every Part was full of Vice,
Yet the whole Mass a Paradise;'

The Fable of the Bees, ed. F. B. Kaye (2 vols, Oxford, 1924; repr. Bloomington, Indiana, 1988) vol. 1, p. 24.

[156] *Philosophy of Right*, §187, note: For society this requires institutions which raise individuals out of their self-centredness to appreciate the collective nature of life as an enterprise of the human spirit. For individuals it also requires education in the widest sense. Mind becomes objective by internalising the culture which provides it with real options, by suppressing or overcoming its 'natural simplicity'. Ironically the external realm is not the true and absolute realm of freedom, this lies within the mental world itself — in art, religion and philosophy — yet it is through undergoing an education provided by the external world of objective spirit — the world of culture as conveyed in society — that we can be educated to the point where we can make the transition to the world of absolute spirit.

[157] Ibid., §188.

[158] See above p. 418, and especially the studies by Lukács, *The Young Hegel*, and Plant, *Hegel*.

The nature of need

The variety of ways in which human beings satisfy their needs fulfills Hegel's notion that society, like other aspects of mind, is to be unified through differentiation and not through homogenization. Thus Hegel's ideal is not (as Marx's) that we should each be able to do all of the jobs that society needed – for this would make us independent and potentially isolate us. Rather we should each do one of the things that society needed, thus creating interdependence, and through that, unity.

Need can be satisfied through external material things which (as property) are owned, and therefore have to be acquired. The acquisition of them involves work. Work is what links need or desire and its object. Individuals do this when they exert effort to acquire some natural thing. But such individual efforts have no implications for a social world. To be *social*, work or labour needs to be separated from the direct satisfaction of *my* desire, and linked instead, through exchange, to the satisfaction of another's desire. In a commercial society the separation of need from desire creates an expanding network of exchanges in which I do something for A who does something for B who does something for C and so on and so forth until the circle is complete. This has the effect of making desire 'objective' or real, in the sense of existing for others. Were we each to satisfy our desires directly through our own work, they (and we) would not exist for one another, and so would fail to achieve objectivity.[159] Moreover although each exchange is egoistically, and even competitively motivated, the overall effect – and one that is reinforced as civil society progresses – is not only to create equality of respect, but to integrate the actors.[160]

To do this there must be many desires, and Hegel turns now to the problem that had so exercised Rousseau: how human needs are, unlike those of animals, not static but dynamic. Humans' needs grow constantly as they invent new conveniences and transform them into necessities. In the end, need becomes detached from biological requirement, and rests on 'opinions' about what we want, opinions that others seek to manipulate in order to profit from them.[161] Hegel has both a more developed sense of how this process works, and a more positive view of it than Rousseau. Human needs are increased firstly by diversifying the range of ways in which they might be satisfied. Thus the need for food can be diversified into a need for sweet and savoury things; a need for sweet things into a need for dairy creams, fruits, honeys of various kinds; the need for dairy creams into ice cream, yoghurt, butter etc.; the need for ice cream into any of the numerous flavours now available. The creation of diversity makes us dissatisfied with what comes to appear as monotony, and to see what had previously been a luxury as a need. This is

---

[159] The idea of determinate existence as 'being for another' is central to Hegel's whole philosophy, see *Logic*, §§91–3. The doctrine is referred to in *Philosophy of Right* §48 (note), & §71, and argued as a necessary moment of consciousness in the passages of the *Phenomenology* discussed above, see e.g. §175. It plays a role in the emergence of the identity of the state too, see below, p. 475.

[160] *Philosophy of Right*, §§189, 196 (work), 192 (exchange). The idea that 'le doux commerce', in some general way promoted social harmony gained increasing acceptance in the eighteenth century. It was only as capitalism took on an increasingly industrial character in the nineteenth century that its own specific class-generating properties became apparent.

[161] *Philosophy of Right*, notes to §§190, 191.

more or less Rousseau's story. But Hegel, drawing on Adam Smith's account of the division of labour, perceives another process taking place.

It is not only needs themselves that are diversified but (in the very process), also the means to them. Thus the business of meeting the subjective need of the consumer of the end product comes to be broken up into a series of 'abstract' needs on the part of the producers of intermediate components. Thus to sell ice cream, the maker will need to buy in from others: tubs or wrappers, fats, milk, flavourings etc. Since these products are not themselves subjectively 'enjoyed', or 'consumed' by actual individuals they are 'abstract' needs. But they are universal, because it is through being linked by these kinds of needs — which are separated from the subjective desire that characterizes personal consumption and enjoyment — that agents can come to recognize the *social*, and not merely the *subjective* character of the system of need-satisfaction.[162] There is no end to this process of refining needs, and at a certain point it results in luxury. Although Rousseau saw a loss of freedom in the proliferation of need, luxury and the resulting dependency; Hegel points out that the elaboration of artificial need entails emancipation from natural need and so has in it 'an aspect of liberation'. This is because to be subject to natural need is to be subject to something external, whereas social needs, even ephemeral ones such as those arising from fashion, are themselves a product of consciousness, which is what we essentially are.[163] Once artificial need can be seen as expressive of what we are (mind, or consciousness) rather than an imposition (on what we are not, i.e. nature), its role can be seen as a freeing or enabling one, rather than, as Rousseau saw it, as constraining or corrupting.

The kinds of work

Work is the means of meeting need. Means of meeting need that have been worked on possess value, which is universalized use or utility.[164] Work is therefore potentially the meeting of another's need (and when actually so, through exchange, becomes objectified need).[165] Given the existence of an exchange-economy, work is need-satisfaction in general, and has the capacity to adapt to the multiplicity of needs continually being thrown up by society. Therefore, within an exchange economy, work is informed by a mind flexible enough to perceive changing needs and to adopt means to meet them.[166]

[162] Ibid., §190 (two ways of multiplying need), §§191–2 (intermediate, abstract needs creating recognition of social nature). The analysis is picked up again at §198, where the role of the division of labour is made clearer. Despite the influence of the more sceptical Steuart, and the idiosyncratic interpretation of Smith in Germany, this stress on the fundamental and largely benign generation of social needs and luxury in the creation of the modern economy is an assertion which dominates Hegel's view. Many of Hume and Smith's Scots contemporaries, including Steuart and Ferguson, were more cautious in their endorsement of the process. See the masterful discussion by Istvan Hont, 'The Rich Country — Poor Country Debate' in Scottish classical political economy', in *Wealth and Virtue*, ed. Istvan Hont and Michael Ignatieff (Cambridge, 1983).

[163] Ibid., §194.

[164] Ibid., §63.

[165] Ibid., §196 Hegel's transition here is extremely compressed. I have done what I can with it.

[166] Ibid., §197.

Ironically Hegel points to another aspect of work in commercial society. This has rather threatening consequences, which, in due course he will acknowledge, but from which Marx was to draw the most cataclysmic implications. The end result of the abstraction of needs and division of labour inherent in the articulation of the production process into distinct operations, is that the kind of labour demanded, whilst at first more specialized, becomes gradually less and less skilled as workers perform smaller and smaller parts of the production process. Eventually the tasks become so subdivided and unskilled they can be done by a machine and the worker is no longer needed.[167]

Capital and class divisions

The satisfaction of need occurs in three different ways giving rise to three characteristic types of activity; they are, agriculture, commerce and industry, and administration. These divisions, or classes, are defined in terms of the nature of their work and the needs they satisfy. Classes include all individuals, employers and employees alike, involved in that particular sector of the economy. Hegel sees different modes of life producing different kinds of personalities, characterized, like mental concepts in terms of immediate, reflective and universal.[168]

The immediate or substantial class is the agricultural sector. It is immediate because it produces directly for need, moreover it is tied to the rhythms of nature in a way that offers little scope for opportunistic, reflective innovation. It is not fundamentally mediated by changing tastes or technology: as a social whole it is universalistic and all-encompassing, but its universality is immediate, not reflective. It is characterized by feeling: custom, tradition and paternalism. Though Hegel recognizes the beginnings of 'industrialized agriculture' he does not think modernization will change the essential nature of agricultural life. Although thus limited, agriculture was essential to the emergence of the state, for it was only with the cultivation of the soil that communities could take on a fixed geographical location, and thus combine the identity of people and space which comprises the state. Subsequently, however, the agricultural class takes on some of the more differentiated characteristics that result from the emergence of other classes.[169]

In the second class, the class of business and production, particularity is made explicit in the reflective, interest-calculating, way of thinking that typifies individuals in it. It operates either at the level of craft workers producing individual needs, through machines producing mass needs, or through commerce which, as exchange, provides potentially for any and all particular needs. There universality is reduced to a property of the whole, which emerges from, but is in tension with, the particular interests rampant here. It is only in a third class, the civil servants, that universal interests and particular are both made explicit and reconciled. It is their task as individuals (and it is also the way they

---

[167] Ibid., §198. Hegel seems to see this as a tendency within particular industries, not, as Marx does, as an ineluctable process of capitalist development itself. It nevertheless poses problems at the general level which Hegel picks up again at §243.

[168] Ibid., §202.

[169] Ibid., §203, and addition.

meet their own private needs) to meet those universal needs of the community which would not be provided for by individual action.[170]

Individuals have a choice in the kind of work they do. This is enormously important since, Hegel claims, it objectively embodies the principle of the will as subjectively free; and he contrasts this choice with societies such as caste societies, or Plato's *Republic* where individuals' work and life-chances are determined by the accident of birth, revealing still a belief that man is determined by nature, not consciousness. Hegel might have observed here that it is the Guardians, the embodiment of reason, who in fact determine the 'accidents of birth' by rigging the ballot behind the scenes. It would be entirely congruent with his belief that earlier philosophies reveal a truth of which they were not themselves quite aware, to see this as an unconscious allegory of the way in which, in the fully developed and rational state, the rational division of classes lies behind, and appears to be the expression of, what appear to be the arbitrary and subjective choices of individuals' wills. [171]

Choosing a way of life and thereby gaining membership of a class is part of two parallel developments. Firstly it provides the individual with a way of particularizing the merely abstract potential for personality and in doing so gives him standing in the community. But secondly it is at the same time part of the process which lifts the individual from the particular, from a concern merely with self, to an awareness of the more universal aspects of human community. This process will culminate in the state.

To be a real as opposed to an abstract person, one must be a member of a class. Hegel suggests that the young hold back from allowing their characters to be determined by such a move. Yet this is to aspire after the kind of abstract freedom which cannot really exist, and which if persisted in will result in alienation and even madness. To become a real personality is to become one particular personality, and not another. Whilst this closes off some possible avenues of development it is foolish to think of this as an imposition on one's freedom.[172] In the modern world, although accidents of birth still affect men's lives to a degree, we have, within the scope of our natural aptitudes, some choice as to how we lead our lives, what kind of work we do. In this respect the modern state allows more freedom to the individual. Because those freedoms are expressed within a rational social order they cannot threaten to destroy the society as Greek society's unreflective freedom was destroyed.[173] The form through which such choices are made actual is property and the maintenance and guarantee of property is the system of justice.

Civil society: the system of justice

Whatever limitations Hegel's philosophy imposes on what can legitimately be the content of legislation, Hegel is very clear that law must conform, in its general principles to certain universal standards. Legality involves clear and knowable laws; it involves giving legal form to all the concepts Hegel has shown to be necessary in his derivation of society from abstract right: personality, property, contract, wrong, punishment, marriage, the family.[174] Since these now derive their existence from an actual legal code,

---

[170] Ibid., §§204, 203.
[171] Ibid., §206.
[172] Ibid., §207.

[173] Ibid., §207, and note to §206.
[174] Ibid., §217.

offences against them (crimes) can the more easily be seen not simply as an infringement of individual right, but an infringement of right, and an injury to society in general.[175] Punishment administered by law, can escape the appearance of subjective revenge which it will otherwise always risk appearing as. Indeed, to avoid this appearance of revenge, the prosecution of criminals is commonly undertaken by the state, or public prosecutor, rather than the injured party. [176] The fact that the conceptual manifestations of right are given embodiment in law, does not mean they have status only as legal realities. In this sense Hegel is no legal positivist. Nevertheless, it is only through being given legal expression that the principles of right can be made objectively real. What this entails is a widely known code of laws.[177] Hegel has harsh criticism for legal systems, such as those of English Common Law, which do not rest on codified law.[178]

Hegel, who has often been charged with responsibility for the extremes of nationalism prevalent in Germany, is in fact at pains to reject the ideas of the 'historical school' of German legal theorists who identified legality with positively existing, and historically defined law. Thinkers such as Müller, Haller and the reactionary Savigny and their associated movements wanted to defend a uniquely German law based on national tradition and precedent. In this they represented the historical and conservative aspects of romanticism's revolt against the rationalistic approach of the Enlightenment, much given to attempts at universalizing legal principles, and reaching their apogee in the Code Napoléon. Here, as elsewhere Hegel can be seen trying to combine divergent aspects of the Enlightenment, universalist rationalism and an awareness of historical particularity. For Hegel, law is the expression of what is essentially rational, i.e. mind and must ultimately conform to rational principles. The mere fact of a law's existence could never in itself, therefore, be sufficient grounds for its retention. In this Hegel is better placed than Burke with whom he shares a reverence for the past as a rational process which has produced the present. For Burke, the past remains mysterious, as does the process by which it produces the present; indeed Burke was a major influence on the German historical school of law whom Hegel is here criticizing.[179] Hegel claims reason must be used to discriminate within our historically acquired experience. The historical origins of a legal system must never be confused with its conceptual status, which is precisely the concrete embodiment of that universal authority required to prevent legal punishment being seen as revenge.

A legal system is, like other elements of Hegel's social system, made actual through the synthesis of the universal and the particular. The application of judgement to particular cases is one aspect of that synthesis; but what is important – 'the fundamental thing' as Hegel puts it – is that this synthesis should be subjectively recognized by the

---

[175] Ibid., §218.

[176] Ibid., §220.

[177] Ibid., §216.

[178] Ibid., §211, and note, §213.

[179] Burke made a profound impression on Müller and was in fact translated into German by his close friend and associate, Friedrich Gentz, Hertz, *German Public Mind*, pp. 53, 206–7. On Burke's European reception see Rodney Preece, 'Edmund Burke and his European Reception', *Eighteenth Century: Theory and Interpretation*, vol. 21, no.3 (1980).

citizen as taking place, hence the importance of public proceedings and a jury system.[180] Justice must be seen to be done as well as done.

What the legal system represents for Hegel is the reunification of the universal and the subjective particular, principles which, though present, were in apparent contradiction in the workings of the economy. But the reunification afforded by law is strictly limited. It is limited to the abstract assertion of right, and its embodiment in those particular cases which come before the courts.[181] That is to say, although a legal code is a formalized, recognized and therefore actual expression of right, the positive enjoyment of those rights by citizens still rests on various contingencies, which cannot themselves be guaranteed by the legal system. This is an implied criticism of the now prevalent liberal view that mere justice is sufficient to sustain community.[182] These deficiencies therefore point to the need for some further institutions within civil society to overcome this opposition between the principle of particularity – individual right, and that of universality (community), without however undermining the now established expression of individual right. To ensure that all members of the society experience this unity to at least some extent there is a public authority (police), and to provide it completely for some, there are corporations.[183] That neither provides complete integration for all, points to the ultimate inability of civil society to reconcile its own tensions, and to the need for something beyond it – 'a power out of ourselves', as Burke had put it – to sustain the collectivity.[184]

Civil society: the police and corporations

The system of laws and its enforcement exists only to protect man in general: man as he is presupposed by civil society, with a minimum of capital, some personal skills and education provided by his family and membership of a particular class. Law thus protects an abstract universal idea of man; it cannot protect individuals who do not possess these characteristics.

Because the rights guaranteed to individuals in civil society are abstract, i.e. there is protection of property (for those who have it) but no property rights (for those who don't), the capacity of individuals to sustain or realize their welfare is dependent on their chance holdings of property, possession of saleable skills and so on with which they can enter the market.[185]

Since the consequences of free individuals' actions, or their voluntary associations will, even when not criminal, impinge on other individuals in ways which are in principle unpredictable, the possibility of wrong to others resulting from them is ever-present. The

---

[180] *Philosophy of Right*, §227–8, esp. notes. The importance of the jury system, and of publicity of proceeding is emphasised by Hegel in this respect.

[181] Hegel's technical terminology here, defeats me. He seems to want to assert both that the legal system is Right's 'determinate mode of being' (§219) *and* that the universality it achieves is only 'that of abstract right.' (§229) Determinate and abstract are strictly antithetical in Hegel's system. Cf. *Logic*, §89 & §164.

[182] See for example the work of Dworkin, Ackerman, Gutman etc. etc.

[183] *Philosophy of Right*, §228.

[184] Hegel picks up these limitations in his transition to the State at ibid., §256.

[185] Ibid., §§230, 237.

456

public authority therefore has a general duty of surveillance and oversight which must go beyond a concern with what is merely criminal.[186] Hegel is concerned both with the external effects on third parties of legitimate market transactions, for example with the potentially monopolistic effects of associations, *and* with the haphazard distribution of the endowments needed to enter the market in the first place. Either may undermine the rights of individuals, and thereby require supervision.[187]

Hegel therefore rejects the notion that the free market is self-regulating. In particular he attacks the version of that doctrine enshrined in the 'law' of the French economist Jean-Baptiste Say, that supply and demand will invariably and involuntarily reach equilibrium. Despite the right of individuals to contract freely with one another, the public authority has the right to intervene to regulate the prices of necessities to ensure they are within the reach of ordinary people. Hegel's argument for this is not very convincing. It is that being necessities, they are needed by everyone and so offered to the community as a whole, rather than to an individual. The community therefore, in the form of the public authority, has the right to stipulate the terms of the offer.[188] Not only individual goods consumed by everyone, but, and here the argument is more convincing, collective goods enjoyed by the whole society – street-lighting, the infrastructure of transport, public health – are rightfully subject to social intervention. Moreover even private goods of a strategic nature, and subject to unpredictable external factors, can take on the character of public goods.[189] Hegel seems to recognize here, what extremist defenders of laissez-faire often forget: that industries can collapse for reasons completely external to what we normally regard as their economic efficiency – foreign wars (or cartels) can temporarily interrupt the supplies of raw materials, and secondly that market interests cannot take into account the strategic importance to the state of particular products.

Whilst it is originally the family (both historically, as clan or tribe, and within the individual's life as the domestic environment) that provides for individuals' material and educational needs, the destruction of the family leaves civil society to fulfil this role. Historically, as the individualism of the commercial world supplants the collective whole, and as the private appropriation of natural resources denies the individual access to unclaimed land and natural capital, civil society isolates and deprives individuals of their natural endowments. Civil society as 'the new family' must ensure that they do not suffer as a result of this by equipping them with the education and skills to survive in their new environment.[190] Society must also stand in for parents who neglect their duties.[191] What Hegel has to say here is quite consistent with his particular brand of liberalism. Although he justifies considerable state supervision of education and upbringing of children, this is because he recognizes, as many liberals fail to, that personality cannot simply be assumed as given, and that education and the formation of personality is an essential prerequisite for the exercise of freedom. On this view, being cavalier about how citizen's personalities are formed is not liberal, it is simply irresponsible.

The most striking claim Hegel makes, however, is that poverty is not something that only occurs as a result of misfortune, the breakdown of the market or parental profligacy.

---

[186] Ibid., §§232–5.
[187] Ibid., §235.
[188] Ibid., §236.

[189] Ibid., §236, addition.
[190] Ibid., §238.
[191] Ibid., §239.

It is, he claims, endemic in the actual processes of a commercial society. For it exists not only amongst those without employment, but also amongst the lowly paid, unskilled workers increasingly produced by that very division of labour which is the principle cause of economic progress and the creation of luxury.[192] The development of the more sophisticated modern economy and the spread of property rights has not only deprived them of the most immediate means of physical existence, through denying them access to the land; it has also deprived them of the means of establishing their status as personalities through the possession of some property which would proclaim their existence in the social world. They develop a sense of resentment at the apparently irrational and chance forces which reduce them to their distressed positions. These people, the 'rabble of paupers', the ancestors of Marx's proletariat, are not simply economically deprived; for poverty alone does not create a rabble. More important, they are cut adrift from the culture in which they live. It is the role of ethical culture to educate men – in the widest sense – to provide them with a personality that fits their world. Hegel observed that modern society was failing to do this for a significant class of people.[193] In his earlier writings Hegel had remarked that to be cut off from society is to be mad, and society very often does so regard individuals who fail to 'belong' in the sense of sharing the values and customs of the group.[194] Individuals denied a status in society are also denied or themselves reject the values a social life can give them. They lose their own self-respect, for self-respect and indeed self-awareness, rely on the recognition accorded one mind by another mind, and society shows no respect to them, nor allows them the means to establish it: property.[195] They therefore see punishment and the laws of the state not as the expression of universal right, but as a 'wrong' done to them by a particularistic and alien group with whom they have no identification.[196] Objectively speaking this, whilst not 'right', is an appropriate response, for as Hegel points out 'he who has no rights has no duties'.[197]

This process cannot be allowed to proceed unchecked, nor can it be left to the haphazard operation of charity. Dealing with poverty – the creation of social dislocation – not merely starvation is, for Hegel, clearly a public responsibility, and one which involves intervention in, and regulation of market forces.[198] Consequently public authorities can control actions, even if they are not essentially illegal, by preventing individuals from harming others in non-criminal ways, for example, by profiteering from the

---

[192] Ibid., §243.

[193] Hegel was not the first to notice this, Adam Smith expressed concern about the moral and psychological effects of repetitive factory work. He also pointed to its dire implications for citizenship. (Smith, *Wealth of Nations*, V, i, f.50, 61)

[194] See especially Plant, *Hegel*, pp. 70–1, 125. Plant sees the relationship between a search for rational coherence, and its opposite — a kind of individual or even social madness, as a major theme of Hegel's.

[195] *Philosophy of Right*, §244.

[196] 'Against nature men can claim no right, but once society is established poverty immediately takes the form of a wrong done by one class against another.' Ibid., §244 (addition). As Marx was to point out, one tactic of society is to claim that the laws of economics are 'natural' and therefore beyond human control; a response which Hegel rejects out of hand.

[197] *Philosophy of Mind*, §486.

[198] *Philosophy of Right*, §240, addition: 'It is not simply starvation which is at issue; the further end in view is to prevent the formation of a pauperised rabble.' Also §242, note.

necessities of life, and by ensuring that accidental disadvantage doesn't ruin an individual's life. Furthermore, not only regulation, but provision can rightfully be undertaken
by public authorities. Consequently the cost of basic foods, the guarantee of a minimum
education and certain basic social rights can be publicly ensured.[199] There is, though, a
limit as to how far social provision may go without destroying the principle of autonomy
which the modern development of civil society has given to the individual, and without
involving public authority too much in the sphere of private choice from which it ought
really to stand apart.[200]

Charity – private or public – offends against the principle of self-sufficiency which
characterizes the individual in civil society, and would simply reinforce their loss of self-
respect. A system of publicly financed employment could provide them with work, but
who would buy their produce? The problem of unemployment is already one of
overproduction, how could it be cured through producing more? [201] Hegel sees no
resources from within society capable of doing more than ameliorate the problem.
Consequently emigration and colonization, to export both surplus goods and surplus
population is a necessary outcome of modern political economy. Apart from this
suggestion, the embryo of Marx and Lenin's theory of economic imperialism, Hegel has
no answer.[202]

The system of needs, and the problem of poverty emphasize the divisive aspects of
civil society. These are a consequence of private right and the individual's status as a
property owner established in the first part of the *Philosophy of Right*. But as Hegel tried
to show there, property was not something that could be assumed as an object; nor was
it simply a relation between individual and thing. It depended for its objective existence
on a nexus of recognition by other individuals. Property thus has not only an individuating
but also a unifying effect. This aspect of modern society enabled him to overcome his
nostalgia for the freedom of Greece and to see that modern societies could offer both
wider individual freedom, and a higher level of political awareness (and indeed for Hegel
these are interdependent) without the alienating consequences he had previously regarded as inevitable. This dual aspect of individuation and inter-dependence can be seen
in the economic phenomenon of the division of labour. The division of tasks into separate
operations divides men up, since each becomes more skilled and specialized at a
particular job. Yet, because each individual operation is pointless outside of the context
of the total process of production, it also unites men by making them mutually interde-

---

[199] Ibid., §§236, 239, 240.

[200] The public authority must draw a balance between the claims of individualists — who argue all
provision should be made through the market, and the claims of those who argue for public provision. Ibid.,
§236, addition. Hegel here reflects a longstanding debate in Germany. Not only Steuart, initially the most
influential economic thinker, but even Smith, given the way he came to be read in Germany, provided
grounds for scepticism that the economy could be self-regulating. K.Tribe, *Governing Economy, the
reformation of German economic discourse, 1750–1840* (Cambridge, 1988) pp. 136, 170–76.

[201] Ibid., §245. Hegel despite sharing the German view that the state has a role as an economic agent,
nevertheless seems to assume it has to act through the normal medium of the market. He does not seem to
have the modern conception of public works, which being infrastructural rather than consumer goods,
roads, sewer networks, etc., do not need to be bought but are financed and consumed socially, and do not
therefore add to the overproduction.

[202] The problem is one that, Hegel notes, does not exist in North America where westward migration
continually relieves civil society established in the east from this pressure. *Philosophy of History*, pp. 85–6.

pendent. Nevertheless this unity is not intended and it is Hegel's purpose now to show how the state emerges as the citizens' subjective awareness of, and commitment to, an objective system of universal right.

The particularity of civil society which threatens to dissolve human association into a competitive selfishness so well characterized by Hobbes is held in check partly by the laws, and partly by what Hegel calls the public authority (often misleadingly translated 'police') which has the task, referred to above, of mitigating the worse consequences of the free economic activity of members. But there is yet another institution, besides classes, and police authority, within civil society, which counters divisiveness and brings men's minds to a consciousness of a unity which is higher than their selfish needs. Whilst the public authority can appear to economic actors as an external, restrictive and imposed force, as indeed can the laws, the corporation is an organization within which men consciously pursue common ends.[203] A corporation is formed from members who earn their livings in sufficiently similar ways to have not only common interests, but common perceptions, through having minds shaped by that way of living. Only skilled workers and producers dedicated to a particular kind of work can form corporations, since only they have work which will differentiate them from others and give them something in common. Thus unskilled workers – the kind increasingly created by the growing division of labour – cannot comprise corporations, or, consequently be full members of civil society, or, as we shall see, have full political rights. The corporation therefore represents the transformation of egoism (particularity) into collectivism (universality), although the collectivity here is a distinctly limited one.[204]

Hegel is thus both wholly opposed to Rousseau's abolition of intermediate social groupings in the name of democratic sovereignty, and against extreme laissez-faire liberalism's hostility to economic associations. Here as elsewhere Hegel, defends a pluralist view. Recognizing the divisive nature of modern market society, he stresses that its survival presupposes spheres of community in which men can find mutual recognition and assistance, and lift their minds above their own selfish interests. Without these 'resting places' of community, the pursuit of gain is, as Aristotle had remarked, limitless. In an anomic society distinction through moneymaking is the only kind of recognition available.[205]

Corporations result from originally egoistic motives as individuals recognize the existence of common aims and the possibility of benefiting through combination. Membership of them results in a greater recognition of the benefits of collectivist principles than civil society would otherwise encourage, or even make possible.[206] Hegel sees this recognition as vital. Although universality is present in the 'hidden hand' operations of the market, it is unconscious, and insufficient to hold a community together. It is in the life of the corporations that individuals first find and consciously realize the claims of collective life which will come to fruition in the state. Hegel can be seen here, rather like J.S. Mill, addressing Rousseau's problem of the lack of civic experience which the large modern state provides for its citizens. Mill seeks to remedy this by stressing the

[203] *Philosophy of Right*, §249.

[204] Ibid., §66.

[205] Ibid., §253, note.

[206] Thus 'The sanctity of marriage and the dignity of Corporation membership are the two fixed points around which the unorganised atoms of civil society revolve'. Ibid., §255, note.

importance of local government. This was hardly possible under German conditions without seeming to undermine the already considerable difficulties posed to national unification by local jurisdictions. Hegel seeks a public role for the private citizen by trying to hold on to the political life of the surviving medieval economic corporations, only then under attack in Germany by the movement for economic liberalism.[207]

The state

Although civil society generates a certain movement of consciousness in the direction of social unity and universality; these are limited by the prevailing principle of individualism. Collective provision of welfare, Hegel thinks, cannot reach the point where it violates the underlying principle of civil society, namely self-sufficiency, and the resulting self-respect.[208] Although it's true that the provision of welfare through corporations escapes this taint, because they are essentially partial and sectional organizations this cannot reach all members of the population – particularly those systematically impoverished, unskilled labourers who are excluded from corporation membership.[209] For the same reasons, corporations cannot be allowed to function completely without external supervision. If they were, the defence of each corporate group's interests could act to the detriment of society as a whole, restricting entry, making jobs hereditary and otherwise offending the freedom of the individual. Yet again, the public authority, whilst it does impose certain self-consciously universal standards on the community, does so as an external authority with which the individual does not personally identify (as he does with his corporation). The expressly universal is not felt as such, and what is felt as universal (the corporation) is not actually so.[210] The unification of the subjective and objective principles, of both individualism and universality is required.[211] The successful functioning of the corporations, and the citizen's identification with social institutions as in some sense his own – on both of which the survival of civil society depends – is in turn dependent on some body which is above the competition and selfishness of the market. This is the state itself. Or rather it is the state in the restricted sense, for all of the institutions we have been discussing have at one time been part of the state, and are contained within it and yet presuppose it.[212]

---

[207] Ibid., addition to §255. Guild organisation and restrictions lasted well into the nineteenth century in the German states, although subject to increasing restriction by the state authorities in the name of freedom of trade. See: F. Hertz, *The German Public Mind in the Nineteenth Century* (London, 1975), pp. 164–5.

[208] *Philosophy of Right*, §245 (b). Presumably creating what has since come to be characterised as a 'dependency culture'.

[209] Ibid., note to §244.

[210] Ibid., §256.

[211] In the *Philosophy of Mind*, §535, Hegel puts it less abstractly: 'The state is the *self-conscious*, ethical substance, the unification of the family principle with that of civil society.'

[212] *Philosophy of Right*, note to §256. Hegel's point here is partly to remind the reader that the *Philosophy of Right* is not meant to be a historical sequence. The last philosophical derivation, the state, does not come into existence *after* the market economy rather the family, civil society and (modern) state are differentiated out from earlier forms of social organisation (such as the clan, or the feudal state) where all these aspects of social consciousness and organisation are still mutually embedded with the resulting injustices, unfreedoms and contradictions.

The state as a synthesis of subjective and objective freedom

At this point it might be useful to step back and consider the relationship of Hegel's conception of the state to the problems generated by those put forward by his predecessors.

Classical theories of the state, deriving principally from Aristotle, involved demonstrating that the state was a natural outgrowth. The family, the village and the polis were all natural and proper contexts for individuals; indeed, one could not be fully a human being outside such contexts. Christian Aristotelianism, epitomised in the writings of St Thomas, perpetuated this view, whilst adding a Christian and transcendent dimension. But the rise of modern science had changed man's conception of nature (and indeed, of himself) from an end-oriented, purposeful process, to, as so brutally presented in Hobbes, a mechanical and essentially meaningless one. This bifurcation of the world into material nature and a thinking, potentially free mind, posed, as we have seen, all sorts of problems for philosophers, problems which Hegel saw reflected in real life in terms of personal alienation, lack of social direction and lack of unity between man and nature, and amongst men. This bifurcation achieved its highest expression in Kant's attempts to articulate the freedom of the will (practical reason), whilst denying the applicability of the category of freedom to the natural world.

Lacking a secure basis for community in a teleological conception of nature, theories of politics in the modern world thus tended to start from the assumption of free individuals; and used the only means plausible, the contract, to account for their association. But this too posed problems. We have seen how difficult it was for Hobbes to give a psychologically convincing account of, let alone justify, the subordination of individual desire to political duty when the two came into conflict. The problem reappears in Locke's equivocation over consent and in his assumption of a 'natural political virtue' which will ensure that men can in fact by trusted to remain within the limits of the law of nature and reasonable expectations in their political judgements.[213] Rousseau recognizes the need for the state to embody freedom in the sense of being a product of men's minds and wills, yet he is so concerned about the demoralizing effects of modern liberty on the personality, that in doing so he produces an artificial reconstruction of the ancient unity of individual and state which has all the potentiality for totalitarian democracy. Rousseau's solution involved giving up the postulated freedom of the liberal individual and assimilating the individual (albeit voluntarily) back into the state again: 'the individual brings his *person* and all his possessions . . . ' (my emphasis).

Hegel recognizes and endorses the distinctively subjective basis of modern individual right.[214] Yet he also recognizes its insufficiency as the basis for a state to which there

---

[213] The phrase is Laslett's. Locke nowhere asserts such a quality, yet it seems necessary to distinguish his position on legitimacy — which is ultimately based on natural law, and a residue of Christian Aristotelianism — from popular sovereignty.

[214] *Philosophy of Right*, notes to §124 and §185. Characteristically though, Hegel sees this individual right not merely as a legal or economic right but as a principle that expresses itself in all fields; in religion as Christianity (particularly Protestantism), in the emotional life as romantic love, as artistic creativity etc.

could be any enduring, and non-selfishly motivated allegiance.[215] The abstract and selfish right of the individual must be supplemented (not suppressed) by the kind of consummate allegiance to the political community so emphasised by Aristotle and the ancients. The structure of the third part of the *Philosophy of Right* is an analogue of Aristotle's argument in Bk I of the *Politics*: dealing successively with the family, the arena of economic exchange – for Aristotle the village association – as Hegel calls it, the system of needs or civil society and finally the state.[216] All this however, is preceded in Hegel, as it could not have been for the classical Greeks, by a discussion of the nature of individual right and of the principles of morality.[217] Hegel sees in the modern state a unique synthesis of the individual freedom *and* community which exist, but separately, in civil society and the family.[218] The *Philosophy of Right* can be seen as an attempt to illuminate the relationship between these different principles and to establish a new, distinctively modern synthesis.

The modern state is the realization of human social freedom in two senses. Firstly, in the very ordinary sense that it allows people a lot of subjective liberty, a lot more than any other social form in history. But secondly, in the more philosophical and Hegelian sense that it, uniquely, he claims, comprises those institutions which enable individuals to externalize their wills (i.e. exercise freedom) without contradicting one another. Hegel believes he has shown this by demonstrating that all other attempts to embody freedom

---

[215] A state established on the basis of sovereign individuals' rights would have to be established on the basis of an (optional) contract. Since such individuals would precede the state their wills would be abstract. But an abstract will, being only form (right, property, contract etc.) without content, is unstable and capricious, and so therefore would be any state resulting from such a will. This is shown by the instability of revolutionary regimes which try, as the French did, to reform society on the basis of *abstract* principles. Ibid., note to §258 first and fourth paras.; and *Phenomenology*, §§587–9. On the other hand, points out Hegel, we should not go to the extreme of Karl Ludwig von Haller, a radical-turned-conservative legal theorist. His monumental work in six volumes, *The Restoration of Political Science*, started to come out in 1816 but was not completed until after Hegel's death, in 1834. Haller elevated custom to the complete exclusion of reason, and regarded the principles of political right as a contingent concatenation of a variety of historical circumstances. For Hegel, this uncritical endorsement of custom 'takes as the essence of the state, not what is substantive but the sphere of accident.' *Philosophy of Right*, note to §268 (final para.) On Haller in general see Hertz, *The German Public Mind*, pp. 204–6.

[216] As German scholars seem long to have recognised, in English see K. – H. Ilting in *Hegel's Political Philosophy, Problems and Perspectives*, ed. Z.A. Pelczynski, (Cambridge, 1971).

[217] The discussion of individual right and morality could not have preceded discussion of the state for the ancients because they recognised no individual right or morality prior to, or outside the state. Plato explicitly denies individual right *Laws* (932a): 'I, as your legislator, do not count either your person or your property as your own: [but] . . . as belonging to your family . . . and still more . . . as belonging to the state.' For the ancients it was virtue, and not right which was the basis of the state, and here the argument applied *a fortiori*. The *Republic* of course, is actually structured around the argument that human virtues cannot be identified or made sense of, except as 'writ large' in the state. For Aristotle too, individuals are primarily 'a part of the state' (*Politics*, 1337, a, §4) and virtuous human life is unrealizeable outside it — except for beasts or Gods. It is only with the collapse of the Greek city state that the idea of virtue became decoupled from the civic role (see esp. S. Wolin, *Politics and Vision*, (Boston, 1960) ch. 3). The question of whether virtue *can* be made sense of outside an ethical community has been revived by those thinkers who criticise the inadequacy of rights-based theories whilst recognising the absence of a positive community of shared ethics. See in particular, Alastair MacIntyre, *After Virtue, a study in moral theory* (London, 1981) and *Whose Justice? Which Rationality?* (London, 1988).

[218] *Philosophy of Right*, §§264–6.

result in inconsistencies, clashes of will (right) and developmental dead-ends of one kind or another. These inconsistencies can be demonstrated logically: as in the *Philosophy of Right*, or else historically which he does in the *Philosophy of History*, or, in that curious combination of the two the *Phenomenology of Mind*. Ultimately, of course, because Hegel conceives of concepts in a dynamic social and historical context, i.e., in actual use by human beings, rather than as symbols on paper with purely static logical properties, the two approaches yield the same result. The formal, philosophical properties of a concept will ultimately be revealed in the history of attempts to realize, or use it. So the full meaning of the concept 'state' can only be arrived at through an awareness of its historical development. Conversely: a historical understanding of the state can only be gained through philosophical reflection on the reasons why it has taken the sequence of forms that it has. Indeed, only by combining the two can we avoid attempting to impose a purely abstract theory onto the living reality of an evolving society, or, at the other extremes, either uncritically accepting all aspects of the present as a necessary product of history, or crippling nostalgia for a time and a world (such as that of ancient Greece) which has long since passed, and which has passed for reasons which are inevitable, and if properly understood, conducive to the further development of the human spirit of freedom. All these tendencies were prevalent in Hegel's time, and it is a mark of his originality that he attempts, and in large degree succeeds, in showing ways out of the dilemma that have subsequently been adopted.

The state is essentially an idea in the minds of the citizens.[219] At one – and only the most inchoate – level, it is the pure feeling of patriotism, although, as always for Hegel, pure feeling is not enough.[220] It is an idea which unifies its subjects and enables them freely and willingly to subordinate their particular interests to that of the larger whole. The existence of a sphere of particular interests, remember, is what distinguishes the modern state from the state of Greek antiquity. The modern state both allows individual freedom, and yet also creates – through nationalism – a feeling of identity with and belonging to the larger unit which would prevent it disintegrating, as did Greece, or being held together by merely legal relationships, as was Rome. In the state individuals have an idea which unites, rather than divides or is imposed on them. The unity of the state is the result of a conscious awareness, unlike that of civil society, which is the paradoxical result of selfish action. The state is conceived of not as some external agency impinging on my individual freedom but as an entity of which I am a real part. It is only if the state is so conceived that the problems which result from basing the state on individual right, can be overcome.[221]

This is an ideal answer to the problems of modern society and economy, but how is it to be realized? What institutional arrangements will ensure that the state possesses the characteristics which Hegel claims must obtain in the fully rational polity? Hegel's answer to this question must be an answer couched, at least in part, in terms of what state institutions would create that kind of perception of itself in the minds of the citizens.

---

[219] Ibid., §260. 'The state is the actuality of concrete freedom [which] consists in . . . personal individuality . . . know[ing] and will[ing] the universal..even recognis[ing] it as their own substantive mind . . . ' Again §274 . . . 'the state, as the mind of a nation, is both law permeating all relationships within the state and also at the same time the manners and consciousness of the citizens.'

[220] Ibid., §268.

[221] Ibid., §§258, 260, 264, 266.

Hegel's task – and that of modern politics – is difficult; for it involves simultaneously satisfying two, only contingently compatible conditions. The first being to construct institutions in accordance with the objective principles of right, and the second to construct institutions which satisfy subjective perceptions of right.[222] This attempt to co-ordinate an objective perception of political right with a sociology of knowledge which would render it acceptable to citizens is a major theme of all modern political thinkers, faintly perhaps in Hobbes – although he thought teaching *Leviathan* to citizens would make them more likely to behave accordingly – but increasingly in Locke, who has to assuage doubts about the consequences of his doctrine being believed, and acutely in Mandeville, Hume and Burke in whom philosophical perception and necessary popular belief are in increasing tension. Because he believes both principles are logically derived from the properties of objective mind Hegel ultimately believes them compatible, but this has to be shown.

The state can be conceived of from two perspectives, internally, in terms of its composition, and externally, in terms of its relationships with other states and its role in history. Hegel initially deals with the first although as we shall see they are related.[223]

The internal structure of the state – the constitution

One cannot provide a constitution for a state, because in an important sense the constitution of the state simply is the whole which constitutes the state.[224] By constitution here Hegel means more than the legal provisions of rule, but the whole assemblage of attitudes and beliefs, dispositions and behaviour which make it possible for the state to be a unity. No state could be brought into existence simply by imposing a set of laws on 'an agglomeration of atomic individuals' – an assertion which the experiences of emergent nations in the twentieth century show clearly enough. Indeed, even if a particular constitution *has* been fabricated at some stage, it is important that it is believed that it was not: but that it was, as Rousseau suggested, a divine gift, or at least the gift of one divinely inspired (the Legislator).[225]

A people must share a pattern of behaviour, a way of life, similar expectations about how each other behaves, how they interact with each other in terms of contractual, social and familial relationships not less than in their political life. Thus the existence of the state in the narrow political sense presupposes the existence of what Hegel has already discussed in the *Philosophy of Right*, that is a system of traditional ethics, comprising the family, social morality and civil society, all of which constitute the state in a wider sense.[226]

---

[222] Ibid., §260: 'concrete freedom consists in this, that personal individuality and its particular interests not only achieve their complete development and gain explicit recognition for their right . . . but . . . they also pass over of their own accord into the interests of the universal, and . . . know and will the universal; they even recognise it as their own substantive mind; . . . '

[223] Ibid., §259.

[224] Ibid., §247.

[225] Ibid., note to §272.

[226] Ibid., note to §256.

That said the focus is now on the form taken by the state in its narrower sense. Hegel believes that to be rational the state must possess particular features which need to be understood. Although Hegel is often linked with the emergence of fascism and the totalitarian state, his view of the state, far from being unitary and homogeneous, stresses pluralism and differentiation. Nevertheless, Hegel was concerned that these pluralistic entities are not conceived of as self-subsistent atoms, mechanically related, like the selfish individuals of utilitarian theory.

This concern with differentiation *and* integration is repeated at the level of the state. The problem of the separation of powers, was a much discussed issue at the time following Locke's insistence on the separation of judiciary from legislature, Montesquieu's famous treatment of the subject in Book XI of *The Spirit of the Laws*, and its embodiment in the epochal constitutional experiment of the eighteenth century, the American Federal Constitution of 1787. Although Hegel agrees that the separation of powers is 'of the highest importance', it is, to him, vital that those powers are not held in isolation, that is, that each *power* is not identified with a particular *institution*.[227]

Hegel's version of the separation of powers distinguishes three powers or processes in the rational state. The legislative power is the power 'to establish the universal' – i.e. general rules governing the conduct of the state's life. Secondly there is the power to determine the relationship of individual cases to the universal, which is the executive power. There is finally what Hegel calls the 'power of subjectivity' – the moment of will which at once unites and enforces the other aspects of the state's activity.[228] This separation of powers, Hegel correctly points out, is a descendent of the classical doctrine of the 'mixed constitution'. But for Hegel its modern formulation resolves certain problems inherent in the tradition. For the ancients, the problem of 'the mixed constitution' seemed insoluble, for they could only conceive of different constitutions as the embodiment of different types of sociologically defined individuals' wills. A constitution, it seemed, had to embody the will of one, the few (rich) or the many (poor); attempts to combine them led to problems of where the balance lay, and the continual danger of class tyranny if one group gained the upper hand. Hegel sees the mixture not as a mixture of classes of men of different social types, but as a mixture of functions and of principles embodied in different social classes and institutions, although in fact historically the one has embodied the principle of monarchy, the few that of the executive and the many that of legislation. If these functions are identified with different social groups they will tend to view their political rights and functions as private privileges, and they can then be held in check only by the principle of honour. That Montesquieu, the most important writer to discuss the subject, attributed 'honour' as a political virtue to monarchy showed to Hegel that it was precisely the disarticulated feudal monarchy he had in mind. On the contrary, thought Hegel, the modern constitutional monarchy can rely on the more objective notion of duty (from office-holder) because the offices in question are coherently interdependent.[229]

---

[227] Ibid., §272 note, 'If the powers of the Legislature and the executive become self-subsistent the destruction of the state is a fait-accompli'. See also §276 addition.

[228] Ibid., §273.

[229] Ibid., §273, note; on the difference between modern 'organic' monarchies and feudal ones see §286 (note).

Because Hegel is dealing not with classes but with principles and functions, he has not the same problem about balancing one with the other and combining them in a single unity; nor is there the same problem about the individuals involved containing in their minds aspects of the other functions performed by the state. If I am characterized in terms of my membership of some objectively defined external characteristic such as wealth, then, as Aristotle points out, that characterization is unitary and unequivocal, I cannot be both rich and poor, or a member of the few and the many, at one and the same time.[230] But if we are talking about people's subjective mental characteristics and the principles which are there embodied, or about their roles in the state, then clearly, in their mental lives, people are capable of taking a number of different points of view into account, and capable of performing a number of different tasks in the state. Whilst I may be predominantly a civil servant, or a member of the legislature, I can still appreciate the problems of someone who is performing other tasks. Through this rational reflection Hegel believes the modern state, whilst a product of, and relying on, the differentiation of tasks, so criticised by an earlier generation, can achieve unity at the level of reflective thought through a proper understanding of the rational part played not only by myself, but by other individuals.[231] Here is where the state is an essentially superior form of consciousness to that produced by civil society. For in civil society the unity achieved is not conscious, on the contrary it results from the conscious competition and adversity of individuals seeking selfish satisfactions. The function of the state is to supersede and contain this selfish freedom within limits; but it can only do so without infringing subjective dimensions of freedom if philosophy assists the state by correcting unattainable ideals of freedom, reflecting on social life, demonstrating its necessity and hence its rationality.

The crown

In accordance with Hegel's view that each institution must share in the powers of the state, the 'crown' is not simply the power of executive decision but also the constitutive authority behind the whole formal legal structure, as well as a focus of the consultation by which proposals are canvassed amongst particular interests[232]

The end of the state is fundamentally to achieve unity of aim and purpose whilst preserving subjective freedom. Since only an individual can provide unity and an expression of unequivocal will, there must be an individual monarch at the apex of the state.[233] Yet, to avoid the end of the *Philosophy of Right* turning full circle as it were, and recreating all the problems posed by the purely abstract individual will, this individual must contain within himself all the logical properties which the *Philosophy of Right* has demonstrated to be necessary to the existence of social and political life. The monarch must therefore be constitutional and not absolute.

---

[230] Aristotle, *Politics*, III, viii, 1279b-1280a.

[231] Schiller's *Letters on the Aesthetic Education of Mankind* is the classic German articulation of this view. See Introduction to this chapter, p. 414.

[232] *Philosophy of Right*, §275.

[233] Ibid., §279.

Hegel's insistence on a monarchy as the culmination of the rational form of the state may seem to modern readers bizarre and misplaced, so it is probably worth dwelling on it a little.

Firstly there must be some source of sovereign authority which allocates and organizes the offices and functions of the state and in virtue of which office-holders exercise authority. Historically, Hegel points out, men seem always to have needed some outside source of sovereignty, whether it is derived superstitiously through 'reading' the entrails of sacrificed animals or the flight of birds or from some other supernatural source, or mythical founder figure.[234] Yet of course the modern state, to be rational and self sufficient, cannot continue to rely on such superstitious and external sources of authority. Why then, can there not be some elected embodiment of sovereignty, a presidential figure?

The reasons for Hegel's dislike of direct democracy account partly for this, and these can be dealt with shortly. But also relevant here is the relationship of the state to civil society. Civil society is characterized by a selfish mentality which is only partly mitigated by the existence of institutions such as the classes and corporations. To elect the sovereign from such atomized or even incorporated individuals would be to make the unifying principle of the state, and in effect the state itself, subject to all the conflicting interests within civil society.[235] To make sovereignty elective would be to surrender the state to the most powerful interest in civil society – 'the state becomes everyone's booty' – Hegel cites Montesquieu and in doing so anticipates Marx's critique of the state-as-parasite in the *18th Brumaire*.[236] As the function of the sovereign is to hold together and restrain these opposing tendencies, it would obviously be impossible for the individual performing this task to be seen by one group of the community as a representative of another. Hegel's objection is at once a development and a criticism of Rousseau. Whilst Hegel thought Rousseau was right to see sovereignty as an expression of will, it cannot be a merely 'general' will, but must be an expression of a truly universal will, and this means it cannot be the direct expression of the will of an actual 'people' – except as organized under a differentiated constitution. For the will of a people otherwise constituted is not

[234] Ibid., §279, note.

[235] Ibid., §281. The principle of heredity saves the state 'from the risk of being drawn down into the sphere of particularity and its caprices, ends, and opinions, and saved too from the war of factions round the throne.' Hegel here seems to ignore the disruptive effect that the reversionary interest can have in an hereditary monarchy. Moreover, Hegel seems to have revised his original republican conception of the state after the 1819 'Karlsbad Decrees' imposing censorship on the universities and academic publications, and the rejection of the reformed constitution in 1820. Hegel's revisions inserted a conception of the state as a separate congeries of institutions (including the restoration monarchy) into a conception of the state as something directly proceeding from the wills of free citizens. See K.–H. Ilting 'Hegel on the State and Marx's Early Critique, in *The State and Civil Society*, ed. Z.A. Pelczynski (Cambridge, 1984) esp. pp. 98ff. Nevertheless the de-facto persistence of heredity in the political world gives his point greater enduring relevance than might be thought. Succession crises are endemic in many developing states with supposedly republican consitutions, and the incipient re-emergence of the hereditary principle which circumvents the problem has occurred in unlikely places: India, North Korea, for example. Nor is this all to be explained by the 'natural' desire to benefit one's offspring or ensure loyal subordinates. Belief in the advantages of the hereditary principle, based not so much on nostalgic legitimism but on the kind of anti-foundationalist reasons given by Hegel have been prominent in some of the newly emergent nation-states of the old Soviet Union.

[236] Ibid., §273.

universal, but subject to natural, superstitious, partial and whimsical impulse. Since it is only as differentiated that a people's will can be universal, the sovereign will cannot be the expression of any particular group's will within that entity. The will of which the sovereign is the expression is arrived at philosophically and expressed only through the complex of institutions that is the state, it cannot be derived from any one, or one group of interests – even a majority.[237]

The sovereign must in some sense be 'above politics', if by politics we mean the conflicts resulting from competing interests. Hobbes seems to recognize this in pointing out that even in a contractual state the sovereign cannot be a party to the contract, this would make him dismissable and destroy sovereignty. So the keystone of the state, the monarch, must owe his position to something altogether outside civil society, and that, for Hegel, is to nature, to the natural process of birth. From one point of view there is a certain irony, as more than one commentator has remarked, in the state, the culmination of human attempts to embody the freedom of the will, having to resort to a principle of heredity drawn from nature, the realm of necessity, in order to achieve its completion.[238]

The formal powers of the crown include the right of pardon in individual cases, the inauguration of business and the command of the armed forces. The second of these is only formally the prerogative of the monarch since Hegel envisages the role of counsellors and advisors here being most active.[239] It is relatively unclear just how much personal power the sovereign is expected to wield. The monarch's power to choose and dismiss advisors is absolute.[240] On the other hand 'the crown' is a legal person, and many of its powers lie in counsellors or officials who are therefore individually answerable for their actions. At times the monarch seems to be a mere formal cipher, someone whose personal qualities are irrelevant, whose assent is only formally necessary to make the action of the state an act of will, someone who merely 'dots the i's and crosses the t's'.[241] On other occasions his role seems more active. Perhaps most so in the case of foreign affairs, for it is here, in relationships with other states that the state is most to be conceived of as an individual and needs the characteristics of an individual to express its will.[242] This is the rationale for the monarch's control over the armed forces, although here again Hegel stresses that what he means by sovereign is not the person of the monarch, simply, but the totality of the state, as fused together and embodied in his office.

Executive

The second power of the state is executive. The crown makes decisions, but the execution or maintenance of them is an executive task. The institutions exercising this power include for Hegel the judiciary and police. Although these authorities operate within civil

---

[237] Ibid., §279, note, and §258 note.

[238] Herbert Marcuse, *Reason and Revolution* (2nd edn., London, 1955), pp. 217–18.

[239] *Philosophy of Right*, §282–3.

[240] Ibid., §283.

[241] Ibid., §279 and note (need for an individual act of will); §280, and addition (dotting 'i's and crossing 't's).

[242] Ibid., §278, note (ii), §§321, 329.

society as well, Hegel tries to indicate that their role in the state underscores his insistence on the difference between it and civil society. Hegel makes a distinction between 'particular interests which are common to everyone', which are the concern of the institutions of civil society, and 'universal interests'. It is tempting to identify this with Rousseau's distinction between the will of all and the general will.[243] Those aspects of the judiciary, public authorities and corporations which are particular interests, or aggregations of them fall into the sphere of civil society, whilst those that relate 'to the maintenance of the state's universal interest' are the concern of the state authorities. In this case it involves supervision of these authorities' activities through the appointment of a certain proportion of 'positions of responsibility in the corporations'. The function of these representatives of the state is to convert the incipient universality of these forms of association resulting from the selfish needs of civil society into a full blown identification with the social unity which is the state.[244] However they must do this without actually controlling them. Hegel does not provide support for fascism viewed as state corporatism any more than for it viewed as the atomization of civil society. Indeed, ever conscious of the low level of Germany's political development, he stresses how important it is that the mass of the citizens should have autonomous forms of civil organization.[245]

Consistent with his rejection of the state as an aggregation (or aggregator) of interests, Hegel does not see the state's participation in these institutions as concerned with mediating between the competing interests that go to make up civil society, a view of the state which pervades much contemporary thought on the role of politics. On the contrary it is the task of the state to lift men's consciousness above that level, to the universal one where they recognize that shared community which transcends these particular interests. In order that those performing this function be freed from concern with selfish needs, Hegel argues that civil servants need to be given security of tenure. The kind of devotion to duty required of them cannot be defined in terms of a contract.[246] It requires instead, the creation of a particular type of personality with a natural inclination to serve the universal interests of the state rather than seek always for personal advantage. Because discharging such a task requires not merely a skill, but a disposition, it cannot be merely a casual 'job'. Civil servants must have made the objective requirements and principles of their organization so much a part of their character as to automatically pursue those ends. Hegel refers to this mentality as a 'culture'. It must therefore be a lifelong vocation. Hegel penetrates much of the peculiar nature of a modern civil service and his characterization anticipates much that Weber has to say in developing the important concept of bureaucracy.[247]

---

[243] As Hegel himself does in the *Logic*, §163n, where he criticises Rousseau for, having made the distinction, failing to recognise that the general will is only the universal notion of will, and the laws 'are the clauses of this will'. Rousseau's politics would have been better if he had recognised that (in accordance with Hegel's *Logic*), the notion of will requires a particularistic articulation to realize its expression as well as a universal (or, in Rousseau's terms, 'General') one. See the note to §258, p. 157 where Hegel attributes the Terror of the French Revolution to this failure to recognise any but the most abstract conception of will.

[244] *Philosophy of Right*, §288–9, and note.

[245] Ibid., §290, addition.

[246] Ibid., §294.

[247] Ibid., §§291–2.

Although Hegel might idealize his civil service, he is not naive enough to allow the rule of law to rest purely on their incorruptibility.[248] The second safeguard is the people organized in their corporations. Members of civil society who also participate in these institutions, and who through such participation come to have an awareness of their universal function and benefits, will act as a check on the activities of civil servants, and on any potential misuse of power. The executive, which Hegel thinks of as constituting the bulk of the middle class, are thus controlled from below by the representatives in the corporations and from above by the sovereign himself.[249]

The legislature

The third power of the state is the legislature, the task of which is to produce general rules (and amend them as necessary), conducive to the well being and happiness of the state, and to grant to the state the supply of necessary goods and services from the citizens.[250] Hegel points out that the distinction between legislation and application of the laws is ultimately a difficult one to make, since the more detailed the determination of the law the less is involved in its application. Ultimately, the full specification of a law would make it so particular that it would only fit one case, and it would be an executive and not a legislative act. This may be seen as an example of the principle of the dialectic: that concepts pass over into their opposites. Hegel uses it here to reinforce his point that the different functions of the state cannot and should not be thought of as rigidly separate; and so cannot be identified with particular institutions: he points out that both the monarchy and the executive have roles to play in the legislative process – in assenting to and advising on legislation.[251]

Hegel again stresses the crucial part played by the emergence of a commercial society and a money economy in enabling the modern state to combine personal freedom with political strength. For such an economy means that the demands of the state on the individual can take the form of taxation rather than the direction of labour to perform particular tasks.[252] In ancient despotisms such as Egypt, in Plato's *Republic* and in feudal

---

[248] He recognises the potential bureaucracies have for forming their own interests, as a 'clique'. Ibid., §295, note.

[249] Ibid., §§295, 297. Hegel's assertion that the bulk of the middle class will constitute state officials and bureaucrats is both a revealing acknowledgement of his political assumptions and an insight into German social conditions, which lacked a numerous and developed *commercial* middle class as found in England and France. (See for example the background sketched in the masterful recent study *Hegelianism* by Toews, esp. p. 15ff.) As stressed in the introductory sections, Hegel acknowledges the central importance of a strong middle class in political development (addition to §297) as well as acknowledging that Germany's lack of one was a major impediment to her political development. (As early as his Essay on the Württemberg estates in *Hegel's Political Writings*, ed. Z.A. Pelczynski (Oxford, 1961).

[250] *Philosophy of Right*, §298–9.

[251] Ibid., §299, note, §300. The extent to which Hegel has in mind the English constitution as a model — almost certainly mediated through writers such as Montesquieu, or the later widely popular Jean De Lolme's *Constitution of England* (1775), — should be obvious. Less remarked on is the fact that Württemburg unusually, had retained its estates in the era of absolutism. See, Toews, *Hegelianism*, p. 17.

[252] *Philosophy of Right*, §299, and note. Notice that Hume had made the same observation about the crucial role of money taxation in the modern state, but had emphasised as a result the strength of the state rather than the freedom of the individual. David Hume, 'Of Commerce', in *Essays* (Oxford, 1963).

societies such as *ancien régime* France through the dreaded *corvée*, the state comman-
deered men's labour in order to achieve its ends. In doing so of course it prevented
individuals from exercising that individual freedom of choice which is such a feature of
modern society. The emergence of a commercial exchange economy enables men to
offer, and the state to demand something universal which will always be in demand –
money – and which the citizens can raise through their own chosen means, thus
preserving their subjective freedom. The one exception is the performance of military
service of which we shall have more to say shortly.

The institutions most closely identified with the legislative power are the estates.
Strictly an estate is a legal condition or rank of the citizens. Calling a representative body
or parliament an estate thus emphasises that the people in it are being recognized
politically, not as individuals but only through those ranks or orders of people already
created by civil society, as Hegel makes clear.[253] There are two houses of the estates.
One represents the agricultural class. Hegel seems to presume agricultural property
continuing to be passed down by entail, as in feudal societies. The agricultural class is
thus very traditional, and Hegel sees it as appropriate that this should be reflected in the
process by which it is represented in the state. Membership of the agricultural house of
the estates is thus hereditary. The second house of the estates represents the commercial
element in civil society and it is elective, based on the corporations. Hegel also agrees
that political parties on the British model form a useful way of recruiting members and
forming alternative administrations. He notes that this works in Britain because all parties
are groups drawn from within the same political class, and thus share a consensus on the
nature of the constitutional 'game'. Because the life of the business part of civil society
is dependent on chance, and fluctuates, Hegel considers the hereditary members of the
first estate more suitable for public office although in his earlier works he favours indirect
election. In general though Hegel considers the British constitution to have retained too
much irrational privilege, whilst on the other hand having gone too far in curbing the
influence of the crown.

There is no emphasis on representation. Hegel's view of the franchise is that it should
be restricted, in order that it is more highly valued by the citizens.[254] Furthermore the
deputies in the estates are not delegates, receiving instructions from their constituents,
but representatives of the nation as a whole who act, as Burke suggested MPs should act,
according to their consciences. The role of the estates is not just, or even primarily, as we
might think, to express in law the people's opinions. For a start the legislative process is
not confined to the estates but is shared with the crown, and the executive.[255] Rather the
estates heighten the subjective identification of the people (through their representatives)
with the state. Its task is integrative rather than interest – aggregative.[256] Hegel does not

---

[253] Ibid., §303, note. Despite his differences with an earlier generation of reformers, Hegel's position on
adapting the estates to modern political conditions was broadly that of the Prussian reformer Karl von
Stien (see Krieger, *The German Idea of Freedom*, pp. 153–4, and Aris, *Political Thought in Germany*, ch.
xiii).

[254] Hegel interestingly anticipates rational-choice theory explanations of voter apathy: 'popular suffrage . . . in large states leads inevitably to electoral indifference, since the casting of a single vote is of no
significance where there is a multitude of electors.' *Philosophy of Right*, §311, note.

[255] Ibid., §300.

[256] Ibid., §301.

see the estates as a channel for some autonomously existing popular will; much less, as is popularly supposed, an essential opposition to the executive. Instead they are part of the educative process, by which the essentially partial and sectarian mentality of civil society is drawn on to appreciate the necessity for a more universal perspective.[257]

On the other hand it is true that the estates also proved a safeguard for the people against the abuse of powers by the other organs of the state, although again, true to his balance-of-powers position, Hegel stresses that this is not a role peculiar to the estates, but one each power in the state exercises, some much more effectively. Moreover this role is not to be taken as implying any superior insight on the part of the Deputies or those electing them, but rather to lead the bureaucracy to avoid incurring criticism by anticipating it. Indeed Hegel goes so far as to say that adopting an attitude of mistrust to officialdom is 'a presupposition characteristic of the rabble'.[258] Rejecting insinuations of popular sovereignty is a major theme of this section of the work. Realizing the rational will is an emergent property of a properly co-ordinated set of powers, in turn organically related to a free civil society. It thus cannot be the product of one particular institution, much less one which is simply an instrument of popular will:

> To know what one wills: and still more to know what the absolute will, Reason, wills, is the fruit of profound apprehension and insight, precisely the things which are not popular. [259]

Another related aspect of his antipathy towards the democratic tendencies in modern society is Hegel's rejection of any individual basis for representation. This had shown itself even in his earlier, perhaps more radical period, in his writings on the German constitution. But now Hegel, still mindful of the path of the French Revolution, is concerned to retain the organic nature of the state, and avoid the representation of atomized isolated individuals: 'a formless mass whose commotion and activity could therefore only be elementary, irrational, barbarous and frightful.'[260]

It is not therefore the individual that is represented in the estates, but the group, the groups which civil society has already produced as a result of its primary need-satisfying activity. Indeed the estates comprise two chambers reflecting the major division within civil society, a hereditary chamber representing the agricultural class and an elected chamber representing the commercial class.[261] Furthermore Hegel clearly envisages representation within the commercial estate on the basis of trade or skill.[262]

---

[257] Ibid., §301, note, and §302. Once again the pedagogical role of government parallels von-Stien's paradoxical concern 'that government was to direct men to be free and how to be free.' Krieger, *German Idea of Freedom*, p. 151.

[258] *Philosophy of Right*, §301, note.

[259] Ibid., §§301 and 303, notes.

[260] Ibid., §303, note; and see above, note 129.

[261] Ibid., §§305–10.

[262] 'Deputies are "representatives" in an organic rational sense, only if they are representatives not of individuals or conglomerates of them, but of one of the essential spheres of society in its large-scale interests.' Ibid., §311, note. Despite this 'functional' conception of constituency Hegel endorses Burke's view that deputies are representatives of the whole, and not delegates of their electors. (§309 note.)

Reflecting on the course of the argument of the *Philosophy of Right* explains this concern with group or class representation. The individual, simply as an individual, has no determinate existence at all. His personality requires to be clothed, as it were, in the subjective attitudes, beliefs and prejudices of a particular existence. This can only be provided for him by existence within a particular class, and by following a particular way of life. It is in and through these that he becomes a person, and through these that he becomes a part of the state. Since these 'particular ways of life' have already found institutional expression in the corporate bodies which characterize the unifying aspects of civil society, it is irrational to represent men as isolated individuals rather than through those organizations and categories which make them the particular men they are and not others.

> The circles of association in civil society are already communities. To picture these communities as once more breaking up into a mere conglomeration of individuals as soon as they enter the field of politics ..is *eo ipso* to hold civil life and political life apart from one another and as it were to hang the latter in the air, because its basis could then only be the abstract individuality of caprice and opinion, and hence it would be grounded in chance and not on what is absolutely stable and justified.[263]

This concern with providing a rational form for men's opinions rather than simply a transparent medium through which individual desires can be communicated, also emerges in Hegel's insistence which we noted that the estates should act as a means of promulgating and spreading public and political awareness. It is reiterated in his concern for creating a 'public opinion', knowledgeable, aware and informed of political issues, which can thus play a part in the formation of policy. One of the great worries of Hegel's generation of reformers had been the lack of any body of informed political opinion in Germany. Hegel had by now transcended any crude desire to apply classical Greek ideals to modern society. But he was still concerned not only to articulate a rational political ideal, but also with how to translate that into a feeling of political community within the nation such that its relationship with the state could be organic and free.[264] Since for a number of reasons, he thought this could not involve the direct participation of all citizens in political decision-making, it was all the more important to keep them informed and reflective about political issues.

Given Germany's political backwardness Hegel is suitably ambivalent about public opinion.[265] As a shared set of beliefs about politics in the widest sense it is, subjectively speaking, constitutive of political community. It is related very closely to Burke's concept of an assemblage of prejudices. It is 'the unorganized way in which a people's opinions and wishes are made known.' But simply because public opinion is unorganized, an inchoate assemblage of 'common sense' believing itself to be complete and sufficient, it follows that it cannot, or should not be translated directly into political action. Thus, on the one hand 'to be independent of public opinion is the first formal condition of achieving anything great or rational whether in life or in science;'[266] but on

---

[263] Ibid., §303, note.

[264] Toews, *Hegelianism*, pp. 33–4.

[265] 'It deserves to be as much respected as despised . . . ' *Philosophy of Right*, §318.

[266] Ibid., §318.

the other: 'The great man of his age is the one who can put into words the will of his age, tell his age what its will is, and accomplish it.'[267]

The state from the outside: the moral autonomy of states in war and international relations

So far, Hegel has been considering the state in its internal aspects only. Yet the state, as the most rational form of objective mind, is a form of individuality. That is to say: it has a unity which Hegel has been concerned to argue must be more than simply the sum of any atomistic conception of the individuals composing it. Like any other individuals the state can only achieve identity through negation.[268] Consequently it is in its relationships to other states that the state, and indeed the individual citizens prove and realize themselves. Ultimately this means in warfare, for it is in warfare that the state proves and maintains its historical existence. In war also the individual is forced to recognize that it is upon the state that he depends for his existence. Moreover it is upon his particular state that he depends for the particular form of life to which his character has moulded itself. No account of the state which regards it as an association merely to secure life and property (such as Hobbes's) could explain or justify such a sacrifice. It is only in the citizen's readiness to sacrifice life for this ideal that the state can survive; and this readiness will only be forthcoming where the citizen sees his very personality as integrally related to the state. More idiosyncratically Hegel also defends war as the actual and necessary expression of the contingency of such finite things as human life, property and particular relations. Since reality is the-coming-to-be of what is present originally only in concept, the contingency of life in particular, and of particular forms of property (although not of the concept of property itself), needs, Hegel thinks, to be enacted in history. The destruction wrought by war is that realization of its contingency.[269] It is in that destruction that the realization that they owe their existence to the state is brought home. In this sense war, like coercion, is not an unmitigated evil, but the practical reassertion of the principle of right at the highest level.[270] The courage of the citizen may well not be enough. The form of social organization as well as the strength of commitment is relevant to the society's historical survival.[271] Those whom Hegel calls 'barbarians' do not necessarily lack the personal courage to fight the European (although he suggests this is so in a number of cases). What they lacked was the social organization to

---

[267] Ibid., §318, addition.

[268] This is an oft-repeated point of Hegel's, he reiterates it in this context at ibid., §331, note: 'A state is as little an actual individual without relations to other states as an individual is actually a person without *rapport* with other persons.' See also §322 'Identity is awareness of one's existence as a unit in sharp distinction to others', and §324, addition.

[269] Ibid., §324, note.

[270] If it were not so, Hegel suggests, we should be unable to distinguish courageous patriots from spirited criminals. This recalls St Augustine's story of the pirate's questions to Alexander the Great: 'What are kingdoms but Great Robber Bands?' St. Augustine, *The City of God*, tr. Bettenson (Harmondsworth, 1972) Bk. IV, ch. 4. The equivalent modern conundrum of distinguishing the terrorist from the freedom fighter is a distinctly more difficult one to answer, but, likewise, can only be answered with a conception of what rightly constitutes a state.

[271] Ibid., §324 and note.

compete.[272] In the modern world, aboriginal peoples, notably in South America, who manage to arrest the imposition of what we call, with far less confidence than Hegel, progress, do so because and inasmuch as they adopt western tactics of leadership, organization and media management.

Even warfare, Hegel points out, has changed to adapt itself to the demands of the new social organization. Just as modern society involves a degree of fragmentation through the division of labour, which is only recovered at a higher level of generality in the mechanism of the market, so in warfare, individual virtues such as courage have become subordinate to those of disciplined group action. [273] In making this point, Hegel stresses the role of thought as the active subject of the historical process. It is, he claims, in order to conform with these developments in consciousness 'that thought has invented the gun', rather than, as we might be tempted to say, that a different evaluation of personal valour in war has been brought about by the invention of the gun.[274]

To recognize a state is to recognize its absolute authority as the guarantor and only actual basis of all the institutions of right established thus far, and it is only in defence of this 'structure of right' that we are justified in risking our lives. States are states inasmuch as they are recognized by other members of the international community, although whether they survive will depend on their internal structures.

The autonomy and sovereignty of states is simply an expression of the fact that there can be no actual structure of right regulating their actions. [275] This does not mean that states ought not to keep their word and adhere to treaties, indeed that is the fundamental principle of international law, but it remains only an 'ought'. Relations between states, because they never generate complex levels of interdependence, never, for Hegel, seem to have the possibility of moving beyond this stage, as relations between individuals clearly do in the early stages of the *Philosophy of Right*.[276] 'There is no praetor to judge between states; at best there may be an arbitrator or mediator, and even he exercises his functions contingently only, i.e. depending on the particular wills of the disputants.'[277] Any state is justified in engaging in conflict with another state if it judges its welfare to have been damaged in some way, and only it can be the judge of that. Like Hobbes's men in the state of nature it could judge this to have occurred as a result of a 'trifle'.[278] States in the international system stand in a very different relationship from that of individuals within a state. A state is a concrete embodiment of what Hegel calls 'ethical substance', it provides an actual and concrete moral environment for men. We are not, as individuals, justified in disturbing this moral environment simply to pursue our own welfare, or even to pursue a subjective or abstract notion of the good. [279] The international environment in which states exist is, however, not 'concrete' in this sense: ' . . . their relations are on the largest scale a maelstrom of external contingency and the inner particularity of passions, private interests and selfish ends, abilities and virtues, vices,

---

[272] Hegel praises the individual courage of Indian soldiers, despite succumbing to numerically inferior forces (ibid., § 327, addition), but expresses contempt for the 'crouching submissiveness' of the native Americans. *Philosophy of History*, p. 81.

[273] *Philosophy of Right*, §328.

[274] Ibid., §328, note.

[275] Ibid., §333.

[276] Ibid., §332.

[277] Ibid., §333, note.

[278] Ibid., §334.

[279] Ibid., §337, note.

force, and wrong.' [280] Consequently there is not nor can be anything to inhibit states from pursuing their own welfare, indeed it is the only criterion of action they have.[281] Ultimately judgements on the actions of states will be made, not by individual morality, tied as it necessarily is to a particular parochial view, but by history.

World history as the history of freedom

World history is thus the final section of the *Philosophy of Right*, and it has already led beyond the sphere of 'objective mind' which is its subject area and into what Hegel calls 'absolute mind'. Objective mind is human consciousness as it exists amongst a particular people, or to put it more conventionally, as their social and political institutions and culture. Absolute mind goes beyond the interactive structures of practical conscious-nesses; it is mind reflecting on itself; in this case reflecting on its own historical development, and the historical fate of particular states.

Absolute mind takes a number of forms (which however share the same content). Art, religion and philosophy are all modes of expression in which mind reflects on its own nature. In art absolute mind takes the immediate form of intuition and is expressed in material objects, in religion that of emotion; but in philosophy that of pure thought.[282] Art and religion thus provide allegories of that truth which it is the task of philosophy to make plain. Religion is 'truth in a veil'.[283] The state is the objectification of the rational truth of which religion provides an emotional certainty, and art an image. It is, inciden-tally, precisely because religion is absolute mind-as-feeling that neither it, nor the church, can be allowed to take precedence over the philosophical state. For feelings are essen-tially indeterminate and volatile. One of the roles of the state is to provide a secure framework to contain, although of course not suppress, religion.[284]

The highest aspect of absolute spirit is philosophy, in which humans, through thought, achieve their highest freedom in being able to reflect on their own consciousness as pure mind. But for Hegel philosophy and history are interwoven, the highest form of knowledge cannot be confined to the two categories into which Hume and the empiricists had divided the world: necessary but abstract truths of philosophy, and the contingent but concrete facts of history. It is Hegel's claim that this alienating legacy must be overcome, that the two can and indeed must be combined, if the world is to be seen as a coherent and not a divided whole. In the first of his mature works Hegel writes:

> The goal, which is absolute knowledge, or spirit knowing itself as spirit, is reached through the recollection of these spiritual forms, both as they are in themselves (philosophical logic) and as they bring about the organization of their existing spiritual domain (in a Phenomenology of spirit). Their preservation, as free existence appearing in the form of the contingent is history; organized systematically in concepts however,

[280] Ibid., §340.

[281] Ibid., §336.

[282] Ibid., §341; *Philosophy of History*, p. 53.

[283] *Philosophy of Right*, §270, addition.

[284] Ibid. See the very important note, and addition to §270.

it is the science of the structure of appearances. Both together, history comprehended in concepts, form the recollection and the totality of absolute spirit.

Therefore the task of philosophy is to reveal the rationality of historical development, and the task of history is to exhibit the process by which the present philosophical world-view came about. The tension between history and philosophy as the two competing hegemonic conceptualizations of the world of consciousness, revealed in the way the changes documented by the history of philosophy undermines philosophy's claims to universality, whilst the inability of historical investigation to provide its own principles of relevance without philosophical insight is, in Hegel, overcome. For history is the history of mind, and philosophy is essentially historical, and developmental.

History, both formally and in content is the process of the growth of human consciousness. The rest, the mere record of blind events succeeding each other, is meaningless, a mere list:

> The history of mind is its own act. Mind is only what it does, and its act is to make itself the object of its own consciousness. In history, its act is to gain consciousness of itself as mind, to apprehend itself in its interpretation of itself to itself.[285]

Hegel characterizes history as we might characterize the moral growth of an individual. We grow by reflecting on, and therefore gaining a perspective on, and stepping beyond the bounds of, an earlier mentality. Our earlier selves become for us, objective items of appraisal, and in doing so we at once incorporate and transcend them. True personal growth is not mere rejection of our past, but recognition, incorporation and supersession.

It is important to understand how Hegel relates this to both meanings of the word history. As we use the word it is often ambiguous. It refers to all those events and actions that comprise the past, but also to the narratives, commentaries and analyses that have been written about them. Hegel refers to these as the objective and subjective aspects of history. Although the whole world consists of various aspects of *Geist* or spirit, it is only in the conscious world, or in man himself that spirit knows itself to be what it is, a conscious substance. Consequently it is only through the developing awareness of actual human beings that the forms and nature of *Geist* can themselves develop and be known.[286] Now what distinguishes mind as spirit, from nature, is precisely this self-consciousness; and history, for Hegel is the history of self consciousness. This must be a continuous history, since once lost, the subjective meaning of a way of life cannot be recovered.[287] Societies such as those of ancient Africa or America which have left us no record of their awareness of themselves over time, have left, and therefore as far as Hegel is concerned,

---

[285] Ibid., §343.

[286] *Philosophy of History*, p. 78.

[287] Archaeological remains, without a written record, reveal only the artefacts, and not the subjective meaning that they, or the culture with which they were associated, conveyed to their users. Prehistory is therefore, on this view, for ever severed from history; and civilization is impossible without continuity. Russel Hoban's *Riddley Walker*, gives a brilliant glimpse into a post-holocaust barbarism where even the continuity provided by the meaning of speech itself has been all but broken, a caesura which is virtually constitutive of barbarism.

have had, no history.[288] History, then is only the advance of human awareness, and not simply a sequence of events. This view of history both provides a principle of inclusion and exclusion for those attempting to write history (only the history of ideas and ideologies is strictly relevant), and explains why philosophy itself is irreducibly historical; thereby suggesting ways in which both history and philosophy as disciplines are ultimately united. It furthermore shows why history in the sense of 'the totality of past events', must effectively collapse into history as 'the sum of written records of past consciousness and the accounts we construct from that material'.

The belief that history is a rational process is sometimes presented by Hegel as though it were an absolute assumption or axiom of historical investigation, brought in from outside it, from philosophy.[289] However Hegel does have arguments from within history itself which attempt to show why the history – at least in the sense of our *knowledge* of the past – must be the history of both intellectual and social progress.

Organized political life, Hegel argues, is a precondition for the development of such awareness and advance. Only in the state can records and a structure of thought sufficient to enable intellectual progress, in the sense of increasing awareness of, and therefore progress from, the past, take place. The state is thus a condition of history.[290] In this sense, Hegel wants to argue that human studies are essentially different from the natural sciences. Our social and political awareness is essentially dialectical, we respond to our own conception of ourselves. The beliefs that we hold about our social world will themselves influence our behaviour, and may render those original beliefs about it redundant by exposing inadequacies in them. Nature on the other hand, Hegel describes as spirit 'sunk in otherness', unaware of itself as spirit. It is appropriate then to bring to the study of nature a mind which is aware only of the apparent logic of phenomena which it deems to be objective facts; and this is the type of mentality (and world) that is presupposed by science. Consequently scientists are not expected to know or understand the development of their own subjects as a precondition for practising them. Philosophers on the other hand deal not with a natural subject, but with our thought processes themselves. These thought processes develop in accordance with a logic which is implicit in the nature of thought itself, but which is only perfectly visible in retrospect. But for history to reveal this it has to have *been* progressive, to have worked out this way it is of course necessary that reflection be constantly active, that the human and historical studies be kept alive, 'that Reason should not sleep'.[291] Any philosopher – or society (for philosophy is simply 'its own time apprehended in thought') – who is ignorant of the history of philosophy is likely to have to repeat it, since philosophical mistakes have to

---

[288] *Philosophy of History*, pp. 91–9 (on Africa). This has some of Hegel's most unpleasantly racist remarks, although attributing mental aspects on the basis of biology is here (as in the discussion of the female mind) fundamentally at odds with his whole approach. On America see ibid., p. 81.

[289] Thus 'The only thought which philosophy brings with it to the contemplation of history, is the simple conception of *Reason*; that reason is the sovereign of the world; that the history of the world, therefore presents us with a rational process.' Within the subject of history itself this is presented as a given, a 'conviction and intuition'; but 'in Philosophy it is no hypothesis. It is there proved by speculative cognition.' Ibid., p. 9.

[290] Ibid., pp. 68–9.

[291] Ibid., p. 11.

be lived through as social forms, or remembered as such, if they are to be avoided in future.

Whilst history may look like a part of nature, operating to laws independent of human consciousness or will, it will, argues Hegel, seem so only to the mind which operates at the level of understanding. To the rational mind, history is something more, it is the working out of the rational purpose and meaning of mind itself, which is, essentially, freedom.[292] But it can only truly become this inasmuch as humans become reflective and develop their self conscious awareness – cumulatively – into progress. It is this which rescues them from the mere repetition which seemed, in days before the theory of evolution, to characterize the world of nature. If true historical progress is only found in the growing awareness of mankind as a conscious subject, the content of that progress is the unfolding of freedom. Since mind is essentially free, unbounded by physical constraints: the growing self-awareness of that mind is the growth of freedom – the making explicit what was implicit.[293] At one level this happens within particular states at particular stages in history, and an appreciation of our own nation in this regard is nationalism.[294] But further reflection on the wider historical context takes us beyond nationalism, to an appreciation of the historical process as a whole, in which the lives of nation-states are mere episodes. In this sense, the understanding of the state in its international and historical context is the point at which objective mind spills over into absolute mind, the philosophy of right becomes world history and the political theory of the state becomes the philosophy of history.[295] The structure of world history manifests this growth of freedom by demonstrating a significantly staged series of political arrangements.

Starting in the east, civilization was first organized around the freedom, or rather caprice, of one individual, the oriental despot, the historical exemplification of the master-slave relationship. It then developed into the slave based democracies of ancient Greece, where freedom was more widespread, but still restricted to a few – to the citizens. The decline of the classical world was inevitable for reasons which have already been well canvassed. In Greece the relationship between citizen and state was too immediate and unreflective, unable to withstand rational scrutiny by figures such as Socrates; its opposite, and so, for Hegel, compliment, found in Rome, was too fixed into rigid and external legal categories. The rise of the modern 'Germanic' (i.e. northern-European) state, if Hegel's account is accepted, sees the extension of freedom to all.[296]

Moral problems of Hegel's vision

One disturbing question raised by Hegel's view of history as the unfolding of reason and freedom is whether whatever has come about in history is rational, and by implication

---

[292] *Philosophy of Right,* §342.

[293] *Philosophy of History,* p. 70.

[294] Ibid., p. 74.

[295] Ibid., p. 78; *Philosophy of Right,* §344.

[296] Ibid., §355–60; *Philosophy of History,* pp. 103–10. Of course inasmuch as it is institutional freedom that is said to be equalised, it is all *males* that Hegel has in mind here, and even so, this does not presuppose equal access to political power.

justifiable. Because the sphere of morality is contained within the state itself, it is inappropriate, Hegel holds, to make moral judgements about the actions of states.[297] Moreover, individuals who are instrumental in changing the course of history cannot be bound by the morality of their age; such a moral code is directed at the preservation of that very social world they are engaged in transforming: 'It is irrelevant and inappropriate . . . to raise moral claims against world-historical acts and agents, they stand outside morality.'

In Hegel's view the world progresses from one phase to another through the action of 'world historical individuals'. Men such as Napoleon, who refuse to be bound by the narrow and outmoded confines of the prevailing standards, and who effect a breakthrough into a new world. Being creatures of their age they are normally unaware of the significance of what they are doing. For the most part Hegel regards them, and other forces which lead to the development of historical change as part of the 'cunning of reason' – a historical relation of Adam Smith's 'Hidden Hand'. Reason produces the necessary effects without the conscious connivance of the individuals who are its unwitting instrument.[298] But again Hegel is here on what turned out to be dangerous ground. For a philosophical historian to retrospectively identify an individual as a 'world-historical actor' is one thing; for a living politician to be possessed of the illusion that he is one, has provided a pretext for all kinds of atrocities. Hegel seeks to prevent such claims by denying that this kind of knowledge is available except in retrospect, it is a way of making sense of the past, and not a technique for tackling the future. The problem is that there is no way of ensuring this will not happen. For the scrupulous Hegelian, as for Hegel himself, philosophy can offer no practical advice, since 'it always comes on the scene too late to give it'.[299] No philosopher can step out of his time, but the temptations of the man of action with a smattering of philosophy to do so have proved irresistible. So, once again Hegel has been held responsible for the development of fascist ideologies, for which the basis in his own writings is to say the least highly questionable. He was, at worst, careless.

Nevertheless, Hegel says some apparently unpleasant things about history. It is the 'court of judgement' of states.[300] Which seems to imply that the historical success or otherwise of states and societies constitutes a higher form of morality. He also says history can be described as 'the slaughter bench at which the happiness of peoples, the wisdom of states, and the virtue of individuals have been sacrificed.'[301] And whilst he regards the general historical perspective as 'a picture of most fearful aspect [that] excites emotions of the profoundest and most hopeless sadness', he nevertheless seeks to persuade us that its outcome is rational and right. Does this amount to a doctrine that might is right?

It is important to notice (although not decisive) that Hegel explicitly denies the proposition that might is right.[302] It is not the mere fact of a particular historical

---

[297] *Philosophy of Right*, §337, note; §345.

[298] Ibid., §344; *Philosophy of History*, pp. 29–33.

[299] *Philosophy of Right*, Preface, p. 12.

[300] Ibid., §340.

[301] *Philosophy of History*, p. 21.

[302] 'World history is not the verdict of mere might . . . [but] the necessary development . . . of the moments of reason and so of the self-consciousness and freedom of mind.' *Philosophy of Right*, §342.

development, be it the use of a philosophy or a state's power that justifies it as rational. It is not because things have come about that they are rational, nor are they rational *tout court*. They are rational if and because they can be shown to play a part in the unfolding of *Geist* or rationality embodied in consciousness. To do this involves approaching history with the intention of making sense of it: 'To he who looks rationally at the world, the world looks rationally back.'[303] But this assumption, that what has happened *can* be shown to be a part of a rational process can, he stresses, at the start, only be a presupposition. Although a necessary working assumption, like the scientific presupposition that all events have a cause, it does not excuse us from having to demonstrate its truth, in each particular case, which it is the job of history to do. As a truth, rather than as a principle of investigation, it is only after the investigation of history that we are justified in asserting the rationality of history.[304] Furthermore, as already mentioned, the rationality of history is only apparent in retrospect. In one of Hegel's most famous images he portrays the kind of philosophical knowledge that reflection on history provides as the 'owl of Minerva', symbol of wisdom: which puts to flight only as dusk falls.[305] It is, unless we have other grounds for believing in 'spirit' as an efficient historical cause, only a form of rationalization, a way of coming to terms with what has been. It is only in retrospect that we can make rational philosophical sense of the world. It is for this reason, Hegel believes, that philosophical systems emerge as the society they depict has passed: Aristotle's *Politics* was written during the rise of the Macedonian Empire which was to end the culture of the Greek city-state; Cicero wrote as feuding would-be emperors destroyed the institutions of Republican Rome; Saint Augustine attempted to fix in religious categories the secular Roman City as it was being dismantled, and Filmer wrote his *Patriarcha* in the midst of the English Civil War which saw fatal attacks on a political order based on actual or imagined paternal authority.

Yet unpalatable as is the preoccupation with historical winners, Hegel's assumption that it is the winning in history that has to be explained, is surely right. If history is to be seen as a process, we need to know why the winners won and the losers lost. If the reasons for this are accidental or irrational then so ultimately, is history (and indeed life). On the other hand if there is a rationale behind success and failure which can be expressed in reasonably general terms, there is surely a sense in which Hegel is at least asking the right questions. Those societies and systems of belief which triumph historically do just that. This does not mean that we as individuals who belong to a particular place and time, have to commend them, although we may find that we have to come to terms with their success. That individuals may resist historical change, and from the noblest of motives, Hegel acknowledges.[306] Yet, short of some absolute standards of right and wrong, a position very rarely adopted by Hegel's empiricist critics, there is little more, in a wider historical context to be said. No doubt a Christian hermit would regard the standards by which we judge the world to be totally misguided, just as society commonly regards the standards of some potentially emerging society in our midst to be totally misguided; each may be able to provide very sophisticated intellectual defences of their worlds.

But in the end the intellectual defence of a world is not enough, it is rationality in action that makes the world in which we live, and if that rationality is inadequate it will be superseded, as Hegel has tried to show that the conception of the state as a family, as a

---

[303] *Philosophy of History*, p. 11.
[304] Ibid., p. 10.

[305] *Philosophy of Right*, Preface, p. 13.
[306] *Philosophy of History*, Introduction, p. 67.

contract and as a system of needs was inadequate. The task of the philosopher as Hegel came to see it was to lay bare the inadequacies of these systems, and to demonstrate the rationality of the world as it now stands by demonstrating – if possible – the necessity of the process which has made it what it is, and us who we are. This is true self knowledge – knowing how we came to be who we are – and with it comes true freedom.

This is not a programme for changing the world, nor even a guide to action. It is curious that the reforming impulse which first led Hegel to his study of society and philosophy should have led to such quietist conclusions. Hegel does not deny the role of individual innovators in history, but as we have seen, their very novelty renders them incapable of being fitted into philosophical systems except retrospectively and in the broadest sense. The world of the present is the world of action, the world of freedom and the world of possibility; the world to which philosophy provides an understanding is the world of the past; neither philosophy nor history can do more than hint at what would be appropriate for the contemporary world.

X

Karl Marx

Introduction: Early life and influences[1]

Karl Marx was born on 5th May 1818 in Trier, in the Rhineland. Although Prussia, of which the Rhineland was a part, had abolished serfdom in the imperial lands, liberalized economic institutions and instituted administrative reform in the early part of the century, these reforms were imposed from above.[2] There was no national parliament and Prussia did not, by and large, possess an articulate or politically minded middle class on which the emergence of liberal politics depends. Public opinion in the Rhineland, however was more developed and liberal and there was concern there with the social issues raised by industrialisation.

Marx's family had traditionally provided the rabbi for the Jewish community there, but his father had converted to Christianity when laws preventing Jews from holding public positions were enforced in 1818. He was educated at home until he was 12 and then attended the local school. An undoubted influence on Marx at this early stage was the Baron von Westphalen, a cultured and politically progressive local notable.

In 1835 Marx went to Bonn University to study law, but his irregular life-style, and pursuit of literature at the expense of his law persuaded his father to send him to Berlin in 1836, having become engaged to Jenny von Westphalen, daughter of the Baron, over the summer. His legal studies there included courses by Gans, a liberal interpreter of Hegel's rational view of law, and the conservative de Savigny who argued (in a rather similar fashion to Burke) that laws took their authority from their positive historical existence. Given these conflicting views it is hardly surprising that Marx became interested in the philosophy of law, and eventually in Hegel. His adoption of Hegelianism was not easy; he had previously written a series of rather mischievous epigrams at Hegel's expense; he wrote of his 'consuming anger at having to make an idol of a view

---

[1] The source for all biographical details is David McLellan, *Karl Marx, his life and thought* (London 1973), hereafter referred to as *KMLT*.

[2] The Stein-Hardenberg reforms were carried out in the first decade of the century largely as a result of a recognition that traditional Prussian military and political institutions had proved unequal to the challenge posed by Napoleon's new national citizens' army. The army and civil service was professionalized, and town government established or strengthened. Although serfdom was abolished on imperial lands, the nobility defended its retention on their own lands. The situation was thus very uneven. For a good brief sketch which bears on the theoretical concerns of the various actors see F. Hertz, *The German Public Mind in the Nineteenth Century* (London, 1975), Ch.1.

that I hated'.[3] Deciding to give up law, Marx began to prepare a doctoral thesis in the hope of obtaining a university lectureship.[4]

The critique of religion as the key to social criticism

The philosophical climate of Germany was dominated at this time by the ideas of Hegel, more especially in Berlin where he had held his final professorship. But Hegel's legacy was equivocal. Hegel had argued that history involved the working out, and making actual, of what was rational. There were two 'Hegelian' tendencies in Germany at the time, one of which, the more conservative, attempted merely to demonstrate that the social and political status quo was indeed rational, that the historical process had been achieved, or, as Marx put it to 'turn philosophy inward'. The other school attempted to 'turn philosophy outward', [5] that is to make an as yet imperfect and irrational social reality conform to a philosophical ideal of rationality. In terms of Hegel's aphorism that the rational is the real, and the real the rational, one party took one side and the other party the other.

The 'Young Hegelians' as the radical Hegelians were called regarded themselves as true disciples of Hegel. They deployed his method which involved an internal critique of the seemingly irrational to reveal its hidden rational kernel within. The area of thought to which they especially applied themselves was the philosophy of religion, which, for a number of reasons, continued to be a very active area in German intellectual life. Hegel's conception of religion as 'truth in a veil' proved powerful and suggestive. Religion was important for Hegel, as, along with art and philosophy, the highest form of spirit, even if it remained the task of philosophy to explain it. It was to this task that the Young Hegelians were devoting themselves.

Yet if Hegel had been clear about the importance of religion, he had been less clear about the exact status of religious truth. Although he regarded himself as a devout Lutheran, his philosophical identification of God with the Absolute Idea, was to say the least, theologically unorthodox. Hegel claimed that his philosophy of religion involved no innovation, 'merely' the transformation into the form of thinking of a content that had previously been provided by faith: 'The object of religion , like that of philosophy, is eternal truth . . . Philosophy is only explicating *itself* when it explicates religion, and when it explicates itself it is explicating religion. For the *thinking* spirit is what penetrates this object, the truth; it is thinking that enjoys the truth and purifies the subjective consciousness. Thus, religion and philosophy coincide.'[6]

A number of conservative commentators and followers of Hegel in the 1820s were prepared to accept Hegel's assurances and to recruit Hegelian philosophy of religion into the Christian apologetics of the restoration regime.[7] However those who perceived a

---

[3] Letter to his father in *Karl Marx Early Texts*, ed. David McLellan (Oxford 1971), subsequently *ET.*, p. 8.

[4] *KMLT*, pp. 1–34.

[5] Quoted from Marx's doctoral thesis, *Marx Before Marxism*, David McLellan (London 1970) p. 66.

[6] G.W.F. Hegel, 'Introduction', *Lectures on the Philosophy of Religion*, ed. Peter C. Hodgson (Berkeley, 1988), pp. 78–9.

[7] John Edward Toews, *Hegelianism* (Cambridge, 1980), pp. 146–51.

tension between the two concepts of the Absolute Idea and the Christian God, were insistently faced with the issue of whether Hegel's claim that there was an identity of content between the two reduced the content of God to the content of Hegel's philosophy, or elevated the metaphysical system of a mere mortal to a parity with the divine plan of the Almighty. Neither alternative endeared Hegel to the orthodox Lutherans and pietists with a deep suspicion of the impact of philosophy on religion, and who were unhappy about the influence enjoyed by Hegelianism in university circles.

It seems to have been at the practical level that the identity between absolute and God broke down. David Freidrich Strauss was a Hegelian village pastor, who tried to reconcile his advanced philosophical ideas with the need to deploy traditional religious representational language and imagery in his Sunday sermons.[8] The struggle to reconcile image and concept led Strauss to write an influential *Life of Jesus* (1835) arguing that the need to believe in a literal flesh and blood Christ belonged to an earlier age: 'Faith in her early stages is governed by the senses, and therefore contemplates a temporal history; what she holds to be true is the external, ordinary event, . . . a fact to be proved by sense-certainty.' With the historical development and sophistication of humankind, however, 'the object of faith is completely changed; instead of a sensible, empirical fact, it has become a spiritual and divine idea which has its confirmation no longer in history but in philosophy.'[9] The incarnation, therefore should be seen not as literal historical truth, but as an allegory of the essentially spiritual essence of mankind – a truth which Hegelianism articulated at the philosophical level. Strauss did not see himself as a radical, indeed in social terms he seems to have been a conservative. His naive attempt to clear up doubts about the compatibility of Hegelianism and religion served however only to confirm them for many.

Worse was to follow. Bruno Bauer, one of the last of the generation of Hegel's pupils, was recruited by the conservative 'Old Hegelians' to answer Strauss' work. After six years of publishing a variety of works Bauer came to conclusions which held little comfort for his sponsors. In his *Critique of the Synoptic Gospels* he argued that Strauss had stepped outside Hegelianism and retained a residual 'mystery' albeit in secular form. For by explaining the historical origin of the ideas comprising the life of Jesus as the projection, by the Jewish Gospel writers, of inherited Jewish mythical ideas, onto the Christ-figure, Strauss had had resort to contingent and arbitrary – in fact 'irrational' factors. Since these sources were unexplained (philosophically) Strauss had not 'closed the gap' between religion and philosophical absolutism by excluding the irrational. For Bauer, far from upsetting the delicate balance between philosophy and religion, Strauss had failed to press the truths of philosophical insight into the nature of religion far enough. The progress of spirit towards the absolute, was, for Bauer, the progress of human consciousness to an awareness of its own agency in the creation of (its) forms of consciousness, including religious forms. The achievement of that awareness constituted the breakthrough which revealed both religion, and Hegelianism as having only an anthropological content. Neither religion, nor Hegelianism was about a transcendent

---

[8] Ibid., pp. 170–71
[9] D. F. Strauss, *The Life of Jesus* (1835), excerpted in *The Young Hegelians*, ed. Lawrence Stapelevich (Cambridge, 1983), p. 50.

beyond, they were about mankind. Hegelianism, which had been taken by many to be 'a mirror of orthodoxy', was now revealed as a 'system of atheism'.[10]

Bauer followed through his philosophical analysis by drawing practical implications. If the successive phases of human consciousness were identified with the creation of cultural and institutional forms, then the breakthrough into full self-consciousness represented the emergence of the radical possibility of human beings self-consciously creating institutions and social structures in the full knowledge of their freedom to do so; and dismantling those – political, religious and social – which had come about during the period when humans were ignorant of the possibility of exercising their control over these things. The gap between the actual and the rational is now seen to require not an effort at mere intellectual synthesis, but the reordering of reality itself: 'Philosophy becomes a critic of the established order . . . philosophy must be active in politics, and whenever the established order contradicts the self-consciousness of philosophy, it must be directly attacked and shaken.'[11]

By now the radical cat was well out of the theological bag, and the issues were becoming openly political. Although initially, neither Strauss nor Bauer seem to have had political motives, the fact was that interest in the philosophy of religion was becoming intimately connected with social and political criticism. Religious criticism could evade censorship, if it was serious-minded enough, and this may have attracted radicals to the genre, but in the non-constitutional monarchy of the time, even politically liberal ideals were treasonable and critical philosophy of any kind was regarded with deep suspicion. The movement as a whole provided a springboard for social and political criticism. Hegelian theology was clearly a threat to the politico-theological orthodoxy underpinning the state. In 1841 the aged Schelling was wheeled out by the new King of Prussia, Frederick William to (as he put it) 'root out the dragon seed of Hegelianism' which was producing so much unorthodox theological speculation.[12] Strauss, Bauer and all of their followers were excluded from university posts. Indeed Bauer, who had provoked his own dismissal, regarded it as a vindication of his analysis of the incapacity of the existing church-state order to handle the new philosophical truths, truths he referred to as 'theoretical terrorism'.[13]

However the movement for reform was very fragmented, for it was unclear what form it should take. Perceptions of injustices were very different in different parts of Germany. Indeed the issue of unification itself was to be one on which reformers differed. Liberal political institutions existed patchily in different areas, and not at all at the national level. A partly modernized feudal agricultural system operated in the east, in the west, in the Rhineland, a brutalized proletariat was already being described by Engels.[14] In Germany there were thus two kinds of battles to be fought – a fact that was to have a profound effect on the development of Marxism as a theory. There was the battle to establish –

---

[10] Toews, *Hegelianism*, pp. 320–3

[11] Ibid., p. 325; Bruno Bauer, *The Trumpet of the Last Judgement*, excerpted in Stepelevich, *Young Hegelians*, p. 184.

[12] *KMLT*, pp. 40–1. 1841 was in fact the year of publication of Ludwig Feuerbach's *Essence of Christianity*. The episode made a great impact on the young Engels, see Terrell Carver, *Marx and Engels: the intellectual relationship* (Brighton, 1983), p. 8.

[13] Teows, *Hegelianism*, pp. 316–18.

[14] Carver, *Marx and Engels*, p. 4.

against the remnants of political and economic feudalism – the institutions of a liberal and commercial state, and there was, for some others at least, the battle to establish a socialist answer to the evils of developing capitalism, the poisoning and maiming of workers and children in unregulated factories, the discharge of untreated poisons, the destruction of familial stability and resulting poverty and degradation already described by Hegel in the *Philosophy of Right*.

The Young Hegelians, now excluded from any possibility of official positions, were free to develop their critical ideas in the most extravagant and diverse ways, and they did so. Most modern discussions of their ideas fail to bring out their increasing desire to shock conventional society and the sheer confrontationalism of their life-style.[15] Their irresponsible and idiosyncratic radicalism was later to be lampooned and ridiculed by Marx in *The Holy Family, or A Critique of Critical Criticism: against Bruno Bauer and Co.* (1845). Yet in important ways they remained within the Hegelian system, Bauer for example presented his conclusions as the true implications of Hegel's ideas.

The pervasiveness of Hegel seems to have influenced Marx in his choice of doctoral dissertation. He chose a study of the materialist philosophies of Democritus, a presocratic, eleatic philosopher, and Epicurus, a Hellenistic philosopher who wrote under the shadow of Aristotle in precisely the same way as the Young Hegelians seemed to be under the shadow of Hegel.[16] Marx may have been further influenced in his choice of subject by the insistence of Bruno Bauer, the senior Young Hegelian, that it was in the post Aristotelian philosophy that the philosophical basis of the modern world was to be found, and not – as orthodox Hegelians suggested – in Christianity which was its religious, and therefore mystified, representation.[17]

Marx certainly adopted the Young Hegelian attempt to reduce religion to philosophy, and incorporated an appendix to his thesis making this clear:

> . . . philosophy will continually shout at her opponents the cry of Epicurus: 'Impiety does not consist in destroying the gods of the crown [i.e. politics], but rather in ascribing to the gods the ideas of the crown.' Philosophy makes no secret of it. The proclamation of Prometheus: 'in one word – I hate all gods' is her own profession, her own slogan against all gods of heaven and earth who do not recognize man's self-consciousness as the highest divinity.[18]

The notion that God and religion were a projection of the human mind was one of the most exciting ideas circulating in Young Hegelian circles. The most famous exponent

---

[15] This was particularly true of the Berlin group know as 'the Free', who included Bruno Bauer and Max Stirner, the anarchist. For an account which brings out well the *louche*, bohemian context see Robert J. Hellman, *Berlin, the Red Room and White Beer, the 'Free' Hegelian Radicals in the 1840s* (Washington, 1990).

[16] McLellan, *Marx Before Marxism* p. 55, and R. Tucker, *Philosophy and Myth in Karl Marx* (London 1961) p. 77 both make the suggestion. But see G. Teeple, 'Marx's Doctoral Dissertation', *History of Political Thought*, XI, 1 (1990) which argues Marx had a much more specific reason for studying these thinkers which was to sort out certain problems in the relationship between idealism and materialism for science.

[17] In all of this too, the Young Hegelians were taking their cue from Hegel who, both in the *Phenomenology*, and in the *Philosophy of Right* (note to §185), had stressed the Hellenistic period as one of the spiritual sources of modernity.

[18] 'Preface' to Marx's Doctoral Dissertation, *ET*, p. 13.

of it was Ludwig Feuerbach whose *Essence of Christianity* was, however, not published until 1841, the year Marx submitted his thesis. In it Feuerbach pressed the development of Hegel's ideas on religion to breaking point; he was, writes one commentator, to Hegel, what the cup of hemlock was to Socrates, [19] and Marx himself acknowledged his debt to Feuerbach in freeing him from the last shackles of idealism. [20]

Feuerbach retained Hegel's method in criticizing philosophy or religion from inside itself, trying to use the content of the doctrine under analysis as itself a method of criticism. [21] His argument is roughly as follows: Christianity can be presented as a series of propositions: God made the world, God made man, God became man, God can save man through love. Orthodox Christianity presents these as a set of historical propositions about mankind in general and an independently existing God. For Hegel these are statements about the relationship between man and an idealist entity called the Absolute Mind. Yet the central truth proclaimed by Christianity is that God became man. This central truth or 'essence' of Christianity is to be used as a key to unlock the real truth of the rest of the Christian message by substituting the term 'man' for the term 'God' in the other central propositions of the doctrine. The central truth, or 'essence' of Christianity (that God become man) was to be understood as an interpretive principle. [22] We then find that the propositions of religion can be resolved into anthropology, they are statements about exclusively *human relationships*: Feuerbach claims that the central truths of Christianity are really statements about the relation between man and his own ideas:

> God is nothing else than the nature of man purified from that which to the human individual appears . . . an evil, so the future life freed from that which appears as a limitation or evil . . . But the separation of the soul from the body, of . . . God from man must be abolished again . . . So our process of analysis has brought us again to the position with which we set out. The beginning, middle and end of religion is MAN.' [23]

Feuerbach is claiming in fact that Christian dogma represents a hidden humanism which can be discovered using the 'essence' of Christianity — the idea that God can become man. The truth behind the veil of religion is that religion is a veiled humanism. So it is not God, but man who *intellectually* creates the world in his language, who creates his picture of himself, his psychological states, and who can resolve the problems there through love for man.

As we have seen the basis of such ideas was common amongst the Young Hegelians. Feuerbach is famous for having given the most thoroughgoing account of them, but there

---

[19] Quoted in S. Hook, *From Hegel to Marx* (New York, 1950) p. 220.

[20] 'They [Feuerbach's] are the only writings since Hegel's *Phenomenology* and *Logic* to contain a real theoretical revolution.' 'Preface' to the *Economic and Philosophical Manuscripts of 1844*, *ET*, p.132, and in Karl Marx, *Early Writings*, ed. L.Colletti (Harmondsworth, 1975), p. 281; hereafter cited as *EW*. Where titles occur in both collections reference will be given to each location.

[21] As did Marx. Consider this from a letter to Ruge in 1843: 'Reason has always existed, but not always in a rational form. Hence the critic can take his cue from every existing form of theoretical and practical consciousness and from this ideal and final goal implicit in the *actual* forms of existing reality he can deduce a true reality.' *EW*, p. 208; *ET*, p.80.

[22] For a more nuanced discussion see Marx W. Wartofsky, *Feuerbach* (Cambridge, 1977), ch.8.

[23] Ludwig Feuerbach, *The Essence of Christianity* (New York and London, 1957) pp. 181, 183, 184.

is no evidence that the *Essence of Christianity* itself had any profound effect on Marx. What did have an effect and was to have the most far-reaching consequences was Feuerbach's extension of his ideas on religion into the field of philosophy.

In his *Principles of the Philosophy of the Future* (1844) Feuerbach starts from the point he had previously left off: he assumes the reduction of theology to anthropology as complete. In the process of this he points out that the attributes of Hegel's 'absolute idea' are in fact identical with the attributes of 'God' (sect 9).

> By the same token that abstraction from all that is sensuous and material was once the necessary condition of theology, so was it also the necessary condition of speculative philosophy, except for the difference that the theological abstraction was, as it were, a sensuous abstraction, because its object although reached by abstraction, was at the same time imagined as a sensuous being, whereas the abstraction of speculative philosophy is an intellectual and ideational abstraction that has only scientific or theoretical, but not practical, meaning. The beginning of Descartes' philosophy, namely the abstraction from sensation and matter, is the beginning of modern speculative philosophy.[24]

Hegel's philosophy, is now to be interpreted in the way the Young Hegelians had interpreted religion; it is, claims Feuerbach, merely a secularized version of religion. Just as religion abstracts and mystifies human relations, so Hegelian philosophy abstracts them, attributing to the abstract categories of thought the properties and qualities of flesh and blood individuals. In contrast to Hegel's claims about history being the activity of the spirit, it is actual physical individuals that make up the world, not abstract categories. True knowledge, immediate knowledge, is based on sensation, and not my sensations alone, but those shared and agreed sensations of a community. Reality for Feuerbach is human inter subjectivity. Truth lies not in the idea but in the totality of human sense-experience.[25]

Here was the exit from the closed garden of Hegelian idealism which Marx and his contemporaries sought. There was much still to be squeezed from Hegel both in terms of using his method and in terms of bringing out the latent truths in his idealism, and there is a sense in which Feuerbach, and indeed Marx, could be said to have remained Hegelians, applying their master's methods to the content of his own philosophy. But from now on , philosophy dealt with the world and 'the world' meant human beings in their sensuously experienced existence.

Early radical journalism

After receiving his doctorate, eventually at the University of Jena and not at Berlin, in 1841, Marx began to write for a radical newspaper, the *Rheinische Zeitung*.[26] Two

[24] Ludwig Feuerbach, *Principles of the Philosophy of the Future* (Indianapolis, N.Y., 1966), p. 13.

[25] Ibid. pp. 70, 71; and see Wartofsky, *Feuerbach*, p. 349ff.

[26] On these see A. McGovern, 'Karl Marx's first political writings, the Rheinische Zeitung 1842–3' in *Demythologizing Marxism*, ed. F. Adelman (The Hague, 1969); and Heinz Lubasz, 'Marx's Initial Problematic: The Problem of Poverty', *Political Studies*, XXIV, 1 (1976).

articles, one dealing with the freedoms of the press and one with legislation on the theft of firewood have particularly attracted attention. The law on press freedom draws on Hegel's argument about law being the rational embodiment of freedom and not being confined to certain groups – in this Marx went no further than advanced liberal views. But in dealing with the issue of 'wood theft' Marx, as he later acknowledged, first confronted the socio-economic issues raised by the transition from a feudal to a bourgeois society, from communal to individually defined rights. Traditionally, in the Rhineland, wood-gathering for fuel was a common right. Just as 'commons' in Great Britain, had been enclosed by Acts of Parliament, reassigning property rights to particular individuals so that the exercise of once 'common right' became a crime, so, now, property rights in Germany were being 'privatized' and people were being prosecuted for exercising what, a short time ago, had been their 'common' right. An anonymous English verse precisely captures the irony of a situation in which minor thefts were punished whilst great ones could be perpetrated by legislation:

> The law is hard on man or woman
> Who steals the goose from off the common
> But lets the greater felon loose
> Who steals the common from the goose!

As Marx was quick to point out, there was no mystery about the source of rural poverty in this situation. It was a direct consequence of the redefinition of property rights which led people to have to pay for things (e.g. fuel), which they had previously been able to gather for free.

Under Marx's editorship, which he gradually assumed in 1842, the paper prospered in the relatively liberal climate of the Rhineland, but it eventually succumbed to the censorship it had so vigorously attacked. Arnold Ruge, one of the original Young Hegelians with private means, suggested publishing another paper in Strasbourg just across the border in France, out of reach of the censor: and Marx was commissioned to write a series of articles, paid in advance. This gave Marx the opportunity to synthesize his thoughts on religion, his criticisms of Hegel and his growing social and political radicalism. He did this through his usual method of a critique.

The critique of Hegel

Marx took Hegel's *Philosophy of Right*, and applied to it the critical tools developed by the Young Hegelian school in their critique of religion. More especially he applied Feuerbach's 'transformational criticism', that is the practice of inverting subject and object in the central theses of a particular philosophy or standpoint. Marx agreed with Feuerbach's central critique of Hegel. Hegel's central philosophical position was that change takes place through contradiction between (or within) concepts or ideas. Particular things, institutions or societies, are exemplifications, at differing levels of adequacy or development, of concepts or ideas. Ultimately it is the need for the idea of the whole, or the totality, to iron out internal contradictions, which determines the existence or failure of particulars. One consequence of this is Hegel's assimilation of logic to causality, so that it is concepts and abstractions which seem to be 'causing' or bringing about real, actual institutions and states in the world. The mentality or outlook of individuals at particular points in time is said to be a manifestation of, or determined by, the movement of 'spirit' or mind in general. Hegel attributed even the invention of firearms to the spirit's need to change the social mentality from that of individual heroism to the more socially disciplined one of modernity.[27]

The general point to emerge from Feuerbach's criticism is that Hegel inverted subject and object: it is individual human beings who have consciousness and thoughts, not an abstract or hypostatized 'thought' or 'consciousness' that gives rise to individuals or their culture. Yet there remained the problem of identifying the nature of these 'individuals' and the process which shaped their consciousness – religious and other. Marx wrote to Ruge 'he (Feuerbach) refers too much to nature and not enough to politics'.[28] If the determinants of 'actual human consciousness' could not be articulated without falling back on some hazy notion of human 'nature', political theory would be in danger of reverting to that unsatisfactory seventeenth and eighteenth-century move of presuming, as given, some idea of human nature which turned out to be a figment of the thinker's imagination, or reading into men's nature the characteristics of the particular society in which he was living.

Furthermore this question of how to arrive at a conception of human nature had implications for how 'religious alienation' was to be overcome: Feuerbach seemed to see his philosophy itself as therapy – rather as psycho-analysis suggests that bringing our subconscious fears and neuroses to the level of awareness will itself loosen their power over us. To Marx, Feuerbach seemed to suggest that the unhappiness of men in the world – the longing and sense of incompleteness that characterized the religious mentality – could be shrugged off simply by getting them to recognize religion for what it was – a projection of a merely human consciousness. Yet even Hegel had originally seen that religion was a response to a dislocation in men's social world.[29] To expect men to give up religion simply because one had explained that it was a projection of their own psyches would be like expecting a patient to stop feeling pain because it had 'only' psychological causes. Marx's criticism of Feuerbach was that in believing that religious alienation could be overcome by simply making people aware of it, by mere exhortation, Feuerbach remained an idealist; for to argue in this way is to ignore the social reasons why people sought consolation in religion in the first place. Interestingly, although denying that religious alienation can be overcome by an act of will, Marx was at this time a voluntarist as far as politics was concerned, and still impressed with the ideals of classical antiquity, writing again to Ruge about Germany he argues:

> man's self-esteem, his sense of freedom, must be re-awakened in the breast of these people. This sense vanished from the world with the Greeks, and with Christianity it took up residence in the blue mists of heaven, but only with its aid can society ever again become a community of men that can fulfill their highest needs, democratic state.[30]

[27] The argument being that firearms rendered individuals such as mounted knights too vulnerable and required war to be conducted by disciplined bodies of troops in formation. See *Philosophy of Right*, §328, n.

[28] Marx to Arnold Ruge, 13 March 1843, *ET*, p. 60.

[29] *The Phenomenology of Spirit*, tr.Baillie, p. 264ff.

[30] Marx to Arnold Ruge, May 1843, *EW*, p. 201; *ET*, p.75.

The problem of how to inspire political ideals was shelved for the moment. The next efforts of Marx were devoted to applying Feuerbach's transformational critique to Hegel's *Philosophy of Right*, or at least that part of it that dealt directly with the state. The result was his *Critique of Hegel's Philosophy of Right*, written between March and August 1843, but unpublished in Marx's lifetime. In it Marx assumes that Hegel's theory of the state, like religion itself, contains the correct content but in a mystified form. Hegel writes as though the 'Idea' differentiates itself into the family and the economy, thus determining their natures:

> The family and civil society are the presuppositions of the state . . . in speculative thought the relationship is inverted. When the idea is made a subject the real subjects become unreal objective phases of the idea and have a completely different significance

Instead of creating the state they are presented as being created by it. Whereas in fact says Marx:

> The state arises from them in an unconscious and arbitrary way. The family and civil society are the dark background from which the light of the state is kindled . . . In Hegel the Idea is given the status of a subject, and the actual relationship of family and civil society to the state is conceived of as its inner imaginative activity . . . But just as religion does not make man but man makes religion so the constitution of the state doesn't make the people, but the people make the constitution, The fact is the state issues from the mass of men existing as members of families and of civil society.[31]

A consequence of reversing this causality so that the state 'arises' from civil society, instead of them both being 'phases' of the idea, is that the state, far from being able, as Hegel supposed it would be, to mediate the antagonisms and conflicts of civil society, would be bound to reflect them. Nor could it control a bureaucratic class which would be bound to interpret the state's interest in terms of its own. Indeed Hegel's representation of the state as standing above the conflicts of society, was, for Marx, a part of the ideological illusion that was necessary to sustain or legitimize the imperfect state. In the Middle Ages the state *was* seen in terms of the categories of civil society, as an assemblage of private rights and properties. At this time the relationship between the state and civil society was clear: 'civil society determined, indeed, comprised the state, people's life and the life of the state were identical. Man was the real principle of the state, but it was *unfree* man.'[32]

Modern society on the other hand turns the state into an abstraction so that it can *claim* that its citizens are free. But the claim is only an abstract one. The modern state, as Hegel noted, gives people general legal freedoms based on an abstract idea of man possessing certain capacities and a certain amount of property, capacities and property which individuals may not, and indeed increasingly did not, possess. The modern state had to be presented as an abstraction, pointed out Marx, because it satisfied only an abstraction of humankind. It is man as he is in civil society that determines the nature of the state,

---

[31] 'Critique of Hegel's *Philosophy of Right* ', *ET*, pp. 61ff.; *EW* , pp.61–2.

[32] Ibid., *ET*, p. 68; *EW*, p.90.

and the man in civil society, as Hegel had shown in the very arrangement of his *Philosophy of Right* is man determined by property rights. Marx develops Hegel in an almost photographic sense turning Hegel's determining concepts into determined ones, his abstract subjects into concrete objects and ultimately his philosophy into economics. Indeed it has been argued with a good degree of plausibility that the structure of part III of Hegel's *Philosophy of Right* provided Marx with the whole plan of campaign for his later economic studies.[33]

However there is still another strand of Marx's early thought that leads him into economics besides his desire to clarify the 'dark forces' operating within civil society, and that strand relates still to religion. For although Marx believed religion to be an illusion, it was an illusion that contained in a distorted way, and so held a clue to, the nature of the society that produced it.

'On the Jewish question': the conceptual breakthrough from religion to economics

In his *Introduction to a Contribution to a Critique of Hegel's Philosophy of Right*, written after the critique, in Paris in late 1843, Marx made clear his view that the resort to religion was an important symptom of deeper and material problems. The criticism of religion had shown that it is man who makes religion and not the other way around; but the men who make religion are particular men who do so as a result of particular historical circumstances. Not only does it follow that the demand to abolish religious illusions is pointless unless something is done about the material circumstances of those people who need to seek fulfilment in the illusory happiness of religion, but, he also suggests, in some of his most memorable prose, that the particular *form* taken by religious belief provides a vital key to understanding the form of the society which produces it:

> This state and this society produce religion, which is *an inverted consciousness of the world*, because they are an *inverted world* . . . . The struggle against religion is therefore indirectly the struggle against *that world* whose spiritual *aroma* is religion.

> *Religious* suffering is at one and the same time the *expression* of real suffering and a protest against real suffering. Religion is the sigh of the oppressed creature, the heart of a heartless world and the soul of soulless conditions. It is the *opium* of the people.

> The abolition of religion as the *illusory* happiness of the people is the demand for their *real* happiness. To call on them to give up their illusions about their condition is to *call on them to give up a condition that requires illusions*. The criticism of religion is therefore in *embryo* the *criticism of that vale of tears* of which religion is the *halo*.[34]

Marx agrees with both Feuerbach and Hegel that although religion is not *literally* true, nevertheless the *content* of religious belief tells us something true about the social world that produces religious beliefs. Indeed Feuerbach, as we have seen, used the content of Christianity, the belief that God came down to man, to discover its hidden message: that

---

[33] J.O'Malley, 'Marx's "Economics" and Hegel's *Philosophy of Right*'. *Political Studies*, XXIV, 1 (1976).

[34] 'Introduction' to 'A Critique of Hegel's *Philosophy of Right* ', *EW*, p. 244; *ET*, p.115.

God is really only a projection of man and man must 'bring God back down to earth again', i.e. convert religious tenets into humanist ones.

This had led a number of Young Hegelians to demand the secularization of the state, for how could men renounce religion when it was embedded in the laws of the state? The political emancipation of the Jews was a standing item on the agenda of German reformists ever since the failure of Hardenberg to achieve it in his 1810 programme. To the liberal the removal of civil disabilities based on religion was a precondition for the emergence of the new universal secular citizen. But did the causality work that way round? Could political emancipation itself produce a secular, emancipated society?

Bruno Bauer had pointed out that demands for Jewish emancipation then being made were demands made in terms which precluded their being granted: to ask for *Jewish* emancipation is to ask for the freeing of a group *defined in religious terms* from religious discrimination. As long as Jewishness is pursued as an identity, Bauer claims, it must attract many of the attitudes and criticisms which history has given it. To deny them this is to deny the Jewish experience. Part of this is their reputation for avarice. Jews have, claims Bauer, through usury, exploited the needs and weaknesses of those left unsupported by the economic corporations which Christian society has produced to mollify the worst effects of commercial society. They didn't create those needs, but they used them. Whilst they cannot be blamed for this, they were in a position to exploit those needs as a consequence of their having adopted a position by which they deliberately excluded themselves from the rest of society, but this exclusion is no honour. It shows only that Jews had refused, unlike other tribes, to meld into the wider society and develop with history. This is the root of the problem. Emancipation can only be achieved, claimed Bauer, not only by abolishing the state's concern with any religious differences, but by exclusive groups themselves renouncing their own religious identities.[35]

Marx takes issue with this in his essay *On the Jewish Question*. For Marx, Bauer does not penetrate to the core of the issue at all. Firstly Bauer asks only for the abolition of the *Christian* state. He treats religious differences as accretions on the state which can be abolished, as Feuerbach suggests, *by an act of (here political) will.* Instead, Marx argues, these religious accretions need to be seen as expressions of the inadequacy of the state *as such.* It is the nature of the state itself, and not just its religious laws that needs analysis and correction. Marx notes that 'the Jewish question' takes different forms in different situations. In Germany where there is no real state at all it takes the form of a religious problem, in France which is a constitutional state it takes the form of a political issue. In America, which is a democracy, a perfect political state, we should expect to find no religious differences. Marx's argument is that if religion is a pathology caused by imperfections in man's earthly life, then its continued existence in even the most perfect *state*, must mean that the modern state as such is imperfect, even in its most perfect form, as democracy: 'the existence of religion is the existence of a defect, the source of this defect can only be sought in the nature of the state itself.[36] So, claims Marx, the question of the relationship between religious emancipation and politics seems to beg the much more general question of the relationship between human emancipation and the state. The declaration of a purely secular state no more frees man from the need

[35] Bruno Bauer, *The Jewish Problem* (1843); excerpted in Stepelevich, *Young Hegelians*, pp. 187–97.
[36] Marx, *On the Jewish Question*, *ET*, p. 91; *EW*, p. 217.

for religion, than the abolition of a property franchise frees man from the need for property.

Marx is here beginning to develop the notion that our view of the political world might be just as much an illusion as our religious views, indeed he goes on to suggest a close structural similarity between the nature of religious illusion and the nature of political illusion fostered by the bourgeois – even the democratic bourgeois – state. The political state is to civil society, what heaven is to earth: just as in political life we assert the abstract rights of man, whilst in commercial life we treat the labourer as an object of gain for ourselves, so in religion we assert the sanctity of the soul whilst treating man on earth as the sinners our religion tells us we are. In each case the ideal compensates for the actual. At least the espousal of Christian *ideals* somehow makes us better, even though we can't live up to them: the religious practice of confession is a formal recognition of this. So, by analogy, the constitution of the liberal state salves our consciences for the plight of those who are impoverished by its actual, economic, reality by giving everyone the same rights and assuring us that we are all legally, i.e. purely formally, equal. So, argues Marx, even the democratic liberal state is imperfect in a way to which religion not only provides a clue, but is actually implicated. 'The state is still a theologian who acts as confessor to the Christian faith – it allows religion to continue as long as it declares its interest.' The democratic state is founded, as an ideal, on the humanized truth of Christianity – that is on the recognition of a common humanity – for it gives formal and political rights to all (men). But because it remains an ideal (the equality is only formal), because there is a discrepancy between the ideal (civic equality and fraternity) and the reality (which is civil society – economic competition, inequality and institutionalised selfishness) there is, thinks Marx, still a need for religion, and a religion which *structurally* represents to its adherents the problems which give rise to the need for it.

> ... political emancipation from religion allows religion – but not privileged religion – to continue in existence. The contradiction in which the adherent of a particular religion finds himself in relation to this citizenship is only *one aspect* of the general *secular contradiction between the political state and civil society*. The final form of the Christian state is one which recognizes itself as the state and disregards the religion of its members. The emancipation of the state from religion is not the emancipation of actual man from religion.[37]

In the second part of this work Marx goes on to make good his claim that the *content* of religious life can actually provide a clue to the social problems which give rise to it; as he put it in his *Introduction to a Contribution to Hegel's Philosophy of Right*: 'It is the immediate task of philosophy which is in the service of history, to unmask self-estrangement in its unholy forms once the holy form of human self-estrangement has been unmasked.'[38] We must then, he insists, look for the nature of Jewishness, not 'in the sabbath Jew', i.e. in the doctrinal content of Judaism, but in the 'everyday Jew', that is to say in the role Jewishness plays in normal 'Christian' society. If we look at the social form that Jewishness takes within Christian societies we find that it comes down to the

[37] Ibid., *EW*, p. 226; *ET*, p.100.
[38] *EW*, p. 244; *ET*, p. 116.

worship of money. That is what the Jew 'represents' to Christian society, and this is precisely why he must be ostracized, the Jew is a symbol to the Christian of what *Christian* society actually is – but cannot be admitted to be. It is because of the moral and psychological tension between the humanitarian and charitable ideal and the avaricious facts of the state's social life that we still need religion, and the *form* that religion takes is to project our ideals into our religious principles, whilst attributing the inhuman reality of our society onto the religion of some other group (indeed a religious group, which are held responsible for the death of the Christian God) in this case the Jews.[39] Indeed, inasmuch as Christian societies have actually become devoted to the pursuit of commercial gain they have already emancipated the Jews by themselves becoming practical Jews: they practise all those activities which are attributed, in theory and prejudice to the Jews themselves. Supposed practical Jewishness, the worship of money, is the reality of Christian material life within commercial society. 'Sunday' Christianity is the humanitarian ideal and illusion which makes that inhuman reality bearable. Marx's insight into the as yet uninvented realm of the subconscious is here extraordinary. By projecting the unacceptable reality of their own society onto the Jews, and punishing them for it, he suggests, Christian society was able to exorcise and make bearable its guilt at the gap between its own ideals and reality.

Money, says Marx, pursuing still the analogy of religion, is a jealous god, it debases all other gods (or ideals) and turns them into commodities. Because money, like God, is itself the measure of value, it takes away the intrinsic value of other things. In practice we increasingly find that objects, qualities and even our real experienced desires, are not acknowledged to be real unless they can be expressed in money terms, and conversely unless I possess money, I cannot enjoy any real existence, for there is no way in which to express myself without it. This makes human worth a function of their wealth, just as in religion we are valued according to the properties of our God. So money functions in civil society just as a God does in religion. The claim of the Christian God that: 'except in me there is no salvation' becomes a truth about the need for money in order to live.[40]

This work has been cited as evidence for Marx's supposed anti-semitism, but only the most superficial reading of it could sustain such an interpretation. Rather, it is an astonishingly brilliant analysis of the workings of the social sub-conscious. Whether the Jews are truly avaricious or not is irrelevant to Marx's thesis, which concerns the way that what is attributed to Jews functions to deflect Christian awareness of the gap between Christian practice and Christian values. Marx is dealing with the belief system of Christian commercial society and only consequently with its religious sociology, and for him it is the fact that Christian society feels the need to *attribute* such characteristics to Jews that is significant. Indeed Marx's argument to some extent relies on the fact that the German for Jewry has a secondary meaning of commerce.[41] Of course if society organized itself in such a way as to force Jews to engage in the kind of behaviour it wished to attribute to them, then this, as Bauer had argued, would merely reinforce Marx's case. But Bauer had attributed this to Jews' and Christians' desire to maintain their separate religious identity, whereas Marx explains this religious identity itself as a product of the moral tensions in a society organized by commercial principles. In fact the laws

---

[39] *Jewish Question*, EW, p. 238; *ET*, p. 99.

[40] Ibid., *EW*, pp. 239–41; *ET*, pp. 112–114; see also the essay 'On Money' in *1844 MSS*, *EW*, pp. 375 ff.; *ET*, p.178.

[41] *KMLT*, p. 86.

concerning usury had of course for long accomplished this; but like other aspects of the relationship between economic and political life which had been brutally clear in the middle ages, the modern state had managed to elevate them to the level of abstract thought.

The notion that money could be viewed as a god, or rather, to put things in their correct relationship, the notion that religion was an allegory of economic life, provided Marx with the final transformation of the Hegelian system. It was the last of the 'veils' hiding the truths that religion had promised mankind. Religion had been re-interpreted as an allegory of philosophy, only for philosophy to be re-interpreted as a realm not of ideas but of actual sensuous existence. Religion had thus in turn provided an allegory of social life and politics. But even the abolition of political imperfection does not abolish the need for religion, showing that it is not political imperfections which give rise to the need for it. However the social form that religious belief takes, provided Marx with the idea that all these layers of illusion, religious, philosophical and political are ultimately projections of the imperfections of man's economic, life. The final truths to be wrung from religion involve the exploration of religion in general, and Christianity in particular, as an allegory of man's material existence. This task was undertaken in a set of documents known today as the 'Paris Manuscripts'.

The first critique of capitalism:
The Paris Manuscripts and 'alienated labour'

Marx had arrived in Paris in the autumn of 1843, bringing with him from Kreuznach the manuscript of *On the Jewish Question*. The reason for going to Paris was the decision to launch Ruge's journal, the *Deutsch-Französische Jahrbücher* from there, rather than Strasburg. Ruge had arrived in August to arrange finance and find contributors, both had proved difficult. In the event the journal did not survive its first issue, containing Marx's essay *On the Jewish Question* and his *Introduction to a Critique of Hegel's Philosophy of Right*. Banned in Prussia, and unable to attract French contributors, the journal fell between two publics, one at which it was aimed and one to which it was available. Meanwhile Marx and Ruge were falling out with each other, Marx's adoption of communism and his bohemian company were offending the moderate and prudish Ruge. The final break occurred over Marx's extravagant criticism of an article Ruge had written on the Silesian weaver's revolt. Marx's optimism over the imminence of revolution was however, and not for the first time, misplaced.[42]

One immensely important consequence of the brief venture was that in November 1843, Marx received an article on the 'Outlines of a Critique of Political Economy' from a young man called Friedrich Engels. Already convinced of the importance of economics, Marx was here overwhelmed by what he saw as a brilliant critical analysis of the most advanced economic thinking of the day, which stimulated and set an agenda for his own work.[43] In the summer of 1844 Marx immersed himself in a study of classical economics,

---

[42] *KMLT*, pp. 77–100.

[43] Marx and Engels had met briefly in 1842, but their intellectual partnership was not to be established until two years later. For a detailed analysis and assessment of the effect of Engels's 'Outline..' on Marx see Terrell Carver, *Marx and Engels*, pp. 32ff.; and his 'Marx — and Engels's Outlines of a Critique of Political Economy', *History of Political Thought*, IV, 3 (1983); also G. Claeys, 'Engels's "Outline..." and the Origins of the Marxist Critique of Capitalism', *History of Political Economy*, xvi (1984).

theories of communism and a renewed attack on Hegel. The result was not only a summary of his whole development so far, but an exploration on which, in the view of some commentators, the rest of his life's work was to be based. Known variously as the 'Paris Manuscripts' and the 'Economic and Philosophical Manuscripts of 1844' they were published only in 1932 and were not widely known in the West until after the Second World War. Since then they have been responsible not only for a reappraisal of Marx's own philosophical and political position, but for a reassessment of the political implications of Marxism. In focussing on Marx's philosophical and humanist ideals, as opposed to the more materialist economic critique of his later years, they have held great appeal for those who sought to combine a Marxist critique of capitalism, with a denunciation of so-called Marxist regimes of the Stalinist model.

The manuscript consists of a short introduction acknowledging his debt to Feuerbach, and expressing Marx's intention to transcend both the criticism of religion and the Hegelian philosophical position which he saw as indistinguishable from it. This is followed by the first manuscript containing a commentary on classical economic doctrines, the relationship of profit to rent, a very short fragment on the relation of capital to labour, further small sections on capitalist competition and on rent and a final important essay on alienated labour. The second manuscript consists of a single essay on private property. The third contains an essay discussing the relationship between private property and labour, and another between private property and communism, another on the division of labour, a short but brilliant essay on money and another final critical essay on Hegel's philosophy as a whole.

It would be foolish to treat these texts as a coherent and finished work. Despite the existence of an introduction there seems little doubt that they were not intended for publication as they stand.[44] The best way to approach them would seem to be to try to relate them to what Marx had already written and see in what way they provided a synthesis or development of those ideas.

The *structure* of the theory informing the Paris Manuscripts is provided by the concept of alienation. The *content* of it is economics, and economics is shown to be the final irreducible content of both religion and speculative philosophy. Let us look first at the concept of alienation.

Alienation

As we have already seen, the concept of alienation was of central importance for Hegel and his followers. For the Young Hegelians religion, as well as being an example of alienation, is an allegory of it, as Feuerbach especially had demonstrated. The Judeo-Christian view of the world as a place to which men had been banished by their God, but from which they would eventually be redeemed by 'God becoming man again' was an allegory of the thought processes involved in alienation. Feuerbach had interpreted the Christian redemption (God becoming man) as the realization that God was a creation of man's mind. The 'realization' that this was the case constituted the return of God, that is the idea of God, to where he belonged, down here on earth as a creation of human

---

[44] Indeed some have argued that as Marx did not even attempt to publish them, they should not be given prominence (see, e.g. M. Evans, *Karl Marx* (London, 1975), pp. 50–2. They are however invaluable in understanding the *development* of Marx's thought.

consciousness. But as we have seen, Marx did not believe that Feuerbach had considered the full implications of his claim that reality lay not in the ideas of man, but in his actual material life. For it seemed to Marx that Feuerbach still dealt with the whole meaning of alienation in terms of ideas or consciousness.

For Marx alienation is not, as in Hegel, a process by which 'mind' projects itself into some 'other' to be eventually overcome by its recognition of this process as its essential reality. Nor, as in Feuerbach, is it only a process by which human individuals project their unhappiness into religion or philosophy, which is then overcome by their recognition that this God or philosophical scheme has no reality outside of their own minds. Alienation for Marx is the *material* process by which man creates things out of nature, comes to be dominated by those creations, but will finally overcome that alienation through recovering control of his own (material) creations. Creativity is thus the central category for Marx, but it is *a) physical* and *b) social* creative activity, not the abstract or individual creation of thought which is central. The creation of ideas, in the form of philosophy or religion is simply a symptom which enables a diagnosis of the form which material alienation has taken. The final truth of Christianity is not merely that man, not God, makes the world *conceptually*, but that he does so *materially* through his own economic activity. Men are continually creating the world, they project themselves into it, by, as Locke had put it 'mixing their labour' with nature. Yet in doing so they lose control of their own creations, and become subject to them, men even create social and economic forms which institutionalize this loss of control – alienation was thus the externalization of human creativity into forms which not only obscured but denied their human, creative origins.

Marx's examination of Hegel's philosophy as a whole, the last time he was to devote a sustained critique to Hegel, makes clear the way in which Marx believed Hegel had got the structure right but the content wrong.

Hegel's whole system is about the 'philosophical mind', a mind which we now know to be itself a product of an alienated society. It is no surprise that an alienated mind should present to us a picture of the world in an alienated form, i.e. as thought, as an abstraction. But philosophy, like religion, although an illusion, provides us with *the structure* of the reality that creates it:

> the greatness of Hegel's *Phenomenology* and its final product, the dialectic of negativity as the moving and creating principle is on the one hand that Hegel conceives of the self-creation of man as a process, objectification as loss of the object as externalization and the transcendence of this externalization . . . he grasps the nature of labour.

It is the content of Hegel that is wrong:

> For Hegel the human essence is the same as self- consciousness, but this is not regarded as itself an expression of man's *real* alienation.[45]

Hegel has the whole thing not so much upside down as inside out. Because he starts with abstract consciousness, actual human consciousness can be presented as an alienation of this abstraction, and the recognition of this process – which merely puts

---

[45] *1844 MSS, EW*, pp. 385–6, 387; *ET*, pp. 164, 165.

everything back inside the head – as realization, the overcoming of alienation. Whereas in fact, argued Marx, it is actual, material men that produce thought. That this is an inadequate view of the whole process can be shown even from within Hegel's own philosophy. For Hegel starts with logic, and the culmination of his discussion of logic leads to his philosophy of nature, thus acknowledging the need for material reality:

> abstract thought that comprehends itself as such knows itself to be nothing. It must abandon itself, as abstraction, and thus arrive at a being that is its exact opposite, nature. The whole *logic* is thus the proof that abstract thought is nothing for itself, the absolute idea is nothing for itself and that only nature is something.

Yet Hegel refuses to acknowledge this, and for him the concept of nature, instead of providing a way out of his purely abstract and idealist system is in turn treated in a purely abstract way *as a set of ideas about nature*: 'thus the whole of Nature, only repeats to him in a sensuous exterior form the abstractions of logic'.[46]

So it appears, that even starting from Hegel's abstract premises, the necessity of acknowledging material nature as a presupposition of abstract thought cannot be denied. But if it is material human beings that are the subject, then the whole developmental process about which Hegel is talking is not a conceptual process, a development of mind, but a material process, a development in some physical sense. The developmental activity of human beings, presented by Hegel as *conceptual* activity, is in fact *practical* activity.

Marx, having already suggested the parallels that could be drawn between our notion of God and the role of money, now draws a similar parallel between money and logic. Just as Hegel's logic creates an illusory reality out of purely abstract – logical – relationships, so does money create an illusory reality out of social relationships. Just as the terms in logic express relationships but cannot of themselves, generate reality, so money expresses value relationships but has no value in itself. The belief that money *does* have a value, so common in commercial society, is itself as much a form of alienation as the philosophical version: the belief that logic can create reality. The whole money system needs to be explained in *other, real* terms for money to have any meaning.[47] Economics which is unrelated to an anthropology or a value-system is simply a set of logical relationships, and whilst the science of economics is interested in the logic of those relationships it does not penetrate beneath the logic to consider the ontology of economics, the meaning of its propositions in material human terms.

Having shown both in general and in some detail how religions and philosophical alienation depict the structure of practical alienation, Marx then goes on to explore in detail the sources of that alienation in contemporary economic life. He does this in two ways. Firstly he continues wherever possible to draw attention to the way in which our religious beliefs can be seen as an allegory of our economic and social life, hence the continual, and otherwise rather mystifying remarks that 'just as in religion . . . so . . . '. Secondly he adopts the role of an anthropologist in the territory of economics. Starting from the claims that economists themselves make, he penetrates behind the logic to the realities of economic life in nineteenth-century capitalism, hence his claim, relating to a lost part of the MS, that:

---

[46] Ibid., *ET*, pp. 175, 177; *EW*, pp. 397, 399.
[47] Ibid., *ET*, p. 161; *EW*, p. 383.

We have started out from the premises of political economy, we have accepted its language and its laws ... From political economy itself, using its own words we have shown that the worker sinks to the level of a commodity ...[48]

Let us first pursue Marx's notion of the parallels between money and the idea of God.[49] Money, like God, is originally an expression of value and a means of exchange between men. It is men's inherent sociability, the fact that their creativity is invariably communal rather than individual (although of course bourgeois society with its cult of the individual genius attempts to make even this individualistic), that leads to the need for exchange in the first place. But money is not the only possible means of exchange or method of sharing creativity, it is a means which presupposes private property. Money represents, not the exchange between humans but the exchange between the private properties of humans. Since money represents private property rather than human individuals, Marx claims that under a system of private properties it is in virtue of their money value that objects come to have value, rather than in virtue of the objects it can buy that money has value. It is because private property dissociates our creations from their social and human context that they come to have value only in terms of money, and in consequence, money, which had seemed to Hegel to universalize particular values, instead merely individuates social value.[50] Money, he suggests is to private property as Christ is to God. What was originally a mediator between us and our God (private property), has taken on a separate existence and become a God, the source of value in its own right:

> Christ originally represents (1) man before God (2) God for man and (3) man for man. In the same way money originally represents (1) private property for private property; (2) society for private property (3) private property for society.

> But Christ is God alienated and man alienated. God continues to have value only in so far as he represents Christ, man continues to have value only in so far as he represents Christ. Likewise with money.[51]

Just as in religion God is the source of all reality, so in economics money is the source of all reality. If I have money I can do and appear to be all sorts of things which I cannot if I do not have money. If I have no money I have no 'effective demand' as the economists say, which means, that as far as society is concerned I have no desires at all, which will probably be very far from the truth.[52] Under a money system all things sooner or later lose human value, that is their use value to individual human beings, and come to represent only the amount of money they can fetch in the market. This then becomes true also of humans, as their labour, which is also a commodity, is exchanged on the market at its lowest price.[53]

---

[48] Ibid., *ET*, p. 133, *EW*, p. 322

[49] Much of this is drawn by Marx from the German communist Hess who wrote a work on the essence of money, see Tucker, *Philosophy and Myth*, pp. 109–110.

[50] Hegel *Philosophy of Right*, §§192–4; Marx, *EW*, p. 261.

[51] 'Excerpts from James Mill's *Elements of Political Economy*', *EW*, p. 261; *ET*, p. 189.

[52] *1844 MSS*, *EW*, pp. 377–8; *ET*, p.180–1.

[53] Ibid., *EW*, p. 283.

The essential characteristic of human beings, their differentiating characteristic from all others, their 'species being', as Marx puts it, adopting a phrase of Feuerbach's, is their ability to create, freely, together, the means of their life. Under a money system this activity is first of all fragmented, for the communal nature of their creativity is invariably individualized by money, but secondly, reduced to a commodity it ceases to have value for itself. This is the situation described by Marx in the most famous and difficult of the manuscripts, the one known as 'Alienated Labour'.

Alienated labour

Marx points out that the classical economists all concentrate their attention on the categories of *exchange*, for example, price, supply and demand. Yet all the forms of exchange which they discuss presuppose private property as a basis for what is being exchanged, and none of them give an account of the nature or origins of private property: it exists, Say remarks, simply by positive law.[54]

Now a rational system of human exchange would be based on the satisfaction of human needs. But what we in fact find is that the system of exchange is based around private property – the exclusive individual possession of objects. Implicit in Marx's analysis is the question: Why do we need private possession and the exclusion of others in order to satisfy need? Is human need identical with private possession, or rather with use, activity, contemplation? If I wish to use an article of machinery do I need to entirely possess it (and so exclude others) in order to satisfy that need? If I wish to play tennis or golf do I need to own the court and so exclude others before I can pursue that activity? If I wish to contemplate a work of art or listen to music, do I need to *buy* the painting or have a private orchestra in order to do so? Such questions are only implicit in Marx's critical approach to the system of private property.[55] It is not his method to contrast capitalism with a-prioristic alternatives (although it is useful to remind ourselves that there are some). On the contrary, Marx is insistent that his analysis is based on the internal workings of the system as portrayed by its apologists – the bourgeois economists. But their central axiom, which they do not themselves analyse is private property:

> Political economy proceeds from the fact of private property. It does not explain
> it . . . . Political economy teaches us nothing about the extent to which these external
> and apparently accidental circumstances are only the expression of a necessary
> development.[56]

Marx argues that economics cannot proceed on the basis of private property by merely assuming that private property is the optimum system for satisfying need, this must be shown. Marx thinks he can show the opposite. The requirement that all our economic activity take the form of exchanges of private property strongly determines the way we organize our productive activity. Nevertheless, this institution of private property, which

---

[54] Ibid., *EW*, pp. 322–3; *ET*, pp.133–4.

[55] But see n.21 above for the immanent method of criticism.

[56] *1844 MSS, EW*, pp. 322–3; pp. 133–4.

so dominates our creative activity, is simply a human convention, a device we ourselves have invented. The economist can say no more about it than this.

Despite its conventionality, private property is what determines our basic and essential activity as human beings: creating things. As a result of this, our own product, our own convention, private property, comes to dominate our way of life.

Marx thinks he can show this in a rigorous fashion in the particular process of production. Consider a labourer working, i.e. creating things, in return for wages. Using direct quotation, Marx shows that according to contemporary economic theory 1) capital is stored up labour, and 2) labour is extracted as profit from the wage of employees by capitalist, and is 3) then used to create more capital through investment. But capital is *defined* by these economists as 'command over labour'.[57] It follows, says Marx, that when a labourer works for a capitalist, and increases the amount of capital available, he is (via profit) increasing the extent to which his life is controlled ('commanded') by capital. His own creation – capital – escapes his control, takes on an independent existence, controlling and limiting his existence, the very structure of alienation. Once again there is a parallel with religion: just as in religion the more man attributes to God the more he detracts from the worth of his own existence, so now in a material form, the more the labourer through his physical activity contributes to the growth of capital, the less worth he has himself, the less he realizes himself through his work. Sometimes, Marx notes with black humour, the worker realizes himself so little that he starves to death.[58]

Despite appearances capitalism is in fact the secular parallel of ascetic religion: it preaches the renunciation of present consumption in the midst of a system designed to create wealth. Instead of distributing and consuming wealth, capitalism concentrates and re-invests it. Instead of using and enjoying life – eating, drinking, buying books, theatre–going, dancing – the capitalist mentality preaches *saving*. This continual putting off of present life-enjoyment until some future heaven is the secular triumph of the repressive religious mentality, the practical realization of the conceptual self-denial which constitutes religious alienation.[59]

It is important not to simply identify alienation with poverty. Marx is of course acutely aware that the consequence of the capitalist system was abject poverty for the majority of workers, and at this time he held that the results of the system must be to increase their *absolute* poverty. Nevertheless it is clear that alienation is not mere physical deprivation, but a structural property of the relationships amongst human beings and between them and nature in their work. Alienation is the distortion of human productive activity. This has a number of aspects.

Alienation from the product

As we have seen, under a system of wage-labour, the worker is alienated *from his product* in the simple sense that it does not belong to him, it belongs to his employer, but also in the more complex sense that the profits from his product will go to increase capital investment, and thus the control of capital over labour. The worker's own labour thus

---

[57] Ibid., *EW*, p. 295.
[58] Ibid., *EW*, p. 324; *ET*, p.135.

[59] Ibid., *EW*, p. 361.

increases his loss of power, for more capital investment increases the division of labour, that is the extent to which tasks in production are divided up, and this gives the capitalist even more control over the labourer, since the breakdown of skilled tasks into simple repetitive ones, reduces the bargaining power of the skilled labourer eventually to the point where his task is so routine it can be done by a machine, with which the labourer is accordingly in competition.[60] Since it is the labourer that produces the machine in the first place, labour is once again in conflict with its own product.

A second aspect of this is that the object on which human labour works, nature, is increasingly transformed by labour into a commodity or capital under the control of the capitalist. As Marx had noticed in his discussion of the laws relating to the thefts of wood, the emergence of bourgeois property rights, the allocation of individual property rights to all the land of a given country had the effect of *creating* a class of paupers who had previously been capable of communally harvesting an area. Parallel to this legal process was the productive process in working up natural objects into products or into capital in the form of machines; in this way the labourer distances himself further and further *from nature*. It is not clear whether this is peculiar to capitalism: this form of alienation would appear to be an essential part of production itself, for production under any circumstances objects must be abstracted from nature through labour.[61]

Alienation from the activity of labour

The major form of alienation is the alienation of productive activity itself, as Marx says, the activity of alienation presupposes the alienation of activity.

> How could the product of the worker's activity confront him as something alien if it were not for the fact that in the act of production he was estranging himself? After all the product is simply the resume of the activity . . . The estrangement of the object of labour merely summarizes the estrangement, the alienation in the activity of labour itself.[62]

This alienation of activity consists in the fact that work, instead of being the free creative expression of human life, becomes a compulsive means to a merely animal one. It is not his essentially human, labouring activity which appears central to the worker's life, but his purely animal functions: 'eating, drinking and procreating, or at most in his dwelling and adornment.'[63] In short the worker works in order to live, he does not live in order to work; he does not see his work as fulfilling his life, but simply as something to be got through in order to live it.

---

[60] Ibid., *EW*, pp. 323–4; *ET*, pp.134–5.

[61] Ibid., *EW*, p. 325; 328; *ET*, pp. 135, 139.

[62] Ibid., *EW*, p. 326; *ET*, p.137.

[63] Ibid., *EW*, p. 327; *ET*, p.138.

Alienation from species being

This second aspect of alienation in a sense presupposes some kind of ethical norm, or value judgement about how human productive life should be lived. This is made more explicit in the third category of alienation Marx deals with, which he points out, derives from the first two. This is alienation from man's species being. Species being is a term used by Feuerbach. In the first chapter of the *Essence of Christianity* he attempted to show how consciousness was related to an awareness of one's essential nature: 'consciousness in the strictest sense is present only in a being to whom his species, his essential being, is an object of thought.'

Now this is true only of man: 'Man is himself at once I and thou; he can put himself in the place of another, for this reason that to him his species, his essential nature, and not merely his individuality, is an object of thought.'[64] Now of course Marx criticised Feuerbach's claim that sensuous consciousness was the central category of humanity; but he retained the idea of 'species being' within his material conception of human kind. Consequently for Marx, man's species being lies not in his mental creativity but in his practical creativity. Yet there is another aspect of Feuerbach's characterization which is carried over and that is the universality which characterizes humanness. Species being involves an element of universality, the ability, to which Feuerbach drew attention, of being *conscious* of anyone who is a member of one's species. For Marx, it is the ability to create universally, i.e. socially, as well as to reflect on the collective nature of that activity that makes man a species being, and the fragmentation of that activity renders it unexpressive of his true species-nature:

> Man makes his life-activity itself an object of his will and consciousness . . . Conscious life-activity directly distinguishes man from animal activity . . . Estranged labour reverses the relationship so that man, just because he is a conscious being, makes his life activity, his *being*, a mere means for his existence.[65]

or again:

> . . . man reproduces himself not only intellectually, in his consciousness, but actively, and actually, and he can therefore contemplate himself in a world he himself has created. In tearing away the object of his production from man, estranged labour therefore tears away from him his *species life*, his true species objectivity . . .[66]

---

[64] Feuerbach, *The Essence of Christianity*, pp. 1–2.

[65] *1844 MSS, EW*, p. 328, *ET*, p. 139.

[66] Ibid., *EW*, p. 329, *ET.* p. 140.

Alienation of man from man

But this rather abstract aspect of alienation from an idealized model of consciously social creativity points the way to a fourth and perhaps more easily appreciated aspect of alienation, which is in a way a specification of the previous one:

> In general, the proposition that man is estranged from his species being means that each man is estranged from the others and that all are estranged from man's essence.

Man's estrangement, like all relationships of man to himself is realized and expressed only in man's relationship to other men.[67]

The practical expression of this species alienation – the alienation of men from each other – can be seen in the categories of political economy analysed by Marx in the preceding manuscripts. It shows itself in the way in which the capitalist treats the labourer as simply a 'factor' of production, subject to laws of supply and demand, without considering the human consequences, of for example unemployment, or the ten, twelve or even fourteen hour working day commonly imposed on labourers in the first half of the nineteenth century; it shows itself in the antagonistic competition between workers for jobs which cuts their rate of pay, and even in the competition between capitalists, in the course of which some will be bankrupted and relegated to the ranks of the workers.

As a reading of the text shows, Marx sometimes claims that alienation has a subjective, identifiable manifestation in the 'feelings' of the worker; but its core lies in an objective pattern of relationships and their effect on man's essential, creative activity. Clearly we are not expected to applaud this state of affairs, yet Marx claims his analysis is objective and value free:

> We started out from an economic fact, the estrangement of the worker and of his production. We gave this fact conceptual form: *estranged, alienated* labour. We have analysed this concept and in so doing merely analysed an economic fact.[68]

Despite this claim to objectivity, the demonstration that man's essential creative nature has suffered dislocation under wage labour involves clear normative as well as purely structural observations.

This issue has had important interpretive and even political implications. If the categories of Marx's initial analysis are based on a value judgement, and if there is clear continuity between this and his later theory, then the claim of the latter to be 'scientific' and in some sense value free looks dubious. On the other hand, if either his early works were not so value based, or there were no such continuity, then, at least on these grounds, the claims of the later work to scientific objectivity are intact. Considerations such as these have led important political positions to depend on the interpretation of these early

---

[67] Ibid., *EW*, pp. 328, 329, 330; *ET*, pp. 139, 140, 141.
[68] Ibid., *EW*, p. 330; *ET*, p.141.

texts and their relationship to his later work.[69] For example a political issue related to this is the degree to which Marxism as a political programme should be concerned with the wide humanistic concern about the quality of human life exhibited in these early works, or whether it is concerned only with the economic structure of society and with political dominance of the working class or its representatives.

One important aspect of this debate relates to the issue of how 'philosophical' these early works are. It is true that Marx is using as evidence, the writings of bourgeois economists. Yet his analysis of how their categories come into existence often betrays still a Hegelian dialectic, rather than a materialist one. For example Marx insists that private property is a causal consequence of alienated labour, and not vice versa:

> Private property derives from an analysis of the concept of alienated labour. i.e. Alienated man . . . it is true that we took the concept of alienated labour from political economy as a result of the movement of private property. But it is clear from an analysis of this concept that, although private property appears as the basis and cause of alienated labour, it is in fact its consequence, just as the Gods were originally not the cause but the effect of the confusion in men's minds. Later however this relationship becomes reciprocal.

Private property Marx sees as 'the material, summarised expression of alienated labour', and yet it is this material relationship which is being determined by the abstract one.[70]

Another issue which relates to how objective, or scientific in an empirical sense Marx's thought is in this period, concerns the sources of his ideas about the proletariat as the class which would abolish the system of alienated labour, and transcend the state.[71] Marx first attributes this role to the proletariat in his *Introduction to the Critique of Hegel's Philosophy*, written immediately after moving to Paris. It has seemed to some central whether Marx derived his concept of the proletariat from empirical observation, or from some internal transformation of the categories of Hegelian philosophy. According to Avineri, the proletariat is the true 'universal class' – which replaces Hegel's illusory one, the bureaucracy – 'Marx arrived at this conclusion (concerning the transcendence of the state) not through an economic or historical study, but by applying Feuerbach's method to Hegel'. Others, for example Althusser, try to dissociate even Marx's early work from the influence of Hegel. A recent commentator claims:

> the Marxian project as a whole can be seen then for what it was: an attempt from the first to found an empirically grounded and practical science of society, rather than a

---

[69] See e.g. Louis Althusser, 'The 1844 Manuscripts of Karl Marx' in *For Marx* (Harmondsworth 1969) pp. 155–160.

[70] *1844 MSS, EW*, pp. 332, 334; *ET*, pp. 143, 144. When Marx came to analyse the historical origins of these categories he insisted that it was the creation of private property, i.e., the separation of serfs and cottagers from their land, that made wage-labour possible. See note 124.

[71] The concern is more than slightly anachronistic, Marx did not mean by 'scientific', what those who discuss the issue, whether critics or defenders, normally mean by the term — i.e. 'derived from empirical observation'. On Marx's conception of science see Paul Thomas, 'Marx and Science', *Political Studies*, XXIV, 1 (1976).

speculative inversion of a ready-made philosophical world-view.[72]

Whilst it is unfair to claim the only proletarians known to Marx at this time were in books,[73] there can be no doubt that up to this point in his life Marx's personal experience of an urban based work force employed on machinery, was very limited. Although Engels started work on his *Condition of the Working Class in England* in the same year as Marx was writing the Paris Manuscripts, Marx wrote without knowledge of the work. Engels' work was written after two years in England helping to manage his father's cotton mill in Manchester, it was based on personal observation and official statistics collected by Factory and Child Commissioners.[74] Marx had no such material available to him in Germany. It has been estimated that the urban industrial working class in Germany at this period comprised only 4 per cent of the population.[75] Nevertheless what industrial development there was was extremely concentrated in the Rhineland, and Marx had already shown keen interest in social questions and the newly created poor there in his articles for the *Rheinishe Zeitung*. There is no doubt also that Marx's readings on the French Revolution where the category of class was commonly employed in historical explanation had sensitized him to its revolutionary potential.[76] Even his short experience of the industrialized working class in Paris, had it seems made a strong impression on him.[77]

Yet it is surely significant that it is in a writing on Hegel (the *Introduction to a critique*) that the proletariat are first allotted a historic role. Hegel himself had of course been immensely exercised by the question of poverty. Urban, industrialized poverty was, on his own admission, the major irrational blot on the enlightened aspect of the modern rational state. Moreover Hegel perceived, and from reading many of the same classical economists as Marx, that it was the economic life of society itself, and not accident or misfortune, that produced poverty. Hegel was not talking only about the industrial proletariat, but also about those displaced and dispossessed country-dwellers defended by Marx in his writings *On Wood Thefts*.[78] The word 'proletariat' was being employed widely in 19th century Germany to describe paupers in the traditional sense, as well as the urban poor generally. They formed between a half and two thirds of the population in parts of Prussia. Marx's notion that the proletariat were the negation of civil society had its roots in German law, parts of which found its way into Hegel's political thought.

---

[72] S. Avineri, *The Social and Political Thought of Karl Marx* (Cambridge, 1970), p. 38, on transformation of bureaucracy into proletariat see pp. 48–65; Althusser postulates an 'epistemological break' dividing Marx's work into an 'ideological' early period. Up to 1845, a transitional period 1845–7 and the mature or scientific works of 1857 and after. *For Marx*, pp. 33–8. The final quote is from Lubasz 'Marx's Initial Problematic', p. 25.

[73] As claimed by Tucker, *Philosophy and Myth*, p. 114.

[74] Frederick Engels, *The Condition of the Working Classes in England* (London, 1969).

[75] *KMLT*, p. 98.

[76] Ibid., pp. 97–8; see also Avineri's discussion of Marx's source, *Social and Political Thought*, pp. 52–7.

[77] *KMLT*, p. 87.

[78] Hegel's 'rabble of paupers' included both those who have lost the 'natural means of acquisition' — i.e. access to the land and natural forms of property (*Philosophy of Right*, §§241 and 217) as well as those whose repetitive and ill paid work leads to 'distress' and a below-subsistence standard of living (ibid., §§243, 244).

Those poor who were either unemployed, or – an increasing number as industrialization progressed – involved in unskilled work, were not, and could not be, members of corporations. As political rights were acquired or exercised through membership of the corporations – from which the poor were excluded – the poor were not in consequence members of the state either. They lived within its physical boundaries but did not enjoy its rights and freedoms.[79] Clearly a state which was producing an increasing number of these people was in the process of producing a population which would soon 'transcend' it. Clearly also in a state in which political status was so identified with corporations and corporate membership of its citizens, the introduction of a universal franchise – giving the vote to corporate-less individuals – could be identified with the abolition of the state considered as a structure of essentially corporate privilege.[80]

This seems clearly to be the historical and intellectual background to Marx's claim, in the *Critique*, that universal suffrage, in effect democracy, would entail the dissolution of both the state and civil society, itself the ancestor of his idea that the proletarian revolution would herald the transcendence, or overcoming of the state.It is because the poor can be identified with no legally defined status group that they are not of the state, they exist only as humans, not as farmers or traders or artisans or craftsmen belonging to guilds. Human emancipation then must be based on the overthrow of any purely state-defined status and the generalization of the condition of those whose only status was their humanity. Marx had already written in his *Critique*, that the answer to modern society's problems lies:

> In the formation of a class with *radical chains*, a class of civil society which is not a class of civil society, a class [here *stande*, meaning a legally defined status group] which is the dissolution of all classes, a sphere which has a universal character because of its universal suffering and which lays claim to no *particular right* because the wrong it suffers is not a *particular wrong* but *wrong in general*; a sphere of society which can no longer lay claim to a *historical* title, but merely to a *human* one which does not stand in one-sided opposition to the consequences but in all-sided opposition to the premises of the German political system; and finally a sphere which cannot emancipate itself without emancipating itself from – and thereby emancipating – all other spheres of society, which is, in a word, the *total loss* of humanity and which can therefore redeem itself only through the *total redemption of humanity*. This dissolution of society as a particular class is the *proletariat*.[81]

In the last of the Paris Manuscripts Marx claims that the emancipation of the proletariat through the democratization of the franchise and the subsequent generalization of their condition must lead to communism. Those who are members of no corporate class in Germany are those with no skill or property of their own, hence their position is one of propertylessness. The emancipation of this class, the universalization of their condition, is the universalization of the condition of propertylessness, or communism. Communism was the secular equivalent of Christian redemption:

> it is the *genuine* resolution of the conflict between man and nature, and between man

---

[79] Lubasz, 'Initial Problematic', p. 27.

[80] 'Critique of Hegel . . .' *EW*, p. 191.

[81] 'Introduction to the critique of Hegel's *Philosophy of Right*,' *EW*, p. 256; *ET*, p.127.

and man, the true resolution of the conflict between existence and being, between objectification and self-affirmation, between freedom and necessity, between individual and species. It is the riddle of history solved and knows itself to be the solution.[82]

Marx's last observation – that communism had both an objective, historical status, as well as a subjective, psychological one is important. It established an important area of investigation for his later work: the question of the relationship between 'objective circumstances' and people's perceptions of them. Revolutions are after all made by groups of people. Their realization that a revolution is possible, is one of the conditions of it actually being so. This awareness of the role of consciousness also lends Marx's discussion of communism here a certain dialectical subtlety.

The first phase of communism, he writes, is likely to be crude. The mentality of those participating in it will be a desire to negate absolutely the previous society. Ironically this will only focus sharper attention on its characteristic institution: physical possessions. Just as the liberation from sexual taboos expresses itself initially not in more genuinely human relationships but in a compulsive promiscuity, so the liberation from private property expresses itself in the compulsive desire to communalize all property which is material and destroy all that is not:

> This communism, inasmuch as it negates the *personality* of man in every sphere, is simply the logical expression of the private property which is this negation. Universal *envy* constituting itself as a power is the hidden form in which *greed* reasserts itself and satisfies itself, but in another way. The thoughts of every piece of private property as such are *at least turned against richer* private property in the form of envy and in the desire to level everything down.

But Marx is optimistic that such communism is very far from the true potentiality available in the act of liberation:

> How little this abolition of private property is a true appropriation is shown by the abstract negation of the entire world of culture and civilization, and the return to the unnatural simplicity of the *poor*, unrefined man who has no needs and who has not even reached the stage of private property, let alone gone beyond it.[83]

True communism, claims Marx, is not simply the crude negation of bourgeois society, and the assertion of an ascetic plebeianism, but its transcendence in a dialectical sense, the preservation of what is of cultural and aesthetic value together with the supersession of the social and psychological forms which prevented all men from enjoying those values because they were expressed in the forms of private property: 'Private property has made us so stupid and one sided that an object is only *ours* when we have it, when it exists for us as capital or when we directly possess, eat, drink, wear, inhabit it, etc.'[84]

Marx wishes to avoid falling back into what he saw as the trap of some of Kant's followers in making this state of affairs a mere ideal, of becoming stuck 'on an ought'. He is convinced that communism is immanent in the historical circumstances of the present, and that the whole of historical development can be shown to be a preparation

---

[82] *1844 MSS, EW*, p. 348; *ET*, p.148.   [84] Ibid., *EW*, p. 351; *ET*, pp.151–2.
[83] Ibid., *EW*, p. 346; *ET*, pp. 146–7.

for its emergence and the return to a non-alienatory human society: 'The entire movement of history is therefore both the *actual* act of creating communism – birth of its empirical existence – and, for its thinking consciousness, the *comprehended* and *known* movement of its *becoming*.'[85]

Marx's economic analysis in the Paris Manuscripts thus provided a solution to alienation through the abolition of private property. The major question posed by Marx's summary of his thought so far was whether his claim that this solution could be firmly located in history could be vindicated. Marx's next work of importance *The German Ideology*, written jointly with Engels in 1845-6, deals with this question.[86]

In the meanwhile Marx was on the move again. The French Government, in response to pressure from Prussia, expelled him on 2 February 1845 and he moved instead to Brussels where he was given a residence permit on condition that he abstain from political activity. Before leaving Paris he had signed a contract for a book on politics and economics, which was eventually to become *Capital*. He had obtained an advance of 1500 francs. An appeal amongst the radical community for the Marx family (Marx had married Jenny von Westphalen in 1842) had produced 1000 francs, and the comfortably-off Engels had assigned to Marx the royalties on his *Condition of the Working Classes in England*. For once in his life Marx was not preoccupied with his own economics.[87]

A theory of history and society

The historical basis of human nature and consciousness:
The Theses on Feuerbach as the programme for the German Ideology

The German Ideology continued the attack on the Young Hegelian school begun in the (published but unremarked) *Holy Family*. Its importance lies largely in that part of it in which Marx attempted to supply the deficiencies of Feuerbach's abstract conception of man by developing an account of the historical processes that shape human's natures. In his unpublished *Theses on Feuerbach* Marx had already sketched out his principal departures from the thinker to whom he owed so much. Although Feuerbach had criticised religion as an esoteric humanism, he had not, according to Marx, seen that 'the human essence is no abstraction inherent in each individual. It is in reality the ensemble of social relations.'[88] Religious belief, and indeed all other beliefs and institutions are the product of a certain form of society.[89] Furthermore, although Feuerbach had also criticised abstract social theorising as a form of alienation akin to religion, and which therefore required, like religion, to be explained as the distorted form of something else, he did not know what to resolve that alienation *into*. As a result, he resolved it into the

---

[85] Ibid., *EW*, p. 348; *ET*, p.148.

[86] *The German Ideology* was not quite the next major work, it was preceded in 1845 by *The Holy Family*, a long and intellectually incestuous critique of the Young Hegelian school, his first collaboration with Engels, and originally intended as a short pamphlet of 15 or so pages (it runs to nearly 300!).

[87] *KMLT*, pp. 136–9.

[88] The *Theses on Feuerbach*, Thesis VI, in *Karl Marx: Selected Writings*, ed. David McLellan (Oxford, 1977), hereafter *SW*, p.157.

[89] Ibid., Thesis VII, *SW*, p.157.

senses, or what he called sensuous contemplation.[90] Abstract theorising in the Hegelian tradition can only be abolished, Marx points out, by translating it into action – it is only as action that theory really exists. In dialectical terms the translation of an idea into action is at once the abolition and transcendence of that idea. Since it is only in action that the proof or adequacy of any conception or idea can be shown, truth must therefore be demonstrated in practical activity rather than in the correspondence of any theory to 'the world' for that world itself must also be an abstraction.[91] The *Theses* end with the famous assertion: 'Philosophers have only *interpreted* the world, in various ways; the point, however, is to *change* it.'[92]

The major point of *The German Ideology* was to demonstrate the inadequacies of those thinkers who remained satisfied with a Feuerbachian analysis. Feuerbach's philosophy itself was the 'German ideology' of the title. In terms of the development of Marx's own ideas by far the most important part is the first section 'On Feuerbach', in which Marx and Engels attempt to show how the idea, already widespread amongst some French and Scottish Enlightenment thinkers, of history as a series of economic stages, can be used to provide a non-arbitrary, non-idealist basis on which to explain the forms of social and political life, and religious and philosophical beliefs. It remains only a sketch, but it is one of the fullest statements of Marx's interpretation of history that we have.[93]

Marx begins by pointing out that the difference between the 'Old', and the radical 'Young' Hegelians in Germany is not fundamental. For they both accepted the primacy of ideas. One believes that conventional ideas are constitutive of reality (their 'true bonds'), the other believes such ideas constrain and limit social development (they are the 'real chains'). Neither acknowledges that ideas are the product of the material circumstances in which men live, and so cannot be changed until their determining circumstances are also changed.

Marx proposes a different starting point:

> The premises from which we start are not arbitrary ones, not dogmas, but real premises from which abstraction can only be made in the imagination. They are the real individuals, their activity and the material conditions under which they live, both those which they find already existing and those produced by their activity. These premises can thus be verified in a purely empirical way.[94]

---

[90] Notice, though, that Marx himself was still doing this in the *1844 MSS*, see *EW*, p. 352 .

[91] *Theses on Feuerbach*, Thesis II., *SW*, p.156. On this see L. Kolakowski 'Karl Marx and the Classical Definition of Truth' in Kolakowski, *Marxism and Beyond* (London 1969).

[92] *Theses on Feuerbach*, Thesis XI, *SW*, p.158.

[93] *The German Ideology*, was written jointly by Marx and Frederick Engels with whom he was, of course, to enjoy a lifelong collaboration. Although communists of the second and third international and, at one time, academic students too, considered their work as an integrated whole, modern scholarship has now in my view established clear distinctions between their positions. See the debate summed up in Terrel Carver, 'Marx, Engels and Scholarship', *Political Studies*, xxxii, 2 (1984); and generally, Norman Levine, *The Tragic Deception, Marx contra Engels* (Oxford and Santa Barbara, 1975); and Carver, *Marx and Engels*, esp., for the German Ideology, pp. 69–78. More specifically on the question of Marx and Engels's contributions to the text of *The German Ideology* see the edition by Wataru Hiromatsu (Tokyo, 1974), discussed by Carver in 'Communism for Critical Critics', *History of Political Thought*, IX, 1 (1988).

[94] *The German Ideology* (London & Moscow, 1964), p. 31.

The notion that there is a 'nature' or 'essence' of man is a mistake, invariably made by earlier political theorists. Hegel's thought had rejected the arbitrary devices of 'states of nature' and a postulated aboriginal human nature. Now, in rejecting Hegelian abstractions, Feuerbachians were falling into the same trap again. The possible choices of such a human 'essence' are numerous: 'Men can be distinguished from animals by consciousness, by religion or anything else you like.' But there is no need, claims Marx, for us to choose a human nature in this arbitrary and theoretically aprioristic way, for there is a sense in which human beings as a matter of practical fact:

> themselves begin to distinguish themselves from animals as soon as they begin to *produce* their means of subsistence, a step which is conditioned by their physical organization. By producing their means of subsistence men are indirectly producing their actual material life.[95]

In the case of humankind then, our nature is determined for us irrespective of philosophers' speculations *by the very fact that humans create themselves* through their productive activity. This dismissal of attempts to theorize about humans' essential natures has two important implications, one methodological, the other practical. Firstly historical analysis must proceed without assumptions about human 'nature' which will invariably be based on unjustifiable and probably ideologically fuelled assumptions. Secondly, if human nature is self-creation, then the outcome of any emancipatory revolution is unpredictable in the sense that it will involve only the freeing of human nature from the social constraints under which it has developed. Only the liberated agents of the revolution themselves could determine what form communist society should or could take, and no social analyst could tell in advance. In the case of history however we can look back and see what sort of humans and what sort of society, and what sort of 'natures' we have, in the past, made for ourselves.

The premise of all history is that men must live before they can make history. This focuses us not onto biological determinism, but onto the social organization of individual survival and social reproduction. The production of the means (tools) necessary to satisfy human needs itself leads to new needs.[96] The third premise is the existence of some means of recreating *men* and *women*, that is the family, and the fourth premise is that the production of material goods necessary for life, and the procreation of future generations, is related not only to nature, but also to other human beings, different modes of satisfying need produce different forms of social co-operation and reproduction. Human history is thus essentially economic history, the study of the interrelationship between these various material premises, and it is only the Scottish historians of civil society – Smith, Ferguson, Steuart et. al. – who have actually written any history at all!

Acknowledging the material basis of history, however, is not the whole of Marx's insight, for these material conditions in turn determine the forms taken by human consciousness. Consciousness is essentially a social product, and the form of society determines the form of consciousness. Any social organization of production involves specialization of tasks, the division of labour, and the consequent differentiation of forms of consciousness, amongst the different kinds of labour. The most significant of these is

---

[95] Ibid., p. 31.
[96] As Rousseau had regretted, and Hegel had accepted. See above pp. 450–1.

the differentiation of intellectual from physical labour, a differentiation which gives rise to such muddles as those of the Young Hegelian school. Once consciousness is separated from practical activity – in the form of philosophers and thinkers who do not have to physically labour for a living, then philosophy is, as Marx says, 'in a position to emancipate itself from the world'. It 'can really flatter itself that it is something other than consciousness of existing practice, that it really represents something other than something real.'[97] Hegelianism, in claiming reality is about *thought* is really a typical piece of special pleading by philosophers! Philosophy is only of use when it turns itself again to the question of what must be *done* and not how the world is to be *interpreted*. It cannot successfully do this until the division of labour is abolished; and the abolition of the division of labour is, for reasons already outlined in the Paris MSS, identical with the abolition of private property. The recovery of truth is identical with the recovery of an undivided, i.e., classless, society. Consequently all this presupposes the establishment of communism.

The political implication of this analysis is that where labour is divided there is a conflict – Marx claims a contradiction – between the interests of one and the interest of the whole, and between one class and another. The nature of these contradictions had already been explored in some detail by Marx in his *Economic and Philosophical Manuscripts*, and to be fair, they had been acknowledged by Hegel. However, in Hegelian thought, the state is represented as the arbiter and enforcer of the general interest as against the interest of groups (or, for Hegel, corporations) or the individual. For Marx it is only *represented* as such. In reality the state is no more cut off from the material circumstances of life than are our ideas about religion. The state is the expression of the dominant social group in the community, and the reason for its social dominance is economic power:

> it follows from this that all struggles within the State, the struggle between democracy, aristocracy, and monarchy, the struggle for the franchise, etc., etc., are merely the illusory forms in which real struggles of the different classes are fought out among one another.[98]

This economic and social dominance is given ideological effect through the production and spread of ideas supportive of that dominance:

> The ideas of the ruling class are in every epoch the ruling ideas . . . The division of labour . . . manifests itself also in the ruling class as the division of mental and material labour, so that inside this class one part appears as the thinkers of the class (its active conceptual ideologists, who make the perfecting of the illusion of the class about itself their chief source of livelihood . . . '

The principal form that this ideology takes is the attempt to represent the interests of that class as the interests of the society as a whole:

> For each new class which puts itself in the place of one ruling before it, is compelled, merely in order to carry out its aim, to represent its interest as the common interest of

---

[97] *German Ideology*, p. 43.　　　　[98] Ibid., p. 45.

all the members of society, that is expressed in an ideal form: it has to give its ideas the form of universality, and represent them as the only rational, universally valid ones.[99]

The ability to perpetuate this illusion cannot be retained indefinitely, it is dependent on the ability of that form of society's economic relationships to function effectively. Political ideals and conflict are thus the surface manifestation of the economic forces which give rise to them; they are not at any fundamental level, the consequence of men holding certain ideals and aims, except inasmuch as those very ideals will be conditioned by material circumstances. This is as true of communism as it is of any other ideal, so, although the ideal of communism has occurred before in history Marx believes it will only be possible to implement it when the material economic circumstances allow, at which point also people's understanding of what communism is will become adequate to the task of implementing it:

> These conditions of life which different generations find in existence, decide also whether or not the periodically recurring revolutionary convulsion will be strong enough to overthrow the basis of the entire existing system. And if these material elements of a complete revolution are not present (namely, on the one hand the existing productive forces, on the other the formation of a revolutionary mass, which revolts not only against separate conditions of society up till then, but against the very 'production of life' till then, the 'total activity' on which it was based), then as far as practical development is concerned it is absolutely immaterial whether the *idea* of this revolution has been expressed a hundred times already, as the history of communism proves.[100]

The whole of the (uncompleted) second half of *The German Ideology* was devoted to a discussion of the inadequacies of theories of communism and socialism which are not based on a proper understanding of the material conditions necessary for its successful implementation.

The Communist Manifesto

Marx had now arrived at a general conception of what an overall theory of society would be, and the *German Ideology*, had outlined it. It was to be a theory which saw social and political life, and their associated beliefs – moral, aesthetic, religious – as a series of complex responses to the 'material conditions of life' – effectively the forms of economic existence. Moreover, true to his critique of Feuerbach, Marx integrated this analysis with a commitment to revolution, of which the *Communist Manifesto* was the most famous expression. The *Manifesto* was also written jointly with Frederick Engels and published a year later than the *The German Ideology*, in February of the revolutionary year of 1848 at the behest of the Communist League, a small organization of German revolutionary exiles. In the *Manifesto* Marx and Engels sought to link their account of economic-historical development to the prospects for revolutionary politics. They did so in two ways: negatively, by distinguishing their communism from other reactionary, bourgeois or

---

[99] Ibid., pp. 61, 62.   [100] Ibid., p. 51.

utopian forms of socialism, and positively by asserting the link between communism and its historical embodiment, the class of proletarians. What, according to Marx and Engels, made a communism identified with the proletariat more than simply an ideal was the fact that the development of capitalism, an undoubted historical reality, required and promoted the development of a proletariat – an industrial working class, which, through the conditions of factory production was to be radicalized and brought more and more in contact with one another, rather than – as agricultural workers – remaining apolitical, dispersed and isolated. They concluded that 'what the bourgeoisie therefore produces, above all, are its own grave diggers. Its fall and the victory of the proletariat are equally inevitable.'[101]

The *Manifesto* was an explicitly polemical work, designed to attract and inspire supporters. At the time of its writing, revolutionary disturbances seemed, and indeed were, imminent all over Europe. However, they did not lead to communism, and even the modest advances made towards democratic government in many European countries were subsequently repressed. Shortly after, in 1852, the Communist League was dissolved and the likelihood of imminent revolution receded.

Between the end of the Communist League and the establishment of the First Communist International in 1864, Marx was supported financially by Engels and by his own work as a journalist commenting on world affairs. It was during this time that he conducted the research and much of the writing for his major theoretical works, the *Grundrisse, A Contribution to a Critique of Political Economy, Theories of Surplus Value* and *Capital* itself.[102] These writings were concerned to elaborate in greater detail both the general relationship between man's productive activity and the various historical forms of social life, and more particularly to understand the processes at work in its dominant contemporary form, capitalism.

The centre of the social theory: Marx's 'guiding thread'– the language of the *Preface to A Critique of Political Economy*

In the Preface to *A Critique of Political Economy*, one of his abandoned attempts to give a general overview of his economic critique of capitalism, Marx records the 'general result' of the reflections on economic history which he had undertaken as a result of his realization, in the *Paris Manuscripts*, of the central role played in human life by economics.[103] The statement is a succinct, and possibly the most famous account of his

---

[101] *The Communist Manifesto*, p. 79, in *The Revolutions of 1848* (Volume 1 of *Karl Marx Political Writings*, ed. David Fernbach (Harmondsworth, 1973).

[102] Only the *Contribution*, and volume I of *Capital*, were in fact published by Marx, the former in 1859, the latter in 1867. The *Grundrisse* was composed in 1857–8, and was written by Marx to clarify for himself the theoretical problems involved in understanding capitalism as a system, it was not meant for publication, and appeared in print in the Soviet Union only in 1939–41. It was virtually unknown in the West until the 1950s and not widely available in English until the 1970s. Apart from its intrinsic interest, one of its major significances lies in establishing a link between Marx's 'philosophical' writings of the Paris period, and the more technically 'economic' work of *Capital*. It therefore has a bearing on the debate over the continuity of Marx's work. *Theories of Surplus Value* are essentially Marx's notes on the history of economic thought which he undertook as a preparatory study for the composition of *Capital*. Made in 1861–3, they were first published between 1967–72.

[103] It is worth noticing by how much Marx failed to achieve his ultimate aim. In the Preface to the *Critique* Marx announced his intention of treating political economy under six sections: capital, landed property,

theory of social change, it introduces many of his technical terms, and bears extended quotation:

> In the social production of their life, men enter into definite relations, that are indispensable and independent of their will, relations of production which correspond to a definite stage of the development of their material productive forces. The sum total of these relations of production constitutes the economic structure of society, the real foundation on which rises a legal and political superstructure and to which correspond definite forms of social consciousness. The mode of production of material life conditions the social, political, and intellectual life processes in general. It is not the consciousness of men that determines their being, but, on the contrary, their social being that determines their consciousness.[104]

The structure of society, and its belief-system or ideology, is then, as follows. The 'material productive forces' of a particular historical epoch give rise to, or, more weakly, 'correspond to' relations of production, law, politics and 'social consciousness'. The relationship of 'productive forces' to these other social phenomena is described by a famous constructional metaphor as one of a supportive 'base' to a 'superstructure'. Notice that the only relationship which is described by a verb as strong as 'determine' is that between the whole economic realm and the realm of 'consciousness'. Other relations are weaker: 'correspond', 'condition'. Moreover the relationship is not one way, Marx will also want to argue that this superstructure is in some kind of sense conducive to the operation of the base. Before looking at what these terms might mean, we should notice also that this account of social structure is applied by Marx to each of a sequence of historical stages: 'in broad terms Asiatic, ancient, feudal, and modern bourgeois modes of production can be designated as progressive epochs in the economic transformation of society.'[105]

There are thus two aspects to Marx's social theory – a structural one which analyses the relationships between economic base and social, legal, political and ideological superstructure, and a dynamic one which sees different contents given to these categories in different historical epochs, and which also seeks to provide an account of the

---

wage-labour, the state, foreign trade and the world market. The *Critique* was meant to be the first two chapters of the first part, on capital. However Marx abandoned this particular start to the project and reworked the material in *Capital*, vol.I. Only one volume of *Capital* was published by Marx himself, although a further two were prepared from notes by Engels. Yet these three volumes amount to only the first of the six sections into which Marx intended to divide his critique of political economy which would accordingly have run to something like eighteen volumes!

[104] Marx, 'Preface to a contribution to a Critique of Political Economy' in *Selected Writings*, ed. McLellan, p. 389. This passage has traditionally been taken as the starting point for discussions of Marx's general theory. However this is something of an interpretive tradition and the passage was accorded no special status by Marx himself. As one commentator has observed, Marx is unique in having his theory so often 'reconstructed in large part, by a close reading of a brief formulation embedded in an autobiographical sketch in a preface to a book that he gladly allowed to go out of print, as superseded by later writings.' Richard W. Miller, 'Producing Change: Work, technology, and power in Marx's theory of history' in *After Marx*, ed. Terence Ball and James Farr (Cambridge, 1984). However outside the 'Preface' Marx occasionally asserts similar general propositions. For a discussion of such passages see G. A. Cohen, *Karl Marx's Theory of History: A Defence* (Oxford, 1978) pp. 142–50.

[105] 'Preface', *SW*, p. 390.

transitions between one epoch and another. As a historian and a social theorist Marx was concerned to demonstrate the 'fit' of his model to the transition between the epochs of feudalism and capitalism – a transition still incomplete in many parts of Europe; and as a political revolutionary he was concerned to demonstrate in advance, how the present epoch of capitalism must give way to socialism. Whilst the behaviour of the economic basis of production could, Marx thought, 'be determined with the precision of natural science'; the behaviour of the superstructure was not exactly predictable, although it was, in the long term, bound to the fate of the economic basis of society.[106] Thus for practical purposes the two kinds of society Marx was most concerned to analyse were feudalism and capitalism. We shall first try to explain the meanings of his terms as applied to these societies, and then show how he understood the transition between them. Tracing the dynamic of the transition from capitalism to socialism will require some investigation of Marx's economics, since, as this transition had not yet taken place, only the scientific theory of the economic determinants of it could be traced with any precision. In order to keep to the historical sequence, and to the development of Marx's own ideas this will be left to last, since it was only fully elaborated in his later writings.

Forces of production and relations of production

By 'forces of production' Marx evidently meant to designate some specifically material element(s) of the productive process that could be clearly distinguished from the socio-economic relations (of production) which correspond to them. Whether or not Marx succeeded in doing this, and whether, if he did, he then sustained this distinction in his own historical and economic analysis has been the subject of huge recent debate. Marx sometimes spells out his theory of historical materialism in terms of a rather crude and mechanical model, where technological change directly and simply determines changes in social organization. At other times, and in Marx's own detailed, if fragmentary presentations of the process of socio-economic change, he is infinitely more nuanced. Although this increased subtlety yields gains in historical plausibility, it does so at some cost to the fit with his 'guiding thread'.

At the crudest level then, the 'forces of production' might be equated with technology, and Marx sometimes says this:

> In acquiring new productive forces men change their mode of production; and in changing their mode of production, in changing their way of earning their living, they change all their social relations. The hand mill gives you society with the feudal lord, the steam mill industrial capitalism. [107]

---

[106] Ibid., p. 389. The sequence of 'epochs', Marx came to see as something not all societies were bound to pass through. At least twice he mentioned the possibility of the Russian village commune-based economy passing directly to modern socialism by being able to appropriate the economic and technical benefits of capitalism developed elsewhere. See the drafts of 'Letter to Vera Sassoulitch' (Feb. 1881) *SW*, p. 577, and the 'Preface' to the Russian edition of the *Communist Manifesto*, *SW*, p. 583.

[107] From *The Poverty of Philosophy* (1847) *SW*, p. 202.

However if forces of production are equated simply with 'level of available tech-nology' then other distinctions implied in the 'guiding thread' statement seem difficult to sustain. Either a) the 'forces of production' as technology seem to be dependent on the mental or intellectual activity or insights of their inventors – contrary to Marx's intention to distinguish between a 'material' base and the 'intellectual life processes', or b) if technology is qualified to mean 'applicable technology' – i.e. applicable given the social circumstances – then the distinction between the 'material forces' and the (supposedly dependent) 'social relations of production' is jeopardized: and if such a distinction cannot be sustained then the one cannot operate causally upon the other.[108]

These objections may not be as fatal as they appear, albeit at a certain cost to the neat simplicity of Marx's abstract presentation of his theory (itself – it should be remembered – described by him as only a 'guiding thread'). For with regard to a), scientific knowledge may be regarded as separate from other intellectual products of a society which are more directly ideological. On this view the 'forces of production' may include 'scientific knowledge', but still exclude other non-material factors such as beliefs about social structure, religion, etc.. This argument is reinforced by the observation that the prevailing polarity in Marx's thought is between 'material' and 'social', and not between 'material' and 'mental'.[109] Although this may save Marx from inconsistency, it seems implausible that human invention in the sciences could operate independently of social, religious and other 'superstructural' mental dimensions.

Secondly, with regard to b), it can be argued that it is not the *conceptual distinction* between material forces and social relations of production that is endangered here, but a particular, and incorrect, account of the *causal relationship* between them. For as we noted in the 'guiding thread' statement, not all the relations Marx asserts are strong enough to establish causal links in any rigorous sense of the term. If, therefore, an account can be found in which relations of production are allowed to qualify the way in which technology can be applied, which yet retains a secure analytic distinction between them, and which still allows for explanations as to how the forces can have 'corresponding' relations, Marx can be said to be making sense.[110] Moreover Marx did clearly intend the possibility of influence operating both ways at different times, since in his account of his 'guiding thread', he talks about relations of production and their legal expression being at one time the 'forms of development of productive forces, and yet later becoming fetters which, as a result of changes in productive forces, have themselves to be transformed.'

[108] By far the most disciplined attempt to wrest coherence from Marx's various accounts of the meanings of 'productive forces' and 'relations of production' is Cohen's *Marx's Theory of History*, esp chs. II, III. This book has proved seminal in setting new standards of rigour in the formulation of Marxian theory and spawned a tremendous secondary literature. Its aim is, however, as Cohen himself admits (p. ix), not so much to discover Marx's own meaning or development, but 'to construct a tenable theory of history which is broadly in accord with what Marx said on the subject', although this hardly does justice to the care with which he documents his argument. For a developed version of the sort of objections raised here to Marx's account see: S. Lukes, 'Can the base be distinguished from the superstructure?' in *The Nature of Political Theory*, ed. David Miller and Larry Siedentop (Oxford, 1983), pp. 103–19

[109] Cohen, *Marx's Theory of History*, pp. 45–7.

[110] The argument is developed at length by Cohen, ch. VI, *Marx's Theory of History*. For particularly lucid critiques see Lukes 'Can the Base be Distinguished from the Superstructure?', and Jon Elster *Making Sense of Marx* (Cambridge, 1985), ch.5. However, see also John Torrance, 'Reproduction and Development, the case for a Darwinian mechanism in Marx's Theory of History,' *Political Studies*, xxxiii, 3(1985).

This question of whether relations of production, or forces of production exercise causal primacy in Marx's theory has also been a matter of enormous contention. At least some of this can be resolved by bearing mind that Marx seemed to want to use relations between these two in order to explain two different social phenomena, occurring under different conditions. Firstly, within a (relatively) established and stable economic epoch (ancient, feudal or capitalist), the relations of production, and the ideological superstructure generally, operated in a way that was conducive to, or as modern analysts would say, 'functional for' the development of the relevant forces of production. Under these conditions causality flows from relations to forces as effects. However, under the unstable conditions of revolution, or the rapid transformation of the forces of production, forces themselves exercise a destructive effect on the old, and a beneficial effect on new relations of production. Here the causality runs from forces to relations. Since it is usually presumed to be the nature (and not the extent) of the productive forces that, for Marx, definitively characterizes the social structure, it seems right to say that ultimately, and fundamentally, the new forces determine their 'corresponding' relations. Moreover this is not at all incompatible with the claim that *within* any established economic mode of production, or epoch, relations can exercise a benign effect on the development of forces.[111]

All this is very abstract, and would benefit from some examples. Unfortunately for any attempts to link his general theory to his analysis, when Marx actually engages in a historical account he is far more sympathetic to the facts of history (as available to him) and inventive in his use of them, than he is concerned to establish one-to-one correspondences between his technical terms and the processes he describes. Not infrequently he allots a major historico-economic role to some apparently contingent event or phenomenon which seems unconnected with the internal economic dynamic of society. For example, the influx of American gold, he claims, in fuelling European inflation, undermined traditional landed proprietors and wage-earners, but strengthened commerce and capitalists generally.[112] However, there is no suggestion that this was in any sense a product of the internal forces of the European economy. (Clearly the activity of colonization might be seen in this way, but the *existence* of already refined new-world precious metals was not, and it is the specific importation of gold and silver that Marx cites as a cause).

---

[111] Conversely, and to further complicate matters: The equivocation in 'revolution . . . or rapid transformation' in the quoted account dodges the issue as to whether it is the *nature* or *extent* of change in the productive forces that affects the relations of production. Marx talks variously about the 'development', 'transformation' and creation of 'new' forces of production. Inasmuch as productive forces can be identified with material technology, where unequivocally 'new' forms can be identified, the distinction between circumstances in which the (new) forces exert a causal influence on the 'old' relations, can be readily distinguished from those in which the (established) forces are being 'developed' by their 'corresponding' relations. For example, the much cited passage about the hand mill and the steam mill, or another, more problematic one — since none of the inventions mentioned seem to be forces of production — where Marx claimed *'Gunpowder, the compass and printing, the three great inventions which ushered in bourgeois society'*. However, if the 'development' of productive forces refers to an incremental process, or even simply to the forces becoming *more productive*, the identification of circumstance in which relations or forces predominate is much less clear. For a detailed discussion see Elster, *Making Sense*, p. 278ff.

[112] *The German Ideology*, p. 73, *Capital*, tr. Moore and Aveling (London, 1908) p. 775.

Feudal society

Nevertheless I shall now try to offer a Marxian account of feudalism as an economic system and to show how Marx's terms can be operationalised to demonstrate both the static 'structural' elements of a particular economic 'epoch', and the 'dynamic' transformational elements involved in a transition from one epoch to another. As I have suggested, this is difficult to do by direct citation from Marx himself, so it will also be important to indicate where Marx's historical account differs from his more general theory. One further problem is that the historical account is incomplete: although Marx three times gives an extended account of the early development of capitalism, in each case he starts from an already *decaying* feudalism and not from its high point.[113] Moreover he commonly contrasts capitalism analytically with *all* previous forms of socio-economic organization (as being generally communal) without distinguishing their particular characteristics, let alone doing so in virtue of their distinctive 'productive forces'.[114] Marx's focus is on how the categories so central to a modern commercial economy – the isolated wage labourer and capital – came to be historical realities, and only incidentally on how the characteristics of feudalism were displaced, let alone how they functioned under the healthy feudal system.

Under the primitive economic conditions and material resources available to human beings in the chaotic aftermath of the Roman Empire, the basic productive forces were agricultural land and human labour. The feudal relationship was essentially the grant of land in return for the performance of service.[115] That service was either the cultivation of the lord's land in the case of villeins, or the provision of military service in the case of individuals of higher status. The social structure was (ideally) pyramidal in that the king granted tenure of estates to his great lords or 'tenants in chief' who in turn had sub-tenants (who may in turn have had sub-sub-tenants) down to the level of the 'immediate producer' or labourer who had only agricultural obligations.[116] Above this level, individuals in each tier were linked to the one above by personal oath or agreement. The 'feu' or 'foedum' involved the grant of land in return for providing military service,

---

[113] The accounts are *The German Ideology*, part I, and *Capital*, part VII, and, more sporadically the *Grundrisse*, tr. and ed. Martin Nicolaus (Harmondsworth, 1973), pp. 459–515.

[114] For example in the sections on pre-capitalist economic forms in the *Grundrisse*, pp. 471 ff., where Marx continually switches between, and generalizes about classical antiquity, tribalism, Germanic (feudalism) and Asiatic despotism. This is not to say he does not make very suggestive and insightful remarks about the differences between them, e.g.: 'The history of classical antiquity is the history of cities, but of cities founded on landed property and on agriculture; Asiatic history is a kind of indifferent unity of town and countryside (the really large cities must be regarded here merely as royal camps, as works of artifice [*Superfötation*] erected over the economic construction proper); the Middle Ages (Germanic Period) begins with the land as the seat of history, whose further development then moves forward in the contradiction between town and countryside; the modern [age] is the urbanization of the countryside, not the ruralization of the city as in antiquity.' *Grundrisse*, p. 479. None of the above, however identifies the 'forces of production' distinguishing the various pre-modern forms.

[115] *Capital*, p. 741.

[116] Although Marx notes that in England there was a mixture of 'great seignorial domains' and 'small peasant properties'. Ibid., vol.I, p. 741. The modern historian agrees here: 'the impression gained from a study of twelfth-century agricultural conditions is of an archipelago of manors in central England

say twenty pike men or five knights for two months of each year, which the lord needed to fulfil his obligations to the next individual up the hierarchy. There is, in feudalism, a great stress on the military needs of society – and clearly in the chaotic conditions of the Dark and early Middle Ages this is understandable. The establishment of civil order, and the exclusion of bandits and invaders was a paramount condition of any production under these circumstances.

This prominent, one might almost say determining aspect of military need, however, does not quite fit Marx's account. Although Marx recognizes military force may be a condition for the successful *conduct* of an economic system, he is quite explicit that such conditions are not themselves a part of the *material conditions of production.*[117] Military feudalism is indeed a social structure which seems to arise above, and provide the conditions for the development (even the viability) of the materially productive unit – the commune, village or manor. But what shapes the militaristic feudal social structure here seems to be not the productive forces *per se*, but the chaotic conditions under which they have to be deployed. However good this is as a historical explanation, this is not what Marx's 'outline account' would have us believe. For that to work, distinctively feudal productive *forces* (raw materials, skills, tools and perhaps technical knowledge) would have to be identified, and these would have to shape the productive, and in turn the legal and political relations distinctive to feudalism. Marx nowhere says what these would be.[118] Moreover if we think of forces of production in terms of technology it is difficult to see in what important ways the forces of production available under feudalism differed from those of classical antiquity.

Any attempt to cash out what Marx's 'forces of production' might have been for feudalism, seems unlikely to succeed. However the sense in which feudal production gives rise to a distinctive 'legal, political and ideological superstructure' can be more plausibly identified. The material basis on which feudalism depended was the appropriation, by a landholding class, of the agricultural product of the serfs or villeins. To achieve this it was vital that landholders restricted the movement of serfs – the actual producers – away from the land. Particularly so as, at various stages under feudalism there may have been marginal uncultivated land available for them to move to.[119] Secondly, since the ability of those higher up the social pyramid to discharge their military obligations (needful for both the survival of the state, and continued economic activity) was dependent on those

surrounded by a sea of freer communities.' Frank Barlow, *The Feudal Kingdom of England, 1042–1216* (Harlow, 1972) p. 275.

[117] Karl Marx, *Theories of Surplus Value* (3 vols, London and Moscow, 1969), vol. I, pp. 287ff. Once we start down this slippery slope, Marx rightly observes, 'it can be shown that *all* human relations and functions, however, and in whatever form they may appear, influence material production and have a more or less decisive influence on it' (ibid., p. 288).

[118] Here I agree with Elster, *Making Sense*, pp. 277–8.

[119] As noted above, there is a case to be made for saying that Marx viewed the growth of precapitalist economies as peculiarly *extensive* rather than *intensive* (Elster, *Making Sense*, p. 273). This would partly excuse Marx's otherwise disturbing (in view of his insistence on historical periodization) tendency to generalise about precapitalist social forms. Also, in presuming a boundary beyond which feudal (exploitative) relations did not obtain, it accounts for the severity of the laws needed to prevent the mobility of labour. If *all* cultivable land were feudalized, what incentive would serfs have to escape? In capitalism too, labour, although it cannot be directly coerced, must be denied access to land (through enclosure or limiting emigration) in order to ensure the availability of 'free' labour to the capitalist.

below them being able to supply their material or military needs, and since this in turn was dependent on sustaining economic units large enough to produce the required surplus, it followed that the 'ruling class' as a group had an interest in disciplining itself not to allow the fragmentation or alienation of its landholdings. Law – as the political expression of these 'relations of production' – therefore enshrined the entailment and (in England) impartibility of estates, and the immobility of unfree labourers.[120] Even if we cannot identify with any precision the 'forces of production' of feudalism, it can be clearly seen that these legally enforced relations of production, by keeping landholdings at the required size, and by keeping labour where it was needed – on that land – are, as Marx argues, the 'forms of development' for feudalism as an economic system as a whole; and that without them the system would have been – as it frequently was in its early development – subject to severe dislocation and erosion.

The transformation of feudalism into capitalism

Now let us consider the claim that the transformation of the forces of production, made possible by the success of feudal production relations and their legal expression, brings about the eventual conversion of the latter in such a way as to once again 'correspond' to new, capitalist forces.

Inasmuch as the feudal economic system was successful it allowed, and indeed encouraged, the development within it of commerce. Whilst a feudal society is dominated by the exchange of personal services, as Marx puts it 'from the boot black up to the King', commerce requires – and so brings about – more flexible forms of exchange involving money.[121] Of course commerce had always existed, but had never exercised the dominant and determining role in an economic system – even the ancient trading nations of Phoenicia and Carthage, were parasitic on, and so determined by, the dominance of ancient agriculture: 'There is in every social formation a particular branch of production which determines the position and importance of all others, and the relations obtaining in this branch accordingly determine the relations of all others as well.'[122] Under feudalism, for example such manufacture as took place was organized on feudal lines, which paralleled the dominant relations in agriculture: it was conducted within guilds. The transformation of a society is effected through the emergence into *dominance* of a new mode of production which then affects others in its wake.[123] Marx's claim that different epochs are characterized by different modes of production is not affected by pointing to the mere *existence* of other economic forms coexisting in subsidiary fashion.

[120] This is an 'ideal type' of feudalism which was of course subject to marked regional variations, and was constantly undergoing change. England was peculiar: 'The rule of primogeniture prevented the creation of a caste nobility and threw many younger sons of gentle birth into the professions and into commerce and industry; and the refusal to shackle the land market helped to keep English society mobile.' Barlow, *The Feudal Kingdom*, p. 318. For a more thoroughgoing (and contentious) view of English peculiarity see Alan MacFarlane, *The Origins of English Individualism* (Oxford, 1978).

[121] *Grundrisse*, p. 465.

[122] *A Contribution to the Critique . . .* p. 212

[123] This seems to be true for earlier transitions. Thus the latifundia of the late Roman Empire can be regarded as proto-manorial forms. However it is not true for socialism. Though feudal economic institutions grow up within late antiquity, and capitalist ones within feudalism, socialist institutions don't grow up

Marx wants to show how the growth and development of commerce transforms and erodes feudal relations. It *can* only grow once feudalism has successfully pacified the environment, and it is encouraged to grow by successful feudal landholders, and others with a surplus to spend on luxuries which the local, manorial economy does not itself produce. Commerce 'erodes' feudalism as a structure because merchants and others involved in commerce need to enter into exchange relationships on a money basis and be free to move around; to do so they must be freed from feudal obligations. The establishment of free commercial 'space' within the feudal network (which as we have seen otherwise required personal and proprietorial immobility) involved the creation of towns, not just as physical concentrations of buildings, but as legal entities with their own 'liberties': markets, 'freemen', all juridically separated from the network of obligations imposed by feudalism. Towns were effectively islands where different, legally sanctioned economic relations, could flourish.

Relations of production obtain between human beings and between human beings and means of production. Marx's concern in each of his accounts of the transition from capitalism to feudalism is to show how, as a matter of historical fact, the two major economic categories taken for granted by the economists of his day came into existence as social facts, namely 'capitalist private property', and 'free labour', and with them the consequent possibility of the one hiring the other through the wage contract.[124] The historical emergence of these two are not separate processes, but different sides of the same coin. For labourers to be 'free' they had to be not only emancipated – unobligated by feudal ties (the part of the story emphasised by bourgeois apologists for capitalism-as-freedom) – but also free, in the more sinister sense of 'deprived of' any means of existence other than the sale of their labour. Freeing labour in both these ways involved disentangling primary producers from the nexus of rights and obligations that constituted feudal relations.[125] Once the labourer had no personal duties to his immediate and local social superiors he could move around in search of work, and once he was deprived of customary rights of access to the means of life – a plot of land, common grazing, wood-gathering etc. which had acted as inducements to keep him in place – he then *had* to move around in search of work. The freeing of the labourer from the land thus simultaneously involved freeing property from the claims of anyone other than the single owner. Once freed from the old relations of production, labour and capital were available to be formulated in the new relations characteristic of capitalism. According to the outline account in the 'Preface' this should be determined by changes in the 'forces of production' but Marx's historical discussion emphasises the role of both economics and force in this development, and it is the latter, he claims that played 'the greater part'.[126]

---

within capitalism (as Mill thought they might, in the form of co-operatives), rather the class that will create socialism does.

[124] So *Capital*, p. 737. Capitalism can only occur where two different conditions of human being exist: 'on the one hand, the owners of money, means of production, means of subsistence, who are eager to increase the sum of values they possess, by buying other people's labour power; on the other hand, free labourers, the sellers of their own labour power.' See also *Grundrisse*, pp. 463–4. In *The German Ideology* the separation of labour from land is embedded more in his account of the growth in the division of labour.

[125] 'The expropriation of the agricultural producer, of the peasant, from the soil, is the basis of the whole process.' *Capital*, p. 739.

[126] *Capital*, p. 737

The two major economic factors that separated labourers from the land in England were, Marx claims, firstly the abolition and disbanding of feudal retainers. This took place both by royal statute under Henry VII, but also voluntarily by a 'new nobility', anxious to capitalize on the Flemish weavers' demand for English wool by converting peasants' arable land into grazing for sheep.[127] The growth of weaving manufacture thus led to simultaneous pressures to depopulate hitherto arable agricultural land *and* to create a demand for a labour force in the towns.[128] A second factor was the dissolution of the monasteries. This again simultaneously 'hurled their inmates into the proletariat' whilst releasing a huge amount of landed property, untrammelled by traditional rights. Land was eagerly acquired as gifts by royal favourites, or purchased by speculative investors, both groups anxious to derive a commercial revenue from their new property, rather than regarding it as a social responsibility in the traditional light. Simultaneously with all this, the ancillary common rights by which independent yeomen cultivators had supplemented their subsistence – rights to gather wood, graze animals, cut peat or turf for heating etc. on common land began to be curtailed. Where cultivators were tenants, for example, their landlords forbade them to keep domestic animals for food. All of which drove them into the labour market since they were left incapable of supporting themselves without selling their labour.[129]

The process was hurried along by violence, both open and under cover of law. The Restoration in England abolished all obligations still owed to the state through feudal land tenures, and instead compensated the state by imposing taxes on the propertyless. This at a stroke concentrated political resources at the centre, and shifted the burden of providing them from the propertied to the landless, accomplishing simultaneously the two characteristic features of the capitalist state – centralization and the privileging of the propertied classes. In the 1688 settlement in England more crown estates were turned into private property, and a free market in land established to assist the operation of capitalist agriculture. Besides these more spectacular episodes of expropriation, there was, from the 15th to the end of the eighteenth century, a continual series of acts of what Marx calls Parliamentary robbery: 'Acts for the enclosure of the Commons, in other words, decrees by which the landlords grant themselves the people's land as private property.'[130] The last great legalized expropriation in Britain of a people's communal property was still under way in the highland clearances of Scotland whilst Marx wrote.[131] Marx cites numerous contemporary analysts – most impressively the Rev. Richard Price, Burke's target in *Reflections* – to show that the known effect, and often the intention, of all these actions was that a previously quasi-self-sufficient peasantry 'will be converted into a body of men who earn their subsistence by working for others, who will be under a necessity of going to market for all they want . . . [and that as a result] there will perhaps

---

[127] The significance of Henry's 'Statute of Retainers' in initiating socio-economic change had been a continuous feature of social theorists since at least Harrington, see, Pocock, *Ancient Constitution and the Feudal Law*, (2nd edn. Cambridge, 1987), pp. 141ff. and 331ff.

[128] *Capital*, pp. 741–2; *The German Ideology*, pp. 71–2.

[129] As noted in the earlier discussion on 'The Law on the theft of wood', Marx's early journalism had highlighted the same process at work in Germany.

[130] *Capital*, p. 748.

[131] As this book was written, a Conservative Government conducted a series of massive 'privatizations' some of which amounted to a similar statute-induced theft of communal property.

be more labour, because there will be more compulsion to it'.[132] Depriving the peasants of free access to raw materials and the 'natural' (i.e. unowned) means of subsistence, forced them to buy and sell these in the market place. This further enmeshes the peasants in a money economy – to participate in which they must themselves earn money, either by producing cash-crops, or selling their labour – and their demand provided a further stimulus to commercial production.[133]

However, in addition to both spontaneous and legally contrived economic pressures, horrendously cruel means were used to terrify and coerce individuals displaced from the land into accepting the strange discipline of wage labouring in manufacturing. Branding, chaining, whipping, mutilation, enslavement and execution were all 'legally' deployed against those who would not or could not find work. The conversion of peasants into an urban proletariat was accomplished both by depriving them of rural resources and driving them from the land, and by coercive 'discipline' in the towns. Yet since rural depopulation constantly ran ahead of the demand for labour in the towns there was often simply no work to be found. At the same time legal regulation of wages – necessary to enable capital to accumulate in its early stages – constantly depressed workers' standards of living, and other laws punished 'combinations' or unions of workers seeking to improve pay or conditions.[134] Marx is at pains to emphasise the active role played by political force in economic change.[135]

The coherence of Marx's account

How does this history bear out Marx's general account? The re-invocation of the 'fetters' metaphor at one point helps to focus this question. Marx writes that the feudal constitution in the country, and the guild organization in the towns prevented the conversion of capital in its feudal forms – usury and commerce – into industrial forms of capital. Feudal and guild forms are examples of relations of production, and they clearly fetter or constrain the use of factors of production in capitalist forms – by inhibiting the mobility of, and access to, capital and labour, and by placing constraints on who might engage in certain forms of economic activity. For this reason early manufacturers sought to locate themselves beyond the reach of these constraints – in sea ports, which were often subject to different legal constraints, or in parts of the countryside beyond feudal control. This is clearly a case of relations of production inhibiting economic developments. But are those developments themselves developments of the 'forces of production'? This seems more doubtful.

Capital is a store of value, at this point in history a sum of money. This is true whether we conceive of it as usurious capital, merchant capital or a manufacturer's outlay. What makes it distinctively capitalist is its being deployed to hire wage labour to produce a commodity for sale on the market.[136] Marx is insistent that capitalism should not be identified with either industry (as opposed to agriculture) or mechanized (as opposed to

---

[132] *Capital*, p. 750, citing Richard Price.

[133] Ibid., pp. 771–2.

[134] Ibid., pp. 758–65.

[135] Ibid., p. 776.

[136] Ibid., p. 311.

manual) manufacture.[137] He argues both of the following: i) that 'with regard to the mode of production itself, manufacture, in its strict meaning, is hardly to be distinguished in its earliest stages from the handicraft trades of the guilds'; *and* ii) that the first form of capitalism was in fact capitalist agriculture, in which the farmer 'makes his own capital breed by employing wage-labourers, and pays a part of the surplus product, in money or in kind, to the landlord as rent'.[138] What Marx gives us as the initial stages of capitalism is essentially a story about the *reorganization of existing forces under new relations,* which are in conflict with the legal constraints established to perpetuate the old ones. In fact Marx identifies capitalism with a specific form of productive organization – the division of labour – whilst disingenuously claiming that this itself amounts to a new power (does Marx mean force?):

> Not only have we here an increase in the productive power of the individual, by means of cooperation, but the creation of a new power, namely the collective power of the masses . . . .

The work of directing, superintending and adjusting, becomes one of the functions of capital, from the moment that labour under the control of capital, becomes cooperative. Once a function of capital, it acquires special characteristics.[139]

As a matter of economic history this may be true, but if it is the organizational role to which it is put that distinguishes the 'capitalist' deployment of capital from its feudal forms, indeed if organizational change itself can be, as he suggests a power or force, it is difficult to see how the distinction between forces and relations of production can be sustained, nor – in the development of capitalism – do we have a picture of how any distinctively material 'force of production' (understood broadly as technology) is pressing against the limits imposed by feudal relations and social forms. Indeed quite the opposite: Marx here not only describes how the tools utilized in manufacture are themselves developed and specialised through the influence of the division of labour characteristic of the capitalist organization of manufacturing, but also insists that the division of labour itself is and can only be understood as the decomposition of handicraft production 'into its successive manual operations'.[140] All the initiative in tooling here seems to flow from changes in the relations – the organization – of production not from changes in 'forces'. Where Marx does mention the role of machinery, its impact on change is indirect, and operates through its effect on scientific thought rather than directly on productive relations![141]

Also of great interest here is the role Marx ascribes to the state. According to some popular accounts of Marx, the political advancement of the bourgeoisie, the class representative of capital, is a battle against the feudal state, and their success is dependent

---

[137] Ibid., p. 341. 'On the whole, machinery played that subordinate part which Adam Smith assigns to it in comparison with the division of labour.' It is worth pointing out that manufacture, is etymologically speaking, the making by hand.

[138] Ibid., pp. 311, 767. This follows Smith and Ricardo, see below pp. 542ff.

[139] Ibid., pp. 316, 321.

[140] Ibid., pp. 333, 330.

[141] 'The sporadic use of machinery in the 17th century was of the greatest importance, because it supplied the great mathematicians of the time with a practical basis and stimulant to the creation of a science of mechanics.' Ibid., p. 341.

on, and a consequence of, their increasing economic importance as a class.[142] But the account in *Capital*, so far from regarding the state as part of the old legal and political superstructure which inhibits, or fetters the development of the new forces and relations of production, actually gives it an important role in the process of capitalist development:

> all [these methods of accumulation] employ the power of the State, the concentrated and organized force of society, to hasten, hothouse fashion, the process of transformation of the feudal mode of production into the capitalist mode, and to shorten the transition. Force is the midwife of every old society pregnant with a new one. It is *itself an economic power*.[143]

Once the political institutions of the state have been taken over by the rising bourgeoisie, it is possible to understand how, consistent with Marx's general theory, the state can be used to facilitate the development of capitalism. This fits with what he says about relations of production (or law and politics as their 'legal expression') being used to *develop* the 'forces of production'. But the claim made in *Capital* seems to involve the state enforcing the development of the capitalist mode of production *before* the political triumph of the bourgeoisie – which according to Marx himself was not achieved in England until 1688.[144] Marx's own historical and economic analysis therefore raises in acute form the question of the degree of autonomy that can be attributed to the realm of politics. It was a question which took on huge practical significance in the light of his attempt to understand the progress of European revolution in 1848–50.

Revolutionary tactics and the state

Between 1847 and 1851 Marx was very involved in revolutionary politics, and the period saw some of his most sustained attempts to apply his theory to the different circumstances that existed in the various European states – but particularly Germany and France – then threatened with revolution. In the course of this Marx developed important modifications to his 'general' theory of politics and revolution, modifications which have had far-reaching implications for Marxist political beliefs and practice in the century since his death.

---

[142] See for example, *The Communist Manifesto*, in *Revolutions of 1848*, p. 69, the famous passage which ends with the claim: 'The executive of the modern state is but a committee for managing the common affairs of the whole bourgeoisie.'

[143] *Capital*, vol. I, p. 776. My italics.

[144] Ibid., pp. 746/7. Marx is not entirely consistent on this. In his article comparing the abortive German revolution of 1848 he identifies 1648/9 as the victory of the bourgeoisie and the bourgeois social order (*N.Rh.Z.* 15.12.1848, in *Revolutions of 1848*, p. 192). In a review of F. Guizot's 'Why did the English Revolution succeed?' written in 1850 he claimed that it was under William III 'the rule of the financial bourgeoisie was given its first legitimation', that 'the momentous development and transformation of bourgeois society in England only began with the consolidation of the constitutional monarchy.' Yet he also claimed there that the characteristically English alliance between the bourgeoisie and the large landowners 'had already arisen under Henry VIII' *and* that the bourgeoisie only 'gained direct political power as a result of the Reform Bill [of 1832]'. 'Review of Guizot's Book on the English Revolution' in *Revolutions of 1848*, pp. 251, 254, 255.

The simplified model: The Manifesto

In Marx's general model – outlined in *The Communist Manifesto* – the development of industrial production, gradually polarizes the population into two classes, bourgeoisie and proletariat. All other classes are residues from earlier modes of production such as peasants, or those belonging to earlier phases of the development of capitalism such as craft artisans or small shopkeepers. Such groups may, like the proletariat, come into conflict with the bourgeoisie, yet this conflict is for them, an essentially reactionary one – they seek to prevent or reverse economic development in order to recover their obsolete economic position.[145] All such groups are gradually abolished by the competitive processes at work under capitalism, forced to give up their independence and sell their labour as wage-earners in order to live; thus only the proletariat is *developed* as capitalism grows. The increasing scale of capitalist production draws the wage-earning proletariat into larger and larger factories; the abolition of traditional skills through the division of labour, and as workers become de-skilled adjuncts to machines, renders all workers uniform. These processes encourage in the proletariat both an awareness of their collective class character and the hopelessness of their situation. The competition from machinery and worsening economic conditions consequent on the increasing instability of the capitalist economy forces them more and more into the political arena under conditions of virtual civil war until the revolution finally breaks out, and the working class, by now the vast majority of the population, seize control of the factories and workshops to run them in the interests, not of profit, but of the whole society.

In these circumstances, with a mature bourgeoisie and a developed (i.e. large and yet universally degraded) proletariat, there will also be found a centralized, homogenized nation–state, an instrument created by the bourgeoisie in their drive for the easy movement of capital, labour and goods which facilitates the growth of the market and the division of labour. Such a state is the political expression of the dominance of the bourgeoisie, indeed, its executive is described by Marx as 'but a committee for managing the affairs of the whole bourgeoisie'. 'Political power, properly so called, is merely the organized power of one class for oppressing another.'[146] A revolution then, is the wresting of political power by one class from another, an event which is the culmination of a historico-economic process which has created the newly dominant class. However Marx's claims about the nature of the proletariat make their revolution, and indeed their development, peculiar.

Earlier dominant classes developed, in company with the class which they exploit, within, but distinct from, the class relations of the immediate previous economic formation. Thus feudal lord and tenant grew up within the collapsing master–slave, or tribal relationship by which Marx variously characterizes the political economy of the classical world. The bourgeoisie and their incipient workers emerge together, in gaps outside the nexus of feudal relations, gaps either accidental or, as in the case of chartered towns, deliberately created. But the proletariat is not the dominant member of a new class relationship within capitalism, it is simply the subordinate half of the existing class

---

[145] *The Communist Manifesto*, in *Revolutions of 1848*, pp. 75, 77.
[146] Ibid., pp. 69, 86.

relationship. Its victory, Marx believed, will establish not another form of class relationship, but a classless society. The proletariat is the 'universal class' because, amongst
other things, it comprises human beings bereft of any particular – i.e. class determining –
characteristics. In this sense its propertylessness, which is the cause of its misery under
capitalism, is the reason why it can represent the salvation of humankind from class
domination.[147] Because class divisions are a function of private property, the propertyless
character of the proletariat entails, for Marx, that a society based on it will be free from
class divisions. Not only that, but if it is true that the state is both caused by, and functions
in order to sustain, the role of the ruling class, the absence of class antagonisms should
lead to the absence of the state. Ultimately then the victory of the proletariat brings about
a classless society, and a classless society, has no role for, and by implication therefore
no state, which will accordingly 'wither away'.[148]

On the other hand the *Manifesto* acknowledges that in the act of revolution the
proletariat will need to establish its 'class' rule over the capitalists as long as any of them
remain, and that the state may form a useful means of doing so, and of completing the
transformation of the forces of production hitherto inhibited by capitalist relations.[149]
Thus Marx's generalized theory of revolution at this time seems to envisage two
sequential attitudes to the state: the initial taking over of it by the proletariat as a means
to ensuring its class dominance, and then, secondly, the destruction of the state through
its sheer irrelevance, once class antagonisms have been transcended through the abolition
of private property.

In this model, revolution respects the neat periodization of history, into epochs
dominated by different classes corresponding to different modes of production – feudal
landowners under feudalism, capitalists under capitalism. Tidily, the transition from one
epoch to another is effected when a newly emerging economically dominant class wrests
political control from the previously dominant class through a revolution. Different
dominant classes establish their own typical political forms – monarchical absolutism
under feudalism, constitutional monarchy or limited republicanism under capitalism.[150]
A fully democratic republic was often identified by Marx with the victory, and even the
dictatorship, of the proletariat itself. But this depended on the social structure of the state
in question. Where the capitalist economy had completed its historical task of converting
the mass of the population into wage labourers, as was the case in England, the institution
of universal suffrage, would be tantamount to revolution since it would effectively place
political power in the hands of the proletariat.[151] Marx's theory of revolution was closely

---

[147] Ibid., p. 78 clearly draws on Marx's earlier, more philosophical analysis.

[148] Ibid., p. 87. The phrase 'the withering away of the state' is actually used by Engels in *Anti Düring*.
The notion that a social institution can be either brought about or 'wither away' depending on whether or
not there is a function for it to perform is a highly controversial aspect of Marx's social thought. See the
discussion above. On the specific methodological points see: Cohen, Elster, Torrence, etc.

[149] *Communist Manifesto*, p. 86: 'The proletariat will use its political supremacy to wrest, by degrees,
all capital from the bourgeoisie, to centralize all instruments of production in the hands of the state, i.e., of
the proletariat organised as the ruling class, and to increase the total of productive forces as rapidly as
possible.'

[150] The account is drawn from *Communist Manifesto*, pp. 75–9, supplemented by various other
writings.

[151] 'Universal suffrage is the equivalent of political power for the working class of England, where the
proletariat forms a large majority of the population'. 'The Chartists', in *Surveys from Exile* (volume 2 of

tied to nineteenth-century struggles to expand or limit the franchise. Marx commonly used this as an index of the class-basis of a regime. His assumption – a not-unreasonable one in mid-century – was that the bourgeoisie would never voluntarily abolish property qualifications for voting. This was why a revolution was needed, and why he claimed in the *Manifesto* that 'the first step in the revolution . . . is to win the battle of [sc. for] democracy', and he often (confusingly for those of us who think we live in democracies) identified democracy with the dictatorship of the proletariat.[152] Marx simply assumed and hoped, as Mill assumed and feared, that an enfranchised labouring class majority, would use their power despotically – as a dictatorship.[153] However, whether the bourgeoisie would concede the vote to the working class, however unlikely, was an empirical question. In later life when working class majorities were enfranchised in Britain, the USA and Holland, Marx observed that the proletariat had there, only to learn to use the legal and political rights they possessed in order to gain effective power.[154] Whether the bourgeoisie would *then* sit quietly back and allow political rights to be used to establish socialism was another matter.

England, simply because it was the country where capitalism, and therefore the polarization between wage labourers and bourgeoisie, was most developed, where the peasantry, and independent artisans had all but disappeared, was untypical in conforming so closely to the ideal model of the *Manifesto*.[155] However, in most continental states capitalism had not progressed so far, the class situation was less tidy, the historical periodization was less clear-cut. As a result revolutionary tactics were more complex.

Karl Marx, Political Writings), ed. David Fernbach (Harmondsworth, 1973), hereafter *SE*, p. 264; and 'England was the only country where the working class was sufficiently developed and organised to turn universal suffrage to its proper account.' 'Report of Marx's speech on the seventh anniversary of the international' in *First International and After* (volume 3 of *Karl Marx, Political Writings*) (Harmondsworth, 1974), p. 270.

[152] *Communist Manifesto*, p. 86.

[153] The term 'dictatorship' had more equivocal overtones in the nineteenth century, before the eras of Mussolini and Hitler. Under the Roman Republic a dictatorship was a specific constitutional device, enabling absolute powers to be exercised in an emergency for a limited period, after which the dictator was answerable for his actions.

[154] *SW*, p. 594, Letter to Hyndman (8 Dec. 1880) and Speech in Amsterdam, (1872).

[155] See, most insistently, *SE*, pp. 277–8, 'Letter to the Labour Parliament'. Even so this had not led to a totally class-transparent political situation. Marx observed that the political alliance forged in England between the already capitalistically operating aristocracy and the emergent bourgeoisie, had prolonged the political life of the landowners and gave her national politics a special complexion, in which the aristocratic Whigs operated government on behalf of the capitalists. *SE*, p. 259, 'Tories and Whigs'. The observation is insisted on in various writings, for example in an article on the 'British Constitution' in the *Neue Oder-Zeitung*, 6 March, 1855: 'The British Constitution is, in fact, only an antiquated and obsolete compromise made between the bourgeoisie, which rules in actual practice, although *not officially*, in all the decisive spheres of bourgeois society, and the landed aristocracy, which forms the *official government*.' *SE*, pp. 281–2. In France by contrast, whatever the peculiarities of the economic development, the bourgeoisie had eventually confronted the feudal nobility in a classic political revolution. The peculiarities of French economic development are hinted at in *The Class Struggles in France*, *SE*, p. 46. Engels, Marx's collaborator on the *Manifesto* commented that 'for the economic development of the bourgeoisie, England is here taken as the typical country; for its political development, France.' *The Communist Manifesto*, p. 69.

Historical variants (i) Germany and the retarded bourgeois revolution

In 1848 Marx, as a German in exile, and leader of an international, if largely German revolutionary movement, was heavily involved in the prospects for revolution in Germany, even returning there briefly in 1848. However he was committed to the view that revolution could not be carried out as an act of mere will – however strong – but only when historical and economic circumstances were right. There are no universally correct tactics for the communists to adopt, all must depend on a correct analysis of the historical circumstances. What these were in Germany had been hinted at in the closing lines of the *Manifesto*. Germany, he wrote, was still expecting its bourgeois revolution. It is, moreover one:

> that is bound to be carried out *under much more advanced conditions* of European civilisation and with a much more developed proletariat, than that of England was in the seventeenth, and of France in the eighteenth century, and because the bourgeois revolution in Germany will be but the prelude to *an immediately following proletarian revolution.*[156]

Marx here anticipates a certain telescoping of the 'normal' historical revolutionary process. France and England had experienced their 'bourgeois' revolutions against feudalism under still predominantly financial, commercial and agricultural bourgeoisies, before the emergence of industrial capitalism or, therefore, a politically significant proletariat. In England this had led to a peculiar alliance in which the aristocracy 'fronted' the bourgeois commercial revolution on the latter's behalf, giving the appearance of political continuity.[157] German economic development however, occurring much later, was excluded from the world market that would have stimulated the development of an indigenous commercial bourgeoisie, and experienced the growth of a purely industrial capitalism in her western regions, whilst still not even a unified state, and yet wholly under the dominance of a feudal political system – Prussia – in the east.[158] Germany had still to experience her bourgeois revolution, although there was already in existence there a proletariat and a proletarian party which was historically opposed to the bourgeoisie. The problem of the attitude of the proletariat to the still pre-bourgeois and fragmented state, and of its tactical attitude towards the still forthcoming bourgeois revolution, required a more complex revolutionary stance than that suggested by the normal model.

Marx initially argued that the workers should support the unification of Germany as a bourgeois liberal state, as a way of dealing with its relative economic backwardness – only a unified state could assist the development of capitalism and only the development of capitalism could assist the growth of the proletariat as a class, and so aid the ultimate

---

[156] Ibid., p. 98 (my emphasis).

[157] 'The Whigs are the *aristocratic representatives* of the bourgeoisie' in return for the exercise of political office . . . 'they make to the middle class, and assist it in conquering, all those concessions which in the course of social and political development have shown themselves to have become *unavoidable* and *undelayable*.' 'Tories and Whigs' *New York Daily Tribune*, 21 August, 1852, in *SE*, p. 256 and see note 155.

[158] 'The programme of the Radical Democratic Party', *N.Rh.Z.*, 7.6. 1848, in *Revolutions of 1848*, p. 123

prospects for a communist revolution. Until then, Marx urged, they should pursue a united front with the bourgeoisie. The *Demands of the Communist Party in Germany* (31 March 1848) argued for a joint programme that was radical in the circumstances but hardly communist: universal suffrage, abolition of feudal dues, transference of peasant tenures to the state, progressive taxation, death duties, state workshops for the unemployed, the nationalization of the banks, large feudal estates and transport. It was, he claimed 'in the interests of the German proletariat, petty bourgeoisie and peasantry to work energetically for the implementation of the above measures.'[159] Marx's policy of participation in the elections of that year caused a split amongst the communists, with Gottschalk and Marx forming separate parties. Marx argued for participation and against disunity amongst the anti-absolutist parties: 'the proletariat has not the right to isolate itself; however hard it may seem, it must reject anything that could isolate it from its allies.'

However, by midsummer, when a timid bourgeois bill, for fear of setting a precedent in abolishing property-rights, suggested compensation for the abolition of feudal rights, Marx was outraged, both at what he regarded as the bourgeoisie's betrayal of the peasants, and at their rendering themselves powerless against the forces of reaction. A series of other compromises by the liberals forced Marx to rethink his analysis of the German situation and the appropriate tactics. Marx compared the revolutionary performance of the German bourgeoisie with that of the French and found them lacking in every respect. For although in each case the revolution had brought about a counter-revolutionary coup:

> In France, however the bourgeoisie took its place at the *head* of the counter-revolution only after it had levelled every barrier which stood in the way of its supremacy as a class. In Germany the bourgeoisie finds itself pressed into the *retinue* of absolute monarchy and feudalism before it has even made sure of the basic conditions for its own freedom and supremacy. In France it stepped forth as a despot and made its own counter-revolution. In Germany it plays the role of a slave, and makes the counter-revolution required by the despots who rule it. In France it conquered in order to humble the people. In Germany it humbles itself in order to prevent the people from conquering. In the whole of history there is no more ignominious example of abjectness than that provided by the *German bourgeoisie*.[160]

The cowardly German bourgeoisie had been so fearful of seizing power on their own that they had continually sought to legitimate their actions by reference to the previous regime. But that regime was an absolutist feudal state, now acting as 'a fetter and a hindrance for the new bourgeois society, with its changed mode of production and changed needs.'[161] Its attempt to legitimate its rule by embedding it in the institutions of the old state – in fact in the monarchy – had the result of depriving the bourgeoisie of the authority and power to effect the very political and legal changes which they needed to pursue their economic interests.[162]

---

[159] Ibid., p. 110.

[160] *N.Rh.Z.*, 7.11.48, Ibid., p. 174.

[161] *N.Rh.Z.*, 10.12.48, Ibid., p. 189.

[162] *N.Rh.Z.*, 15.12.48, Ibid., p. 191, and more fully, 16.12.48, Ibid., pp. 197–8.

However, the inadequacies of the German bourgeoisie were no accident. They were rooted in material circumstances, in the 'more advanced conditions' under which it had to make its revolution, and about which Marx had written in the *Manifesto*. Those more advanced conditions referred to the already considerable development of manufacturing capital – largely in the Rhineland – and hence the emergence of a proletarian class – *before* the bourgeoisie had effected their historical showdown with the old feudal order. Unlike the English and the French, the German bourgeoisie:

> Saw itself threateningly confronted by the proletariat, and all those sections of the urban population related to the proletariat in interests and ideas, at the very moment of its own threatening confrontation with feudalism and absolutism. As well as having this class *behind* it, it saw *in front of* it the enmity of all Europe . . . irresolute against each of its opponents, taken individually, because it always saw the other one to the front of it or to the rear; inclined from the outset to treachery against the people and compromise with the crowned representatives of the old society, because it itself already belonged to the old society; . . . .[163]

Caught, as it were, between two historical stools, the German bourgeoisie was afraid to overthrow absolutism for fear of being unable, without its help, to resist socialism. They had even forfeited the support of an obvious ally – the peasants. They had reached, concluded Marx, a historical impasse, there was nothing to be done about them, they were incapable of making their own revolution: 'a purely bourgeois revolution . . . is impossible in Germany'. Only a feudal counter-revolution or what Marx calls a social-republican revolution is possible.[164] Since the bourgeoisie were incapable of undertaking or sustaining their own bourgeois revolution, there was little point in communists pursuing, as Marx had hitherto urged, a united front with them. The tactics of revolution therefore needed rethinking.

Permanent revolution

Forced into exile in London from both Germany and France, Marx reviewed the tactics of revolution in the winter of 1849–50. The result was a policy document for the members of the Communist League on the continent. In it Marx criticised his previous policy of supporting the bourgeoisie, and allowing the workers to be led and dominated by them. Instead the workers' party must now, he thought, reorganize and establish its autonomy 'so that it is not exploited and taken in tow by the bourgeoisie as in 1848'.[165] In this report, as elsewhere, Marx develops a conception of the revolutionary process as a kind of ratchet, in which the transition from feudal absolutism to republicanism is brought about, not at once, but in a series of steps, each of which corresponds to a constitutional settlement encapsulating the political victory of a particular fraction of the bourgeoisie as a whole. The next notch on the ratchet in Germany, he thought, corresponded to the revolutionary pressure from the democratic petty bourgeoisie, excluded from the settlement between the big liberal bourgeoisie and the feudal landowners. If the bourgeois

---

[163] *N.Rh.Z.*, 15.12.48, Ibid., pp. 193–4.   [164] *N.Rh.Z.*, 31.12.48, Ibid., p. 212.

[165] 'Address to the Central Committee of the Communist Party' in Ibid., pp. 320, 324.

democrats could gain their limited political demands – designed only to 'make the existing society as tolerable and comfortable for themselves as possible' and to buy off the workers with welfare provision – they too would desert their erstwhile allies, the radical workers, and so Marx warned 'the treacherous role that the German liberal bourgeoisie played against the people in 1848 will be assumed in the coming revolution by the democratic petty bourgeoisie'.[166] Thus once the petty bourgeoisie have achieved their aims of constitutional welfare liberalism, they will wish the movement of the revolutionary ratchet to cease and settle in the notch of a property-guaranteeing welfare republic.

A key to the success or failure of this tactic was the policy toward the peasants – a class which did not exist in England. Petty-bourgeois democrats wanted to abolish the feudal estates and give them to individual peasants as smallholdings, creating a rural property-owning petty-bourgeoisie to increase their support in the country. The workers' policy instead, thought Marx, should support the formation of state farming collectives, creating both a rural proletariat and the experience of collective property.[167] Whilst the bourgeoisie have an interest in arresting the momentum of the revolution at this point, the workers' interests lie in sustaining it:

> to make the revolution permanent until all the more or less propertied classes have been driven from their ruling positions, until the proletariat has conquered state power and until the association of the proletarians has progressed sufficiently far – not only in one country but in all the leading countries of the world – that competition ceases and at last the decisive forces of production are concentrated in the hands of the workers.[168]

A final crucial part of this strategy lay in the unification of Germany, then still a patchwork of autonomous states dominated by Prussia. Despite his general hostility to the state, and his desire to see it wither away *after* the revolution, Marx saw that the revolutionary transformation of a unified state would be much easier to effect than pursuing revolutionary power piecemeal in each locality. The revolutionary workers' party must therefore keep an independent and centralized political organization, run their own candidates, establish a parallel government structure, and arm the workers: it should pursue a policy of cooperation with the bourgeoisie only when in its interests (i.e. in destroying feudal institutions), and oppose them when their interests differ.[169] Whilst the proletariat was not yet strong enough to seize power for itself, it was strong enough to force the petty bourgeoisie to go further than it wished, and so strengthen the long-term position of the workers. The slogan Marx coined for this tactic was The Permanent Revolution!

This analysis and these tactics were to have immense historical importance. European Russia, at the end of the nineteenth century arguably bore a strong resemblance to Germany in the 1850s, still a quasi-feudal autocracy, still without its bourgeois revolution, still with a large notionally free peasantry, Russia was nevertheless undergoing the transformation to capitalism under even more 'advanced conditions', importing some of

---

[166] Ibid., pp. 322–3, 321.
[167] Ibid., p. 328.
[168] Ibid., pp. 323–4.
[169] Ibid., pp. 326–7, 322.

the largest and most advanced industrial processes directly from the west to create a locally large proletariat. Yet because all this was dependent on foreign capital, she was without a strong indigenous bourgeoisie. When Russian Bolsheviks, using proletarian political forces in a weakly capitalized economy, pursued a bourgeois revolution against a feudal Tsarist autocracy in the hope that, with international help, they could sustain the revolutionary movement to the point where it became a socialist one, they were therefore drawing on a tactic with Marx's own authority behind it.

However, as revolutionary activity died down in the 1850s Marx himself gradually abandoned both these tactics and the immediate revolutionary expectations that underpinned them. His perspective on the forthcoming revolution became longer and longer. In April 1850 he still thought the later and smaller annual upswing in business trends an encouraging sign, and a 'temporary revival . . . which will only delay the development of the crisis a little'. By October he writes 'If the new cycle of industrial development which began in 1848 takes the same course as that of 1843–7, the crisis will break out in 1852.' But privately he was even prepared to split the Communist League on the issue of the immediate prospects for a workers' revolution. Marx told his colleagues they should say to the workers: 'If you want to change conditions and make yourselves capable of government, you will have to undergo fifteen, twenty or fifty years of civil war.' If the proletariat came to power prematurely, under present conditions they would only be able to implement a petty-bourgeois programme.[170]

During the summer Marx had acquired a reading ticket for the reading room of the British Museum and had embarked on a ten-year long study of economics that was to immensely deepen his understanding of capitalism, but also temper his immediate hopes of revolution. It was, however, to result in his most famous work, *Capital*.

Historical variants (ii) France, the 18th Brumaire and the state as parasite

The idea of the state as an instrument of class rule was good polemic, but it suggested a degree of instrumentality which is difficult to square with the policing role which the state was sometimes required to exercise over even the ruling class. For example, feudal restrictions were beneficial for feudalism as a whole, but they inhibited individual feudal lords from following their self-interest, eventually preventing them from transforming themselves into capitalists! Again, it may be in the interests of the survival of capitalism as a system, and of capitalists as a class, to place certain restrictions on the rapacity of capitalist exploitation (by for example limiting the maximum hours of work, or contributing to the education of the work force), but it is not necessarily in the interests of individual capitalists to do so unless all are similarly constrained. In the case of France, Marx frequently goes much further, and suggests that the state can exercise a degree of autonomy which makes it a distinct actor in the situation.

The massive state apparatus of France was a result of her particular historical development. In attempting to dismantle the complex web of power in the *ancien régime*,

---

[170] *Neue Rheinische Zeitung Revue*, 4 (April, 1850) and 5–6 (Oct.1850). Minutes of the Central Committee Meeting, 15th September 1850, all in *Revolutions of 1848*, pp. 283, 297, 341.

the French Revolution had been forced to 'develop what absolute monarchy had commenced, the centralization and organization of state power.' Furthermore the fragmented nature of the French bourgeoisie had led to not one but a series of revolutions in which factions within the bourgeoisie vied with each other for power, and each subsequent revolutionary episode in France's history had required of its victor the further development and perfection of the state apparatus to retain its fragile grip on power.[171] The state in France appears 'high above society', it is 'a parasitical [excrescence upon] civil society', a 'frightful parasitic body'.[172] Moreover, in the form of Bonapartism – the more or less autocratic rule of an individual embodiment of the national will – it appears to take on an existence independent of any particular class. In fact here, the fragmentation and relative weakness of the bourgeois classes means that the executive power in the state can – and not only can but needs to – usurp the legislative arm through which the ruling class controls the apparatus: 'it was the only form of government possible at a time when the bourgeoisie had already lost, and the working class had not yet acquired, the faculty of ruling the nation.'[173]

But Marx's political analysis is committed to the view that there is an underlying class basis to all important political phenomena. What can be the social significance of Louis Bonaparte's coup? If republicanism represented the class rule of the bourgeoisie, what class could the overthrow of that regime and its substitution by an autocrat represent?

Marx described the complex history and convoluted class politics of the period 1848-51 before concluding that the coup 'is the victory of the executive over the legislative power'. In republican states or even constitutional monarchies the executive is presented as the doer of the will expressed in the legislature. For the executive to gain control of the state suggests interesting possibilities about how even democratic state forms could dominate, as opposed to express the will of their citizens. However, pregnant as this explanation is, it still seems to render Bonaparte's regime independent of any social class basis. The state, instead of being a means of preparing for, or exercising the rule of the bourgeoisie, which Marx claims was its role under previous regimes, now 'seems to have attained a completely autonomous position', it is 'a frightful parasitic body, which surrounds the body of French society like a caul'.[174] However, the autonomy is only apparent: state power does not hover in mid-air. Bonaparte represents the most numerous class of French society, the *small peasant proprietors*. Marx's explanation of how this can be so fills out much detail of the way his theory of socio-economic development relates to politics and the state, as well as the role of ideology.

Attachment to the idea of the Napoleonic hero, to the memory of the man who saved a nation from self-destructive revolution, did indeed play a role in Louis' success. Marx argues at the end of the work that one function of reviving such now outdated ideals will be to exorcise them, and free the French nation from a misguided belief in such solutions to its problems so that it can face up to the realities of the situation. This recalls the way in which Marx described religious emancipation removing the flowers concealing the

---

[171] 'The Civil War in France' First Draft, in *Ist International*, pp. 247–9, *18th Brumaire,* in *SE*, p. 237

[172] 'Civil War in France', in *Ist International*, pp. 208, 247, *18th Brumaire,* in *SE*, p. 237.

[173] 'Civil War in France', in *Ist International*, p. 208.

[174] *18th Brumaire*, in *SE*, p. 238, 237. The caul is the membrane surrounding the intestinal cavity, or any tight-fitting net-like envelope, such as that of a wig.

political and social chains that bind us, so that we can see and recognize them for what they are.[175] Acting out national myths, Marx argues, exposes their incapacity to deal with a changed world.

The 'Napoleonic ideals' which Louis holds out again so apparently effectively to the French nation, offered a return to the politico-economic strategy of his uncle, the first Napoleon. What was this strategy? The original French Revolution had emancipated the French peasant from his servile status and made him a freeholder, owning his own small plot of land outright. As property-owners the new, free peasants had interests in common with the other property-owners – the urban bourgeoisie, and so sided with them against the landed aristocracy on the one hand, and the extreme propertyless workers on the other. It was on this broad bourgeois-property constituency that Napoleon I had relied. But fifty years on, whilst some peasants had succeeded in the new environment, most were failing. The process of competition with larger, more productive agricultural units, the consolidation of landholdings by some and the slide into bankruptcy or debt by the many, meant that the peasant ideal of self-employed proprietorship was no longer sustainable. Peasants, their properties mortgaged to purchase the capital needed to keep up with modern farming, are not any longer working for themselves; the small-holding is simply 'a pretext that allows the capitalist to draw profits, interest and rent from the soil, whilst leaving the tiller himself to work out how to extract the wage for his labour'.[176] The interests of the peasants and the bourgeoisie, once united against feudal power, were now opposed. How then did the new Napoleon seek to reconcile them? It was here that a second Napoleonic idea – and institution – played a role.

The first Napoleon had created, on the basis of universal taxation, a massive state, dominated by a national army. Marx explains this both by pointing out how conducive peasant society is to the creation of such a state, and by stressing its function in ameliorating certain problems posed by a free peasant economy. Firstly a society of smallholding peasants is not integrated, it does not generate secondary social groupings or those intermediate centres of power which Montesquieu had pointed to as the basis of liberal political institutions in modern monarchies. Being largely self-sufficient there is nothing to link peasant households with one another, or with the other institutions of society or the economy. They are, Marx observed, in a famous simile, like a sack of potatoes, held together only by what encloses them. In more technical terms, whilst they are objectively a class – being all related in the same way to the means of production – they do not subjectively feel themselves to be a class.[177] Being uniformly weak and isolated in this way they form the ideal social basis for a powerful, centralized state which experiences no resistance from alternative social institutions or powers. However, a peasant society not only *allows* a strong and therefore large state, it finds it beneficial. Peasants' family small-holdings cannot provide employment for all their children: both

---

[175] In the *Introduction to a Critique of Hegel's Philosophy of Right, Early Writings*, p. 244. In the *18th Brumaire* Marx argued that Napoleonic ideals are 'the hallucinations of its [the peasant small-holder's] death agony' but that 'this parody of empire was necessary to free the mass of the French nation from the burden of tradition and to bring out the antagonism between the state power and society in its pure form.' *18th Brumaire*, in *SE*, p. 244.

[176] Ibid., p. 242.

[177] Ibid., pp. 243, 239.

the army and the minor positions of the state bureaucracy provide necessary employment as 'a kind of respectable charity'. However the circumstances of the original Napoleon and those under his nephew differ greatly. Under Napoleon I the taxes used to pay for the army represented a kind of investment – for the army was used to establish an empire which was variously plundered or used to create new markets for French products, stimulating home investment and economic development. But now, without an empire, or any real return on that investment, the army and the rest of the state apparatus is a parasitic caste, which consumes taxation without creating any real wealth (or even pillaging it from other countries). Its sole function now is to maintain order within the state – in fact to repress the distressed peasantry. For the demands of order are now the demands to respect the property of the advanced capitalists, the financiers, large-scale commerce and industrialists, in fact those groups whose profits and loans so depress the living standards of the peasants. Despite this objective conflict with the interests of the peasants, the memory of Empire and illusion of military grandeur still promotes peasant support for the militarily strong-state ideal.[178]

Peasant support for Louis Bonaparte rests therefore on the illusion that he can represent the same policies which served the interests of the peasants under Napoleon I. Objectively the development of the French economy makes this impossible. This development has also produced tensions between the different groups or factions within the bourgeoisie. No one single class or fraction of a class is individually capable of seizing and exercising political power, hence the apparent independence of the state. The state apparatus grows strong as the bourgeoisie fails – through internal weakness – to be able to articulate and impose its own interests. Hence also the apparently vacillating nature of Bonaparte's policies, as he tried to live up to the ideal of being the saviour of the nation by placating each group in turn. Effective placation involves making material concessions, and each concession made to one group requires depriving another: 'Bonaparte would like to appear as the patriarchal benefactor of all classes . . . He would like to steal the whole of France in order to be able to give it back to France' or rather, to be able to sell it back to France and finance the state apparatus.[179] Marx is convinced that the whole regime is a conjuring trick, but one that has a rational explanation in terms both of social myths, and of class forces.

Bonapartism – the political dominance of the executive – represents, Marx suggests, a particular and recurrent phenomenon in capitalism, one that is a possibility whenever the class structure is sufficiently fragmented that no single group can express its interests through the legislature and its supposed control over the executive. However, in parliamentary regimes, there will always be limits as to how long such a 'conjuring trick' can be sustained, for the illusory pursuit of national interest, or the successive placation of different and competing class interests is carried on within limits which are set by the capacities of the capitalist economic system. In the end it is the failure of the economy to provide politicians with the means to buy themselves into favour that dispels the illusion. An understanding of the limitations and dynamics of the capitalist economy was

---

[178] Ibid., pp. 243–4.
[179] Ibid., pp. 246–7.

therefore central to Marx's claim that ultimately, political possibilities were limited by economics. It was that understanding that *Capital* was designed to provide.

Capital: The economic analysis of capitalism

In order to distinguish capitalism as an economic system Marx contrasted its characteristic relations with other possible and historical modes of economic exchange and meanings of value. Whilst all societies engage in exchange, by no means all exchange is capitalist. Simple forms of exchange begin and end with use value – the desire to enjoy the peculiar properties of a particular good. Capitalism begins and ends with exchange value – money, credit, a bank balance, which is not inherently consumable. The purpose of capitalist relations is to increase exchange value, not to enjoy use. It is a kind of fetishist, compulsive behaviour on a social scale.

The simplest form of exchange is barter: you have something I want, I have something you want. We agree to swap. What we each seek is the use-value embodied in the objects of the exchange. The aim of the economic relationship is to enjoy the sensuous use of the object sought. Even if money is brought into the equation as the means by which exchange is effected it does not affect the start and end point of the process which, in each case is a use-value:

$$C[ommodity]1 > M[oney] > C[ommodity]2$$

But capitalism doesn't operate in this way. Capitalism starts and ends with capital – money – accumulated exchange value. The object of capitalist exchange is not to exchange one use-value for a different one. It is to start and end with exchange value – only more at the end than at the start. The commodity, the use value, is merely a means to this end. The logic of capitalism is not to create use-values, it is to subject them, as means, to a process devoted to the increase of exchange value:

$$M[oney] > \text{Factors of Production} > \text{Production} > \text{Commodity} > \Delta M[oney]$$

However since use values are intimately related to the satisfaction of human need, the subjection of use-values to the process of increasing exchange values involves the subjection of human need to this process also.

As an anthropologist and social observer Marx clearly thought such behaviour quite odd, if not compulsive. Why should anyone want to *systematically* accumulate more and more exchange value? As a social system capitalism was a bizarre kind of asceticism, in which hard working entrepreneurs laboured to increase their wealth in order to reinvest and . . . increase their wealth. However, as an economist, and even more as a revolutionary committed to its overthrow, Marx wanted to *understand* the process by which capitalism produced this profit. Nor was he alone in this.

The labour theory of value, and the problem of exploitation

As far back as the days of the Paris Manuscripts, Marx had determined to pursue his analysis of capitalism through a critique of the categories deployed by the classical 'bourgeois' (as Marx called them) economists themselves.[180] A central tenet of these theorists was the labour theory of value (hereafter LTV), which states that in one way or another the value of a product is consistently related to labour units. Marx's commitment to the categories of the classical economists is partly a reflection of his overall 'critical method', which owed much to the influence of Feuerbach. Marx argued outwards as it were, from within particular ways of thinking – Hegelianism, religion, now economics – exploring their logic and exposing their contradictions. In resolving these contradictions or irrationalities he constructed his own position. But Marx was also committed to the labour theory of value because it was central to Marx's claim that capitalist profits arose from the exploitation of labour.

Many of the problems encountered by both Marx and the classical economists in deploying the LTV resulted from the fact that economic theory was needed to explain both the growth *and* the distribution of the social product; and central to an understanding of both these was the analysis of profit. For profit was seen as a return to a particular social group (capitalists) and so part of the story of distribution, as well as being a part of the story of growth. One particular, and already rejected theory, which, however often reappears in vulgar versions of Marx's work, is mercantilism, the notion that profit results from unequal exchanges. This view was originally put forward in the context of international trade, explaining growth in national wealth as the result of one-sided trade. This is inconsistent with any notion of overall growth, since it explains profit merely by (unfair) redistribution within a given total value. The idea that capitalist profit results from unequal exchange is a persistent one, yet it is a difficult one to apply within a domestic economy once it is acknowledged that profits under capitalism do indeed result in growth. The difficulty is compounded by the apparent fact that under capitalism goods and services (including labour itself) are 'freely' exchanged in the market. For if, as was widely believed, market prices, at least in the long term, reflected true (i.e. labour) values, then exchanges were always of equivalent values. It was then unclear how exchanges could be unequal, how profit arose, or growth occurred.

To rephrase the problem in class-historical terms, the fact of class exploitation was clear under previous economic orders: slavery and feudalism each rested on obvious and blatant compulsion. In the case of the latter the ruling class's physical appropriation of the surplus product was a visible fact, as grain was wheeled away from the peasant's land and put into the lord's, or the church's barns. In the case of capitalism, however, there appeared no compulsion, and no physical product was taken away from anyone else without their voluntary consent. If all voluntary exchanges took place at their true values how was profit possible? In tackling these problems Marx based his analysis on a review of his predecessors' thinking, in particular Adam Smith and David Ricardo. Whilst it is widely acknowledged that Marx writes about these matters with a certain political animus, it is of course, worth remembering also that Smith and Ricardo were similarly motivated, thus the attempt to provide an analysis of the origin of value, and

---

[180] For example in the *1844 MSS* he insisted: 'We have started out from the premises of political economy. We have accepted its language and its laws . . . From political economy itself, using its own words, we have shown that the worker sinks to the level of a commodity . . . the misery of the worker is in inverse proportion to the power and volume of his production; . . .' etc. etc. *Early Writings*, p. 322. In the *Grundrisse* too, the categories of bourgeois economics provide a starting point, rather than naive 'real' categories such as population, which are in fact abstractions. *Grundrisse*, Introduction, pp.100–8.

hence growth, was not a purely scholarly endeavour but was entangled in theories designed to discredit certain political positions and the classes holding them, namely mercantilism (Smith), and agricultural protectionism (Ricardo).

Adam Smith

Adam Smith had argued that in simple hunting and gathering economies objects of exchange would indeed be bartered in proportions that reflected the amounts of labour needed to acquire or produce them. Thus, to use Smith's example, if a deer takes twice as long to hunt and catch (or requires twice as many people), as a beaver, two beavers will be worth one deer. The value of a commodity is here directly determined by the amount of labour embodied in it.[181]

However, as economies became more complex, in the sense of instituting the private ownership of land and capital, Smith thought this 'embodied labour' theory of value would cease to hold. True, commodities continued to *have* (exchange) value only because labour was required to produce them – even vital things like air and water, as long as they don't require labour inputs, don't have exchange value – but as economies became more complex their value no longer reflected *only* their labour inputs. For example, in a farming community, once land is privately owned, Smith points out, rent will have to be paid to the landowner out of the price of the crop. And if we assume labourers who have nothing to live on but their weekly wage, someone with money will be needed to advance their wages and the cost of the seed until the time when the harvest enables the investment to be realized. As a result, in complex economies, 'natural' prices (which equal value, but may differ from short term, market-fluctuations in actual price) are a result of the sum of these inputs. This is a new theory of value: an added-up 'cost-of production' theory, which is also a theory of social distribution in that the wages of labour, rent and profit on capital are all distributed to different classes as components of a total product. Each of the 'three great constituent orders' of society – labourers, landowners and capitalists – take a share of the ensuing value. The result, however, still relates labour to value in that the value of the resulting product is determined, claims Smith, by the amount of labour it can 'command'.[182]

This move to an 'adding up', or 'accounting' theory of value, Marx comments, sacrificed the original labour-based analysis of value for one which was mere description. For at an empirical level, as the matter appears to the capitalist, prices are indeed the sum of the various costs he has to incur in production. But the value of money itself varies, and cannot be constitutive of value without some independent account of how *its* value is determined. At some kind of deeper level labour must, and indeed is still acknowledged to play a decisive role as the measure of value, as is clear in Smith's original theory of

---

[181] Adam Smith, *An Enquiry into the Nature and Causes of the Wealth of Nations* (Ed. Campbell, Skinner and Todd), 2 vols (Oxford, 1976), vol. I, Bk.1, ch. vi, p. 65. This, of course, assumes some (and roughly equal) demand for beavers and deer in the first place, an aspect of the equation which earlier economists did not much concern themselves with, since they assumed, and for the most part rightly so, unsatisfied demand for the agricultural commodities they were primarily concerned with. Demand levels become crucial in more advanced economies.

[182] Ibid., pp. 67–8.

value, and as his revised notion that value is 'command over labour' also still conceded. For Marx, the problem with Smith, was that this later, 'exoteric' or superficial account of price as the sum of costs of production, does not explain the other, inner processes of economic creativity based on embodied labour, and Smith never integrated the two accounts, thus permitting his value theory and price theory to fall apart.[183]

Other aspects of Smith's theory set an agenda of problems for Marx's immediate predecessor, Ricardo. Under appropriate conditions, Smith thought that high wages were beneficial to the economy and productive of growth. No economy could be thought to be in a good state unless the majority of its members – the less well off – were 'tolerably well fed, cloathed and lodged'. High wages were 'an encouragement of industry' producing labourers who were 'more active, diligent, and expeditious' than where wages were low.[184] Higher wages increased costs and therefore also the 'natural price' of goods (– for this was arrived at by 'adding up' the component parts of it), but they did not, thought Smith, except in the very long term (see below) adversely affect profits. Smith however, was not primarily concerned with the question of how the economic product was distributed amongst the different classes, but with how economies grow, and become more productive overall. The central mechanism here, for Smith, was the division of labour. By encouraging and organizing specialization, entrepreneurs could enable operatives to become more skilled at particular parts of a productive process, and so produce more in a given time.[185] However it only became worthwhile trying to increase production in this way if larger markets could be reached. Hence his famous dictum that 'the division of labour is limited by the extent of the market',[186] and hence too, his equally famous denunciation of restraints on trade which artificially limited the size of the market, and in consequence the division of labour and so its productivity.

Productivity was expressed through greater profits, for value was 'command over labour' and profit (or more precisely the ratio between profit and wages levels) was what commanded labour, although as we saw above, in Marx's view Smith failed to show how [money] prices and values were related. Finally, for Smith, as for all classical economists, there was a life-cycle to economies, and growth was a phase not capable of being indefinitely extended: for the accumulation of capital investment, together with the competition amongst merchants or capitalists within particular trades would, he thought, lead to an inevitable decline in the rate of profit and therefore growth.[187]

---

[183] 'The one task interests him as much as the other and since both proceed independently of one another, this results in completely contradictory ways of presentation: the one expresses the intrinsic connections more or less correctly, the other, with the same justification — and without any connection to the first method of approach — expresses the *apparent* contradictions without any internal relation.' Karl Marx, *Theories of Surplus Value*, 3 vols (London, 1969), vol. II, p. 165.

[184] Smith, *Wealth Of Nations*, vol. I, viii, pp. 96, 99.

[185] So central was this to Smith that he opened the whole work with a chapter devoted to the subject and the observation: 'The greatest improvement in the productive powers of labour, and the greater part of the skill, dexterity and judgement with which it is anywhere directed or applied, seem to have been the effects of the division of labour.' Ibid., Bk. I, i, p. 13.

[186] The title of chapter iii of *Wealth Of Nations*, p. 31.

[187] Ibid., Bk. I, ix, p. 108.

David Ricardo

For Marx, it was Smith's great successor and critic, David Ricardo, who exposed more clearly than anyone else the contradictions – both social and intellectual – inherent in the capitalist economy.[188] Ricardo, a successful stockbroker, was initially recruited by James Mill as a pamphleteer in the anti-corn law debates of 1814–15. Ricardo's argument was that allowing the free trade in, and the importation of corn (and hence lower food prices) would increase profits and assist economic growth. Conversely, protection for corn would only benefit landowners, allowing rents to grow at the expense of both profits and wages. If, as Ricardo believed, investment were better served by higher profits or wages than by higher rents (because of different spending and investment patterns by the classes of capitalists and workers as opposed to landlords) then investment (and hence growth) would be maximized by ensuring that more of the total product went to capitalists as profit, or workers as wages, than to landowners, as rent. To establish this position he needed to show that Adam Smith's price theory was incorrect. For, if it were true that prices were simply the result of 'adding up' the factor costs, then clearly the claim that wage increases did not affect prices, or that increased rent depressed profits could not be sustained.

Partly at least in pursuit of these aims, Ricardo committed himself to rehabilitating Smith's original 'labour-input' theory of value, which was he thought 'really the foundation of the exchangeable value of all things'.[189] Ricardo noted, and rejected, Smith's switch from 'embodied labour' to 'command over labour' as the measure of value. He comments that these two measures could only be consistent 'if the reward of the labourer were always in proportion to what he produced' which, on Smith's own account of the difference between the primitive and private-property based economy, it is not.[190] But if the two are not consistent and Smith was right to apply two value theories to the two different periods, this implied not only that 'value' means one thing at one stage of development, and something different at another, but that the same product (containing the same amount of labour) was worth different amounts at different times. This not only seems odd within the context of a 'labour theory of value', but goes against the grain of the whole thrust of classical value theory which sought an invariable standard of value against which other things could be measured. Smith's original formulation of the theory of value was, thought Ricardo, right: 'that it is the comparative quantity of commodities which labour will produce that determines their . . . value, and not the comparative quantities of commodities which are given to the labourer in exchange for his labour.'[191]

This clearly acknowledged what was veiled and only implicit in Smith: that once simple hunting economies were superseded, labour was paid less than the full value (in

---

[188] Marx thought Ricardo the most fearlessly honest of the 'bourgeois' economists, as a result the incoherencies in Ricardo's thought faithfully reflected the incoherencies in his subject matter. Marx, *TSV*, II, p. 166.

[189] David Ricardo *The Principles of Political Economy and Taxation* (London & N.Y., 1973), p. 7.

[190] Ibid., p. 7.

[191] Ibid., p. 9.

the original sense of labour-input) of what it produced. But to sustain this position Ricardo had to show that the original labour-input theory of value could work in a complex, private-property based economy, and this involved showing that rent and profit were in some consistent way determined by labour, even though rent, at least, was not a component part of value. The denial that the advent of property rights changed the applicability of the labour theory of value, entailed that the new factor costs incurred under private property were either not part of the *value* of products, or could be subsumed under labour. The implication Ricardo drew was that rent was no part of the value of a product, but a sheer surplus enjoyed by those who benefited from possessing more productive land.

Ricardo's model of agriculture

To demonstrate this point Ricardo produced a simplified model – one of the first extended formalized models in the history of economic thought – in which he envisaged an economy, devoted to the production of corn, through the deployment of two inputs: labour and land.[192] Ricardo observed that rent is possible *at all* because a) land is privately owned and a scarce, productive resource; and b) land is naturally differentially fertile. However, the value of its product, and therefore *the amount* of rent that particular parcels of land will command, is set by the amount of labour required to produce a given product – here, corn – under the least favourable circumstances which the market will still purchase, i.e. at the margins of economic cultivability.

This will become clearer as the model is developed. Consider an increase in the demand for corn. If the best land is already in use – a reasonable assumption – this will bring into cultivation more, but less productive, units of land, and has the effect of producing less additional harvest for each additional unit of land. There is *more*, but not as much more as there had been for the last addition. In all but name Ricardo identifies what economists now call decreasing marginal productivity. A graph showing how proportionally less extra corn is produced for each extra investment of land will slope downward as total production increases (fig. 1, 1).[193]

The most marginal plot of land capable of supporting the labour expended on it, will, by definition, produce the least corn of all those under cultivation, or to put it another way, it will, in terms of the labour expended to produce a given amount of corn, be the most expensive. Assuming adequate demand, it will set the price of corn, again in terms

---

[192] Although commonly presented as 'the corn model' it is not in fact clear that Ricardo originally envisaged this as a 'one product economy'. Although he wants, for the most part, to ignore the impact of other economic factors on the corn-growing sector, he claims that the argument holds for the application of additional units of *capital* to a given acreage of cultivation, as well as the extension of cultivation to more marginal land. In fact, as Piero Sraffa showed, whether he realised it or not, Ricardo's proofs logically presume an isolated, single-product economy. *The Works and Correspondence of David Ricardo*, ed. P. Sraffa (10 vols, London, 1951–2) vol. I, Introduction. pp. xlff.

[193] For simplicity's sake I have assumed (as does Ricardo *Principles*, pp. 35 ff.) that the margin is the *extensive* one — i.e., that the extent of cultivation is being increased to include poorer and poorer soils. The same argument would hold if the margin was an *intensive* one, i.e. if more and more labour were being applied to a fixed amount of land, resulting in less and less increase in productivity as less marginally effective labour inputs were added.

Figure 1: Ricardo's analysis of rent, profit and wages

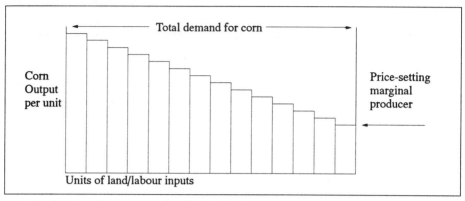

1 Production of corn per unit of land, showing decreasing productivity of marginal land

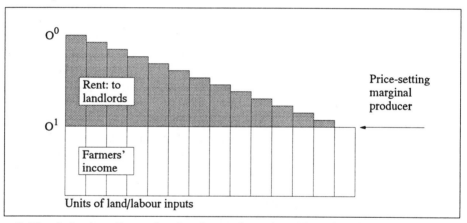

2 The derivation of rent, showing the surplus enjoyed by units of production within the margin, enabling landlords to charge rent.

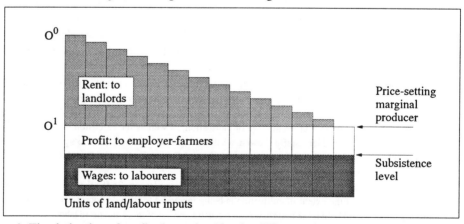

3 The derivation of profit: determined by the difference between subsistence level and the product of the marginal unit.

of labour input, for all other corn too. This is an equalizing effect of the market. The marginal producer cannot *charge* more because it *cost* him more to produce – any more than a buyer could expect to purchase more cheaply from a producer on more fertile land. So, conversely, all other producers will also be able to sell their crop at the price commanded by the marginal one, even though their corn is cheaper to produce. They do not want, and have no need, to sell cheaper (for the same reason the marginal producer cannot sell dearer). This appears to undermine the role of labour as a determinant of value, since different labour inputs (on differentially fertile plots of land) do not give rise to differently priced products. The market has the effect of rendering indifferent, or equalizing out the price effects of the labour inputs to particular portions of the total harvest.[194] However, although no differential prices are set by the labour costs of *individual* producers, the *general* price level *is* set by labour: *It is the labour costs of the most marginal viable producer that determines the value of everyone else's product.*

Most importantly for Marx, this showed that even if the labour theory of value were only literally true at one point in the economy (i.e. at the margin), it could still play a central role in determining prices throughout, and also, as we shall now see, in the distribution of the social product amongst the different classes.

Ricardo's model also explained the existence of rent (and of the social class of rentiers) in a way that is consistent with the LTV. The fact that it is the labour costs of the marginal producer that determines the value of everyone else's product enables these others to realize a surplus equal to the difference between the productivity of their own land, and the productivity of the most marginal piece it is worth farming.[195] Ricardo calls this difference rent, which he defines as 'that portion of the produce of the earth which is paid to the landlord for the use of the original and indestructible powers of the soil.' We have seen why this difference should exist. Why should it be paid as a sum from tenants to landlords? (Indeed – why should there *be* landlords?) The reason is not difficult to see.[196]

Anyone owning a piece of highly productive land (near the left hand end of the graph (1, 2)) would realize $O^1 - O^0$ over and above the general price level (O^1) for crops raised on their land. Since even at the marginal price level a living is to be had, such better placed owners need not bother to work themselves, they could let the farm out at a rent equal to or slightly below the difference which would effectively transfer the surplus to themselves. Given that there are people without land (for assume all land is privately owned) or employment, there would be takers for such offers. The class of people called landlords, brought about by the possibility of their deriving an income as rent, was explained by Ricardo's analysis quite consistently with the labour theory of value: he showed, indeed insisted on the centrality of the fact, that the value of corn was not

---

[194] This is an important phenomenon of the market which Marx utilizes to great effect when explaining the way a market in capital equalizes profits. See below: pp. 154–5.

[195] Ricardo, *Principles*, p. 37.

[196] Ricardo is here (pp. 34–6) talking about the differential productivity of *land*, but he then quite self-consciously generalizes the point in a way that suggests — and may well have been suggestive to Marx — that some portion of the prices realised by the more productive *manufacturer* will — conceptually at least — comprise rent as well: 'The exchangeable value of all commodities, . . . manufactured, or the produce of mines, or . . . land, is always regulated . . . by the quantity of labour necessarily bestowed . . . by those who continue to produce them under the most unfavourable circumstances, . . . ' Ibid., p. 37.

determined by rent, but that its price (and therefore its value) was set by labour operating under the least favourable productive circumstances.[197] Ricardo therefore performed the seemingly impossible feat of maintaining the labour theory of value by showing that whilst rent was not a part of the value of a product, it *was* determined by labour. This vindicated the general role of the labour-input theory of value in a private-property based agricultural economy. Smith had therefore been wrong to assume that because rent was a component *cost of production*, it was a component of *value*. Although, under private property relations it is indeed part of the *cost* of production, it is a pure surplus, which produced no benefit to anyone except the landlord. This conceptual separation of value from cost-of production was of crucial importance for Marx's analysis. It also had important, and as some immediately saw, politically divisive implications. Landlords as a class contribute to the cost (but not to the *value* of a product), they simply enjoy a kind of windfall benefit, consequent on their chance ownership of 'the original and indestructible powers of the soil', their interests in deriving an income from portions of price to which no value has been contributed are 'always opposed to the interest of every other class of society'.[198]

The last stage of Ricardo's argument went on to establish in a similar analytical way, how the category of profit, and indeed show how the class of capitalist farmers, employing labour, comes about.

The existence of profit

Ricardo accepted the argument of his contemporary, Thomas Malthus. Malthus had argued that in the long run labourers' wages will always hover around subsistence, since if they fall below, labourers will die of starvation or at least fail to reproduce, and the resulting shortage of labour will then raise wages; whilst if wages rise above subsistence, workers will have larger families and the glut of labourers will depress the wage rate.[199] This ghoulish equilibrium convinced Ricardo that, except in the unlikely event that economic growth – and so the demand for labour – constantly outstripped population growth, wages in the long run would be at or around subsistence. As long as access to land is unhindered, the marginal plot will then be that which supports a subsistence. But once access to land is limited, through private ownership, there is no guarantee what the marginal plot will yield, although it could hardly be below subsistence.

If, as is most likely, the level of corn required to sustain a labourer and family at subsistence is below the product of the most marginal plot under cultivation, then even the most marginal cultivator, might in principle be able to hire someone to do some of the labour for him, given that there are people without access to land who need to sell their labour to live. Indeed, if even he can do it, then the better off tenant farmers (whose

---

[197] 'The reason why raw produce rises in comparative value is because more labour is employed in the production of the last portion obtained, and not because a rent is paid to the landlord. The value of corn is regulated by the quantity of labour bestowed on its production on that quality of land, or with that portion of capital which pays no rent.' Ibid., pp. 38, 41.

[198] Ibid., p. 33.

[199] Ibid., pp. 52–3, Thomas Robert Malthus, *Principles of Political Economy* (2nd edn. 1836 [repr.1986, Fairfield, N.J.]), pp. 222–3.

existence was established in stage one of the model) throughout the economy will also be able to do so, and make a profit (Fig 1, 3). Profit is thus determined by the difference between the productivity at the margin of cultivation, and the wage necessary to sustain life; or more generally, between the productivity of the price-determining unit of labour and its cost – again a crucial insight for Marx. Where the possibility for profit exists, a new class of people can come into being – those who employ and set others to work, and who deploy machinery – capitalists. Thus: landlords rent land which is more productive than the marginal plot to (capitalist) farmers, who can hire labourers as long as the productivity of a labourer exceeds the subsistence wage needed to pay him.

Ricardo's account both explained the social origins of different groups within the private-property agrarian economy – landlord, farmer and labourer – and offered an economic analysis of their returns: explaining both the origin of rent, and the relationship between rent and profit as products of private property and the operation of market mechanisms. Moreover he does all this using labour as the crucial determinant in the analysis. He had also established, what were, for Marx, two important insights, consistent with the labour theory of value: one was that values and costs of production might diverge, and secondly that profit derived in some way from the difference between the price and value-determining unit of labour. He did not claim labour inputs determined value, costs of production or profits in any direct, 1:1 way, but that they did do so in ways that derived and diverged *in a consistent and predictable way* from labour inputs. He thus held together, what Marx had criticised Smith for allowing to fall apart, namely the analysis of value and the cost-of-production and, moreover, he did so in a way that suggested a central and causative role for labour inputs.

Policy implications of Ricardo's analysis

Clear policy implications followed from Ricardo's understanding of the distinction between rent and profit and their operation in the economy. He noted that the application of more capital (or labour) could decrease the extensive margin of cultivation, reducing the rent sector of the economic product (see diagram). Ricardo thought labour benefitted both from cheaper (i.e. less labour-costly) food, and from the increased application of capital which determined a labourer's employment opportunities.[200] Rent, however, was not only an unproductive sector, but when more of the social product went to rent, less went to capital through profit, and to labour through wages. Ricardo's model demonstrated that if, for any reason, demand for corn rises, rent will increase and profits fall as more marginally productive land is brought under cultivation (in 1, 3, the graph is extended to the right). This was the effect of the operation of the corn laws: in prohibiting the importation of foreign corn they increased the domestic demands on relatively unproductive land. With respect to the implications for economic growth, if it were also true (as Ricardo believed) that because of capitalists greater propensity to invest, it was profit and not rent that fuelled growth in the industrial sector, then the corn laws not only tended to depress profits in the agricultural sector, they also inhibited industrial growth and the benefits that followed from it.

---

[200] Ricardo, *Principles*, p. 41.

Ricardo's theory of the declining rate of profit

Although Ricardo's argument originated as a brilliant polemical attack on the land-owning lobby in the British Parliament, his theory had more disturbing long term consequences. For him, as for Malthus, ineluctable natural factors, and not just the artificiality of the Corn Laws determined an eventual decline in the rate of profit.

As we have seen, Ricardo rejected Smith's claim that wage increases would simply and directly raise price levels. If they don't, Smith's account of the decline in the rate of profit resulting from competing entrepreneurs bidding up the price of labour, is untenable. Ricardo's theory implied not only a different theory of long term price formation, in which wage increases were a result and not a cause of (food) price increases, but a different theory of growth and stagnation. A growing economy produces (by increasing demand for labour) a larger population. As a result, either more marginal land, or more labour, or more capital must be employed to feed that labour. Any of these increases at the margin will enable higher rent to be charged by intra-marginal landowners, and this rent is always passed on to the consumer, via the price-setting role of the most expensive producer. But if the price of corn rises, labourers' wages must (being at or near subsistence) rise too, and since profit-and-wages constitute a residual totality, any rise in wages must lead to a decrease in profits (rather than, as Smith suggested, simply and innocuously raising money prices).[201] As more unproductive land or more labour is deployed to feed the increased population, the rate of profit not only in agriculture, but in the economy as a whole, will fall. For investment opportunities in manufacturing are also tied to labour costs, which are in turn tied to the rising cost of corn.

Marx's problem: does the labour theory of value hold in manufacturing economies?

The problem with sustaining the LTV was that as economies became more complex, labour inputs persistently seemed to diverge in more and more alarming ways from costs. A theory of value that bore no relationship to costs – to the market prices widely believed to be tied to them – or profits, was something of an irrelevance. Indeed this was what had forced Smith to abandon his original theory of cost-price as labour-inputs. True, Ricardo had shown the importance of the labour theory of value even when most production costs diverged from their labour inputs, by showing the strategic price-setting role of the labour costs at the margin. But was this only true in an agricultural economy where the role of capital was marginal? Its applicability to more advanced sectors of the economy, as he himself recognized, raised similar problems at another level of complexity. This was even more true for Marx who was predominantly concerned with a manufacturing industrial economy.

Both Ricardo and Smith argued that the 'natural price' of a commodity was in some sense or other its normal cost of production. But both also acknowledged that the market price, might, for all sorts of reasons – to do with variations in supply and demand – diverge temporarily from this natural price. However, as Ricardo saw, the growing

---

[201] Ibid., p. 21: 'There can be no rise in the value of Labour without a fall in the value of profits. If corn is to be divided between the Farmer and the Labourer, the larger the proportion that is given to the latter the less will remain for the former. So, if cloth or cotton goods be divided . . . '

diversity of the industrial sector raised the question of whether such cost-prices and labour-values could be related to each other in any systematic way at all. For, if labour inputs truly determined value, or profits, how could the variations in the capital to labour ratios of firms with roughly similar productivity or profits be accounted for? Whilst, as Ricardo pointed out, it was true enough, and consistent with an 'embodied labour' theory of value that 'If men employed no machinery in production but labour only . . . the exchangeable value of their goods would be precisely in proportion to the quality of labour employed',[202] and true too that 'if they employed fixed capital of the same value and durability, then, too, the value of the commodities would be the same' it was not true that when labour-capital mixes varied, the prices of the resulting products – or the profits of those industries – varied in the same proportion. If this phenomenon could not be explained then the link between labour inputs, and 'normal prices' as cost-of-production, would be broken, and the labour theory of value – so important to Marx's theory of exploitation – would be rendered quite untenable.

To illustrate the point, suppose there are two industries, each with an overall investment of one hundred pounds. Competition for investment and in the credit system will ensure that the return on that hundred pounds is (roughly) the same, at least where industries are to survive; let us say it is 10%.[203] But obviously the composition of the investments – that is the ratio of their labour to their capital costs – will likely be different. Let us say it is 20:80 in favour of capital in one and equal in the other, 50:50. If each makes 10% profit overall, the relationship of this total cost price to the value of the *labour* inputs will be $(20 + 80 + 10):20 = 5.5$ in one case and $(50 + 50 + 10):50 = 2.2$ in the other. Thus where different firms, let alone different industrial sectors, possessed different capital/labour ratios there appeared to be no direct relationship between value (either as profit or as total cost-price) and labour input. Ricardo tries to explain this by variations in the periodicity of capital – that is, by differences in how long the capital must be invested before producing a return, but his explanation, as Marx points out, seems to confuse a number of different possible causes.[204] Ricardo failed to resolve the LTV with the fact of the variety of capital-labour mixes, argued Marx, largely because Ricardo and his followers failed to distinguish between the two concepts of *surplus value* and *profit*.[205] There is, after all, a sense in which Adam Smith's adding up theory was right.

Profit enters into the *production costs of commodities*, it is rightly included in the 'natural price' of commodities by Adam Smith, because, in conditions of capitalist production, the commodity – in the long run, on the average – is not brought to market if it does not yield the cost price, which is equal to the value of the advances plus the average profit.[206]

In other words average profit must be part of the 'normal costs of production' since if a producer cannot make the going rate of profit he will go out of business – he would be better off buying shares in the business of someone who can! To save the relevance of the LTV, what Marx now had to show was that the costs of particular enterprises including this 'going rate of profit', as well as the formation of this 'going rate of profit' itself, all bore a consistent relationship to the labour inputs of production. Marx's

---

[202] Ibid., p. 19.

[203] Ibid., p. 70.

[204] Ibid., p. 23; Marx, *TSV*, II, p. 178–9.

[205] *TSV*, III, p. 85.

[206] Ibid., III, p. 83.

argument was to try and show that LTV held in a complex economy despite the variety of capital:labour ratios in the different enterprises or industrial sectors. He tried to show that labour values did determine cost prices, and thus that the LTV, far from being rendered irrelevant by the increasing complexity of the capitalist economy, was essential to an understanding of capitalist price formation and profits.

The ideological import of Ricardo's analysis

Marx also persisted in his attempts to show that economic phenomena were primarily historico-social phenomena – a product of the particular relations of production obtaining within a particular historical period, and not the result of timeless universal 'natural' laws. The tendency which he had noted in *The German Ideology* of ruling classes to present their own ideology as a universal truth persisted under capitalism, and, in his view, within economics. For Marx, Ricardo's analysis represented particular interests: '*those of industrial capital against landed property*'.[207]

One such 'universal law' which Marx rejected was Malthus' explanation as to why labourers' wages must always be at or around subsistence. This, Marx argued, was not a natural phenomenon, but a socio-historical one: a consequence of rural depopulation hastened by the private enclosure of once-common land, combined with the constant tendency for capital to increase faster than the demand for labour. Labour's wages are at subsistence because the peculiar circumstances of development in a capitalist economy – in particular the private ownership of all means of production – ensures a constant supply of individuals with no way of supporting themselves but by wage labour, and also ensures that there will never be enough employment for all. Artificially created competition between the labourers – itself a capitalist institution – tends always to push wages down to the minimum that will support life. Subsistence wages were therefore a social and not a natural phenomenon.

The darkest secret of capitalism: the origin of profit, was to be explained, thought Marx, in the difference between the price of labour-power as a commodity, and the value that labour creates in the workplace. As long as the value created by a day's labour exceeded its cost to the capitalist (= the price of a subsistence wage), the capitalist could extract surplus value, and, if he was doing so competitively – in such a way as to enable him to sell his product – he could make a profit. This much was implicit in Ricardo, although for understandable ideological reasons it was not stressed by him.[208] Marx wanted to make it explicit.

The following example illustrates the simplest version of Marx's account of exploitation in a single isolated firm.

---

[207] Ibid., III, p. 85, emphasis in original.

[208] To be fair to Ricardo — which Marx, of course had no interest in being, Ricardo did, in the later editions of his *Principles*, not only express serious doubts about the effects of mechanization on labourers' wages, but gave essentially the same analysis of capitalist competition as Marx. Ricardo. *Principles*, Chapter xxxi. These implications had however, already been drawn by a group of radical English economists known as the Ricardian Socialists. See works by W. Stafford, *Socialism, Radicalism and Nostalgia* (Cambridge, 1987); and G. Claeys, *Machinery, Money and the Millenium, 1815–1860* (Cambridge, 1987).

Suppose an industry where in a given period:

k (the investment = total outlay of the capitalist) is 100
c (constant capital, i.e., raw materials, amortization of physical plant) is 80
v (variable capital, i.e., wages) is 20
sv (surplus value, the amount of value available to the capitalist at the end of the production, derived from an independently determined s/v, see below) is 20
s/v (rate of exploitation, this is an expression of the amount of value in excess of his wages a labourer produces in a working day. Thus if, as it commonly was before the ten hour act, the working day was twelve or fourteen hours, and the labourer contributed value equivalent to his or her wages in the first six (or seven hours) then the rate of exploitation was, as here assumed) 100%

V (value of product created, $c + v + sv$, 80 + 20 + 20) = 120
the cost of production ($c + v$) 100
profit (value less cost of production) 20

This example shows Marx's central categories in the analysis of value, but it is clearly too simple. The determination of the rate of exploitation is arbitrarily fixed and surplus value and profit are the same, in other words it is implied here that the market will be able to realize (= the entrepreneur will be able to sell) the product at a price equal to the value created, for which there is no warrant in the model. There is no explanation of the external forces operating on the firm. Secondly, and related to these unrealistic assumptions, the determinant of profit seems to be v. If profit = $V(c + v + sv)$ – cost of production ($c + v$), then profit = sv, but sv is a function of labour inputs and the rate of exploitation, which is another way of saying that capitalists would appear to be able to make more profit by increasing the labour factor of production relative to the capital element, and this seems counter-intuitive. After all one cannot make something more valuable simply by spending more time (more labour) making it!

The problem was thus to explain how the economic environment determined these various otherwise arbitrary factors. In particular to understand how competition amongst capitalists for capital, and the values of the labour inputs, filtered through the price mechanism in a sufficiently consistent fashion to sustain the viability of the labour theory of value whilst at the same time solving Ricardo's conundrum as to how different organic compositions of capital (different mixes of labour and machinery) could produce similar rates of profit.

To pose the problem in this way is to suggest that these were, for Marx, intellectual puzzles. They were, of course, more than this. For Marx, solving them in one way rather than another had important political implications. In particular, being able to vindicate the labour theory of value enabled him to assert, and explain clearly, the exploitative nature of capital. Of central importance to Marx's account, and central both to Marx's politics, and his theory of economic breakdown, is the claim that *value is created in production and only realized in exchange.*[209] This tenet is used to defend the claim that the kind of reforms common in social democratic countries, which are based not on the collective ownership of the means of production, but on the redistribution of the final

---

[209] 'The structure of distribution is completely determined by the structure of production. . . is itself a product of production', *Grundrisse*, p.95.

social product can never seriously overcome class divisions, let alone accomplish socialism, which requires instead the reorganization of production itself. The exchange system is thus ancillary and subsidiary to the production process itself, which is where surplus value arises and where the nature of the economy is fundamentally determined. This coincides with Marx's criticism that the 'liberty' of the specifically *capitalist* market is essentially a sham. It is inside the firm or business enterprise – where relationships are authoritarian – and not in the market – where they appear voluntary – that value is created, surplus extracted and social relations determined.

Solving the 'transformation' problem, that is showing that (and how) prices and profits could only be understood as transformations of underlying labour values and so could be related to the exploitation of labour was thus crucial to Marx's political, and polemical purpose. Marx had been convinced since at least 1844 that capital is 'alienated labour'. Showing that the operation of capitalism, as an economic system, involved the systematic appropriation of labour inputs was, in a sense, a technical demonstration of this lifelong belief. Marx's tactic was to show that labour inputs do determine values, and subsequently prices, but he knew they did not do so directly, or simply. They do so at first collectively *via* the market in capital by establishing a general rate of exploitation in the economy which is then read off, in the short term, as a rate of return on capital (interest) which is a component of the prices in individual industries. The analysis of a capitalist economy thus involves first an analysis of value production (which establishes the total rate of profit in the economy) and then an analysis of the cost of production. Demonstrating this involves a slightly complex table as Marx distinguishes the value system from the price system, yet tries to show how the latter can only be understood as a function of the former.

Consider three industries with different ratios between their capital (c) and labour inputs (v): 80/20, 10/25 and 30/15. Assume a rate of exploitation of 100% so that each labour input produces an equal amount of surplus value. The value of the resulting outputs will be 120 (80 + 20 + 20), 60 (10 + 25 + 25) and 60 (30 + 15 + 15). The organic composition of their original capital, that is the ratio of their labour (variable capital) to other capital costs is 4, 4 and 2, and their rate of profit, in accordance with the labour theory of value will be the ratio of surplus value to the total capital employed: $sv/(c + v)$. Expressed as a percentage in each case this will be 20% (20/[80 + 20]), 71.4% (25/[10 + 25]) and 33.3% (15/[30 + 15]). The rates of profit vary consistently and inversely with the organic composition of capital, expressing the fact that it is from labour alone that the capitalist must make his profit.

If the situation outlined above were translated directly into prices it could not persist long where there was a free market in capital and easy entry to a particular sector, for all investment would be attracted to the most profitable industry, and competition would then prevent the full value being realized, eroding its realizable surplus until it bottomed out at the average return. It is the market in capital, which, rather like the market in corn in Ricardo's model, equalizes out the returns to the various producers, although here, instead of production at the margin determining price, it is the average return on capital that determines its price (i.e. the rate of interest).[210] Since, in general all capitalists must

---

[210] Ricardo saw the need for such a figure, and sought it in that commodity which had the average production mix of labour and capital, which he thought was gold. Piero Sraffa showed this century how it could be done by constructing an imaginary commodity by averaging out the mixes of all significant

cover the cost of their capital, this is part of the cost of production prices of all industries. This is a historical process too, since it is only as an actual capital market comes into being that this average return comes to impinge on economic factors by establishing real alternatives to capital use which are expressed in prices.

In order to transform these 'values' into the true realized profits of particular industries, therefore, a knowledge of the average rate of return on investment was indispensable. But this in turn was an aggregate of the ratio of surplus values to capital obtaining in the different industries in the value system – which Marx believed (incorrectly) could not be calculated without using the labour theory of value. The centrality of the LTV in the understanding and operation of the capitalist economy was thus vindicated for Marx, even in the most complex economies.

Value and prices

Assume an economy with five industries, each with a total investment (k) of 100, and with a shared rate of exploitation, but with different labour-capital mixes, and different rates of amortization of capital:

1. Values

Industry	(A) constant capital (c)	(B) variable capital (v)	(C) surplus value (s)	(D) c used up in t^1 (c^1)	(E) production values $(c^1 + v + s)$
1	80	20	20	50	90
2	70	30	30	50	110
3	60	40	40	52	132
4	85	15	15	40	70
5	95	5	5	10	20
Totals for the economy	390	110	110	202	422
Per cent (of k)	78	22	22	n/a	n/a

[Adapted from Howard and King]

This table expresses the value of the products in each industry or sector of the economy. Values are arrived at in a Smithean fashion by summing, using however, the labour-unit values involved in production. However, these values do not yet represent the cost of production or 'natural prices'. For, Marx argues, given the existence of a capital market, all successful capitals must pay an average return on capital, and thus for every 100

---

commodities in the economy. See M. C. Howard and J. E. King, *The Political Economy of Marx* (2nd edn, Harlow, 1985), pp. 140ff. for a discussion of the significance of Sraffa's work.

[211] I have found Howard and King, *The Political Economy of Marx* (2nd edn, Harlow, 1985), to be the best account of Marx's economic thought which is (just) accessible to the non-economist. The tables are adapted, with permission, from their chapter 6. Also helpful and less technical is Ronald L. Meek, *Studies in the Labour Theory of Value* (London, 1973).

invested 22 must be added to the normal cost of production. This figure is arrived at by summing the surplus values derived from each industrial sector in column C and expressing this as a percentage of the total investment. The 'normal prices' can now be derived.

2. Prices

Industry	(F) cost price $(c^1 + v)$	(G) avge profit (22%)	(H) price of production	(I) price minus value (E, above) $(c^1 + v + $ avge. profit)
1	70	22%	92	+ 2
2	80	22%	102	− 8
3	92	22%	114	−18
4	55	22%	77	+ 7
5	15	22%	37	+17
Totals	312	—	422	0

The (internal) cost price of each industry is derived from the amortization of fixed capital (the proportion used up in the given period) and the labour costs, but the total price of production includes both that and the required average profit on the whole investment ($k = 100$ in each case). Once again, it must be remembered that Marx, like his classical colleagues acknowledged that supply and demand may lead market prices to temporarily deviate from this 'natural price'. Because the overall rate of profit is derived from the surplus value obtaining in each industry, that is from v and the rate of exploitation, the rate of amortization is, thinks Marx, immaterial to it. Secondly, although there may be individuals prepared to forfeit this return on their capital to indulge a desire, say, to produce in eccentric fashions, Marx assumed that overall, credit, and the competition for capital, will impose on all firms the need to produce this return. The 'transformation problem', the transformation of values into prices, was a historical process, something that was effected more and more completely as all areas of production were drawn into the capital market.

Total values equal total prices of production, although they are differently composed (sum columns E, H). Values (E) vary according to the different amount of constant and variable capital consumed and the difference yielded by the rate of exploitation applied to different amounts of variable capital (labour). Costs of production (F) differ from values simply by the amount of surplus value produced by the labour force. Prices of production differ from cost prices by the average rate of profit because each industry must pay that interest annually on the whole 100 of its tied up investment, whether consumed in that year or not. The prices of production vary from the values systematically as the capital/labour ratio varies from the median. In the case of that firm or industry whose capital/labour ratio was identical to the average in the economy as a whole the price of production and value would be identical. Thus the sum of all the differences between the prices of production and the values is 0.

In industries with a high labour/capital mix (such as industry 3) values will be considerably higher than prices of production: this may be just a fact of life about that particular area of production, but because of the equalization effect of competing capital, the overall profit will be the same. Those high values do affect profit, but only in aggregate through the total surplus value (total column B) in the value system. They do not enter simply and directly into the profits of that industry.

Capitalist competition

All this is consistent with the long term tendency, noted by Ricardo, for capital to find its highest return.[212] It was important for Marx to show, as in the above example, that profit is a result of normal capitalist production which derives ultimately from the difference between the value of labour-power in the market (real wages), and the value labour is capable of producing under average production conditions. In other words profit ultimately derives from the capacity of capital *in general* and as a system, to extract a surplus from labour, and not from the capacity of particular entrepreneurs to be more successful than others. Under these 'normal conditions', '*profit results not from selling the commodity above its value, but from selling it above the value of the advances the capitalist made.*'[213]

However, there is another possible source of profit, and that is the advantage which an innovating entrepreneur enjoys over his competitors. This is available because the 'normal price' of any commodity is determined 'not by the *quantity of labour* which the individual commodity costs, but by the quantity which *the* commodity costs that is produced under the *average* conditions of the sphere'. It is an obvious objection to the LTV that you cannot make something more valuable simply by expending more labour on it. However, by the same token you do not have to sell it cheaper because you have expended *less* labour than other producers. Competition, both Smith and Ricardo – and Marx, took almost for granted, performs an essential role in keeping down the amount of labour required to produce anything, to a norm, the 'socially necessary labour time'. But as Ricardo began to see, this competition amongst capitalists might have more than a merely regulatory role.

Whilst it is the capacity to exploit labour-power that enables the entrepreneur to realize profit, even when commodities are sold *at or below* their values, innovating entrepreneurs can sell commodities at market prices which realize profits above even their surplus values. An entrepreneur who devises a mode of production which requires only two labourers, where four are required by his competitors, will, other things being equal, halve his labour costs. But the price he can realize in the market will still be determined by the 'average socially necessary labour costs' – i.e. by the average production costs of his competitors – allowing him to realize the difference between his costs and theirs, as well as the 'normal profit' analysed above. This is a quite different source of profit, reminiscent of Ricardo's extended notion of rent, where 'exchangeable value . . . is always regulated, not by the less quantity of labour that will suffice for their production under circumstances highly favourable . . . but by the greater quantity of labour necessarily bestowed on their production by those who have no such facilities . . . '.[214]

---

[212] Ricardo, *Principles*, p. 70.

[213] Marx, *TSV*, III, p. 81.

[214] Ricardo, *Principles*, p. 37.

The pursuit of such extraordinary profits is the motive which spurs entrepreneurs on to innovate. However, the competitive advantage enjoyed by any innovator cannot last. Competition amongst capitalists ensures that they either follow the innovator in cutting their costs, or go out of business. The consequences of this competitive process are both economic and social.

Economically, the new equilibrium capital-labour ratio achieved will inevitably (on Marx's account) have a smaller labour component – remember it was by cutting labour costs that the initial advantage was gained. But since normal profits are determined by the rate of surplus value obtaining in the economy as a whole, and surplus value derives only from the labour component of production, it follows that either the rate of exploitation of the residual labour must be increased, or the rate of profit must fall, or more likely, both. Because normal profit arises from labour (not from capital), and because the process of capitalist competition continually reduces the labour component of the investment mix, competition must lead to a fall in the rate of profit. Ultimately, Marx argues, it will fall to the point where there will be no incentive to invest at all. This is not because the economy is poor, on the contrary it is immensely rich – in productive capacity, because the process of capitalist competition will have accumulated huge productive resources in machinery and organizational complexity. The economy grinds to a halt because it is not profitable, not because it is not productive. This is a classic example of the relations of production here – profit, competition and the investment process – inhibiting the operation of the forces of production – highly mechanized, or even automated, production lines.

Social consequences reinforce this breakdown of the relations of production. The process of capitalist competition produces losers as well as winners, it thus increasingly polarizes society into big capitalists and those who must find employment. Capitalist competition and development also involves the constant search for ways of shedding labour. It thus constantly creates unemployment. This lowers wages, since labourers must bid them down in their competition for work. The more capitalism develops, the more such workers it produces.

A combination of these social and economic factors will, Marx confidently believed, eventually produce the breakdown of the capitalist economic system. A spectre that haunted classical economics was the possibility of a systematic disequilibrium between supply and demand. Say's law stated that supply and demand, would, in aggregate, always balance in a closed economy.[215] But it was as much an article of faith as a law. Even if it were true in a stationary economy, it was inconsistent with growth. Marx's analysis predicted that as productive capacity grew, effective demand would fall. The same process which increased production, decreased the numbers of workers with money in their pockets to buy it. The end result was a crisis of overproduction in which the market failed to absorb the products of industry and so denied the capitalists the ability to realize their profits. Socially, the concentration of production also concentrated workers in larger and larger factories and workplaces, enabling them to act effectively politically when the economic breakdown finally occurred.

---

[215] Jean-Baptiste Say, 1767–1832. In his discussion of overproduction Marx refers to this assumption of equilibrium as 'childish babble'. *TSV*, II, p. 502.

Conclusion

As in the case of Marx's historical model, the above account is a simplification, an 'ideal type'. Here, however, we have Marx's authority for claiming that the way to understand capitalism involved understanding the model. For in his view the logic of capitalism was to insinuate its own structures and relationships in the place of all others; as a result Marx thought that reality would more and more conform to the model. There can be no doubt that the processes described by Marx are indeed at work in capitalism. The social processes described, the increasing capitalization, the routinization of work and the concentration of production in large centres, does reflect nineteenth-century develop-ments in the major sectors of the industrial revolution – particularly spinning and weaving, coal-mining and iron-working, and shipbuilding. It was in these areas that an industrial proletariat with radical and collectivist political beliefs indeed developed and for a time threatened to overthrow both the economic system of property relations and the political superstructure which provided the conditions for its operation. However, capitalism has proved more resilient than Marx could ever have believed. Its capacity to invent and diversify, indeed to create whole new industrial sectors, has continually falsified Marx's assertion about the inevitable decline in profitability – the keystone of Marx's claim to have made socialism, or at least the collapse of capitalism, a scientific inevitability. Furthermore its capacity to survive the advent of universal suffrage has thrown serious doubt on Marx's later political sociology and revived in a more complex form the eighteenth-century concern with the stability and management of political opinion.

   In assessing Marx's thought it is increasingly common to stress his moral and philosophical critique of capitalism whilst rejecting as essentially obsolete his historical materialism and his economic analysis. Nevertheless we should probably not be too hasty. There is a sense in which some of Marx's insights, the importance of the role of class, the importance of understanding the relationship between economic institutions and their cultural environment, the difficulty of sustaining growth in advanced industrial economies, the politically mobilizing effect of economic development, all of these we take so much for granted that we forget that it was Marx who did so much to put them on the agenda. Moreover, economic fashions come and go. Because economics is presented as more like the natural sciences than the humanities, its practitioners tend to be less aware of the history of their subject, and less aware of the ephemerality of their categories. Conventional economists can make one think that taking Marx's economic categories seriously is like the serious study of flat-earth doctrines. Yet there is, at a minimum, a case to be made for taking it seriously as a rival explanation of the phenomena, and it is a case which looks much stronger from a Third World perspective than from some positions in the First. Even some of Marx's more technical economics may not be so outmoded as commentators liked to think.[216] Western euphoria over the

---

[216] The 'Fundamental Marxian Theorem', that positive profits are only possible where the rate of exploitation is positive, seems to have been rescued. M. Morishima, 'The Fundamental Marxian Theorem: a reply to Samuelson', *Journal of Economic Literature*, 12 (1974); and further Morishima and G. Cataphores, *Value, Exploitation and Growth* (Maidenhead, 1978).

downfall of the tyrannical regimes of Eastern Europe and Asia is only too likely – there as well as in the West – to result in an uncritical acceptance of capitalist and market mechanisms. Yet the most intractable problems facing the world at this time – environmental pollution, starvation and the resulting mass population movements – are problems to which the individualist and unguided operation of capitalist markets hold no solution. We may, despite ourselves, still need Marx's insights into the historical and global context of capitalism as a specific social form, to gain a judgmental perspective on an economics that claims to be purely formal and neutral, whilst it is deployed as an ideological tool to justify 'free market' policies.

Defenders of the free market commonly celebrate its embodiment of freedom by pointing out that distributions and decisions which result from the market are not authoritarian in the sense that they are not imposed on a minority in the way political decisions are.[217] Marx seems to have envisaged a communist society as one in which, whilst most allocative decisions would not need to be made, because it would be a non-acquisitive society of plenty, such decisions as remained to be made would be made collectively, i.e.politically. It is a paradox of Marx's thought that whilst his major focus is on impersonal economic processes and his ultimate aim recover them for politics, that in doing so, he should so devalue the limited safeguards which our political tradition has created, and that regimes arising in his name should have been able to utterly disregard them as mere bourgeois rights. Yet the major problems of late capitalism seem to require collective solutions, and they will only be forthcoming if we can sustain, indeed enhance the legitimacy of collectivist ideals and solutions which in turn require political decision-making processes. To do this against the tide of libertarianism we need to understand the limitations of a capitalist market order, and Marx's heritage is still a vital intellectual resource for this. It is one to which, particularly in view of the Soviet and Eastern European experience, we are still too close, whether critics or sympathizers, to appraise coolly.

Modern societies are formally democratic. In many undeveloped countries of the world this is untrue, or only intermittently, or imperfectly so. However, the capacity of even the most advanced countries to combine what would have seemed to all earlier thinkers the elusive combination of stability and democracy is vitally dependent on being able to satisfy public opinion's expectations and its conception of what is just and right.[218] This is done by a combination of moulding that opinion to accept what is the case, and moulding the case to the opinion. Too large a gap and the most apparently stable state can fall into anarchy or tyranny. All the thinkers studied in this book have shared the essentially modern recognition that the capacities of states to survive depend ultimately on their having the resources either to meet what opinion demands or to mould that opinion to accept reality. Despite the welcome collapse of self styled 'Marxist' regimes in Eastern Europe, it is far from clear that capitalism will continue to have the capacity to do one or other of these things. If and when it fails we shall need other resources. Marx's thought is now an undeniable part of our intellectual heritage, as any survey of political ideas in the twentieth century would reveal. However, one suspects it is as a

---

[217] For example F.A. Hayek, 'The Principles of a Liberal Social Order', in *Studies in Philosophy, Politics and Economics* (London, 1967).

[218] I do not mean that modern populations have an over-scrupulous concern with transcendental values: What is 'just and right' most often refers to expectations about their own living standards.

critique of capitalism, not as a programme for socialism that Marx will continue to attract interest and inspire thinking.

The temptation to appraise Marx's thought in terms of our own needs or fears is much stronger than it is for most of the other thinkers in this book. Yet there is a sense in which Marx is still an heir of the Enlightenment in a way that it is very difficult for us to be today. The original Enlighenment aspiration to emancipate human thinking from prejudice, its attack on privileged or esoteric knowledge and the faith and hope that the understanding thus achieved could be turned unequivocally to human advantage, has always been an awkward one to apply to politics. Marx's conception of a revolution carried out by emancipated universal individuals – with crystal clear insight into social reality and nothing to lose but their chains – solving the riddle of history, and knowing themselves to be the solution – represents a kind of activist incarnation of the Enlightenment's otherwise essentially epistemological programme. In that revolution the perceptions of the actors and their objective historical circumstances, became fused through their action in a unique emancipatory moment, the coherence of which was supposedly guaranteed by Marx's insight into the social forces giving rise to them. The scale of his – and indeed of Hegel's – intellectual effort in drawing together and rendering relatively coherent sociological, economic, epistemological and political processes and insights is quite extraordinary. Yet it is an effort which by any standards – intellectual or practical, must be judged a failure. Moreover it is an effort which seems unlikely to be repeated, not only because each of these disciplines has become vastly more complex since Marx's day, and requires a lifetime's study to master, but also in the end because we are simply more pessemistic about the possibilities of acheiving any kind of politically transparent knowledge, and more cautious in the claims we make about the relations between knowledge and control. However, the story of political theories constructed under such conditions belongs to another century, and another book.

Bibliography

Chapter I Thomas Hobbes

A) Original works

i) By Hobbes

The English Works of Thomas Hobbes, ed. Sir W. Molesworth (11 vols, London, 1839–45).
An Answer to a book published by Dr Bramhall, late bishop of Derry . . . (E.W., vol. IV).
Behemoth, ed. F. Tönnies (2nd edn. repr. intr. M.M.Goldsmith London, 1969).
Considerations upon the reputation, Loyalty, Manners and religion of Thomas Hobbes, E.W., vol. IV.
De Cive.
De Corpore.
Dialogue between a Philosopher and a Student of the Common Laws of England, E.W., vol. VI.
The Elements of Law, ed. Tonnies, 2nd edn., intr. M.M.Goldsmith (London, 1969).
Leviathan, ed. W.G. Pogson-Smith (Oxford, 1909),
Leviathan, ed. C.B. Macpherson (Harmondsworth, 1968),
Leviathan, ed. Richard Tuck (Cambridge, 1991).
Leviathan, ed. Michael Oakeshott (Oxford, 1946).
The Life of Mr Thomas Hobbes of Malmsbury (repr. Exeter, 1979).
The Question Concerning Liberty , Necessity, and Chance, clearly stated and debated . . . E.W., vol. V.

ii) By other authors

St. Augustine, *The City of God* (Harmondsworth, 1972).
Aubrey, John, ed. O.L. Dick, *Aubrey's Brief Lives* (Harmondsworth, 1972).
Balguy, John *A Letter to a Deist* (1726).
Bodin, Jean *The Six Books of the Commonwealth* (1576) ed. & tr. M.J. Tooley (Oxford, 1967).
Bramhall, Bishop John *The Catching of Leviathan* (1658).
Cicero, Marcus Tullius, *The Laws.*
Dudley, Edmund *The Tree of Commonwealth*, ed. Brodie (Cambridge, 1948) [written 1509–10].
Eachard, John *Mr Hobbs's State of Nature Considered* (London, 1672).
Grotius, Hugo *De Iuri Belli ac Pacis*, [The Rights of War and Peace, 1625].
Hume, David *A Treatise of Human Nature*, (Oxford, 1888[1739]).
Hunton, Philip *A Treatise of Monarchy* (1643).
James I, *The Trewe Law of Free Monarchies* (1598).
Lilburne, John *The Afflicted Man's out-cry* (1653).
Lucy, Bishop William *Observations, Censures and Confutations of . . . Mr Hobbes* (1663).
Montaigne, Michel *The Essayes of Michael Lord of Montaigne*, tr. John Florio (London & N.Y., 1928 [1610]).
Wilkins, Bishop John *An Essay towards a Real Character and a Philosophical Language* (1668).

Collections containing excerpts from political writers of Hobbes's time:
Gardiner, S.R. ed., *Constitutional Documents of the Puritan Revolution, 1625–1660* (Oxford, 1906).
Wooton, D., *Divine Right and Democracy* (Harmondsworth, 1986).
Erskine-Hill, Howard and Storey, Graham *Revolutionary Prose of the English Civil War* (Cambridge, 1983).

B) Secondary works

i) Bibliographical

MacDonald, Hugh and Hargreaves, Mary *Thomas Hobbes: A Bibliography* (London, 1952).
Sacksteder, William, *Hobbes Studies 1879–1979: A Bibliography* (Bowling Green, Ohio, 1982).

ii) Biographical

Rogow, A. A., *Thomas Hobbes* (New York, 1986).

iii) Full length studies

Baumgold, Deborah *Hobbes's Political Theory* (Cambridge, 1988).
Brandt, Frithiof *Thomas Hobbes' Mechanical Conception of Nature* (London, 1928).
Gauthier, David P., *The Logic of Leviathan* (Oxford, 1969),
Goldsmith, M.M., *Hobbes's Science of Politics* (New York, 1966).
Hampton, Jean *Hobbes and the Social Contract Tradition* (Cambridge, 1986).
Hood, F.C., *The Divine Politics of Thomas Hobbes: an interpretation of Leviathan* (Oxford, 1964).
Johnston, D., *The Rhetoric of Leviathan* (Princeton, 1986).
Kavka, Gregory S., *Hobbesian Moral and Political Theory* (Princeton, 1986).
King, Preston *The Ideology of Order* (London, 1974).
Macpherson, C.B. ,*The Political Theory of Possessive Individualism* (Oxford, 1962).
McNeilly, F.S., *Anatomy of Leviathan* (London, 1968).
Oakeshott, Michael *Hobbes on Civil Association* (London, 1975).
Peters, R.S., *Hobbes* (Harmondsworth, 1967).
Raphael, D.D., *Hobbes: Morals and Politics* (London, 1977).
Shapin, Steven and Schaffer, Simon *Leviathan and the Air Pump: Hobbes Boyle and the Experimental Life*
     (Princeton, 1985).
Skinner, Quentin *The Foundations of Modern Political Thought*, 2 vols. (Cambridge, 1978), vol. 2,
Sorell, Thomas *Hobbes* (London, 1986).
Spragens, Thomas *The Politics of Motion: The World of Thomas Hobbes* (Lexington, 1973).
State, S.A., *Hobbes and the Debate over Natural Law and Religion* (New York and London, 1991).
Strauss, Leo *Natural Right and History* (Chicago and London, 1950).
— *The Political Philosophy of Thomas Hobbes: Its Basis and its Genesis*, tr. Sinclair (Chicago, 1952).
Taylor, A.E., *Thomas Hobbes* (London, 1908).
Watkins, J.W.N., *Hobbes's System of Ideas: A study in the political significance of philosophical theories*
     (London, 1965).
Warrender, Howard *The Political Philosophy of Hobbes* (Oxford, 1957).

iv) Specialist journals and collections devoted to Hobbes

The Hobbes Newsletter; since 1988, *Hobbes Studies.*
Bend, J.G. van der, ed., *Thomas Hobbes, his view of Man* (Amsterdam, 1982).
Brown, K.C., ed., *Hobbes Studies* (Oxford, 1965),
Cranston, M., and Peters, R.S., ed., *Hobbes and Rousseau* (New York, 1972).
Dietz, Mary G., ed., *Thomas Hobbes and Political Theory* (Lawrence, Kansas, 1990).
Hampsher-Monk, I.W., ed., *History of Political Thought*, XI, 4 (1990) Hobbes Issue.

Rodgers, G.A.G., and Alan Ryan, ed., *Perspectives on Thomas Hobbes* (Oxford, 1988).
Ross, R., Schneider, H., and Waldeman, T., ed., *Thomas Hobbes in His Time* (Minneapolis, 1974).

v) Important articles and chapters on Hobbes

Ashcraft, Richard 'Hobbes's Natural Man', *Journal of Politics*, 33 (1971).
— 'Political Theory and Practical Action: A Reconsideration of Hobbes's State of Nature', *Hobbes Studies*, I (1988).
Ball, T., 'Hobbes's Linguistic Turn', *Polity*, 17 (1985).
Barry, Brian 'Warrender and his Critics', *Philosophy*, XLII, (1968).
Baumgold, Deborah 'Subjects and Soldiers: Hobbes on Military Service', *History of Political Thought*, IV, 1 (1983).
Condren, Conal 'On the Rhetorical Foundations of *Leviathan*', *History of Political Thought*, XI, 4 (1990).
Eisenach, Eldon J., 'Hobbes on Church, State, and Religion, *History of Political Thought* , III, 2 (1982).
— *Two Worlds of Liberalism: religion and politics in Hobbes, Locke and Mill* (Chicago, 1981).
Farr, James 'Hobbes and the Politics of Biblical Interpretation', in Dietz, ed., *Hobbes and Political Theory*.
Gert, B., 'Hobbes and Psychological Egoism', *Journal of the History of Ideas*, XXVII (1967).
Glover, Willis B., 'God and Thomas Hobbes', in Brown ed., *Hobbes Studies*.
Goldie, Mark 'The Reception of Hobbes', in *The Cambridge History of Political Thought 1450–1700*, ed. J.H. Burns with Mark Goldie (Cambridge, 1991).
Goldsmith, M.M., 'Hobbes's Mortall God', *History of Political Thought*, I, 1 (1980).
— 'Hobbes on Liberty', *Hobbes Studies*, Vol. II (1989).
Greenleaf, W.H., 'Hobbes, the problem of interpretation', in Cranston and Peters, ed., *Hobbes and Rousseau*.
Hanson D.W., 'The Meaning of Demonstration in Hobbes's Science', *History of Political Thought* XI, 4 (1990).
Malcolm, Noel 'Hobbes and the Royal Society' in Rodgers and Ryan, ed., *Perspectives . . .*
— 'Hobbes and Spinoza' in *The Cambridge History of Political Thought, 1450–1700*, ed. Burns and Goldie.
Mclean, Iain 'The Social Contract Supergame', *Political Studies*, 28 (1981).
Lott, Tommy L., 'Hobbes's Mechanistic Psychology', in *Thomas Hobbes His View of Man*, ed. J.G.van der Bend (Amsterdam, 1982).
MacGillivray, Royce 'Thomas Hobbes's History of the English Civil War: A study of *Behemoth*', *Journal of the History of Ideas*, 31 (1970).
Macpherson, C.B., 'Hobbes's Bourgeois Man', in Brown ed., *Hobbes Studies*.
McNeilly, F.S., 'Egoism in Hobbes', *Philosophical Quarterly*, 16 (1966),
Marshall, J., 'The Ecclesiology of the Latitude men 1660–89: Stillingfleet, Tillotson, and 'Hobbism', *Journal of Ecclesiastical History* 36 (1985).
Meilander, Gilbert, '"A Little Monarchy": Hobbes on the Family', *Thought*, 53 (1978).
Missner, Marshall 'Skepticism and Hobbes's Political Philosophy', *Journal of the History of Ideas*, 44 (1983).
Okin, Susan Moller '"The Sovereign and his Counsellours:" Hobbes's Reevaluation of Parliament', *Political Theory*, 10 (1982).
Orwin, Clifford 'On the Sovereign Authorisation', *Political Theory*, 3, 1 (1975).
Pacchi, Arrigo 'Hobbes and the Problem of God', in Rodgers and Ryan, *Perspectives . . . .*
Pateman, Carole '"God Hath Ordained to Man a Helper"; Hobbes, Patriarchy and Conjugal Right', *British Journal of Political Science*, 19, 4 (1989).
Pocock, J.G.A., 'Time, History and Eschatology in the thought of Thomas Hobbes', in Pocock, *Politics Language and Time* (Chicago and London, 1971).
Rossini, G., 'The criticism of rhetorical historiography and the ideal of scientific method: History, nature and science in the political language of Thomas Hobbes' in A. Pagden ed., *The Languages of Political Theory in Early Modern Europe* (Cambridge, 1987).
Ryan, Alan 'Hobbes and Individualism', in Rogers and Ryan, ed., *Perspectives . . . .*
Sacksteder, William 'Hobbes: man the maker', in van der Bend, ed., *Thomas Hobbes: His view of Man*.
Schochet, Gordon J., 'Intending (political) obligation: Hobbes and the voluntary Basis of Society', in Dietz, ed., *Thomas Hobbes and Political Theory*.
Skinner, Quentin 'The Ideological Context of Hobbes's Political Thought', *Historical Journal*, 9 (1966).

Skinner, Quentin 'Conquest and Consent: Thomas Hobbes and the Engagement Controversy', in *The Interregnum : The Quest for a Settlement, 1646–1660* ed. E.G. Aylmer (London, 1972).
— 'Thomas Hobbes on the Proper Signification of Liberty' *Transaction of the Royal Historical Society* 5th Ser., 40 (1990).
— 'Thomas Hobbes: rhetoric and the construction of morality', *Proceedings of the British Academy*, 76 (1991).
Slomp, G., 'Hobbes, Thucydides, and the Three Greatest Things', *History of Political Thought*, XI, 4 (1990).
Springborg, Patricia 'Leviathan and the Problem of Ecclesiastical Authority', *Political Theory*, III, 3 (1975).
Stewart, J.B., 'Hobbes Among the Critics', *Political Science Quarterly*, LXXIII (1958) (547–65) .
Taylor, A.E., 'The Ethical Doctrine of Hobbes', *Philosophy* (1938) reprinted in *Modern Political Theory from Hobbes to Marx, key debates* ed. J. Lively, and A. Reeve, (London and New York, 1989).
Thomas, Keith 'The Social Origins of Hobbes's Political Thought', in Brown ed., *Hobbes Studies*.
Tuck, Richard 'Hobbes and Locke on Toleration', in Dietz ed., *Thomas Hobbes and Political Theory*.
— 'Hobbes' in *Plato to Nato*, intr. B.Redhead (London, 1984).
— 'Optics and Sceptics, : the Philosophical Foundations of Hobbes's Political Thought, in Leites, E., *Conscience and Casuistry in Early Modern Europe* (Cambridge, 1988).
Watkins, J.W.N., 'Philosophy and Politics in Hobbes., in K.C.Brown (ed) *Hobbes Studies* (Cambs, Mass., 1965).
Wood, Neal 'Hobbes and the Crisis of the Aristocracy', *History of Political Thought*, I, 3 (1986).

vi) Background

Bowle, John *Hobbes and his Critics* (London, 1951).
Capp, B.S., *The Fifth Monarchy Men: a study in seventeenth-century English millenarianism.* (1972).
Coltman, Irene *Private Men and Public Causes* (Oxford, 1962).
Daly, James 'The idea of Absolute Monarchy in Seventeenth-Century England', *Historical Journal*, 21 (1978).
Foot, P., 'Morality as a system of Hypothetical Imperatives', *Philosophical Review*, 81 (1972).
Franklin, Julian H., *John Locke and the Theory of Sovereignty, mixed monarchy and the right of resistance in the political thought of the English Revolution* (Cambridge, 1978).
Hall, A. Rupert 'Gunnery, Science, and the Royal Society', in *The Uses of Science in the Age of Newton*, ed. J.G. Burke (Berkeley, 1983).
Hampsher-Monk, I.W., 'Putney, Property and Professor Macpherson: The Political Theory of the Levellers', *Political Studies*, XXIV (1976).
Hill, Christopher *The World Turned Upside Down* (1972).
Mintz, S., *The Hunting of Leviathan* (Cambridge, 1962).
Olard, Richard *Clarendon and his Friends* (Oxford, 1988).
Pocock, J.G.A., *The Ancient Constitution and the Feudal Law*, (2nd. revised edn., Cambridge, 1987).
Popkin, Richard H., *The History of Scepticism from Erasmus to Spinoza* (Berkeley, L.A. & London, 1979).
Roots, Ivan *The Great Rebellion* (London, 1966).
Russell, Conrad *The Crisis of Parliaments* (Oxford, 1971).
Searle, John R., 'How to derive 'ought' from 'is'', *Philosophical Review*, 73 (1964), and in Philippa Foot (ed) *Theories of Ethics* (Oxford, 1967).
Skinner, Quentin 'The Origins of the Calvinist Theory of Revolution', in Barbara C.Malament ed., *After the Reformation, essays in honour of J.H. Hexter* (Manchester, 1980).
Somerville, J.P., 'Ideology Property and the Constitution', in R. Cust and A. Hughes, ed., *Conflict in Early Stuart England* (London, 1989).
— *Politics and Ideology in England 1603–1640* (London, 1986).
Taylor, Michael *The Possibility of Cooperation* (Cambridge, 1987).
Tierney, Brien *Religion, Law and the Growth of Constitutional Thought* (Cambridge, 1982).
Tuck, Richard *Natural Rights Theories, their origin and development* (Cambridge, 1979).
— 'The Ancient Law of Freedom': John Selden and the Civil War', in John Morrill, ed., *Reactions to the English Civil War* (London and Basingstoke, 1982).
Leeuwen, Henry van *The Problem of Certainty in English Thought 1630–1690* (The Hague, 1963).
Wallace, John M., 'The Engagement Controversy, 1649–52, an annotated list of pamphlets', *Bulletin of the New York Public Library*, 68 (1964).

Weston, C.C., 'Co-ordination: a radicalising principle in Stuart Politics', in M. Jacob and J. Jacob, ed., *The Origins of Anglo-American Radicalism* (London, 1984).
— and Greenberg, J.R., *Subjects and Sovereigns: The Grand Controversy over Legal Sovereignty in Stuart England* (Cambridge, 1983).
Wolin, Sheldon *Politics and Vision*, (Boston, 1960).
Yale, D.E.C., 'Hobbes and Hale on Law, Legislation and the Sovereign', *Cambridge Law Journal*, 31 (1972).

Chapter II John Locke

A) Original works

i) By Locke

Locke's Two Treatises of Government, ed. Peter Laslett (Cambridge, 1960).
John Locke: Two Tracts on Government, ed. Philip Abrams (Cambridge, 1967).
A Letter Concerning Toleration, (Indianapolis, 1955 [1689]).
A Letter Concerning Toleration, ed. John Horton and Susan Mendus (London, 1991).
Essays on the Law of Nature, ed. W. von Leyden (Oxford, 1954, 1988).
Some Considerations of the Lowering of Interest, and raising of the Value of Money (1692).
Correspondence of John Locke, ed. De Beer (8 vols, Oxford, 1978).
The Library of John Locke, John Harrison and Peter Laslett, (2nd edn., Oxford, 1971).

ii) By other authors

Capel, Sir Henry *A Character of Popery and Arbitrary Government*,
Falkland and Culpepper, 'His Majesty's Answer to the Nineteen Propositions' (1642).
Filmer, Sir Robert *Patriarcha and other Political Writings*, ed. Peter Laslett (Oxford, 1949).
Lawrence, William *The Right of Primogeniture* (1681).
Sidney, Algernon *Discourses Concerning Government* , ed. Thomas G. West (Indianapolis, 1990[1698]).
Slayter, William *Genethliacon* (1630).
Smith, Adam *The Wealth of Nations* (2 vols, Oxford, 1976).
Williams, E.N., *The Eighteenth-Century Constitution* (Cambridge, 1970).
Wolfe D.M., ed., *Leveller Manifestoes of the Puritan Revolution* (London, 1967).

B) Secondary works

i) Bibliographical

The Locke Newsletter carries regular bibliographical updates.

ii) Biographical

Cranston, M. *John Locke a Biography* (London, 1957, repr. Oxford, 1985).
Fox-Bourne, H.R. *The Life of John Locke* (2 vols, 1876),

iii) Full length studies

Aaron, Richard *John Locke*, (3rd edn., Oxford, 1971).
Ashcraft, Richard *Revolutionary Politics & Locke's Two Treatises of Government* (Princeton, 1986).
— *Locke's Two Treatises of Government* (London, 1987).
Cox, R.H., *Locke on War and Peace* (Oxford, 1966).
Dunn, John *The Political Thought of John Locke* (Cambridge, 1969).
— *Locke* (Oxford, 1984).

Franklin, Julian *John Locke and the Theory of Sovereignty* (Cambridge, 1978).
Gough, J.W., *John Locke's Political Philosophy: Eight Studies* (Oxford, 1950).
Grant, Ruth *John Locke's Liberalism* (Chicago, 1987).
Kendall, Willmoore *John Locke and the Doctrine of Majority Rule* (Urbana, Ill., 1941).
Leyden, W. von *Hobbes and Locke* (London, 1981).
Macpherson, C.B., *The Political Theory of Possessive Individualism* (Oxford, 1962).
Parry, Geraint *John Locke* (London, 1978).
Polin, Raymond *La Politique Morale de John Locke* (Paris, 1960).
Seliger, Martin *The Liberal Politics of John Locke* (London, 1968).
Tarcov, Nathan *Locke's Education for Liberty* (Chicago, 1984).
Tuck, Richard *Natural Rights Theories* (Cambridge, 1979).
Tully, James *A Discourse on Property, John Locke and his adversaries* (Cambridge, 1980).
Wood, Neal *The Politics of Locke's Philosophy: A social study of 'An Essay Concerning Human Understanding'* (Berkeley, 1983).
— *John Locke and Agrarian Capitalism* (Berkeley, 1984).
Yolton, John *John Locke and the Way of Ideas* (Oxford, 1956).
— *Locke, an Introduction* (Oxford, 1985).

iv) Specialist journals and collections devoted to Locke

The Locke Newsletter (York, England).
Harpman, Edward J., ed., *John Locke's Two Treatises of Government, new interpretations*, (Lawrence, Kansas, 1992).
Schochet, Gordon ed., *Life, Liberty and Property: Essays on Locke's Political Ideas* (Belmont, Ca., 1971).
Yolton, John ed., *John Locke, Problems and Perspectives* (Cambridge, 1969).

v) Important articles and chapters on Locke

Albritton, Robert 'The Politics of Locke's Philosophy', *Political Studies*, 24, 3 (1976).
Ashcraft, Richard 'Locke's State of Nature: Historical Fact or Moral Fiction?', *American Political Science Review* , 62 (1968).
— and Goldsmith, M.M., 'Locke, revolution principles and the formation of whig ideology', *Historical Journal*, 26, 4 (1983).
Berlin, Isaiah 'Locke and Professor Macpherson', *Political Quarterly*, 35 (1964) and in *Modern Political Theory from Hobbes to Marx*, ed. Lively and Reeve (London, 1989).
Coleman, Janet 'Dominium in Thirteenth and Fourteenth-Century Political Thought and its Seventeenth-Century Heirs: John of Paris and John Locke', *Political Studies*, XXXIII, 1 (1985).
Colman, J., John Locke's Moral Philosophy (Edinburgh, 1983).
Day, J.P., 'Locke on Property' *Philosophical Quarterly*, 16 (1966).
Dunn, John 'Consent in the political theory of John Locke', *Historical Journal*, 10, 2 (1967).
— 'Justice and the interpretation of Locke's Political Theory', *Political Studies*, XII, 2 (1964).
— 'From applied theology to social analysis: the break between John Locke and the Scottish Enlightenment', in *Wealth and Virtue: The Shaping of Political Economy in the Scottish Enlightenment*, ed. Istvan Hont and Michael Ignatieff (Cambridge, 1983).
— 'The Concept of "trust" in the politics of John Locke', in *Philosophy in History*, ed., R. Rorty, J.B. Schneewind, and Q. Skinner (Cambridge, 1984).
Edie, C.A., 'Succession and Monarchy: the Controversy of 1678–1681', *American Historical Review*, LXX (1964–5).
Gale, G., 'John Locke on territoriality: an unnoticed aspect of the Second Treatise', *Political Theory*, 1 (1973).
Gauthier, David 'The role of inheritance in Locke's Political Theory' *Canadian Journal of Economics and Political Science* 32 (1966).
Glenn, Gary D., 'Inalienable rights and Locke's argument for limited government: Political implicationso of a right to suicide', *Journal of Politics*, 46 (1984).
Goldie, Mark 'John Locke and Anglican Royalism', *Political Studies*, XXXI, 1 (1983).
Hampsher-Monk, I. W., 'Tacit Concept of Consent in Locke's *Two Treatises of Government*: A note on citizens travellers and Patriarchalism', *Journal of the History of Ideas* XL, no.1 (1979).
— 'Resistance and economy in Dr Anglim's Locke', *Political Studies*, XXVI, 1 (1978).

Hundert, E.J., 'The Making of Homo Faber: John Locke between Ideology and History', *Journal of the History of Ideas* , 33 (1972).

Hinton, R.W.K., 'Husbands, Fathers and Conquerers', *Political Studies*, XV (1967), and XVI (1968).

Hughes, M., 'Lock on Taxation and Suffrage', *History of Political Thought*, XI, 3 (1990).

Kraynak, Robert 'John Locke: from Absolutism to Toleration', *American Political Science Review*, 74 (1980).

Laslett, Peter 'The English Revolution and Locke's *Two Treatises of Government'*, *Cambridge Historical Journal*, XII (1956).

Monson, Charles H. Jr., 'Locke and his interpreters', *Political Studies*, 6 (1958).

Karl Olivekrona, 'Appropriation in the State of Nature: Locke on the Origin of Property, *Journal of the History of Ideas*, 35 (1974).

— 'The Term "Property" in Locke's Two Treatises of Government', *Archiv für Rechts – und Sozialphilosophie*, LXI/1 (1975).

Parry, Geraint 'Individuality, Politics and the Critique of Paternalism in John Locke', *Political Studies*, XII, 2 (1964).

Pitkin, Hannah 'Obligation and Consent', *American Political Science Review*, 59 & 60 (1965–6).

Poole, Ross 'Locke and the Bourgeois State', *Political Studies*, XXVIII, 2 (1980).

Riley, Patrick 'On finding an equilibrium between Consent and Natural Law in Locke's Political Philosophy', *Political Studies*, 22 (1974).

Ryan, Alan 'Locke and the Dictatorship of the Bourgeoisie', *Political Studies*, XIII, 2 (1965).

Tarcov, Nathan 'Locke's *Second Treatise* and the 'Best Fence against Rebellion'', *Review of Politics*, 43 (1981).

Tully, James, 'Locke' ch. 21 in *The Cambridge History of Political Thought, 1450–1700, ed. Burns and Goldie* (Cambridge, 1991).

Waldron, J. 'Locke, Tully and the Regulation of Property', *Political Studies*, XXXII, 1 (1984).

Yolton, John 'Locke on the Law of Nature', *Philosophical Review*, 67 (1958).

vi) Background

Ashley, M.*The Glorious Revolution of 1688* (London, 1966).

Aylmer, G. 'The Meaning and Definition of "property" in seventeenth century England', *Past and Present*, 86 (1980),

Daley, James *Sir Robert Filmer and English Political Thought* (Toronto, 1979).

Franklin J.H., (tr. & ed.), *Constitutionalism and Resistance in the Sixteenth Century: Three Treatises by Hotman, Beza and Mornay* (NewYork, 1969).

Goldie, Mark, 'The Roots of True Whiggism', *History of Political Thought*, I (1980).

— 'The Revolution of 1689 and the Structure of Political Argument' *Bulletin of Research in the Humanities*, 83 (1980).

Gough, J.W., *The Social Contract: A Critical Study of its Development* (Oxford, 1957).

— 'James Tyrrell, Whig Historian and Friend of John Locke', *Historical Journal*, 19 (1976).

Greenleaf, W.H., *Order, Empiricism and Politics* (Oxford, 1964).

Hampsher-Monk, I.W., 'John Thelwall and the eighteenth-century radical response to political economy', *Historical Journal*, 34, 1 (1991).

Kenyon, J.P., *The Popish Plot,* (London, 1972).

— 'The Revolution of 1688, Resistance and Contract', in *Historical Perspectives, Studies in Honour of J.H.Plumb*, ed. N.McKendrick (London, 1974).

Plumb, J.H., *The Growth of Political Stability in England 1675–1725* (London, 1967).

Pocock, J.G.A., *The Ancient Constitution and the Feudal Law,* (2nd edn., Cambridge, 1987).

Schochet, Gordon *Patriarchalism in Political Thought* (New York, 1975),

Scott, Jonathan *Algernon Sidney and the Restoration Crisis 1677- 1683* (Cambridge, 1991).

Sharp, Andrew 'John Lilburne and the Long Parliament's *Book of Declarations*: A Radical's Exploitation of the Words of Authorities', *History of Political Thought*, IX, 1 (1988).

Skinner, Quentin 'The Origins of the Calvinist Theory of Revolution', in *After the Reformation, Essays in Honour of J.H.Hexter*, Barbara C. Malament, ed. (Manchester, 1980).

Somerville, Johann P., 'The Norman Conquest in Early Stuart Political Thought', *Political Studies*, XXIV, 2 (1986).

Stone, Lawrence 'Children and the Family', in Lawrence Stone, *The Past and the Present Revisited* (London, 1987).

Washburn, Wilcomb E., 'The moral and Legal Justification for Dispossessing the Indians', in *Seventeenth Century America: Essays in Colonial History*, ed. James Morton Smith (Chapel Hill, 1959).

Weston, Corinne.C., 'The Case for Sir Robert Holbourne Reasserted', *History of Political Thought* , VIII, 3 (1987).

Western, J.R., *Monarchy and Revolution: The English State in the 1680s* (London, 1972).

Chapter III David Hume

A) Original works

i) By Hume

The Philosophical Works of David Hume, ed. T.H. Green, and T.H. Grose. (4 vols, London, 1874–5).

A Treatise of Human Nature, ed. L.A.Selby-Bigge (Oxford, 1965 [1888]).

Enquiries, Concerning Human Understanding and thePrinciples of Morals ed. L.A.Selby-Bigge (Oxford, 1902).

Essays, Moral, Political and Literary (Oxford, 1963).

The Letters of David Hume, ed. J.Y.T. Greig (2 vols., Oxford, 1932).

New Letters of David Hume, ed., Klibansky, R., and Mossner, E.C. (Oxford, 1954).

ii) By other authors

Smith, Adam *An Enquiry into the Nature and Causes of the Wealth of Nations*, 2 vols. (Oxford, 1976) ed. R.H. Campbell,

A.S. Skinner and W.B. Todd.

Collections containing other useful contemporary material

Rendall, Jane *The Origins of the Scottish Enlightenment, 1707–1776* (London, 1978).

Selby-Bigge, L.A., *British Moralists, being selections from writers principally of the Eighteenth Century* (New York, 1965 [Oxford, 1897]).

Schneewind, J.B., *Moral Philosophy from Montaigne to Kant*, vol 2. (2 vols, Cambridge, 1990).

B) Secondary works

i) Bibliographical

Jessop, T.E., *A Bibliography of David Hume and Scottish Philosophy, from Francis Hutcheson to Lord Balfour* (New York, 1966).

Hall, R., *A Hume Bibliography from 1930* (York, 1971).

—*Fifty Years of Hume Scholarship: a Bibliographical Guide* (Edinburgh, 1978), updated in *Hume Studies.*.

ii) Biographical

Christensen, J., *Practising Enlightenment: Hume and the Formation of a Literary Career* (Madison, 1987).

Mossner, E.C. *The Life of David Hume* (Oxford, 1954).

iii) Full length studies

Ardal, P., *Passion and Value in Humes' Treatise* (Edinburgh, 1966).
Barfoot, M.M., *Hume and the Culture of Science in Early Eighteenth-Century Britain* (Oxford, 1989).
Bongie, Laurence, L. *David Hume Prophet of the Counter-revolution* (Oxford, 1965).
Forbes, Duncan *Hume's Philosophical Politics* (Cambridge, 1975).
Haakonssen, Knud *The Science of a Legislator: the natural jurisprudence of David Hume and Adam Smith* (Cambridge, 1981).
Harrison, Jonathan *Hume's Theory of Justice* (Oxford, 1981).
Jones, Peter *Hume's Sentiments, their Ciceronian and French Context* (Edinburgh, 1982).
Kemp-Smith, Norman *The Philosophy of David Hume: A critical Study of its Origin and Central Doctrines* (London, 1941).
Letwin, Shirley *The Pursuit of Certainty* (London, 1965).
Livingstone, Donald W., *Hume's Philosophy of Common Life* (Chicago, 1984).
Miller, David *Philosophy and Ideology in Hume's Political Thought*, (Oxford, 1981).
Norton, David Fate *David Hume, Common-Sense Moralist, Sceptical Metaphysician* (Princeton, 1982).
Phillipson, Nicholas *Hume* (London, 1989).
Robertson, J., *The Scottish Enlightenment and the Militia Issue* (Edinburgh, 1985).
Stewart, J.B., *The Moral and Political Philosophy of David Hume* (New York, 1963).
Stroud, B., *Hume* (London, 1978).
Taylor, W., *Francis Hutcheson and David Hume as predecessors of Adam Smith* (Durham, N.C., 1965).
Whelan, Frederick G. *Order and Artifice in Hume's Political Philosophy* (Princeton, 1985).

iv) Specialist journals and collections devoted to Hume

Hume Studies.
Chappell, V.C., ed. *Hume* (London, 1966).
Livinstone, D.W. and King, J.T., ed., *Hume: A Re-Evaluation* (New York, 1976).
Morice, G.P., ed., *David Hume: Bicentenary Papers* (Edinburgh, 1977).
Norton, D.F., *et al.*, ed., *McGill Hume Studies* (San Diego, 1979).

v) Important articles and chapters on Hume

Cipaldi, Nicholas 'Hume as a Social Scientist', *Review of Metaphysics*, 32 (1978).
Day, J., 'Hume on Justice and Allegiance', *Philosophy*, 40 (1965).
Farr, James 'Hume, Hermeneutics and History: A Sympathetic Account' *History and Theory*, 17 (1978).
Forbes, Duncan 'Politics and History in David Hume' *Historical Journal*, 6 (1963).
Hiskes, Richard 'Does Hume have a Theory of Social Justice' *Hume Studies*, 3 (1977).
Mossner, E.C., 'Was Hume a Tory Historian', *Journal of the History of Ideas*, II (1941).
Moore, James 'Hume's Political Science and the Classical Republican Tradition', *The Canadian Journal of Political Science* X, 4 (1977).
Pocock, J.G.A., 'Hume and the American Revolution: dying thoughts of a North Briton' in *McGill Hume Studies*, and in *Virtue Commerce and History.*.
Wertz, S.K., 'Hume, History and Human Nature', *Journal of the History of Ideas*, XXXVI (1975).

vi) Background

Burnyeat, Miles, ed., *The Sceptical Tradition* (Berkeley, 1983).
Clarke, J.C.D., *English Society 1688-1832* (Cambridge, 1985).
Dickinson, H.T., *Liberty and Property: Political ideology in Eighteenth-Century Britain* (London, 1977).
Ferreira, M. Jamie *Scepticism and Reasonable Doubt, the British Naturalist Tradition* (Oxford, 1986).
Phillipson, Nicholas 'The Scottish Enlightenment' in R. Porter and M.Teich, *The Enlightenment in National Context* (Cambridge, 1981).

Pocock, J.G.A., 'Varieties of Whiggism from Exclusion to Reform' in *Virtue Commerce and History* (Cambridge, 1985).
Sher, R.B., *Church and University in the Scottish Enlightenment* (Edinburgh, 1985).
Stewart. M.A. *Studies in the Philosophy of the Scottish Enlightenment* (Oxford, 1990).

Chapter IV Jean-Jacques Rousseau

A) Original works

i) By Rousseau

Political Writings of Rousseau, ed. and intr. C.E.Vaughan, (2 vols, Cambridge, 1915).
The Confessions of Jean-Jacques Rousseau, tr & intr. J.M.Cohen (Harmondsworth, 1957[1953]).
Emile, trs. Barbara Foxley (London & N.Y, 1911).
The Social Contract and the Discourses, tr. and. intr. G.D.H. Cole, revised and augmented J.H. Brumfitt and John C. Hall (London and New York, 1973).
The First and Second Discourses, together with the replies to critics and Essay on the Origin of Languages, Ed & trs.Victor Gourevitch (NY, 1986).
'Preface to *Narcisse*', *Political Theory,* 6 no. 4, Nov.1978; and in Gourevitch, ed.
Religious Writings, ed. R. Grimsley (Oxford, 1970).
The Indispensible Roussseau, ed. John Hope-Mason (London, 1979).

ii) By other authors

d'Alembert, Jean & Diderot, Denis *L'Encyclopédie, ou Dictionnaire Raisonné,* (Paris, 1751).
d'Alembert, Jean tr. & intr R.N.Schwab with W.E.Rex.*Preliminary Discourse to the Encyclopaedia of Diderot* (Indianapolis and NY, 1963).
Montesquieu, Charles Secondat, Baron *The Spirit of the Laws* tr. Nugent (New York, 1949).
Smith, Adam, *The Theory of Moral Sentiments,* ed. DD.Raphael and A.L.MacFie (Oxford, 1976).
Voltaire, *Philosophical Dictionary,* ed. & tr. T. Besterman (Harmondsworth, 1971).

B) Secondary works

i) Bibliographical

Gay, Peter 'Reading About Rousseau', in P. Gay, *The Party of Humanity.*

ii) Biographical

Cranston, M., *Jean-Jacques The Early Life and Works of Jean-Jacques Rousseau (London, 1983).*
Crocker, L., *Jean-Jacques Rousseau* (2 vols, New York, 1968–73).

iii) Full length studies

Berman, Marshall *The Politics of Authenticity* (London, 1971).
Brooome, J. H., *Rousseau: a study of his thought* (London, 1973).
Cameron, D., *The Social Thought of Rousseau and Burke* (London, 1973).
Cassirer, E., *The Question of Jean-Jacques Rousseau* (2nd edn., New Haven, 1989).
Charvet, J., *The Social Problem in the Philosophy of Rousseau* (Cambridge, 1974).
Chapman, J., *Rousseau – Totalitarian or Liberal?* (New York, 1956).
Cobban, A., *Rousseau and the Modern State* (2nd edn., London, 1964).

Cohler, A. M., *Rousseau and Nationalism* (New York, 1970).
Colletti, L., *From Rousseau to Lenin* (London, 1972).
Crocker, L., *Rousseau's Social Contract: An interpretive essay* (Cleveland, 1968).
Fralin, R., *Rousseau and Representation* (New York, 1978).
Green, F. C., *Jean-Jacques Rousseau: A Critical Study of his Life and Writings* (Cambridge, 1955).
Grimsley, R., *The Philosophy of Rousseau* (London, 1973).
— *Jean-Jacques Rousseau* (Brighton, 1983).
Hall, J.C., *Rousseau, an introduction to his Political Philosophy* (London, 1973).
Hampson, Norman *Will and Circumstance, Montesquieu, Rousseau and the French Revolution* (London, 1983).
Hendel, C. W., *Jean-Jacques Rousseau, Moralist* (2 vols, London, 1934).
Horowitz, A., *Rousseau, Nature, and History* (Toronto, 1987).
Masters, R. D., *The Political Philosophy of J.-J. Rousseau* (Princeton, 1968).
Miller, J., *Rousseau; Dreamer of Democracy* (New Haven, 1984).
Noone, J. B., *Rousseau's Social Contract* (Athens, Ga., 1980).
Osborn, A. M., *Rousseau and Burke* (London, 1940).
Roche, K.F., *Rousseau Stoic and Romantic* (London, 1974).
Shklar, Judith *Men and Citizens, a study of Rousseau's Social Theory* (Cambridge, 1969).
Schwartz, J., *The Sexual Politics of Jean-Jacques Rousseau* (Chicago, 1984).
Starobinski, Jean *Le Transparence et l'Obstacle* (Paris, 1970, trs . A. Goldhammer, Chicago and London, 1971)
Talmon, J. L., *The Origins of Totalitarian Democracy* (London, 1952).
Volpe, G. della *Rousseau and Marx* (London, 1978).
Wokler R., *The Social Thought of Jean-Jacques Rousseau* (1987).

iv) Specialist journals and collections of essays devoted to Rousseau

Annales de la Societé Jean-Jacques Rousseau.
Besterman, Theodore, ed., *Studies on Voltaire and the Eighteenth Century*, often carries articles on Rousseau.
Cranston, M. and Peters, R., ed., *Hobbes and Rousseau* (New York, 1972).
Harvey, Simon Hobson, Marian Kelley, David and Taylor, Samuel S.B., ed. *Reappraisals of Rousseau, studies in honour of R.A. Leigh* (Manchester, 1980)
Leigh, R. A., ed., *Rousseau after Two-Hundred Years* (Cambridge, 1982).
Daedalus, 3 (1978), *Rousseau for Our Time.*
Political Theory, 6, no. 4 (1978) Rousseau Issue.

v) Important articles and chapters on aspects of Rousseau's thought

Bloom, Alan 'The Education of Democratic Man: Emile', *Daedalus* (1978).
Charvet, John 'Rousseau and the idea of community', *History of Political Thought*, 1 (1980) [see reply by R. Wokler in the same issue].
Echeverria, D., 'Pre-revolutionary Influence of Rousseau's *Contrat Social*', *Journal of the History of Ideas*, XXXIII (4).
Fireside, H., 'The Concept of the Legislator in Rousseau's Social Contract' *Review of Politics* , 32 (1970).
Fralin, R., 'The Evolution of Rousseau's View of Representative Government', *Political Theory*, 6, 4 (1978).
— 'Rousseau and community: the role of moeurs in social change', *History of Political Thought*, 7 (1986), 131–50.
Hope Mason, John 'Reading Rousseau's First Discourse', *Studies on Voltaire and the Eighteenth Century*, 249 (1987).

Jones, W. T., 'Rousseau's General Will and the Problem of Consent', *Journal of the History of Philosophy*, 25 (1987).

Kateb, G., 'Aspects of Rousseau's political thought', *Political Science Quarterly*, 76 (1961).

Kelley, C., 'To persuade without convincing: the language of Rousseau's Legislator', *American Journal of Political Science*, 32, 2 (1987).

Keohane, N., 'The Masterpiece of policy in our century – Rousseau on the Morality of the Enlightenment', *Political Theory*, 6, 4 (1978).

Levin, M., 'Rousseau and Independence', *Political Studies*, 18 (1970).

Macadam, J.I., 'The Discourse on Inequality and the Social Contract', *Philosophy* (1972).

Marshall, T.E., 'Rousseau and Enlightenment', *Political Theory*, 6, 4 (1978).

Noble, R., 'Freedom and Sentiment in Rousseau's Philosophical Anthropology', *History of Political Thought*, IX, 2 (1988).

Noone J.B., 'The Social Contract and ideas of Sovereignty in Rousseau', *Jolurnal of Politics.*, 32 (1970).

Plamenatz J., 'On Le Forcera d'Etre Libre', in *Hobbes and Rousseau*, ed. Cranston and Peters.

Rosenfeld D., 'Rousseau's Unanimous Contract and the Doctrine of Popular Sovereignty', *History of Political Thought*, VIII, 1 (1987).

Sabine, J., 'Two democratic traditions', *Philosophical Review* (1952).

Shklar, Judith 'Rousseau's Two Models, Sparta and the Age of Gold, ' *Political Science Quarterly*, LXXXI, 1 (1966).

— 'Rousseau's Images of Authority' in *Hobbes and Rousseau*, ed. Cranston and Peters.

Skillen, A., 'Rousseau and the Fall of Social Man', *Philosophy* (1975).

Volpe, G. della 'The Marxist critique of Rousseau', *New Left Review*, 59 (1970).

Waldman, T., 'Rousseau on the general will and the legislator', *Political Studies*, 8 (1960).

Weiss, P., 'Rousseau and Women's Nature', *Political Theory*, 15, 1 (1987).

Wokler, Robert 'The *Discourse sur les sciences et les arts* and its offspring: Rousseau in reply to his critics' in *Reappraisals of Rousseau*, ed. Simon Harvey et al.

— 'Rousseau's Perfectibilian Libertarianism' in *The Idea of Freedom*, ed. A. Ryan (Oxford, 1979)

— 'Rousseau and Marx', in *The Nature of Political Theory*, ed. D. Miller and L. Siedentop (Oxford, 1983).

vi) Background

Cassirer, Ernst *The Philosophy of the Enlightenment* (Princeton, 1951[1932]).

Cranston, M., *Philosophers and Pamphleteers: Political Theorists of the Enlightenment* (Oxford, 1985).

Gay, Peter *The Enlightenment: An Interpretation* (2 vols London, 1970[1966]).

Hampson, Norman *Will and Circumstance: Montesquieu, Rousseau and the French Revolution* (London, 1983).

Hazard, Paul *European Thought in the Eighteenth Century* (Harmondsworth, 1965[Paris, 1946]).

Keohane, N.O., *Philosophy and the State in France, the Renaissance to the Enlightenment* (Princeton, 1980).

Martin, Kingsley *French Liberal Thought in the Eighteenth Century* (2nd ed., London 1954 [1929]).

Pocock J.G.A., 'Virtue rights and manners, a model for historians of political thought' in Pocock, *Virtue Commerce and History, Essays on Political Thought and History, Chiefly in the Eighteenth Century* (Cambridge, 1985).

Riley, Patrick *The General Will Before Rousseau* (Princeton, 1986).

Taylor, S.S.B., 'Rousseau's Reputation in Contemporary France', *Studies in Voltaire and the Eighteenth-Century*, XXVII (1963).

Wade, Ira O., *The Structure and Form of the French Enlightenment* (2 vols, Princeton, 1977).

— *The Intellectual Origins of the French Enlightenment* (Princeton, 1971).

Wokler, Robert 'The Ape Debates in Enlightenment Anthropology', *Studies in Voltaire and the Eighteenth-Century*, XCXII (1980).

Chapter V 'Publius': *The Federalist*

A) *Original works and documents*

i) *By authors of* The Federalist

The Federalist or, The New Constitution, 'Publius' (Alexander Hamilton, James Madison and John Jay), ed. & intr., Max Beloff (Oxford, 1987[1948]).
The Federalist, ed. J.E. Cooke (Middletown, Conn., 1961).
Hamilton, Alexander *The Papers of Alexander Hamilton*, ed. H.C. Seyrett (New York, 1961).
Madison, James *Papers of James Madison*, ed., R.A. Rutland et al. (Chicago, 1973).
The Mind of the Founder: sources in the Political Thought of James Madison, ed. & intr. Marvin Meyers (Hanover & London, 2nd edn., 1981[1973]).

ii) *By other authors*

Aristotle, *Politics*.
Blackstone, Sir William, *Commentaries on the Laws of England* (15th edn., London, 1809).
Cicero *De Officiis*.
De Lolme, J.L., *The Constitution of England* (London, 1810).
Hume, D., *Essays, Moral, Political and Literary* (Oxford, 1963).
Jefferson, Thomas *The Political Writings of Thomas Jefferson, representative selections*, ed & intr. Edward Dumbald (Indianapolis, 1955).
Machiavelli, *Discourses*.
Montesquieu, Charles Secondat, Baron de, *The Spirit of the Laws*, tr. Thomas Nugent, intr. Fr Neumann (NY.1949).
Montesquieu, Charles Secondat, Baron de *Considerations on the Causes of the Greatness of the Romans and their Decline* ed. & tr. David Lowenthal (NY, 1965).
Paine, Tom, *Common Sense* in *Complete Works* 2 vols ed. Philip S. Foner.
Priestley, Joseph, *An Essay on the First Principles of Government* (2nd edn., 1771).
Robbins, Caroline, *Two English Republican Tracts* (Cambridge, 1969).
Smith, Adam, *The Wealth of Nations*.

Collections containing other useful contemporary material
The Anti-Federalist, ed. Herbert J. Storing, selected by Murray Dry (Chicago, 1985)).
The Antifederalists, ed. Cecilia M. Kenyon (Boston, 1985 [Indianapolis, 1966]).
Farrand, Max, ed., *The records of the Federal Convention of 1787*, 4 vols. (New Haven, 1966[1937]).
Pole, J.R., ed., *The Revolution in America 1754–88* (London 1970).

B) *Secondary works*

i) *Full length studies*

Epstien, David, *The Political Theory of the Federalist* (Chicago, 1984).
Stourzh, G., *Alexander Hamilton and the Idea of Republican Government* (Stanford, 1970).
White, Morton *Philosophy, The Federalist, and the Constitution* (Oxford, 1987).

ii) *Specialist journals and collections devoted to the Federalist*

Ball, Terence and Pocock, J.G.A., ed., *Conceptual Change and the Constitution* (Lawrence, Ka., 1988).
Quarterly Journal of the Library of Congress 37 (1980) [Madison memorial issue].

iii) *Important articles and chapters on the Federalist*

Adair, Douglas, '"Experience Must be our Only Guide"': History, Democratic Theory and the United States Constitution' in R.A. Billington ed., *The Reinterpretation of Early American History* (San Marino, 1966).

Adair, Douglas, 'That Politics may be reduced to a Science: David Hume, James Madison and the Tenth Federalist' *Huntington Library Quarterly* 20 (1957) and in *Fame and the Founding Fathers*, ed. Colbourn.

Adair, Douglass 'The Tenth Federalist Revisited' in *Fame and the Founding Fathers*, ed. T. Colbourn (N.Y., 1974).

Hobson, Charles F. 'The Negative on State Laws: James Madison, the Constitution, and the Crisis of Republican Government' *William and Mary Quarterly*, XXXVI, 2 (1979).

Hutson, James H., 'The Creation of the Constitution: Scholarship at a standstill, *Reviews in American History*, 12 (1984).

Ketcham, Ralph, 'Notes on James Madison's Sources' *Midwest Journal of Political Science* 1 (i) (1957).

Kobylka, Joseph F. & Carter, Bradley Kent 'Madison, *The Federalist*, and the Constitutional Order: Human Nature and Institutional Structure.' *Polity*, XX (1987).

Mason, Alpheus T. 'The Federalist – A Split Personality' *American Historical Review*, 57 (1952).

Meyers, Marvin 'Founding and Revolution: a commmentary on Publius-Madison' in S. Elkins, and E. McKetrick, ed., *The Hofstadter Aegis* (N.Y., 1974).

Morgan, Edmund 'Safety in Numbers: Madison, Hume and the Tenth *Federalist*' *Huntingdon LIbrary Quarterly*, XLIX (1986).

Morgan, Robert 'Madison's Theory of Representation in the Tenth *Federalist*', *Journal of Politics*, XXXVII (1974).

Morgan, Robert 'Madison's analysis of the sources of political authority' *American Political Science Review*, LXXV (1981).

Rakove, Jack N. 'The Madisonian Moment' *University of Chicago Law Review* LV (1988).

Rakove, Jack N. 'The Madisonian Theory of Rights'. *William and Mary Law Review*, XXXI (1990).

Riemer, N., 'The Republicanism of James Madison' *Political Science Quarterly*, 69 (1954).

Shklar, Judith N. 'Alexander Hamilton and the language of poitical science' in A. Pagden (ed.) *The Languages of Political Theory in Early-Modern Europe*.

iv) *Background*

Adams, W. Paul, 'Republicanism in Political Rhetoric before 1776' *Political Science Quarterly* LXXXV (1970).

Appleby, Joyce, 'Republicanism and Ideology', *American Quarterly* vol. 37, no. 4.

Arendt, Hannah *On Revolution* (N.Y.1965).

Bailyn, Bernard, 'Central Themes of the American Revolution, an Interpretation' in Stephen G. Kurtz and James H. Hutson, eds., *Essays on the American Revolution* (Williamsburg Va. and New York, 1973).

Bailyn, Bernard. *The Ideological Origins of the American Revolution* (Camb. Mass, 1967).

Banning, Lance 'Republican Ideology and the Triumph of the Constitution 1789–1793' *William and Mary Quarterly* 3rd ser., XXXI (1971).

Banning, Lance 'James Madison and the dynamics of the Constitutional Convention' *Political Science Reviewer* XVII (1987).

Banning, Lance 'Some Second Thoughts on Virtue and the Course of Revolutionary Thinking' in T. Ball and J.G.A. Pocock ed., *Conceptual Change and the Constitution*.

Beard, Charles A. *An Economic Interpretation of the Constitution* (Priceton, 1956).

Berthoff, Roland, and John M. Murrin, 'Feudalism, Communalism and the Yeoman Freeholder' in S.G. Kurt and J.H. Hutson (ed.) *Essays on the American Revolution* (Chapel Hill, 1973).

Bushman, R.L., '"This New Man"; Dependence and Independence, 1776' in *Uprooted Americans* (Boston, 1979), ed. Bushman, et.al.

Diamond, Martin 'The Declaration and the Constitution: Liberty, Democracy, and the Founders' *The Public Interest* (No. 41, Fall 1973).

Duffy, M., 'The Making of the Constitution' in *The American Constitution, the first 200 Years*, 1787–1987 ed., Joe Smith (Exeter, 1987).

Dunn, John, 'The Politics of Locke in England and America' in J. Yolton (ed.) *John Locke, Problems and Perspectives* (Cambs., 1969).

Fletcher, F.T.H., *Montesquieu and English Politics* (1750–1800) (London, 1939; repr., Philadelphia, 1980).

Forbes, Duncan, *Hume's Philosophical Politics* (Cambs, 1975).

Goldsmith, M.M., and R.Ashcraft, 'Locke, Revolution Principles and the formation of Whig Ideology' *Historical Journal*, 26, 4 (1983).

Hamowy, R., 'Jefferson and the Scottish Enlightenment: A Critique of Garry Wills' Inventing America: Jefferson's Declaration of Independence,' *William and Mary Quarterly*, 3rd Ser., 36 (1979).

Hampsher-Monk, Iain 'Civic Humanism and Parliamentary Reform: The Case of the Society of the Friends of the People' *Journal of British Studies* 18 (Spring 1979).

— 'British and European Background to the Ideas of the Constitution' in Joseph Smith ed., *The American Constitution: the first 200 years 1787–1987* Exeter Studies in History, no.16 (Exeter, 1987).

Handlin, O, and M.Handlin, 'James Burgh and American Revolutionary Theory' *Proceedings, Mass. Historical Society* 73 (1961).

Hartz, Louis, *The Liberal Tradition in America* (N.Y., 1955).

Hyneman, C.S., and D.S.Lutz (eds.) *American Political Writing During the Founding Era, 1760–1805* (Indianapolis, 1983).

Kramnick, Isaac, *Bolingbroke and His Circle: The Politics of Nostalgia in the Age of Walpole* (Camb., Mass., 1968).

— 'Republican Revisionism Revisited', *American Historical Review, 87 (1982)* .

— 'The "Great National Discussion": the Discourse of Politics in 1787' *William and Mary Quarterly*, XLIV (1987).

Lutz, Donald S., 'The Relative influence of European Writers on Late-Eighteenth Century American Political Thought', *The American Political Science Review* vol. 78 (1984).

McCoy, Drew 'James Madison and Visions of American Nationality' in Jack P.Greene, Ed., *The American Revolution: its Character and Limits* (N.Y., 1987).

Manicas, P.T., 'Montesquieu and the Eighteenth-Century Vision of the State' *History of Political Thought* II, 2 (1981).

Moore, J.M., 'Hume's Political Science and the Classical Republican Tradition.' *Canadian Journal of Political Science* x (1977).

Morgan, Edmund 'The Puritan Ethic and the American Revolution' *W & M Qy* XXIV, 1 (1967).

Morison, S.E., *The Oxford History of the American People* (London, 1965).

Morris, Richard, B. 'The Confederation Period and the American Historian' *William and Mary Quarterly*, 13 (1956).

Murin, John M., '"The Great Inversion" or "Court Versus Country"' in J.G.A. Pocock, *Three British Revolutions, 1641, 1688, 1776* (Princeton, 1980).

Plumb, J.H., *The Growth of Political Stability in England* 1675–1725 (London, 1967).

Pocock, J.G.A., 'Machiavelli, Harrington, and English Political Ideologies in the Eighteenth Century', in Pocock, *Politics Language and Time.* (London and New York, 1974).

— 'Civic Humanism and its Role in Anglo American Thought' in *Politics Language and Time.*

— *The Machiavellian Moment: Florentine Political Thought and the Atlantic Republican Tradition* (Princeton, 1975).

— 'The Machiavellian Moment Revisited: A study in history and ideology', *Journal of World History* (1981).

— *Three British Revolutions 1641, 1688, 1776* (Princeton, 1980).

— 'Virtue Rights and Manners, A Model for Historians of Political Thought' in *Virtue Commerce and History.*

— 'Hume and the American Revolution: the dying thoughts of a North Briton' in *Virtue, Commerce and History, Essays on Political Thought and History, Cheifly in the Eighteenth Century* (Cambridge, 1985).

Richter, Melvin, *The Political Theory of Montesquieu* (London, 1977).

Robertson, John, 'The Scottish Enlightenment at the Limits of the Civic Tradition' in eds. Istvan Hont and Michael Ignatieff *Wealth and Virtue: The Shaping of Political Economy in the Scottish Enlightenment.* (Cambridge:1983).

Rossiter, Clinton *Seedtime of the Republic* (N.Y., 1953).

— *1787 The Grand Convention* (London & N.Y., 1966).

Schmitt, G.J., and R.H.Webking 'Revolutionaries, Antifederalists and Federalists: comments on Gordon Wood's understanding of the American Founding.' *The Political Science Reviewer*, 9 (1979).

Shalhope, R.E., 'Republicanism and Early American Historiography' *William and Mary Quarterly*, 3rd Ser. (XXXIX, 1982).

— 'Towards a Republican Synthesis: the Emergence of an Understanding of Republicanism in American Historiography' *W & M Qy* (xix, 1972).

Smith, Joseph (ed.) *The American Constitution, the First Two Hundred Years* (Exeter Studies in History, no.16) (Exeter, 1987).

Spurlin, P.M., *Montesquieu in America 1760–1801* (Baton Rouge, La., 1940).

Walton, Craig, 'Hume and Jefferson on the Uses of History', in D. Livingstone and J. King, ed., *Hume a Re-evaluation* (Illinois, 1976).

Weston, C.C., 'Co-ordination – a Radicalising Principle in Stuart Politics' in M. & J. Jacob (eds.) *The Origins of Anglo-American Radicalism* (London, 1984).

— and J.R.Greenberg *Subjects and Sovereigns* (Cambs., 1981).

Winch, Donald, *Adam Smith's Politics: An Essay in Historiographic Revision,* (Cambs.1978).

Wood, Gordon S., *The Creation of the American Republic 1776–1787* (Chapel Hill, N.C., 1969).

Chapter VI Edmund Burke

A) Original works

i) By Burke

The Works of the Right Honourable Edmund Burke, (6 vols, later 8, London, 1889: the 'Bohn Library Edition').

The Writings and Speeches of Edmund Burke, General editor Paul Langford (Oxford, Clarendon Press, 1981 – continuing) Vols 2, 5, and 8 published, volume 8 contains *Reflections . . . .*

The Correspondence of Edmund Burke, General editor Thomas W. Copeland (10 vols, Cambridge and Chicago, 1958–78).

A Notebook of Edmund Burke, ed. H. V. F. Somerset (Cambridge, 1957).

A Philosophical Enquiry into the Origin of our Ideas of the Sublime and Beautiful, intr. and ed., J.T. Boulton (London and N.Y., 1958).

Reflections on the Revolution in France, ed. and intr. Conor Cruise O'Brien (Harmondsworth, 1968).

Reflections on the Revolution in France, ed. and intr. J.G.A. Pocock (Indianapolis & Cambridge, 1987), by far the best introduction.

Single volume selections of Burke's writings.

The Political Philosophy of Edmund Burke, ed. I. W. Hampsher-Monk (Harlow, 1987).

Edmund Burke on Politics and Society, ed. B. W. Hill (London).

Edmund Burke, ed. Isaac Kramnick (Englewood Cliffs, 1974).

ii) By other authors

Aristotle, *Politics.*

Barruel, Abbé *Memoirs Illustrating the History of Jacobinism* (3 vols, London, 1797).

Coleridge, S.T., *Biographia Literaria* (2 vols, Oxford, 1939).

Locke, John *An Essay Concerning Human Understanding,* ed. and intr. P.H. Nidditch, (Oxford, 1975)

Marx, Karl *The 18th Brumaire of Napolean Bonaparte,* in *Surveys from Exile,* ed. D. Fernbach (Harmondsworth, 1973).

Montesquieu, *The Spirit of the Laws.*

Millar, William *Observations concerning the Origin of the Distinction of Ranks in Society* (Bristol, 1990[1771].

Paine, Tom *Rights of Man* (Harmondsworth, 1984 [1791]).

Price, Richard *Observations on Civil Liberty,* (London, 1776).

— 'General Introduction and Supplement to the Two Tracts on Civil Liberty . . . etc.' (London, 1778) both in *Richard Price and the Ethical Foundations of the American Revolution: Selections from his pamphlets,* ed. & intr. Bernard Peach (Durham, N.C., 1979).

Robertson, William *A View of the Progress of Society in Europe,* ed. Felix Gilbert (Chicago, 1972[1769]).

Smith, Adam *Wealth of Nations* (2 Vols, Oxford, 1976).

Tucker, Josiah *A Treatise Concerning Civil Government* (London, 1781).

iii) Collections containing other useful contemporary material

Cobban, Alfred *The Debate on the French Revolution, 1789–99* (London, 1950).

Stewart, John Hall *A Documentary History of the French Revolution* (New York, 1951).

B) Secondary works

i) Bibliographical

Bryant, D. C., 'Edmund Burke: a generation of scholarship and discovery', *Journal of British Studies,* 2 (1962) (bibliographic review).

Gandy, C.I., and Stanlis, Peter J., *Edmund Burke a Bibliography of secondary Studies to 1982* (New York, 1983).

Todd, William B., *A Bibliography of Edmund Burke* (London, 1964).

Reflections, provoked a huge literary response at the time, there is a bibliography:

Pendelton, Gayle Trusdel 'Towards a Bibliography of the *Reflections,* and *Rights of Man* Controversy', *Bulletin of Research in the Humanities,* 85 (1982).

ii) Biographical

Ayling, S., *Edmund Burke: his life and opinions* (London, 1988).

Magnus, Sir Philip *Edmund Burke* (London, 1939).

Prior, James *Memoir of the Life and Character of the Right Honourable Edmund Burke* (London, 1824).

iii) Full length studies

Boulton, J., *The Language of Politics in the Age of Wilkes and Burke* (London, 1963).

Cameron, D. R., *The Social Thought of Rousseau and Burke* (London, 1973).

Canavan, F., *The Political Reason of Edmund Burke* (Durham, N.C., 1960).

Chapman, G. W., *Edmund Burke, the practical imagination* (Cambridge, Mass., 1967).

Cobban, A., *Edmund Burke and the Revolt against the Eighteenth Century* (London, 1960).

Cone, Carl B., *Edmund Burke and the Nature of Politics* (2 vols, Lexington, 1957–64).

Copeland, T. W., *Edmund Burke: Six Essays* (London, 1960).

Courtney, C.P., *Montesquieu and Burke* (Oxford, 1963).

Dreyer, F., *Burke's Politics: a Study in Whig Orthodoxy* (Waterloo, Ontario, 1979).

Fennessy, R. R., *Burke, Paine and the Rights of Man: A Difference of Political Opinion* (The Hague, 1963).

Freeman, M., *Edmund Burke and the Critique of Political Radicalism* (Oxford, 1980).

Kramnick, Isaac *The Rage of Edmund Burke: Portrait of an ambivalent Conservative* (New York, 1977).

Lock, F.P., *Burke's Reflections on the Revolution in France* (London, 1985).

Maccun, J., *The Political Philosophy of Burke* (London, 1913).

Macpherson, C. B., *Edmund Burke* (Oxford, 1980).

Mahoney, T.D., *Edmund Burke and Ireland* (Cambridge, Mass., 1960).

Mansfield, Harvey, (jr) *Statesmanship and Party Government* (Chicago, 1965).

O'Gorman, F., *Edmund Burke, his political Philosophy* (London, 1973).

Osborne, A.M., *Rousseau and Burke a study of the Idea of Liberty in Eighteenth-Century Thought* (London, 1940).

Parkin, C.H., *The Moral Basis of Burke's Political Thought* (Cambridge, 1956).
Smith, B.J., *Politics and Remembrance, republican themes in Machiavelli, Burke, and Tocqueville* (Princeton, 1985).
Stanlis, P. J., *Burke and the Natural Law* (Ann Arbor, 1958).
Wilkins, B. T., *The Problem of Burke's Political Philosophy* (Oxford, 1967).

iv) Specialist journals

Burke Newsletter (to 1958) *Studies in Burke and his time* (to 1978), *Eighteenth Century – theory and interpretation.*

v) Important articles and chapters on aspects of Burke's thought

Brewer, J., 'Rockingham, Burke and Whig political argument', *Historical Journal*, 18 (1975).
Campbell, J. A., 'Edmund Burke: Argument from circumstance in *Reflections . . .* ', *Studies in Burke and his Time*, 12, 2 (1970–1).
Canavan, F., 'Burke on Prescription in Government', *Review of Politics* , V, 35 (1973).
Carnall, G., 'Burke as Modern Cicero', in *The Impeachment of Warren Hastings*, ed. G. Carnall and C. Nicholson (Edinburgh, 1989).
Copeland, T. W., 'The reputation of Edmund Burke', *Journal of BritishStudies*, 1 (1962).
Courtney, C. P., 'Edmund Burke and the Enlightenment', in *Statesmen, Scholars, and Merchants*, ed. A.Whiteman, J. S. Bromley, and P. G. M. Dickinson (Oxford, 1973).
Davidson, J. F., 'Natural law and International Law in Edmund Burke', *The Review of Politics*, XXI (1959).
Dinwiddy, J., 'Utility and Natural Law in Burke's Thought: a reconsideration', *Studies in Burke and his Time*, 16, 2 (1974–5).
Einaudi, M., 'The British Background of Burke's Political Thought', *Political Science Quarterly*, XLIX (December, 1934).
Fasel, G., '"The Soul that Animated": the role of property in Burke's thought', *Studies in Burke and his Time*, 17, 1 (1976).
Freeman, M., 'Edmund Burke and the sociology of revolution', *PoliticalStudies*, XXV (1977).
Goodwin, A., 'The Political Genesis of Burke's *Reflections . . .* ', *Bulletin of the John Rylands Library*, 50, 2 (1968).
Hampsher-Monk, I.W., 'Rhetoric and Opinion in the Politics of Edmund Burke', *History of Political Thought* IX, 3 (1988).
Kilcup, R. W., 'Reason and the basis of morality in Burke', *Journal of the History of Philosophy*, 17, 3 (1979).
Kramnick, I., 'The Left and Edmund Burke', *Political Theory*, 11, 2 (1983).
Lucas, P., 'Burke's doctrine of prescription, ' *Historical Journal*, 11 (1968).
Macpherson, C. B., 'Edmund Burke', *Proceedings of the Royal Society of Canada*, 53 (1959).
Melvin, J., 'Burke on theatricality and revolution', *Journal of the History of Ideas*, 36 (1975).
Mosher, M.J., 'The skeptic's Burke: Reflections on the Revolution in France, 1790–1990', *PoliticalTheory*, 19, 3 (1991).
Paulson, R., 'Burke's Sublime and the Representation of Revolution', in *Culture and Politics from Puritanism to the Enlightenment*, ed. Perez Zagorin (Los Angeles, 1980).
Pocock, J. G. A., 'Burke and the Ancient constitution' in Pocock, *Politics, Language and Time.*
— 'The political economy of Burke's analysis of the French Revolution' in Pocock, *Virtue, Commerce, and History.*
— 'The varieties of Whiggism from Exclusion to Reform: a history of ideology and discourse' in Pocock, *Virtue, Commerce, and History.*
Smith, R. A., 'Burke's Crusade against the French Revolution: principles and prejudices', *Burke Newsletter*, 7, 3 (1966).
Underdown, T.P., *'Bristol and Burke'* (Bristol, 1961).
Wecter, D., 'Burke's Theory Concerning Words, Images and Emotions', *Proceedings of the Moder Language Association*, LX (March 1940).
Western, J. R., 'Edmund Burke's view of history', *Review of Politics*, 23 (1961).
Wieser, D. K., 'The Imagery of Burke's *Reflections*', *Studies in Burke and his Time*, 16, 3 (1975).
Wood, N., 'The Aesthetic dimension of Burke's Political Thought', *Journal of British Studies*, 4, 1 (1964).

vi) Background

Aftalion, Florin *The French Revolution: An Economic Interpretation* (Cambridge and Paris, 1990).
Berman, David 'The Irish Counter-Enlightenment', in *The Irish Mind, exploring intellectual traditions*, ed. Richard Kearney (Dublin, 1985).
Brewer, John *Party Ideology and Popular Politics at the Accession of George III* (Cambridge, 1976).
Claeys, G., *Thomas Paine : social and political thought* (London, 1989).
Clark, J. C. D., *English Society, 1688–1832* (Cambridge, 1986).
Deane, Seamus *The French Revolution and Enlightenment in England 1789–1832* (Cambridge, Mass., 1988).
Dozier, Robert R., *For King, Constitution and Country: the English Loyalists and the French Revolution* (Lexington, 1983).
Hole, Robert *Pulpits, Politics, and Public Order in England 1760–1832* (Cambridge, 1989).
Jones, R.Ben *The French Revolution* (London, 1967).
Goodwin, Albert *The Friends of Liberty, the English Democratic Movement in the Age of the French Revolution* (London, 1979).
Lefebvre, Georges *The French Revolution from its Origins to 1793*, tr. Evanson (London, 1962).
O'Gorman, Frank *The Whig Party and the French Revolution* (London, 1967).
Philp, Mark *Paine*, (Oxford, 1990).
— *The French Revolution and British Popular Politics*, (Cambridge, 1991).
Schofield, T.P., 'Conservative Political Thought in Britain in Response to the French Revolution' *Historical Journal*, XXIX (1986).
Smith, Olivia *The Politics of Language, 1791–1819* (Oxford, 1984).
Smith, R. J., *The Gothic Bequest: Medieval institutions in British thought, 1688–1863* (Cambridge, 1987).

Chapter VII Jeremy Bentham

A) Original works

i) Collected editions

The Works of Jeremy Bentham, published under the superintendence of . . . John Bowring (11 vols Edinburgh, 1838–43).
Jeremy Bentham's Economic Writings, ed. W. Stark (3 vols London, 1952–4).
The Collected Works of Jeremy Bentham, ed. J.H. Burns, J.R. Dinwiddy, and F. Rosen (London, 1968 –) (in progress).

ii) Single works

A Fragment on Government and An Introduction to the Principles of Morals and Legislation ed. W. Harrison (Oxford, 1948).
A Fragment on Government, ed. F.C. Montague (Oxford, 1891).
A Fragment on Government, ed. Ross Harrison (Cambridge, 1988).
An Introduction to the Principles of Morals and Legislation, ed. J.H. Burns and H.L.A. Hart (London, 1982).
The Handbook of Political Fallacies, ed. Harold Larrabee, intr. Crane Brinton (New York, 1952).
Selections from Bentham's writings:
Everett, C.W. *Jeremy Bentham* (London, 1966).
Goldworth, A., 'Bentham on the measurement of subjective states' *Bentham Newsletter*, 2 (1979).
Mack, Mary *A Bentham Reader* (New York, 1969).
Parekh, Bhikhu *Bentham's Political Thought* (London, 1973).

iii) By other authors

Beccaria, Cesare, *An Essay on Crimes and Punishments* tr. H. Paolucci (Indianapolis, 1963).
Blackstone, Sir Wm. *Commentaries on the Laws of England* (4 vols, Oxford, 1765–9, many reprints).
Chastellux, F.J.de *An Essay on Public Happiness* (2 vols.) (London, 1774; repr. New York, 1969).

Helvetius, C.A. *De l'Esprit, or essays on the mind and its several faculties* (London, 1807).
Mill, James, *An Essay on Government* (Indianapolis and New York, 1955).
Montesquieu, C.L.de Secondat, Baron *The Spirit of the Laws* (tr. Nugent) NEW CAMBS EDN, NY, 1949).
Paley, Wm. *Principles of Moral and Political Philosophy* (London, 1785, many edns.).

B) Secondary works

i) Bibliographical

Jackson, Donald (with others), 'The Bentham Bibliography' serially in *The Bentham Newsletter*, Nos. 1 (1945–60 (in fact to 65)), 2 (1966–78), 4 (1901–44), 6 (Bentham's works and pre-1900) 7 (additions).

ii) Full length studies

Baumgardt, David, *Bentahma and the Ethics of Today* (New York, 1966).
Boralevi, Lea Campos *Bentham and the Oppressed* (Berlin, 1984).
Dinwiddy, John *Bentham,* (Oxford, 1989).
Harrison, Ross *Bentham,* (London, 1983).
Hume, L.J., *Bentham and Bureaucracy* (Cambs., 1981).
Letwin, S., *The Pursuit of Certainty* (Cambs., 1965).
Long, D., *Bentham on Liberty* (Toronto, 1977).
Lyons, D., *In the Interests of the Governed: A Study of Bentham's Philosophy of Utility and Law* (Oxford, 1973).
Mack, Mary *Jeremy Bentham: An Odyssey of Ideas 1748–1792* (London, 1962).
Manning, D.H., *The Mind of Jeremy Bentham* (London, 1968).
Ogden, C.K., *Bentham's Theory of Fictions* (London, 1932).
Plamenatz, J., *The English Utilitarians* (Oxford, 1958).
Postema, Gerald J., *Bentham and the Common Law Tradition.* (Oxford, 1986).
Rosen, Frederick *Jeremy Bentham and Representative Democracy* (Oxford, 1983).
Rosenblum, Nancy *Bentham's Theory of the State* (Harvard, 1978).
Steintrager, James *Bentham* (London, 1977).

iii) Specialist journals and collections devoted to Bentham

The Bentham Newsletter, now incorporated in *Utilitas*.
Keeton, G.W., and Schwartzenberger, G., ed., *Jeremy Bentham and the Law* (London, 1948).
Jeremy Bentham Bicentenary Celebrations (London, 1948).
James, M.H., ed., *Northern Ireland Legal Quarterly,* XXIV (1973).
Hart, H.L.A., *Essays on Bentham* (Oxford, 1982).
Parekh, Bhikhu ed., *Jeremy Bentham: Ten Critical Essays.* (London, 1974)

iv) Important articles and chapters on Bentham

Ball, Terence 'Utilitarianism, Feminism and the Franchise' *History of Political Thought* I, i (1980).
Burns. J.H., 'Utilitarianism and Democracy', *The Philosophical Quarterly*, 9 (1959).
— 'Bentham and the French Revolution', *Trs. R.Hist.Soc*, 5th ser., XVII (1966).
— 'The Fabric of Felicity: the Legislator and the Human Condition', Inaugural lecture, University College, (London, 1967).
— 'Bentham on Sovereignty: an exploration', *Northern Irland Legal Qu'y* XXIV (1973).
Burkholder, L., 'Tarleton on Bentham's Fragment on Government', *Political Studies,* vol 21 (1973).
Dinwiddy, John 'Bentham's Transition to Political Radicalism 1809–10', *Journal of the History of Ideas,* XXXV (1975).
— 'Bentham on private ethics and the principle of utility', *Revue International de Philosophie*, 141 (1982).

Fry, G.K., 'Bentham and public administration', *Pubic Administration Bulletin*, 24 (1977).
Goldworth, A., 'The Meaning of Bentham's Greatest Happiness Principle' *Jol. Hist. Phil.* (VII (1969).
Hamburger, J., *James Mill and the Art of Revolution* (New Haven, 1963).
Hart, H.L.A. 'Bentham' *Proc.Br.Acad.*, xlviii (1960, and in *Essays on Bentham*).
Himmelfarb, G., 'Bentham scholarship and the Bentham "problem"', *Jol. Modern History*, XLI (1969).
— 'On reading Bentham Seriously', *Studies in Burke and his Time*, XIV (1972–3).
Hume, L.J., 'Bentham's Panopticon: an administrative history', *Historical Studies*, XV and XVI (1973–4).
— 'Bentham's Theory of Fictions', *The Bentham Newsletter*, 3 (1979).
— 'Revisionism in Bentham Studies', *The Bentham Newsletter*, 1 (1978).
— 'Jeremy Bentham and the Nineteenth Century Revolution in Government', *Historiical Jol.*, X (1967).
James, M.H., 'Public Interest and Majority Rule in Bentham's Democratic Theory', *Political Theory*, IX (1981).
Leiberman, David 'From Bentham to Benthamism', *Historical Journal*, XXXVIII (1985).
Milo, Ronald 'Bentham's Principle', *Ethics* (84, 1973–4).
Parekh, Bhikhu 'Bentham's Theory of Equality', *Political Studies* XVIII (1970).
Rosen, F., 'Jeremy Bentham and Democratic Theory', *The Bentham Newsletter*, 3 (1979).
Rosenblum, Nancy L 'Bentham's Social Psychology for Legislators' *Political Theory* 1 (1973).
Schwartz, P., 'Bentham's influence in Spain, Portugal and Latin America', *The Bentham Newsletter*, 1 (1978).
Shackleton, R., 'The Greatest Happiness of the Greatest Number', *Studies in Voltaire and the Eighteenth Century*, XC (1972).
Stark, Werner 'Liberty and Equality or: Jeremy Bentham as an economist' I: Bentham's Doctrine'.
— 'Bentham as an Economist II: Bentham's Influence' *Economic Journal*, 56 (1946).
Steintrager, James 'Bentham on Religion', *The Bentham Newsletter*, 4 (1980).
Tarleton, Charles D., 'The Overlooked Strategy of Bentham's *Fragment on Government*,' *Political Studies*, XX (December, 1972) and see Burkholder.
Twining, W.L., and P.E., 'Bentham on Torture', *Bentham and Legal Theory*, ed. James, M.H., *N. Ireland Legal Quarterly*, XXIV (1973).

v) Background

Finer, S.E., 'The Transmission of Benthamite Ideas 1820–1850' in *Studies in the Growth of Nineteenth-Century Government*, ed. G.Sutherland (London, 1972).
Halévy, Elie *The Growth of Philosophic Radicalism* (London, 1928).
Hamburger, James *James Mill and the Art of Revolution* (New Haven, 1963).
Lieberman, David, *The province of Legislation Determined: Legal Theory in Eighteenth Century Britain* (Cambridge, 1989).
Pearson, Robert and Williams, Geraint, *Political Thought and Public Policy in the Nineteenth Century, an introduction* (Longman, 1984).
Thomas, William *The Philosophical Radicals: Nine Studies in Theory and Practice, 1817–1841* (Oxford, 1979)

Chapter VIII John Stuart Mill

A) Original works

i) By Mill

Collected Works of John Stuart Mill ed. J.M. Robson, (29 vols, Toronto and London, 1963–89).
Dissertations and Discussions, Political, Philosophical, and Historical, 2nd edn., (3 vols, London, 1867).
Autobiography, ed. J.Stillinger (Oxford, 1971).
Utilitarianism, On Liberty and Considerations on Representative Government, ed. H.B. Acton (London, 1972[1910]).
On Liberty and other writings, ed. Stefan Collini (Cambridge, 1989).
Mill on Bentham and Coleridge, ed. F.R. Leavis (London, 1967).

ii) By other authors

Coleridge, S.T., *On the Constitution of the Church and State* (London, 1972 [1830]).
Humboldt, W. von, *The Limits of State Action*, ed. J.W. Burrow (Cambridge, 1969).
Macaulay, Thomas Babington 'Mill's Essay on Government' in *Complete works* (12 vols. London, 1897).
Ricardo, D., *Principles of Political Economy and Taxation* (London, 1817).
Smith, Adam *The Theory of the Moral Sentiments*, ed. D.D. Raphael, and A.L. Macfie (Oxford, 1976).
Stephen, James Fitzjames *Liberty, Equality, Fraternity*, ed. R.J. White, (Cambridge, 1967[London, 1873]).
Tocqueville, Alexis de *Democracy in America*, (2 vols. New York, 1961 [first trs. 1835]).

B) Secondary works

i) Bibliographical

Bibliography of the Published Writings of John Stuart Mill ed. Ney MacMinn, J.R.Hainds and J.M.McCrimmon (Evanston, 1945).
Bibliography of Works on John Stuart Mill, Michael Laine (Toronto and London, 1982).

ii) Biographical

Bain, Alexander *John Stuart Mill: A Criticism with Personal Recollections* (London, 1882).
Hayek, F.A. *John Stuart Mill and Harriet Taylor: Their Friendship and Subsequent Marriage* (London, 1951).
Mill, J.S., *Autobiography*, ed. J.Stillinger (Oxford, 1971).
Packe, M, st. J., *The Life of John Stuart Mill* (London, 1954).
Pappé, H.O., *John Stuart Mill and the Harriet Taylor Myth* (London and Cambridge, 1960).

iii) Full length studies

Anschutz, R.P., *The Philosophy of J.S. Mill* (Oxford, 1953).
Berger, F.R., *Happiness, Justice and Freedom: The Moral and Political Philosophy of John Stuart Mill* (Berkeley, 1984).
Cowling, M., *Mill and Liberalism* (Cambridge, 1963), excerpted in Schneewind (ed).
Gray, J., *Mill on Liberty: a Defence* (London, 1983).
Halliday, J., *John Stuart Mill* (London, 1976).
Hamburger, James *Intellectuals in Politics: John Stuart Mill and the Philosophical Radicals* (New Haven, 1965).
Himmelfarb, G., *On Liberty and Liberalism: the Case of John Stuart Mill* (New York, 1974).
Hollander, Samuel *The Economics of John Stuart Mill* (2 vols, Oxford, 1985).
Letwin, S.R., *The Pursuit of Certainty* (Cambridge, 1965).
McCloskey, H.J., *John Stuart Mill: A Critical Study* (London, 1971).
Mazlish, B., *James and John Stuart Mill* (N.Y., 1975).
Mueller, J.W., *John Stuart Mill and French Thought* (Urbana, Ill., 1956).
Neff, E., *Carlyle and Mill* (New York, 1926).
Plamenatz, J., *The English Utilitarians* (Oxford, 1958).
Rees, John *John Stuart Mill's On Liberty* (Oxford, 1985).
Robson, J.M., *The Improvement of Mankind* (Toronto and London, 1968).
Ryan, A., *The Philosophy of John Stuart Mill* (London, 1970).
—*J.S.Mill* (London, 1974).
Schwartz, Pedro *The New Political Economy of J.S. Mill* (London, 1973).
Spitz, D., *On Liberty* (N.Y., 1975).
Stephen, L., *The English Utilitarians* (3 vols., London, 1900).
Ten, L.C., *Mill on Liberty* (Oxford, 1980).
Thomas, William, *Mill* (Oxford, 1985).

Thompson, Dennis F., *John Stuart Mill and Representative Government* (Princeton, 1976).
Woods, T., *Poetry and Philosophy: A Study in the Thought of John Stuart Mill* (London, 1961).

iv) Specialist journals and collections devoted to Mill

The Mill Newsletter, 1965–1989, now succeeded by *Utilitas*.
Laine, M., ed., *A cultured mind: essays on J.S. Mill presented to J.M. Robson* (Toronto, 1991).
Robson, J.M., and Laine, M., ed., *James and John Stuart Mill: Papers of the Centenary Conference*, (Toronto, 1976).
Schneewind, J.B., ed., *Mill: A collection of critical essays* (London, 1970).

v) Important articles and chapters on Mill

Annas, Julia 'Mill and the subjection of Women', *Philosophy*, 52 (1977).
Burns, J.H., 'J.S. Mill and Democracy, 1829–1861', in *Political Studies*, vol. V (1957) and in Schneewind (ed).
Capaldi, N., 'Mill's Forgotten Science of Ethology', *Social Theory and Practice*, 2 (1973).
Cumming, R.D. 'Mill's History of his Ideas' *Journal of the History of Ideas*, 25 (1964).
Eisenach, E.J., 'Mill's *Autobiography* as Political Theory', *History of Political Thought*, VIII, 1 (1987).
Gray, John 'John Stuart Mill on Liberty, Utility and Rights', in *Nomos: Human Rights*, ed., J.W. Chapman, and J.R. Pennock, (New York and London, 1981).
Halliday, J., 'Some Recent Interpretations of John Stuart Mill', *Philosophy*, XLIII, no.163 (1968); and in Schneewind (ed.).
Levi, A.W., 'The Mental Crisis of J.S. Mill', *Psychoanalytic Review*, 32 (1945).
Lewisohn, D.H., 'Mill and Comte on the methods of Social Science', *Journal of the History of Ideas*, 33 (1972).
Mabbott, J., 'Interpretations of Mill's *Utilitarianism*', *Philosophical Quarterly* , 6 (1956).
Mandelbaum, M., 'Two Moot Issues in Mill's *Utilitarianism*', in Schneewind (ed.).
Mazlish, B., 'Mill's Liberalism' *Philosophical Quarterly*, 13 (1963).
Pappé, H.O., 'Mill and Tocqueville', *Journal of the History of Ideas*, 25 (1964).
Rees, John C., 'A Re-reading of Mill on Liberty', *Political Studies*, VIII (1960).
— 'The thesis of the two Mills', *Political Studies*, XXV, (1977).
Robson, J.M., 'John Stuart Mill's Theory of Poetry', *University of Toronto Quarterly*, 39 (1960) and in Schneewind (ed).
Urmson, J.O., 'The Moral Philosphy of J.S. Mill', in Foot (ed.).
— 'Interpretations of Mill's *Utilitarianism*', in Foot (ed.).
Viner, J., 'Bentham and J.S.Mill: the Utilitarian Background', in Viner, *The Long View and the Short* (Glencoe, 1958).

vi) Background

Burrow, J.W., *Whigs and Liberals* (Oxford, 1988).
Burston, W.H., *James Mill on Philosophy and Education* (London, 1973).
Collini, S., Winch, D., and Burrow, J., *That Noble Science of Politics: A study of Nineteenth-Century Intellectual History* (Cambridge, 1983).
Devlin, Patrick *The Enforcement of Morals* (London, 1965) repr. in part in Spitz (ed.).
Feyerabend, P., 'Against Method', *Minnesota Studies in the Philosophy of Science*', 4 (1970).
Foot, P., (ed.) *Theories of Ethics* (Oxford, 1967).
Hamburger, J. *James Mill and the Art of Revolution* (New Haven, 1963).
Kelly, G.A., 'Parnassan Liberalism', *History of Political Thought* VIII (1987).
Parfit D., *Reasons and Persons* (Oxford, 1984).
Pocock, J.G.A .,'The Political Economy of Burke's Analysis of the French Revolution', in Pocock, *Virtue Commerce and History* (Cambridge, 1985).
Smart, J.J., and Williams, B., *Utilitarianism For and Against* (Cambridge, 1973).
Thomas, William *The Philosophical Radicals: Nine Studies in Theory and Practice, 1817–1841* (Oxford, 1979).

Winch, D., 'The System of the North: Dugald Stewart and his Pupils', in *That Noble Science...*, ed. Collini et. al.
Woodcock, M., 'Educational principles and political thought: the case of James Mill', *History of Political Thought*, 1, 3 (1980).

Chapter IX G.W.F. Hegel

A) Original works

i) By Hegel

Early Theological Writings, ed. T. M. Knox (Chicago, 1948).
Hegel's Phenomenology of Spirit, tr. A.V.Miller, ed. & intr. J.N. Findlay (Oxford, 1977).
Hegel's Political Writings, ed. Z. A. Pelczynski (Oxford, 1961).
Logic, tr. W. Wallace (Oxford, 1975).
Philosophy of Mind, tr. W. Wallace (Oxford, 1971).
The Philosophy of Right, ed. & tr. T.M. Knox, (Oxford, 1952).
Elements of the Philosophy of Right, tr. H.B. Nisbet, ed. Allen W. Wood (Cambridge, 1991).
Philosophy of History, tr. J. Sibree (New York, 1956).

ii) By other authors

St. Augustine, *The City of God*, tr. Bettenson (Harmondsworth, 1972).
Bayle, Pierre *Historical and Critical Dictionary* (1696).
DeLolme, Jean *Constitution of England* (1775).
Descartes, René*The Philosophical Works of Descartes*, tr. E. Haldane and G.R.T. Ross (2 vols, New York, 1955[Cambridge, 1931]).
Bolingbroke, Viscount St. John, Henry *Letters on the Study and use of History*, Letter III, in *Lord Bolingbroke, Historical Writings*, ed. Isaac Kramnick (Chicago and London, 1972).
Herder, J.G., *Essay on the Origin of Language* in *Herder on Social and Political Culture*, ed. F.M. Barnard (Cambridge, 1969)
Hume, David *Essays* (Oxford, 1963).
Kant, Immanuel *Critique of Pure Reason*, tr. N. Kemp-Smith (2nd., corrected edn., London, 1933).
 Groundwork of the Metaphysics of Morals, Tr. H.J. Paton (New York & London, 1964[1948]).
Kant, Political Writings, ed. Hans Reiss (2nd edn., Cambridge, 1991).
Locke, John *An Essay Conerning Human Understanding*, ed. P. Niddich (Oxford, 1975).
Mandeville, Bernard *The Fable of the Bees*, ed. F.B. Kaye (2 vols, Oxford, 1924, [repr. Bloomington, Indiana, 1988]).
Montesquieu, Charles Secondat, Baron de, *Spirit of the Laws,*
Schiller, Friedrich *On the Aesthetic Education of Man*, tr. Reginald Snell (London, 1954 [1801]).
Steuart, Sir James *An Enquiry into the Principles of Political Economy*, ed. Andrew Skinner (2 Vols, Chicago, 1966).

B) Secondary works

i) Bibliographical

Schmidt, James, S., 'Recent Hegel Literature', *Telos*, 46 (1980–1).
Weiss, Frederick, G., 'Hegel: A Bibliography of Books in English, Arranged Chronologically', in *The Legacy of Hegel: Proceedings of the Marquette Hegel Symposium 1970* (The Hague, 1973).

ii) Full length studies

Avineri, S. *Hegel's Theory of the Modern State* (Cambridge, 1972).
Berry, C., *Hume, Hegel and Human Nature* (The Hague, 1982).
Findlay, J.N., *Hegel: a Re-examination* (London, 1962).
Gray, J. Glenn *Hegel and Greek Thought* (New York, 1941, [repr., retitled *Hegel's Hellennic Ideal*, 1968]).
Harris, H.S., *Hegel's Development: Toward the Sunlight (1770-1801)* (Oxford, 1972).
Hegel's Development: Night Thoughts (Jena, 1801- 06) (Oxford, 1983).
Hinchman, Lewis *Hegel's Critique of Enlightenment* (Gainsville, 1984).
Hyppolite, J., *Studies on Marx and Hegel* (New York, 1969),
Inwood, M.J., *Hegel* (London, 1983).
Kelly, G.A., *Hegel's Retreat from Eleusis: Studies in Political Thought* (Princeton, 1978).
Kojève, Alexandre *An Introduction to the Reading of Hegel*, trs. James H. Nichols (New York, 1969).
Lukacs, G.*The Young Hegel*, tr. RodneyLivingstone (London, 1975).
Marcuse, H., *Reason and Revolution, Hegel and the Rise of Social Theory* (2nd edn. London, 1955 [1941]).
O'Brien, G.D., *Hegel on Reason and History* (Chicago, 1975).
Plant, R., *Hegel* (London, 1973).
Riedel, Manfred, *Between Tradition and Revolution: the Hegelian Transformation of Political Philosophy*, tr. W. Wright (Cambridge, 1984).
Rosen, Stanley *G.W.F. Hegel: An Introduction to the Science of Wisdom* (New Haven, 1974).
Hegel's Dialectic and its Criticism (Cambridge, 1982).
Ritter, Joachim *Hegel: Essays on the Philosophy of Right and the French Revolution*, trs. Richard Dien Winfield (Cambridge, Mass., 1982).
Schacht, Richard 'The Background of Hegel's Metaphysics' in Shacht, *Hegel and After, Studies in Continental Philosophy between Kant and Sartre* (Pittsburgh, 1975).
Shklar, Judith *Freedom and Independence, political aspects of Hegel's Phenomenology* (Cambridge, 1976).
Singer, P., *Hegel* (Oxford, 1983).
Smith, S.B., *Hegel's Critique of Liberalism* (Chicago, 1989).
Taylor, C., *Hegel and Modern Society* (Cambridge, 1979).
Hegel (Cambridge, 1975).
Toews, J.E., *Hegelianism: The Path Toward Dialectical Humanism, 1805-1841* (Cambridge, 1980).

iii) Specialist journals and collections devoted to Hegel

Bulletin of the Hegel Society of Great Britain, 1980– (Biennially).
The Legacy of Hegel: Proceedings of the Marquette Hegel Symposium 1970 (The Hague, 1973).
Kaufmann, W., ed., *Hegel's Political Philosophy* (New York, 1970).
MacIntyre, A., ed., *Hegel: A Collection of Critical Essays* (New York, 1972).
Pelczynski, Z. A., ed., *Hegel's Political Philosophy: Problem and Perspectives* (Cambridge, 1971).
The State and Civil Society: Studies in Hegel's Political Philosophy (Cambridge, 1984).
Steinkraus, W.E., ed., *New Studies in the Philosophy of Hegel*, (New York, 1971).
Verene, D.D., ed., *Hegel's Social and Political Thought* (Atlantic Heights, N.J and Brighton, 1979).

iv) Important articles and chapters on Hegel

Beck, L.W., 'The Reformation, the Revolution and the Restoration in Hegel's Political Philosophy', *Journal of the History of Philosophy*, 12 (1976).
Brudner, A., 'Constitutional Monarchy as the Divine Regime: Hegel's Theory of the Just State', *History of Political Thought*, II, i (1981).
Christi, F.R., 'Hegel on Possession and Property', *Candian Journal of Social and Political Theory* 2 (1978).
'Hegel and Roman Liberalism' *History of Political Thought* V, ii (1984).
'The *Hegelsche Mitte* and Hegel's Monarch', *Political Theory*, 11, 4 (1983).
Landes, J.B., 'Hegel's Conception of the Family', *Polity*, 14 (1981).

Maletz, Donald J., 'Hegel's "Introduction" to the *Philosophy of Right'*, *Interpretation*, 13 (1985).
'Hegel on Right as actualised will', *Political Theory*, 17, 1 (1989).
Nicholson, P., 'Hegel on Crime', *History of Political Thought*, III, i (1982).
Plant, R., 'Hegel and Political Economy', *New Left Review*, 103–4 (1977).
Schacht, Richard 'The Background of Hegel's Metaphysics', in Schacht, *Hegel and After,* .
Schmidt, J., 'A Paideia for the *'Burger als Bourgeois'*: The Concept of Civil Society in Hegel's Political Thought', *History of Political Thought*, II, iii (1981).
Seade, E.D. de, 'State and History in Hegel's concept of a people', *Journal of the History of Ideas*, 40 (1979).
Smith, Stephen B., 'What is "Right" in Hegel's *Philosophy of Right?' American Political Science Review*, 83 (1989).
Steinberger, P.J., 'Hegel as a Social Scientist', *American Political Science Review*, 71 (1977).
'Hegel on Marriage and Politics', *Politial Studies* , XXXIV, 4 (1986).
Stillman, P., 'Hegel's Critique of Liberal Theories of Rights', *American Political Science Review*, 71 (1977).
'Hegel's idea of Punishment', *Journal of the History of Philosophy*, 12 (1976).
'Property Freedom and individuality in Hegel's and Marx's political thought', *NOMOS*, XXII (1980).
Yack, B., 'The rationality of Hegel's concept of monarchy', *American Political Science Review*, 74 (1980).

v) Background

Aris, Rheinhold *History of Political Thought in Germany, 1789–1815* (London, 1965 [1936]).
Berlin, Isaiah 'The Sciences and the Humanities', in *Against the Current* (Harmondsworth, 1982).
Bruford, W.H., *Germany in the Eighteenth Century: the Social Background of the Literary Revival* (Cambridge, 1971).
Buckland, W.W., *A Textbook of Roman Law* (3rd ed. revised by Peter Stien, Cambridge, 1975).
Butler, E.M., *The Tyranny of Greece over Germany* (Cambridge, 1935).
Hertz, F., *The German Public Mind in the Nineteenth Century*.
Hazard, Paul *European Thought in the Eighteenth Century* (Harmondsworth, 1965[1946]).
Gay, Peter *The Enlightenment, An Interpretation* (2 vols, London, 1970).
Hawthorn, Geoffry *Enlightenment and Despair* (2nd edn., Cambridge, 1987),
Hont, Istvan 'The Rich Country – Poor Country Debate' in Scottish classical political economy', in *Wealth and Virtue*, ed. Istvan Hont and Michael Ignatieff (Cambridge, 1983).
Kelly, G.A., *Idealism, Politics, and History: Sources of Hegelian Thought* (Cambridge, 1969).
Körner, S., *Kant* (Harmondsworth, 1955).
Kreiger, Leonard *The German Idea of Freedom* (Boston, 1957).
MacIntyre, Alastair *After Virtue, a study in moral theory* (London, 1981).
Whose Justice?, Which Rationality? (London, 1988).
Nisbet, H. B., *Herder and the Philosophy of Science* (Cambridge, 1970).
Richards, R. J., 'The influence of the sensationalistic tradition in early theories of the evolution of behaviour', *Journal of the History of Ideas*, XL, 1 (1979).
Riley, Patrick 'On Kant as the most Adequate of the Social Contract Theorists', *Political Theory*, 1, 4 (1973).
Preece, Rodney 'Edmund Burke and his European Reception', *Eighteenth Century: Theory and Interpretation*, vol. 21, no.3 (1980).
Scruton, Roger *Kant* (Oxford, 1982)..
Tribe, Keith *Governing Economy, the reformation of German economic discourse, 1750–1840* (Cambridge, 1988).

Chapter X Karl Marx

A) Original Works

i) By Marx

The complete standard edition is the *Marx-Engels-Werke* (Berlin, 1956–64). There is an English language *Collected Works* in progress (London, 1975 –) There are a number of easily available English-language selections of which the most complete, from which I have quoted wherever possible, is:

The Penguin Marx Library, General Editor: Quinton Hoare.

Early Writings, tr. R. Livingstone and G. Benton, intr. Lucio Colletti (Harmondworth, 1975).

Political Writings vol. I, The Revolutions of 1848, intr. David Fernbach (Harmondsworth, 1973).

Political Writings vol. II, Surveys from Exile, ed. & intr. David Fernbach (Harmondsworth, 1973).

Political Writings vol. III, The First International and After ed. & intr. David Fernbach (Harmondsworth, 1973).

Grundrisse: Foundations of the Critique of Political Economy, tr. & Forward, Martin Nicolaus (Harmondsworth, 1973).

Capital (3 vols.) tr. David Fernbach (Harmondsworth, 1979).

Other useful collections.

Karl Marx: Early Texts, tr. & ed. David McLellan (Oxford, 1971).

Karl Marx: Selected Writings ed. David McLellan (Oxford, 1977).

Marx-Engels Selected Works (Moscow, 1958).

Marx-Engels Basic Writings on Politics and Philosophy, ed. L. Feuer (New York, 1959).

Karl Marx: A Reader ed. Jon Elster (Cambridge, 1986).

I have also cited or used the following single works which do not appear, at least in their entirety, in the above selections:

The German Ideology (with Frederick Engels) (London and Moscow, 1965).

Theories of Surplus Value (3 vols.) tr. Emile Burns (London, 1969–72).

A Contribution to the Critique of Political Economy tr. S.W. Ryazanskaya, ed. Maurice Dobb) (Moscow, 1970).

ii) By other authors

Bruno Bauer, *The Jewish Problem* (1843).

Engels, Frederick *The Condition of the Working Classes in England* (London, 1842).

— *Anti-Düring*.

Feuerbach, Ludwig *Principles of the Philosophy of the Future* (Indianapolis, N.Y., 1966).

— *The Essence of Christianity* (New York and London, 1957).

Hegel, G.W.F. 'Introduction', *Lectures on the Philosophy of Religion*, ed. Peter C. Hodgson (Berkeley, 1988).

— *Phenomenology of Spirit*, tr. Miller (Oxford, 1979).

— *Philosophy of Right*, tr. Knox (Oxford, 1952).

Malthus, Robert *Principles of Political Economy* (2nd edn. 1836 [repr.1986, Fairfield, N.J.]), .

Ricardo, David *The Principles of Political Economy and Taxation* (London & N.Y., 1973).

Smith, Adam *An Enquiry into the Nature and Causes of the Wealth of Nations* (ed. Campbell, Skinner and Todd) (2 vols Oxford, 1976).

Strauss, D.F., *The Life of Jesus* (1835).

Collections containing other useful contemporary material

The Young Hegelians, ed. Lawrence Stapelevich (Cambridge, 1983).

B) Secondary Works

i) Bibliographical

Carver, Terrell, 'Guide to Further Reading' Appendix to Berlin, *Karl Marx* (4th ed. Oxford, 1978).
Lachs, J. *Marxist Philosophy, A Bibliographical Guide* (Chapel Hill, 1976).
McLellan, David, 'Select Critical Bibliography' in *Karl Marx his Life and Thought*.
Rubel, Maximilian 'Bibliographie Marxologique' *Etudes de Marxologie*, 1959–65. (Covers mostly the period up to the Second International, although the economic titles reach 1960).

ii) Biographical

The now standard work on which I have relied for all biographical details is McLennan, D., *Karl Marx his Life and Thought* (London, 1973).
Berlin, I., *Karl Marx* (3rd edn., Oxford, 1973).
Meyring, F., *Karl Marx* (tr. 1936, Anne Arbor, 1962).

iii) Full length studies

Althusser, Louis, *For Marx* (Harmondsworth, 1969).
Avineri, S., *The Social and Political Thought of Karl Marx* (Cambridge, 1970).
Berki, R.N., *Insight and Vision: The Problem of Communism in Marx's Thought* (London, 1983).
Carver, Terrell, *Marx and Engels: the intellectual relationship* (Brighton, 1983).
Marx's Social Theory (Oxford, 1982).
Callinicos, A., *Marxism and Philosophy* (Oxford, 1983).
Cohen, G.A. *Marx's Theory of History: a defence* (Oxford, 1978).
Draper, Hal, *Marx's Theory of Revolution* (2 vols New York, 1977)).
Elster, Jon, *Making Sense of Marx* (Cambridge and Paris, 1985).
Evans, Michael, *Karl Marx* (London, 1975).
Gilbert, Alan, *Marx's Politics, Communists and Citizens* (Oxford, 1981).
Hook, Sidney, *From Hegel to Marx* (New York, 1950).
Howard, M.C. and King, J.E., *The Political Economy of Marx* (2nd edn., Harlow, 1985).
Hunt, Richard N., *The Political Ideas of Marx and Engels: Marxism and Totalitarian Democracy* (Pittsburg, 1974.
Kamenka, E., *The Ethical Foundations of Marxism* (London, 1962).
Kolakowski, L., *Main Currents of Marxism* tr. Falla (3 vols Oxford, 1978).
Levine, Norman *The Tragic Deception, Marx contra Engels* (Oxford and Santa Barbara, 1975).
MacIntyre, A., *Marxism and Christianity* (London, 1968).
McLellan, D., *Marx Before Marxism* (London 1970).
— *The Young Hegelians and Karl Marx* (London, 1969).
McMurtry, J., *The Structure of Marx's World View* (Princeton, 1978).
Maguire, J., *Marx's Theory of Politics* (Cambridge, 1978).
Mandel, Ernest, *The Formation of the Economic Thought of Karl Marx* (New York, 1971).
R. Miliband, 'Marx and the State' *The Socialist Register* (1965) ed. Miliband and J. Saville.
Meek, Ronald L., *Studies in the Labour Theory of Value* (London, 1973).
— *Smith, Ricardo, and Marx* (London, 1977).
Meszaros, Istvan, *Marx's Theory of Alienation* (London, 1970).
Morishima and G. Cataphores, *Value, Exploitation and Growth* (Maidenhead, 1978).
Ollman, B., *Alienation* (Cambridge, 1971).
Plamenatz, J., *German Marxism and Russian Communism* (London, 1954).
Karl Marx's Philosophy of Man (Oxford, 1975).

Roemer, John, *Analytical Marxism* (Cambridge and Paris, 1986).
Rubel, Maximilian, *Rubel on Marx*, ed., O'Malley, Joseph, and Algozin, Keith (Cambridge, 1981).
Shaw, W., *Marx's Theory of History* (Stanford, 1978).
Singer, Peter, *Marx* (Oxford, 1980).
Sowell, Thomas, *Marxism, Philosophy and Economics* (London, 1986).
Thomas, Paul, *Karl Marx and the Anarchists* (London, 1980).
Tucker, R., *Philosophy and Myth in Karl Marx* (London 1961).
The Marxian Revolutionary Idea (London, 1970).
Walker, Angus *Marx, his theory and its context* (London, 1978).
Wood, Allen *Karl Marx* (London, 1981).

iv) Specialist journals and collections devoted to Marx

Specialist journals tend to specialize in Marx*ism* rather than Marx studies, but the *New Left Review*, and *Telos* both carry high quality articles. Publishing mostly French language articles is *Etudes de Marxologie*.

Avineri, S. ed., *Varieties of Marxism* (The Hague, 1977).
Ball, Terence and Farr, James, eds. *After Marx* (Cambridge, 1984).
Hobsbawm, Eric, J. ed., *The History of Marxism, 1: Marxism in Marx's Day* (Brighton, 1982).

v) Important articles and chapters on Marx

Althusser, L., 'Marx's Relation to Hegel' in L. Althusser *Politics and History* and *Essays in Self Criticism*.
Ball, Terence 'Marx and Darwin: A Reconsideration' *Political Theory*, 7 (1979).
Bloom, S., 'The Withering away of the State', *Journal of the History of Ideas* vii (1946).
Carling, A., 'Rational Choice Marxism' *New Left Review*, 160 (1986).
Carver, Terrell, 'Marx – and Hegel's Logic' *Political Studies* xxiv (1976).
— 'Marx, Engels and the Dialectic' *Political Studies* xxviii (1980).
— 'Marx – and Engels's 'Outlines of a Critique of Political Economy'', *History of Political Thought*, IV, 3 (1983).
— 'Communism for Critical Critics', *History of Political Thought* IX, 1 (1988).
Claeys, G. 'Engels' Outlines of a Critique of Political Economy (1843) and the Origins of the Marxist Critique of Capitalism,' *History of Political Economy*, xvi (1984).
Cunliffe, J. 'Marx, Engels and The Party' *History of Political Thought* II2 (1981).
— 'Marx's Politics – The Tensions of The Communist Manifesto' *Political Studies* xxx, no. 4 (1982).
Draper, H., 'Marx and the dictatorship of the proletariat' *Etudes de Marxologie* 6 (1962).
Elster, J., 'Cohen on Marx's Theory of History' *Political Studies* xxviii, no.1 (1980).
Gilbert, A., 'Social Theory and Revolutionary Activity in Marx', *American Political Science Review*, 73 (1979).
Levin, M., 'Deutschmarx: Marx, Engels and the German Question', *Political Studies* 29 (1981).
— 'Marx, Engels, and the generalised Class State' *History of Political Thought* VI.3.
Liebich, A., 'On the Origins of a Marxist Theory of Bureaucracy in the Critique of Hegel's Philosophy of Right' *Political Theory* vol 10 no.1 (1982).
Lubasz, Heinz, 'Marx's Initial Problematic: The Problem of Poverty' *Political Studies* xxiv (1976).
Lukes, Steven, 'Can the base be distinguished from the superstructure?' in Seidentop and Miller (ed.) *The Nature of Political Theory* (Oxford, 1983).
Miller, Richard W., 'The Consistency of Historical Materialism' *Philosophy and Public Affairs* 4 (1975).
— 'Producing Change: Work, technology and power in Marx's theory of history' in *After Marx*, ed. Terence Ball and James Farr (Cambridge, 1984).
Morishima, M., 'The Fundamental Marxian Theorem: a reply to Samuelson', *Journal of Economic Literature*, 12 (1974).
O'Malley, J., 'Marx's 'Economics' and Hegel's Philosophy of Right: An Essay in Marx's Hegelianism' *Political Studies* xxiv (1976).
Rubel, Maximilian, 'Notes on Marx's Conception of Democracy' *New Politics* 1 no.2 (1962).

Stedman-Jones, G., 'Engels and the Genesis of Marxism' *New Left Review*, cvi (1977).
Suchting, W., ' "Productive Forces" and "Relations of Production" in Marx', *Analyse und Kritik*, 4, 2 (1982).
Thomas, Paul, 'Marx and Science', *Political Studies*, XXIV, 1 (1976).
Torrance, J., 'Reproduction and Development: a Case for a Darwinian Mechanism in Marx's Theory of History.' *Political Studies* xxxiii, no.3 (1985).
Kolakowski, L., 'Karl Marx and the Classical Definition of Truth' in Kolakowski, *Marxism and Beyond* (London 1969).
Lubasz, Heinz, 'Marx's Initial Problematic: The Problem of Poverty', *Political Studies*, XXIV, 1 (1976).
McGovern, A., 'Karl Marx's first political writings, the Rheinische Zeitung 1842-3' in *Demythologizing Marxism*, ed. F. Adelman (The Hague, 1969).
O'Malley, J., 'Marx's "Economics" and Hegel's *Philosophy of Right*'. *Political Studies*, XXIV, 1 (1976).
Teeple, G., 'Marx's Doctoral Dissertation', *History of Political Thought*, XI, 1 (1990).

vi) Background

Barlow, Frank, *The Feudal Kingdom of England, 1042-1216* (Harlow, 1972).
Hayek, F.A., 'The Principles of a Liberal Social Order', in *Studies in Philosophy, Politics and Economics* (London, 1967).
Hellman, Robert J., *Berlin, the Red Room and White Beer, the 'Free' Hegelian Radicals in the 1840s* (Washington, 1990).
Hertz, F., *The German Public Mind in the Nineteenth Century* (London, 1975).
MacFarlane, Alan, *'The Origins of English Individualism* (Oxford, 1978).
Toews, John Edward, *Hegelianism* (Cambridge, 1980).
Wartofsky, Marx W., *Feuerbach* (Cambridge, 1977).

Index